COUNTY COURTHOUSE BOOK

COUNTY COURTHOUSE BOOK

2nd Edition

Elizabeth Petty Bentley

GENEALOGICAL PUBLISHING CO. Inc.

CONTENTS

INTRODUCTION

The data in this compilation is based largely upon information received in response to questionnaires sent to over 4,700 counties, cities, and towns across the country. I was gratified to receive responses from nearly 65 percent of the agencies polled (as noted by asterisks preceding those entries). In my questionnaire I requested verification of address, telephone number, and the jurisdiction's date of organization and provenance. Of the major record groups that are of significant interest to genealogists and other researchers, I selected four—land records, naturalization records, vital records, and probate records—and asked that for each category my correspondent identify the particular office researchers should contact and note the dates covered by its holdings. I also requested information about the fees for an index search and photocopying, whether there was a minimum charge, and whether there were restrictions on the records' use (such as proof of relationship for vital records).

Some correspondents supplied more information than was requested, and I have included this additional data wherever possible, such as the actual street address, in addition to the mailing address, and phone numbers for specific offices as distinguished from a main switchboard number. I was not able, however, to include information on other record groups which were often held by these same offices: bonds, marks and brands, voter registrations, licenses, fictitious names, name changes, school records, divorces, guardianships, adoptions, and criminal and civil court proceedings.

The address of a specific office is given in the first appropriate record category only if its address is different from the main address. Where the notation "Contact Recorder," "Contact Clerk," etc., appears, these officials are to be contacted at the main address. Where a clerk or other official is listed by name, it isn't usually necessary to contact only that person, but to address his or her office.

In a few instances, where the form was filled out by only one of two or three agencies responsible for the various records, or I was able to glean only partial information from secondary sources, the entry will appear incomplete. In these instances, and in instances where there was no response at all, the reader can refer to the summary of judicial organization at the beginning of each state's listing and to other jurisdictions in the state to determine the pattern of record-keeping and the average fees for the area. Note especially whether neighboring counties reported having naturalization records. I made a special effort to elicit information on naturalizations from those jurisdictions that previously claimed to have none, and I was surprised at the number that now report finding some. Most naturalizations are now recorded by the Immigration and Naturalization Service, so those that were recorded earlier in the general court dockets, often undifferentiated and unindexed, are rarely consulted now and mostly forgotten. Vital records are also somewhat under-reported, since some offices did not realize that I meant to include marriages in that category. Many states have relegated the recording of twentieth-century births, deaths, and marriages to a state office, whose address can be found in my book *The Genealogist's Address Book*. Also note the information regarding a jurisdiction's creation (usually carved out of a larger geographical area). Events that occurred in a locality before the current jurisdiction assumed its present boundaries should also be sought in the town, county, territory, or state from which the younger jurisdiction was formed, because the governing body that retained the area's original name usually retained all the records created before the split. (Note that territorial records are held by the federal government.)

This present directory is aimed primarily at facilitating research that is done by mail, not in person, so I have deliberately omitted listing office hours, per diem reading-room fees, or charges for second copies of the same document, or for unassisted photocopying (usually somewhat less than for photocopies prepared by the staff for mailing). Most agencies allow, and even encourage, individuals to come and view their records in person. However, they may require positive identification, and they usually restrict the availability of fragile originals and curtail browsing in files which contain confidential information, such as adoptions or illegitimate births. It's always advisable to phone ahead for an appointment before visiting, especially to town offices. But if a personal visit is impossible, mailed requests should be kept very specific when addressed to understaffed and underfunded offices that are primarily geared to creating current records, not answering historical and genealogical inquiries. Ask only for copies of specific records, giving as much identifying information as possible. Some agencies provide a search service, but it is usually limited to determining whether a specific record exists, not searching every Smith will and deed to see if a daughter who married a Jones is mentioned in one. If you have that kind of a project, it's best to hire a professional genealogist or a title search company. Local genealogical or historical societies usually maintain lists of researchers and their fees.

For their efforts in my behalf I would like to thank Michael Tepper, Editor-in-Chief of the Genealogical Publishing Company, Marian Hoffman, the librarians at Western New England College Law Library, and the hundreds of nameless correspondents who took the time to research their holdings and answer my letter.

I hope that future editions of this work will contain more information, based on an even greater response from the agencies themselves. I would welcome additions and corrections to the present text from any readers who may find omissions or errors.

Elizabeth Petty Bentley
The Village Bookstore
45 Southwick Rd.
Westfield, MA 01085

COUNTY COURTHOUSE BOOK

ALABAMA

Capital: Montgomery. Statehood: 14 December 1819 (southern part claimed in Louisiana Purchase of 1803, the rest included in the Territory of Mississippi in 1798, became a territory in 1817)

Court System

Alabama's Municipal Courts handle city ordinance violations and misdemeanors. District Courts hear some civil actions, misdemeanors, traffic and juvenile matters. Probate Courts are convened in each county. Appeals from these three courts go to the Circuit Courts, which sit in each county.

First Judicial Circuit: Choctaw, Clarke and Washington counties; Second Judicial Circuit: Butler, Crenshaw and Lowndes counties; Third Judicial Circuit: Barbour and Bullock counties; Fourth Judicial Circuit: Bibb, Dallas, Hale, Perry and Wilcox counties; Fifth Judicial Circuit: Chambers, Macon, Randolph and Tallapoosa counties; Sixth Judicial Circuit: Tuscaloosa County; Seventh Judicial Circuit: Calhoun and Cleburne counties; Eighth Judicial Circuit: Morgan County; Ninth Judicial Circuit: Cherokee and DeKalb counties; Tenth Judicial Circuit: Jefferson County; Eleventh Judicial Circuit: Lauderdale County; Twelfth Judicial Circuit: Coffee and Pike counties; Thirteenth Judicial Circuit: Mobile County; Fourteenth Judicial Circuit: Walker County; Fifteenth Judicial Circuit: Montgomery County; Sixteenth Judicial Circuit: Etowah County; Seventeenth Judicial Circuit: Greene, Marengo and Sumter counties; Eighteenth Judicial Circuit: Clay, Coosa and Shelby counties; Nineteenth Judicial Circuit: Autauga, Chilton and Elmore counties; Twentieth Judicial Circuit: Henry and Houston counties; Twenty-first Judicial Circuit: Escambia County; Twenty-second Judicial Circuit: Covington County; Twenty-third Judicial Circuit: Madison County; Twenty-fourth Judicial Circuit: Fayette, Lamar and Pickens counties; Twenty-fifth Judicial Circuit: Marion and Winston counties; Twenty-sixth Judicial Circuit: Russell County; Twenty-seventh Judicial Circuit: Marshall County; Twenty-eighth Judicial Circuit: Baldwin County; Twenty-ninth Judicial Circuit: Talladega County; Thirtieth Judicial Circuit: Blount and Saint Clair counties; Thirty-first Judicial Circuit: Colbert County; Thirty-second Judicial Circuit: Cullman County; Thirty-third Judicial Circuit: Dale and Geneva counties; Thirty-fourth Judicial Circuit: Franklin County; Thirty-fifth Judicial Circuit: Conecuh and Monroe counties; Thirty-sixth Judicial Circuit: Lawrence County; Thirty-seventh Judicial Circuit: Lee County; Thirty-eighth Judicial Circuit: Jackson County; Thirty-ninth Judicial Circuit: Limestone County.

Appeals from the Circuit Courts go to either the Court of Criminal Appeals at Montgomery or the Court of Civil Appeals at Montgomery or other locations at the court's discretion. Some appeals from the Circuit Courts and all those from the Appeals Courts go to the Supreme Court, which sits at Montgomery or elsewhere.

Courthouses

Autauga County Courthouse
Fourth and Court Streets
PO Box 488
Prattville, AL 36067-0488
Phone (205) 365-2281
County organized 1818 from Montgomery County

*Baldwin County Courthouse
Courthouse Square
PO Box 239
Bay Minette, AL 36507-0239
Phone (205) 937-9561
County organized 1809 from Washington County
Land records: From 1810
Naturalization records: No naturalization records
Vital records: No vital records
Probate records: From 1810
No probate search service; copies: $1.00 per page, no minimum

Barbour County Courthouse
1800 Fifth Avenue, North
PO Box 398
Clayton, AL 36016
Phone (205) 775-3203
County organized 1832 from Pike County and Original Territory

Benton County
(see Calhoun County)

Bibb County Courthouse
Centreville, AL 35042
Phone (205) 926-4747
County organized 1818 from Monroe and Montgomery counties

*Blount County Courthouse
220 Second Avenue, East
PO Box 668
Oneonta, AL 35212-9111
Phone (205) 625-4222
County organized 1818 from Montgomery County
Land records: Contact Warren Weaver, Archivist, PO Box 45, Oneonta, AL 35121
Naturalization records: No naturalization records
Vital records: Marriages from 1820 to date; contact Archivist
Probate records: Contact Archivist

Bullock County Courthouse
PO Box 71
Union Springs, AL 36089-0071
Phone (205) 738-2250
County organized 1866 from Barbour, Macon, Montgomery and Pike counties

*Butler County Courthouse
700 Courthouse Square
PO Box 756
Greenville, AL 36037-2326
Phone (205) 382-3512
County organized 1819 from Conecuh and Montgomery counties
Land records: From 1853
Vital records: Births and deaths from 1899 to 1919
Probate records: From 1853; copies: $1.00 (includes search), no minimum

*Calhoun County Administrative Building
1702 Noble Street, Suite 102
Anniston, AL 36201
Phone (205) 236-8231 Probate Court
County organized 1832 from Creek Cession, name changed from Benton County 1858
Land records: Deeds from 1865
Naturalization records: No naturalization records
Vital records: Marriages from 1834
Probate records: Probate records, probate minutes from 1850s
No probate search service; copies: 50¢ per page

*Chambers County Courthouse
Court Square
Lafayette, AL 36862
Phone (334) 644-1224
County organized 1832 from Creek Cession
Land records: Contact Ruth Crump, 212 South Fifth Avenue, Lanett, AL 36863
Naturalization records: Contact Ruth Crump
Vital records: Contact Ruth Crump
Probate records: Contact Ruth Crump

*Cherokee County Courthouse
Main Street
Centre, AL 35960
Phone (205) 927-3363; (205) 927-3378

County organized 1836 from Cherokee Cession
Land records: Deeds and mortgages 1882 to present
Vital records: Marriages, but no births
Probate records: Yes
No probate search service; copies: $1.00 per page

Chilton County Courthouse
Second Avenue North
PO Box 557
Clanton, AL 35045-0057
Phone (205) 755-1551
County organized 1868 from Bibb, Perry, Autauga and Shelby counties; name changed from Baker County in 1874

*Choctaw County Courthouse
117 South Mulberry
Butler, AL 36904-2523
Phone (205) 459-2417
County organized 1847 from Sumter and Washington counties
Land records: From 1873
Probate records: From 1873
No probate search service; copies: 50¢ per page

*Clarke County Courthouse
117 Court Street
PO Box 548
Grove Hill, AL 36451-0548
Phone (205) 275-3251; (205) 275-3507
County organized 1812 from Washington County
Land records: Contact Probate Office
Naturalization records: No naturalization records
Vital records: No vital records
Probate records: Contact Probate Office
No probate search service; copies: $1.00 per page for each of the first ten pages and 50¢ for each additional page

*Clay County Courthouse
Courthouse Square
PO Box 187
Ashland, AL 36251
Phone (205) 354-2198
County organized 1866 from Talladega and Randolph counties
Land records: Contact Revenue Commission, (205) 354-7310
Naturalization records: Contact Circuit Clerk, (205) 354-7926
Probate records: Contact Judge, (205) 354-2198
No probate search service; copies: 25¢ per page, no minimum

*Cleburne County Courthouse
406 Vickery Street
Heflin, AL 36264
Phone (205) 463-5655; (205) 463-2651

County organized 1866 from Calhoun and Randolph counties
Land records: No land records
Naturalization records: No naturalization records
Vital records: No vital records
Probate records: Yes
No probate search service; copies: $1.00 per page

*Coffee County Courthouse
230 Court Street
Elba, AL 36323
Phone (205) 897-2211; (205) 897-2954
County organized 1841 from Dale County
Land records: Some from 1823
Naturalization records: No naturalization records
Vital records: Marriages from 1877
Probate records: Wills from early 1900s, probate minutes from 1861; contact Judge William O. Gammill
No probate search service; copies: varies, usually about $1.00 per page, no minimum

*Colbert County Courthouse
201 North Main Street
Tuscumbia, AL 35674-2042
Phone (205) 383-6353; (205) 383-4272
County organized 1867 from Franklin County
Land records: From 1867
Naturalization records: No naturalization records
Vital records: No vital records
Probate records: From 1861
No probate search service; copies: 50¢ per page, $2.00 for certified copies, no minimum

Conecuh County Courthouse
Court Square
Evergreen, AL 36401
Phone (205) 578-1221; (205) 578-2095
County organized 1818 from Monroe County

*Coosa County Courthouse
PO Box 218
Rockford, AL 35136
Phone (205) 362-5721; (205) 377-2420; (205) 377-4919
County organized 1832 from Creek Cession
Land records: From 1834
Vital records: Marriages from 1834 (published through 1865)
Probate records: From 1834
No probate search service; copies: $1.00 per page by mail, 50¢ in person (if researcher makes copies)

Covington County Courthouse
1 Court Square
Andalusia, AL 36420

Phone (205) 222-3189; (205) 222-4313
County organized 1821 from Henry County

*Crenshaw County Courthouse
Glenwood Avenue
Luverne, AL 36049
Phone (334) 335-6568, ext. 101 Probate Office
County organized 1866 from Covington, Butler, Coffee, Lowndes and Pike counties
Land records: From 1866
Naturalization records: No naturalization records
Vital records: Some vital records at County Health Office
Probate records: Contact Probate Office, Glenwood Avenue, PO Box 328, Luverne, AL 36049-0328
Probate search service: $5.00; copies: $1.00 each, $2.00 for certified copies, no minimum

*Cullman County Commission
c/o Ms. Dean Jacobs, Clerk/ Administrator
500 Second Avenue, S.W.
PO Box 698
Cullman, AL 35056-0698
Phone (205) 739-3530
County organized 1877 from Blount, Morgan and Winston counties
Land records: Contact Revenue Commissioner, Louis Moore
Naturalization records: From 1883 to 1912; contact Circuit Clerk, Sandra Smith
Vital records: Contact Cullman County Health Department, PO Box 1678, Cullman, AL 35056
Probate records: Contact Probate Judge, Betty Brewer
Charges for probate search and copy services vary

*Dale County Courthouse
PO Box 246
Ozark, AL 36360-0246
Phone (205) 774-2754; (205) 774-6025
County organized 1824 from Covington and Henry counties
Land records: From 1884 (earlier records destroyed in fire)
Naturalization records: No naturalization records
Vital records: From 1884
Probate records: From 1884
No probate search service; copies: $1.00 per page, no minimum

*Dallas County Courthouse
105 Lauderdale Street
PO Box 997
Selma, AL 36702-0997
Phone (334) 874-2500

County organized 1818 from Montgomery County
Land records: Contact Probate Judge, Recording Office
Vital records: Contact Dallas County Health Department, Selma, AL
Probate records: Contact Probate Judge's Office; copies: $1.50 per page for each of the first twenty pages and $1.00 for each additional page, $2.00 for certification

DeKalb County Courthouse
300 Grand Avenue, South
Fort Payne, AL 35967
Phone (205) 845-0404
County organized 1836 from Cherokee Cession

Elmore County Courthouse
PO Box 280
Wetumpka, AL 36092-0280
Phone (205) 567-2571
County organized 1866 from Montgomery, Coosa and Autauga counties, and from Tallapoosa County in 1867
Land records: Yes
Vital records: Marriages
Probate records: Yes; copies: 50¢ per page

Escambia County Courthouse
Belleville Avenue
PO Box 848
Brewton, AL 36427-0848
Phone (205) 867-3252; (205) 867-6261
County organized 1868 from Baldwin and Conecuh counties

Etowah County Courthouse
800 Forrest Avenue
Gadsden, AL 35901-3641
Phone (205) 546-2821
County organized 1867 from Blount, Calhoun, Cherokee, DeKalb, Marshall and Saint Clair counties, formerly Baine County
Land records: Contact Bobby M. Junkins, Judge of Probate, PO Box 187, Gadsden, AL 35902
Naturalization records: Contact Judge of Probate
Vital records: Contact Judge of Probate
Probate records: Contact Judge of Probate

Fayette County Courthouse
113 North Temple Avenue
PO Box 509
Fayette, AL 35555-0509
Phone (205) 932-4519
County organized 1824 from Marion and Pickens counties
Land records: Contact Probate Office

Naturalization records: Contact Probate Office
Vital records: No births or deaths
Probate records: Contact Probate Office

Franklin County Courthouse
410 Jackson Street
PO Box 1438
Russellville, AL 35653
Phone (205) 332-1210
County organized 1818 from Cherokee Cession
Land records: Contact Judge Hal Kirby
Naturalization records: No naturalization records
Vital records: No vital records
Probate records: Contact Judge Hal Kirby
Probate search service: $4.00; copies: $1.00 per page for each of the first ten pages and 50¢ for each additional page if the staff looks them up

Geneva County Probate Office
Recording Clerk, R. Milton
PO Box 430
Geneva, AL 36340-0340
Phone (205) 684-2276
County organized 1868 from Coffee, Dale and Henry counties
Land records: From 1898
Vital records: Marriages from 1898
Probate records: From 1898
No probate search service; copies: $1.00 per page

Greene County Courthouse
440 Morrow Avenue
PO Box 790
Eutaw, AL 35462
Phone (205) 372-3340
County organized 1819 from Marengo and Tuscaloosa counties
Land records: Deeds and mortgages from 1820
Naturalization records: No naturalization records
Vital records: No vital records
Probate records: From 1820
Probate search service: $2.00; copies: 50¢ per page, $2.50 if certified, minimum $2.00 by correspondence

Hale County Courthouse
1001 Main Street
PO Box 396
Greensboro, AL 36744-0396
Phone (334) 624-8740; (334) 624-4257
County organized 1867 from Greene, Marengo and Perry counties

Henry County Courthouse
PO Box 337
Abbeville, AL 36310-0337
Phone (205) 585-3257; (205) 585-2753

County organized 1819 from Conecuh County

Houston County Courthouse
100 North Oates Street
Dothan, AL 36302-6406
Phone (205) 793-1114; (205) 677-4700
County organized 1903 from Dale, Geneva and Henry counties

Jackson County Courthouse
Courthouse Square
PO Box 128
Scottsboro, AL 35768
Phone (205) 574-3116; (205) 574-2231
County organized 1819 from Cherokee Cession
Land records: From 1830, including mortgages and miscellany; contact R. I. Gentry, Judge of Probate
Vital records: Scattered unindexed births from 1920 to 1934, unindexed births and deaths from 1892 to 1896, marriages from 1851; contact Judge of Probate
Probate records: From 1850; contact Judge of Probate
No probate search service; copies: $1.00 per page, no minimum

Jefferson County Courthouse
716 North 21st Street
Birmingham, AL 35263-0068
Phone (205) 325-5512
County organized 1819 from Blount County
Land records: Deeds and mortgages from 1812; contact Probate Court, Probate Records Room; copies: $1.00 per page plus SASE, $2.00 per document for certification
Vital records: Marriages from 1818; contact Probate Court; copies: $1.00 per page plus SASE, $2.00 per document for certification
Probate records: From 1818; contact Probate Record Room
No probate search service without date; copies: $1.00 per page plus SASE, $2.00 per document for certification, no minimum

Lamar County Courthouse
Pond Street
PO Box 338
Vernon, AL 35592-0338
Phone (205) 695-9119
County organized 1867 from Marion, Pickens and Fayette counties
Land records: Yes
Probate records: Yes

Lauderdale County Courthouse
South Court Street
PO Box 1059
Florence, AL 35631-1059

Phone (205) 760-5800; (205) 766-5180
County organized 1818 from Cherokee Cession
Land records: Yes
Naturalization records: No naturalization records
Vital records: Marriages only
Probate records: Yes
No probate search service; copies: $1.00 per page, no minimum

*Lawrence County Courthouse
14330 Court Street
Moulton, AL 35650
Phone (205) 974-0663; (205) 974-2439 Probate Judge's Office; (205) 974-1757 Historical Commission
County organized 1818 from Cherokee Cession
Probate records: Probate Judge's Office
No probate search service (contact Lawrence County Historical Commission, 698 Main Street, PO Box 728, Moulton, AL 35650)

Lee County Courthouse
South Ninth Street
PO Box 666
Opelika, AL 36801-0666
Phone (205) 745-4641; (205) 745-9767
County organized 1866 from Chambers and Macon counties

*Limestone County Archives
310 West Washington Street
Athens, AL 35611
Phone (205) 233-6404
County organized 1818 from Cherokee and Chickasaw cessions
Land records: From 1818 to 1900
Naturalization records: From 1818 to 1900
Vital records: From 1881 to 1919
Probate records: From 1818 to 1900
The Archives is the official depository for the Probate Court, Circuit Court, County Commission, Board of Education, Tax Assessor and Board of Registrars. It also has a collection of private, church and organizational records. They have family name files as well as historic photographs and other collections

*Lowndes County Courthouse
PO Box 5
Hayneville, AL 36040
Phone (205) 584-2365 Probate Office; (205) 584-2331
County organized 1830 from Butler and Dallas counties
Land records: Yes; copies: $1.00 per page
Naturalization records: No naturalization records

Vital records: Marriages from the 1830s; certified copies: $1.00 per page plus $3.00 for certification
Probate records: Yes; copies: $1.00 per page

*Macon County Courthouse
Judge of Probate
Suite 101
Tuskegee, AL 36083
Phone (334) 724-2611
County organized 1832 from Creek Cession
Land records: From 1832
Vital records: Marriages from 1832
Probate records: From 1832
Probate search service: $5.00; copies: $1.00 per page

Madison County Courthouse
717 Randolph Avenue, SE
Huntsville, AL 35801-3606
Phone (205) 532-3330
County organized 1808 from Cherokee Cession

*Marengo County Courthouse
101 East Coats Avenue
Linden, AL 36748-1546
Phone (205) 295-5226; (205) 295-8709
County organized 1818 from Choctaw Cession
Land records: Deed and mortgage records from 1818
Naturalization records: No naturalization records
Vital records: No vital records
Probate records: Wills, administrations and guardianships
Probate search service: $5.00; copies: $1.00 per page, no minimum

*Marion County Courthouse
Military Street
Hamilton, AL 35570
Phone (205) 921-2471; (205) 921-7451
County organized 1818 from Indian Lands
Land records: Contact Annette Bozeman, Judge of Probate, PO Box 1687, Courthouse, Hamilton, AL 35570
Naturalization records: Contact Judge of Probate
Vital records: Contact Judge of Probate
Probate records: Contact Judge of Probate

*Marshall County Courthouse
425 Gunter Avenue
Guntersville, AL 35976
Phone (205) 571-7767; (205) 571-7768; (205) 571-7764 Probate
County organized 1836 from Blount County and Cherokee Cession

*Mobile County Probate Court
PO Box 7
Mobile, AL 36601
Phone (334) 690-8508 Probate Court; (334) 690-4737 FAX, Probate Court
County created by proclamation 18 December 1812 by Governor Holmes of the Mississippi Territory; on 13 April 1813 Major General James Wilkinson took possession of Mobile when the Spanish, who did not recognize the Louisiana Purchase, surrendered at Fort Charlotte
Land records: Deeds from 25 May 1813 through 12 September 1958, real property records from 12 September 1958 to date (earliest land record is a Spanish Land Grant circa 1715), miscellaneous books from 12 Jan 1819 through 12 September 1958 (including early records of slave sales as well as some contracts for house and building plans); contact Ms. Judith A. Busby, Supervisor, Micrographics/Record/Archive Departments
Naturalization records: From September 1906 from Immigration and Naturalization, PO Box 1526, Mobile, AL 36633
Vital records: No births and deaths; white marriage licenses from 3 March 1813, colored marriage licenses from 29 May 1865; contact Micrographics/Record/Archive Departments
Probate records: Will books from 22 September 1812 to date, judicial records from 1819 (containing wills, estate cases, any judicial occurrence); contact Micrographics/Record/Archive Departments
No probate search service; copies: $1.00 per page for each of the first ten pages and 50¢ per page thereafter per instrument; pay by money order or cashier's check only

*Monroe County Courthouse
PO Box 8
Monroeville, AL 36461-0008
Phone (334) 743-4107 Probate Office; (334) 575-7433 Heritage Museums
County organized 1815 from Creek Cession of 1814 and Washington County
Land records: Mortgages and deeds from about 1830; contact Matthew W. Rhodes, Archivist, Monroe County Heritage Museums, PO Box 1637, Monroeville, AL 36461-1637
Probate records: Wills, estates and inventories from about 1830; contact Probate Records Office or Heritage Museums

Montgomery County Courthouse
251 South Lawrence Street
PO Box 1667

Montgomery, AL 36195-2501
Phone (205) 832-4950
County organized 1816 from Monroe County

*Morgan County Courthouse
302 Lee Street, N.E.
PO Box 668
Decatur, AL 35602-0668
Phone (205) 350-9600; (205) 350-4678 Probate Office
County organized 1818 from Indian Lands; name changed from Cotaco County in 1821
Land records: Deeds, mortgages, plats, original land survey from 1819 to date; contact Probate Office, 302 Lee Street, N.E., PO Box 848, Decatur, AL 35602
Vital records: Incomplete births and deaths from 1893 to 1912, marriages from 1821 to date (black marriages from 1865 to the 1920s); contact Probate Office. Births and deaths from 1908; contact Alabama Department of Public Health, Center for Health Statistics, PO Box 5625, Montgomery, AL 36130-5625
Probate records: Wills from 1819 to date
No probate search service; copies: $1.00 per page (records indexed in-house, but indices are not available in a published form, except through private compilations by the local genealogical society)

*Perry County Courthouse
PO Box 478
Marion, AL 36756-0478
Phone (205) 683-2210; (205) 683-2211
County organized 1819 from Tuscaloosa County
Land records: Yes
Naturalization records: Yes
Vital records: No birth or death records
Probate records: Yes

*Pickens County Courthouse
PO Box 370
Carrollton, AL 35447
Phone (205) 367-2010
County organized 1820 from Tuscaloosa County
Land records: From 1876
Naturalization records: No naturalization records
Vital records: No vital records
Probate records: From 1876
No probate search service; copies: 50¢ per page, no minimum

*Pike County Courthouse
PO Box 1008
Troy, AL 36081
Phone (334) 566-1246
County organized 1821 from Henry and Montgomery counties

Land records: From 1830
Naturalization records: No naturalization records
Probate records: Some wills and estate records
No probate search service; copies: 50¢ per page, no minimum

*Randolph County Courthouse
Main Street
PO Box 328
Wedowee, AL 36278-0328
Phone (205) 357-4933 Probate Judge; (205) 357-4551
County organized 1832 from Creek Cession
Land records: From early 1900s; contact Probate Judge
Probate records: From early 1900s; contact Probate Judge

*Russell County Courthouse
14th Street
PO Box 700
Phenix City, AL 36868-0700
Phone (205) 297-1347
County organized 1832 from Creek Cession
Land records: Real estate deeds, mortgages, etc.
Naturalization records: No naturalization records
Vital records: Marriages
Probate records: Wills, guardianships, veterans' discharges, bonds, miscellaneous
No probate search service; copies: $1.00 per page, no minimum

*Saint Clair County Courthouse
Sixth Avenue
PO Box 397
Ashville, AL 35953-0397
Phone (205) 594-5114; (205) 594-5116; (205) 594-2120 Office of Judge of Probate
County organized 1818 from Shelby County
Land records: From 1818
Vital records: Marriages from 1818 to date; contact Johnnie H. Bagwell, Probate Clerk, PO Box 220, Ashville, AL 35953-0220
Probate records: Estate records from 1818; contact Probate Clerk

*Shelby County Courthouse
Main Street
Columbiana, AL 35051-1627
Phone (205) 669-3713 Judge of Probate; (205) 669-4895; (205) 669-4651
County organized 1818 from Montgomery County
Land records: Deeds and mortgages; contact Recording Office, PO Box 825, Columbiana, AL 35051

Probate records: Contact Judge of Probate, PO Box 825, Columbiana, AL 35051

*Sumter County Courthouse
Circuit Clerk's Office
PO Box 936
Livingston, AL 35470-0936
Phone (205) 652-7281 Probate Judge; (205) 652-2291 Circuit Clerk; (205) 652-2424 Tax Collector; (205) 652-7972 County Health Department
County organized 1832 from Choctaw Cession
Land records: Contact Edmond Bell, Tax Collector, PO Box 277, Livingston, AL 35470
Vital records: Contact County Health Department
Probate records: Contact Judge Willie Pearl Watkins Rice, PO Box 1040, Livingston, AL 35470

Talladega County Courthouse
Court Square
PO Box 755
Talladega, AL 35160-0755
Phone (205) 362-4175
County organized 1832 from Creek Cession

Tallapoosa County Courthouse
Dadeville, AL 36853
Phone (205) 825-4266; (205) 825-4268
County organized 1832 from Chicksaw Cession

*Tuscaloosa County Courthouse
714 Greensboro Avenue
Tuscaloosa, AL 35401-1847
Phone (205) 349-3870
County organized 1818 from Indian Lands
Land records: From 1818
Naturalization records: No naturalization records
Vital records: Marriages from 1823
Probate records: From 1821; contact Record Room Probate Office
No probate search service; copies: $1.00 per page, no minimum

*Walker County Courthouse
19th Street
PO Box 749
Jasper, AL 35501-0749
Phone (205) 384-5531; (205) 384-3404; (205) 384-7281 Judge of Probate
County organized 26 December 1823 from Marion and Tuscaloosa counties
Land records: From about 1877; contact Rick Allison, Judge of Probate, PO Box 502, Jasper, AL 35502-0502; copies: $1.00 per page
Naturalization records: No naturalization records

Vital records: Marriages from about
    1877; contact Judge of Probate;
    copies: $2.50 each, $1.00 for
    certification
Probate records: From about 1877;
    contact Judge of Probate; copies:
    $1.50 per page

*Washington County Courthouse
PO Box 549
Chatom, AL 36518
Phone (205) 847-2201; (205) 847-2208
*County organized 1800, original county,
    formed from Mississippi Territory*
Vital records: Marriages from 1826
Probate records: Yes
Probate search service: $5.00 per
    surname from Mrs. Barbara Waddell,
    PO Box 421, Chatom, AL 36518,
    (205) 847-3156; copies: $1.00 per
    page

Wilcox County Courthouse
PO Box 656
Camden, AL 36726
Phone (205) 682-4881; (205) 682-4126
*County organized 1819 from Dallas and
    Monroe counties*

Winston County Courthouse
PO Box 309
Double Springs, AL 35553-0309
Phone (205) 489-5219; (205) 489-5533
*County organized 1858 from Walker
    County*

ALASKA

*Capital: Juneau. Statehood: 3 January
1959 (ceded by Russia by treaty in 1867,
organized in 1884, obtained territorial
status in 1884)*

Court System

Magistrate Courts in many Alaskan cities handle small civil cases, small claims
and misdemeanors. District Courts handle
larger civil actions and misdemeanors. The
first Judicial District Court sits at Juneau
and Ketchikan. The Second Judicial District jurisdiction is handled by the Superior
Court. The Third Judicial District Court sits
at Anchorage and Homer. And the Fourth
Judicial District Court sits at Fairbanks.

Fifteen Superior Courts have jurisdiction over all civil and criminal matters, including probate, guardianship, and domestic relations. They are included in the four
Judicial Districts: First Judicial District (the
"Panhandle" area in southeastern Alaska);
Second Judicial District (Northwest Alaska
and the North Slope region); Third Judicial District (Aleutian Chain, the Bristol
Bay region, the greater Anchorage region,
Kenai Peninsula, Kodiak, Matanuska Valley and the Prince William Sound-Copper
River region); Fourth Judicial District (in-
terior Alaska).

A Court of Appeals in Anchorage and
Fairbanks hears appeals from the Superior
Courts, and a Supreme Court in Anchorage, Fairbanks, Juneau and occasionally in
other locations is the court of last resort.

The following boroughs or reservations
were organized after statehood in lieu of
counties: Aleutian Islands, Anchorage,
Angoon, Barrow, Bethel, Bristol Bay,
Cordova-McCarthy, Fairbanks, Haines,
Juneau, Kenai-Matanuska-Susitna, Nome,
Outer Ketchikan, Prince of Wales, Seward,
Sitka, Skagway-Yakutat, Southeast
Fairbanks, Upper Yukon, Valdez-Chitina-
Whittier, Wade-Hampton, Wrangell-Peters-
burg, and Yukon-Koyukuk.

Courthouses

*First Judicial District
Court and Office Building
Juneau, AK 99811
Phone (907) 465-3420
Land records: Contact Bureau of Land
    Management, Washington, DC, or The
    National Archives—Pacific-Northwest
    Region, Seattle, WA, or Bureau of

Land Management, Anchorage
    Federal Office Building, 701 C Street,
    Anchorage, AK 99513, or Division of
    Lands, Department of Natural
    Resources, Anchorage, AK 99501
Naturalization records: No naturalization
    records
Vital records: No vital records
Probate records: Yes
Probate search service: $3.00 by
    correspondence only; copies: 20¢ per
    page from paper originals, $1.25 per
    page from microfilm originals, no
    minimum

Second Judicial District
Box 100
Nome, AK 99762-0100
Phone (907) 443-5216
Land records: Contact Bureau of Land
    Management, Washington, DC, or The
    National Archives—Pacific-Northwest
    Region, Seattle, WA, or Bureau of
    Land Management, Anchorage
    Federal Office Building, 701 C Street,
    Anchorage, AK 99513, or Division of
    Lands, Department of Natural
    Resources, Anchorage, AK 99501

*Third Judicial District
303 K Street
Anchorage, AK 99501-2083
Phone (907) 264-0401
Land records: Contact Bureau of Land
    Management, Washington, DC, or The
    National Archives—Pacific-Northwest
    Region, Seattle, WA, or Bureau of
    Land Management, Anchorage
    Federal Office Building, 701 C Street,
    Anchorage, AK 99513, or Division of
    Lands, Department of Natural
    Resources, Anchorage, AK 99501
Naturalization records: No naturalization
    records
Vital records: Contact Sandra
    Weatherman, Supervisor; marriages
    and deaths are not open to the public
    for fifty years, births for 100 years;
    inquirer must prove relationship to the
    subject of inquiry prior to the fifty- or
    100-year period
Probate records: Contact Kathleen
    Harrington, Probate Master
Probate search service: varies; copies:
    20¢ per page, $5.00 for certified
    copies, $7.00 for authenticated copies,
    no minimum; requests must be in
    writing, including as much
    information as possible.

*Fourth Judicial District
604 Barnette Street, Room 342
Fairbanks, AK 99701-4569
Phone (907) 452-9317
Land records: Contact Bureau of Land
    Management, Washington, DC, or The
    National Archives—Pacific-Northwest

Region, Seattle, WA, or Bureau of
Land Management, Anchorage
Federal Office Building, 701 C Street,
Anchorage, AK 99513, or Division of
Lands, Department of Natural
Resources, Anchorage, AK 99501, or
Fairbanks Recorder's Office, 210
Cushman, Fairbanks, AK 99701
Naturalization records: Contact U.S.
District Court, 101 12th Avenue,
Fairbanks, AK 99701
Vital records: Contact Courthouse,
Coroner's Office, 604 Barnette Street,
Fairbanks, AK 99701
Probate records: Contact Courthouse,
Probate Office, 604 Barnette Street,
Fairbanks, AK 99701
Probate search service: $3.00; copies:
20¢ per page, $3.00 for certified
copies.

ARIZONA

*Capital: Phoenix. Statehood: 14 February
1912 (annexed through the Treaty of
Guadalupe-Hidalgo, 1848, and the
Gadsden Purchase, 1853, organized as a
territory in 1863)*

Court System

Arizona's Municipal Courts and Justices
of the Peace handle civil actions and misdemeanors. Superior Courts in each county
have jurisdiction over probate and domestic relations. Appeals are made to one of
two Courts of Appeal. Division One includes Apache, Coconino, La Paz,
Maricopa, Mohave, Navajo, Yavapai and
Yuma counties and sits at Phoenix and elsewhere as needed. Division Two includes
Cochise, Gila, Graham, Greenlee, Pima,
Pinal and Santa Cruz counties and sits in
Tucson and elsewhere. The state's Supreme
Court is the court of last resort and sits in
Phoenix.

Courthouses

Apache County Courthouse
75 West Cleveland Street
PO Box 667
Saint Johns, AZ 85936
Phone (602) 337-4364
*County organized 1879 from Mohave
County*

*Cochise County Superior Court
PO Drawer CK
Bisbee, AZ 85603
Phone (520) 432-9364
*County organized 1881 from Pima
County*
Land records: Contact Recorder
Naturalization records: Contact Denise
Lundin Glass, Clerk of the Superior
Court
Naturalization records search service:
$11.00 per year or source; copies: 50¢
per page, $11.00 for certification, no
minimum
Vital records: Yes
Vital records search service: $11.00 per
year or source; copies: 50¢ per page,
$11.00 for certification, no minimum
Probate records: Yes
Probate search service: $11.00 per year
or source; copies: 50¢ per page,
$11.00 for certification, no minimum

*Coconino County Courthouse
100 East Birch
Flagstaff, AZ 86001-4696
Phone (602) 779-6585 County
Recorder's Office
*County organized 1891 from Yavapai
County*
Land records: Contact County Recorder's
Office; copies: $1.00 per page, $3.00
per document for certification
Naturalization records: No naturalization
records
Vital records: No vital records
Probate records: From 1891; contact
Superior Court's Office
Probate search service: $3.00 per year;
copies: 50¢ per page, $3.00 minimum

Gila County Courthouse
1400 East Ash Street
Globe, AZ 85501-1414
Phone (602) 425-3231
*County organized 1881 from Maricopa
and Pinal counties*

*Graham County Courthouse
800 Main Street
Safford, AZ 85546-2828
Phone (602) 428-3310; (602) 428-3250
*County organized 1881 from Apache
and Pima counties*
Land records: Contact Recorder
Probate records: Contact Amelia Sainz,
Clerk of the Superior Court
Probate search service: $11.50 per year;
copies: $1.25 per page, no minimum

*Greenlee County Courthouse
Webster Street
PO Box 1027
Clifton, AZ 85533
Phone (602) 865-3872; (602) 865-4242
*County organized 1909 from Graham
County*
Probate records: Yes
Probate search service: $3.00 per year;
copies: 50¢ per page, no minimum

LaPaz County Courthouse
PO Box 729
Parker, AZ 85344
Phone (602) 669-6134
*County organized 1983 from Yuma
County*

**Maricopa County Central Court
Building**
201 West Jefferson Street
Phoenix, AZ 85003
Phone (602) 262-3916; (602) 262-3011
*County organized 1871 from Yavapai
and Yuma counties*

*Mohave County
Clerk of Superior Court

401 East Spring Street
Kingman, AZ 86401
Phone (602) 753-9141
*County organized 1864, original county,
and in 1871 annexed Pah-Ute
County, which had been organized in
1865*
Land records: Contact Mohave County
Recorder
Naturalization records: No naturalization
records
Vital records: Marriages and divorces;
contact Clerk
Probate records: Contact Clerk
Probate search service: $3.00 per year;
copies: 50¢ per page, no minimum

Navajo County Courthouse
PO Box 668
Holbrook, AZ 86025
Phone (602) 524-6161
County organized 1870, original county

*Pima County Courthouse
131 West Congress Street
Tucson, AZ 85701-1707
Phone (602) 792-8011
County organized 1870, original county
Land records: Property ownership
records from 1924; contact The
Assessor's Office. The Pima County
Recorder has grantor/grantee index
from 1912 (statehood) in the "old"
Courthouse, 115 North Church,
Tucson, AZ 85701
Naturalization records: Contact Office of
Immigration and Naturalization, 300
West Congress Street, Tucson, AZ
85701
Vital records: Marriage licenses; contact
Clerk of the Superior Court, Probate
Division, Pima County Superior
Courts Building, 110 West Congress,
Tucson, AZ 85701-1317. Births and
deaths: contact Pima County Health
and Welfare, 150 West Congress,
Tucson, AZ 85701; copies: $11.50
plus $3.50 postage for certified copies
of marriage licenses
Probate records: Contact Clerk of the
Superior Court
Probate search service: $11.50; copies:
$1.15 per page, rounded up to next
quarter dollar, $1.25 minimum, plus
$3.50 postage

*Pinal County Courthouse
PO Box 827
Florence, AZ 85232-0827
Phone (602) 868-5801; (602) 868-6296
Probate Desk
*County organized 1875 from Pima
County*
Land records: Contact Recorder or
Assessor
Probate records: Contact Alma Jennings
Haught, Clerk of the Superior Court,

PO Box 889, Florence, AZ 85232-
0889
Probate search service: $11.50 per source
(each docket book for records before
1985 or computer index from 1985 to
date); copies: $1.15 per page
(cashier's check or money order only),
no minimum

*Santa Cruz County Courthouse
Court Street and Morley Avenue
PO Box 1265
Nogales, AZ 85628-1265
Phone (602) 287-2221; (602) 287-9297
*County organized 1899 from Pima
County*
Naturalization records: From 18 July
1899 through 25 May 1984; copies:
$1.15 per page, rounded up to next
quarter dollar, $1.25 minimum, plus
$3.50 postage
Vital records: Marriage licenses and
applications; certified copies: $11.50
each plus $3.50 postage
Probate records: From 9 May 1899
Probate search service: $3.00 per year;
copies: $1.15 per page, $1.25
minimum, plus $3.50 postage

Yavapai County Courthouse
225 Gurley
Prescott, AZ 86301-3803
Phone (602) 445-7450
County organized 1860, original county

Yuma County Courthouse
168 South Second Avenue
PO Box 1112
Yuma, AZ 85364-0191
Phone (602) 782-4534
County organized 1864, original county

ARKANSAS

*Capital: Little Rock. Statehood: 15 June
1836 (Arkansas Territory organized 1819
from parts of Louisiana and Missouri
territories)*

Court System

Arkansas has several courts of limited
jurisdiction: Police Courts, City Courts,
Municipal Courts, Courts of Common
Pleas, and County Courts. The last have
jurisdiction in county taxes, county expen-
ditures and claims against the county as
well as bastardy proceedings and juvenile
cases.

Twenty-four Chancery and Probate
Courts, sitting in each county, have jurisdiction in land disputes, domestic relations,
probate matters and adoptions. Twenty-four
Circuit Courts also meet in each county and
have jurisdiction over civil and criminal
cases. First Judicial Circuit: Cross, Lee,
Monroe, Phillips, Saint Francis and Woodruff counties; Second Judicial Circuit:
Clay, Craighead, Crittenden, Greene, Mississippi and Poinsett counties; Third Judicial Circuit: Jackson, Lawrence, Randolph
and Sharp counties; Fourth Judicial Circuit:
Madison and Washington counties; Fifth
Judicial Circuit: Franklin, Johnson and
Pope counties; Sixth Judicial Circuit: Perry
and Pulaski counties; Seventh Judicial Cir-
cuit: Grant, Hot Spring and Saline coun-
ties; Eighth Judicial Circuit: Hempstead,
Lafayette, Miller and Nevada counties;
Ninth Judicial Circuit-East: Clark and Pike
counties; Ninth Judicial Circuit-West:
Howard, Little River and Sevier counties;
Tenth Judicial Circuit: Ashley, Bradley,
Chicot, Desha and Drew counties; Eleventh
Judicial Circuit-East: Arkansas County;
Eleventh Judicial Circuit-West: Jefferson
and Lincoln counties; Twelfth Judicial Cir-
cuit: Crawford and Sebastian counties;
Thirteenth Judicial Circuit: Calhoun, Cleve-
land, Columbia, Dallas, Ouachita and
Union counties; Fourteenth Judicial Circuit:
Baxter, Boone, Marion and Newton counties; Fifteenth Judicial Circuit: Conway,
Logan, Scott and Yell counties; Sixteenth
Judicial Circuit: Cleburne, Fulton, Independence, Izard and Stone counties; Seventeenth Judicial Circuit-East: Prairie and
White counties; Seventeenth Judicial Circuit-West: Lonoke County; Eighteenth Judicial Circuit-East: Garland County; Eighteenth Judicial Circuit-West: Montgomery
and Polk counties; Nineteenth Judicial Circuit: Benton and Carroll counties; Twentieth Judicial Circuit: Faulkner, Searcy and
Van Buren counties.

Six District Courts of Appeal sit in any of their respective county seats. District One: Clay, Craighead, Crittenden, Cross, Greene, Lee, Mississippi, Monroe, Phillips, Poinsett, Saint Francis and Woodruff counties; District Two: Baxter, Boone, Cleburne, Faulkner, Fulton, Independence, Izard, Jackson, Lawrence, Lonoke, Marion, Newton, Prairie, Randolph, Searcy, Sharp, Stone, Van Buren and White counties; District Three: Benton, Carroll, Crawford, Franklin, Johnson, Madison, Pope, Sebastian and Washington counties; District Four: Clark, Conway, Garland, Grant, Hempstead, Hot Spring, Howard, Lafayette, Little River, Logan, Miller, Montgomery, Nevada, Pike, Polk, Saline, Scott, Sevier and Yell counties; District Five: Arkansas, Ashley, Bradley, Calhoun, Chicot, Cleveland, Columbia, Dallas, Desha, Drew, Jefferson, Lincoln, Ouachita and Union counties; District Six: Perry and Pulaski counties. A Supreme Court meets in Little Rock.

Courthouses

*Arkansas County Courthouse
101 Court Square
PO Box 719
DeWitt, AR 72042
Phone (501) 946-4321; (501) 673-7311
County organized 1813, original county
Land records: Yes
Naturalization records: Yes
Vital records: Yes
Probate records: Yes

*Ashley County Courthouse
205 East Jefferson Street
Hamburg, AR 71646
Phone (501) 853-5243
County organized 1848 from Union and Drew counties
Land records: From 1849; Circuit Clerk's Office, (501) 853-5113
Naturalization records: No naturalization records
Vital records: Marriages from 1848; contact Sonya Meeks, County Clerk
Probate records: From 1921; index of some before that year; contact County Clerk
No probate search service; copies: 50¢ per page; courthouse burned in 1921

*Baxter County Courthouse
Mountain Home, AR 72653-4065
Phone (501) 425-3475
County organized 1873 from Fulton County
Land records: From 1895
Naturalization records: No naturalization records

Vital records: Marriages and deaths that were recorded
Probate records: From 1895
No probate search service; copies: 25¢ per page, no minimum; adoptions and juvenile records are not public record; courthouse burned in the late 1800s

*Benton County Courthouse
Bentonville, AR 72712-0699
Phone (501) 271-1015 Circuit Clerk and Recorder; (501) 271-1013 County Clerk
County organized 1836 from Washington County
Land records: From 1837 to date; contact Circuit Clerk and Recorder
Land records search service: $3.00; copies: 50¢ per page
Naturalization records: From 1907 to 1929; contact Mary L. Slinkard, County and Probate Clerk
Naturalization records search service: $3.00; copies: 50¢ per page
Vital records: Marriages from 1868 to date; contact County and Probate Clerk
Vital records search service: $3.00; copies: 50¢ per page
Probate records: From 1859 to date, wills from 1837 to date; contact County and Probate Clerk
Probate search service: $3.00; copies: 50¢ per page

Boone County Courthouse
PO Box 846
Harrison, AR 72602-0846
Phone (501) 741-5760; (501) 741-8428
County organized 1869 from Carroll and Marion counties

Bradley County Courthouse
Warren, AR 71671
Phone (501) 226-3853
County organized 1840 from Union County

*Calhoun County Circuit Clerk
PO Box 626
Hampton, AR 71744-0626
Phone (501) 798-2517
County organized 1850 from Dallas, Ouachita and Union counties
Land records: From 1851
Naturalization records: No naturalization records
Vital records: No vital records
Probate records: From 1862
No probate search service; copies: 25¢ per page (50¢ for 11" x 17"), no minimum

*Carroll County Courthouse
210 West Church Street
Berryville, AR 72616-4233

Phone (501) 423-2967
County organized 1833 from Izard County
Land records: From the late 1860s; contact Circuit Clerk
Naturalization records: No naturalization records
Vital records: Marriages; contact County Clerk (Circuit Clerk for divorces)
Probate records: Contact County Clerk
No probate search service; copies: 25¢ each, $3.00 for certified copies, minimum $5.00 if typed

*Chicot County Courthouse
Lake Village, AR 71653
Phone (501) 265-2208
County organized 1823 from Arkansas County
Land records: Contact Harvey Adams, Assessor
Naturalization records: Contact Little Rock, AR 72201
Vital records: No vital records
Probate records: Contact Chicot County Clerk, Lake Village, AR 71653
No probate search service; copies: $3.00 each, $5.00 for certified copies, no minimum; must have a year

*Clark County Courthouse
Arkadelphia, AR 71923
Phone (501) 246-5847; (501) 246-4491
County organized 1818 from Arkansas County
Probate records: Contact Lynda C. Franklin, County and Probate Clerk
Probate search service: no charge; copies: $1.00 per page, $3.00 per certified document, 32¢ postage

*Clay County Courthouse
PO Box 306
Piggott, AR 72454-0306
Phone (501) 598-2667; (501) 598-2813 County and Probate Clerk's Office; (501) 598-2524 Circuit Court Clerk's Office
County organized 1873 from Randolph and Greene counties
Land records: Contact Circuit Court Clerk's Office
Naturalization records: No naturalization records
Vital records: No vital records
Probate records: Contact Charles Pollard, Clay County Clerk and Probate Clerk

*Cleburne County Courthouse
Courthouse Square
PO Box 543
Heber Springs, AR 72543
Phone (501) 362-8149
County organized 1883 from White, Van Buren and Independence counties

Land records: Contact Judith E. Russell, County and Circuit Clerk
Naturalization records: No naturalization records
Vital records: No vital records
Probate records: Contact Judith E. Russell, County and Circuit Clerk
Probate search service: $3.00; copies: 25¢ per page, $3.00 minimum; enclose SASE

*Cleveland County Courthouse
PO Box 368
Rison, AR 71665-0368
Phone (501) 325-6902; (501) 325-6521
County organized 1873 as Dorsey County, renamed 5 March 1885 as Cleveland County, and by provision of the organic act, portions of the counties of Lincoln, Jefferson, Dallas, and Bradley were integrated in the new county
Land records: Yes
Vital records: Marriages only
Probate records: Yes

*Columbia County Courthouse
Magnolia, AR 71753
Phone (501) 234-2542
County organized 1852 from Lafayette County
Land records: Contact Circuit Clerk
Naturalization records: Contact Federal Court
Vital records: Marriage licenses; contact County Clerk
Probate records: Contact County Clerk
Probate search service: $2.00; copies: 50¢ per page

Conway County Courthouse
Morrilton, AR 72110-3427
Phone (501) 354-4506; (501) 354-2561
County organized 1825 from Pulaski County

*Craighead County Courthouse
511 South Main Street
Jonesboro, AR 72401-2849
Phone (501) 933-4500
County formed 19 February 1859 from parts of Greene, Mississippi and Poinsett counties
Land records: Contact Judge Roy C. "Red" Bearden
Vital records: Contact Judge Bearden
Probate records: Contact Judge Bearden; copies: 25¢ per page

*Crawford County Courthouse
Van Buren, AR 72956-5765
Phone (501) 474-1511
County organized 1820 from Pulaski County
Land records: Contact Circuit Clerk

Naturalization records: No naturalization records in Courthouse
Vital records: Marriages; contact County Clerk
Probate records: Contact County Clerk
No probate search service; copies: 50¢ per page, $5.00 for certified copies, no minimum; send SASE; courthouse burned in 1876

*Crittenden County Courthouse
Marion, AR 72364
Phone (501) 739-4434
County organized 1825 from Phillips County
Land records: Contact Circuit Clerk's Office
Naturalization records: No naturalization records
Vital records: Marriage licenses; contact County Clerk's Office
Probate records: Contact County Clerk's Office

*Cross County Courthouse
705 East Union Street
Wynne, AR 72396-3039
Phone (501) 238-3373
County organized 15 November 1862 from Crittenden, Poinsett and Saint Francis counties
Land records: Deeds from 1863; contact Office of Circuit Clerk
Naturalization records: No naturalization records
Vital records: Marriages from 1863; contact County Clerk; copies of license: no charge for verification, $5.00 for certified copy
Probate records: From 1864; contact County Clerk
No probate search service; copies: $1.00 per page

Dallas County Courthouse
Fordyce, AR 71742
Phone (501) 352-3371
County organized 1845 from Clark and Hot Spring counties

Desha County Courthouse
PO Box 188
Arkansas City, AR 71630-0188
Phone (501) 877-2426
County organized 1838 from Arkansas County

Drew County Courthouse
210 South Main
Monticello, AR 71655-4731
Phone (501) 367-3574
County organized 1846 from Arkansas County

*Faulkner County Courthouse
Conway, AR 72032

Phone (501) 450-4911 Circuit Clerk's Office
County organized 1873 from Pulaski County
Land records: Contact Circuit Clerk's Office, PO Box 9, Conway, AR 72033
Naturalization records: No naturalization records
Vital records: No vital records
Probate records: Contact County Clerk's Office
Probate search service: $2.00 (long search); copies: 25¢ per page

*Franklin County Courthouse
211 West Commercial
Ozark, AR 72949
Phone (501) 667-3607 County and Probate Clerk
County organized 1837 from Crawford County
Land records: From 1860; contact Circuit Clerk's Office
Naturalization records: Contact Circuit Clerk's Office
Vital records: Marriages from 1850; contact County Clerk's Office; copies: $1.00 plus SASE
Probate records: From 1886, unindexed; contact County Clerk's Office
No probate search service; copies: $1.00 plus SASE; County and Probate Clerk also has Quorum Court Records, Ministerial Records, Articles of Incorporation, Record of Administrator's Settlements, Real Estate Tax Books, etc.

*Fulton County Courthouse
PO Box 485
Salem, AR 72576-0278
Phone (501) 895-3310 County Clerk's Office
County organized 1842 from Izard County
Land records: From 1879 to date
Naturalization records: No naturalization records
Vital records: No vital records
Probate records: From 1870 to date (courthouse fire in 1890 destroyed records); searches and copies not available in the fragile, old records bound in unindexed books

*Garland County Courthouse
501 Ouachita Avenue
Hot Springs, AR 71901-5154
Phone (501) 622-3600; (501) 622-3630 Circuit Clerk; (501) 622-3610 County Clerk
County organized 1873 from Hot Spring County
Land records: Deeds; contact Circuit Clerk, Room 207
Vital records: Marriages; contact Nancy Johnson, County and Probate Clerk,

Room 103; certified copies: $5.00 each for marriages (includes search). Divorces; contact Circuit Clerk

Probate records: Probates, adoptions (sealed) and guardianships; contact County Clerk

Probate search service: no charge; copies: $1.00 per page

Grant County Courthouse
PO Box 364
Sheridan, AR 72150
Phone (501) 942-2551; (501) 942-2631
County organized 1869 from Jefferson County

*Greene County Courthouse
PO Box 364
Paragould, AR 72451-0364
Phone (501) 239-4097; (501) 239-6330 Circuit Clerk; (501) 239-6345 County Clerk
County organized 1833 from Lawrence County
Land records: From 1876; contact Circuit Clerk
Naturalization records: No naturalization records
Vital records: Marriages from 1876; contact County Clerk, PO Box 62, Paragould, AR 72450
Probate records: From 1876; contact County Clerk; copies: $1.00 each, no minimum

*Hempstead County Courthouse
Hope, AR 71801
Phone (501) 777-6164
County organized 1818 from Arkansas County
Land records: Contact Collectors-County Clerk
Naturalization records: Contact County and Circuit Clerk
Vital records: Marriages; contact County Clerk
Probate records: Contact County Clerk
Probate search service: charges vary, depending on time spent; copies: 50¢ per page, no minimum

*Hot Spring County Courthouse
Third and Locust
Malvern, AR 72104
Phone (501) 332-2291 County Clerk
County organized 1829 from Clark County
Land records: From 1829
Naturalization records: No naturalization records
Vital records: No vital records
Probate records: From 1829
Probate search service: charges vary

Howard County Courthouse
421 North Main Street

Nashville, AR 71852-2008
Phone (501) 845-3585; (501) 845-5916
County organized 1873 from Pike County

Independence County Courthouse
1982 East Main Street
Batesville, AR 72501-3135
Phone (501) 793-2720
County organized 1820 from Arkansas County

Izard County Courthouse
Melbourne, AR 72556
Phone (501) 368-4328; (501) 368-4316
County organized 1825 from Independence County

*Jackson County Courthouse
PO Box 641
Newport, AR 72112-0641
Phone (501) 523-7400
County organized 1829 from Independence County
Land records: Contact Jerry Carlew, Jackson County Judge
Naturalization records: Yes
Vital records: Yes; restrictions on adoption records and juvenile records
Probate records: Yes

*Jefferson County Courthouse
PO Box 6317
Pine Bluff, AR 71601
Phone (501) 541-5360; (501) 541-5322
County organized 1829 from Arkansas and Pulaski counties
Land records: Contact Clerk; copies: 25¢ per page
Naturalization records: Contact Clerk; copies: 25¢ per page
Vital records: Contact Clerk; copies: 25¢ per page
Probate records: Contact Clerk; copies: 25¢ per page

*Johnson County Clerk
PO Box 57
Clarksville, AR 72830
Phone (501) 754-3967
County organized 1833 from Pope County
Land records: Tax books; contact County Clerk. Copy of tax books, assessment books, plat maps; contact Assessor. Deeds, mortgages, oil and gas leases; contact Circuit Clerk. Current tax books; contact Sheriff and Collector
Naturalization records: Contact Circuit Clerk for a few very old records; contact District Courts for all others
Vital records: Marriages from 1855; contact County Clerk. Veteran discharge records; contact Circuit Clerk

Probate records: Wills, administrations, guardianships; contact County Clerk
Probate search service: $5.00; copies: 25¢ per page, $5.00 minimum. The County Clerk also has voter registration, minister credentials, doctors' and nurses' credentials, articles of incorporation, county officials' commissions, affidavit for collection of small estates by distributees

*Lafayette County Courthouse
PO Box 754
Lewisville, AR 71845
Phone (501) 921-4878 Circuit Clerk; (501) 921-4633 County Clerk
County organized 1827 from Hempstead County
Land records: Deeds, civil and chancery records; contact Mrs. June Stevens, Circuit Clerk, PO Box 986, Lewisville, AR 71845; certified copies: $3.00 plus 80¢ per page, survey plats $6.00 each
Naturalization records: No naturalization records
Vital records: Marriage licenses; contact Mrs. Diane Fletcher, County Clerk, PO Box 945, Lewisville, AR 71845; certified copies: $5.00 each
Probate records: Probate, small estate, assumed name, county court cases; contact County Clerk
No probate search service; copies: from 40¢ to $1.00 plus certification and postage

*Lawrence County Courthouse
PO Box 553
Walnut Ridge, AR 72476-0553
Phone (501) 886-2167; (501) 886-1112 Circuit Clerk; (501) 886-1111 County Clerk
County organized 1815 from New Madrid County, Missouri
Land records: Deeds; contact Circuit Clerk's Office, PO Box 581, Walnut Ridge, AR 72476
Probate records: Contact County Clerk's Office, PO Box 526, Walnut Ridge, AR 72476; copies: $1.00–$2.00

*Lee County Courthouse
15 East Chestnut Street
Marianna, AR 72360-2302
Phone (501) 295-2339
County organized 1873 from Phillips and Monroe counties
Land records: Deeds; contact Circuit Clerk. Tax books (only); contact County Clerk's Office
Naturalization records: No naturalization records
Vital records: Marriages; contact County Clerk; copies: 25¢ each, $5.00 if certified

Probate records: Contact County Clerk's Office

Probate search service: no charge for index search; copies: $1.00 per page; staff limited, public invited to do searches

*Lincoln County Courthouse
Star City, AR 71667
Phone (501) 628-4147
County organized 1871 from Arkansas, Bradley, Desha, Drew and Jefferson counties
Land records: Deeds, etc.; contact Circuit Clerk and Recorder
Vital records: No vital records
Probate records: Contact County and Probate Clerk
Probate search service: $3.00; copies: 25¢ per page, $5.00 for certified copies

*Little River County Courthouse
Ashdown, AR 71822
Phone (501) 898-3362; (501) 898-5021
County organized 1867 from Hempstead County
Land records: Contact Circuit Clerk
Naturalization records: No naturalization records
Vital records: No vital records
Probate records: Contact County Clerk
Probate search service: $3.00; copies: 50¢ per page, no minimum

*Logan County Courthouse
Paris, AR 72855
Phone (501) 963-2618 County Clerk; (501) 963-2164 Circuit Clerk
County organized 1871 from Franklin County; name changed from Sarber County in 1875
Land records: From 1877; contact Circuit Clerk
Naturalization records: No naturalization records
Vital records: No vital records
Probate records: From 1877; contact County Clerk
No probate search service; copies: 25¢ per page, no minimum, no photocopies available of records prior to 1940, transcriptions only

*Lonoke County Courthouse
PO Box 431
Lonoke, AR 72086
Phone (501) 676-6403
County organized 1873 from Pulaski and Jefferson counties
Land records: Yes
Naturalization records: No naturalization records
Vital records: No vital records
Probate records: Yes; copies: $1.00 per page, $5.00 for certified copies

*Madison County Courthouse
PO Box 37
Huntsville, AR 72740-0037
Phone (501) 738-6721
County organized 1836 from Washington County
Land records: Deeds from 1848, mortgages from 1883; contact Circuit Clerk
Naturalization records: No naturalization records
Vital records: Marriage licenses from 1901; contact County Clerk. Deaths from 1848–1972 (previously recorded in the Deed Books); contact Circuit Clerk
Probate records: From 1860; contact County Clerk
No probate search service; copies: 25¢ per page, $3.00 for certified copy, no minimum

*Marion County Courthouse
County and Circuit Clerk
Yellville, AR 72687
Phone (501) 449-6226
County organized 1835 from Izard County
Land records: From late 1887 to date
Land records search service: $6.00; copies: $50¢ per page
Naturalization records: No naturalization records
Probate records: From late 1887 to date
Probate search service: $6.00; copies: 50¢ per page

*Miller County Courthouse
400 Laurel Street
Texarkana, AR 75502
Phone (501) 774-1500
County organized 1862 from Lafayette County, abolished 1863, reestablished 1874
Land records: Contact Circuit Clerk (Judy Langley)
Naturalization records: No naturalization records
Vital records: No births or deaths
Probate records: Contact County Clerk (Ann Nicholas)
Probate search service: no charge; copies: $1.00 per page, $5.00 for certified copies, no minimum, send SASE

*Mississippi County Courthouse
Blytheville, AR 72315
Phone (501) 763-3212
County organized 1883 from Crittenden County
Land records: Contact Assessor's Office
Naturalization records: No naturalization records
Vital records: No vital records
Probate records: Contact County Clerk's Office

Probate search service: no charge; copies: 25¢ per page, no minimum

Monroe County Courthouse
123 Madison Street
Clarendon, AR 72029-2742
Phone (501) 747-3921
County organized 1839 from Phillips and Arkansas counties

Montgomery County Courthouse
PO Box 717
Mount Ida, AR 71957-0717
Phone (501) 867-3114
County organized 1842 from Clark County

*Nevada County Courthouse
Prescott, AR 71857
Phone (501) 887-3115
County organized 1871 from Hempstead County
Land records: From 1871; contact Circuit Clerk, PO Box 552, Prescott, AR 71857
Naturalization records: From 1871; contact Circuit Clerk
Vital records: No vital records
Probate records: From 1871; contact County Clerk, PO Box 618, Prescott, AR 71857
No probate search service; copies: $1.00 each, $5.00 for certified copies

*Newton County Courthouse
PO Box 410
Jasper, AR 72641
Phone (501) 446-5125
County organized 1842 from Carroll County
Land records: From 1870s, unindexed
Naturalization records: No naturalization records
Vital records: No vital records
Probate records: From 1870s

*Ouachita County Courthouse
PO Box 644
Camden, AR 71701
Phone (501) 836-4116
County organized 1842 from Clark County
Land records: Contact Assessor's Office and Circuit Clerk's Office
Naturalization records: No naturalization records
Vital records: No vital records
Probate records: Contact County Clerk's Office
Probate search service: 50¢ per page; copies: 50¢ per page; enclose fees with request

Perry County Courthouse
PO Box 358

Perryville, AR 72126-0358
Phone (501) 889-5126 County Clerk
County organized 1840 from Pulaski County

*Phillips County Courthouse
Helena, AR 72342
Phone (501) 338-9102
County organized 1820 from Arkansas County
Land records: From 1873; contact Linda White, County and Probate Clerk, 626 Cherry Street, Suite 202, Helena, AR 72342-3399
Land records search service: $5.00; copies: 25¢ per page
Naturalization records: No naturalization records
Vital records: Marriages from 1831; contact Linda White, County and Probate Clerk, 626 Cherry Street, Suite 202, Helena, AR 72342-3399
Vital records search service: $5.00; copies: 25¢ each, $5.00 for certified copies
Probate records: From 1821; contact Linda White, County and Probate Clerk, 626 Cherry Street, Suite 202, Helena, AR 72342-3399; contact Kay Benz, County Clerk
Probate search service: $5.00; copies: 25¢ per page

Pike County Courthouse
Murfreesboro, AR 71958
Phone (501) 285-2414; (501) 285-2231
County organized 1833 from Carroll and Clark counties

Poinsett County Courthouse
Harrisburg, AR 72432
Phone (501) 578-5333; (501) 578-5408
County organized 1838 from Greene County

*Polk County Courthouse
507 Church Street
Mena, AR 71953-3257
Phone (501) 394-3312 County Clerk; (501) 394-8123
County organized 1844 from Montgomery County
Vital records: Marriages from 1893
Probate records: From 1920; contact Pat Myers, County Clerk
No probate search service; copies: 25¢ per page, no minimum

Pope County Courthouse
Russellville, AR 72801
Phone (501) 968-7487
County organized 1829 from Pulaski County

Prairie County Courthouse
PO Box 278

Des Arc, AR 72040-0278
Phone (501) 256-3741
County organized 1846 from Monroe County

*Pulaski County Courthouse
405 West Markham
Little Rock, AR 72201-1407
Phone (501) 372-8330 County Clerk
County organized 1818 from Arkansas County
Land records: From 1819; contact Jacquetta Alexander, Circuit Clerk
Vital records: Marriage licenses; contact County Clerk, Room 108
Probate records: contact County Clerk
Probate search service: $3.00 per name; copies: 75¢ for the first page and 38¢ for each additional page; need date (year) case was opened

*Randolph County Courthouse
201 Marr Street
Pocahontas, AR 72455-3322
Phone (501) 892-5264
County organized 1835 from Lawrence County
Land records: From 1836
Naturalization records: No naturalization records
Probate records: From 1836; copies: 25¢ per page, 15¢ to 20¢ for copies of papers in files (since paper is smaller), no minimum

*Saint Francis County Courthouse
313 South Izard Street
Forrest City, AR 72335-3856
Phone (501) 261-1725
County organized 1827 from Phillips
Land records: Yes
Naturalization records: Yes
Vital records: Yes
Probate records: From 1900s; contact County Clerk
Probate search and copy fees vary

*Saline County Courthouse
Benton, AR 72015
Phone (501) 776-5630 County Clerk's Office
County organized 1835 from Pulaski County
Land records: Deeds from 1836; contact Circuit Clerk's Office
Naturalization records: No naturalization records
Vital records: No vital records
Probate records: From 1836, tax records from 1890
No probate search service; copies: 50¢ per page, no minimum

*Scott County Courthouse
County Clerk's Office
PO Box 1578

Waldron, AR 72958-1578
Phone (501) 637-2155
County organized 1833 from Crawford and Pope counties
Land records: Yes
Naturalization records: Yes
Vital records: Yes
Probate records: Yes

*Searcy County Courthouse
Marshall, AR 72650
Phone (501) 448-3554
County organized 1838 from Marion County
Land records: Deeds from 1878
No land records search service
Vital records: Births from 1919 to 1920, deaths from 1919 to 1921, marriages from 1881
No vital records search service
Probate records: From 1879
No probate search service; copies: 10¢ per page, no minimum

Sebastian County Courthouse
Fort Smith, AR 72901
Phone (501) 783-6139
County organized 1851 from Crawford County

*Sevier County Courthouse
De Queen, AR 71832
Phone (501) 642-2425; (501) 642-2852
County organized 1828 from Hempstead County
Land records: Contact Circuit Clerk
Naturalization records: No naturalization records
Vital records: No births or deaths
Probate records: Contact County Clerk
Probate search service: no charge; copies: $1.00 per page if request includes book and page numbers, no minimum

Sharp County Courthouse
Ash Flat, AR 72513
Phone (501) 994-7338
County organized 1868 from Izard County

*Stone County Court Clerk
PO Drawer 120
Mountain View, AR 72560
Phone (501) 269-3271
County organized 1873 from Independence and Izard counties
Land records: From 1873
Naturalization records: No naturalization records
Vital records: Marriages from 1873
Probate records: From 1873
Probate search service: $2.00; copies: 50¢ each, $2.00 minimum; "will do as we have time."

*Union County Courthouse
El Dorado, AR 71730
Phone (501) 864-1940 Circuit Clerk;
    (501) 864-1910 County Clerk
County organized 1829 from Hempstead
    and Clark counties
Land records: Contact Circuit Clerk
Naturalization records: No naturalization
    records
Vital records: No vital records
Probate records: Contact County Clerk
Probate search service: $1.00 per name;
    copies: $1.00 per page plus SASE

*Van Buren County Courthouse
PO Box 80
Clinton, AR 72031-0080
Phone (501) 745-4140
County organized 1833 from
    Independence County
Land records: Deeds, mortgages, etc.,
    from late 1860s
Naturalization records: No naturalization
    records
Vital records: Marriage licenses; certified
    copies: $5.00
Probate records: From 1903; copies: 25¢
    each from paper original, 50¢ each
    from microfilm original, plus SASE

Washington County Courthouse
2 North College Street
Fayetteville, AR 72701-5309
Phone (501) 521-8400; (501) 521-6400
County organized 1828 from Crawford
    County

*White County Courthouse
300 North Spruce
Searcy, AR 72143-7720
Phone (501) 268-2950
County organized 1835 from Pulaski,
    Jackson and Independence counties
Land records: Deeds, mortgages, etc.;
    contact Circuit Clerk
Naturalization records: No naturalization
    records
Vital records: Marriages; contact County
    Clerk; copies: $1.00 each, $5.00 for
    certified copies. Divorces; contact
    Circuit Clerk
Probate records: Contact County Clerk
Probate search service: no charge;
    copies: $1.00 per page, $3.00 for
    certified copies, no minimum; copies
    are typed due to the condition of the
    records

*Woodruff County Courthouse
500 North Third
Augusta, AR 72006-2056
Phone (501) 347-5206
County organized 1862 from White
    County
Land records: From 1862
Naturalization records: No naturalization
    records

Vital records: No vital records
Probate records: From 1868; copies:
    $1.00 per page, no minimum

*Yell County Courthouse
PO Box 219
Danville, AR 72833
Phone (501) 495-2414 Carolyn Morris,
    Circuit and County Clerk
County organized 1840 from Pope
    County
Land records: From circa 1868
Vital records: From circa 1868
Vital records search service: "as time
    permits"
Probate records: From circa 1868
No probate search service; copies: 25¢
    per page, certified copies $3.00.
    Courthouse burned in 1865

Capital: Sacramento. Statehood: 9
September 1850 (annexed after the Treaty
of Guadalupe-Hidalgo, 1848)

Court System

California's Municipal Courts and
Justice Courts handle civil disputes, small
claims, misdemeanors and infractions.
Superior Courts have jurisdiction over all
felonies as well as civil and criminal cases,
juvenile, probate and family law, etc., and
sit at the county seats.

Courts of Appeal are divided into six
districts. First District at San Francisco:
Alameda, Contra Costa, Del Norte,
Humboldt, Lake, Marin, Mendocino, Napa,
San Francisco, San Mateo, Solano and
Sonoma counties; Second District at Los
Angeles and Ventura: Los Angeles, Santa
Barbara and Ventura counties; Third
District at Sacramento: Alpine, Amador,
Butte, Calaveras, Colusa, El Dorado,
Glenn, Lassen, Modoc, Mono, Nevada,
Placer, Plumas, Sacramento, San Joaquin,
Shasta, Sierra, Siskiyou, Sutter, Tehama,
Trinity, Yolo and Yuba counties; Fourth
District at San Diego, San Bernardino and
Santa Ana: Imperial, Inyo, Orange,
Riverside, San Bernardino and San Diego
counties; Fifth District at Fresno: Fresno,
Kern, Kings, Madera, Mariposa, Merced,
San Luis Obispo, Stanislaus, Tulare and
Tuolumne counties; Sixth District at San
Jose: Monterey, San Benito, Santa Clara
and Santa Cruz counties. The Supreme
Court sits in San Francisco, Los Angeles
and Sacramento, with special sessions
elsewhere.

Courthouses

*Alameda County Courthouse
1225 Fallon Street
Oakland, CA 94612-4216
Phone (415) 272-6070; (415) 272-6790
County organized 1853 from Contra
    Costa and Santa Clara counties
Land records: From 1853; contact
    County Recorder, Room 100
Naturalization records: From 11 April
    1853; contact County Clerk, Room
    105
Vital records: From 1905; contact County
    Recorder
Probate records: From 1853; contact
    County Clerk

Probate search service: $1.75 per year; copies: 50¢ per page plus $1.75 for certification

*Alpine County Library/Archives
PO Box 187
Markleeville, CA 96120-0187
Phone (916) 694-2120
County organized 1864 from Calaveras, Amador, El Dorado, Mono and Tuolumne counties
Land records: From 1864 to date
Naturalization records: From 1848 to 1947
Vital records: From 1900 (some earlier records not indexed or complete)
Probate records: Index from 1864 to 1924
No probate search service; copies: 25¢ per page, no minimum. Newer records are kept in office of origin, but the Archives can route requests to the proper place for an answer

*Amador County Courthouse
108 Court Street
Jackson, CA 95642-2308
Phone (209) 223-6463
County organized 1854 from Calaveras County
Land records: Yes; copies: $2.00 for the first page and 50¢ for each additional page, $1.00 for certification
Naturalization records: Contact Court Clerk
Vital records: Births from 1873, deaths from 1872, and marriages; contact County Clerk and Recorder; copies: $13.00 each for births and marriages, $9.00 each for deaths
Probate records: Contact Court Clerk

Butte County Courthouse
25 County Center Drive
Oroville, CA 95965-3316
Phone (916) 538-7551
County organized 1850, original county

*Calaveras County Government Center
County Recorder or Superior Court
891 Mountain Ranch Road
San Andreas, CA 95249
Phone (209) 754-6372 County Recorder; (209) 754-6310 Superior Court
County organized 1850, original county
Land records: Contact Karen Varni, County Recorder
Naturalization records: Contact Superior Court
Vital records: Contact County Recorder
Probate records: Contact Superior Court

*Colusa County Courthouse
546 Jay Street
Colusa, CA 95932-2443

Phone (916) 458-4660; (916) 458-5146
County organized 1850, original county (records included in Butte County for the first few years)
Land records: Contact County Recorder
Naturalization records: Contact County Clerk-Recorder
Vital records: Contact County Recorder
Probate records: Contact County Clerk
Probate search service: $1.75 per year of search; copies: 50¢ per page, no minimum

Contra Costa County Courthouse
725 Court Street
Martinez, CA 94553-1233
Phone (415) 372-4010; (415) 372-2950
County organized 1850, original county

*Del Norte County Courthouse
450 H Street
Crescent City, CA 95531-4021
Phone (707) 464-4139; (707) 464-7205 County Clerk; (707) 464-7216 County Recorder
County organized 1857 from Klamath County
Land records: Contact John D. Alexander, County Clerk-Recorder, Room 182; copies: 50¢ per page, $1.75 for certification
Vital records: Marriage licenses; contact County Clerk-Recorder; certified copies: $12.00 each
Probate records: Contact County Clerk-Recorder; copies: 50¢ per page, $1.75 for certification

*El Dorado County Courthouse
495 Main Street
Placerville, CA 95667-5628
Phone (916) 621-6426 County Clerk's Office; (916) 621-5719 County Assessor's Office; (916) 621-5490 County Recorder's Office
County organized 1850, original county
Land records: Contact Recorder's Office or Assessor's Office, 360 Fair Lane, Placerville, CA 95667
Naturalization records: Contact Clerk's Office
Vital records: Births and deaths; contact Recorder's Office
Probate records: Contact Clerk's Office
No probate search service; copies: 50¢ per page, no minimum

*Fresno County Courthouse
1100 Van Ness, Room 401
Fresno, CA 93721
Phone (209) 488-3253 Clerk of the Court; (209) 488-1830 County Recorder
County organized 1856 from Mariposa and Merced counties
Land records: Contact County Recorder,

Hall of Records, 2281 Tulare Street, Room 201, Fresno, CA 93721
Land records search service: $5.00
Naturalization records: Contact Clerk of the Court
Vital records: Contact County Recorder
Vital records search service: $5.00
Probate records: Contact Clerk of the Court

*Glenn County Courthouse
526 West Sycamore Street
PO Box 391
Willows, CA 95988-0391
Phone (916) 934-6412 County Clerk-Recorder's Office; (916) 934-6407 County Superior Court's Office
County organized 1891 from Colusa County
Land records: From 1891; contact County Clerk-Recorder's Office
No land records search service; copies: $1.00 for the first page and 50¢ for each additional page per document
Naturalization records: Before 1931; contact County Superior Court's Office
Naturalization records search service: $5.00 per file or name; copies: 50¢ per page
Vital records: Births, deaths and marriages from 1905, plus a few delayed birth registrations going back to 1887; contact County Clerk-Recorder's Office; certified copies: $13.00 each for births and marriages, $9.00 each for deaths
Probate records: Contact County Superior Court's Office

*Humboldt County Courthouse
825 Fifth Street
Eureka, CA 95501-1172
Phone (707) 445-7620; (707) 445-7217
County organized 1853 from Trinity County, and in 1874 annexed part of Klamath County, which was formed in 1851
Land records: Contact County Assessor
Naturalization records: Contact County Clerk
Vital records: Contact County Recorder or County Clerk
Probate records: Contact County Clerk
Probate search service: $1.75 per name per year; copies: 50¢ per page, no minimum; certification: $1.75; enclose SASE

Imperial County Courthouse
852 Broadway
El Centro, CA 92243-2312
Phone (619) 339-4374; (612) 339-4256
County organized 1907 from San Diego County

*Inyo County Courthouse
Drawer N
Independence, CA 93526
Phone (619) 878-2411
County organized 1866 from Tulare
   County
Land records: From 1866
Naturalization records: From 1866 to
   1971
Vital records: Births and deaths from
   1905, marriages from 1875; contact
   Beverly J. Harry, Clerk-Recorder, PO
   Drawer F, Independence, CA 93526;
   copies: $11.00 each for births and
   marriages, $7.00 each for deaths
Probate records: From 1866
Probate search service: 50¢ per name per
   year; copies: 50¢ for the first page and
   25¢ for each additional page;
   certification: $1.75, no minimum

*Kern County Administration and
   Court Building
1415 Truxtun Avenue
Bakersfield, CA 93301-5222
Phone (805) 861-2621 County Clerk's
   Office; (805) 861-2181 County
   Recorder's Office
County organized 1866 from Los
   Angeles and Tulare counties
Land records: Contact County Recorder,
   Hall of Records, 1655 Chester
   Avenue, Bakersfield, CA 93301
Naturalization records: Contact Gale S.
   Enstad, County Clerk's Office
Vital records: Contact Hall of Records
Probate records: Contact County Clerk's
   Office
Probate search service: $1.75 per name
   per year; copies: 50¢ per page, $1.75
   for certification, 50¢ minimum

*Kings County Government Center
1400 West Lacey Boulevard
Hanford, CA 93230
Phone (209) 582-3211
County organized 1893 from Tulare
   County
Land records: From 1894
Naturalization records: From 1894 to
   1957
Vital records: From 1904
Probate records: From 1894
No probate search service; copies: 50¢
   per page, $1.75 minimum if file is in
   warehouse

Lake County Courthouse
255 North Forbes Street
Lakeport, CA 95453-4731
Phone (707) 263-2231; (707) 263-2372
County organized 1861 from Tuolumne
   County

*Lassen County Courthouse
220 Lassen Street

Susanville, CA 96130
Phone (916) 251-8234 County Clerk/
   Recorder, (916) 257-3480 FAX,
   County Clerk/Recorder
County organized 1864 from Plumas
   and Shasta counties
Land records: From 1857; contact
   Theresa Nagel, County Clerk/
   Recorder
Naturalization records: From about 1867
   to 1974; contact County Clerk/
   Recorder
Vital records: Births and deaths from
   1864, marriages from 1864
   (incomplete); contact County Clerk/
   Recorder
Probate records: From 1864; contact
   County Clerk/Recorder
Probate search service: $5.00 per case;
   copies: $1.50 for the first page and
   50¢ for each additional page, no
   minimum; please send SASE

Los Angeles County Courthouse
111 North Hill Street
Los Angeles, CA 90012-3117
Phone (213) 868-9711; (213) 974-5401
County organized 1850, original county

Madera County Courthouse
209 West Yosemite Avenue
Madera, CA 93637-3534
Phone (209) 675-7907; (209) 675-7721
County organized 1893 from Fresno
   County

Marin County Hall of Justice and
   Civic Center
San Rafael, CA 94903
Phone (415) 499-6063; (415) 499-6407
County organized 1850, original county

Mariposa County Courthouse
5088 Bullion Street
PO Box 247
Mariposa, CA 95338-0247
Phone (209) 966-5784; (209) 966-2005
County organized 1850, original county

*Mendocino County Courthouse
North State and Perkins Streets
PO Box 148
Ukiah, CA 95482
Phone (707) 463-4221 Clerk of the
   Board; (707) 463-4376 County
   Recorder; (707) 463-4664 Superior
   Court
County organized 1850, original county
Land records: Contact Marsha A. Young,
   County Recorder
Naturalization records: Contact Superior
   Court, PO Box 996, Ukiah, CA 95482
Vital records: Contact County Recorder
Probate records: Contact Superior Court

*Merced County
County Courts Building
(627 West 21st Street—location)
2222 M Street (mailing address)
Merced, CA 95340-3729
Phone (209) 385-7623; (209) 385-7434
County organized 1855 from Mariposa
   County
Land records: Contact County Recorder
Naturalization records: Contact Clerk of
   the Superior Court
Vital records: Contact Recorder's Office
Probate records: Contact Clerk of the
   Superior Court
Probate search service: $5.00; copies:
   50¢ per page, $1.75 for certification,
   no minimum; include SASE

*Modoc County Courthouse
200 Court Street
Alturas, CA 96101-4026
Phone (916) 233-3939
County organized 1874 from Siskiyou
   County
Land records: Contact Recorder's Office
Naturalization records: Contact Clerk
Vital records: Contact Recorder
Probate records: Contact Clerk
Probate search service: no charge;
   copies: 50¢ per page, no minimum

*Mono County Courthouse
Main Street
PO Box 537
Bridgeport, CA 93517-0537
Phone (619) 932-7911
County organized 1861 from Calaveras
   and Fresno counties
Land records: Contact Recorder's Office
Naturalization records: Contact
   Recorder's Office
Vital records: Contact Recorder's Office
Probate records: Contact Recorder's
   Office
Probate search service: $2.00 per year;
   copies: $1.00 per page, minimum
   $2.00

*Monterey County Courthouse
240 Church Street
PO Box 1819
Salinas, CA 93902
Phone (408) 755-5030; (408) 755-5035
   County Tax Assessor; (408) 647-7730
   Clerk of the Superior Court (Salinas);
   (408) 647-7730 Clerk of the Superior
   Court (Monterey)
County organized 1850, original county
Land records: Contact County Tax
   Assessor, PO Box 570, Salinas, CA
   93902
Naturalization records: Contact Clerk of
   the Superior Court (Salinas office
   only)
Vital records: Contact County Recorder,
   PO Box 29, Salinas, CA 93902

Probate records: Contact Clerk of the Superior Court in Salinas or at the Branch Courthouse on the Monterey Peninsula (Courthouse, 1200 Aguajito Road, Monterey, CA 93940), depending on the residence of the decedent

Probate search service: $5.00 per year; copies: 75¢ per page, no minimum

Napa County Courthouse
1195 Third Street
Napa, CA 94559-3001
Phone (707) 253-4481
County organized 1850, original county

*Nevada County Courthouse Annex
201 Church Street
Nevada City, CA 95959-2504
Phone (916) 265-1293
County organized 1851 from Yuba County
Land records: From 1851 to date; contact Recorder's Office, Box 6100, Nevada City, CA 95959
Naturalization records: From 1851 to the early 1900s; contact Searls Library, Church Street, Nevada City, CA 95959
Vital records: From 1851 to date; contact Recorder's Office
Probate records: From 1851 to date; contact Bruce C. Bolinger, County Clerk, Box 6126, Nevada City, CA 95959
Probate search service: $5.00; copies: 50¢ per page

*Orange County Courthouse
700 Civic Center Drive, West
PO Box 238
Santa Ana, CA 92701-4022
Phone (714) 834-2200; (714) 834-2500 Recorder; (714) 834-2225 Clerk
County organized 1889 from Los Angeles County
Land records: Contact Recorder
Naturalization records: No naturalization records
Vital records: Contact Recorder
Probate records: Contact Clerk, PO Box 838, Santa Ana, CA 92702
Probate search service: $1.75 per year; copies: 50¢ per page, $1.75 for certified copies, no minimum; include SASE. "If you do not know the correct amount needed, leave it blank and write 'not to exceed $____' on the check. We will fill in the amount necessary."

*Placer County Courthouse
PO Box 5228
Auburn, CA 95604-5228
Phone (916) 823-4471 County Clerk; (916) 823-4621 Recorder

County organized 1851 from Yuba and Sutter counties
Land records: Contact County Recorder, 175 Fulweiler Avenue, Auburn, CA 95603
Naturalization records: Naturalization papers from 1852 to 1893 and from 1903 to 1906, Declarations of Intention from 1893 to 1906 and from 1913 to 1939, Certificates of Citizenship (District Court from 1874 to 1879, County Court from 1876 to 1897, and Superior Court from 1897 to 1903), Petitions and Records from 1906 to 1942, Petitions for Naturalization 1943 to 1960; contact County Clerk
Vital records: Marriages; contact County Recorder; copies: $5.00 each
Probate records: From late 1800s; contact County Clerk (Probate Clerk)
Probate search service: $1.75 (from 1974 to present), additional $1.75 per year per name (prior to 1974); copies: 50¢ for the first page, 25¢ for each additional page of the same document, 10¢ per page for each additional copy of same document, no minimum. "Supply all info possible when requesting a search of our records."

*Plumas County Courthouse
520 West Main Street
Quincy, CA 95971
Phone (916) 283-6380 Assessor; (916) 283-6218 Clerk-Recorder; (916) 283-6305 County Clerk/Recorder
County organized 1854 from Butte County
Land records: Contact Assessor, PO Box 11016
Land records search service: $1.75 per year; copies: 50¢ per page, $1.00 per page if copy entails research, $1.75 for certification
Naturalization records: Contact Museum, PO Box 10776
Vital records: Contact Clerk-Recorder, PO Box 10706
Vital records search service: $1.75 per year; certified copies: $13.00 each for births and marriages, $9.00 each for deaths
Probate records: Contact Judith A. Wells, County Clerk/Recorder, PO Box 10207
Probate search service: $1.75 per year; copies: 50¢ per page, $1.00 per page if copy entails research, $1.75 for certification

*Riverside County Courthouse
Executive Office
4075 Main Street, Room 310
Riverside, CA 92501
Phone (909) 275-5536; (909) 275-1949 County Recorder (land records); (909)

275-1900 County Recorder (vital records); (909) 275-1970 Probate Section
County organized 1893 from San Bernardino and San Diego counties
Land records: Contact County Recorder, County Administrative Center, 4080 Lemon Street, PO Box 751, Riverside, CA 92502
Naturalization records: No naturalization records
Vital records: Contact County Recorder
Probate records: Contact Probate Section

*Sacramento County Courthouse
720 Ninth Street
Sacramento, CA 95814
Phone (916) 440-5522 Clerk; (916) 440-6334 Recorder
County organized 1850, original county
Land records: Contact Clerk/Recorder, 901 G Street, Sacramento, CA 95814
Vital records: Contact Clerk/Recorder
Probate records: Contact County Clerk's Office
Probate search service: $1.75 per name; copies: 50¢ per page, $1.75 per document for certification. "Fees change periodically. If unsure of the amount needed you may write a check payable to the 'Sacramento County Clerk' leaving the dollar amount blank and writing 'Not to exceed $5.00' on the check. Do not send cash."

*San Benito County Courthouse
440 Fifth Street, #206
Hollister, CA 95023-3843
Phone (408) 637-3786
County organized 1874 from Monterey County
Land records: From 1850s (transcribed from Monterey County until 1870s)
Naturalization records: Some from 1874 and some not available to the public
Vital records: From 1874, but not mandatory until 1905
Probate records: From 1874
Probate search service: $1.75 per year searched; 50¢ per page (Clerk's office), $2.00 for the first page and $1.00 for each additional page (Recorder's Office), no minimum. "Specific questions should be made either to the Clerk's Office or Recorder's Office."

909-884-1858

*San Bernardino County Courthouse
351 North Arrowhead Avenue
San Bernardino, CA 92415
Phone (714) 387-3921
County organized 1853 from Los Angeles County
Land records: From 1854; contact Recorder's Office

Handwritten annotations at top of page: 387-8306, Land Records, from 1905 no Robbock, 909-387-8306, 387-8314, death, 387-3944, 909-

Vital records: From 1880; contact
    Recorder's Office
Probate records: From 1856; contact
    County Clerk
Probate search service: $1.75 per source;
    50¢ per page, no minimum

San Diego County Courthouse
220 West Broadway Street
San Diego, CA 92101
Phone (619) 236-2984
County organized 1850, original county

San Francisco County Courthouse
400 Van Ness Avenue
San Francisco, CA 94102-4607
Phone (415) 554-4114
County organized 1850, original county

*San Joaquin County Courthouse
222 East Weber Avenue
Stockton, CA 95202-2702
Phone (209) 468-2630 County Assessor's
    Office; (209) 468-2355 Records Unit;
    (209) 468-3939 Clerk/Recorder's
    Office
County organized 1850, original county
Land records: Contact County Assessor's
    Office, 24 South Hunter Street,
    Stockton, CA 95202
Naturalization records: Contact Records
    Unit, Superior Court, Courthouse,
    Room 303; copies: 50¢ per page,
    payable in advance
Vital records: Marriage licenses; contact
    Clerk/Recorder's Office, 24 South
    Hunter Street, Third Floor, Stockton,
    CA 95202
Probate records: Contact Records Unit;
    copies: 50¢ per page, payable in
    advance

***San Luis Obispo County Government
    Center**
San Luis Obispo, CA 93408
Phone (805) 549-5245
County organized 1850, original county
Land records: Contact County Clerk-
    Recorder, County Government Center,
    Room 102
Naturalization records: Contact Superior
    Court, 1035 Palm Street, Room 385,
    San Luis Obispo, CA 93408
Vital records: Contact County Clerk
    Recorder, 1144 Monterey Street, San
    Luis Obispo, CA 93408
Probate records: Contact Superior Court

*San Mateo County
Hall of Justice and Records
401 Marshall Street
Redwood City, CA 94063-1636
Phone (415) 363-4000, ext. 4711
*County organized 1856 from San
    Francisco County*

Naturalization records: Contact
    Recorder's Office
Vital records: Contact Recorder's Office
Probate records: Contact Probate Unit
Probate search service: $1.75; copies:
    50¢ per page

***Santa Barbara County Clerk-
    Recorder-Assessor**
Hall of Records
1100 Anacapa Street
Santa Barbara, CA 93101
Phone (805) 568-2250 County Clerk/
    Recorder
County organized 1850, original county
Land records: Contact County Clerk/
    Recorder, PO Box 159, Santa Barbara,
    CA 93102-0159
Naturalization records: Contact Superior
    Court, Attn: Certification, PO Box
    21107, Santa Barbara, CA 93121-1107
Vital records: Contact County Clerk/
    Recorder
Probate records: Contact Superior Court
Probate search service: $1.75 per name
    per year; copies: 50¢ per page, no
    minimum; inquiries should be sent by
    correspondence

*Santa Clara County Clerk
191 North First Street
San Jose, CA 95113
Phone (408) 299-2966 (9:00-4:00)
County organized 1850, original county
Land records: Contact Assessor, 70 West
    Hedding Street, San Jose, CA 95110
Naturalization records: From 1850 to
    1970; contact Stephen V. Love,
    County Clerk
Vital records: Contact Recorders, 70
    West Hedding Street
Probate records: From 1800; contact
    County Clerk
Probate search service: $4.00 per year;
    copies: 50¢ per page, no minimum

*Santa Cruz County Courthouse
701 Ocean Street
Santa Cruz, CA 95060-4027
Phone (408) 424-2465 Assessor; (408)
    425-2175 Special Services; (408) 454-
    2800 County Clerk/Recorder
*County incorporated 18 February 1850,
    original county*
Land records: Contact Robert C.
    Petersen, Assessor, Room 130
Naturalization records: Contact Special
    Services, Room 210D
Vital records: Contact Richard W. Bedal,
    Recorder and Registrar of Voters,
    Room 230
Probate records: Contact Richard W.
    Bedal, County Clerk, Room 110
Probate search service: $1.75 per year;
    copies: 50¢ per page, no minimum;
    enclose SASE

*Shasta County Courthouse
1500 Court Street
Redding, CA 96001-1662
Phone (916) 225-5631; (916) 225-5641
County organized 1850, original county
Land records: Contact County Assessor
Naturalization records: Contact Ann
    Reed, County Clerk, PO Box 880,
    Redding, CA 96009 (Mon.–Fri. 8:00–
    5:00)
Vital records: Contact County Recorder
Probate records: Contact County Clerk
Probate search service: $1.75 per year
    searched; copies: 50¢ per page, no
    minimum

*Sierra County Courthouse
Courthouse Square
PO Box D
Downieville, CA 95936-0398
Phone (916) 289-3295
*County organized 1852 from Yuba
    County*
Land records: From 1852 to date; contact
    County Recorder
Naturalization records: From 1852 to
    date; contact Court Administrator, PO
    Box 95, Downieville, CA 95936
Vital records: Births from 1857 to date,
    deaths from 1864 to date, marriages
    from 1852 to date; contact County
    Recorder; certified copies: $13.00
    each for births and marriages, $9.00
    each for deaths (includes search)
Probate records: From 1852 to date;
    contact Court Administrator

*Siskiyou County Clerk
PO Box 338
Yreka, CA 96097-9910
Phone (916) 842-8084
*County organized 1852 from Klamath
    and Shasta counties, and in 1874
    annexed part of Klamath County,
    which was formed in 1851*
Land records: Contact Assessor
Naturalization records: Contact County
    Clerk
Vital records: Contact County Recorder
Probate records: Contact County Clerk
Probate search service: $1.75 per year;
    copies: 50¢ per page, no minimum;
    "If files are stored, it may take some
    time to retrieve them."

*Solano County Courthouse
600 Union Avenue
Fairfield, CA 94533
Phone (707) 429-6412 County Clerk
County organized 1850, original county
Land records: Contact County Recorder,
    580 Texas Street, Fairfield, CA 94533
Naturalization records: No naturalization
    records
Vital records: No vital records
Probate records: Contact County Clerk

Probate search service: $1.75 per name per year; copies: 50¢ per page, no minimum

*Sonoma County Superior and Municipal Court
600 Administration Drive
PO Box 11187
Santa Rosa, CA 95406-5000
Phone (707) 527-1100; (707) 527-2651 County Recorder's Office; (707) 527-3800 County Clerk's Office
County organized 1850, original county
Land records: Contact County Recorder's Office, 585 Fiscal Drive, Santa Rosa, CA 95406
Naturalization records: Only limited information
Vital records: Contact Recorder's Office
Probate records: Contact Superior Court
Probate search service: $15.00 per hour, $5.00 minimum

*Stanislaus County Courthouse
800 11th Street
Modesto, CA 95354
Phone (209) 558-6419 Clerk-Recorder and Clerk's Office; (209) 558-6310 Recorder's Office
County organized 1854 from Tuolumne County
Land records: Contact Karen Mathews, County Clerk-Recorder, 912 Eleventh Street, PO Box 1670, Modesto, CA 95353-1670
Naturalization records: Contact County Clerk-Recorder
Vital records: Births, deaths and marriages; certified copies: $13.00 each for births and marriages, $9.00 each for deaths
Probate records: Contact Superior Court, Room 222
No probate search service; copies: 50¢ for the first page, 30¢ for each additional page, $1.75 per page for certification, plus SASE

*Sutter County Courthouse
4636 Second Street
Yuba City, CA 95991-5524
Phone (916) 741-7134 Recorder; (916) 741-7120
County organized 1850, original county
Land records: From 1849; contact Recorder, 466 Second Street, Yuba City, CA 95991
Vital records: From 1873; contact Recorder

*Tehama County Courthouse
633 Washington Street
Red Bluff, CA 96080-0250
Phone (916) 527-3350
County organized 1856 from Butte, Colusa and Shasta counties

Land records: From 1856; contact Mary Alice George, County Clerk and Recorder
Naturalization records: From the late 1800s; no longer in the County Clerk and Recorder's Office, contact the state
Vital records: Births and deaths from 1889, marriages from 1856; contact County Clerk and Recorder
Probate records: Contact Clerk of Superior Court
No probate search service

*Trinity County Courthouse
101 Court Street
PO Box 1258
Weaverville, CA 96093
Phone (916) 623-4000; (916) 623-1222
County organized 1850, original county
Land records: Contact Barbara M. Rhodes, County Clerk/Recorder, PO Box 1258, Weaverville, CA 96093-1258
Naturalization records: Contact Clerk/Recorder
Vital records: Contact Clerk/Recorder
Probate records: Contact Clerk/Recorder
No probate search service; copies: 50¢ per page, no minimum; case number preferred but not required

*Tulare County Courthouse
County Civic Center
Visalia, CA 93291-4593
Phone (209) 733-6377 County Clerk-Recorder; (209) 733-6374 Superior Court
County organized 1852 from Mariposa County
Land records: From 1854; contact County Clerk-Recorder's Office, Room 203
Land records search service: $10.00 per name; copies: $1.00 for the first page and 50¢ for each additional page of the same document, $1.00 for certification
Naturalization records: Contact Superior Court, Room 201
Vital records: Births, deaths and marriages; certified copies: $16.00 each for births, $9.00 each for deaths, $13.00 each for marriages
Probate records: From 1854; contact Superior Court
Probate search service: $5.00 per name; copies: 50¢ per page, $1.75 for certified copies, no minimum

Tuolumne County Courthouse
2 South Green Street
Sonora, CA 95370-4617
Phone (209) 533-5675; (209) 533-5555
County organized 1850, original county

*Ventura County Courthouse
800 South Victoria Avenue
Ventura, CA 93009-5317
Phone (805) 654-2292 Recorder; (805) 654-2269 County Clerk (naturalization records); (805) 654-2264 County Clerk (probate records)
County organized 1 January 1873 from Santa Barbara County
Land records: Contact Recorder
Naturalization records: From 1873 to 1987; contact County Clerk
Vital records: Contact Recorder
Probate records: Contact County Clerk
Probate search service: $1.75 per year; copies: 50¢ for the first page, 30¢ for each additional copy at the same time from same original; "Need to have fee before service can be rendered."

*Yolo County Courthouse
725 Court Street
Woodland, CA 95695
Phone (916) 666-8010 Archives; (916) 666-8130 County Clerk/Recorder; (916) 666-8170 County Courts
County organized 1850, original county
Land records: Deed books from 1849 to 1927, homestead declarations from 1861 to 1932, land patents from 1859 to 1932, mortgages (real and personal property) and indexes from 1850 to 1932, separate property and sole traders from 1876 to 1914; contact Marilyn Thompson, Yolo County Archives, 226 Buckeye Street, Woodland, CA 95695 (hours: Tue. 9:00-noon and 12:30-3:00). Current records; contact Tony Bernhard, County Clerk/Recorder (725 Court Street, Room 105—location), PO Box 1130 (mailing address), Woodland, CA 95776
Land records search service by Archives: for a fee. No land records search service by County Clerk/Recorder; certified copies available
Naturalization records: From 1870 to 1951; contact Archives
Vital records: Register of births from 1878 to 1903, death index from 1870 to 1918, deaths, burial and removal permits 1870 to 1918, marriage index from 1863 to 1914; contact Archives. Current records; contact County Clerk/Recorder
Vital records search service by Archives: for a fee. No vital records search service by County Clerk/Recorder; certified copies available
Probate records: Probate case files from 1879 to 1939; contact Archives. Current records; contact County Courts
Probate search service by Archives: for a fee. No probate search service by County Courts

*Yuba County Courthouse
215 Fifth Street
Marysville, CA 95901-5737
Phone (916) 741-6341 County Clerk;
    (916) 741-6258
County organized 1850, original county
Land records: Contact Frances Fairey,
    County Clerk/Recorder, 935 14th
    Street, Marysville, CA 95901
Naturalization records: Contact County
    Clerk/Recorder
Vital records: Contact County Clerk/
    Recorder
Probate records: Contact Clerk of the
    Superior Court
Probate search service: $5.00 per case;
    copies: 50¢ per page

COLORADO

*Capital: Denver. Statehood: 1 August 1876
(annexed as a result of the Louisiana
Purchase, 1803, and the Treaty of
Guadalupe-Hidalgo, 1848, became a
territory in 1861)*

Court System

Colorado's Municipal Courts handle
ordinance violations and traffic matters.
The County Courts hear civil cases,
misdemeanors, felony preliminaries and
small claims. Seven Water Courts, in
Greeley, Pueblo, Alamosa, Montrose,
Glenwood Springs, Steamboat Springs, and
Durango, determine water rights.

Twenty-two District Courts sit in each
of the counties and handle domestic
relations, civil and criminal cases, and
(except in Denver) probate and juvenile
matters. First Judicial District: Gilpin and
Jefferson counties; Second Judicial District:
City and County of Denver; Third Judicial
District: Huerfano and Las Animas
counties; Fourth Judicial District: El Paso
and Teller counties; Fifth Judicial District:
Clear Creek, Eagle, Lake and Summit
counties; Sixth Judicial District: Archuleta,
La Plata and San Juan counties; Seventh
Judicial District: Delta, Gunnison,
Hinsdale, Montrose, Ouray and San Miguel
counties; Eighth Judicial District: Jackson
and Larimer counties; Ninth Judicial
District: Garfield, Pitkin and Rio Blanco
counties; Tenth Judicial District: Pueblo
County; Eleventh Judicial District: Chaffee,
Custer, Fremont and Park counties; Twelfth
Judicial District: Alamosa, Conejos,
Costilla, Mineral, Rio Grande and
Saguache counties; Thirteenth Judicial
District: Kit Carson, Logan, Morgan,
Phillips, Sedgwick, Washington and Yuma
counties; Fourteenth Judicial District:
Grand, Moffat and Routt counties; Fifteenth
Judicial District: Baca, Cheyenne, Kiowa
and Prowers counties; Sixteenth Judicial
District: Bent, Crowley and Otero counties;
Seventeenth Judicial District: Adams
County; Eighteenth Judicial District:
Arapahoe, Douglas, Elbert and Lincoln
counties; Nineteenth Judicial District: Weld
County; Twentieth Judicial District:
Boulder County; Twenty-first Judicial
District: Mesa County; Twenty-second
Judicial District: Dolores and Montezuma
counties.

The Denver Probate Court and the
Denver Juvenile Court serve that city. A
Court of Appeals sits in Denver and
occasionally at Colorado Springs and
Grand Junction. The Supreme Court sits at
Denver.

Courthouses

*Adams County Courthouse
450 South Fourth Street
Brighton, CO 80601-3123
Phone (303) 659-2120
*County organized 1901 from Arapahoe
County, and annexed part of Denver
County in 1909*
Land records: Contact County Clerk and
    Recorder
Naturalization records: From 1905 to
    1954; contact Colorado State Archives
Vital records: No vital records. Marriages
    from 1902 to 1975; contact Colorado
    State Archives
Probate records: Contact District Court
No probate search service; copies: 75¢
    per page

*Alamosa County Courthouse
Fourth and San Juan
PO Box 178
Alamosa, CO 81101
Phone (719) 589-5887 County
    Information; (719) 589-4996 Courts
*County organized 1913 from Costilla
County*
Land records: Yes
Naturalization records: Yes
Vital records: Yes
Probate records: Court records; contact
    Courts, Alamosa County Courthouse,
    702 Fourth Street, Alamosa, CO
    81101

*Arapahoe County Courthouse
5606 South Court Place
Littleton, CO 80120
Phone (303) 798-4592; (303) 798-4593
County organized 1861, original county
Land records: Contact Jane K.
    Wullbrandt, Clerk of the County Court
Naturalization records: Contact Clerk of
    the County Court
Vital records: Marriages from 1903 to
    1966; contact Colorado State Archives
Probate records: Contact Clerk of the
    County Court

*Archuleta County Combined Courts
PO Box 148
Pagosa Springs, CO 81147
Phone (970) 264-5932 Combined Courts;
    (970) 264-2673 San Juan Basin
    Health
*County organized 1885 from Conejos
County*
Land records: Contact (970) 264-5656
Naturalization records: Contact (970)
    247-2304

Vital records: Contact San Juan Basin
Health
Probate records: Contact Combined
Courts

*Baca County Courthouse
741 Main Street
PO Box 116
Springfield, CO 81073-0116
Phone (719) 523-4555; (719) 523-6532
*County organized 1889 from Las
Animas County*
Land records: From 1889; contact Sheila
Ingle, Baca County Clerk
Vital records: Some from 1917, more
consistently starting in the 1920s;
contact Betty Nutt, 732 College,
Springfield, CO 81073. Marriages
from 1889 to 1937; contact Colorado
State Archives
Probate records: From 1911; contact
Linda Gibson, Clerk of District Court
Probate search service: no fee; copies:
75¢ per page, no minimum

*Bent County Courthouse
725 Bent Avenue
Las Animas, CO 81054
Phone (719) 456-2009 County Clerk and
Recorder's Office; (719) 456-2223
FAX, County Clerk and Recorder's
Office; (719) 456-1353 Clerk of
Court; (719) 456-0040 FAX, Clerk of
Court
*County organized 1870 from
Greenwood County, which was
organized in 1874 and abolished in
1878 by being divided between Bent
and Elbert counties*
Land records: From 1888 to date; contact
County Clerk and Recorder's Office,
PO Box 350, Las Animas, CO 81054-
0350
No land records search service; copies:
$1.25 per page, $1.00 additional for
certification
Vital records: Marriage licenses from
1888 to date; contact County Clerk
and Recorder's Office; copies: $12.00
for the first copy of births or deaths
and $6.00 for each additional copy of
the same record purchased on the
same day (restricted to immediate
relatives), $2.00 each for marriage
licenses, $1.00 for certification
Probate records: From 1888 to date;
contact Clerk of Court
Probate search service: $8.00 per name

*Boulder County District Court
PO Box 4249
Boulder, CO 80306-4249
Phone (303) 441-3516 County Clerk;
(303) 441-4740 Clerk of Court; (303)
441-3750 Probate
County organized 1861, original county

Land records; Contact County Clerk, PO
Box 471, Boulder, CO 80306
Naturalization records: From 1865 to
1929; contact Colorado State Archives
Vital records: Marriages from 1868 to
1959; contact Colorado State Archives
Probate records; contact Clerk of Court

*Chaffee County Courthouse
104 Crestone
PO Box 699
Salida, CO 81201-0699
Phone (719) 539-6031 County Court
Clerk; (719) 539-2218 County
Commissioners; (719) 539-4016
County Assessor; (719) 539-4004
County Clerk and Recorder; (719)
539-2311 City of Salida
*County organized 1861 from Lake
County*
Land records: Contact County Assessor
No land records search service; copies:
50¢ to $2.00 depending on size
Naturalization records: Contact County
Clerk and Recorder
No naturalization records search service;
copies: 50¢ to $2.00 depending on
size
Vital records: Contact City of Salida
Probate records: Contact County Court
Clerk
No probate search service; copies: 50¢ to
$2.00 depending on size

*Cheyenne County Courthouse
51 South First Street
PO Box 696
Cheyenne Wells, CO 80810-0696
Phone (719) 767-5649
*County organized 1889 from Bent and
Elbert counties*
Naturalization records: Contact Betty
Jean Schweers, Clerk of the
Combined Courts
Vital records: No births
Probate records: Contact Clerk of the
Combined Courts
No probate search service; copies: 75¢
per page

Clear Creek County Courthouse
Fifth and Argentine
PO Box 2000
Georgetown, CO 80444-2000
Phone (303) 569-3273; (303) 534-5777
County organized 1861, original county
Vital records: Marriages from 1864 to
1959; contact Colorado State Archives

*Conejos County Courthouse
Main Street
PO Box 127
Conejos, CO 81129
Phone (719) 376-5927
County organized 1861, original county
Land records: From 1900

Naturalization records: Contact Conejos
County Court Clerk, Conejos, CO
81129
Vital records: Contact Court Clerk
Probate records: Contact Court Clerk

Costilla County Courthouse
Main Street
PO Box 100
San Luis, CO 81151
Phone (719) 672-3681; (719) 672-3962
County organized 1861, original county

*Crowley County Courthouse
Sixth and Main
Ordway, CO 81063
Phone (719) 267-4468; (719) 267-4643
*County organized 1911 from Bent
County*

Custer County Courthouse
205 South Sixth Street
Westcliffe, CO 81252
Phone (719) 267-4468; (719) 783-2441
*County organized 1877 from Fremont
County*
Naturalization records: From 1876 to
1906; contact Colorado State Archives

*Delta County Courthouse
501 Palmer, Suite 338
Delta, CO 81416
Phone (303) 874-4416 Combined Courts
*County organized 1883 from Gunnison
County*
Land records: Contact County Clerk and
Recorder
Vital records: Contact County Clerk and
Recorder. Marriages from 1883 to
1960; contact Colorado State Archives
Probate records: Contact Combined
Courts
No probate search service; copies: 75¢
per page

*Denver County City-County Building
1437 Bannock Street
Denver, CO 80216
Phone (303) 575-2628; (303) 575-2641
*County organized 1901 from Adams
County*
Land records: From 1800
Naturalization records: County
naturalization records from 1862 to
1915 and District Court naturalization
records from 1877 to 1920; contact
Colorado State Archives
Vital records: Marriages from 1883 to
1960; contact Colorado State
Archives. Births and deaths; contact
Vital Statistics Room, Denver General
Hospital

Dolores County Courthouse
PO Box 614

Dove Creek, CO 81324-0614
Phone (303) 677-2258; (303) 677-2383
County organized 1881 from Ouray County

*Douglas County Courthouse
301 South Wilcox Street
Castle Rock, CO 80104-2440
Phone (303) 660-7446
County organized 1861, original county
Land records: Real estate records from 1864; contact County Clerk and Recorder (no search service; copies: $1.25 per page)
Naturalization records: From 1856 to 1920; contact Colorado State Archives
Vital records: Marriages from 1864 to 1959 and from 1982 to 1984; contact Colorado State Archives

Eagle County Justice Center
605 East Chambers Road
PO Box 597
Eagle, CO 81631
Phone (303) 328-6373; (303) 328-7311
County organized 1883 from Summit County
Naturalization records: From 1884 to 1938; contact Colorado State Archives

Elbert County Courthouse
751 Ute Street
Kiowa, CO 80117
Phone (303) 621-2131; (303) 621-2080
County organized 1874 from Douglas and Greenwood counties, the latter of which was organized in 1874 and abolished in 1878 by being divided between Bent and Elbert counties
Naturalization records: From 1875 to 1931; contact Colorado State Archives
Vital records: Marriages from 1874 to 1967; contact Colorado State Archives

*El Paso County Judicial Building
20 East Vermijo
Colorado Springs, CO 80903-2214
Phone (719) 630-2898
County organized 1861, original county
Vital records: Marriages from 1861 to 1917; contact Colorado State Archives
Probate records: Yes
Probate search service: $8.00 per name; copies: 75¢ per page; no phone calls, correspondence only

*Fremont County Clerk and Recorder
615 Macon, Room 100
Canon City, CO 81212
Phone (719) 275-1522 County Clerk and Recorder
County organized 1861, original county
Land records: Real property; contact Norma Hatfield, County Clerk and Recorder

*Garfield County Courthouse
109 Eighth Street
Glenwood Springs, CO 81601-3362
Phone (303) 945-2377 County Clerk and Recorder
County organized 1883 from Summit County
Land records: From 1883; contact Mildred Alsdorf, County Clerk, Suite 200
No land records search service
Vital records: Births, deaths and marriage licenses from 1884 to date; contact County Clerk; certified copies: $12.00 each for births and deaths (includes search; some early birth and death records are very hard to find, and you have to be a member of the family or have permission to get a copy); $3.50 each for marriage licenses (includes search)
Probate records: Contact Suite 104

*Gilpin County Courthouse
203 Eureka Street
PO Box 366
Central City, CO 80427-0366
Phone (303) 582-5522; (303) 572-0567
County organized 1861, original county
Land records: Contact Gilpin County Assessor's Office
Naturalization records: From 1854 to 1941; contact Colorado State Archives
Vital records: Marriages from 1864 to 1907 and from 1931 to 1932; contact Colorado State Archives
Probate records: Contact Court Clerk, Gail Murray, PO Box 426, Central City, CO 80427
Probate search service: $80.00

Grand County Courthouse
308 Byers Street
Box 192
Hot Sulphur Springs, CO 80451
Phone (303) 725-3347
County organized 1874 from Summit County

*Gunnison County Courthouse
200 East Virginia Avenue
Gunnison, CO 81230-2248
Phone (303) 641-3500 Clerk of the Court; (303) 641-2038 County Recorder; (303) 641-3244 Director of Social Services
County organized 1877 from Lake County
Land records: From 20 April 1877; contact County Recorder; copies: $1.25 per page, must have book and page number or reception number or exact date with grantor and grantee names
Naturalization records: From 1890 to 1942; contact Clerk of the Court;

copies: 75¢ per page, no fee for searches
Vital records: Marriages from 1 December 1877; contact County Recorder; copies: $2.00 per page, $6.00 for certified copies, inquiry must contain names and dates. Vital records from 1910 (some early records may be missing); contact Director of Social Services. Marriages from 1881 to 1896; contact Colorado State Archives
Probate records: From 1900; contact Clerk of the Courts
Probate search service: no charge; copies: 75¢ per page, no minimum

*Hinsdale County Combined Courthouse
PO Box 245
Lake City, CO 81235
Phone (303) 944-2227
County organized 1874 from Conejos County
Vital records: Marriages from 1876 to 1965; contact Colorado State Archives
Probate records: Yes
No probate search service; copies: 75¢ each, no minimum

Huerfano County Courthouse
400 Main Street
Walsenburg, CO 81089-2034
Phone (719) 738-1290; (719) 738-2370
County organized 1861, original county

*Jackson County Courthouse
PO Box 337
Walden, CO 80480-0337
Phone (303) 723-4363; (303) 723-4334
County organized 1909 from Grand County
Land records: Contact County Clerk and Recorder's Office
Vital records: Contact County Registrar, Bonnita E. Ary, Walden, CO 80480
Probate records: Contact County Court Clerk, Walden, CO 80480

*Jefferson County Hall of Justice
1701 Arapahoe Street
Golden, CO 80401-6199
Phone (303) 278-6197; (303) 278-6135 Clerk of the District Court
County organized 1861, original county
Naturalization records: From 1862 to 1955; contact Colorado State Archives
Vital records: Marriages from 1974 to 1976; contact Colorado State Archives
Probate records: Contact Clerk of the District Court, Attn: Probate
Probate search service: $5.00 per name; copies: 75¢ per page, $1.00 for certification, no minimum

Kiowa County Courthouse
200 East 13th Street
PO Box 353
Eads, CO 81036
Phone (303) 438-5531; (303) 438-5421
County organized 1889 from Cheyenne and Bent counties

*Kit Carson County Courthouse
251 16th Street
Burlington, CO 80807
Phone (719) 346-5524 District Court Clerk; (719) 346-8638 County Clerk and Recorder
County organized 1889 from Elbert County
Land records: Contact County Clerk and Recorder, PO Box 249, Burlington, CO 80807-0249
Vital records: Births and deaths; contact District Court Clerk. Marriage licenses; contact County Clerk and Recorder. Marriages from 1889 to 1982 (index only); contact Colorado State Archives
Probate records: Contact District Court Clerk, PO Box 547, Burlington, CO 80807-0547

*Lake County Combined Courts
Fifth and Harrison Avenue
PO Box 55
Leadville, CO 80461
Phone (719) 486-0334; (719) 486-0535
County organized 1861, original county; name changed from Carbonate in 1879
Naturalization records: From 1860s to about 1945
Vital records: Marriages from 1874 to 1888; contact Colorado State Archives
Probate records: From 1860
No probate search service; copies: 75¢ per page, no minimum

La Plata County Courthouse
1060 Second Avenue
Durango, CO 81301-5157
Phone (303) 247-2004; (303) 259-4000
County organized 1874 from Conejos and Lake counties
Naturalization records: From 1877 to 1903; contact Colorado State Archives

*Larimer County Courthouse
200 South Oak
Fort Collins, CO 80522
Phone (303) 498-7000; (303) 498-7918 Clerk of District Court
County organized 1861, original county
Land records: Contact Clerk of District Court, PO Box 2066, Fort Collins, CO 80522; copies: 75¢ per page
Naturalization records: From 1907 to 1929; contact Colorado State Archives
Vital records: Marriages from 1865.

Marriages from 1867 to 1959; contact Colorado State Archives
Probate records: From 1878; contact Clerk of District Court; copies: 75¢ per page

Las Animas County Courthouse
First and Maple
PO Box 773
Trinidad, CO 81082
Phone (719) 846-2221; (719) 846-3481
County organized 1866 from Huerfano County

*Lincoln County Courthouse
PO Box 67
Hugo, CO 80821
Phone (719) 743-2455; (719) 743-2444
County organized 1889 from Elbert County
Land records: Contact Roxana L. Devers, County Clerk
Naturalization records: Contact Jan Bandy, Court Clerk, PO Box 128, Hugo, CO 80821. Naturalization records from 1889 to 1894; contact Colorado State Archives
Vital records: From 1915; contact Bonnie Thompson, Registrar, PO Box 533, Hugo, CO 80821
Probate records: Contact Court Clerk
No probate search service; copies: 75¢ per page, no minimum

*Logan County Courthouse Annex
Third and Ash
Sterling, CO 80751
Phone (303) 522-1572; (303) 522-0888; (303) 522-6565 District Court Courthouse; (303) 522-3741 Northeast Colorado Health Department
County organized 1887 from Weld County
Land records: Contact County Clerk, Courthouse, Sterling, CO 80751, (303) 522-1544
Naturalization records: Contact District Court Courthouse, PO Box 71, Sterling, CO 80751
Vital records: Births and deaths; contact Northeast Colorado Health Department, PO Box 3300, Sterling, CO 80751. Marriages; contact County Clerk
Probate records: Contact District Court
Probate search service: no charge; copies: 75¢ per page for filed documents

*Mesa County Courthouse
544 Rood Avenue
Grand Junction, CO 81501
Phone (303) 244-1670 Chief Deputy, Recording Division
County organized 1883 from Gunnison County

Land records: From 1883 to date; Gincy French, Chief Deputy, Recording Division, Mesa County Courthouse (Sixth and Rood Avenue—location), PO Box 20,000 (mailing address), Grand Junction, CO 81502-5007
No land records search service; copies: $1.25 per page plus $1.00 per document for certification
Naturalization records: Contact Clerk of the District Court, 544 Rood Avenue, Grand Junction, CO 81501
Vital records: Births and deaths; contact Health Department, 515 Patterson Road, Grand Junction, CO 81501. Marriages from 1883 to date; contact Chief Deputy, Recording Division; copies: $2.00 each plus $1.00 for certification
Probate records: Contact Clerk of the District Court

*Mineral County Courthouse
North First Street
PO Box 70
Creede, CO 81130-0070
Phone (719) 658-2575; (719) 658-2440
County organized 1893 from Hinsdale County
Land records: Contact Clerk, Assessor and Treasurer
Naturalization records: Contact Clerk of District Court
Vital records: Contact Clerk of District and County Court
Probate records: Contact Clerk of District Court

*Moffat County Courthouse
221 West Victory Way
Craig, CO 81625-2732
Phone (303) 824-8254 Court; (303) 824-5484 County Clerk
County organized 1911 from Routt County
Land records: Contact Jessie L. Rowley, County Clerk; copies: $1.25 each
Naturalization records: No naturalization records
Vital records: Limited vital records
Probate records: Contact Alice Embury, District Court
No probate search service; copies: 75¢ per page, no minimum

*Montezuma County Courthouse
109 West Main Street
Cortez, CO 81321-3154
Phone (303) 565-3728 Clerk; (303) 565-1111 District Court
County organized 1889 from La Plata County
Land records: From 1889; contact Clerk, Room 108
Vital records: From 1879; contact Clerk
Probate records: Contact District Court, Room 210

*Montrose County Courthouse
320 South First Street
PO Box 1289
Montrose, CO 81402-1289
Phone (303) 249-4364; (303) 249-7755
*County organized 1883 from Gunnison
County*
Land records; Contact Ruth Heath,
County Clerk and Recorder; copies:
$1.25 per page, $5.00 per sheet for
plats or documents larger than 8¹/₂" x
14"
Naturalization records: Contact District
Court
Vital records: Births and deaths; contact
County Clerk and Recorder; certified
copies: $15.00 for the first copy of
births or deaths and $6.00 for each
additional copy ordered at the same
time, $2.00 for marriage licenses
Probate records: Contact District Court

*Morgan County Courthouse
Fort Morgan, CO 80701
Phone (303) 867-8266 District Court;
(303) 867-4918 Northeast Colorado
Health Department; (303) 867-5616
County Clerk and Recorder
*County organized 1889 from Weld
County*
Land records: Contact County Clerk, PO
Box 1399, Fort Morgan, CO 80701
Naturalization records: Contact District
Court, 400 Warner Street, Fort
Morgan, CO 80701
Vital records: Contact Northeast
Colorado Health Department, 228
West Railroad Avenue, Fort Morgan,
CO 80701. Marriages from 1889 to
date; contact Fay A. Johnson, County
Clerk and Recorder, PO Box 1399,
Fort Morgan, CO 80701
Probate records: Contact District Court,
PO Box 130, Fort Morgan, CO 80701
Probate search service: no charge;
copies: 75¢ per page, certification 75¢
per page, no minimum

*Otero County Courthouse
13 West Third Street
PO Box 511
La Junta, CO 81050-0511
Phone (719) 384-8701 Deputy Clerk and
Recorder; (719) 384-7080 Land Use
Administrator's Office; (719) 384-
4951 Clerk of the Court; (719) 384-
2584 County Health Department;
(719) 384-4221 FAX
*County organized 1889 from Bent
County*
Land records: Deeds, original subdivision
plats, etc.; contact Deputy Clerk and
Recorder, Clerk and Recorders Office,
Room 210. Maps; contact Kathy
Ehrlich, Land Use Administrator's
Office, Room 208

Naturalization records: Contact Clerk of
the Court, District Court, Room 207
Vital records: Marriages; contact Deputy
Clerk and Recorder. Deaths; contact
Receptionist, County Health
Department, Room 111. Marriages
from 1889 to 1916; contact Colorado
State Archives
Probate records: Contact Deputy Clerk
and Recorder

*Ouray County Courthouse
541 Fourth
PO Box C
Ouray, CO 81427-0615
Phone (303) 325-4405; (303) 325-4961
*County organized 1877 from Hinsdale
County; name changed from
Uncompahgre County in 1883*
Land records: Ownerships; contact
County Clerk's Office
Naturalization records: Contact Clerk of
the Court
Vital records: Marriages; contact County
Clerk's Office. Births and deaths;
contact County Treasurer. Marriages
from 1881 to 1959; contact Colorado
State Archives
Probate records: Contact Clerk of Court
Office

Park County Courthouse
300 Fourth Street
PO Box 220
Fairplay, CO 80440-0220
Phone (303) 836-2433; (303) 838-7509
County organized 1861, original county

*Phillips County Courthouse
221 South Interocean Avenue
Holyoke, CO 80734-1534
Phone (303) 854-3279; (303) 854-3131
*County organized 1889 from Logan
County*
Land records: Yes
Naturalization records: Yes
Vital records: Yes
Probate records: Yes

*Pitkin County Courthouse
506 Main Street
Aspen, CO 81611-2923
Phone (303) 920-5180
*County organized 1881 from Gunnison
County*
Land records: Contact Clerk and
Recorder's Office; copies: $1.25 per
page, $5.00 for plats
Naturalization records: No naturalization
records
Vital records: Births and deaths prior to
1907; contact Grantee-Grantor
Records. Marriages from 1881 to
1984; contact Colorado State Archives
Probate records: Contact Courts

*Prowers County Courthouse
301 South Main
PO Box 1046
Lamar, CO 81052-1046
Phone (719) 336-2209 County Assessor's
Office; (719) 336-7416 District Court
or County Court; (719) 336-2606
Annex Building
*County organized 1889 from Bent
County*
Land records: Contact County Assessor's
Office
Naturalization records: Contact District
Court
Vital records: Contact Annex Building,
1001 South Main, PO Box 336
Probate records: Contact District Court
or County Court

Pueblo County Judicial Building
211 West Tenth Street
Pueblo, CO 81003-2905
Phone (719) 546-5037; (719) 543-3550
County organized 1861, original county
Naturalization records: District Court
naturalization records from 1883 to
1949; contact Colorado State Archives
Vital records: Marriages from 1963 to
1965; contact Colorado State Archives

*Rio Blanco Combined Courts
PO Box 1150
Meeker, CO 81641
Phone (303) 878-5622 Court; (303) 878-
5068 Clerk and Recorder
*County organized 1889 from Garfield
County*
Land records: Contact County
Courthouse, 555 Main Street, Meeker,
CO 81641
No land records search service; copies:
$1.25 per page
Vital records: Births, deaths and marriage
licenses; contact Clerk and Recorder,
County Courthouse, PO Box 1067,
Meeker, CO 81641
No vital records search service; copies:
$12.00 for births and deaths, $2.00 for
marriage licenses
Probate records: From 1891; contact
Combined Courts
Probate search service: no charge (but
depends on available time); copies:
75¢ per page from paper originals,
$1.00 per page from microfilm
originals, plus postage; no minimum;
send written request with payment and
SASE

*Rio Grande County Courts
PO Box W
Del Norte, CO 81132
Phone (719) 657-3394; (719) 657-3334
*County organized 1874 from Conejos
County*
Land records: From Rio Grande County

Clerk and Recorder, PO Box 160, Del Norte, CO 81132
Naturalization records: Contact Rio Grande Courts
Vital records: Contact West End, Chula Vista Medical Center, 17228 West Highway 160, Del Norte, CO 81132 or East End of Valley, Vivian Allison, 416 Second Avenue, Monte Vista, CO 81144
Probate records: Contact Rio Grande Courts
Probate search service: $5.00; copies: 75¢ per page, $5.00 for certification, no minimum

Routt County Courthouse
522 Lincoln Avenue
PO Box 773117
Steamboat Springs, CO 80477
Phone (303) 879-5020; (303) 879-0108
County organized 1877 from Grand County

*Saguache County Combined Courts
PO Box 164
Saguache, CO 81149-0164
Phone (719) 655-2512 County Clerk and Recorder
County organized 1866 from Costilla County
Land records: Contact Marlene L. Pruitt, County Clerk and Recorder, 501 Fourth Street, PO Box 176, Saguache, CO 81149-0176
Naturalization records: From 1869 to 1940; contact Colorado State Archives
Probate records: Contact Combined Courts

*San Juan County Courthouse
PO Box 466
Silverton, CO 81433
Phone (303) 387-5671
County organized 1876 from La Plata County
Land records: Contact County Clerk
Naturalization records: No naturalization records
Vital records: Marriages; contact County Clerk. Births and deaths; contact Office of the Town Clerk, Silverton, CO 81433

San Miguel County Courthouse
305 West Colorado
PO Box 919
Telluride, CO 81435
Phone (303) 728-3891; (303) 728-3954
County organized 1861 from Ouray County

*Sedgwick County Courthouse
315 Cedar Street
PO Box 50

Julesburg, CO 80737
Phone (303) 474-3627 Courts; (303) 474-3346 Clerk's Office; (303) 474-0954 FAX
County organized 1889 from Logan County
Land records: Contact County Clerk
Naturalization records: No naturalization records
Vital records: Contact Mrs. Linda Hartwell, Registrar of Vital Statistics, 204 East Ninth, Julesburg, CO 80737
Probate records: Contact County and District Court, Courthouse, Julesburg, CO 80737

*Summit County Courthouse
Clerk and Recorder or Combined Courts
Breckenridge, CO 80424
Phone (303) 453-2561 Clerk and Recorder; (303) 453-2272 Combined Courts
County organized 1861, original county
Land records: Contact Clerk and Recorder
Naturalization records: Contact Combined Courts
Vital records: Contact Clerk and Recorder
Probate records: Contact Combined Courts

Teller County Courthouse
PO Box 959
Cripple Creek, CO 80813-0959
Phone (719) 689-2574; (719) 689-2482
County organized 1899 from Fremont County

*Washington County Courthouse
150 Ash
Akron, CO 80720-1510
Phone (303) 345-2756; (303) 345-2701
County organized 1887 from Weld and Arapahoe counties
Land records: Contact County Clerk and Recorder, PO Box L, Akron, CO 80720
Vital records: Contact Emma Howard, Registrar of Vital Statistics, 251 Hickory, Akron, CO 80720
Probate records: Contact Willadene Burley, PO Box 455, Akron, CO 80720
Probate search service: no charge; copies: 75¢ per page, $1.00 for certified copies, 75¢ minimum

Weld County Courthouse
915 10th Avenue
Greeley, CO 80631-3811
Phone (303) 356-4000
County organized 1861, original county

Yuma County Courthouse
PO Box 347
Wray, CO 80758-0347
Phone (303) 332-5809
County organized 1889 from Washington County

CONNECTICUT

Capital: Hartford. Statehood: 9 January 1788 (chartered 1662, relinquished western lands in 1786 and Western Reserve in 1800)

Court System

In 1978 Connecticut was divided into twelve Judicial Districts consisting of one or more of the state's one hundred sixty-nine towns: Ansonia-Milford (A), Danbury (D), Fairfield (F), Hartford-New Britain (H), Litchfield (L), Middlesex (M), New Haven (NH), New London (NL), Stamford-Norwalk (S), Tolland (T), Waterbury (Wa), and Windham (Wi).

The following is a list of Connecticut towns and their respective districts: Andover (T), Ansonia (A), Ashford (Wi), Avon (H), Barkhamstead (L), Beacon Falls (A), Berlin (H), Bethany (NH), Bethel (D), Bethlehem (L), Bloomfield (H), Bolton (T), Bozrah (NL), Branford (NH), Bridgeport (F), Bridgewater (L), Bristol (H), Brookfield (D), Brooklyn (Wi), Burlington (H), Canaan (L), Canterbury (Wi), Canton (H), Chaplin (Wi), Cheshire (NH), Chester (M), Clinton (M), Colchester (NL), Colebrook (L), Columbia (T), Cornwall (L), Coventry (T), Cromwell (M), Danbury (D), Darien (S), Deep River (M), Derby (A), Durham (M), Eastford (Wi), East Granby (H), East Haddam (M), East Hampton (M), East Hartford (H), East Haven (NH), East Lyme (NL), Easton (F), East Windsor (H), Ellington (T), Enfield (H), Essex (M), Fairfield (F), Farmington (H), Franklin (NL), Glastonbury (H), Goshen (L), Granby (H), Greenwich (S), Griswold (NL), Groton (NL), Guilford (NH), Haddam (M), Hamden (NH), Hampton (Wi), Hartford (H), Hartland (L), Harwinton (L), Hebron (T), Kent (L), Killingly (Wi), Killingworth (M), Lebanon (NL), Ledyard (NL), Lisbon (NL), Litchfield (L), Lyme (NL), Madison (NH), Manchester (H), Mansfield (T), Marlborough (H), Meriden (NH), Middlebury (Wa), Middlefield (M), Middletown (M), Milford (A), Monroe (F), Montville (NL), Morris (L), Naugatuck (Wa), New Britain (H), New Canaan (S), New Fairfield (D), New Hartford (L), New Haven (NH), Newington (H), New London (NL), New Milford (L), Newtown (D), Norfolk (L), North Branford (NH), North Canaan (L), North Haven (NH), North Stonington (NL), Norwalk (S), Norwich (NL), Old Lyme (NL), Old Saybrook (M), Orange (A), Oxford (A), Plainfield (Wi),

Plainville (H), Plymouth (H), Pomfret (Wi), Portland (M), Preston (NL), Prospect (Wa), Putnam (Wi), Redding (D), Ridgefield (D), Rocky Hill (H), Roxbury (L), Salem (NL), Salisbury (L), Scotland (Wi), Seymour (A), Sharon (L), Shelton (A), Sherman (D), Simsbury (H), Somers (T), Southbury (Wa), Southington (H), South Windsor (H), Sprague (NL), Stafford (T), Stamford (S), Sterling (Wi), Stonington (NL), Stratford (F), Suffield (H), Thomaston (L), Thompson (Wi), Tolland (T), Torrington (L), Trumbull (F), Union (T), Vernon (T), Voluntown (NL), Wallingford (NH), Warren (L), Washington (L), Waterbury (Wa), Waterford (NL), Watertown (Wa), Westbrook (M), West Hartford (H), West Haven (NH), Weston (S), Westport (S), Wethersfield (H), Willington (T), Wilton (S), Winchester (L), Windham (Wi), Windsor (H), Windsor Locks (H), Wolcott (Wa), Woodbridge (NH), Woodbury (Wa), Woodstock (Wi).

Probate Courts within each district have original jurisdiction over estate matters. Appeals are taken to the Superior Court in the same Judicial District, which also handles all other civil and criminal cases. An Appellate Court and a Supreme Court sit in Hartford.

Counties and Districts

*Ansonia-Milford District Courthouse
14 West River Street
Milford, CT 06460
Phone (203) 878-5791
District organized 1978
Land records: Foreclosure records only; copies: 50¢ each, $2.00 for certification
Naturalization records: No naturalization records
Vital records: No vital records
Probate records: No probate records

*Danbury District Courthouse
146 White Street
Danbury, CT 06810
Phone (203) 797-4416
District organized 1978
Land records: No land records
Naturalization records: No naturalization records
Vital records: No vital records
Probate records: No probate records

*Fairfield County Courthouse
1061 Main Street
Bridgeport, CT 06604
Phone (203) 579-6527
Fairfield County organized 1666, original county; district organized 1978

Land records: No land records
Naturalization records: No naturalization records
Vital records: No vital records
Probate records: No probate records

Hartford-New Britain District Courthouse
95 Washington Street
Hartford, CT 06106-4406
Phone (203) 566-3170 Chief Clerk's Office
Hartford County organized 1666, original county; district organized 1978

*Litchfield Superior Court
PO Box 247, West Street
Litchfield, CT 06759
Phone (203) 567-0885
Litchfield County organized 1751 from Hartford and Fairfield counties; district organized 1978
Land records: No land records
Naturalization records: No naturalization records
Vital records: No vital records
Probate records: No probate records

*Middlesex Superior Court
Judicial District Courthouse
1 Court Street
Middletown, CT 06457-3374
Phone (203) 343-6400
Middlesex County organized 1785 from Hartford, New London and New Haven counties; district organized 1978
Land records: No land records
Naturalization records: No naturalization records
Vital records: No vital records
Probate records: No probate records

*New Haven District Courthouse
235 Church Street
New Haven, CT 06510-0998
Phone (203) 789-7908
New Haven County organized 1666, original county; district organized 1978
Land records: No land records
Naturalization records: No naturalization records
Vital records: Divorces (civil and criminal cases)
Probate records: No probate records

New London District Courthouse
70 Huntington Street
New London, CT 06320
Phone (203) 443-5363 Chief Clerk's Office
New London County organized 1666, original county; district organized 1978

*Stamford-Norwalk District Courthouse
123 Hoyt Street
Stamford, CT 06905
Phone (203) 965-5315
District organized 1981 (in its present form)
Land records: No land records (only records of litigation)
Naturalization records: No naturalization records
Vital records: No vital records
Probate records: No probate records

*Tolland District Courthouse
69 Brooklyn Street
Rockville, CT 06066-3643
Phone (203) 875-6294
Tolland County organized 1785 from Windham County; district organized 1978
Naturalization records: No naturalization records, removed several years ago and sent to Federal Archives in Waltham

*State of Connecticut Judicial Department
Judicial District of Waterbury
300 Grand Street
Waterbury, CT 06702
Phone (203) 757-8306
District organized 1978
Land records: No land records
Naturalization records: No naturalization records
Vital records: No vital records
Probate records: No probate records

Windham District Courthouse
155 Church Street
PO Box 191
Putnam, CT 06260
Phone (203) 928-7749 Chief Clerk's Office
Windham County organized 1726 from Hartford and New London counties; district organized 1978

Towns and Cities

Birth records are restricted in Connecticut; a copy of a certificate can be obtained only by the person whose name appears on the certificate if eighteen years of age or older, a minor's parent or guardian, or a member of a legally incorporated genealogical society. If the last, a copy of a current, signed membership card must accompany all requests for certificates. However, microfilm copies of births, deaths, and marriages prior to 1900 are on deposit at the Connecticut State Library, 231 Capitol Avenue, Hartford, CT 06106. Naturalization records from some of Connecticut's Municipal Courts were transferred to the

U.S. District Courts for Connecticut and were subsequently transferred to the National Archives along with naturalization records from the Federal Courts for Connecticut (Record Group 21 and Record Group 200). The State Library retains records of pre-1790 naturalizations and photocopies of some records from Middlesex and New London Superior Courts as well as microfilm copies of some of the Municipal, County Court, and Court of Common Pleas records.

The State Library has most of the original estate papers prior to 1900 and some of later date, mostly on microfilm.

*Town of Andover
Town Office Building
School Road
Andover, CT 06232
Phone (203) 742-0188 Town Clerk and Registrar of Vital Statistics; (203) 649-2223 Judge of Probate Court
Town incorporated 18 May 1848 from Coventry, Hebron and Lebanon. Probate district constituted 27 June 1851 from Hebron (contains the records of Hebron from May session 1789 to 27 June 1851)
Land records: Contact Marie R. Burbank, Town Clerk and Registrar of Vital Statistics
Naturalization records: No naturalization records
Vital records: Contact Town Clerk and Registrar of Vital Statistics
Probate records: Contact Elaine N. Camposeo, Judge of Probate Court, 158 Bolton Center Road, Bolton, CT 06043

City of Ansonia
City Hall
253 Main Street
Ansonia, CT 06401
Phone (203) 734-8034 City Clerk, Town Clerk and Registrar of Vital Statistics; (203) 734-1277 Judge of Probate Court
Town incorporated April 1889 from Derby. City incorporated January session 1893. Probate district constituted 4 July 1858 from New Haven
Land records: Contact Florence K. Hoinski, City Clerk, Town Clerk and Registrar of Vital Statistics
Vital records: Contact City Clerk, Town Clerk and Registrar of Vital Statistics
Probate records: Contact Clifford D. Hoyle, Judge of Probate Court

*Town of Ashford
Knowlton Memorial Town Hall
25 Pompey Hollow Road
Ashford, CT 06278

Phone (203) 429-7044 Town Clerk and Registrar of Vital Statistics
Town incorporated October 1714. Probate district constituted 4 June 1830 from Pomfret
Land records: Contact Barbara B. Metsack, Town Clerk and Registrar of Vital Statistics; copies: $1.00 per page, $3.00 for maps
Naturalization records: No naturalization records
Vital records: Contact Town Clerk and Registrar of Vital Statistics
Probate records: Before 1832; contact Town Clerk and Registrar of Vital Statistics

Town of Avon
Town Hall
60 West Main Street
Avon, CT 06001
Phone (203) 677-2634 Town Clerk and Registrar of Vital Statistics; (203) 677-2634 Judge of Probate Court
Town incorporated May 1830 from Farmington. Probate district constituted May session 1844 from Farmington
Land records: Contact Town Clerk and Registrar of Vital Statistics
Vital records: Contact Town Clerk and Registrar of Vital Statistics
Probate records: Contact D. Stephen Gaffney, Judge of Probate Court

*Town of Barkhamstead
Town Office Building
67 Ripley Hill Road, Route 318
PO Box 185
Pleasant Valley, CT 06063-0185
Phone (203) 379-8665 Town Clerk and Registrar of Vital Statistics; (203) 379-8665 Judge of Probate Court
Town incorporated October 1779. Probate district constituted 5 June 1834 from New Hartford (contains the records of New Hartford from 27 May 1825 to 5 June 1834)
Land records: Contact Nancy N. Winn, Town Clerk and Registrar of Vital Statistics
Naturalization records: Contact Curtis K. Case, Judge of Probate Court
Vital records: Contact Town Clerk and Registrar of Vital Statistics
Probate records: Contact Judge of Probate Court

*Town of Beacon Falls
10 Maple Avenue
Beacon Falls, CT 06403
Phone (203) 729-8254 Town Clerk and Registrar of Vital Statistics; (203) 729-4571, ext. 220 Judge of Probate Court
Town incorporated June 1871 from Bethany, Oxford, Seymour and

Naugatuck. Probate district constituted 4 July 1863 from Waterbury

Land records: Contact Paula D. Balanda, Town Clerk and Registrar of Vital Statistics

Vital records: Contact Town Clerk and Registrar of Vital Statistics

Probate records: Contact Robert M. Siuzdak, Judge of Probate Court, Town Hall, 229 Church Street, Naugatuck, CT 06770

*Town of Berlin

(240 Kensington Road, Berlin, CT—location)

PO Box 1 (mailing address)

Kensington, CT 06037

Phone (203) 828-7075 Town Clerk and Registrar of Vital Statistics; (203) 826-2696 Judge of Probate Court

Town incorporated May 1785 from Farmington, Wethersfield and Middletown. Probate district constituted 2 June 1824 from Farmington, Hartford and Middletown

Land records: Contact Joanne G. Ward, Town Clerk and Registrar of Vital Statistics

Naturalization records: Contact Walter A. Clebowicz, Judge of Probate Court, Courthouse, 177 Columbus Boulevard, New Britain, CT 06051

Vital records: Contact Town Clerk and Registrar of Vital Statistics

Probate records: Contact Judge of Probate Court

*Town of Bethany

Town Hall

40 Peck Road

Bethany, CT 06524-3338

Phone (203) 393-0820 Town Clerk and Registrar of Vital Statistics; (203) 393-3744 Judge of Probate Court

Town incorporated May 1832 from Woodbridge. Probate district constituted 4 July 1854 from New Haven

Land records: Contact Joan C. Simpson, Town Clerk and Registrar of Vital Statistics

Naturalization records: No naturalization records

Vital records: Contact Town Clerk and Registrar of Vital Statistics. Vital records before 1852; contact Town of Woodbridge, Town Clerk and Registrar of Vital Statistics, Town Hall, 11 Meetinghouse Lane, Woodbridge, CT 06525

Probate records: Contact Guy D. Yale, Judge of Probate Court

Town of Bethel

Town Hall

5 Library Place

PO Box 3

Bethel, CT 06801-0003

Phone (203) 794-8505 Town Clerk and Registrar of Vital Statistics; (203) 794-8508 Judge of Probate Court

Town incorporated May 1855 from Danbury. Probate district constituted 4 July 1859 from Danbury

Land records: Contact Jane D. Shannon, Town Clerk and Registrar of Vital Statistics

Vital records: Contact Town Clerk and Registrar of Vital Statistics

Probate records: Contact Martin J. Lawlor, Jr., Judge of Probate Court

Town of Bethlehem

(Main Street)

254 Lakes Road

Bethlehem, CT 06751

Phone (203) 266-7510 Town Clerk and Registrar of Vital Statistics; (203) 263-2417 Judge of Probate Court

Town incorporated May 1787 from Woodbury and known as "North Purchase." Probate district constituted October session 1719 from Hartford, Fairfield and New Haven

Land records: Contact Lucy N. Palangio, Town Clerk and Registrar of Vital Statistics

Vital records: Contact Town Clerk and Registrar of Vital Statistics

Probate records: Contact Mary D. Donaldson, Judge of Probate Court, 281 Main Street South, Town Office Building, Woodbury, CT 06798

*Town of Bloomfield

800 Bloomfield Avenue

PO Box 337

Bloomfield, CT 06002

Phone (203) 769-3507 Town Clerk and Registrar of Vital Statistics; (203) 769-3549 Judge of Probate Court

Town incorporated May 1835 from Windsor. Probate district constituted 5 January 1983 from Hartford

Land records: Contact Marguerite Phillips, Town Clerk and Registrar of Vital Statistics

Vital records: Contact Town Clerk and Registrar of Vital Statistics

Probate records: Contact Steven Zelman, Judge of Probate Court

*Town of Bolton

222 Bolton Center Road

Bolton, CT 06043

Phone (203) 649-8066 Town Clerk and Registrar of Vital Statistics

Town incorporated October 1720. Probate district constituted 27 June 1851 from Hebron (contains the records of Hebron from May session 1789 to 27 June 1851)

Land records: Contact Susan M. DePold, Town Clerk and Registrar of Vital Statistics; copies: $1.00 per page

Naturalization records: No naturalization records

Vital records: Contact Town Clerk and Registrar of Vital Statistics; certified copies: $5.00 each

Probate records: Contact Elaine N. Camposeo, Judge of Probate Court; copies: $5.00 for pages 1–5, $1.00 for each additional page

Town of Bozrah

Town Hall

Bozrah, CT 06334

Phone (203) 889-2689 Town Clerk and Registrar of Vital Statistics; (203) 859-0852 Judge of Probate Court

Town incorporated May 1786 from Norwich. Probate district constituted 3 June 1843 from Norwich

Land records: Contact Anna Mair, Town Clerk and Registrar of Vital Statistics

Vital records: Contact Town Clerk and Registrar of Vital Statistics

Probate records: Contact Helene L. Bloom, Judge of Probate Court, 179 Lake Road, Bozrah, CT 06334

*Town of Branford

1019 Main Street

PO Box 150

Branford, CT 06405

Phone (203) 488-6305 Town Clerk and Registrar of Vital Statistics; (203) 488-0318 Judge of Probate Court

Town named 1653. Probate district constituted 21 June 1850 from Guilford

Land records: Contact Georgette A. Laske, Town Clerk and Registrar of Vital Statistics

Vital records: Contact Town Clerk and Registrar of Vital Statistics

Probate records: Contact John E. Donegan, Judge of Probate Court, 1019 Main Street, PO Box 638, Branford, CT 06405

City of Bridgeport

City Hall, Room 124

45 Lyon Terrace

Bridgeport, CT 06604

Phone (203) 576-7207 Town Clerk and Registrar of Vital Statistics; (203) 333-4165 Judge of Probate Court

Town incorporated May 1821 from Stratford and Fairfield. City incorporated May session 1836. Probate district constituted 4 June 1840 from Stratford (contains the records of Stratford from May session 1782 to 4 June 1840, and the

records of Easton, which include the records of Weston, Easton being a district of its own from 22 July 1875 until 4 March 1878)
Land records: Contact Hector Diaz, Town Clerk and Registrar of Vital Statistics
Vital records: Contact Town Clerk and Registrar of Vital Statistics
Probate records: Contact Raymond C. Lyddy, Judge of Probate Court, McLevy Hall, 202 State Street, Bridgeport, CT 06604

Town of Bridgewater
Town Hall
Main Street
Bridgewater, CT 06752
Phone (203) 354-5102 Town Clerk and Registrar of Vital Statistics; (203) 355-6029 Judge of Probate Court
Town incorporated May 1856 from New Milford. Probate district constituted May session 1787 from Woodbury, Sharon and Danbury
Land records: Contact Grace V. Meddaugh, Town Clerk and Registrar of Vital Statistics
Vital records: Contact Town Clerk and Registrar of Vital Statistics
Probate records: Contact Suzanne L. Powers, Judge of Probate Court, Town Hall, 10 Main Street, New Milford, CT 06776

*City of Bristol
City Hall
111 North Main Street
Bristol, CT 06010
Phone (203) 584-7656 City Clerk and Registrar of Vital Statistics; (203) 564-7650 Judge of Probate Court
Town incorporated May 1785 from Farmington. City incorporated January session 1911. Probate district constituted 4 June 1830 from Farmington
Land records: Contact Florence McAuliffe, City Clerk and Registrar of Vital Statistics
Vital records: Contact City Clerk and Registrar of Vital Statistics
Probate records: Contact Andre D. Dorval, Judge of Probate Court

*Town of Brookfield
Brookfield Municipal Center
Pocono Road
PO Box 5106
Brookfield, CT 06804-5106
Phone (203) 775-7313 Town Clerk and Registrar of Vital Statistics; (203) 775-3700 Judge of Probate Court
Town incorporated May 1788 from Danbury, New Milford and Newtown. Probate district constituted 19 June 1850 from Newtown

Land records: Contact Ruth B. Burr, Town Clerk and Registrar of Vital Statistics
Naturalization records: No naturalization records
Vital records: Contact Town Clerk and Registrar of Vital Statistics
Probate records: Contact Jeffrey W. Reinen, Judge of Probate Court, Town Hall, Pocono Road, Brookfield, CT 06804

*Town of Brooklyn
Town Hall
PO Box 356
Brooklyn, CT 06234
Phone (203) 774-9543 Town Clerk and Registrar of Vital Statistics; (203) 774-5973 Judge of Probate Court
Town incorporated May 1786 from Pomfret and Canterbury. Probate district constituted 4 June 1833 from Pomfret and Plainfield
Land records: Contact Leona A. Mainville, Town Clerk and Registrar of Vital Statistics; copies: $1.00 per page, $1.00 for certification
Vital records: Contact Town Clerk and Registrar of Vital Statistics
Probate records: Contact James K. Kelley, Judge of Probate Court

Town of Burlington
Town Hall
Route 4
Burlington, CT 06013
Phone (203) 673-2108 Town Clerk and Registrar of Vital Statistics; (203) 673-2108 Judge of Probate Court
Town incorporated May 1806 from Bristol. Probate district constituted 3 June 1834 from Farmington
Land records: Contact Kathleen K. Zabel, Town Clerk and Registrar of Vital Statistics, 200 Spielman Highway, Burlington, CT 06013
Vital records: Contact Town Clerk and Registrar of Vital Statistics
Probate records: Contact Charles W. Bauer, Judge of Probate Court

*Town of Canaan
Town Hall
107 Main Street
Falls Village, CT 06031
Phone (203) 824-0707 Town Clerk and Registrar of Vital Statistics; (203) 824-7114 Judge of Probate Court
Town incorporated October 1739. Probate district constituted 6 June 1846 from Sharon
Land records: Contact Mary Mittaud, Town Clerk and Registrar of Vital Statistics
Vital records: Contact Town Clerk and Registrar of Vital Statistics

Probate records: Contact Diana J. Matheson, Judge of Probate Court, Town Hall, North Canaan, PO Box 905, Canaan, CT 06018

*Town of Canterbury
PO Box 27
Canterbury, CT 06331
Phone (203) 546-9377 Town Clerk and Registrar of Vital Statistics
Town incorporated October 1703 from Plainfield. Probate district constituted 27 May 1835 from Plainfield
Land records: Contact Marilyn E. Burris, Town Clerk and Registrar of Vital Statistics
Naturalization records: Yes
Vital records: Contact Town Clerk and Registrar of Vital Statistics
Probate records: Contact Juliette S. Stadnicki, Judge of Probate Court, Town Office Building, PO Box 26, Canterbury, CT 06331

Town of Canton
Town Hall
Collinsville, CT 06022
Phone (203) 693-4112 Town Clerk and Registrar of Vital Statistics; (203) 693-8684 Judge of Probate Court
Town incorporated May 1806 from Simsbury. Probate district constituted 7 June 1841 from Simsbury
Land records: Contact Shirley C. Krompegal, Town Clerk and Registrar of Vital Statistics, 4 Market Street, PO Box 168, Collinsville, CT 06022
Vital records: Contact Town Clerk and Registrar of Vital Statistics
Probate records: Contact Raymond B. Green, Judge of Probate Court, PO Box 175, Collinsville, CT 06022

*Town of Chaplin
Town Hall
Route 198
PO Box 286
Chaplin, CT 06235
Phone (203) 455-9455 Town Clerk and Registrar of Vital Statistics; (203) 455-9455 Judge of Probate Court
Town incorporated 1822 from Windham. Probate district constituted 7 June 1850 from Windham
Land records: From 1822 to date; contact Jane S. Hampton Smith, Town Clerk and Registrar of Vital Statistics; copies: $1.00 per page
Vital records: Some from early 1800s, complete from 1895 to date; contact Town Clerk and Registrar of Vital Statistics
Probate records: Contact Reid Samuelson, Judge of Probate Court

Town of Cheshire
Town Hall
84 South Main Street
Cheshire, CT 06410
Phone (203) 272-2293 Town Clerk and
Registrar of Vital Statistics; (203)
272-8247 Judge of Probate Court
*Town incorporated May 1780 from
Wallingford. Probate district
constituted 27 May 1829 from
Wallingford*
Land records: Contact Mae R. Tabor,
Town Clerk and Registrar of Vital
Statistics
Vital records: Contact Town Clerk and
Registrar of Vital Statistics
Probate records: Contact Raymond F.
Voelker, Judge of Probate Court

Town of Chester
Town Office Building
65 Main Street
Chester, CT 06412
Phone (203) 526-0006 Town Clerk and
Registrar of Vital Statistics; (203)
526-0007 Judge of Probate Court
*Town incorporated May 1836 from
Saybrook. Probate district constituted
May session 1780 from Guilford*
Land records: Contact Debra Germini
Calamari, Town Clerk and Registrar
of Vital Statistics
Naturalization records: Contact Helen B.
(Bonnie) Bennet, Judge of Probate
Court
Vital records: Contact Town Clerk and
Registrar of Vital Statistics
Probate records: Contact Judge of
Probate Court

*Town of Clinton
549 Main Street
Clinton, CT 06413
Phone (203) 669-9101 Town Clerk and
Registrar of Vital Statistics; (203)
669-6447 Judge of Probate Court
*Town incorporated May 1838 from
Killingworth. Probate district
constituted 5 July 1862 from
Killingworth*
Land records: Contact Karen Lee
Marsden, Town Clerk and Registrar of
Vital Statistics; copies: $1.00 per
page, $1.00 per document for
certification
Naturalization records: No naturalization
records
Vital records: Contact Town Clerk and
Registrar of Vital Statistics; certified
copies: $5.00 each
Probate records: Contact William Dunn,
Judge of Probate Court, Town Hall,
PO Box 130, Clinton, CT 06413

*Town of Colchester
Town Hall
40 Norwich Avenue

Colchester, CT 06415
Phone (203) 537-7215 Town Clerk and
Registrar of Vital Statistics; (203)
537-7290 Judge of Probate Court
*Town incorporated 1698, named
October 1699. Borough incorporated
May session 1824. Probate district
constituted 29 May 1832 from East
Haddam (contains records of East
Haddam from October session 1741
to 29 May 1832)*
Land records: Contact Patricia A.
LaGrega, Town Clerk and Registrar of
Vital Statistics
Naturalization records: No naturalization
records
Vital records: Contact Town Clerk and
Registrar of Vital Statistics
Probate records: Contact Kevin Kennedy,
Judge of Probate Court, Town Office
Building, Colchester, CT 06415

Town of Colebrook
Town Hall
Route 183
PO Box 5
Colebrook, CT 06021
Phone (203) 379-2922 Town Clerk and
Registrar of Vital Statistics; (203)
379-5576 Judge of Probate Court
*Town incorporated October 1779.
Probate district constituted 31 May
1838 from Norfolk*
Land records: Contact N. Coyce Nelson,
Town Clerk and Registrar of Vital
Statistics
Vital records: Contact Town Clerk and
Registrar of Vital Statistics
Probate records: Contact Alan M. Barber,
Judge of Probate Court, Town Hall,
338 Main Street, Winsted, CT 06098

*Town of Columbia
Yeomans Hall
Route 87
PO Box 165
Columbia, CT 06237
Phone (203) 228-3284 Town Clerk and
Registrar of Vital Statistics; (203)
649-8066 Judge of Probate Court
*Town incorporated May 1804. Probate
district constituted 27 June 1851
from Hebron (contains the records of
Hebron from May session 1789 to 27
June 1851)*
Land records: From 1804 to date (prior
records in the Town of Lebanon);
contact Eleanor V. Vickers, Town
Clerk and Registrar of Vital Statistics;
copies: $1.00 per page, $1.00 for
certification
Vital records: From 1804 to date; contact
Town Clerk and Registrar of Vital
Statistics; certified copies: $5.00
(births are restricted)
Probate records: From 1851 to date;
contact Elaine N. Camposeo, Judge of

Probate Court, 222 Bolton Center
Road, Bolton, CT 06043; copies:
$1.00 per page, $1.00 for certification

Town of Cornwall
Town Office
Pine Street
PO Box 87
Cornwall, CT 06753
Phone (203) 672-6651 Town Clerk and
Registrar of Vital Statistics; (203)
672-2677 Judge of Probate Court
*Town incorporated May 1740. Probate
district constituted 15 June 1847
from Litchfield*
Land records: Contact Barbara C. Dakin,
Town Clerk and Registrar of Vital
Statistics
Vital records: Contact Town Clerk and
Registrar of Vital Statistics
Probate records: Contact Margaret D.
Cooley, Judge of Probate Court

*Town of Coventry
Town Office Building
1712 Main Street
PO Box 189
Coventry, CT 06238
Phone (203) 742-7966 Town Clerk and
Registrar of Vital Statistics; (203)
742-6791 Judge of Probate Court
*Town incorporated May 1712. Probate
district constituted 19 June 1849
from Hebron*
Land records: From 1712; contact Ruth
E. Benoit, Town Clerk and Registrar
of Vital Statistics
No land records search service: copies:
$1.00 per page
Vital records: From 1712; contact Town
Clerk and Registrar of Vital Statistics;
certified copies: $5.00 each (births are
restricted)
Probate records: Contact David C.
Rappe, Judge of Probate Court, Town
of Coventry (District), PO Box 189,
Coventry, CT 06238

*Town of Cromwell
41 West Street
Cromwell, CT 06416
Phone (203) 632-3440 Town Clerk and
Registrar of Vital Statistics; (203)
347-7424 Judge of Probate Court
*Town incorporated May 1851 from
Middletown. Probate district
constituted May session 1752 from
Hartford, Guilford and East Haddam*
Land records: From 1851 to date; contact
Bernard Neville, Town Clerk and
Registrar of Vital Statistics
Naturalization records: No naturalization
records
Vital records: From 1851 to date; contact
Town Clerk and Registrar of Vital
Statistics
Probate records: Contact Joseph D.

Marino, Judge of Probate Court, Marino Professional Building, 94 Court Street, Middletown, CT 06457

*City of Danbury
City Hall
155 Deer Hill Avenue
Danbury, CT 06810
Phone (203) 797-4531 City Clerk and Registrar of Vital Statistics; (203) 797-4521 Judge of Probate Court
Town settled 1687, named October 1697, incorporated May 1702. City incorporated January session 1889. Town and city consolidated 1 January 1965. Probate district constituted May session 1744 from Fairfield
Land records: Contact Marjorie L. Cerveniski, City Clerk and Registrar of Vital Statistics
Vital records: Contact City Clerk and Registrar of Vital Statistics
Probate records: Contact Dianne E. Yamin, Judge of Probate Court

Borough of Danielson
(see Town of Killingly)

*Town of Darien
Town Hall
2 Renshaw Road
Darien, CT 06820
Phone (203) 656-7307 Town Clerk and Registrar of Vital Statistics; (203) 656-7342 Judge of Probate Court
Town incorporated May 1820 from Stamford. Probate district constituted 18 May 1921 from Stamford
Land records: Contact Marilyn M. Van Sciver, Town Clerk and Registrar of Vital Statistics
Naturalization records: No naturalization records
Vital records: Contact Town Clerk and Registrar of Vital Statistics
Probate records: Contact William H. Atkinson, Judge of Probate Court

*Town of Deep River
Town Hall
174 Main Street
Deep River, CT 06417
Phone (203) 526-6024 Town Clerk and Registrar of Vital Statistics; (203) 526-6026 Judge of Probate Court
Town settled 1635 as Saybrook, united with Connecticut December 1644, name changed to Deep River 1 July 1947. Probate district constituted 5 January 1949 from Saybrook
Land records: Contact Jeanne G. Nickse, Town Clerk and Registrar of Vital Statistics
Naturalization records: No naturalization records

Vital records: Contact Town Clerk and Registrar of Vital Statistics
Probate records: Contact Patricia L. Damon, Judge of Probate Court

City of Derby
City Hall
35 Fifth Street
Derby, CT 06418
Phone (203) 734-9207 City Clerk and Registrar of Vital Statistics; (203) 734-1277 Judge of Probate Court
Town named May 1675, incorporated 13 May 1775. City incorporated 7 June (January session) 1893. Town and city consolidated 7 June 1893. Probate district constituted 4 July 1858 from New Haven
Land records: Contact Marion C. Molloy, City Clerk and Registrar of Vital Statistics
Vital records: Contact City Clerk and Registrar of Vital Statistics
Probate records: Contact Clifford D. Hoyle, Judge of Probate Court, City Hall, Ansonia, CT 06401

*Town of Durham
Town Hall
Town House Road
PO Box 428
Durham, CT 06422
Phone (203) 349-3452 Town Clerk and Registrar of Vital Statistics; (203) 347-7424 Judge of Probate Court
Town named May 1704, incorporated October 1708. Probate district constituted May session 1752 from Hartford, Guilford and East Haddam
Land records: Contact Marjorie C. Hatch, Town Clerk and Registrar of Vital Statistics
Naturalization records: Contact Joseph D. Marino, Judge of Probate Court, Marino Professional Building, 94 Court Street, Middletown, CT 06457
Vital records: Contact Town Clerk and Registrar of Vital Statistics
Probate records: Contact Judge of Probate Court

*Town of East Granby
Town Hall
9 Center Street
East Granby, CT 06026
Phone (203) 653-6528 Town Clerk and Registrar of Vital Statistics; (203) 653-3434 Judge of Probate Court
Town incorporated June 1858 from Granby and Windsor Locks. Probate district Number 040 established 4 July 1865 from Granby
Land records: Contact Elisabeth W. Birmingham, Town Clerk and Registrar of Vital Statistics, PO Box TC, East Granby, CT 06026-0459; copies: $1.00 per page

Vital records: Contact Town Clerk and Registrar of Vital Statistics; copies: $5.00 each
Probate records: Contact Paul A. Ridgeway, Judge of Probate Court, PO Box 542, East Granby, CT 06026-0542

*Town of East Haddam
Town Office Building
Goodspeed Plaza
East Haddam, CT 06423
Phone (203) 873-5027 Town Clerk and Registrar of Vital Statistics; (203) 873-5028 Judge of Probate Court
Town incorporated May 1734 from Haddam. Probate district constituted October session 1741 from Hartford (the records of East Haddam, previous to 29 May 1832, are in Colchester)
Land records: From 1704 to date; contact Mildred E. Quinn, Town Clerk and Registrar of Vital Statistics
Vital records: From 1704 to date; contact Town Clerk and Registrar of Vital Statistics
Probate records: From 1832 to date; contact Paul Buhl, Judge of Probate Court, East Haddam Town Office, River House, East Haddam, CT 06423

*Town of East Hampton
Town Hall
20 East High Street
East Hampton, CT 06424
Phone (203) 267-2519 Town Clerk and Registrar of Vital Statistics; (203) 267-9262 Judge of Probate Court
Town incorporated as Chatham October 1767 from Middletown. Probate district constituted 1 June 1824 from Middletown and East Haddam (the records of Chatham, previous to 6 January 1915, are in Portland)
Land records: Contact Pauline L. Markham, Town Clerk and Registrar of Vital Statistics
Naturalization records: No naturalization records
Vital records: Contact Town Clerk and Registrar of Vital Statistics
Probate records: From 1915; contact Anne C. McKinney, Judge of Probate Court

*Town of East Hartford
Town Hall
740 Main Street
East Hartford, CT 06108
Phone (203) 291-7230 Town Clerk and Registrar of Vital Statistics; (203) 291-7278 Judge of Probate Court
Town incorporated October 1783 from Hartford. Probate district constituted May 1887 from Hartford

Land records: Contact Anne R. Fornabi, Town Clerk and Registrar of Vital Statistics

Naturalization records: No naturalization records

Vital records: Contact Town Clerk and Registrar of Vital Statistics

Probate records: Contact Ann Kennedy Fulco, Judge of Probate Court

*Town of East Haven
250 Main Street
East Haven, CT 06512
Phone (203) 468-3201 Town Clerk and Registrar of Vital Statistics
Town incorporated May 1785 from New Haven. Probate district constituted 5 January 1955 from New Haven
Land records: Contact Elizabeth C. Leary, Town Clerk and Registrar of Vital Statistics
No land records search service; copies: $1.00 per page
Naturalization records: No naturalization records
Vital records: Contact Town Clerk and Registrar of Vital Statistics
No vital records search service: copies: births subject to limitations
Probate records: Contact Thomas J. Giaimo, Judge of Probate Court, Town Hall, East Haven, CT 06512

*Town of East Lyme
Town Hall
108 Pennsylvania Avenue
PO Box 519
Niantic, CT 06357
Phone (203) 739-6931 Town Clerk and Registrar of Vital Statistics; (203) 739-6931 Judge of Probate Court
Town incorporated May 1839 from Lyme and Waterford. Probate district constituted 2 June 1843 from New London
Land records: Contact Esther B. Williams, Town Clerk and Registrar of Vital Statistics; copies: $1.00 per page
Naturalization records: No naturalization records
Vital records: Contact Town Clerk and Registrar of Vital Statistics; certified copies: $5.00 each
Probate records: Contact Leo J. McNamara, Judge of Probate Court; copies: $1.00 per page

Town of East Windsor
Town Hall
11 Rye Street
PO Box 213
Broad Brook, CT 06016
Phone (203) 623-9467 Town Clerk and Registrar of Vital Statistics; (203) 644-2511 Judge of Probate Court

Town incorporated May 1768 from Windsor. Probate district constituted May session 1782 from Hartford and Stafford
Land records: Contact Claire S. Badstubner, Town Clerk and Registrar of Vital Statistics
Vital records: Contact Town Clerk and Registrar of Vital Statistics
Probate records: Contact William E. Grace, Judge of Probate Court, Town Hall, South Windsor, CT 06074

Town of Eastford
Town Office Building
Westford Road
PO Box 296
Eastford, CT 06242
Phone (203) 974-1885 Town Clerk and Registrar of Vital Statistics; (203) 974-1885 Judge of Probate Court
Town incorporated May 1847 from Ashford. Probate district constituted 21 June 1849 from Ashford
Land records: Contact Emily Y. Bunnell, Town Clerk and Registrar of Vital Statistics
Vital records: Contact Town Clerk and Registrar of Vital Statistics
Probate records: Contact Stewart M. Tatem, Judge of Probate Court, Town Office Building, Westford Road, Eastford, CT 06242

Town of Easton
Town Hall
225 Center Road
Easton, CT 06612
Phone (203) 268-6291 Town Clerk and Registrar of Vital Statistics; (203) 452-5068 Judge of Probate Court
Town incorporated May 1845 from Weston. Probate district constituted 7 January 1959 from Bridgeport (Bridgeport contains the records of Easton, which include the records of Weston, Easton being a district of its own from 22 July 1875 until 4 March 1878)
Land records: Contact Carl Milnar, Town Clerk and Registrar of Vital Statistics
Vital records: Contact Town Clerk and Registrar of Vital Statistics
Probate records: Contact John P. Chiota, Judge of Probate Court, Town Hall, 5866 Main Street, Trumbull, CT 06611

*Town of Ellington
55 Main Street
PO Box 187
Ellington, CT 06029
Phone (203) 875-3190 Town Clerk and Registrar of Vital Statistics; (203) 872-0519 Judge of Probate Court
Town incorporated May 1786 from East Windsor. Probate district constituted

31 May 1826 from East Windsor and Stafford
Land records: Contact Cynthia J. Lacaprucia, Town Clerk and Registrar of Vital Statistics
No land records search service
Vital records: Contact Town Clerk and Registrar of Vital Statistics
No vital records search service
Probate records: Contact Thomas F. Rady, III, Judge of Probate Court, 14 Park Place, PO Box 268, Rockville, CT 06066

*Town of Enfield
820 Enfield Street
Enfield, CT 06082
Phone (203) 745-0371, ext. 310 Town Clerk and Registrar of Vital Statistics; (203) 745-0371, ext. 359 Judge of Probate Court
Town named and incorporated by Massachusetts 1683, annexed to Connecticut May 1749. Probate district constituted 26 May 1831 from East Windsor
Land records: Contact Suzanne F. Olechnicki, Jr., Town Clerk and Registrar of Vital Statistics
Naturalization records: No naturalization records
Vital records: Contact Town Clerk and Registrar of Vital Statistics
Probate records: Contact Susan L. Warner, Judge of Probate Court (adoption and guardianship records subject to restrictions)

*Town of Essex
Town Hall
29 West Avenue
Essex, CT 06426
Phone (203) 767-4344 Town Clerk and Registrar of Vital Statistics; (203) 767-4347 Judge of Probate Court
Town incorporated 13 September 1852 as Old Saybrook, taken from Saybrook, name changed to Essex 8 July 1854. Probate district constituted as Old Saybrook 4 July 1853 from Saybrook and included what are now the three towns of Essex, Old Saybrook and Westbrook (name changed to Essex in 1859; contains Old Saybrook probate records from 4 July 1853 to 4 July 1859)
Land records: Contact Betty J. Gaudenzi, Town Clerk and Registrar of Vital Statistics
Vital records: Contact Town Clerk and Registrar of Vital Statistics
Probate records: Contact Deborah M. Holcomb, Judge of Probate Court

*Town of Fairfield
Town Hall

611 Old Post Road
Fairfield, CT 06430
Phone (203) 256-3090 Town Clerk and Registrar of Vital Statistics; (203) 256-3041 Judge of Probate Court
Town settled 1639, named 1645, included in Connecticut Colony May 1685. Probate district constituted May session 1666 as a county court
Land records: From 1639 (original early records stored in Hartford); contact Marguerite H. Toth, Town Clerk and Registrar of Vital Statistics
No land records search service
Naturalization records: No naturalization records
Vital records: From 1639 (original early records stored in Hartford); contact Town Clerk and Registrar of Vital Statistics
No vital records search service (births are restricted)
Probate records: Contact Daniel Caruso, Judge of Probate Court, 725 Old Post Road, Fairfield, CT 06430

*Town of Farmington
Town Hall
1 Monteith Drive
Farmington, CT 06034-0948
Phone (203) 673-8200 Town Clerk and Registrar of Vital Statistics; (203) 673-8250 Judge of Probate Court
Town incorporated and named December 1645. The town of Farmington, Borough of Unionville and Borough of Farmington were consolidated in 1947. Probate district constituted January 1769 from Hartford
Land records: Contact Edgar A. King, Town Clerk and Registrar of Vital Statistics
Naturalization records: No naturalization records
Vital records: Contact Town Clerk and Registrar of Vital Statistics
Probate records: Contact J. David Morrissey, Judge of Probate Court

*Borough of Fenwick
(see Town of Old Saybrook)

*Town of Franklin
Town Hall
Meeting House Hill Road
RFD 1
North Franklin, CT 06254
Phone (203) 642-7352 Town Clerk and Registrar of Vital Statistics; (203) 887-2160 Judge of Probate Court
Town incorporated May 1786 from Norwich. Probate district constituted October 1748 from New London
Land records: Contact Grace B. Sterry, Town Clerk and Registrar of Vital Statistics

Naturalization records: Contact Linda M. Salafia, Judge of Probate Court, City Hall, 100 Broadway, Norwich, CT 06360
Vital records: Contact Town Clerk and Registrar of Vital Statistics
Probate records: Judge of Probate Court

*Town of Glastonbury
2155 Main Street
Glastonbury, CT 06033-0377
Phone (203) 652-7616 Town Clerk and Registrar of Vital Statistics; (203) 652-7629 Judge of Probate Court
Town incorporated May 1693 from Wethersfield. Probate district constituted 8 January 1975 from Hartford
Land records: Contact Edward J. Friedeberg, Town Clerk and Registrar of Vital Statistics
Vital records: Contact Town Clerk and Registrar of Vital Statistics
Probate records: Contact Donald Hamer, Judge of Probate Court

Town of Goshen
Town Office Building
North Street
PO Box 54
Goshen, CT 06756
Phone (203) 491-3647 Town Clerk and Registrar of Vital Statistics; (203) 489-2215 Judge of Probate Court
Town incorporated October 1739. Probate district constituted 16 June 1847 from Litchfield
Land records: Contact Lorraine M. Franzi, Town Clerk and Registrar of Vital Statistics
Vital records: Contact Town Clerk and Registrar of Vital Statistics
Probate records: Contact Joseph J. Gallicchio, Judge of Probate Court, Municipal Building, 140 Main Street, Torrington, CT 06790

Town of Granby
Town Hall
15 North Granby Road
Granby, CT 06035
Phone (203) 653-4817 Town Clerk and Registrar of Vital Statistics; (203) 653-3740 Judge of Probate Court
Town incorporated October 1786 from Simsbury. Probate district constituted May session 1807
Land records: Contact Carol J. Smith, Town Clerk and Registrar of Vital Statistics
Vital records: Contact Town Clerk and Registrar of Vital Statistics
Probate records: Contact Arline R. Mooney, Judge of Probate Court

*Town of Greenwich
Town Hall

101 Field Point Road
PO Box 2540
Greenwich, CT 06836
Phone (203) 622-7897 Town Clerk and Registrar of Vital Statistics; (203) 622-7879 Judge of Probate Court
Town settled 1640, submitted to Connecticut 6 October 1656. Probate district constituted 4 July 1853 from Stamford
Land records: Contact Carmella C. Budkins, Town Clerk and Registrar of Vital Statistics
Naturalization records: No naturalization records
Vital records: Contact Town Clerk and Registrar of Vital Statistics
Probate records: Contact David R. Tobin, Judge of Probate Court, Town Hall, 101 Field Point Road, Greenwich, CT 06830

*Town of Griswold
Town Hall
32 School Street
Jewett City, CT 06351-2398
Phone (203) 376-7064 Griswold Town Clerk and Registrar of Vital Statistics; (203) 376-7063 Jewett City Town Clerk; (203) 376-0216 Judge of Probate Court
Town incorporated October 1815 from Preston. Borough incorporated January session 1895. Probate district constituted 3 January 1979 from Norwich
Land records: Contact Ellen Dupont, Griswold Town Clerk and Registrar of Vital Statistics or Valerie Pudua, Jewett City Town Clerk
Vital records: Contact Griswold Town Clerk and Registrar of Vital Statistics; certified copies: $5.00 each
Probate records: Contact George Kennedy, Judge of Probate Court

*Town of Groton
Town Hall
45 Fort Hill Road
Groton, CT 06340
Phone (203) 441-6640 Town Clerk and Registrar of Vital Statistics; (203) 446-4102 City Clerk; (203) 441-6655 Judge of Probate Court
Town incorporated 10 May 1705 from New London. City incorporated 4 May 1964. Probate district constituted 25 May 1839 from Stonington
Land records: Contact Barbara Tarbox, Town Clerk and Registrar of Vital Statistics; copies $1.00 per page plus $1.00 if certified
Naturalization records: No naturalization records
Vital records: Births, deaths and marriages; contact Town Clerk and

Registrar of Vital Statistics; copies: 25¢ per page, $5.00 per certified copy (births are restricted)

Probate records: From 1839 to date; contact Frederick W. Palm, Jr., Judge of Probate Court; copies: $1.00 per page; certified copies: $5.00 for the first two pages and $2.00 for each additional page

*Town of Guilford
Town Hall
31 Park Street
Guilford, CT 06437
Phone (203) 453-8001 Town Clerk and Registrar of Vital Statistics; (203) 453-8006 Judge of Probate Court
Town settled 1639, named 6 July 1643. Probate district constituted October session 1719 from New Haven and New London
Land records: Contact Shirley R. Bohan, Town Clerk and Registrar of Vital Statistics
No land records search service (by state statute); copies: $1.00 per page
Vital records: Births, deaths and marriages from 1639; contact Town Clerk and Registrar of Vital Statistics
No vital records search service (by state statute); copies: $1.00 uncertified
Probate records: Contact Shirley M. Sabine, Judge of Probate Court
No probate search service (by state statute); copies: $1.00 per page

Town of Haddam
Town Office Building
Route 154
PO Box 87
Haddam, CT 06438
Phone (203) 345-8531 Town Clerk and Registrar of Vital Statistics; (203) 345-8531, ext. 9 Judge of Probate Court
Town incorporated 8 October 1668. Probate district (Higganum, Haddam Neck) constituted 3 June 1830 from Middletown and Chatham
Land records: Contact Ann P. Huffstetler, Town Clerk and Registrar of Vital Statistics
Vital records: Contact Town Clerk and Registrar of Vital Statistics
Probate records: Contact Charles F. Riordan, Judge of Probate Court, Town Office Building, 30 Field Park Drive, Haddam, CT 06438

Town of Hamden
Memorial Town Hall
2372 Whitney Avenue
Hamden, CT 06518
Phone (203) 287-2517, Town Clerk and Registrar of Vital Statistics; (203) 248-3561 Judge of Probate Court

Town incorporated May 1786 from New Haven. Probate district constituted 8 January 1945 from New Haven
Land records: Contact ext. 511 Nancy S. Hurlburt, Town Clerk and Registrar of Vital Statistics
Vital records: Contact Town Clerk and Registrar of Vital Statistics
Probate records: Contact Salvatore L. Diglio, Judge of Probate Court

*Town of Hampton
Town Office Building
164 Main Street
PO Box 143
Hampton, CT 06247
Phone (203) 455-9132 Town Clerk and Registrar of Vital Statistics
Town incorporated October 1786 from Windham, Pomfret, Brooklyn, Canterbury and Mansfield. Probate district constituted 2 June 1836 from Windham
Land records: Contact Margaret A. Fox, Town Clerk and Registrar of Vital Statistics
Vital records: Contact Town Clerk and Registrar of Vital Statistics
Probate records: Contact Jeannine Lamont, Judge of Probate Court

*City of Hartford
Municipal Building
550 Main Street
Hartford, CT 06103
Phone (203) 543-8581 Town and City Clerk; (203) 543-8538 Registrar of Vital Statistics; (203) 522-1813 Judge of Probate Court
Town colonized 1635 as a Dutch trading post organized out of Nieuw Amsterdam and called "House of Hope," name changed to Hartford in 1637, incorporated 1784. City incorporated May session 1784. Town and city consolidated April 1896. Probate district constituted May session 1666 as a county court
Land records: Contact Daniel M. Carey, Town and City Clerk, Town Clerk's Office, 2020 Broad Street, Hartford, CT 06114; copies: $1.00 for the first page, 50¢ for each additional page, $1.00 per document for certification
Vital records: Births, deaths and marriage licenses; contact Alexander Marcellino, Registrar of Vital Statistics, Bureau of Vital Statistics; copies: $5.00 per certified copy
Probate records: Contact Robert K. Killian, Jr., Judge of Probate Court

Town of Hartland
Town Office Building
South Road
East Hartland, CT 06027

Phone (203) 653-3542 Town Clerk and Registrar of Vital Statistics; (203) 653-9710 Judge of Hartland Probate District
Town incorporated May 1761. Probate district constituted 3 June 1836 from Granby
Land records: Contact Peder T. Pedersen, Town Clerk and Registrar of Vital Statistics
Vital records: Contact Town Clerk and Registrar of Vital Statistics
Probate records: Contact Beatrice Y. Isabelle, Judge of Hartland Probate District, Town Office Building Annex, East Hartland, CT 06027

*Town of Harwinton
Town Offices
100 Bentley Drive
Harwinton, CT 06791
Phone (203) 485-9613 Town Clerk and Registrar of Vital Statistics; (203) 485-1403 Judge of Probate Court
Town incorporated October 1737. Probate district constituted 27 May 1835 from Litchfield
Land records: Contact Patricia K. Williamson, Town Clerk and Registrar of Vital Statistics; copies: $1.00 per page
Vital records: Contact Town Clerk and Registrar of Vital Statistics; certified copies: $5.00 each (births are restricted)
Probate records: Contact John W. Pickard, Judge of Probate Court; copies: $5.00 for from one to five pages and $1.00 for each additional page

*Town of Hebron
Town Office Building
15 Gilead Street
PO Box 156
Hebron, CT 06248
Phone (203) 228-9406 Town Clerk and Registrar of Vital Statistics; (203) 228-9406 Judge of Probate Court
Town incorporated 26 May 1708. Probate district constituted May session 1789 from Windham, East Haddam and East Windsor (the records of Hebron, prior to 27 June 1851, are in Andover)
Land records: From 1708 to date; contact Marian Celio, Town Clerk and Registrar of Vital Statistics; copies: $1.00 for the first page and 50¢ for each additional page, $1.00 for certification
Naturalization records: No naturalization records
Vital records: From 1708 to date; contact Town Clerk and Registrar of Vital Statistics; certified copies: $5.00 each

Probate records: From 1851 to date; contact Kathleen M. Sawyer, Judge of Probate Court

*Town of Kent
Town Hall
41 Kent Green Boulevard
PO Box 678
Kent, CT 06757
Phone (203) 927-3433 Town Clerk and Registrar of Vital Statistics; (203) 927-3729 Judge of Probate Court
Town incorporated 1739. Probate district constituted 26 May 1831 from New Milford
Land records: From 1739 to date; contact Marian F. Pacocha, Town Clerk and Registrar of Vital Statistics
No land records search service; copies: $1.00 per page
Naturalization records: No naturalization records
Vital records: Contact Town Clerk and Registrar of Vital Statistics
No vital records search service; certified copies: $5.00 each
Probate records: Contact Barbara L. Miller, Judge of Probate Court, Town Hall, Kent, CT 06757
No probate search service; copies 25¢ per page, $1.00 per page for certified copies

*Town of Killingly
Town Hall
127 Main Street
PO Box 6000
Killingly, CT 06239-0900
Phone (203) 774-8601, ext. 109 Killingly Town Clerk and Registrar of Vital Statistics; (203) 774-8601, ext. 120 Judge of Probate Court
Town of Killingly incorporated May 1708. Borough incorporated May session 1854. Probate district constituted 4 June 1830 from Pomfret and Plainfield
Land records: From early 1700s to date for both Killingly and Danielson, which is a borough within the Town of Killingly; contact Joan A. Cyr, Killingly Town Clerk and Registrar of Vital Statistics
Land records search service: $5.00; copies $1.00 per page
Naturalization records: No naturalization records
Vital records: From early 1700s to date; contact Killingly Town Clerk and Registrar of Vital Statistics; copies: $5.00 each
Probate records: Contact Charles P. Ferland, Judge of Probate Court

*Town of Killingworth
Town Office Building
323 Route 81

Killingworth, CT 06417
Phone (203) 663-1616 Town Clerk and Registrar of Vital Statistics; (203) 663-1276 Judge of Probate Court
Town named May 1667. Probate district constituted 3 June 1834 from Saybrook (now Chester)
Land records: Contact Susan S. Adinolfo, Town Clerk and Registrar of Vital Statistics
Naturalization records: No naturalization records
Vital records: Contact Town Clerk and Registrar of Vital Statistics
Probate records: Contact Judith P. Lentz, Judge of Probate Court, 323 Route 81, Killingworth, CT 06419

*Town of Lebanon
Town Hall
Route 207
Lebanon, CT 06249
Phone (203) 642-7319 Town Clerk and Registrar of Vital Statistics; (203) 642-7429 Judge of Probate Court
Town incorporated October 1700. Probate district constituted 2 June 1826 from Windham
Land records: Contact Joyce A. McGillicuddy, Town Clerk and Registrar of Vital Statistics
Naturalization records: Contact George P. Randall, Judge of Probate Court
Vital records: Contact Town Clerk and Registrar of Vital Statistics
Probate records: Contact Judge of Probate Court
No probate search service; copies: $1.00 per page

*Town of Ledyard
Town Hall
741 Colonel Ledyard Highway
PO Box 38
Ledyard, CT 06339
Phone (203) 464-8740, ext. 229 Town Clerk and Registrar of Vital Statistics; (203) 464-8740, ext. 219 Judge of Probate Court
Town incorporated June 1836 from Groton. Probate district constituted 6 June 1837 from Stonington (the records of Ledyard from May 1666 to October 1766 are in New London; from October 1766 to 6 June 1837 in Stonington)
Land records: Contact Patricia Karns, Town Clerk and Registrar of Vital Statistics
Vital records: Contact Town Clerk and Registrar of Vital Statistics
Probate records: Contact Gertrude B. Smith, Judge of Probate Court

Town of Lisbon
Town Office Building
Newent Road

Lisbon, CT 06351
Phone (203) 376-2708 Town Clerk and Registrar of Vital Statistics; (203) 887-2160 Judge of Probate Court
Town incorporated May 1786 from Norwich. Probate district constituted October 1748 from New London
Land records: Contact Barbara Burzycki, Town Clerk and Registrar of Vital Statistics
Vital records: Contact Town Clerk and Registrar of Vital Statistics
Probate records: Contact Linda M. Salafia, Judge of Probate Court, City Hall, 100 Broadway, Norwich, CT 06360

*Town of Litchfield
Town Office Building
74 West Street
Litchfield, CT 06759
Phone (203) 567-9461 Town Clerk and Registrar of Vital Statistics; (203) 567-8065 Judge of Probate Court
Town of Litchfield incorporated May 1719. Litchfield Borough incorporated January session 1879. Bantam Borough incorporated January session 1915. Probate district constituted October session 1742 from Hartford, Woodbury and New Haven
Land records: Contact Eveilyn N. Goodwin, Town Clerk and Registrar of Vital Statistics
Vital records: Contact Town Clerk and Registrar of Vital Statistics
Probate records: Contact Arleen G. Keegan, Judge of Probate Court

*Town of Lyme
Town Hall
Route 156, Lyme PO
Lyme, CT 06371
Phone (203) 434-7733 Town Clerk and Registrar of Vital Statistics; (203) 434-7733 Judge of Probate Court
Town named May 1667, set off from Saybrook (now Deep River) 1665. Probate district constituted 5 July 1869 from Old Lyme (probate records concerning Lyme, from 1 May 1666 to 4 June 1830, are in New London; from 4 June 1830 to 4 July 1869, are in Old Lyme; from 4 July 1869 to date, are in Lyme)
Land records: Contact Ruth N. Perry, Town Clerk and Registrar of Vital Statistics
Vital records: Contact Town Clerk and Registrar of Vital Statistics
Probate records: Contact William Koch, Jr., Judge of Probate Court

*Town of Madison
Madison Town Campus
8 Campus Drive

Madison, CT 06443
Phone (203) 245-5672 Town Clerk and Registrar of Vital Statistics; (203) 245-5661 Judge of Probate Court
Town incorporated May 1826 from Guilford. Probate district constituted 22 May 1834 from Guilford
Land records: Contact Betty Anne Lynch, Town Clerk and Registrar of Vital Statistics
Vital records: Contact Town Clerk and Registrar of Vital Statistics
Probate records: Contact George G. McManus, Jr., Judge of Probate Court, Town Hall, PO Box 205, Madison, CT 06443

Town of Manchester
Town Hall
41 Center Street
Manchester, CT 06040
Phone (203) 647-3037 Town Clerk and Registrar of Vital Statistics; (203) 647-3227 Judge of Probate Court
Town incorporated May 1823 from East Hartford. Probate district constituted 3 June 1836 from Granby
Land records: Contact Edward J. Tomkiel, Town Clerk and Registrar of Vital Statistics
Vital records: Contact Town Clerk and Registrar of Vital Statistics
Probate records: Contact William E. FitzGerald, Judge of Probate Court, Hall of Records, 66 Center Street, Manchester, CT 06040

Town of Mansfield
Audrey P. Beck Building
4 South Eagleville Road
Storrs, CT 06268
Phone (203) 429-3302 Town Clerk and Registrar of Vital Statistics; (203) 429-3313 Judge of Probate Court
Town incorporated October 1702 from Windham. Probate district constituted 30 May 1831 from Windham
Land records: Contact Joan E. Gerdsen, Town Clerk and Registrar of Vital Statistics
Vital records: Contact Town Clerk and Registrar of Vital Statistics
Probate records: Contact George Hill, Judge of Probate Court

*Town of Marlborough
North Main Street
PO Box 29
Marlborough, CT 06447
Phone (203) 295-0713 Town Clerk and Registrar of Vital Statistics; (203) 295-9547 Judge of Probate Court
Town incorporated October 1803 from Colchester. Probate district constituted 11 June 1846 from

Colchester, Hebron and Glastonbury
Land records: Contact Ethel M. Fowler, Town Clerk and Registrar of Vital Statistics
Vital records: Contact Town Clerk and Registrar of Vital Statistics
Probate records: Contact William J. Heslin, III, Judge of Probate Court, Town Hall, PO Box 29, 26 North Main Street, Marlborough, CT 06447

*City of Meriden
City Hall
142 East Main Street
Room 124
Meriden, CT 06450
Phone (203) 630-4030 City and Town Clerk and Registrar of Vital Statistics; (203) 630-4025 FAX, City and Town Clerk and Registrar of Vital Statistics; (203) 235-4325 Judge of Probate Court
Town incorporated May 1806. City incorporated May session 1867. Town and city consolidated 1923. Probate district constituted 3 June 1836 from Wallingford
Land records: Contact Irene G. Massé, City Clerk, Town Clerk and Registrar of Vital Statistics
No land records search service; copies: $1.00 per page, $1.00 per document for certification
Vital records: Births, deaths and marriages; contact City Clerk, Town Clerk and Registrar of Vital Statistics; certified copies: $5.00 (births are restricted)
Probate records: Contact John Papandrea, Judge of Probate Court, City Hall, Room 113

Town of Middlebury
Town Hall
1212 Whittemore Road
Middlebury, CT 06762
Phone (203) 758-2557 Town Clerk and Registrar of Vital Statistics; (203) 755-1127 Judge of Probate Court
Town incorporated October 1807 from Waterbury, Woodbury and Southbury. Probate district constituted May session 1779 from Woodbury
Land records: Contact Alicia H. Ostar, Town Clerk and Registrar of Vital Statistics
Vital records: Contact Town Clerk and Registrar of Vital Statistics
Probate records: Contact James J. Lawlor, Judge of Probate Court, City Hall Annex, Chase Building, 236 Grand Street, Waterbury, CT 06702

*Town of Middlefield
Town Administration Building
393 Jackson Hill Road
PO Box 179

Middlefield, CT 06455
Phone (203) 349-7116 Town Clerk and Registrar of Vital Statistics; (203) 347-7424 Judge of Probate Court
Town incorporated June 1866 from Middletown. Probate district constituted May session 1752 from Hartford, Guilford and East Haddam
Land records: Contact Linda R. DeMaio, Town Clerk and Registrar of Vital Statistics; copies: $1.00 per page
Vital records: Contact Town Clerk and Registrar of Vital Statistics; certified copies: $5.00 each
Probate records: Contact Joseph D. Marino, Judge of Probate Court, Marino Professional Building, 94 Court Street, Middletown, CT 06457

*City of Middletown
Municipal Building
DeKoven Drive and Court Street
PO Box 1300
Middletown, CT 06457
Phone (203) 344-3459 City and Town Clerk, and Leon Vinci, Registrar of Vital Statistics; (203) 347-7424 Judge of Probate Court
Town incorporated 11 September 1651, named November 1653. City incorporated May session 1784. Town and city consolidated 1923. Probate district constituted May session 1752 from Hartford, Guilford and East Haddam
Land records: Contact Anthony Sbona, City and Town Clerk, and Leon Vinci, Registrar of Vital Statistics
Vital records: Contact City and Town Clerk, and Leon Vinci, Registrar of Vital Statistics
Probate records: Contact Joseph D. Marino, Judge of Probate Court, Marino Professional Building, 94 Court Street, Middletown, CT 06457

*City of Milford
Parsons Complex
70 West River Street
Milford, CT 06460
Phone (203) 783-3210 Town Clerk and Registrar of Vital Statistics; (203) 783-3205 Judge of Probate Court
Town settled 1639 under New Haven, named 24 November 1640, united with Connecticut Colony 1664. City incorporated 15 June (January session) 1959. Town and city consolidated 1959. Probate district constituted 30 May 1832 from New Haven
Land records: Contact Alan H. Jepson, City Clerk, Town Clerk and Registrar of Vital Statistics
No land records search service
Naturalization records: No naturalization records

Vital records: Contact City Clerk, Town
Clerk and Registrar of Vital Statistics
No vital records search service (births are
restricted)
Probate records: Contact Bernard F. Joy,
Judge of Probate Court

*Town of Monroe
Town Hall
7 Fan Hill Road
Monroe, CT 06468
Phone (203) 452-5417 Town Clerk and
Registrar of Vital Statistics; (203)
452-5068 Judge of Probate Court
*Town incorporated May 1823 from
Huntington (now Shelton). Probate
district constituted 7 January 1959
from Bridgeport*
Land records: Contact Thelma Kay
Inderdohnen, Town Clerk and
Registrar of Vital Statistics
Naturalization records: No naturalization
records
Vital records: Contact Town Clerk and
Registrar of Vital Statistics
Probate records: Contact John P. Chiota,
Judge of Probate Court, Town Hall,
5866 Main Street, Trumbull, CT
06611

Town of Montville
Town Hall
310 Norwich-New London Road
Uncasville, CT 06382
Phone (203) 848-1349 Town Clerk and
Registrar of Vital Statistics; (203)
848-9847 Judge of Probate Court
*Town incorporated 12 October 1786
from New London. Probate district
constituted 27 June 1851 from New
London*
Land records: Contact Margaret E.
Skinner, Town Clerk and Registrar of
Vital Statistics
Naturalization records: No naturalization
records
Vital records: Contact Town Clerk and
Registrar of Vital Statistics
Probate records: Contact Linda Mott,
Judge of Probate Court

*Town of Morris
Morris Town Offices
Morris Community Hall
3 East Street
PO Box 66
Morris, CT 06763
Phone (203) 567-5387 Town Clerk and
Registrar of Vital Statistics; (203)
567-8065 Judge of Probate Court
*Town incorporated June 1859 from
Litchfield. Probate district constituted
October session 1742 from Hartford,
Woodbury and New Haven*
Land records: Contact Ann E. Carr, Town
Clerk and Registrar of Vital Statistics

Naturalization records: Contact Arleen G.
Keegan, Judge of Probate Court,
Town Office Building, 74 West Street,
Litchfield, CT 06759
Vital records: Contact Town Clerk and
Registrar of Vital Statistics
Probate records: Contact Judge of
Probate Court

*Town of Naugatuck
Town Hall
229 Church Street
Naugatuck, CT 06770
Phone (203) 729-4571, ext. 265 Town
Clerk and Registrar of Vital Statistics;
(203) 729-4571, ext. 220 Judge of
Probate Court
*Town incorporated May 1844 from
Waterbury, Bethany and Oxford.
Borough incorporated January
session 1893. Borough and town
consolidated 1895. Probate district
constituted 4 July 1863 from
Waterbury*
Land records: Contact Sophie K. Morton,
Town Clerk and Registrar of Vital
Statistics
Vital records: Contact Town Clerk and
Registrar of Vital Statistics
Probate records: Contact Robert M.
Siuzdak, Judge of Probate Court

*City of New Britain
City Hall
27 West Main Street
New Britain, CT 06051
Phone (203) 826-3344, Town Clerk and
Registrar of Vital Statistics; (203)
826-2696 Judge of Probate Court
*Town incorporated May 1850 from
Berlin. City incorporated May
session 1870. Probate district
constituted 2 June 1824 from
Farmington, Hartford and
Middletown*
Land records: Contact City Clerk, Town
Clerk and Registrar of Vital Statistics
Vital records: Contact Town Clerk and
Registrar of Vital Statistics; copies:
$5.00 each
Probate records: Contact Walter J.
Clebowicz, Judge of Probate Court,
Court House, 117 Columbus
Boulevard, New Britain, CT 06051

*Town of New Canaan
Town Hall
77 Main Street
New Canaan, CT 06840
Phone (203) 972-2323 Town Clerk and
Registrar of Vital Statistics; (203)
972-7500 Judge of Probate Court
*Town incorporated May 1801 from
Norwalk and Stamford. Probate
district constituted 22 June 1937
from Norwalk*

Land records: From 1802; contact Mary
L. Ritter, Town Clerk and Registrar of
Vital Statistics
Naturalization records: No naturalization
records
Vital records: From 1802; contact Town
Clerk and Registrar of Vital Statistics
Probate records: Contact Richard E.
Burke, Judge of Probate Court, Town
Hall, PO Box 326, New Canaan, CT
06840

Town of New Fairfield
Town Hall
Route 39
PO Box 8896
New Fairfield, CT 06812
Phone (203) 746-8110 Town Clerk and
Registrar of Vital Statistics; (203)
746-8160 Judge of Probate Court
*Town incorporated May 1740. Probate
district constituted 8 January 1975
from Danbury*
Land records: Contact Diana M. Peck,
Town Clerk and Registrar of Vital
Statistics
Vital records: Contact Town Clerk and
Registrar of Vital Statistics
Probate records: Contact Peter R. Larkin,
Judge of Probate Court

*Town of New Hartford
Town Hall
Main Street
New Hartford, CT 06057
Phone (203) 379-5037 Town Clerk and
Registrar of Vital Statistics; (203)
379-3254 Judge of Probate Court
*Town incorporated October 1738.
Probate district constituted 27 May
1825 from Simsbury (the records of
New Hartford, previous to 5 June
1834, are in Barkhamsted)*
Land records: Contact Patricia J.
Halloran, Town Clerk and Registrar of
Vital Statistics
Naturalization records: No naturalization
records
Vital records: Contact Town Clerk and
Registrar of Vital Statistics
Probate records: Contact Norman E.
Rogers, Jr., Judge of Probate Court

*City of New Haven
Kennedy Mitchell Hall of Records
200 Orange Street
Room 204
New Haven, CT 06510
Phone (203) 946-8339 or 7343 City and
Town Clerk; (203) 946-8085 Registrar
of Vital Statistics; (203) 946-4880
Judge of Probate Court
*Town settled April 1634, named August
1640, incorporated 1784. City
incorporated January session 1784.
Town and city consolidated*

November 1895. Probate district constituted May session 1666 as a county court

Land records: Contact Sally J. Brown, City and Town Clerk

Naturalization records: No naturalization records

Vital records: Contact Michael V. Lynch, Registrar of Vital Statistics, 165 Church Street, Room 154, New Haven, CT 06510

Probate records: Contact John A. Keyes, Judge of Probate Court, 200 Orange Street, Fourth Floor, New Haven, CT 06510

*City of New London

181 State Street

New London, CT 06320

Phone (203) 447-5205 City Clerk, Town Clerk and Registrar of Vital Statistics; (203) 443-7121 Judge of Probate Court

Town settled 1646, named 11 March 1658, incorporated January 1784. City incorporated January session 1784. Town and city are co-extensive. Probate district constituted May session 1666 as a county court

Land records: Contact Clark van der Lyke, City Clerk, Town Clerk and Registrar of Vital Statistics

Naturalization records: No naturalization records

Vital records: Contact City Clerk, Town Clerk and Registrar of Vital Statistics

Probate records: Contact Matthew Green, Judge of Probate Court, Municipal Building, 181 State Street, New London, CT 06320

Town of New Milford

Town Hall

PO Box 360

New Milford, CT 06776

Phone (203) 355-6020 Town Clerk and Registrar of Vital Statistics; (203) 355-6029 Judge of Probate Court

Town incorporated October 1712. Probate district constituted May session 1787 from Woodbury, Sharon and Danbury

Land records: Contact Anna E. Chapin, Town Clerk and Registrar of Vital Statistics

Vital records: Contact Town Clerk and Registrar of Vital Statistics

Probate records: Contact Suzanne L. Powers, Judge of Probate Court, Town Hall, 10 Main Street, New Milford, CT 06776

Town of Newington

131 Cedar Street

Newington, CT 06111

Phone (203) 666-4661, ext. 231 Town Clerk and Registrar of Vital Statistics;

(203) 666-4661 Judge of Probate Court

Town incorporated 10 July 1871 from Wethersfield. Probate district constituted 8 January 1975 from Hartford

Land records: Contact Roberta N. Jenkins, Town Clerk and Registrar of Vital Statistics

Vital records: Contact Town Clerk and Registrar of Vital Statistics

Probate records: Contact Michael A. DellaFera, Judge of Probate Court

Town of Newtown

Edmond Town Hall

45 Main Street

Newtown, CT 06470

Phone (203) 426-8131, ext. 244 Town Clerk and Registrar of Vital Statistics; (203) 426-8131 Judge of Probate Court

Town incorporated October 1711. Borough incorporated May session 1824. Probate district constituted May session 1820 from Danbury

Land records: Contact Cynthia S. Curtis, Town Clerk and Registrar of Vital Statistics

Vital records: Contact Town Clerk and Registrar of Vital Statistics

Probate records: Contact Merlin E. Fisk, Judge of Probate Court

*Town of Norfolk

Maple Avenue

PO Box 552

Norfolk, CT 06058

Phone (203) 542-5679 Town Clerk and Registrar of Vital Statistics; (203) 542-5134 Judge of Probate Court

Town incorporated October 1758. Probate district constituted May session 1779 from Simsbury and Litchfield

Land records: Contact Anne R. Moses, Town Clerk and Registrar of Vital Statistics

Vital records: Contact Town Clerk and Registrar of Vital Statistics

Probate records: Contact Linda F. Riiska, Judge of Probate Court, Maple Avenue, Norfolk, CT 06058

*Town of North Branford

Town Hall

1599 Foxon Road

PO Box 287

North Branford, CT 06471

Phone (203) 481-5369 Town Clerk and Registrar of Vital Statistics; (203) 481-0829 Judge of Probate Court

Town incorporated May 1831 from Branford. Probate district constituted 14 April 1937 from Guilford and Wallingford

Land records: Contact Lisa A. Valenti,

Town Clerk and Registrar of Vital Statistics

No land records search service; copies: $1.00 per page

Naturalization records: No naturalization records

Vital records: Contact Town Clerk and Registrar of Vital Statistics; copies: $5.00 each

Probate records: Contact Frank J. Forgione, Judge of Probate Court

*Town of North Canaan

Town Hall

100 Pease Street

PO Box 338

Canaan, CT 06018

Phone (203) 824-7246 Town Clerk and Registrar of Vital Statistics; (203) 824-7114 Judge of Probate Court

Town incorporated May 1858 from Canaan. Probate district constituted 6 June 1846 from Sharon

Land records: Contact Carolyn C. O'Connor, Town Clerk and Registrar of Vital Statistics, PO Box 338

Vital records: Contact Town Clerk and Registrar of Vital Statistics

Probate records: Contact Diana J. Matheson, Judge of Probate Court, Town Hall, North Canaan, PO Box 905, Canaan, CT 06018

Town of North Haven

Town Hall

18 Church Street

North Haven, CT 06473

Phone (203) 239-5321, ext. 541 Town Clerk and Registrar of Vital Statistics; (203) 239-5321, ext. 569 Judge of Probate Court, Town Hall, 18 Church Street, PO Box 175, North Haven, CT 06473-0175

Town incorporated October 1786 from New Haven. Probate district constituted 5 January 1955 from New Haven

Land records: Contact Amelia P. Kennedy, Town Clerk and Registrar of Vital Statistics

Vital records: Contact Town Clerk and Registrar of Vital Statistics

Probate records: Contact Edward T. Falsey, Jr., Judge of Probate Court, Town Hall, 18 Church Street, PO Box 175, North Haven, CT 06473-0175

Town of North Stonington

Town Hall

Main Street

PO Box 91

North Stonington, CT 06359

Phone (203) 535-2877 Town Clerk and Registrar of Vital Statistics, and Judge of Probate Court

Town incorporated May 1807 from Stonington. Probate district

constituted 4 June 1835 from Stonington

Land records: Contact Patricia P. McGowan, Town Clerk and Registrar of Vital Statistics, and Judge of Probate Court

Vital records: Contact Town Clerk and Registrar of Vital Statistics, and Judge of Probate Court

Probate records: Contact Town Clerk and Registrar of Vital Statistics, and Judge of Probate Court

City of Norwalk
125 East Avenue
PO Box 5152
Norwalk, CT 06851
Phone (203) 854-7746 Town Clerk and Registrar of Vital Statistics; (203) 854-7900 City Clerk; (203) 847-1443 Judge of Probate Court
Town incorporated 11 September 1651. City incorporated January session 1893. Town and city consolidated January 1913. Probate district constituted May session 1802 from Fairfield and Stamford
Land records: Contact Mary O. Keegan, Town Clerk and Registrar of Vital Statistics
Vital records: Contact Town Clerk and Registrar of Vital Statistics
Probate records: Contact John E. Vallerie, Jr., Judge of Probate Court, 105 Main Street, PO Box 2009, Norwalk, CT 06852

City of Norwich
City Hall
100 Broadway
Room 241
Norwich, CT 06360
Phone (203) 886-2381 City Clerk, Town Clerk and Registrar of Vital Statistics; (203) 887-2160 Judge of Probate Court
Town settled 1659, accepted as legal township May 1662. City incorporated May session 1784. Town and city consolidated 1 January 1951. Probate district constituted October 1748 from New London
Land records: Contact Beverly C. Muldoon, City Clerk, Town Clerk and Registrar of Vital Statistics
Vital records: Contact City Clerk, Town Clerk and Registrar of Vital Statistics
Probate records: Contact Linda M. Salafia, Judge of Probate Court, City Hall, 100 Broadway, Norwich, CT 06360

*Town of Old Lyme
Memorial Town Hall
52 Lyme Street
PO Box 338

Old Lyme, CT 06371
Phone (203) 434-1655 Town Clerk and Registrar of Vital Statistics; (203) 434-1406 Judge of Probate Court
Town set off from Saybrook 13 February 1665, incorporated May 1855 as South Lyme, taken from Lyme, name changed 1857. Name of probate district changed from Lyme to Old Lyme 24 July 1868 (probate records concerning Old Lyme, from 1 May 1666 to 4 June 1830, are in New London; from 4 June 1830 to date, are in Old Lyme)
Land records: Contact Irene A. Carnell, Town Clerk and Registrar of Vital Statistics
Naturalization records: No naturalization records
Vital records: Contact Town Clerk and Registrar of Vital Statistics
Probate records: Contact Sylvia L. Peterson, Judge of Probate Court

*Town of Old Saybrook
302 Main Street
Old Saybrook, CT 06475
Phone (203) 395-3135 Town Clerk and Registrar of Vital Statistics; (203) 395-3128 Judge of Probate Court
Town incorporated 8 July 1854, includes Fenwick Borough, incorporated January session 1899. Probate district constituted 4 July 1859 from Essex (Old Saybrook probate records between 1666 and 1719 are in New London and New Haven; records between 1719 and 1780 are in Guilford; records between 1780 and 1853 are in Chester; records between 1853 and 1859 are in Essex; records from 1859 to the present are in Old Saybrook)
Land records: Contact Sarah V. Becker, Town Clerk and Registrar of Vital Statistics
Vital records: Contact Town Clerk and Registrar of Vital Statistics
Probate records: Contact Dorothy W. Rhodes, Judge of Probate Court, Town Hall, Main Street, Old Saybrook, CT 06475

*Town of Orange
Town Hall
617 Orange Center Road
Orange, CT 06477
Phone (203) 795-0751 Town Clerk and Registrar of Vital Statistics; (203) 795-0426 Judge of Probate Court
Town incorporated May 1822 from Milford and West Haven. Probate district constituted 8 January 1975 from New Haven
Land records: Contact Jean W. Mitchell, Town Clerk and Registrar of Vital Statistics

Vital records: Contact Town Clerk and Registrar of Vital Statistics
Probate records: Contact Robert W. Carangelo, Judge of Probate Court, High Plains Community Center, 525 Orange Center Road, Orange, CT 06477

*Town of Oxford
486 Oxford Road
Oxford, CT 06483
Phone (203) 888-2543 Town Clerk and Registrar of Vital Statistics; (203) 888-2543 Judge of Probate
Town incorporated October 1798 from Derby and Southbury. Probate district constituted 4 June 1846 from New Haven
Land records: Contact Constance E. Koskelowski, Town Clerk and Registrar of Vital Statistics
Vital records: Contact Town Clerk and Registrar of Vital Statistics
Probate records: Contact John W. Fertig, Jr., Judge of Probate Court, Town Hall, Oxford, CT 06483

*Town of Plainfield
Town Hall
8 Community Avenue
Plainfield, CT 06374
Phone (203) 564-4075, ext. 48 Town Clerk and Registrar of Vital Statistics; (203) 564-4071, ext. 45 Judge of Probate Court
Town incorporated as Quinabaug May 1699, named Plainfield October 1700. Probate district constituted May session 1747 from Windham
Land records: Contact Town Clerk and Registrar of Vital Statistics
Naturalization records: Yes
Vital records: Contact Town Clerk and Registrar of Vital Statistics
Probate records: Contact Kathleen Sendley Barry, Judge of Probate Court, Town Hall, 8 Community Avenue, Plainfield, CT 06374

*Town of Plainville
Municipal Center
1 Central Square
Plainville, CT 06062
Phone (203) 793-0221 Town Clerk and Registrar of Vital Statistics; (203) 793-0221, Judge of Probate Court
Town incorporated July 1869 from Farmington. Probate district constituted May 1909 from Farmington
Land records: Contact Peter T. Lennon, Town Clerk and Registrar of Vital Statistics
No land records search service; copies: $1.00 per page
Naturalization records: No naturalization records

Vital records: Contact Town Clerk and Registrar of Vital Statistics; certified copies: $5.00 each

Probate records: Contact Heidi Famiglietti, Judge of Probate Court, Municipal Center, 1 Central Square, Plainville, CT 06062; copies: $5.00 per document, up to five pages, certified copies $5.00 for the first two pages and $1.00 for each additional page

*Town of Plymouth
Town Hall
19 East Main Street
Terryville, CT 06786
Phone (203) 585-4039 Town Clerk and Registrar of Vital Statistics; (203) 585-4014 Judge of Probate Court
Town incorporated May 1795 from Watertown. Probate district constituted 31 May 1833 from Waterbury
Land records: Contact Janet P. Scoville, Town Clerk and Registrar of Vital Statistics (no title search allowed by state statutes)
Naturalization records: No naturalization records
Vital records: Contact Town Clerk and Registrar of Vital Statistics
Probate records: Contact Sonja DeSousa, Judge of Probate Court, Town Hall, 19 East Main Street, Terryville, CT 06786

*Town of Pomfret
5 Haven Road
Pomfret Center, CT 06259
Phone (203) 974-0343 Town Clerk and Registrar of Vital Statistics; (203) 974-0186 Judge of Probate Court
Town incorporated and named May 1713. Probate district constituted May session 1752 from Windham and Plainfield (the records of Pomfret were burned 5 January 1754)
Land records: Contact Nora V. Johnson, Town Clerk and Registrar of Vital Statistics
Vital records: Contact Town Clerk and Registrar of Vital Statistics
Probate records: Contact Cecile D. Stoddard, Judge of Probate Court

*Town of Portland
Town Hall
265 Main Street
PO Box 71
Portland, CT 06480
Phone (203) 342-2880 Town Clerk and Registrar of Vital Statistics; (203) 342-2880 Judge of Probate Court
Town incorporated May 1841 from Chatham. Probate district constituted

22 April 1913 from Chatham (contains the records of the district of Chatham previous to 6 January 1915)
Land records: Contact Bernadette M. Dillon, Town Clerk and Registrar of Vital Statistics
Vital records: Contact Town Clerk and Registrar of Vital Statistics
Probate records: Contact Richard J. Euliani, Judge of Probate Court, Town Hall, 265 Main Street, Portland, CT 06480

Town of Preston
Town Hall
RFD 1, Route 2
Preston, CT 06360
Phone (203) 887-9821 Town Clerk and Registrar of Vital Statistics; (203) 887-2160 Judge of Probate Court
Town incorporated October 1687. Probate district constituted October 1748 from New London
Land records: Contact Janet Perkins, Town Clerk and Registrar of Vital Statistics
Vital records: Contact Town Clerk and Registrar of Vital Statistics
Probate records: Contact Linda M. Salafia, Judge of Probate Court, City Hall, 100 Broadway, Norwich, CT 06360

*Town of Prospect
Town Office Building
36 Center Street
Prospect, CT 06712-1699
Phone (203) 758-4461 Town Clerk and Registrar of Vital Statistics; (203) 272-8247 Judge of Probate Court
Town incorporated May 1827 from Cheshire and Waterbury. Probate district constituted 27 May 1829 from Wallingford
Land records: Contact Patricia M. Vaillancourt, Town Clerk and Registrar of Vital Statistics; copies: $1.00 per page
Vital records: Births, deaths and marriages; contact Town Clerk and Registrar of Vital Statistics; copies: $5.00 each (births are restricted)
Probate records: Contact Raymond F. Voelker, Judge of Probate Court, Cheshire Town Hall, 84 South Main Street, Cheshire, CT 06410

*Town of Putnam
Town Hall
126 Church Street
Putnam, CT 06260
Phone (203) 963-6807 Town Clerk and Registrar of Vital Statistics; (203) 963-6868 Judge of Probate Court
Town incorporated May 1855 from

Killingly, Pomfret and Thompson. Probate district constituted 5 July 1856 from Thompson
Land records: Contact Lillian M. Newth, Town Clerk and Registrar of Vital Statistics
Land records search service: $3.00 per name; copies: $1.00 per page
Vital records: Contact Town Clerk and Registrar of Vital Statistics
Vital records search service: $3.00 per name; copies: $1.00 each, $5.00 for certified copies
Probate records: Contact Nicholas A. Scola, Judge of Probate Court, 126 Church Street, Putnam, CT 06260

*Town of Redding
Town Office Building
Route 107
Redding, CT 06875
Phone (203) 938-2377 Town Clerk and Registrar of Vital Statistics; (203) 938-2326 Judge of Probate Court
Town incorporated May 1767 from Fairfield. Probate district constituted 24 May 1834 from Danbury and Fairfield
Land records: Contact Patricia A. Creigh, Town Clerk and Registrar of Vital Statistics
Vital records: Contact Town Clerk and Registrar of Vital Statistics
Probate records: Contact Richard L. Emerson, Judge of Probate Court, Town Hall, Route 107, PO Box 1125, Redding, CT 06875

Town of Ridgefield
Town Hall
400 Main Street
Ridgefield, CT 06877
Phone (203) 438-7301 Town Clerk and Registrar of Vital Statistics; (203) 438-7301, ext. 7 Judge of Probate Court
Town settled 1708, incorporated October 1709. Town and borough consolidated 11 May 1921. Probate district constituted 10 June 1841 from Danbury
Land records: Contact Dora Cassavechia, Town Clerk and Registrar of Vital Statistics
Vital records: Contact Town Clerk and Registrar of Vital Statistics
Probate records: Contact Romeo G. Petroni, Judge of Probate Court

City of Rockville
(see Town of Vernon)

Town of Rocky Hill
Town Hall
699 Old Main Street
PO Box 657

Rocky Hill, CT 06067
Phone (203) 563-1451, ext. 71 Town Clerk and Registrar of Vital Statistics; (203) 666-4661, ext. 231 Judge of Probate Court
Town incorporated May 1843 from Wethersfield. Probate district constituted 8 January 1975 from Hartford
Land records: Contact Marion H. Palmer, Town Clerk and Registrar of Vital Statistics
Vital records: Contact Town Clerk and Registrar of Vital Statistics
Probate records: Contact Michael A. DellaFera, Judge of Probate Court, Town Hall, 131 Cedar Street, Newington, CT 06111

Town of Roxbury
PO Box 203
Roxbury, CT 06783-0203
Phone (203) 354-3328 Town Clerk and Registrar of Vital Statistics; (203) 354-7164 Judge of Probate Court
Town incorporated October 1796 from Woodbury. Probate district constituted 6 June 1842 from Woodbury
Land records: Contact Peter A. Hurlbut, Town Clerk and Registrar of Vital Statistics
Vital records: Contact Town Clerk and Registrar of Vital Statistics
Probate records: Contact Mildred A. Erwin, Judge of Probate Court, Town Hall South Street, Roxbury, CT 06783

*Town of Salem
Town Office Building
270 Hartford Road
Route 85
Salem, CT 06415
Phone (203) 859-3875 Town Clerk and Registrar of Vital Statistics; (203) 859-1184 FAX, Town Clerk and Registrar of Vital Statistics; (203) 859-3873 Judge of Probate Court
Town incorporated May 1819 from Colchester, Lyme and Montville. Probate district constituted 9 July 1841 from Colchester and New London
Land records: Contact Cynthia B. Rowin, Town Clerk and Registrar of Vital Statistics
Vital records: Contact Town Clerk and Registrar of Vital Statistics
Probate records: Contact William C. Kollman, II, Judge of Probate Court

Town of Salisbury
Town Hall
Main Street
Salisbury, CT 06068
Phone (203) 435-9511 Town Clerk and Registrar of Vital Statistics; (203) 435-9513 Judge of Probate Court
Town incorporated October 1741. Probate district constituted 16 June 1847 from Sharon
Land records: Contact Laura H. Johnson, Town Clerk and Registrar of Vital Statistics
Vital records: Contact Town Clerk and Registrar of Vital Statistics
Probate records: Contact Richard T. Fitzgerald, Judge of Probate Court

Town of Scotland
Town Hall
9 Devotion Road (a.k.a. Route 97)
PO Box 122
Scotland, CT 06264
Phone (203) 423-9634 Town Clerk and Registrar of Vital Statistics; (203) 456-3593, ext. 239 Judge of Probate Court
Town incorporated May 1857 from Windham. Probate district constituted October session 1719 from Hartford and New London
Land records: Contact Nancy O'Connor, Town Clerk and Registrar of Vital Statistics
Vital records: Contact Town Clerk and Registrar of Vital Statistics
Probate records: Contact Patrick M. Prue, Judge of Probate Court, Town Building, PO Box 34, Willimantic, CT 06226

Town of Seymour
Town Hall
1 First Street
Seymour, CT 06483
Phone (203) 888-0519 Town Clerk and Registrar of Vital Statistics; (203) 734-1277 Judge of Probate Court
Town incorporated May 1850 from Derby. Probate district constituted 4 July 1858 from New Haven
Land records: Contact Norma E. Drummer, Town Clerk and Registrar of Vital Statistics
Vital records: Contact Town Clerk and Registrar of Vital Statistics
Probate records: Contact Clifford D. Hoyle, Judge of Probate Court, City Hall, Ansonia, CT 06401

*Town of Sharon
Town Hall
Main Street
PO Box 224
Sharon, CT 06069-0224
Phone (203) 364-5224 Town Clerk; (203) 364-5514 Judge of Probate
Town incorporated October 1739. Probate district constituted October session 1775 from Litchfield
Land records: Contact Town Clerk; copies $1.00 per page
Vital records: Yes

Probate records: Contact the Honorable Suzanne Xanthos, Probate Court, Town Hall

Town of Shelton
54 Hill Street
PO Box 364
Shelton, CT 06484
Phone (203) 735-3363 Town Clerk and Registrar of Vital Statistics; (203) 734-8462 Judge of Probate Court
Town incorporated January 1789 from Stratford. City incorporated January session 1915. Town and city are co-extensive. Probate district constituted May 1889 from Bridgeport and Derby (name changed from Huntington to Shelton, 29 August 1919)
Land records: Contact Beverly M. Brown, Town Clerk and Registrar of Vital Statistics
Vital records: Contact Town Clerk and Registrar of Vital Statistics
Probate records: Contact Maurice J. Martin, Judge of Probate Court, 40 White Street, Shelton, CT 06484

*Town of Sherman
Mallory Town Hall
Route 39
PO Box 39
Sherman, CT 06784
Phone (203) 354-5281 Town Clerk and Registrar of Vital Statistics; (203) 355-1821 Judge of Probate Court
Town incorporated October 1802 from New Fairfield. Probate district constituted 4 June 1846 from New Milford
Land records: From 1802 to date; contact Carol L. Havens, Town Clerk and Registrar of Vital Statistics
Naturalization records: No naturalization records
Vital records: From 1853 (some earlier) to date; contact Town Clerk and Registrar of Vital Statistics
Probate records: From 1846 to date; contact Barbara J. Ackerman, Judge of Probate Court

*Town of Simsbury
Belden Town Office Building
933 Hopmeadow Street
PO Box 495
Simsbury, CT 06070
Phone (203) 651-3751 Town Clerk and Registrar of Vital Statistics or Judge of Probate
Town named May 1670. Probate district constituted May session 1769 from Hartford
Land records: Contact Carolyn Keily, Town Clerk and Registrar of Vital Statistics; copies: $1.00 per page
Vital records: Contact Town Clerk and

Registrar of Vital Statistics; copies: $5.00 each (births are restricted)

Probate records: Contact Glenn E. Knierim, Judge of Probate

*Town of Somers
Town Hall
600 Main Street
PO Box 308
Somers, CT 06071
Phone (203) 763-0841 Town Clerk and Registrar of Vital Statistics; (203) 749-7012 Judge of Probate Court
Town named July 1734, annexed to Connecticut May 1749. Probate district constituted 3 June 1834 from Ellington
Land records: Contact Claire L. Walker, Town Clerk and Registrar of Vital Statistics; copies: $1.00 per page
Naturalization records: No naturalization records
Vital records: Contact Town Clerk and Registrar of Vital Statistics; certified copies: $5.00 each
Probate records: Contact Francis W. Devlin, Jr., Judge of Probate Court, Town Hall, 600 Main Street, Somers, CT 06071

Town of South Windsor
Town Hall
1540 Sullivan Avenue
South Windsor, CT 06074
Phone (203) 644-2511 Town Clerk and Registrar of Vital Statistics or Judge of Probate Court
Town incorporated May 1845 from East Windsor. Probate district constituted May session 1782 from Hartford and Stafford
Land records: Contact Marilyn W. Burger, Town Clerk and Registrar of Vital Statistics
Vital records: Contact Town Clerk and Registrar of Vital Statistics
Probate records: Contact William E. Grace, Judge of Probate Court

*Town of Southbury
Town Hall
501 Main Street, South
Southbury, CT 06488
Phone (203) 262-0657 Town Clerk and Registrar of Vital Statistics; (203) 262-0641 Judge of Probate Court
Town incorporated May 1787 from Woodbury. Probate district constituted 4 January 1967
Land records: From 1787 to date (includes South Britain); contact Joyce K. Hornbecker, Town Clerk and Registrar of Vital Statistics; copies: $1.00 per page, $2.00 for maps
Vital records: Contact Town Clerk and Registrar of Vital Statistics

Probate records: From 1967; contact Mary Kay Flaherty, Judge of Probate District of Southbury, Town Hall Annex, 421 Main Street, PO Box 674, Southbury, CT 06488

*Town of Southington
Town Office Building
75 Main Street
Southington, CT 06489
Phone (203) 276-6211 Town Clerk and Registrar of Vital Statistics; (203) 276-6253 Judge of Probate Court
Town incorporated October 1779 from Farmington. Town and borough consolidated 1947. Probate district constituted 24 May 1825 from Farmington
Land records: Contact Leslie G. Cotton, Town Clerk and Registrar of Vital Statistics.
Vital records: Contact Town Clerk and Registrar of Vital Statistics
Probate records: Contact Carl J. Sokolowski, Judge of Probate Court, Town Office Building, 75 Main Street, PO Box 165, Southington, CT 06489

*Town of Sprague
1 Main Street
PO Box 162
Baltic, CT 06330-0162
Phone (203) 822-3001 Town Clerk and Registrar of Vital Statistics; (203) 887-2160 Judge of Probate Court
Town incorporated May 1861 from Lisbon and Franklin. Probate district constituted October 1748 from New London
Land records: Contact Mary M. Stefon, Town Clerk and Registrar of Vital Statistics; copies: $1.00 per page, $1.00 for certification
Naturalization records: Contact Linda M. Salafia, Judge of Probate Court, City Hall, 100 Broadway, Norwich, CT 06360
Vital records: Contact Town Clerk and Registrar of Vital Statistics; certified copies: $5.00 each
Probate records: Judge of Probate Court

Town of Stafford
Warren Memorial Town Hall
PO Box 11
Stafford Springs, CT 06076
Phone (203) 684-2532 Town Clerk and Registrar of Vital Statistics; (203) 684-3423 Judge of Probate Court
Town settled 1719. Borough incorporated May session 1873. Probate district constituted May session 1759 from Hartford and Pomfret
Land records: Contact Pauline Laskow, Town Clerk and Registrar of Vital Statistics

Vital records: Contact Town Clerk and Registrar of Vital Statistics
Probate records: Contact Thomas J. Fiore, Judge of Probate Court, Town Hall, Stafford Springs, CT 06076

Town of Stafford Springs
PO Box 91
Stafford Springs, CT 06076
Phone (203) 684-3827 Town Clerk; (203) 684-3423 Judge of Probate Court
Probate district constituted May session 1759 from Hartford and Pomfret
Land records: Contact Kathleen M. Walsh, Town Clerk
Vital records: Contact Town Clerk
Probate records: Contact Thomas J. Fiore, Judge of Probate Court, Town Hall, Stafford Springs, CT 06076

City of Stamford
Stamford Government Center
888 Washington Boulevard
PO Box 891
Stamford, CT 06904-0891
Phone (203) 977-4056 City and Town Clerk and Registrar of Vital Statistics; (203) 323-2149 Judge of Probate Court
Town settled 1641 under New Haven jurisdiction, named Town of Stamford 1642, submitted to Connecticut October 1662. City of Stamford (comprising central portion of Town of Stamford) incorporated January session 1893; henceforth City of Stamford became a composite part of Town of Stamford, resulting in two separate governments. Town and city consolidated 15 April 1949 and named City of Stamford. Probate district constituted May session 1728 from Fairfield
Land records: Contact Lois PontBriant, City and Town Clerk and Registrar of Vital Statistics
Vital records: Contact City and Town Clerk and Registrar of Vital Statistics
Probate records: Contact Paul D. Shapero, Judge of Probate Court, Town Hall, 175 Atlantic Street, Stamford, CT 06901

*Town of Sterling
114 Plainfield Pike
PO Box 157
Oneco, CT 06373
Phone (203) 564-2657 Town Clerk and Registrar of Vital Statistics; (203) 564-4103 Judge of Probate Court
Town incorporated 4 May 1794 from Voluntown. Probate district constituted 17 June 1852 from Plainfield
Land records: Contact Catherine S. Nurmi, Town Clerk and Registrar of Vital Statistics

Vital records: Contact Town Clerk and Registrar of Vital Statistics
Probate records: Contact Signe L. Nowosadko, Judge of Probate Court

*Town of Stonington
Town Hall Building
152 Elm Street
PO Box 352
Stonington, CT 06378
Phone (203) 535-5060 Town Clerk and Registrar of Vital Statistics; (203) 535-5090 Judge of Probate Court
Town settled 1649, named 1666. Borough incorporated May session 1801. Probate district constituted October session 1766 from New London
Land records: Contact Ruth Waller, Town Clerk and Registrar of Vital Statistics
Vital records: Contact Town Clerk and Registrar of Vital Statistics
Probate records: Contact Paul E. Cravinho, Judge of Probate Court, Town Hall Building, PO Box 312, Stonington, CT 06378

*Town of Stratford
Town Hall
Room 101
2725 Main Street
Stratford, CT 06497
Phone (203) 385-4020 Town Clerk and Registrar of Vital Statistics; (203) 385-4023 Judge of Probate Court
Town settled 1639. Probate district constituted May session 1782 from Fairfield (the records of Stratford, previous to 4 June 1840, are in Bridgeport)
Land records: Contact Town Clerk and Registrar of Vital Statistics; copies: $1.00 for the first page and 50¢ for each additional page, $5.00 for maps
Naturalization records: No naturalization records
Vital records: Contact Town Clerk and Registrar of Vital Statistics
Probate records: Contact F. Paul Kurmay, Judge of Probate Court, Town Hall, 2725 Main Street, Stratford, CT 06497

*Town of Suffield
Town Hall Building
83 Mountain Road
PO Box 238
Suffield, CT 06078
Phone (203) 668-3880 Town Clerk and Registrar of Vital Statistics; (203) 668-3835 Judge of Probate Court
Town incorporated May 1674 by Massachusetts, annexed to Connecticut May 1749. Probate district constituted May session 1821 from Hartford and Granby

Land records: Contact Dorothy K. McCarty, Town Clerk and Registrar of Vital Statistics; copies: $1.00 per page, except early land records cannot be copied because the light destroys the ink
Vital records: Contact Town Clerk and Registrar of Vital Statistics; certified copies: $5.00 each
Probate records: Contact Beverly T. Patterson, Judge of Probate Court

*Town of Thomaston
Town Hall Building
158 Main Street
Thomaston, CT 06787
Phone (203) 283-4141 Town Clerk and Registrar of Vital Statistics; (203) 283-4874 Judge of Probate Court
Town incorporated July 1875 from Plymouth. Probate district constituted June 1882 from Waterbury
Land records: Contact Catherine P. DuPont, Town Clerk and Registrar of Vital Statistics
Vital records: Contact Town Clerk and Registrar of Vital Statistics
Probate records: Contact Susan Kaniewski, Judge of Probate Court

Town of Thompson
Town Office Building
PO Box 899
Route 12
North Grosvenor Dale, CT 06255
Phone (203) 923-9900 Town Clerk and Registrar of Vital Statistics; (203) 923-2203 Judge of Probate Court
Town incorporated May 1785 from Killingly. Probate district constituted 25 May 1832 from Pomfret
Land records: Contact Rachel C. Haggerty, Town Clerk and Registrar of Vital Statistics
Vital records: Contact Town Clerk and Registrar of Vital Statistics
Probate records: Contact Aileen A. Witkowski, Judge of Probate Court, Town Office Building, PO Box 74, North Grosvenor Dale, CT 06255

Town of Tolland
Hicks Memorial Municipal Center
21 Tolland Green
Tolland, CT 06084
Phone (203) 871-3630 Town Clerk and Registrar of Vital Statistics; (203) 871-3640 Judge of Probate Court
Town named May 1715, incorporated May 1722. Probate district constituted 4 June 1830 from Stafford
Land records: Contact Elaine G. Bugbee, Town Clerk and Registrar of Vital Statistics
Vital records: Contact Town Clerk and Registrar of Vital Statistics

Probate records: Contact George A. Baker, Judge of Probate Court, Town Hall, 21 Tolland Green, PO Box 667, Tolland, CT 06084

*City of Torrington
Municipal Building
140 Main Street
Torrington, CT 06790
Phone (203) 489-2241 Town and City Clerk and Registrar of Vital Statistics; (203) 489-2215 Judge of Probate Court
Town incorporated October 1740. City incorporated 1 October (January session) 1923. Town and city consolidated 1923. Probate district constituted 16 June 1847 from Litchfield
Land records: From 1732 to date; contact Joseph L. Quartiero, Town and City Clerk and Registrar of Vital Statistics
Naturalization records: No naturalization records
Vital records: From 1732 to date; contact City Clerk, Town Clerk and Registrar of Vital Statistics
Probate records: From 1847 to date; contact Joseph J. Gallicchio, Judge of Probate Court

*Town of Trumbull
Town Hall
5866 Main Street
Trumbull, CT 06611
Phone (203) 452-5035 Town Clerk and Registrar of Vital Statistics; (203) 452-5068 Judge of Probate Court
Town incorporated October 1797 from Stratford. Probate district constituted 7 January 1959 from Bridgeport
Land records: Contact Linda M. Lungi, Town Clerk and Registrar of Vital Statistics
Naturalization records: Contact John P. Chiota, Judge of Probate Court
Vital records: Contact Town Clerk and Registrar of Vital Statistics; certified copies: $5.00 each
Probate records: Contact Judge of Probate Court

*Town of Union
Route 171
1024 Buckley Highway
Union, CT 06076
Phone (203) 684-3770 Town Clerk and Registrar of Vital Statistics; (203) 684-3423 Judge of Probate Court
Town incorporated October 1734. Probate district constituted May session 1759 from Hartford and Pomfret
Land records: Contact Heidi O. Bradrick, Town Clerk and Registrar of Vital Statistics

Vital records: Contact Town Clerk and
   Registrar of Vital Statistics
Probate records: Contact Thomas J.
   Fiore, Judge of Probate Court, Town
   Hall, Stafford Springs, CT 06076

*Town of Vernon
Memorial Building
14 Park Place
PO Box 245
Rockville, CT 06066
Phone (203) 872-8591 Town Clerk and
   Registrar of Vital Statistics; (203)
   872-0519 Judge of Probate Court
*Town incorporated October 1808 from
   Bolton. Town of Vernon and City of
   Rockville consolidated 1 July 1965.
   Probate district constituted 31 May
   1826 from East Windsor and Stafford*
Land records: From 1808; contact Terri
   A. Krawczyk, Town Clerk and
   Registrar of Vital Statistics
No land records search service (must
   supply name and date of occurrence);
   copies: $1.00 per page
Vital records: From 1869; contact Town
   Clerk and Registrar of Vital Statistics
No vital records search service (must
   supply name and date of occurrence);
   certified copies: $5.00 each (births are
   restricted)
Probate records: Contact Thomas F.
   Rady, III, Judge of Probate Court, 14
   Park Place, PO Box 268, Rockville,
   CT 06066

Town of Voluntown
Town Hall
Main Street
PO Box 96
Voluntown, CT 06384
Phone (203) 376-4089 Town Clerk and
   Registrar of Vital Statistics; (203)
   887-2160 Judge of Probate Court
*Town incorporated May 1721. Probate
   district constituted October 1748
   from New London*
Land records: Contact Mary Anne
   Nieminen, Town Clerk and Registrar
   of Vital Statistics
Vital records: Contact Town Clerk and
   Registrar of Vital Statistics
Probate records: Contact Linda M.
   Salafia, Judge of Probate Court, City
   Hall, 100 Broadway, Norwich, CT
   06360

*Town of Wallingford
Municipal Building
45 South Main Street
PO Box 427
Wallingford, CT 06492
Phone (203) 294-2145 Town Clerk and
   Registrar of Vital Statistics; (203)
   294-2100 Judge of Probate Court
Town named May 1670. Town and

*borough consolidated 1 January
   1958. Probate district constituted
   May session 1776 from New Haven
   and Guilford*
Land records: Contact Town Clerk and
   Registrar of Vital Statistics; copies:
   50¢ per page
Vital records: Contact Town Clerk and
   Registrar of Vital Statistics; copies:
   $5.00 each (births are restricted)
Probate records: Contact Philip Wright,
   Jr., Judge of Probate Court

*Town of Warren
Town Hall
Sackett Hill Road
PO Box 25
Warren, CT 06754
Phone (203) 868-0090 Town Clerk and
   Registrar of Vital Statistics; (203)
   567-8065 Judge of Probate Court
*Town incorporated May 1786 from
   Kent. Probate district constituted
   October session 1742 from Hartford,
   Woodbury and New Haven*
Land records: Contact Carolyn E.
   Reynolds, Town Clerk and Registrar
   of Vital Statistics, PO Box 1025,
   Warren, CT 06754
Naturalization records: Contact Arleen G.
   Keegan, Judge of Probate Court,
   Town Office Building, 74 West Street,
   Litchfield, CT 06759
Vital records: Contact Town Clerk and
   Registrar of Vital Statistics
Probate records: Contact Judge of
   Probate Court

*Town of Washington
Bryan Memorial Town Hall
Washington Depot, CT 06794
Phone (203) 868-2786 Town Clerk and
   Registrar of Vital Statistics; (203)
   868-7974 Judge of Probate
*Town incorporated January 1779 from
   Woodbury, Litchfield, Kent and New
   Milford. Probate district constituted
   22 May 1832 from Litchfield and
   Woodbury*
Land records: Contact Doris K. Welles,
   Town Clerk and Registrar of Vital
   Statistics; copies: $1.00 per page
Vital records: Contact Town Clerk and
   Registrar of Vital Statistics; copies:
   $1.00 per page (births are restricted)
Probate records: Contact Victoria M.
   Cherniske, Judge of Probate, Bryan
   Memorial Town Hall, PO Box 295,
   Washington Depot, CT 06794; copies:
   $1.00 per page

City of Waterbury
City Hall
235 Grand Street
Waterbury, CT 06702
Phone (203) 574-6806 Town Clerk or

Assistant Registrar of Vital Statistics;
   (203) 574-6741 City Clerk; (203) 755-
   1127 Judge of Probate Court
*Town incorporated May 1686. City
   incorporated May session 1853.
   Town and city consolidated 1902.
   Probate district constituted May
   session 1779 from Woodbury*
Land records: Contact Gloria M. Gallo,
   Town Clerk, or John J. Buckley, City
   Clerk, City Hall Annex, Chase
   Building, 236 Grand Street,
   Waterbury, CT 06702
Vital records: Contact Dolores D. Shortt,
   Assistant Registrar of Vital Statistics
Probate records: Contact James J.
   Lawlor, Judge of Probate Court, City
   Hall Annex, Chase Building, 236
   Grand Street, Waterbury, CT 06702

*Town of Waterford
Town Hall
15 Rope Ferry Road
Waterford, CT 06385
Phone (203) 442-0553 Town Clerk and
   Registrar of Vital Statistics; (203)
   443-7121 Judge of Probate Court
*Town incorporated October 1801 from
   New London. Probate district
   constituted May session 1666 as a
   county court*
Land records: Contact Robert M. Nye,
   Town Clerk and Registrar of Vital
   Statistics
Vital records: Contact Town Clerk and
   Registrar of Vital Statistics and Town
   Historian
Probate records: Contact Matthew
   Greene, Judge of Probate Court,
   Municipal Building, 181 State Street,
   New London, CT 06320

*Town of Watertown
Town Hall
37 DeForest Street
Watertown, CT 06795
Phone (203) 945-5230 Town Clerk and
   Registrar of Vital Statistics; (203)
   (203) 945-5237 Judge of Probate
   Court
*Town incorporated May 1780 from
   Waterbury. Probate district
   constituted 3 June 1834 from
   Waterbury*
Land records: Contact Dolores LaRosa,
   Town Clerk and Registrar of Vital
   Statistics
Vital records: Contact Town Clerk and
   Registrar of Vital Statistics
Probate records: Contact Carey R.
   Geghan, Judge of Probate Court

*Town of West Hartford
Town Hall
50 South Main Street
West Hartford, CT 06107

Phone (203) 523-3100 Town Clerk and Registrar of Vital Statistics; (203) 523-3174 Judge of Probate Court
Town incorporated May 1854 from Hartford. Probate district constituted 5 January 1983 from Hartford
Land records: From 1854; contact Nan L. Glass, Town Clerk and Registrar of Vital Statistics, Room 313
Land records search service: no charge for search for individual records, but no genealogical searches; copies: $1.00 per page, $1.50 for certification
Naturalization records: No naturalization records
Vital records: Births, deaths and marriages from 1854; contact Town Clerk and Registrar of Vital Statistics
Vital records search service: no charge for search for individual records, but no genealogical searches; certified copies: $5.00 each (births are restricted)
Probate records: From 1983; contact John A. Berman, Judge of Probate Court, Town Hall, 50 South Main Street, West Hartford, CT 06107

City of West Haven
City Hall
355 Main Street
West Haven, CT 06516
Phone (203) 934-3421 Town Clerk and Registrar of Vital Statistics or Judge of Probate Court
Town incorporated 24 June 1921 from Orange. City incorporated 27 June 1961. Probate district constituted 4 January 1943 from New Haven
Land records: Contact Daniel J. Krevolin, City Clerk, Town Clerk and Registrar of Vital Statistics
Vital records: Contact City Clerk, Town Clerk and Registrar of Vital Statistics
Probate records: Contact E. Michael Heffernan, Judge of Probate Court

*Town of Westbrook
PO Box G
1163 Boston Post Road
Westbrook, CT 06498
Phone (203) 399-3044 Town Clerk and Registrar of Vital Statistics; (203) 399-5661 Judge of Probate Court
Town incorporated May 1840 from Saybrook (Deep River). Probate district constituted 4 July 1854 from Old Saybrook
Land records: Contact Tanya D. Lane, Town Clerk and Registrar of Vital Statistics
Vital records: Contact Town Clerk and Registrar of Vital Statistics
Probate records: Contact Constance J. Vogell, Judge of Probate Court, Town Hall, Westbrook, CT 06498

Town of Weston
Town Hall
56 Norfield Road
PO Box 1007
Weston, CT 06883
Phone (203) 222-2682 Town Clerk and Registrar of Vital Statistics; (203) 226-8311 Judge of Probate Court
Town incorporated October 1787 from Fairfield. Probate district constituted May session 1835 (Bridgeport district contains the records of Easton, which include the records of Weston, Easton being a district of its own from 22 July 1875 until 4 March 1878)
Land records: Contact Helen M. Rosendahl, Town Clerk and Registrar of Vital Statistics
Vital records: Contact Town Clerk and Registrar of Vital Statistics
Probate records: Contact Earl F. Capuano, Judge of Probate Court, Town Hall, 110 Myrtle Avenue, Westport, CT 06881

*Town of Westport
Town Hall
110 Myrtle Avenue
PO Box 549
Westport, CT 06881
Phone (203) 226-8311 Town Clerk and Registrar of Vital Statistics or Judge of Probate Court
Town incorporated 28 May 1835 from Fairfield, Norwalk and Weston. Probate district constituted May session 1835 at the time of the incorporation of the town of Westport (the territory was taken from Fairfield, Norwalk and Weston)
Land records: Contact Joan M. Hyde, Town Clerk and Registrar of Vital Statistics
Naturalization records: No naturalization records
Vital records: Contact Town Clerk and Registrar of Vital Statistics
Probate records: Contact Earl F. Capuano, Judge of Probate Court

*Town of Wethersfield
Town Hall
505 Silas Deane Highway
Wethersfield, CT 06109
Phone (203) 721-2880 Town Clerk and Registrar of Vital Statistics; (203) 665-1285 Judge of Probate Court
Town settled 1634, named 1637, incorporated May 1822. Probate district constituted 8 January 1975 from Hartford
Land records: Contact Dorcas McHugh, Town Clerk and Registrar of Vital Statistics; copies: $1.00 each
Vital records: Births, deaths and marriages; contact Town Clerk and

Registrar of Vital Statistics; copies: $5.00 each (births are restricted)
Probate records: Contact Sheila Hennessey, Judge of Probate Court, Town Hall, 66 Cedar Street, Newington, CT 06111

*Town of Willington
40 Old Farms Road
West Willington, CT 06279
Phone (203) 429-9965 Town Clerk and Registrar of Vital Statistics; (203) 871-3640 Judge of Probate Court
Town incorporated May 1727. Probate district constituted 4 June 1830 from Stafford
Land records: From 1727 to date; contact Patricia Godbout, Town Clerk and Registrar of Vital Statistics
Naturalization records: No naturalization records
Vital records: From 1727 to date; contact Town Clerk and Registrar of Vital Statistics
Probate records: Contact George A. Baker, Judge of Probate Court, Town Hall, 21 Tolland Green, PO Box 667, Tolland, CT 06084

*Town of Wilton
Town Hall
238 Danbury Road
Wilton, CT 06897
Phone (203) 834-9205 Town Clerk and Registrar of Vital Statistics; (203) 847-1443 Judge of Probate Court
Town incorporated May 1802 from Norwalk. Probate district constituted May session 1802 from Fairfield and Stamford
Land records: Contact Mary H. Duffy, Town Clerk and Registrar of Vital Statistics
Vital records: Contact Town Clerk and Registrar of Vital Statistics
Probate records: Contact John E. Vallerie, Jr., Judge of Probate Court, 105 Main Street, PO Box 2009, Norwalk, CT 06852

*Town of Winchester
Town Hall
338 Main Street
Winsted, CT 06098
Phone (203) 379-2713 Town Clerk and Registrar of Vital Statistics; (203) 379-5576 Judge of Probate Court
Town incorporated May 1771. City of Winsted incorporated January session 1915. Probate district constituted 31 May 1838 from Norfolk
Land records: Contact William T. Riiska, Town Clerk and Registrar of Vital Statistics
Vital records: Contact Town Clerk and Registrar of Vital Statistics

Probate records: Contact Alan M. Barber, Judge of Probate Court

*Town of Windham
Town Building
979 Main Street
PO Box 94
Willimantic, CT 06226
Phone (203) 456-3593, ext. 215 Town Clerk and Registrar of Vital Statistics; (203) 456-0659 FAX, Town Clerk and Registrar of Vital Statistics; (203) 456-3593, ext. 239 Judge of Probate Court
Town incorporated May 1692. City of Willimantic incorporated January 1893. Town of Windham and City of Willimantic consolidated 1 July 1983. Probate district constituted October session 1719 from Hartford and New London
Land records: Contact Ann M. Bushey, Town Clerk and Registrar of Vital Statistics; copies: $1.00 for the first page and 50¢ for each additional page
Naturalization records: No naturalization records
Vital records: Contact Town Clerk and Registrar of Vital Statistics; copies: $1.00 each, $5.00 for certified copies (births are restricted)
Probate records: Contact Patrick M. Prue, Judge of Probate Court, Town Building, PO Box 34, Willimantic, CT 06226; copies: $1.00 each, $5.00 minimum

*Town of Windsor
Town Hall
PO Box 472
Windsor, CT 06095
Phone (203) 285-1902 Town Clerk and Registrar of Vital Statistics
Town settled 26 September 1633, named February 1637. Probate district constituted 4 July 1855 from Hartford
Land records: Contact Mary Hogan, Town Clerk and Registrar of Vital Statistics; copies: $1.00 for the first page and 50¢ for each additional page
Naturalization records: No naturalization records
Vital records: Contact Town Clerk and Registrar of Vital Statistics; certified copies: births $15.00 each, deaths and marriages $5.00 each (prior to 1880: 50¢ per page uncertified, $1.00 for certification)
Probate records: Contact Brian Griffin, Judge of Probate Court

*Town of Windsor Locks
Town Office Building
50 Church Street
PO Box L
Windsor Locks, CT 06096

Phone (203) 627-1441 Town Clerk and Registrar of Vital Statistics; (203) 627-1450 Judge of Probate Court
Town incorporated May 1854 from Windsor. Probate district constituted 4 January 1961 from Hartford
Land records: Contact William R. Hamel, Town Clerk and Registrar of Vital Statistics
No land records search service
Vital records: Contact Town Clerk and Registrar of Vital Statistics
No vital records search service
Probate records: Contact William C. Leary, Judge of Probate Court
No probate records search service

*Town of Wolcott
Town Hall
10 Kenea Avenue
Wolcott, CT 06716
Phone (203) 879-8100, ext. 15 Town Clerk and Registrar of Vital Statistics; (203) 755-1127 Judge of Probate Court
Town incorporated May 1796 from Waterbury and Southington. Probate district constituted May session 1779 from Woodbury
Land records: Contact Elaine L. King, Town Clerk and Registrar of Vital Statistics
Naturalization records: No naturalization records
Vital records: Contact Town Clerk and Registrar of Vital Statistics
Probate records: Contact James J. Lawlor, Judge of Probate Court, City Hall Annex, Chase Building, 236 Grand Street, Waterbury, CT 06702

*Town of Woodbridge
Town Hall
11 Meetinghouse Lane
Woodbridge, CT 06525
Phone (203) 389-3422 Town Clerk and Registrar of Vital Statistics
Town incorporated January 1784 from New Haven and Milford. Probate district constituted 7 January 1987 from New Haven
Land records: Contact Stephanie Ciarleglio, Town Clerk and Registrar of Vital Statistics
Naturalization records: Contact Robert Horowitz, Judge of Probate Court
Vital records: Contact Town Clerk and Registrar of Vital Statistics
Probate records: Contact Judge of Probate Court

*Town of Woodbury
275 Main Street South
PO Box 369
Woodbury, CT 06798
Phone (203) 263-2144 Town Clerk and

Registrar of Vital Statistics; (203) 263-2417 Judge of Probate Court
Town named May 1673. Probate district constituted October session 1719 from Hartford, Fairfield and New Haven
Land records: Contact Jane H. Sandulli, Town Clerk and Registrar of Vital Statistics
No land records search service; copies: $1.00 per page
Naturalization records: No naturalization records
Vital records: Contact Town Clerk and Registrar of Vital Statistics
No vital records search service; copies: $1.00 per page (births are restricted)
Probate records: Contact Mary D. Donaldson, Judge of Probate Court, 281 Main Street South, Town Office Building, Woodbury, CT 06798
No probate search service; copies: $1.00 per page

Town of Woodmont
PO Box 5033
Woodmont, CT 06460
Phone (203) 874-7229 Town Clerk; (203) 783-3205 Judge of Probate Court
Borough incorporated January session 1903. Probate district constituted 30 May 1832 from New Haven
Land records: Contact Janice R. Slater, Town Clerk
Vital records: Contact Town Clerk
Probate records: Contact Bernard F. Joy, Judge of Probate Court

*Town of Woodstock
Town Office Building
Route 169
PO Box 123
Woodstock, CT 06281
Phone (203) 928-6595 Town Clerk and Registrar of Vital Statistics; (203) 928-2223 Judge of Probate Court
Town settled 1686, named New Roxbury, name changed March 1690 to Woodstock, annexed to Connecticut May 1749. Probate district constituted 30 May 1831 from Pomfret
Land records: Contact Judy W. Alberts, Town Clerk and Registrar of Vital Statistics
Vital records: Contact Town Clerk and Registrar of Vital Statistics
Probate records: Contact Nancy M. Gale, Judge of Probate Court, Town Hall, 415 Route 169, Woodstock, CT 06281

DELAWARE

Capital: Dover. Statehood: 7 December 1787 (separated from Pennsylvania in 1776)

Court System

Delaware's Alderman's Courts, by town or city charter, have jurisdiction over minor civil cases, minor misdemeanors, municipal and traffic matters. The Municipal Court of Wilmington has jurisdiction over misdemeanors, municipal violations, preliminary hearings for felonies and drug-related misdemeanors, plus traffic violations. Nineteen Justice of the Peace Courts throughout the state handle civil actions, some misdemeanors, motor vehicle cases (except felonies), and landlord-tenant cases. Family Courts in each county seat handle, among other matters, divorce, annulment, separate maintenance, property settlement, custody, adoptions, and termination of parental rights. Courts of Common Pleas in each county seat handle some civil actions and misdemeanors. The Delaware Court of Chancery, which sits at each county seat, handles equity cases, guardianships, trusts and estates. The Superior Court has general jurisdiction and sits at each county seat. The Supreme Court sits at Dover and receives appeals.

Courthouses

*Kent County Administration Building
414 Federal Street
Dover, DE 19901-3615
Phone (302) 736-2040; (302) 736-2060
    Recorder of Deeds; (302) 736-2233
    Register of Wills
County organized 1680 from Horre Kill District, which was organized in 1664; name changed from Saint Jones County in 1682
Land records: Contact Recorder of Deeds
Vital records: Births, deaths and marriage licenses; contact State of Delaware, Department of State, Division of Historical and Cultural Affairs, Bureau of Archives and Records Management, Hall of Records, Dover, DE 19901
Probate records: Wills and estates; contact Register of Wills

*New Castle County Courthouse
800 French Street

Wilmington, DE 19801-3590
Phone (302) 571-4011
County organized 1673, original county
Land records: Contact Recorder of Deeds (302) 571-7550
Naturalization records: No naturalization records
Vital records: No vital records
Probate records: Contact New Castle County Register of Wills, Public Building, 11th and King Streets, Wilmington, DE 19801, (302) 571-7545
No probate search service; copies: $1.00 per page

Sussex County Courthouse
The Circle
PO Box 505
Georgetown, DE 19947-0505
Phone (302) 856-5601
County organized 1680 from Horre Kill District, which was organized in 1664, name changed from Deale County in 1682
Land records: Contact Recorder of Deeds
Probate records: Contact Delaware State Archives

DESERET

(see Utah)

DISTRICT OF COLUMBIA

Authorized as a federal district in 1790 from parts of Maryland and Virginia; Alexandria retroceded to Virginia in 1846

Court System

The Superior Court of the District of Columbia has five divisions: Civil, Criminal, Family, Probate and Tax. The Family Division has jurisdiction over juveniles, divorce, custody and support, paternity, adoption, commitment of the mentally ill, etc. The District of Columbia Court of Appeals has some primary jurisdiction and hears appeals from the Superior Court.

Courthouse

District of Columbia Courthouse
500 Indiana Avenue, N.W.
Washington, DC 20001-2131
Phone (202) 879-1010
Organized 1790 from Prince George's and Montgomery counties, Maryland, and (until retroceded in 1846) from Fairfax County, Virginia

FLORIDA

Capital: Tallahassee. Statehood: 3 March 1845 (annexed as part of the Louisiana Purchase, 1803, and the Adams-Onis Treaty, 1819, became a territory in 1822)

Court System

Florida's County Courts handle some civil actions, small claims, misdemeanors, ordinance violations, felony preliminaries and traffic. Circuit Courts meet in each county and have jurisdiction over felonies and actions over $5,000, plus juvenile cases, domestic relations, probate, guardianship, mental health and equity. First Judicial Circuit: Escambia, Okaloosa, Santa Rosa and Walton counties; Second Judicial District: Franklin, Gadsden, Jefferson, Leon, Liberty and Wakulla counties; Third Judicial District: Columbia, Dixie, Hamilton, Lafayette, Madison, Suwannee and Taylor counties; Fourth Judicial District: Clay, Duval and Nassau counties; Fifth Judicial District: Citrus, Hernando, Lake, Marion and Sumter counties; Sixth Judicial District: Pasco and Pinellas counties; Seventh Judicial District: Flagler, Putnam, Saint Johns and Volusia counties; Eighth Judicial District: Alachua, Baker, Bradford, Gilchrist, Levy and Union counties; Ninth Judicial District: Orange and Osceola counties; Tenth Judicial District: Hardee, Highlands and Polk counties; Eleventh Judicial District: Dade County; Twelfth Judicial District: DeSoto, Manatee and Sarasota counties; Thirteenth Judicial District: Hillsborough County; Fourteenth Judicial District: Bay, Calhoun, Gulf, Holmes, Jackson and Washington counties; Fifteenth Judicial District: Palm Beach County; Sixteenth Judicial District: Monroe County; Seventeenth Judicial District: Broward County; Eighteenth Judicial District: Brevard and Seminole counties; Nineteenth Judicial District: Indian River, Martin, Okeechobee and Saint Lucie counties; Twentieth Judicial District: Charlotte, Collier, Glades, Hendry and Lee counties.

Five District Courts of Appeal have appellate jurisdiction. First District at Tallahassee: First, Second, Third, Fourth, Eighth and Fourteenth Judicial Circuits; Second District at Lakeland: Sixth, Tenth, Twelfth, Thirteenth and Twentieth Judicial Circuits; Third District at Miami: Eleventh and Sixteenth Judicial Circuits; Fourth District at West Palm Beach: Fifteenth, Seventeenth and Nineteenth Judicial circuits; Fifth District at Daytona Beach: Fifth, Seventh, Ninth and Eighteenth Judicial Circuits. The Supreme Court, which sits at Tallahassee, is the court of last resort.

Courthouses

*Alachua County Courthouse
201 East University Avenue
PO Box 2877
Gainesville, FL 32602-2877
Phone (904) 374-3643; (904) 374-5210
County organized 1824 from Duval and Saint Johns counties
Land records: From 1826
Naturalization records: No naturalization records
Vital records: Marriages only from 1837
Probate records: From early 1800s
Probate search service: $1.00 per year per name, $4.00 minimum; copies: $1.00 per page, $2.00 for certified copies, $1.00 minimum

*Baker County Courthouse
55 North Third Street
Macclenny, FL 32063-2101
Phone (904) 259-3575; (904) 259-3613
County organized 1861 from New River County
Land records: Contact Clerk of Courts
Land records search service: $1.00 per year; copies: $1.00 per page
Naturalization records: Contact Clerk of Courts
Naturalization records search service: $1.00 per year; copies: $1.00 per page
Vital records: from 1877; contact Clerk of Courts
Vital records search service: $1.00 per year; copies: $1.00 per page
Probate records: Contact Clerk of Courts
Probate search service: $1.00 per year; copies: $1.00 per page

*Bay County Courthouse
300 East Fourth Street
PO Box 2269
Panama City, FL 32402-2269
Phone (904) 785-0231
County organized 1913 from Calhoun and Washington counties; name changed from New River County in 1861
Land records: Contact Clerk of Circuit Court
Naturalization records: No naturalization records
Vital records: Marriages and deaths; contact Clerk of Circuit Court
Probate records: Contact Clerk of Circuit Court

*Bradford County Courthouse
PO Drawer B
Starke, FL 32091-1286
Phone (904) 964-6280
County organized 1858 from New River County
Land records: Contact Property Appraiser, ext. 216
Vital records: Marriages; contact ext. 267
Probate records: From March 1875; contact Ray Norman, Clerk of the Court, ext. 297
Probate search service: $1.00 per year; copies: $1.00 per page, $2.00 for certified copies, no minimum

*Brevard County Courthouse
PO Box H
Titusville, FL 32781
Phone (407) 269-8122
Saint Lucie County organized 1844 from Mosquito County, name changed to Brevard County in 1855 (present-day Saint Lucie County organized from Brevard County in 1905)
Land records: Contact Clerk of Courts
Naturalization records: No naturalization records
Vital records: No vital records
Probate records: Contact Clerk of Courts
Probate search service: $1.00 per year of search; copies: $1.00 per page, no minimum

*Broward County Government Center
115 South Andrews Avenue, Room 114
Fort Lauderdale, FL 33301-1801
Phone (407) 357-7286, Search Department; (305) 357-5632 Probate Clerk
County organized 1915 from Dade and Palm Beach counties
Land records: Yes
Naturalization records: No naturalization records
Vital records: No vital records
Probate records: Contact Probate Clerk, Broward County Courthouse, 201 S.E. Sixth Street, Room 230, Fort Lauderdale, FL 33301
Probate search service: $1.00 per year per name; copies: $1.00 per page, $1.00 for certification, no minimum; include period of time to be searched

Calhoun County Courthouse
425 East Central Avenue
Blountstown, FL 32424-2242
Phone (904) 674-5061; (904) 674-4545
County organized 1838 from Jackson County

*Charlotte County Courthouse
Barbara T. Scott
Clerk of the Circuit Court

Room 141
PO Box 1687
Punta Gorda, FL 33950
Phone (813) 637-2115
County organized 1921 from DeSoto County
Land records: From 1921
Naturalization records: No naturalization records
Vital records: Marriages from 1921
Probate records: From 4 July 1921
Probate search service: $1.00 per year; copies: 25¢ each for unrecorded records, $1.00 each for recorded records, no minimum

*Citrus County Courthouse
110 North Apopka Avenue
Inverness, FL 34450-4299
Phone (904) 637-9410 Clerk of the Circuit Court
County organized 1887 from Hernando County
Land records: From 1887; contact Betty Strifler, Clerk of the Circuit Court, Room 101
Naturalization records: No naturalization records
Vital records: Marriages from 1887; contact Clerk of the Circuit Court. Deaths; contact Department of Health
Probate records: Contact Clerk of the Circuit Court

*Clay County Courthouse
PO Box 698
Green Cove Springs, FL 32043-0698
Phone (904) 284-6300
County organized 1858 from Duval County
Land records: From 1835 (except from 1858 to 1872)
Naturalization records: Some naturalization records in Circuit Court minutes, 1858 to date
Vital records: No vital records
Probate records: From 1858
No probate search service; copies: $1.00 per page, no minimum; some old records are not indexed

Collier County Courthouse
3301 Tamiami Trail
Naples, FL 33962-4902
Phone (813) 774-8999
County organized 1923 from Lee and Monroe counties

*Columbia County Courthouse
Clerk of Courts
145 North Hernando Street
PO Drawer 2069
Lake City, FL 32056-2069
Phone (904) 755-4100; (904) 752-1264 Clerk
County organized 1832 from Alachua County

Land records: Deeds from 1 January 1875, plats from 1886, mortgages from 7 December 1872; Contact P. DeWitt Cason, Clerk of Courts
Naturalization records: No naturalization records
Vital records: Marriages from 1876, delayed births from 1943
Probate records: Estate files from 1895, dockets from 1871, guardianships from 1868
Probate search service: $1.00 per year; copies: $1.00 per page (to 8½" x 14"), $5.00 per page (over 8½" x 14"), $1.00 for certification, no minimum; visitors welcome

Dade County Courthouse
73 West Flagler, Room 242
Miami, FL 33130
Phone (305) 375-5124
County organized 1836 from Monroe County

*DeSoto County Courthouse
PO Box 591
Arcadia, FL 33821
Phone (813) 494-3773
County organized 1887 from Manatee County
Land records: Deeds, etc.; contact Clerk
Vital records: Marriage licenses; contact Clerk
Probate records: Contact Clerk
Probate search service: $1.00 per year; copies: $1.00 per page, no minimum

Dixie County Courthouse
Highway 351
PO Box 551
Cross City, FL 32628
Phone (904) 498-3385; (904) 498-7021
County organized 1921 from Lafayette County

*Duval County Courthouse
330 East Bay Street
Jacksonville, FL 32202-2909
Phone (904) 630-2028 Clerk's Office and Recording Department
County organized 1822 from Saint Johns County
Land records; Contact Henry W. Cook, Clerk of the Circuit and County Courts
Land records search service: $1.00 per year of index
Probate records: contact Clerk of the Circuit and County Courts
Probate search service: $1.00 per year of index

Escambia County Courthouse
223 South Palafox Place
Pensacola, FL 32501-5845
Phone (904) 436-5500; (904) 436-5783
County organized 1822, original county

Flagler County Courthouse
PO Box 787
Bunnell, FL 32010-0787
Phone (904) 437-2218
County organized 1917 from Saint Johns and Volusia counties

Franklin County Courthouse
PO Box 340
Apalachicola, FL 32320-0340
Phone (904) 653-8861
County organized 1832 from Jackson County

Gadsden County Courthouse
PO Box 1649
Quincy, FL 32353-1649
Phone (904) 875-4700
County organized 1823 from Jackson County

*Gilchrist County Courthouse
PO Box 37
Trenton, FL 32693-0037
Phone (904) 463-3170
County organized 1925 from Alachua County
Land records: Contact Cindy
Land records search service: $1.00 per name per year for requests in writing
Vital records: Contact Joan
Vital records search service: $1.00 per name per year for requests in writing
Probate records: Contact Tracie
Probate search service: $1.00 per name per year for requests in writing

*Glades County Courthouse
PO Box 10
Moore Haven, FL 33471-0010
Phone (813) 946-0949
County organized 1921 from DeSoto County
Land records: From 1921
Probate records: Contact Clerk of Circuit Court
Probate search service: $1.00 per year; copies: $1.00 per page, no minimum

*Gulf County Courthouse
1000 Fifth Street
Port Saint Joe, FL 32456-1648
Phone (904) 227-1141; (904) 229-6113
County organized 1925 from Calhoun County
Land records: Yes
Naturalization records: No naturalization records
Vital records: No vital records
Probate records: Yes
Probate search service: $1.00 per year; copies: $1.00 per page, no minimum; requests must be in writing and include payment

Hamilton County Courthouse
PO Box 789
Jasper, FL 32052
Phone (904) 792-1220; (904) 792-1288
County organized 1827 from Duval
County

*Hardee County Courthouse
Clerk of Courts
PO Box 1749
Wauchula, FL 33873
Phone (813) 773-4174
County organized 1921 from DeSoto
County
Land records: Yes
Naturalization records: No naturalization
records
Vital records: No vital records
Probate records: Yes
Probate search service: $1.00 per year;
copies: $1.00 per page, no minimum

Hendry County Courthouse
PO Box 1760
La Belle, FL 33935-1760
Phone (813) 675-5227; (813) 675-5217
County organized 1923 from Calhoun
County

*Hernando County Courthouse
20 North Main Street
Brooksville, FL 34601
Phone (904) 754-4201
County organized 1843 from Benton
County, which no longer exists but
was organized 1843 from Alachua
County
Land records: Contact Patricia
Hargraves, Clerk of the Circuit Court,
Recording Department, Room 215
Land records search service: $1.00 per
year; copies: $1.00 per page, $1.00
minimum
Vital records: Contact Health
Department, Brooksville, FL 34601
Probate records: Contact Marie Shaw,
Clerk's Office, Probate Department
Probate search service: $1.00 per year;
copies: $1.00 per page, $1.00
minimum

*Highlands County Courthouse
430 South Commerce Avenue
Sebring, FL 33870-3701
Phone (813) 386-6565
County organized 1921 from DeSoto
County
Land records: From 1921; contact Clerk,
Recording Division
Naturalization records: No naturalization
records
Vital records: No vital records
Probate records: From 1921; contact
Clerk, Probate Division
Probate search service: $1.00 per year;
copies: $1.00 per page, no minimum

*Hillsborough County Courthouse
419 Pierce Street
PO Box 1110
Tampa, FL 33601-1110
Phone (813) 272-5000 Courthouse
switchboard; (813) 272-5750 County
Administrator; (813) 276-8100
(automated voice system for property
records information—touch 4) Clerk
of Circuit Court; (813) 272-6100
Property Appraiser
County organized 1834 from Alachua
and Monroe counties
Land records: Contact Mr. Richard Ake,
Clerk of Circuit Court. Current
records; contact Mr. Alton "Bud"
Parker, Property Appraiser
Vital records: Births from 1950; contact
Hillsborough County Health
Department, Office of Vital Statistics,
PO Box 5735, Tampa, FL 33675-
5135, (813) 272-6931
Probate records: Contact Clerk of Circuit
Court
Probate search service: $1.00 per person
per year; copies: $1.00 per page,
$3.00 minimum (three years or more)

*Holmes County Courthouse
(201 North Oklahoma Street—location)
PO Box 397 (mailing address)
Bonifay, FL 32425-2243
Phone (904) 547-1100; (904) 547-1101;
(904) 547-1102
County organized 1848 from Walton
and Calhoun counties
Land records: From 1901; copies $1.00
each
Probate records: Some patent deed
records from late 1800s
Probate search service: $1.00 per year;
copies: 15¢ per page, $1.00 for
certified copies, no minimum

*Indian River County Courthouse
(2000 16th Avenue, Vero Beach, FL
32960—location)
PO Box 1028 (mailing address)
Vero Beach, FL 32961-1028
Phone (407) 770-5185
County organized 1925 from Saint
Lucie County
Land records: Contact Jeffrey K. Barton,
Clerk of Circuit Court, Recording
Division
Land records search service: $1.00 per
year
Vital records: Marriage licenses; contact
Clerk of Circuit Court, Civil Division
Vital records search service: $1.00 per
year
Probate records: Contact Clerk of Circuit
Court, Civil Division
Probate search service: $1.00 per year

Jackson County Courthouse
PO Box 510

Marianna, FL 32446-0510
Phone (904) 482-3354
County organized 1822 from Escambia
County, and in 1834 annexed Fayette
County, which was organized in 1832

*Jefferson County Courthouse
PO Box 547
Monticello, FL 32344
Phone (904) 342-0218 ext. 32 Clerk of
Court; (904) 342-0218 ext. 25
Marriage Clerk; (904) 342-0218 ext.
28 Probate Clerk; (904) 342-0222
FAX
County organized 1827 from Leon
County
Land records: Property transactions from
1827; Contact Eleanor B. Hawkins,
Clerk of Court, Room 10
Land records search service: $1.00 per
year; copies: $1.00 per page
Vital records: Marriage licenses from
1827; contact Joyce Alpine, Marriage
Clerk
Vital records search service: $1.00 per
year; copies: $1.00 per page
Probate records: Contact Shelby
Thompson, Probate Clerk
Probate search service: $1.00 per year;
copies: $1.00 per page

Lafayette County Courthouse
PO Box 88
Mayo, FL 32066-0088
Phone (904) 294-1600
County organized 1856 from Madison
County

*Lake County Courthouse
315 West Main Street
Tavares, FL 32778-3813
Phone (904) 343-9800; (904) 742-4117
Recording Division
County organized 1887 from Orange
and Sumter counties
Land records: Deeds; contact Clerk of
Circuit Court, Recording Division, PO
Box 7800, Tavares, FL 32778
Vital records: Marriages; contact Clerk of
Circuit Court, Executive Division
Probate records: Contact Clerk of Circuit
Court, Probate Division
Probate search service: $1.00 per year;
copies: $1.00 per page

*Lee County Justice Center
PO Box 2469
Fort Myers, FL 33902-2469
Phone (813) 335-2283 Probate Division
County organized 1887 from Monroe
County
Land records: Contact Clerk of Courts
Probate records: From 1889; contact
Clerk of Courts, Probate Division
Probate search service: no charge;
copies: $1.00 per page, no minimum

*Leon County Courthouse
Tallahassee, FL 32302
Phone (904) 488-7534 Clerk of Circuit
    Court (Recording); (904) 487-2300
    Clerk of Circuit Court (Marriage and
    Divorce); (904) 487-3146 County
    Public Health Unit; (904) 488-7667
    Clerk of Circuit Court (Probate)
*County organized 1824 from Gadsden
    County*
Land records: From 1825; contact Clerk
    of Circuit Court (Recording)
Naturalization records: No naturalization
    records
Vital records: Marriages from 1825;
    contact Clerk of Circuit Court
    (Marriage and Divorce). Births and
    deaths; contact Leon County Public
    Health Unit
Probate records: From 1825; contact
    Clerk of Circuit Court (Probate)
Probate search service: $1.00 per year;
    copies: $1.00 per page, no minimum

*Levy County Courthouse
PO Box 610
Bronson, FL 32621-0610
Phone (904) 486-5229
*County organized 1845 from Alachua
    and Marion counties*
Land records: Contact Clerk of Court,
    PO Drawer 610, Bronson, FL 32621
Probate records: Contact Clerk of Court
Probate search service: $1.00 per name;
    copies: $1.00 per page

Liberty County Courthouse
PO Box 399
Bristol, FL 32321-0399
Phone (904) 643-2272; (904) 643-5404
*County organized 1855 from Franklin
    and Gadsden counties*

Madison County Courthouse
PO Box 237
Madison, FL 32340-0237
Phone (904) 973-6221; (904) 973-4176
*County organized 1827 from Jefferson
    County*

*Manatee County
Historical Records Library
1405 Fourth Avenue, West
Bradenton, FL 34205
Phone (813) 741-4070
*County organized 1855 from
    Hillsborough County*
Land records: From 1842 to 1977,
    mortgage and land deed books, real
    estate tax sales and records, old maps
    and plat maps
Vital records: Marriage registries
Probate records: From 1853 to 1994
Probate search service: no charge;
    copies: $1.00 per page

*Marion County
Clerk of the Circuit Court
110 N.W. First Avenue
PO Box 1030
Ocala, FL 32670-1030
Phone (904) 622-0242
*County organized 1844 from Alachua
    County*
Land records: From 1845; contact
    Frances E. Thigpin, Clerk of the
    Circuit Court
Probate records: From 1845
Probate search service: $1.00 per year;
    copies: $1.00 per page, $2.00 for
    certified copies, no minimum

*Martin County Courthouse
100 East Ocean Boulevard
Stuart, FL 33494
Phone (407) 288-5400; (407) 288-5576
    Clerk of Circuit Court
*County organized 1925 from Palm
    Beach County*
Land records: Contact Marshal Stiller,
    Clerk of Circuit Court
Land records search service: $1.00 per
    year; copies: $1.00, plats $5.00
Vital records: marriage licenses; contact
    Clerk of Circuit Court
Vital records search service: $1.00 per
    year; copies: $1.00

*Monroe County Courthouse
500 Whitehead Street
Key West, FL 33040
Phone (305) 294-4641
*County organized 1823 from Saint
    Johns County*
Land records: Contact Danny L.
    Kalhage, Clerk, PO Box 1980, Key
    West, FL 33041
Vital records: Deaths; contact Clerk
Probate records: Contact Clerk
Probate search service: $1.00 per year,
    per name; copies: $1.00 per page,
    $2.00 for certified copies, no
    minimum

*Nassau County Courthouse
PO Box 456
Fernandina Beach, FL 32034-0456
Phone (904) 261-5724; (904) 261-6127
*County organized 1824 from Duval
    County*
Land records: From 1840; contact Ms.
    Nancy Beasley, Deputy Clerk
Naturalization records: No naturalization
    records
Vital records: Marriages from 1887;
    contact Margie Armstrong, Deputy
    Clerk
Probate records: From 1872; contact Ms.
    June Stewart, Deputy Clerk
Probate search service: $1.00 per year;
    copies: $1.00 per page

*Okaloosa County Courthouse
PO Drawer 1359
Crestview, FL 32536
Phone (904) 682-2711
*County organized 1915 from Santa
    Rosa and Walton counties*
Land records: Deeds, mortgages,
    judgments, plats, etc.
Naturalization records: No naturalization
    records
Vital records: Marriages only
Probate records: From 1915
Probate search service: $1.00 per year;
    copies: $1.00 per page, $1.00 extra for
    certification

Okeechobee County Courthouse
304 N.W. Second Street
Okeechobee, FL 33472
Phone (813) 763-3193; (813) 763-6441
*County organized 1917 from Osceola
    and Palm Beach counties*

*Orange County Courthouse
37 North Orange Avenue, Suite 1030
Orlando, FL 32801
Phone (407) 836-5115 Land Records;
    (407) 836-2625 Vital Records; (407)
    836-2058 Clerk of the Circuit Court
*County organized 1824 from Indian
    lands; name changed from Mosquito
    County in 1845*
Land records: Contact 100 East Pine
    Street, Orlando, FL 32801
Vital records: Contact 832 West Central
    Boulevard, Orlando, FL 32805
Probate records: From 1873 to date;
    contact Clerk of the Circuit Court
Probate search service: $1.00 per year;
    copies: $1.00 per page, $1.00
    additional per document for
    certification, no minimum

*Osceola County Courthouse
12 South Vernon Avenue
Kissimmee, FL 34741-5491
Phone (407) 847-1300 Clerk of the
    Circuit Court; (407) 870-1409 Health
    Department
*County organized 1887 from Brevard
    and Orange counties*
Land records: Deeds, mortgages,
    satisfactions, etc.; Contact Mel Wills,
    Jr., Clerk of the Circuit Court; copies:
    $1.00 per page (up to 8½" x 14"),
    $1.00 for certification
Naturalization records: Contact Clerk of
    the Circuit Court
Vital records: Marriages; contact Clerk of
    the Circuit Court. Births and deaths;
    contact Health Department (Vital
    Statistics)
Probate records: Wills, probate of estates,
    guardianships, trusts; contact Clerk of
    the Circuit Court; copies: $1.00 per
    page (up to 8½" x 14"), $1.00 for
    certification

Palm Beach County Courthouse
301 North Olive
PO Drawer H
West Palm Beach, FL 33401-4705
Phone (407) 820-2697; (407) 820-2754
County organized 1909 from Dade County

*Pasco County Courthouse
38053 East Live Oak Avenue
Dade City, FL 33525
Phone (904) 521-4424; (813) 847-2411
County organized 1887 from Hernando County
Land records: Contact Jed Pittman, Clerk of Circuit Court, PO Drawer 338, New Port Richey, FL 34656-0338
Naturalization records: Contact Clerk of Circuit Court
Vital records: Contact Clerk of Circuit Court
Probate records: Contact Clerk of Circuit Court

*Pinellas County Courthouse
Official Records Department
315 Court Street
Clearwater, FL 34616-5192
Phone (813) 464-4876
County organized 1911 from Hillsborough County
Land records: From 1912 and old Hillsborough records that pertain to property that is now in Pinellas County; contact Karleen F. DeBlaker, Clerk of the Circuit Court
Naturalization records: No naturalization records
Vital records: Marriages from 1912 and death certificates which have been recorded in connection with the sale of real estate
Probate records: From 1912; contact Karleen F. DeBlaker, Clerk of the Circuit Court
Probate search service: $1.00 per year; copies: $1.00 per page, $2.00 for certified copies, no minimum

Polk County Courthouse
PO Box 988
Bartow, FL 33830
Phone (813) 534-4000; (813) 533-1161
County organized 1861 from Brevard and Hillsborough counties

*Putnam County Courthouse
PO Box 758
Palatka, FL 32078-0758
Phone (904) 329-0330 Archivist; (904) 329-0258 Recording; (904) 329-0350 Marriage Department
County organized 13 January 1849 from Alachua, Duval, Marion, Mosquito (now Orange) and Saint Johns counties

Land records: From 1849; contact Recording, 518 Saint Johns Avenue, Palatka, FL 32078
Naturalization records: From 1849 to 1910; contact Janice S. Mahaffey, Archivist, Archives Office, PO Box 1976, Palatka, FL 32078-1976 (after 1915 contact the Bureau of Vital Statistics in Jacksonville)
Vital records: Marriage records from 1849; contact Marriage Department
Probate records: Contact Archives Department or Law Department
Probate search service from Law Department: $1.00 per year; copies: $1.00 per page. Probate search service from Archives Department: $5.00; copies: 25¢ per page

*Saint Johns County Courthouse
4010 Lewis Speedway
PO Box 300
Saint Augustine, FL 32085-0300
Phone (904) 823-2333
County organized 1822, original county
Land records: From 1820; contact Carl "Bud" Markel, Clerk of Courts, PO Drawer 300, Saint Augustine, FL 32085
Land records search service: $1.00 per year; copies: $1.00 per page, $1.00 per document for certification
Naturalization records: No naturalization records
Vital records: Marriages from 1840 (some years in 1800s missing); contact Clerk of Courts
Vital records search service: $1.00 per year; copies: $1.00 per page, $1.00 per document for certification
Probate records: From 1845 (some years in 1800s destroyed by fire); contact Clerk of Courts
Probate search service: $1.00 per year; copies: $1.00 per page, $1.00 per document for certification

Saint Lucie County Courthouse
221 South Indian River Drive
Fort Pierce, FL 33450
Phone (407) 465-8000
County organized 1844 from Mosquito County; name changed to Brevard County in 1855 (present-day Saint Lucie County organized from Brevard County in 1905)

*Santa Rosa County Courthouse
801 Caroline S.E.
PO Box 148
Milton, FL 32570-4978
Phone (904) 623-0135 ext. 2181/2182 Archives; (904) 623-0135 ext. 2110 Deed Room
County organized 1845 from Escambia County

Land records: From July 1869 to date (all earlier records destroyed by fire)
Naturalization records: No naturalization records
Vital records: Marriages from 1869 to date, marriage applications from 1922 to date
Probate records: From 1869 to date

*Sarasota County Courthouse
2000 Main Street
Sarasota, FL 34237
Phone (813) 951-5206
County organized 1921 from Manatee County
Land records: Deeds and mortgages; contact Clerk of Circuit Court, Recording Department, Room 101
Vital records: Contact Recording Department
Probate records: Contact Clerk of Circuit Court, Probate Department, Room 119

*Seminole County Courthouse
301 North Park Avenue
Sanford, FL 32771
Phone (407) 323-4330 ext. 4407 Land Records; (407) 323-4330 ext. 4376 Probate Division
County organized 1913 from Orange County
Land records: Contact Clerk of the Circuit Court, Land Records, PO Drawer C, Sanford, FL 32772-0659
No land records search service; copies: $1.00 per page (money order or cashier's checks acceptable) plus SASE
Naturalization records: No naturalization records
Vital records: Marriage licenses and a few death certificates having to do specifically with land recordings; contact Clerk of the Circuit Court
Probate records: Contact Clerk of the Circuit Court, Probate Division
Probate search service: $1.00 per year; copies: $1.00 per page, no minimum

Sumter County Courthouse
209 North Florida Street
Bushnell, FL 33513-9308
Phone (904) 793-2601; (904) 793-0215
County organized 1853 from Marion and Orange counties

*Suwannee County Courthouse
Clerk of Circuit Court
200 South Ohio Avenue
Live Oak, FL 32060
Phone (904) 364-3498 Clerk's Office; (904) 364-3437 Recording Division
County organized 1858 from Columbia County
Land records: From 1859
Naturalization records: No naturalization records

Vital records: Delayed birth certificates and death certificates
Probate records: From 1859
Probate search service: $1.00 per year, per name; copies: $1.00 per recorded instrument, 15¢ per unrecorded instrument, no minimum

*Taylor County Courthouse
PO Box 620
Perry, FL 32347-0620
Phone (904) 584-3285; (904) 584-3531 Clerk of Circuit Court
County organized 1856 from Madison County
Land records: Contact Clerk of Circuit Court Office
Probate records: Contact Clerk of Circuit Court Office

*Union County Courthouse
55 Main Street, West
Lake Butler, FL 32054-1637
Phone (904) 496-2621; (904) 496-3711
County organized 1921 from Bradford County
Land records: Contact Clerk
Naturalization records: No naturalization records
Vital records: No vital records
Probate records: Contact Clerk
Probate search service: $1.00 per year; copies: $1.00 per page, no minimum

*Volusia County Courthouse
120 West Indiana Avenue
PO Box 43
De Land, FL 32720-4210
Phone (904) 736-5915
County organized 1854 from Saint Lucie County
Land records: Contact Clerk, Recording Department
Naturalization records: Limited to name and date only; contact Clerk
Vital records: Marriages and divorces; contact Clerk
Probate records: Contact Clerk
Probate search service: $1.00 per year, per name; copies: $1.00 per page, no minimum

*Wakulla County Courthouse
PO Box 337
Crawfordville, FL 32326-0337
Phone (904) 926-3331; (904) 926-3341
County organized 1843 from Leon County

Walton County Courthouse
PO Box 1260
De Funiak Springs, FL 32434-1260
Phone (904) 892-3131; (904) 892-3137
County organized 1824 from Jackson County

*Washington County Courthouse
203 West Cypress
Chipley, FL 32428-1821
Phone (904) 638-0281
County organized 1825 from Jackson and Walton counties
Land records: Contact Clerk of the Circuit Court, PO Box 647, Chipley, FL 32428-0647; copies: $1.00 per page plus $1.00 for certification
Vital records: Marriages only; contact Clerk of the Circuit Court; copies: $1.00 per page plus $1.00 for certification
Probate records: Contact Clerk of the Circuit Court
Probate search service: $1.00 per year, per name; copies: $1.00 per page, no minimum

FRANKLIN

(see North Carolina and Tennessee)

GEORGIA

Capital: Atlanta. Statehood: 2 January 1788 (chartered by England in 1732, ceded western lands to Alabama and Mississippi in 1802, southern boundary settled in 1866)

Court System

Georgia has 361 Municipal Courts with local jurisdiction. The Municipal Court of Columbus has countywide jurisdiction in civil and some landlord-tenant cases as well as misdemeanor guilty pleas and preliminary hearings. The City Court of Atlanta deals with traffic violations. The Civil Courts of Bibb and Richmond counties exist in lieu of the original City Courts there and sit at the county seats. The County Recorder's Courts in Chatham, DeKalb, Gwinnett and Muscogee counties are courts of limited jurisdiction. There is a Magistrate Court in each of the counties to deal with criminal and civil matters, as well as a Juvenile and a Probate Court. The State Courts sit in each county seat and deal with some civil actions and misdemeanors.

The Superior Courts are the courts of general trial jurisdiction and sit at each county seat. They are divided into forty-five circuits. Alapha Judicial Circuit: Atkinson, Berrien, Clinch, Cook and Lamar counties; Alcovy Judicial Circuit: Newton and Walton counties; Appalachian Judicial Circuit: Fannin, Gilmer and Pickens counties; Atlanta Judicial Circuit: Fulton County; Atlantic Judicial Circuit: Bryan, Evans, Liberty, Long, McIntosh and Tattnall counties; Augusta Judicial Circuit: Burke, Columbia and Richmond counties; Blue Ridge Judicial Circuit: Cherokee and Forsyth counties; Brunswick Judicial Circuit: Appling, Camden, Glynn, Jeff Davis and Wayne counties; Chattahoochee Judicial Circuit: Chattahoochee, Harris, Marion, Muscogee, Talbot and Taylor counties; Cherokee Judicial Circuit: Bartow and Gordon counties; Clayton Judicial Circuit: Clayton County; Cobb Judicial Circuit: Cobb County; Conasauga Judicial Circuit: Murray and Whitfield counties; Cordele Judicial Circuit: Ben Hill, Crisp, Dooly and Wilcox counties; Coweta Judicial Circuit: Carroll, Coweta, Heard, Meriwether and Troup counties; Dougherty Judicial Circuit: Dougherty County; Douglas Judicial Circuit: Douglas County; Dublin Judicial Circuit: Johnson, Laurens, Treutlen and Twiggs counties; Eastern Judicial Circuit: Chatham County; Flint Judicial Circuit: Butts, Henry, Lamar and Monroe counties;

Griffin Judicial Circuit: Fayette, Pike, Spalding and Upson counties; Gwinnett Judicial Circuit: Gwinnett County; Houston Judicial Circuit: Houston County; Lookout Mountain Judicial Circuit: Habersham, Rabun, Stephens, Towns and Union counties; Northeastern Judicial Circuit: Dawson, Hall, Lumpkin and White counties; Northern Judicial Circuit: Elbert, Franklin, Hart, Madison and Oglethorpe counties; Ocmulgee Judicial Circuit: Baldwin, Greene, Hancock, Jasper, Jones, Morgan, Putnam and Wilkinson counties; Oconee Judicial Circuit: Bleckley, Dodge, Montgomery, Pulaski, Telfair and Wheeler counties; Ogeechee Judicial Circuit: Bulloch, Effingham, Jenkins and Screven counties; Pataula Judicial Circuit: Clay, Early, Miller, Quitman, Randolph, Seminole and Terrell counties; Piedmont Judicial Circuit: Banks, Barrow and Jackson counties; Rockdale Judicial Circuit: Rockdale County; Rome Judicial Circuit: Floyd County; South Georgia Judicial Circuit: Baker, Calhoun, Decatur, Grady and Mitchell counties; Southern Judicial Circuit: Brooks, Colquitt, Echols, Lowndes and Thomas counties; Southwestern Judicial Circuit: Lee, Macon, Schley, Stewart, Sumter and Webster counties; Stone Mountain Judicial Circuit: DeKalb County; Tallapoosa Judicial Circuit: Haralson, Paulding and Polk counties; Tifton Judicial Circuit: Irwin, Tift, Turner and Worth counties; Toombs Judicial Circuit: Glascock, Lincoln, McDuffie, Taliaferro, Warren and Wilkes counties; Waycross Judicial Circuit: Bacon, Brantley, Charlton, Coffee, Pierce and Ware counties; Western Judicial Circuit: Clarke and Oconee counties. The Court of Appeals and the Supreme Court of Georgia sit in Atlanta.

Courthouses

Appling County Courthouse
100 Oak Street
Baxley, GA 31513-2028
Phone (912) 367-4335; (912) 367-8100
County organized 1818 from Creek Cession

*Atkinson County Courthouse
PO Box 855
Pearson, GA 31642
Phone (912) 422-3552; (912) 422-3343
County organized 1917 from Coffee and Clinch counties
Land records: Contact Clerk of Court
Naturalization records: Contact Clerk of Court
Vital records: Contact Probate Judge
Probate records: From 1919; contact Probate Judge

Probate search service: $3.00; copies: 25¢ each, $3.00 for certified copies, no minimum

*Bacon County Courthouse
PO Box 376
Alma, GA 31510-0376
Phone (912) 632-7661; (912) 632-4915
County organized 1914 from Appling, Pierce and Ware counties
Land records: Contact Rena Hutto, Clerk of Superior Court
Vital records: Contact Jerri Jackson, Probate Judge, PO Box 146, Alma, GA 31510
Probate records: Contact Jerri Jackson, Probate Judge
Probate search service: $3.00; copies: $3.00, $3.00 minimum

Baker County Courthouse
PO Box 10
Newton, GA 31770
Phone (912) 734-5394; (912) 734-5294
County organized 1825 from Early County

*Baldwin County Courthouse
Milledgeville, GA 31061
Phone (912) 453-4807; (912) 453-4007
County organized 1803 from Creek Indian Lands and Hancock, Washington and Wilkinson counties
Land records: Contact Clerk's Office
Naturalization records: No naturalization records
Vital records: Births and deaths from 1917, marriages from 1806; contact Probate Court, PO Box 964, Milledgeville, GA 31061
Probate records: Wills and estates from 1806; contact Probate Court
Probate search service: no charge; copies: 25¢ per page, $4.00 for certified copies, no minimum

*Banks County Courthouse
PO Box 130
Homer, GA 30547
Phone (404) 673-2320
County organized 1858 from Franklin and Habersham counties
Vital records: Births, deaths and marriages
Probate records: Wills and estates
Probate search service: $3.00; copies: 25¢ per page, $3.00 for certified copies

*Barrow County Courthouse
30 North Broad Street
Winder, GA 30680
Phone (404) 307-3000
County organized 1914 from Gwinnett, Jackson and Walton counties

Land records: Deeds; contact Syble H. Brock, Clerk of Superior Court
Naturalization records: No naturalization records
Vital records: Contact Janet T. Cape, Probate Court
Probate records: Contact Probate Court

*Bartow County Courthouse
PO Box 543
Cartersville, GA 30120
Phone (404) 382-5275; (404) 382-4766; (404) 382-6676 Bartow County Genealogical Society
County organized 1832 from Indian Lands; name changed from Cass County in 1861
Land records: Books A & B missing, C to P many gaps, P to present intact; contact Superior Court Clerk
No land records search service (contact Jean Belew, President, Bartow County Genealogical Society, PO Box 993, Cartersville, GA 30120-0993)
Naturalization records: A few scattered naturalization records in Superior Court Minutes; contact Superior Court Clerk
Vital records: Marriages from 1832, births and deaths from 1919; contact Judge, Probate Court
Probate records: Wills from 1836, probate from 1853; contact Judge, Probate Court
Probate search service: no charge; copies: $1.00 per page, no minimum

Ben Hill County Courthouse
PO Box 1163
Fitzgerald, GA 31750
Phone (912) 423-3944; (912) 423-2455
County organized 1906 from Irwin and Wilcox counties

Berrien County Courthouse
PO Box 446
Nashville, GA 31639-0446
Phone (912) 686-5213; (912) 686-5421
County organized 1856 from Coffee, Irwin and Lowndes counties

*Bibb County Courthouse
601 Mulberry Street
PO Box 4708
Macon, GA 31298
Phone (912) 743-7494; (912) 749-6527
County organized 1822 from Houston, Jones, Monroe and Twiggs counties
Land records: Contact Aline Byrd, Clerk of Court, 275 Second Street, Macon, GA 31201
Vital records: Births and deaths; contact Theresa Aultman, County Health Department, 175 Emery Highway, Macon, GA 31201

Probate records: Contact William J. Self, II, Probate Judge

*Bleckley County Courthouse
306 S.E. Second Street
Cochran, GA 31014-1622
Phone (912) 934-7942; (912) 934-4516
County organized 1912 from Pulaski County
Land records: Contact Diane Brown, Clerk of Court
Probate records: Contact Robert F. Johnson, Probate Judge

*Brantley County Courthouse
PO Box 207
Nahunta, GA 31553
Phone (912) 462-5192; (912) 462-5256
County organized 1920 from Charlton, Pierce and Wayne counties
Vital records: Yes
Probate records: Yes
Probate search service: $3.00

*Brooks County Courthouse
PO Box 665
Quitman, GA 31643-0665
Phone (912) 263-4747 Clerk, Superior Court; (912) 263-7585 County Health Department; (912) 263-5567 Judge, Probate Court
County organized 1858 from Lowndes and Thomas counties
Land records: Contact Ms. Elizabeth D. Baker, Clerk, Brooks County Superior Court, PO Box 630, Quitman, GA 31643
Vital records: Contact Brooks County Health Department, PO Box 447, Quitman, GA 31643
Probate records: Contact Remer C. Edmondson, Judge, Brooks County Probate Court, PO Box 665, Quitman, GA 31643
No probate search service; copies: $3.00, no minimum

*Bryan County Courthouse
PO Box 757
Pembroke, GA 31321
Phone (912) 653-4721; (912) 653-4912
County organized 1793 from Chatham, Effingham and Liberty counties
Land records: Contact Clerk of Superior Court
Vital records: Contact Probate Court
Probate records: Yes
Probate search service: $3.00; copies: 50¢ per page, $3.00 for certified copies

*Bulloch County Courthouse
PO Box 1005
Statesboro, GA 30458
Phone (912) 765-9009 Clerk of Superior

Court; (912) 764-3800 County Health Department; (912) 489-8749 Probate Court
County organized 1796 from Bryan and Screven counties
Land records: Deeds; contact Clerk of Superior Court, 1 North Main Street, Statesboro, GA 30458
Vital records: Births and deaths: contact Bulloch County Health Department, 1 West Altman Street, PO Box 666, Statesboro, GA 30459. Marriages; contact Lee H. DeLoach, Judge, Probate Court, PO Box 1009, Statesboro, GA 30458
Probate records: Estates and guardianships; contact Judge, Probate Court
Probate search service: no charge; copies: 25¢ per page, no minimum; SASE helpful

*Burke County Courthouse
PO Box 62
Waynesboro, GA 30830-0062
Phone (404) 554-3000; (404) 554-2324
County organized 1777 from Saint George Parish
Land records: Deeds and land records; contact Office of Clerk of Superior Court, PO Box 803, Waynesboro, GA 30830
Vital records: Contact Bobbie N. Odom, Clerk, Burke County Probate Court, PO Box 322, Waynesboro, GA 30830
Probate records: Contact Burke County Probate Court
Probate search service: no charge; copies: 25¢ per page, no minimum; no records before 24 January 1856, when courthouse burned

*Butts County Courthouse
PO Box 320
Jackson, GA 30233
Phone (404) 755-3298; (404) 775-8215; (404) 775-8204 Probate Court
County organized 1825 from Henry and Monroe counties
Land records: Contact Clerk of Superior Court, PO Box 320, Jackson, GA 30233
Vital records: Contact Probate Court, PO Box 91, Jackson, GA 30233
Probate records: Contact Probate Court
Probate search service: no charge; copies: 25¢ per page, $1.00 minimum; enclose SASE

*Calhoun County Courthouse
PO Box 87
Morgan, GA 31766
Phone (912) 849-2115; (912) 849-2715
County organized 1854 from Baker and Early counties

Land records: Contact Clerk of Superior Court
Vital records: Contact Probate Court
Probate records: Contact Probate Court
Probate search service: $3.00 (includes cost of copies)

Camden County Courthouse
PO Box 578
Woodbine, GA 31569
Phone (912) 576-5601
County organized 1777 from Saint Mary, Saint Thomas parishes

Campbell County
(see Fulton County)

*Candler County Courthouse
(Courthouse Square—location)
PO Box 636 (mailing address)
Metter, GA 30439-1605
Phone (912) 685-2835
County organized 1914 from Bulloch, Emanuel and Tattnall counties
Land records: Contact Pam Holland, Clerk, Candler County Board of Commissioners, 705 North Lewis Street, Metter, GA 30439
Naturalization records: Contact Clerk
Vital records: Contact Clerk
Probate records: Contact Clerk

*Carroll County Courthouse
PO Box 1620
Carrollton, GA 30117-1620
Phone (404) 830-5840 Probate; (404) 830-5830 Clerk
County organized 1826 from Indian Lands and Paulding County
Land records: Deeds from 1828; contact Clerk of Superior Court Office
Vital records: Contact Health Department
Probate records: Wills; contact Probate Court
No probate search service (contact private researcher)

Cass County
(see Bartow and Gordon counties)

Catoosa County Courthouse
206 East Nashville Street
Ringgold, GA 30736-1712
Phone (404) 935-3511; (404) 935-2500
County organized 1853 from Walker and Whitfield counties

Charlton County Courthouse
100 Third Street
Folkston, GA 31537-3706
Phone (912) 496-2230; (912) 496-2549
County organized 1854 from Camden and Ware counties

Chatham County Courthouse
133 Montgomery
Savannah, GA 31401-3230
Phone (912) 944-4900; (912) 944-4641
County organized 1777 from Saint Phillips and Christ Church parishes

*Chattahoochee County Courthouse
Board of County Commissioners
PO Box 299
Cusseta, GA 31805
Phone (706) 989-3603 Probate Court; (706) 989-3602 Board of County Commissioners
County organized 1854 from Marion and Muscogee counties
Land records: Contact Clerk, Superior Court, PO Box 120, Cusseta, GA 31805
Vital records: Contact Vital Records Custodian, PO Box 119, Cusseta, GA 31805
Probate records: Contact Judge, Probate Court, PO Box 119, Cusseta, GA 31805
Probate search service: $3.00; copies: 25¢ per page, $3.00 minimum

Chattooga County Courthouse
PO Box 211
Summerville, GA 30747
Phone (404) 857-1813; (404) 857-4796
County organized 1838 from Floyd and Walker counties

*Cherokee County Justice Center
90 North Street
Canton, GA 30114-2725
Phone (404) 479-0541 Probate Court; (404) 479-5384; (404) 479-1953
County organized 1832 from Cherokee Lands and Carroll, DeKalb, Habersham, Hall and Swinnett counties
Land records: From 1832; contact Office of Clerk of Superior Court
Vital records: Deaths from 1928, marriages from 1841; contact Probate Court, Suite 340
Probate records: Estates from 1832; contact Probate Court

Christ Church Parish
(see Chatham County)

*Clarke County Courthouse
325 East Washington Street
Athens, GA 30601-2776
Phone (404) 354-2850; (404) 354-2660
County organized 1801 from Greene and Jackson counties
Land records: Contact Clerk of Superior Court
No land records search service; copies $1.00 each (assisted)

Vital records: Marriages from 1803; contact Probate Court. Births and deaths from 1900s; contact Clarke County Health Department
Probate records: From 1802; contact Probate Court
No probate search service; copies: 25¢ per page

*Clay County Courthouse
PO Box 550
Fort Gaines, GA 31751-0550
Phone (912) 768-2445; (912) 768-2631
County organized 1854 from Early and Randolph counties
Land records: Yes
Naturalization records: No naturalization records
Vital records: Yes
Probate records: Yes

*Clayton County Courthouse
121 South McDonough
Jonesboro, GA 30236-3694
Phone (404) 477-3395 Clerk of Superior Court; (404) 477-3301 Vital Records; (404) 477-3299 Estates
County organized 1858 from Fayette and Henry counties
Land records: Contact Clerk of Superior Court
Vital records: From 1919; contact Probate Court of Clayton County; copies: $10.00 for the first page and $5.00 each additional page
Probate records: From 1859; contact Probate Court of Clayton County
Probate search service: no charge (estates); copies: 25¢ per page, no minimum

Clinch County Courthouse
100 Court Square
Homerville, GA 31634-1415
Phone (912) 487-5523; (912) 487-2667
County organized 1850 from Lowndes and Ware counties

*Cobb County Courthouse
30 Waddell Street
Marietta, GA 30090-9640
Phone (404) 429-3109 Probate; (404) 429-3142 Land
County organized 1832 from Cherokee County
Land records: Contact Jay C. Stephenson, Clerk of Superior Court
Vital records: Contact Probate Court/ Department of Human Resources
Probate records: Contact Probate Court

*Coffee County Courthouse
101 South Peterson Avenue
Douglas, GA 31533
Phone (912) 384-5213; (912) 384-4799

County organized 9 February 1854 from Clinch, Irwin, Telfair and Ware counties
Land records: Contact Clerk of Superior Court (does not do title work, but will furnish a copy of a deed if sufficient information is given)

Colquitt County Courthouse
PO Box 886
Moultrie, GA 31776
Phone (912) 985-3088; (912) 985-1324
County organized 1856 from Lowndes and Thomas counties

*Columbia County Courthouse
PO Box 58
Appling, GA 30802
Phone (706) 541-1254; (706) 541-4001
County organized 1790 from Richmond County
Naturalization records: No naturalization records
Vital records: Births and deaths from 1927, marriages from 1790; contact Melissa Eidson, Probate Court
Vital records search service: $5.00 minimum in advance
Probate records: From 1790; contact Probate Court
Probate search service: $5.00 minimum in advance

Cook County Courthouse
103 North Hutchinson
Adel, GA 31620-2417
Phone (912) 896-3941; (912) 896-7717
County organized 1918 from Berrien County

Coweta County Estate Court
22 East Broad Street
Newnan, GA 30264
Phone (404) 253-2558; (404) 253-2668
County organized 1826 from Indian Lands and DeKalb and Meriwether counties

Crawford County Courthouse
PO Box 420
Knoxville, GA 31050-0420
Phone (912) 836-3434; (912) 836-3328
County organized 1822 from Houston, Macon, Marion and Talbot counties

Crisp County Courthouse
Cordele, GA 31015
Phone (912) 273-2887; (912) 273-2672
County organized 1905 from Dooly County

Dade County Courthouse
PO Box 417
Trenton, GA 30752-0417

Phone (404) 657-4414; (404) 657-4778
County organized 1837 from Walker County

Dawson County Courthouse
PO Box 192
Dawsonville, GA 30534
Phone (404) 265-2271; (404) 265-3164
County organized 1857 from Gilmer and Lumpkin counties

*Decatur County Courthouse
PO Box 234
Bainbridge, GA 31717
Phone (912) 248-3025 Clerk of Court; (912) 248-3016; (404) 371-2000
County organized 1823 from Gilmer and Lumpkin counties
Land records: Contact Clerk of Court
Vital records: Marriages; contact Probate Court, PO Box 234, Bainbridge, GA 31717
Probate records: Wills and estates; contact Probate Court
Probate search service: $1.50 per name; certified copies: $4.50

*DeKalb County Courthouse
556 North McDonough Street
Decatur, GA 30030-3356
Phone (404) 371-2718; (404) 371-2000
County organized 1822 from Fayette, Gwinnett, Henry and Newton counties
Land records: Yes
Vital records: Yes

Dodge County Courthouse
PO Box 818
Eastman, GA 30123-0818
Phone (912) 374-3775; (912) 374-4361
County organized 1870 from Montgomery, Pulaski and Telfair counties

*Dooly County Courthouse
PO Box 322
Vienna, GA 31092-0322
Phone (912) 268-4217; (912) 268-4228
County organized 1821 from Indian Lands
Land records: Yes
Naturalization records: Yes
Vital records: Yes
Probate records: Yes

*Dougherty County Courthouse
225 Pine Avenue
Albany, GA 31701-2561
Phone (912) 431-2198
County organized 1853 from Baker County
Land records: Deeds; contact Clerk of Court, Room 126 or PO Box 1827, Albany, GA 31702-1827

No land records search service; copies: $1.00 per page, $2.00 for oversize copies, $2.50 for the first certified page and 50¢ for each additional certified page
Naturalization records: Contact Clerk of Court
No naturalization records search service
Vital records: Contact Clerk of Court
No vital records search service
Probate records: Contact Clerk of Court
No probate search service

*Douglas County Courthouse
6754 Broad Street
Douglasville, GA 30134-4501
Phone (404) 949-2000
County organized 1870 from Campbell and Carroll counties
Land records: Contact Clerk of Superior Court
Naturalization records: No naturalization records
Vital records: Contact Probate Court
Probate records: Contact Probate Court
Probate search service: Yes; copies: no charge for one or two copies, $4.00 plus 25¢ per page for certified copies, no minimum

*Early County Courthouse
PO Box 525
Blakely, GA 31723-0525
Phone (912) 723-3454; (912) 723-3033
County organized 1818 from Creek Indian Lands
Land records: Yes
Vital records: Yes
Probate records: Yes
Probate search service: $3.00; copies: $3.00 for certification plus 25¢ per page

Echols County Courthouse
PO Box 118
Statenville, GA 31648
Phone (912) 559-7526; (912) 559-6538
County organized 1858 from Clinch and Lowndes counties

*Effingham County Courthouse
PO Box 387
Springfield, GA 31329-0307
Phone (912) 754-6071
County organized 1777 from Saint Mathew and Saint Phillips parishes
Land records: Contact Elizabeth Z. Hursey, Clerk Superior Court
Vital records: Contact Frances Y. Seckinger, Judge, Probate Court
Probate records: Contact Judge, Probate Court
Probate search service: $3.00; copies: 25¢ per page, $3.00 minimum

Elbert County Courthouse
Elberton, GA 30635
Phone (404) 283-1320; (404) 283-4702
County organized 1790 from Madison and Wilkes counties

Emanuel County Courthouse
PO Box 787
Swainsboro, GA 30401-0787
Phone (912) 237-7091; (912) 237-3881
County organized 1812 from Bulloch and Montgomery counties

*Evans County Courthouse
PO Box 711
Claxton, GA 30417
Phone (912) 739-4080; (912) 739-1141
County organized 1914 from Bulloch and Tattnall counties
Land records: From 1915 to date; contact Clerk of Superior Court, PO Box 845, Claxton, GA 30417
Naturalization records: No naturalization records
Vital records: From 1915 to date; contact Probate Court, PO Box 852, Claxton, GA 30417
Probate records: From 1915 to date; contact Probate Court, PO Box 852, Claxton, GA 30417

*Fannin County Probate Court
PO Box 245
Blue Ridge, GA 30513
Phone (404) 632-3011
County organized 1854 from Gilmer and Union counties
Land records: From 1854
Naturalization records: No naturalization records
Vital records: Deaths from 1927, births (some delayed certificates) from 1861
Probate records: From 1868
Probate search service: $10.00 (unlimited search); copies: 25¢ per page, no minimum; searches are done as time permits

*Fayette County Courthouse
145 Johnson Avenue
Fayetteville, GA 30214-2157
Phone (404) 461-9555; (404) 461-6041
County organized 1821 from Indian Lands and Henry County
Vital records: From 1890 to date; contact Clerk, Probate Court
Probate records: From 1890 to date; contact Clerk, Probate Court
Probate search service: $3.00; no copying service, contact the Archives for copies

*Floyd County Courthouse
3 Government Plaza
Rome, GA 30161

Phone (404) 291-5136; (404) 291-5110
County organized 1832 from Chattooga, Cherokee and Paulding counties
Land records: Yes
Naturalization records: Yes
Vital records: Yes
Probate records: Yes

*Forsyth County Courthouse
100 Courthouse Square
Cumming, GA 30130-0128
Phone (404) 781-2140; (404) 781-2100
County organized 1832 from Cherokee and Lumpkin counties

Franklin County Courthouse
PO Box 70
Carnesville, GA 30521
Phone (404) 384-2403; (404) 384-2514
County organized 1784 from Cherokee Lands

*Fulton County Courthouse
136 Pryor Street, S.W.
Atlanta, GA 30303-3519
Phone (404) 730-5313
County organized 1853 from Campbell and DeKalb counties, on 1 January 1932 annexed Campbell County (organized 1828 from Carroll, Cherokee, Coweta, DeKalb and Fayette counties) and Milton County (organized 1857 from Cherokee, Cobb and Forsyth counties)
Land records: Yes
Naturalization records: Yes
Vital records: Yes
Probate records: Yes

*Gilmer County Courthouse
1 Westside Square
Ellijay, GA 30540-1071
Phone (404) 635-4763
County organized 1832 from Cherokee and Union counties
Land records: Contact Clerk of Superior Court
Vital records: From 1927; contact Probate Judge
Probate records: From 1837; contact Probate Judge
No probate search service; copies: 25¢ each, $3.00 for certified copies, 25¢ minimum

Glascock County Courthouse
PO Box 231
Gibson, GA 30810
Phone (404) 598-3241; (404) 598-2084
County organized 1857 from Warren County

*Glynn County Courthouse
701 H Street
Courthouse Square
Brunswick, GA 31520

Phone (912) 267-5626 Probate Court; (912) 267-5628 FAX, Probate Court
County organized 1777 from Saint David and Saint Patrick parishes
Vital records: Marriage licenses from the late 1800s; contact Linnie M. Torkildsen, Senior Deputy Clerk, Probate Court, PO Box 938, Brunswick, GA 31521
Vital records search service: no charge; copies 25¢ per page, $4.00 for certification of the first page and 25¢ for each additional page, no minimum
Probate records: Wills, estates, administrators' returns, inventories from the late 1800s; contact Probate Court
Probate search service: no charge; copies: 25¢ per page, $4.00 for certification of the first page and 25¢ for each additional page, no minimum

Gordon County Courthouse
PO Box 580
Calhoun, GA 30701
Phone (404) 629-7314; (404) 629-3795
County organized 1850 from Cass, Floyd and Murray counties

*Grady County Courthouse
250 North Broad Street
Cairo, GA 31728-4101
Phone (912) 377-4621 Probate; (912) 377-1512 County Commissioners
County organized 1906 from Decatur and Thomas counties
Land records: Yes
Naturalization records: No naturalization records
Vital records: No vital records
Probate records: Yes
Probate search service available, send SASE; copies: $3.00 per page

*Greene County Courthouse
113 C North Main
Greensboro, GA 30642-1107
Phone (404) 453-7789; (404) 453-7716
County organized 1786 from Oglethorpe, Washington and Wilkes counties
Land records: Contact Cindy Baugh, Chief Clerk
Naturalization records: Contact Chief Clerk
Vital records: Contact Chief Clerk
Probate records: Contact Chief Clerk

Gwinnett County Courthouse
240 Oaks Street
Lawrenceville, GA 30245-4828
Phone (404) 962-1565; (404) 962-1400
County organized 1818 from Cherokee Lands and Hall and Jackson counties

Habersham County Courthouse
PO Box 227
Clarkesville, GA 30523-0227
Phone (404) 754-2013; (404) 754-6264
County organized 1818 from Cherokee Lands and Franklin County

*Hall County Courthouse
Gainesville, GA 30503
Phone (404) 531-6921; (404) 531-6925
County organized 1819 from Cherokee Lands and Franklin and Jackson counties
Vital records: Marriage licenses only; contact Probate Court, Room 123; certified copies: $4.00
Probate records; contact Probate Court
Probate search service: $2.00; copies: 25¢ per page; send SASE

*Hancock County Courthouse
Courthouse Square
Sparta, GA 31087
Phone (706) 444-5343 Probate; (706) 444-5746
County organized 1793 from Greene and Washington counties
Land records: Contact Clerk of Superior Court
Vital records: Births and deaths from 1927 (very few births before 1927)
Probate records: From 1793
Probate search service: $3.00 (to verify availability), $8.00 for research before 1900; copies: 25¢ per page

Haralson County Courthouse
PO Box 488
Buchanan, GA 30113-0488
Phone (404) 628-5038; (404) 646-5528
County organized 1856 from Carroll and Polk counties

*Harris County Courthouse
PO Box 528
Hamilton, GA 31811
Phone (404) 628-5038; (404) 628-4944
County organized 1827 from Muscogee and Troup counties
Probate records: Yes
No probate search service; "County offices do not search *any records*; contact a professional genealogist or visit the Archives in Atlanta to see records on microfilm."

*Hart County Courthouse
PO Box 128
Hartwell, GA 30643
Phone (404) 376-2565; (404) 376-3944
County organized 1853 from Elbert and Franklin counties
Land records: Yes
Vital records: Restricted to persons and parents

Probate records: Contact Probate Judge's
Office, Courthouse Annex
Probate search service: $3.00; copies:
25¢ per page, $3.00 minimum

*Heard County Courthouse
North River Street
PO Box 478
Franklin, GA 30217
Phone (706) 675-3301 Clerk of Superior
Court; (404) 675-3353 Probate Court;
(404) 675-3821 Commissioner
*County organized 1830 from Carroll,
Coweta and Troup counties*
Land records: From 1894; contact Clerk
of Superior Court
Vital records: Marriages and deaths from
1894; contact Probate Court; certified
copies: $10.00 each for births and
deaths, $4.00 each for marriages
Probate records: From 1894; contact
Probate Court; copies: 25¢ per page,
$3.00 minimum

*Henry County Courthouse
Courthouse Square
McDonough, GA 30253
Phone (404) 954-2121 Clerk of Superior
Court; (404) 954-2303 Probate Court
*County organized 1821 from lands
acquired from the Creek Nation*
Land records: Contact Sara E. Taylor,
Clerk of Superior Court
Vital records: Contact Judge Del Buttrill,
Probate Court, Lawrenceville Street,
McDonough, GA 30253

Houston County Courthouse
200 Carl Vinson Parkway
Warner Robins, GA 31088-5808
Phone (912) 987-2880; (912) 922-4471
*County organized 1821 from Indian
Lands*

*Irwin County Courthouse
PO Box 287
Ocilla, GA 31774-0287
Phone (912) 468-5138 Probate Court;
(912) 469-5356 Superior Court
*County organized December 1818 from
Indian Lands (ceded from the Creek
Nation in treaties of 1814 and 1818)*
Land records: Contact Mrs. Raymond
Paulk, Clerk of Superior Court, PO
Box 186, Ocilla, GA 31774; copies:
$3.00 minimum
Naturalization records: Contact Clerk of
Superior Court
Vital records: Births and deaths from
1919; contact Clarence Smith, Probate
Judge, Probate Court, PO Box 566,
Ocilla, GA 31774; certified copies:
$10.00 each; birth records restricted
for family only
Probate records: Contact Probate Judge

Probate search service: $3.00; copies:
25¢ per page, $3.25 minimum

*Jackson County Courthouse
85 Washington Street
Jefferson, GA 30549
Phone (706) 367-1199
*County organized 1796 from Franklin
County*
Land records: Yes
No land records search service; no copies
available by mail
Vital records: From 1919, marriages from
1806 to date
Probate records: Yes

Jasper County Courthouse
Monticello, GA 31064
Phone (404) 468-6705; (404) 468-2812
*County organized 1807 from Baldwin,
Newton and Walton counties; name
changed from Randolph County in
1812 (present-day Randolph County
was organized in 1828)*

*Jeff Davis County Courthouse
Hazlehurst, GA 31539
Phone (912) 375-5836; (912) 375-4263
*County organized 1905 from Appling
and Coffee counties*
Land records: Contact Clerk of Court
Naturalization records: Contact Clerk of
Court
Vital records: Contact Probate Judge
Probate records: Contact Probate Judge

Jefferson County Courthouse
PO Box 658
Louisville, GA 30434-0658
Phone (912) 625-3141; (912) 625-3332
*County organized 1796 from Burke and
Warren counties*

*Jenkins County Courthouse
PO Box 797
Millen, GA 30442-0797
Phone (912) 982-5581 Probate Judge;
(912) 982-2563 Commissioners'
Office
*County organized 1905 from Bulloch,
Burke, Emanuel and Screven
counties*

Johnson County Courthouse
PO Box 269
Wrightsville, GA 31096-0269
Phone (912) 864-3316; (912) 864-3388
*County organized 1858 from Emanuel,
Laurens and Washington counties*

*Jones County Courthouse
PO Box 1359
Gray, GA 31032
Phone (912) 986-6671 Superior Court

Clerk's Office; (912) 986-6668
Probate Court; (912) 986-6405
*County organized 1807 from Baldwin,
Bibb and Putnam counties*
Land records: From 1807; Contact
Superior Court Clerk's Office
Naturalization records: No naturalization
records
Vital records: Births from 1871
(indexed), deaths from 1917 and
marriages from 1811; contact Probate
Court; certified copies: $10.00 each
for births and deaths (restricted to
relatives, indexes not open for
searches), $4.00 each for marriages
Probate records: Wills from 1809, Court
Dockets from 1829, Minutes from
1808
Probate search service: no charge;
copies: 25¢ per page

Kinchafoonee County
(see Webster County)

*Lamar County Courthouse
326 Thomaston Street
Barnesville, GA 30204-1612
Phone (404) 358-5146; (404) 358-5149
FAX Commissioners; (404) 358-5145
Clerk of Court; (404) 358-1483
Health Department; (404) 358-5155
Judge
*County organized 1920 from Monroe
and Pike counties*
Land records: Contact Robert Abbott,
Clerk of Court
Naturalization records: Contact Clerk of
Court
Vital records: Contact Health
Department, Yvonne Melvin
Probate records: Contact Kathryn B.
Martin, Judge
No probate search service; copies: $3.00,
no minimum; must have genuine
reason for interest

*Lanier County Courthouse
100 Main Street
Lakeland, GA 31635
Phone (912) 482-3594 Clerk of Superior
Court; (912) 482-3668 Probate Judge
*County organized 1920 from Berrien,
Clinch and Lowndes counties*
Land records: Contact Martha B.
Neugent, Clerk of Superior Court
Naturalization records: Contact Clerk of
Superior Court
Vital records: Births, deaths and marriage
licenses; contact Judy B. Mullis,
Probate Judge
Vital records search service: $10.00;
copies: Births and deaths $10.00
(confidential and limited to family
members); marriage licenses $4.00
Probate records: Contact Probate Judge

*Laurens County Courthouse
PO Box 2098
Dublin, GA 31040
Phone (912) 272-2566; (912) 272-4755
County organized 1807 from
Montgomery, Washington and
Wilkinson counties
Vital records: Marriage records
Probate records: From 1809
Probate search service: $10.00; copies:
25¢ per page, no minimum

Lee County Courthouse
PO Box 56
Leesburg, GA 31763-0056
Phone (912) 759-6953; (912) 759-6875
County organized 1826 from Indian
Lands and Dooly County

*Liberty County Courthouse
PO Box 829
Hinesville, GA 31313
Phone (912) 876-3635; (912) 876-2164
County organized 1777 from Saint
Johns Parish
Land records: From 1756; contact Clerk
of Superior Court
Vital records: Contact Nancy K.
Aspinwall, Judge, Probate Court/
Liberty County, PO Box 28,
Hinesville, GA 31313
Probate records: Contact Judge, Probate
Court

Lincoln County Courthouse
PO Box 340
Lincolnton, GA 30817-0340
Phone (404) 359-4444
County organized 1796 from Wilkes
County

*Long County Courthouse
Ludowici, GA 31316
Phone (912) 545-2131; (912) 545-2143
County organized 1920 from Liberty
County
Land records: Contact Clerk of Superior
Court, PO Box 458, Ludowici, GA
31316
Naturalization records: No naturalization
records
Vital records: Contact Frances G.
DeLoach, Judge, Probate Court, PO
Box 426, Ludowici, GA 31316-0426;
copies: $10.00; proof of relationship
required
Probate records: Contact Probate Court

*Lowndes County Courthouse
PO Box 1349
Valdosta, GA 31603-1349
Phone (912) 333-5116; (912) 333-5103
Probate
County organized 1825 from Irwin
County

Land records: Contact Clerk of Superior
Court
Vital records: Contact Lowndes County
Health Department
Probate records: Yes
No probate search service; copies:
depends on type of records, 25¢
minimum

*Lumpkin County Courthouse
280 Courthouse Hill
Dahlonega, GA 30533
Phone (404) 864-3847 Probate Judge;
(404) 864-3736 Clerk of Superior
Court; (706) 864-5298 FAX, Clerk of
Superior Court
County organized 1832 from Cherokee,
Habersham and Hall counties
Land records: Deeds, surveys; contact
Edward E. Tucker, Clerk of Superior
Court, 279 Courthouse Hill,
Dahlonega, GA 30533-1142; copies:
$1.00 per page for 8½" x 11", $2.00
per page for 8½" x 11", plus $1.00
postage
Vital records: Births from 1921, deaths
from 1928, marriage licenses from the
1830s; contact Ralph Jones, Probate
Judge, 278 Courthouse Hill,
Dahlonega, GA 30533
Vital records search service: births and
deaths are closed to the public, but
with correct name and date, the office
will look them up at no charge, open
to relatives; copies: 25¢ per page,
certified copies $10.00 each for births
and deaths, $3.00 each for marriage
licenses
Probate records: Contact Probate Judge

*Macon County Courthouse
PO Box 216
Oglethorpe, GA 31068
Phone (912) 472-7685
County organized 1837 from Houston
and Marion counties
Vital records: Contact Mack S. McCarty,
Probate Judge
Probate records: Contact Probate Judge

*Madison County Courthouse
PO Box 147
Danielsville, GA 30633-0147
Phone (404) 795-3351
County organized 1811 from Clarke,
Elbert, Franklin, Jackson and
Oglethorpe counties
Land records: Contact Tax
Commissioners and Tax Assessor's
Office
Vital records: Contact Probate Office
Probate records: Contact Probate Office
No probate search service (due to
understaffing)

Marion County Courthouse
PO Box 481

Buena Vista, GA 31803-0481
Phone (912) 649-5542; (912) 649-2603
County organized 1827 from Lee,
Muscogee and Stewart counties

*McDuffie County Courthouse
PO Box 28
Thomson, GA 30824
Phone (706) 595-2100; (706) 595-2134
Clerk of Superior Court; (706) 595-
2124 Probate Court
County organized 17 October 1870 from
Columbia and Warren counties
Land records: Contact Clerk of Superior
Court, PO Box 158, Thomson, GA
30824
Vital records: Contact Probate Court, PO
Box 2028, Thomson, GA 30824
Probate records: Contact Probate Court

McIntosh County Courthouse
PO Box 453
Darien, GA 31305
Phone (912) 437-6636; (912) 437-6671
County organized 1793 from Liberty
County

*Meriwether County Superior Court
PO Box 160
Greenville, GA 30222
Phone (404) 672-4416 Superior Court;
(404) 672-4952 Probate Clerk
County organized 1827 from Troup
County
Land records: Yes
Vital records: Marriages; contact Laurie
B. Harrison, Probate Clerk,
Meriwether County Probate Office,
PO Box 608, Greenville, GA 30222
Probate records: From 1828 to date;
contact Probate Clerk

Miller County Courthouse
115 South First Street
Colquitt, GA 31737-1284
Phone (912) 758-3456; (912) 758-2731
County organized 1856 from Baker and
Early counties

Milton County
(see Fulton County)

Mitchell County Courthouse
PO Box 187
Camilla, GA 31730-0187
Phone (912) 336-8094; (912) 336-5352
County organized 1857 from Baker
County

*Monroe County Courthouse
PO Box 817
Forsyth, GA 31029-0817
Phone (912) 994-2175; (912) 994-2035;
(912) 994-7022 Clerk of Superior

Court Office; (912) 994-7036 Probate Judge

County organized 1821 from Indian Lands

Land records: Deeds; contact Clerk of Superior Court Office; copies: $2.25

Naturalization records: Contact Clerk of Superior Court Office

Vital records: Marriages; contact Office of the Probate Judge; copies: $2.00

Probate records: Contact Office of the Probate Judge

Probate search service: $3.00; copies: $3.50, no minimum

*Montgomery County Courthouse
PO Box 295
Mount Vernon, GA 30445-0295
Phone (912) 583-2363; (912) 583-4401 Clerk of Superior Court; (912) 583-2681 Probate Court
County organized 1793 from Washington County
Land records: Contact Clerk of Superior Court, PO Box 311, Mount Vernon, GA 30445
Naturalization records: Contact Clerk of Superior Court
Vital records: Contact Probate Court, PO Box 302, Mount Vernon, GA 30445
Probate records: Contact Probate Court

*Morgan County Courthouse
Clerk of Superior Court
Hancock & Jefferson
Madison, GA 30650
Phone (706) 342-1373 Probate
County organized 1807 from Baldwin and Jasper counties
Land records: Contact Elaine Mealer, Clerk of Superior Court
Probate records: Contact Mike Bracewell, Probate Court, Morgan County Courthouse, Hancock & Jefferson, Madison, GA 30650

Murray County Courthouse
Third Avenue
Chatsworth, GA 30705-0023
Phone (404) 695-3812; (404) 695-2932
County organized 1832 from Cherokee County

Muscogee County Courthouse
1000 Tenth Street
Columbus, GA 31901-2617
Phone (404) 571-4847; (404) 571-4860
County organized 1826 from Creek Lands and Harris, Lee and Marion counties

*Newton County Courthouse
1124 Clark Street
Covington, GA 30209-3155
Phone (404) 784-2045 Probate Court; (404) 784-2035 Clerk, Superior Court

County organized 1821 from Henry, Jasper, Morgan and Walton counties

Land records: From 1822; contact Clerk, Superior Court

Naturalization records: No naturalization records

Vital records: Births and deaths from 1927, marriages from 1822; contact Probate Court; copies: $10.00 each

Probate records: From 1822; contact Probate Court

Probate search service: no charge; copies: $4.00, no minimum; request should be in writing

Oconee County Courthouse
PO Box 145
Watkinsville, GA 30677-0145
Phone (404) 769-5167; (404) 769-5120
County organized 1875 from Clarke County

*Oglethorpe County Courthouse
PO Box 70
Lexington, GA 30648
Phone (404) 743-5350
County organized 1793 from Clarke, Greene and Wilkes counties
Land records: From 1794; contact Geneva Stamey, Clerk of Superior Court, Oglethorpe County Courthouse, PO Box 68, Lexington, GA 30648
Vital records: Births from 1919, deaths from 1927, marriages from 1794; contact Judge Beverly W. Nation, Oglethorpe County Probate Court
Probate records: Wills and estates from 1794
Probate search service: $3.00; copies: 25¢ per page, $3.00 for certified copies, $3.25 minimum

Paulding County Courthouse
Courthouse Square
116 Main Street
Dallas, GA 30132-1441
Phone (404) 445-2115; (404) 445-8871
County organized 1832 from Cherokee Lands and Carroll and Cobb counties

Peach County Courthouse
PO Box 468
Fort Valley, GA 31030-0468
Phone (912) 825-2313; (912) 825-2535
County organized 1924 from Houston and Macon counties

*Pickens County Courthouse
211-1 North Main Street
Jasper, GA 30143-9501
Phone (404) 692-2515; (404) 692-3556
County organized 1853 from Cherokee and Gilmer counties

Vital records: Yes
Probate records: Yes
Probate search service: $1.00; copies: $3.00, $3.00 minimum

Pierce County Courthouse
PO Box 646
Blackshear, GA 31516
Phone (912) 449-5011; (912) 449-6648
County organized 1857 from Appling and Ware counties

Pike County Courthouse
PO Box 377
Zebulon, GA 30295-0377
Phone (404) 567-8734; (404) 567-3406
County organized 1822 from Monroe and Upson counties

Polk County Courthouse
PO Box 268
Cedartown, GA 30125-0268
Phone (404) 748-2234; (404) 748-1305
County organized 1851 from Floyd and Paulding counties

*Pulaski County Courthouse
PO Box 29
Hawkinsville, GA 31036-0029
Phone (912) 783-2061; (912) 783-4154
County organized 1808 from Dodge, Dooly, Houston and Laurens counties
Land records: Contact Clerk of Superior Court
Vital records: Contact Judge, Probate Court
Probate records: Contact Judge, Probate Court
Probate search service: $3.00; copies: $3.00

Putnam County Courthouse
Eatonton, GA 31024
Phone (404) 485-5476; (404) 485-5826
County organized 1807 from Baldwin County

Quitman County Courthouse
PO Box 7
Georgetown, GA 31754
Phone (912) 334-2224; (912) 334-9000
County organized 1858 from Randolph and Stewart counties

*Rabun County Courthouse
Probate Court
PO Box 346
Clayton, GA 30525
Phone (404) 782-3614
County organized 1819 from Cherokee Land and Habersham County
Land records: Contact Clerk of Superior Court, PO Box 893, Clayton, GA 30525

Naturalization records: No naturalization
  records
Vital records: Births from 1869, deaths
  from 1930, and marriages from 1820;
  contact Probate Court; copies: $10.00
  each for births and deaths, $4.00 each
  for marriages; must show death
  certificate of person in order to obtain
  birth certificate
Probate records: From 1820; contact
  Probate Court
Probate search service: $10.00 (not
  refundable, must have name of
  person, name of record requested, and
  date of record); copies: 25¢ per page
  when mailed

Randolph County Courthouse
Court Street
PO Box 98
Cuthbert, GA 31740
Phone (912) 732-2671; (912) 732-6440
*County organized 1828 from Baker and
  Lee counties (an earlier county of the
  same name was renamed Jasper
  County in 1812)*

*Richmond County Building
530 Greene Street
Augusta, GA 30911
Phone (706) 821-2460 Clerk of Superior
  Court; (706) 821-2434 Probate Court
*County organized 1777 from Saint Paul
  Parish*
Land records: Contact Clerk of Superior
  Court
Vital records: Marriage licenses; contact
  Lelia R. Botnick, Clerk of Probate
  Court, 401 City-County Municipal
  Building (11), Augusta, GA 30911
Probate records: Contact Probate Court,
  Room 401
Probate search service: no charge;
  copies: 25¢ per page

*Rockdale County Courthouse
922 Court Street
Conyers, GA 30207-4540
Phone (404) 922-7750
*County organized 1870 from Henry and
  Newton counties*
Vital records: Births and deaths from
  1920 to date; contact Clerk of Probate
  Court, Room 107
Vital records search service: $10.00;
  Births are covered under the privacy
  act, but deaths are public if
  relationship can be established
Probate records: Estates from 1871 to
  date; contact Probate Court
Probate search service: $10.00; copies
  25¢ each

Saint David Parish
(see Glynn County)

Saint George Parish
(see Burke County)

Saint Johns Parish
(see Liberty County)

Saint Mary Parish
(see Camden County)

Saint Mathew Parish
(see Effingham County)

Saint Patrick Parish
(see Glynn County)

Saint Paul Parish
(see Richmond County)

Saint Phillips Parish
(see Chatham and Effingham counties)

Saint Thomas Parish
(see Camden County)

Schley County Courthouse
PO Box 352
Ellaville, GA 31806-0352
Phone (912) 937-2905; (912) 937-2609
*County organized 1857 from Marion
  and Sumter counties*

Screven County Courthouse
216 Mims Road
Sylvania, GA 30467
Phone (912) 564-2783; (912) 564-7535
*County organized 1793 from Burke and
  Effingham counties*

*Seminole County Courthouse
PO Box 458
Donalsonville, GA 31745-0458
Phone (912) 524-5256 Probate Court;
  (912) 524-2525 Clerk of Superior
  Court
*County organized 1920 from Decatur
  and Early counties*
Land records: Contact Clerk of Superior
  Court, PO Box 672, Donalsonville,
  GA 31745
Vital records: Contact Probate Court, PO
  Box 63, Donalsonville, GA 31745
Probate records: Contact Probate Court
Probate search service: depends on what
  is requested; certified copies: $3.00
  plus 50¢ per page, $5.00 minimum

Spalding County Courthouse
132 East Solomon Street
Griffin, GA 30223-3312
Phone (404) 228-9900
*County organized 1851 from Henry,
  Fayette and Pike counties*

Stephens County Courthouse
PO Box 386
Toccoa, GA 30577-0386
Phone (404) 886-2828; (404) 886-9491
*County organized 1905 from Franklin
  and Habersham counties*

Stewart County Courthouse
PO Box 157
Lumpkin, GA 31815-0157
Phone (912) 838-4394; (912) 838-6769
*County organized 1830 from Randolph
  County*

*Sumter County Courthouse
PO Box 246
Americus, GA 31709
Phone (912) 924-7693 Clerk, Probate
  Court; (912) 924-3090
*County organized 1831 from Lee
  County*
Vital records: Marriages; contact Clerk,
  Probate Court; copies: 25¢ per page,
  $4.00 for certified copies, plus SASE
Probate records: Contact Clerk, Probate
  Court; copies: 25¢ per page

Swinnett County
(see Cherokee County)

Talbot County Courthouse
PO Box 155
Talbotton, GA 31827-0155
Phone (404) 665-8866; (404) 665-3220
*County organized 1827 from Crawford,
  Harris, Macon, Marion and
  Muscogee counties*

*Taliaferro County Courthouse
PO Box 114
Crawfordville, GA 30631
Phone (706) 456-2494; (706) 456-2123
  Clerk's Office; (706) 456-2253
  Probate Office
*County organized 1825 from Greene,
  Hancock, Oglethorpe, Warren and
  Wilkes counties*
Land records: Contact Clerk's Office
Vital records: Births; contact Probate
  Office
Probate records: Contact Probate Office

Tattnall County Courthouse
PO Box 387
Reidsville, GA 30453
Phone (912) 557-6719; (912) 557-4335
*County organized 1801 from Liberty
  and Montgomery counties*

*Taylor County Courthouse
PO Box 278
Butler, GA 31006-0278
Phone (912) 862-3336; (912) 862-3357
  Clerk

County organized 1852 from Macon, Marion and Talbot counties

Land records: From 1852 to date; contact Dianne C. Renfroe, Clerk, Probate and Magistrate Courts, Deputy Registrar-Vital Records, PO Box 536, Butler, GA 31006

Naturalization records: No naturalization records

Vital records: From 1927 to date (confidential, restricted to family members); contact Clerk

Probate records: From 1852 to date; contact Clerk; copies: 20¢ per page

Telfair County Courthouse
Courthouse Square
McRae, GA 31055
Phone (912) 868-6038; (912) 868-5688
County organized 1807 from Appling and Wilkinson counties

*Terrell County Courthouse
PO Box 525
Dawson, GA 31742-0525
Phone (912) 995-5515; (912) 995-4476
County organized 1856 from Lee and Randolph counties

Land records: Contact Clerk of Superior Court

Naturalization records: Contact Clerk of Court

Vital records: Contact Probate Judge

Probate records: Contact Probate Judge

Probate search service: $3.00; copies: 25¢ per page, $1.50 for certified copies

*Thomas County Courthouse
PO Box 1582
Thomasville, GA 31799
Phone (912) 226-3373; (912) 226-0516; (912) 225-4116 Probate Court
County organized 1825 from Baker, Decatur, Irwin and Lowndes counties

Land records: Contact Superior Clerk of Court's Office

Naturalization records: No naturalization records

Vital records: Contact County Health Department

Probate records: Contact Sallylu H. Hart, Judge, Probate Court

Probate search service: $3.00 in person only, not by mail; copies: $1.00 per page in person only, no minimum

Tift County Courthouse
PO Box 826
Tifton, GA 31793-0826
Phone (912) 382-4515; (912) 386-7850
County organized 1905 from Berrien, Irwin and Worth counties

Toombs County Courthouse
Lyons, GA 30436

Phone (912) 526-8696; (912) 526-3311
County organized 1905 from Emanuel, Montgomery and Tattnall counties

Towns County Courthouse
PO Box 178
Hiawassee, GA 30546
Phone (404) 896-3467; (404) 896-2130
County organized 1856 from Rabun and Union counties

*Treutlen County Courthouse
PO Box 88
Soperton, GA 30457-0088
Phone (912) 529-3342; (912) 529-3664
County organized 1917 from Emanuel and Montgomery counties

Land records: From 1919

Naturalization records: No naturalization records

Vital records: From 1919

Probate records: From 1919

Probate search service: no charge; copies: 25¢ per page, no minimum

Troup County Courthouse
900 Dallas Street
La Grange, GA 30241
Phone (404) 882-6642; (404) 883-1600
County organized 1826 from Indian Lands and Carroll County

*Turner County Courthouse
PO Box 191
Ashburn, GA 31714
Phone (912) 567-2151 Probate Judge; (912) 567-2011 Clerk Superior Court; (912) 567-2334 Tax Assessor
County organized 1905 from Dooly, Irwin, Wilcox and Worth counties

Land records: Contact Sylvia Lamb, Tax Assessor, and Linda House, Clerk Superior Court

Vital records: Contact Dorothy I. Coker, Vital Records Registrar

Vital records search service: $10.00 (index only open to the public); copies: first copy included in search fee, $5.00 for each additional copy (restricted to relatives)

Probate records: Contact Dorothy I. Coker, Probate Judge

Probate search service: $10.00; copies: $1.00 per page

Twiggs County Courthouse
PO Box 202
Jeffersonville, GA 31044-0202
Phone (912) 945-3390; (912) 945-3629
County organized 1809 from Wilkinson County

*Union County Courthouse
Rt. 8
Blairsville, GA 30512-9808

Phone (404) 745-2654; (404) 745-2611
County organized 1832 from Cherokee Lands and Lumpkin County

Land records: From 1860s

Vital records: Births and deaths from 1919, marriages from 1833

Probate records: Wills, administrations, etc. from 1835

Probate search service: $3.00; copies: $1.00 per page, no minimum

*Upson County Courthouse
PO Box 889
Thomaston, GA 30286
Phone (706) 647-7015; (706) 647-7012; (706) 647-8176 Tax Assessor's Office; (706) 647-5847 Clerk of Court; (706) 647-7149 Health Department
County organized 1824 from Crawford and Pike counties

Land records: Contact Tax Assessor's Office

Naturalization records: Contact Clerk of Court

Vital records: Contact County Health Department

Probate records: Contact Probate Judge's Office

*Walker County Courthouse
PO Box 445
Lafayette, GA 30728-0445
Phone (404) 638-3044; (404) 638-1437
County organized 1833 from Murray County

Land records: Deeds; contact Clerk of Court. Appraisal records; contact Property Records Office

Vital records: Marriage licenses; contact Walker County Health Department; copies: $3.00 each

Probate records: From 1882; contact Probate Judge's Office

Probate search service: $3.00; copies: 25¢ each, $3.00 for certified copies, no minimum

*Walton County Courthouse
Court Street Annex 1
PO Box 585
Monroe, GA 30655
Phone (404) 267-1301
County organized 1803 from Cherokee Lands and Henry and Jackson counties

Land records: From 1819

Naturalization records: From 1819

Vital records: From 1819

Probate records: From 1819

No probate search service; copies: 25¢

*Ware County Courthouse
Waycross, GA 31501
Phone (912) 287-4315; (912) 287-4340 Clerk of Superior Court's Office
County organized 1824 from Appling County

Land records: Contact Clerk of Superior
    Court's Office, PO Box 776,
    Waycross, GA 31501
Naturalization records: Contact Clerk of
    Superior Court's Office
Vital records: Marriages from 1874;
    contact Probate Court, Room 105
Probate records: Wills, administrations,
    guardianships from 1874; contact
    Probate Court
Probate search service: no charge;
    copies: 25¢ per page, no minimum

Warren County Courthouse
PO Box 46
Warrenton, GA 30828-0046
Phone (404) 465-2227; (404) 465-2171
*County organized 1793 from Columbia,
    Richmond and Wilkes counties*

*Washington County Courthouse
PO Box 271
Sandersville, GA 31082
Phone (912) 552-3304; (912) 552-2325
*County organized 1784 from Indian
    Lands*
Land records: Contact Clerk of Superior
    Court
Naturalization records: Contact
    Washington County Health
    Department
Vital records: Contact Washington
    County Health Department
Probate records: From 1828; contact
    Probate Court, PO Box 669,
    Sandersville, GA 31082
Probate search service: no charge;
    copies: $1.00, no minimum

Wayne County Courthouse
PO Box 1093
Jesup, GA 31545
Phone (912) 427-2252; (912) 427-3789
*County organized 1803 from Indian
    Lands and Appling, Camden and
    Glynn counties*

Webster County Courthouse
PO Box 29
Preston, GA 31824-0029
Phone (912) 828-3615; (912) 828-5775
*County organized 1853 from Stewart
    County; name changed from
    Kinchafoonee in 1856*

*Wheeler County Courthouse
PO Box 477
Alamo, GA 30411
Phone (912) 568-7133; (912) 568-7135
*County organized 1912 from
    Montgomery County*
Land records: Yes
Naturalization records: Yes
Vital records: Marriages; contact Jeannie
    Davis, Probate Clerk. Births and

deaths; contact County Health
    Department
Probate records: Estate records; contact
    Probate Clerk

White County Courthouse
PO Box 185
Cleveland, GA 30528-0185
Phone (404) 865-4141; (404) 865-2235
*County organized 1857 from
    Habersham County*

*Whitfield County Courthouse
PO Box 248
Dalton, GA 30722-0248
Phone (404) 278-4707; (404) 278-8717
*County organized 1851 from Murray
    and Walker counties*
Vital records: Yes; copies: $3.00
Probate records: Yes
Probate search service: no charge

Wilcox County Courthouse
Abbeville, GA 31001
Phone (912) 467-2220; (912) 467-2737
*County organized 1857 from Dooly,
    Irwin and Pulaski counties*

*Wilkes County Courthouse
23 East Court Street
Washington, GA 30673
Phone (706) 678-2523
*County organized 1777 from original
    territory*
Land records: Land grants (not deeds);
    contact Probate Court, Room 422
Land records search service: $3.00 plus
    SASE
Vital records: Births and deaths from
    1927 (not public records), marriages
    from 1800; contact Probate Court
Probate records: From 1777; contact
    Probate Court

*Wilkinson County Courthouse
PO Box 201
Irwinton, GA 31042
Phone (912) 946-2222; (912) 946-2236
*County organized 1803 from Creek
    Cession*
Vital records: Births and deaths from
    1919, marriages from 1823 to 1828
    and from 1865 to date; contact Clerk
    of Probate Court; copies: 25¢ per page
Probate records: Wills from 1820 to date;
    contact Clerk of Probate Court;
    copies: 25¢ per page

*Worth County Courthouse
201 North Main
Sylvester, GA 31791-2100
Phone (912) 776-8205 Clerk's Office;
    (912) 776-8207 Probate Court
*County organized 1853 from Dooly and
    Irwin counties*

Land records: From 1892; contact
    Clerk's Office, Room 13
Vital records: Births and deaths from
    1919, marriages from 1854; contact
    Virginia Andrews, Probate Court;
    certified copies: $10.00 (cashier's
    check or money order only)
Probate records: From 1853, wills from
    1863; contact Virginia Tanner, Probate
    Court, Room 12
Probate search service: $3.00 per name;
    copies: 25¢ per page, $4.00 for
    certified copies, $1.00 minimum plus
    postage (cashier's check or money
    order only)

HAWAII

Capital: Honolulu. Statehood: 21 August 1959 (annexed in 1898, became a territory on 30 April 1900)

Court System

Hawaii's Tax Appeal Court and Land Court have statewide special jurisdiction and sit at Honolulu. Four District Courts handle some civil actions, small claims, landlord-tenant disputes, misdemeanors, traffic violations and felony preliminaries. Four Circuit Courts handle civil matters, domestic relations, probate, felonies, and juvenile matters. First Circuit: Honolulu County, the Kalaupapa settlement in Kalawao, Molokai and all other islands not covered by other circuits; Second Circuit: Maui County except the Kalaupapa settlement in Kalawao, Molokai; Third Circuit: Hawaii County; Fifth [sic] Circuit: Kauai County. An Intermediate Court of Appeals and the state's Supreme Court sit at Honolulu.

Courthouses

Hawaii Land Court
426 South Queen Street
Honolulu, HI 96809
Phone (808) 548-6423

First Circuit Courthouse
Kaahumanu Hale
777 Punchbowl Street
PO Box 619
Honolulu, HI 96813
Phone (808) 548-5441; (808) 523-4141;
 (808) 548-7669
Honolulu County organized 1905

*Second Circuit Court
2145 Main Street, Suite 106
Wailuku, HI 96793
Phone (808) 244-2929
Maui County organized 1905
Land records: Yes
Vital records: Yes
Probate records: Yes

Third Circuit Courthouse
State Building
75 Aupini Street
PO Box 1007
Hilo, HI 96720
Phone (808) 961-7220; (808) 961-8255;
 (808) 961-7226
Hawaii County organized 1905

Fifth Circuit Courthouse
3059 Umi Street
Lihue, HI 96766
Phone (808) 245-4317; (808) 245-4785
Kauai County organized 1905

IDAHO

Capital: Boise. Statehood: 3 July 1890 (became sole U.S. possession by treaty with Great Britain in 1846, was part of Oregon Territory in 1848, Washington Territory in 1853, and became a separate territory in 1863)

Court System

Idaho's District Courts sit at each county seat and have original jurisdiction over civil, personal injury, domestic relations, criminal, felony and other matters, including appeals from the Magistrate's Division of District Courts, which hear some civil actions and cases concerning property liens, probate, small claims, misdemeanors, traffic, juveniles, etc. First Judicial District: Benewah, Bonner, Boundary, Kootenai and Shoshone counties; Second Judicial District: Clearwater, Idaho, Latah, Lewis and Nez Perce counties; Third Judicial District: Adams, Canyon, Gem, Owyhee, Payette and Washington counties; Fourth Judicial District: Ada, Boise, Elmore and Valley counties; Fifth Judicial District: Blaine, Cassia, Gooding, Jerome, Lincoln, Minidoka, and Twin Falls counties; Sixth Judicial District: Bannock, Bear Lake, Caribou, Franklin, Oneida and Power counties; Seventh Judicial District: Bingham, Bonneville, Butte, Clark, Custer, Fremont, Jefferson, Lemhi, Madison and Teton counties. The Idaho Supreme Court sits at Boise and elsewhere.

Courthouses

*Ada County Courthouse
650 Main Street
Boise, ID 83702-5960
Phone (208) 383-1200; (208) 383-4417
*County organized 1864 from Boise
 County*
Land records: From 1865; contact Ada
 County Recorder; copies: $1.00 per
 page
Naturalization records: No naturalization
 records
Vital records: No vital records

*Adams County Courthouse
PO Box 48
Council, ID 83612-0048
Phone (208) 253-4233; (208) 253-4561

*County organized 1911 from
Washington County*
Land records: From about 1900
Naturalization records: No naturalization
records
Probate records: From 1911
Probate search service: depends on what
is requested; copies: $1.00 per page,
no minimum

*Bannock County Courthouse
PO Box 4016
Pocatello, ID 83205-4016
Phone (208) 236-7380; (208) 236-7342;
(208) 236-7352 District Court Clerks
*County organized 1893 from Oneida
and Bear Lake counties*
Land records: From 1893
Naturalization records: From 1903 to
1917, declarations of intention from
1893 to 1906
Probate records: Contact District Court
Clerks
Probate search service: no charge;
copies: $1.00 per page, no minimum

*Bear Lake County Courthouse
7 East Center Street
PO Box 190
Paris, ID 83261
Phone (208) 945-2557; (208) 945-2212
*County organized 1875 from Oneida
County*

*Benewah County Courthouse
Saint Maries, ID 83861-2042
Phone (208) 245-3241; (208) 245-2234
*County organized 1915 from Kootenai
County*
Land records: Yes
Naturalization records: Yes
Vital records: Yes
Probate records: Yes
No probate search service; copies: $1.00
per page (all records have been
microfilmed by the Family History
Library in Salt Lake City)

*Bingham County Courthouse
501 Maple
Blackfoot, ID 83221-2961
Phone (208) 785-5005
*County organized 1885 from Oneida
County*
Land records: From 1865
Naturalization records: From 1892 to
about 1969
Vital records: Births and deaths from
1907 to 1911, marriages from 1865
Probate records: From 1894
Probate search service: no charge;
copies: $1.00 per page, $1.00 for
certification, no minimum

*Blaine County Courthouse
PO Box 400

Hailey, ID 83333-0400
Phone (208) 788-4574; (208) 788-4290
*County organized 1895 from Alturas
County, which was organized in 1864
and abolished in 1895, and whose
records were deposited with Blaine
County, along with those of Logan
County, which was organized in 1889
and abolished in 1895*
Vital records: From 1907 to 1913
Probate records: Yes
No probate search service; copies: $1.00
if recorded, 25¢ if not recorded, no
minimum

*Boise County Courthouse
PO Box 126
Idaho City, ID 83631
Phone (208) 383-1209; (208) 392-4431
County organized 1907, original county
Land records: From 1860s; contact
Recorder's Office, Box 157, Idaho
City, ID 83631-0157
Naturalization records: Some
naturalization records from 1865 to
1916; contact Clerk of Court
Vital records: No vital records
Probate records: From 1865; contact
Clerk of Court
Probate search service: no charge;
copies: $1.00 per page, $10.00
minimum

*Bonner County Courthouse
215 South First
Sandpoint, ID 83664-1305
Phone (208) 265-1432
*County organized 1907 from Kootenai
County*
Land records: From 1907; copies: $1.00
per page, $1.00 per document for
certification
Naturalization records: Some
naturalization records from 1890s to
1920s; copies: $1.00 per page, $1.00
per document for certification
Vital records: Births from 1907 to 1911,
deaths from 1707 to 1911 and 1986 to
present, marriages from 1907; copies:
$1.00 per page, $1.00 per document
for certification
Probate records: From 1907
Probate search service: no charge;
copies: $1.00 per page, $1.00 per
document for certification, no
minimum

Bonneville County Courthouse
605 North Capital Avenue
Idaho Falls, ID 83402-3582
Phone (208) 529-1340; (208) 529-1350
*County organized 1911 from Bingham
County*

*Boundary County Courthouse
PO Box 419

Bonners Ferry, ID 83805-0419
Phone (208) 267-5504; (208) 267-2242
*County organized 1915 from Bonner
County*
Land records: Yes
Naturalization records: Confidential
Vital records: Confidential
Probate records: Yes
No probate search service; copies: 50¢
per page

*Butte County Courthouse
PO Box 737
Arco, ID 83213-0737
Phone (208) 527-3021
*County organized 1917 from Bingham,
Blaine and Jefferson counties*
Land records: From 1917
Naturalization records: From 1909
Vital records: From 1917
Probate records: From 1917
Probate search service: $5.00; copies:
$1.00

Camas County Courthouse
PO Box 430
Fairfield, ID 83327-0430
Phone (208) 764-2238; (208) 764-2242
*County organized 1917 from Blaine
County*

*Canyon County Courthouse
1115 Albany Street
Caldwell, ID 83605-3542
Phone (208) 454-7300; (208) 454-7555
County Recorder
*County organized 10 November 1892
from Owyhee and Ada counties*
Land records: Only by deeded owner's
name; copies: $1.00 per page, $1.00
per instrument for certification
Naturalization records: Books 1 & 2,
1893 to 1906; copies: $1.00 per page,
no certification available
Vital records: Births from May 1907
through June 1911, deaths from June
1907 through March 1912, marriages;
copies: $1.00 per page, $1.00 per
instrument for certification
Probate records: From 1892
No probate search service; will search a
five-year period or specific year;
copies: $1.00 per page, $1.00 per
instrument for certification

*Caribou County Courthouse
159 South Main Street
Soda Springs, ID 83276-1427
Phone (208) 547-4324
*County organized 1919 from Bannock
and Oneida counties*
Land records: Yes
Vital records: Marriages
Probate records: Yes
No probate search service; copies: $1.00
per page

*Cassia County Courthouse
1459 Overland Avenue
Burley, ID 83318-1862
Phone (208) 678-5240; (208) 678-4367
County organized 1879 from Oneida County
Land records: From 1878; contact Recorder
Naturalization records: Contact Recorder
Vital records: Births and deaths from 1907 through 1911 only, marriages from 1879 to date; contact Recorder
Probate records: Estate files from January 1919; contact Magistrate Division
No probate search service; copies: $1.00 per page, no minimum

*Clark County Courthouse
PO Box 205
Dubois, ID 83423-0205
Phone (208) 529-1345; (208) 374-5304
County organized 1919 from Fremont County
Land records: Yes
Naturalization records: Yes
Vital records: Yes
Probate records: Yes

*Clearwater County Courthouse
PO Box 586
Orofino, ID 83544-0586
Phone (208) 476-5596; (208) 476-5615; (208) 476-3127 FAX
County organized 1911 from Nez Perce County
Land records: Deeds, mortgages, leases, etc.
Naturalization records: No naturalization records
Vital records: Marriages from 1911
Probate records: Yes
Probate search service: $6.00; copies: $1.00 per page

Custer County Courthouse
PO Box 597
Challis, ID 83226
Phone (208) 879-2359; (208) 879-2325
County organized 1881 from Alturas County

*Elmore County Courthouse
150 South Fourth East
Mountain Home, ID 83647-3097
Phone (208) 587-2133 Court; (208) 587-2129 Commissioners; (208) 587-2130 Recorder; (208) 587-2126 Assessor
County organized 1889 from Alturas County
Land records: By legal description: contact James Haydon, Assessor, Drawer A, Mountain Home, ID 83647; by name: contact Delores Robison, Recorder, 150 South Fourth East, Mountain Home, ID 83647

Naturalization records: From 1889 to 1908 only
Vital records: From 1907 to 1911 only
Probate records: Yes
No probate search service; copies: $1.00 per page; searches must be made in person

*Franklin County Courthouse
39 West Oneida
PO Box 231
Preston, ID 83263-1234
Phone (208) 852-0877; (208) 852-1090
County organized 1913 from Oneida County
Probate records: Yes
Probate search service: depends on extent of search; copies: $1.00 per page

*Fremont County Courthouse
151 West First North
Saint Anthony, ID 83445-1403
Phone (208) 624-7401 Court; (208) 624-7332 Clerk of the District Court, Ex-officio Auditor and Recorder; (208) 624-4607 FAX
County organized 1893 from Bingham and Lemhi counties
Land records: From 1893
Naturalization records: Yes
Vital records: From 1906 to 1917 (spotty)
Probate records: From 1893
Probate search service: $17.00; copies: $1.00 per page, no minimum

*Gem County Clerk
415 East Main Street
Emmett, ID 83617-3049
Phone (208) 365-4561
County organized 1915 from Boise and Canyon counties
Land records: From 1915 (some records recorded a little earlier, but possibly not available)
Naturalization records: No naturalization records
Vital records: Marriages and divorces from 1915, no births
Probate records: From 1915
Probate search service: no charge; copies: $1.00 per page, $1.00 for certification, no minimum

*Gooding County Courthouse
PO Box 417
Gooding, ID 83330-0417
Phone (208) 934-4261; (208) 934-4221; (208) 934-4841 Recorders Office
County organized 1913 from Lincoln County
Land records: From 1913 to date; contact Alberta Sites or Helen Piatt, Recorders Office; copies: $1.00 per page plus $1.00 if certified
Naturalization records: From 1913 to

1941; contact Recorders Office; copies: $1.00 per page plus $1.00 if certified
Vital records: Marriages only; contact Recorders Office; copies: $1.00 per page plus $1.00 if certified
Probate records: To 1970; contact Recorders Office. After 1970; contact court offices; copies: $1.00 per page plus $1.00 if certified

Idaho County Courthouse
320 West Main Street
Grangeville, ID 83530-1948
Phone (208) 983-2776; (208) 983-2751
County organized 1864, original county

*Jefferson County Courthouse
134 North Clark
PO Box 275
Rigby, ID 83442-1462
Phone (208) 745-7756
County organized 12 January 1914 from Fremont County
Land records: Contact (208) 745-9215
Naturalization records: To 1940
Vital records: No vital records
Probate records: Contact (208) 745-7736

*Jerome County Courthouse
PO Box 407
Jerome, ID 83338-0407
Phone (208) 324-8811
County organized 1919 from Gooding and Lincoln counties
Land records: Contact Greg Heinrich, Assessor
Probate records: Contact Cheryl Watts, Clerk
No probate search service; copies: $1.00 per page

*Kootenai County Courthouse
501 Government Way
Coeur d'Alene, ID 83814-2915
Phone (208) 664-2918; (208) 769-4400
County 1864 from a portion of Nez Perce County, but was not organized or officered until 1881
Land records: From 1881
No land records search service; copies: $1.00 per page, $1.00 per certification
Naturalization records: Declarations of intention and naturalizations from 1882 through 1939
Vital records: Births and deaths from 1907 to 1911, marriages from 1881
Probate records: Contact Kootenai County District Court, Civil Department, 324 West Garden Avenue, Coeur d'Alene, ID 83814
No probate search service; copies: $1.00 per page, $1.00 for certification; make checks or money orders payable to the Clerk of the District Court

*Latah County Courthouse
PO Box 8068
Moscow, ID 83843-0568
Phone (208) 882-4432; (208) 882-8580
County organized 1888 from Kootenai
County
Land records: From 1888
Naturalization records: No naturalization
    records
Vital records: Births and deaths from
    1907 to 1911
Probate records: Yes
Probate search service: $4.00; copies:
    $1.00 per page, no minimum; include
    name and date of death

*Lemhi County Courthouse
206 Courthouse Drive
Salmon, ID 83467-3943
Phone (208) 756-3115; (208) 756-2815
County organized 1869 from Idaho
County
Land records: Contact Clerk
Naturalization records: Contact Clerk
Vital records: Marriages and divorces;
    contact Clerk
Probate records: Contact Magistrate
    Court
Probate search service: no charge;
    copies: $1.00 per page, no minimum

*Lewis County Courthouse
Cathy Larson, Clerk
PO Box 39
Nezperce, ID 83543
Phone (208) 937-2661
County organized 1911 from Nez Perce
County
Land records: Contact Assessor's Office
    for tract index
Naturalization records: No naturalization
    records
Vital records: No vital records
Probate records: Contact District Court
No probate search service; copies: $1.00
    per page, no minimum

*Lincoln County Courthouse
PO Box A
Shoshone, ID 83352-0800
Phone (208) 886-2173; (208) 886-7641
County organized 1895 from Alturas
County
Land records: From 1895; contact Clerk
Naturalization records: From 1895 to
    1930; contact Clerk
Vital records: Births and deaths from
    1907 to 1911, marriages from 1895;
    contact Clerk
Probate records: From 1900; contact
    Clerk
Probate search service: no charge;
    copies: $1.00 per page

*Madison County Courthouse
PO Box 389

Rexburg, ID 83440-0389
Phone (208) 356-9383; (208) 356-3662
County organized 1913 from Fremont
and Teton counties
Land records: Yes
Naturalization records: Some older
    naturalization records
Probate records: Contact Magistrate
    Court
Probate search service: $10.00; copies:
    $1.00 per page

*Minidoka County Courthouse
715 G Street
PO Box 474
Rupert, ID 83350-0474
Phone (208) 436-9511 County Recorder;
    (208) 436-7186 Clerk of the
    Magistrate Court
County organized 1913 from Lincoln
County
Land records: Contact County Recorder
Land records search service: no charge;
    copies: $1.00 per page, $1.00 per unit
    for certification
Naturalization: No naturalization records
Vital records: Marriages only
Probate records: Contact Clerk of the
    Magistrate Court

*Nez Perce County Courthouse
PO Box 896
Lewiston, ID 83501-0896
Phone (208) 799-3040; (208) 799-3090
County organized 1864 from Shoshone
County
Land records: Contact County Assessor
Probate records: From 1900
Probate search service: no charge;
    copies: $1.00 per page plus $1.00 for
    certification, no minimum

Oneida County Courthouse
10 Court Street
Malad City, ID 83252-0191
Phone (208) 766-4285; (208) 766-4116
County organized 1864, original county

*Owyhee County Courthouse
PO Box 128
Murphy, ID 83650
Phone (208) 495-2806; (208) 495-2421
County organized 1863, original county
Land records: From 1865
Naturalization records: From 1904
Vital records: Births and deaths from
    1907 to 1911, marriages from 1886 to
    1893
Probate records: From 1865
Probate search service: no charge;
    copies: $1.00 per page, $2.00 for
    certified copies, no minimum

*Payette County Courthouse
1130 Third Avenue North

Payette, ID 83661-2473
Phone (208) 642-6000; (208) 642-6010
County organized 1917 from Canyon
County
Land records: Contact Clerk
Naturalization records: Contact Clerk
Vital records: Contact Clerk
Probate records: Contact Clerk

*Power County Courthouse
543 Bannock Street
American Falls, ID 83211-1200
Phone (208) 226-7610; (208) 226-7611
County organized 1913 from Bingham
and Blaine counties
Land records; Contact County Clerk
Naturalization records; Contact County
    Clerk
Vital records: Marriages; contact County
    Clerk
Probate records: Contact County Clerk
No probate search service; copies: $1.00
    per page

*Shoshone County Courthouse
PO Box 1049
Wallace, ID 83873-1049
Phone (208) 752-1264; (208) 752-1266;
    (208) 752-3331 Commissioner's
    Office
County organized 1864, original county
Land records: From 1871; contact Clerk
Naturalization records: From about 1906;
    contact Clerk
Vital records: From 1907 to 1911;
    contact Clerk
Probate records: From 1885; contact
    Clerk
Probate search service: no charge;
    copies: $1.00 per page, no minimum

*Teton County Courthouse
89 North Main
PO Box 756
Driggs, ID 83422
Phone (208) 354-2905
County organized 1915 from Fremont
County
Land records: Yes
Naturalization records: Very early
Vital records: Marriage licenses only
Probate records: Yes

*Twin Falls County Courthouse
PO Box 126
Twin Falls, ID 83303-0126
Phone (208) 736-4004
County organized 1907 from Cassia
County
Land records: Yes
Vital records: Marriages only; certified
    copies: $2.00
Probate records: Yes
No probate search service; copies: $1.00
    per page

*Valley County Courthouse
PO Box 737
Cascade, ID 83611-0737
Phone (208) 382-4150 Court; (208) 382-4297 Recorder; (208) 382-4955 FAX
County organized 1917 from Boise County
Land records: From July 1917; contact Valley County Recorder
Probate records: From 1917; contact Valley County District Court Clerk
No probate search service; copies: $1.00 per page, no minimum

*Washington County Courthouse
PO Box 670
Weiser, ID 83672-0670
Phone (208) 549-2092
County organized 1879 from Boise County
Land records: From 1879; contact Lisa McKnight, Deputy Recorder
Naturalization records: Certificates of naturalization from 27 September 1903 to 25 September 1906, intent from March 1885 to 12 December 1929; contact Deputy Recorder; no copying available, information must be written down in person
Vital records: Births from 13 May 1907 to 17 June 1911, deaths from 18 August 1907 to 19 June 1911, marriages from 19 June 1879; contact Deputy Recorder
Probate records: From 1879; contact Deputy Recorder
No probate search service; copies: $1.00 per page, $2.00 for certified copies, no minimum

ILLINOIS

Capital: Springfield. Statehood: 3 December 1818 (ceded by England in the Treaty of Paris, 1783, settled claims with Virginia, Connecticut and Massachusetts in 1786, was part of the Northwest Territory in 1787, Indiana Territory in 1800, and became a separate territory in 3 February 1809)

Court System

Illinois' Court of Claims sits in Chicago and Springfield and is a quasi-judicial part of the legislative branch, having jurisdiction on all claims against the state. Twenty-two Circuit Courts have general jurisdiction and sit at the county seats and elsewhere, as needed. First Judicial Circuit: Alexander, Jackson, Johnson, Massac, Pope, Pulaski, Saline, Union and Williamson counties; Second Judicial Circuit: Crawford, Edwards, Franklin, Gallatin, Hamilton, Hardin, Jefferson, Lawrence, Richland, Wabash, Wayne and White counties; Third Judicial Circuit: Bond and Madison counties; Fourth Judicial Circuit: Christian, Clay, Clinton, Effingham, Fayette, Jasper, Marion, Montgomery and Shelby counties; Fifth Judicial Circuit: Clark, Coles, Cumberland, Edgar and Vermilion counties; Sixth Judicial Circuit: Champaign, DeWitt, Douglas, Macon, Moultrie and Piatt counties; Seventh Judicial Circuit: Greene, Jersey, Macoupin, Morgan, Sangamon and Scott counties; Eighth Judicial Circuit: Adams, Brown, Calhoun, Cass, Mason, Menard, Pike and Schuyler counties; Ninth Judicial Circuit: Fulton, Hancock, Henderson, Knox, McDonough and Warren counties; Tenth Judicial Circuit: Marshall, Peoria, Putnam, Stark and Tazewell counties; Eleventh Judicial Circuit: Ford, Livingston, Logan, McLean and Woodford counties; Twelfth Judicial Circuit: Will County; Thirteenth Judicial Circuit: Bureau, Grundy and LaSalle counties; Fourteenth Judicial Circuit: Henry, Mercer, Rock Island and Whiteside counties; Fifteenth Judicial Circuit: Carroll, Jo Daviess, Lee, Ogle and Stephenson counties; Sixteenth Judicial Circuit: DeKalb, Kane and Kendall counties; Seventeenth Judicial Circuit: Boone and Winnebago counties; Eighteenth Judicial Circuit: DuPage County; Nineteenth Judicial Circuit: Lake and McHenry counties; Twentieth Judicial Circuit: Monroe, Perry, Randolph, Saint Clair and Washington counties; Twenty-first Judicial Circuit: Iroquois and Kankakee counties; and Circuit Court of Cook County.

Five District Appellate Courts sit at Chicago, Elgin, Ottawa, Springfield and Mount Vernon. The Illinois Supreme Court sits at Springfield and Chicago.

Courthouses

*Adams County Courthouse
521 Vermont Street
Quincy, IL 62301-2901
Phone (217) 223-6300 Clerk of the Circuit Court
County organized 1825 from Pike County. Highland County organized from Adams and Marquette counties in 1847 and eliminated in 1848. Marquette County organized 1843 from Adams County and eliminated in 1847.
Land records: From early 1800s; contact County Recorder
Vital records: Births and deaths from 1878, marriages from 1825; contact County Clerk
Probate records: From 1830; contact Glen F. Hultz, Clerk of the Circuit Court
Probate search service: $4.00 per year; copies: $1.00 for the first page, 50¢ for each of the next nineteen pages and 25¢ for each additional page, $1.00 for certification

Alexander County Courthouse
2000 Washington Avenue
Cairo, IL 62914-1717
Phone (618) 734-0509; (618) 734-3947
County organized 1819 from Johnson County

*Bond County Courthouse
PO Box 407
Greenville, IL 62246-1088
Phone (618) 664-3208; (618) 664-0449
County organized 1817 from Madison County
Land records: From 1850
Vital records: Births and deaths from 1877, marriages from 1817
Probate records: From 1825
No probate search service; copies: 50¢ per page, $2.00 minimum

*Boone County Courthouse
601 North Main Street
Belvidere, IL 61008-2708
Phone (815) 544-3103 Clerk and Recorder; (815) 544-0371 Circuit Clerk
County organized 1837 from Winnebago County
Land records: Contact Recorder, Suite 202

Naturalization records: Contact Circuit
Clerk, Suite 301
Vital records: Contact County Clerk,
Suite 202
Probate records: Contact Circuit Clerk

*Brown County Courthouse
PO Box 142
Mount Sterling, IL 62353
Phone (217) 773-2311; (217) 773-3421
*County organized 1839 from Schuyler
County*
Land records: Contact County Clerk
Naturalization records: Contact Circuit
Clerk
Vital records: Contact County Clerk
Probate records: Contact Circuit Clerk

*Bureau County Courthouse
700 South Main
Princeton, IL 61356
Phone (815) 875-2014; (815) 875-3239
*County organized 1837 from Putnam
County*
Land records: Contact County Clerk
Naturalization records: Contact Circuit
Clerk Office
Vital records: Births, deaths and
marriages; contact County Clerk
(access to birth records is restricted to
the person himself or his parents,
unless the person is proven deceased
by presentation of a death record;
applicant must show proof of
relationship)
Probate records: Contact Circuit Clerk
Office

*Calhoun County Courthouse
County Clerk
PO Box 187
Hardin, IL 62047-0187
Phone (618) 576-2351
*County organized 1825 from Pike
County*
Land records: From 1825; contact
County Recorder
Naturalization records: From 1825;
contact Circuit Clerk, PO Box 486,
Hardin, IL 62047, (618) 576-2451
Vital records: Births and deaths from
1878, marriages from 1825 (indexed
through 1979); contact County Clerk
Probate records: From 1825; contact
Circuit Clerk
Probate search service: $4.00; copies:
10¢ short, 25¢ long, plus postage

*Carroll County Courthouse
PO Box 152
Mount Carroll, IL 61053-0152
Phone (815) 244-9171
*County organized 1839 from Jo Daviess
County*
Land records: From 1839; contact
County Recorder

Naturalization records: Contact Clerk of
the Circuit Court; copies: $4.00 per
year
Vital records: From 1877; contact County
Clerk; copies: $5.00 each
Probate records: Contact Clerk of the
Circuit Court
Probate search service: $4.00 per year;
copies: $1.00 for the first page, 50¢
for each of the next nineteen pages
and 25¢ for each additional page,
$2.00 for certification, no minimum

*Cass County Courthouse
Virginia, IL 62691
Phone (217) 452-7225 Circuit Clerk;
(217) 452-7217 County Clerk
*County organized 1837 from Morgan
County*
Naturalization records: Contact Circuit
Clerk
Vital records: Births and marriages;
contact County Clerk; copies $5.00
(includes search)

*Champaign County Clerk's Office
204 East Elm Street
Urbana, IL 61801-3363
Phone (217) 384-3720
*County organized 1833 from Vermilion
County*
Vital records: Births and deaths from
1878, marriages from 1833

*Christian County Courthouse
PO Box 647
Taylorville, IL 62568-0190
Phone (217) 824-4810 Circuit Clerk;
(217) 824-4969 County Clerk
*County organized 1839 from
Sangamon, Montgomery and Shelby
counties*
Land records: Contact Terry Ryan,
County Clerk/Recorder
Naturalization records: Contact Robert
Zueck, Circuit Clerk
Vital records: Contact County Clerk
Probate records: Contact Circuit Clerk

Clark County Courthouse
Marshall, IL 62441
Phone (217) 826-8713; (217) 826-8311
*County organized 1819 from Crawford
County*

Clay County Courthouse
PO Box 160
Louisville, IL 62858-0160
Phone (618) 665-3626
*County organized 1824 from Lawrence,
Wayne and Fayette counties*

*Clinton County Courthouse
Courthouse Square
Carlyle, IL 62231-1840

Phone (618) 594-2464
*County organized 1824 from
Washington, Bond and Fayette
counties*
Land records: Contact County Clerk
Naturalization records: Contact Circuit
Clerk
Vital records: Contact County Clerk
Probate records: Contact Circuit Clerk

*Coles County Courthouse
Charleston, IL 61920
Phone (217) 348-0501 County Clerk;
(217) 348-0516 Circuit Clerk
*County organized 1830 from Clark and
Edgar counties*
Land records: From 1830; contact Betty
Coffrin, County Clerk, PO Box 207,
Charleston, IL 61920
Land records search service: $5.00 per
five-year search, per name, per
document, $1.00 per additional year;
supply full name, years to be
searched, kind of document(s), and
your relationship
Vital records: Births from 1879 (but not
required until 1916), deaths from 1879
(but not required until 1916),
marriages from 1830; contact County
Clerk
Vital records search service: $7.00 for a
five-year search and $1.00 for each
additional year; certified copies:
$7.00, $2.00 for each additional copy
requested at the same time (access to
birth records after 1916 is restricted to
the person himself or his parents,
unless the person is proven deceased
by presentation of a death record)
Probate records: Contact Circuit Clerk,
PO Box 38, Charleston, IL 61920
No probate search service; copies: 50¢
per page

*Cook County Courthouse
118 North Clark Street
Chicago, IL 60602-1304
Phone (312) 443-6000; (312) 443-6398;
(312) 629-6601 Archives; (312) 443-
5013 FAX, Archives; (312) 443-6441
Circuit Court Clerk; (312) 443-5024
FAX, Circuit Court Clerk
*County organized 1831 from Putnam
County*
Land records: From Chicago Fire of
1871; contact County Recorder's
Office. Abstracts prior to 1871;
contact Chicago Title Insurance
Company. Government land patents:
contact Illinois State Archives
Naturalization records: From 1871 to
1903 from both County Court and
Criminal Court and from 1871 to
1929 from both Circuit Court and
Superior Court; contact Philip J.
Costello, Archivist, Clerk of the
Circuit Court of Cook County,

Archives Department, Richard J. Daley Center, Room 1113, Chicago, IL 60602

Probate records: Will index from 1850, Documented Record of Wills from 1851, Abstract of Probate Proceedings from 1861, all other probate records from 1871; contact Aurelia Pucinski, Circuit Court Clerk, County Bureau, Probate Division, Richard J. Daley Center, Room 1202, Chicago, IL 60602. Deceased estate indexes from 1871 to 1967, will indexes from 1871 to 1970, minors indexes from 1871 to 1967, incompetents indexes from 1911 to 1965; contact Archives.

Probate search service: $6.00 per year; copies: $2.00 for the first page, 50¢ for each of the next nineteen pages and 25¢ for each additional page or $2.00 for the first three certified and $1.00 for each additional certified page, plus postage

*Crawford County Courthouse
PO Box 602
Robinson, IL 62454-0602
Phone (618) 546-1212
County organized 1816 from Edwards County
Land records: From 1816; contact Ruth E. Knoblett, County Clerk/Recorder
Vital records: Births and deaths from 1877, marriages from 1816; contact County Clerk/Recorder
Vital records search service: $5.00 (extensive searches referred to Robinson Public Library District, 606 North Jefferson Street, Robinson, IL 62454); copies: $2.00 each, $5.00 for the first certified copy, $2.00 for each additional certified copy of the same record
Probate records: Contact Circuit Clerk's Office, PO Box 222, Robinson, IL 62454

*Cumberland County Courthouse
PO Box 146
Toledo, IL 62468-0146
Phone (217) 849-2631 County Clerk and Recorder's Office; (217) 849-2968 FAX, County Clerk and Recorder's Office
County organized 1843 from Coles County
Land records: Deeds; contact Priscilla Schrock, County Clerk and Recorder's Office
Land records search service: $10.00; certified copies: $5.00 to $10.00 for the first copy, $2.00 for each additional copy
Vital records: Marriage licenses

*DeKalb County Administration
110 East Sycamore Street

Sycamore, IL 60178-1448
Phone (815) 895-7149 Clerk's Office; (815) 895-7156 Recorder's Office
County organized 1837 from Kane County
Land records: Deeds, plat maps, land atlases; contact Sharon L. Holmes, County Clerk and Recorder
Naturalization records: From 1853 to 1906 and a small part of 1906 to 1908 (indexed), and a few additional early naturalization records; contact County Clerk and Recorder; copies: $2.00
Vital records: Birth indexes from 1878 through 1915 (incomplete) and from 1916 to date (no personal access by visitors), death indexes from 1878 through 1915 (incomplete) and from 1916 to date, marriage indexes from 1837 to date; contact County Clerk and Recorder; copies: $8.00 for certified copies of records from 1916 (access to births restricted to the person named, his parents or legal representative), $3.00 for uncertified copies of records before 1916. Marriages 1837-1877; contact Sheila Larson, Society Genealogist, The Historical & Genealogical Society of DeKalb County, Illinois, 240 S. Emmett St., Genoa, IL 60135.
Vital records search service from The Historical & Genealogical Society: $5.00 per surname plus LSASE with two stamps (includes search of ten other indexed materials as well)
Probate records: Contact Maureen Josh, Circuit Court Clerk, DeKalb County Courthouse, 133 West State Street, Sycamore, IL 60178

*DeWitt County Courthouse
201 West Washington
PO Box 439
Clinton, IL 61727-0439
Phone (217) 935-2119 County Clerk and Recorder
County organized 1839 from McLean and Macon counties
Land records: From 1839; contact Joye Floyd, County Clerk and Recorder
Naturalization records: From 1880; contact County Clerk and Recorder
Vital records: From 1916; contact County Clerk and Recorder; copies $5.00 (births restricted after 1916)
Probate records: Contact Circuit Clerk's Office
No probate search service; certified copies: $2.00 and $4.00, no minimum

Douglas County Courthouse
401 South Center
PO Box 67
Tuscola, IL 61953-0067
Phone (217) 253-4121; (217) 253-2411

County organized 1859 from Coles County

*DuPage County Courthouse
421 North County Farm Road
Wheaton, IL 60187-3978
Phone (312) 682-7000; (312) 682-7035; (312) 682-7100 Clerk's Office
County organized 1839 from Cook County
Land records: Contact Recorder of Deeds
Naturalization records: To 1945; contact Circuit Clerk's Office, 505 North County Farm Road, Wheaton, IL 60187
Naturalization records search service: no charge for search by special deputy clerks (Genealogical Section); copies: $2.00 for the first page, 50¢ for each of the next nineteen pages and 25¢ for each additional page
Vital records: Contact County Clerk and Health Department
Probate records: Contact Circuit Court Clerk
Probate search service: $4.00 per name per year; copies: $2.00 for the first page, 50¢ for each of the next nineteen pages and 25¢ for each additional page, no minimum

*Edgar County Courthouse
Paris, IL 61944
Phone (217) 465-4151 County Clerk and Recorder
County organized 1823 from Clark County
Land records: From 1827; contact Rebecca R. Kraemer, County Clerk and Recorder
Land records search service: $7.00 for search of 1827–1873 Grantee/Grantor index (includes copy of index pages), other searches referred to Edgar County Genealogy Library; copies of deeds: $1.00 per page (to be billed), $7.00 for certification
Naturalization records: Contact Mrs. Nancy Martin, Circuit Court Clerk's Office, 115 West Court Street, Room "M", Paris, IL 61944
Vital records: Births and deaths from 1877, marriages from 1823 (before 1878 marriages give only names of bride and groom and date of marriage); contact County Clerk and Recorder; copies: $1.00 per page, $7.00 for certification
Probate records: Contact Circuit Court Clerk's Office

*Edwards County Courthouse
Albion, IL 62806
Phone (618) 445-2115
County organized 1814 from Madison and Gallatin counties

Land records: Contact County Clerk
Naturalization records: Contact Circuit Clerk, (618) 445-2016
Vital records: Contact County Clerk
Probate records: Contact Circuit Clerk
Probate search service: $4.00 per year; copies: 30¢ per page; send SASE and payment in advance

*Effingham County Courthouse
PO Box 628
Effingham, IL 62401-0628
Phone (217) 342-6535 County Recorder and County Clerk; (217) 342-3577 FAX County Clerk; (217) 342-4065 Circuit Clerk
County organized 1831 from Fayette and Crawford counties
Land records: From 1833; contact County Recorder, 101 North Fourth Street, Suite 201 or PO Box 628; copies: $1.00
Naturalization records: Contact Circuit Clerk, PO Box 586, Effingham, IL 62401
Naturalization records search service (requests in writing only): $4.00 per year; copies: 50¢ for each of the first nineteen pages and 25¢ for each additional page
Vital records: Births and deaths from 1878, marriages from 1833 (filing of births and deaths were not required in the state until 1918); contact Robert L. Behrman, County Clerk; copies: $7.00 per certified copy, $2.00 for each additional copy of same record (access to birth records is restricted to the person himself or his parents, unless the person is proven deceased by presentation of a death record)
Probate records: Contact Circuit Clerk
Probate search service (requests in writing only): $4.00 per year; copies: 50¢ for each of the first nineteen pages and 25¢ for each additional page

*Fayette County Courthouse
221 South Seventh Street
Vandalia, IL 62471
Phone (618) 283-5009 Circuit Clerk; (618) 283-5000 County Clerk
County organized 1821 from Bond, Jefferson, Wayne and Clark counties
Land records: From 1821; contact Isabelle B. Brandt, County Clerk and Recorder, PO Box 401, Vandalia, IL 62471
Land records search service: $5.00 for twenty-year search (includes copy)
Vital records: Births and deaths from 1877 ("few and far between before 1916"), marriages from 1821 (before 1878 the records show only the bride's and groom's names, date of marriage and who performed the

marriage); contact Isabelle B. Brandt, County Clerk and Recorder; certified copies: $5.00 each (includes twenty-year search)
Probate records: Wills and estate records from 1834; contact Marsha Wodtka, Circuit Clerk

*Ford County Courthouse
200 West State Street
Paxton, IL 60957
Phone (217) 379-2721
County organized 1859 from Vermilion County
Land records: Deeds, mortgages and releases; contact Ronald A. Rasmus, County Clerk and Recorder, Room 101
Naturalization records: Contact Circuit Clerk's Office
Vital records: Births, marriages and deaths; contact County Clerk and Recorder
Probate records: Contact Circuit Clerk

*Franklin County Courthouse
Benton, IL 62812
Phone (618) 438-3221 County Clerk; (618) 438-3311
County organized 1818 from White and Gallatin counties
Land records: Deeds and mortgages; contact Dave Dobill, County Clerk and Recorder, PO Box 475, Benton, IL 62812; copies: $1.00 for the first two pages, 50¢ for each additional page
Naturalization records: Contact Circuit Clerk
Vital records: Births, deaths and marriages; contact County Clerk; copies: $2.00 each, $5.00 for certified copies
Probate records: Contact Circuit Clerk's Office

*Fulton County Courthouse
100 North Main
Lewistown, IL 61542-1409
Phone (309) 547-3041, ext. 43 or 705 County Clerk and Recorder
County organized 1823 from Pike County
Land records: Grantee records from 1823, grantor records from 1856, tract index from the 1820s; contact Randal L. Rumler, County Clerk and Recorder, PO Box 226, Lewistown, IL 61542; copies: 50¢ per page
Naturalization records: Contact Circuit Clerk's Office; records may be researched but not photocopied
Vital records: Births and deaths from 1878, marriages from 1824; contact County Clerk; certified copies: $7.00 for the first copy (includes search); $2.00 for each additional copy

Probate records: From about 1850: contact Circuit Clerk's Office
Probate search service: no charge; copies: 50¢ per page, no minimum

*Gallatin County Courthouse
PO Box 550
Shawneetown, IL 62984-0550
Phone (618) 269-3025
County organized 1812 from Randolph County
Land records: From 1813; contact County Clerk; copies: 25¢ per page, possible search fee
Vital records: Births and deaths from 1878, marriages from 1830; contact County Clerk; certified copies: $5.00 for the first copy, $2.00 for each additional copy
Probate records: Probate records and wills from 1814; contact Circuit Clerk, PO Box 249, Shawneetown, IL 62984
Probate search service: depends on how much searching; copies: 25¢ per page, $2.00 minimum

*Greene County Courthouse
519 North Main
Carrollton, IL 62016
Phone (217) 942-5443
County organized 1821 from Madison County
Land records: Deeds from 1821; contact Deborah Banghart, County Clerk and Recorder, County Clerk's Office
Naturalization records: Contact Circuit Clerk's Office
Vital records: Births and deaths from December 1877, marriages from 1821 (indexed from 1845 to 1858 and from 5 May 1870 to 31 January 1901); contact County Clerk's Office
Vital records search service: $8.00; access to birth records is restricted to the person himself or his parents, unless the person is proven deceased by presentation of a death record, and members of Illinois genealogical societies may look at indexes prior to 1916 if they present a membership card
Probate records: Contact Circuit Clerk's Office
Probate search service: no charge; copies: 25¢ per page, no minimum

*Grundy County Courthouse
111 East Washington Street
Morris, IL 60450-2268
Phone (815) 941-3222
County organized 1841 from LaSalle County
Land records: From 1841; contact County Recorder
Naturalization records: From 1859 to 1906

Vital records: Births and deaths from 1878, marriage records from 1841; contact County Clerk
Probate records: Wills from 1836
Probate search service: $7.00; copies: $1.00 per page, no minimum

*Hamilton County Courthouse
McLeansboro, IL 62859
Phone (618) 643-2721
County organized 1821 from White County
Land records: From 1851 (possibly some from 1830); contact Lavella Cradlock, County Clerk
Naturalization records: No index; contact Circuit Clerk's Office
Vital records: Births and deaths from 1878, marriages from 1821; contact County Clerk (for births, need child's name, date of birth, father's name, mother's maiden name)
Probate records: From 1830; contact Circuit Clerk's Office
Probate search service: $2.00; copies: 75¢ per side when mailed

*Hancock County Courthouse
PO Box 39
Carthage, IL 62321
Phone (217) 357-2515; (217) 357-3911
County organized 1825 from Pike County and unorganized territory
Land records: Yes
Naturalization records: Yes
Vital records: Yes; copies: $7.00 (includes search)
Probate records: Yes

*Hardin County Courthouse
Elizabethtown, IL 62931
Phone (618) 287-2251
County organized 1839 from Pope County
Land records: From 1884; contact County Clerk
Land records search service: $10.00; copies 25¢ per page
Naturalization records: No naturalization records
Vital records: From 1884; contact County Clerk; certified copies: $5.00
Probate records: From 1884; contact Clerk of the Circuit Court
Probate search service: $5.00; copies: 25¢ per page (certified copies higher)

*Henderson County Courthouse
Oquawka, IL 61469
Phone (309) 867-3121 Circuit Clerk; (309) 867-2911 County Recorder
County organized 1841 from Warren County
Land records: From 1841; contact County Recorder's Office

Naturalization records: From 1850 to 1920; contact Circuit Clerk's Office
Vital records: Births and deaths from 1878, marriages from 1841; contact County Recorder's Office
Probate records: From 1841; contact Circuit Clerk's Office
Probate search service: no charge; copies: 25¢ per page, no minimum

*Henry County Courthouse
Cambridge, IL 61238
Phone (309) 937-2426 County Clerk/Recorder; (309) 937-3305 Clerk of the Circuit Court
County organized 1825 from Fulton County
Land records: From the 1800s; contact Shari Graham, deputy Recorder, County Recorder's Office
No land records search service; copies: $1.00 per page (must supply document number)
Naturalization records: From the late 1800s to 1950; contact Debra J. Doss Bumann, Clerk of the Circuit Court, Fourteenth Judicial Circuit, Cambridge, IL 61238
Naturalization records search service: $4.00 per name; copies: $2.00 per case from automated system, 50¢ per page from non-automated system, $2.00 per document for certification
Vital records: Births, deaths and marriages from the late 1800s but not required by law until after 1916; contact Martha S. Sawyer, County Clerk/Recorder, County Clerk's Office, 100 South Main Street, Cambridge, IL 61238
Vital records search service: $5.00; certified copies: $7.00 for the first copy, $2.00 for each additional copy of the same record (access to births after 1916 restricted to the person named or their legal guardian)
Probate records: From the late 1800s to date; contact Clerk of the Circuit Court
Probate search service: $4.00 per name; copies: $2.00 per case from automated system, 50¢ per page from non-automated system, $2.00 per document for certification

*Iroquois County Courthouse
550 South Tenth Street
Watseka, IL 60970-1810
Phone (815) 432-6960 County Clerk; (815) 432-6950 Clerk of the Circuit Court; (815) 432-6953 FAX, Clerk of the Circuit Court
County organized 1833 from Vermilion County
Land records: From 1839, indexed by buyer or seller and date of transaction; contact John M. Kuntz, County Clerk,

1001 East Grant Street, Watseka, IL 60970; copies: $2.00
Naturalization records: No naturalization records
Vital records: Births and deaths from 1878, indexed by name and date, and marriages from 1868, indexed by bride or groom and date; copies: $3.00 each, $7.00 for certified copies; indexes closed to the public after 1916
Probate records: From about 1862, better indexes from about 1927; contact Earl Lober, Clerk of the Circuit Court

*Jackson County Courthouse
Walnut Street
Murphysboro, IL 62966
Phone (618) 684-2153 Circuit Clerk; (618) 684-2151 County Clerk
County organized 1816 from Randolph and Johnson counties
Land records: From 1873
Naturalization records: No naturalization records
Vital records: Births and deaths from 1874, marriages from 1843; copies: $1.00 each for records before 1916, $7.00 each for records after 1916 (must be certified)
Probate records: From 1843
No probate search service; copies: 50¢ per page

*Jasper County Courthouse
100 West Jordan Street
Newton, IL 62448-1973
Phone (618) 783-2524; (618) 783-3124
County organized 1831 from Crawford and Clay counties
Land records: Contact Clerk; copies: 50¢ per page, $2.00 to $5.00 for certification
Naturalization records: Contact Clerk; copies: 50¢ per page, $2.00 to $5.00 for certification
Vital records: Contact Clerk; copies: 50¢ per page, $2.00 to $5.00 for certification
Probate records: Contact Clerk; copies: 50¢ per page, $2.00 to $5.00 for certification

*Jefferson County Courthouse
Mount Vernon, IL 62864
Phone (618) 242-5400 County Clerk
County organized 1819 from Edwards and White counties
Land records: From 1819; contact Donald K. Rector, County Clerk and Recorder, Room 105
Naturalization records: A few from 1880 through 1930; contact Gene Bolerjack, Circuit Clerk, PO Box 1266, Mount Vernon, IL 62864
Vital records: Births from 1878, deaths from 1877, marriages from 1830; contact County Clerk

Probate records: Wills from 1866 to date, probate records from 1830 to date; contact Circuit Clerk's Office

*Jersey County Courthouse
201 West Pearl Street
Jerseyville, IL 62052-1675
Phone (618) 498-5571, ext. 113 County Clerk
County organized 1839 from Greene County
Land records: Original land grant records from 1830, field notes from 1856, Road Record A from 1839, grantor-grantee records (deeds, mortgages, etc.) from 1839, plats of towns and sub-divisions from 1839; contact Recorder's Office
Naturalization records: From 1839 to 1848 and from 1854 to 1903; contact Linda J. Crotchett, County Clerk
Vital records: Births and deaths from 1 January 1875 (indexes to 1916 open to the public), marriages (females indexed 1839–1876); contact County Clerk, Office of Vital Records, PO Box 216, Jerseyville, IL 62052
Vital records search service: $5.00 (includes first copy if found); additional copies of the same record: $2.00 each

*Jo Daviess County Courthouse
330 North Bench Street
Galena, IL 61036
Phone (815) 777-0037 Circuit Clerk; (815) 777-0161 County Clerk; (815) 777-9694 Recorder
County organized 1827 from Mercer, Henry and Putnam counties
Land records: From 1829 (tract index starts 1920s); contact Recorder
Naturalization records: From 1800s; contact Recorder
Vital records: Births and deaths from 1877 (not public record after 1916), marriages from 1830; contact County Clerk, First Floor; copies: $7.00 each
Probate records: From 1850; contact Circuit Clerk, Second Floor
Probate search service: $4.00 by mail; copies: 25¢ per page, 25¢ minimum

*Johnson County Courthouse
PO Box 96
Vienna, IL 62995
Phone (618) 658-3611; (618) 658-4751 Probate
County organized 1812 from Randolph County
Land records: Yes; copies: $1.00 each
Naturalization records: No naturalization records
Vital records: Yes
Vital records search service: $5.00;

certified copies: $7.00 each (includes search)
Probate records: Yes

*Kane County Courthouse
100 South Third Avenue
Geneva, IL 60134-2722
Phone (312) 232-3413; (312) 232-3429 Daniel J. Rosier, Records Manager, Circuit Court
County organized 1836 from LaSalle County
Naturalization records: From 1800 to 1943 (not complete due to fire)
Probate records: From 1800
Probate search service: $4.00 per year; copies: $1.00 for the first page, 50¢ for each of the next ten pages, and 25¢ for each additional page, no minimum

*Kankakee County Courthouse
450 East Court Street
Kankakee, IL 60901-3997
Phone (815) 939-8836 County Clerk; (815) 937-2990
County organized 1853 from Iroquois and Will counties
Vital records: Births from 1878 to date, deaths from 1877 to date, marriages from 1853 to date; contact County Clerk, 189 East Court Street, Kankakee, IL 60901; certified copies: $7.00 for the first copy and $2.00 for each additional copy of the same record (records after 1900 are restricted)

*Kendall County Courthouse
109 West Ridge Street
PO Box M
Yorkville, IL 60560-0549
Phone (312) 553-4183; (312) 553-4112 County Clerk and Recorder; (312) 553-4104 County Clerk
County organized 1841 from LaSalle and Kane counties
Land records: Contact County Clerk and Recorder, 110 Fox Street, Yorkville, IL 60560
Naturalization records: Contact Circuit Clerk
Vital records: Contact County Clerk and Recorder
Probate records: Contact Circuit Clerk
Probate search service: $4.00 per year in advance

*Knox County Courthouse
200 South Cherry Street
Galesburg, IL 61401-4912
Phone (309) 343-3121
County organized 1825 from Fulton County
Land records: Contact Recorder's Office

Naturalization records: Contact Circuit Clerk's Office
Vital records: Contact County Clerk
Probate records: Contact Circuit Clerk

Lake County Courthouse
18 North County Street
Waukegan, IL 60085-4339
Phone (312) 360-6600
County organized 1839 from McHenry County

*LaSalle County Clerk
707 Etna Road
PO Box 430
Ottawa, IL 61350-0430
Phone (815) 433-1281 Office of the Circuit Clerk; (815) 434-8202 County Clerk
County organized 1831 from Putnam and Vermilion counties
Land records: Deeds from 1835; contact Eugene Novotney, Office of the Recorder of Deeds; copies: $1.00 per page
Naturalization records: From the mid-1800s; contact David Carey, Office of the Circuit Clerk, LaSalle County Courthouse, 119 West Madison Street, Ottawa, IL 61350
Vital records: Births and deaths from 1877, marriages from 1832; contact Mary Jane Wilkinson, County Clerk; copies: $7.00 each (includes search)
Probate records: From 1830; contact Circuit Clerk
Probate search service: $4.00 per year; copies: 25¢ per page, $4.00 minimum

*Lawrence County Courthouse
Lawrenceville, IL 62439
Phone (618) 943-2346; (618) 943-5126 County Recorder
County organized 1821 from Crawford and Edwards counties
Land records: Contact Nancy J. Hoke, County Recorder
Land records search service: $10.00
Naturalization records: To 1957; contact Mary Lou Moore, Circuit Clerk
Vital records: Births from 1877, deaths from 1878, marriages from 1821; contact Nancy J. Hoke, County Clerk; copies: $2.00 before 1916, $5.00 after 1916 (must be certified), proof of relationship required
Probate records: Contact Mary Lou Moore, Circuit Clerk, (618) 943-2815
Probate search service: $4.00 per year searched (include names, years and what you want); copies: $1.00 for the first page, 50¢ for each of the next nineteen pages and 25¢ for each additional page

*Lee County Courthouse
PO Box 385
Dixon, IL 61021-0385
Phone (815) 288-3309; (815) 288-3298; (815) 284-5234 County Circuit Clerk
County organized 1839 from Ogle County
Land records: Contact Nancy Nelson, County Clerk and Recorder; copies: $1.00
Naturalization records: Contact L. Jean Hammil, County Circuit Clerk
Vital records: Births from 1878 (with a few delayed births back to 1856), deaths from 1877, marriages from 1839; contact County Clerk and Recorder; certified copies: $7.00 for the first copy, $2.00 for each additional copy
Probate records: Contact County Circuit Clerk

*Livingston County Courthouse
Pontiac, IL 61764
Phone (815) 844-5166
County organized 1837 from LaSalle and McLean counties
Land records: From 1837; contact County Clerk; copies: $2.00 each, $5.00 for certified copies
Naturalization records: From 1837 through the early 1900s; contact Circuit Clerk
Vital records: Births from 1856, deaths from 1878, marriages from 1837; contact County Clerk; certified copies: $5.00 each
Probate records: From 1837; contact Circuit Clerk
Probate search service: $4.00 per year; copies: $1.00 for the first page, 50¢ for each of the next nineteen pages and 25¢ for each additional page, no minimum; request search in writing

Logan County Courthouse
Lincoln, IL 62656
Phone (217) 732-4148
County organized 1839 from Sangamon County

*Macon County Courthouse
253 East Wood Street
Decatur, IL 62523-1488
Phone (217) 424-1438; (217) 424-1305
County organized 1829 from Shelby County
Land records: Contact Recorder of Deeds
Naturalization records: Contact Circuit Clerk
Vital records: Contact County Clerk
Probate records: Contact Circuit Clerk
Probate search service: $5.00; copies: 30¢ first page, 10¢ each additional page

Macoupin County Courthouse
PO Box 39
Carlinville, IL 62626
Phone (217) 854-3211; (217) 854-3214
County organized 1829 from Madison and Greene counties

*Madison County Courthouse
155 North Main Street
Edwardsville, IL 62025
Phone (618) 692-6200, ext. 4521 Probate Division; (618) 692-6290 County Clerk; (618) 692-6240 Clerk of the Circuit Court
County organized 1812 from Saint Clair County
Naturalization records: From 1816; contact Lovejoy Library, SIU, Edwardsville, IL 62025 (records from 1816 to 1900); contact Willard V. Portell, Clerk of the Circuit Court (records from 1900)
Vital records: Births from late 1800s, deaths from 1878, marriages from 1813; contact Evelyn M. Bowles, Madison County Clerk
Probate records: From about 1815; contact Probate Division, Attn: Clerk

Marion County Courthouse
PO Box 637
Salem, IL 62881-0637
Phone (618) 548-1179; (618) 548-3400
County organized 1823 from Fayette and Jefferson counties

*Marshall County Courthouse
122 North Prairie
PO Box 278
Lacon, IL 61540-1216
Phone (309) 246-6325 County Clerk and Recorder
County organized 1839 from Putnam County
Land records: Contact Marjorie A. Rossetti, County Clerk and Recorder
No land records search service; copies: 50¢ per page, $1.00 per page if mailed
Naturalization records: Contact PO Box 98
Naturalization records search service: $4.00
Vital records: Contact County Clerk and Recorder
Vital records search service: $5.00 (includes one copy, but no copies are available for records containing a social security number)
Probate records: Contact PO Box 98
Probate search service: $4.00; copies: 50¢ each

*Mason County Courthouse
PO Box 90
Havana, IL 62644-0090
Phone (309) 543-6661; (309) 543-6619 Circuit Clerk

County organized 1841 from Tazewell County
Land records: From 1841; contact County Clerk, PO Box 77
Naturalization records: Contact Circuit Clerk
Vital records: Births and deaths from 1878, marriages from 1841 (records prior to 1916 are accessible to members of genealogical societies, but after 1916 births are available only to the person himself or his parents, unless the person is proven deceased by presentation of a death record)
Probate records: Contact Circuit Clerk
Probate search service: $4.00 per year; copies: 50¢ for each of the first nineteen pages and 25¢ for each additional page, no minimum

*Massac County Courthouse
PO Box 429
Metropolis, IL 62960-0429
Phone (618) 524-9359 Circuit Clerk; (618) 524-5213 County Clerk
County organized 1843 from Pope and Johnson counties
Land records: From 1843; contact John Oldham, County Clerk
Naturalization records: Contact Circuit Clerk
Vital records: Births from 1864, deaths from 1878, marriages from 1843; contact County Clerk
Probate records: Contact Circuit Clerk
No probate search service; certified copies: $5.00 each

*McDonough County Courthouse
Macomb, IL 61455
Phone (309) 833-2474; (309) 837-4889 County Clerk
County organized 1826 from Schuyler County
Land records: Contact County Clerk and Recorder
Naturalization records: Contact Circuit Clerk
Vital records: Births, deaths and marriages; contact County Clerk and Recorder; copies: $5.00 each (includes search), $7.00 each after 1916 (must be certified)
Probate records: Contact Circuit Clerk

*McHenry County Courthouse
2200 North Seminary Avenue
Woodstock, IL 60098-2639
Phone (815) 338-2040 Switchboard
County organized 1836 from Cook County
Land records: Deeds and mortgages; contact Recorder; copies: $2.00 for the first copy, 50¢ for each additional copy of the same document
Naturalization records: From 11 September 1851; contact County

Clerk (for abstracted and published Declarations of Intention contact McHenry County Illinois Genealogical Society, c/o McHenry District Library, 1011 North Green Street, McHenry, IL 60050)

Vital records: Births from 1877, deaths from 1878 (both incomplete before 1916), marriages from 1837; contact County Clerk; certified copies: $7.00 for the first copy and $2.00 for each additional copy of the same record made at the same time

Probate records: From 1836; contact Circuit Court Clerk's Office

No probate search service; copies: $2.00 for the first page, 50¢ for each of the next nineteen pages and 25¢ for each additional page

*McLean County Courthouse
202 North Main Street
Bloomington, IL 61701-2400
Phone (309) 888-5001; (309) 888-5170 Recorder; (309) 888-5190 County Clerk; (309) 888-5300 Circuit Clerk
County organized 1830 from Tazewell County
Land records: Contact Recorder, Room 105
Naturalization records: Contact Circuit Clerk, Law and Justice Center, 104 West Front Street, Bloomington, IL 61701
Vital records: Births and deaths from 1878 (deaths indexed through 1964, but no family information on deaths until about 1912), marriages from 1831 (indexed through 1935, no family information until about 1878, filings not required until 1916); contact County Clerk, Law and Justice Center, 104 West Front Street, Room 704, PO Box 2400, Bloomington, IL 61701
Vital records search service: $5.00 (none by phone); certified copies: $5.00
Probate records: Contact Circuit Clerk

*Menard County Courthouse
PO Box 456
Petersburg, IL 62675
Phone (217) 632-2415 County Clerk; (217) 632-2615 Clerk of the Circuit Court
County organized 1839 from Sangamon County
Land records: From 1839 to date; contact Marjorie O'Brien, County Clerk
Land records search service: $10.00; copies: $1.00 each
Vital records: Births from 1877 to 1952, deaths from 1877 to date, and marriage licenses from 1839 to date; copies: $1.00 per document, $5.00 for certification
Probate records: Contact David Hitchcock, Clerk of the Circuit Court

Probate search service: $4.00 per year, payable in advance (personal check not accepted); copies: $1.00 for the first page, 50¢ for each of the next nineteen pages and 25¢ for each additional page plus estimated postage, $2.00 for certification, billed after search is completed

Mercer County Courthouse
100 S.E. Third Street
Aledo, IL 61231
Phone (309) 582-7012
County organized 1825 from Pike County

*Monroe County Courthouse
Waterloo, IL 62298
Phone (618) 939-8681
County organized 1816 from Randolph and Saint Clair counties
Land records: Deeds; contact County Clerk; copies: $1.00 per page
Naturalization records: Contact Circuit Clerk
Vital records: Contact County Clerk; certified copies: $7.00 (includes search)
Probate records: Contact Circuit Clerk
No probate search service; copies: 20¢ per page, no minimum

*Montgomery County Courthouse
Hillsboro, IL 62049
Phone (217) 532-9530
County organized 1821 from Bond and Madison counties
Land records: Contact Clinton F. Kimbro, County Clerk
Naturalization records: Contact Roy Herte, Circuit Clerk
Vital records: Births and deaths from 1877, marriages from 1821; contact County Clerk; certified copies: $5.00 if exact name and date are supplied
Probate records: Contact Circuit Clerk

*Morgan County Courthouse
300 West State Street
PO Box 1286
Jacksonville, IL 62650
Phone (217) 243-8581 County Clerk's Office
County organized 1823 from Sangamon County
Land records: From 1823; contact Barbara J. Gross, County Clerk and Recorder; copies: 50¢ each from paper originals, $1.00 each from microfilm originals
Vital records: Births and deaths from 1878 (parents' names were required as of 1911), birth and death index from 1878 to 1916, marriages from 1828 (parents' names were required as of 1911), marriage index from 1828 to

1916; certified copies: $7.00 each, subject to restrictions

*Moultrie County Courthouse
Sullivan, IL 61951
Phone (217) 728-4521; (217) 728-4389 County Clerk and Recorder, (217) 728-8178 FAX, County Clerk and Recorder
County organized 1843 from Macon and Shelby counties
Land records: Contact Arlene Aschermann, County Clerk and Recorder
No land records search service
Naturalization records: Contact Circuit Clerk's Office
Vital records: Contact County Clerk and Recorder; copies: $5.00 for the first copy, $2.00 for each additional copy of the same record
Probate records: Contact Circuit Clerk's Office

*Ogle County Courthouse
Washington and South Fourth Streets
Oregon, IL 61061
Phone (815) 732-3201
County organized 1836 from Jo Daviess County
Land records: From 1836; contact County Recorder's Office, PO Box 357, Oregon, IL 61061
Land records search service: $5.00 per name (give approximate year); copies: $1.00 each
Naturalization records: Contact Ogle County Circuit Clerk's Office, PO Box 337, Oregon, IL 61061
Vital records: Births from 1860, deaths from 1878, and marriages from 1836; contact County Clerk's Office
Vital records search service: $5.00 per name (includes copy)
Probate records: Contact County Circuit Clerk's Office
Probate search service: $4.00 per year by statute; copies: from 10¢ to $1.00 per page (depends on the size of the search)

*Peoria County Courthouse
324 Main Street
Peoria, IL 61602
Phone (309) 672-6056
County organized 1825 from Fulton County
Land records: Grantee index only; contact Recorder of Deeds
Naturalization records: Contact Circuit Clerk
Vital records: Contact County Clerk
Probate records: Contact Circuit Clerk
No probate search service; copies: 50¢ for each of the first twenty pages and 25¢ for each additional page (policies may change)

*Perry County Courthouse
1 Public Square
Pinckneyville, IL 62274
Phone (618) 357-5116
*County organized 1827 from Randolph
and Jackson counties*
Land records: Contact County Clerk,
Government Building, 1¹/₂ miles south
on I-127
Naturalization records: Contact Circuit
Clerk, Courthouse, First Floor
Vital records: Contact County Clerk
Probate records: Contact Circuit Clerk

*Piatt County Courthouse
101 West Washington
Monticello, IL 61856-1149
Phone (217) 762-9487 County Clerk;
(217) 762-4966 Circuit Clerk
*County organized 1841 from De Witt
and Macon counties*
Land records: Contact County Clerk, PO
Box 150, Monticello, IL 61856
Naturalization records: Sketchy
naturalization records from 1858
through 1928
Vital records: Births and deaths from late
1800s (very few, most from 1916),
marriages from 1841; contact County
Clerk
Probate records: Guardianships sketchy
from mid 1800s, possibly written into
old Court Docket books; contact
Circuit Clerk
Probate search service: no charge;
copies: 20¢ per page (prior to 1964) or
$1.00 for the first page and 50¢ per
each additional page (after 1964), no
minimum

*Pike County Courthouse
Pittsfield, IL 62363
Phone (217) 285-6812
*County organized 1821 from Madison,
Bond and Clark counties*
Land records: From 1839; contact Roger
E. Yaeger, County Clerk
Naturalization records: From 1859;
contact Ben R. Johnson, Circuit Clerk
Vital records: Births and deaths from
1877, marriages from 1827; contact
County Clerk
Probate records: From 1831; contact
Circuit Clerk
Probate search service: $5.00 per name;
certified copies: $5.00

*Pope County Courthouse
Golconda, IL 62938
Phone (618) 683-4466 County Clerk;
(618) 683-3941 Circuit Clerk
*County organized 1816 from Johnson
and Gallatin counties*
Land records: From 1816; contact Evelyn
F. Hogg, County Clerk
Naturalization records: From 1865 to
1896; contact Circuit Clerk

Vital records: Births from 1877 (few
delayed records from 1862), deaths
from 1878, marriages from 1816;
contact County Clerk; copies: $5.00
(includes search)
Probate records: From 1816 to 1950;
contact County Clerk. Probate records
from 1951; contact Circuit Clerk
Probate search service: $5.00; copies:
25¢ each, $5.00 for certified copies,
$5.00 minimum

Pulaski County Courthouse
PO Box 218
Mound City, IL 62963-0218
Phone (618) 748-9360
*County organized 1843 from Johnson
County*

*Putnam County Courthouse
Hennepin, IL 61327
Phone (815) 925-7129
*County organized 1825 from Fulton
County*
Land records: From 1831; contact
County Recorder
Land records search service: $10.00 per
name (includes copy)
Naturalization records: Contact County
Circuit Clerk
Vital records: Births and deaths from
1877, marriages from 1831; contact
County Recorder
Vital records search service (through
1910): $5.00 (includes certified copy,
if found); vital records after 1910
subject to restrictions
Probate records: Estates; contact County
Circuit Clerk

*Randolph County Courthouse
1 Taylor Street
Chester, IL 62233-0309
Phone (618) 826-2712; (618) 826-2510
County Clerk and Recorder; (618)
826-3750 FAX, County Clerk and
Recorder
*County organized 1795 from Saint Clair
County*
Land records: From 1724 to date
(indexed from 1853 to date); contact
William E. Rabe, County Clerk and
Recorder
Land records search service: $5.00;
copies $1.00 each, $7.00 for
certification
Naturalization records: Some; contact
County Clerk and Recorder or Circuit
Clerk's Office
Vital records: Births from 1857, deaths
from 1878, marriages from 1805
Vital records search service: $5.00;
copies $1.00 each, $7.00 for
certification
Probate records: Contact Circuit Clerk's
Office

*Richland County Courthouse
103 West Main Street
Olney, IL 62450-2170
Phone (618) 392-3111
*County organized 1841 from Clay and
Lawrence counties*
Land records: General Entry Book from
1841; contact Michael T. Buss,
County Clerk
Naturalization records: Naturalization
Index (General); contact Circuit
Clerk's Office
Vital records: Births and deaths from
1878, marriages from 1841; contact
County Clerk
Probate records: Contact Circuit Clerk's
Office

*Rock Island County Courthouse
2105 15th Street
Rock Island, IL 61201
Phone (309) 786-4451 Circuit Clerk
*County organized 1831 from Jo Daviess
County*
Naturalization records: From 1872 to
1962; contact Marilyn Esslinger,
Circuit Clerk
Naturalization records search service:
$4.00 per person

*Saint Clair County Courthouse
10 Public Square
Belleville, IL 62220-1623
Phone (618) 277-6600
*County organized 1790 from Northwest
Territory*
Land records: Contact Dick
Weilmuenster, Mapping and Platting
Naturalization records: To 1900
Vital records: Contact Sam Flood,
County Clerk; copies: births $8.60
(includes search), deaths and
marriages $7.00 (includes search)
Probate records: Contact C. Barney
Metz, Circuit Clerk

*Saline County Courthouse
Harrisburg, IL 62946
Phone (618) 253-7641; (618) 253-8197
*County organized 1847 from Gallatin
County*
Land records: Yes
Naturalization records: Limited
naturalization records
Vital records: Yes
Probate records: Yes
Probate search service: $5.00 per year;
copies: 25¢ per page, no minimum; all
requests by mail

*Sangamon County Courthouse
800 East Monroe
Springfield, IL 62701-1926
Phone (217) 753-6600
*County organized 1821 from Bond and
Madison counties*

Vital records: Births and deaths from 1877, marriages from 1988; contact Maralee Lindley, County Clerk

Probate records: Contact Candice D. Trees, Clerk of the Circuit Court, Sangamon County Building, Springfield, IL 62701

Probate search service: no charge; copies: $1.00 for the first page, 50¢ for each of the next eighteen pages, and 25¢ for each additional page, $4.00 minimum

*Schuyler County Courthouse
Rushville, IL 62681
Phone (217) 322-6226; (217) 322-4734
County organized 1825 from Pike and Fulton counties
Land records: From 1825
Naturalization records: From 1859; contact Jacqueline M. Rebman, Clerk of the Circuit Court
Vital records: Births and deaths from 1877, marriages from 1825
Probate records: From 1827; contact Clerk of the Circuit Court
Probate search service: $4.00 per year; copies: $1.00 for the first page, 50¢ for each of the next nineteen pages and 25¢ for each additional page, no minimum

*Scott County Courthouse
Winchester, IL 62694
Phone (217) 742-3173; (217) 742-3178
County organized 1839 from Morgan County
Land records: Yes
Naturalization records: Yes
Vital records: Births from 1860, deaths from 1877, marriages from 1839
Vital records search service: $5.00 per name with written request
Probate records: Yes

*Shelby County Courthouse
Shelbyville, IL 62565
Phone (217) 774-4421
County organized 1827 from Fayette County
Land records: From 1833; contact Dwight Campbell, County Clerk
Naturalization records: No naturalization records
Vital records: Births from 1848 to date, deaths from 1878 to date, marriages from 1827 to date; contact County Clerk
Probate records: Contact Circuit Clerk's Office

*Stark County Courthouse
130 West Main
PO Box 97
Toulon, IL 61483-0097
Phone (309) 286-5911

County organized 1839 from Knox and Putnam counties
Land records: From 1839; contact Linda K. Peyll, County Clerk and Recorder
Naturalization records: Very few naturalization records; contact Circuit Clerk
Vital records: Births from 1855, deaths from 1878, marriages from 1839; contact County Clerk and Recorder; copies: $3.00
Probate records: Contact Circuit Clerk
No probate search service; copies: $1.00 for the first page and 50¢ for each additional page

*Stephenson County Courthouse
15 North Galena Avenue
Freeport, IL 61032-4348
Phone (815) 235-8289
County organized 1837 from Winnebago and Jo Daviess counties
Land records: From 1837
Naturalization records: From 1850 to 1960
Vital records: From 1887
Probate records: From 1850
No probate search service; copies: from $5.00 to $10.00

*Tazewell County Clerk
McKenzie Building
Fourth and Court Streets
Pekin, IL 61554
Phone (309) 477-2264 County Clerk, (309) 477-2210 Recorder of Deeds; (309) 477-2214 Circuit Clerk or Probate
County organized 1827 from Fayette County
Land records: Somewhat incomplete from the 1830s (public domain records in Illinois State Archives); contact Robert A. Lutz, Recorder of Deeds
No land records search service (but Tazewell County Genealogical Society, PO Box 312, Pekin, IL 61555-0312 will search for $5.00 per surname plus SASE)
Naturalization records: From 1850s
Vital records: Births from 1854, deaths from 1878, marriages from 1869; contact County Clerk; copies: $5.00 for the first copy, $2.00 for each additional copy of the same record
Probate records: From 1830s; contact Pam Gardner, Clerk of the Circuit Court, PO Box 69, Pekin, IL 61555-0069
No probate search service (requests forwarded to Tazewell County Genealogical Society, PO Box 312, Pekin, IL 61555-0312); copies: $1.00 for the first page, 50¢ for each of the next nineteen pages and 25¢ for each additional page, $2.00 for certification

Union County Courthouse
PO Box H
Jonesboro, IL 62952
Phone (618) 833-5913; (618) 833-5711
County organized 1818 from Johnson County

*Vermilion County Courthouse Annex
6 North Vermilion Street
Danville, IL 61832-5879
Phone (217) 431-2605; (217) 431-2615
County organized 1826 from Edgar County
Land records: From 1826
Vital records: Births from 1858, deaths from 1877, marriages from 1926; contact Lynn Foster, County Clerk; certified copies: $7.00 each (access subject to restrictions)
Probate records: Contact Circuit Clerk's Office, 7 North Vermilion Street, Danville, IL 61832
Probate search service: no charge for a specific year, $4.00 for each year searched (request must be in writing)

*Wabash County Courthouse
Mount Carmel, IL 62863
Phone (618) 262-5362; (618) 262-4561
County organized 1824 from Edwards County
Land records: From 1857; contact Marie L. Kolb, County Clerk
Naturalization records: From 1877
Vital records: Births and deaths from 1877
Probate records: From 1857
Probate search service: no charge if found; copies: 25¢ per page, $10.00 minimum (with extra returned)

*Warren County Courthouse
Monmouth, IL 61462
Phone (309) 734-8592
County organized 1825 from Pike County
Land records: From 1834; contact County Clerk
Naturalization records: Contact Beverly E. Davis, Warren County Circuit Clerk, (309) 734-5179
Vital records: Births and deaths from about 1876, but are random until 1916; contact County Clerk; copies: 50¢ per page before 1916, $7.00 for certified copies after 1916
Probate records: From 1830; contact Circuit Clerk
Probate search service: $5.00; copies: 50¢ per page, $2.00 for certified copies, no minimum

*Washington County Courthouse
Nashville, IL 62263
Phone (618) 327-3612; (618) 327-8314
County organized 1818 from Saint Clair County

Land records: From 1821
Naturalization records: From 1865
Vital records: Births and deaths from 1877, marriages from 1832; certified copies: $5.00 each
Probate records: From 1865
Probate search service: $4.00 per year

*Wayne County Courthouse
PO Box 187
Fairfield, IL 62837-0187
Phone (618) 842-5182
County organized 26 March 1819 from Edwards County, reduced to its present size by an Act on 23 December 1895. Part of the courthouse burned on 17 November 1886, destroying many records of the Recorder's Office
Land records: From 1887; contact County Clerk
Naturalization records: Contact Circuit Clerk
Vital records: From 1887; contact County Clerk; certified copies: $5.00 each (includes search)
Probate records: Contact Circuit Clerk

*White County Courthouse
Carmi, IL 62821
Phone (618) 382-7211
County organized 1815 from Gallatin County
Land records: From 1816; contact County Clerk, PO Box 339, Carmi, IL 62821
Vital records: Births and deaths from 1878, marriages from 1816; contact County Clerk
Probate records: Contact Circuit Clerk

Whiteside County Courthouse
400 North Cherry Street
Morrison, IL 61270-2605
Phone (815) 786-4451; (815) 772-7201
County organized 1836 from Jo Daviess and Henry counties

Will County Courthouse
14 West Jefferson Street
Joliet, IL 60431-1302
Phone (815) 727-8542; (815) 740-4615
County organized 1836 from Cook and Iroquois counties

*Williamson County Courthouse
200 Jefferson Street
Marion, IL 62959-3061
Phone (618) 997-1301
County organized 1839 from Franklin County
Land records: Contact County Clerk, PO Box 1108, Marion, IL 62959
Naturalization records: Contact Circuit Clerk; copies not permitted
Vital records: Contact County Clerk

Probate records: Contact Circuit Clerk
Probate search service: $4.00 per year; copies: $1.00 for the first page, 50¢ for each of the next nineteen pages and 25¢ for each additional page, no minimum

*Winnebago County Courthouse
400 West State Street
Rockford, IL 61101-1212
Phone (815) 987-2522; (815) 987-3050 County Clerk
County organized 1836 from Jo Daviess County
Land records: Contact County Recorder, (815) 987-3100
Vital records: Contact County Clerk
Probate records: Contact Circuit Clerk, (815) 987-3148
Probate search service: $4.00 per year; copies: $1.00 for the first page, 50¢ for each of the next nineteen pages and 25¢ for each additional page

*Woodford County Courthouse
115 North Main Street
Eureka, IL 61530
Phone (309) 467-2822
County organized 1841 from Tazewell and McLean counties
Land records: Yes
Land records search service: $5.00 per name with year; copies: $1.00
Naturalization records: Contact Circuit Clerk
Vital records: Births and deaths from 1877, marriages from 1841
Vital records search service: $5.00 per name with year; copies: $1.00; relationship required for births and deaths
Probate records: Contact Circuit Clerk

INDIANA

Capital: Indianapolis. Statehood: 11 December 1816 (annexed as a result of the Treaty of Paris, 1783, was part of the Northwest Territory in 1787, and became a separate territory 7 May 1800)

Court System

Indiana has seventy-eight city and town courts with local jurisdiction. The Small Claims Court of Marion County sits at Indianapolis, as does the Marion Municipal Court. A separate Probate Court for Saint Joseph County sits in South Bend. County Courts exist in forty-nine of the ninety-two counties and meet at the county seats to hear contract and tort disputes, misdemeanors, traffic and local ordinance violations and some criminal matters. The Superior Courts are courts of general jurisdiction and sit in the county seats of forty-seven counties, where they deal with law, equity, domestic relations, felonies, misdemeanors, preliminary hearings, and sometimes juvenile matters. The Marion and Vanderburgh Courts have probate divisions. The Circuit Courts handle all civil and criminal matters except where exclusive jurisdiction is conferred on a lower court in a county. The Circuit Courts sit in each county seat, but two circuits contain two counties: Dearborn-Ohio and Jefferson-Switzerland. The Court of Appeals sits at Indianapolis and is divided into four districts. The Supreme Court at Indianapolis is the court of last resort.

Courthouses

*Adams County Courthouse
112 South Second
Decatur, IN 46733-1618
Phone (219) 724-2600
County organized 1835 from Warren County
Land records: Contact Recorder
Naturalization records: Contact Clerk
Vital records: Contact Health Department
Probate records: Contact Clerk
Probate search service: no charge; copies: $1.00 per page, no minimum

Allen County Courthouse
City-County Building
Fort Wayne, IN 46802-1804
Phone (219) 428-7602; (219) 428-7245
County organized 1823 from Indian Lands

*Bartholomew County Courthouse
234 Washington Street
Columbus, IN 47201
Phone (812) 379-1610; (812) 379-1600
Clerk's Office; (812) 379-1675 FAX,
Clerk's Office; (812) 379-1503
Archives; (812) 379-1520
*County organized 1821 from Indian
Lands*
Land records: Original and early owners
of land and Tract Book index; contact
Mary Ellen Sweet Grossman, County
Clerk's Office, PO Box 924,
Columbus, IN 47202-0924. All other
land records; contact County Recorder
Naturalization records: Contact Clerk's
Office or Courthouse Archives, Mary
Frances Urbahn's Room
Vital records: Marriage licenses from
March 1821 to date, marriage
applications (called marriage records)
from February 1882 to date; contact
Clerk's Office. Births and deaths from
1882; contact Bartholomew County
Vital Statistics, 440 Third Street, Suite
303, Columbus, IN 47201
Probate records: From 1821; contact
Clerk's Office
Probate search service: no charge;
copies: $1.00 per page (billable), no
minimum

Benton County Courthouse
700 East Fifth Street
Fowler, IN 47944-1556
Phone (317) 884-0370; (317) 884-0930
*County organized 1840 from Indian
Lands*

*Blackford County Courthouse
Hartford City, IN 47348-2251
Phone (317) 348-2901; (317) 348-3213
*County organized 1838 from Jay
County*
Land records: Contact Assessor
Naturalization records: Contact Clerk
Probate records: Contact Clerk
No probate search service; copies: 25¢
per page plus postage, $1.00 for
certification, no minimum; researchers
welcome to search for themselves

Boone County Courthouse
1 Courthouse Square
Lebanon, IN 46052-2161
Phone (317) 482-0530; (317) 482-3510
*County organized 1830 from Indian
Lands*

*Brown County Courthouse
PO Box 85
Nashville, IN 47448
Phone (812) 988-7557 Circuit Court;
(812) 988-4796 Clerk's Office; (812)
988-2788 Auditor's Office
*County organized 1836 from Monroe,
Jackson and Bartholomew counties*

Land records: Grantor/grantee records
from 1873 (earlier records destroyed
by fire); contact Recorder; copies:
$2.00 per page
Naturalization records: No more than
half a dozen entries from 1860
through 1890; contact Clerk; copies:
$2.00 per page
Vital records: Births and deaths from
1882 (except deaths missing from
1899 to 1907); contact Health
Department
Probate records: From 1836 to 1945
(abstracted and indexed by every
name in 1992 publication by the
Brown County Historical Society);
contact Clerk
Probate search service: no charge;
copies: $2.00 per page plus postage,
no minimum; all genealogical
inquiries sent to the Clerk's Office or
the Health Department are sent to
Helen H. Reeve, Brown County
Historical Society, 6431 South
Christiansburg Road, Columbus, IN
47201

*Carroll County Courthouse
101 West Main Street
Delphi, IN 46923
Phone (317) 564-3711; (317) 564-4485
*County organized 1828 from Indian
Lands*
Land records: Contact Phyllis Ellis,
Recorder
Naturalization records: Contact Clerk;
copies: $1.00 per page
Vital records: Marriages from 1828 to
date; contact Beth L. Myers, Clerk.
Births and deaths; contact Harriett
Jones, Health; copies from Clerk:
$1.00 per page
Probate records: Contact Clerk; copies:
$1.00 per page

*Cass County Courthouse
200 Court Park
Logansport, IN 46947-3114
Phone (219) 753-7740
*County organized 1828 from Indian
Lands*
Land records: Contact Charlene "Chod"
Gibson, County Auditor
Naturalization records: Contact County
Clerk
Vital records: Contact County Health
Department
Probate records: Contact County Clerk

Clark County Courthouse
Court Avenue
Jeffersonville, IN 47130-4063
Phone (812) 283-4451
*County organized 1801 from Knox
County*

*Clay County Courthouse
Brazil, IN 47834
Phone (812) 448-1365; (812) 448-8727
*County organized 1825 from Indian
Lands*
Land records: Contact Recorder's Office
Naturalization records: From 1850;
contact Clerk's Office
Vital records: Contact Health Office
Probate records: From 1850; contact
Clerk's Office
Probate search service: $3.00 for ten
years; copies: $1.00 per page, no
minimum; make request in writing
and include payment

*Clinton County Courthouse
Frankfort, IN 46041
Phone (317) 659-6320 Recorder; (317)
659-6320, ext. 29 Archivist
*County organized 1830 from Indian
Lands*
Land records: From 1830; contact
Shirley R. Wells, Recorder, 270
Courthouse Square, Frankfort, IN
46041; copies: $1.00 per page plus
SASE
Naturalization records: From 1882 to
1896; contact Archivist, c/o Clerk,
Clinton Circuit Court, 265 Courthouse
Square, Frankfort, IN 46041-1993;
copies: 25¢ to $1.00 each plus SASE,
$2.00 for certified copies
Vital records: Marriages from 1830 to
date, some early marriage consents
from 1850 to 1882, marriage
applications from 1882 to date;
contact Archivist; copies: 25¢ to $1.00
each plus SASE, $2.00 for certified
copies. Births and deaths from 1882 to
date (indexed through 1920); contact
County Board of Health, 211 North
Jackson Street, Frankfort, IN 46041;
copies: $1.00 each plus SASE, $2.00
for certified copies (proof required)
Probate records: From 1830 to date;
contact Archivist
No probate search service; copies: 25¢ to
$1.00 each plus SASE, $2.00 for
certified copies

*Crawford County Courthouse
PO Box 375
English, IN 47118-0375
Phone (812) 338-2565
*County organized 1818 from Harrison
County*
Vital records: Marriages from 1828;
contact Clerk's Office. Births and
deaths from 1899; contact Health
Department
Probate records: Yes
No probate search service; copies: 25¢
per page plus postage, $2.00 for
certified copies, $1.00 minimum

Daviess County Courthouse
Washington, IN 47501
Phone (812) 254-1090
County organized 1816 from Indian Lands

*Dearborn County Courthouse
215B West High Street
Lawrenceburg, IN 47025-1662
Phone (812) 537-1040
County organized 1803, original county
Land records: Contact Recorder
Naturalization records: Contact Clerk
Vital records: Contact Health
Probate records: Contact Clerk
Probate search service: no charge if simply to see if will is on record, no service for further research; copies: $1.00 per page

*Decatur County Courthouse
150 Courthouse Square, Suite 5
Greensburg, IN 47240-2091
Phone (812) 663-2570 Auditor's Office; (812) 663-4681 Recorder's Office; (812) 663-8223 Clerk's Office; (812) 663-8301 Board of Health
County organized 1821 from Indian Lands
Land records: Land transfers from 1843 to 1844, from 1851 to 1878, and from 1891 to date; contact Auditor's Office. Deed recording from 1821 to date; contact Recorder's Office
Naturalization records: Contact Indiana State Library, 140 North Senate Avenue, Indianapolis, IN 46204
Vital records: Contact Board of Health, 801 North Lincoln Street, Greensburg, IN 47240
Probate records: Contact Clerk's Office
Probate search service: no charge if not extensive; copies: $1.00 per page

DeKalb County Courthouse
Auburn, IN 46706
Phone (219) 925-2764; (219) 925-0912
County organized 1835 from Allen County

Delaware County Courthouse
100 West Main Street
PO Box 1089
Muncie, IN 47305
Phone (317) 747-7780; (317) 747-7726
County organized 1827 from Indian Lands

*Dubois County Courthouse
1 Courthouse Square
Jasper, IN 47546
Phone (812) 481-7035 Clerk
County organized 1817 from Orange and Perry counties
Land records: Contact Auditor and Recorder

No land records search service; copies: $1.00 per page, $5.00 for copies from plat book
Naturalization records: From 1839; contact Janet Sendelweck, Clerk, Dubois Circuit and Superior Courts
No naturalization records search service; copies: $1.00 per page
Vital records: Births and deaths; contact Health Department, Courthouse Annex
No vital records search service; copies: $1.00 per page
Probate records: From 1839; contact Clerk's Office and Records Library
No probate search service (abstractors and attorneys do them normally); copies: $1.00 per page, no minimum

*Elkhart County Courthouse
Goshen, IN 46526
Phone (219) 535-6430; (219) 535-6471 FAX, (219) 535-6474 Recorder; (219) 535-6718 Auditor; (219) 535-6433 Clerk
County organized 1830 from Indian Lands
Land records: Contact Auditor's Office, Administration Building, 117 North Second Street, Goshen, IN 46526. Deeds; contact Recorder's Office, Administration Building
Vital records: Marriages from the early 1830s; contact Randall Yohn, Clerk of Circuit Court. Births and deaths from 1882 (births not required until October 1907); contact County Health Department, 315 South Second Street, Elkhart, IN
Probate records: From the early 1830s; contact Clerk of Circuit Court
Probate search service: no charge; copies: $1.00 per page, $1.00 for certification

*Fayette County Courthouse
401 Central Avenue
Connersville, IN 47331-1903
Phone (317) 825-8987; (317) 825-1813; (317) 825-4938
County organized 1818 from Wayne County

Floyd County Courthouse
New Albany, IN 47150
Phone (812) 948-5455; (812) 948-5411
County organized 1819 from Harrison and Clark counties

*Fountain County Courthouse
Covington, IN 47932
Phone (317) 793-3301; (317) 793-2192
County organized 1825 from Montgomery County
Land records: Contact Assessor
Naturalization records: Contact Clerk

Vital records: Contact Fountain-Warren Health Department, 210 South Perry Street, Attica, IN 47918
Probate records: Yes
No probate search service; copies: $1.00 per page, $1.00 for certification, no minimum

*Franklin County Courthouse
459 Main Street
Brookville, IN 47012-1405
Phone (317) 647-4186; (317) 647-5131 Recorder; (317) 647-4631 Auditor; (317) 647-5111 Clerk's Office; (317) 647-4322 County Health Department; (317) 647-4031 Brookville Library; (317) 232-3689 Indiana State Library (Genealogy Section)
County organized 1811 from Clark and Dearborn counties
Land records: Deeds from 1811 to date (indexed, original tract books; contact Recorder. County Maps; contact Auditor. Earliest Tract Book, land entries from Cincinnati, Indianapolis and Jefferson districts; contact Brookville Library. Land entries from 1803 to date; contact Indiana State Library, 140 North Senate Avenue, Indianapolis, IN 46204-2296
Land records search service from Brookville Library: no charge for minimal search; copies: 25¢ per double-sided page
Naturalization records: From 1820 in miscellaneous order books; contact Clerk's Office. Original naturalization records; contact Indiana State Library. Index only from 1820; contact Brookville Library, 919 Main Street, Brookville, IN 47012. Naturalization records from 1820 to date; contact Indiana State Library.
Naturalization records search service from Clerk's Office: no charge for minimal search (contact local researchers for extended searches); copies: $1.00 per page. Naturalization records search service from Brookville Library: no charge for minimal search; copies: 25¢ per double-sided page
Vital records: Births and deaths from 1882 to date (not complete for early years); contact County Health Department, Courthouse Annex, 459 Main Street, Brookville, IN 47012; copies: $2.00 each (includes search, must know year and supply proof or relationship for births, no personal checks accepted). Marriages from 1811 to date (indexed); contact Clerk's Office. Births and deaths from 1882 to 1920 (indexed), index to marriages from 1811 to 1920, index to marriage transcripts from 1882 to 1920; contact Brookville Library.

Births and deaths from 1882; contact Indiana State Library

Vital records search service from Clerk's Office: no charge for minimal search (contact local researchers for extended searches); copies: $1.00 per page. Vital records search service from Brookville Library: no charge for minimal search; copies: 25¢ per double-sided page

Probate records: Probate and wills from 1811 to date (indexed); contact Clerk's Office. Wills from 1813 to 1936; contact Brookville Library. Wills from 1811 to date; contact Indiana State Library

Probate search service from Clerk's Office: no charge for minimal search (contact local researchers for extended searches); copies: $1.00 per page. Probate search service from Brookville Library: no charge for minimal search; copies: 25¢ per double-sided page

*Fulton County Courthouse
815 Main Street
Rochester, IN 46975-1546
Phone (219) 223-4339; (219) 223-2911; (219) 223-2881 Health Department
County organized 1835 from Indian Lands
Land records: Contact Auditor
Naturalization records: Contact Clerk
Vital records: Contact Health Department, 175 South 50 East, Rochester, IN 46975
Probate records: Contact Circuit Court

*Gibson County Courthouse
101 North Main
Princeton, IN 47670
Phone (812) 386-8401 Clerk's Office
County organized 1813 from Knox County
Land records: Contact Recorder's Office; copies: $1.00 per page, $5.00 for certification
Naturalization records: Some naturalization records; contact Clerk's Office
Vital records: Marriages from 1813 (no information on parents until 1882); contact Clerk's Office. Births and deaths from 1882; contact Health Office, Courthouse Annex, 800 South Prince Street, Princeton, IN 47670; copies: $2.00 each
Probate records: Contact Clerk's Office
No probate search service; copies: $1.00 per page, $1.00 for certification, no minimum; need some dates to go by, no personal checks

*Grant County Courthouse
101 East Fourth Street

Marion, IN 46952
Phone (317) 664-5527; (317) 668-8871 County Complex Switchboard; (317) 668-8121 Circuit Court Clerk
County organized 1831 from Delaware County
Land records: Contact Recorder/Auditor, Grant County Complex, 401 South Adams, Marion, IN 46953
Naturalization records: A few; contact Karen Bostic Weaver, Circuit Court Clerk; copies: $1.00 per page, $1.00 for certification
Vital records: Births and deaths; contact Health Department, County Complex
Probate records: Contact Circuit Court Clerk; copies: $1.00 per page, $1.00 for certification

Greene County Courthouse
Bloomfield, IN 47424
Phone (812) 384-4325; (812) 384-8532
County organized 1821 from Knox County

*Hamilton County Courthouse
Noblesville, IN 46060
Phone (317) 776-9675; (317) 773-6110; (317) 776-9619 County Recorder
County organized 1823 from Hancock and Marion counties
Land records: Contact Sharon K. Cherry, County Recorder
Naturalization records: Contact Kathy Richardson, County Clerk
Vital records: From 1882; contact Registrar, Hamilton County Health Department, 940 North Tenth Street, Noblesville, IN 46060. Marriages; contact County Clerk.
Probate records: Contact County Clerk
Probate search service: no charge; copies: 50¢ each; "We accept written requests, however our work load is so heavy we find it difficult to get the searches done in speedy fashion."

*Hancock County Courthouse
Greenfield, IN 46140
Phone (317) 462-1107; (317) 462-1106; (317) 462-1105 Auditor; (317) 462-1109 or 462-1110 County Clerk; (317) 462-1125 Health Department
County organized 1827 from Madison County
Land records: Contact Marilyn W. Counter, Auditor
Naturalization records: Contact County Clerk, 9 East Main Street, Room 201, Greenfield, IN 46140
Vital records: Marriages and divorces; contact County Clerk. Births and deaths; contact Health Department
Probate records: Contact County Clerk
Probate search service: no charge; copies: $1.00 per page, no mailing fee

Harrison County Courthouse
300 North Capital Avenue
Corydon, IN 47112-1333
Phone (812) 738-8141; (812) 738-8927
County organized 1808 from Northwest Territory

Hendricks County Courthouse
PO Box 349
Danville, IN 46122
Phone (317) 745-9271; (317) 745-9207
County organized 1823 from Indian Lands

*Henry County Courthouse
New Castle, IN 47362-4219
Phone (317) 529-4304 Recorder; (317) 529-6401 Clerk of Henry Circuit and Superior Courts; (317) 521-1401 Health Department
County organized 1821 from Delaware County
Land records: From 1823; contact Linda Winchester, Recorder
Naturalization records: Contact Linda Ratcliff, Clerk of Henry Circuit and Superior Courts
Vital records: Births and deaths from 1882; contact Health Department
Probate records: From 1822; contact Clerk of Henry Circuit and Superior Courts
No probate search service; copies: $1.00 per page, no minimum

Howard County Courthouse
Kokomo, IN 46901
Phone (317) 456-2200; (317) 456-2204
County organized 1844 from Indian Lands; name changed from Richardville County in 1846

Huntington County Courthouse
Huntington, IN 46750
Phone (219) 356-3520; (219) 356-0692
County organized 1832 from Grant County

Jackson County Courthouse
Brownstown, IN 47220
Phone (812) 358-6133; (812) 358-6116
County organized 1815 from Washington County
Vital records: Contact County Board of Health, Jackson County Hospital, Second Floor, 200 South Walnut Street, Seymour, IN 47274

*Jasper County Courthouse
115 West Washington Street
Rensselaer, IN 47978-2888
Phone (219) 866-4930 Auditor; (219) 866-4926 Clerk
County organized 1835 from Indian Lands

Land records: Yes
Naturalization records: Contact State Archives, where county records were deposited
Vital records: From 1865; contact Clerk's Office
Probate records: From 1853; contact Clerk's Office
Probate search service: no charge; copies: 25¢ per page

*Jay County Courthouse
Portland, IN 47371
Phone (219) 726-4572 Recorder; (219) 726-4951 Clerk; (219) 726-8080 Health Office; (219) 726-4331 Jay Circuit Court
County organized 1835 from Randolph County
Land records: Deeds/land records from 1830s; contact Recorder
Naturalization records: Contact Clerk, Jay Circuit Court
Vital records: Marriages from 1837; contact Clerk, Jay County Court; copies: $1.00 each. Births and deaths from 1882; contact Health Office; copies: $3.00 each
Probate records: From the early 1840s; contact Clerk, Jay Circuit Court, Attn: Linda Kirkpatrick
Probate search service: $1.00 for each surname, plus postage; copies: $1.00 for the first page and 35¢ for each additional page, plus postage

*Jefferson County Courthouse
Madison, IN 47250
Phone (812) 265-8922 Clerk's Office; (812) 265-8902 Treasurer's Office; (812) 265-8910 Recorder; (812) 265-1942 Health Department
County organized 1810 from Indian Lands, chartered 1811
Land records: Contact Treasurer's Office and the Recorder
Naturalization records: Contact Clerk's Office
Vital records: Contact Health Department. Marriages; contact Donna Jackson, County Clerk, Room 203
Probate records: Wills from 1811; contact County Clerk

Jennings County Courthouse
Vernon, IN 47282
Phone (812) 346-5977
County organized 1816 from Indian Lands

*Johnson County Courthouse
5 West Jefferson
Franklin, IN 46131
Phone (317) 736-3720
County organized 1822 from Indian Lands

Land records: From 1823; contact County Recorder's Office, Annex Building, 86 West Court Street, Franklin, IN 46131; copies: $1.00 each
Naturalization records: From 1867 to 1908; contact Microfilm Department, 80 South Jackson Street, Franklin, IN 46131-2309
Vital records: Marriages from 1823 to date, marriage licenses from 1830; contact Microfilm Department. Births and deaths from 1882; contact Johnson County Health Department, Annex Building, 86 West Court Street, Franklin, IN 46131
Vital records search service from Microfilm Department: no charge, but must have a "range of years for a specific person"; copies: $1.00 per page plus SASE. Vital records search service from Health Department: no charge; copies: $5.00 each (must be accompanied by a copy of the applicant's current driver's license as identification)
Probate records: From 1826; contact Microfilm Department
Probate search service: no charge, but must have a "range" of years for specific person; copies: $1.00 per page plus SASE, no minimum

*Knox County Courthouse
PO Box 906
Vincennes, IN 47591-5338
Phone (812) 885-2521
County organized 1790 from Northwest Territory
Land records: Contact Brenda Hall, County Recorder
Naturalization records: Contact Lisa Clark/Benock, Clerk
Vital records: Contact County Board of Health, 624 Broadway Street
Probate records: Contact Clerk
Probate search service: no charge; copies: $1.00 per page, $1.00 for certified copies, no minimum

*Kosciusko County Courthouse
100 West Center Street
Warsaw, IN 46580-2846
Phone (219) 267-4444
County organized 1835 from Indian Lands
Land records: From 1845
Naturalization records: From 1855 to 1929; contact Clerk, Kosciusko Circuit Court, 121 North Lake Street, Warsaw, IN 46580
Vital records: Marriages from 1882; contact Clerk's Office
Probate records: From 1836; contact Clerk's Office
Probate search service: no charge; copies: $1.00 per page, no minimum

*LaGrange County Courthouse
105 North Detroit Street
LaGrange, IN 46761
Phone (219) 463-3442 Clerk of the Circuit Court
County organized 1832 from unorganized territory in Elkhart County
Land records: Contact County Auditor, LaGrange County Office Building, 114 West Michigan Street, LaGrange, IN 46761-1853; copies: $1.00 per page, $2.00 for certified copies
Naturalization records: Contact Suellen J. Mickem, Clerk of the Circuit Court. Microfilm copies; Contact State Archives, Public Records Commission, 402 West Washington Street, Room W472, Indianapolis, IN 46204; copies: $1.00 per page, $2.00 for certified copies
Vital records: Marriages from 1832 to date; contact Clerk of the Circuit Court; copies: $1.00 per page, $2.00 for certified copies. Births and deaths; contact Health Department, LaGrange County Office Building, 114 West Michigan Street, LaGrange, IN 46761
Probate records: From 1840 to date; contact Clerk of the Circuit Court
No probate search service; copies: $1.00 per page, $2.00 for certified copies; genealogy is done only when there is time

Lake County Courthouse
2293 North Main
Crown Point, IN 46307-1854
Phone (219) 738-2020; (219) 755-3000
County organized 1836 from Porter and Newton counties

LaPorte County Courthouse
LaPorte, IN 46350
Phone (219) 326-6808
County organized 1832 from Indian Lands

*Lawrence County Courthouse
Bedford, IN 47421
Phone (812) 275-7543 County Clerk
County organized 1818 from Orange County
Land records: From 1819; contact County Recorder's Office, Room 21
Naturalization records: Contact Indiana Commission on Public Records, 402 West Washington Street, Indianapolis, IN 46204
Vital records: Births and deaths from 1882; contact Department of Public Health, 2419 Mitchell Road, Bedford, IN 47421; copies: $1.00 each. Marriages from 1818; contact County Clerk's Office, Room 31; copies: $1.00 each, $2.00 for certified copies.

Probate records: From 1818; contact County Clerk's Office

Probate search service: no charge; copies: $1.00 per page, send SASE

*Madison County Government Center
16 East Ninth Street
Anderson, IN 46016-1538
Phone (317) 641-9470 Commissioner's Office
County organized 1823 from Fayette County
Land records: Contact Emley Hallgarth, Board of County Commissioners Office
Naturalization records: Contact Board of County Commissioners Office
Vital records: Contact Board of County Commissioners Office
Probate records: Contact Board of County Commissioners Office

*Marion County Courthouse
City-County Building
Indianapolis, IN 46204-3307
Phone (317) 236-4010; (317) 236-3200
County organized 1821 from Ohio County
Land records: Contact County Assessor, 1141 City-County Building
Vital records: Contact Division of Health and Hospital, 222 East Ohio, Indianapolis, IN 46204
Probate records: Contact 17th Floor, City-County Building
No probate search service; copies: $1.00 per page, no minimum

*Marshall County Courthouse
501 North Center Street
Plymouth, IN 46563-1707
Phone (219) 936-8922 Circuit Court Clerk; (219) 936-8893 FAX, Circuit Court Clerk
County organized 1836 from Indian Lands
Land records: Contact Recorder, County Building, 112 West Jefferson Street, Plymouth, IN 46563
Naturalization records: Until these records became part of the Federal Court system; contact State Archives
Vital records: Marriages only; contact Circuit Court Clerk, 211 West Madison Street, Plymouth, IN 46563. Births from 1 Jan 1882 to date (some destroyed by fire before 1907) and deaths from 1900; contact Health Department, 112 West Jefferson, Plymouth, IN 46563; copies: $3.00 for the first copy of births and $1.00 for each additional copy, $4.00 for the first copy of deaths and $2.00 for each additional copy (must show proof of relationship)
Probate records: Contact Circuit Court Clerk

Probate search service: $10.00 if done professionally; copies: $1.00 per page, no minimum; searches will not be done without dates

*Martin County Courthouse
PO Box 170
Shoals, IN 47581-0170
Phone (812) 247-3651
County organized 1820 from Indian Lands
Land records: Contact County Recorder's Office
Vital records: From 1882; contact Dr. Donald Beemblossom
Probate records: From 1820
Probate search service: no charge; copies: $1.00 per page, $2.00 for certified copies, no minimum

Miami County Courthouse
35 South Broadway
Peru, IN 46970-2231
Phone (317) 472-3901; (317) 472-2344
County organized 1832 from Cass County

*Monroe County Justice Building
PO Box 547
Bloomington, IN 47402-0547
Phone (812) 333-3600; (812) 333-3543 Health Department
County organized 1818 from Orange County
Land records: Contact Recorder's Office, Court House, Bloomington, IN 47401
Naturalization records: From 1908 to 1918; contact County Clerk's Office, Justice Building
Naturalization records search service: no charge for index search for a single name, $25.00 for a more complete search; copies: $1.00 per page
Vital records: Contact Health Department, 119 West Seventh Street, Bloomington, IN 47404; certified copies: $5.00 for births, $6.00 for deaths (births restricted to the individual named, parent, guardian, grandparent, sibling, spouse or child, with photocopy of driver's license for identification)
Probate Records: Wills and probates from 1818 to date; contact County Clerk
Probate search service: no charge for index search for a single name, $25.00 for a more complete search; copies: $1.00 per page

*Montgomery County Courthouse
100 East Main Street
Crawfordsville, IN 47933
Phone (317) 364-6430 Clerk; (317) 364-6440 Health Department; (317) 364-6415 Recorder

County organized 1823 from Indian Lands
Land records: Contact Delores Paddack, Recorder
Naturalization records: Contact Cindy Edmiston, Clerk, Montgomery Circuit and County Court, PO Box 768, Crawfordsville, IN 47933
Vital records: Marriages; contact Clerk; copies: $1.00 per page, $2.00 for certified copies (specify photocopy or typed copy). Births and Deaths; contact Health Department, 307 Binford Street, Crawfordsville, IN 47933
Probate records: Contact Clerk
Probate search service: no charge; copies: $1.00 per page, no minimum

Morgan County Courthouse
Martinsville, IN 46151
Phone (317) 342-1020; (317) 342-1025
County organized 1821 from Delaware County

Newton County Courthouse
PO Box 143
Kentland, IN 47951
Phone (219) 474-6081
County organized 1857 from Jasper County

*Noble County Courthouse
101 North Orange Street
Albion, IN 46701-1049
Phone (219) 636-2128; (219) 636-7877; (219) 636-2672 County Recorder; (219) 636-2736 County Clerk
County organized 1835 from Elkhart County
Land records: Deeds, mortgages, assignments, releases, powers of attorney, real estate contracts, annexations, surveys, cemetery deeds, plats, bonds, etc., from 1834 to date; contact Mary Ann Houser, County Recorder, 101 North Orange Street, PO Box 75, Albion, IN 46701; copies: $1.00 per page, $2.00 for copies larger than 9" x 15", $5.00 for certification
Naturalization records: Contact Indiana State Archives, 140 North Senate Avenue, Room 117, Indianapolis, IN 46204
Vital records: Birth and death records; contact Health Department, PO Box 13, Albion, IN 46701, (219) 636-2191
Probate records: Contact County Clerk, 101 North Orange, Second Floor Courthouse, Albion, IN 46701

*Ohio County Courthouse
Main Street
Rising Sun, IN 47040
Phone (812) 438-2062; (812) 438-3264 Assessor; (812) 438-3369 Recorder;

(812) 438-2610 Clerk; (812) 438-2551 Health Department
County organized 1844 from Dearborn County
Land records: From 1844; contact Assessor or Recorder
Naturalization records: From 1844; contact Clerk
Vital records: From 1882; contact Health Department
Probate records: From 1844; contact Clerk
No probate search service; copies 50¢ and $1.00 each, no minimum

Orange County Courthouse
Paoli, IN 47454
Phone (812) 723-2411; (812) 723-2649
County organized 1815 from Crawford and Washington counties

*Owen County Courthouse
PO Box 86
Spencer, IN 47460
Phone (812) 829-2796; (812) 829-2325
County organized 1819 from Sullivan County, with addition from Greene County in August 1821
Land records: From 1819; contact Recorder
Naturalization records: From 1819; contact Clerk, Owen Circuit Court
Vital records: Marriages from 1819; contact Clerk. Vital records from 1882; contact County Health Board
Probate records: From 1819; contact Clerk, Owen Circuit Court
Probate search service: no charge; copies $1.00 per page, no minimum

*Parke County Courthouse
Rockville, IN 47872
Phone (317) 569-5671; (317) 569-5132
County organized 1821 from Indian Lands
Land records: From 1832; contact County Recorder
Naturalization records: Scattered naturalization records from 1832; contact County Clerk
Vital records: From 1900; contact County Department of Health
Probate records: From 1832; contact County Clerk

*Perry County Courthouse
Clerk of Circuit Court
Cannelton, IN 47520
Phone (812) 547-7048; (812) 547-3741
County organized 1814 from Harrison and Warrick counties
Land records: Contact Clara A. Jarboe, County Recorder, 2219 Payne Street, Tell City, IN 47586
Naturalization records: Contact Clerk of Circuit Court

Vital records: Contact County Health Department, Courthouse Annex, Eighth Street, Cannelton, IN 47520
Probate records: Contact Clerk of Circuit Court
Probate search service: $1.00 per page; copies: $1.00 per page, $2.00 for certified copies

*Pike County Courthouse
Ninth and Main Streets
Petersburg, IN 47567
Phone (812) 354-6026 Court; (812) 354-6025 Clerk
County organized 1816 from Indian Lands
Land records: Contact Auditor's Office
Vital records: Contact Health Office
Probate records: Contact Clerk's Office
Probate search service: no charge; copies: $1.00 per page, no minimum; "Be sure records requested would be found in this county. Many randomly write all counties when searching for such information."

Porter County Courthouse
16 East Lincoln Way
Valparaiso, IN 46383-5636
Phone (219) 464-8661
County organized 1835 from Indian Lands

*Posey County Courthouse
PO Box 745
Mount Vernon, IN 47620
Phone (812) 838-1302; (812) 838-1306
County organized 1814 from Knox County
Land records: Contact County Recorder's Office; copies: $1.00 per page
Naturalization records: Some early ones are in Probate Order Books in the County Clerk's Office, some are in Civil Records Books in the Indiana State Library; some docket books and actual papers are in the Indiana State Archives
Vital records: Births and deaths; contact Posey County Health Department
Probate records: Contact County Clerk's Office; copies: $1.00 per page

Pulaski County Courthouse
Winamac, IN 46996
Phone (219) 946-3851; (219) 946-3653
County organized 1835 from Cass County

*Putnam County Courthouse
Greencastle, IN 46135
Phone (317) 653-5315; (317) 653-2648
County organized 1821 from Indian Lands
Land records: From 1821; contact Recorder's Office

Naturalization records: Contact Clerk's Office
Vital records: From 1882; contact Board of Health
Probate records: From 1825; contact Clerk's Office
Probate search service: $2.00; copies: $1.00 per page, $1.00 minimum

*Randolph County Courthouse
Winchester, IN 47394
Phone (317) 584-7070
County organized 1818 from Wayne County
Land records: Early land records, patent deeds, plat maps for towns and cemeteries; contact Recorder's Office, First Floor; copies: $1.00 per page
Naturalization records: Some in Civil Court books, others removed to Indiana State Library
Vital records: Births and deaths from 1882 (although not mandatory until about 1908, indexed by year); contact Health Department, 211 South Main Street. Marriages (some only partially indexed) from 1819 to 1882 (no applications) and from 1882 (with name and birthplaces of parents, ages, and other information); contact Clerk's Office, Third Floor; copies: $3.00 for births, $4.00 for deaths
Probate records: Wills, probate books, guardianship records; contact Clerk's Office
No probate search service (inquiries, other than prepaid orders for copies, are forwarded to Randolph County Historical/Genealogical Society, Rt. 3, Box 61, Winchester, IN 47394); copies: $1.00 per page, $2.00 per certified copy

*Ripley County Courthouse
PO Box 177
Versailles, IN 47042-0177
Phone (812) 689-6226; (812) 689-6115
County organized 1816 from Indian Lands
Land records: From 1818; contact County Recorder
Naturalization records: From 19th century; contact Circuit Court Clerk
Vital records: Births and deaths from 1880s; contact Ripley County Health Department. Marriages from 1818; contact Circuit Court Clerk
Probate records: Wills and probate records from 1818; contact Circuit Court Clerk
No probate search service; copies: $1.00 per page, $2.00 for certified copies, no minimum

*Rush County Courthouse
101 East Second Street
Rushville, IN 46173

Phone (317) 932-2078; (317) 932-3791; (317) 932-2086 Clerk of Circuit Court
County organized 1821 from Franklin County
Land records: From 1822; contact Recorder's Office, Room #8
Naturalization records: Very few naturalization records; contact Clerk of Circuit Court, PO Box 429, Rushville, IN 46173
Vital records: Contact County Health Department, First Floor, Courthouse
Probate records: From 1822; contact Clerk of Circuit Court
Probate search service for names given only; copies: $1.00 per page, no minimum; "No record sent before paid for; furnish SASE."

*Saint Joseph County Courthouse
101 South Main Street
South Bend, IN 46601
Phone (219) 284-9551; (219) 284-9534
County organized 1830 from Indian Lands
Land records: Deeds, mortgages, liens, plat books, final estates from 1830; contact Recorder's Office, County-City Building, South Bend, IN 46601
Naturalization records: From middle 1830s through about 1955; contact Clerk's Office
Vital records: Births from 1902 (does not issue certificates, only abstracts) and deaths from 1882; contact Vital Records, Saint Joseph County Health Department, Eighth Floor/County-City Building, South Bend, IN 46601. Marriages from 1832 and divorces; contact Clerk's Office
Vital records search service from Health Department: $5.00 for from one to six names; copies: $1.00 each
Probate records: From 1830; contact Clerk's Office
Probate search service: no charge; copies: $1.00 per page, no minimum

*Scott County Courthouse
1 East McClain Avenue
Scottsburg, IN 47170
Phone (812) 752-8420; (812) 752-3765; (812) 752-4769; (812) 752-8408 County Auditor
County organized 1820 from Clark and Jackson counties
Land records: Contact County Auditor
Vital records: Contact County Health Department; copies: $5.00
Probate records: Contact Clerk
No probate search service; copies: $1.00 per page in books

*Shelby County Courthouse
South Harrison Street
Shelbyville, IN 46176

Phone (317) 398-6151; (317) 392-6320
County organized 1821 from Indian Lands
Land records: From 1821; contact County Clerk's Office. Deeds from 1821; contact Recorder's Office
No land records search service from County Clerk's Office; no copies from large books. Copies available from Recorder's Office
Naturalization records: From 1821 (most of them in Civil and Probate books); contact County Clerk's Office
No naturalization search service; no copies from large books
Vital records: Marriages from 1821; contact County Clerk's Office. Births and deaths from 1882; contact Health Department, 53 West Polk Street
No vital records search service from County Clerk's Office; no copies from large books
Probate records: From 1821; contact County Clerk's Office
No probate search service; no copies from large books

*Spencer County Courthouse
PO Box 12
Rockport, IN 47635-0012
Phone (812) 649-2481; (812) 649-4916; (812) 649-4866, ext. 12 Genealogy Room Librarian
County organized 1818 from Warrick County
Land records: deeds or land records; contact Recorder's Office. Deeds from November 1818 to 1886, grantor/grantee indexes from 1818 to 1888; contact Becky Middleton, Genealogy Room Librarian, Spencer County Public Library, 210 Walnut Street, Rockport, IN 47635-1398
Naturalization records: Contact Clerk's Office; copies: $1.00 per page. Naturalization records from July 1852 to 1903; contact Genealogy Room Librarian
Vital records: Contact Health Department, Attention: Dallas. Index to births 1882 to 1920, index to deaths 1882 to 1936, marriages from March 1818 to December 1921; contact Genealogy Room Librarian
Health Department copies: $5.00 each
Probate records: Contact Clerk's Office. Probate records from November 1833 to December 1921, guardianships from 1871 to 1885, wills from 1833 to 1933; contact Genealogy Room Librarian; copies: $1.00 per page

*Starke County Courthouse
Knox, IN 46534
Phone (219) 772-9146; (219) 772-9128
County organized 1835 from Marshall County

Land records: Yes
Naturalization records: Yes
Vital records: Yes
Probate records: Yes

*Steuben County Courthouse
55 South Public Square
Angola, IN 46703
Phone (219) 665-9364 Circuit Court; (219) 665-7712 Superior Court; (219) 665-2361 County Clerk
County organized 1835 from Indian Lands
Land records: Contact County Recorder
Naturalization records: Only a few naturalization records; contact County Clerk, PO Box 327, Angola, IN 46703
Vital records: Contact Steuben County Health Department, 5 Martha Street, Angola, IN 46703
Probate records: Contact County Clerk
No probate search service; copies: $1.00 per page, $2.00 for certified copies, no minimum; "We need date."

Sullivan County Courthouse
Sullivan, IN 47882
Phone (812) 268-4411; (812) 268-5677
County organized 1816 from Knox County

*Switzerland County Courthouse
Vevay, IN 47043
Phone (812) 427-3410; (812) 427-3175
County organized 1814 from Indian Lands
Land records: Deeds from 1816; contact Rita Sullivan, Registrar, Switzerland County Health Department, PO Box 14, Vevay, IN 47043
Vital records: Births and deaths from 1882, marriages from 1814; contact Registrar
Probate records: Wills from 1823, probates 1831; contact Registrar

*Tippecanoe County Office Building
20 North Third Street
Lafayette, IN 47901-1211
Phone (317) 423-9343; (317) 423-9215
County organized 1826 from Montgomery County
Land records: Contact Ruth Shedd, Recorder
Naturalization records: Contact Sarah S. Brown, Clerk, or Tippecanoe County Historical Association (TCHA), 909 South Street, Lafayette, IN 47901, (317) 742-8411
Vital records: Births and deaths from 1882 to 1907; contact Tippecanoe County Board of Health, 20 North Third Street, Lafayette, IN 47901. Marriages; contact Clerk or TCHA, which has originals up to 1971

Probate records: Contact Clerk or TCHA for early originals

Probate search service: $10.00 per surname (clerk will refer requests to Tippecanoe County Area Genealogical Society (TIPCOA), 909 South Street, Lafayette, IN 47901); copies: 15¢ per page plus SASE

*Tipton County Courthouse
Tipton, IN 46072
Phone (317) 675-2795
County organized 1844 from Hamilton County
Probate records: From 1800s
Probate search service: no charge; copies: $1.00 per page; "extensive research referred to a lady who does research."

*Union County Courthouse
26 West Union
Liberty, IN 47353-1350
Phone (317) 458-6121; (317) 458-5263 FAX
County organized 1821 from Wayne County
Land records: From 1815; contact Recorder
Naturalization records: From 1821; contact Clerk of Circuit Court
Vital records: Marriages from 1821; contact Clerk of Circuit Court. Births from 1882 and deaths from 1907; contact Health
Probate records: From 1821; contact Clerk of Circuit Court
Probate search service: no charge; copies: $1.00 per page, no minimum

*Vanderburgh County Courthouse
Courts Building
(825 Sycamore Street, Evansville, IN 47708-1831—location)
PO Box 3356 (mailing address)
Evansville, IN 47732-3356
Phone (812) 435-5160
County organized 1818 from Indian Lands
Land records: Contact County Recorder
Naturalization records: Contact County Clerk
Vital records: Contact Health Department
Probate records: Contact Probate Department, Vanderburgh County Clerk
No probate search service; copies: $1.00 per page, no minimum

*Vermillion County Courthouse
Newport, IN 47966
Phone (317) 492-5003 Recorder; (317) 492-3500 Clerk of Circuit Court; (317) 832-3622 County Health Department
County organized 1824 from Parke County

Land records: Deeds; contact Martha Mott, Recorder, PO Box 145, Newport, IN 47966
Naturalization records: Contact Lavonna Mattick, Clerk of Circuit Court, 47th Judicial District; copies: $1.00 per page
Vital records: Marriages; contact Clerk of Circuit Court. Births and deaths; contact County Health Department, 825 South Main Street, Clinton, IN 47842; copies: $1.00 per page from Clerk of Circuit Court
Probate records: Contact Clerk of Circuit Court
No probate search service; copies: $1.00 per page

*Vigo County Courthouse
Third and Wabash
Terre Haute, IN 47807
Phone (812) 238-8211
County organized 1818 from Indian Lands
Land records: Contact Nancy Barnhart, Recorder, Recorder's Office, Vigo County Annex. Early land entries from "Tract Book" 1816 to 1821, index to grantors and grantees from March 1818 to May 1860, indexes from May 1860 to December 1887, deeds from 1816 to August 1886; contact Vigo County Public Library, Special Collections/Archives, 1 Library Square, Terre Haute, IN 47807.
Naturalization records: Contact Patricia R. Mansard, County Clerk, Clerk's Office, Courthouse, Room 22, PO Box 8449, Terre Haute, IN 47808-8449. Naturalization records from January 1856 to September 1906 (with index from 1818 to 1906); contact Vigo County Public Library
Vital records: Births and deaths; contact Department of Health, Vital Statistics, Vigo County Annex. Delayed births from June 1941 to October 1978, index to deaths from 1882 to 1920, marriage licenses from April 1818 through 19 June 1921, index to marriage licenses from 1818 to 1850 and from 1853 to 1916, marriage affidavits from December 1871 to January 1908, marriage supplements from March 1882 to April 1905, marriages from February 1910 to March 1916; contact Vigo County Public Library. Marriages from 1921 to date; contact Clerk's Office
Probate records: Contact Clerk's Office; copies: $1.00 per page. Index to settled estates and guardianships from 1819 to 1927, guardians' and administrators' records from February 1897 to November 1918, probate order books from October 1818 to November 1918, will records from

November 1818 to 1918; contact Vigo County Public Library; copies: 15¢ per page plus postage

*Wabash County Courthouse
1 West Hill
Wabash, IN 46992
Phone (219) 563-0661
County organized 1832 from Huntington County
Land records: Contact Auditor
Naturalization records: Contact Clerk of Circuit Court
Vital records: Contact Board of Health (proof of relationship required for copies of births)
Probate records: Contact Clerk of Circuit Court
Probate search service: no charge; copies: $1.00 per page, no minimum

*Warren County Courthouse
125 North Monroe
Williamsport, IN 47993-1198
Phone (317) 762-3510
County organized 1827 from Indian Lands
Land records: Contact Recorder's Office
Naturalization records: Contact Clerk's Office, Suite 11
Vital records: Marriages only; contact Clerk's Office. Births and deaths; contact Fountain-Warren Health Department, 210 South Perry, Attica, IN 47918
Probate records: Contact Clerk's Office

Warrick County Courthouse
Boonville, IN 47601
Phone (812) 897-3580
County organized 1813 from Indian Lands

*Washington County Courthouse
Salem, IN 47167
Phone (812) 883-5748
County organized 1813 from Indian Lands
Land records: Contact Clerk's Office
Naturalization records: Contact Clerk's Office
Vital records: Contact Clerk's Office
Probate records: Contact Clerk's Office

*Wayne County Courthouse
PO Box 1172
Richmond, IN 47375-1172
Phone (317) 973-9200; (317) 973-9235 Recorder's Office; (317) 973-9220 Clerk's Office; (317) 973-9245 Health Department
County organized 1810 from Indian Lands
Land records: Contact Recorder's Office, 401 East Main, Richmond, IN 47374

Naturalization records: Contact Clerk's Office

Vital records: Contact Health Department, 401 East Main, Richmond, IN 47374. Marriages (before 1882 did not keep "parental info"); contact Clerk's Office

Probate records: Contact Clerk's Office

No probate search service unless date range is supplied; copies: $1.00 per page, $2.00 for certified copies, no minimum

Wells County Courthouse
Main and Market
Bluffton, IN 46714
Phone (219) 824-2320
County organized 1835 from Huntington and Allen counties

*White County Courthouse
PO Box 260
Monticello, IN 47960
Phone (219) 583-7032
County organized 1834 from Carroll County
Land records: Contact County Recorder and County Auditor
Naturalization records: No naturalization records
Vital records: Contact County Health Department
Probate records: Contact Clerk, White Circuit Court
Probate search service: no charge; copies: $1.00 per page, no minimum

*Whitley County Courthouse
101 West Van Buren Street
Columbia City, IN 46725-2402
Phone (219) 248-3102; (219) 248-3106 County Recorder
County organized 1835 from Huntington County
Land records: From 1838; contact County Recorder, Second Floor, Room 18
Naturalization records: From 1853
Vital records: From 1853
Probate records: From 1853
No probate search service; copies: $1.00 per page, no minimum

IOWA

Capital: Des Moines. Statehood: 28 December 1846 (annexed as a result of the Louisiana Purchase, 1803, was part of the Missouri Territory from 1812 to 1821, mostly unorganized from 1821 to 1834, part of the Michigan Territory from 1834 to 1836, part of Wisconsin Territory from 1836 to 1838, when it became a separate territory)

Court System

Iowa has eight District Courts of general jurisdiction, which sit in each county seat. First Judicial District: Allamakee, Black Hawk, Buchanan, Chickasaw, Clayton, Delaware, Dubuque, Fayette, Grundy, Howard and Winneshiek counties; Second Judicial District: Boone, Bremer, Butler, Calhoun, Carroll, Cerro Gordo, Floyd, Franklin, Greene, Hamilton, Hancock, Hardin, Humboldt, Marshall, Mitchell, Pocahontas, Sac, Story, Webster, Winnebago, Worth and Wright counties; Third Judicial District: Buena Vista, Cherokee, Clay, Crawford, Dickinson, Emmet, Ida, Kossuth, Lyon, Monona, O'Brien, Osceola, Palo Alto, Plymouth, Sioux and Woodbury counties; Fourth Judicial District: Audubon, Cass, Fremont, Harrison, Mills, Montgomery, Page, Pottawattamie and Shelby counties; Fifth Judicial District: Adair, Adams, Clarke, Dallas, Decatur, Guthrie, Jasper, Lucas, Madison, Marion, Polk, Ringgold, Taylor, Union, Warren and Wayne counties; Sixth Judicial District: Benton, Iowa, Johnson, Jones, Linn and Tama counties; Seventh Judicial District: Cedar, Clinton, Jackson, Muscatine and Scott counties; Eighth Judicial District: Appanoose, Davis, Des Moines, Henry, Jefferson, Keokuk, Lee, Louisa, Mahaska, Monroe, Poweshiek, Van Buren, Wapello and Washington counties. The Supreme Court and Court of Appeals have appellate jurisdiction.

Courthouses

*Adair County Courthouse
Greenfield, IA 50849
Phone (515) 743-2445
County organized 1851 from Cass County
Land records: Contact Recorder's Office
Naturalization records: A few naturalization records; contact Clerk of Court

Vital records: Births from 1880 (few from 1921 to 1941 when certificates were sent directly to the state office), deaths from 1880 (none from 1921 to 1941), marriages from 1880; contact Clerk of Court
Probate records: Contact Clerk of Court
Probate search service: $1.00; copies: 25¢ each, $1.00 minimum

*Adams County Courthouse
Corning, IA 50841
Phone (515) 322-3744 County Recorder; (515) 322-4711
County organized 1851 from Taylor County
Land records: From 1855; contact Mary Miller, County Recorder, PO Box 28, Corning, IA 50841
Naturalization records: From 1880; contact Myrna Brown, Clerk of District Court, PO Box 484, Corning, IA 50841
Vital records: From 1880; contact Clerk of Court; certified copies: $10.00 each
Probate records: From 1880; contact Clerk of Court

*Allamakee County Courthouse
Waukon, IA 52172
Phone (319) 568-6351
County organized 1847 from Clayton County
Land records: From 1851; contact Recorder or Auditor
Naturalization records: From 1850 to 1890; contact Carl R. Christianson, Clerk of District Court
Vital records: Births and deaths from 1880, marriages from 1849; contact Clerk of District Court
Probate records: From 1852; contact Clerk of District Court
Probate search service: $10.00; copies: 50¢ each, no minimum; "If search in probate is lengthy, cost of search goes up."

*Appanoose County Courthouse
Centerville, IA 52544
Phone (515) 856-6101
County organized 1843 from Davis County
Land records: From 1850; contact Recorder's Office
Naturalization records: From 1884 to 1929; contact Clerk of Court
Vital records: Births and deaths from 1880; contact Clerk of Court
Probate records: From 1847; contact Clerk of Court
Probate search service: no charge; copies: 25¢ per page, no minimum; "Most of the research that is uncertified is referred to our local Genealogy Society."

*Audubon County Courthouse
318 Leroy
Audubon, IA 50025
Phone (712) 563-4275
County organized 1851 from Cass and Black Hawk counties
Land records: Contact County Recorder (by owner's name) or County Auditor (by legal description)
Naturalization records: Contact Evelyn Wiges, Clerk of District Court, Courthouse, 318 Leroy, #6, Audubon, IA 50025
Vital records: Contact Clerk of District Court
Probate records: Contact Clerk of District Court
Probate search service: $6.00; copies: 50¢ per page, no minimum

*Benton County Courthouse
PO Box 719
Vinton, IA 52349
Phone (319) 472-2766
County organized 1837 from Indian Lands
Land records: Contact Recorder's Office
Naturalization records: From 1860; contact Clerk of the District Court
Vital records: From 1880; contact Clerk of the District Court
Probate records: From 1860; contact Clerk of the District Court
Probate search service: $6.00; copies: 25¢ per page, $1.00 minimum

*Black Hawk County Courthouse
316 East Fifth Street
Waterloo, IA 50703-4712
Phone (319) 291-2500; (319) 291-2468 Auditor; (319) 291-2472 Recorder; (319) 291-2482 Clerk of Court
County organized 1843 from Delaware County
Land records: From about 1860; contact County Auditor (plat room deed transfer books, atlas–1937) or County Recorder (grantee/grantor books, atlas–1896, records from 1854)
Naturalization records: From 1869 to 1926; contact Clerk of Court
Naturalization search service: $6.00
Vital records: Births, deaths and marriages from 1880 (except from 1936 to 1941 records in Des Moines); contact Clerk of Court
Vital records search service: $6.00; copies: 25¢ each
Probate records: From 1880; contact Clerk of Court
Probate search service: no charge; copies: 50¢ per page, 50¢ minimum; "Some records show origination in Buchanan County."

*Boone County Courthouse
201 State Street
Boone, IA 50036
Phone (515) 433-0561 Clerk of Court's Office
County organized 1846 from Polk County
Naturalization records: Some naturalization records from 1867; contact Clerk of Court
Vital records: Births and deaths from 1880, marriages from 1851; contact Clerk of Court; certified copies: $10.00
Probate records: From about 1850
Probate search service: no charge; copies: 50¢ per page, $10.00 for certification, no minimum; "We do these searches only when we have time."

*Bremer County Courthouse
Waverly, IA 50677
Phone (319) 352-5040 Recorder; (319) 352-5661 Clerk of Court
County organized 1851 from Winnebago Indian Reserve
Land records: Contact Recorder
Naturalization records: Contact Clerk of Court, PO Box 328, Waverly, IA 50677
Vital records: Contact Clerk of Court; certified copies: $10.00 each
Probate records: Contact Clerk of Court
Probate search service: no charge; copies: 50¢ per page, $5.00 minimum

*Buchanan County Courthouse
PO Box 259
Independence, IA 50644
Phone (319) 334-2196
County organized 1837 from Delaware County
Land records: Contact Recorder's Office
Naturalization records: From about 1875 to 1923; contact Clerk of District Court
Vital records: Births and deaths from 1 July 1880, marriages from 1848; contact Clerk of District Court
Probate records: From 1854; contact Clerk of District Court
Probate search service: no charge (must have SASE); copies: 50¢ per page, $10.00 for certified copies, no minimum

*Buena Vista County Courthouse
Storm Lake, IA 50588
Phone (712) 749-2546
County organized 1851 from Sac and Clay counties
Land records: Contact Recorder and Auditor Offices
Naturalization records: Contact Clerk of Court's Office, PO Box 1186, Storm Lake, IA 50588-1186; copies: 50¢ per page, $10.00 for certified copies

Vital records: From 1880; contact Clerk of Court's Office; copies: 50¢ per page, $10.00 for certified copies
Probate records: From 1880; contact Clerk of Court's Office; copies: 50¢ per page, $10.00 for certified copies

*Butler County Courthouse
428 Sixth Street
Allison, IA 50602
Phone (319) 267-2487 Clerk of Court; (319) 267-2670 Auditor
County organized 1851 from Buchanan and Black Hawk counties
Land records: Contact County Auditor
Naturalization records: Contact Clerk of Court
Vital records: Contact Clerk of Court
Probate records: Contact Clerk of Court
Probate search service: no charge; copies: 50¢ per page, no minimum

*Calhoun County Courthouse
Rockwell City, IA 50579
Phone (712) 297-7741 Auditor; (712) 297-8121 Recorder; (712) 297-7500 Assessor; (712) 297-8122 Clerk of Court; (712) 297-7111 Treasurer
County organized 1851 from Greene County; name changed from Fox County in 1853
Land records: Contact Judy Howrey, Auditor, or Marty Minnick, Recorder
Land records search service: no charge (extensive searches referred to Calhoun County Genies, c/o Mrs. Beverly Courter, 226 North Grant Street, Rockwell City, IA 50579); copies: 25¢ each
Naturalization records: Contact Shirley Redenius, Clerk of Court
Vital records: Contact Clerk of Court
Probate records: Contact Clerk of Court
Probate search service: no charge; copies: 50¢ per page, no minimum

Carroll County Courthouse
PO Box 867
Carroll, IA 51401-0867
Phone (712) 792-4327
County organized 1851 from Guthrie County

*Cass County Courthouse
Atlantic, IA 50022
Phone (712) 243-2105
County organized 1851 from Pottawatamie County
Land records: Contact Recorder
Naturalization records: Only early naturalization records; contact Clerk
Vital records: From 1880; contact Clerk
Probate records: Contact Clerk
Probate search service: no charge; copies: 25¢ per page, no minimum

*Cedar County Courthouse
Tipton, IA 52772
Phone (319) 886-2101
County organized 1837 from Wisconsin Territory
Land records: From 1839; contact County Recorder
Naturalization records: Some naturalization records but not well indexed; contact Clerk of Court, PO Box 111, Tipton, IA 52772
Vital records: Births and deaths from 1880, marriages from 1839; contact Clerk of Court; certified copies: $6.00 each
Probate records: From 1836
Probate search service: $10.00 per name; copies: 50¢ per page, $10.00 for certified copies

*Cerro Gordo County Courthouse
Mason City, IA 50401-3254
Phone (515) 421-3056 Recorder; (515) 424-6431 Clerk of Court
County organized 1851 from Floyd County
Land records: Contact Recorder
Naturalization records: Contact Clerk of Court
Vital records: Contact Clerk of Court
Probate records: Contact Clerk of Court

*Cherokee County Courthouse
Cherokee, IA 51012
Phone (712) 225-6744 Clerk of Courts; (712) 225-6704 Auditor
County organized 1851 from Crawford County
Land records: Contact County Auditor's Office
Land records search service: $10.00; copies: 50¢ per page
Naturalization records: Contact Clerk of Courts
Naturalization records search service: $10.00; copies: 50¢ per page
Vital records: From 1880 to date; contact Clerk of Courts
Vital records search service: $10.00 (includes certified copy)
Probate records: Contact Clerk of Courts
Probate search service: $10.00; copies: 50¢ per page, no minimum

*Chickasaw County Courthouse
New Hampton, IA 50659
Phone (515) 394-2106
County organized 1851 from Fayette County
Land records: From 1866; contact Gloria Hauser, County Auditor, Courthouse Box 311
Naturalization records: From 1858 to 1906; contact Clerk of Court
Vital records: Births from 1880, deaths from 1880 to 1919 and from 1941, marriages from 1853; contact Clerk of Court
Probate records: From 1880; contact Clerk of Court
Probate search service: $6.00; copies: 50¢ per page, no minimum; "Supply all information possible."

*Clarke County Courthouse
North Main Street
Osceola, IA 50213
Phone (515) 342-2213
County organized 1846 from Lucas County
Land records: From 1866
Naturalization records: Very few naturalization records
Vital records: From 1880
Probate records: From late 1800s
Probate search service: $3.00; copies: 25¢ per page, $3.00 minimum; "Cover letter must accompany request with all information needed."

*Clay County Courthouse
PO Box 4104
Spencer, IA 51301
Phone (712) 262-4335
County organized 1851 from Indian Lands
Land records: Contact Recorder's Office, Clay County Administration Building, Spencer, IA 51301
Naturalization records: From 1866; contact Clerk
No naturalization search service; copies: 25¢ per page
Vital records: Births and deaths from 1880, marriages from 1866; contact Clerk
No vital records search service; copies: 25¢ per page
Probate records: From 1871; contact Clerk
No probate search service; copies: 25¢ per page

*Clayton County Courthouse
Elkader, IA 52043
Phone (319) 245-2204
County organized 1837 from Dubuque County
Land records: Contact County Recorder
Naturalization records: Contact County Clerk
Vital records: Contact County Clerk
Probate records: Contact County Clerk
Probate search service: $6.00; copies: 50¢ per page

*Clinton County Courthouse
PO Box 157
Clinton, IA 52732-0157
Phone (319) 243-6210
County organized 1837 from Dubuque County

Land records: From 1846; contact Recorder
Naturalization records: From 1859; contact Clerk
Vital records: Births and deaths from 1880, marriages from 1840; contact Clerk; certified copies: $6.00
Probate records: From 1854; contact Clerk
Probate search service: no charge; copies: 50¢ per page, no minimum

*Crawford County Courthouse
PO Box 546
Denison, IA 51442-0546
Phone (712) 263-2242
County organized 1851 from Shelby County
Land records: Contact Recorder
Naturalization records: Contact Karen Kahl, Clerk
Vital records: Contact Clerk; certified copies: $6.00
Probate records: Contact Clerk
No probate search service; "Nothing done over telephone."

*Dallas County Courthouse
801 Court Street
Adel, IA 50003-1447
Phone (515) 993-4789
County organized 1846 from Polk County
Land records: Contact County Auditor
Naturalization records: No naturalization records
Vital records: Births and deaths from 1880 (except some omissions from 1921 through 1941), marriages from 1850
Probate records: From 1860
Probate search service: no charge; copies: 50¢ per page, $1.00 minimum

*Davis County Courthouse
Bloomfield, IA 52537
Phone (515) 664-2011
County organized 1843 from Van Buren County
Land records: Contact County Recorder
Vital records: Births and deaths from 1880, marriages from 1840; contact Clerk of District Court
Probate records: From 1840; contact Clerk of District Court
Probate search service: $6.00; certified copies: $6.00; "Make check or money order payable to the Clerk District Court and enclose a SASE."

*Decatur County Courthouse
207 North Main
Leon, IA 50144
Phone (515) 446-4331
County organized 1846 from Appanoose County

Land records: From 1874; contact
Recorder's Office
Naturalization records: Very few
naturalization records from early
1900s; contact Clerk of Court
Vital records: Births and deaths from
1880, marriages from 1874; contact
Clerk of Court
Probate records: From 1880; contact
Clerk of Court
Probate search service: no charge;
copies: $1.00 per page, $10.00 for
certified copies, no minimum; "We do
not run Xerox copies on our old
books, as it breaks the backs down."

*Delaware County Courthouse
Manchester, IA 52057
Phone (319) 927-4942; (319) 927-4665
*County organized 1837 from Dubuque
County*
Land records: Contact County Recorder
or County Auditor
Naturalization records: Contact Clerk of
District Court
Vital records: Contact Clerk of District
Court
Probate records: Contact Clerk of District
Court
Probate search service: no charge;
copies: 50¢ per page, no minimum

*Des Moines County Courthouse
513 North Main Street
PO Box 158
Burlington, IA 52601
Phone (319) 753-8262
*County organized 1834 from Wisconsin
Territory*
Land records: Contact Recorder
Naturalization records: From 1856 to
1906 and 1928 to 1955; contact Clerk
of District Court
Vital records: Births from 1880, deaths
from 1880 to 1910 (no index) and
from July 1941; contact Clerk of
District Court
Probate records: From 1835; contact
Clerk of District Court
No probate search service; contact Mrs.
Louise Strable, 719 South 12th,
Burlington, IA 52601

Dickinson County Courthouse
Spirit Lake, IA 51360
Phone (712) 336-1138
*County organized 1851 from Kossuth
County*

*Dubuque County Courthouse
720 Central
Dubuque, IA 52001-7053
Phone (319) 589-4418
*County organized 1834 from Wisconsin
Territory*
Land records: Contact Clerk of Court

Naturalization records: Contact Clerk of
Court
Vital records: Contact Clerk of Court
Probate records: Contact Clerk of Court

Emmet County Courthouse
Estherville, IA 51334
Phone (712) 362-4261
*County organized 1851 from Kossuth
and Dickinson counties*

*Fayette County Courthouse
West Union, IA 52175
Phone (319) 422-6061
*County organized 1837 from Clayton
County*
Land records: Contact Recorder; copies:
50¢ per page
Naturalization records: Contact Clerk;
copies: 50¢ per page
Vital records: Contact Clerk; copies: 50¢
per page
Probate records: Contact Clerk
Probate search service: no charge;
copies: 50¢ per page, no minimum

*Floyd County Courthouse
101 South Main Street
Charles City, IA 50616
Phone (515) 228-7111
*County organized 1851 from Chickasaw
County*
Land records: Contact Marilee Monroe,
County Recorder (very early records)
Naturalization records: From 1800s;
contact Barbara Fuls, Clerk of Court
Vital records: Births and deaths from
1880, marriages from 1854; contact
Clerk of Court; certified copies:
$10.00
Probate records: From 1854; contact
Clerk of Court
No probate search service

Franklin County Courthouse
12 First Avenue, N.W.
Hampton, IA 50441-0026
Phone (515) 456-5626
*County organized 1851 from Chickasaw
County*

Fremont County Courthouse
PO Box 549
Sidney, IA 51652-0549
Phone (712) 374-2031
*County organized 1847 from
Pottawattamie County*

*Greene County Courthouse
Jefferson, IA 50129
Phone (515) 386-2516 Auditor's or
Clerk's Office
*County organized 1851 from Dallas
County*
Land records: Contact Auditor's Office

Naturalization records: Contact Clerk's
Office
Vital records: Contact Clerk's Office
Probate records: Contact Clerk's Office

*Grundy County Courthouse
706 G Avenue
Grundy Center, IA 50638
Phone (319) 824-5229
*County organized 1851 from Black
Hawk County*
Land records: From 1855; contact
Recorder
Naturalization records: From April 1870;
contact Clerk of Court
Vital records: Births from July 1877
(incomplete through 1880 and from
1921 to 1941), deaths from 1880
(incomplete to 1921, none from 1921
to 1941); contact Clerk of Court
Probate records: From August 1856, first
complete probate November 1870;
contact Clerk of Court
Probate search service: $10.00; copies:
50¢ per page; $10.00 minimum per
index search

Guthrie County Courthouse
Guthrie Center, IA 50115
Phone (515) 747-3415
*County organized 1851 from Jackson
County*

*Hamilton County Courthouse
2300 Superior Street (South Highway 17)
Webster City, IA 50595-3158
Phone (515) 832-4640; (515) 832-9535
County Recorder; (515) 832-9600
Clerk of Court
*County organized 1856 from Webster
County*
Land records: Contact County Recorder's
Office
Naturalization records: First and second
papers (no applications) from 1880 to
1910, petition and records from May
1910 to September 1921, declarations
of intention from October 1921 to
January 1930; contact Darlene L.
Dingman, Clerk of Court, PO Box
845, Webster City, IA 50595-0845
Naturalization records search service:
$10.00 (includes cost of certified
copy); copies: 50¢ per page (if no
search is needed)
Vital records: Births and deaths from
1880 to date, marriages from 1857 to
date; contact Clerk of Court, Attn:
Vital Records
Vital records search service: $10.00
(includes cost of certified copy)
Probate records: From about 1857 to
date; contact Clerk of Court
Probate search service: $10.00 (includes
cost of certified copy); copies: 50¢ per
page (if no search is needed)

*Hancock County Courthouse
855 State Street
Garner, IA 50438-1645
Phone (515) 923-2532
County organized 1851 from Wright County
Land records: From 1865; contact County Auditor's Office
Naturalization records: Not very many; contact Clerk of Court's Office
Vital records: From 1880; contact Clerk of Court's Office
Probate records: From 1880; contact Clerk of Court's Office
Probate search service: $2.00; certified copies: $6.00

*Hardin County Courthouse
Eldora, IA 50627
Phone (515) 858-3461, ext. 336 County Recorder; (515) 858-2328 Clerk of the District Court
County organized 1851 from Black Hawk County
Land records: Original land entries 1852, deeds from 1852 to date, book of plats 1892, 1903, 1916 and current, mortgage records from 1852 to date; contact County Recorder, Attn: Genealogy, PO Box 443, Eldora, IA 50627; copies: 50¢ per page
Naturalization records: Limited naturalization records from 1860 to 1940; contact Diane L. Ryerson, Clerk of the District Court, Attn: Genealogy, PO Box 495, Eldora, IA 50627
Vital records: Births from 1880 to 1932 and from 1942 to date, deaths from 1880 to 1920 and from 1942 to date, marriages from 1854 to date; contact County Clerk's Office
Probate records: From 1850s; contact County Clerk's Office
Probate search service: $6.00 per name; copies: 25¢ per page, $6.00 for certified copies, $6.00 minimum

Harrison County Courthouse
Logan, IA 51546
Phone (712) 644-2665
County organized 1851 from Pottawattamie County

Henry County Courthouse
Mount Pleasant, IA 52641
Phone (319) 385-8480
County organized 1836 from Wisconsin Territory

*Howard County Courthouse
Cresco, IA 52136
Phone (319) 547-2661
County organized 1851 from Chickasaw and Floyd counties
Land records: From 1867; contact County Auditor

Naturalization records: From 1880; contact Clerk of District Court
Vital records: From 1880; contact Clerk of District Court
Probate records: From 1880; contact Clerk of District Court
Probate search service: $10.00 per name; "Include dates (from? to?), names (also maiden names when necessary), parents' names, cities."

*Humboldt County Courthouse
Dakota City, IA 50529
Phone (515) 332-1806 Clerk of Court; (515) 332-1571 Auditor; (515) 332-3693 Recorder
County organized 1851 from Webster County
Land records: Contact Auditor (from 1881) or Recorder (deeds begin in 1856)
Naturalization records: From May 1871; contact Clerk of Court
Vital records: Births and deaths from July 1880
Probate records: From 1880
No probate search service

*Ida County Courthouse
401 Moorehead Street
Ida Grove, IA 51445-1429
Phone (712) 364-2626 County Auditor; (712) 364-2628 Clerk of District Court; (712) 364-2220 County Recorder
County organized 1851 from Cherokee County
Land records: Contact County Auditor or County Recorder
Naturalization records: Contact Clerk of District Court
Vital records: Contact Clerk of District Court
Probate records: Contact Clerk of District Court
Probate search service: $6.00; copies: $6.00, certified $10.00, no minimum

Iowa County Courthouse
PO Box 126
Marengo, IA 52301
Phone (319) 642-3914
County organized 1843 from Washington County

Jackson County Courthouse
201 West Platt
Maquoketa, IA 52060-2243
Phone (319) 652-4946
County organized 1837 from Wisconsin Territory

*Jasper County Courthouse
PO Box 666
Newton, IA 50208-0666

Phone (515) 792-3255
County organized 1846 from Mahaska County
Land records: From 1870
Naturalization records: From early 1900s
Vital records: Births and deaths from 1880, marriage licenses from 1849
Probate records: From 1850
Probate search service: no charge; copies: 50¢ per page

*Jefferson County Courthouse
PO Box 984
Fairfield, IA 52556-0984
Phone (515) 472-3454
County organized 1839 from Indian Lands
Land records: From 1839; contact Clerk of District Court
Naturalization records: Incomplete naturalization records; contact Clerk of District Court
Vital records: From 1880; contact Clerk of District Court
Probate records: Contact Clerk of District Court
Probate search service: no charge; copies: 25¢ per page, no minimum

*Johnson County Courthouse
417 South Clinton Street
PO Box 2510
Iowa City, IA 52240
Phone (319) 356-6060 Clerk of Court; (319) 356-6095 County Recorder
County organized 1837 from Des Moines County
Land records: Contact County Recorder's Office, Johnson County Administration Building, 913 South Dubuque Street, PO Box 1350, Iowa City, IA 52244
Naturalization records: From 1880s to 1900s; contact Clerk of Court (no searches or copies available by mail)
Vital records: Births and deaths from 1 July 1880, marriages from 1 July 1839; contact Clerk of Court
Vital records search service: $6.00 (includes free certified copy)
Probate records: From 1843; contact Clerk of Court
Probate search service: $6.00, includes copies

*Jones County Courthouse
500 West Main
Anamosa, IA 52205
Phone (319) 462-2477 County Recorder; (319) 462-4341 Clerk of Court
County organized 1837 from Wisconsin Territory
Land records: Contact County Recorder
Vital records: Contact Clerk of Court
Probate records: Contact Clerk of Court

*Keokuk County Courthouse
Sigourney, IA 52591
Phone (515) 622-2210; (515) 622-2540
County organized 1844 from Washington County
Land records: From 1845
Naturalization records: From 1851
Vital records: Births and deaths from 1880, marriages from 1844
Probate records: From 1854
Probate search service: $6.00; copies: $1.00 per page, $6.00 minimum; "Give as much information as possible."

Kossuth County Courthouse
Algona, IA 50511
Phone (515) 295-3240
County organized 1851 from Webster County

Lee County Courthouse
701 Avenue F
Fort Madison, IA 52627
Phone (319) 372-3523
County organized 1836 from Des Moines County

*Linn County Courthouse
Third Avenue Bridge
Cedar Rapids, IA 52401
Phone (319) 398-3411 Clerk of Court
County organized 1837 from Wisconsin Territory
Land records: Contact County Recorder, 930 First Street, S.W., Cedar Rapids, IA 52404
Vital records: Contact Clerk of Court, PO Box 1468, Cedar Rapids, IA 52406-1468; certified copies: $10.00 each (only available to immediate family)
Probate records: Contact Clerk of Court
No probate search service: copies: 25¢ per page, 25¢ minimum; "We forward many requests to Linn County Heritage Society."

Louisa County Courthouse
Wapello, IA 52653
Phone (319) 523-4541
County organized 1836 from Des Moines County

*Lucas County Courthouse
Chariton, IA 50049
Phone (515) 774-4421
County organized 1846 from Monroe County
Land records: Contact Recorder or Auditor or Assessor
Naturalization records: Discontinued about 1929–30; contact Clerk of District Court
Vital records: From 1880 (except from 1935 to 1940); contact Clerk of District Court

Probate records: Contact Clerk of District Court
Probate search service: $6.00; copies: $1.00 per page

*Lyon County Courthouse
Rock Rapids, IA 51246
Phone (712) 472-2623
County organized 1851 from Woodbury County; name changed from Buncombe County in 1862
Land records: Contact County Recorder or County Auditor
Naturalization records: Contact Clerk of Court
Vital records: Contact Clerk of Court
Probate records: Contact Clerk of Court
Probate search service: no charge; copies: 25¢ per page, no minimum; "Must have names and dates as close as possible."

*Madison County Courthouse
PO Box 152
Winterset, IA 50273-0152
Phone (515) 462-4451 Clerk of Court; (515) 462-3771 County Recorder
County organized 1844 from Polk County
Land records: From 1850; contact County Recorder; copies: $1.00 per page
Vital records: Births and deaths from 1880, marriages from 1855; contact Clerk of Court
Probate records: From 1852; contact Clerk of Court
Probate search service: no charge; copies: 25¢ per page plus postage, no minimum

*Mahaska County Courthouse
106 South First Street
Oskaloosa, IA 52577
Phone (515) 643-7786
County organized 1843 from Indian Lands
Land records: From 1845; contact County Recorder
Naturalization records: From about 1880; contact Clerk of Court
Vital records: From 1880; contact Clerk of Court
Probate records: From 1845; contact Clerk of Court
Probate search service: $6.00; copies: $1.00 per page from old records or microfilm originals, 25¢ per page for current records, $6.00 minimum

*Marion County Courthouse
PO Box 497
Knoxville, IA 50138-0497
Phone (515) 828-2211
County organized 1845 from Washington County

Land records: From 1845
Naturalization records: Contact Clerk of Court
Vital records: Contact Clerk of Court
Probate records: Contact Clerk of Court
No probate search service; copies: 20¢ per page in county, $1.00 per instrument outside of county, no minimum; "If order is quite large and the postage is going to be quite high, then we ask for postage."

*Marshall County Courthouse
Marshalltown, IA 50158
Phone (515) 754-6373 Clerk of Court
County organized 1846 from Jasper County
Land records: Contact County Recorder
No land records search service
Naturalization records: Contact Clerk of Court
Vital records: Contact Clerk of Court
No vital records search service; certified copies: $10.00 each
Probate records: Contact Clerk of Court
No probate search service; copies: 50¢ per page, no minimum; "If there is an exact date; no charge for search."

*Mills County Courthouse
Glenwood, IA 51534
Phone (712) 527-4880
County organized 1851 from Pottawattamie County
Land records: From 1853; contact Auditor; copies: 50¢ per page; "Our early record books are bound books and we do not make copies."
Naturalization records: Contact Recorder
Vital records: Contact Clerk
Probate records: Contact Clerk
No probate search service; copies: 50¢ each, no minimum

*Mitchell County Courthouse
508 State Street
Osage, IA 50461
Phone (515) 732-5861 Recorder; (515) 732-3726 Clerk of District Court
County organized 1851 from Chickasaw County
Land records: From 1854 to date; contact Lois D. Eidness, Recorder
Naturalization records: From 1857 to 1951; contact Clerk of District Court
Vital records: Births from July 1880 to date, deaths from 1880 to date, marriages from 1855 to date; contact Clerk of District Court
Probate records: Contact Clerk of District Court
Probate search service: no charge; copies: 50¢ per page, no minimum

*Monona County Courthouse
610 Iowa Avenue

PO Box 53
Onawa, IA 51040
Phone (712) 423-2575
County organized 1851 from Harrison County
Land records: Yes
Naturalization records: Contact Clerk of Court's office
Vital records: Contact Clerk of Court's Office
Probate records: Contact Clerk of Court's Office
No probate search service; copies: 25¢ per page from paper originals, 75¢ per page from microfilm originals, no minimum

*Monroe County Courthouse
Albia, IA 52531
Phone (515) 932-5212
County organized 1843 from Wapello County
Land records: Contact Office of County Recorder
Naturalization records: Contact Office of Clerk of Court
Vital records: Contact Office of Clerk of Court; copies: $1.00
Probate records: Contact Office of Clerk of Court
Probate search service: $6.00; copies: 25¢ per page, no minimum

*Montgomery County Courthouse
Red Oak, IA 51566-0469
Phone (712) 623-4986
County organized 1851 from Polk County
Probate records: Contact Clerk of District Court
No probate search service; contact Fran Woodworth, Red Oak Public Library, Second and Washington, Red Oak, IA 51566

*Muscatine County Courthouse
Muscatine, IA 52761
Phone (319) 263-6511; (319) 264-3622 FAX
County organized 1836 from Des Moines County
Land records: Contact Auditor's Office and Recorder's Office
Naturalization records: Sketchy early naturalization records; contact Clerk's Office
Vital records: From 1890; contact Clerk's Office
Probate records: Contact Clerk's Office
Probate search service: no charge; copies: 50¢ ("if we make them"), no minimum

O'Brien County Courthouse
Primghar, IA 51245
Phone (712) 757-3255

County organized 1851 from Cherokee County

*Osceola County Courthouse
300 Seventh Street
Sibley, IA 51249-1695
Phone (712) 754-3345 Recorder; (712) 754-3743 FAX, Recorder; (712) 754-3595 Clerk of District Court; (712) 754-2480 FAX, Clerk of District Court
County organized 1851 from Woodbury County
Land records: Deeds, mortgages and releases (earliest dated 1869); contact Arlene Kuehl, Recorder
Land records search service: no charge, as time alows; copies: $1.00 per page, $2.00 per document for certification
Naturalization records: From the early 1880s; contact Eileen Grave, Clerk of District Court, 300 Seventh Street, PO Box 156, Sibley, IA 51249
No naturalization records search service; copies: 25¢ per page, $10.00 for certified copies
Vital records: Births, deaths and marriages from the early 1880s; contact Clerk of District Court
No vital records search service; copies: 25¢ per page, $10.00 for certified copies
Probate records: From the early 1880s; contact Clerk of District Court
No probate search service; copies: 25¢ per page, $10.00 for certified copies, no minimum

*Page County Courthouse
112 East Main Street
Clarinda, IA 51632
Phone (712) 542-3130 County Recorder; (712) 542-3219 County Auditor; (712) 542-3214 Clerk of Court
County organized 1847 from Pottawattamie County
Land records: Actual recorded instrument and indexes; contact County Recorder. Transfer books and plat books; contact County Auditor; copies: 50¢ per document
Naturalization records: Contact Clerk of Court; copies: 50¢ per document
Vital records: Contact Clerk of Court; copies: 50¢ per document
Probate records: Contact Clerk of Court; copies: 50¢ per document

*Palo Alto County Courthouse
11th and Broadway
Emmetsburg, IA 50536
Phone (712) 852-3701 Recorder's Office; (712) 852-3603 Clerk of Court
County organized 1851 from Kossuth County
Land records: From about 1860; contact Recorder's Office

Naturalization records: From 1871; contact Clerk of Court
Vital records: From 1880; contact Clerk of Court
Probate records: From 1864; contact Clerk of Court

*Plymouth County Courthouse
215 Fourth Avenue, S.E.
Le Mars, IA 51031
Phone (712) 546-4215
County organized 1851 from Woodbury County
Land records: From 1856; contact Richard L. Kenyon, Clerk District Court
No land records search service; contact Northwest Iowa Genealogical Society Chapter (IGS), Le Mars Public Library, 46 First Street, S.W., Le Mars, IA 51031
Naturalization records: From 1871; contact Clerk District Court
No naturalization records search service (contact Northwest Iowa Genealogical Society Chapter)
Vital records: Births from 1871, deaths from 1880, marriages from 1860; contact Clerk District Court
No vital records search service (contact Northwest Iowa Genealogical Society Chapter)
Probate records: From 1870; contact Clerk District Court
No probate search service (contact Northwest Iowa Genealogical Society Chapter); copies: 50¢ each, no minimum

*Pocahontas County Courthouse
Pocahontas, IA 50574
Phone (712) 335-4404 Recorder; (712) 335-3361 Auditor
County formed in part from the extensive limits of Buchanan and in part from those of Fayette, created in 1851 from Humboldt and Greene counties, attached for governmental purposes in succession to Polk, Boone and Webster counties, surveyed during 1853-1855, formally organized in March 1859
Land records: Deeds from mid 1856; contact Recorder's Office. Plat Books; contact Auditor's Office; copies: 25¢ each
Naturalization records: From 1867 through about 1926 (many are incomplete); contact James D. Bartosh, Clerk of District Court
Vital records: Births, deaths, and marriages (missing for 1905); contact Clerk of District Court
Vital records search service: $6.00; certified copies: $10.00 each
Probate records: Contact Clerk of District Court

Probate search service: no charge for twenty-year span (extensive searches referred to Laurens Genies Chapter (IGS), c/o Pocahontas Public Library, 14 Second Avenue, N.W., Pocahontas, IA 50574); copies: 25¢ or 50¢ per page, depending on the size of paper, no minimum; "We will look up a record for genealogy purposes for a search fee of $6 when the request is reasonable and *if* the information sought has specific dates and names so that we don't have to spend a lot of time, such as when the request is vaguely submitted, i.e., 'I *think* it was *about*.'"

*Polk County Courthouse
500 Mulberry
Des Moines, IA 50309
Phone (515) 286-3160 County Recorder; (515) 286-3845 County Records Supervisor
County organized 1846 from Indian Lands
Land records: Contact Timothy J. Brien, County Recorder, c/o Administrative Office Building, 111 Court Avenue, Room 250, Des Moines, IA 50309-2294
Naturalization records: Through 1928; contact William Albright, County Records Supervisor, Room 115
Vital records: Births from 1880 to 1920 and from 1941 to date, deaths from 1888 to 1907 and from 1941 to date, marriages from 1846 to date; contact County Records Supervisor. Births, deaths and marriages; contact Iowa Department of Public Health, Vital Records Bureau, Lucas State Office Building, Des Moines, IA 50319-0075; copies: $10.00 each, plus SASE, payable in advance
Probate records: From 1907 to date (if a case is closed and five years have passed, files will be on microfilm); contact County Records Supervisor; copies: 20¢ per page for file copies, 50¢ per page for microfilm copies, $4.00 minimum for microfilm copies, plus SASE, payable in advance

*Pottawattamie County Courthouse
227 South Sixth Street
Council Bluffs, IA 51501-4208
Phone (712) 328-5604
County organized 1848 from Indian Lands
Land records: Contact Auditor's Office
Naturalization records: From 1890 to 1901; contact Clerk's Office
Vital records: Births and deaths from 1880 through 1921 and from 1941 to date, marriages from 1846 to date; contact Clerk of the District Court. Births and deaths from 1921 through

1941; contact Iowa Department of Public Health, Vital Records Bureau, Lucas State Office Building, Des Moines, IA 50319-0075
Vital records search service from Clerk of the District Court: $10.00 (includes certified copy). Vital records search service from Iowa Department of Public Health: $10.00 each
Probate records: From the late 1800s to date; contact Clerk's Office

*Poweshiek County Courthouse
Montezuma, IA 50171
Phone (515) 623-5644 County Recorder or County Clerk of Court; (515) 623-5443 County Auditor
County organized 3 April 1843 from Keokuk, Iowa and Mahaska counties
Land records: From 1850 to date; contact County Recorder; copies: 25¢ per page
Naturalization records: Discontinued in early 1990s; contact County Clerk of Court; copies: $1.00 per page, $10.00 for certified copies
Vital records: From 1880 to date; contact County Clerk of Court; copies: $1.00 per page, $10.00 for certified copies (restricted to relatives or attorneys)
Probate records: From 1840s to date; contact County Clerk of Court; copies: 25¢ per page, $10.00 per document for certified copies

*Ringgold County Courthouse
Mount Ayr, IA 50854
Phone (515) 464-3234; (515) 464-3231 Recorder's Office
County organized 1855 from Taylor County
Land records: Contact County Recorder's Office
Naturalization records: Very few naturalizations from the early 1900s; contact Cindy Johnson, Clerk of the District Court
Vital records: Births, deaths and marriages from 1880; contact Clerk of the District Court ("All our vital records are on microfilm at our County library.")
Probate records: From 1915
Probate search service: no charge, as time permits; copies: 50¢ per page, $10.00 for certified copies

*Sac County Courthouse
PO Box 368
Sac City, IA 50583-0368
Phone (712) 662-7791; (712) 662-7978 FAX
County organized 1851 from Greene County
Land records: Contact County Recorder
Naturalization records: Very few naturalization records

Vital records: From 1888
Probate records: From 1888
Probate search service: $10.00 per search; copies: 25¢ per page

*Scott County Courthouse
416 West Fourth Street
Davenport, IA 52801-1187
Phone (319) 326-7902 Davenport Public Library; (319) 326-8650 Vital Records
County organized 1837 from Wisconsin Territory
Land records: Auditor's Office Land Transfer Books from 1871 to 1918, deed records (land) from 1838 to 1885, deed records (original entries) from 1839 to 1854 and from 1885 to 1913, grantor/grantee index (deeds and mortgages) from 1838 to 1900, town lot deed record from 1855 to 1886; contact Special Collections Room, Davenport Public Library, 321 Main Street, Davenport, IA 52801
Land records search service: limited to 30 minutes; copies of specific records: $3.00 for the first ten pages and 50¢ for each additional page, $3.00 minimum
Naturalization records: Declarations of intention from 1856 to 1924, naturalization documents from 1848 to 1906, naturalization records from 1856 to 1906; contact Special Collections Room
Vital records: Births and deaths from 1880, marriages from 1838; contact Vital Records; certified copies: $10.00 each. Birth records from 1880 to 1911, birth returns from 1880 to 1927, death certificates from 1880 to 1897 (but some portions missing), death records from 1880 to 1931, marriage applications from 1869 to 1892, marriage certificates from 1836 to 1925 (some to 1935), marriage records from 1838 to 1910 and 1917 to 1926, marriage register from 1880 to 1903; contact Special Collections Room
Vital records search service from Special Collections Room: limited to 30 minutes; copies of specific records: $3.00 for the first ten pages and 50¢ for each additional page, $3.00 minimum
Probate records: Administrators' bonds from 1880 to 1885, executors' bonds from 1877 to 1885, guardians' bonds from 1873 to 1886, index from 1838 to 1962, probate appearance docket from 1866 to 1927, probate packets from 1838 to 1947, probate records (transcribed) from 1838 to 1920 and from 1924 to 1925, register of heirs and estates from 1865 to 1923, will records from 1873 to 1895 and from 1921 to 1926, wills (original) from

1838 to February 1930; contact Special Collections Room

Probate search service: limited to 30 minutes; copies of specific records: $3.00 for the first ten pages and 50¢ for each additional page, $3.00 minimum

*Shelby County Courthouse
Harlan, IA 51537
Phone (712) 755-5543 Clerk of Court
County organized 1851 from Cass County
Land records: Contact Linda Jacobsen, County Recorder
Naturalization records: Not very complete; contact Shannon Goeser, Clerk of Court, PO Box 431, Harlan, IA 51537-0431
Vital records: Births and deaths from 1880, marriages from 1853; contact Clerk of Court; certified copies: $10.00 each
Probate records: Contact Clerk of Court
Probate search service: no charge; copies: 50¢ per page, no minimum

*Sioux County Courthouse
Orange City, IA 51041
Phone (712) 737-2216 County Auditor
County organized 1860 from Plymouth County
Land records: Contact County Auditor or County Recorder
Naturalization records: Contact Clerk of District Court
Vital records: Contact Clerk of District Court
Probate records: Contact Clerk of District Court
No probate search service; copies: 25¢ per page

Story County Courthouse
Nevada, IA 50201
Phone (515) 382-6581
County organized 1846 from Jasper, Polk and Boone counties

*Tama County Courthouse
PO Box 306
Toledo, IA 52342-0306
Phone (515) 484-3721
County organized 1843 from Boone and Benton counties
Land records: Contact Assessor's Office
Naturalization records: Contact Tama County Museum, 200 North Broadway, PO Box 84, Toledo, IA 52342
Vital records: Births and deaths from 1880, marriages from 1850; contact Clerk of Court or Tama County Museum (proof of relationship required for certified copies of births, deaths and marriages)

Probate records: From 1890; contact Clerk of Court or Tama County Museum; copies: 25¢ per page, no minimum

*Taylor County Courthouse
Bedford, IA 50833
Phone (712) 523-2095
County organized 1847 from Page County
Land records: Contact County Recorder's Office
Naturalization records: From 1850
Vital records: From 1880
Probate records: From 1858
Probate search service: $6.00; copies: 50¢ each, no minimum

*Union County Courthouse
Creston, IA 50801-2403
Phone (515) 782-7616 Recorder; (515) 782-7315
County organized 1851 from Clarke County
Land records: Contact Recorder's Office; copies: $1.00 per document, payable in advance
Naturalization records: Contact Clerk of Court
Vital records: Contact Clerk of Court
Probate records: Contact Clerk of Court
Probate search service: $6.00; copies: 50¢ each, no minimum; "Payment must accompany request."

*Van Buren County Courthouse
Fourth and Dodge
Keosauqua, IA 52565
Phone (319) 293-3240 Recorder; (319) 293-3129 Auditor; (319) 293-3108 Clerk of Court
County organized 1836 from Des Moines County
Land records: From 1837 to date; contact Recorder and Auditor
Land records search service: no charge (as time allows); copies: 25¢ per page
Vital records: Births and deaths from 1880 to date, marriages from 1837 to date; contact Clerk of Court
Probate records: Wills from 1837 to date; contact Clerk of Court

*Wapello County Courthouse
101 West Fourth Street
Ottumwa, IA 52501
Phone (515) 683-0060
County organized 1843 from Indian Lands
Land records: Contact Recorder
Vital records: Contact Clerk of Court
Vital records search service: $6.00 (must have a "tangible reason" to obtain birth certificates)

*Warren County Courthouse
PO Box 379
Indianola, IA 50125-0379
Phone (515) 961-1033
County organized 1846 from Polk County
Land records: Contact Recorder's Office
Naturalization records: From 1862; contact Deb Lockwood, Clerk of District Court
Vital records: Births and deaths from 1880, marriages from 1850; contact Clerk of District Court
Probate records: From 1858; contact Clerk of District Court
Probate search service: no charge; copies: 25¢ per page, $1.00 minimum; "Must request in writing."

*Washington County Courthouse
PO Box 889
Washington, IA 52353
Phone (319) 653-7727 County Recorder; (319) 653-7742 Clerk of Court
County organized 1837 from Wisconsin Territory
Land records: From 1840; contact County Recorder
Land records search service: $5.00 for a search of grantor-grantee indexes for a short period of years; copies: 25¢ per page
Naturalization records: Some unindexed naturalization records
Vital records: Births and deaths from 1880, marriages from 1844; contact Clerk of Court; copies: $1.00 each, $6.00 for certified copies
Probate records: From 1856
Probate search service: no charge

*Wayne County Courthouse
PO Box 435
Corydon, IA 50060
Phone (515) 872-1676 Recorder's Office; (515) 872-2264 Clerk of Court
County organized 1846 from Appanoose County
Land records: From the 1850s; contact Recorder's Office
Naturalization records: Some in Recorder's Office, some in Clerk of Court's Office
No naturalization records search service (scattered among the records)
Vital records: Births and deaths from the 1880s, marriages from 1851; contact Clerk of Court. A few birth certificates for people born outside of Wayne County; contact Recorder's Office
No vital records search service from Clerk of Court; copies available only if name and correct date are supplied. Vital records search service from Recorder's Office: no charge if supplied with an approximate date

Probate records: From the 1850s; contact
Clerk of Court
No probate search service

Webster County Courthouse
703 Central Avenue
Fort Dodge, IA 50501-3853
Phone (515) 576-7115
*County organized 1853 from Yell and
Risley counties, both of which were
organized in 1851 and abolished in
1853*

Winnebago County Courthouse
Forest City, IA 50436
Phone (515) 582-4520
*County organized 1847 from Kossuth
County*

*Winneshiek County Courthouse
201 West Main
Decorah, IA 52101-1713
Phone (319) 382-2469 Clerk of Court;
(319) 382-3486 Recorder
*County organized 1847 from Indian
Lands*
Land records: Contact Recorder
Naturalization records: Contact Clerk of
Court
Vital records: Contact Clerk of Court
Probate records: Contact Clerk of Court
No probate search service; copies: 50¢
(except $1.00 from old books), no
minimum

*Woodbury County Courthouse
101 Courthouse
Sioux City, IA 51101
Phone (712) 279-6616
*County organized 1851 from Indian
Lands*
Land records: From 1809; contact
County Auditor, 103 Courthouse,
Sioux City, IA 51101
Naturalization records: From 1870 to
1932
Vital records: From 1880 (excluding
adoptions and single parent births)
Probate records: From 18 June 1868;
contact County Clerk
Probate search service: no charge;
copies: 50¢ per page, no minimum

Worth County Courthouse
Northwood, IA 50459
Phone (515) 324-2840
*County organized 1851 from Mitchell
County*

*Wright County Courthouse
PO Box 306
Clarion, IA 50525-0306
Phone (515) 532-3113
*County organized 1851 from Webster
County (Polk County, then Boone,*

then Webster), set up 1855
Land records: From 1850 to date; contact
Clerk of District Court. Other land
records; contact Auditor, PO Box 147
No land records search service; contact
Wright County Genealogical
Searchers Chapter (IGS), PO Box
225, Clarion, IA 50525
Naturalization records: From the 1860s
to date; contact Clerk of District Court
No naturalization records search service;
contact Wright County Genealogical
Searchers Chapter
Vital records: From 1880; contact Clerk
of District Court
No vital records search service; contact
Wright County Genealogical
Searchers Chapter; no copying service
Probate records: From 1880; contact
Clerk of District Court
No probate search service; contact
Wright County Genealogical
Searchers Chapter; copies: 25¢ per
page

KANSAS

*Capital: Topeka. Statehood: 29 January
1861 (annexed as part of the Louisiana
Purchase, 1803, territory created by the
Kansas-Nebraska Act, 1854)*

Court System

Kansas has about 384 Municipal Courts
of limited jurisdiction. The thirty-one Dis-
trict Courts, sitting at each county seat, have
general jurisdiction over civil and criminal
matters, and probate. First Judicial District:
Atchison and Leavenworth counties; Sec-
ond Judicial District: Jackson, Jefferson,
Pottawatomie and Wabaunsee counties;
Third Judicial District: Shawnee County;
Fourth Judicial District: Anderson, Coffey,
Franklin and Osage counties; Fifth Judicial
District: Chase and Lyon counties; Sixth
Judicial District: Bourbon, Linn and Mi-
ami counties; Seventh Judicial District:
Douglas County; Eighth Judicial District:
Dickinson, Geary, Marion and Morris coun-
ties; Ninth Judicial District: Harvey and
McPherson counties; Tenth Judicial Dis-
trict: Johnson County; Eleventh Judicial
District: Cherokee, Crawford and Labette
counties; Twelfth Judicial District: Cloud,
Jewell, Lincoln, Mitchell, Republic and
Washington counties; Thirteenth Judicial
District: Butler, Elk and Greenwood coun-
ties; Fourteenth Judicial District:
Chautauqua and Montgomery counties;
Fifteenth Judicial District: Cheyenne,
Logan, Rawlins, Sheridan, Sherman, Tho-
mas and Wallace counties; Sixteenth Judi-
cial District: Clark, Comanche, Ford, Gray,
Kiowa and Meade counties; Seventeenth
Judicial District: Decatur, Graham, Norton,
Osborne, Phillips and Smith counties; Eigh-
teenth Judicial District: Sedgwick County;
Nineteenth Judicial District: Cowley
County; Twentieth Judicial District: Barton,
Ellsworth, Rice, Russell and Stafford coun-
ties; Twenty-first Judicial District: Clay and
Riley counties; Twenty-second Judicial
District: Brown, Doniphan, Marshall and
Nemaha counties; Twenty-third Judicial
District: Ellis, Gove, Rooks and Trego
counties; Twenty-fourth Judicial District:
Edwards, Hodgeman, Lane, Ness, Pawnee
and Rush counties; Twenty-fifth Judicial
District: Finney, Greeley, Hamilton,
Kearny, Scott and Wichita counties;
Twenty-sixth Judicial District: Grant,
Haskell, Morton, Seward, Stanton and
Stevens counties; Twenty-seventh Judicial
District: Reno County; Twenty-eighth Ju-
dicial District: Ottawa and Saline counties;
Twenty-ninth Judicial District: Wyandotte

County; Thirtieth Judicial District: Barber, Harper, Kingman, Pratt and Sumner counties; Thirty-first Judicial District: Allen, Neosho, Wilson and Woodson counties. A Court of Appeals and the state's Supreme Court have appellate jurisdiction.

Courthouses

*Allen County Courthouse
1 North Washington
Iola, KS 66749-2841
Phone (316) 365-7491
County organized 1855, original county
Land records: Contact Register of Deeds
Naturalization records: Contact Clerk of District Court
Vital records: Contact City Clerk, City Hall, 2 West Jackson, Iola, KS 66749
Probate records: Contact Janel Shaul, Clerk of District Court
No probate search service ("However, if you have a date, we can check to see if there is an estate filed."); copies: 25¢ per page plus postage, no minimum

*Anderson County Courthouse
100 East Fourth Avenue
Garnett, KS 66032-1503
Phone (913) 448-6841
County organized 1855, original county
Land records: Contact Register of Deeds
Naturalization records: Contact District Court Clerk
Probate records: Contact District Court Clerk

*Atchison County Courthouse
423 North Fifth
Atchison, KS 66002-1861
Phone (913) 367-1653
County organized 1855, original county
Land records: From 1855; contact Register of Deeds
Land records search service: $8.00; copies: 25¢ each, $1.00 for certified copies
Naturalization records: From 1855 to date
Vital records: Births and deaths from 1891 to 1911 (sketchy, formerly belonged to a doctor); contact County Clerk's Office; certified copies: $6.00 each (requests should be in writing)
Probate records: From 1855 to date

*Barber County Courthouse
120 East Washington Street
Medicine Lodge, KS 67104-1421
Phone (316) 886-3961
County organized 1873 from Harper County

*Barton County Courthouse
Great Bend, KS 67530
Phone (316) 792-7391
County organized 1867 from Ellsworth County
Probate records: Yes
Probate search service: $9.00 per hour; copies: 35¢ per page (Xerox), 50¢ per page (microfilm), no minimum; "It is very important for us to have correct spellings and accurate dates."

*Bourbon County Courthouse
Fort Scott, KS 66701-1304
Phone (316) 223-3800 Barbara Wood, County Clerk; (316) 223-0780 District Court
County organized 1855, original county
Vital records: Marriages and divorces; contact District Court. Deaths from 1898 to 1911; contact Konantz-Cheney Funeral Home, 15 Wall, Fort Scott, KS 66701. Deaths from 1890 to 1911; contact Cheney-Witt Memorial Chapel, 201 South Main, Fort Scott, KS 66701.

Brown County Courthouse
Hiawatha, KS 66434
Phone (913) 742-2581
County organized 1855, original county

Butler County Courthouse
El Dorado, KS 67042
Phone (316) 321-1960
County organized 1855, original county

*Chase County Courthouse
Cottonwood Falls, KS 66845
Phone (316) 273-6423
County organized 1859 from Butler County
Land records: Contact Register of Deeds

*Chautauqua County Courthouse
215 Chautauqua
Sedan, KS 67361-1326
Phone (316) 725-5800; (316) 725-5830 Register of Deeds; (316) 725-5870 Clerk of District Court
County organized 1875 from Howard County, which was organized in 1855 (named Godfrey and changed to Seward in 1867) and abolished at the time of its division into Chautauqua and Elk counties
Land records: Contact Register of Deeds
Naturalization records: No naturalization records
Vital records: No vital records
Probate records: Contact Clerk of District Court
No probate search service; copies: 25¢ each

Cherokee County Courthouse
PO Box 14
300 East Maple
Columbus, KS 66725
Phone (316) 429-2159
County organized 1855 from unorganized territory; name changed from McGee County between 1860 and 1870

*Cheyenne County Historical Society
(Courthouse Basement)
PO Box 611
Saint Francis, KS 67756-0611
Phone (913) 332-2401
County organized 1886 from Rawlins County
Land records: Contact Office of the Register of Deeds, PO Box 907, Saint Francis, KS 67756
Naturalization records: Contact Office of the Clerk of the District Court, PO Box 646, Saint Francis, KS 67756
Vital records: Births from 1885 to 1895, deaths (all), marriages from 1885 to 1920
Probate records: Contact Office of the Clerk of the District Court
No probate search service; contact Marilyn Holzwarth, PO Box 671, Saint Francis, KS 67756; copies: 25¢ per page, 25¢ minimum

*Clark County Courthouse
Ashland, KS 67831
Phone (316) 635-2813; (316) 635-2812 Register of Deeds; (316) 635-2753 Clerk of the District Court
County organized 1873 from Ford County
Land records: Contact Register of Deeds, PO Box 222, Ashland, KS 67831
Naturalization records: Contact Clerk of the District Court, PO Box 790, Ashland, KS 67831
Probate records: Contact Clerk of the District Court

*Clay County Courthouse
PO Box 98
Clay Center, KS 67432-0098
Phone (913) 632-2552
County organized 1857, original county
Land records: Contact Register of Deeds, PO Box 63, Clay Center, KS 67432
Naturalization records: Contact Kayla Ernsting, Clerk of the District Court, PO Box 203, Clay Center, KS 67432. Many early records transferred to Clay County Historical Society Museum, 2121 Seventh Street, Clay Center, KS 67432.
Vital records: From 1885 to 1911; contact County Clerk. Many early records transferred to Clay County Historical Society Museum, 2121

Seventh Street, Clay Center, KS
67432.
Vital records search service: $5.00
minimum
Probate records: Contact Clerk of the
District Court
Probate search service: $9.00 per hour;
copies: 25¢ per page

*Cloud County Courthouse
811 Washington
Concordia, KS 66901-3415
Phone (913) 243-4319
*County organized 1860 from
unorganized territory; name changed
from Shirley County in 1861*
Land records: Contact Register of Deeds
Naturalization records: Contact Clerk of
the District Court, PO Box 314,
Concordia, KS 66901
Vital records: To 1911; contact County
Clerk
Probate records: Contact Clerk of the
District Court
Probate search service: $2.00 per search;
copies: 25¢ per page, no minimum

*Coffey County Courthouse
110 South Sixth
Burlington, KS 66839
Phone (316) 364-2191
*County organized 1855 from Kiowa
County*
Land records: Contact Register of Deeds
Naturalization records: Contact District
Court; copies: 15¢ per page
Vital records: Births and deaths from
1892 to 1910; contact County Clerk's
Office. Marriage licenses; contact
District Court. Certified copies: $1.15
each
Probate records: Contact District Court
Probate search service: as time permits;
copies: from 15¢ to $1.00 per page,
$1.00 minimum plus SASE

*Comanche County Courthouse
201 South New York
Coldwater, KS 67029
Phone (316) 582-2152 Register of Deeds;
(316) 582-2361 County Clerk
*County organized 1875 from Kiowa
County*
Land records: From 1883; contact
Guyneth Snyder, Register of Deeds,
PO Box 576, Coldwater, KS 67029;
copies: $1.50 per page
Vital records: From 1891 to 1912;
contact Alice Smith, County Clerk,
PO Box 776, Coldwater, KS 67029-
0776

Cowley County Courthouse
Winfield, KS 67156
Phone (316) 221-4066
*County organized 1867; name changed
from Hunter County*

*Crawford County Courthouse
PO Box 249
Girard, KS 66743-0249
Phone (316) 724-6115; (316) 724-8158
Register of Deeds; (316) 724-8823
FAX, Register of Deeds
*County organized 1867 from Bourbon
and Cherokee counties*
Land records: Contact Jeanette Nepote,
Register of Deeds, PO Box 44, Girard,
KS 66743
Naturalization records: Contact District
Court Office
Vital records: Births and deaths from
1886 to 1911; contact Dan Brunetti,
County Clerk; certified copies: $3.00
each. Marriage licenses; contact
District Court Office
Probate records: Contact District Court
Office

*Decatur County Courthouse
194 South Penn
Oberlin, KS 67749-2243
Phone (913) 475-2132
*County organized 1873 from Norton
County*
Land records: From 1885
Naturalization records: Initial papers
from 1881 to 1906, petitions and
records from 1901 to 1929, first
papers from 1880 to 1894
Vital records: Births from 10 November
1885 to 6 July 1911 (with some gaps),
deaths from 5 December 1885 to 31
July 1911 (with some gaps), marriages
from 21 February 1880 (with some
gaps)
Probate records: From 2 March 1900
No probate search service ("The Decatur
County Historical Society will do
research"); copies: 25¢ per page (8½" x
11"), 30¢ (17" x 11") plus certification

*Dickinson County Courthouse
PO Box 248
Abilene, KS 67410
Phone (913) 263-3774; (913) 263-3073
Linda Jones, Register of Deeds
County organized 1855, original county
Land records: From 1859 (deeds,
mortgages, land patents, oil & gas
leases and other miscellaneous
documents); contact Karen J.
Freeman, Clerk, Register of Deeds
Office
Land records search service: no charge;
copies: 25¢ per page from paper
originals, $1.00 per page from
microfilm originals
Naturalization records: Some
naturalization records; contact District
Court
Vital records: Births from 1895 to 1911,
deaths from 1901 to 1911; contact
County Clerk's Office. Marriages
from the 1870s; contact District Court

Probate records: From the 1870s; contact
District Court
Probate search service: usually no
charge; copies: $1.00 per page, no
charge; "Have correct names and the
dates as close as you can to the time
that you are searching for."

Doniphan County Courthouse
Troy, KS 66087
Phone (913) 985-3513
County organized 1855, original county

*Douglas County Courthouse
111 East 11th
Lawrence, KS 66044-2912
Phone (913) 841-7700
County organized 1855, original county
Land records: Contact Sue Neustifter,
Register of Deeds
Naturalization records: From 1865 to
1920; contact Sherlyn Sampson,
Deputy Clerk of District Court
Probate records: Contact Deputy Clerk of
District Court
Probate search service: $9.00 per hour;
copies: 25¢ per page, no minimum;
"Money must be estimated and paid in
advance; request must be in writing or
in person."

*Edwards County Courthouse
312 Massachusetts
Kinsley, KS 67547-1059
Phone (316) 659-3121
*County organized 1874 from Kiowa
County*
Land records: Contact Register of Deeds
Naturalization records: Contact County
Clerk
Vital records: Contact County Clerk
Probate records: Contact District Court
Clerk

*Elk County Courthouse
127 North Pine
Howard, KS 67349
Phone (316) 374-2490
*County organized 1875 from Howard
County, which was organized in 1855
(named Godfrey and changed to
Seward in 1867) and abolished at the
time of its division into Chautauqua
and Elk counties*
Land records: Contact Neva L. Walter,
Register of Deeds, PO Box 476,
Howard, KS 67349
Land records search service: $5.00;
copies 25¢ plus postage
Vital records: Contact Register of Deeds
Vital records search service: $5.00;
copies 25¢ plus postage
Probate records: Contact Nadine Fickle,
Clerk of the District Court, PO Box
306, Howard, KS 67349
Probate search service: $3.00 plus extra

time; copies: 25¢ (standard size), $1.00 (oversized), no minimum

*Ellis County Courthouse
1204 Fort Street
Hays, KS 67601-3831
Phone (913) 628-9410 County Clerk;
(913) 628-9450 Register of Deeds;
(913) 628-9415 District Court
County organized 1867 from unorganized territory
Land records: Contact Register of Deeds, 1204 Fort Street, PO Box 654, Hays, KS 67601
Naturalization records: Contact County District Court, PO Box 8, Hays, KS 67601
Vital records: Contact County Clerk, 1204 Fort Street, PO Box 720, Hays, KS 67601
Probate records: Contact County District Court

*Ellsworth County Courthouse
Ellsworth, KS 67439
Phone (913) 472-3022 Register of Deeds
County organized 1867 from Saline County
Land records: From 1872; contact Register of Deeds, PO Box 306, Ellsworth, KS 67439; copies: $1.00 per page
Naturalization records: Contact Peggy Svaty, District Court, Ellsworth, KS 67439
Probate records: From 1881; contact District Court
Probate search service: no charge; copies: 35¢ per page, no minimum; "Written requests only."

Finney County Courthouse
PO Box M
Garden City, KS 67846-0450
Phone (316) 276-3051
County organized 1883 from Arapahoe and Foote counties; Garfield County was annexed to Finney County in 1893

Ford County Courthouse
Dodge City, KS 67801
Phone (316) 227-3184
County organized 1873 from unorganized territory

Franklin County Courthouse
Ottawa, KS 66067
Phone (913) 242-1471
County organized 1855, original county

*Geary County Courthouse
Eighth and Franklin
Junction City, KS 66441
Phone (913) 238-3912; (913) 762-5221

County organized 1876 from Riley County; name changed from Davis County in 1889
Land records: Contact Register of Deeds, Geary County Courthouse Annex
Naturalization records: Contact Clerk of the District Court
Probate records: Contact Clerk of the District Court
Probate search service: $9.00 per hour; copies: $1.00 per page, no minimum

*Gove County Courthouse
PO Box 128
Gove, KS 67736-0128
Phone (913) 938-2300
County organized 1880 from Rooks County
Land records: Contact Register of Deeds
Naturalization records: Contact Clerk of District Court
Vital records: Births and deaths to 1911
Probate records: Contact Clerk of District Court
No probate search service; no minimum

Graham County Courthouse
410 Pomeroi
Hill City, KS 67642-1645
Phone (913) 674-5433
County organized 1881 from Rooks County

Grant County Courthouse
108 South Glen
Ulysses, KS 67880-2551
Phone (316) 356-1335
County organized 1873 from Finney and Kearny counties

*Gray County Courthouse
PO Box 487
Cimarron, KS 67835
Phone (316) 855-3618
County organized 1887 from Finney and Ford counties
Land records: Contact Register of Deeds
Naturalization records: Contact Clerk of District Court
Vital records: Contact Clerk of District Court
Probate records: Contact Clerk of District Court

*Greeley County Courthouse
PO Box 277
Tribune, KS 67879-0277
Phone (316) 376-4256
County attached to Hamilton County for judicial purposes in March 1886, organized 6 November 1888
Land records: Contact Register of Deeds, PO Box 12, Tribune, KS 67879
Naturalization records: Yes
Vital records: Yes

Probate records: Contact Clerk of the District Court, PO Box 516, Tribune, KS 67879

*Greenwood County Courthouse
311 North Main
Eureka, KS 67045
Phone (316) 583-8121; (316) 583-8124 FAX
County organized 1855, original county
Land records: Patent and deed records from 1850s; contact Register of Deeds
Naturalization records: Mostly complete
Vital records: From 1885 to 1911
Probate records: Contact County Clerk or Clerk of the Court or Office of the Magistrate Judge
No probate search service; copies: 25¢; genealogical inquiries to the County Clerk are referred to the Greenwood County Historical Society (117 North Main, Eureka, KS 67045), which accepts donations for its volunteer services

*Hamilton County Courthouse
219 North Main
PO Box 1167
Syracuse, KS 67878
Phone (316) 384-6925 Register of Deeds;
(316) 384-5629 County Clerk
County organized 1873 from unorganized territory
Land records: Contact Vivian Roberts, Register of Deeds; copies: $1.00 per page
Probate records: Contact Beverly Holdren, County Clerk; copies: $1.00 per page

*Harper County Courthouse
Anthony, KS 67003
Phone (316) 842-5336 Register of Deeds;
(316) 842-5555 County Clerk
County organized 1879 from Kingman County
Land records: Contact Register of Deeds
Land records search service: no charge; copies: $1.00 per page
Vital records: Before 1911 (incomplete); contact City Clerk, Anthony, KS 67003
Probate records: Contact County District Court
Probate search service: no charge; copies: 25¢ per page, $1.00 for certification, no minimum

*Harvey County Courthouse
PO Box 687
Newton, KS 67114
Phone (316) 284-6800
County organized 1872 from McPherson and Sedgwick counties
Land records: Contact Register of Deeds
Naturalization records: Yes

Vital records: Yes
Probate records: Contact District Court

Haskell County Courthouse
Sublette, KS 67877
Phone (316) 675-2263
County organized 1887 from Finney County

Hodgeman County Courthouse
Jetmore, KS 67854
Phone (316) 357-6421
County organized 1873 from Indian Lands

*Jackson County Courthouse
Courthouse Square
Holton, KS 66436
Phone (913) 364-2891; (913) 364-3591 Register of Deeds
County organized 1855 from Calhoun County
Land records: Deeds, mortgages, etc. from 1959 [sic], school records from 1883 to 1966; contact Carol Bickford, Register of Deeds
Naturalization records: Contact Clerk of District Court
Vital records: Marriages from 1854; contact Clerk of the District Court
Probate records: From 1854; contact Clerk of District Court
Probate search service: $9.00 per hour; copies: 25¢ per page, no minimum

*Jefferson County Courthouse
PO Box 321
Oskaloosa, KS 66066-0321
Phone (913) 863-2272 County Clerk; (913) 863-2070 Jefferson County Genealogical Society, Inc.
County organized 1855, original county
Land records; Contact County Clerk
Vital records: Contact Jefferson County Genealogical Society, Inc., Research Center, Highway 59, Old Jefferson Town, PO Box 174, Oskaloosa, KS 66066-0174
Probate records: Contact County Clerk

*Jewell County Courthouse
307 North Commercial
Mankato, KS 66956-2025
Phone (913) 378-3121 County Clerk; (913) 378-3951 Register of Deeds; (913) 378-3651 District Court
County organized 1867 from Mitchell County
Land records: Land ownership from when land patented, assessment rolls from 1871, school records from 1884; contact Register of Deeds
Land records search service: no charge; copies: $1.00 per page plus postage
Naturalization records: From 1872 to 1937; contact County District Court

Vital records: Unofficial register of births, marriages and deaths (only births are indexed) from 1886 to 1894; contact Register of Deeds. Marriages from 1871; contact County District Court
Probate records: From 1871; contact County District Court
Probate search service: no charge; copies: 25¢ per page plus postage, no minimum

*Johnson County Courthouse
Santa Fe and Kansas
Olathe, KS 66061
Phone (913) 782-5000; (913) 764-8484, ext. 6174, Archives and Records Management; (913) 791-5000 FAX, Archives and Records Management; (913) 764-8484, ext. 5571 Clerk of the District Court, Probate Division
County organized 1855, original county
Land records: Yes
Naturalization records: From 1872 to 1952; contact Gerald A. Motsinger, Director, Archives and Records Management, Johnson County Administration Building, Johnson County Square, 111 South Cherry Street, Suite 500, Olathe, KS 66061-3441
Naturalization records search service from Archives and Records Management: no charge; copies: 25¢ each
Vital records: Marriages from 1857 to 1971; contact Archives and Records Management
Vital records search service from Archives and Records Management: no charge; copies: 25¢ each
Probate records: Contact Clerk of the District Court, Probate Division. Wills from 1878 to 1969; contact Archives and Records Management
Probate search service from Archives and Records Management: no charge; copies: 25¢ each

*Kearny County Courthouse
Lakin, KS 67860
Phone (316) 355-6422
County organized 1873 from Finney County
Land records: Contact Register of Deeds, PO Box 42, Lakin, KS 67860
Naturalization records: Contact Clerk of the District Court, PO Box 64, Lakin, KS 67860
Vital records: Births, deaths and marriages from 1900 to 1910; contact County Clerk, PO Box 86, Lakin, KS 67860
Probate records: Contact Clerk of the District Court
Probate search service: $9.00 per hour; copies: 25¢ per page, no minimum

*Kingman County Courthouse
Kingman, KS 67068
Phone (316) 532-2521; (316) 532-5151 Clerk of District Court; (316) 532-3111 City Clerk and Register of Deeds
County organized 1874 from unorganized territory
Land records: Open to the public on the fourth floor of the courthouse (no search services)
Naturalization records: Contact Clerk of District Court
Vital records: Births; contact City Clerk. Deaths; contact Register of Deeds
Probate records: Contact Clerk of District Court
Probate search service: $9.00 per hour; copies: 25¢ per page, $2.00 minimum

*Kiowa County Courthouse
211 East Florida
Greensburg, KS 67054-2211
Phone (316) 723-3366; (316) 723-3317 Clerk of District Court
County organized 1886 from Comanche and Edwards counties, abolished in 1875, and recreated in 1886 from Comanche and Edwards counties
Land records: Contact Faye Hargadine, Register of Deeds, or Evelyn Grimm, Clerk
Naturalization records: No naturalization records
Vital records: Contact Register of Deeds
Probate records: Contact Billie Huckriede, Clerk of District Court
Probate search service: $9.00 per hour; copies: 25¢ per page plus SASE, no minimum

*Labette County Courthouse
517 Merchant
Oswego, KS 67356
Phone (316) 795-2138 Clerk; (316) 795-4931 Register of Deeds; (316) 795-4533 District Court
County organized 1867 from Neosho County
Land records: From 1869; contact Register of Deeds
Vital records: Births from 1885 to 1896, deaths from 1885 to 1889; contact County Clerk, PO Box 387, Oswego, KS 67356
Probate records: Contact District Court
No probate search service; copies: 25¢ per page

*Lane County Courthouse
PO Box 188
Dighton, KS 67839-0788
Phone (316) 397-5552 District Court
County organized 1873 from Finney County
Land records: From 1885; contact Probate Court

Naturalization records: From 1885 to 1935

Vital records: From 1885 to 1915, marriage licenses from 1885

Probate records: Estates from 1885

Probate search service: $8.00 per hour; copies: 25¢ per page plus postage

*Leavenworth County Courthouse
Fourth and Walnut
Leavenworth, KS 66048
Phone (913) 684-0400 District Court
County organized 1855, original county
Land records: Contact Register of Deeds
Naturalization records: Very few records available ("as courthouse fire in 1911 destroyed a great many of them.")
Vital records: Marriages; contact Clerk of District Court
Probate records: Contact Clerk of District Court
Probate search service: no charge at present; copies: 25¢ per page, $1.00 for certified copies, no minimum; "If copies are requested by mail, payment should be by money order, not cash or personal check."

*Lincoln County Courthouse
Lincoln, KS 67455
Phone (913) 524-4757
County organized 1867 from Ellsworth County
Land records: Yes
Naturalization records: Yes
Vital records: Marriages
Probate records: Yes

*Linn County Courthouse
315 Main
PO Box 350
Mound City, KS 66056-0601
Phone (913) 795-2660 District Court
County organized 1855, original county
Land records: Contact Register of Deeds Office
Searches referred to Linn County Historical and Genealogical Society
Naturalization records: Very limited information; contact Judicial Building
Probate records: Contact Judicial Building
Probate search service: $10.00 per hour by Linn County Historical and Genealogical Society, $5.00 for trip to the courthouse; copies: 10¢ per page

*Logan County Courthouse
710 West Second
Oakley, KS 67748-1251
Phone (913) 672-4224 Register of Deeds; (913) 672-3654 Clerk of District Court
County organized 1887 from the entirety of Saint John County, which was established 13 March 1881 out of

what previously had been in the eastern part of Wallace County
Land records: Contact Register of Deeds Office
Probate records: Contact Clerk of District Court
Probate search service: contact Abstracters' Office; copies: 25¢ per page, $1.00 minimum

*Lyon County Courthouse
402 Commercial
Emporia, KS 66801-4000
Phone (316) 342-4950
County organized 1857 from Madison County (which was abolished at the time it was divided between Lyon and Greenwood counties); name changed from Breckinridge County in 1862
Land records: Contact Lyon County Clerk's Office
Naturalization records: Contact County District Court
Probate records: Contact County District Court
Probate search service: $6.60 per hour; copies: 50¢ per page, no minimum; "Most things take one hour; send $6.60 in advance; Lyon County Historical Society might help you."

*Marion County Courthouse
Marion, KS 66861
Phone (316) 382-2185
County organized 1855 from Chase County
Land records: Contact Dorothy Lawrence, Register of Deeds
Vital records: From 1885 to 1911; contact Marquetta Eilerts, County Clerk (research: $3.00)
Probate records: Contact Geraldine Seibel, Clerk of District Court
No probate search service; copies: 25¢ per page, 15¢ for ten or more

*Marshall County Courthouse
1201 Broadway
Marysville, KS 66508-1844
Phone (913) 562-5361 County Clerk; (913) 562-3226 Register of Deeds; (913) 562-5301 Clerk of District Court
County organized 1855, original county
Land records: Land records, school records, veterans' discharges; contact Register of Deeds
Naturalization records: Contact Clerk of District Court, PO Box 86, Marysville, KS 66508
Naturalization records search service: $9.00 per hour, $2.25 minimum; copies: 50¢ for the first page, 25¢ for each additional page, $1.00 for certification
Vital records: Births from November

1885 to August 1911, deaths from May 1889 to August 1911 (except 1890 and 1891); contact County Clerk
Probate records: Contact Clerk of District Court
Probate search service: $9.00 per hour, $2.25 minimum; copies: 50¢ for the first page, 25¢ for each additional page, $1.00 for certification

*McPherson County Courthouse
PO Box 425
McPherson, KS 67460-0425
Phone (316) 241-3656
County organized 1867 from unorganized territory
Vital records: From 1888 to 1905; contact County Clerk

*Meade County Courthouse
PO Box 278
Meade, KS 67864-0278
Phone (316) 873-8700
County organized 1873 from unorganized territory; proclamation November 1855
Land records: Contact Register of Deeds, PO Box 399, Meade, KS 67864
Probate records: Contact Clerk of District Court, PO Box 623, Meade, KS 67864

*Miami County Courthouse
120 South Pearl
Paola, KS 66071
Phone (913) 294-3976
County organized 1855; name changed from Lykins County
Land records: Yes
Naturalization records: Yes
Vital records: Yes
Probate records: Yes
No probate search service; "Please contact Genealogy Society Research, PO Box 123, Paola, KS 66071, Attn: Vera Dakin; we have released our records to them through The Church of Jesus Christ of Latter-day Saints, and they also have additional resources."

*Mitchell County Courthouse
111 South Hersey
Beloit, KS 67420
Phone (913) 738-3854 Register of Deeds; (913) 738-5844 FAX, Register of Deeds; (913) 738-3644 County Highway Department; (913) 738-3753 District Court; (913) 738-3652 County Clerk's Office
County formed 1870 from Kirwin Land District
Land records: Contact Susanne Thompson, Register of Deeds, PO Box 6, Beloit, KS 67420; copies: $1.00 each. Plats and maps (limited); contact County Highway Department

Naturalization records: From about 1876; contact District Court

Vital records: Marriage licenses from about 1876; contact District Court

Probate records: From about 1876; contact District Court

*Montgomery County Courthouse
Independence, KS 67301
Phone (316) 331-2180 Register of Deeds; (316) 331-4510 County Appraiser; (316) 331-4840 County Clerk; (316) 331-2550 Clerk of the Court
County organized 1867 from Labette County
Land records: Contact Jeannie Burton, Register of Deeds or Bill Hendrix, County Appraiser
Naturalization records: Contact Charlotte A. Scott, County Clerk
Vital records: Births and deaths from 1887 to 1911; contact County Clerk; certified copies: $3.00 each
Probate records: Contact Glenda Hubbard, Clerk of the Court, Montgomery County Judicial Center, 300 East Main, Independence, KS 67301

Morris County Courthouse
Council Grove, KS 66846
Phone (316) 767-5518
County organized 1855 from Madison County

*Morton County Courthouse
PO Box 1116
Elkhart, KS 67950-1116
Phone (316) 697-2157 County Clerk; (316) 697-2159 FAX, County Clerk; (316) 624-6865 Methodist Mexican American Affairs
County constructed out of the territory belonging to Seward County in 1883, and comprising the territory defined originally as Kansas County (1873), except that it extends three miles further east; it was organized 20 February 1886; prior to 1887, it was attached to Hamilton County for judicial purposes
Land records: Contact County Register of Deeds, PO Box 756, Elkhart, KS 67950
Naturalization records: Contact Methodist Mexican American Affairs, 311 North Grand, Liberal, KS 67901
Vital records: Contact Mary C. Gilmore, County Clerk, 1025 Morton, PO Box 1116, Elkhart, KS 67950-1116
Probate records: Contact District Court, PO Box 825, Elkhart, KS 67950
Probate search service: $9.00 per hour; copies: 25¢ per page, no minimum

*Nemaha County Courthouse
607 Nemaha

Seneca, KS 66538
Phone (913) 336-2170; (913) 336-2146 District Court
County organized 1855, original county
Land records: From 1858 to date; copies: 25¢ each for 8½" x 11" (35¢ two-sided), 35¢ each for 8½" x 14" (50¢ two-sided)
Naturalization records: Limited records from 1859 to 1946; contact District Court
Vital records: From 1885 through 1911; contact County Clerk's Office; certified copies: $2.00 each. Marriage licenses from 1832 to date; contact District Court; certified copies: $1.25 each
Probate records: From 1857 to date; contact District Court
Probate search service: $9.00 per hour; copies: 25¢ each, $1.00 for certification

*Neosho County Courthouse
PO Box 138
Erie, KS 66733
Phone (316) 244-3800
County organized 1855 from Labette County
Land records: From 1867; contact Leora N. Smith, Register of Deeds; copies: $1.00 per page from large bound books, 25¢ per page from small books, $1.00 for certified copies
Naturalization records: Contact District Clerk's Office; copies: 25¢ per page, $1.00 for certified copies
Vital records: Very few births; contact County Clerk's Office. Marriages from 1867 to date; contact District Clerk's Office; copies: 25¢ per page, $1.00 for certified copies
Probate records: From 1867; contact District Clerk's Office; copies: 25¢ per page, $1.00 for certified copies

*Ness County Courthouse
202 West Sycamore Street
Ness City, KS 67560-1558
Phone (913) 798-2401
County organized June 1880 from Ness [sic] County
Land records: Contact Register of Deeds, PO Box 127, Ness City, KS 67560
Naturalization records: Contact Clerk of District Court or District Magistrate Judge, PO Box 445, Ness City, KS 67560
Vital records: Marriages; contact Clerk of Courts (may be received from the Clerk of the District Magistrate Judge)
Probate records: Contact District Magistrate Judge (has affidavits of death in some earlier cases)
Probate search service: no charge; copies: 25¢ per page, no minimum

*Norton County Courthouse
PO Box 70
Norton, KS 67654-0070
Phone (913) 877-5710 County Clerk; (913) 877-5765 Register of Deeds; (913) 877-5720 Clerk of the District Court
County organized 1872 from unorganized territory
Land records: Contact Register of Deeds
Naturalization records: Contact Clerk of the District Court
Vital records: Contact Clerk of the District Court
Probate records: Contact Clerk of the District Court

*Osage County Courthouse
717 Topeka Avenue
Lyndon, KS 66451
Phone (913) 828-4812
County organized 1855, original county; name changed from Weller County 11 February 1859
Land records: From 1859; contact Register of Deeds Office
Naturalization records: From 1906 to 1929; contact Clerk of the District Court
Vital records: Births, deaths and marriages from 1885 to 1912; contact County Clerk. Marriage licenses from 1960; contact Clerk of the District Court
Probate records: From 1875; contact Clerk of the District Court
Probate search service: $8.00 per hour; copies: 15¢ per page, $1.00 per page for certification, no minimum

*Osborne County Courthouse
West Main Street
Osborne, KS 67473
Phone (913) 346-5911 Clerk of the District Court; (913) 346-2452 Register of Deeds
County organized 1867 from Mitchell County
Land records: From 1870; contact Register of Deeds
Land records search service: $2.00 for searches under thirty minutes, otherwise $5.00 per hour; copies 25¢ per page
Naturalization records: From 1876; contact Clerk of the District Court
Vital records: Marriages from 1872; contact Clerk of the District Court
Probate records: From 1880; contact Clerk of the District Court
Probate search service: $9.00 per hour; copies: 25¢ per page, no minimum

Ottawa County Courthouse
Minneapolis, KS 67467
Phone (913) 392-2279

County organized 1866 from Saline County

Pawnee County Courthouse
715 Broadway
Larned, KS 67550-3054
Phone (316) 285-3721
County organized 1872 from Rush and Stafford counties

*Phillips County Courthouse
301 State Street
Phillipsburg, KS 67661
Phone (913) 543-6875 Registrar of Deeds; (913) 543-6830 Clerk of the District Court
County organized 1872 from Kirwin Land District
Land records: Contact Registrar of Deeds
Naturalization records: Some naturalization records; contact Clerk of the District Court. Some naturalization records; contact Decatur County.
Vital records: Marriages and adoptions; contact Clerk of the District Court
Probate records: Contact Clerk of the District Court

*Pottawatomie County Courthouse
Westmoreland, KS 66549
Phone (913) 457-3314
County organized 1857 from Indian Lands
Land records: Contact Register of Deeds
Naturalization records: Contact Clerk of the District Court
Vital records: Births and deaths from 1857 to 1900; contact County Clerk. Marriages; contact Clerk of the District Court
Probate records: Contact Clerk of the District Court
Probate search service: $2.00 per name, as time permits; copies: 25¢ per page, $2.00 for certified copies, $1.00 minimum

Pratt County Courthouse
Pratt, KS 67124
Phone (316) 672-7761
County organized 1870 from Stafford County

*Rawlins County Courthouse
607 Main Street
Atwood, KS 67730-1839
Phone (913) 626-3351; (913) 626-3394 Delores A. Luedke
County organized 1873 from Kirwin Land District
Land records: Contact Register of Deeds
Land records search service: c/o Delores A. Luedke, PO Box 42, Atwood, KS 67730: for donation to The Rawlins

County Genealogical Society Reader Printer Fund
Naturalization records: Contact Clerk of District Court
Naturalization records search service: c/o Delores A. Luedke
Vital records: A few; contact City Clerk, 106 South Third, Atwood, KS 67730
Vital records search service: c/o Delores A. Luedke
Probate records: Yes
Probate search service: c/o Delores A. Luedke

*Reno County Courthouse
206 West First Street
Hutchinson, KS 67501-5245
Phone (316) 694-2942 Register of Deeds; (316) 694-2934 County Clerk
County organized 1872 from Sedgwick County
Land records: From 1872; contact Register of Deeds; copies: $1.00 per page
Naturalization records: Contact District Court (to be checked by local abstract company or the persons themselves)
Vital records: Births and deaths from 1890 to 1910; contact Roxanne Wheatley, County Clerk; certified copies: $2.00 each
Probate records: Contact District Court (to be checked by local abstract company or the persons themselves)
No probate search service; no copy service

Republic County Courthouse
Rt. 1
Belleville, KS 66935-9801
Phone (913) 527-5691
County organized 1868 from Washington and Cloud counties

*Rice County Courthouse
101 West Commercial
Lyons, KS 67554
Phone (316) 257-2232
County organized 1867 from Reno County
Land records: Contact Register of Deeds
Naturalization records: Contact Clerk of the District Court
Probate records: Contact Clerk of the District Court

Riley County Courthouse
110 Courthouse Plaza
Manhattan, KS 66502-6018
Phone (913) 537-0700
County organized 1855 from Wabaunsee County

*Rooks County Courthouse
115 North Walnut Street

Stockton, KS 67669-1663
Phone (913) 425-6718 Clerk of the District Court
County organized 1872 from Kirwin Land District
Vital records: Births and deaths from 1888 to 1905 (not indexed), marriages from 1888; contact Virginia Doughty, Clerk of the District Court
Probate records: From 1880; contact Clerk of the District Court
Probate search service: $9.00 per hour; copies: 25¢ per page

*Rush County Courthouse
715 Elm Street
La Crosse, KS 67548
Phone (913) 222-3312 Register of Deeds; (913) 222-2718 District Court
County organized 1874 from unorganized territory
Land records: Contact Register of Deeds; copies: $1.00 per instrument
Naturalization records: Contact County District Court, PO Box 387, La Crosse, KS 67548; copies: 25¢ each
Vital records: Marriage licenses; contact County District Court; "On marriage licenses we need the name and approximate date."
Probate records: Contact County District Court
Probate search service: $9.00 per hour if it is an extensive search; copies: 25¢ each, no minimum; "On probates we need the name."

Russell County Courthouse
Russell, KS 67665
Phone (913) 483-4641
County organized 1867 from Ellsworth County

Saint John County
(see Logan County)

*Saline County Courthouse
300 West Ash
Salina, KS 67401-2396
Phone (913) 826-6540; (913) 826-6570 Register of Deeds; (913) 926-6610 County Clerk of the District Court
County organized 1860, original county
Land records: From 1860 to date; contact Register of Deeds
Probate records: Contact County Clerk of the District Court

*Scott County Courthouse
303 Court Street
Scott City, KS 67871-1122
Phone (316) 872-2420
County organized 1873 from Finney County
Land records: Contact Appraiser

Naturalization records: Contact Finney County Courthouse
Vital records: Contact County Clerk
Probate records: Contact District Court Clerk
No probate search service; copies: 25¢ per page

*Sedgwick County Courthouse
525 North Main
Wichita, KS 67203
Phone (316) 268-7474
County organized 1867 from Butler County
Probate records: Contact Clerk, Room 925
No probate search service; copies: 25¢ per page, $1.00 for certification, no minimum

*Seward County Courthouse
415 North Washington
Liberal, KS 67901-3462
Phone (316) 624-0211
County laid out, along with Kansas and Stevens counties, in 1873 from Indian Lands; the legislature passed an act fixing the boundaries of the three counties on 7 March 1875; in 1883 the three counties became one, with Seward county extending to the Colorado-Kansas line
Land records: Yes
Land records search service: $3.00 per name search on U.C.C. filings, otherwise $6.00 per hour; copies: 50¢ each
Vital records: Contact City Hall, 325 North Washington, Liberal, KS 67901
Probate records: Contact District Court
No probate search service, "You search your own records or have an abstract company do the searching."

*Shawnee County Courthouse
200 S.E. Seventh
Topeka, KS 66603-3922
Phone (913) 233-8200, ext. 4020 Register of Deeds; (913) 233-8200, ext. 4625 County Clerk; (913) 233-8200, ext. 5156 Probate
County organized 1855, original county
Land records: Contact Register of Deeds
Vital records: Births and deaths from 1894 to 1911, marriages from February 1856 through 10 June 1906; contact County Clerk's Office, Room 107
Probate records: Contact Joyce D. Reeves, Clerk of the District Court, Room 209
Probate search service: $9.00 per hour; copies: 50¢ per page, no minimum; "Release of Copy Request must be signed."

Sheridan County Courthouse
PO Box 899
Hoxie, KS 67740-0899
Phone (913) 675-3361
County organized 1873 from unorganized territory

*Sherman County Courthouse
Goodland, KS 67735
County organized 1873 from Kirwin Land District
Land records: Contact Register of Deeds, 813 Broadway, Room 104, Goodland, KS 67735
Probate records: Contact District Court, 813 Broadway, Room 201, Goodland, KS 67735

*Smith County Courthouse
218 South Grant Street
Smith Center, KS 66967-2708
Phone (913) 282-5160 Register of Deeds; (913) 282-5150 Clerk of the District Court; (913) 282-5110 County Clerk
County organized 1872 from unorganized territory
Land records: Contact Register of Deeds
Naturalization records: Contact Clerk of the District Court
Vital records: From 1891 to 1897; contact County Clerk
Probate records: Contact Clerk of the District Court
Probate search service: no charge; copies: 25¢ per page, no minimum

Stafford County Courthouse
Saint John, KS 67576
Phone (316) 549-3509
County organized 1879 from unorganized territory

*Stanton County Courthouse
Johnson, KS 67855
Phone (316) 492-2140
County created in 1873, later abolished and made part of Hamilton County; in 1887 Stanton County was reorganized from Hamilton County
Land records: Contact Register of Deeds
Naturalization records: Some naturalization records; contact Clerk of District Court Office
Vital records: Contact City Clerk (some early dates with County Clerk)
Probate records: Contact Clerk of District Court
Probate search service: $9.00 per hour; copies: 25¢ per page, no minimum

*Stevens County Courthouse
200 East Sixth Street
Hugoton, KS 67951-2652
Phone (316) 544-2541

County laid out, along with Kansas and Seward counties, in 1873 from Indian Lands; the legislature passed an act fixing the boundaries of the three counties on 7 March 1875; in 1883 the three counties became one, with Seward county extending to the Colorado-Kansas line; Stevens County was reorganized by 1886
Land records: Contact County Clerk
Vital records: Contact Clerk of District Court
Probate records: Contact Clerk of District Court
No probate search service; copies: 10¢ per page; "Requests for copies must be in writing."

*Sumner County Courthouse
500 North Washington
Wellington, KS 67152-4064
Phone (316) 326-3395 Sibyl P. Whipple, County Clerk; (316) 326-2041 Register of Deeds; (316) 326-2811 City Clerk; (316) 326-5936 Probate Department
County organized 1867 from Cowley County
Land records: Contact Register of Deeds
Naturalization records: Contact District Court (Probate Department)
Vital records: Births and deaths; contact Wellington City Clerk, City Administration Building, Wellington, KS 67152
Probate records: Contact District Court (Probate Department)
Probate search service: $6.60 per year; copies: 25¢ per page, no minimum

*Thomas County Courthouse
300 North Court Street
Colby, KS 67701-2494
Phone (913) 462-2561
County organized 1873 from Kirwin Land District; organized with elected officials in October 1885
Land records: From 1885; contact County Clerk or Register of Deeds
Land records search service: $10.00 per hour; copies: 25¢ per page plus postage
Naturalization records: Through 1977
Vital records: From 1885 through June 1910; contact County Clerk. Marriage licenses; contact Clerk of Court
County Clerk's vital records search service: $10.00 per hour; copies: 25¢ per page plus postage
Probate records: Contact Clerk of District Court
Probate search service: $9.00 per hour if takes a lot of time; copies: 25¢ per page, $1.00 for certification, no minimum; "Not all things can be copied."

*Trego County Courthouse
216 Main Street
Wa Keeney, KS 67672-2102
Phone (913) 743-5773; (913) 743-6622
Register of Deeds; (913) 743-2461
FAX
County organized 1879 from Ellis County
Land records: From homestead or patent; contact Clerk of the District Court
Probate records: Contact Clerk of the District Court

*Wabaunsee County Courthouse
215 Kansas Street
Alma, KS 66401-9797
Phone (913) 765-3414
County organized 1855 from Riley and Morris counties
Land records: Contact Register of Deeds' Office
Naturalization records: Very few naturalization records (not complete); contact District Court Office
Vital records: Contact Register of Deeds' Office
Probate records: Contact District Court Office
No probate search service ("Contact the Wabaunsee County Abstract Office, Alma, KS 66401"); copies: 25¢ per page, no minimum

*Wallace County Courthouse
Sharon Springs, KS 67758
Phone (913) 852-4282
County was created in 1868 from Indian Lands and was part of a territory that went to Wa Keeney, now the county seat of Trego County; Wallace was established with its present boundaries in 1881, but no form of county government was created until 1886.
Land records: Deeds and mortgages from 1887 to date; contact Register of Deeds-County Clerk, Appraiser and Treasurer
Naturalization records: Contact Court Offices
Vital records: Births, deaths and marriages from 1895 to 1911; contact County Clerk. Marriage licenses from 1887 to date and coroner's records from 1888 to date; contact District Court Clerk.
Probate records: From 1908 to date; contact District Court Clerk

*Washington County Courthouse
Washington, KS 66968-1928
Phone (913) 325-2974 County Clerk; (913) 325-2381 Clerk of the District Court
County organized 1855, original county
Land records: Contact Register of Deeds

Naturalization records: Contact Clerk of the District Court
Vital records from 1887 to 1911 only; contact County Clerk
Probate records: Contact Clerk of the District Court
No probate search service; copies: 10¢ to 50¢ each, no minimum

Wichita County Courthouse
Leoti, KS 67861
Phone (316) 375-2731
County organized 1873 from Indian Lands

*Wilson County Courthouse
Fredonia, KS 66736
Phone (316) 378-2186
County organized 1855, original county
Land records: Contact Register of Deeds Office
Naturalization records: No naturalization records
Probate records: Contact Clerk of the Court Office
No probate search service ("You may look for yourself"); copies: 25¢ per page, no minimum

*Woodson County Courthouse
105 West Rutledge
Yates Center, KS 66783-1497
Phone (316) 625-8635 Register of Deeds; (316) 625-8670 FAX, Register of Deeds and County Clerk; (316) 625-8605 or 8606 County Clerk; (316) 625-8610 or 8611 Clerk of the District Court; (316) 625-8674 FAX, Clerk of the District Court
County organized 1855, original county
Land records: Contact Register of Deeds; copies: 25¢ per page; FAX: $1.00 per page to receive a FAX, $5.00 to send a single page, $9.00 for two pages, $12.00 for three pages, $14.00 for four pages, $1.00 for each additional page
Naturalization records: No naturalization records
Vital records: Births, deaths and marriages from 1885 to 1910; contact County Clerk; copies: $1.00 for the first page and 50¢ for each additional page; FAX: $1.00 per page to receive, $5.00 to send a single page, $9.00 for two pages, $12.00 for three pages, $14.00 for four pages, $1.00 for each additional page. Deaths from 1940; contact Register of Deeds; copies: 25¢ per page; FAX: $1.00 per page to receive, $5.00 to send a single page, $9.00 for two pages, $12.00 for three pages, $14.00 for four pages, $1.00 for each additional page. Marriages from 1860 to date; contact Clerk of the District Court; copies: 25¢ each;

FAX: no charge to receive, $3.00 to send a single page, $1.00 for each additional page
Probate records: Contact Clerk of the District Court
Probate search service: $9.00 minimum; copies: 25¢ per page; FAX: no charge to receive, $3.00 to send a single page, $1.00 for each additional page

*Wyandotte County Courthouse
710 North Seventh Street
Kansas City, KS 66101-3047
Phone (913) 573-2800
County organized 1859, original county
Probate records: Yes
Probate search service: no charge; copies: 25¢ per page if court file in office, $2.00 per page from microfilm originals, no minimum

KENTUCKY

Capital: Frankfort. Statehood: 1 June 1792 (organized as a county of Virginia in 1776, separated 1783)

Court System

Kentucky's fifty-nine District Courts, sitting in each county seat, have jurisdiction over most misdemeanors, uncontested probate matters, and juvenile cases. First Judicial District: Fulton and Hickman counties; Second Judicial District: McCracken County; Third Judicial District: Christian County; Fourth Judicial District: Hopkins County; Fifth Judicial District: Crittenden, Union and Webster counties; Sixth Judicial District: Daviess County; Seventh Judicial District: Logan and Todd counties; Eighth Judicial District: Warren County; Ninth Judicial District: Hardin County; Tenth Judicial District: Hart and LaRue counties; Eleventh Judicial District: Green, Marion, Taylor and Washington counties; Twelfth Judicial District: Henry, Oldham and Trimble counties; Thirteenth Judicial District: Garrard, Jessamine and Lincoln counties; Fourteenth Judicial District: Bourbon, Scott and Woodford counties; Fifteenth Judicial District: Carroll, Grant and Owen counties; Sixteenth Judicial District: Kenton County; Seventeenth Judicial District: Campbell County; Eighteenth Judicial District: Harrison, Nicholas, Pendleton and Robertson counties; Nineteenth Judicial District: Bracken, Fleming and Mason counties; Twentieth Judicial District: Greenup and Lewis counties; Twenty-first Judicial District: Bath, Menifee, Montgomery and Rowan counties; Twenty-second Judicial District: Fayette County; Twenty-third Judicial District: Estill, Lee and Owsley counties; Twenty-fourth Judicial District: Johnson, Lawrence and Martin counties; Twenty-fifth Judicial District: Clark and Madison counties; Twenty-sixth Judicial District: Harlan County; Twenty-seventh Judicial District: Knox and Laurel counties; Twenty-eighth Judicial District: Pulaski and Rockcastle counties; Twenty-ninth Judicial District: Adair, Casey, Cumberland and Monroe counties; Thirtieth Judicial District: Jefferson County; Thirty-first Judicial District: Floyd County; Thirty-second Judicial District: Boyd County; Thirty-third Judicial District: Perry County; Thirty-fourth Judicial District: McCreary and Whitley counties; Thirty-fifth Judicial District: Pike County; Thirty-sixth Judicial District: Knott and Magoffin counties; Thirty-seventh Judicial District: Carter, Elliott and Morgan counties; Thirty-eighth Judicial District: Butler, Edmonson, Hancock and Ohio counties; Thirty-ninth Judicial District: Breathitt, Powell and Wolfe counties; Fortieth Judicial District: Clinton, Russell and Wayne counties; Forty-first Judicial District: Clay, Jackson and Leslie counties; Forty-second Judicial District: Calloway County; Forty-third Judicial District: Barren and Metcalfe counties; Forty-fourth Judicial District: Bell County; Forty-fifth Judicial District: McLean and Muhlenberg counties; Forty-sixth Judicial District: Breckinridge, Grayson and Meade counties; Forty-seventh Judicial District: Letcher County; Forty-eighth Judicial District: Franklin County; Forty-ninth Judicial District: Allen and Simpson counties; Fiftieth Judicial District: Boyle and Mercer counties; Fifty-first Judicial District: Henderson County; Fifty-second Judicial District: Graves County; Fifty-third Judicial District: Anderson, Shelby and Spencer counties; Fifty-fourth Judicial District: Boone and Gallatin counties; Fifty-fifth Judicial District: Bullitt County; Fifty-sixth Judicial District: Caldwell, Livingston, Lyon and Trigg counties; Fifty-seventh Judicial District: Nelson County; Fifty-eighth Judicial District: Marshall County; Fifty-ninth Judicial District: Ballard and Carlisle counties.

The fifty-six Circuit Courts, sitting in each county seat, have general jurisdiction, including all cases of real estate title questions, contested probate matters, and appellate jurisdiction over the District Courts. The Judicial Circuits are the same as the Judicial Districts except that the First Judicial Circuit includes the First and Fifty-ninth Judicial Districts; the Tenth Judicial Circuit includes the Tenth and Fifty-seventh Judicial Districts; and the Forty-second Judicial Circuit includes the Forty-second and Fifty-eighth Judicial Districts. The Court of Appeals and the seven Districts of the Supreme Court exercise appellate jurisdiction.

Courthouses

*Adair County Courthouse
Columbia, KY 42728
Phone (502) 384-2801
County organized 1802 from Green County
Probate records: Contact Clerk
Probate search service: $2.00; copies: $1.00 per page, no minimum

Allen County Courthouse
PO Box 336
Scottsville, KY 42164-0036
Phone (502) 237-3706
County organized 1815 from Barren and Warren counties

Anderson County Courthouse
151 South Main Street
Lawrenceburg, KY 40342-1174
Phone (502) 839-3041
County organized 1827 from Franklin, Mercer and Washington counties

*Ballard County Courthouse
PO Box 145
Wickliffe, KY 42087
Phone (502) 335-5168 County Clerk
County organized 1842 from Hickman and McCracken counties
Land records: Contact Lynn W. Lane, County Clerk, PO Box 145, Wickliffe, KY 42087
Vital records: Births and deaths; contact County Health Center, PO Box 357, La Center, KY 42056
Probate records: Wills; contact County Clerk

*Barren County Courthouse
103 Courthouse Square
Glasgow, KY 42141-2812
Phone (502) 651-3783
County organized 1799 from Green and Warren counties
Land records: Yes
Naturalization records: Yes
Vital records: Yes
Probate records: Yes

*Bath County Courthouse
PO Box 39
Owingsville, KY 40360
Phone (606) 674-2613
County organized 1811 from Montgomery County
Land records: From 1811
Naturalization records: No naturalization records
Vital records: No vital records
Probate records: From 1811
Probate search service: depends on index; copies: $3.00 per document, $3.00 minimum

*Bell County Courthouse
PO Box 156
Pineville, KY 40977-0156
Phone (606) 337-6143
County organized 1867 from Harlan and Knox counties
Land records: Yes
Naturalization records: No naturalization records
Vital records: Marriages only
Probate records: Yes

*Boone County Courthouse
PO Box 874
Burlington, KY 41005
Phone (606) 334-2108
County organized 1799 from Campbell County

Land records: Deeds from 1799; contact Clerk

Naturalization records: From about 1835 to 1900; contact Clerk

Vital records: Marriages from 1799; contact Clerk; copies: $1.00 each, $5.00 for certified copies

Probate records: Wills, inventories, etc., from 1799; contact Clerk

Probate search service: $10.00 per hour; copies: 50¢ per page plus SASE, no minimum

Bourbon County Courthouse
Paris, KY 40361
Phone (606) 987-2430
County organized 1786 from Fayette County

Boyd County Courthouse
2800 Louisa Street
Catlettsburg, KY 41129-1116
Phone (606) 739-5116
County organized 1860 from Carter, Greenup and Lawrence counties

*Boyle County Courthouse
Main Street
Danville, KY 40422
Phone (606) 238-1110; (606) 238-1111; (606) 238-1112
County organized 1842 from Lincoln and Mercer counties (having the same county seat as the now-abolished Kentucky County, which was organized in 1776 from Fincastle County, Virginia)
Land records: Deeds from 1842 and mortgages; contact County Clerk's Office
No land records search service
Vital records: Marriage licenses
No vital records search service
Probate records: Wills from 1842 to 1978; contact County Clerk's Office. Probate records from 1978; contact Boyle District Court Clerk's Office
No probate search service; County Clerk's copies: 50¢ per page, no minimum

*Bracken County Courthouse
Brooksville, KY 41004
Phone (606) 735-2952 County Clerk
County organized 1797 from Campbell and Mason counties
Land records: From 1797 to date; contact Karen Rumford, County Clerk, PO Box 147, Brooksville, KY 41004; copies: 50¢ each
Naturalization records: No naturalization records
Vital records: No vital records
Probate records: From 1797
No probate search service (contact Miss Margaret Whitehead, Wallin Avenue,

Brooksville, KY 41004); copies: 50¢ each

Breathitt County Courthouse
Main Street
Jackson, KY 41339
Phone (606) 666-4035
County organized 1839 from Clay, Estill and Perry counties

*Breckinridge County Courthouse
Hardinsburg, KY 40143
Phone (502) 756-6166 Archives
County organized 1800 from Hardin County
Land records: Contact County Archives
Land records search service: $5.00 per hour; copies: 25¢ per page, $3.00 minimum
Probate records: Contact County Archives
Probate search service: $5.00 per hour; copies: 25¢ per page, $3.00 minimum

*Bullitt County Courthouse
Shepherdsville, KY 40165
Phone (502) 543-2262
County organized 1797 from Jefferson and Nelson counties
Land records: Contact Nina Mooney, County Clerk, PO Box 6, Shepherdsville, KY 40165
Probate records: From 1796 through 1977; contact County Clerk. Probate records from 1978; contact Jean Hatzell, Circuit Clerk
No probate search service; copies: $3.50 per instrument

*Butler County Courthouse
PO Box 448
Morgantown, KY 42261
Phone (502) 526-5676
County organized 1810 from Logan and Ohio counties
Land records: Contact R. Dallas Embry, County Clerk
Naturalization records: No naturalization records
Vital records: Marriages
Probate records: Contact Circuit Clerk
No probate search service; copies: 25¢ per page

Caldwell County Courthouse
100 East Market Street
Princeton, KY 42445-1675
Phone (502) 365-6754
County organized 1809 from Livingston County

*Calloway County Courthouse
101 South Fifth Street
Murray, KY 42071-2567
Phone (502) 753-2920

County organized 1821 from Hickman County

*Campbell County Courthouse
24 West Fourth Street
Newport, KY 41071-1063
Phone (606) 292-3838
County organized 1794 from Harrison, Mason and Scott counties
Land records: Contact County Clerk's Office, Newport Courthouse, Fourth and York Streets, Newport, KY 41071
Naturalization records: Contact County Clerk's Office
Vital records: Contact County Clerk's Office
Probate records: Contact County Clerk's Office

*Carlisle County Courthouse
Bardwell, KY 42023
Phone (502) 628-5451
County organized 1886 from Ballard County
Land records: From 1886; contact County Clerk
Vital records: Marriages; contact County Clerk
Probate records: Contact Circuit Clerk

*Carroll County Courthouse
Carrollton, KY 41008-1099
Phone (502) 732-4487
County organized 1838 from Gallatin, Henry and Trimble counties
Land records: Deeds from 1838
Vital records: Marriages from 1839
Probate records: Contact Circuit Court Offices
Probate search service: $3.50 per name; copies: 25¢ per page

*Carter County Courthouse
Grayson, KY 41143
Phone (606) 474-5188
County organized 1838 from Greenup and Lawrence counties
Land records: Contact Hugh R. McDavid, County Clerk, Room 232
Land records search service: $5.00 for one to three years, $10.00 for three to ten years; copies: $1.00 per page, $5.00 for certified copies
Vital records: Marriages; contact County Clerk. Other vital records: Contact County Health Department
Vital records search service: $5.00 for one to three years, $10.00 for three to ten years; copies: $1.00 per page, $5.00 for certified copies
Probate records: Contact County Clerk
Probate search service: $5.00 for one to three years, $10.00 for three to ten years; copies: $1.00 per page, $5.00 for certified copies

Casey County Courthouse
Liberty, KY 42539
Phone (606) 787-6471
*County organized 1807 from Lincoln
County*

*Christian County Courthouse
511 South Main Street
Hopkinsville, KY 42240-2368
Phone (502) 887-4105
*County organized 1797 from Logan
County*
Land records: From 1797
Naturalization records: No naturalization
records
Vital records: No vital records
Probate records: From 1797
Probate search service: $5.00; copies:
25¢ per page, $1.00 minimum

*Clark County Courthouse
Winchester, KY 40391
Phone (606) 745-0200
*County organized 1793 from Bourbon
and Fayette counties*
Land records: From 1793 to date; contact
County Clerk
Naturalization records: No naturalization
records
Vital records: No births or deaths
Probate records: Contact County Clerk
Probate search service: $3.00; copies:
50¢ per page or $3.00 per document,
no minimum; "We do not have
someone that does the genealogy
research full time."

*Clay County Courthouse
PO Box 463
Manchester, KY 40962-0463
Phone (606) 598-3663
*County organized 1807 from Floyd,
Knox and Madison counties*
Probate records: From 1978
No probate search service; copies: 15¢
per page

*Clinton County Courthouse
Albany, KY 42602
Phone (606) 387-5234
*County organized 1836 from
Cumberland and Wayne counties*
Land records: Contact County Clerk
Probate records: Contact Circuit Clerk

*Crittenden County Courthouse
107 South Main Street
Marion, KY 42064-1507
Phone (502) 965-3403
*County organized 1842 from Livingston
County*
Land records: Contact Crittenden County
PVA or County Court Clerk Offices
Vital records: Contact County Health
Department, 402 North Walker Street,
Marion, KY 42064

Probate records: Contact County District
Court
No probate search service; copies: 25¢
per page

*Cumberland County Courthouse
PO Box 275
Burkesville, KY 42717-0826
Phone (502) 864-3726; (502) 864-5884
FAX
*County organized 1799 from Green
County*
Land records: Deeds from 1799; contact
Cumberland County Clerk
Naturalization records: No naturalization
records
Vital records: Marriages from 1882
(older ones burned); contact
Cumberland County Clerk
Probate records: Wills and estate
settlements from 1814; contact
Cumberland County Clerk
Probate search service: no charge;
copies: $2.00 per instrument; $2.00
minimum

*Daviess County Courthouse
PO Box 609
Owensboro, KY 42302-0609
Phone (502) 685-8434
*County organized 1815 from Ohio
County*
Land records: Yes
Naturalization records: No naturalization
records
Vital records: Marriages
Probate records: Older probate records
and wills
No probate search service; copies: $2.00
per instrument under three pages

*Edmonson County Courthouse
Brownsville, KY 42210
Phone (502) 597-2819
*County organized 1825 from Grayson,
Hart and Warren counties*
Land records: From early 1800s; contact
Clerk's Office
Probate records: From early 1800s;
contact Circuit Clerk's Office
Probate search service: $2.50 per person;
copies: 50¢ per page (up to legal size),
75¢ (large size), no minimum

*Elliott County Courthouse
PO Box 225
Sandy Hook, KY 41171-0710
Phone (606) 738-5421
*County organized 1869 from Carter,
Lawrence and Morgan counties*
Land records: Deeds from 1869
Naturalization records: No naturalization
records
Vital records: Marriages from 1934
Probate records: From 1957 to 1978
(courthouse burned in 1957). Probate

records from 1978; contact Circuit
Clerk's Office
No probate search service; copies: $1.00
per page

*Estill County Courthouse
Main Street
Irvine, KY 40336
Phone (606) 723-5156; (606) 723-5158
for record inquiries; (606) 723-5108
FAX
*County organized 1808 from Clark and
Madison counties*
Land records: Contact County Clerk
Naturalization records: No naturalization
records
Vital records: Marriages; contact County
clerk
Probate records: Contact County Clerk.
Current probate records; contact
Circuit Clerk
Probate search service by County Clerk:
$5.00 per name per category; copies:
$1.00 per page, $5.00 for certified
copies, no minimum; "We do not
allow customers to make copies
themselves."

*Fayette County Courthouse
162 East Main Street
Lexington, KY 40507-1318
Phone (606) 253-3344
*County organized 1780 from Kentucky
County*
Land records: From 1794
Naturalization records: No naturalization
records
Vital records: Marriages from 1803
Probate records: Wills from 1793;
contact Archives. Probate records
from the 1960s and 1970s; contact
Circuit Clerk
No probate search service; copies: 50¢
per page; "We do not perform this
type of research, we pass these
requests on to a local genealogist."

*Fleming County Courthouse
Court Square
Flemingsburg, KY 41041
Phone (606) 845-7571; (606) 845-8801
Archivist; (606) 845-8461 County
Clerk's Office
*County organized 1798 from Mason
County*
Land records: Deeds from 1798; contact
Mrs. Caren Dawn Curotto Prater,
Archivist; copies: $2.00 per page, plus
Archivist's fee, plus postage
Naturalization records: From 1850s;
contact Archivist
Vital records: Marriages from 1798;
contact Archivist; copies: $2.00 per
page, plus Archivist's fee, plus
postage
Probate records: Wills, settlements,
inventories and appraisements from

1798; contact Archivist; copies: $2.00 per page, plus Archivist's fee, plus postage

Floyd County Courthouse
Prestonsburg, KY 41653
Phone (606) 886-9193
County organized 1800 from Fleming, Mason and Montgomery counties

*Franklin County Courthouse
Saint Clair Street
Frankfort, KY 40601
Phone (502) 875-8702
County organized 1795 from Mercer, Shelby and Woodford counties
Land records: Contact County Clerk's Office, Courthouse Annex
Naturalization records: No naturalization records
Vital records: Marriages; contact County Clerk's Office
Probate records: Contact District Court Clerk's Office

Fulton County Courthouse
PO Box 126
Hickman, KY 42050-0126
Phone (502) 236-2727
County organized 1845 from Hickman County

Gallatin County Courthouse
Warsaw, KY 41095
Phone (606) 567-5411
County organized 1799 from Franklin and Shelby counties

*Garrard County Courthouse
Lancaster, KY 40444
Phone (606) 792-3531
County organized 1797 from Lincoln, Madison and Mercer counties
Land records: Contact Shelton Moss, County Court Clerk
Naturalization records: Contact County Court Clerk
Vital records: Contact County Court Clerk
Probate records: Contact County Court Clerk
No probate search service; copies: $2.50 per document

Grant County Courthouse
Williamstown, KY 41097
Phone (606) 824-3321
County organized 1820 from Pendleton County

Graves County Courthouse
902 West Broadway
Mayfield, KY 42066-2021
Phone (502) 247-6110

County organized 1824 from Hickman County

*Grayson County Courthouse
100 Court Square
Leitchfield, KY 42754
Phone (502) 259-3201
County organized 1810 from Hardin and Ohio counties
Land records: From 1896
Vital records: Marriages from 1896
Probate records: Contact Circuit Clerk
No probate search service; copies: 25¢ per page, $3.50 for certified copies

*Green County Courthouse
203 West Court Street
Greensburg, KY 42743-1522
Phone (502) 932-5386
County organized 1793 from Lincoln and Nelson counties
Land records: From 1793; contact County Court Clerk; copies: $1.50 each plus postage
Naturalization records: No naturalization records
Vital records: Marriages from 1793; contact County Court Clerk; copies: $1.50 each plus postage
Probate records: From 1793; contact County Court Clerk
Probate search service: $2.00; copies: $1.50 each plus postage

Greenup County Courthouse
Greenup, KY 41144
Phone (606) 473-7455
County organized 1804 from Mason County

*Hancock County Administration Building
Hawesville, KY 42348
Phone (502) 927-6117 County Clerk; (502) 927-8095 County Archives
County organized 1829 from Breckinridge, Daviess and Ohio counties
Land records: From 1829; contact County Clerk's Office
Naturalization records: From 1850 to 1860; contact County Archives
Probate records: From 1829 to 1975; contact County Clerk's Office. Probate records from 1975; contact Circuit Clerk's Office, Old Courthouse, Hawesville, KY 42348
Probate search service: $4.00 per hour; copies: 50¢ per page, $3.50 for certified copies, $4.00 minimum

*Hardin County Government Building
Elizabethtown, KY 42701
Phone (502) 765-2171
County organized 1793 from Nelson County

Land records: From 1793; contact County Clerk
Probate records: From 1793; contact County Clerk
No probate search service; "It is necessary to employ a private researcher for search of *any* Hardin County records; the county does not have any personnel to do this work."

Harlan County Courthouse
First and Central Streets
Harlan, KY 40831
Phone (606) 573-2600
County organized 1819 from Knox County

*Harrison County Courthouse Annex
Cynthiana, KY 41031
Phone (606) 234-2232
County organized 1794 from Bourbon and Scott counties
Land records: Contact Ralph E. Coppage, Clerk
Vital records: From 1794; contact Clerk
Probate records: From 1794
Probate search service: variable ("research done by local citizen"); copies: 50¢ per page, 50¢ minimum

Hart County Courthouse
PO Box 277
Munfordville, KY 42765-0277
Phone (502) 524-2751
County organized 1819 from Barren and Hardin counties

*Henderson County Courthouse
Henderson, KY 42420
Phone (502) 826-3906
County organized 1799 from Christian County

*Henry County Fiscal Court
PO Box 202
New Castle, KY 40050
Phone (502) 845-5707
County organized 1799 from Shelby County

*Hickman County Courthouse
Clinton, KY 42031
Phone (502) 653-2131 County Court Clerk
County organized 1822 from Caldwell and Livingston counties
Land records: From 1822; contact Sophia Barclay, County Court Clerk
Naturalization records: Five citizenship records from 1843; contact County Court Clerk
Vital records: Marriages from 1822, "1854–1906 very scattered in both birth and death records in a book (1850–1860 in a box)"; contact County Court Clerk

Probate records: From 1822; contact
County Court Clerk

Probate search service: "depends on how
many people and the length of time it
takes to go through the dates that are
asked for"; copies: $2.00 per
document if mailed, 25¢ per page if
working in our office, no minimum

Hopkins County Courthouse
Madisonville, KY 42431
Phone (502) 821-8294
*County organized 1807 from Henderson
County*

*Jackson County Courthouse
PO Box 700
McKee, KY 40447
Phone (606) 287-7800
*County organized 1858 from Clay,
Estill, Madison, Owsley, Laurel and
Rockcastle counties*

Jefferson County Courthouse
Louisville, KY 40202
Phone (502) 625-6161
*County organized 1780 from Kentucky
County*

*Jessamine County Courthouse
Nicholasville, KY 40356
Phone (606) 885-4161 County Clerk
*County organized 1799 from Fayette
County*
Land records: From 1799; contact Eva L.
McDaniel, County Clerk
Naturalization records: No naturalization
records
Vital records: No vital records
Probate records: Contact County Clerk

*Johnson County Courthouse
Paintsville, KY 41240
Phone (606) 789-2557 County Court
Clerk; (606) 789-8181 Circuit Clerk's
Office
*County organized 1843 from Floyd,
Lawrence and Morgan counties*
Land records: Contact Betty Jo Conley,
County Court Clerk
Vital records: Contact County Court
Clerk
Probate records: Contact Vickie Rice,
Circuit Clerk's Office, Court Street,
Paintsville, KY 41240

*Kenton County Courthouse
Covington, KY 41012
Phone (606) 491-0702 Covington Office;
(606) 356-2972 Independence Office
*County organized 1840 from Campbell
County*
Land records: From 1860; contact
County Clerk, Covington Office, PO
Box 1109, Covington, KY 41012.

Land records from 1840; contact
County Clerk, Independence Office,
PO Box 38, Independence, KY 41051
Probate records: From 1860; contact
Covington Office. Probate records
from 1840; contact Independence
Office

Knott County Courthouse
Hindman, KY 41822
Phone (606) 785-5651
*County organized 1884 from Breathitt,
Floyd, Letcher and Perry counties*

*Knox County Courthouse
Circuit Court Clerk's Office
102 Cole Court
Barbourville, KY 40906
Phone (606) 546-3568; (606) 546-3075
Circuit Court Clerk
*County organized 1800 from Lincoln
County*
Land records: Deeds
Naturalization records: No naturalization
records
Vital records: No vital records
Probate records: Wills
Probate search service: $2.00; copies:
$2.00 per instrument, no minimum

*LaRue County Courthouse
Hodgenville, KY 42748
Phone (502) 358-3544
*County organized 1843 from Hardin
County*
Land records: Deeds from 1843; copies
$1.00 each
Naturalization records: No naturalization
records
Vital records: Marriage licenses from
1843; copies $1.00 each
Probate records: Wills (incomplete)
No probate search service; copies: $1.00

Laurel County Courthouse
London, KY 40741
Phone (606) 864-5158
*County organized 1826 from Clay,
Knox, Rockcastle and Whitley
counties*

*Lawrence County Courthouse
122 South Main Cross
Louisa, KY 41230-1331
Phone (606) 638-4108
*County organized 1822 from Floyd and
Greenup counties*
Land records: From early 1800s
Naturalization records: No naturalization
records
Vital records: Marriages only
Probate records: Yes
Probate search service: $5.00; copies:
50¢ (letter size), 75¢ (legal size),
$1.00 (ledger), 50¢ minimum

*Lee County Courthouse
PO Box 551
Beattyville, KY 41311-0417
Phone (606) 464-2596
*County organized 1870 from Breathitt,
Estill, Owsley and Wolfe counties*
Land records: Deeds and mortgages from
1870; contact Russell Stamper, Clerk
Vital records: Marriages from 1870;
contact Clerk
Probate records: From 1870; contact
Clerk
No probate search service; copies: 25¢
per page, 25¢ minimum

Leslie County Courthouse
Hyden, KY 41749
Phone (606) 672-2193
*County organized 1878 from Clay,
Harlan and Perry counties*

*Letcher County Courthouse
Whitesburg, KY 41858-1145
Phone (606) 633-2432
*County organized 1842 from Harlan
and Perry counties*
Land records: Yes
Naturalization records: Yes
Vital records: Marriage records only
Probate records: Before 1978 only

*Lewis County Courthouse
PO Box 129
Vanceburg, KY 41179-0129
Phone (606) 796-3062
*County organized 1807 from Mason
County*
Land records: From 30 April 1807;
contact Shirley A. Hinton, Lewis
County Clerk
Probate records: From 30 April 1807
Probate search service: $3.50; copies:
$1.50 per instrument, no minimum

Lincoln County Courthouse
Stanford, KY 40484
Phone (606) 365-2601
*County organized 1780 from Kentucky
County*

*Livingston County Courthouse
Court Street
Smithland, KY 42081
Phone (502) 928-2162
*County organized 1798 from Christian
County*
Land records: Deeds and mortgages from
1800
Vital records: Marriages from 1898
Probate records: From 1800 to 1978
No probate search service; copies: vary
in price, $2.00 minimum

*Logan County Courthouse
Russellville, KY 42276

Phone (502) 726-6061; (502) 726-6621 County Clerk; (502) 726-8179 County Archives
County organized 1792 from Lincoln County
Land records: Deeds; contact County Clerk Office
Probate records: Before 1977; contact County Clerk Office. Probate records from 1977 to 1987; contact Evelyn Graham, Clerk, Logan County Archives, 182 Tom Graham Road, Russellville, KY 42278
No probate search service; copies: 25¢ per page, no minimum

*Lyon County Courthouse
PO Box 350
Eddyville, KY 42038-0350
Phone (502) 388-2331
County organized 1854 from Caldwell County
Land records: From 1854 to date
No land records search service
Probate records: From 1854 to date
No probate search service

*Madison County Courthouse
101 West Main Street
Richmond, KY 40475-1415
Phone (606) 624-4703 County Court Clerk; (606) 623-3071 FAX, County Court Clerk
County organized 1786 from Lincoln County
Land records: Yes
No land records search service (contact Katherine Vockery, 128 Redwood Drive, Richmond, KY 40475, (606) 623-0862, or David Green, c/o Richmond Supply Company, 517 Leighway Drive, Richmond, KY 40475, (606) 623-1398)
Vital records: No vital records
Probate records: Yes
No probate search service

Magoffin County Courthouse
PO Box 530
Salyersville, KY 41465-0530
Phone (606) 349-2216
County organized 1860 from Floyd, Johnson and Morgan counties

*Marion County Courthouse
Lebanon, KY 40033
Phone (502) 692-2651
County organized 1834 from Washington County
Land records: From 1863; contact Eddie Lee, County Court Clerk
Vital records: From 1863; contact County Court Clerk
Probate records: From 1863 to 1978; contact County Court Clerk. Probate records from 1978; contact Circuit Court Clerk

Probate search service: no charge; copies: 25¢ per page; "Our courthouse was burned in 1863, during the Civil War, and all records were lost."

Marshall County Courthouse
Benton, KY 42025
Phone (502) 527-3323
County organized 1842 from Calloway County

*Martin County Courthouse
PO Box 485
Inez, KY 41224-0485
Phone (606) 298-3336
County organized 1870 from Floyd, Johnson, Lawrence and Pike counties
Land records: Deeds and mortgages; certified copies: $5.00 each
Naturalization records: No naturalization records
Vital records: Marriage licenses
Probate records: Yes
No probate search service; copies: $1.00 per page, $1.00 minimum plus SASE

*Mason County Courthouse
Maysville, KY 41056
Phone (606) 564-3341
County organized 1789 from Bourbon County
Land records: From 1789 to 1988; contact Clerk
Naturalization records: From 1789; contact Clerk
Vital records: Contact County Health Department
Probate records: From 1789; contact Clerk
Probate search service: $3.00; copies: $2.00 each, no minimum

McCracken County Courthouse
600 Washington Street
Paducah, KY 42003
Phone (502) 444-4700
County organized 1825 from Hickman County

McCreary County Courthouse
PO Box 579
Whitley City, KY 42653
Phone (606) 376-2411
County organized 1912 from Pulaski, Wayne and Whitley counties

*McLean County Courthouse
Calhoun, KY 42327
Phone (502) 273-3082
County organized 1854 from Daviess, Muhlenberg and Ohio counties
Land records: Deeds from 1854
Naturalization records: Found only in Court Order Books, only a few in this county

Vital records: No vital records
Probate records: From 1854
No probate search service; copies: 25¢ per page if book number and page given, $3.50 for certified copies; "Equity files and civil suits found in Circuit Court Clerk Office."

*Meade County Courthouse
PO Box 614
Brandenburg, KY 40108
Phone (502) 422-2152 County Clerk
County organized 1824 from Breckinridge and Hardin counties
Land records: From 1824 to date
Vital records: Births and deaths from 1824 to 1911; contact Division of Archives and Records Management, PO Box 537, 300 Coffee Tree Road, Frankfort, KY 40601. Marriages from 1824 to 1976; contact Meade County Public Library, Brandenburg, KY 40108. Marriages from 1976; contact Katherine Mercer, County Clerk; copies $2.00 each, $5.00 for certified copies
Probate records: Wills from 1824; contact County Clerk
No probate search service; copies: $2.00 each, $5.00 for certified copies

*Menifee County Courthouse
PO Box 123
Frenchburg, KY 40322-0123
Phone (606) 768-3512
County organized 1869 from Bath, Montgomery, Morgan, Powell and Wolfe counties
Land records: From 1869
Vital records: Contact County Health Department
Probate records: Contact Tom Peck, Circuit Clerk
No probate search service (contact Barbara Ingram, PO Box 114, Frenchburg, KY 40322)

*Mercer County Courthouse
Main Street
PO Box 426
Harrodsburg, KY 40330
Phone (606) 734-6313
County organized 1786 from Lincoln County
Land records: Contact County Clerk
Land records search service: $5.00; copies 50¢ each
Naturalization records: No naturalization records
Vital records: No vital records
Probate records: Contact County Clerk

Metcalfe County Courthouse
Edmonton, KY 42129
Phone (502) 432-4821
County organized 1860 from Adair,

*Barren, Cumberland, Green and
Monroe counties*

Monroe County Courthouse
Tompkinsville, KY 42167
Phone (502) 487-5471
*County organized 1820 from Barren
and Cumberland counties*

*Montgomery County Courthouse
PO Box 414
Mount Sterling, KY 40353
Phone (606) 498-8700
*County organized 1797 from Clark
County*
Land records: Deeds and mortgages from
1800
Naturalization records: No naturalization
records
Vital records: Marriages from 1864
Probate records: Wills from 1779; "All
probate packages in Frankfort" (see
Meade County)
No probate search service; copies: 50¢
per page plus postage, no minimum

*Morgan County Courthouse
West Liberty, KY 41472
Phone (606) 743-3949
*County organized 1823 from Bath and
Floyd counties*
Land records: Yes
Naturalization records: No naturalization
records
Vital records: Yes
Probate records: Yes
Probate search service: $4.00 for a period
of twenty years; copies: 50¢ per page
plus postage, no minimum

Muhlenberg County Courthouse
Greenville, KY 42345
Phone (502) 338-1441
*County organized 1799 from Christian
and Logan counties*

*Nelson County Clerk
Old Records
311 East Stephen Foster
Bardstown, KY 40004
Phone (502) 348-1820; (502) 348-1832
Old Records Researcher
*County organized 1785 from Jefferson
County*
Land records: Deeds from 1785,
processioners' reports from 1779 to
1785; Contact Pat Craven, Old
Records, PO Box 312, Bardstown, KY
40004
Land records search service: no charge
for limited, specific request, $10.00
per hour with minimum of $50.00
(includes copies and postage) for
more extensive research; copies: $5.00
plus SASE for up to five pages

Naturalization records: Few
naturalization records in county order
books; contact Old Records
Naturalization records search service: no
charge for limited, specific request,
$10.00 per hour with minimum of
$50.00 (includes copies and postage)
for more extensive research; copies:
$5.00 plus SASE for up to five pages
Vital records: No vital statistics
Probate records: Wills from 1785,
appraisals, sales and settlements from
1785 to 1978; contact Old Records
Probate search service: no charge for
limited, specific request, $10.00 per
hour with minimum of $50.00
(includes copies and postage) for
more extensive research; copies: $5.00
plus SASE for up to five pages

*Nicholas County Courthouse
Douglas Fryman, County Clerk
PO Box 227
Carlisle, KY 40311
Phone (606) 289-3730
*County organized 1800 from Bourbon
and Mason counties*
Land records: Deeds and mortgages from
1800
Land records search service: no charge
for one record; copies: SASE plus
$5.00 per document up to three pages,
and $1.50 for each additional page
Naturalization records: No naturalization
records
Vital records: Marriage records only
from 1800; copies: $2.00 each
Probate records: Wills, settlements,
inventories and appraisements from
1800
Probate search service: no charge if you
have a name and an approximate date
for one record; copies: SASE plus
$5.00 per document up to three pages,
and $1.50 for each additional page

*Ohio County Courthouse
Hartford, KY 42347
Phone (502) 298-3673
*County organized 1799 from Hardin
County*
Naturalization records: No naturalization
records
Vital records: No vital records
Probate records: From 1826 to 1972
Probate search service: $3.50 per item;
copies: 50¢ each, $2.00 minimum if
mailed, plus record search fee

*Oldham County Courthouse
La Grange, KY 40031
Phone (502) 222-9311
*County organized 1824 from Henry,
Jefferson and Shelby counties*
Land records: Yes
Vital records: Marriages

Probate records: Wills
Probate search service; copies: 25¢ per
page plus postage and handling; $2.00
minimum

*Owen County Courthouse
Owenton, KY 40359
Phone (502) 484-2213
*County organized 1819 from Franklin,
Gallatin, Pendleton and Scott
counties*
Land records: From 1819
Probate records: From 1819 to 1978

Owsley County Courthouse
Booneville, KY 41314
Phone (606) 593-5735
*County organized 1843 from Breathitt,
Clay and Estill counties*

*Pendleton County Courthouse
PO Box 129
Falmouth, KY 41040-0129
Phone (606) 654-3380
*County organized 1799 from Bracken
and Campbell counties*
Land records: From 1799; contact Carol
W. Ockerman, County Clerk
Naturalization records: Contact Circuit
Clerk's Office
Vital records: Contact Health Department
Probate records: From 1799; contact
Carol W. Ockerman, County Clerk
Probate search service: cost varies;
copies: $1.00 per page

*Perry County Courthouse
PO Box 150
Hazard, KY 41701-0150
Phone (606) 436-4614
*County organized 1821 from Clay and
Floyd counties*
Land records: From 1821
Naturalization records: No naturalization
records
Vital records: Marriages from 1821
Probate records: Some probate records to
1977
No probate search service; copies: 50¢
per page, no minimum

*Pike County Courthouse
320 Main Street
Pikeville, KY 41501-1118
Phone (606) 432-6240
*County organized 1821 from Floyd
County*
Land records: From 1821; contact Lillian
Pearl Elliott, Clerk, PO Box 631,
Pikeville, KY 41502
No land records search service (must
supply book and page or name);
copies: $5.00 for the first two pages
and 50¢ for each additional page of
the same instrument

Vital records: Birth and death index from 1911 to 1949, marriages from 1821 to date; contact Clerk

No vital records search service (must supply book and page or name); copies: $5.00 each for marriages plus 50¢ postage (no copies of births)

Probate records: From 1821 to 1978; contact Clerk

No probate search service (must supply book and page or name); copies: $5.00 for the first two pages and 50¢ for each additional page of the same instrument

Powell County Courthouse
Stanton, KY 40380
Phone (606) 663-4390
County organized 1852 from Clark, Estill and Montgomery counties

*Pulaski County Courthouse
PO Box 724
Somerset, KY 42502-0724
Phone (606) 679-2042
County organized 1799 from Green and Lincoln counties
Land records: From 1799; copies: $3.50
Naturalization records: No naturalization records
Vital records: Marriages from 1799; copies: $2.00 each
Probate records: Wills from 1799; contact Willard Hansford, Clerk
No probate search service; copies: $3.50 per instrument, $5.00 for certified copies

*Robertson County Courthouse
Mount Olivet, KY 41064
Phone (606) 724-5212
County organized 1867 from Bracken Harrison, Mason and Nicholas counties
Land records: Contact County Clerk
Vital records: Contact County Health Department
Probate records: Contact Circuit Clerk
No probate search service; copies: 5¢

*Rockcastle County Courthouse
Mount Vernon, KY 40456
Phone (606) 256-2831
County organized 1810 from Knox, Lincoln, Madison and Pulaski counties
Land records: From 1873; contact Norma Houk, County Clerk, PO Box 365, Mount Vernon, KY 40456
Vital records: From 1873; contact County Clerk
Probate records: Contact Circuit Clerk's Office

Rowan County Courthouse
Morehead, KY 40351

Phone (606) 784-5212
County organized 1856 from Fleming and Morgan counties

Russell County Courthouse
Jamestown, KY 42629
Phone (502) 343-2125
County organized 1826 from Adair, Cumberland and Wayne counties

*Scott County Courthouse
Georgetown, KY 40324
Phone (502) 863-7875 County Clerk
County organized 1792 from Woodford County
Land records: Deeds from 1784 (very few that early); contact County Clerk
Naturalization records: Mixed—hard to find; contact County Clerk
Vital records: No vital records
Probate records: Wills, administration bonds, settlements, appraisals, sale bills; contact County Clerk
Probate search service: no charge; copies: $2.00 per page, $2.00 minimum; "The courthouse burned in 1833 and 1837, destroying *all* marriages and lots of wills and deeds. What was left was recopied just as it was, with blank areas on lots of pages. All loose probate papers were destroyed or thrown away. The county court order books are mostly intact. They start 1792, indexed in back of book. Not all names were indexed, guardianship appointments are in there. Early deed index—up to 1837—is by last name only. It is cross-indexed, grantor-grantee."

*Shelby County Courthouse
501 Washington Street
Shelbyville, KY 40065-1119
Phone (502) 633-4410
County organized 1792 from Jefferson County
Land records: Contact Clerk
Land records search service: SASE for cost estimate
Naturalization records: Contact Clerk
Naturalization records search service: SASE for cost estimate
Vital records: Contact Clerk
Vital records search service: SASE for cost estimate
Probate records: Contact Clerk
Probate search service: SASE for cost estimate

*Simpson County Archives
206 North College Street
Franklin, KY 42134
Phone (502) 586-8161 Courthouse; (502) 586-4228 Archives
County organized 1819 from Allen, Logan and Warren counties

Land records: From 1882; contact Archives, repository for older court records. Current records; contact County Clerk, PO Box 268, Franklin, KY 42134
Naturalization records: contact Archives
Vital records: contact Archives. Current records; contact County Clerk
Probate records: contact Archives. Current records; contact County Clerk

*Spencer County Courthouse
321 Main Street
Taylorsville, KY 40071
Phone (502) 477-8121
County organized 1824 from Bullitt, Nelson and Shelby counties
Land records: Contact Robin Greenwell, Clerk
Naturalization records: Yes
Vital records: Yes
Probate records: Yes

Taylor County Courthouse
Campbellsville, KY 42718
Phone (502) 465-6677
County organized 1848 from Green County

Todd County Courthouse
Elkton, KY 42220
Phone (502) 265-2363
County organized 1820 from Christian and Logan counties

*Trigg County Courthouse
Cadiz, KY 42211
Phone (502) 522-6661
County organized 1820 from Caldwell and Christian counties
Land records: Contact Wanda H. Thomas, County Clerk, PO Box 1310, Cadiz, KY 42211
Naturalization records: Contact Judge Edw. H. Johnstone, Princeton, KY 42445
Vital records: Contact County Health Department, Cadiz, KY 42211
Probate records: Contact Judge Chappell Wilson, Cadiz, KY 42211
No probate search service; copies: 25¢ each

*Trimble County Courthouse
Bedford, KY 40006
Phone (502) 255-7196; (502) 255-7174 County Clerk (Mon-Tue & Thur-Sat)
County organized 1837 from Gallatin, Henry and Oldham counties
Land records: Deeds from 1837 (indexed); copies: 25¢ per page plus postage
Vital records: Marriage records from 1862; contact Violet Jennings, County Clerk, Rt. 1, Box 127A, Pendleton,

KY 40055-9511. Marriages before 1863; contact Kentucky Historical Society (300 Broadway, Old Capitol Annex, Frankfort, KY 40601— location), PO Box H (mailing address), Frankfort, KY 40602-2108

Vital records search service from County Clerk: $7.50 per hour plus copying costs and postage

Probate records: Yes; copies: 25¢ per page plus postage

Union County Courthouse
Morganfield, KY 42437
County organized 1811 from Henderson County

*Warren County Courthouse
429 East Tenth Street
Bowling Green, KY 42101-2250
Phone (502) 843-4146
County organized 1797 from Logan County
Land records: From 1797; contact County Clerk
Probate records: From 1797 to 1978; contact County Clerk. Probate records from 1978; contact Circuit Clerk, 925 Center Street, Bowling Green, KY
Probate search service: no charge; copies: 25¢ per page

Washington County Courthouse
PO Box 446
Springfield, KY 40069-0446
Phone (606) 336-3471
County organized 1792 from Nelson County

*Wayne County Courthouse
PO Box 565
Monticello, KY 42633
Phone (606) 348-6661
County organized 1801 from Cumberland and Pulaski counties
Land records: Yes
Naturalization records: No naturalization records
Vital records: Marriages only
Probate records: Yes

*Webster County Courthouse
Dixon, KY 42409
Phone (502) 639-5042; (502) 639-5170 Webster County Historical and Genealogical Society
County organized 1860 from Henderson, Hopkins and Union counties
Vital records: Births, deaths and marriages; contact Betty J. Branson, Editor and Corresponding Secretary, Webster County Historical and Genealogical Society (Webster County Courthouse—location), PO Box 215 (mailing address), Dixon, KY 42409

*Whitley County Courthouse
Main Street
Williamsburg, KY 40769
Phone (606) 549-6002 County Clerk;
   (606) 549-2790 FAX, County Clerk;
   (606) 549-2973 Clerk of Circuit Court
County organized 1818 from Knox County
Land records: Contact Tom Rains, County Clerk, PO Box 8, Williamsburg, KY 40769-0008
Probate records: Contact Gary W. Barton, Clerk of Circuit Court, PO Box 329, Williamsburg, KY 40769-0329

Wolfe County Courthouse
PO Box 400
Campton, KY 41301-0400
Phone (606) 668-3515
County organized 1860 from Breathitt, Morgan, Owsley and Powell counties

*Woodford County Courthouse
103 South Main Street
Versailles, KY 40383
Phone (606) 873-3421
County organized 1789 from Fayette County
Land records: Yes
Naturalization records: Yes
Vital records: Yes
Probate records: Yes

LOUISIANA

Capital: Baton Rouge. Statehood: 18 July 1812 (annexed as part of the Louisiana Purchase, 1803, organized as the Territory of Orleans in 1804)

Court System

Louisiana's parishes are roughly equivalent to other states' county designations. In 1804 the area was divided into two parts: the District of Louisiana and the Territory of New Orleans. In 1805 it was divided into twelve counties: Orleans, German Coast, Acadia, Lafourche, Iberville, Pointe Coupee, Attakapas, Opelousas, Natchitoches, Rapides, Ouachita (sometimes written Washita) and Concordia. In 1807 the Orleans Territory was divided into nineteen parishes, prior to being admitted to the Union in 1812. Today, the Mayor's Court, Municipal Court of New Orleans, Traffic Court of New Orleans, City Courts, Justice of the Peace Courts and Parish Courts are the state's courts of limited jurisdiction, handling municipal and city violations, some civil actions, and criminal offenses not punishable by hard labor. Three Juvenile Courts sit in Caddo, Jefferson and Orleans parishes, and there is an East Baton Rouge Family Court.

Forty-one District Courts, sitting in each parish seat, have general trial jurisdiction and have exclusive jurisdiction over real property and probate. Orleans District: Orleans Parish; First Judicial District: Caddo Parish; Second Judicial District: Bienville, Claiborne and Jackson parishes; Third Judicial District: Lincoln and Union parishes; Fourth Judicial District: Morehouse and Ouachita parishes; Fifth Judicial District: Franklin, Richland and West Carroll parishes; Sixth Judicial District: East Carroll, Madison and Tensas parishes; Seventh Judicial District: Catahoula and Concordia parishes; Eighth Judicial District: Winn Parish; Ninth Judicial District: Rapides Parish; Tenth Judicial District: Natchitoches Parish; Eleventh Judicial District: De Soto Parish; Twelfth Judicial District: Avoyelles Parish; Thirteenth Judicial District: Evangeline Parish; Fourteenth Judicial District: Calcasieu Parish; Fifteenth Judicial District: Acadia, Lafayette and Vermilion parishes; Sixteenth Judicial District: Iberia, Saint Martin and Saint Mary parishes; Seventeenth Judicial District: Lafourche Parish; Eighteenth Judicial District: Iberville, Pointe Coupee and West Baton Rouge parishes; Nineteenth Judicial District: East Baton Rouge Parish; Twentieth Judicial District: East Feliciana and West Feliciana parishes; Twenty-first Judicial District: Livingston, Saint Helena and Tangipahoa parishes; Twenty-second Judicial District: Saint Tammany and Washington parishes; Twenty-third Judicial District: Ascension, Assumption and Saint James parishes; Twenty-fourth Judicial District: Jefferson Parish; Twenty-fifth Judicial District: Plaquemines Parish; Twenty-sixth Judicial District: Bossier and Webster parishes; Twenty-seventh Judicial District: Saint Landry Parish; Twenty-eighth Judicial District: La Salle Parish; Twenty-ninth Judicial District: Saint Charles Parish; Thirtieth Judicial District: Vernon Parish; Thirty-first Judicial District: Jefferson Davis Parish; Thirty-second Judicial District: Terrebonne Parish; Thirty-third Judicial District: Allen Parish; Thirty-fourth Judicial District: Saint Bernard Parish; Thirty-fifth Judicial District: Grant Parish; Thirty-sixth Judicial District: Beauregard Parish; Thirty-seventh Judicial District: Caldwell Parish; Thirty-eighth Judicial District: Cameron Parish; Thirty-ninth Judicial District: Red River Parish; Fortieth Judicial District: Saint John the Baptist Parish. A Court of Appeals and a Supreme Court handle the appeals.

Courthouses

Acadia Parish Courthouse
PO Box 1342
Crowley, LA 70527-1342
Phone (318) 783-3107
Parish organized 1886 from Saint Landry Parish

Allen Parish Courthouse
PO Box G
Oberlin, LA 70655-2007
Phone (318) 639-4396
Parish organized 1910 from Calcasieu Parish

*Ascension Parish Courthouse
PO Box 192
Donaldsonville, LA 70346
Phone (504) 473-9866
Parish organized 1807 from Acadia County
Land records: Conveyances from 1833; contact Mr. James Regira or Ms. Margaret Martin
Naturalization records: From 1857; contact Mr. James Regira or Ms. Margaret Martin
Vital records: No vital records
Probate records: From 1820; contact Kermit Hart Bourque, Clerk of Court
Probate search service: $7.00 for each index search plus $2.00 for each entry

found; copies: $1.00 for each of the first five copies, 75¢ for each of the next fifteen copies and 50¢ for each additional copy, no minimum

*Assumption Parish Courthouse
PO Box 249
Napoleonville, LA 70390
Phone (504) 369-6653
Parish organized 1807 from Lafourche County

Avoyelles Parish Courthouse
Marksville, LA 71351
Phone (318) 253-7523
Parish organized 1807, original parish

*Beauregard Parish Courthouse
PO Box 100
De Ridder, LA 70634
Phone (318) 463-8595 Clerk of Court
Parish organized 1912 from Calcasieu Parish
Land records: Contact Ronald L. Nichols, Clerk of Court
Naturalization records: Contact Clerk of Court
Vital records: Marriages; contact Clerk of Court
Probate records: Contact Clerk of Court

*Bienville Parish Clerk of Court
601 Locust Street, Room 100
Arcadia, LA 71001
Phone (318) 263-2123
Parish organized 1848 from Claiborne Parish
Land records: From 1848
Naturalization records: No naturalization records
Vital records: No vital records
Probate records: From 1848
Probate search service: $5.00; copies: 50¢ each, no minimum

*Bossier Parish Clerk of Court
26th Judicial District
PO Box 369
Benton, LA 71006
Phone (318) 965-2336
Parish organized 1843 from Claiborne Parish
Land records: Yes
Land records search service: call for estimate; copies: $1.00 per page
Vital records: Marriages only
Vital records search service: call for estimate; copies: $1.00 per page
Probate records: Yes
Probate search service: call for estimate; copies: $1.00 per page

Caddo Parish Courthouse
501 Texas Street
Shreveport, LA 71101-5401

Phone (318) 226-6911
Parish organized 1838 from Natchitoches Parish

*Calcasieu Parish Courthouse
James R. Andrus, Clerk of Court
PO Box 1030
Lake Charles, LA 70602-1030
Phone (318) 437-3550
Parish organized 1840 from Saint Landry Parish
Land records: From 1910 (earlier records destroyed by fire)
Land records search service: $10.00 per name; copies: $1.00 per page, plus $5.00 to certify each document
Vital records: Marriage index from 1910
Vital records search service: $10.00 per name; copies: $1.00 per page, plus $5.00 to certify each document
Probate records: From 1910
Probate search service: $10.00 per name; copies: $1.00 per page, plus $5.00 to certify each document

*Caldwell Parish Courthouse
Columbia, LA 71418
Phone (318) 649-2681
Parish organized 1838 from Catahoula and Ouachita parishes
Land records: Yes
Naturalization records: Yes
Vital records: Yes
Probate records: Yes

*Cameron Parish Courthouse
Courthouse Square
PO Box 549
Cameron, LA 70631
Phone (318) 775-5316 Clerk's Office
Parish organized 1832 from Calcasieu and Vermilion parishes
Land records: From 1874; contact Clerk of Court, PO Box 549, Cameron, LA 70631-0549
Naturalization records: No naturalization records
Vital records: No vital records
Probate records: From 1874; contact Clerk of Court
Probate search service: no charge; copies: $1.00 per page, no minimum; "We need a letter of request for copies or to search the records; must file original or certified copy from another Louisiana Clerk of Court Office."

*Catahoula Parish Courthouse
PO Box 198
Harrisonburg, LA 71340-0198
Phone (318) 744-5497
Parish organized 1808 from Rapides County
Land records: From 1808
Naturalization records: No naturalization records

Vital records: No vital records
Probate records: From 1846
Probate search service: $15.00; copies:
    $1.00 per page, $5.00 for certification

Claiborne Parish Courthouse
Homer, LA 71040
Phone (318) 927-2222
Parish organized 1828 from
    Natchitoches Parish

Concordia Parish Courthouse
Vidalia, LA 71373
Phone (318) 336-4204
Parish organized 1807, original parish

*DeSoto Parish Clerk's Office
W.A. Porter, Jr., Clerk of Court
Joy E. Guy, Chief Deputy Clerk of Court
PO Box 1206
Mansfield, LA 71052
Phone (318) 872-3110
Parish organized 1843 from
    Natchitoches Parish
Land records: From 1843
Naturalization records: No naturalization
    records
Vital records: Marriage licenses
Probate records: Yes
Probate search service: $10.00 per hour
    ("But we do not do these for lack of
    time"); copies: $1.00 per page; "No
    one in Mansfield does research."

*East Baton Rouge Parish Courthouse
222 Saint Louis Street
Baton Rouge, LA 70802-5817
Phone (504) 389-3950
Parish organized 1810 from Spanish
    West Florida
Land records: From 1782 (Spanish West
    Florida)
Naturalization records: No naturalization
    records
Vital records: No vital records
Probate records: From 1782 (Spanish
    West Florida)
Probate search service: $22.00 per name;
    copies: 50¢ per page, $2.20 per
    certification; $2.50 minimum mail-out
    charge

East Carroll Parish Courthouse
400 First
Lake Providence, LA 71254-2616
Phone (318) 559-2256
Parish organized 1877 from Carroll
    Parish

*East Feliciana Parish Courthouse
PO Box 595
Clinton, LA 70722
Phone (504) 683-5145
Parish organized 1824 from Feliciana
    Parish

Land records: Conveyances, donations,
    mortgages, suits from 1825
Naturalization records: A few
    naturalization records, early 1800s
Vital records: No vital records
Probate records: From 1825
No probate search service; copies: $1.00
    each, no minimum; "Depending on
    the amount of research involved, there
    may not be a fee. If it is involved
    there is someone that will search the
    records for $8.00 per hour plus copy
    cost. Direct inquiries to Amanda S.
    Thomas."

Evangeline Parish Courthouse
Courthouse Building
Ville Platte, LA 70586
Phone (318) 363-5651
Parish organized 1908 from Saint
    Landry Parish

Franklin Parish Courthouse
210 Main Street
Winnsboro, LA 71295-2708
Phone (318) 435-9429
Parish organized 1843 from Catahoula,
    Madison and Ouachita parishes

Grant Parish Courthouse
Colfax, LA 71417
Phone (318) 627-9907
Parish organized 1869 from Rapides
    and Winn parishes

*Iberia Parish Courthouse
PO Drawer 12010
New Iberia, LA 70562-2010
Phone (318) 365-7282
Parish organized 1868 from Saint
    Martin and Saint Mary parishes
Land records: Conveyance records from
    1868 to date; contact Patrick Saunier,
    Clerk of Court; copies: 50¢ per page,
    $5.50 per document for certification
Naturalization records: From 1884;
    contact Clerk of Court
Vital records: Marriage licenses only
    from 1868; certified copies: $6.00
    each
Probate records: From 1868; contact
    Clerk of Court

Iberville Parish Courthouse
PO Box 423
Plaquemine, LA 70765
Phone (504) 687-5160
Parish organized 1807 from Iberville
    County

*Jackson Parish Courthouse
500 East Courthouse Avenue
Jonesboro, LA 71251
Phone (318) 259-2424

Parish organized 1845 from Claiborne,
    Ouachita and Union parishes
Land records: From 1880; contact Ann B.
    Walsworth, Clerk of Court, PO
    Drawer 730, Jonesboro, LA 71251
Probate records: From 1880; contact
    Clerk of Court
Probate search service: $2.00 per name
    per ten years; copies: $1.10 for the
    first copy and 55¢ for each additional
    copy, $5.00 minimum by mail

*Jefferson Parish Courthouse
Second and Derbiney Street
Gretna, LA 70053
Phone (504) 364-2900 Clerk of Court
Parish organized 1825 from Orleans
    Parish
Land records: Contact Clerk of Court,
    PO Box 10, Gretna, LA 70054
Probate records: Contact Clerk of Court
No probate search service; copies: 75¢
    per page, $1.50 minimum

*Jefferson Davis Parish Courthouse
PO Box 799
Jennings, LA 70546
Phone (318) 824-1160
Parish organized 1912 from Calcasieu
    Parish
Land records: From 1913; contact Clerk
    of Court
Naturalization records: No naturalization
    records
Vital records: No births, marriages from
    1913; contact Clerk of Court
Probate records: From 1913; contact
    Clerk of Court
Probate search service: no charge;
    copies: $1.00 per page, no minimum;
    "All records are public except
    adoption and juvenile records."

*Lafayette Parish Courthouse
PO Box 2009
Lafayette, LA 70502
Phone (318) 233-0150
Parish organized 1823 from Attakapas
    and Saint Martin parishes
Land records: From 1823; O. C. Guilliot,
    contact Clerk of Court
Probate records: From 1823; contact
    Clerk of Court
No probate search service; copies: 50¢
    per page

*Lafourche Parish Annex Building
309 West Third Street
PO Box 818
Thibodaux, LA 70301
Phone (504) 447-4841 Clerk of Court
Parish organized 1807 from Lafourche
    County
Land records: From 1808; contact
    Vernon H. Rodrigue, Clerk of Court;
    copies: $1.10 per page from large

books, otherwise 50¢ per page, $2.20 per document for certification
Naturalization records: Yes
Vital records: From 1808; contact Clerk of Court; copies: $1.10 per page
Probate records: From 1808; contact Clerk of Court
Probate search service: $5.50; copies: 55¢ per page

*LaSalle Parish Courthouse
PO Box 1372
Jena, LA 71342-1372
Phone (318) 992-2101
Parish organized 1910 from Catahoula Parish
Land records: Contact Clerk of Court
Probate records: Contact Clerk of Court
Probate search service: $12.00 per name, $5.50 thereafter; copies: 50¢ per page, no minimum; "Please send a deposit with request."

*Third Judicial District Court of Louisiana
Lincoln Parish Clerk of Court
(100 Texas Avenue—location)
PO Box 924 (mailing address)
Ruston, LA 71273-0924
Phone (318) 251-5130
Parish organized 1873 from Bienville, Claiborne, Jackson and Union parishes
Land records: Yes
Land records search service: $10.00; copies: $1.00 per page, $2.00 for certified copies
Vital records: Marriage licenses
Vital records search service: $10.00; copies: $1.00 per page, $2.00 for certified copies
Probate records: Yes
Probate search service: $10.00; copies: $1.00 per page, $2.00 for certified copies

Livingston Parish Courthouse
Livingston, LA 70754
Phone (504) 686-2266
Parish organized 1832 from Saint Helena Parish

Madison Parish Courthouse
100 North City Street
Tallulah, LA 71282
Phone (318) 574-0655
Parish organized 1838 from Concordia Parish

*Morehouse Parish Courthouse
Fourth District Court
100 East Madison Avenue
Bastrop, LA 71220-3824
Phone (318) 281-3343 Clerk of Court
Parish organized 1844 from Ouachita Territory

Land records: Deeds and mortgages from 1844; contact Lillian R. Boyd, Clerk of Court
Naturalization records: From 1871 to 1901; contact Clerk of Court
Probate records: From 1870; contact Clerk of Court
Probate search service: $10.00; copies: $1.00 per page plus SASE, $2.00 for certification, no minimum

*Natchitoches Parish Courthouse
PO Box 799
Natchitoches, LA 71458-0799
Phone (318) 352-2714
Parish organized 1807 from Natchitoches County
Land records: Contact Clerk of Court
Land records search service: $10.00 minimum
Naturalization records: Contact Clerk of Court
Naturalization records search service: $10.00 minimum
Vital records: No vital records
Probate records: Contact Clerk of Court
Probate search service: $10.00 minimum

Orleans Parish Courthouse
1300 Perdido Street
New Orleans, LA 70112-2114
Phone (504) 586-4322
Parish organized 1807 from Orleans County

Ouachita Parish Courthouse
300 Saint John Street
Monroe, LA 71201-7326
Phone (318) 323-5188
Parish organized 1807 from Ouachita County

*Plaquemines Parish Courthouse
Clerk of Court
PO Box 129
Pointe a la Hache, LA 70082
Phone (504) 333-4377
Parish organized 1807 from Orleans County
Land records: Yes
Naturalization records: No naturalization records
Vital records: Marriages
Probate records: Yes
No probate search service; copies: 50¢ per page, no minimum

Pointe Coupee Parish Courthouse
PO Box 86
New Roads, LA 70760-0086
Phone (504) 638-9596
Parish organized 1807 from Pointe Coupee County

*Rapides Parish Courthouse
PO Drawer 952
Alexandria, LA 71309-0952
Phone (318) 473-8153
Parish organized 1807 from Rapides County
Land records: From 1864; contact Clerk, Sheriff, Assessor
Land records search service: $11.00 per name per index (as time permits); copies: 50¢ per page, $2.00 for certification
Naturalization records: From 1864; contact Carolyn C. Jones Ryland, Clerk of Court
Naturalization records search service: $11.00 per name per index (as time permits); copies: 50¢ per page, $2.00 for certification
Vital records: Marriages from 1864; contact Clerk of Court
Vital records search service: $11.00 per name per index (as time permits); copies: 50¢ per page, $2.00 for certification
Probate records: From 1864; contact Clerk of Court
Probate search service: $11.00 per name per index (as time permits); copies: 50¢ per page, $2.00 for certification; "Offices do not do research; contact local genealogists. The courthouse and all records were burned during the Civil War. Therefore we have no records prior to 1864."

*Red River Parish Clerk of Court
615 East Carrol
PO Box 485
Coushatta, LA 71019-0485
Phone (318) 932-6741
Parish organized 1871 from Bienville, Bossier, Caddo, DeSoto and Natchitoches parishes
Land records: Contact Judith W. Huckabay
Probate records: Yes
Probate search service: $5.00; copies: 50¢ per page, $1.00 minimum

Richland Parish Courthouse
PO Box 668
Rayville, LA 71269
Phone (318) 728-4878
Parish organized 1852 from Carroll, Franklin, Morehouse and Ouachita parishes

*Sabine Parish Courthouse
PO Box 419
Many, LA 71449
Phone (318) 256-6223
Parish organized 1843 from Natchitoches Parish
Land records: Conveyance records from 1843

Naturalization records: No naturalization
  records
Vital records: Marriages from 1843
Vital records search service (give
  groom's and bride's names): $5.00;
  copies: $5.00 each
Probate records: From 1843
Probate search service (give name and
  year of death): $5.00; copies: $5.00
  each

Saint Bernard Parish Courthouse
8201 West Judge Perez Drive
Chalmette, LA 70043-1611
Phone (504) 277-6371
*Parish organized 1807 from Orleans
  County*

Saint Charles Parish Courthouse
River Road
Hahnville, LA 70057
Phone (504) 783-6246
*Parish organized 1807 from German
  Coast County*

*Saint Helena Parish Courthouse
PO Box 308
Greensburg, LA 70441-0308
Phone (504) 222-4514
*Parish organized 1810 from Feliciana
  County*
Land records: Yes
Vital records: Marriages
Probate records: Yes
No probate search service; copies: 50¢
  each, no minimum

*Saint James Parish Courthouse
5800 La 44
Convent, LA 70723
Phone (504) 562-7496
Parish organized 1807, original parish
Land records: Contact Clerk of Court,
  PO Box 63, Convent, LA 70723
Vital records: Contact Clerk of Court
Probate records: Contact Clerk of Court
Probate search service: $10.00; copies:
  75¢ per page, no minimum

**Saint John the Baptist Parish
  Courthouse**
1801 West Pirlwelleux
La Place, LA 70068-4118
Phone (504) 652-5311
*Parish organized 1807 from German
  Coast County*

*Saint Landry Parish Clerk of Court
Twenty-Seventh Judicial District
PO Box 750
Opelousas, LA 70570-0750
Phone (318) 942-5606 Clerk of Court;
  (318) 948-7265 FAX, Clerk of Court
*Parish organized 1807 from Opelousas
  County (1805–1807), encompassing*

*most of Southwestern Louisiana
prior to 1840; Imperial Saint Landry
Parish comprised the modern
parishes of Acadia, Allen,
Beauregard, Cameron, Calcasieu,
Evangeline, Jefferson Davis, and
present-day Saint Landry*
Land records: from 1805 to date
  (including Opelousas County).
  Opelousas Colonial Post (1764–1805);
  contact Clerk's Archives for microfilm
  copies (originals deposited at the
  Louisiana State Archives)
Naturalization records: From 1824 to
  1912
Vital records: Marriages from 1808 to
  date
Probate records: From 1807 to date

*Saint Martin Parish Courthouse
PO Box 308
Saint Martinville, LA 70582-0009
Phone (318) 394-2210
*Parish organized 1815 from Attakapas
  County*
Land records: Yes
Naturalization records: Yes
Vital records: Marriages only
Probate records: Yes

Saint Mary Parish Courthouse
PO Box 1231
Franklin, LA 70538
Phone (318) 828-4100
*Parish organized 1811 from Attakapas
  County*

*Saint Tammany Parish Courthouse
510 East Boston
Covington, LA 70433-2945
Phone (504) 898-2430 Clerk of Court
*Parish organized 1810 from Feliciana
  County*
Land records: From 1810; contact Clerk
  of Court, ask for vault records
Naturalization records: No naturalization
  records
Vital records: No vital records
Probate records: From 1810; contact
  Clerk of Court, ask for civil records
No probate search service; copies: 50¢
  per page, no minimum

*Tangipahoa Parish Clerk of Court
PO Box 667
Amite, LA 70422
Phone (504) 748-4146
*Parish organized 1869 from Livingston,
  Saint Helena, Saint Tammany and
  Washington parishes*
Land records: From 1820
Naturalization records: From 1911 to
  1928
Vital records: No vital records
Probate records: From 1850
Probate search service: $10.00 per name;
  copies: $1.00 per page, no minimum

Tensas Parish Courthouse
PO Box 78
Saint Joseph, LA 71366-0078
Phone (318) 766-3921
*Parish organized 1843 from Concordia
  Parish*

*Terrebonne Parish Clerk of Court
Attn: Copy Request
PO Box 1569
Houma, LA 70361-1569
Phone (504) 872-0466 Clerk of Court;
  (504) 868-5660
*Parish organized 1822 from Lafourche
  Parish*
Land records: From June 1806; contact
  I. Robert (Bobby) Boudreaux, Clerk
  of Court
Naturalization records: From December
  1907 to December 1927; contact
  Clerk of Court
Vital records: Marriages from October
  1814; contact Clerk of Court
Probate records: From September 1807;
  contact Clerk of Court
Probate search service: no charge;
  copies: 75¢ per page, $5.00 for
  certification; "Give as much
  information as possible to aid search."

*Union Parish Clerk of Court
Courthouse Building
Farmerville, LA 71241
Phone (318) 368-3055
*Parish organized 1839 from Ouachita
  Parish*
Land records: Yes
Naturalization records: No naturalization
  records
Vital records: Yes
Probate records: Yes
Probate search service: no charge;
  copies: 75¢ each, no minimum

*Vermilion Parish Clerk of Court
PO Box 790
Abbeville, LA 70511-0790
Phone (318) 898-1992
*Parish organized 1844 from Lafayette
  Parish*
Land records: From 1884; contact Public
  Service Department
Naturalization records: No naturalization
  records
Vital records: No vital records
Probate records: From 1884; contact
  Civil Suit Library
No probate search service; copies: $1.00
  each; "Must get abstracter or do
  searches in person unless it is very
  small."

*Vernon Parish Courthouse
PO Box 40
Leesville, LA 71496-0040
Phone (318) 238-1384

Parish organized 1871 from Natchitoches, Rapides and Sabine parishes
Land records: From 1871
Probate records: From 1871
Probate search service: $15.00; copies: $1.00 each, no minimum

*Washington Parish Courthouse
PO Box 607
Franklinton, LA 70438-0607
Phone (504) 839-4663 Franklinton; (504) 732-7189 Bogalusa
Parish organized 1819 from Saint Tammany Parish
Land records: From 1897 (because of a fire in March of that year, which destroyed all earlier records); contact Johnny D. Crain, Clerk of Court and Ex-Officio Recorder, 22nd Judicial District Court
Vital records: Marriages only; contact Clerk of Court
Probate records; Contact Clerk of Court

Webster Parish Courthouse
410 Main Street
Minden, LA 71055-3325
Phone (318) 371-0366
Parish organized 1871 from Bienville, Bossier and Claiborne parishes

*West Baton Rouge Parish Clerk of Court
PO Box 107
Port Allen, LA 70767
Phone (504) 383-4755
Parish organized 1807 from Baton Rouge Parish
Land records: Yes
Naturalization records: No naturalization records
Vital records: Marriages
Probate records: Yes
Probate search service: no charge; copies: $1.00 per page, no minimum; "An index search of probate records will be conducted when time is available."

West Carroll Parish Courthouse
PO Box 630
Oak Grove, LA 71263-0630
Phone (318) 428-3390
Parish organized 1877 from Carroll Parish

West Feliciana Parish Courthouse
PO Box 1921
Saint Francisville, LA 70775
Phone (504) 635-3864
Parish organized 1824 from Feliciana Parish

*Winn Parish Courthouse
101 Main Street
Winnfield, LA 71483
Phone (318) 628-5824; (318) 628-3515 Clerk of Court
Parish organized 1852 from Catahoula, Natchitoches and Rapides parishes
Land records: From 1886 to date; Contact Donald E. Kelley, Clerk of Court, Room 103
Vital records: Marriage licenses from 1886 to date; contact Clerk of Court
Probate records: From 1886 to date; contact Clerk of Court
Probate search service: $10.00 per name for a ten-year search; 50¢ per page, $3.00 minimum for mailing copies

MAINE

Capital: Augusta. Statehood: 15 March 1820 (was part of Massachusetts from 1639 to 1820, established boundary with Canada, 1842)

Court System

Each of Maine's counties has a Probate Court which sits at the county seat. The Maine Administrative Court sits in the District Court or Superior Court and handles cases involving real estate licenses. Thirteen District Courts sit in each county seat and elsewhere and hear some civil actions and non-felony criminal cases. District One: the eastern and western sections of Aroostook County; District Two: the central and southern sections of Aroostook County; District Three: the southern and western sections of Penobscot County; District Four: the northern and southern sections of Washington County; District Five: the central and southern sections of Hancock County and all of Waldo County; District Six: the eastern section of Cumberland County and all of Knox, Lincoln and Sagadahoc counties; District Seven: the northern and southern sections of Kennebec County; District Eight: the southern section of Androscoggin County; District Nine: the northern and southern sections of Cumberland County; District Ten: the eastern, western and southern sections of York County; District Eleven: the northern section of Androscoggin County and the northern and southern sections of Oxford County; District Twelve: Franklin and Somerset counties; District Thirteen: the central and northern sections of Penobscot County and all of Piscataquis County.

The Superior Court sits at each county seat and has original jurisdiction over all matters that are not dealt with by the lower courts. The Supreme Judicial Court hears appeals in Portland and Bangor.

Counties

*Androscoggin County Courthouse
2 Turner Street
Auburn, ME 04210-5953
Phone (207) 784-8390 County Commissioners Office; (207) 782-0191 Register of Deeds; (207) 782-0281 Register of Probate
County organized 18 March 1854 from

Cumberland, Kennebec, Lincoln and Oxford counties
Land records: Contact Jeannine Bergeron, Register of Deeds; copies: $1.00 per page
Naturalization records: No naturalization records
Vital records: No vital records (contact cities of Auburn and Lewiston, and towns of Durham, Greene, Leeds, Lisbon, Livermore, Livermore Falls, Mechanic Falls, Minot, Poland, Sabbattus, Turner and Wales)
Probate records: Contact Robert Couturier, Register of Probate
Probate search service: no charge; copies: $1.00 for the first page and 50¢ for each additional page, no minimum

*Aroostook County Courthouse
(Northern District)
Court Street
PO Box 787
Houlton, ME 04730-0787
Phone (207) 493-3318; (207) 834-3925 Register of Deeds; (207) 532-1500 Register of Deeds (South); (207) 532-7317 Register of Probate (North); (207) 532-1502 Register of Probate (South)
County organized 16 March 1839 from Penobscot and Washington counties; 21 March 1843 annexed part of Penobscot County; 12 Mar 1844 annexed parts of Piscataquis and Somerset counties
Land records: From 1808; contact Louise Caron (Northern Aroostook County, north of Caribou), Register of Deeds, Fort Kent, ME 04743 or Mary C. Bennett (Southern Aroostook County, south of Caribou), Register of Deeds, Aroostook County Commissioners, Caribou Courthouse, 240 Sweden Street, Caribou, ME 04736; copies: 25¢ per page (if done in person), 50¢ per page (if done by registry personnel), $1.00 per page (if mailed)
Vital records: No vital records (contact cities of Caribou and Presque Isle, towns of Allagash, Amity, Ashland, Bancroft, Blaine, Bridgewater, Castle Hill, Caswell, Chapman, Crystal, Dyer Brook, Eagle Lake, Easton, Fort Fairfield, Fort Kent, Frenchville, Grand Isle, Hamlin, Hammond, Haynesville, Hersey, Hodgdon, Houlton, Island Falls, Limestone, Linneus, Littleton, Ludlow, Madawaska, Mapleton, Mars Hill, Masardis, Merrill, Monticello, New Canada, New Limerick, New Sweden, Oakfield, Orient, Perham, Portage Lake, Saint Agatha, Saint Francis, Sherman, Smyrna, Stockholm, Van Buren, Wade, Wallagrass, Washburn,

Westfield, Westmanland, Weston and Woodland, plantations of Cary, Cyr, E, Garfield, Glenwood, Macwahoc, Moro, Nashville, Oxbow, Reed, Saint John and Winterville, and Maine State Archives for unorganized areas of Central Aroostook, Connor, Northwest Aroostook, South Aroostook and Square Lake)
Probate records: Contact Cecilia B. Rhoda, Register of Probate (North) or Joanne Carpenter, Register of Probate (South)

*Cumberland County Courthouse
142 Federal Street
Portland, ME 04101-4151
Phone (207) 871-8380; (207) 871-8389 Register of Deeds; (207) 773-2931 Register of Probate
County organized 19 June 1760 from York County
Land records: Contact James J. Walsh, Register of Deeds
Vital records: No vital records (contact cities of Portland, South Portland and Westbrook, and towns of Baldwin, Bridgton, Brunswick, Cape Elizabeth, Casco, Cumberland, Falmouth, Freeport, Gorham, Gray, Harpswell, Harrison, Long Island, Naples, New Gloucester, North Yarmouth, Pownal, Raymond, Scarborough, Sebago, Standish, Windham and Yarmouth)
Probate records: Contact Linwood E. Graffam, Register of Probate

*Franklin County Courthouse
Main Street
Farmington, ME 04938
Phone (207) 778-5889 Register of Deeds; (207) 778-5888 Register of Probate
County organized 20 March 1838 from Cumberland, Kennebec, Oxford and Somerset counties
Land records: Contact Susan A. Black, Register of Deeds
Vital records: No land records (contact towns of Avon, Carrabassett Valley, Carthage, Chesterville, Eustis, Farmington, Industry, Jay, Kingfield, Madrid, New Sharon, New Vineyard, Phillips, Rangeley, Strong, Temple, Weld and Wilton, plantations of Coplin, Dallas, Rangeley and Sandy River, and unorganized areas of East Central Franklin, North Franklin, South Franklin and Wyman)
Probate records: Contact Joyce S. Morton, Register of Probate
No probate search service; copies: $1.00 for the first page and 50¢ for each additional page, no minimum

*Hancock County Courthouse
60 State Street
Ellsworth, ME 04605-1926

Phone (207) 667-9542; (207) 667-8353 Register of Deeds; (207) 667-8434 Register of Probate
County organized 25 June 1789 from Lincoln County
Land records: Contact Marilyn Hanscom, Register of Deeds
Vital records: No vital records (contact City of Ellsworth, towns of Amherst, Aurora, Bar Harbor, Blue Hill, Brooklin, Brooksville, Bucksport, Castine, Cranberry Isles, Dedham, Deer Isle, Eastbrook, Franklin, Frenchboro, Gouldsboro, Great Pond, Hancock, Lamoine, Mariaville, Mount Desert, Orland, Osborn, Otis, Penobscot, Sedgwick, Sorrento, Southwest Harbor, Stonington, Sullivan, Surry, Swan's Island, Tremont, Trenton, Verona, Waltham and Winter Harbor, and unorganized areas of Central Hancock and East Hancock)
Probate records: Contact Margaret Lunt, Register of Probate
Probate search service: no charge; copies: $1.00 for the first page and 50¢ for each additional page; "Send any info they are looking for; where person last resided and date of death."

*Kennebec County Courthouse
95 State Street
Augusta, ME 04330-5611
Phone (207) 622-0971; (207) 622-0431 Register of Deeds; (207) 622-7558 Register of Probate
County organized 20 February 1799 from Cumberland and Lincoln counties
Land records: Contact Norma Buck Mann, Register of Deeds
Vital records: No vital records (contact cities of Augusta, Gardiner, Hallowell and Waterville, towns of Albion, Belgrade, Benton, Chelsea, China, Clinton, Farmingdale, Fayette, Litchfield, Manchester, Monmouth, Mount Vernon, Oakland, Pittston, Randolph, Readfield, Rome, Sidney, Vassalboro, Vienna, Wayne, West Gardiner, Windsor, Winslow and Winthrop, and Unorganized Area of Unity)
Probate records: Contact Donna B. Grant, Register of Probate
No probate search service; copies: $1.00 for the first page and 50¢ for each additional page, no minimum

*Knox County Courthouse
62 Union Street
Rockland, ME 04841
Phone (207) 594-0422 Register of Deeds; (207) 596-2240 Sixth District Court; (207) 594-0427 and (207) 594-0444 Register of Probate

County organized 5 March 1860 from Lincoln and Waldo counties

Land records: From early 1700s; contact Belle Crane, Register of Deeds

Naturalization records: Contact Sixth District Court, 62 Union Street, Rockland, ME 04841

Vital records: No vital records (contact City of Rockland, towns of Appleton, Camden, Cushing, Friendship, Hope, Isle au Haut, North Haven, Owl's Head, Rockport, Saint George, South Thomaston, Thomaston, Union, Vinalhaven, Warren and Washington, and Plantation of Matinicus Island)

Probate records: Adoptions from 1860; contact Linda J. Wotton, Register of Probate

No probate search service; copies: $1.00 for the first page and 50¢ for each additional page, no minimum; "Inquiries should be made to the individual department."

*Lincoln County Courthouse
High Street
Wiscasset, ME 04578
Phone (207) 882-6311; (207) 882-7341 Register of Deeds; (207) 882-7392 Register of Probate

County organized 19 June 1760 from York County

Land records: Contact Register of Deeds

Naturalization records: Contact Jean E. Huber, Register of Deeds

Vital records: No vital records (contact towns of Alna, Boothbay, Boothbay Harbor, Bremen, Bristol, Damariscotta, Dresden, Edgecomb, Jefferson, Newcastle, Nobleboro, Somerville, South Bristol, Southport, Waldoboro, Westport, Whitefield and Wiscasset, and Plantation of Monhegan)

Probate records: Contact Thomas A. Berry, Register of Probate

No probate search service; copies: $1.00 per page

*Oxford County Courthouse
26 Western Avenue
PO Box 179
South Paris, ME 04281-1417
Phone (207) 743-6359; (207) 743-6211 (East) Register of Deeds; (207) 935-2565 (West) Register of Deeds; (207) 743-6671 Register of Probate

County organized 4 March 1805 from Cumberland and York counties

Land records: Contact Jane Rich, Eastern District, Register of Deeds or Jean Watson, Western District, Register of Deeds

Naturalization records: Contact Superior Court

Vital records: No vital records (contact towns of Andover, Bethel, Brownfield,

Buckfield, Byron, Canton, Denmark, Dixfield, Fryeburg, Gilead, Greenwood, Hanover, Hartford, Hebron, Hiram, Lovell, Mexico, Newry, Norway, Otisfield, Oxford, Paris, Peru, Porter, Roxbury, Rumford, Stoneham, Stow, Sumner, Sweden, Upton, Waterford, West Paris and Woodstock, plantations of Lincoln and Magalloway, and unorganized areas of Milton and North Oxford)

Probate records: From 1795; contact Theodore R. Tracy, Register of Probate

Probate search service: no charge; copies: $1.00 for the first page and 50¢ for each additional page of each document, no minimum; "We do not have time for extensive searches; we must have specific names."

*Penobscot County Courthouse
97 Hammond Street
Bangor, ME 04401-4996
Phone (207) 942-8797 Register of Deeds; (207) 942-8769 Register of Probate

County organized 16 February 1816 from Hancock County

Land records: Contact Susan F. Bulay, Register of Deeds, PO Box 2070, Bangor, ME 04402-2070

No land records search service; copies: $1.00 per page

Vital records: No vital records (contact cities of Bangor, Brewer and Old Town, towns of Alton, Bradford, Bradley, Burlington, Carmel, Charleston, Chester, Clifton, Corinna, Corinth, Dexter, Dixmont, East Millinocket, Eddington, Edinburg, Enfield, Etna, Exeter, Garland, Glenburn, Greenbush, Greenfield, Hampden, Hermon, Holden, Howland, Hudson, Kenduskeag, Lagrange, Lakeville, Lee, Levant, Lincoln, Lowell, Mattawamkeag, Maxfield, Medway, Milford, Millinocket, Mount Chase, Newburgh, Newport, Orono, Orrington, Passadumkeag, Patten, Plymouth, Springfield, Stacyville, Stetson, Veazie, Winn and Woodville, plantations of Carroll, Drew, Prentiss, Seboeis and Webster, and unorganized areas of Argyle, Kingman, North Penobscot and Penobscot Indian Island Reservation)

Probate records: Contact Susan M. Almy, Register of Probate

Probate search service: $10.00; copies: $1.00 for the first page and 50¢ for each additional page

*Piscataquis County Courthouse
51 East Main Street
Dover-Foxcroft, ME 04426-1306
Phone (207) 564-2161; (207) 564-2411

Register of Deeds; (207) 564-2431 Register of Probate

County organized 23 March 1838 from Penobscot and Somerset counties

Land records: Contact Priscilla P. Bolduc, Register of Deeds

Naturalization records: Contact Lisa Richardson, Superior Court

Vital records: No vital records (contact towns of Abbot, Atkinson, Beaver Cove, Bowerbank, Brownville, Dover-Foxcroft, Greenville, Guilford, Medford, Milo, Monson, Parkman, Sangerville, Sebec, Shirley, Wellington and Willimantic, plantations of Kingsbury and Lake View, and unorganized areas of Blanchard, Northeast Piscataquis and Northwest Piscataquis)

Probate records: Contact Judith A. Raymond, Register of Probate

No probate search service; copies: $1.00 for the first page and 50¢ for each additional page, no minimum

*Sagadahoc County Courthouse
(752 High Street—location)
PO Box 246 (mailing address)
Bath, ME 04530-0246
Phone (207) 443-8200; (207) 443-8214 Register of Deeds; (207) 443-9733 Clerk of Courts; (207) 443-8218 Register of Probate

County organized 4 April 1854 from Lincoln County

Land records: From 1826; contact Barbara J. Trott, Register of Deeds; copies: $1.00 per page

Naturalization records: Some old naturalization records; contact Clerk of Courts

Vital records: No vital records (contact City of Bath and towns of Arrowsic, Bowdoin, Bowdoinham, Georgetown, Phippsburg, Richmond, Topsham, West Bath and Woolwich)

Probate records: From 1854; contact Noreen R. Cohen, Register of Probate

Probate search service: $10.00 per estate; copies: $1.00 for the first page and 50¢ for each additional page, no minimum

*Somerset County Courthouse
Court Street
Skowhegan, ME 04976-9801
Phone (207) 474-9861; (207) 474-3421 Register of Deeds; (207) 474-3322 Register of Probate

County organized 1 March 1809 from Kennebec County

Land records: Land transfers; contact Marguerite Farrin, Register of Deeds

Naturalization records: May be available through Superior Court Clerk

Vital records: No vital records (contact towns of Anson, Athens, Bingham,

Cambridge, Canaan, Caratunk, Cornville, Detroit, Embden, Fairfield, Harmony, Hartland, Jackman, Madison, Mercer, Moose River, Moscow, New Portland, Norridgewock, Palmyra, Pittsfield, Ripley, Saint Albans, Skowhegan, Smithfield, Solon and Starks, plantations of Brighton, Dennistown, Highland, Pleasant Ridge, The Forks and West Forks, and unorganized areas of Central Somerset, Northeast Somerset and Seboomook Lake)

Probate records: From 1809 (microfiche); contact Alison M. Hawes, Register of Probate

No probate search service; copies: $1.00 for the first page and 50¢ for each additional page, no minimum; "Parties must do own search or hire genealogist."

*Waldo County Courthouse

73 Church Street
Belfast, ME 04915-1705
Phone (207) 338-3282; (207) 338-1710 Register of Deeds; (207) 338-2780 Register of Probate

County organized 7 February 1827 from Hancock County

Land records: Contact Deloris Page, Register of Deeds

No land records search service; copies: $1.00 per page

Vital records: No vital records (contact City of Belfast, towns of Belmont, Brooks, Burnham, Frankfort, Freedom, Islesboro, Jackson, Knox, Liberty, Lincolnville, Monroe, Montville, Morrill, Northport, Palermo, Prospect, Searsmont, Searsport, Stockton Springs, Swanville, Thorndike, Troy, Unity, Waldo and Winterport)

Probate records: Contact Joanne Crowley, Register of Probate

Probate search service: no charge; copies: $1.00 for the first page and 50¢ for each additional page

*Washington County Courthouse

Court Street
PO Box 297
Machias, ME 04654-0297
Phone (207) 255-3127; (207) 255-6512 Register of Deeds; (207) 255-6591 Register of Probate; (207) 255-3326 Clerk of Superior Court

County organized 25 June 1789 from Lincoln County

Land records: Contact Sharon Strout, Register of Deeds

Naturalization records: Contact Marilyn Braley, Clerk of Superior Court

Vital records: No vital records: (contact cities of Calais and Eastport, towns of Addison, Alexander, Baileyville,

Baring, Beals, Beddington, Centerville, Charlotte, Cherryfield, Columbia, Columbia Falls, Cooper, Crawford, Cutler, Danforth, Deblois, Dennysville, East Machias, Harrington, Jonesboro, Jonesport, Lubec, Machias, Machiasport, Marshfield, Meddybemps, Milbridge, Northfield, Pembroke, Perry, Princeton, Robbinston, Roque Bluffs, Steuben, Talmadge, Topsfield, Vanceboro, Waite, Wesley, Whiting and Whitneyville, plantations of Codyville and Grand Lake Stream, unorganized areas of East Central Washington, North Washington, and Indian Township Reservations of Passamaquoddy and Passamaquoddy Pleasant Point)

Probate records: Contact Barbara Johnson, Register of Probate

*York County Courthouse

1 Court Street
Alfred, ME 04002
Phone (207) 324-1571; (207) 324-1574 Register of Deeds; (207) 324-1577 Register of Probate

County organized 20 November 1652, original county (originally called Yorkshire County, when Massachusetts assumed jurisdiction in 1658 to 1691)

Land records: From the early 1600s to date; contact Lois M. Muse, Register of Deeds, PO Box 339, Alfred, ME 04002-0339; copies: $1.25 per page

Vital records: No vital records (contact cities of Biddeford and Saco, and towns of Acton, Alfred, Arundel, Berwick, Buxton, Cornish, Dayton, Eliot, Hollis, Kennebunk, Kennebunkport, Kittery, Lebanon, Limerick, Limington, Lyman, Newfield, North Berwick, Ogunquit, Old Orchard Beach, Parsonsfield, Sanford, Shapleigh, South Berwick, Waterboro, Wells and York)

Probate records: Contact Lorraine Lemay Hutchins, Register of Probate, PO Box 339, Alfred, ME 04002

Probate search service: "We don't really have time to do in-depth searches; we can look up estates, but not a large quantity"; copies: $1.00 for the first page and 50¢ for each additional page of the same document, no minimum

Cities, Towns and Plantations

(All cities, towns and plantations deposited copies of their vital statistics, 1782–1922, with the Maine State Archives, L.M.A. Building, State House Station, Number 84, Augusta, ME 04333, (207) 287-5795, Jeffrey Brown, Archivist)

Town of Abbott

PO Box 120
Abbott, ME 04406
Settled 1805; incorporated as a town 31 January 1827 (Piscataquis County)
Vital records: From 1900

Town of Acton

PO Box 510
Acton, ME 04001
Phone (207) 636-3839 Selectmen's Office
Settled 1772; set off from Shapleigh and incorporated as a town 6 March 1830; set off part to Shapleigh 22 March 1831 (York County)
Vital records: From 1860

Adams

(see Crawford)

*Town of Addison

PO Box 142
Addison, ME 04606
Phone (207) 483-4678
Settled 1780; incorporated as a town 1797 (Washington County)
Land records: Tax records from the early 1900s to date; contact Town Office; copies: 25¢ each
Naturalization records: No naturalization records
Vital records: From 1834 to date; contact Town Office; certified copies: $7.00 each
Probate records: No probate records

Aetna

(see Etna)

Town of Albany (disorganized)

Settled 1784; incorporated as a town 20 June 1803; set off part to Waterford 1811; repealed incorporation 29 October 1937; surrendered organization 20 November 1937 (Oxford County)
Vital records: From 1794–1944; contact Maine State Archives

*Town of Albion

PO Box 287
Albion, ME 04910
Phone (207) 437-2900 Selectmen's Office
Incorporated as town of Fairfax 9 March 1804; annexed part of Winslow 1810; annexed part of Clinton 1814; set off part to form China 5 June 1818; changed name to Lygonia 10 March 1821; changed name to Albion 25 February 1824; territory at north annexed 31 January 1835; established boundary with China 13 March 1839; annexed

part of Unity 30 March 1853; set off
part to Benton 14 March 1863
(Kennebec County)
Vital records: From 1700s

Town of Alexander
Rt. 1, Box 1550
Alexander, ME 04694
*Settled 1810; incorporated as a town 19
January 1825; annexed part of
Cooper 22 February 1838; set off
part to Crawford 2 April 1859
(Washington County)*
Vital records: From 1784 to 1926 and
from 1975

Town of Alfred
Saco Road
PO Box 138
Alfred, ME 04002
Phone (207) 324-3521 Selectmen's
Office
*Settled 1764; set off from Sanford and
designated a district 4 February
1794; incorporated as a town 25
February 1808; set off part to
Sanford 23 February 1828; annexed
part of Waterboro 22 July 1847 (York
County)*
Vital records: From 1803

Town of Allagash
Rt. 1, Box 137
Allagash, ME 04774
Phone (207) 398-3198
*Organized as a plantation 14 June
1886; repealed organization 28
March 1933; reorganized as town
(Aroostook County)*
Vital records: From 1892 (many missing)

Almond
(see Orneville)
(Piscataquis County)

***Town of Alna**
Rt. 194
PO Box 265
Alna, ME 04535
Phone (207) 586-5313
*Settled 1663; set off from Wiscasset and
incorporated as town of New Milford
25 June 1794; annexed part of
Newcastle 1795; changed name to
Alna 28 February 1811; annexed
part of Jefferson 1816; established
north boundary 19 June 1820;
annexed parts of Jefferson and
Whitefield 26 January 1824, repealed
19 February 1907; established
boundary with Jefferson 23 February
1828; set off part to Wiscasset 25
February 1839; set off part to
Dresden 20 March 1841 (Lincoln
County)*

Land records: No land records
Naturalization records: No naturalization
records
Vital records: From 1795; contact Maine
State Archives, L.M.A. Building, State
House Station, Number 84, Augusta,
ME 04333
Probate records: No probate records

Town of Alton
Rt. 1, Box 379
Old Town, ME 04468
Phone (207) 394-2601 Selectmen's
Office
*Settled 1810; set off from Argyle and
incorporated as a town 9 March
1844; set off parts to Old Town 27
February 1863 and 17 February
1871 (Penobscot County)*
Vital records: From 1859

Town of Amherst
Star Route 31
Ellsworth, ME 04605
*Settled 1805; set off from Mariaville
and incorporated as a town 5
February 1831 (Hancock County)*
Vital records: From 1783

Town of Amity
General Delivery
North Amity, ME 04465
*Settled 1825; incorporated as a town 19
March 1836 (Aroostook County)*
Vital records: From 1862

Town of Andover
PO Box 219
Andover, ME 04216
Phone (207) 392-3302
*Settled 1780; incorporated as town of
East Andover 23 June 1804; changed
name to Andover 13 June 1820
(Oxford County)*
Vital records: From 1795

Andover West Surplus
(see Newry)

Town of Anson
PO Box 298
North Anson, ME 04958
Phone (207) 696-3979 Selectmen's
Office
*Settled 1775; incorporated as a town 1
March 1798; set off part to Industry
10 February 1823; annexed part of
Embden 28 January 1828; set off
part to New Portland 6 March 1830;
annexed part of New Vineyard 18
March 1840; set off North Anson 20
March 1845, reannexed 13 March
1855 (Somerset County)*
Vital records: From 1798

Town of Appleton
PO Box 622
Union, ME 04862
Phone (207) 785-4722
*Settled 1775; incorporated as a town 28
January 1829; annexed part of Hope
7 February 1843 (Knox County)*
Vital records: From 1774

Argyle (unorganized area)
*Settled 1810; set off from Argyle
Plantation and incorporated as a
town 19 March 1839; set off part to
Old Town 22 March 1843; set off
part to form Alton 9 March 1844;
repealed incorporation 15 April 1937
(Penobscot County)*
Vital records: From 1876–1892; contact
Maine State Archives

Argyle Plantation
(see Argyle)

Town of Arrowsic
Rt. 127
Star Rt. 2, Box 61A
Arrowsic, ME 04530
Phone (207) 443-4609
*Settled 1625; set off from Georgetown
and incorporated as a town 2 March
1841 (Sagadahoc County)*
Vital records: From 1741

***Town of Arundel**
RR 1, 1375 Old Limerick Road
Kennebunkport, ME 04046
Phone (207) 985-4201 Municipal Clerk;
(207) 985-7589 FAX
*Set off from Kennebunkport and
incorporated as town of North
Kennebunkport 1 April 1915;
changed name to Arundel 9
September 1957 (York County; see
also Kennebunkport, York County,
which was called Arundel from 1719
to 1821)*
Land records: No land records
Naturalization records: No naturalization
records
Vital records: From 1916
Probate records: No probate records

Town of Ashland
Bridgham Street
PO Box A
Ashland, ME 04732
Phone (207) 435-2311 Manager's Office
or Selectmen's Office
*Settled 1835; incorporated as town of
Ashland 18 February 1862; changed
name to Dalton 18 February 1869;
changed name to Ashland 3
February 1876; annexed Sheridan
Plantation (formerly Buchanan) 19
March 1901 (Aroostook County)*
Vital records: From 1863

*Town of Athens
PO Box 4137
Athens, ME 04912
Phone (207) 654-3471
Settled 1782; incorporated as a town 7
March 1803; annexed part of
Hartland 8 February 1821; annexed
parts of Brighton 15 March 1838 and
18 March 1862 (Somerset County)
Vital records: Births, deaths and
marriages from 1900; contact Sandra
A. Linkletter, Town Clerk; copies:
$7.00 for the first copy and $3.00 for
each additional copy

*Town of Atkinson
102 North Stagecoach Road
Atkinson, ME 04426
Phone (207) 564-7273
Settled 1804; incorporated as a town 12
February 1819; annexed part of
Orneville 21 February 1837
(Piscataquis County)
Vital records: From 1766 (some from
1722); contact Debra Andrews, Clerk
Vital records search service: $25.00
minimum

City of Auburn
45 Spring Street
Auburn, ME 04210
Phone (207) 786-2421
Settled 1786; set off from Minot and
incorporated as a town 24 February
1842; established boundary with
Minot 20 March 1844; annexed part
of Danville 19 February 1859;
annexed remainder of Danville 26
February 1867; incorporated as a
city 12 February 1868; adopted city
charter 22 February 1869; enacted
annexation to Lewiston 25 January
1870, but rejected on referendum;
annexed part of Minot 20 February
1873 (Androscoggin County)
Vital records: From 1751

*City of Augusta
16 Cony Street
Augusta, ME 04330
Phone (207) 626-2310 City Clerk
Established 1628 as the Cushnoc
Trading Post; built Fort Western on
the site of the old trading post 1754;
erected first dwelling 1759; divided
the old town 1797, the "hook"
retaining the name of Hallowell and
Cushnoc becoming Harrington; set
off from Hallowell and incorporated
as town of Harrington 20 February
1797; changed name to Augusta 9
June 1797; became shire town of
Kennebec County in 1799 and the
seat of government in 1831; set off
part to Winthrop 1810; set off parts
to Hallowell 1812 and 1813;
incorporated as a city 23 July 1849;

adopted city charter 20 August 1849;
set off part to form part of Kennebec
(present-day Manchester) 12 August
1850; set off part to Hallowell 9 April
1852; annexed part of Manchester 9
April 1856 (Kennebec County)
Vital records: From 1780 (missing
original volumes of births from 1932
to 1936 and from 1937 to 1963,
deaths from 1932 to 1934 and from
1936 to 1942 and from 1943 to 1963,
marriages from 1932 to 1963); contact
Madeline Cyr, City Clerk
Vital records search service: no charge
(illegitimate births and causes of death
are restricted); copies: $1.00 for an
attested copy, $7.00 for the first
certified copy and $3.00 for each
additional certified copy of the same
record

Town of Aurora
Star Route 31
Aurora, ME 04408
Settled 1805; incorporated as town of
Hampton 1 February 1831; changed
name to Aurora 6 February 1833
(Hancock County)
Vital records: From 1945

Town of Avon
PO Box 13
Phillips, ME 04966
Settled 1779; incorporated as a town 22
February 1802; set off part to Strong
26 March 1853 (Franklin County)
Vital records: From 1766

*Town of Baileyville
27 Broadway Street
PO Box 370
Woodland, ME 04694
Phone (207) 427-3442; (207) 427-6200
FAX
Incorporated as a town 11 February
1828; annexed part of Princeton 26
July 1847 (Washington County,
sometimes known as Woodland, not
to be confused with Woodland,
Aroostook County)
Land records: No land records
Naturalization records: No naturalization
records
Vital records: Births, deaths and
marriages from 1861 to date; contact
Eve Roberts, Deputy Town Clerk;
certified copies: $7.00 each
Probate records: No probate records

Town of Baldwin
Rt. 1, Box 433
West Baldwin, ME 04091
Phone (207) 625-3581 Selectmen's
Office
Settled 1735; incorporated as a town 23
June 1802; set off part to Hiram 28

February 1821; set off part to form
Sebago 10 February 1826; set off
parts to Sebago 26 January 1827 and
28 March 1837; set off part to Hiram
7 March 1844; set off part to Sebago
15 February 1871 (Cumberland
County)
Vital records: From 1790s

Ballstown
(see Jefferson)

Town of Bancroft
RFD, Box 80
Wytopitlock, ME 04497
Settled 1830; organized as a plantation
21 February 1878; incorporated as a
town 5 February 1889; set off part to
Weston 26 February 1907 (Aroostook
County)
Vital records: From 1892

*City of Bangor
73 Harlow Street
Bangor, ME 04401
Phone (207) 945-4400 City Clerk
Settled 1768; incorporated as a town 25
February 1791; incorporated as a
city 12 February 1834; helped make
up a deficiency in the Waldo Patent 5
February 1800; adopted charter 24
February 1834; set off part to form
Veazie 26 March 1853; annexed part
of Veazie 29 January 1889
(Penobscot County)
Land records: No land records
Naturalization records: No naturalization
records
Vital records: Births from 1775, deaths
from 1800, marriages from 1834;
contact City Clerk
Vital records search service: $2.00 per
year; certified copies: $7.00 each
Probate records: No probate records

Town of Bar Harbor
93 Cottage Street
Bar Harbor, ME 04601
Phone (207) 288-4098 Town Clerk
Settled 1786; incorporated as town of
Eden 22 February 1796; set off part
to Trenton 27 June 1849; changed
name to Bar Harbor 5 March 1918
under law of 25 March 1913
(Hancock County)
Vital records: From 1796

Town of Baring
PO Box 349
Baring, ME 04694
Settled 1786; incorporated as a town 19
January 1825; set off part to form
Meddybemps 20 February 1841;
repealed incorporation 18 February
1841; reorganized as a plantation 16

September 1961; reincorporated as a town (Washington County)
Vital records: From 1892 to 1931 and from 1941

*Barnard Plantation
Brownville, ME 04414
Set off from Williamsburg and incorporated as a town 8 February 1834; repealed incorporation 7 Feb 1877; reorganized as a plantation 15 March 1895 (Piscataquis County)
Vital records: From 1921 (fire destroyed most documents)

Bartlett Island
(see Mount Desert)

Batchelders Grant
Set off part to form part of Stoneham 31 January 1834; set off part to form Mason 3 February 1843 (Oxford County)

*City of Bath
55 Front Street
Bath, ME 04530
Phone (207) 443-4282 City Clerk
Settled 1664; set off from Georgetown and incorporated as a town 17 February 1781; established boundary with Phippsburg 7 March 1840; set off part to form West Bath 14 February 1844; incorporated as a city 4 June 1847; annexed part of West Bath 16 March 1855 (Sagadahoc County)
Vital records: From 1757

Town of Beals
PO Box 93
Beals, ME 04611
Set off from Jonesport and incorporated as a town 7 April 1925 (Washington County)
Vital records: From 1925

Town of Beaver Cove
PO Box 2000
Greenville, ME 04441
Organized as a plantation 17 March 1975; incorporated as a town (Piscataquis County)
Vital records: From 1975

Town of Beddington
HCR 72, Box 78B
Beddington, ME 04622
Incorporated as a town 31 January 1833 (Washington County)
Vital records: From 1792

City of Belfast
71 Church Street
Belfast, ME 04915

Phone (207) 338-3063 City Clerk
Settled 1769; incorporated as a town 29 June 1773; set off part to form part of Searsport 13 February 1845; incorporated as a city 17 August 1850 (Waldo County)
Vital records: From 1892

Town of Belgrade
PO Box 96
Belgrade, ME 04917
Phone (207) 495-2258
Settled 1774; incorporated as a town 3 February 1796; annexed part of Sidney 1798; annexed parts of Dearborn 29 January 1834 and 22 March 1839; annexed part of Rome 10 February 1845; set off part to Mount Vernon 16 July 1846; annexed part of Rome 25 March 1897 (Kennebec County)
Vital records: From 1758

Town of Belmont
HCR 80, Box 132
Belmont, ME 04915
Phone (207) 342-5722 Municipal Office
Settled 1790; previously named Green; incorporated as a town 5 February 1814; set off part to form Morrill 3 March 1855 (Waldo County)
Vital records: From 1855

Town of Benedicta (disorganized)
Settled 1834; incorporated as a town 1 February 1873, now in unorganized territory (Aroostock County)
Vital records: From 1928

Town of Benton
1145 Clinton Avenue
Benton, ME 04901
Settled 1775; set off from Clinton and incorporated as town of Sebasticook 16 March 1842; annexed part of Unity Gore 26 July 1847; changed name to Benton 19 June 1850; part set off to Clinton 24 March 1853; annexed part of Albion 14 March 1863; set off part to Fairfield 27 February 1873 (Kennebec County)
Vital records: From 1841

Town of Berlin (disorganized)
Formerly known as 6 AP (Franklin County)
Vital records: 1846 only

Town of Berwick
PO Box 696
Berwick, ME 03901
Settled 1627; set off from Kittery and incorporated as a town 9 June 1713; set off part to Kittery 1716; set off part to form South Berwick 12

February 1814; set off part to form North Berwick 22 March 1831; set off part to South Berwick 18 March 1841; set off part to North Berwick 22 February 1875; set off part to South Berwick 5 February 1881 (York County)
Vital records: From 1701

*Town of Bethel
PO Box 108
Bethel, ME 04217
Phone (207) 824-2669
Settled 1774; incorporated as a town 10 June 1796; set off part to form part of Hanover 14 February 1843; annexed part of Hanover 31 July 1849 (Oxford County)
Land records: Yes
Naturalization records: No naturalization records
Vital records: From 1745
Probate records: No probate records

*City of Biddeford
205 Main Street
Biddeford, ME 04005
Phone (207) 284-9307 City Clerk
Settled 1630; incorporated 5 July 1653; set off part to form district of Pepperrellborough (present-day Saco) 15 June 1762; incorporated as a city 10 February 1855 (York County)
Land records: From 1653 to 1855; contact Charles L. Butler, Jr., President, The Biddeford Historical Society, PO Box 200, Biddeford, ME 04005
Vital records: From 1745; contact Clerk. From 1653 to 1891; contact The Biddeford Historical Society

Town of Bingham
PO Box 136
Bingham, ME 04920
Phone (207) 672-5519 Selectman's Office
Settled 1784; incorporated as a town 6 February 1812 (Somerset County)
Vital records: From 1759

Black
(see Friendship)

Town of Blaine
PO Box 190
Blaine, ME 04734
Phone (207) 425-2611
Settled 1842; incorporated as a town 10 February 1874 (Aroostook County)
Vital records: From 1892

Blanchard Plantation
Settled 1813; incorporated as a town 17

March 1831; became a plantation 20 August 1951; now in unorganized territory (Piscataquis County)
Vital records: From 1800s; contact Maine State Archives

Bloomfield
Settled 1771; set off from Canaan and incorporated 5 February 1814; annexed part of Fairfield 22 February 1858; annexed to Skowhegan 4 March 1861, under law of 19 February 1861 (Somerset County)

*Town of Blue Hill
Main Street
PO Box 433
Blue Hill, ME 04614
Phone (207) 374-2281 Selectmen's Office; (207) 374-5741 Town Clerk
Settled 1762; incorporated as a town 2 February 1789; annexed part of Sedgwick 5 February 1831; set off part to Penobscot 7 April 1845 (Hancock County)
Land records: Contact Town Office
Vital records: From 1700; contact Clerk's Office

*Town of Boothbay
PO Box 106
Boothbay, ME 04537
Phone (207) 633-2051
Settled 1630; incorporated as a town 3 November 1764; set off part to form Townsend (present-day Southport) 12 February 1842; set off part to form Boothbay Harbor 16 February 1889 (Lincoln County)
Land records: Contact Assessors' Office
Naturalization records: No naturalization records
Vital records: From 1763; contact Joan M. Rittall, Town Clerk
Probate records: No probate records

*Town of Boothbay Harbor
19 Townsend Avenue
PO Box 117
Boothbay Harbor, ME 04538
Phone (207) 633-2144 Town Clerk
Settled 1630; set off from Botthbay and incorporated as a town 16 February 1889 (Lincoln County)
Land records: No land records
Vital records: From 1889
Probate records: No probate records

Town of Bowdoin
Rt. 2, Box 181
Bowdoinham, ME 04008
Phone (207) 666-3066
Settled 1725; incorporated as a town 21 March 1788; set off part to form

Thompsonborough (present-day Lisbon) 22 June 1799; set off part to Lisbon 31 January 1826 and reannexed 17 February 1827; set off part to Lisbon 7 March 1834 (Sagadahoc County)
Vital records: From 1763

*Town of Bowdoinham
School Street
PO Box 85
Bowdoinham, ME 04008
Phone (207) 666-5531
Settled 1725; incorporated as a town 18 September 1762; annexed part of Gardinerston (present-day Pittston) 4 February 1799; annexed Richmond Plantation (see Richmond) 1779; set off part (Cathance Neck) to Topsham 1788; annexed part of Litchfield 1817; set off part to form Richmond 10 February 1823; annexed part of Topsham 16 March 1830 (Sagadahoc County)
Land records: No land records
Naturalization records: No naturalization records
Vital records: From 1764
Probate records: No probate records

Town of Bowerbank
Rt. 2, Box 47
Dover-Foxcroft, ME 04426
Settled 1825; incorporated as a town 4 February 1839; repealed incorporation 15 February 1869; organized as a plantation 27 November 1888; ratified organization 5 March 1895; incorporated as a town 28 February 1907; annexed part of Sebec 7 April 1927 (Piscataquis County)
Vital records: From 1832

Town of Bradford
PO Box 26
Bradford, ME 04410
Phone (207) 327-2121
Settled 1803; incorporated as a town 12 March 1831 (Penobscot County)
Vital records: From 1862

*Town of Bradley
41 Main Road
PO Box 502
Bradley, ME 04411
Phone (207) 827-7725 Manager
Settled 1817; incorporated as a town 3 February 1835; annexed gore bounded by Bradley, Clifton and Eddington 10 February 1859 (Penobscot County)
Land records: From the 1900s
Naturalization records: Scattered
Vital records: From the late 1800s
Probate records: No probate records

Bradley's Grant
(see Stow)

*Town of Bremen
PO Box 171
Medomak, ME 04551
Phone (207) 529-5945 Town Clerk
Settled 1625; set off from Bristol and incorporated as a town 19 February 1828; annexed part of Waldoboro 6 March 1830; established boundary with Bristol 6 March 1830; set off parts to Waldoboro 11 March 1853 and 27 March 1856 (Lincoln County)
Vital records: From 1756

*City of Brewer
City Clerk
City Hall
80 North Main Street
Brewer, ME 04412-2010
Phone (207) 989-7050 City Clerk
Settled 1770; set off from Orrington and incorporated as a town 22 February 1812; annexed parts of Orrington, Dedham and Bucksport 10 April 1841; set off part to Eddington 30 June 1846; set off part to form Holden 13 April 1852; set off part to Eddington 16 March 1855; incorporated as a city 30 March 1889 under law of 2 February 1889 (Penobscot County)
Vital records: From 1812

Town of Bridgewater
Mian Street
Bridgewater, ME 04735
Phone (207) 429-9856
Settled 1827; incorporated as a town 2 March 1858 (Aroostook County)
Vital records: From 1894

*Town of Bridgton
1 Chase Common
Bridgton, ME 04009
Phone (207) 647-8786
Settled 1769; incorporated as a town 7 February 1794; set off part to form Harrison 8 March 1805; set off part to form part of Naples 4 March 1834; annexed part of Denmark 7 March 1842; annexed part of Fryeburg 2 August 1847; annexed part (Texas) of Denmark 2 August 1847; set off part to Naples 29 February 1856; set off parts to Harrison 20 February 1866 and 30 January 1877 (Cumberland County)
Vital records: From 1892 to date; contact Julie M. Mowatt, Clerk; copies: $7.00 for the first copy and $3.00 for each additional copy

Brighton Plantation
PO Box 126
Athens, ME 04912-0126

Settled 1801; incorporated as town of North Hill 20 June 1816; changed name to Brighton 29 January 1827; set off parts to Athens 15 March 1838 and 18 March 1862; repealed incorporation 6 March 1895; surrendered incorporation 8 April 1895; organized as a plantation 18 April 1895 (Somerset County)
Vital records: From 1840

Town of Bristol
PO Box 147
Bristol, ME 04539
Phone (207) 563-5270 Selectmen's Office
Settled 1625; incorporated as a town 21 June 1765; established bounds 19 June 1766; set off part to Nobleboro 1815; set off part to form Bremen 19 February 1828; established boundary with Bremen 6 March 1830; set off part to form part of Damariscotta 26 July 1847; set off part to form South Bristol 26 March 1915 (Lincoln County)
Vital records: From 1765

Town of Brooklin
Reach Road
Brooklin, ME 04616
Phone (207) 359-8394 Selectmen's Office
Settled 1763; set off from Sedgwick and incorporated as town of Port Watson 9 June 1849; changed name to Brooklin 23 July 1849 (Hancock County)
Vital records: From 1835

Town of Brooks
Rt. 2, Box 120
Brooks, ME 04921
Phone (207) 722-3254
Settled 1798; incorporated as a town 10 December 1816; annexed part of Monroe 23 January 1833; set off part to Swanville 5 March 1841; set off parts to Monroe 15 March 1844 and 17 February 1883 (Waldo County)
Vital records: From 1892

Town of Brooksville
Town House
Rt. 1, Box 56
Brooksville, ME 04617
Phone (207) 326-4518
Settled 1760; set off from Castine, Penobscot and Sedgwick and incorporated as a town 13 June 1817 (Hancock County)
Vital records: From 1817

Town of Brookton (disorganized)
Incorporated 2 March 1883; repealed incorporation 24 February 1941 (Washington County)
Vital records from 1871 to 1892; contact Maine State Archives

*Town of Brownfield
PO Box 100
Brownfield, ME 04010
Phone (207) 935-2007
Settled 1765; incorporated as a town 20 February 1802; set off part to Fryeburg 20 February 1807; set off part to form Denmark 20 February 1807; annexed part of Porter 20 February 1807; set off part to Denmark 2 March 1821; annexed parts of Porter 19 February 1831 and 11 February 1832; set off part to Hiram 23 April 1852; annexed part of Porter 17 March 1855; set off part to Denmark 13 March 1907 (Oxford County)
Land records: Contact Wanda Bartlett, Town Clerk/Registrar
Naturalization records: No naturalization records
Vital records: From 1802 (some were lost in the fire of 1947); contact Town Clerk/Registrar
Probate records: No probate records

*Town of Brownville
PO Box 659
Brownville, ME 04414
Settled 1795; incorporated as a town 3 February 1824 (Piscataquis County)
Land records: No land records
Naturalization records: No naturalization records
Vital records: Births, etc. from 1892; contact Jacqueline Roy, Town Clerk; certified copies: $7.00 each
Probate records: No probate records

Town of Brunswick
28 Federal Street
Brunswick, ME 04011
Phone (207) 725-7132 Town Clerk
Settled 1625; incorporated as a town 24 June 1737; annexed parts of North Yarmouth 1739 and 1740; annexed parts of Freeport 1790, 28 January 1833, 15 February 1839 and 24 August 1850; incorporated as a city 29 March 1858 but rejected by voters; incorporated as a city 7 February 1885 (Cumberland County)
Vital records: From 1735

Buchanan
(see Ashland)

*Town of Buckfield
PO Box 179
Buckfield, ME 04220

Phone (207) 336-2521 Selectmen's Office
Settled 1776; incorporated as a town 16 March 1793; set off part to Paris 19 February 1828; annexed part of Sumner 12 March 1856; annexed parts of Hartford 25 March 1856 and 11 March 1862 (Oxford County)
Land records: Yes
Naturalization records: No naturalization records
Vital records: From 1700
Probate records: No probate records

Town of Bucksport
Main Street
PO Drawer
Bucksport, ME 04416
Phone (207) 469-7368 Town Clerk
Settled 1764; incorporated as town of Buckstown 27 June 1792; set off part to Orrington 1816; changed name to Bucksport 12 June 1817; established boundary Orrington 28 February 1821; set off part to Brewer 10 April 1841; set off part to Orrington 20 August 1850; set off part to Dedham 18 March 1909 (Hancock County)
Vital records: From 1775

Buckstown
(see Bucksport)

Town of Burlington
PO Box 36
Burlington, ME 04417
Incorporated as a town 8 March 1832; annexed part of Lowell 26 July 1847; annexed part of Two Mile Strip (a tract north of Lowell and Burlington) 10 March 1885 (Penobscot County)
Vital records: From 1769

*Town of Burnham
PO Box 55
Burnham, ME 04922
Phone (207) 948-2369 Selectmen's Office; (207) 487-5090 Town Clerk
Settled 1795; formerly called Twentyfivemile Pond Plantation; set off part to Unity 1813; set off part to Joy (present-day Troy) 1819; incorporated as a town 4 February 1824; annexed part of Warsaw (present-day Pittsfield) 17 March 1821; established boundary with Unity 17 January 1868; annexed part of Clinton Gore 26 February 1873 (Waldo County)
Land records: Contact Selectmen's Office, Town Office, Rt. 1, Box 760, Burnham, ME 04922
Naturalization records: No naturalization records
Vital records: 1892 to date (very few prior to 1892); contact Caroline

Mitchell, Town Clerk
Probate records: No probate records

Town of Buxton
Town Clerk
RR 3, Box 225A
Gorham, ME 04038
Phone (207) 929-6171 Town Clerk
Settled 1748; incorporated as a town 14 July 1772; set off part to Standish 17 February 1824 (York County)
Vital records: From 1773

*Town of Byron
HC 62, Box 408
Byron, ME 04275-9715
Phone (207) 364-3194 Town Clerk
Incorporated as a town 24 January 1833 (Oxford County)
Vital records: From 1814; contact Town Clerk

City of Calais
Church Street
Calais, ME 04619
Phone (207) 454-2521 City Clerk
Settled 1779; incorporated as a town 16 June 1809; incorporated as a city 18 November 1850 under a law of 24 August 1850 (Washington County)
Vital records: From 1824

Calf Island
(see Frenchboro and Swan's Island)

Town of Cambridge
Rt. 1, Box 162
Cambridge, ME 04923
Settled 1804; set off from Ripley and incorporated as a town 8 February 1834; annexed part of Wellington 27 February 1885 (Somerset County)
Vital records: From 1792

Town of Camden
Rt. 2
PO Box 1207
Camden, ME 04843
Settled 1769; incorporated as a town 17 February 1791; annexed part of Warren 10 February 1836; set off part to form Rockport 25 February 1891; set off parts to Rockport 4 March 1891 and 28 March 1893 (Knox County)
Vital records: From 1783

*Town of Canaan
PO Box 68
Canaan, ME 04924
Phone (207) 474-8682
Settled 1770; incorporated as a town 18 June 1788; set off part to form Bloomfield 5 February 1814; set off part to form Milburn (present-day Skowhegan) 5 February 1823; annexed part of Warsaw (present-day Pittsfield) 9 February 1824; annexed parts of Pittsfield 12 March 1830 and 27 February 1841; annexed parts of Hartland 24 February 1838 and 17 July 1849; annexed part of Clinton 24 July 1849, repealed annexation 8 August 1850 (Somerset County)
Vital records: From 1776

*Town of Canton
PO Box 607
Canton, ME 04221
Phone (207) 597-2920 Selectmen's Office
Settled 1792; incorporated as a town 5 February 1821 from Jay; set off parts to Jay 27 January 1823, 3 February 1824, 4 March 1831 and 28 February 1864; parts of Hartford annexed 24 February 1838, 25 February 1839 and 8 August 1850; set off part to Peru 2 April 1859 (Oxford County)
Land records: No land records
Naturalization records: No naturalization records
Vital records: From 1818 to 1866 and from 1891 to date
Probate records: No probate records

*Town of Cape Elizabeth
Town Hall
320 Ocean House Road
PO Box 6260
Cape Elizabeth, ME 04107-0060
Phone (207) 799-7665 Town Clerk
Settled 1630; set off from Falmouth and erected as a district 1 November 1765; incorporated as a town 23 August 1775; set off part to Westbrook 1852; set off part to form South Portland 15 March 1895 (Cumberland County)
Land records: No land records
Naturalization records: No naturalization records
Vital records: From 1895 to date
Probate records: No probate records

Cape Porpoise
(see Kennebunkport)

Cape-Porpus
(see Kennebunkport)

Town of Caratunk
PO Box 44
Caratunk, ME 04925
Settled 1810; organized as a plantation 1840; incorporated as a town (Somerset County)
Vital records: From 1854

*City of Caribou
25 High Street
Caribou, ME 04736
Phone (207) 493-3324
Settled 1839; incorporated as town of Lyndon 5 April 1859; annexed Eatons Grant, Sheridan and Forestville 12 February 1869; changed name to Caribou 26 February 1869; changed name to Lyndon 9 March 1869; changed name to Caribou 8 February 1877; set off part to Connor 18 March 1881; incorporated as a city 23 February 1967 (Aroostook County)
Land records: No land records
Naturalization records: No naturalization records
Vital records: From 1892; contact City Clerk; copies: $7.00 each
Probate records: No probate records

Town of Carmel
Main Road
PO Box 114
Carmel, ME 04419
Phone (207) 848-3361 Manager
Settled 1798; incorporated as a town 21 June 1811; annexed part of Etna 19 February 1866 (Penobscot County)
Vital records: From 1760

Town of Carrabassett Valley
Town Office
Carrabassett, ME 04947
Phone (207) 235-2645
Incorporated as a town 23 September 1972 (Franklin County)

Carroll Plantation
Rt. 1, Box 1900
Springfield, ME 04487
Settled 1831; incorporated as a town 20 March 1845; surrendered incorporation 28 June 1937 under law of 26 March 1937; organized as a plantation (Penobscot County)
Vital records: From 1928

Town of Carthage
HCR 67
Dixfield, ME 04224
Phone (207) 562-8874
Settled 1803; incorporated as a town 20 February 1826 (previously known as 4 AP, as which set off part to Dixfield 6 February 1822 and annexed it again 1 February 1827); set off part to form Plantation Number 4, 17 July 1849 (Franklin County)
Vital records: From 1812

*Cary Plantation
PO Box 1271
Houlton, ME 04730

Settled 1824; organized as Plantation Number 11, Range 1, 30 June 1859; ratified organization 21 February 1878; organized as Cary Plantation 27 January 1883; ratified organization 5 March 1895 (Aroostook County)
Land records: No land records
Naturalization records: No naturalization records
Vital records: From 1862
Probate records: No probate records

Town of Casco
PO Box 60
Casco, ME 04015
Settled 1771; set off from Raymond and incorporated as a town 18 March 1841; annexed part of Raymond 7 March 1842; annexed part of Poland 20 March 1858; annexed Dingley Islands and Songo Gore 28 January 1876 (Cumberland County)
Vital records: From 1841

*Town of Castine
Court Street
PO Box 204
Castine, ME 04421
Phone (207) 326-4502
Settled 1626; set off from Penobscot and incorporated as a town 10 February 1796; set off part to form part of Brooksville 13 June 1817; annexed parts of Penobscot 1817, 12 February 1839 and 14 March 1927 (Hancock County)
Land records: Yes
Naturalization records: No naturalization records
Vital records: From 1796
Probate records: Yes

Town of Castle Hill
Pulcifer Street
PO Box 211
Mapleton, ME 04757
Phone (207) 764-3755
Settled 1843; incorporated as a town 25 February 1903 (Aroostook County)
Vital records: From 1855

Town of Caswell
HC 62
Limestone, ME 04750
Organized as a plantation 14 April 1879; incorporated as a town (Aroostook County)
Vital records: From 1898

Cathance Neck
(see Bowdoinham)

Town of Centerville
RFD, Box 142
Columbia Falls, ME 04623

Incorporated as a town 16 March 1842; annexed part of Columbia 24 February 1859; set off part to Northfield 11 March 1915 (Washington County)
Vital records: From 1770

Central Aroostook (unorganized area)
(Aroostook County)

Central Hancock (unorganized area)
(Hancock County)

Central Somerset (unorganized area)
(Somerset County)

Chandler's Gore
(see Livermore and Hartford)

Chandlerville
(see Detroit)

Town of Chapman
PO Box 211
Mapleton, ME 04757
Organized as a plantation 27 April 1824; ratified organization 14 February 1879; incorporated as a town 11 March 1915 (Aroostook County)
Vital records: From 1868

Town of Charleston
PO Box 102
Charleston, ME 04422
Phone (207) 285-3637
Settled 1795; incorporated as town of New Charleston 16 February 1811; changed name to Charleston 23 February 1827 (Penobscot County)
Vital records: From 1809

Town of Charlotte
Rt. 1, Box 334
Charlotte, ME 04666
Settled 1807; organized 21 March 1821; incorporated as a town 19 January 1825; set off part to form part of Meddybemps 20 February 1841 (Washington County)
Vital records: From 1816

*Town of Chelsea
Rt. 6, Box 1320
Gardiner, ME 04345
Phone (207) 582-4802
Settled 1759; set off from Hallowell and incorporated as a town 1 March 1850 under act of 17 August 1850; set off part to Pittston 20 February 1855 (Kennebec County)
Land records: Yes
Naturalization records: No naturalization records

Vital records: From 1782
Probate records: No probate records

Town of Cherryfield
Rt. 1, Box 3
Cherryfield, ME 04622
Phone (207) 546-2376
Settled 1757; incorporated as a town 9 February 1816; annexed part of Steuben 6 February 1826; annexed part of Columbia 12 February 1881 (Washington County)
Vital records: From 1845

Town of Chester
Rt. 1
Lincoln Center, ME 04458
Settled 1823; incorporated as a town 26 February 1834 (Penobscot County)
Vital records: From 1788

Town of Chesterville
Rt. 2, Box 4190
Farmington, ME 04938
Phone (207) 778-2433
Settled 1782; incorporated as a town 20 February 1802; annexed part of Wilton 1811; annexed part of Vienna 2 August 1847 (Franklin County)
Vital records: From 1785

Town of China
Pond Road
Rt. 1, Box 970
South China, ME 04358
Phone (207) 445-2014
Settled 1774; town of Harlem incorporated 3 February 1796; annexed part of Winslow 1813; China formed 5 June 1818 from parts of Harlem, Albion and Winslow; annexed remainder of Harlem 15 January 1882; set off part to Vassalboro 18 February 1829; established boundary with Palermo 15 March 1830; established boundary with Albion 13 March 1839 (Kennebec County)
Vital records: From 1785

Town of Clifton
PO Box 249
East Eddington, ME 04428
Formerly called Jarvis Gore; settled 1812; part set off to Eddington 31 January 1823; incorporated as town of Maine 7 August 1848; changed name to Clifton 9 June 1849 (Penobscot County)
Vital records: From 1848

*Town of Clinton
Railroad Street
Rt. 2, Box 2440
Clinton, ME 04927

Phone (207) 426-8511; (207) 426-9194

Settled 1775; incorporated as a town 28 February 1795; set off part to Fairfax (present-day Albion) 1814; annexed part of Pittsfield 6 March 1830; set off part to form Benton 16 March 1842; set off part to Canaan 24 July 1849 and reannexed 8 August 1850; annexed part of Benton 24 March 1853; annexed part of Clinton Gore 26 February 1873 (Kennebec County)

Vital records: From 1797

Clinton Gore
(see Burnham and Clinton)

Codyville Plantation
Rt. 6
Topsfield, ME 04490
Organized as a plantation 14 April 1845 (Washington County)
Vital records: From 1892

Cold Stream Settlement
(see Lowell)

Town of Columbia
PO Box 22
Columbia, ME 04623
Phone (207) 483-2365
Settled 1770; incorporated as a town 8 February 1796; set off parts to Harrington 1818 and 5 February 1823; annexed part of 19 MD BPP (wild land township) 17 February 1834; annexed part of Jonesboro 8 February 1838; annexed part of 19 MD BPP 18 March 1840; set off part to Centerville 24 February 1859; set off part to form Columbia Falls 25 March 1863; set off part to Cherryfield 12 February 1811 (Washington County)
Vital records: From 1752

Town of Columbia Falls
PO Box 66
Columbia Falls, ME 04623
Phone (207) 483-4067
Settled 1780; set off from Columbia and incorporated as a town 25 March 1863 (Washington County)
Vital records: From 1860

Concord
Settled 1780; incorporated as a town 25 January 1821; established western boundary 21 January 1823; annexed part of 1R2 BKP WKR (Pleasant Ridge Plantation) 28 January 1829; set off part to Pleasant Ridge 9 February 1860; repealed incorporation and organized as a plantation 15 March 1921; repealed

organization 22 March 1935; surrendered organization 6 July 1935 (Somerset County)

Connor (unorganized area)
Organized 1877; annexed part of Caribou and ratified organization 18 March 1881; ratified organization 9 March 1883; incorporated as a town 12 July 1913 under act of 18 March 1913 (Washington County)

*Town of Cooper
HC 68, Box 151B
Cooper, ME 04638
Phone (207) 454-7703
Settled 1812; incorporated as a town 6 February 1822; set off part to Alexander 22 February 1838; set off part to form part of Meddybemps 20 February 1841 (Washington County)
Land records: No land records
Naturalization records: No naturalization records
Vital records: From 1878
Probate records: No probate records

Coplin Plantation
PO Box 91
Stratton, ME 04982
Organized as a plantation 5 February and 5 March 1895 (Franklin County)
Vital records: From 1895

*Town of Corinna
PO Box L
Corinna, ME 04928
Phone (207) 278-4234 Town Clerk
Settled 1815; incorporated as a town 11 December 1816; established boundary with Dexter 26 January 1852 (Penobscot County)
Land records: Yes
Naturalization records: No naturalization records
Vital records: From 1797
Probate records: No probate records

Town of Corinth
Town Hall, Exeter Road
PO Box 10
East Corinth, ME 04427
Phone (207) 285-3271
Settled 1792; incorporated as a town 21 June 1811 (Penobscot County)
Vital records: From 1785

Town of Cornish
Maple Street
PO Box 346
Cornish, ME 04020
Phone (207) 625-4324
Settled 1776; incorporated as a town 27 February 1794; established boundary

with Parsonsfield 12 February 1876 (York County)
Vital records: From 1857

*Town of Cornville
West Ridge Road
Rt. 1, Box 3050
Cornville, ME 04976
Phone (207) 474-3275
Settled 1794; incorporated as a town 24 February 1798; set off parts to Milburn (present-day Skowhegan) 23 February 1831, 29 January 1833 and 2 March 1833; annexed Mile-and-a-half Strip, a tract of land south of the north line of the Kennebec Purchase, 1907 (Somerset County)
Vital records: From 1772; contact Town Clerk

Coxhall
(see Lyman)

Cranberry
(see Friendship)

*Town of Cranberry Isles
Islesford, ME 04646
Phone (207) 244-5943
Settled 1761; set off from Mount Desert and incorporated as a town 16 March 1830; annexed part of Mount Desert 13 June 1849 (Hancock County)
Land records: No land records
Naturalization records: No naturalization records
Vital records: From 1783 (scant until 1892); contact Irene M. Bartlett, Clerk
Probate records: No probate records

Town of Crawford
Rt. 1, Box 1045
Crawford, ME 04694
Incorporated as town of Adams 11 February 1828; changed name to Crawford 23 February 1828; annexed part of Alexander 2 April 1859 (Washington County)
Vital records: From 1827

Criehaven
(see Matinicus Isle Plantation)

*Town of Crystal
PO Box 383
Island Falls, ME 04747
Phone (207) 463-2770
Settled 1839; organized 1840; ratified organization 21 February 1878; ratified 5 March 1895; incorporated as a town 21 March 1901; set off part to Sherman 17 February 1881 (Aroostook County)

Land records: Yes
Naturalization records: No naturalization records
Vital records: From 1893
Probate records: No probate records

Town of Cumberland
PO Box 128
Cumberland, ME 04021
Phone (207) 829-5559
Set off from North Yarmouth and incorporated as a town 2 April 1822 under act of 19 March 1821; set off part to Portland 14 February 1889 (Cumberland County)
Vital records: From 1720

Town of Cushing
PO Box 10
Cushing, ME 04563-0010
Phone (207) 354-2375
Settled 1733; incorporated as a town 30 January 1789; set off part to form Saint George 7 February 1803; annexed part of Warren 1807; set off part to Thomaston 1809; annexed part of Friendship 5 February 1834; set off part to Friendship 20 February 1839; set off part to Thomaston 21 February 1891 (Knox County)
Vital records: From 1735

Town of Cutler
PO Box 236
Cutler, ME 04626
Phone (207) 259-3693
Settled 1765; incorporated as a town 26 January 1826 (Washington County)
Vital records: From 1844

Cyr Plantation
HCR 63, Box 58
Van Buren, ME 04785
Ratified organization as a plantation 12 March 1870 (Aroostook County)
Vital records: From 1892

Dallas Plantation
PO Box 92
Rangeley, ME 04970
Changed name from Plantation Number 2 and 3 to Dallas Plantation 25 February 1845; changed name to Rangely Plantation 18 March 1852; organized as Dallas Plantation 5 March 1895 (Franklin County)
Vital records: From 1892

Dalton
(see Ashland)

*Town of Damariscotta
Church Street
PO Box 218
Damariscotta, ME 04543

Phone (207) 563-5168 Selectmen's Office
Settled 1640; set off from Bristol and Nobleboro and incorporated as a town 15 March 1848 under act of 26 July 1847 (Lincoln County)
Vital records: From 1848

*Town of Danforth
Central Street
PO Box 117
Danforth, ME 04424
Phone (207) 448-2321
Settled 1829; incorporated as a town 17 March 1860; annexed part of Weston 4 March 1885; annexed part of Eaton 15 February 1887 (Washington County)
Land records: No land records
Naturalization records: No naturalization records
Vital records: From 1860; contact Town Clerk
No vital records search service; copies: 20¢ each, $7.00 for certified copies
Probate records: No probate records

Town of Danville (now part of City of Auburn)
Settled 1764; called Danville-Old Danville from 1781 to 1864; Danville and Pejepscot from 1775 to 1867; incorporated as town of Pejepscot 6 March 1802; name changed to Danville 1 February 1818; set off parts to Durham 5 February 1821 and 11 February 1823; annexed part of Poland 24 March 1852; set off part to Auburn 19 February 1859; set off remainder to Auburn 26 February 1867 (Androscoggin County)
Vital records: From 1751 to 1834

Town of Dayton
Rt. 2, Box 437A
Hollis Center, ME 04042
Phone (207) 499-7526
Settled 1753; set off from Hollis and incorporated as a town 7 April 1854 (York County)
Land records; contact Town Clerk
Naturalization records: No naturalization records
Vital records: From 1854; contact Town Clerk
Probate records: No probate records

Dearborn
Settled 1782; incorporated 22 February 1812; set off parts to Waterville 1815, 21 January 1822 and 28 February 1826; set off parts to Belgrade 29 January 1834 and 22 March 1839; set off part to form part of Smithfield 29 February 1840; surrendered

organization 20 April 1841; remainder annexed to Waterville 17 March 1843 (Somerset County)

Town of Deblois
PO Box 32D
Deblois, ME 04622
Incorporated as a town 4 March 1852 (Washington County)
Vital records: From 1855

*Town of Dedham
PO Box 1248
East Holden, ME 04429
Phone (207) 843-6217
Settled 1810; incorporated as a town 7 February 1837; set off part to Brewer 10 April 1841; established boundary with Orland and Ellsworth 31 July 1847; set off part to Ellsworth 23 April 1852; annexed part of Bucksport 18 March 1909 (Hancock County)
Vital records: From 1787

Town of Deer Isle
Church Street
PO Box 43
Deer Isle, ME 04627
Phone (207) 348-6060 Selectmen's Office
Settled 1762; incorporated as a town 2 February 1789; established boundary 29 February 1868; set off part to form Isle Au Haut 28 February 1874; set off part to form Stonington 18 February 1897 (Hancock County)
Vital records: From 1768

Deering
Settled 1628; set off from Falmouth and Westbrook and incorporated as a town 16 February 1871; incorporated as a city 5 March 1889; annexed to Portland 6 February 1899 (Cumberland County)
Vital records: Marriages from 1871 to 1899

Town of Denmark
PO Box 90
Denmark, ME 04022
Phone (207) 452-2163
Formed from Fryeburg Academy Grant (Pleasant Mountain Gore), Fosters Gore and part of Brownfield and incorporated as a town 20 February 1807; annexed part of Fryeburg 1813; annexed part of Brownfield 2 March 1821; set off part to Sebago 12 March 1830; set off part to Bridgton 7 March 1842; set off part (Texas) to Bridgton 2 August 1847; annexed part of Brownfield 13 March 1907 (Oxford County)
Vital records: From 1807

Dennistown Plantation
HCR 76, Box 125
Jackman, ME 04945
Ratified organization as a plantation 5 March 1895 (Somerset County)
Vital records: From 1840

Town of Dennysville
King Street, Box 142
Dennysville, ME 04628
Phone (207) 726-4663 Municipal Offices
Settled 1786; incorporated as a town 13 February 1818; set off part to form Pembroke 4 February 1832 (Washington County)
Vital records: From 1790

Town of Detroit
PO Box 147
Detroit, ME 04929
Phone (207) 257-4488
Incorporated as town of Chandlerville 19 February 1828; changed name to Detroit 18 March 1841; established boundary with Plymouth 29 February 1844; set off part to Pittsfield 12 March 1855 (Somerset County)
Vital records: From 1780

*Town of Dexter
PO Box 313
Dexter, ME 04930-0313
Phone (207) 924-7351
Settled 1801; incorporated as a town 17 June 1816; established boundary with Corinna 26 January 1852; chartered as a city 7 February 1895 but act rejected by voters (Penobscot County)
Land records: No land records
Naturalization records: No naturalization records
Vital records: From 1900 (earlier records destroyed by fire)
Probate records: No probate records

Dickeyville
(see Frenchville)

Dingley Islands
(see Casco)

Town of Dixfield
PO Box O
Dixfield, ME 04224
Phone (207) 562-8151
Settled 1795; incorporated as a town 21 June 1803; annexed part of 4 AP (present-day Carthage) 6 February 1822 and set it off again 1 February 1827 (Oxford County)
Vital records: From 1803

*Town of Dixmont
Rt. 1, Box 180
Dixmont, ME 04932
Phone (207) 234-2294
Settled 1799; incorporated as a town 1807 (Penobscot County)
Vital records: From 1700

Town of Dover-Foxcroft
34 East Main Street
Dover-Foxcroft, ME 04426
Incorporated as towns 19 January 1822 (Dover) and 28 February 1812 (Foxcroft); united towns 23 March 1915, effective 1 March 1922 (Piscataquis County)
Vital records: From 1792

DR1 WELS
(see Fort Fairfield)

*Town of Dresden
PO Box 30, Route 27
Dresden, ME 04342
Phone (207) 737-4335 Selectman's Office
Settled 1750; set off from Wiscasset and incorporated as a town 25 June 1794; annexed part of Alna 20 March 1841; set off Perkins (Swan Island in Kennebec River) 24 June 1847 (Lincoln County)
Land records: Yes
Naturalization records: No naturalization records
Vital records: From 1771
Probate records: No probate records

Drew Plantation
HCR 60
Wytopitlock, ME 04497
Settled 1825; set off part to Prentiss 1 March 1869; set off part to Reed 5 March 1889 and reannexed it 28 March 1903; incorporated as a town 5 April 1921; repealed incorporation 24 March 1933; organized as a plantation 1934 (Penobscot County)
Vital records: From 1853

Town of Durham
Rt. 2, Box 1908
Lisbon Falls, ME 04252
Phone (207) 353-2561
Settled 1763; incorporated as a town 17 February 1789; annexed parts of Danville 5 February 1821 and 11 February 1823 (Androscoggin County)
Vital records: From 1744

Dutton
(see Glenburn)

Town of Dyer Brook
Rt. 1, Box 87-C
Island Falls, ME 04747
Phone (207) 757-8302
Organized as a plantation 1863; reorganized 14 July 1880; incorporated as a town 21 March 1891 (Aroostook County)
Vital records: From 1895

E Plantation
PO Box 94
Blaine, ME 04734
Organized as a plantation 26 September 1898 (Aroostook County)
Vital records: From 1936

Township E
(see Madrid)

Town of Eagle Lake
Main Street
PO Box 287
Eagle Lake, ME 04739
Phone (207) 444-5511
Settled 1840; organized as a plantation 1856, ratified organization 12 March 1870 and 5 March 1895; incorporated as a town 30 June 1911 under act of 16 March 1911 (Aroostook County)
Vital records: From 1867

East Central Franklin (unorganized area)
(Franklin County)

East Central Washington (unorganized area)
(Washington County)

East Hancock (unorganized area)
(Hancock County)

East Livermore
(see Livermore Falls)

Town of East Machias
Municipal Building
PO Box 117
East Machias, ME 04630
Phone (207) 255-8598
Settled 1763; set off from Machias and incorporated as town 24 January 1826; changed name to Machisses 12 February 1840; changed name to East Machias 6 April 1841 (Washington County)
Vital records: From 1709

*Town of East Millinocket
53 Main Street
East Millinocket, ME 04430
Phone (207) 746-3551 Town Clerk

Incorporated as a town 21 February 1907 (Penobscot County)
Vital records: From 1907

East Pond Plantation
(see Norridgewock and Smithfield)

East Thomaston
(see Rockland)

Town of Eastbrook
Rt. 1, Box 467
Franklin, ME 04634
Settled 1800; incorporated as a town 8 February 1837; annexed part of Waltham 27 January 1872 (Hancock County)
Vital records: From 1892

Eastmans Grant
(see Stow)

Town of Easton
Main Street
PO Box 127
Easton, ME 04740
Phone (207) 488-6652
Settled 1865; incorporated as a town 24 February 1865 (Aroostook County)
Vital records: From 1892

City of Eastport
78 High Street
Eastport, ME 04631
Phone (207) 853-2300 City Clerk
Settled 1772; incorporated as a town 24 February 1798; set off part to form Lubec 3 March 1811; Dudleys or Allens Island annexed 19 July 1847; incorporated as a city 3 March 1893 (Washington County)
Vital records: From 1778

Eaton
Settled 1829; incorporated 25 January 1873; set off part to form Forest City and remainder annexed to Danforth 15 February 1887 (Washington County)

Eatons Grant
(see Caribou)

*Town of Eddington
PO Box 99
East Eddington, ME 04428
Phone (207) 843-5233
Settled 1787; incorporated as a town 22 February 1811; annexed part of Jarvis Gore (present-day Clifton) 31 January 1823; annexed parts of Brewer 30 June 1846 and 16 March 1855 (Penobscot County)

Vital records: Births from 1797 to 1821, 1828, 1830, 1834, 1837, 1844, from 1864 to 1890, and from 1923 to 1938, deaths from 1810 to 1817, from 1864 to 1873, 1888, and from 1923 to 1934, and marriages from 1802 to 1822, 1843, from 1846 to 1850, from 1852 to 1894, and from 1897 to 1934; copies: $1.00 plus SASE

Eden
(see Bar Harbor)

*Town of Edgecomb
PO Box 139
Edgecomb, ME 04556
Phone (207) 882-7018
Settled 1744; incorporated as a town 9 March 1774; set off part to form Westport 5 February 1828 (Lincoln County)
Vital records: From 1774; contact Town Clerk

Town of Edinburg
HCR 66, Box 118
Howland, ME 04448
Settled 1827; incorporated as a town 31 January 1835 (Penobscot County)
Vital records: From 1835

Town of Edmunds (disorganized)
Settled 1775; incorporated 7 February 1828; annexed parts of Trescott 7 February 1828 and 7 March 1899; repealed incorporation 29 March 1937 (Washington County)
Vital records: From 1806 to 1895

Eighty Rod Strip
(see New Gloucester, Poland and Raymond)

*Town of Eliot
141 State Road
Eliot, ME 03903
Phone (207) 439-1813
Separated from Kittery and incorporated as a town 3 March 1810; annexed parts of Kittery 8 February 1826 (repealed) and annexed same part 7 February 1829 (York County)
Vital records: From 1810

Elliotsville Plantation
Settled 1820; incorporated as town of Elliotsville 19 February 1835; annexed part of Wilson 10 August 1848; repealed incorporation 26 March 1858; organized as a plantation 3 January 1887; ratified organization 5 March 1895 (Piscataquis County)
Vital records: From 1913

City of Ellsworth
City Hall
PO Box 586
Ellsworth, ME 04605
Phone (207) 667-2563 City Clerk
Settled 1763; incorporated as a town 26 February 1800; annexed parts of Surry and Trenton 3 March 1809; set off part to Surry 28 February 1821 and reannexed it 17 February 1829; established boundary with Dedham and Orland 31 July 1847; annexed part of Dedham 23 April 1852; incorporated as a city 27 February 1869 under act of 6 February 1869 (Hancock County)
Vital records: From 1800s

Town of Embden
PO Box 3160
North Anson, ME 04958
Settled 1779; incorporated as a town 22 June 1804; set off part to Anson 28 January 1828 (Somerset County)
Vital records: From 1783

*Town of Enfield
PO Box 28
Enfield, ME 04433
Phone (207) 732-4270
Settled 1820; incorporated as a town 31 January 1835 (Penobscot County)
Land records: Yes
Naturalization records: No naturalization records
Vital records: From 1857
Probate records: No probate records

*Town of Etna
Town Hall, Shadow Lane
PO Box G
Etna, ME 04434
Phone (207) 269-3551
Settled 1807; incorporated as town of Aetna 15 February 1820; changed name almost immediately to Etna; set off part to form Plymouth 21 February 1826; set off part to Carmel 19 February 1866 (Penobscot County)
Vital records: From 1742

*Town of Eustis
PO Box 350
Stratton, ME 04982
Phone (207) 246-4401
Organized with other territory as Jackson 1850; organized as Eustis 1857; incorporated as a town 18 February 1871 (Franklin County)
Land records: Contact Town Clerk
Naturalization records: No naturalization records
Vital records: From about 1890 (others burned); contact Town Clerk
Probate records: No probate records

Town of Exeter
PO Box 59
Exeter, ME 04435
Phone (207) 379-2191
Settled 1801; incorporated as a town 16 February 1811 (Penobscot County)
Vital records: From 1808

Fairfax
(see Albion)

*Town of Fairfield
Lawrence Avenue
PO Box 149
Fairfield, ME 04937
Phone (207) 453-7346 Town Clerk
Settled 1774; incorporated as a town 18 June 1788; set off parts to Norridgewock 21 February 1834 and 16 April 1841; set off part to Bloomfield 22 February 1858; annexed part of Benton 27 February 1873 (Somerset County)
Vital records: From 1788; contact Thelma Brooks, Deputy Town Clerk; copies: small charge, standard charge for certified copies

*Town of Falmouth
271 Falmouth Road
Falmouth, ME 04105
Phone (207) 781-5253 Town Clerk
Settled 1632; incorporated as a town 12 November 1718; set off part to form district of Cape Elizabeth 1 November 1765; set off part to form Portland 4 July 1786; set off part to form Stroudwater (present-day Westbrook) 14 February 1814; annexed part of Westbrook 1819; set off part to Westbrook 31 January 1825; annexed parts of Westbrook 11 February 1828 and 22 March 1831; set off parts to Westbrook 24 February 1835, 21 March 1836 and 25 March 1853; set off part to form Deering town 16 February 1871 (Cumberland County)
Land records: Inventory records 1840, from 1843 to 1851, and from 1853 to 1888, assessments from 1876 to 1888 and from 1890 to 1896, inventories, valuations and assessments 1889, from 1891 to 1893, from 1896 to 1923, and from 1938 to 1947, inventories and valuations 1889, valuations from 1812 to 1817, 1821, 1825, 1830, from 1836 to 1840, 1843, 1851, 1890, 1894, and from 1924–1946, valuations and assessments from 1947 to 1967, annual assessment rolls from 1926 to date, individual property record cards from 1960 to date
Naturalization records: No naturalization records

Vital records: Records of births from 1718 to 1739 and from 1784 to 1881 and from 1883 to 1977, records of deaths from 1851 to 1974, records of marriages from 1813 to 1974, marriage intentions from 1733 to 1763 and 1849 to 1855 and 1858 to 1958
Probate records: No probate records

*Town of Farmingdale
Town Hall
175 Maine Avenue
Gardiner, ME 04345
Phone (207) 582-2225
Settled 1759; set off from Gardiner, Hallowell and West Gardiner and incorporated as a town 3 April 1852; set off part to West Gardiner 19 March 1853; set off part to Manchester 15 March 1870 (Kennebec County)
Vital records: From 1852

Town of Farmington
147 Lower Main Street
Farmington, ME 04938
Phone (207) 778-6538 Town Clerk
Settled 1776; incorporated as a town 1 February 1794; annexed part of Industry 29 July 1850; annexed part of Strong 16 March 1853 (Franklin County)
Vital records: From 1741

Town of Fayette
Kents Hill, ME 04349
Phone (207) 685-4373
Settled 1779; incorporated as a town 28 February 1795; set off part to Mount Vernon 1802 (Kennebec County)
Vital records: From 1785

Forest City
Settled 1829; set off from Eaton and incorporated 15 February 1887; repealed incorporation 1 March 1924 under act of 16 March 1923 (Washington County)

Forestville
(see Caribou)

The Forks Plantation
Rt. 201
The Forks, ME 04985
Organized as a plantation 20 March 1895 (Somerset County)
Vital records: From 1800s

Forkstown
(see Haynesville)

Town of Fort Fairfield
79 Main Street
PO Box 102

Fort Fairfield, ME 04742
Phone (207) 472-3881
Settled 1816; incorporated as a town 11 March 1858; annexed part of DR1 WELS 16 February 1866; annexed Sarsfield (or Plymouth) 12 February 1867 (Aroostook County)
Vital records: From 1847

*Town of Fort Kent
111 West Main Street
Fort Kent, ME 04743
Phone (207) 834-3090
Settled 1841; incorporated as a town 23 February 1869 (Aroostook County)
Vital records: From 1892

Fosters Gore
(see Denmark)

Fox Isle
(see North Haven)

Foxcroft
(see Dover-Foxcroft)

Fox's Grant
(see Peru)

Town of Frankfort
Main Street
PO Box 57
Frankfort, ME 04438
Phone (207) 223-5546
Settled 1760; incorporated as a town 25 June 1799; set off part to form Prospect and part to form Hampden 24 February 1794; set off part to Hampden 1816; set off part to Swanville 21 February 1832; set off part to form part of Searsport 13 February 1845; set off part to form Winterport 12 March 1860; set off part to Monroe 21 February 1863; set off part to Winterport 18 February 1867 (Waldo County)
Vital records: From 1903

Town of Franklin
PO Box 209
Franklin, ME 04634
Phone (207) 565-3663 Selectman's Office
Settled 1784; incorporated as a town 24 June 1825; annexed part of 9 SD BPP (wild land township) 14 March 1837; annexed part of Hancock 18 February 1852; annexed part of 10 SD BPP (wild land township) 16 March 1857 (Hancock County)
Vital records: From 1813

Franklin Plantation (disorganized)
Settled 1820; formerly called Plantation

Number 2; organized 1841; set off parts to Sumner 22 February 1844 and 12 February 1863; set off part to Peru 21 February 1885; abolished 21 February 1899 and annexed to Rumford and Peru (Oxford County)
Vital records: From 1842 to 1892

Town of Freedom
Rt. 1, Box 860
Freedom, ME 04941
Phone (207) 382-6177
Settled 1794; incorporated as a town 11 June 1813; established boundary with Montville 10 February 1836 (Waldo County)
Vital records: From 1777

Freeman (disorganized)
Settled 1797; incorporated 4 March 1808; set off part to form part of North Salem (Salem) 10 January 1823; set off part to form New Portland 7 February 1833; repealed incorporation 9 April 1937; surrendered organization 1 January 1938 (Franklin County)

Town of Freeport
4 Main Street
Freeport, ME 04032
Phone (207) 865-4745 Town Clerk
Settled 1750; set off from North Yarmouth and incorporated as a town 14 February 1789; set off part to Brunswick 1790; set off part to form Pownal 3 March 1808; set off parts to Brunswick 28 January 1833, 15 February 1839 and 24 August 1850 (Cumberland County)
Vital records: From 1789

Town of Frenchboro
32 Harborside Drive
Frenchboro, ME 04635
Phone (207) 334-2933
Incorporated as town of Islandport 11 February 1857; repealed incorporation 27 March 1858; organized as Long Island Plantation; set off Calf Island and West Black Island to Swan's Island 22 February 1901; incorporated as Town of Frenchboro (Hancock County)
Vital records: From 1900

Town of Frenchville
Main Street
PO Box 185
Frenchville, ME 04745
Phone (207) 543-7301
Incorporated as town of Dickeyville 23 February 1869; changed name to Frenchville 26 January 1871; set off part to form Saint Agatha 17 March 1899; set off part to Saint Agatha 14 March 1827 (Aroostook County)
Vital records: From 1869

*Town of Friendship
HCR 68, Box 439
Friendship, ME 04547
Phone (207) 832-7644
Settled 1770; incorporated as a town 25 February 1807; set off part to Cushing 5 February 1834; annexed part of Cushing 20 February 1839; annexed Otter, Cranberry, Halls, Harbor, Black and Heron Islands 28 February 1867 (Knox County)
Land records: Yes
Naturalization records: No naturalization records
Vital records: From 1900 (earlier records destroyed by fire)

Town of Fryeburg
2 Lovewell's Pond Road
Fryeburg, ME 04037
Settled 1762; set off part to New Hampshire 1766; incorporated as a town 11 January 1777; annexed part of Brownfield 20 February 1807; set off part to Denmark 1813; set off part to Bridgton 2 August 1847 (Oxford County)
Vital records: From 1777

Fryeburg Academy Grant
Set off part to form Denmark 20 February 1807. Set off part to Stoneham 31 January 1884; annexed remainder to Mason 25 March 1911 (the northern part of Mason, the south line passing over the summit of Caribou Mountain, Oxford County)

Fryeburg Addition
(see Stow)

*City of Gardiner
City Hall
6 Church Street
Gardiner, ME 04345
Phone (207) 582-4460 City Clerk
Settled 1760; set off from Pittston and incorporated as a town 17 February 1803; annexed part of Hallowell 24 February 1834; incorporated as a city 11 August 1849; adopted city charter 26 November 1849; set off part to form West Gardiner 8 August 1850; set off part to form part of Farmingdale 3 April 1852 (Kennebec County)
Land records: Contact Assessor's Office
Naturalization records: No naturalization records
Vital records: From 1800; contact City Clerk
Probate records: No probate records

Gardinerston
(see Pittston)

*Garfield Plantation
Rt. 1, Box 100
Ashland, ME 04732
Organized as a plantation 13 April 1885; ratified organization 5 March 1895 (Aroostook County)
Land records: No land records
Vital records: From 1892

*Town of Garland
PO Box 36
Garland, ME 04939
Phone (207) 924-6615
Settled 1802; incorporated as a town 16 February 1811 (Penobscot County)
Land records: Contact Town Office
Naturalization records: No naturalization records
Vital records: From early 1900s; contact Susan Grant, Town Clerk's Office, PO Box 196, Garland, ME 04939
Probate records: No probate records

*Town of Georgetown
PO Box 436
Georgetown, ME 04548
Phone (207) 371-2820
Settled 1607; incorporated as a town 13 June 1716; annexed Parkers Island and land west of Kennebec River 1738; annexed part (Small Point) of North Yarmouth 1741; set off part to form Woolwich 20 October 1759; set off part to form Bath 17 February 1781; set off part to form Phippsburg 26 January 1814; set off part to form Arrowsic 2 March 1841 (Sagadahoc County)
Naturalization records: No naturalization records
Vital records: From 1750 (includes areas which are now towns of Arrowsic, Bath, Phippsburg and Westport); contact Catherine Collins, Town Clerk

Gerry
(see Windsor)

*Town of Gilead
Rt. 2, Box 1310
Bethel, ME 04217
Phone (207) 836-2032 Selectmen's Office; (207) 824-2908 Bethel Historical Society
Settled 1780; incorporated as a town 23 June 1804 (Oxford County)
Land records: No land records
Naturalization records: No naturalization records
Vital records: From 1757; contact Randall H. Bennett, Curator of Collections, Bethel Historical Society,

Inc., 14 Broad Street, PO Box 12, Bethel, ME 04217-0012
Probate records: No probate records

Town of Glenburn
Lakeview Road
Rt. 1, Box 1375
Bangor, ME 04401
Phone (207) 947-6623; (207) 942-2905 Town Clerk-Assessor
Settled 1805; incorporated as town of Dutton 29 January 1822; changed name to Glenburn 18 March 1837; set off part to form part of Kenduskeag 20 February 1852; set off part to Old Town 28 March 1929 (Penobscot County)
Vital records: From 1800

Glenwood
(see Haynesville)

Glenwood Plantation
Wytopitlock, ME 04497
Incorporated as town of Glenwood 14 February 1867; repealed incorporation 28 February 1868; organized as a plantation 15 March 1877 (Aroostook County)
Vital records: From 1866

*Town of Gorham
270 Main Street
Gorham, ME 04038
Settled 1736; incorporated as a town 30 October 1764; annexed parts of Standish 19 February 1831 and 14 March 1839; annexed part of Scarboro 4 March 1864 (Cumberland County)
Land records: No land records
Vital records: From 1721; certified copies: $7.00 each

*Town of Gouldsboro
PO Box 68
Prospect Harbor, ME 04669
Phone (207) 963-5589
Settled 1700; incorporated as a town 16 February 1789; annexed part (West Bay Stream) of 7 SD BPP 28 February 1845; annexed part (Sowle Tract) of 7 SD BPP 26 February 1870; annexed part of Hancock 26 February 1870; set off part to form Winter Harbor 21 February 1895; annexed part of 7 SD BPP 8 March 1905 (Hancock County)
Vital records: From 1772; contact Yvonne P. Wilkinson, Town Clerk/ Registrar

Grand Falls Plantation (disorganized)
Settled 1830; organized as a plantation 16 November 1878 (Penobscot County)

*Town of Grand Isle
Main Street
PO Box 197
Grand Isle, ME 04746
Phone (207) 895-3420
Settled 1805; incorporated as town of Grant Isle 2 March 1869; changed name to Grand Isle 9 February 1872 (Aroostook County)
Vital records: From 1892

Grand Lake Stream Plantation
PO Box 82
Grand Lake Stream, ME 04637
Organized as a plantation 11 February 1897 (Washington County)

Grant Isle
(see Grand Isle)

Town of Gray
Dry Mills Road
PO Box 258
Gray, ME 04039
Phone (207) 657-3339
Settled 1750; incorporated as a town 19 June 1778 (Cumberland County)
Vital records: From 1700s

Grays Surplus
(see Raymond)

Town of Great Pond
Great Pond Road
Aurora, ME 04408
Organized as Plantation Number 33 MD 5 March 1895; changed name to Great Pond 1 October 1969; incorporated as a town (Hancock County)
Vital records: From 1894

Green
(see Belmont)

*Town of Greenbush
PO Box 210
Olamon, ME 04467
Phone (207) 732-3644
Settled 1812; incorporated as a town 28 February 1834 (Penobscot County)
Land records: Some
Naturalization records: No naturalization records
Vital records: From 1834
Probate records: No probate records

*Town of Greene
West Main Street
Rt. 1, Box 130
Greene, ME 04236
Phone (207) 946-5146
Settled 1773; set off from Lewiston and incorporated as a town 18 June 1788; established boundary with Lewiston and Lisbon 6 February 1826; established boundary with Wales 22 March 1843; set off part to Lewiston 20 April 1852; set off part to Webster (present-day Sabattus) 7 February 1895 (Androscoggin County)
Vital records: From 1748

Town of Greenfield (disorganized)
Settled 1812; incorporated as a town 29 January 1834 (Penobscot County)
Vital records: From 1850s; contact Maine State Archives

Greenvale Plantation
(see Sandy River Plantation)

*Town of Greenville
PO Box 1109
Greenville, ME 04441
Settled 1824; organized 1831 as Haskell; incorporated as a town 6 February 1836; annexed part of Wilson 10 August 1848 (Piscataquis County)
Vital records: From 1820

Town of Greenwood
PO Box 181
Locke Mills, ME 04255
Phone (207) 875-2773
Settled 1802; incorporated as a town 2 February 1816; set off part to Woodstock 17 February 1893 (Oxford County)
Vital records: From 1797

*Town of Guilford
PO Box 355
Guilford, ME 04443
Phone (207) 876-2202
Settled 1806; organized 8 October 1812; incorporated as a town 8 February 1816; annexed part of Parkman 15 February 1878; annexed part of Sangerville 23 February 1889 (Piscataquis County)
Land records: Mortgages from 1857 to 1904, tax abatements from 1912 to 1949 and from 1955 to 1961, tax collectors sales from 1845 to 1839; contact Michelle Nichols, Town Clerk
Vital records: Birth records from 1892 to date (indexed), death records from 1892 to date (indexed), death certificates from 1897 to 1949, marriage intentions from 1892 to 1939, marriage records from 1892 to date (indexed); contact Town Clerk
Vital records search service: $10.00 per hour; certified copies: $7.00 for the

first copy and $3.00 for each additional copy of the same record (burial location not available unless listed on death certificate, contact Peter Neal, Sexton, PO Box 750, Guilford, ME 04443)

*City of Hallowell
1 Winthrop Street
Hallowell, ME 04347
Phone (207) 623-4021
Settled 1754; incorporated as a town 26 April 1771; set off part to form Augusta 20 February 1797; annexed parts of Augusta 1812 and 1813; annexed parts of Winthrop 1813 and 1814; established boundary with Litchfield 16 February 1825; set off part to Gardiner 24 February 1834; set off part to Pittston 29 February 1844; set off part to form part of Kennebec (present-day Manchester) 12 August 1850; set off part to form Chelsea 17 August 1850; incorporated as a city 17 February 1852 under act of 29 August 1850; set off part to form part of Farmingdale 3 April 1852; annexed part of Augusta 9 April 1852; annexed part of Manchester 24 February 1860; set off part to Manchester 15 March 1870; annexed part of Manchester 22 March 1870 (Kennebec County)
Land records: Yes
Vital records: From 1761; certified copies: $7.00 for the first copy and $2.00 for each additional copy of the same record

Halls
(see Friendship)

Town of Hamlin
HCR 62, Box 38
Van Buren, ME 04785
Ratified organization as a plantation 12 March 1870 and 5 March 1895; set off part to Van Buren 19 February 1907; incorporated as a town 27 March 1976 (Aroostook County)
Vital records: From 1892

Hamlin's Grant
(see Woodstock)

Town of Hammond
PO Box 632
Houlton, ME 04730
Organized as a plantation 17 February 1886; ratified organization 5 March 1895; organized as a town (Aroostook County)
Vital records: From 1885

*Town of Hampden
106 Western Avenue
Hampden, ME 04444
Phone (207) 862-3034
Settled 1768; set off from Frankfort and incorporated as a town 24 February 1794; helped make up a deficiency in the Waldo Patent 5 February 1800; annexed part of Frankfort 1816; annexed part of Newburgh 31 January 1823; annexed part of Hermon 5 February 1831; annexed part of Newburgh 21 February 1832 (Penobscot County)
Vital records: From 1892; contact Paula M. Newcomb, Town Clerk
Vital records search service: $5.00 per hour

Hampton
(see Aurora)

Town of Hancock
PO Box 68
Hancock, ME 04640
Phone (207) 422-3393 Selectmen's Office
Settled 1764; set off from 8 SD BPP (wild land township, organized 26 June 1877, reorganized 13 May 1896, surrendered organization 14 March 1913), Sullivan and Trenton and incorporated as a town 21 February 1828; set off part to Franklin 18 February 1852; set off part to Gouldsboro 26 February 1870; set off part (Marlboro) to Lamoine and annexed part of Lamoine 9 April 1929 (Hancock County)
Vital records: From 1828

Town of Hanover
PO Box 33
Hanover, ME 04237
Settled 1774; formed from Howards Gore and part of Bethel and incorporated as a town 14 February 1843; set off part to Bethel 31 July 1849 (Oxford County)
Vital records: From 1791

Harbor
(see Friendship)

Hardwood
(see Mount Desert)

Harlem
(see China and Winslow)

*Town of Harmony
PO Box 14
Harmony, ME 04942

Settled 1796; incorporated as a town 15 June 1803 (Somerset County)
Vital records: From 1764

Town of Harpswell
Orr's Island, ME 04066
Phone (207) 833-5822
Settled 1720; set off from North Yarmouth and constituted as a district 25 January 1758; incorporated as a town 23 August 1775; annexed part of Phippsburg (Ragged Island) 5 February 1891 (Cumberland County)
Vital records: From 1740s

Town of Harrington
PO Box 165
Princeton, ME 04643
Settled 1765; incorporated as a town 17 June 1797; annexed part of Columbia 1818; set off part to Steuben 5 February 1823; annexed part of Columbia 5 February 1823; set off part to form Milbridge 14 July 1848 (Washington County)
Vital records: From 1771

*Town of Harrison
Front Street
PO Box 300
Harrison, ME 04040
Phone (207) 583-2241
Settled 1792; set off from Otisfield and Bridgton and incorporated as a town 8 March 1805; set off part to form part of Naples 4 March 1834; annexed parts of Bridgton 20 February 1866 and 30 January 1877 (Cumberland County)
Land records: Contact Evelyn M. Pike, Clerk
Naturalization records: No naturalization records
Vital records: Births from 1806 to 1871 and from 1892, deaths from 1851, marriages from 1853, marriage intentions from 1858; contact Clerk
Probate records: No probate records

*Town of Hartford
Rt. 1, Box 200
Hartford, ME 04221
Phone (207) 388-2674
Settled 1783; incorporated as a town 13 June 1798; part of Plantation Number 1 annexed 1807; part of Chandler's Gore annexed 11 March 1834; set off parts to Canton 24 February 1838, 25 February 1839 and 8 August 1850; set off parts to Buckfield 25 March 1856 and 11 March 1862 (Oxford County)
Land records: Contact Kathleen Hutchins, Town Clerk
Land records search service: $7.00 per

hour, $5.00 minimum; certified copies: $8.00 each

Naturalization records: No naturalization records

Vital records: From 1800; contact Town Clerk

Vital records search service: $7.00 per hour, $5.00 minimum; certified copies: $8.00 each

Probate records: No probate records

*Town of Hartland
11 Academy Street
PO Box 280
Hartland, ME 04943
Phone (207) 938-4401 Selectmen's Office
Settled 1800; Organized 11 October 1811; incorporated as a town 7 February 1820; set off part to Athens 8 February 1821; set off part to Saint Albans 15 March 1821; set off part to Canaan 24 February 1838; annexed part of Saint Albans 7 August 1846; set off part to Canaan 17 July 1849; set off part to Pittsfield 11 March 1852 (Somerset County)
Vital records: From 1885; contact Patricia J. Walker, Town Clerk/ Registrar

Haskell
(see Greenville)

Town of Haynesville
Rt. 2A, Danforth Road
Haynesville, ME 04446
Phone (207) 448-2239
Settled 1828; formed from Haynesville (2R2 WELS), Leavitt Plantation, Forkstown (3R2 WELS) and Glenwood Plantation (western half of Township 9 Greenwoods Survey) and incorporated as a town 18 February 1876; established north boundary 7 February 1877 (Aroostook County)
Vital records: From 1892

Town of Hebron
Rt. 1, Box 645
Hebron, ME 04238
Settled 1774; incorporated as a town 6 March 1792; established bounds 1804; annexed part of Paris 1817; set off part to form Oxford 27 February 1829 (Oxford County)
Vital records: From 1700

Town of Hermon
Billings Road
Rt. 3, Box 1206
Bangor, ME 04401
Phone (207) 848-3485 Manager
Settled 1790; helped make up a deficiency in the Waldo Patent 5

February 1800; incorporated as a town 14 June 1814; set off part to Hampden 5 February 1831 (Penobscot County)
Vital records: From 1872

Heron
(see Friendship)

Town of Hersey
Rt. 1, Box 145
Patten, ME 04765
Settled 1839; incorporated as a town 25 January 1873 (Aroostook County)
Vital records: From 1862

Hibberts Gore (unorganized)
(Lincoln County)

Highland Plantation
HCR 68, Box 425
North New Portland, ME 04961
Changed name from Plantation Number 2, Range 2, West of the Kennebec River (2R2 BKP WKR) to Highland Plantation 18 February 1871 (Somerset County)
Vital records: From 1972 [sic]

Hill
(see Winterville Plantation)

Town of Hiram
Rt. 2, Box 5049
Hiram, ME 04041
Phone (207) 625-4663 Selectmen's Office
Settled 1774; constituted as a district 21 February 1807; incorporated as a town 14 June 1814; annexed parts of Baldwin 28 February 1821 and 7 March 1844; annexed part of Brownfield 23 April 1852 (Oxford County)
Vital records: From 1815

Town of Hodgdon
Rt. 4, Box 95
Houlton, ME 04730
Phone (207) 532-6498 Manager's Office
Settled 1824; incorporated as a town 11 February 1832 (Aroostook County)
Vital records: From 1837

Town of Holden
PO Box 490
East Holden, ME 04429
Phone (207) 843-5151
Settled 1770; set off from Brewer and incorporated as a town 13 April 1852 (Penobscot County)
Vital records: From 1752

Town of Hollis
PO Box 9
Hollis, ME 04042
Phone (207) 929-8552 Town Clerk
Settled 1753; incorporated as town of Phillipsburg 27 February 1798; annexed part of Limington 1798; changed name to Hollis 22 January 1812; set off part to form Dayton 7 April 1854; established boundary with Waterboro 23 February 1865; annexed part of Waterboro 19 February 1866 (York County)
Vital records: From 1781

*Town of Hope
HC 62, Box 1
Hope, ME 04847
Phone (207) 763-4199
Settled 1782; incorporated as a town 23 June 1804; set off part to Appleton 7 February 1843 (Knox County)
Vital records: From 1740

Town of Houlton
21 Water Street
Houlton, ME 04730
Phone (207) 532-7111 Administration
Settled 1805; organized 21 April 1826; incorporated as a town 8 March 1831; annexed part of Williams College Grant 11 February 1834 (Aroostook County)
Vital records: From 1892

Howard
(see Willimantic)

Howards Gore
(see Hanover)

*Town of Howland
PO Box 386
Howland, ME 04448-0386
Phone (207) 732-3513; (207) 732-4112
Settled 1820; incorporated as a town 10 February 1826; set off part to form Mattamiscontis 8 March 1839; established boundary with Maxfield 12 August 1850 (Penobscot County)
Land records: Yes
Naturalization records: No naturalization records
Vital records: From 1821
Probate records: No probate records

Town of Hudson
PO Box 3
Hudson, ME 04449
Phone (207) 327-1284
Settled 1800; organized 1824; incorporated as town of Kirkland 25 February 1825; changed name to Hudson 17 March 1855; set off part

*to Old Town 26 March 1929
(Penobscot County)*
Vital records: From 1856

Huntressville
(see Lowell)

Hurricane Isle
*Settled 1765; set off from Vinalhaven
and incorporated 7 February 1878;
repealed incorporation 29 March
1921; surrendered organization 9
July 1921; part annexed to North
Haven 17 June 1937 under act of 4
March 1913; part annexed to
Vinalhaven 17 June 1937 under act
of 19 March 1937 (Knox County)*

Independence
(see Kingman)

Indian Island Reservation
(see Penobscot Indian Island
    Reservation)

**Indian Township Reservation of
    Passamaquoddy**
PO Box 503
Princeton, ME 04668
(Washington County)
Vital records: From 1970

**Indian Township Reservation of
    Passamaquoddy Pleasant Point**
PO Box 343
Perry, ME 04667
(Washington County)

Town of Industry
Rt. 1, Box 1308
Farmington, ME 04938
Phone (207) 778-5050
*Settled 1793; incorporated as a town 20
June 1803; annexed part of New
Sharon 1813; annexed part of New
Vineyard 1815; annexed part of
Starks 21 January 1822; annexed
part of Anson 10 February 1823;
annexed parts of New Vineyard 21
March 1844 and 7 August 1846; set
off part to Farmington 29 July 1850;
set off part to New Sharon 19 March
1952 (Franklin County)*
Vital records: From 1738

Town of Island Falls
PO Box 100
Island Falls, ME 04747
Phone (207) 463-2246
*Settled 1843; organized 6 September
1858; incorporated as a town 27
February 1872 (Aroostook County)*
Vital records: From 1910

Islandport
(see Frenchboro)

Town of Isle au Haut
PO Box 36
Isle au Haut, ME 04645
Phone (207) 335-5001
*Settled 1772; set off from Deer Isle and
incorporated as a town 28 February
1874 (Knox County)*
Vital records: From 1875

Town of Isleboro
PO Box 75
Islesboro, ME 04848
Phone (207) 734-2253
*Settled 1769; incorporated as a town 30
January 1789 (Waldo County)*
Vital records: From 1789

Isles of Shoals
(see Kittery)

*Town of Jackman
PO Box 269
Jackman, ME 04945
Phone (207) 668-2111
*Organized as a plantation 5 March
1895; incorporated as a town 17
March 1958 (Somerset County)*
Vital records: From 1892

Jackson
(see Eustis)

Town of Jackson
Town Hall
Rt. 1, Box 2770
Brooks, ME 04921
Phone (207) 722-3439
*Settled 1798; organized 1812;
incorporated as a town 12 June 1818
(Waldo County)*
Vital records: From 1809

Jarvis Gore
(see Clifton)

*Town of Jay
99 Main Street
Jay, ME 04239
Phone (207) 897-6785 Town Manager
*Settled 1776; incorporated as a town 26
February 1795; annexed part of
Letter A 1810; set off part to form
Canton 5 February 1821; parts of
Canton annexed 27 January 1823, 3
February 1824, 4 March 1831 and 28
February 1864 (Franklin County)*
Land records: Yes
Naturalization records: No naturalization
    records
Vital records: From early 1700s
Probate records: No probate records

Town of Jefferson
PO Box 237
Jefferson, ME 04348
Phone (207) 549-7401
*Settled 1770; previously known as
Ballstown; incorporated as a town 24
February 1807; set off part to form
Whitefield 19 June 1809; set off part
to Alna 1816; set off part to Alna 26
January 1824, repealed 19 February
1907; established boundary with
Washington, Waldoboro, Newcastle
and Alna 23 February 1828; annexed
part of Patricktown (present-day
Somerville) 11 February 1829; set off
part to Newcastle 11 March 1858
(Lincoln County)*
Vital records: From 1757

Town of Jonesboro
Rt. 1, Box 29
Jonesboro, ME 04648
Phone (207) 434-5141 Selectmen's
    Office
*Settled 1763; incorporated as a town 4
March 1809; set off part to form
Jonesport 3 February 1832; set off
part to Columbia 8 February 1838;
set off part to Machias 22 February
1838; set off part to form Roque
Bluffs 12 March 1891 (Washington
County)*
Vital records: From 1766

Town of Jonesport
PO Box 137
Jonesport, ME 04649
Phone (207) 497-5926
*Settled 1764; set off from Jonesboro
and incorporated as a town 3
February 1832; set off part to form
Beals 7 April 1925 (Washington
County)*
Vital records: From 1872

Joy
(see Troy)

Town of Kenduskeag
PO Box 308
Kenduskeag, ME 04450
Phone (207) 884-7947
*Settled 1801; set off from Glenburn and
Levant and incorporated as a town
20 February 1852 (Penobscot
County)*
Vital records: From 1852

Kennebec
(see Manchester)

*Town of Kennebunk
1 Summer Street
Kennebunk, ME 04043
Phone (207) 985-3675 Town Clerk

Settled 1650; set off from Wells and incorporated as a town 24 June 1820, effective 31 July 1820; set off part to Wells 21 February 1868 (York County)

Land records: Property ownership; contact Tax Assessor's Office

Vital records: From 1820 (with some previous information from 1729, when Kennebunk was part of Wells); contact Ethelyn S. Marthia, CmC, Town Clerk

Vital records search service: $5.00 per hour for the first hour or significant part thereof (requires proof of relationship)

*Town of Kennebunkport
Elm Street
PO Box 566
Kennebunkport, ME 04046
Phone (207) 962-4243 Town Clerk
Settled 1629; incorporated as town of Cape-Porpus or Cape Porpoise 5 July 1653; came under the jurisdiction of Saco 1688; changed name to Arundel 10 June 1719; changed name to Kennebunkport 19 February 1821; set off part to form North Kennebunkport (present-day Arundel) 1 April 1915 (York County)
Vital records: From 1678

Kilmarnock
(see Medford)

*Town of Kingfield
Rt. 1, Box 1585
Kingfield, ME 04947
Phone (207) 265-4637 Selectman's Office
Settled 1806; incorporated as a town 24 January 1816 (Franklin County)
Land records: No land records
Naturalization records: No naturalization records
Vital records: Some from 1816, most from 1892 (except for a few marriages)
Probate records: No probate records

Kingman Plantation (disorganized)
Organized as McCrillis 4 July 1859; reorganized as Independence 28 March 1866; incorporated as town of Kingman 25 January 1873; repealed incorporation and reorganized as a plantation 13 April 1935 under act of 6 April 1935 (Penobscot County)
Vital records: From 1874 to 1892

Kingsbury Plantation
HC 31, Box 53
Kingsbury Plantation, ME 04990
Incorporated as a town 22 March 1836;

repealed incorporation 24 February 1885; organized as a plantation 20 July 1886; ratified organization 5 March 1895 (Piscatquis County)
Vital records: From 1836

Kingville
(see Troy)

Kirkland
(see Hudson)

*Town of Kittery
PO Box 808
Kittery, ME 03904
Phone (207) 439-1633; (207) 439-0452
Settled 1623; incorporated as a town 20 November 1652; annexed Isles of Shoals (three islands) 1696; set off part to form Berwick 9 June 1713; annexed part of Berwick 1716; set off part to form Eliot 1 March 1810; set off part to Eliot 8 February 1826 (repealed); set off same part to Eliot 7 February 1829 (York County)
Vital records: Births, deaths and marriages from 1674 to date; contact Maryann Place, Town Clerk. From 1892 to 1926; contact Maine State Archives. From 1923 to date; contact Office of Vital Statistics (221 State Street—location), State House, Station 11 (mailing address), Augusta, ME 04333-0011
Vital records search service from Town Clerk: $1.00 per person (supply as much information as possible—names, dates, places, parents); certified copies: $7.00 for the first record and $3.00 for each additional record

Town of Knox
Rt. 2, Box 1697
Thorndike, ME 04986-9642
Settled 1800; incorporated as a town 12 February 1819; annexed part of Thorndike 1 February 1831; annexed part of Montville 13 February 1833 (Waldo County)
Vital records: From 1777

Town of Lagrange
PO Box 106
Lagrange, ME 04453
Incorporated as a town 11 February 1832 (Penobscot County)
Vital records: From 1833

Lake View Plantation
Rt. 2, Box 218A
Milo, ME 04463
Organized as a plantation 16 June

1892; ratified organization 5 March 1895 (Piscataquis County)
Vital records: From 1892

Town of Lakeville
PO Box 63
Springfield, ME 04487
Settled 1855; organized as a plantation 29 February 1868; organized as a town (Penobscot County)
Vital records: From 1862

*Town of Lamoine
Rt. 2
Ellsworth, ME 04605
Phone (207) 667-2242 Selectman's Office
Settled 1763; set off from Trenton and incorporated as a town 11 February 1870, effective 1 March 1870; set off part to Hancock and annexed part of Hancock (Marlboro) 9 April 1929 (Hancock County)
Land records: From 1873 to date; contact Town Clerk
Naturalization records: No naturalization records
Vital records: From 1870 to date; contact Town Clerk. From 1849; contact Town of Trenton; copies from Lamoine Town Clerk: $7.00 each

Leavitt Plantation
(see Haynesville)

Town of Lebanon
Rt. 1, Box 828
East Lebanon, ME 04027
Phone (207) 457-1171 Selectmen's Office
Settled 1743; incorporated as a town 17 June 1767; annexed unincorporated land 1785; annexed part of Sanford 1787; set off part to Shapleigh 1793; annexed part of Shapleigh 23 February 1825 (York County)
Vital records: From 1765

Lee
(see Monroe)

*Town of Lee
Town Office
PO Box 308
Lee, ME 04455
Phone (207) 738-2134
Settled 1824; incorporated as a town 3 February 1832 (Penobscot County)
Vital records: From 1780

*Town of Leeds
Town House
PO Box 206
Leeds, ME 04263
Phone (207) 524-5171

Settled 1779; incorporated as a town 16 February 1801; annexed part of Livermore 1802; annexed part of Monmouth 1809; set off part to Wayne 1810; set off part to Wales 16 March 1855; set off parts to Webster (present-day Sabattus) and Wayne 2 April 1859 (Androscoggin County)
Land records: Contact Jane Wheeler, Deputy Clerk
Naturalization records: No naturalization records
Vital records: Births, deaths, and marriages from 1785; contact Deputy Clerk; certified copies: $7.00 for the first copy and $3.00 for each additional copy of the same record
Probate records: No probate records

Town of Levant
PO Box 220
Levant, ME 04456-0220
Phone (207) 884-7788 Town Clerk
Settled 1789; incorporated as a town 14 June 1813; set off part to form part of Kenduskeag 20 February 1852 (Penobscot County)
Vital records: From 1769

City of Lewiston
City Building
Lewiston, ME 04240
Phone (207) 784-2951
Settled 1770; set off part to form Greene 18 June 1788; incorporated as a town 18 February 1795; established boundary with Lisbon and Greene 6 February 1826; annexed parts of Greene and Webster 20 April 1852; incorporated as a city 15 March 1861; adopted charter 16 March 1863; enacted annexation of Auburn 25 January 1870 but rejected on referendum; set off part to Webster (present-day Sabatus) 7 February 1895, reannexed 8 March 1895 (Androscoggin County)
Vital records: From 1750

*Town of Liberty
PO Box 116
Liberty, ME 04949
Phone (207) 589-4318
Settled 1800; incorporated as a town 31 January 1827; established boundary 21 February 1830; annexed part of Montville 21 February 1876 (Waldo County)
Vital records: From 1856

Town of Limerick
Town Hall
Main Street
Rt. 2, Box 878
Limerick, ME 04048
Phone (207) 793-2655

Settled 1775; incorporated as a town 6 March 1787; annexed part of Limington 2 March 1870 (York County)

Town of Limestone
27 Church Street
Limestone, ME 04750
Phone (207) 325-4704
Settled 1847; incorporated as a town 26 February 1869 (Aroostook County)
Vital records: From 1862

Town of Limington
PO Box 240
Limington, ME 04049
Phone (207) 637-2171
Settled 1670; incorporated as a town 9 February 1792; set off part to Hollis 1798; established boundary with Waterboro 23 February 1865; set off part to Limerick 2 March 1870 (York County)
Vital records: From 1792

*Town of Lincoln
75 Main Street
Lincoln, ME 04457
Phone (207) 794-3372
Settled 1825; incorporated as a town 30 January 1829 (Penobscot County)
Land records: No land records
Naturalization records: No naturalization records
Vital records: From 1856 (index from 1829); contact Town Clerk
Vital records search service: $5.00 per name per ten-year period; copies: 25¢ each
Probate records: No probate records

Lincoln Plantation
HCR 10
Wilson Mills, ME 04293
Organized as a plantation 15 September 1875 (Oxford County)
Vital records: From 1890s

Town of Lincolnville
RR 1 Box 4660
Lincolnville, ME 04849
Phone (207) 763-3555
Settled 1780; incorporated as a town 23 June 1802 (Waldo County)
Land records: Yes
Naturalization records: No naturalization records
Vital records: From 1786
Probate records: No probate records

*Town of Linneus
Rt. 2, Box 2500
Houlton, ME 04730
Phone (207) 532-6182 Manager's Office

Incorporated as a town 19 March 1836 (Aroostook County)
Land records: Yes
Naturalization records: No naturalization records
Vital records: From 1784
Probate records: No probate records

*Town of Lisbon
24 Main Street
PO Box 8
Lisbon Falls, ME 04252
Phone (207) 353-3000, ext. 112
Settled 1725; set off from Bowdoin and incorporated as town of Thompsonborough 22 June 1799; changed name to Lisbon 20 February 1802; annexed Little River Plantation 4 March 1808; annexed part of Bowdoin 31 January 1826 and set it off again 17 February 1827; established boundary with Lewiston and Greene 6 February 1826; annexed part of Bowdoin 7 March 1834; set off part to form Webster (present-day Sabattus) 7 March 1840; annexed part of Webster 26 July 1847; part set off to Webster 19 February 1863 (Androscoggin County, includes village of Lisbon Falls)
Land records: No land records
Naturalization records: No naturalization records
Vital records: From 1782; contact Twila D. Lycette, CMC, Town Clerk; copies: $3.00 for the first uncertified copy or $7.00 for the first certified copies (both include a five-year search), $3.00 for each additional copy of the same record
Probate records: No probate records

Town of Lisbon Falls
(see Lisbon)

Town of Litchfield
Rt. 1, Box 1280
Litchfield, ME 04350
Phone (207) 268-4721
Settled 1776; organized 24 September 1793 as Smithfield; incorporated as a town 18 February 1795; set off part to Bowdoinham 1817; established boundary with Richmond 14 February 1824; established boundary with Hallowell 16 February 1825; set off part to Wales 20 January 1827; set off part to Wales 31 January 1828 (amended 23 February 1828); set off part to form part of Kennebec (present-day Manchester) 12 August 1850; set off part to Wales 12 March 1856; set off part to West Gardiner 22 March 1856; set off part to

Webster (present-day Sabattus) 14 February 1867 (Kennebec County)
Vital records: From 1785

Little River Plantation
(see Lisbon)

Town of Littleton
Rt. 1, Box 70
Monticello, ME 04760
Phone (207) 538-9862
Settled 1835; incorporated as a town 18 March 1856 (Aroostook County)
Vital records: From 1892

*Town of Livermore
Rt. 2, Box 2450
Livermore Falls, ME 04254
Phone (207) 897-3207 Selectmen's Office
Settled 1770; incorporated as a town 28 February 1795; set off part to Leeds 1802; set off part to Wayne 8 February 1821; annexed part of Chandler's Gore 7 March 1834; set off part to form East Livermore (present-day Livermore Falls) 20 March 1843 (Androscoggin County)
Vital records: From 1762

*Town of Livermore Falls
2 Main Street
Livermore Falls, ME 04254
Phone (207) 897-3321 Treasurer-Clerk; (207) 897-3800 Clerk of Courts
Set off from Livermore and incorporated as town of East Livermore 20 March 1843; changed name to Livermore Falls 15 March 1929, adopted 3 March 1930 (Androscoggin County)
Land records: Contact Jane Castonguay
Naturalization records: Contact Sue Copeland, Clerk of Courts
Vital records: From 1892; contact Kristal A. Flagg
Probate records: Contact Clerk of Courts

Long Island Plantation
(see Frenchboro)

Town of Long Island
Town Hall
Long Island, ME 04050
Phone (207) 766-5820
Set off from Portland 1993 (Cumberland County)

Town of Lovell
PO Box 236
Center Lovell, ME 04016
Settled 1777; incorporated as a town 15 November 1800; set off part to form

Town of Lowell
PO Box 55
Enfield, ME 04433
Settled 1819; incorporated as town of Huntressville 9 February 1837; changed name to Lowell 22 March 1838; annexed part of Pages Mills settlement (Two Mile Strip, a tract north of Lowell and Burlington) 20 February 1841; annexed Cold Stream Settlement or The Strip 17 March 1842; annexed part of Passadumkeag 17 March 1842; set off part to Burlington 28 July 1847 (Penobscot County)
Vital records: From 1854

*Town of Lubec
40 School Street
Lubec, ME 04652
Phone (207) 733-2241 Town Clerk (Mon, Wed & Fri 10:00–1:00)
Settled 1780; incorporated as a town 21 June 1811, set off from Eastport, both formerly known as Number 8; annexed part of Trescott 3 July 1847; set off part to Eastport 19 July 1847 (Washington County)
Vital records: From 1819 through 1920; contact Town Clerk; certified copies: $7.00 each

Town of Ludlow
Rt. 1, Box 180
Houlton, ME 04730
Phone (207) 532-7743
Settled 1825; organized with New Limerick as a plantation 1830; set off New Limerick 18 March 1837; incorporated as a town 21 March 1864 (Aroostook County)
Vital records: From 1840

Lunt's Upper and Lower Grants
(see Peru)

Lygonia
(see Albion)

*Town of Lyman
1 South Waterboro Road
Lyman, ME 04005
Phone (207) 499-7562 Municipal Office
Settled 1767; incorporated as town of Coxhall 11 March 1778; incorporation suspended by legislative resolves 1 October 1778 and 5 June 1779; resolves repealed 24 April 1780; changed name to Lyman 26 February 1803 (York County)
Vital records: From 1780

Lyndon
(see Caribou)

Town of Machias
70 Court Street
PO Box 418
Machias, ME 04654
Phone (207) 255-8683 Town Clerk
Settled 1763; organized 26 April 1770; incorporated as a town 23 June 1784; divided to form West Machias, East Machias and Machiasport 24 June 1826; name of West Machias changed to Machias 12 March 1830; annexed part of Jonesboro 22 February 1838; set off part to form Whitneyville 10 February 1845; set off part to form Marshfield 30 June 1846 (Washington County)
Vital records: From 1773

Town of Machiasport
PO Box 295
Machiasport, ME 04655
Settled 1763; set off from Machias and incorporated as a town 26 January 1826 (Washington County)
Vital records: From 1859

Machisses
(see East Machias)

*Macwahoc Plantation
Kingman Post Office
Kingman, ME 04451
Phone (207) 765-2581
Settled 1830; organized as a plantation 16 December 1851 (Aroostook County)
Vital records: From 1851; contact Denise Worster, Clerk

*Town of Madawaska
98 Saint Thomas Street
Madawaska, ME 04756
Phone (207) 728-6351
Incorporated as a town 24 February 1869 (Aroostook County)
Vital records: From 1871; contact Town Clerk

*Town of Madison
26 Weston Avenue
PO Box 190
Madison, ME 04950
Phone (207) 696-5622 Town Clerk
Settled 1780; incorporated as a town 7 March 1804; set off part to Norridgewock 30 July 1846 (Somerset County)
Land records: Contact Robin Locke, Deputy Tax Collector
Vital records: From 1892; contact Lisa F. Paine, Town Clerk-Treasurer
Probate records: No probate records

Town of Madrid
Rt. 1
Phillips, ME 04966
*Settled 1807; incorporated as a town 29
    January 1836; annexed part of
    Township E 16 February 1872
    (Franklin County)*
Vital records: From 1789

*Magalloway Plantation
Town Clerk
HCR 10, Box 260
Errol, NH 03579
Phone (207) 486-3247 Town Clerk
*Organized as a plantation 1883 (Oxford
    County)*
Vital records: From 1952; contact Mrs.
    Beverly Cameron, Town Clerk

Maine
(see Clifton)

Malta
(see Windsor)

Town of Manchester
Readfield Road
PO Box 263
Manchester, ME 04351
Phone (207) 622-1894
*Formed from parts of Augusta,
    Hallowell, Litchfield, Readfield and
    Winthrop and incorporated as town
    of Kennebec 12 August 1850;
    annexed part of Readfield 7
    February 1852; set off part to
    Readfield 26 February 1852; set off
    part to Winthrop 30 March 1852;
    established boundary 24 April 1852;
    set off part to Readfield 1 April 1854;
    changed name to Manchester 18
    April 1854; set off part to Augusta 9
    April 1856; set off part to Hallowell
    24 February 1860; annexed part of
    Hallowell 15 March 1870; annexed
    part of Farmingdale 15 March 1870;
    set off part of Hallowell 22 March
    1870; set off part to Winthrop 14
    February 1873 (Kennebec County)*
Vital records: From 1808

Mansel
(see Tremont)

Town of Mapleton
Pulcifer Street
PO Box 211
Mapleton, ME 04757
Phone (207) 764-3754
*Settled 1842; ratified organization as a
    plantation 21 February 1878;
    incorporated as a town 5 March 1880
    (Aroostook County)*
Vital records: From 1864

Town of Mariaville
Rt. 4
Ellsworth, ME 04605
*Settled 1802; organized 1820; annexed
    part of Mariaville South (present-day
    Waltham) 25 February 1825; set off
    part to 14 MD BPP (present-day
    Waltham) 20 February 1829; set off
    part to form Amherst 5 February
    1831; set off part to form Waltham
    29 January 1833; incorporated as a
    town 29 February 1836; set off part
    to form Tilden 17 July 1850 and
    reannexed 23 March 1852 (Hancock
    County)*
Vital records: From 1875

Marlboro
(see Hancock and Lamoine)

Town of Mars Hill
Rt. 1, Box 13, Fort Fairfield Road
Mars Hill, ME 04758
Phone (207) 425-3731
*Settled 1844; organized 1866;
    incorporated as a town 21 February
    1867 (Aroostook County)*
Vital records: From 1786

Town of Marshfield
HCR 71, Box 37
Machias, ME 04654
*Settled 1763; set off from Machias and
    incorporated as a town 30 June 1846
    (Washington County)*
Vital records: From 1700s

*Town of Masardis
PO Box 6
Masardis, ME 04759
Phone (207) 435-2841
*Settled 1833; incorporated as a town 21
    March 1839 (Aroostook County)*
Vital records: From 1918

Mason
*Settled 1826; set off from Batchelders
    Grant and incorporated as a town 3
    February 1843; annexed Fryeburg
    Academy Grant 25 March 1911;
    repealed incorporation 6 April 1935;
    surrendered organization 6 July 1935
    (Oxford County)*

Matinicus Isle Plantation
PO Box 258
Matinicus, ME 04851
*Organized as a plantation 22 October
    1840; set off Criehaven 3 March
    1897 (Knox County)*
Vital records: From 1840

Mattamiscontis
Settled 1829; set off from Howland and

*incorporated as a town 8 March
    1839; repealed incorporation 21
    February 1907 and surrendered
    organization (Penobscot County)*

Town of Mattawamkeag
PO Box 260
Mattawamkeag, ME 04459
Phone (207) 736-2464
*Incorporated as a town 14 February
    1860 (Penobscot County)*
Vital records: From 1860

Town of Maxfield
Rt. 1, Box 128
Lagrange, ME 04453
Phone (207) 732-3627
*Settled 1814; incorporated as a town 6
    February 1824; established boundary
    with Howland 12 August 1850
    (Penobscot County)*
Vital records: From 1825

Maysville
(see Presque Isle)

McCrillis
(see Kingman)

*Town of Mechanic Falls
90 Lewiston Street
PO Box 130
Mechanic Falls, ME 04256
Phone (207) 345-2871
*Settled 1769; set off from Minot and
    Poland and incorporated as a town
    22 March 1893 (Androscoggin
    County)*
Land records: Contact Town Clerk
Naturalization records: No naturalization
    records
Vital records: From 1893; contact Town
    Clerk
Probate records: No probate records

Town of Meddybemps
Rt. 214
Meddybemps, ME 04657
*Formed from parts of Cooper, Charlotte
    and Baring and incorporated as a
    town 20 February 1841 (Washington
    County)*
Vital records: From 1936

Town of Medford
PO Box 72
Lagrange, ME 04453
Phone (207) 732-4079
*Settled 1808; incorporated as town of
    Kilmarnock 31 January 1824;
    changed name to Medford 21 March
    1856; repealed incorporation 1 April
    1940; reorganized as a plantation
    1942; surrendered organization 30*

March 1945; reincorporated as a
town 23 October 1967 (Piscataquis
County)
Vital records: From 1844

*Town of Medway
School Street
HCR 86, Box 320
Medway, ME 04460
Phone (207) 746-9531 Selectmen's
Office
*Settled 1838; organized 1852;
established boundary 17 February
1874; incorporated as a town 8
February 1875 (Penobscot County)*
Vital records: From 1856; contact B. M.
Hartford, Town Clerk

Town of Mercer
Rt. 2, Box 900
Norridgewock, ME 04957
*Settled 1784; incorporated as a town 22
June 1804; annexed part of Starks 2
March 1835; set off part to form part
of Smithfield 29 February 1840; set
off part to New Sharon 6 April 1840;
set off parts to Norridgewock 26 July
1849 and 12 January 1852; annexed
part of Starks 22 February 1865
(Somerset County)*
Vital records: From 1769

Town of Merrill
PO Box 54
Smyrna Mills, ME 04780
Phone (207) 757-8286
*Settled 1840; organized 1876; ratified
organization 5 March 1895;
incorporated as a town 4 March 1911
(Aroostook County)*
Vital records: From 1893

Town of Mexico
32 Main Street
PO Box 251
Mexico, ME 04257
Phone (207) 364-7971 Town Officers
*Settled 1780; incorporated as a town 13
February 1818; annexed part of
Roxbury 28 March 1857 (Oxford
County)*
Vital records: From 1818

Town of Milbridge
PO Box 66
Milbridge, ME 04658
Phone (207) 546-2422
*Settled 1765; set off from Harrington
and incorporated as a town 14 July
1848; annexed parts of Steuben 12
February 1876 and 18 March 1907
(Washington County)*
Vital records: From 1848

Milburn
(see Skowhegan)

Town of Milford
Davenport Street
PO Box 336
Milford, ME 04461
Phone (207) 827-2072
*Incorporated as a town 28 February
1833 (Penobscot County)*
Vital records: From 1864

Town of Millinocket
197 Penobscot Avenue
Millinocket, ME 04462
Phone (207) 723-8506 Town Clerk
*Incorporated as a town 16 March 1901
(Penobscot County)*
Vital records: From 1898

*Town of Milo
PO Box 218
Milo, ME 04463
Phone (207) 943-2202
*Settled 1803; incorporated as a town 21
January 1823 (Piscataquis County)*
Land records: No land records
Naturalization records: No naturalization
records
Vital records: From 1833
Probate records: No probate records

Milton
(see Orneville)
(Piscataquis County)

Milton
*Organized 26 April 1842; set off part to
Woodstock 24 March 1853;
surrendered organization April 1939
(Oxford County)*

Town of Minot
PO Box 67
Minot, ME 04258
*Settled 1769; set off from Poland and
incorporated as a town 18 February
1802; set off part to form Auburn 24
February 1842; established boundary
with Auburn 20 March 1844; set off
part to Auburn 20 February 1873; set
off part to form part of Mechanic
Falls 22 March 1893 (Androscoggin
County)*
Vital records: From 1786

Monhegan Plantation
PO Box 313
Monhegan Island, ME 04852
*Organized as a plantation 4 September
1839 (Lincoln County)*
Vital records: From 1841

Town of Monmouth
Municipal Office
PO Box 270
Monmouth, ME 04295
Phone (207) 933-2206

*Incorporated as a town 20 January
1792; set off part to Leeds 1809; set
off part to Winthrop 1813; set off
part to Wales 16 March 1855
(Kennebec County)*
Vital records: From 1774

Town of Monroe
Belfast Road
PO Box 646
Monroe, ME 04951
Phone (207) 525-3515
*Settled 1800; organized as Lee 1812;
incorporated as town of Monroe 12
February 1818; set off part to Brooks
23 January 1823; altered boundary
14 February 1824; annexed part of
Brooks 15 March 1844; annexed part
of Frankfort 21 February 1863;
annexed part of Brooks 17 February
1883 (Waldo County)*
Vital records: From 1778

Town of Monson
PO Box 308
Monson, ME 04464
*Settled 1818; incorporated as a town 8
February 1822 (Piscataquis County)*
Vital records: From 1635

Montgomery
(see Troy)

Town of Monticello
PO Box 99
Monticello, ME 04760
Phone (207) 538-9500 Manager's Office
*Settled 1830; incorporated as a town 29
July 1846 (Aroostook County)*
Vital records: From 1860

Town of Montville
Rt. 2, Box 860
Thorndike, ME 04986
Phone (207) 589-4302 Town Clerk
*Settled 1780; incorporated as a town 18
February 1807; set off part to Knox
13 February 1833; established
boundary with Freedom 10 February
1836; set off part to Liberty 21
February 1876 (Waldo County)*
Vital records: From 1785

Town of Moose River
HCR 76, Box 1240
Jackman, ME 04945
*Settled 1820; organized as a plantation
16 October 1852; reorganized 21
December 1903; incorporated as a
town 28 August 1957 (Somerset
County)*
Vital records: From late 1800s

Moro Plantation
Rt. 1, Box 36
Smyrna Mills, ME 04780

Settled 1837; organized as Rockabema 1850; reorganized as Moro 1860 (Aroostook County)
Vital records: From 1896

Town of Morrill
Rt. 1, Box 2410
Morrill, ME 04952
Settled 1790; set off from Belmont and incorporated as a town 3 March 1855; annexed The Gore 4 April 1941 (Waldo County)
Vital records: From 1781

Town of Moscow
Rt. 1, Box 1440
Bingham, ME 04920
Phone (207) 672-4834
Settled 1773; incorporated as a town 30 January 1816 (Somerset County)
Vital records: From 1771

Mount Abraham
(see Salem)

*Town of Mount Chase
Route 159
PO Box 318
Patten, ME 04765
Phone (207) 528-2255
Settled 1838; incorporated as a town 21 March 1864; repealed organization 22 March 1935; surrendered incorporation 1 March 1936; organized as a plantation 6 April 1936, incorporated as a town 9 March 1979 (Penobscot County)
Land records: Current tax maps
Naturalization records: No naturalization records
Vital records: From 1871 (only a few before 1892)
Probate records: No probate records

Town of Mount Desert
Municipal Office
Sea Street
Northeast Harbor, ME 04662
Phone (207) 276-5531 Town Clerk
Settled 1613; organized 30 March 1776; incorporated as a town 17 February 1789; set off part to form Cranberry Isles 16 March 1830; set off Bartlett Island, Hardwood and Robinson Islands to form Seaville 18 March 1838; set off part to form Mansel (present-day Tremont) 3 June 1848; set off part to Cranberry Isles 13 June 1849; annexed part of Seaville 24 February 1859 (Hancock County)
Vital records: From 1806

*Town of Mount Vernon
Rt. 1, Box 3340
Mount Vernon, ME 04352

Phone (207) 293-2379 Town Clerk
Settled 1774; incorporated as a town 28 June 1792; annexed parts of Fayette, Readfield and Goshen (present-day Vienna) 1802; annexed part of Rome 1814; set off part to Readfield 25 February 1825; annexed part of Vienna 28 January 1826; set off and annexed parts of Readfield 13 February 1845; annexed part of Belgrade 16 July 1846; annexed part of Vienna 11 March 1853 (Kennebec County)
Vital records: From 1788

*Town of Naples
PO Box 6
Naples, ME 04055
Phone (207) 693-6364
Settled 1790; formed from parts of Bridgton, Harrison, Otisfield, Raymond and Sebago and incorporated as a town 4 March 1834; annexed part of Sebago 20 February 1845; annexed part of Otisfield 27 July 1848; annexed parts of Sebago 17 July 1849 and 27 March 1852; annexed part of Bridgton 29 February 1856 (Cumberland County)
Vital records: From 1834

Nashville Plantation
Rt. 1, Box 162
Ashland, ME 04732
Organized as a plantation 17 April 1889; ratified organization 5 March 1895 (Aroostook County)
Vital records: From 1889

*Town of New Canada
Rt. 1, Box 802
Fort Kent, ME 04743
Organized as a plantation 9 November 1881; incorporated as a town 27 February 1976 (Aroostook County)
Vital records: From 1892; contact Clerk and Registrar Office

New Charleston
(see Charleston)

*Town of New Gloucester
Lower Gloucester Street
PO Box 82
New Gloucester, ME 04260
Phone (207) 926-4126 Selectmen's Office
Settled 1738; incorporated as a town 9 March 1774; annexed part of Thompson Pond Plantation 1816; annexed unorganized land (Eighty Rod Strip) 23 March 1838 (Cumberland County)

Vital records: From 1700
Vital records search service: fee charged only for extended search; copies: 50¢ per page, $7.00 per record for certified copies

*Town of New Limerick
Town Office Box 2
New Limerick, ME 04761
Phone (207) 532-3303
Settled 1775; organized with Ludlow as a plantation 1830; set off from Ludlow and incorporated as a town 18 March 1837 (Aroostook County)
Land records: Contact Louise Wetmore, Clerk
Naturalization records: No naturalization records
Vital records: From 1892; contact Clerk
Probate records: Contact Clerk

New Milford
(see Alna)

Town of New Portland
PO Box 629
New Portland, ME 04954-0629
Settled 1783; organized 1805; incorporated as a town 9 March 1808; annexed part of Anson 6 March 1830; annexed part of Freeman 7 February 1833; annexed part of New Vineyard 4 March 1834, set off by repeal 12 March 1835 (Somerset County)
Vital records: From 1770

Town of New Sharon
Main Street
Rt. 1, Box 1950
New Sharon, ME 04955
Phone (207) 778-4046 Selectman's Office
Settled 1782; incorporated as a town 20 June 1794; set off part to Industry 1813; annexed part of Mercer 6 April 1840; annexed part of Industry 19 March 1852 (Franklin County)
Vital records: From 1797; contact Ellen Griswold, Clerk/Registrar, PO Box 7, New Sharon, ME 04955

Town of New Sweden
East Road, Box 149
New Sweden, ME 04762
Settled 1870; organized 6 April 1876; incorporated as a town 29 January 1895 (Aroostook County)
Vital records: From 1872

*Town of New Vineyard
PO Box 29
New Vineyard, ME 04956
Phone (207) 652-2222
Settled 1791; incorporated as a town 22

February 1802; set off part to
Industry 1815; set off part to New
Portland 4 March 1834 and
reannexed by repeal 12 March 1835;
set off part to Anson 18 March 1840;
set off parts to Industry 21 March
1844 and 7 August 1846; annexed
part of Strong 28 March 1856
(Franklin County)
Naturalization records: No naturalization
records
Vital records: From 1892; certified
copies: $10.00 each

*Town of Newburgh
Rt. 1, Box 1513
Hampden, ME 04444
Phone (207) 234-4151 Town Clerk
Settled 1794; incorporated as a town 15
February 1819; set off parts to
Hampden 31 January 1823 and 21
February 1832; helped make up a
deficiency in the Waldo Patent 5
February 1800 (Penobscot County)
Land records: No land records
Naturalization records: No naturalization
records
Vital records: From 1814 to date; contact
Libby E. Lois, Clerk
Vital records search service: $10.00;
certified copies: $7.00 each
Probate records: No probate records

*Town of Newcastle
River Road
PO Box 386
Newcastle, ME 04553
Phone (207) 563-3441
Settled 1630; established as a district 19
June 1753; incorporated as a town
23 August 1775; set off part to New
Milford (present-day Alna) 1795;
established boundary with Jefferson
23 February 1828; annexed part of
Jefferson 11 March 1858 (Lincoln
County)
Land records: No land records
Naturalization records: Yes
Vital records: From 1754
Probate records: No probate records

Town of Newfield
Town Hall
PO Box 81
West Newfield, ME 04095
Phone (207) 793-8832
Settled 1778; incorporated as a town 26
February 1794; annexed part of
Shapleigh 30 June 1846 (York
County)
Vital records: From 1897

*Town of Newport
31 Water Street
Newport, ME 04953
Phone (207) 368-4410 Manager; (207)
368-5778 Clerk of Court

Settled 1807; incorporated as a town 14
June 1814 (Penobscot County)
Land records: Contact Town
Naturalization records: Contact Jane
Sawyer, Clerk of Court, Newport
District Court, 16 Water Street,
Newport, ME 04953
Vital records: From 1892; contact Town
Clerk
Probate records: Contact Clerk of Court

*Town of Newry
General Delivery
Newry, ME 04261
Phone (207) 824-3123
Settled 1781; incorporated as a town 15
June 1805; annexed parts of Andover
West Surplus and Grafton 29 March
1837; established boundary with
Andover West Surplus (wild land
township) 22 February 1842;
established boundary with Grafton
(wild land township) 22 February
1842 (Oxford County)
Land records: A few in the 1960s, pretty
consistent from 1970s to date
Naturalization records: No naturalization
records
Vital records: From 1805; contact Sylvia
R. Gray, Administrative Assistant
Vital records search service: $6.00 per
hour, $6.00 minimum, payable in
advance (no walk-in searches);
certified copies: $7.00 for the first
copy and $3.00 for each additional
copy of the same record
Probate records: No probate records

Town of Nobleboro
Rt. 1
PO Box 168
Nobleboro, ME 04555
Phone (207) 563-8816
Settled 1730; incorporated as a town 20
November 1788; annexed part of
Bristol 1815; set off part to form part
of Damariscotta 26 July 1847
(Lincoln County)
Vital records: From 1788

Town of Norridgewock
PO Box 7
Norridgewock, ME 04957
Phone (207) 634-2252
Settled 1773; incorporated as a town 18
June 1788; set off part to Milburn
(present-day Skowhegan) 2 February
1828; annexed part of Fairfield 21
February 1834; annexed part of East
Pond Plantation 11 February 1836;
annexed part of Fairfield 16 April
1841; annexed part of Madison 30
July 1846; annexed parts of Mercer
26 July 1849 and 12 January 1852;
annexed part of Smithfield 27 March
1852; set off part to Skowhegan 9

April 1856; annexed part of Starks
28 February 1907 (Somerset County)
Vital records: From 1620

North Anson
(see Anson)

*Town of North Berwick
Main Street
PO Box 422
North Berwick, ME 03906
Phone (207) 676-3353 Selectmen's
Office
Settled 1630; set off from Berwick and
incorporated as a town 22 March
1831; annexed part of Berwick 22
February 1875 (York County)
Vital records: From 1831

North Franklin (unorganized area)
(Franklin County)

*Town of North Haven
PO Box 525
North Haven, ME 04853
Phone (207) 867-4433 Selectmen's
Office
Settled 1765; set off from Vinalhaven
and incorporated as town of Fox Isle
30 June 1846 under law of 1 March
1846; changed name to North Haven
13 July 1847; annexed part of
Hurricane Isle 17 June 1937 under
act of 4 March 1913 (Knox County)
Land records: Yes
Naturalization records: Yes
Vital records: From 1843
Probate records: No probate records

North Hill
(see Brighton Plantation)

North Kennebunkport
(see Arundel)

North Oxford (unorganized area)
(Oxford County)

North Penobscot (unorganized area)
(Penobscot County)

North Salem
(see Salem)

North Washington (unorganized area)
(Washington County)

Town of North Yarmouth
130 Walnut Hill Road
Cumberland Center, ME 04021
Phone (207) 829-3705
Incorporated as a town 20 February

1680; annexed unincorporated land 1734; set off parts to Brunswick 1739 and 1740; set off part (Small Point) to Georgetown 1741; set off part to form Harpswell 25 January 1758; set off part to form Freeport 14 February 1789; set off part to Pownal 1813; annexed part of Pownal 1816; set off part to form Cumberland 19 March 1821; set off part to form Yarmouth 20 August 1849 (Cumberland County)
Vital records: From 1720

Northeast Piscataquis (unorganized area)
(Piscataquis County)

Northeast Somerset (unorganized area)
(Somerset County)

Town of Northfield
HCR 71, Box 224
Northfield, ME 04654
Incorporated as a town 21 March 1838; annexed part of Centerville 11 March 1915 (Washington County)
Vital records: From 1798

Town of Northport
Mounted Route
Belfast, ME 04915
Phone (207) 338-3819 Selectmen's Office
Settled 1780; incorporated as a town 13 February 1796 (Waldo County)
Vital records: From 1896

Northwest Aroostook (unorganized area)
(Aroostook County)

Northwest Piscataquis (unorganized area)
(Piscataquis County)

Town of Norway
116 Main Street
Norway, ME 04268
Phone (207) 743-6651
Incorporated as a town 9 March 1797; annexed part of Paris 18 March 1859; set off part to Paris 2 March 1861
Vital records: From 1700

Town of Oakfield
PO Box 69
Oakfield, ME 04763
Phone (207) 757-8479
Settled 1831; organized 17 April 1866; ratified organization 21 February 1878 and 5 March 1895;

incorporated as a town 24 February 1897 (Aroostook County)
Vital records: From 1882

*Town of Oakland
Cascade Mill Road
PO Box 187
Oakland, ME 04963
Phone (207) 465-7357
Settled 1764; incorporated as town of West Waterville 26 February 1873 from Waterville; changed name to Oakland 10 March 1883 (Kennebec County)
Naturalization records: No naturalization records
Vital records: From 1896; contact Town Clerk; certified copies: $7.00 each
Probate records: No probate records

Town of Ogunquit
School Street
PO Box 883
Ogunquit, ME 03907
Phone (207) 646-9546 Town Clerk
Incorporated as a town 1980 (York County)

Old Danville
(see Danville)

Old Orchard
(see Old Orchard Beach)

*Town of Old Orchard Beach
Town Hall
PO Box 234
Old Orchard Beach, ME 04064
Phone (207) 934-5721 Town Clerk
Settled 1631; set off from Saco and incorporated as town of Old Orchard 20 February 1883; changed name to Old Orchard Beach 13 July 1929 under act of 23 March 1929; annexed part of Saco 16 April 1927 (York County)
Vital records: Births, deaths and marriages from 1883

*City of Old Town
51 North Brunswick Street
Old Town, ME 04468-1497
Phone (207) 827-6148 City Clerk
Settled 1774; set off from Orono and incorporated as a town 16 March 1840; annexed part of Argyle Plantation 22 March 1843; annexed parts of Alton 27 February 1863 and 17 February 1871; incorporated as a city 30 March 1891 under act of 19 February 1891; annexed part of Hudson 26 March 1929; annexed part of Glenburn 28 March 1929 (Penobscot County)
Vital records: From 1820 (only compiled

records and marriage index available to the public, because originals in poor condition); contact Patricia A. Ramsey, MMC, City Clerk
Vital records search service: no charge; copies: 50¢ per page (requires proof of relationship on any records after 1892)

Town of Orient
Orient, ME 04471
Phone (207) 448-7729
Settled 1830; incorporated as a town 9 April 1856 (Aroostook County)
Vital records: From 1892

*Town of Orland
School House Road
PO Box 67
Orland, ME 04472
Phone (207) 469-3186 Selectmen's Office
Settled 1764; incorporated as a town 21 February 1800; established boundary with Ellsworth and Dedham 31 July 1847 (Hancock County)
Vital records: From 1765; contact Town Clerk

Orneville
Incorporated as town of Milton 31 January 1832; set off part to Atkinson 21 February 1837; changed name to Almond 19 February 1841; changed name to Orneville 24 January 1843; repealed incorporation 8 April 1939 (Piscataquis County)

*Town of Orono
59 Main Street
PO Box 130
Orono, ME 04473
Phone (207) 866-2556
Settled 1774; incorporated as a town 12 March 1806; set off part to form Old Town 16 March 1840 (Penobscot County)
Vital records: From 1806

*Town of Orrington
PO Box 159
Orrington, ME 04474
Phone (207) 825-3340 Manager's Office
Incorporated as a town 21 March 1788; set off part to form Brewer 22 February 1812; annexed part of Buckstown (present-day Bucksport) 1816; established boundary with Bucksport 28 February 1821; set off part to Brewer 10 April 1841; annexed part of Bucksport 20 August 1850 (Penobscot County)
Land records: Tax records and some deeds

Naturalization records: No naturalization records
Vital records: From 1788
Probate records: No probate records

Town of Osborn
HCR 31, Box 99
Ellsworth, ME 04605
Organized as Plantation Number 21 MD BPP 5 March 1895; changed name to Osborn 4 April 1923; law incorporating town of Osborn passed 11 February 1976 (Hancock County)
Vital records: From 1938

*Town of Otis
Rt. 4, Box 167AA
Ellsworth, ME 04605
Phone (207) 537-2211
Settled 1808; incorporated as a town 19 March 1835 (Hancock County)
Vital records: From 1835

Town of Otisfield
Rt. 2, Box 1160
Oxford, ME 04270
Settled 1776; incorporated as a town 19 February 1798; annexed Phillips Gore 9 February 1803; set off part to form Harrison 8 March 1805; annexed part of Thompson Pond Plantation 8 March 1830; set off part to Oxford 17 March 1830; set off part to form part of Naples 4 March 1834; set off part to Naples 27 July 1848; annexed part of Poland 20 March 1858 (Oxford County)
Vital records: From 1798

Otter
(see Friendship)

*Town of Owl's Head
PO Box 128
Owl's Head, ME 04854
Phone (207) 594-7434 Selectmen's Office
Settled 1719; set off from South Thomaston and incorporated as a town 9 July 1921 under law of 9 April 1921 (Knox County)
Vital records: From 1921

Oxbow Plantation
Oxbow, ME 04764
Settled 1840; organized 1840; organized as a plantation 1870; ratified organization 5 March 1895 (Aroostook County)
Vital records: From 1940

*Town of Oxford
High Street
Oxford, ME 04270
Phone (207) 539-4431

Settled 1774; set off from Hebron and incorporated as a town 27 February 1829; annexed part of Otisfield 17 March 1830; annexed part of Paris 8 March 1838 (Oxford County)
Land records: Yes
Naturalization records: No naturalization records
Vital records: From 1892
Probate records: No probate records

Pages Mills
(see Lowell)

Town of Palermo
Palermo, ME 04354
Phone (207) 993-2296
Settled 1778; incorporated as a town 23 June 1804; established boundary with China 15 March 1830; set off part to Washington 11 April 1854 (Waldo County)
Vital records: From 1908

*Town of Palmyra
PO Box 6
Palmyra, ME 04965
Phone (207) 938-4871
Settled 1800; incorporated as a town 20 June 1807; set off part to Pittsfield 12 February 1824; set off part to Pittsfield 23 February 1828 (Somerset County)
Land records: Fairly complete back to incorporation
Naturalization records: No naturalization records
Vital records: From 1800 (not complete prior to 1892)
Probate records: No probate records

*Town of Paris
1 East Main Street
South Paris, ME 04281
Phone (207) 743-2501 Selectmen's Office
Settled 1779; incorporated as a town 20 June 1793; set off part to Hebron 1817; annexed part of Woodstock 10 February 1825; annexed part of Buckfield 19 February 1928; set off part to Oxford 8 March 1838; set off part to Woodstock 23 March 1841; set off part to Norway 18 March 1859; annexed part of Norway 2 March 1861; annexed part of Woodstock 9 March 1880 (Oxford County)
Land records; contact Town Clerk
Naturalization records: No naturalization records
Vital records: From 1700; contact Town Clerk; certified copies: $7.00 for the first copy, $3.00 for each additional copy
Probate records: No probate records

Town of Parkman
Rt. 1, Box 181-B
Guilford, ME 04443
Settled 1810; incorporated as a town 29 January 1822; annexed part of Wellington 23 March 1841, repealed 10 March 1842; set off part to Guilford 15 February 1878 (Piscataquis County)
Vital records: From 1782

*Town of Parsonsfield
PO Box 30
Kezar Falls, ME 04047
Phone (207) 625-4558 Selectmen's Office
Settled 1772; incorporated as a town 29 August 1785; established boundary with Cornish 12 February 1876 (York County)
Vital records: From 1762

Patricktown
(see Somerville)

Town of Passadumkeag
PO Box 45
Passadumkeag, ME 04475
Settled 1819; incorporated as a town 31 January 1835; set off part to Lowell 17 March 1842 (Penobscot County)
Vital records: From 1844

Town of Patten
PO Box 260
Patten, ME 04765
Phone (207) 528-2215
Settled 1828; incorporated as a town 16 April 1841 (Penobscot County)
Vital records: From 1821

Pejepscot
(see Danville)

Town of Pembroke
Rt. 2, Box 32
Pembroke, ME 04666
Settled 1770; set off from Dennysville and incorporated as a town 4 February 1832 (Washington County)
Vital records: From 1831

Town of Penobscot
HC 79, Box 147
Orland, ME 04472
Phone (207) 326-4364 Selectmen's Office
Settled 1760; incorporated as a town 23 February 1787; set off part to form Castine 10 February 1796; set off part to form part of Brooksville 13 June 1817; set off parts to Castine 1817 and 12 February 1839; set off part to Surry 31 January 1843; annexed part of Surry 28 February

1845; annexed part of Blue Hill 7 April 1845; annexed part of Sedgwick 16 March 1857; set off part to Castine 14 March 1927 (Hancock County)
Vital records: From 1732

Penobscot Indian Island Reservation (unorganized area)
Community Building
Indian Island, ME 04468
(Penobscot County)
Vital records: From 1962

Pepperrellborough
(see Saco)

Town of Perham
PO Box 69
Perham, ME 04766-0069
Settled 1860; organized as a plantation 1860; reorganized 1867; ratified organization 21 February 1878; incorporated as a town 26 March 1897 (Aroostook County)
Vital records: From 1855

Perkins (disorganized)
Settled 1663; formerly known as Swan Island (in Kennebec River); set off from Dresden and incorporated 24 June 1847; repealed incorporation 26 March 1917; surrendered organization 1 March 1918 (Franklin County)
Vital records: From 1849 to 1916

Town of Perry
Municipal Building
Shore Road
Perry, ME 04667
Phone (207) 853-4161
Settled 1780; incorporated as a town 12 February 1818 (Washington County)
Vital records: From 1780

*Town of Peru
Rt. 1, Box 1315
Peru, ME 04290
Phone (207) 562-4627
Organized as Number 1, Partridgetown, 23 March 1812 from Thompson's Grant, Fox's Grant, Lunt's Upper and Lower Grants; incorporated as a town 5 February 1821; set off part to Rumford 8 February 1825; part of Canton annexed 2 April 1859; part of Franklin Plantation annexed 21 February 1885; set off part to Rumford 21 February 1895; part of Canton annexed 12 April 1895; part of Franklin Plantation annexed 21 February 1899 (Oxford County)
Vital records: From 1812; contact Olga K. Richardson, Clerk

Town of Phillips
PO Box 66
Phillips, ME 04966
Phone (207) 639-3561
Settled 1791; incorporated as a town 25 February 1812; set off part to form part of Salem 10 January 1823; annexed part of 6 AP (Berlin) 17 March 1842 (Franklin County)
Vital records: From 1762

Phillips Gore
(see Norway and Otisfield)

Phillipsburg
(see Hollis)

Town of Phippsburg
HCR 31, Box 25
Phippsburg, ME 04562
Phone (207) 389-2653 Selectman's Office
Settled 1607; set off from Georgetown and incorporated as a town 26 January 1814; established boundary with Bath 7 March 1840; set off part (Ragged Island) to Harpswell 5 February 1891; annexed various islands 28 March 1903; set off various islands 15 March 1905; annexed various islands 19 March 1917 (Sagadahoc County)
Vital records: From 1807

*Town of Pittsfield
16 Park Street
Pittsfield, ME 04967
Phone (207) 487-3136
Settled 1794; organized as Plymouth Gore 1815; incorporated as town of Warsaw 19 June 1819; set off part to Twentyfivemile Pond Plantation (present-day Burnham) 17 March 1821; set off part to Canaan 9 February 1824; annexed part of Palmyra 12 February 1824; changed name to Pittsfield 14 February 1824; annexed part of Palmyra 23 February 1828; set off part to Clinton 6 March 1830; set off parts to Canaan 12 March 1830 and 27 February 1841; annexed part of Hartland 11 March 1852; annexed part of Detroit 12 March 1855 (Somerset County)
Vital records: From 1815; contact Town Clerk
Vital records search service: $10.00 per hour (fee by quarter hour increments, must have Town Clerk's assistance to find records after 1892); copies: 25¢ per page; $7.00 for certified copies
Probate records: No probate records

Town of Pittston
Rt. 2
Gardiner, ME 04345
Phone (207) 582-4438 Selectmen's Office
Settled 1759; formerly called Gardinerston; incorporated as a town 4 February 1779; set off part to Bowdoinham 4 February 1779; set off part to form Gardiner 17 February 1803; annexed part of Hallowell 29 February 1844; annexed part of Chelsea 20 February 1855; set off part to form Randolph 4 March 1887 (Kennebec County)
Vital records: From 1777

Plantation Number 1
(see Hartford)

Plantation Number 2
(see Franklin Plantation)

Plantation Number 2, Range 2, West of the Kennebec River
(see Highland Plantation)

Plantation Number 4
(see Carthage)

Plantation Number 8
(see Lubec)

Plantation Number 11, Range 1
(see Cary Plantation)

Plantation Number 14
Organized as a plantation 5 March 1895
Vital records: From 1875

Plantation Number 21
c/o Princeton Town Clerk
Depot Street
PO Box 408
Princeton, ME 04668
Organized as a plantation 5 March 1895
Vital records: From 1892

Plantation Number 21 MD BPP
(see Osborn)

Plantation Number 33 MD
(see Great Pond)

Pleasant Mountain Gore
(see Denmark)

Pleasant Ridge Plantation
HCR 65, Box 80
Bingham, ME 04920
Settled 1786; organized as a plantation 17 October 1840; ratified

organization 5 March 1895; set off
part to Concord 28 January 1829;
annexed part of Concord 9 February
1860 (Somerset County)
Vital records: From 1852

Plymouth
(see Fort Fairfield)

Town of Plymouth
PO Box 35
Plymouth, ME 04969
Phone (207) 257-4646
Settled 1815; set off from Etna and
incorporated as a town 21 February
1826; established boundary with
Detroit 29 February 1844 (Penobscot
County)
Vital records: From 1795

Plymouth Gore
(see Pittsfield)

*Town of Poland
PO Box 38
Poland, ME 04273
Phone (207) 998-4601
Settled 1768; incorporated as a town 17
February 1795; set off part to form
Minot 18 February 1802; annexed
part of Thompson Pond Plantation 8
March 1830; annexed part of Eighty
Rod Strip (area between New
Gloucester and Poland and between
New Gloucester and Raymond) 20
March 1838; set off part to Danville
24 March 1852; set off part to
Otisfield 20 March 1858; set off part
to Casco 20 March 1858; set off part
to form part of Mechanic Falls 22
March 1893 (Androscoggin County)
Land records: Yes
Naturalization records: No naturalization
records
Vital records: From 1700
Probate records: No probate records

Port Watson
(see Brooklin)

Town of Portage Lake
PO Box 255
Portage Lake, ME 04768
Organized as a plantation 1872; ratified
organization 5 March 1895;
reorganized 7 March 1905;
incorporated as a town 24 March
1909 (Aroostook County)
Vital records: From 1875

Town of Porter
Main Street
Kezar Falls, ME 04047
Phone (207) 625-8344

Settled 1784; incorporated as a town 20
February 1807; set off parts to
Brownfield 20 February 1807, 19
February 1831, 11 February 1832
and 17 March 1855 (Oxford County)
Vital records: From 1892

City of Portland
389 Congress Street
Portland, ME 04101
Phone (207) 874-8300; (207) 874-8481
Set off from Falmouth and incorporated
as a town 4 July 1786; incorporated
as a city 22 March 1833 under law of
28 February 1832; annexed part of
Westbrook 3 April 1845; annexed
part of Cumberland 14 February
1889; annexed Deering 6 February
1899; set off Long Island 1993
(Cumberland County)
Vital records: From 1712

Town of Pownal
Rt. 1
Pownal, ME 04069
Phone (207) 688-4431 Selectman's
Office
Settled 1680; set off from Freeport and
incorporated as a town 3 March
1808; annexed part of North
Yarmouth 1813; set off part to North
Yarmouth 1816 (Cumberland
County)
Vital records: From 1800

Pownalborough
(see Wiscasset)

Prentiss Plantation (disorganized)
Settled 1838; incorporated as a town 27
February 1858; annexed part of
Drew 1 March 1869; repealed
incorporation 14 February 1939;
surrendered incorporation 30
October 1939; organized as a
plantation 5 February 1940,
disorganized in 1990 (Penobscot
County)
Vital records: From 1841; contact Maine
State Archives

*City of Presque Isle
12 Second Street
PO Box 1148
Presque Isle, ME 04769
Phone (207) 764-2520 City Clerk
Settled 1828; incorporated as a town 4
April 1859; annexed Maysville 14
April 1883 under law of 14 February
1883; incorporated as a city 1
January 1940 under law of 8 March
1939 (Aroostook County)
Naturalization records: No naturalization
records
Vital records: Births, deaths and

marriages from 1892 to date; contact
Konni Munson, City Clerk
Vital records search service: $5.00
minimum; copies: $7.00 for the first
copy and $3.00 for each additional
copy of the same record

Town of Princeton
Depot Street
PO Box 408
Princeton, ME 04668
Phone (207) 796-2744
Settled 1815; incorporated as a town 3
February 1832; set off part to
Baileyville 26 July 1847 (Washington
County)
Vital records: From 1861

Town of Prospect
Rt. 1, Box 200
Stockton Springs, ME 04981
Phone (207) 567-3661 Selectman's
Office
Settled 1759; set off from Frankfort and
incorporated as a town 24 February
1794; set off part to form part of
Searsport 13 February 1845; set off
part to form Stockton (present-day
Stockton Springs) 13 March 1857
(Waldo County)
Vital records: From 1756

Putnam
(see Washington)

Town of Randolph
c/o Town Office
128 Water Street
Randolph, ME 04345
Phone (207) 582-5808
Settled 1759; set off from Pittston and
incorporated as town of West Pittston
4 March 1887; changed name to
Randolph 17 March 1887 (Kennebec
County)
Vital records: From 1898

*Town of Rangeley
PO Box 1070
Rangeley, ME 04970
Phone (207) 864-3326; (207) 864-3327
Town Clerk
Settled 1815; incorporated as a town 29
March 1855 (Franklin County)
Land records: No land records
Naturalization records: No naturalization
records
Vital records: From 1795; contact Ivy
Berry, Clerk; copies: must have proof
of relationship
Probate records: No probate records

Rangeley Plantation
Rangeley, ME 04970
Organized as a plantation 1859; ratified

organization 5 March 1895
(Franklin County)
Vital records: From 1910

Town of Raymond
Town Office
Route 85
Raymond, ME 04071
Phone (207) 655-4742 Town Clerk
Settled 1771; incorporated as a town 21
June 1803; set off part to form part
of Naples 4 March 1834; annexed
unincorporated land 1835 and set it
off 1838; annexed part of Eighty Rod
Strip (area between New Gloucester
and Poland and between New
Gloucester and Raymond) 20 March
1838; annexed part of gore between
Gray and Raymond 4 March 1839;
set off part to form Casco 18 March
1841; set off part to Casco 7 March
1842; annexed Gray Surplus (land
between Raymond and Gray) and
gore on cape between Standish and
Raymond 22 March 1859; annexed
part of Standish 24 February 1869;
annexed territory between Gray and
Raymond 31 January 1885
(Cumberland County)
Vital records: From 1745

Town of Readfield
Town Office
PO Box 97
Readfield, ME 04355
Phone (207) 685-4939 Town Clerk
Settled 1760; incorporated as a town 11
March 1791 from Winthrop; set off
part to Mount Vernon 1802; set off
part to Winthrop 1810; annexed part
of Wayne 25 Jan 1821; annexed part
of Mount Vernon 25 February 1825;
set off and annexed parts of Mount
Vernon 13 February 1845; set off
part to form part of Kennebec
(present-day Manchester) 12 August
1850; annexed parts of Kennebec 26
February 1852 and 1 April 1854
(Kennebec County)
Vital records: From 1777

*Reed Plantation
PO Box 9
Wytopitlock, ME 04497
Phone (207) 456-7546
Settled 1830; ratified organization as a
plantation 21 February 1878;
annexed part of Drew 5 March 1889
and set it off again 28 March 1903
(Aroostook County)
Land records: Yes
Naturalization records: No naturalization
    records
Vital records: From 1892
Probate records: No probate records

Town of Richmond
Gardiner Street
PO Box 159
Richmond, ME 04357
Phone (207) 737-4305
Settled 1725; annexed Richmond
Plantation to Bowdoinham 1779; set
off from Bowdoinham and
incorporated 10 February February
1823; established boundary with
Litchfield 14 February 1824
(Sagadahoc County)
Vital records: From 1782

Richmond Plantation
(see Richmond)

Town of Ripley
Rt. 3, Box 1470
Dexter, ME 04930
Settled 1804; incorporated as a town 11
December 1816; set off part to form
Cambridge 8 February 1834; set off
part to Saint Albans 15 March 1862
(Somerset County)
Vital records: From 1783

Town of Robbinston
PO Box 44
Robbinston, ME 04671
Settled 1787; incorporated as a town 18
February 1811 (Washington County)
Vital records: From 1857

Robinson Island
(see Mount Desert)

Rockabema
(see Moro Plantation)

*City of Rockland
4 Union Street
PO Box 546
Rockland, ME 04841
Phone (207) 594-0304 City Clerk
Settled 1719; set off from Thomaston
and incorporated as town of East
Thomaston 28 July 1848; annexed
part of Thomaston 17 July 1849;
changed name to Rockland 17 July
1850; set off part to Thomaston 5
April 1852; incorporated as a city 3
June 1854 under law of 17 April
1854 (Knox County)
Land records: No land records
Naturalization records: No naturalization
    records
Vital records: From 1803 to 1854;
    contact Town of Thomaston. From
    1854 to date; contact City Clerk
Vital records search service: $3.00 per
    search; certified copies: $7.00 each
Probate records: No probate records

*Town of Rockport
Town Office
Main Street
Rockport, ME 04856
Phone (207) 236-9648
Settled 1769; set off from Camden and
incorporated as town 25 February
1891; annexed parts of Camden 4
March 1891 and 28 March 1893
(Knox County)
Vital records: From 1791

*Town of Rome
Rt. 2, Box 1469
Norridgewock, ME 04957
Phone (207) 397-4011; (207) 397-3072
    Town Clerk
Settled 1780; incorporated as a town 7
March 1804; set off part to Mount
Vernon 1814; set off parts to Vienna
1815 and 25 January 1840; set off
parts to Belgrade 10 February 1845
and 25 March 1897 (Kennebec
County)
Land records: Contact Selectmen's
    Office
Vital records: From 1776; contact Town
    Clerk

Town of Roque Bluffs
Rt. 1
Machias, ME 04654
Settled 1763; set off from Jonesboro
and incorporated as a town 12
March 1891 (Washington County)
Vital records: From 1892

*Town of Roxbury
PO Box 24
Roxbury, ME 04275
Phone (207) 364-3982 Selectman's
    Office
Incorporated as a town 17 March 1835;
set off part to Mexico 28 March 1857
(Oxford County)
Vital records: From 1892

Town of Rumford
Municipal Building
Rumford, ME 04276
Phone (207) 364-3001 Town Clerk
Settled 1777; incorporated as a town 21
February 1800 (previously known as
New Pennacook); annexed parts of
Peru 8 February 1825 and 21
February 1895; annexed part of
Franklin Plantation 21 February
1899 (Oxford County)
Vital records: From 1800

Town of Sabattus
Main Street
PO Box 12
Sabattus, ME 04280
Phone (207) 375-4331 Selectman's
    Offices

Settled 1774; set off from Lisbon and incorporated as town of Webster 7 March 1840; set off part to Lisbon 26 July 1847; set off part to Lewiston 20 April 1852; annexed part of Leeds 2 April 1859; annexed part of Lisbon 19 February 1863; annexed parts of Litchfield and Wales 14 February 1867; annexed part of Lewiston 7 February 1895, set it off again 8 March 1895; annexed part of Greene 7 February 1895; changed name to Sabattus 13 March 1971 (Androscoggin County)
Vital records: From 1892

*City of Saco
11 Cutts Avenue
Saco, ME 04072
Phone (207) 284-4831 City Clerk
Settled 1623; had jurisdiction of Kennebunkport 1688; set off from Biddeford and constituted as district of Pepperrellborough 15 June 1762; incorporated as a town 23 August 1775; changed name to Saco 23 February 1805; annexed part of Scarboro 27 March 1841; incorporated as a city 18 February 1867 under law of 5 February 1867; set off part to form Old Orchard (present-day Old Orchard Beach) 20 February 1883; set off part to Old Orchard Beach 16 April 1927 (York County)
Land records: From 1653 to 1855; contact Charles L. Butler, Jr., President, The Biddeford Historical Society, PO Box 200, Biddeford, ME 04005
Naturalization records: No naturalization records
Vital records: From 1717; contact Clerk. Vital records from 1653 to 1855; contact The Biddeford Historical Society
Probate records: No probate records

Town of Saint Agatha
Town Hall
Saint Agatha, ME 04772
Phone (207) 543-7305
Set off from Frenchville and incorporated as a town 17 March 1899; annexed part of Frenchville 14 March 1927 (Aroostook County)
Vital records: From 1889

*Town of Saint Albans
PO Box 100
Saint Albans, ME 04971-0100
Phone (207) 938-4568 Selectmen's Office
Settled 1800; incorporated as a town 14 June 1813; annexed part of Hartland 15 March 1821; set off part of

Hartland 7 August 1846; annexed part of Ripley 15 March 1862 (Somerset County)
Vital records: Births, deaths and marriages from 1785; contact Stacey A. Desrosiers, Town Clerk; certified copies: $10.00 for the first copy and $4.00 for each additional copy

Town of Saint Francis
PO Box 98
Saint Francis, ME 04774
Phone (207) 398-3175; (207) 398-3373
Organized as a plantation 12 March 1870; incorporated as a town 31 January 1966 (Aroostook County)
Vital records: From 1892

Town of Saint George
PO Box 131
Tenants Harbor, ME 04860
Phone (207) 372-6363
Settled 1751; set off from Cushing and incorporated as a town 7 February 1803; defined boundary 14 March 1842; set off part to South Thomaston 24 February 1865 (Knox County)
Vital records: From 1700

Saint George Plantation
(see Thomaston)

Saint John Plantation
Rt. 3, Box 440
Fort Kent, ME 04743
Organized as a plantation 12 March 1870 (Aroostook County)
Vital records: From 1885

Salem (unorganized)
Settled 1791; formed from parts of Freeman, Phillips and Mount Abraham (wild land township) and incorporated 10 January 1823 as North Salem; changed name to Salem 28 February 1834 (Franklin County)

Sandy River Plantation
HCR
Rangeley, ME 04970
Organized as a plantation 23 March 1905; annexed Greenvale Plantation 23 March 1905 (Franklin County)
Vital records: From 1895

Town of Sanford
267 Main Street
Sanford, ME 04073
Phone (207) 324-1080
Settled 1740; incorporated as a town 27 February 1768; annexed unincorporated land 1786; set off

part to Lebanon 1787; set off part to Shapleigh 1787; set off part to form Alfred 4 February 1794; annexed part of Shapleigh 1820; annexed part of Alfred 23 February 1828 (York County)
Vital records: From 1769

Town of Sangerville
PO Box 188
Sangerville, ME 04479
Incorporated as a town 13 June 1814; set off part to Guilford 23 February 1889 (Piscataquis County)
Vital records: From 1793

Sarsfield
(see Fort Fairfield)

Town of Scarborough
Oak Hill
PO Box 360
Scarborough, ME 04074
Phone (207) 883-6616
Settled 1630; incorporated as a town 14 July 1658; set off part to Saco 27 March 1841; set off part to Gorham 4 March 1864 (Cumberland County)
Vital records: From 1725

Town of Searsmont
PO Box 56
Searsmont, ME 04973
Phone (207) 342-5411
Settled 1804; incorporated as a town 5 February 1814 (Waldo County)
Vital records: From 1854

*Town of Searsport
PO Box 499
Searsport, ME 04974
Phone (207) 548-6372
Settled 1770; formed from Belfast, Frankfort and Prospect and incorporated as a town 13 February 1845 (Waldo County)
Vital records: From 1801; contact Claudia R. Mercer, Town Clerk
Vital records search service: $10.00 per hour

Seaville
Set off from Mount Desert (Bartlett Island, Hardwood and Robinson Islands) and incorporated 18 March 1838; annexed to Mount Desert and Tremont 24 February 1859 (Hancock County)

*Town of Sebago
PO Box 237
East Sebago, ME 04029
Phone (207) 787-2457 Selectmen's Office

Settled 1790; set off from Baldwin and incorporated as a town 10 February 1826; annexed part of Baldwin 26 January 1827; annexed part of Denmark 12 March 1830; set off part to form part of Naples 4 March 1834; annexed part of Baldwin 28 March 1837; set off part to Naples 20 February 1845, 17 July 1849 and 27 March 1852; annexed part of Baldwin 15 February 1871 (Cumberland County)
Land records: Yes
Land records search service: no fee for simple research
Naturalization records: No naturalization records
Vital records: From 1892
Vital records search service: no fee for simple research

Sebasticook
(see Benton)

*Town of Sebec
Town Clerk
PO Box 57
Sebec, ME 04481
Phone (207) 564-8367; (207) 564-3474
Settled 1803; incorporated as a town 28 February 1812; set off part to Bowerbank 7 April 1927 (Piscataquis County)
Vital records: From 1811

Seboeis Plantation
HCR 66, Box 230
Howland, ME 04448
Organized as a plantation 8 April 1890; ratified organization 5 March 1895 (Penobscot County)
Vital records: From about 1890; contact Myra Haskell, PO Box 232, Howland, ME 04448

Seboomook Lake (unorganized)
(Somerset County)

*Town of Sedgwick
North Sedgwick Road
PO Box 46
Sedgwick, ME 04676
Phone (207) 359-2275
Settled 1763; incorporated as a town 14 January 1789; set off part to form part of Brooksville 13 June 1817; set off part to Blue Hill 5 February 1831; set off part to form Brooklin 9 June 1849; set off part to Penobscot 16 March 1857 (Hancock County)
Vital records: From 1789; contact Town Clerk

Town of Shapleigh
PO Box 26
Shapleigh, ME 04076

Phone (207) 636-2839 Town Clerk
Settled 1772; incorporated as a town 5 March 1785; set off part to Sanford 1787; set off part to Lebanon 1793; set off part to Shapleigh 1820; set off part to Lebanon 23 February 1825; set off part to form Acton 6 March 1830; annexed part of Acton 22 March 1831; set off part to Newfield 30 June 1846; annexed part of Waterboro 14 March 1854 (York County)
Vital records: From 1784

Sheridan
(see Caribou)

Sheridan Plantation
(see Ashland)

Town of Sherman
PO Box 96
Sherman Mills, ME 04776
Phone (207) 365-4260
Settled 1832; incorporated as a town 28 January 1862; annexed part of Silver Ridge 24 February 1870; annexed part of Crystal 17 February 1881 (Aroostook County)
Vital records: From 1800

Town of Shirley
Box 40, Main Street
Shirley, ME 04485
Settled 1825; incorporated as a town 4 March 1834; annexed part of Wilson 10 August 1848 (Piscataquis County)
Vital records: From 1797

Town of Sidney
Middle Road
Rt. 3, Box 491
Augusta, ME 04330
Phone (207) 547-3340
Settled 1760; incorporated as a town 30 January 1792 from Vassalboro; set off part to Belgrade 1798 (Kennebec County)
Vital records: From 1772

Silver Ridge Plantation (disorganized)
Settled 1858; organized as a plantation 20 July 1863; ratified organization 24 February 1868; set off part to Sherman 24 February 1870; ratified organization 21 February 1878; surrendered organization 28 February 1941 (Aroostook County)
Vital records: From 1859 to 1891; contact Maine State Archives

Town of Skowhegan
90 Water Street
Skowhegan, ME 04976

Phone (207) 474-3423 Town Clerk
Settled 1770; set off from Canaan and incorporated as town of Milburn 5 February 1823; annexed part of Norridgewock 2 February 1828; annexed parts of Cornville 23 February 1831, 29 January 1833 and 2 March 1833; changed name to Skowhegan 25 March 1836; annexed part of Norridgewock 9 April 1856; annexed Bloomfield 4 March 1861, under law of 19 February 1861 (Somerset County)
Vital records: From 1780

Smithfield
(see Litchfield)

Town of Smithfield
PO Box 9
Smithfield, ME 04978
Phone (207) 362-4772
Settled 1784; set off from Dearborn and Mercer, and incorporated with East Pond Plantation as a town 29 February 1840; set off part to Norridgewock 27 March 1852 (Somerset County)
Vital records: From 1775

Town of Smyrna
PO Box 54
Smyrna, ME 04780
Settled 1830; incorporated as a town 7 March 1839 (Aroostook County)
Vital records: From 1869

*Town of Solon
Ferry Street
PO Box 214
Solon, ME 04979
Phone (207) 643-2541; (207) 643-2812 Town Clerk's Office
Settled 1782; incorporated as a town 23 February 1809 (Somerset County)
Vital records: From 1700; contact Mary A. Jackson, Town Clerk

*Town of Somerville
PO Box 1948
Coopers Mills, ME 04341
Phone (207) 549-3828
Set off part to Jefferson 11 February 1829, when known as Patricktown; established easterly line 8 March 1855; incorporated as a town 25 March 1858; repealed incorporation 17 April 1937; surrendered organization 1 February 1938; organized as a plantation 14 March 1938; incorporated as a town 6 February 1974 (Lincoln County)
Vital records: Births, deaths and marriages from 1798; contact Clerk

Songo Gore
(see Casco)

Town of Sorrento
HCR 32, Box 161
Sorrento, ME 04677
Phone (207) 422-6889 Selectman's
Office
*Settled 1762; set off from Sullivan and
incorporated as a town 8 March 1895
(Hancock County)*
Vital records: From 1859

South Aroostook (unorganized area)
(Aroostook County)

Town of South Berwick
PO Box 236
South Berwick, ME 03908
*Settled 1643; set off from Berwick and
incorporated as a town 12 February
1814; annexed part of York 15
February 1834; annexed parts of
Berwick 18 March 1841 and 5
February 1881 (York County)*
Vital records: From 1763

Town of South Bristol
Town Hall
PO Box 65
South Bristol, ME 04568
Phone (207) 563-3977
*Settled 1625; set off from Bristol and
incorporated as a town 3 July 1915
under law of 26 March 1915
(Lincoln County)*
Vital records: From 1916

South Franklin (unorganized area)
(Franklin County)

South Oxford (unorganized area)
(Oxford County)

*City of South Portland
25 Cottage Road
South Portland, ME 04106
Phone (207) 767-7601
*Settled 1630; set off from Cape
Elizabeth and incorporated as a town
15 March 1895; incorporated as a
city 5 December 1898 under law of
22 March 1895 (Cumberland
County)*
Vital records: From 1748

*Town of South Thomaston
PO Box 147
South Thomaston, ME 04858
Phone (207) 596-6584
*Settled 1719; set off from Thomaston
and incorporated as a town 28 July
1848; annexed part of Saint George
24 February 1865; set off part to*

*form Owl's Head 9 July 1921 (Knox
County)*
Land records: Yes
Naturalization records: No naturalization
records
Vital records: From 1780; copies: 20¢
each, $7.00 for certified copies
Probate records: No probate records

Southeast (unorganized)

Town of Southport
PO Box 53
Newagen, ME 04552
Phone (207) 633-3318 Selectmen's
Office
*Settled 1630; set off from Boothbay and
incorporated as town of Townsend 12
February 1842; changed name to
Southport 12 June 1850 (Lincoln
County)*
Vital records: From 1842

Town of Southwest Harbor
Main Street
PO Box 151
Southwest Harbor, ME 04679
Phone (207) 244-5404 Manager
*Settled 1770; set off from Tremont and
incorporated as a town 21 February
1905 (Hancock County)*
Vital records: From 1905

Town of Springfield
PO Box 13
Springfield, ME 04487
Phone (207) 738-2176
*Settled 1830; incorporated as a town 12
February 1834 (Penobscot County)*
Vital records: From 1834

Square Lake (unorganized area)
(Aroostook County)

Town of Stacyville
PO Box 166
Sherman Station, ME 04777
Phone (207) 365-4195
*Settled 1850; organized as a plantation
30 July 1860; ratified organization 7
March 1883 and 5 March 1895;
incorporated as a town 13 March
1953 (Penobscot County)*
Vital records: Births from 1891, deaths
from 1892, marriages and marriage
intentions from 1860

Town of Standish
PO Box 597
Standish, ME 04084
Phone (207) 642-3461; (207) 642-3466
*Settled 1785; incorporated as a town 30
November 1784; annexed part of
Buxton 17 February 1824; set off*

*parts to Gorham 19 February 1831
and 14 March 1839; set off part to
Raymond 24 February 1869
(Cumberland County)*
Vital records: From 1770

Town of Starks
Rt. 1, Box 300
Starks, ME 04911
Phone (207) 696-8069
*Settled 1774; incorporated as a town 28
February 1795; set off part to
Industry 21 January 1822; set off
parts to Mercer 2 March 1835 and 22
February 1865; set off part to
Norridgewock 28 February 1907
(Somerset County)*
Vital records: From 1787

Sterlington
(see Union)

*Town of Stetson
PO Box 85
Stetson, ME 04488-0085
Phone (207) 296-3232; (207) 296-3232
FAX
*Settled 1800; incorporated as a town 28
January 1831 (Penobscot County)*
Vital records: From 1803; contact Carol
Laplant, Clerk

Town of Steuben
Unionville Road
PO Box 26
Steuben, ME 04680
Phone (207) 546-7209; (207) 546-7538
*Settled 1760; incorporated as a town 27
February 1795; annexed part of
Harrington 5 February 1823; set off
part to Cherryfield 6 February 1826;
set off parts to Milbridge 12
February 1876 and 18 March 1907
(Washington County)*
Vital records: From 1769

Town of Stockholm
North Main Street
Rt. 1, Box 16
Stockholm, ME 04783
Phone (207) 896-5659 Town Office;
(207) 896-5759 Town Clerk
*Organized 23 March 1895; incorporated
as a town 30 June 1911 under law of
27 February 1911 (Aroostook
County)*
Land records: Contact Kathy Lausier,
Registrar, Town Office, School Street,
Stockholm, ME 04783
Naturalization records: No naturalization
records
Vital records: Births, deaths and
marriages from 1897; contact
Albertine Dufour, Clerk's Office
Vital records search service: $5.00 per

hour, $5.00 minimum (definite proof of relationship required)
Probate records: No probate records

Stockton
(see Stockton Springs)

*Town of Stockton Springs
PO Box 339
Stockton Springs, ME 04981
Phone (207) 567-3404 Selectmen's Office
Settled 1750; set off from Prospect and incorporated as town of Stockton 13 March 1857; changed name to Stockton Springs 5 February 1889 (Waldo County)
Land records: No land records
Naturalization records: No naturalization records
Vital records: From 1766
Probate records: No probate records

*Town of Stoneham
PO Box 91
East Stoneham, ME 04231
Set off from Fryeburg Academy Grant and Batchelders Grant and incorporated as a town 31 January 1834; changed name to Usher 19 February 1841; renamed Stoneham 11 March 1843 (Oxford County)
Land records: Yes
Naturalization records: No naturalization records
Vital records: From 1837 (missing many from 1837 to 1893)
Probate records: No probate records

*Town of Stonington
Main Street
PO Box 9
Stonington, ME 04681
Phone (207) 367-2351 Manager
Settled 1762; set off from Deer Isle and incorporated as a town 18 February 1897 (Hancock County)
Vital records: From 1897

*Town of Stow
Star Route 68, Box 199A
North Fryeburg, ME 04058
Phone (207) 697-2007
Settled 1770; formed from Fryeburg Addition, Eastmans Grant and Bradley's Grant and incorporated as a town 28 January 1833 (Oxford County)
Land records: Yes
Naturalization records: No naturalization records
Vital records: From 1890
Probate records: No probate records

Town of Strong
PO Box 322
Strong, ME 04983
Phone (207) 684-4005
Settled 1784; incorporated as a town 31 January 1801; set off part to Farmington 16 March 1853; annexed part of Avon 26 March 1853; set off part to New Vineyard 28 March 1856 (Franklin County)
Vital records: From 1767

Stroudwater
(see Westbrook)

*Town of Sullivan
HCR 32, Box 8A
Sullivan, ME 04664
Phone (207) 422-6282 Selectmen's Office; (207) 422-4785 FAX
Settled 1762; incorporated as a town 16 February 1789; set off part to form part of Hancock 21 February 1828; set off part to form Sorrento 8 March 1895; annexed part of 7 SD BPP 11 March 1899 (Hancock County)
Vital records: From 1892 (prior to that sparse)

Town of Summit (unorganized)
(Penobscot County)

Town of Sumner
Town Office
Sumner, ME 04292
Phone (207) 388-2866 Town Clerk and Selectmen's Office (Tue 11:00–7:00, Thur 9:00–1:00, Fri 9:00–noon)
Settled 1783; incorporated as a town 13 June 1798; annexed part of Plantation Number 2 (present-day Franklin Plantation) 20 March 1838; annexed part of Franklin Plantation 22 February 1844; set off part to Buckfield 12 March 1856; annexed part of Franklin Plantation 12 February 1863 (Oxford County)
Vital records: From 1733

Town of Surry
North Bend Road
PO Box 147
Surry, ME 04684
Phone (207) 667-5912
Settled 1785; incorporated as a town 21 June 1803; set off part to Ellsworth 3 March 1809; annexed part of Ellsworth 28 February 1821; set off part to Ellsworth 17 February 1829; annexed parts of Penobscot 31 January 1843 and 28 February 1845 (Hancock County)
Vital records: From 1790

Swan Island
(see Perkins)

*Town of Swan's Island
c/o Monica Cease, Town Clerk
PO Box 1
Minturn, ME 04659
Phone (207) 526-4361
Organized 1834; incorporated as a town 26 March 1897; annexed Calf Island and West Black Island 22 February 1901 (Hancock County)
Land records: Yes
Naturalization records: Yes
Vital records: From 1850 (deaths missing from 1877 to 1880 and from 1881 to 1892, marriages missing from 1869 to 1879)
Probate records: No probate records

Town of Swanville
Rt. 2, Box 325
Belfast, ME 04915
Settled 1774; incorporated as a town 19 February 1818; set off part to Waldo 10 February 1824; annexed part of Frankfort 21 February 1832; annexed part of Brooks 5 March 1841 (Waldo County)
Vital records: From 1812

Town of Sweden
(Route 93, Sweden—location)
Harrison, ME 04040
Phone (207) 647-3944 Selectmen's Office
Settled 1784; set off from Lovell and incorporated as a town 26 February 1813 (Oxford County)
Vital records: From 1953

Town of Talmadge
PO Box 9
Waite, ME 04492
Incorporated as a town 8 February 1875 (Washington County)
Vital records: From 1850

*Town of Temple
PO Box 549
Temple, ME 04984
Phone (207) 778-6680
Settled 1796; incorporated as a town 20 June 1803; annexed part of Wilton 28 March 1831 (Franklin County)
Vital records: From 1784; contact Town Clerk

Texas
(see Bridgton and Denmark)

The Gore
(see Morrill)

The Strip
(see Lowell)

Town of Thomaston
Main Street
PO Box 299
Thomaston, ME 04861
Phone (207) 354-6107
Settled 1719; set off from Warren and Saint George Plantation and incorporated as a town 20 March 1777; annexed part of Warren 28 June 1798; annexed part of Cushing 1809; set off part to form East Thomaston (present-day Rockland) 28 July 1848; set off part to form South Thomaston 28 July 1848; set off part to East Thomaston (present-day Rockland) 17 July 1849; annexed part of Rockland 5 April 1852; established boundary with Warren 12 February 1864; annexed part of Cushing 21 February 1891 (Knox County)
Vital records: From 1775

Thompson Pond Plantation
(see New Gloucester, Otisfield and Poland)

Thompsonborough
(see Lisbon)

Thompson's Grant
(see Peru)

*Town of Thorndike
Route 220
PO Box 10
Thorndike, ME 04986-0010
Phone (207) 568-3653
Settled 1772; incorporated as a town 15 February 1819; set off part to Knox 1 February 1831 (Waldo County)
Land records: Contact Town Clerk
Naturalization records: Contact Town Clerk
Vital records: From 1776; contact Town Clerk

Tilden
Set off from Mariaville and incorporated as a town 17 July 1850; reannexed 23 March 1852 (Hancock County)

*Town of Topsfield
Rt. 1, Box 56
Topsfield, ME 04490
Incorporated as a town 24 February 1838; surrendered incorporation 9 October 1939; became an organized plantation; surrendered organization 18 February 1941; became an

unorganized township; incorporated as a town 7 March 1960 (Washington County)
Vital records: From 1834; contact Town Office

Town of Topsham
22 Elm Street
Topsham, ME 04086
Phone (207) 729-1540 Town Clerk
Settled 1730; incorporated as a town 4 February 1764; annexed part of Bowdoinham (Cathance Neck) 1788; set off part to Bowdoinham 16 March 1830 (Sagadahoc County)
Vital records: From 1892

Townsend
(see Southport)

Town of Tremont
c/o Community Building
PO Box 65
Bernard, ME 04612
Phone (207) 244-7204
Settled 1762; set off from Mount Desert and incorporated as town of Mansel 3 June 1848; established boundary 14 July 1848; changed name to Tremont 8 August 1848; annexed part of Seaville 24 February 1859; set off part to form Southwest Harbor 21 February 1905 (Hancock County)
Vital records: From 1825

Town of Trenton
PO Box 293-A
Trenton, ME 04605
Phone (207) 667-7207
Settled 1763; incorporated as a town 16 February 1789; set off part to Ellsworth 1809; set off part to form part of Hancock 21 February 1828; annexed part of Eden (present-day Bar Harbor) 27 June 1849; set off part to form Lamoine 11 February 1870 (Hancock County)
Vital records: From 1786

Town of Trescott (disorganized)
Settled 1780; incorporated 7 February 1827; set off parts to Edmunds 7 February 1828 and 7 March 1899; set off part to Lubec 3 July 1847 (Washington County)
Vital records: From 1799 to 1892

*Town of Troy
Rt. 1, Box 1970
Troy, ME 04987
Phone (207) 948-2283 Town Office; 948-2524 Town Clerk
Incorporated as town of Kingville 22 February 1812; changed name to Joy 1 March 1814; annexed part of

Twentyfivemile Pond Plantation (present-day Burnham) 1819; changed name to Montgomery 23 January 1826; changed name to Troy 10 February 1827 (Waldo County)
Land records: contact Town Office
Naturalization records: No naturalization records
Vital records: A few prior to 1840, mostly complete from 1840 to 1892, more complete from 1892 to date; contact Janet C. Cropley, Town Clerk; certified copies: $7.00 each (proof of relationship may be required)
Probate records: No probate records

*Town of Turner
PO Box 152
Turner, ME 04282
Phone (207) 225-3417 Selectmen's Office
Settled 1690; incorporated as a town 7 July 1786 (Androscoggin County)
Land records: Yes
Naturalization records: No naturalization records
Vital records: From 1776 (index from 1740)
Probate records: No probate records

Twentyfivemile Pond Plantation
(see Burnham)

Two Mile Strip
(see Burlington and Lowell)

*Town of Union
PO Box 186
Union, ME 04862-0186
Phone (207) 785-3658
Settled 1774; organized as Sterlington 3 May 1786; incorporated as a town 20 October 1786; set off part to form Putnam (present-day Union) 27 February 1811; annexed unincorporated land 1817 (Knox County)
Vital records: From 1789

Unity (unorganized area)
Organized as a plantation; set off part to Albion 30 March 1853; established boundary with Burnham 17 January 1868; surrendered organization 24 February 1941 (Kennebec County)

*Town of Unity
PO Box 416
Unity, ME 04988
Phone (207) 948-3763 Selectmen's Office
Settled 1782; incorporated as a town 22 June 1804; annexed part of Twentyfivemile Pond Plantation (present-day Burnham) 1813;

annexed unincorporated land 1817; established boundary 10 February 1821; established boundary with Burnham 17 January 1868 (Waldo County)
Vital records: From 1790

Unity Gore
(see Sebasticook)

Town of Upton
PO Box 645
Upton, ME 04261
Incorporated as a town 9 February 1860 (Oxford County)
Vital records: From 1830

Usher
(see Stoneham)

Town of Van Buren
65 Main Street
Van Buren, ME 04785
Phone (207) 868-2886
Settled 1791; ratified organization 12 March 1870; incorporated as a town 11 February 1881; annexed part of Hamlin 19 February 1907 (Aroostook County)
Vital records: From 1838

Town of Vanceboro
PO Box 25
Vanceboro, ME 04491
Phone (207) 788-3819
Incorporated as a town 4 March 1874 (Aroostook County)
Vital records: From 1814

*Town of Vassalboro
PO Box 187
North Vassalboro, ME 04962
Phone (207) 872-2826
Settled 1760; incorporated as a town 26 April 1771; set off part to form Sidney 30 January 1792; annexed part of China 18 February 1829 (Kennebec County)
Land records: No land records
Naturalization records: No naturalization records
Vital records: Current records; contact Vicki J. Schad. Early records from 1764; contact Maine State Archives
Probate records: No probate records

*Town of Veazie
1084 Main Street
Veazie, ME 04401
Phone (207) 947-2781
Settled 1769; set off from Bangor and incorporated as a town 26 March 1853; set off part to Bangor 29 January 1889 (Penobscot County)

Vital records: From 1853 to date; contact Town Clerk. Vital records: Before 1853; contact Bangor City Clerk, 73 Harlow Street, Bangor, ME 04401

*Town of Verona
Town Clerk
PO Box 1940
Bucksport, ME 04416
Phone (207) 469-7965
Incorporated as a town 18 February 1861 (Hancock County)
Vital records: From 1900

Town of Vienna
Kimball Pond Road
PO Box 17
Vienna, ME 04360
Phone (207) 293-2087 Selectman's Office
Settled 1786; previously known as Goshen or Wyman; incorporated as a town 20 February 1802; set off part to Mount Vernon 1802; annexed part of Rome 1815; set off part to Mount Vernon 28 January 1826; annexed part of Rome 25 January 1840; set off part to Chesterville 2 August 1847; set off part to Mount Vernon 11 March 1853 (Kennebec County)
Vital records: From 1752

Town of Vinalhaven
Vinalhaven, ME 04863
Phone (207) 863-4471; (207) 863-2077 Town Clerk
Settled 1765; incorporated as a town 25 June 1789; set off part to form North Haven 30 June 1846 under law of 1 March 1846; set off part to form Hurricane Isle 7 February 1878; annexed part of Hurricane Isle 17 June 1937 under act of 19 March 1937 (Knox County)
Vital records: From 1785

Town of Wade
Rt. 1, Box 79-A
Washburn, ME 04786
Settled 1846; organized 1859; reorganized 2 May 1874; ratified organization 4 February 1879 and 5 March 1895; incorporated as a town 12 July 1913 under law of 4 March 1913 (Aroostook County)
Vital records: From 1899

Town of Waite
PO Box 37
Waite, ME 04492
Settled 1832; incorporated as a town 22 February 1876 (Washington County)
Vital records: From 1892

Town of Waldo
Rt. 1, Box 2410
Morrill, ME 04952
Organized 6 July 1821; annexed part of Swanville 10 February 1824; annexed part of gore between Waldo and Knox 23 February 1836; incorporated as a town 17 March 1845 (Waldo County)
Vital records: From 1892

Waldo Patent
Granted 13 March 1630 by the Plymouth Council; included all of Waldo County except towns of Burnham and Troy

Town of Waldoboro
Rt. 1, Box 264
Waldoboro, ME 04572
Phone (207) 832-5369 Manager's Office
Settled 1740; incorporated as a town 29 June 1773; established boundary with Jefferson 23 February 1828; set off part to Bremen 6 March 1830; annexed parts of Bremen 11 March 1853 and 27 March 1856 (Lincoln County)
Vital records: From 1892

Town of Wales
Center Road
Rt. 1, Box 1765
Sabattus, ME 04280
Phone (207) 375-8881
Settled 1773; organized 1803; incorporated as a town 1 February 1816; annexed parts of Litchfield 20 January 1827 and 31 January 1828 (amended 23 February 1828); established boundary with Greene 22 March 1843; annexed parts of Leeds and Monmouth 16 March 1855; annexed part of Litchfield 12 March 1856; set off part to Webster (present-day Sabattus) 14 February 1867 (Androscoggin County)
Vital records: From 1730s

*Town of Wallagrass
PO Box 10
Soldier Pond, ME 04781
Phone (207) 834-2263
Ratified organization as a plantation 12 March 1870; organized as a town 26 March 1986 (Aroostook County)
Vital records: From 1866

Town of Waltham
Star Route 31
Ellsworth, ME 04605
Settled 1804; formerly known as Mariaville South and 14 MD BPP; set off part to Mariaville 25 February 1825; annexed part of Mariaville 20

February 1829; set off from Mariaville and incorporated as a town 29 January 1833; set off part to Eastbrook 27 January 1872 (Hancock County)
Vital records: From 1850

*Town of Warren
PO Box 116
Warren, ME 04864
Phone (207) 273-2421
Settled 1736; incorporated as a town 7 November 1776; set off part to form part of Thomaston 20 March 1777; set off part to Thomaston 28 June 1798; set off part to Cushing 1807; set off part to Camden 10 February 1836; established boundary with Thomaston 12 February 1864 (Knox County)
Land records: Yes
Naturalization records: No naturalization records
Vital records: From 1795

Warsaw
(see Pittsfield)

Town of Washburn
Main Street
PO Box 504
Washburn, ME 04786
Phone (207) 455-8485
Settled 1826; incorporated as a town 25 February 1861 (Aroostook County)
Vital records: From 1885

Town of Washington
Rt. 105
PO Box 408
Washington, ME 04574
Phone (207) 845-2897
Settled 1775; set off from Union and incorporated as town of Putnam 27 February 1811; changed name to Washington 31 January 1823; established boundary with Jefferson 23 February 1828; annexed part of Palermo 11 April 1854 (Knox County)
Vital records: From 1800

*Town of Waterboro
PO Box 130
Waterboro, ME 04087
Phone (207) 247-5166 Town Clerk
Settled 1768; incorporated as a town 6 March 1787; set off part to Alfred 22 July 1847; set off part to Shapleigh 14 May 1854; established boundaries with Limington and Hollis 23 February 1865; set off part to Hollis 19 February 1866 (Knox County)
Land records: No land records

Vital records: From 1787; contact Town Clerk
Probate records: No probate records

Town of Waterford
c/o Town Office
Waterford, ME 04088
Phone (207) 583-4403
Settled 1775; incorporated as a town 2 March 1797; annexed part of Albany 1811 (Oxford County)
Vital records: From 1762

City of Waterville
City Hall
Waterville, ME 04901
Phone (207) 873-7131
Settled 1764; incorporated as a town 23 June 1802 from Winslow; annexed parts of Dearborn 1815, 21 January 1822 and 28 February 1826, and remainder 17 March 1843; set off part to form West Waterville 26 February 1873; incorporated as a city 28 February 1883; incorporation effective 23 January 1888 (Kennebec County)
Vital records: From 1813

Town of Wayne
Lovejoy Pond Road
Rt. 1, Box 515
Wayne, ME 04284
Phone (207) 685-4983; (207) 685-3818 Town Clerk
Settled 1773; incorporated as a town 12 February 1798; annexed part of Leeds 1810; set off part to Winthrop 1816; set off part to Readfield 25 Jan 1821; annexed part of Livermore 8 February 1821; set off parts to Winthrop 13 March 1839 and 19 April 1852; annexed part of Leeds 2 April 1859 (Kennebec County)
Vital records: From 1770

Webster
(see Sabattus)

Webster Plantation
PO Box 144
Springfield, ME 04487
Settled 1843; organized as a plantation 1 September 1856 (Penobscot County)
Vital records: From 1840

Town of Weld
Carthage Road
Rt. 1, Box 210
Weld, ME 04285
Phone (207) 585-2348 Selectmen's Office
Settled 1800; incorporated as a town 8 February 1816 (Franklin County)

Vital records: From 1761

Town of Wellington
HCR 31, Box 250
Harmony, ME 04982
Settled 1814; incorporated as a town 23 February 1828; set off part to Parkman 23 March 1841 and reannexed by repeal 10 March 1842; set off part to Cambridge 27 February 1885 (Piscataquis County)
Vital records: From 1823

Town of Wells
Rt. 109
PO Box 147
Wells, ME 04090
Phone (207) 646-2882 Town Clerk
Settled 1640; incorporated as a town 5 July 1653; set off part to form Kennebunk 24 June 1820; annexed part of Kennebunk 21 February 1868 (York County)
Vital records: From 1600s

Town of Wesley
HCR 71, Box 301
Wesley, ME 04686
Incorporated as a town 24 January 1833 (Washington County)
Vital records: From 1776

Town of West Bath
Rt. 1, Box 881
West Bath, ME 04530
Phone (207) 443-4342 Selectmen's Office
Set off from Bath and incorporated as a town 14 February 1844; set off part to Bath 16 March 1855 (Sagadahoc County)
Vital records: From 1845

West Black Island
(see Frenchboro and Swan's Island)

West Central Franklin (unorganized area)
(Franklin County)

West Forks Plantation
PO Box 5
West Forks, ME 04985
Incorporated as a town 31 March 1893; organized as a plantation (Somerset County)
Vital records: From 1898

*Town of West Gardiner
Spears Corner Road
Rt. 3, Box 1500
Gardiner, ME 04345
Phone (207) 724-3945

Settled 1759; set off from Gardiner and incorporated as a town 8 August 1850; set off part to form part of Farmingdale 3 April 1852; annexed part of Farmingdale 19 March 1853; annexed part of Litchfield 22 March 1856 (Kennebec County)
Vital records: From 1848

Town of West Paris
PO Box 247
West Paris, ME 04289
Phone (207) 674-2701
Incorporated as a town 28 August 1957 (Oxford County)
Vital records: From 1958

West Pittston
(see Randolph)

West Waterville
(see Oakland)

*City of Westbrook
PO Box 648
Westbrook, ME 04092
Settled 1628; set off from Falmouth and incorporated as town of Stroudwater 14 February 1814; changed name to Westbrook 9 June 1814; set off part to Falmouth 1819; annexed part of Falmouth 31 January 1825; set off part to Falmouth 11 February 1828 and 22 March 1831; annexed parts of Falmouth 24 February 1835 and 21 March 1836; set off part to Portland 3 April 1845; annexed part of Cape Elizabeth 1852; annexed part of Falmouth 25 March 1853; set off part to form Deering 16 February 1871; incorporated as a city 1 March 1889; incorporation effective 24 February 1891 (Cumberland County)
Land records: No land records
Naturalization records: No naturalization records
Vital records: From 1892. Marriages from 1799 to 1892; contact Walker Memorial Library, 800 Main Street, Westbrook, ME 04092
Probate records: No probate records

Town of Westfield
Drawer C
Westfield, ME 04787
Phone (207) 425-5951
Settled 1839; incorporated as a town 7 March 1905; annexed gore 15 March 1921 (Aroostook County)
Vital records: From 1892

Town of Westmanland
Rt. 1, Box 125
Stockholm, ME 04783
Ratified organization as a plantation 5

March 1895; organized as a town (Aroostook County)
Vital records: From 1892

Town of Weston
PO Box 28
Danforth, ME 04424
Settled 1825; incorporated as a town 17 March 1835; annexed adjacent territory 19 February 1855; set off part to Danforth 4 March 1885; annexed part of Bancroft 26 February 1907 (Aroostook County)
Vital records: From 1814

Town of Westport
Rt. 2, Box 330
Wiscasset, ME 04578
Settled 1774; set off from Edgecomb and incorporated as a town 5 February 1828 (Lincoln County)
Vital records: From 1761

Town of Whitefield
PO Box 58
North Whitefield, ME 04353
Phone (207) 549-5175
Settled 1770; set off from Ballstown (present-day Jefferson) and incorporated as a town 19 June 1809; set off part to Gerry (present-day Windsor) 8 March 1821 and set off part to Alna 26 January 1824, both repealed 19 February 1907 (Lincoln County)
Vital records: From 1748

Town of Whiting
PO Box 101
Whiting, ME 04691
Settled 1780; incorporated as a town 15 February 1825 (Washington County)
Vital records: From 1814

Whitney (unorganized)

Town of Whitneyville
Whitneyville, ME 04692
Settled 1763; set off from Machias and incorporated as a town 10 February 1845 (Washington County)
Vital records: From 1861

Williams College Grant
(see Houlton)

Williamsburg
Settled 1806; incorporated as a town 21 June 1820; set off part to form Barnard 8 February 1834; repealed incorporation 8 February 1939 (Piscataquis County)

Town of Willimantic
Rt. 2, Box 149
Guilford, ME 04443
Settled 1849; incorporated as town of Howard 22 February 1881; changed name to Willimantic 3 February 1883 (Piscataquis County)
Vital records: From 1859

Wilson
Incorporated as a town 29 March 1836; divided and annexed to Shirley, Greenville and Elliottsville 10 August 1848 (Piscataquis County)

Town of Wilton
PO Box 541
Wilton, ME 04294
Phone (207) 645-4961 Town Manager
Settled 1789; incorporated as a town 22 June 1803; set off part to Chesterville 1811; set off part to Temple 28 March 1831 (Franklin County)
Vital records: From 1765

*Town of Windham
8 School Road
Windham, ME 04062
Settled 1735; organized 18 June 1735; incorporated as a town 12 June 1762 (Cumberland County)
Vital records: From the mid-1800s (earlier records destroyed in fire); contact Town Clerk
Vital records search service: $3.00

Town of Windsor
Rt. 1
Windsor, ME 04363
Phone (207) 445-2998; (207) 549-5543 Town Clerk
Settled 1790; incorporated as town of Malta 3 March 1809; annexed part of Whitefield 8 March 1821; changed name to Gerry 10 March 1821; changed name to Windsor 19 January 1822; 1821 annexation from Whitefield repealed 19 February 1907 (Kennebec County)
Vital records: From 1797; contact Richard H. Gray, Clerk

Town of Winn
PO Box 102
Winn, ME 04495
Phone (207) 736-7111
Settled 1820; incorporated as a town 21 March 1857 (Penobscot County)
Vital records: From 1872

*Town of Winslow
16 Benton Avenue
Winslow, ME 04901
Phone (207) 872-2777 Town Clerk
Settled 1764; incorporated as a town 26

April 1771; set off part to form Waterville 23 June 1802; set off part to Fairfax (present-day Albion) 1810; set off part to Harlem 1813; set off part to form part of China 5 June 1818 (Kennebec County)
Land records: Yes
Naturalization records: No naturalization records
Vital records: From 1759; certified copies: $7.00 each
Probate records: No probate records

Town of Winter Harbor
PO Box 98
Winter Harbor, ME 04693
Phone (207) 963-2235
Set off from Gouldsboro and incorporated as a town 21 February 1895 (Hancock County)
Vital records: From 1895

Town of Winterport
School Street
PO Box 559
Winterport, ME 04496
Phone (207) 223-4433
Settled 1760; set off from Frankfort and incorporated as a town 12 March 1860; annexed part of Frankfort 18 February 1867 (Waldo County)
Vital records: From 1860

Winterville Plantation
General Delivery
Winterville, ME 04788
Settled 1846; organized as a plantation 1884; ratified organization 5 March 1895; changed name to Hill 28 March 1903; changed name to Winterville 22 February 1903 (Aroostook County)
Vital records: From 1876

Town of Winthrop
57 Main Street
Winthrop, ME 04364
Phone (207) 377-2286 Town Clerk
Settled 1760; incorporated as a town 26 April 1771; set off part to form Readfield 11 March 1791; set off parts to Hallowell 1813 and 1814; annexed parts of Readfield and Augusta 1810; annexed part of Monmouth 1813; annexed parts of Wayne 1816 and 13 March 1839; set off part to form part of Kennebec (present-day Manchester) 12 August 1850; annexed part of Wayne 19 April 1852; annexed part of Kennebec 30 March 1853; annexed part of Manchester 14 February 1873 (Kennebec County)
Vital records: From 1720

Town of Wiscasset
Bath Road
PO Box 328
Wiscasset, ME 04578
Phone (207) 882-6331 Town Clerk
Settled 1663; incorporated as town of Pownalborough 13 February 1760; set off parts to form Dresden and Alna 25 June 1794; changed name to Wiscasset 10 June 1802; annexed part of Alna 25 February 1839 (Lincoln County)
Vital records: From 1752

*Town of Woodland
Woodland Center Road
Rt. 1, Box 83B
Caribou, ME 04736
Phone (207) 498-6133
Organized as a plantation 1861; ratified organization 21 February 1878; incorporated as a town 5 March 1880 (Aroostook County, not to be confused with Baileyville, Washington County, which is sometimes known as Woodland)
Vital records: From 1892

*Town of Woodstock
26 Monk Avenue
PO Box 317
Bryant Pond, ME 04219
Phone (207) 665-2668
Settled 1793; incorporated as a town 17 February 1815; set off part to Paris 10 February 1825; annexed part of Paris 23 March 1841; annexed part of Milton 24 March 1853; annexed Hamlin's Grant 13 February 1873; set off part to Paris 9 March 1880; annexed part of Greenwood 17 February 1893 (Oxford County)
Land records: Yes
Naturalization records: No naturalization records
Vital records: From 1860
Probate records: No probate records

*Town of Woodville
HC 65, Box 5058
Lincoln, ME 04457-9416
Phone (207) 746-9298
Settled 1832; organized as a plantation 1854; incorporated as a town 28 February 1895 (Penobscot County)
Vital records: From 1900

*Town of Woolwich
Rt. 1, Box 1660
Nequasset Road
Woolwich, ME 04579
Phone (207) 442-8723 Town Clerk; (207) 442-8859 FAX
Settled 1638; resettled 1734; set off from

Georgetown and constituted a district 20 October 1759; incorporated as a town 23 August 1775 (Sagadahoc County)
Land records: No land records
Naturalization records: No naturalization records
Vital records: Births, deaths and marriages from 1752; contact Town Clerk
Vital records search service: no charge; copies: 25¢ per page, $7.00 for the first certified copy and $3.00 for each additional certified copy of the same record

Wyman (unorganized area)
(A wild land township in Franklin County, not to be confused with Wyman, a former name for Vienna, Kennebec County)

*Town of Yarmouth
79 Main Street
PO Box 907
Yarmouth, ME 04096
Phone (207) 846-9036
Settled 1680; set off from North Yarmouth and incorporated as a town 20 August 1849 under law of 8 August 1849 (Cumberland County)
Lane records: No land records
Naturalization records: No naturalization records
Vital records: From 1815; copies: $7.00 each
Probate records: No probate records

*Town of York
PO Box 9
York, ME 03909
Settled 1624; incorporated as a town 22 November 1652; set off part to South Berwick 15 February 1834 (York County)
Vital records: From 1715

7 SD BPP (unorganized)
Wild land township; set off part (West Bay Stream) to Gouldsboro 28 February 1845; set off part (Sowle Tract) to Gouldsboro 26 February 1870; set off part to Sullivan 11 March 1899; set off part (Sowle Tract) to Gouldsboro 8 March 1905 (Hancock County)

MARYLAND

Capital: Annapolis. Statehood: 28 April 1788 (proprietary colony established 1632, Mason-Dixon Line settled 1763–1767)

Court System

Maryland has twenty-three counties, but Baltimore City, which is an independent city, is not contained within a county. The Maryland Tax Court has statewide jurisdiction. The Maryland Orphans' Courts deal with matters involving probate, guardianships, orphans, etc., and are established in Baltimore City and in each county except Montgomery and Harford, where the Circuit Court exercises the same authority.

The Maryland District Courts sit at each county seat and Baltimore City and handle some civil actions, felony thefts, misdemeanors, and ordinance violations. District One: Baltimore City; District Two: Dorchester, Somerset, Wicomico and Worcester counties; District Three: Caroline, Cecil, Kent, Queen Anne's and Talbot counties; District Four: Calvert, Charles and Saint Mary's counties; District Five: Prince George's County; District Six: Montgomery County; District Seven: Anne Arundel County; District Eight: Baltimore County; District Nine: Harford County; District Ten: Carroll and Howard counties; District Eleven: Frederick and Washington counties; District Twelve: Allegany and Garrett counties.

The Circuit Court of Maryland has unlimited trial jurisdiction and sits in each county seat and Baltimore City. First Judicial Circuit: Dorchester, Somerset, Wicomico and Worcester counties; Second Judicial Circuit: Caroline, Cecil, Kent, Queen Anne's and Talbot counties; Third Judicial Circuit: Baltimore and Harford counties; Fourth Judicial Circuit: Allegany, Garrett and Washington counties; Fifth Judicial Circuit: Anne Arundel, Carroll and Howard counties; Sixth Judicial Circuit: Frederick and Montgomery counties; Seventh Judicial Circuit: Calvert, Charles, Prince George's and Saint Mary's counties; Eighth Judicial Circuit: Baltimore City. The Court of Special Appeals of Maryland and the six circuits of the Court of Appeals of Maryland hear appeals.

Courthouses

*Allegany County Courthouse
30 Washington Street
Cumberland, MD 21502-3043
Phone (301) 777-5922
County organized 1789 from Washington County

*Anne Arundel County Circuit Court
PO Box 71
Annapolis, MD 21404-1930
Phone (410) 222-1397; (410) 222-1425 Circuit Court; (410) 222-1430 Register of Wills
County organized 1650, original county
Land records: Contact Robert P. Duckworth, Clerk of Circuit Court, PO Box 71—Church Circle, Annapolis, MD 21404; copies: 50¢ per page, $3.00 for certification
Naturalization records: No naturalization records
Vital records: No vital records
Probate records: Contact Mr. George Nutwell, Register of Wills, 101 South Street, Annapolis, MD 21401

Baltimore City Courthouse
100 North Holiday Street
Baltimore, MD 21202-3417
Phone (410) 396-3100
City organized 1729, made independent from Baltimore County in 1851
Land records: Contact Land Records Division, 100 North Calvert Street, Room 610, Baltimore, MD 21202-3417
Probate records: Contact Register of Wills, 111 North Calvert Street, Baltimore, MD 21202

*Baltimore County Circuit Court
401 Bosley Avenue
Towson, MD 21204
Phone (410) 887-2601 Clerk
County organized 1659, original county (Baltimore City made independent of the county in 1851)
Land records: Contact Clerk of Circuit Court

*Calvert County Courthouse
175 Main Street
Prince Frederick, MD 20678
Phone (410) 535-1600
County organized 1650, original county
Land records: From 1882; contact Audrey B. Evans, Clerk of Circuit Court
Naturalization records: No naturalization records
Vital records: No vital records
Probate records: From 1882; contact Margaret H. Phipps, Register of Wills
No probate search service; copies: 50¢ each, no minimum

*Caroline County Courthouse
PO Box 207
Denton, MD 21629-0207
Phone (410) 479-1811 Clerk of Circuit Court; (410) 479-0717 Register of Wills
County organized 1773 from Dorchester and Queen Anne's counties
Land records: From 1773; contact Clerk of Circuit Court, PO Box 458, Denton, MD 21629
No land search service; certified copies $5.00 each
Naturalization records: From 1773 to 1945; contact Clerk of Circuit Court
No naturalization search service (most records transferred to The Hall of Records in Annapolis); certified copies $5.00 each
Vital records: Marriages from 1773; contact Clerk of Circuit Court; certified copies $5.00 each
Probate records: Wills from 1688, estate proceedings from 1852; contact Register of Wills, PO Box 416, Denton, MD 21629
Probate search service: no charge; copies: 50¢ per page, no minimum

*Carroll County Courthouse
55 North Court Street
Westminster, MD 21157
Phone (410) 876-2085
County organized 1836 from Baltimore and Frederick counties
Land records: Contact Larry W. Shipley, Clerk of Circuit Court
Probate records: Contact Reese Starner, Registrar of Wills
No probate search service; copies: 50¢ each, no minimum

*Cecil County Commissioners
Room 101, County Office Building
Elkton, MD 21921
Phone (301) 398-0200
County organized 1674 from Kent County
Land records: Contact William C. Bruckman, Clerk to Circuit Court, Room 108
Vital records: Contact Betty Morris, Room 324, County Health Department
Probate records: From 1674; contact Lillian D. Rogers, Registrar of Wills, Room 307
No probate search service; copies: 25¢ per page (closed estates), 50¢ per page (open estates), no minimum

*Charles County Government Offices
PO Box B
La Plata, MD 20646-0167
Phone (301) 932-3201 Circuit Court; (301) 870-3001 Circuit Court; (301) 645-3345 Register of Wills; (301) 870-3879 Register of Wills
County organized 1658, original county
Land records: Contact Clerk of Circuit

Court, PO Box 970, La Plata, MD 20646

Naturalization records: No naturalization records

Vital records: Marriages only from 1886 to date; contact Clerk of Circuit Court

Probate records: Contact Register of Wills, PO Box 3080, La Plata, MD 20646

No probate search service; copies: 50¢ per page, $1.00 minimum; "We must have reference number."

Dorchester County Courthouse
PO Box 26
Cambridge, MD 21613-0026
Phone (301) 228-1700
County organized 1668, original county

*Frederick County Courthouse
100 West Patrick Street
Frederick, MD 21701
Phone (301) 694-1960 Clerk of the Circuit Court; (301) 663-3722 Register of Wills
County organized 1748 from Prince George's County
Land records: From 1748; contact Charles C. Keller, Clerk of the Circuit Court; copies 50¢ per page
Naturalization records: From 1801 to 1906; contact Clerk of the Circuit Court
Vital records: Marriages from 1778, index of names for whom licenses were issued from 1778 to 1865; certified copies: $5.00 each
Probate records: Wills from 1744, administration accounts from 1750; contact Register of Wills

*Garrett County Courthouse
203 South Fourth Street
Oakland, MD 21550-1535
Phone (301) 334-8970; (301) 334-1937 Circuit Clerk; (301) 334-8111 County Health Department; (301) 334-1999 Registrar of Wills
County organized 1872 from Allegany County
Land records: Contact David K. Martin, Circuit Clerk
Naturalization records: From 1872 to 1930; contact Circuit Court
Vital records: Contact County Health Department
Probate records: Contact Joseph DiSimone, Registrar of Wills
No probate search service; copies: 50¢ each, no minimum; "Please direct all correspondence to records of each department."

*Harford County Courthouse
20 West Courtland Street
Bel Air, MD 21014-3833

Phone (410) 838-6000
County organized 1773 from Baltimore County
Land records: From 1779; contact Charles G. Hiob, III, Clerk of the Circuit Court
Probate records: Contact Harry L. W. Hopkins, Jr., Register of Wills, Room 3-04, Third Floor
Probate search service: no charge "but due to our small staff, we do not have the time to search for records, only possibly during summer months if we have summer help"; copies: 50¢ per page, no minimum

Howard County Courthouse
3430 Courthouse Drive
Ellicott City, MD 21043-4300
Phone (410) 992-2025
County organized 1851 from Baltimore County

*Kent County Courthouse
Cross Street
Chestertown, MD 21620
Phone (301) 778-4600
County organized 1642, original county
Land records: From 1656; contact Mark L. Mumford, Clerk of Court
Naturalization records: No naturalization records
Vital records: No vital records
Probate records: From 1669; contact Janet Ashley, Register of Wills
Probate search service: no charge at present; copies: 50¢ per page, no minimum, $5.00 per certified copy; "Wills from 1669 to 1798 are on microfilm here and cannot be copied. To obtain copies for that period, write to Maryland State Archives."

Montgomery County Courthouse
101 Monroe Street
Rockville, MD 20850-2540
Phone (301) 251-2500
County organized 1776 from Frederick County

*Prince George's County Administration Building
Upper Marlboro, MD 20772-3050
Phone (301) 952-4576; (301) 952-3352 Clerk of Circuit Court (Land); (301) 952-3318 Clerk of Circuit Court (Naturalization); (301) 952-3250 Register of Wills
County organized 1695 from Calvert and Charles counties
Land records: Contact Clerk of Circuit Court
Naturalization records: Contact Clerk of Circuit Court's Office
Probate records: Contact Register of

Wills, PO Box 368, Upper Marlboro, MD 20772
No probate search service; copies: 50¢ per page, no minimum

*Circuit Court for Queen Anne's County Courthouse
Centreville, MD 21617
Phone (410) 758-1773
County organized 1706 from Talbot County
Land records: From 1706; contact Scott MacGlashan, Clerk
No land search service; copies 50¢ per page once liber and folio numbers of specific records are provided
Vital records: Marriages from 1927; contact Clerk. Marriages from 1817 to 1926; contact Maryland State Archives, 350 Rowe Boulevard, Annapolis, MD 21401. Births and deaths; contact Division of Vital Records, 4201 Patterson Avenue, PO Box 68760, Baltimore, MD 21215-0020
Probate records: Contact Register of Wills, 107 North Liberty Street, Centreville, MD 21617

*Saint Mary's County Courthouse
PO Box 653
Leonardtown, MD 20650
Phone (301) 475-4568; (301) 475-4558 Clerk of the Circuit Court; (301) 475-4561 Vital Records; (301) 475-5566 Register of Wills
County organized 1637, original county
Land records: From 1827; contact Mary R. Bell, Clerk of the Circuit Court, PO Box 308, Leonardtown, MD 20050
Vital records: Marriages only from 1794
Probate records: Contact Register of Wills, PO Box 102, Leonardtown, MD 20650
Probate search service: no charge; copies: 50¢ per page

*Somerset County Courthouse
30512 Prince William Street
Princess Anne, MD 21853
Phone (410) 651-1555 Clerk of the Circuit Court; (410) 651-1696 Register of Wills
County organized 1666, original county
Land records: From 1665; contact I. Theodore Phoebus, Clerk of the Circuit Court
No land records search service; copies: 50¢ per page
Vital records: Marriages from 1797; contact Clerk of the Circuit Court
No vital records search service: copies: 50¢ per page
Probate records: Contact Register of Wills
No probate search service; copies: 50¢ per page

*Talbot County Courthouse
Easton, MD 21601
Phone (301) 822-2401
County organized 1662 from Kent County
Land records: Contact Clerk of the Circuit Court
Naturalization records: No naturalization records
Vital records: No vital records
Probate records: Contact Register of Wills
No probate search service; copies: 50¢ each, no minimum; "Do not provide index search other than reference number."

*Washington County Courthouse
Summit Avenue
Hagerstown, MD 21740
Phone (301) 733-8660; (301) 739-3612 Register
County organized 1776 from Frederick County
Land records: From 1776; contact Clerk of Court
Naturalization records: From 1787 to 1979; contact Clerk of Court
Vital records: Index of marriages only from 1799 to 1886; contact Clerk of Court
Probate records: Contact Marvin Toms, Register

*Wicomico County Circuit Court
PO Box 198
Salisbury, MD 21803-0198
Phone (410) 543-6551
County organized 1867 from Somerset and Worcester counties
Land records: From 1867
Naturalization records: From 1879 to 1975
Vital records: Marriage licenses only
Probate records: Contact Register of Wills, Courthouse, Salisbury, MD 21801

*Worcester County Courthouse
Snow Hill, MD 21863
Phone (410) 632-1194
County organized 1742 from Somerset County
Land records: Yes
Naturalization records: No naturalization records
Vital records: Marriages
Probate records: Yes

MASSACHUSETTS

Capital: Boston. Statehood: 6 February 1788 (settled 1620, became a charter colony in 1629)

Court System

The Trial Court of Massachusetts was organized in 1978 and consists of seven departments: Superior Court Department, District Court Department, Boston Municipal Court Department, Probate and Family Court Department, Land Court Department, Juvenile Court Department and Housing Court Department. The Superior Court Department sits in each county and has original jurisdiction over all criminal and civil matters except those under the original exclusive jurisdiction of other courts.

The District Court Department has general jurisdiction and is divided into five regions, consisting of thirteen or more divisions. Region One: parts of Barnstable, Bristol, Dukes, Nantucket, Norfolk and Plymouth counties; Region Two: parts of Essex, Norfolk and Suffolk counties; Region Three: parts of Essex and Middlesex counties; Region Four: parts of Middlesex, Norfolk and Worcester counties; Region Five: parts of Berkshire, Franklin, Hampden, Hampshire and Worcester counties.

The Probate and Family Court Department has a division in each county. The Land Court Department has jurisdiction throughout the state and sits primarily at Boston. The Massachusetts Appeals Court and the Massachusetts Supreme Judicial Court hear appeals.

Counties

*Barnstable County Courthouse
Route 6A
Barnstable, MA 02630
Phone (508) 362-2511, ext. 594 Register of Probate
County organized 1685 from Old Plymouth Colony
Land records: Contact Registrar of Deeds, County Registry of Deeds, County Complex, Main Street, Barnstable, MA 02630
Naturalization records: Card file with names of individuals who have been naturalized (no original records);

contact Superior Court, Clerk of Courts
Vital records: Contact individual town and city clerks
Probate records: From 1686; contact Frederic P. Clauseen, Register of Probate, Probate and Family Court Department, Main Street, PO Box 346, Barnstable, MA 02630-0346; attested copies: $1.50 per page, no minimum

*Berkshire County Courthouse
76 East Street
Pittsfield, MA 01201-5304
Phone (413) 448-8424 Commissioner's Office; (413) 442-6941 Register, Probate and Family Court
County organized 1760 from Hampshire County
Land records: Contact Middle District Registry of Deeds
Naturalization records: Contact Superior Court
Vital records: Contact individual town and city clerks
Probate records: From 1760 (divorces from 1924, changes of name, and adoptions); contact Guy A. Pellegrinelli, Jr., Register, Probate and Family Court, 44 Bank Row, Pittsfield, MA 01201
Probate search service: "Depends on involvement"; copies: 50¢ per page, no minimum

Berkshire Northern District
65 Park Street
Adams, MA 01220
Land records: Contact Registry of Deeds

Berkshire Southern District
Great Barrington, MA 01230
Land records: Contact Registry of Deeds

Bristol County Courthouse
9 Court Street
Taunton, MA 02780-3223
Phone (508) 823-6588; (508) 993-2603 Registry of Deeds (Southern District)
County organized 1685 from Old Plymouth Colony
Land records: Contact Registry of Deeds (Southern District), 25 North Sixth Street, New Bedford, MA 02740
Vital records: Contact individual town and city clerks
Probate records: Contact Probate and Family Court Department, 11 Court Street, PO Box 567, Taunton, MA 02780

Attleboro District Courthouse
North Main Street
Attleboro, MA 02703

Bristol Fall River District
441 North Main Street
Fall River, MA 02720

*Dukes County Courthouse
Edgartown District Court
PO Box 190
Edgartown, MA 02539-0190
Phone (617) 627-5535
County organized 1695 from Martha's Vineyard
Land records: Contact Beverly King, Register of Deeds, PO Box 54, Edgartown, MA 02539
Naturalization records: Contact Joseph E. Sallitte, Jr., Clerk of Courts, Edgartown, MA 02539
Vital records: A few vital records available in the courthouse, but most available at relevant town clerks' offices
Probate records: From 1696; contact Emily H. Rose, Register, Probate and Family Court, Dukes County Division, PO Box 338, Edgartown, MA 02539
Probate search service: no charge; copies: 50¢ per page, $1.50 if attested, no minimum

*Essex County Courthouse
65 Washington Street
Salem, MA 01970-3503
Phone (508) 741-0200; (508) 741-0201 Probate and Family Court Department
County organized 1643, original county
Land records: Contact Registry of Deeds
Vital records: Contact individual town and city clerks
Probate records: Contact Registry of Probate, Probate and Family Court Department, 36 Federal Street, Salem, MA 01970; certified copies: $1.50 per page

Essex Northern District
381 Common Street
Lawrence, MA 01840

Lynn District Court
580 Essex Street
Lynn, MA 01901
Probate records: Yes

*Franklin County Courthouse
425 Main Street
Greenfield, MA 01301-3313
Phone (413) 772-0239 Registry of Deeds; (413) 774-5535 Superior Court; (413) 774-7011 Registry of Probate
County organized 1811 from Hampshire County
Land records: Hampshire Abstract records 1663–1786 and Franklin County records to present; contact Registry of Deeds, Courthouse, 425 Main Street, PO Box 1495, Greenfield, MA 01302; copies: 75¢ per page for records, $1.00 per page for plans
Naturalization records: Contact Superior Court, Courthouse, 425 Main Street, PO Box 1573, Greenfield, MA 01302
Vital records: Contact individual town and city clerks
Probate records: Contact Registry of Probate, PO Box 290, Greenfield, MA 01302
Probate search service: no charge; copies: 50¢ per page, no minimum; "Provide estate name and approximate year."

*Hampden County Probate and Family Court
50 State Street
PO Box 559
Springfield, MA 01102-0559
Phone (413) 748-7760 Probate and Family Court
County organized 1812 from Hampshire County
Land records: Contact Registry of Deeds
Naturalization records: Yes
Vital records: Contact individual town and city clerks
Probate records: Contact Thomas P. Moriarty, Jr., Register of Probate

*Hampshire County Hall of Records
33 King Street
Northampton, MA 01060
Phone (413) 584-3637 Land Records and Registry of Deeds; (413) 586-8500 Probate and Family Court
County organized 7 May 1662 from Middlesex County
Land records: Contact Marianne Donohue, Register, Land Records and Registry of Deeds
Naturalization records: Contact Superior Court, Hampshire County Courthouse, 15 Gothic Street, Northampton, MA 01060
Vital records: Contact individual town and city clerks (Amherst, Belchertown, Chesterfield, Cummington, Easthampton, Goshen, Granby, Hadley, Hatfield, Huntington, Middlefield, Northampton, Pelham, Plainfield, South Hadley, Southampton, Ware, Westhampton, Williamsburg and Worthington)
Probate records: Contact Probate and Family Court Department, 33 King Street, Northampton, MA 01060

*Middlesex County Courthouse
Cambridge, MA 02141-1755
Phone (508) 494-4003; (617) 727-2816 State Archives

County organized 1643, original county
Land records: Contact Register of Deeds, 208 Cambridge Street, Cambridge, MA 02141-0005
Vital records: Contact individual town and city clerks
Probate records: From 1872; contact Donna M. Lambert, Registrar of Probate, Middlesex Probate and Family Court, Attn. Copy Department, 208 Cambridge Street, Cambridge, MA 02141-0005. Probate records from 1648 to 1871; contact State Archives, 220 Morrissey Boulevard (Columbia Point), Boston, MA 02125
Probate search service from Registrar of Probate: no charge; copies: 50¢ per page for unofficial copies or $1.50 per attested page; no minimum

Middlesex Northern District
360 Gorham Street
Lowell, MA 01852
Phone (508) 458-8474

*Nantucket Town and County Building
16 Broad Street
Nantucket, MA 02554
Phone (508) 228-6800; (508) 228-7250 Register of Deeds; (508) 228-2559 Superior Court; (508) 228-7216 Town Clerk; (508) 228-2669 Probate and Family Court Department
County organized 1695, original county; town organized 1687 (Sherburn, 1713; Tuckannock, 1795) (town comprises the whole of Nantucket County)
Land records: Contact Sandra M. Chadwick, Register of Deeds
Naturalization records: Contact Patricia R. Church, Superior Court
Vital records: Contact Town Clerk, Town Building, Broad Street, Nantucket, MA 02554
Vital records search service: no charge; copies: 35¢ (8½" x 11"), 50¢ (11" x 17")
Probate records: Contact Probate and Family Court Department, PO Box 1116, Nantucket, MA 02554

Norfolk County Courthouse
614 High Street
Dedham, MA 02026-1833
Phone (617) 326-1600; (617) 326-7200 Probate and Family Court Department
County organized 1793 from Suffolk County
Land records: Contact Superior Court, Registry of Deeds
Vital records: Contact individual town and city clerks
Probate records: Contact Probate and Family Court Department, PO Box 269, 649 High Street, Dedham, MA 02026

*Plymouth County Commissioners
Court Street
Plymouth, MA 02360
Phone (617) 747-1350 County
    Commissioners; (508) 830-9200
    Registry of Deeds; (508) 747-6911
    Office of the Clerk of Courts; (617)
    727-2816 Judicial Archives
*County organized 1685 from Old
    Plymouth Colony*
Land records: Deeds from 1620 to 1692;
    contact County Commissioners, 11
    South Russell Street, Plymouth, MA
    02360; copies: send SASE with
    request for manuscript, transcript or
    both if available, and you will be
    given a cost quotation (50¢ per page,
    $2.00 minimum). Deeds after 1692,
    contact John D. Riordan, Esq.,
    Registry of Deeds, 11 North Russell
    Street, PO Box 3535, Plymouth, MA
    02361-3535.
Naturalization records: Francis R.
    Powers, Clerk of Courts
Vital records: Births, deaths and
    marriages from 1636 to 1686. Vital
    records: Contact individual town and
    city clerks
Probate records: From 1620 to 1692;
    contact County Commissioners;
    copies: send SASE with request for
    manuscript, transcript or both if
    available, and you will be given a cost
    quotation (50¢ per page, $2.00
    minimum). Wills and inventories of
    estates from about 1685 through 1881;
    contact Judicial Archives,
    Massachusetts State Archives, 220
    Morrissey Boulevard (Columbia
    Point), Boston, MA 02125.

Brockton District
72 Belmont Street
Brockton, MA 02401
Phone (508) 583-8250
Probate records: Contact Probate and
    Family Court Division

Suffolk County Courthouse
Old Court House, Government Center
Pemberton Square
Boston, MA 02148
Phone (617) 725-8000; (617) 725-8575
    Registry of Deeds; (617) 775-8300
    Probate and Family Court Department
County organized 1643, original county
Vital records: Contact individual town
    and city clerks
Probate records: Contact Supreme
    Judicial Court for Suffolk County,
    Archives and Record Preservation
    Project, 1300 New Court House,
    Room 1400, Boston, MA 02108,
    (617) 725-8044 or (617) 725-8045

*Worcester County Courthouse
2 Main Street
Worcester, MA 01608-1116

Phone (508) 798-7700; (508) 798-7713
    Registry of Deeds; (508) 756-2441
    Probate and Family Court Department
*County incorporated 2 April 1731 with
    the Town of Brookfield from
    Hampshire County, the towns of
    Lancaster, Leicester, Lunenburg,
    Rutland, Shrewsbury, Southborough,
    Westborough and Worcester from
    Middlesex County, and the towns of
    Mendon, Oxford, Sutton, Uxbridge
    and Woodstock (which revolted and
    was received into Connecticut in
    1748) from Suffolk County*
Land records: Contact Worcester
    Registry of Deeds
Vital records: Contact individual town
    and city clerks
Probate records: Contact Probate and
    Family Court Department

Worcester Northern District
Fitchburg Courthouse
84 and 100 Elm Street
Fitchburg, MA 01420
Land records: Contact Fitchburg Registry
    of Deeds, 84 Elm Street, Fitchburg,
    MA 01420

Towns and Cities

(Deeds, naturalizations and probates are
kept on the county level, but vital statistics
and property tax records are kept in each
municipality)

*Town of Abington
33 Randolph Street
North Abington, MA 02351
Phone (617) 982-2112
*Organized 1712 from Bridgewater
    (Plymouth County)*
Land records: Contact Assessors' Office
Naturalization records: No naturalization
    records
Vital records: Contact Town Clerk's
    Office; copies: $5.00 each
Probate records: No probate records

Town of Acton
Acton, MA 01720
*Organized 1735 from Concord
    (Middlesex County)*

Acushena
(see Town of Dartmouth)

Town of Acushnet
Acushnet, MA 02743
*Organized 1860 from Fairhaven (Bristol
    County)*

Town of Adams
Adams, MA 01220

*Organized 1778 (East Hoosuck)
    (Berkshire County)*

Agawam
(see Town of Ipswich)

*Town of Agawam
Agawam, MA 01001
Phone (413) 786-0400, ext. 215
*Organized 1855 from West Springfield
    (Hampden County)*
Land records: No land records
Naturalization records: No naturalization
    records
Vital records: Births, deaths and
    marriages; copies: $5.00 each
Probate records: No probate records

Agawam Plantation
(see Town of Wareham)

Town of Alford
5 Alford Center Road
Alford, MA 01230
*Organized 1773 from Great Barrington
    (Berkshire County)*

Allston
(see City of Boston)

Town of Amesbury
Amesbury, MA 01913
*Organized 1668 from Salisbury (Essex
    County)*

*Town of Amherst
Amherst, MA 01002
Phone (413) 256-4035
*Organized 1759 from Hadley
    (Hampshire County)*
Land records: No land records
Naturalization records: No naturalization
    records
Vital records: Some from 1732; contact
    Town Clerk, Bangs Community
    Center, 70 Boltwood Walk, Amherst,
    MA 01002; certified copies: $5.00
    each
Probate records: No probate records

*Town of Andover
Town Clerk's Office
36 Bartlet Street
Andover, MA 01810
Phone (508) 470-3800
Organized 1646 (Essex County)
Land records: No land records
Naturalization records: No naturalization
    records
Vital records: Births, deaths and
    marriages; certified copies: $5.00 each
Probate records: No probate records

*Town of Arlington
Arlington, MA 02174
Organized 1807 from Cambridge (West Cambridge, 1867) (Middlesex County)
Land records: No land records
Naturalization records: No naturalization records
Vital records: Births, deaths and marriages; contact Corinne M. Rainville, Town Clerk; copies: $6.00 each
Probate records: No probate records

*Town of Ashburnham
Town Hall
Ashburnham, MA 01430
Phone (508) 827-4102
Organized 1765 (Dorcester-Canada) (Worcester County)
Land records: No land records
Naturalization records: No naturalization records
Vital records: Yes
Probate records: No probate records

Ashburnton
(see Town of Ashby)

Town of Ashby
Main Street
Ashby, MA 01431
Organized 1767 from Ashburnton, Fitchburg and Townsend (Middlesex County)

Town of Ashfield
Eleanor M. Ward, Town Clerk
Town Hall
Main Street
PO Box 213
Ashfield, MA 01330
Phone (413) 628-4441
Organized 1765 (Huntstown Plantation) (Franklin County)

*Town of Ashland
101 Main Street
Ashland, MA 01721
Phone (508) 881-0100
Incorporated 1846 from Framingham, Holliston and Hopkinton (Middlesex County)
Land records: No land records
Naturalization records: No naturalization records
Vital records: Contact David F. Teller, Town Clerk
Probate records: No probate records

Ashuelet Equivalent
(see Town of Dalton)

*Town of Athol
584 Main Street
Athol, MA 01331

Phone (508) 249-4551 Town Clerk's Office
Incorporated 6 March 1762 (Payquage Plantation) (Worcester County)
Land records: No land records
Naturalization records: No naturalization records
Vital records: Births, deaths and marriages; contact Town Clerk's Office; certified copies: $5.00 each

City of Attleboro
City Hall
Attleboro, MA 02703
Organized 1694 from Rehoboth (Bristol County)

Attleborough
(see Town of North Attleborough)

Town of Auburn
Auburn, MA 01501
Organized 1778 from Leicester, Oxford, Sutton and Worcester (Ward, 1837) (Worcester County)

*Town of Avon
Buckley Center
Avon, MA 02322
Phone (508) 588-0414
Organized 1888 (Norfolk County)
Land records: No land records
Naturalization records: No naturalization records
Vital records: Births, deaths and marriages; contact Clerk's Office; certified copies: $10.00 each
Probate records: No probate records

Town of Ayer
Ayer, MA 01432
Organized 1871 from Groton and Shirley (Middlesex County)

Barecove
(see Town of Hingham)

*Town of Barnstable
364 Main Street
Hyannis, MA 02601
Phone (508) 790-6240 Town Clerk's Office; (508) 775-3344 FAX, Town Clerk's Office
Organized 1638; incorporated 1639 (Barnstable County)
Land records: No land records
Naturalization records: No naturalization records
Vital records: Births deaths and marriages; contact Linda E. Leppanen, Town Clerk, First Floor; certified copies: $5.00 each (includes search)
Probate records: No probate records

*Town of Barre
Barre, MA 01005
Phone (508) 355-2504
Organized 1753 from Rutland (Rutland District, 1774; Hutchinson, 1776) (Worcester County)
Land records: No land records
Naturalization records: No naturalization records
Vital records: Contact Town Clerk
Probate records: No probate records

Town of Becket
Becket, MA 01223
Organized 1765 (Number 4 Plantation) (Berkshire County)

*Town of Bedford
10 Mudge Way
Bedford, MA 01730
Phone (617) 275-0083
Organized 1729 from Billerica and Concord (Middlesex County)
Vital records: Contact Doreen Trenbley, Town Clerk

*Town of Belchertown
2 Jabish Street
PO Box 607
Belchertown, MA 01007
Phone (413) 323-0400
Organized 1761 (Cold Spring Plantation) (Hampshire County)
Land records: No land records
Naturalization records: No naturalization records
Vital records: From 1734 to date; contact Town Clerk
Probate records: No probate records

Town of Bellingham
4 Mechanic Street
Bellingham, MA 02019
Organized 1719 from Dedham, Mendon and Wrentham (Norfolk County)

*Town of Belmont
Belmont, MA 02178
Phone (617) 489-8200 General Information; (617) 489-8201 Town Clerk's Office
Organized 1859 from Waltham, Watertown and West Cambridge (Arlington) (Middlesex County)
Land records: No land records
Naturalization records: No naturalization records
Vital records: Contact Town Clerk's Office
Probate records: No probate records

*Town of Berkley
1 North Main Street
Berkley, MA 02779
Phone (508) 822-3348

Organized 1735 from Dighton and Taunton (Bristol County)
Land records: No land records
Naturalization records: No naturalization records
Vital records: Contact Carolyn Awalt, Town Clerk/Treasurer
Probate records: No probate records

*Town of Berlin
Berlin, MA 01503
Phone (508) 838-2442
Organized 1784 from Bolton and Marlborough (Worcester County)
Land records: Contact Assessors' Office
Naturalization records: No naturalization records
Vital records: Contact Town Clerk
Probate records: No probate records

*Town of Bernardston
PO Box 435
Church Street
Bernardston, MA 01337
Phone (413) 648-9342
Organized 1762 as Falltown Plantation (Franklin County)
Land records: No land records
Naturalization records: No naturalization records
Vital records: Contact John A. Senior, Town Clerk
Vital records search service: no fee for cursory search, negotiable fee for in-depth search; certified copies: $5.00 each
Probate records: No probate records

Bernardstone's Grant
(see Town of Florida)

*City of Beverly
City Hall
Beverly, MA 01915
Organized 1668 from Salem (Essex County)
Land records: No land records
Naturalization records: No naturalization records
Vital records: Contact City Clerk; copies: 25¢ per page, $2.00 for abstract, $6.00 for certificate (open to inspection prior to 1920)
Probate records: No probate records

Town of Billerica
Billerica, MA 01821
Organized 1655 (Middlesex County)

*Town of Blackstone
Municipal Center
15 Saint Paul Street
Blackstone, MA 01504-2295
Phone (508) 883-1500

Organized 1845 from Mendon (Worcester County)
Land records: Contact Assessors
Naturalization records: No naturalization records
Vital records: Contact Town Clerk
Vital records search service: no charge; certified copies: $5.00 each
Probate records: No probate records

*Town of Blandford
Main Street
Blandford, MA 01008
Organized 1741 (Suffield Equivalent, Glasgow) (Hampden County)
Land records: Yes
Naturalization records: Yes
Vital records: Yes
Probate records: No probate records

Boardman's Farm
(see Town of Lunenburg)

*Town of Bolton
PO Box 278
Bolton, MA 01740
Phone (508) 779-2771
Organized 1738 from Lancaster (Worcester County)
Land records: No land records
Naturalization records: No naturalization records
Vital records: Contact Town Clerk
Probate records: No probate records

City of Boston
City Hall
Boston, MA 02201
Organized 1630 (Suffolk County, includes Allston, Brighton, Charlestown, Dorchester, Hyde Park, Jamaica Plain, Mattapan, Roslindale, Roxbury, South Boston and West Roxbury)

*Town of Bourne
Bourne, MA 02532
Phone (508) 759-0613
Organized 1884 from Sandwich (Barnstable County)
Land records: No land records
Naturalization records: No naturalization records
Vital records: Contact Town Clerk
Probate records: No probate records

*Town of Boxborough
Boxborough, MA 01719
Phone (508) 263-1116
Organized 1783 from Harvard, Littletown and Stow (Middlesex County)
Land records: Yes
Naturalization records: No naturalization records

Vital records: Some records impounded; copies: $3.00 each
Probate records: No probate records

*Town of Boxford
Boxford, MA 01921
Phone (508) 887-8181
Organized 1694 (Essex County)
Land records: No land records
Naturalization records: No naturalization records
Vital records: Contact Town Clerk's Office
Probate records: No probate records

*Town of Boylston
84 Main Street
Boylston, MA 01505
Phone (508) 869-2234
Organized 1786 from Shrewsbury (Worcester County)
Land records: Contact Assessors' Office (older records stored in Library Vault)
Naturalization records: No naturalization records
Vital records: Contact Town Clerk's Office (older records stored in Library Vault)
Probate records: No probate records

Town of Bradford
Organized 1675 from Southern, annexed to Haverhill, 1897

Town of Braintree
Braintree, MA 02184
Organized 1640 from Boston (Norfolk County)

Town of Brewster
Brewster, MA 02631
Organized 1803 from Harwich (Barnstable County)

*Town of Bridgewater
Bridgewater, MA 02324
Phone (508) 697-0921
Organized 1656 (Plymouth County)
Land records: Yes
Naturalization records: No naturalization records
Vital records: Contact Town Clerk
Vital records search fee: $5.00; copies: 20¢ per page (impounded records are restricted)

Town of Brighton
Organized 1817 from Cambridge, annexed to Boston, 1874

Town of Brimfield
Brimfield, MA 01010
Organized 1714 (Hampden County)

City of Brockton
City Hall
Brockton, MA 02401
Organized 1821 from Bridgewater
(North Bridgewater) (Plymouth
County)

Town of Brookfield
Brookfield, MA 01506
Organized 1673 (Worcester County)

*Town of Brookline
333 Washington Street
Brookline, MA 02147
Organized 1705 from Boston (Norfolk
County)

*Town of Buckland
17 State Street
Buckland, MA 01370
Phone (413) 625-6330
Organized 1779 from No-town
Plantation and Charlemont
(Franklin County)
Land records: No land records
Naturalization records: No naturalization
records
Vital records: From 1777 (after town
fire) to date; contact Janice D.
Purington, Town Clerk
Probate records: No probate records

Bullock's Grant
(see Town of Florida)

*Town of Burlington
Burlington, MA 01803
Phone (617) 270-1660
Organized 1799 from Woburn
(Middlesex County)
Land records: No land records
Naturalization records: No naturalization
records
Vital records: Contact Town Clerk
Probate records: No probate records

*City of Cambridge
City Hall
Cambridge, MA 02139
Phone (617) 349-4300
Organized 1631 (Newe Towne)
(Middlesex County)
Land records: No land records
Naturalization records: No naturalization
records
Vital records: Contact City Clerk
Probate records: No probate records

Cambridge Village
(see City of Newton)

Town of Canton
Canton, MA 02021

Organized 1797 from Stoughton
(Norfolk County)

Cape Ann
(see City of Gloucester)

Town of Carlisle
Carlisle, MA 01741
Organized 1780 from Acton, Billerica,
Chelmsford and Concord (Middlesex
County)

Town of Carver
Carver, MA 02330
Organized 1790 from Plympton
(Plymouth County)

Town of Charlemont
Beda A. Langevin, Town Clerk
Main Street
Charlemont, MA 01339
Phone (413) 339-4335
Organized 1765 (Franklin County)

Town of Charlestown
Organized 1630, annexed to Boston,
1874

Charlestowne Village
(see City of Woburn)

*Town of Charlton
40 Main Street
Charlton, MA 01507
Phone (508) 248-5900; (508) 248-2054
Assessor; (508) 248-2051 Town Clerk
Organized 1754 from Oxford (Worcester
County)
Land records: Contact Assessor
Naturalization records: Contact Town
Clerk
Vital records: Contact Town Clerk
Probate records: No probate records

*Town of Chatham
Chatham, MA 02633
Organized 1712 (Manamoit Village)
(Barnstable County)
Land records: No land records
Naturalization records: No naturalization
records
Vital records: Contact Town Clerk
Probate records: No probate records

Town of Chelmsford
Chelmsford, MA 01824
Organized 1655 (Middlesex County)

City of Chelsea
City Hall
Chelsea, MA 02150
Organized 1739 from Boston
(Winnissimet, Rumney Marsh and
Pullin Point) (Suffolk County)

Town of Cheshire
Cheshire, MA 01225
Organized 1793 from Adams,
Lanesborough, Windsor and New
Ashford District (Berkshire County)

Town of Chester
Chester, MA 01011
Organized 1765 (Murrayfield)
(Hampden County)

Town of Chesterfield
Chesterfield, MA 01012
Phone (413) 296-4771
Organized 1762 (New Hingham
Plantation) (Hampshire County)

City of Chicopee
City Hall
Chicopee, MA 01013
Organized 1848 from Springfield
(Hampden County)

Town of Chilmark
Chilmark, MA 02535
Organized 1694 (Dukes County)

Town of Clarksburg
Clarksburg, MA 01247
Organized 1798 (Berkshire County)

Clayton
(see Town of New Marlborough)

Town of Clinton
Clinton, MA 01510
Organized 1850 from Lancaster
(Worcester County)

Coaksett
(see Town of Dartmouth)

Cohannett
(see City of Taunton)

Town of Cohasset
Cohasset, MA 02025
Organized 1770 from Hingham
(Norfolk County)

Colchester
(see Town of Salisbury)

Cold Spring Plantation
(see Town of Belchertown)

*Town of Colrain
9 Jacksonville Road
PO Box 31
Colrain, MA 01340
Phone (413) 624-3454
Organized 1761 (Franklin County)

Land records: Current Assessors' Records; contact Assessor

Naturalization records: No naturalization records

Vital records: From 1741 to 1796, from 1803 to 1839 and from 1848 to date; Contact Judith D. Sullivan, Town Clerk; certified copies: $5.00 each

Probate records: No probate records

Town of Concord
Concord, MA 01742
Organized 1635 (Musketequid) (Middlesex County)

*Town of Conway
Virginia A. Knowlton, Town Clerk
Town Hall
PO Box 240
Conway, MA 01341
Phone (413) 369-4235
Organized 1767 from Deerfield (Franklin County)

Land records: No land records

Naturalization records: No naturalization records

Vital records: Yes

Probate records: No probate records

Cottage City
(see Town of Oak Bluffs)

*Town of Cummington
Cummington, MA 01026
Phone (413) 634-5354
Organized 1779 from Number 5 Plantation (Hampshire County)

Land records: No land records

Naturalization records: No naturalization records

Vital records: Contact Town Clerk

Probate records: No probate records

Town of Dalton
462 Main Street
Dalton, MA 01226
(413) 684-6103
Organized 1784, formerly known as Ashuelet Equivalent (Berkshire County)

Land records: No land records

Naturalization records: No naturalization records

Vital records: Contact Barbara L. Suriner, Town Clerk

Vital records search service: $10.00–$15.00; certified copies: $5.00 each

Probate records: No probate records

Town of Dana
Organized 1801 from Greenwich, Hardwick and Petersham, annexed to Petersham, 1927

Town of Danvers
Danvers, MA 01923
Organized 1752 from Salem (Salem Village, Middle Parishes) (Essex County)

*Town of Dartmouth
400 Slocum Road
North Dartmouth, MA 02747
Phone (508) 999-0700
Organized 1664 (Acushena, Ponaganesett, Coaksett) (Bristol County)

Land records: No land records

Naturalization records: No naturalization records

Vital records: Contact Town Clerk

Vital records search service: no charge unless search is extensive; certified copies: $5.00 each

Probate records: No probate records

Town of Dedham
Dedham, MA 02026
Organized 1636 (Norfolk County)

*Town of Deerfield
William H. Leno, Town Clerk
2 Park Street
South Deerfield, MA 01373
Phone (413) 665-2130
Organized 1673 (Franklin County)

Land records: Some owner of record map and plots; contact Assessors' Office

Naturalization records: No naturalization records

Vital records: Births, deaths and marriages from 1675 to date; certified copies: $3.00 each

Probate records: No probate records

Town of Dennis
Drawer D
South Dennis, MA 02660
Organized 1793 from Yarmouth (Barnstable County)

Town of Dighton
Dighton, MA 02715
Organized 1712 from Taunton (Bristol County)

Town of Dorchester
Organized 1630, annexed to Boston, 1870

Dorcester-Canada
(see Town of Ashburnham)

*Town of Douglas
PO Box 661
Douglas, MA 01516-0661
Phone (508) 476-4000
Organized 1746 (New Sherbourn) (Worcester County)

Land records: Contact Assessors' Office

Naturalization records: No naturalization records

Vital records: Contact Town Clerk; copies: $5.00 each

Probate records: No probate records

*Town of Dover
PO Box 250
Dover, MA 02030
Phone (508) 785-1719 Town Clerk
First recorded settlement in 1640; established as the Springfield Parish of Dedham in 1748; incorporated as District Dedham in 1748; organized 1784 from Dedham; incorporated as a town in 1836 (Norfolk County)

Land records: No land records

Naturalization records: No naturalization records

Vital records: Births and deaths from 1784 to date, marriages from 1788 to date, marriage intentions from 1785 to date; contact Town Clerk; certified copies: $5.00 (no restrictions except for impounded records)

Probate records: No probate records

*Town of Dracut
Town Hall
62 Arlington Street
Dracut, MA 0¹826
Organized 26 February 1701 (Middlesex County)

Land records: No land records

Naturalization records: No naturalization records

Vital records: Contact Town Clerk

Probate records: No probate records

*Town of Dudley
40 Schofield Avenue
Dudley, MA 01571
Phone (508) 949-8004 Town Clerk
Organized 2 February 1732 from part of Oxford and certain common lands (Worcester County)

Land records: No land records

Naturalization records: No naturalization records

Vital records: Births, deaths and marriages from the early 1700s to date; contact Ora E. Nierodzinski, Town Clerk; certified copies: $5.00 each

Probate records: No probate records

Town of Dunstable
Dunstable, MA 01827
Organized 1673 (Middlesex County)

Town of Duxbury
Duxbury, MA 02332
Organized 1637 (Plymouth County)

East Boston
(see City of Boston)

*Town of East Bridgewater
PO Box 387
East Bridgewater, MA 02333
Phone (508) 378-1606
*Organized 1823 from Bridgewater
(Plymouth County)*
Land records: Contact Assessors' Office
Naturalization records: No naturalization
records
Vital records: Contact Town Clerk's
Office
Probate records: No probate records

Town of East Brookfield
East Brookfield, MA 01515
*Organized 1920 from Brookfield
(Worcester County)*

East Hoosuck
(see Town of Adams)

*Town of East Longmeadow
East Longmeadow, MA 01028
Phone (413) 525-5400
*Organized 1894 from Longmeadow
(Hampden County)*
Land records: No land records
Naturalization records: No naturalization
records
Vital records: Contact Town Clerk
Probate records: No probate records

East Sudbury
(see Town of Wayland)

Town of Eastham
Eastham, MA 02642
*Organized 1646 (Nawsett) (Barnstable
County)*

*Town of Easthampton
Town Hall
43 Main Street
Easthampton, MA 01027
Phone (413) 529-1460
*Organized 1785 from Northampton and
Southampton (Hampshire County)*
Land records: Contact Assessors' Office,
1 Northampton Street, Easthampton,
MA 01027
Naturalization records: No naturalization
records
Vital records: From 1785 to date; contact
Town Clerk's Office; copies: $2.00 for
the long form, $1.00 for the short
form (some records after 1900 are
restricted)
Probate records: No probate records

Town of Easton
Easton, MA 02334
*Organized 1725 from Norton (Bristol
County)*

*Town of Edgartown
Town Hall
70 Main Street
Edgartown, MA 02539
Phone (508) 627-6100
*Organized 1671 (Great Harbour)
(Dukes County)*
Land records: No land records
Naturalization records: No naturalization
records
Vital records: Yes
Probate records: No probate records

*Town of Egremont
PO Box 368
South Egremont, MA 01258
Phone (413) 528-0182
Organized 1760 (Berkshire County)
Land records: No land records
Naturalization records: No naturalization
records
Vital records: From 1853 to date; Contact
Town Clerk's Office, Town Hall
Probate records: No probate records

The Elbows Plantation
(see Town of Palmer)

Town of Enfield
*Organized 1816 from Belchertown,
Greenwich and Hampshire, annexed
to Belchertown, New Salem, Pelham
and Ware, 1938*

*Town of Erving
Theresa Dodge, Town Clerk
12 East Main Street
Erving, MA 01344
Phone (413) 544-2765
*Organized 1838 (includes Miller's Falls,
Franklin County)*

Ervingshire
(see Town of Wendell)

Ervingshire Tract
(see Town of Orange)

*Town of Essex
Town Hall
Essex, MA 01929
*Organized 1819 from Ipswich (Essex
County)*
Land records: No land records
Naturalization records: No naturalization
records
Vital records: From 1844 to date; contact
Sally A. Soucy, Town Clerk
Probate records: No probate records

City of Everett
City Hall
Everett, MA 02149
*Organized 1870 from Malden
(Middlesex County)*

Town of Fairhaven
Fairhaven, MA 02719
*Organized 1812 from New Bedford
(Bristol County)*

City of Fall River
City Hall
Fall River, MA 02722
*Organized 1803 from Freetown (Troy,
1834) (Bristol County)*

Falltown Plantation
(see Town of Bernardston)

*Town of Falmouth
Falmouth, MA 02540
Phone (508) 548-7611
Organized 1694 (Barnstable County)
Land records: No land records
Naturalization records: No naturalization
records
Vital records: From 1668 to date
Probate records: No probate records

City of Fitchburg
718 Main Street
Fitchburg, MA 01420
*Organized 1764 from Lunenberg
(Worcester County)*
Land records: No land records
Naturalization records: No naturalization
records
Vital records: From 1850; contact City
Clerk. From 1764 to 1850; contact
Fitchburg Historical Society, 50 Grove
Street, PO Box 953, Fitchburg, MA
01420; copies from City Clerk: $5.00
each
Probate records: No probate records

Town of Florida
Post Office
Drury, MA 01343
*Organized 1805 from Barnardstone's
Grant and Bullock's Grant
(Berkshire County)*

Town of Foxborough
Foxborough Town Hall
40 South Street
Foxborough, MA 02035
Phone (508) 543-6278 voice or FAX,
Town Hall; (508) 543-1215 Assessors'
Office; (508) 543-1208 Town Clerk's
Office
*Organized 1778 from Stoughton,
Stoughtonham, Walpole and
Wrentham (Sharon) (Norfolk
County)*
Land records: Deeds; contact Assessors'
Office
Naturalization records: No naturalization
records
Vital records: Births, deaths and
marriages; contact Town Clerk's
Office

Vital records search service: $10.00 for five or more years; copies: $5.00 each plus SASE for long form, $4.00 plus SASE for short form (impounded records are restricted, and certified documents cannot be faxed),
Probate records: No probate records

Town of Framingham
Framingham, MA 01701
Organized 1675 (Middlesex County)

Town of Franklin
Franklin, MA 02038
Organized 1778 from Wrentham (Norfolk County)

Town of Freetown
Freetown, MA 02702
Organized 1683 (Bristol County)

Gageborough
(see Town of Windsor)

City of Gardner
City Hall
Gardner, MA 01440
Organized 1785 from Ashburnham, Templeton, Westminster and Winchendon (Worcester County)

Town of Gay Head
Gay Head, MA 02535
Organized 1855 (Dukes County)

Town of Georgetown
Georgetown, MA 01830
Organized 1838 from Rowley (Essex County)

Gerry
(see Town of Phillipston)

*Town of Gill
RFD Gill, Box 313D
Turners Falls, MA 01376
Phone (413) 863-8103
Organized 1793 from Greenfield (Franklin County)
Land records: No land records
Naturalization records: No naturalization records
Vital records: Births, deaths and marriages; contact Harriet A. Tidd, Town Clerk
Probate records: No probate records

Glasgow
(see Town of Blandford)

City of Gloucester
9 Dale Avenue
Gloucester, MA 01930-5998
Phone (508) 281-9720 Tue–Wed 9:00–noon

Settled in 1623; incorporated as Town of Gloucester (Cape Ann) in 1642; incorporated as a city in 1873 (Essex County)
Land records: Deeds and leases from 1664 to 1981, personal and real property from 1672 to 1953+
Naturalization records: From 1885 to 1900
Vital records: From 1634 to date; contact Judith Peterson, Archivist, c/o City Clerk's Office
Vital records search service: $17.00 per hour
Probate records: No probate records

The Gore
(see Town of Monroe)

Town of Goshen
Goshen, MA 01032
Phone (413) 268-7856
Organized 1781 from Chesterfield (Hampshire County)

Town of Gosnold
Gosnold, MA 02713
Organized 1864 from Chilmark (Dukes County)

*Town of Grafton
Grafton, MA 01519
Phone (508) 839-4722
Organized 1735 (originally Hassanamisco, reserved for the Indians when the town of Sutton was granted) (Worcester County)
Land records: No land records
Naturalization records: No naturalization records
Vital records: Births, deaths and marriages
Probate records: No probate records

Town of Granby
Granby, MA 01033
Phone (413) 467-7178
Organized 1768 from South Hadley (Hampshire County)

Town of Granville
Granville, MA 01034
Organized 1754 (Hampden County)

Town of Great Barrington
Great Barrington, MA 01230
Organized 1761 from Sheffield (Berkshire)

Great Harbour
(see Town of Edgartown)

Greene's Harbour
(see Town of Marshfield)

*Town of Greenfield
14 Court Square
Greenfield, MA 01301
Phone (413) 772-1555
Organized 1753 from Deerfield (Franklin County)
Land records: No land records
Naturalization records: Contact Maureen T. Winseck, Town Clerk
Vital records: Contact Town Clerk
Probate records: No probate records

Town of Greenwich
Organized 1754 (Quabin Plantation), annexed to Hardwick, New Salem, Petersham and Ware, 1938

*Town of Groton
PO Box 669
Groton, MA 01450
Phone (508) 448-1100 Town Clerk
Organized 1655 (Middlesex County)
Land records: No land records
Naturalization records: No naturalization records
Vital records: Contact Town Clerk
Probate records: No probate records

Town of Groveland
Groveland, MA 01830
Organized 1850 from Bradford (Essex County)

*Town of Hadley
Hadley, MA 01035
Phone (413) 584-1590
Organized 1661 (New Plantation) (Hampshire County)
Land records: No land records
Naturalization records: No naturalization records
Vital records: Contact Town Clerk
Probate records: No probate records

*Town of Halifax
499 Plymouth Street
Halifax, MA 02338
Phone (617) 293-7970
Organized 1734 from Middleborough, Pembroke and Plympton (Plymouth County)
Land records: No land records
Naturalization records: No naturalization records
Vital records: From 1734 to date; contact Town Clerk
Probate records: No probate records

Town of Hamilton
Hamilton, MA 01936
Incorporated 21 June 1793 from Ipswich (Essex County)

*Town of Hampden
Hampden, MA 01036
Phone (413) 566-3214
Organized 1878 from Wilbraham (Hampden County)
Land records: No land records
Naturalization records: No naturalization records
Vital records; contact Rita Vail
Probate records: No probate records

Hampshire
(see Town of Enfield)

Town of Hancock
Rt. 43, Hancock Road
Williamstown, MA 01267
Organized 1776 (Jericho Plantation) (Berkshire County)

*Town of Hanover
550 Hanover Street
Hanover, MA 02339
Phone (617) 826-2691
Organized 14 June 1727 from Abington and Scituate (Plymouth County)
Land records: No land records
Naturalization records: No naturalization records
Vital records: Contact Town Clerk's Office
Probate records: No probate records

*Town of Hanson
Hanson, MA 02341
Phone (617) 293-5259 Assessors' Office; (617) 293-2772 Town Clerk
Organized 1820 from Pembroke (Plymouth County)
Land records: Contact Assessors' Office
Naturalization records: No naturalization records
Vital records: Contact Town Clerk
Probate records: No probate records

Town of Hardwick
Hardwick, MA 01037
Organized 1739 (Lambstown Plantation) (Worcester County)

Hartsville
(see Town of New Marlborough)

Hartwood Plantation
(see Town of Washington)

Town of Harvard
13 Ayer Road
Harvard, MA 01451-1411
Organized 1732 from Groton, Lancaster and Stow (Worcester County)

Town of Harwich
Harwich, MA 02645

Organized 1694 (Stauckett) (Barnstable County)

Harwick
(see Town of New Braintree)

Hassanamisco
(see Town of Grafton)

*Town of Hatfield
59 Main Street
Hatfield, MA 01038
Phone (413) 247-9211
Organized 1670 from Hadley (Hampshire County)
Land records: No land records
Naturalization records: No naturalization records
Vital records: Yes
Probate records: No probate records

City of Haverhill
City Hall
Haverhill, MA 01830
Organized 1641 (Essex County)

Town of Hawley
Robert Alexander, Town Clerk
Pudding Hollow
Hawley, MA 01339
Phone (413) 339-5518
Organized 1792 (Number 7 Plantation) (Franklin County)

*Town of Heath
Main Street
Heath, MA 01346
Phone (413) 337-4934
Organized 1785 from Charlemont (Franklin County)
Land records: No land records
Naturalization records: No naturalization records
Vital records: Contact Karen Thereault, Town Clerk; certified copies: $5.00 each
Probate records: No probate records

*Town of Hingham
7 East Street
Hingham, MA 02043
Phone (617) 741-1455 Board of Assessors; (617) 741-1410 Town Clerk and Genealogy Department
Organized 1635 (Barecove) (Plymouth County)
Land records: Contact Board of Assessors
Naturalization records: No naturalization records
Vital records: From 1635 to date; contact Mrs. Lyn M. Baxter, CMC, Town Genealogy Researcher, c/o Town Clerk's Office

Vital records search service: $20.00; certified copies: $5.00 each
Probate records: Contact Board of Assessors

*Town of Hinsdale
PO Box 803
Hinsdale, MA 01235
Phone (413) 655-2301; (413) 655-8807 FAX
Organized 1804 from Partridgefield and Dalton (Berkshire County)
Vital records: Births, deaths and marriages from about 1845; contact Dawn Frissell, Town Clerk
Vital records search service: $6.00; copies: $3.00 to $5.00 (some records restricted)

*Town of Holbrook
50 North Franklin Street
Holbrook, MA 02343
Phone (617) 767-4314 Town Clerk's Office
Organized 29 February 1872 from Randolph (Norfolk County)
Land records: No land records
Naturalization records: No naturalization records
Vital records: Contact Town Clerk's Office; certified copies: $5.00 each (includes search)
Probate records: No probate records

*Town of Holden
Town Hall
1196 Main Street
Holden, MA 01520-1092
Phone (508) 829-0265 Town Clerk
Organized 1741 from Worcester (Worcester County)
Land records: No land records
Naturalization records: No naturalization records
Vital records: From 1741 to date; contact Kathleen M. Peterson, Town Clerk
Vital records search service: $6.00; certified copies: $6.00
Probate records: No probate records

*Town of Holland
Holland, MA 01521
Phone (413) 245-7108
Organized 1783 from South Brimfield (Wales) (Hampden County)
Land records: No land records
Naturalization records: No naturalization records
Probate records: No probate records

*Town of Holliston
703 Washington Street
Holliston, MA 01746
Phone (508) 429-0601 Town Clerk
Organized 1724 from Sherborn (Middlesex County)

Land records: No land records
Naturalization records: No naturalization records
Vital records: Contact Nancy L. Norris, Town Clerk's Office
Vital records search service: $3.00; certified copies: $5.00
Probate records: No probate records

City of Holyoke
City Hall
Holyoke, MA 01040
Organized 1850 from West Springfield (Hampden County)

Town of Hopedale
PO Box 7
Hopedale, MA 01747
Organized 1886 from Milford (Worcester County)

Town of Hopkinton
Hopkinton, MA 01748
Organized 1715 (Moguncoy) (Middlesex County)

*Town of Hubbardston
Hubbardston, MA 01452
Phone (508) 928-5244 Town Clerk
Organized 1767 from Rutland (Worcester County)
Land records: No land records
Naturalization records: No naturalization records
Vital records: From the 1700s to date; contact Elaine Olly, Town Clerk
Vital records search service: by appointment only
Probate records: No probate records

Town of Hudson
Hudson, MA 01749
Organized 1866 from Marlborough and Stow (Middlesex County)

Town of Hull
Hull, MA 02045
Organized 1644 (Plymouth County)

Huntstown Plantation
(see Town of Ashfield)

*Town of Huntington
Huntington, MA 01050
Phone (413) 667-3260 Town Clerk's Office; (413) 667-8859 FAX, Town Clerk's Office
Organized 1773 from Murrayfield (Norwich) (Hampshire County)
Land records: Contact Assessors' Office
Naturalization records: No naturalization records
Vital records: Contact Judith A. Guyette, Town Clerk, 50 Searle Road,

Huntington, MA 01050
Probate records: No probate records

Hutchinson
(see Town of Barre)

Hyde Park
(see City of Boston)

Indian Town Plantation
(see Town of Stockbridge)

*Town of Ipswich
Ipswich, MA 01938
Phone (508) 356-6600 Town Clerk
Organized 1634 (Agawam) (Essex)
Land records: No land records
Naturalization records: No naturalization records
Vital records: Contact Town Clerk, Public Library, Ipswich, MA 01938
Probate records: No probate records

Ipswich Canada Plantation
(see Town of Winchendon)

Jamaica Plain
(see City of Boston)

Jericho Plantation
(see Town of Hancock)

Kingsfield
(see Town of Warren)

*Town of Kingston
23 Green Street
PO Drawer E
Kingston, MA 02364
Phone (617) 585-0509 Assessors' Office; (617) 585-0502 Town Clerk's Office
Organized 1726 from Plymouth (Plymouth County)
Land records: Contact Assessors' Office
Naturalization records: No naturalization records
Vital records: Contact Town Clerk's Office
Probate records: No probate records

*Town of Lakeville
346 Bedford Street
Lakeville, MA 02347
Phone (508) 947-3400
Organized 1853 from Middleborough (Plymouth County)
Land records: No land records
Naturalization records: No naturalization records
Vital records: From 1853 to date; contact Sandra J. Horton, Town Clerk; certified copies: $5.00 each
Probate records: No probate records

Lambstown Plantation
(see Town of Hardwick)

*Town of Lancaster
Lancaster, MA 01523
Organized 1653 (Worcester County)
Land records: From 1948 to date; contact Assessors' Office
Naturalization records: No naturalization records
Vital records: Contact Town Clerk or Town Library
Probate records: No probate records

*Town of Lanesboro
Newton Memorial Town Hall
83 North Main Street
PO Box 1492
Lanesboro, MA 01237-1492
Phone (413) 442-1167; (413) 443-5811 FAX
Organized 1765 (New Framingham Plantation) (Berkshire County)
Land records: Partial listing of deeds from 1960 to date
Naturalization records: No naturalization records
Vital records: From 1843 to date; contact Judith A. Gallant, town Clerk
Probate records: No probate records

Lanesborough
(see Town of Cheshire)

*City of Lawrence
City Hall
Lawrence, MA 01840
Phone (508) 794-5803
Organized 1847 from Andover and Methuen (Essex County)
Land records: No land records
Naturalization records: No naturalization records
Vital records: Contact City Clerk
Vital records search service: $10.00 per search; copies: $5.00 each
Probate records: No probate records

*Town of Lee
Memorial Hall
PO Box 630
32 Main Street
Lee, MA 01238-1612
Phone (413) 243-5505
Organized 1777 from Great Barrington (Berkshire County)
Land records: No land records
Naturalization records: No naturalization records
Vital records: Contact Patricia D. Carlino, Town Clerk
Probate records: No probate records

Town of Leicester
Leicester, MA 01524
Organized 1714 (Worcester County)

*Town of Lenox
Town Hall
6 Walker Street
Lenox, MA 01240
Phone (413) 637-5506 Town Clerk
Incorporated 1767 from Richmont
(Berkshire County)
Land records: No land records
Naturalization records: No naturalization
records
Vital records: Contact Lorita Bosworth,
Town Clerk
Probate records: No probate records

*City of Leominster
City Hall
25 West Street
Leominster, MA 01453
Phone (508) 534-7536
Organized 1740 from Lancaster
(Worcester County)
Land records; contact City Clerk
Naturalization records: No naturalization
records
Vital records: Births, deaths and
marriages; contact City Clerk;
certified copies: $3.00 each
Probate records; contact City Clerk

*Town of Leverett
Town Hall
9 Montague Road
PO Box 178
Leverett, MA 01054
Phone (413) 548-9150; (617) 536-5740
The New England Historic
Genealogical Society
Organized 1774 from Sunderland
(Franklin County)
Land records: No land records
Naturalization records: No naturalization
records
Vital records: From 1732 to 1843;
contact Walter Corbin Manuscript
Collection, The New England Historic
Genealogical Society, 99–101
Newbury Street, Boston, MA 02116.
From 1844 to date; contact D'Ann
Sauer Kelty
Probate records: No probate records

*Town of Lexington
Lexington, MA 02173
Phone (617) 861-2770
Organized 1713 from Cambridge
(Middlesex County)
Land records: No land records
Naturalization records: No naturalization
records
Vital records: From 1850 to date; contact
Town Clerk; copies: $5.00 each
Probate records: No probate records

Town of Leyden
Mary Lou Barton, Town Clerk
Greenfield Road
Leyden, MA 01301

Phone (413) 774-4111
Organized 1784 from Bernardston
(Franklin County)

*Town of Lincoln
Lincoln, MA 01773
Phone (617) 259-8850
Organized 1754 from Concord,
Lexington and Weston (Middlesex
County)
Land records: No land records
Naturalization records: No naturalization
records
Vital records: Contact Town Clerk
Probate records: No probate records

Town of Littleton
Littleton, MA 01460
Organized 1715 (Nashoba) (Middlesex
County)

Littletown
(see Town of Boxborough)

Town of Longmeadow
Longmeadow, MA 01106
Organized 1783 from Springfield
(Hampden County)

Loudon
(see Town of Otis)

City of Lowell
City Hall
Lowell, MA 01852
Organized 1826 from Chelmsford
(Middlesex County)

Town of Ludlow
Ludlow, MA 01056
Organized 1774 from Springfield
(Hampden County)

Lunenberg
(see Town of Fitchburg)

Town of Lunenburg
Lunenburg, MA 01462
Organized 1728 from Turkey Hills,
Woburn, Dorchester and Boardman's
Farm (Worcester County)

*City of Lynn
City Hall
3 City Hall Square
Lynn, MA 01901
Phone (617) 598-4000, ext. 245 City
Clerk's Office
Organized 1635 (Saugus) (Essex
County)
Land records: No land records
Naturalization records: No naturalization
records

Vital records: Contact City Clerk's
Office, Room 201
Probate records: No probate records

Town of Lynnfield
Lynnfield, MA 01940
Organized 1782 from Lynn (Essex
County)

City of Malden
City Hall
Malden, MA 02148
Organized 1649 (Middlesex County)

Manamoit Village
(see Town of Chatham)

*Town of Manchester
Manchester, MA 01944
Organized 1645 from Salem (Essex
County)
Land records: No land records
Naturalization records: No naturalization
records
Vital records: From 1844 (sketchy before
then); contact Town Clerk's Office
Probate records: No probate records

*Town of Mansfield
Town Hall
50 West Street
Mansfield, MA 02048
Phone (508) 261-7345
Organized 1770 from Norton;
incorporated 1775 (Bristol County)
Land records: No land records
Naturalization records: No naturalization
records
Vital records: From 1771 to date; contact
Judith F. Scott, Town Clerk; copies:
$5.00 each
Probate records: No probate records

*Town of Marblehead
Abbot Hall
Marblehead, MA 01945
Phone (617) 631-0528
Organized 1629; incorporated 1649
(Essex County)
Land records: No land records
Naturalization records: No naturalization
records
Vital records: Contact Town Clerk
Probate records: No probate records

*Town of Marion
Town Clerk's Office
2 Spring Street
Marion, MA 02738
Phone (508) 748-3502
Organized 1852 from Rochester
(Plymouth County)
Land records: No land records
Naturalization records: No naturalization
records

Vital records: From 1852; certified
    copies: $2.00 each
Probate records: No probate records

*City of Marlborough
City Hall
140 Main Street
Marlborough, MA 01752
Phone (508) 460-3775
Organized 1660 (Middlesex County)
Naturalization records: No naturalization
    records
Vital records: From 1850s to date, two
    early books for the 1600s and 1700s
    whose records cannot be certified

*Town of Marshfield
Town Hall
870 Moraine Street
Marshfield, MA 02050
Phone (617) 834-5563 Town Hall; (617)
    834-5585 Assessors' Department;
    (617) 834-5535 Town Clerk; (617)
    834-7329 Town Historian
*Incorporated 2 March 1640; early
    names: Green's Harbour and
    Rexhame (Plymouth County)*
Land records: Contact Assessors'
    Department
Naturalization records: No naturalization
    records
Vital records: Some from the 1630s;
    contact Town Clerk or Cynthia H.
    Krusell, Town Historian; certified
    copies: $10.00 each
Probate records: No probate records

Town of Mashpee
PO Box 1108
Mashpee, MA 02649
Organized 1763 (Barnstable County)

Mattacheeset
(see Town of Yarmouth)

Mattapan
(see City of Boston)

*Town of Mattapoisett
16 Main Street
PO Box 89
Mattapoisett, MA 02739-0089
Phone (508) 758-4103 Town Clerk; (508)
    758-3030 FAX, Town Clerk
*Organized 1857 from Rochester
    (Plymouth County)*
Naturalization records: No naturalization
    records
Vital records: Contact Lois K. Ennis,
    CMMC, CMC, Town Clerk

Town of Maynard
Maynard, MA 01754
*Organized 1871 from Stow and Sudbury
    (Middlesex County)*

*Town of Medfield
Medfield, MA 02052
Phone (508) 359-8505
*Organized 1650 from Dedham (Norfolk
    County)*
Land records: No land records
Naturalization records: No naturalization
    records
Vital records: From 1651 to date
Probate records: No probate records

City of Medford
City Hall
Medford, MA 02155
Organized 1630 (Middlesex County)

Town of Medway
155 Village Street
Medway, MA 02053
*Organized 1713 from Medfield (Norfolk
    County)*

City of Melrose
City Hall
Melrose, MA 02176
*Organized 1850 from Malden
    (Middlesex County)*

Town of Mendon
PO Box 54
Mendon, MA 01756
Organized 1667 (Worcester County)

Town of Merrimac
Merrimac, MA 01860
*Organized 1876 from Amesbury (Essex
    County)*

Town of Methuen
Methuen, MA 01844
*Organized 1725 from Haverhill
    (Middlesex County)*

Middle Parishes
(see Town of Danvers)

*Town of Middleborough
10 Nickerson Avenue
Middleborough, MA 02346
Phone (508) 946-2415
*Organized 1669 (Namassackett)
    (Plymouth County)*
Land records: Contact Assessors' Office
Naturalization records: No naturalization
    records
Vital records: From 1669 to date: contact
    Town Clerk's Office
Vital records search service: $5.00 per
    name
Probate records: No probate records

Town of Middlefield
Middlefield, MA 01243
Phone (413) 623-8966

*Organized 1783 from Becket, Chester,
    Washington, Partridgefield,
    Worthington and Prescott's Grant
    (Hampshire County)*

*Town of Middleton
Memorial Hall
Middleton, MA 01949
Phone (508) 774-6927
*Organized 1728 from Andover, Boxford,
    Salem and Topsfield (Essex County)*
Land records: No land records
Naturalization records: No naturalization
    records
Vital records: From 1704 to date; contact
    Office of the Town Clerk
Probate records: No probate records

Middletowne
(see Town of Tisbury)

Town of Milford
Town Clerk
Milford, MA 01757
*Organized 1780 from Mendon
    (Worcester County)*

Mill River
(see Town of New Marlborough)

*Town of Millbury
Millbury, MA 01527
Phone (508) 865-9110
*Organized 1813 from Sutton (Worcester
    County)*
Land records: No land records
Naturalization records: No naturalization
    records
Vital records: From 1813
Probate records: No probate records

Miller's Falls
(see Town of Erving)

Town of Millis
Millis, MA 02054
*Organized 1885 from Medway (Norfolk
    County)*

Town of Millville
Millville, MA 01529
*Organized 1916 from Blackstone
    (Worcester County)*

Town of Milton
Milton, MA 02186
*Organized 1662 from Dorchester
    (Norfolk County)*

Moguncoy
(see Town of Hopkinton)

*Town of Monroe
Town Clerk
Monroe Bridge, MA 01350
Organized 1822 from Row and The Gore (Franklin County)
Vital records: Contact Christina Brothers, Town Clerk

*Town of Monson
Monson, MA 01057
Phone (413) 267-4115
Organized 1760 from Brimfield (Hampden County)
Land records: No land records
Naturalization records: No naturalization records
Vital records: From 1755 to date
Vital records search service: $11.02 per hour; copies: $5.00 each (restrictions on impounded records)
Probate records: No probate records

Town of Montague
Raymond J. Zukowski, Town Clerk
1 Avenue A
Turners Falls, MA 01376
Phone (413) 863-4421
Organized 1754 from Sunderland (Franklin County)

Town of Monterey
Monterey, MA 01245
Organized 1847 from Tyringham (Berkshire County)

*Town of Montgomery
Town Clerk
Town Hall
Main Road
Montgomery, MA 01085
Phone (413) 862-4478
Organized 1780 from Westfield, Norwich and Southampton (Hampden County)

*Town of Mount Washington
Rt. 3, Box 67A
Mount Washington, MA 01258
Phone (413) 528-2839
Organized 1779 (Tauconnuck Mountain Plantation) (Berkshire County)
Land records: No land records
Naturalization records: No naturalization records
Vital records: Births, deaths and marriages from the 1790s to date but with lots of gaps; contact Town Clerk
Vital records search service: $5.00; copies 20¢ each, some restriction on actual certificates
Probate records: No probate records

Murrayfield
(see Town of Chester and Town of Huntington)

Musketequid
(see Town of Concord)

Myrefield
(see Town of Rowe)

*Town of Nahant
Nahant, MA 01908
Phone (617) 581-0018; (617) 581-0212 Assessor
Incorporated 1853 from Lynn (Essex County)
Land records: Contact Assessor
Naturalization records: No naturalization records
Vital records: Contact Harriet C. Steeves, Town Clerk
Probate records: No probate records

Namassackett
(see Town of Middleboro)

Town of Nantucket
(see Nantucket County Courthouse)
Organized 1687 (Sherburn, 1713; Tuckannock, 1795) (comprises the whole of Nantucket County)

Naquag Tract
(see Town of Rutland)

Narragansett Number 2 Plantation
(see Town of Westminster)

Narragansett Number 6 Plantation
(see Town of Templeton)

Nashoba
(see Town of Littleton)

Town of Natick
Natick, MA 01760
Organized 1650 (Middlesex County)

Nawsett
(see Town of Eastham)

Town of Needham
1471 Highland Avenue
Needham, MA 02192-0909
Phone (617) 455-7510 Town Clerk; (617) 449-4569 FAX, Town Clerk
Organized 1711 from Dedham (Norfolk)
Vital records: From 1711 to date; contact Theodora K. Eaton, CMC, Town Clerk

Town of New Ashford
New Ashford, MA 01237
Organized 1781 (Berkshire County)

New Ashford District
(see Town of Cheshire)

City of New Bedford
City Hall
New Bedford, MA 02740
Organized 1787 from Dartmouth (Bristol County)

*Town of New Braintree
New Braintree, MA 01531
Phone (508) 867-2071
Organized 1751 from Harwick and Brookfield (Worcester County)

New Cambridge
(see City of Newton)

New Framingham Plantation
(see Town of Lanesboro)

New Hingham Plantation
(see Town of Chesterfield)

New Lisburn Tract
(see Town of Pelham)

*Town of New Marlborough
PO Box 99
Mill River, MA 01244
Phone (413) 229-8116
Organized 1759; consists of the villages of Southfield, Mill River, Clayton, Hartsville and New Marlborough (Berkshire County)
Land records: No land records
Naturalization records: No naturalization records
Vital records: Births from 1734, deaths from 1750, marriages from 1766; contact Margaret W. Smith, CMC, Town Clerk

New Medfield
(see Town of Sturbridge)

New Medfield Tract
(see Town of Sturbridge)

New Plantation
(see Town of Hadley)

Town of New Salem
Helen A. Wetherby
Town Clerk
CPO Box 121
New Salem, MA 01355
Phone (413) 544-2731
Organized 1753 (Franklin County)

New Sherbourn
(see Town of Douglas)

*Town of Newbury
Newbury, MA 01951
Organized 1635 (Wessacucon) (Essex County)
Land records: No land records
Naturalization records: No naturalization records
Probate records: No probate records

City of Newburyport
City Hall
Newburyport, MA 01950
Organized 1764 from Newbury (Essex County)

Newe Towne
(see City of Cambridge)

City of Newton
City Hall
Newton, MA 02159
Organized 1691 (Cambridge Village, New Cambridge) (Middlesex County)

Nichewoag Plantation
(see Town of Petersham)

No-name Plantation
(see Town of Buckland)

Town of Norfolk
Norfolk, MA 02056
Organized 1870 from Franklin, Medway, Walpole and Wrentham (Norfolk County)

*City of North Adams
City Hall
North Adams, MA 01247
Organized 1878 from Adams (Berkshire County)
Land records: No land records
Naturalization records: No naturalization records
Vital records: From 1777; contact City Clerk's Office
Probate records: No probate records

Town of North Andover
North Andover, MA 01845
Organized 1855 from Andover (Essex County)

*Town of North Attleborough
PO Box 871
North Attleborough, MA 02761
Phone (508) 699-0108
Incorporated 14 June from Attleborough (Bristol County)
Land records: No land records
Naturalization records: No naturalization records
Vital records: Births, deaths and

marriages from June 1887; contact Town Clerk; copies (typed abstracts, not photocopies): $5.00 each
Probate records: No probate records

North Bridgewater
(see City of Brockton)

Town of North Brookfield
North Brookfield, MA 01535
Organized 1812 from Brookfield (Worcester County)

North Chelsea
(see Town of Winthrop and City of Revere)

Town of North Reading
North Reading, MA 01864
Organized 1853 from Reading (Middlesex County)

*City of Northampton
City Hall
210 Main Street
Northampton, MA 01060
Phone (413) 586-6950, ext. 222
Organized 1656 (Hampshire County)
Land records: No land records
Naturalization records: No naturalization records
Vital records: Births, deaths and marriages; contact City Clerk
Probate records: No probate records

Town of Northborough
Northborough, MA 01532
Organized 1766 from Westborough (Worcester County)

*Town of Northbridge
Northbridge, MA 01588
Phone (508) 234-2001
Organized 1772 from Uxbridge (Worcester County)
Land records: No land records
Naturalization records: No naturalization records
Vital records: Contact Town Clerk
Probate records: No probate records

Town of Northfield
Mary C. Taferner, Town Clerk
Main Street
Northfield, MA 01360
Phone (413) 498-2901
Organized 1714 (Squakeag Plantation) (Franklin County)

Town of Norton
Norton, MA 02766
Organized 1710 from Taunton (Bristol County)

*Town of Norwell
PO Box 295
345 Main Street
Norwell, MA 02061
Phone (617) 659-8072 Town Clerk
Organized 1849 from Scituate (South Scituate, 1888) (Plymouth County)
Land records: Contact Assessors' Office
Naturalization records: No naturalization records
Vital records: Contact Town Clerk
Probate records: No probate records

Norwich
(see Town of Huntington and Town of Montgomery)

*Town of Norwood
Norwood, MA 02062
Organized 1872 from Dedham and Walpole (Norfolk County)
Land records: No land records
Naturalization records: No naturalization records
Probate records: No probate records

Number 1 Plantation
(see Town of Tyringham)

Number 2 Plantation
(see Town of Westminster)

Number 3 Plantation
(see Town of Sandisfield and Town of Worthington)

Number 4 Plantation
(see Town of Becket)

Number 5 Plantation
(see Town of Cummington)

Number 6 Plantation
(see Town of Templeton)

Number 7 Plantation
(see Town of Hawley)

*Town of Oak Bluffs
PO Box 2490
Oak Bluffs, MA 02557
Phone (508) 693-5515
Organized 1880 from Edgartown as Cottage City (Dukes County)
Land records: No land records
Naturalization records: No naturalization records
Vital records: From 1880; contact Diane R. Kenney, Town Clerk
Vital records search service: $5.00; copies: 20¢ each, $5.00 for certified copies
Probate records: No probate records

*Town of Oakham
Oakham, MA 01068
Phone (508) 882-5549
*Organized 1762 from Rutland
(Worcester County)*
Land records: No land records
Naturalization records: No naturalization
records
Vital records: Contact Town Clerk
Probate records: No probate records

*Town of Orange
6 Prospect Street
Orange, MA 01364
Phone (413) 544-2254
*Organized 1783 from Athol, Royalston,
Warwick and Ervingshire Tract
(Franklin County)*
Land records: No land records
Naturalization records: No naturalization
records
Vital records: Contact Shirley L. Page,
Town Clerk
Probate records: No probate records

*Town of Orleans
19 School Road
Orleans, MA 02653
Phone (508) 240-3700
*Organized 1797 from Eastham
(Barnstable County)*
Land records: Contact Assessors' Office
Naturalization records: No naturalization
records
Vital records: Contact Town Clerk
Probate records: No probate records

*Town of Otis
Otis, MA 01253
Phone (413) 269-0101
*Organized 1773 from Tryingham
Equivalent (Loudon, 1810)
(Berkshire County)*
Land records: Contact Assessors' Office
Naturalization records: No naturalization
records
Vital records: Contact Town Clerk's
Office
Probate records: No probate records

*Town of Oxford
Memorial Hall
325 Main Street
Oxford, MA 01540-0273
Phone (508) 987-6032 Town Clerk; (508)
987-6048 FAX, Town Clerk
Incorporated 1713 (Worcester County)
Land records: Deeds from 1969 and
assessors' maps; contact Assessors'
Office.
Naturalization records: No naturalization
records
Vital records: Contact Lori A. Kelley,
Town Clerk; certified copies: $5.00
each
Probate records: No probate records

*Town of Palmer
Town Administration Building
Palmer, MA 01069
Phone (413) 283-2608 Town Clerk
*Organized 1752 as The Elbows
Plantation, incorporated 1776 as
Town of Palmer (Hampden County)*
Land records: Contact Board of
Assessors
Naturalization records: No naturalization
records
Vital records: Contact Town Clerk;
copies: $3.00 per page
Probate records: No probate records

Parsons
(see Town of West Newbury)

Partridgefield
(see Town of Hinsdale, Town of
Middlefield and Town of Peru)

Pawmett Tract
(see Town of Truro)

*Town of Paxton
Town Hall
Paxton, MA 01612
Phone (508) 799-7347
*Organized 1765 from Leicester and
Rutland (Worcester County)*
Land records: No land records
Naturalization records: No naturalization
records
Vital records: Contact June T. Herron,
Town Clerk
Probate records: No probate records

Payquage Plantation
(see Town of Athol)

*City of Peabody
City Hall
Peabody, MA 01960
Phone (508) 532-3000
*Organized 1855 from Danvers as South
Danvers; 1868 as Town of Peabody;
1916 as City of Peabody (Essex
County)*
Land records: No land records
Naturalization records: No naturalization
records
Vital records: Contact City Clerk's
Office, 24 Lowell Street, Peabody,
MA 01960
Probate records: No probate records

*Town of Pelham
RR 2
351 Amherst Road
Amherst, MA 01002
Phone (413) 253-7129
*Organized 1743 (New Lisburn Tract)
(Hampshire County)*

Land records: Original proprietors'
records from 1738 to about 1805 only
Naturalization records: No naturalization
records
Vital records: From 1738 to date; contact
Town Clerk
Vital records search service: no charge
(Robert Lord Keyes, 40 South Valley
Road, Amherst, MA 01002)
Probate records: No probate records

Town of Pembroke
Pembroke, MA 02359
*Organized 1712 from Duxbury
(Plymouth County)*

Town of Pepperell
Pepperell, MA 01463
*Organized 1753 from Groton
(Middlesex County)*

Town of Peru
PO Box 479
Hinsdale, MA 01235
*Organized 1771 (Partridgefield, 1806)
(Berkshire County)*

Town of Petersham
Petersham, MA 01366
*Organized 1754 (Nichewoag Plantation)
(Worcester County)*

Town of Phillipston
Rt. 1 Athol
Phillipston, MA 01331
*Organized 1786 from Athol and
Templeton (Gerry, 1814) (Worcester
County)*

City of Pittsfield
City Hall
Pittsfield, MA 01201
*Organized 1761 (Pontoosuck
Plantation) (Berkshire County)*

*Town of Plainfield
344 Main Street
Plainfield, MA 01070
Phone (413) 634-5420
*Organized 1785 from Cummington
(Hampshire County)*
Land records: No land records
Naturalization records: No naturalization
records
Vital records: Contact Town Clerk
Probate records: No probate records

Town of Plainville
Plainville, MA 02762
*Organized 1905 from Wrentham
(Norfolk County)*

*Town of Plymouth
11 Lincoln Street
Plymouth, MA 02360
Phone (508) 830-4050
Organized 1620 (Plymouth County)
Land records: No land records
Naturalization records: No naturalization
  records
Vital records: Contact Town Clerk's
  Office; certified copies: $5.00 each
Probate records: No probate records

*Town of Plympton
Town House
Plympton, MA 02367
Phone (617) 585-3220
*Organized 1707 from Plymouth
  (Plymouth County)*
Land records: No land records
Naturalization records: No naturalization
  records
Vital records: Contact Town Clerk's
  Office
Probate records: No probate records

Pompositticut Plantation
(see Town of Stow)

Ponaganesett
(see Town of Dartmouth)

Pontoosuck Plantation
(see City of Pittsfield)

Town of Prescott
*Organized 1822 from Pelham and New
  Salem, annexed back to Pelham and
  New Salem, 1938*

Prescott's Grant
(see Town of Middlefield)

Town of Princeton
Princeton, MA 01541
*Organized 1759 from Rutland
  (Worcester County)*

*Town of Provincetown
Provincetown, MA 02657
Phone (508) 487-7013
Organized 1727 (Barnstable County)
Land records: No land records
Naturalization records: No naturalization
  records
Vital records: Births, deaths and
  marriages from the early 1800s to
  date; contact Sheila Silva, Town Clerk
Probate records: No probate records

Pullin Point
(see City of Chelsea)

Quabin Plantation
(see Town of Greenwich)

Quansigamond Plantation
(see City of Worcester)

*City of Quincy
City Hall
1305 Hancock Street
Quincy, MA 02169
Phone (617) 376-1000
*Organized 1792 from Braintree and
  Dorchester (Norfolk County)*
Land records: Property record cards for
  real estate and personal property;
  contact Assessors' Office
Naturalization records: No naturalization
  records
Vital records: Births and deaths; contact
  City Clerk's Office
Probate records: No probate records

Town of Randolph
Randolph, MA 02368
*Organized 1793 from Braintree
  (Norfolk County)*

*Town of Raynham
Raynham, MA 02767
*Organized 1731 from Taunton (Bristol
  County)*
Vital records: Contact Helen B.
  Lounsbury, Town Clerk

Town of Reading
Reading, MA 01867
*Organized 1644 from Lynn (Middlesex
  County)*

*Town of Rehoboth
14F8R Peck Street
Rehoboth, MA 02769-3099
Phone (508) 252-6502 Town Clerk; (508)
  252-5342 FAX, Town Clerk
Organized 1645 (Bristol County)
Land records: No land records
Naturalization records: No naturalization
  records
Vital records: Contact Suzanne Withers,
  CMC/AAE, Town Clerk
Vital records search service: $6.00 (prior
  to 1900); copies: 50¢ per page
  (printout from microfilm, when
  available), $5.00 for certified copies
  (not a photocopy)
Probate records: No probate records

City of Revere
City Hall
Revere, MA 02151
*Organized 1846 from Chelsea (North
  Chelsea) (Suffolk County)*

Rexhame
(see Town of Marshfield)

*Town of Richmond
1529 State Road
PO Box 81
Richmond, MA 01254
Phone (413) 698-3315
*Organized 1765 (Richmont) (Berkshire
  County)*
Land records: No land records
Naturalization records: No naturalization
  records
Vital records: Contact Town Clerk
Probate records: No probate records

Richmont
(see Town of Lenox and Town of
  Richmond)

Roadtown Plantation
(see Town of Shutesbury)

*Town of Rochester
Rochester, MA 02770
*Organized 1686 (Scippicam) (Plymouth
  County)*
Land records: No land records
Naturalization records: No naturalization
  records
Vital records: Yes
Probate records: No probate records

*Town of Rockland
Rockland, MA 02370
Phone (617) 871-1874
*Organized 1874 from Abington
  (Plymouth County)*

*Town of Rockport
Rockport, MA 01966
Phone (508) 546-6894
*Organized 1840 from Gloucester (Essex
  County)*
Land records: No land records
Naturalization records: No naturalization
  records
Vital records: Yes
Probate records: No probate records

Roslindale
(see City of Boston)

Row
(see Town of Monroe)

*Town of Rowe
Zoar Road
Rowe, MA 01367
Phone (413) 339-5520
*Organized 1785 (Myrefield) (Franklin
  County)*
Vital records: Contact L. Norma Brown,
  Town Clerk

*Town of Rowley
Rowley, MA 01969

Organized 1639 (Essex County)
Vital records: Yes
Vital records search service: $5.00;
   copies: 20¢ per page

Town of Roxbury
Organized 1630, annexed to Boston, 1868

Roxbury Canada Plantation
(see Town of Warwick)

Royalshire Tract
(see Town of Royalston)

*Town of Royalston
PO Box 118
Royalston, MA 01368-0118
Phone (508) 249-6283
Organized 1765 (Royalshire Tract) (Worcester County)
Land records: No land records
Naturalization records: No naturalization
   records
Vital records: From the mid-1700s to
   date; contact Town Clerk; certified
   copies: $3.00 each
Probate records: No probate records

Rumney Marsh
(see City of Chelsea)

Town of Russell
Russell, MA 01071
Organized 1792 from Westfield and Montgomery (Hampden County)

*Town of Rutland
Rutland, MA 01543
Phone (508) 886-4104
Organized 1714 (Naquag Tract) (Worcester County)
Land records: No land records
Naturalization records: No naturalization
   records
Vital records: Contact Town Clerk's
   Office
Probate records: No probate records

Rutland District
(see Town of Barre)

*City of Salem
City Hall
Salem, MA 01970
Phone (508) 745-9595
Organized 1626 (Essex County)
Land records: No land records
Naturalization records: No naturalization
   records
Vital records: From 1600s to date;
   contact City Clerk
Probate records: No probate records

Salem Village
(see Town of Danvers)

*Town of Salisbury
Salisbury, MA 01950
Organized 1639 (Colchester) (Essex County)
Land records: No land records
Naturalization records: No naturalization
   records
Vital records: Yes
Probate records: No probate records

*Town of Sandisfield
Sandisfield, MA 01255
Phone (413) 258-4711
Organized 1762 (Number 3 Plantation) (Berkshire County)
Land records: No land records
Naturalization records: No naturalization
   records
Vital records: Contact Town Clerk
Probate records: No probate records

*Town of Sandwich
Sandwich Archives and Historical Center
145 Main Street
Sandwich, MA 02563
Phone (508) 888-0340 Archivist
Settled 1637 (Barnstable County)
Land records: Assessors' records from
   1790 to date; contact Barbara L. Gill,
   Archivist
Naturalization records: No naturalization
   records
Vital records: From the 17th century to
   date; contact Archivist
Vital records search service: $10.00 per
   hour; copies: 20¢ per page
Probate records: No probate records

*Town of Saugus
Town Hall
298 Central Street
Saugus, MA 01906
Phone (617) 231-4101
Organized 1815 from Lynn (Essex County)
Land records: No land records
Vital records: Yes
Probate records: No probate records

Town of Savoy
720 Main Road
Savoy, MA 01256
Organized 1797 (Berkshire County)

Scippicam
(see Town of Rochester)

*Town of Scituate
Town Hall
Scituate, MA 02066
Phone (617) 545-8744

Organized 1633 (Plymouth County)
Land records: Early land records of the
   town
Naturalization records: No naturalization
   records
Vital records: Births, deaths and
   marriages from 1625 to date; contact
   Town Clerk's Office
Vital records search service: $5.00 per
   hour; certified copies: $5.00 each
Probate records: No probate records

Town of Seekonk
Seekonk, MA 02771
Organized 1812 from Rehoboth (Bristol County)

*Town of Sharon
90 South Main Street
Sharon, MA 02067
Phone (617) 784-1505
Organized 1765 from Stoughton (Stoughtonham) (Norfolk County)
Land records: No land records
Naturalization records: No naturalization
   records
Vital records: Contact Town Clerk
Probate records: No probate records

*Town of Sheffield
Sheffield, MA 01257
Phone (413) 229-2335 Selectmen's
   Office
Organized 1733 (Berkshire County)
Land records: No land records
Naturalization records: No naturalization
   records
Vital records: From 1733 to 1810 and
   from 1843 to date; contact Town
   Clerk
Probate records: No probate records

Town of Shelburne
51 Bridge Street
Shelburne Falls, MA 01370
Phone (413) 625-0301
Organized 1768 from Deerfield (includes Shelburne Falls, Franklin County)
Land records: No land records
Naturalization records: No naturalization
   records
Vital records: Contact Beverly Neeley,
   Town Clerk
Probate records: No probate records

Shelburne Falls
(see Town of Shelburne)

Town of Sherborn
Sherborn, MA 01770
Organized 1674 (Middlesex County)

Sherburn
(see Town of Nantucket)

*Town of Shirley
Municipal Building
PO Box 782
Shirley, MA 01464
Phone (508) 425-2610
*Organized 1753 from Groton
    (Middlesex County)*
Land records: No land records
Naturalization records: No naturalization
    records
Vital records: From 1753 to date; contact
    Town Clerk
Probate records: No probate records

Town of Shrewsbury
Shrewsbury, MA 01545
Organized 1720 (Worcester County)

*Town of Shutesbury
Town Hall
Community Center
Shutesbury, MA 01072
Phone (413) 259-1204
*Organized 1761 (Roadtown Plantation)
    (Franklin County)*
Vital records: Contact Roberta V.
    Bouffard, Town Clerk

*Town of Somerset
Somerset, MA 02726
Phone (508) 646-2818
*Organized 1790 from Swansea (Bristol
    County)*
Vital records: Yes
Vital records search service: $10.00;
    copies: $2.00 each

*City of Somerville
City Hall
93 Highland Avenue
Somerville, MA 02143
Phone (617) 625-6600, ext. 3100
    Assessor's Office; (617) 625-6600,
    ext. 4100 City Clerk's Office
*Organized 1864 from Charlestown;
    incorporated 1872 (Middlesex
    County)*
Land records: From 1958 to date; contact
    Assessor's Office
Naturalization records: No naturalization
    records
Vital records: Contact City Clerk's Office
Probate records: No probate records

South Abington
(see Town of Whitman)

South Boston
(see City of Boston)

South Brimfield
(see Town of Holland and Town of
    Wales)

South Danvers
(see City of Peabody)

*Town of South Hadley
116 Main Street
South Hadley, MA 01075
Phone (413) 538-5023
*Organized 1753 from Hadley
    (Hampshire County)*
Land records: No land records
Naturalization records: No naturalization
    records
Vital records: From 1843
Probate records: No probate records

South Reading
(see Town of Wakefield)

South Scituate
(see Town of Norwell)

Town of Southampton
PO Box 397
Southampton, MA 01073-0397
Phone (413) 527-4741
*Organized 1753 from Northampton
    (Hampshire County)*

Town of Southborough
Southborough, MA 01772
*Organized 1727 from Marlborough
    (Worcester County)*

Town of Southbridge
Southbridge, MA 01550
*Organized 1816 from Charlton, Dudley
    and Sturbridge (Worcester County)*

Southern
(see Town of Bradford)

Southfield
(see Town of New Marlborough)

*Town of Southwick
Southwick, MA 01077
Phone (413) 569-5504
*Organized 1770 from Westfield
    (Hampden County)*
Land records: No land records
Naturalization records: No naturalization
    records
Vital records: From 1860 to date; contact
    John Zanolli, Town Clerk
Probate records: No probate records

*Town of Spencer
Spencer, MA 01562

*Organized 1753 from Leicester
    (Worcester County)*

City of Springfield
City Hall
Springfield, MA 01103
Organized 1641 (Hampden County)

Squakeag Plantation
(see Town of Northfield)

Stauckett
(see Town of Harwich)

Town of Sterling
Sterling, MA 01564
Organized 1781 (Worcester County)

*Town of Stockbridge
Town Hall
6 Main Street
PO Box 417
Stockbridge, MA 01262-0417
Phone (413) 298-4714
*Organized 1739 (Indian Town
    Plantation) (Berkshire County)*
Land records: No land records
Naturalization records: No naturalization
    records
Vital records: Contact Jorja-Ann P.
    Marsden, Town Clerk
Vital records search service: $5.00;
    certified copies: $5.00 each (some
    impounded records restricted)
Probate records: No probate records

Town of Stoneham
Stoneham, MA 02180
*Organized 1725 from Charlestown
    (Middlesex County)*

Town of Stoughton
Stoughton, MA 02072
*Organized 1726 from Dorchester
    (Norfolk County)*

Stoughtonham
(see Town of Foxborough and Town of
    Sharon)

*Town of Stow
Stow, MA 01775
Phone (508) 897-4514; (508) 897-5996
    Ancient Documents Committee
*Organized 1683 (Pompositticut
    Plantation) (Middlesex County)*
Vital records: Contact Mrs. Barbara
    Siplee, Ancient Documents
    Committee

*Town of Sturbridge
PO Box 645
Sturbridge, MA 01566
Phone (508) 347-2510

Organized 1738 (New Medfield Tract), called New Medfield prior to 1738 (Worcester County)
Land records: No land records
Naturalization records: No naturalization records
Vital records: From 1730 to date; contact Town Clerk
Vital records search service: $5.00; copies: $5.00 each

Town of Sudbury
Sudbury, MA 01776
Organized 1693 (Middlesex County)

Suffield Equivalent
(see Town of Blandford)

*Town of Sunderland
12 School Street
Sunderland, MA 01375-9503
Phone (413) 665-2989
Organized 1714 (Swampfield) (Franklin County)
Vital records: Contact Rosemary O'Hagan, Town Clerk

*Town of Sutton
Sutton, MA 01590
Phone (508) 865-8725
Organized 1714 (Worcester County)
Land records: Yes
Naturalization records: No naturalization records
Vital records: From 1704
Probate records: No probate records

Swampfield
(see Town of Sunderland)

*Town of Swampscott
Swampscott, MA 01907
Phone (617) 596-8856
Organized 1852 from Lynn (Essex County)
Land records: No land records
Naturalization records: No naturalization records
Vital records: Births, deaths and marriages; contact Town Clerk
Vital records searches by appointment only; copies: $10.00 each
Probate records: No probate records

Town of Swansea
Swansea, MA 02777
Organized 1667 from Rehoboth (Wannamoisett) (Bristol County)

Tauconnuck Mountain Plantation
(see Town of Mount Washington)

City of Taunton
City Hall
Taunton, MA 02780
Organized 1639 (Cohannett) (Bristol County)

Town of Templeton
Town Clerk
Templeton, MA 01436
Organized 1762 (Narragansett Number 6 Plantation) (Worcester County)

Town of Tewksbury
Tewksbury, MA 01876
Organized 1734 from Billerica (Middlesex County)

The Elbows Plantation
(see Town of Palmer)

The Gore
(see Town of Monroe)

Town of Tisbury
Tisbury, MA 02568
Organized 1671 (Middletowne) (Dukes County)

Town of Tolland
S.R. Box 146
Tolland, MA 01034
Organized 1810 from Granville (Hampden County)

Town of Topsfield
Topsfield, MA 01983
Organized 1648 from Ipswich (Essex County)

Town of Townsend
Memorial Hall
Main Street (Turkey Hills)
Box 597
Townsend, MA 01469
Organized 1732 from Southern (Middlesex County)

Troy
(see City of Fall River)

Town of Truro
Truro, MA 02666
Organized 1709 (Pawmett Tract) (Barnstable County)

Tryingham Equivalent
(see Town of Otis)

Tuckannock
(see Town of Nantucket)

Turkey Hills
(see Town of Lunenburg)

Town of Tyngsborough
Tyngsborough, MA 01879
Organized 1789 from Dunstable (Middlesex County)

*Town of Tyringham
Town Hall
116 Main Road
Tyringham, MA 01264
Settled 1739; organized 1762 (Number 1 Plantation) (Berkshire County)
Land records: Contact Assessors' Office
Naturalization records: No naturalization records
Vital records: Contact Janice O. Curtiss, Town Clerk
Probate records: No probate records

Town of Upton
Upton, MA 01568
Organized 1735 from Hopkinton, Mendon, Sutton and Uxbridge (Worcester County)

Town of Uxbridge
Uxbridge, MA 01569
Organized 1727 from Mendon (Worcester County)

Town of Wakefield
Wakefield, MA 01880
Organized 1812 from Reading (South Reading) (Middlesex County)

*Town of Wales
Hollow Road
PO Box 834
Wales, MA 01081
Phone (413) 245-7571; (413) 245-3260 Assessors' Office
Organized 1762 from Brimfield (South Brimfield) (Hampden County)
Land records: Contact Assessors' Office
Vital records: Contact Town Clerk

Town of Walpole
Walpole, MA 02081
Organized 1724 from Dedham (Norfolk County)

City of Waltham
City Hall
Waltham, MA 02154
Organized 1738 from Watertown (Middlesex County)

Wannamoisett
(see Town of Swansea)

Ward
(see Town of Auburn)

Town of Ware
Ware, MA 01082
Phone (413) 967-4471
Organized 1761 (Ware River Parish)
(Hampshire County)

Ware River Parish
(see Town of Ware)

Town of Wareham
Wareham, MA 02571
Organized 1739 from Rochester and
Agawam Plantation (Plymouth
County)

Town of Warren
Warren, MA 01083
Organized 1742 from Brimfield,
Brookfield and Kingsfield (Western,
1834) (Worcester County)

*Town of Warwick
Evelyn Fournier, Town Clerk
12 Athol Road
Warwick, MA 01364
Phone (508) 544-6315
Formerly known as Roxbury Canada
Plantation; incorporated as Town of
Warwick 17 February 1763 (Franklin
County)

Town of Washington
Washington, MA 01223
Organized 1777 (Hartwood Plantation)
(Berkshire County)

*Town of Watertown
149 Main Street
Watertown, MA 02172
Phone (607) 972-6486
Organized 1630 (Middlesex County)
Land records: No land records
Naturalization records: No naturalization
    records
Vital records: Yes
Probate records: No probate records

*Town of Wayland
Wayland, MA 01778
Phone (508) 358-7701
Organized 1780 from Sudbury (East
Sudbury, 1835) (Middlesex County)
Land records: No land records
Naturalization records: No naturalization
    records
Vital records: From 1830 to date; contact
    Town Clerk; certified copies: $5.00
    each
Probate records: No probate records

*Town of Webster
Town Hall
Webster, MA 01570
Organized 1832 from Dudley and
Oxford (Worcester County)
Land records: No land records
Naturalization records: No naturalization
    records
Vital records: From 1832 to date; contact
    Town Clerk's Office; copies: $5.00
    per page
Probate records: No probate records

Town of Wellesley
Wellesley, MA 02181
Organized 1881 from Needham
(Norfolk County)

*Town of Wellfleet
300 Main Street
Wellfleet, MA 02667
Organized 1763 from Eastham
(Barnstable County)
Land records: No land records
Naturalization records: No naturalization
    records
Vital records: Contact Town Clerk's
    Office
Probate records: No probate records

Town of Wendell
Anna M.C.B. Hartjens, Town Clerk
Town Hall
Wendell, MA 01379
Phone (413) 544-6652
Organized 1781 from Shutesbury and
Ervingshire (Franklin County)

*Town of Wenham
Wenham, MA 01984
Phone (508) 468-5520 Town Clerk
Organized 1643 (Essex County)
Land records: No land records
Naturalization records: No naturalization
    records
Vital records: From 1850; contact Town
    Clerk. Before 1850; contact James
    Duncan Phillips Library of the
    Peabody Essex Museum, East India
    Square, Salem, MA 01970-3773.
    Some records; contact Wenham
    Historical Association and Museum,
    Inc., 132 Main Street, Wenham, MA
    01984; certified copies from Town
    Clerk: $5.00 each
Probate records: No probate records

Wessacucon
(see Town of Newbury)

Wessaguscus
(see Town of Weymouth)

*Town of West Boylston
120 Prescott Street
West Boylston, MA 01583
Phone (508) 835-6093 Assessors; (508)
    835-6240 Town Clerk
Organized 1808 from Boylston, Holden
and Sterling (Worcester County)
Land records: Contact Town Assessors
Naturalization records: No naturalization
    records
Vital records: Contact Barbara M.
    Deschenes, Town Clerk
Probate records: No probate records

Town of West Bridgewater
West Bridgewater, MA 02379
Organized 1822 from Bridgewater
(Plymouth County)

*Town of West Brookfield
Town Hall
Main Street
West Brookfield, MA 01585
Phone (508) 867-7264 Board of
    Assessors; (508) 867-9830 Tax
    Collector; (508) 867-6758 Town Clerk
Organized 1848 from Brookfield
(Worcester County)
Land records: Tax records from 1803,
    valuation and taxes books from 1861
    to date, plot maps from 1984 to date,
    some deeds after 1902; contact Peggy
    J. Walker, Board of Assessors. Some
    tax records from 1803 to 1838 on
    microfilm; contact Susan M. Harry,
    Tax Collector
Vital records: From 1848 to date (prior to
    1849, Brookfield Volume); contact
    Nancy L. Korzec, Town Clerk, PO
    Box 372, West Brookfield, MA
    01585-0372
Vital records search service: $5.00
    (limited to 15 minutes, includes
    certificate if found)

West Cambridge
(see Town of Arlington, Town of
    Belmont and Town of Winchester)

West Hoosuck Plantation
(see Town of Williamstown)

*Town of West Newbury
381 Main Street
West Newbury, MA 01985
Phone (508) 363-1100 Town Clerk
Organized 1819 from Newbury
(Parsons) (Essex County)
Vital records: Contact Town Clerk

West Roxbury
(see City of Boston)

*Town of West Springfield
West Springfield, MA 01089
Phone (413) 263-3012
Organized 1774 from Springfield
(Hampden County)
Land records: No land records
Naturalization records: No naturalization
  records
Vital records: Contact Town Clerk's
  Office
Probate records: No probate records

Town of West Stockbridge
West Stockbridge, MA 01266
Organized 1774 from Stockbridge
(Berkshire County)

Town of West Tisbury
West Tisbury, MA 02575
Organized 1892 from Tisbury (Dukes
County)

*Town of Westborough
Westborough, MA 01581
Organized 1717 from Marlborough
(Worcester County)
Land records: No land records
Naturalization records: No naturalization
  records
Vital records: Contact Town Clerk's
  Office
Probate records: No probate records

Western
(see Town of Warren)

*City of Westfield
City Hall
59 Court Street
Westfield, MA 01085
Organized 1669 from Springfield
(Hampden County)
Vital records: Births, deaths and
  marriages; contact City Clerk's Office

Town of Westford
Westford, MA 01886
Organized 1729 from Chelmsford
(Middlesex County)

Town of Westhampton
Westhampton, MA 01027
Phone (413) 527-0463
Organized 1778 from Northampton
(Hampshire County)

*Town of Westminster
Westminster, MA 01473
Phone (508) 874-7406
Organized 1759 (Narragansett Number
2 Plantation) (Worcester County)
Land records: From 1728; contact
  Assessors' Office
Naturalization records: No naturalization
  records

Vital records: From 1738; contact Town
  Clerk
Probate records: No probate records

*Town of Weston
Town House Road
Weston, MA 02193
Organized 1713 from Watertown
(Middlesex County)
Vital records: Contact G. Grube, Town
  Clerk's Office; certified copies: $5.00
  each

*Town of Westport
816 Main Road
Westport, MA 02790
Phone (508) 636-1000
Organized 1787 from Dartmouth
(Bristol County)
Land records: No land records
Naturalization records: No naturalization
  records
Vital records: From 1787 to date; contact
  Town Clerk
Vital records search service: $2.00 per
  name; certified copies: $5.00 each

Town of Westwood
Westwood, MA 02090
Organized 1897 from Dedham (Norfolk
County)

Town of Weymouth
Weymouth, MA 02188
Organized 1635 (Wessaguscus) (Norfolk
County)

*Town of Whately
346 Haydenville Road
Whately, MA 01093
Phone (413) 665-4584
Organized 1771 from Hatfield (Franklin
County)
Land records: No land records
Naturalization records: No naturalization
  records
Vital records: From 1850 to date; contact
  Mrs. Virginia C. Allis, Town Clerk
Probate records: No probate records

*Town of Whitman
Town Hall
54 South Avenue
PO Box 426
Whitman, MA 02382
Phone (617) 447-7607 Town Clerk
Organized 1875 from Abington and East
Bridgewater (South Abington)
(Plymouth County)
Land records: No land records
Naturalization records: No naturalization
  records
Vital records: Contact Pamela A. Martin,
  Town Clerk
Vital records search service: $10.00;

certified copies: $5.00 each (need
  identification for restricted,
  impounded records)
Probate records: No probate records

Town of Wilbraham
Wilbraham, MA 01095
Organized 1763 from Springfield
(Hampden County)

Town of Williamsburg
Williamsburg, MA 01096
Phone (413) 268-8400
Organized 1771 from Hatfield
(Hampshire County)

*Town of Williamstown
Williamstown, MA 01267
Phone (413) 458-9341
Organized 1765 as West Hoosuck
Plantation (Berkshire County)
Land records: Contact Assessors' Office
Naturalization records: No naturalization
  records
Vital records: From 1860 to date (earlier
  records destroyed in fire); contact
  Town Clerk's Office; copies: 20¢ per
  page, $5.00 for certified copies
Probate records: No probate records

*Town of Wilmington
Town Hall
121 Glen Road
Wilmington, MA 01887
Phone (508) 658-2030
Organized 1730 from Reading and
Woburn (Middlesex County)
Land records: No land records
Naturalization records: No naturalization
  records
Vital records: From 1730 to date; contact
  Kathleen M. Scanlon, Town Clerk
Probate records: No probate records

*Town of Winchendon
Winchendon, MA 01475
Organized 1764 (Ipswich Canada
Plantation) (Worcester County)
Land records: Early proprietor's records;
  contact Town Clerk
Naturalization records: No naturalization
  records
Vital records: Contact Town Clerk
Probate records: No probate records

Town of Winchester
Winchester, MA 01890
Organized 1850 from Medford, Woburn
and West Cambridge (Middlesex
County)

Town of Windsor
Windsor, MA 01270
Organized 1771 (Gageborough)
(Berkshire County)

Winnissimet
(see City of Chelsea)

Town of Winthrop
Winthrop, MA 02152
Organized 1846 from Chelsea (North Chelsea) (Suffolk County)

***City of Woburn**
City Hall
10 Common Street
Woburn, MA 01801-4139
Phone (617) 932-4400
Organized 1642 (Charlestowne Village) (Middlesex County)
Land records: No land records
Naturalization records: No naturalization records
Vital records: Contact Office of City Clerk
Probate records: No probate records

Wollonopaug
(see Town of Wrentham)

Town of Woodstock
(see Worcester County)

City of Worcester
City Hall
Worcester, MA 01608
Organized 1684 (Quansigamond Plantation) (Worcester County)

***Town of Worthington**
PO Box 247
Worthington, MA 01098
Phone (413) 238-5577
Organized 1768 (Number 3 Plantation) (Hampshire County)
Land records: Tax maps, recent deeds, valuation books from 1850; contact Town Clerk
Naturalization records: No naturalization records
Vital records: Births, deaths and marriages; contact Town Clerk
Vital records search service: $20.00 per hour; certified copies: $6.00 each
Probate records: No probate records

Town of Wrentham
Wrentham, MA 02093
Organized 1673 (Wollonopaug) (Norfolk County)

***Town of Yarmouth**
1146 Route 28
South Yarmouth, MA 02664
Phone (508) 398-2231; (508) 398-2365 FAX
Organized 1639 (Mattacheeset) (Barnstable County)
Land records: No land records

Naturalization records: No naturalization records
Vital records: From 1600; contact George F. Barabe, Town Clerk
Vital records search service: $10.39 per hour for genealogical requests; copies: 20¢ per page, $5.00 for certified copies
Probate records: No probate records

MICHIGAN

Capital: Lansing. Statehood: 26 January 1877 (ceded to the U.S. in 1783, part of the Northwest Territory in 1787, part of Indiana Territory in 1800, became a separate territory 11 January 1805 with extensions in 1818 and 1834)

Court System

Michigan has Municipal Courts in East Detroit, Grosse Pointe, Grosse Pointe Farms, Grosse Pointe Park, Grosse Pointe Shores and Grosse Pointe Woods. Probate Courts sit at each county seat and at other locations. However, eight counties have joined to form four Probate Court districts: Alger-Schoolcraft, Clare-Gladwin, Emmet-Charlevoix and Mecosta-Osceola. Ninety-eight District Courts sit throughout the state and deal with some civil matters, misdemeanors, preliminary examinations, evictions, foreclosures, etc. The Court of Claims hears claims against the state. The Recorder's Court of Detroit handles criminal felonies.

Fifty-five Circuit Courts have general jurisdiction and sit in each county seat. The following Circuits include more than one county: Fifth Judicial Circuit: Barry and Eaton counties; Eighth Judicial Circuit: Ionia and Montcalm counties; Eleventh Judicial Circuit: Alger, Luce and Schoolcraft counties; Twelfth Judicial Circuit: Baraga, Houghton and Keweenaw counties; Thirteenth Judicial Circuit: Antrim, Grand Traverse and Leelanau counties; Nineteenth Judicial Circuit: Benzie and Manistee counties; Twenty-third Judicial Circuit: Iosco and Oscoda counties; Twenty-sixth Judicial Circuit: Alcona, Alpena, Montmorency and Presque Isle counties; Twenty-seventh Judicial Circuit: Newaygo and Oceana counties; Twenty-eighth Judicial Circuit: Missaukee and Wexford counties; Twenty-ninth Judicial Circuit: Clinton and Gratiot counties; Thirty-second Judicial Circuit: Gogebic and Ontonagon counties; Thirty-third Judicial Circuit: Charlevoix and Emmet counties; Thirty-fourth Judicial Circuit: Arenac, Ogemaw and Roscommon counties; Forty-first Judicial Circuit: Dickinson, Iron and Menominee counties; Forty-sixth Judicial Circuit: Crawford, Kalkaska and Otsego counties; Forty-ninth Judicial Circuit: Mecosta and Osceola counties; Fiftieth Judicial Circuit: Chippewa and Mackinac counties; Fifty-first Judicial Circuit: Lake and Mason counties; Fifty-fifth Judicial

Circuit: Clare and Gladwin counties. The Court of Appeals and Supreme Court have appellate jurisdiction.

Courthouses

*Alcona County Courthouse
106 Fifth Street
Harrisville, MI 48740-9789
Phone (517) 724-6802 County Register of Deeds; (517) 724-5374 County Clerk; (517) 724-6880 County Probate Court
County organized 1840 from Alpena County; officially organized 1869
Land records: Contact County Register of Deeds, PO Box 269, Harrisville, MI 48740
Naturalization records: From 1869 to the 1930s; contact Gayle E. Simmons, County Clerk, PO Box 308, Harrisville, MI 48740; copies: $1.00 per page
Vital records: Births from 1869 to date (very few), deaths and marriages from 1869 to date; contact County Clerk; copies: $1.00 per document, $5.00 for certification (restrictions on viewing births)
Probate records: Contact County Probate Court
Probate search service: no charge; copies: $1.00 per document, 25¢ per page for files, etc.

*Alger County Courthouse
101 Court Street
Munising, MI 49862-1103
Phone (906) 387-2076
County organized 1885 from Schoolcraft County
Land records: From 1885; contact Donald W. Kinnunen, County Clerk; copies: $1.00 per page
Naturalization records: From about 1885; contact County Clerk; copies: 25¢ per page
Vital records: Some births and deaths from 1884, some marriages from 1885; contact County Clerk; certified copies: $5.00 for the first copy and $2.00 for each additional copy of the same record
Probate records: From about 1885; contact Probate Court
Probate search service: no charge; copies: 25¢ per page, $3.00 for certified copies

*Allegan County Courthouse
113 Chestnut Street
Allegan, MI 49010-1332
Phone (616) 673-0390 Deputy Register of Deeds; (616) 673-0450 Deputy

County Clerk; (616) 673-0250 Probate Court
Territory embracing Allegan County was first claimed by the British who ceded it to France in 1763. It was seized by George Rogers Clark in the name of Virginia on 1 March 1784, and was organized in 1805 from Wayne County. At this time, Allegan County was considered part of Indiana. On 21 August 1821, the Ottawa Indians conveyed their interest to the federal government by the Treaty of Chicago. The county was a portion of the region which the legislative council of the Territory of Michigan declared in November 1826 to be attached to and composed a part of Lenawee County. In April 1827, an Act formed the territory thus annexed to Lenawee County into the Township of Saint Joseph. On 4 November 1829, Ranges 11 and 12 were made a part of Saint Joseph County; Ranges 13 to 17 frl., inclusive, were made a part of Cass County. On 2 March 1831, the present confines of the county were set off into a separate county by the name of Allegan. On 29 March 1833, a law was enacted, "that all the district of country which has been set off into a separate county by the name of Allegan, shall be attached to the County of Kalamazoo for all legal purposes whatsoever." In 1834 the county seat was located at Allegan Village. An act which took effect 1 September 1835 again separated Allegan County from Kalamazoo County when it was organized into four townships: Newark Township, containing what is now Laketown, Saugatuck, Ganges, Casco, Fillmore, Manlius, Clyude and Lee; Allegan Township, containing what is now Overisel, Heath, Valley, Cheshire, Salem, Monterey, Allegan and Trowbridge; Otsego Township, containing what is now Dorr, Hopkins, Watson and Otsego; and Plainfield Township, containing what is now Leighton, Wayland, Martin and GunPlain
Land records: Contact Linda L. Wilson, Deputy Register of Deeds
Vital records: Births from 24 Jan 1867, deaths from 13 Feb 1867, and marriages from 17 Dec 1835; contact Deputy County Clerk
Vital records search service: $7.00 for the first three years, $3.00 for each additional year per person and event (includes a certified copy of the record, if found)
Probate records: Contact Probate Court
Probate search service: no charge;

copies: 50¢ per page for "conformed copies"; no minimum

*Alpena County Courthouse
720 West Chisholm Street
Alpena, MI 49707-2429
Phone (517) 356-0115 County Clerk; (517) 356-6559 FAX, County Clerk
Anamickee County organized 1840 from Mackinac and unorganized territory (Saginaw); County organized 7 February 1857, with the township containing Fremont, renamed the City of Alpena on 2 February 1859, composing the entire county
Land records: Contact Carole Sommerfield, Register of Deeds
Naturalization records: From 1871; contact Blondine Smolinski, County Clerk
Vital records: Births from 1869 to date, deaths and marriages from 1871 to date; contact County Clerk; certified copies: $5.00 for the first copy and $2.00 for each additional copy of the same record (driver's license required for ID)
Probate records: Contact Judge Douglas A. Pugh, County Annex Building, Alpena, MI 49707

*Antrim County Courthouse
PO Box 520
Bellaire, MI 49615
Phone (616) 533-8607
County organized 1840 from Mackinac County; name changed from Meegise County in 1843
Land records: Contact Register of Deeds Office
Naturalization records: From 1873 to 1955; contact County Clerk
Vital records: From 1876; contact County Clerk
Probate records: Contact Probate Court, PO Box 276, Bellaire, MI 49615

Arenac County Courthouse
PO Box 747
Standish, MI 48658
Phone (517) 846-4626
County organized 1883 from Bay County

*Baraga County Courthouse
L'Anse, MI 49946-1085
Phone (906) 524-6183
County organized 1875 from Houghton County
Probate records: Yes
Probate search service: "All records beginning with 1875 under office instruction/supervision; $1.00 per page; certified copies are at the regular fee."

*Barry County Courthouse
Hastings, MI 49058
Phone (616) 948-4824 Register of Deeds; (616) 948-4810 County Clerk; (616) 948-4842 Probate Court
County organized 1829 from Eaton County
Land records: From 1836; contact Register of Deeds, PO Box 7, Hastings, MI 49058
Naturalization records: Contact State Archives of Michigan, Michigan Bureau of History, Department of State, 717 West Allegan Street, Lansing, MI 48918
Vital records: Births and deaths from 1867, marriages from 1839 (but few recorded before 1867); contact County Clerk; copies: $10.00 for the first copy and $3.00 for each additional copy of the same record ("Births may not be researched; with proof of relationship a staff member (time permitting) will look up one or two")
Probate records: From November 1863; contact Pamela A. Miller, Probate Register, Probate Court, 220 West Court Street, Hastings, MI 49058
Probate search service: no charge ("We do not have any individual who does this on a regular basis, and consequently we cannot estimate when we will be able to provide information"; copies: $1.00 per page "as long as the documents do not need to be microfilmed"); "We strongly recommend that if people wish to search our ledgers they call in to check the court schedule, as we have very limited space, and the attorneys' room is the only place we have for our microfilm reader."

*Bay County Courthouse
515 Center Avenue
Bay City, MI 48708-5941
Phone (517) 895-4280
County organized 1857 from Saginaw and Midland counties
Land records: Contact Registrar of Deeds
Naturalization records: Contact State Archives of Michigan, Michigan Bureau of History, Department of State, 717 West Allegan Street, Lansing, MI 48918
Vital records: Deaths and marriages; contact County Clerk; copies: 25¢ each, $8.50 for certified copies of old records that must be typed
Probate records: Contact Probate Court

*Benzie County Government Center
PO Box 398
Beulah, MI 49617
Phone (616) 882-9674 County Planning Office; 882-9675 Probate Registrar
In 1859 the Township of Crystal Lake in

Grand Traverse County included all of what is now Benzie County; county of Benzie formed 1863 and attached to Grand Traverse County for civic and municipal purposes; organized by an act of the legislature 30 March 1869
Land records: Contact County Planning Office (has records of historical homes, photos, locations, etc.)
Naturalization records: Contact Jean Bowers, County Clerk
Vital records: Births from 6 March 1868, deaths from 27 April 1868, marriages from 25 May 1869; contact County Clerk; copies: $5.00 for the first copy and $2.00 for each additional copy of the same record made at the same time; "Researcher should be able to describe the family research being done, some form of identification.")
Probate records: Contact Kimberly Ireton, Register of Probate
No probate search service; copies: 35¢ per page, no minimum

*Berrien County Courthouse
811 Port Street
Saint Joseph, MI 49085-1156
Phone (616) 983-7111
County organized 1829 from Indian lands
Land records: From 1831; contact Register of Deeds Office; copies: $1.00 per page, $3.00 for plats, $1.00 for certification
Naturalization records: From about 1842; contact M. Louise Stine, County Clerk, County Clerk's Office; copies: $3.00 per page
Vital records: Births and deaths from 1867 to date (Death Liber B has limited access because of fragile condition), marriages from 1834; contact County Clerk's Office; certified copies: $10.00 for the first copy or three-year search; "To view a birth since 1900, an heir must show proof of death such as death certificate or obituary notice."
Probate records: Wills, deceased trusts, estates, guardianships, etc., from 1837 to date; contact Ollie M. Hull, Probate Register, Probate Court
Probate search service: no charge; copies: $1.00 per page plus SASE, $10.00 for the first page of a certified copy and $1.00 for each additional page, no minimum

*Branch County Courthouse
31 Division Street
Coldwater, MI 49036-1904
Phone (517) 279-8411
County organized 1829 from Saint Joseph County (formerly attached for judicial purposes only)

Land records: Contact Register of Deeds Office
Naturalization records: Contact County Clerk's Office
Vital records: Deaths from 1867, marriages from 1833; contact County Clerk's Office; copies: $13.00 for the first copy and $4.00 for each additional copy of the same document made at the same time
Probate records: Contact Probate Court
No probate search service; copies: $1.00 per page, no minimum

*Calhoun County Courthouse
315 West Green Street
Marshall, MI 49068-1518
Phone (616) 781-0730 Clerk-Register
County organized 1829 from Indian lands
Land records: From 1833; contact Anne B. Norlander, Clerk-Register
Naturalization records: From 1918 to 1970 (by appointment; copies: $1.00 per page)
Vital records: Deaths and marriages from 1867 (by appointment; copies: $10.00)

*Cass County Courthouse
120 North Broadway
Cassopolis, MI 49031-1398
Phone (616) 445-8621
County organized 1829 from Indian lands
Land records: Real estate records from 1829; contact Register of Deeds Office
Naturalization records: From 1929 to 1952
Vital records: Births and deaths from 1867, marriages from 1830; contact County Clerk's Office
Probate records: From 1829; contact Probate Court
Probate search service: no charge at this time; copies: $1.00 per page

*Charlevoix County Building
Charlevoix, MI 49720
Phone (616) 547-7200
County organized 1869 from Manitou and Otsego counties
Land records: Contact Register of Deeds
Naturalization records: From 1880
Vital records: From 1868
Probate records: Contact Probate Court
No probate search service; certified copies: $3.00 each, no minimum

*Cheboygan County Courthouse
870 South Main Street
PO Box 70
Cheboygan, MI 49721
Phone (616) 627-8808
County organized 1840 from Antrim County

Land records: From 1855
Naturalization records: From 1878
Vital records: From 1867
Probate records: Contact Probate Court

*Chippewa County Courthouse
319 Court Street
Sault Sainte Marie, MI 49783-2183
Phone (906) 635-6300 County Clerk;
(906) 635-6325 FAX, County Clerk
*County organized 1826 from Mackinac
County; a census was taken by
Sheriff John Hulbert in 1827 for the
County of Chippewa; the Michigan
Manual states that the county was
organized in 1843*
Vital records: Births and deaths from
1869 to date, marriages from 1827 to
date; contact Margaret L. Kaunisto,
County Clerk
Vital records search service: $5.00 for
each twenty years; certified copies:
$5.00 for the first copy and $3.00 for
each additional copy

*Clare County Courthouse
PO Box 438
Harrison, MI 48625-0438
Phone (517) 539-7131; (517) 539-7109
Probate Court
*County set off 1840 from Isabella
County; first named Kay-Ka-Knee;
name changed to Clare in 1843;
courthouse burned 12 July 1877*
Land records: From 1871; contact Donna
M. Carr, Register of Deeds
Naturalization records: From 1900
Vital records: Births from 1870, deaths
and marriages from 1871; contact
Donna M. Carr, Clerk
Probate records: From 1876; contact
Honorable Thomas P. McLaughlin,
Probate Judge
No probate search service; copies: $1.00
per page, $10.00 for certified copies,
no minimum *(קๆๆ)*

*Clinton County Courthouse
100 East State Street
Saint Johns, MI 48879-1571
Phone (517) 224-5270 Register of Deeds
Office; (517) 224-5140 Clerk's Office;
(517) 224-5190 Probate Court
*County organized 1831 from
Shiawassee County*
Land records: From 1837; contact
Register of Deeds Office, PO Box
435, Saint Johns, MI 48879-0435
Naturalization records: From 1870;
contact County Clerk
Vital records: Births and deaths from
1867, marriages from about 1839;
contact County Clerk
Vital records search service: $10.00 per
name for a three-year search (includes
one certified copy); copies: $10.00 for

the first certified copy and $3.00 for
each additional certified copy made at
the same time of any births or of
deaths or marriages after 1933, $1.00
for uncertified copies of deaths or
marriages before 1933 (births
restricted to researchers who are heirs,
have the full name and birth date and
can prove that the registrant is
deceased)
Probate records: From 1840; contact
Probate Court
Probate search service: no charge;
copies: $1.00 per page, no minimum;
"Probate Court should be contacted
prior to coming in to assure the
availability of a researcher."

*Crawford County Courthouse
200 West Michigan Avenue
Grayling, MI 49738-1745
Phone (517) 348-2841
County organized 1818, original county
Land records: Yes
Vital records: Deaths and marriages
(births are no longer public record)
Probate records: Yes
No probate search service; copies: $1.00
per record copy, no minimum

*Delta County Courthouse
310 Ludington Street
Escanaba, MI 49829-4057
Phone (906) 786-1763
*County organized 9 March 1843 from
Schoolcraft County*
Land records: From 1863; contact
Register of Deeds
Naturalization records: From 1866;
contact County Clerk
Vital records: From 1867; contact County
Clerk
Probate records: Contact Probate Court
Probate search service: $10.00; copies:
$1.50 per page, $3.00 for certified
copies, $10.00 minimum

*Dickinson County Courthouse
705 South Stephenson Avenue
PO Box 609
Iron Mountain, MI 49801
Phone (906) 774-0988
*County organized 1891 from Marquette
County*
Land records: From 1891 (by legal
description only, not street addresses);
contact Register of Deeds
Naturalization records: Before June
1970; contact County Clerk's Office
Vital records: Births from 1891, deaths
and marriages from 1891 (a separate
death index for the years 1934 and on
is available; separate marriage index
for years 1891 to present indexed
under groom's name only); contact
Dolly L. Cook, County Clerk, County

Clerk's Office; certified copies: $5.00
each (no out-of-county personal
checks accepted, includes ten-year
search); "Births are no longer
considered public record"; available to
"the individual who is the subject of
the birth record, a parent named in the
birth record, an heir, a legal
representative or legal guardian or a
court of competent jurisdiction;" to
view a birth record "they must show
some proof the person is deceased and
they are an heir" by being able to
"describe or display the family
research being done and the records
sought; to prove heirship must show
copy of death certificate, obituary or
funeral card."
Probate records: Contact Probate Court
No probate search service; certified
copies: $5.00 each; "Out-of-county
personal checks are not accepted."

*Eaton County Courthouse
1045 Independence
Charlotte, MI 48813-1033
Phone (517) 543-7500
*County organized 1837 from Kalamazoo
County*
Vital records: Deaths from 1867 through
1970, marriages from 1838 through
1970; contact Linda M. Twitchell,
County Clerk
Vital records search service: contact
Joyce Leiken, Eaton County
Genealogical Society, 100 West
Lawrence Avenue, Charlotte, MI
48813; copies: $1.00 for the first page
and 50¢ for each additional page,
$5.00 for the first certified copy and
$2.00 for each additional certified
copy (very early birth records
available for inspection with clerk's
assistance in locating ancestors; "must
sign form and show proper
identification")

*Emmet County Courthouse
1457 Atkins Road
Petoskey, MI 49770-3242
Phone (616) 348-1744
*County organized 1853 from Mackinac
County*
Land records: From 1852
Naturalization records: From 1867,
immigration records early 1800s
Vital records: Deaths and marriages from
1867; certified copies: $5.00 (births
restricted, death record requested for
proof of heirship)
Probate records: From 1857
No probate search service; copies: 25¢
each, no minimum; "Requests to be in
writing with SASE."

*Genesee County Courthouse
Flint, MI 48502
Phone (810) 257-3228 County Clerk;
    (810) 257-3464 FAX, County Clerk
County organized 1835 from Oakland
    County
Naturalization records: State Archives of
    Michigan, Michigan Bureau of
    History, Department of State, 717
    West Allegan Street, Lansing, MI
    48918
Vital records: Births, deaths and
    marriages from 1867 to date; contact
    County Clerk, Room 202; copies:
    $2.00 per page, $10.00 for the first
    certified copy and $5.00 for each
    additional certified copy (births
    restricted to records over 100 years
    old or if proof of death is presented)

*Gladwin County Courthouse
401 West Cedar Avenue
Gladwin, MI 48624-2088
Phone (517) 426-7551 Register of Deeds
    Office; (517) 426-7351 County Clerk;
    (517) 426-7451 Probate Court Office;
    (517) 426-4281 FAX, Courthouse
County organized 1855 from
    unorganized territory
Land records: Contact Register of Deeds
    Office
Naturalization records: State Archives of
    Michigan, Michigan Bureau of
    History, Department of State, 717
    West Allegan Street, Lansing, MI
    48918
Vital records: Births from 1875 to 1972,
    and deaths and marriages from 1875
    to date; contact Laura E. Flach,
    County Clerk
Vital records search service: $1.00 per
    name per five-year period; copies: 25¢
    each, $7.00 for the first certified copy
    and $3.00 for each additional certified
    copy of the same record (requires
    driver's license number or social
    security number, death certificate for
    births, and relationship to person for
    births or deaths)
Probate records: Contact Probate Court
    Office

*Gogebic County Courthouse
200 North Moore Street
Bessemer, MI 49911
Phone (906) 667-0381 Register of Deeds
    Office; (906) 663-4518 County Clerk/
    Register of Deeds; (906) 663-4090
    FAX, County Clerk/Register of
    Deeds; (906) 667-0421 Probate Court
County organized 1887 from Ontonagon
    County
Land records: Contact Register of Deeds
    Office; copies: $1.00 per page
Naturalization records: Contact State
    Archives of Michigan, Michigan
    Bureau of History, Department of

State, 717 West Allegan Street,
    Lansing, MI 48918
Vital records: Births ("1887—the staff
    will check the index for eligible
    people"), deaths and marriages;
    contact Richard J. Brown, County
    Clerk/Register of Deeds; certified
    copies: $7.00 for the first copy and
    $2.00 for each additional copy of the
    same record made at the same time
    (births restricted, proof of death
    required)
Probate records: Contact Probate Court

*Grand Traverse County Courthouse
400 Boardman Avenue
Traverse City, MI 49684
Phone (616) 922-4748 Register of Deeds;
    (616) 922-4760 County Clerk; (616)
    922-4640 Probate Court; (616) 922-
    4710 Circuit Court Records
County organized by an act approved 7
    April 1851, from a part of Mackinaw
    previously called Omena; enlarged
    1856 to include Benzie and Leelanau
    counties
Land records: Contact Register of Deeds
Naturalization records: Contact County
    Clerk
Vital records: Contact County Clerk
Probate records: Contact Probate Court

*Gratiot County Courthouse
Ithaca, MI 48847
Phone (517) 875-5215; (517) 875-5231
    Probate Court
County organized 1855 from Saginaw
    County
Land records: From 1847; contact
    Register of Deeds ("will assist with
    research but will not answer mail or
    telephone requests")
Naturalization records: Contact State
    Archives of Michigan, Michigan
    Bureau of History, Department of
    State, 717 West Allegan Street,
    Lansing, MI 48918
Vital records: Births and deaths from
    1867, marriages from 1855; contact
    County Clerk; copies: $10.00 each
Probate records: From 1857; contact
    Probate Court, 214 East Center Street,
    Ithaca, MI 48847
Probate search service: no charge;
    copies: $1.00 per page (microfilm),
    $3.00 per page certification

*Hillsdale County Courthouse
29 North Howell Street
Hillsdale, MI 49242
Phone (517) 437-3391
County organized 1835 from Lenawee
    County
Land records: Contact Register of Deeds
Naturalization records: Few
    naturalization records available
Vital records: Births and deaths from

1867, marriages from 1844; contact
    Clerk; copies: $3.00 for non-certified
    copies needing to be typed, $1.00 for
    photocopies, $10.00 for certified
    copies
Probate records: Contact Judge of
    Probate
No probate search service; copies: $1.00
    per page

*Houghton County Courthouse
401 East Houghton Avenue
Houghton, MI 49931-2016
Phone (906) 482-1150 County Clerk
County organized 19 March 1845 from
    parts of Marquette, Schoolcraft and
    Ontonagon counties
Land records: From 1847 (indexed);
    contact Nancy Fenili, Clerk/Register
    Deeds, County Clerk's Office; copies:
    $5.00 each (includes five-year search)
Naturalization records: From 1848
    (indexed); contact County Clerk's
    Office
Uncertified copies: $5.00 each (includes
    five-year search)
Vital records: Births and deaths from
    1867, marriages from 1855; contact
    County Clerk's Office; copies: $5.00
    each (includes three-year search of
    unindexed records or five-year search
    of indexed records) (births available
    only to the subject named, parent,
    legal representative, guardian or heir)
Probate records: Estate records from
    1872; contact County Clerk's Office;
    copies: $5.00 each (includes three-
    year search of unindexed records or
    five-year search of indexed records)

*Huron County Courthouse
250 East Huron Avenue
Bad Axe, MI 48413-1317
Phone (517) 269-9942
County organized 1840 from Sanilac
    and Tuscola counties
Land records: Contact Fran Holdwick,
    Register of Deeds; copies: $1.00 per
    page
Naturalization records: From 1867 to
    1953; contact Helen M. Lemanski,
    County Clerk; copies: $1.00 per page
Vital records: Deaths from 1867,
    marriages from 1850; contact County
    Clerk; certified copies: $10.00 each
Probate records: Contact Judge David L.
    Clabuesch
No probate search service; copies: 50¢
    per page from paper originals, $1.00
    per page from microfilm originals,
    $10.00 for certification plus $1.00 per
    page, no minimum

*Ingham County Courthouse
366 South Jefferson Street
PO Box 179
Mason, MI 48854

Phone (517) 676-0240
County organized 1838 from unorganized territory
Land records: Yes
Naturalization records: No naturalization records
Vital records: Deaths from 1867, marriages from 1837. City of East Lansing has deaths from 1907; certified copies only from the county: $5.00 for the first copy and $2.00 for each additional copy of the same document made at the same time
Probate records: Yes

*Ionia County Courthouse
Ionia, MI 48846
Phone (616) 527-5322
County organized 1837 from unorganized territory
Land records: Contact Register of Deeds
Naturalization records: Contact State Archives of Michigan, Michigan Bureau of History, Department of State, 717 West Allegan Street, Lansing, MI 48918
Vital records: Births, deaths from 1867, marriages from 1837; contact County Clerk; copies: $1.00 each, except for births, which are $10.00 for the first record or search and $3.00 for each additional copy or search included in the same request; "must state relationship; birth record access requires death certificate."
Probate records: Contact Probate Court

Iosco County Courthouse
PO Box 838
Tawas City, MI 48764-0838
Phone (517) 362-3497
County organized 1840 from unorganized territory; name changed from Kanotin County in 1843

*Iron County Courthouse
2 South Sixth Street
Crystal Falls, MI 49920-1413
Phone (906) 875-3121
County organized 1885 from Marquette County
Land records: Contact Register of Deeds or Equalization
Naturalization records: Contact State Archives of Michigan, Michigan Bureau of History, Department of State, 717 West Allegan Street, Lansing, MI 48918
Vital records: Deaths and marriages from 1885; contact County Clerk; copies: 25¢ per page plus $2.00 for each record researched
Probate records: Contact Judge of Probate, Probate Register
Probate search service: $10.00 to $20.00; copies: 25¢ each, $3.00 for certified copies, $5.00 minimum

*Isabella County Courthouse
200 North Main Street
Mount Pleasant, MI 48858-2321
Phone (517) 772-0911
County organized 1831 from unorganized territory
Land records: From 24 November 1851
Naturalization records: From 21 March 1861 to 5 April 1965
Vital records: Deaths from 1867, marriages from 1860
Probate records: closed to the public

*Jackson County Courthouse
312 South Jackson
Jackson, MI 49201
Phone (517) 788-4268 (312 South Jackson); (517) 788-4265 (Tower Building); (517) 788-4350 Register of Deeds
County organized 1832 from Washtenaw County
Land records: Contact G. S. McDevitt, Register of Deeds, Tower Building, 120 West Michigan Avenue, Jackson, MI 49201
Naturalization records: Contact Jean Kahn, County Clerk, Tower Building
Vital records: Births, deaths and marriages from 1867; contact County Clerk; copies: 50¢ or $1.00 each, depending on size, $5.00 for the first certified copy and $2.00 for each additional certified copy; "access to original records is discouraged; office staff handle these or make copies."
Probate records: Contact Judge Fred Sill

*Kalamazoo County Courthouse
201 West Kalamazoo
Kalamazoo, MI 49007-3734
Phone (616) 383-8840
County organized 1829 from Saint Joseph County
Land records: Contact Register of Deeds
Vital records: Contact County Clerk
Probate records: From 1932 to date; contact Andrew R. Carlson, Probate Court, 2227 West Michigan Avenue, Kalamazoo, MI 49007
Probate search service: no charge; copies: $1.00 per page

*Kalkaska County Governmental Center
605 North Birch Street
PO Box 780
Kalkaska, MI 49646-9436
Phone (616) 258-4176; (616) 258-3330 Probate Court
County organized 1870 from Crawford County
Land records: Deeds from 1856 (on microfilm); contact John Hall, Register of Deeds; copies: $1.00 each; "We also have an abstract office, the

books can be used for $45.00 per hour."
Probate records: From 1874; contact Hon. Odell B. Carlisle, Judge, Probate Court
Probate search service: no charge; copies: 30¢ each plus postage

Kay-Ka-Knee County
(see Clare County)

*Kent County Administration Building
300 Monroe Avenue, N.W.
Grand Rapids, MI 49503-2206
Phone (616) 336-3550
County organized 1836 from unorganized territory
Land records: Contact Register of Deeds
Naturalization records: From 1871; contact State Archives of Michigan, Michigan Bureau of History, Department of State, 717 West Allegan Street, Lansing, MI 48918
Vital records: Births and deaths from 1867, marriages from 1845; contact County Clerk's Office
Probate records: Contact Probate Court, 320 Ottawa, N.W., Grand Rapids, MI 49503

*Keweenaw County Courthouse
Eagle River, MI 49924
Phone (906) 337-2229
County organized 11 March 1861 from Houghton County
Land records: Contact Equalization Department
Naturalization records: Contact County Clerk
Vital records: Deaths and marriages from 1869; contact County Clerk; certified copies: $3.00 each
Probate records: Contact Probate Court
Probate search service: no charge; copies: $3.00 for the first page and $1.00 for each additional page, no minimum

*Lake County Courthouse
PO Box B
Baldwin, MI 49304-0902
Phone (616) 745-4641
County organized 1870 from Osceola County
Land records: From 1870; contact Register of Deeds
Vital records: Deaths and marriages from 1870; contact County Clerk; copies: $1.00 per page, $5.00 for certified copies
Probate records: From 1871; contact Probate Register, PO Box 308, Baldwin, MI 49304
Probate search service: no charge; copies: $1.00 per page; $3.00 per certified page, no minimum

*Lapeer County Courthouse
Lapeer, MI 48446
Phone (810) 667-0211 Register of Deeds;
(810) 667-0356
County organized 1837 from Oakland and Saint Clair counties
Land records: From 1835; contact Register of Deeds, 279 North Court, Lapeer, MI 48446; copies: $1.00 per page
Naturalization records: From 1843; contact County Clerk, 255 Clay, Lapeer, MI 48446; certified copies: $7.00 each
Vital records: Births and deaths from 1867, marriages from 1833; contact County Clerk; certified copies: $7.00 each
Probate records: From 1837; contact Probate Court, 255 Clay, Lapeer, MI 48446
Probate search service: no charge; copies: 25¢ per page, no minimum

*Leelanau County Courthouse
Leland, MI 49654
Phone (616) 256-9682 Register of Deeds; (616) 256-9824 County Clerk; (616) 256-9803 Deputy Probate Register
County organized 1863 from Grand Traverse County
Land records: From 1851; contact Barbara Kirt, Register of Deeds; copies: $1.00 per page
Naturalization records: From 1883 to 1929; contact Dorothy L. Wunderlich, County Clerk
Vital records: Deaths and marriages from 1867; contact County Clerk
Vital records search service: $5.00; certified copies: $5.00 for the first copy and $2.00 for each additional copy of the same document made at the same time (birth requests require proof of death and proof of heir, regardless of age)
Probate records: From 1874; contact Julie Orr, Deputy Probate Register
Probate search service: no charge; copies: 25¢ per page for photocopies, $1.00 for the first page of a certified copy and $1.00 for each additional page, no minimum

*Lenawee County Courthouse
300 North Main
Adrian, MI 49221
Phone (517) 264-4538 Register of Deeds Office; (517) 264-4599 County Clerk's Office
County organized 1822 from Indian lands
Land records: Contact Register of Deeds Office
Naturalization records; contact Lou Ann Bluntschly, County Clerk, 425 North Main Street, Adrian, MI 49221

Vital records: Births and deaths from 1867, marriages from 1852; contact County Clerk
Vital records search service: $5.00 for the first five years and $1.00 for each additional year; certified copies: $10.00 each
Probate records: Deceased estates, guardianships, secret marriages from 1827; contact Probate Court, Room 201
Probate search service: no charge; copies: $1.00 for the first page and 50¢ for each additional page, $10.00 for the first page of certified copies and $3.00 for each additional page, no minimum; "If making inquiries of both Clerk's Office and Register of Deed and Probate, send separate letters."

*Livingston County Courthouse
200 East Grand River
Howell, MI 48843-2399
Phone (517) 546-0500 County Clerk
County laid out 21 March 1833 from Shiawassee and Washtenaw counties; organized 24 March 1836 composed of the townships of Green Oak (which included Brighton), Hamburg (which included Genoa), Putnam (which included Marion), Unadilla (which included Iosco), and Howell (which included the present Oceola, Deerfield, Cohactah, Conway, Handy and Tyrone)
Land records: From 1837; contact Register of Deeds, PO Box 332, Howell, MI 48844; copies: $1.00 per page, "have tract"
Vital records: Births and deaths from 1867, marriages from 1836; contact David E. Teggerdine, County Clerk; certified copies: $5.00 for the first copy and $2.00 for each additional copy of the same record (in order to obtain births, genealogists must document direct lineage with birth certificates, death certificates or marriage licenses)
Probate records: From 1838; contact Probate Court
Probate search service: no charge; copies: $1.00 per page, no minimum

*Luce County Courthouse
East Court Street
Newberry, MI 49868
Phone (906) 293-5521
County organized 1887 from Chippewa County
Land records: From 1885
Naturalization records: Contact State Archives of Michigan, Michigan Bureau of History, Department of State, 717 West Allegan Street, Lansing, MI 48918

Vital records: Births from 4 June 1886, deaths from 8 June 1886, marriages from 14 July 1887; copies: $1.00 per page, $10.00 for the first certified copy and $3.00 for each additional certified copy of the same record
Probate records: From 1888
Probate search service: $15.00; copies: $1.00 per page, $10.00 per certified page

*Mackinac County Courthouse
100 Marley Street
Saint Ignace, MI 49781-1457
Phone (906) 643-7300
County organized 1818, original county, formerly called Michilimackinac County
Land records: Contact Dawn Nelson, Equalization Department
Naturalization records: Contact Mary Kay Temlyn, Clerk's Office
Vital records: Deaths from 1873, marriages from 1867; contact Clerk's Office; certified copies: $5.00 for the first copy and $2.00 for each additional copy of same document
Probate records: Contact Judy Ryerse
Probate search service: no charge "search only as time allows"; copies: 25¢ per page, $10.00 for the first page of certified copies and $1.00 for each additional page

*Macomb County Courthouse
40 North Main Street
Mount Clemens, MI 48043
Phone (810) 469-5120 County Clerk/ Register of Deeds; (810) 469-6927 FAX, County Clerk; (810) 469-5290 Probate Court
County organized 1818, original county
Land records: Contact Carmella Sabaugh, County Clerk and Register of Deeds
Vital records: Births and deaths from 1867 (death index only from 1889), marriages from 1819 to date; contact County Clerk and Register of Deeds; certified copies: $10.00 for the first copy and $3.00 for each additional copy of the same record; "Genealogists may inspect a particular certificate if heirship can be proved; heirship also necessary to purchase a certified copy of a deceased relative's birth registration." Deaths only from 1925; contact Eastpointe (formerly known as East Detroit).
Probate records: From 1830; contact Probate Court, 21850 Dunham Road, Mount Clemens, MI 48043
Probate search service: no charge (need specific parameters); copies: 35¢ per page from paper originals, 50¢ per page from microfilm originals, no minimum

*Manistee County Courthouse
415 Third Street
Manistee, MI 49660-1606
Phone (616) 723-3331
County organized 1855 from Wexford County
Land records: From 1856; contact Register of Deeds
Naturalization records: From 1867; contact Clerk
Vital records: From 1867; contact Clerk
Probate records: From 1880; contact Probate Staff
Probate search service: $5.00 (includes one certified copy if found); copies: $1.00 for the first copy and 25¢ for each additional copy, $1.00 minimum

*Marquette County Courthouse
232 West Baraga Avenue
Marquette, MI 49855-4710
Phone (906) 228-1525
County organized 9 March 1843 from Schoolcraft County
Land records: From the early 1800s
Naturalization records: Contact State Archives of Michigan, Michigan Bureau of History, Department of State, 717 West Allegan Street, Lansing, MI 48918
Vital records: Deaths from 1867, marriages from December 1850 (except from January 1882 to 1892)
Vital records search service: $2.00 for each additional year searched beyond three years; certified copies only: $5.00 for the first copy (includes initial three-year search) and $2.00 for each additional copy made at the same time
Probate records: From 1856

*Mason County Courthouse
Ludington, MI 49431
Phone (616) 843-8202
County organized 1855 from Ionia County
Land records: Contact Mary Kolaski, Register of Deeds
Naturalization records: Contact State Archives of Michigan, Michigan Bureau of History, Department of State, 717 West Allegan Street, Lansing, MI 48918
Vital records: Contact Ivan J. Anthony, County Clerk
Probate records: Contact Mark D. Raven, Probate Judge

*Mecosta County Courthouse
400 Elm Street
Big Rapids, MI 49307-1849
Phone (616) 592-0783
County organized 11 February 1859 from Newaygo and Osceola counties
Land records: Contact Register of Deeds

Office, PO Box 718, Big Rapids, MI 49307
Naturalization records: Contact State Archives of Michigan, Michigan Bureau of History, Department of State, 717 West Allegan Street, Lansing, MI 48918
Vital records: Births and deaths from 1867, marriages from 1859; copies: $7.00 for the first copy and $3.00 for each additional copy of the same record
Probate records: From 1859 (deceased estates, guardianships, mentally ill persons, adoption orders, poor persons, wills, juvenile records)
Probate search service: no charge; copies: $1.00 per page, $3.00 for certified copies, no minimum; "Please submit written requests."

*Menominee County Courthouse
839 Tenth Avenue
Menominee, MI 49858
Phone (906) 863-9968
County organized 1863 from Marquette County
Land records: Contact Register of Deeds; copies: $1.00 each
Naturalization records: From 1868; contact Register of Deeds; copies: $1.00 each
Vital records: Deaths and marriages from 1868; contact County Clerk; copies: $5.00 each
Probate records: Contact Probate Court
Probate search service: "They search the indexes"; copies: $5.00 for the first page, $2.00 for each additional page

*Midland County Building
220 West Ellsworth Street
Midland, MI 48640
Phone (517) 832-6739; (517) 832-6820 Register of Deeds; (517) 832-6880 Probate Court
County organized 1850 from Saginaw County
Land records: Contact Register of Deeds Office
Naturalization records: Contact County Clerk
Vital records: Deaths and marriages from 1867; contact County Clerk; copies: 50¢ for deaths and marriages, $7.00 for the first certified copy and $3.00 for each additional certified copy of the same record made at the same time (birth records available as a last resort and eligibility must be proved to obtain a certified copy)
Probate records: Contact Probate Court
No probate search service; copies: 25¢ each, $10.00 for the first page of certified copies and $1.00 for each additional page

*Missaukee County Courthouse
Lake City, MI 49651
Phone (616) 839-4967; (616) 839-2266 Probate Court
County organized 1840 from unorganized territory
Land records: From 1871; contact County Clerk and Register of Deeds
Naturalization records: From 1871; contact County Clerk and Register of Deeds
Vital records: Deaths and marriages from 1871; contact County Clerk and Register of Deeds
No vital records search service; copies (requests must include name and date): $1.00 per Xerox copy (no copies allowed from old books) or $1.00 per page from microfilm, $5.00 for the first certified copy (typed) and $2.00 for each additional certified copy; "If a mail request it is required the researchers list relationship and sign their requests.")
Probate records: From 1873; contact Probate Court
Probate search service: no charge; copies: $1.00 per page/microfilm copy

*Monroe County Courthouse
106 East First
Monroe, MI 48161-2143
Phone (313) 243-7081
County organized 1817, original county
Land records: Contact Register of Deeds
Vital records: Deaths from 1867, marriages from 1818; contact County Clerk; copies: $3.00 for the first copy and $2.00 for each additional copy of same record; "Death record is requested for proof of heirship if a birth record is requested, and staff does searching of births"
Probate records: From 1817; contact Probate Court Office
Probate search service: no charge; copies: $3.00 for the first page and $1.00 for each additional page, no minimum; "Call or write for appointment."

*Montcalm County Courthouse
Stanton, MI 48888
Phone (517) 831-5226
County organized 1831 from Isabella County; set aside as an independent political unit by the Michigan Legislature 29 March 1850
Land records: Contact Register/Abstract
Naturalization records: No naturalization records, sent to Lansing Historical Museum
Vital records: Deaths and marriages from 1867 (with proper ID, may look at a particular birth record if subject is deceased); contact County Clerk's Office; certified copies: $5.00 for the

first copy and $2.00 for each additional copy of the same record
Probate records: Contact Probate Court Office

Montmorency County Courthouse
PO Box 415
Atlanta, MI 49709
Phone (517) 785-4794
County organized 1881 from Alpena County
Vital records: Deaths and marriages from 1881; copies: $2.00 each, $5.00 for certified copies (need proper ID with picture or two other kinds without)

*Muskegon County Courthouse
990 Terrace Street
Muskegon, MI 49442-3301
Phone (616) 724-6221
County organized 1859 from Newaygo County
Land records: From 1859; contact Register of Deeds Office. Hackley Public Library has deeds and indexes to 1886 on microfilm.
Naturalization records: From 1941; contact County Clerk. Naturalization records from 1859 to 1941; contact State Archives of Michigan, Michigan Bureau of History, Department of State, 717 West Allegan Street, Lansing, MI 48918. Hackley Public Library has naturalization records from 1859 to 1906 on microfilm.
Vital records: Births (closed), deaths from 1867, marriages from 1859; contact County Clerk. Hackley Public Library has birth record index 1867-1949 and records to 1917, death record index from 1867 to 1949 and records to 1918, marriage record index from 1859 to 1949 and records to 1912 on microfilm; copies: $5.00 for the first copy and $2.00 for each additional copy of same record, $10.00 for birth records; "Must complete state-approved form upon request to establish heirship; picture ID required; Clerk's Office would prefer use of materials at Hackley before using their offices."
Probate records: From 1859; contact Probate Court Office
No probate search service; copies: 25¢ per page

*Newaygo County Building
1087 Newell Street
White Cloud, MI 49349
Phone (616) 689-7235
County organized 1840 from unorganized territory
Land records: Contact Register of Deeds
Naturalization records: Contact Circuit Court

Vital records: Deaths from 1867, marriages from 1851; contact County Clerk; certified copies: $7.00 each; "Form must be filled out (ID, etc.); for births since 1900, must show proof of death"
Probate records: Contact Probate Court

*Oakland County Courthouse
1200 North Telegraph Road
Pontiac, MI 48053-1008
Phone (313) 858-0560 Register of Deeds; (313) 858-0260
County organized 1819, original county
Land records: Contact Lynn D. Allen, County Clerk-Register of Deeds, Register of Deeds Office, 1200 North Telegraph Road, Department 480, Pontiac, MI 48341-0480
Naturalization records: From 1867 to 1985; contact Lynn D. Allen, County Clerk-Register of Deeds, County Clerk's Office, 1200 North Telegraph Road, Department 413, Pontiac, MI 48341-0413; copies: $10.00 for the first copy and $5.00 for each additional copy
Vital records: Births (unavailable to the public), deaths from 1867 (staff must do the search after 1960), marriages from 1837 (staff must do the search after 1960); contact County Clerk's Office; copies: $10.00 for the first copy and $5.00 for each additional copy. Madison Heights City has deaths from 1955. Rochester Hills City has deaths from 1985. Troy City has deaths from 1897.

*Oceana County Courthouse
PO Box 153
Hart, MI 49420
Phone (616) 873-4328
County organized 1831 from Newaygo County
Land records: From 15 January 1846; contact Joseph Merten, Register of Deeds; copies: $1.00 per page
Naturalization records: From 1856 (very sketchy); contact Phyllis Schlee, County Clerk
Vital records: Births and deaths from 1867, marriages from 1856; contact County Clerk; copies: $7.00 for the first copy and $3.00 for the second copy; "Must fill out a form and have read Procedures Governing the Inspection of Vital Records Documents, and indicate which records are sought; if birth records, must prove they are an heir and show proof of death"
Probate records: Contact Georgia Dennison, Probate Register, Probate Court, PO Box 129, Hart, MI 49420
No probate search service; copies: $1.00 per page

*Ogemaw County Courthouse
West Branch, MI 48661
Phone (517) 345-0215
County organized 1875 from Iosco County
Land records: Contact Register of Deeds
Naturalization records: From 1876; contact Clerk
Vital records: Deaths from 1876, marriages from 1887; contact Clerk; copies: 50¢ each, $5.00 for the first certified copy and $2.00 for each additional certified copy (births restricted)
Probate records: Contact Judge Eugene Turkelson

*Ontonagon County Courthouse
725 Greenland Road
Ontonagon, MI 49953-1423
Phone (906) 884-4255 Clerk/Register of Deeds
County organized 9 March 1843 from Michilimackinac and Chippewa counties
Land records: From formation; contact Register of Deeds; copies: $1.00 per page
Naturalization records: From formation; contact County Clerk
Vital records: Deaths from 12 June 1867, marriages from 9 February 1853; contact County Clerk; copies: $5.00 for the first copy and $2.00 for each additional copy made at the same time (a written statement regarding heirship is required for birth records)
Probate records: From formation; contact Probate Register
Probate search service: no charge; copies: 25¢ per page, $3.00 certified

*Osceola County Courthouse
301 West Upton Avenue
Reed City, MI 49677-1149
Phone (616) 832-5818; (616) 832-6102 County Clerk; (616) 832-6104 Vital Records
County organized 1869 from Missaukee County
Vital records; births from 1869, deaths from 1870, marriages from 1869; contact Karen J. Bluhm, County Clerk; copies: $1.00 each, $7.00 for the first certified copy and $3.00 for each additional certified copy

*Oscoda County Courthouse
PO Box 399
Mio, MI 48647
Phone (517) 826-3241
County organized 1840 from unorganized territory
Land records: Contact Equalization Department or Register of Deeds
Naturalization records: Contact County Clerk

Vital records: Deaths from July 1880, marriages from April 1881 (index books are very fragile); contact County Clerk

Vital records search service: $3.00; copies: $1.00 (photocopies not available on some vital records prior to 1934 or 1942; information may be hand-copied for some of these records), $10.00 for the first certified copy and $2.00 for each additional certified copy

Probate records: Contact Probate Court Registrar

No probate search service; certified copies: $3.00 for the first copy and $1.00 for each additional copy, no minimum

*Otsego County Courthouse
225 West Main Street
Gaylord, MI 49735-1348
Phone (517) 732-6484
County organized 1875 from Crawford County
Land records: Contact Evelyn Pratt, County Clerk and Register of Deeds, Room 203

Vital records: Deaths and marriages from 1875; contact County Clerk; copies: $5.00 for the first copy and $2.00 for each additional copy; "If a birth record is requested, a document proving death is required, unless it is obvious the person is deceased."

Probate records: Contact Probate Court

*Ottawa County Courthouse
414 Washington Street
Grand Haven, MI 49417-1443
Phone (616) 846-8310 County Clerk; (616) 846-8138 FAX, County Clerk
County organized 29 December 1837 from part of Kent County
Land records: Contact Register of Deeds, PO Box 265, Grand Haven, MI 49417

Naturalization records from 1910 to 1962; contact Daniel C. Krueger, County Clerk, Room 301

Vital records: Deaths from 1867, marriages from 1848; contact County Clerk

Vital records search service: no charge; certified copies: $10.00 for the first copy and $3.00 for each additional copy made at the same time (births open before 1908, restricted after 1908)

Probate records: Contact Probate Court, 12120 Fillmore, West Olive, MI 494601

*Presque Isle County Courthouse
151 East Huron Street
PO Box 110
Rogers City, MI 49779-1316

Phone (517) 734-3288
County organized 1840 from unorganized territory
Land records: Contact Register of Deeds Office

Naturalization records: Contact County Clerk's Office

Vital records: Deaths and marriages from 1871; contact County Clerk's Office; copies: $1.00 each, $5.00 for certified copies; "ID is requested and whether the researcher is a relative; birth record viewing requires that the record be of a deceased relative."

Probate records: Contact Probate Court Registrar

*Roscommon County Courthouse
Roscommon, MI 48653
Phone (517) 275-5931 Register of Deeds; (517) 275-5923 County Clerk; (517) 275-5221 Probate Court
County organized 1875 from Crawford County
Land records: Contact Register of Deeds, PO Box 98, Roscommon, MI 48653

Naturalization records: Contact County Clerk, PO Box 98, Roscommon, MI 48653

Vital records: Births and deaths from 1874, marriages from 1875; contact County Clerk; copies: 50¢ per page, $5.00 for the first certified copy and $2.00 for each additional certified copy of same record; "Must be able to relate facts relative to their family—discuss the research, etc.")

Probate records: Contact Probate Court, PO Box 607, Roscommon, MI 48653

No probate search service; copies: $3.00 for the first page and $1.00 for each additional page, no minimum

*Saginaw County Courthouse
111 South Michigan
Saginaw, MI 48602-2019
Phone (517) 790-5270 Register of Deeds; (517) 790-5251 County Clerk; (517) 790-5320 Probate Court
County organized 1835 from unorganized territory
Land records: Contact Register of Deeds

Naturalization records: No naturalization records

Vital records: Contact County Clerk

Probate records: Contact Probate Court; copies: $1.00 per page

*Saint Clair County Courthouse
201 McMorran Boulevard
Port Huron, MI 48060-4006
Phone (810) 985-2275 Register of Deeds; (810) 985-2200 County Clerk/ Registrar
County organized 28 March 1820, original county

Land records: From 1822 to date; contact Register of Deeds

No land records search service; copies: $1.00 each

Naturalization records: From 1864 to 1985; contact Marion Sargent, County Clerk/Registrar

Vital records: Deaths from 1880, marriages from 1833; contact County Clerk ("We do not copy records; certified copies—$5.00, 2nd copy—$2.00, same record"; require "driver's license or other pictured ID; must also fill out and sign form entitled Procedures Governing the Inspection of Vital Records Documents.")

Probate records: Contact Marylyn L. Robbins, Probate Register, Probate Office

Probate search service: no charge; copies: $1.00 each, $3.00 for the first certified copy and $1.00 for each additional certified copy; "Who, what, where, when, if possible."

*Saint Joseph County Clerk's Office
PO Box 189
Centreville, MI 49032-0189
Phone (616) 467-5602 County Clerk
County organized 1829 from Indian lands
Land records: Contact Register of Deeds, PO Box 388, Centreville, MI 49032

Naturalization records: From 1850s to 1860s; contact Pattie S. Bender, County Clerk; copies: $1.00 per page (cannot be certified)

Vital records: Births and deaths from 1867, marriages from 1830; contact County Clerk's Office

Vital records search service: $10.00 for a ten-year search (includes one copy); copies: $3.00 for each additional copy made at the same time (births are restricted to the registrant or to properly identified heirs of deceased registrants)

Probate records: Contact Probate Court, PO Box 190, Centreville, MI 49032

*Sanilac County Courthouse
60 West Sanilac Avenue
Sandusky, MI 48471-1060
Phone (313) 648-2313 Register of Deeds; (313) 648-3212 County Clerk; (313) 648-3221 Probate Court
Executive proclamation of 28 March 1820 proclaimed the county's boundaries, then attached to Oakland County and later to Saint Clair County and included part of Huron County
Land records: Contact Esther Lee, Register of Deeds Office

Naturalization records: Contact State Archives of Michigan, Michigan Bureau of History, Department of

State, 717 West Allegan Street, Lansing, MI 48918

Vital records: Births, deaths and marriages from 1867; contact Linda I. Kozakay, County Clerk; copies: $5.00 each, $10.00 for the first certified copy and $3.00 for each additional certified copy (with proper identification, births restricted to those over 100 years old)

Probate records: Contact Genevieve Hall, Probate Court, General Division

*Schoolcraft County Courthouse
300 Walnut Street
Manistique, MI 49854-1414
Phone (906) 341-3618
County organized 9 March 1843 from Michilimackinac and Chippewa counties

Vital records: Births and deaths from about 1867, marriages from 1849; contact Room 164; copies: $10.00 for the first copy and $3.00 for each additional copy (births restricted to researchers who are able to document their relationship to a deceased registrant)

*Shiawassee County Courthouse
Corunna, MI 48817
Phone (517) 743-2279
County organized 1822 from Indian lands

Land records: From 1836; contact Kaye Grubba, Register of Deeds

Naturalization records: From 1867; contact John Pajtas, County Clerk

Vital records: From 1867; contact County Clerk

Probate records: From 1836; contact Probate Judge James Clatterbaugh

Probate search service: no charge; copies: $1.00 per page

*Tuscola County Courthouse
440 North State Street
Caro, MI 48723-1555
Phone (517) 672-3840 Register of Deeds; (517) 672-3780 County Clerk; (517) 672-3850 Probate Court
County organized 1851 from Saginaw County

Land records: From 1852; contact Ginny McLaren, Register of Deeds; copies: $1.00 per page

Naturalization records: From 1852; contact Margie A. White, County Clerk; no copies

Vital records: Births (not public) and deaths from 1867, marriages from 1852; contact County Clerk; certified copies: $10.00 each, $3.00 for verification of records

Probate records: Contact W. Wallace Kent, Jr., Probate Judge

Probate search service: no charge; copies: $1.00 per page

*Van Buren County Courthouse
212 East Paw Paw Street
Paw Paw, MI 49079-1496
Phone (616) 657-8218 County Clerk; (616) 657-7573 FAX, County Clerk
County organized 1829 from unorganized territory

Land records: From 1836; contact Shirley K. Jackson, County Clerk

Naturalization records: From 1846 (very limited); contact County Clerk

Vital records: Births and deaths from 1867, marriages from 1836

Vital records search service: $1.00 per liber per name; certified copies: $7.00 for the first copy and $3.00 for each additional copy made at the same time (must present picture ID, births available only to the registrant, parents, guardian or legal representative or heir of deceased)

Probate records: From 1839; contact Probate Court

Probate search service: no charge; copies: $1.00 per page from microfilm, no minimum

*Washtenaw County Courthouse
101 East Huron
PO Box 8645
Ann Arbor, MI 48107-8645
Phone (313) 994-2500; (313) 994-2515 Land Records; (313) 994-2502 Vital Records; (313) 994-2474 Probate Court
County organized 1826, original county

Land records: From 1824; contact Peggy M. Haines, County Clerk/Register of Deeds

Naturalization records: Contact State Archives of Michigan, Michigan Bureau of History, Department of State, 717 West Allegan Street, Lansing, MI 48918

Vital records: Deaths from 1867 to date, marriages from 1833 through 1969 for genealogy; contact County Clerk/ Register of Deeds

Vital records search service: $3.00 minimum for five-years search (includes a single copy, if found); copies: $10.00 for the first copy and $3.00 for each additional copy made at the same time (all births and records from 1970 to date are confidential and require current ID, verification of legitimate interest and a certified copy of a death certificate in the case of requests for birth records)

Probate records: From 1828; contact Judge John N. Kirkendall, Probate Court, Estate Division

Probate search service: no charge; copies: $1.00 per page

*Wayne County
City-County Building
Detroit, MI 48226-3413
Phone (313) 224-0286 County Executive; (313) 224-5854 Register of Deeds; (313) 224-6262 County Clerk; (313) 224-5706 Probate Register
County organized 15 August 1796, original county

Land records: Contact Forest E. Youngblood, Register of Deeds, 101 City-County Building, Detroit, MI 48226

Vital records: Births, deaths from 1867 to 1820 and from 1920 to date for all areas except Detroit; contact Teola P. Hunter, County Clerk, 211 City-County Building, Detroit, MI 48226. Detroit City has deaths from 1930 to 1983 on microfiche (anything before or after requires staff search)

Vital records search service: $3.00; copies: $17.00 for the first certified copy and $3.50 for each additional certified copy, $11.50 for uncertified marriages (births restricted to the person named, their parent or legal guardian)

Probate records: Contact Lorraine H. Weber, Probate Register, 1305 City-County Building, Detroit, MI 48226

Probate search service: $3.00 per search; copies: $2.00 per page, no minimum

*Wexford County Courthouse
437 East Division
Cadillac, MI 49601
Phone (616) 779-9450 County Clerk; (616) 779-0292 FAX, County Clerk
County organized 1840 from unorganized territory

Land records: Contact Register of Deeds

Naturalization records: Some naturalization records from about 1850, but they are hard to find; contact Elaine L. Richardson, County Clerk, PO Box 490, Cadillac, MI 49601

Vital records: Births, deaths and marriages; contact County Clerk

Vital records search service: $5.00 for a three-year search and $2.00 for each additional year; copies: $1.00 for deaths from 1934 or marriages from 1920, $10.00 for certified copies prior to those dates, births restricted to the individual named, parents, or heirs with proof

Probate records: Contact Probate Court

No probate search service; copies: $1.00 per page, $10.00 for certified copies, no minimum

MINNESOTA

Capital: Saint Paul. Statehood: 11 May 1858 (part annexed in 1783 and part by the Louisiana Purchase, 1803, was in the Northwest Territory in 1787, Indiana Territory in 1800, and became a separate territory in 1849)

Court System

Minnesota's County and Municipal Courts were eliminated by 1987, having merged with the District Court, which has general jurisdiction and sits in each county seat. First Judicial District: Carver, Dakota, Goodhue, Le Sueur, McLeod, Scott and Sibley counties; Second Judicial District: Ramsey County; Third Judicial District: Dodge, Fillmore, Freeborn, Houston, Mower, Olmsted, Rice, Steele, Wabasha, Waseca and Winona counties; Fourth Judicial District: Hennepin County; Fifth Judicial District: Blue Earth, Brown, Cottonwood, Faribault, Jackson, Lincoln, Lyon, Martin, Murray, Nicollet, Nobles, Pipestone, Redwood, Rock and Watonwan counties; Sixth Judicial District: Carlton, Cook, Lake and Saint Louis counties; Seventh Judicial District: Becker, Benton, Clay, Douglas, Mille Lacs, Morrison, Otter Tail, Stearns, Todd and Wadena counties; Eighth Judicial District: Big Stone, Chippewa, Grant, Kandiyohi, Lac qui Parle, Meeker, Pope, Renville, Stevens, Swift, Traverse, Wilkin and Yellow Medicine counties; Ninth Judicial District: Aitkin, Beltrami, Cass, Clearwater, Crow Wing, Hubbard, Itasca, Kittson, Koochiching, Lake of the Woods, Mahnomen, Marshall, Norman, Pennington, Polk, Red Lake and Roseau counties; Tenth Judicial District: Anoka, Chisago, Isanti, Kanabec, Pine, Sherburne, Washington and Wright counties. The Court of Appeals and Supreme Court hear appeals.

Courthouses

*Aitkin County Courthouse
209 Second Street, N.W.
Aitkin, MN 56431-1257
Phone (218) 927-2102, ext. 336 County Recorder; (218) 927-2102, ext. 350 Court Administrator's Office
County organized 1857 from Cass and Itasca counties
Land records: Contact Everett Davies, County Recorder

Naturalization records: Contact Court Administrator's Office or Minnesota Historical Society Research Center, 345 Kellogg Boulevard, West, Saint Paul, MN 55102-1906
Vital records: Births and deaths; contact County Recorder. Marriages; contact Court Administrator's Office
Probate records: Contact Court Administrator's Office
Probate search service: $8.00 per hour; copies: $5.00 per document, $10.00 per certified document

Anoka County Courthouse
325 East Main Street
Anoka, MN 55303-2401
Phone (612) 421-4760
County organized 1857 from Hennepin County, annexed Manomin County in 1869
Naturalization records: Contact Minnesota Historical Society Research Center, 345 Kellogg Boulevard, West, Saint Paul, MN 55102-1906

*Becker County Courthouse
Detroit Lakes, MN 56501
Phone (218) 847-7659
County organized 1858 from Indian lands
Land records: Yes
Naturalization records: Contact Minnesota Historical Society Research Center, 345 Kellogg Boulevard, West, Saint Paul, MN 55102-1906
Vital records: Yes
Probate records: Yes
Probate search service: no charge; copies: 25¢ per page (if court order), $3.50 for the first page and 25¢ for each additional page, $5.00 for the first certified page and 25¢ for each additional certified page, no minimum

*Beltrami County Courthouse
619 Beltrami Avenue, N.W.
Bemidji, MN 56601-3041
Phone (218) 759-4170 County Recorder; (218) 759-4531 Court Administrator; (218) 759-4174 County Treasurer
County organized 1866 from unorganized territory
Land records: Contact County Recorder
Naturalization records: Contact Court Administrator or Minnesota Historical Society Research Center, 345 Kellogg Boulevard, West, Saint Paul, MN 55102-1906
Vital records: Contact County Treasurer
Probate records: Contact Court Administrator

Benton County Courthouse
531 Drew Street
Foley, MN 56329
Phone (612) 968-6254
County organized 1849, original county
Naturalization records: Contact Minnesota Historical Society Research Center, 345 Kellogg Boulevard, West, Saint Paul, MN 55102-1906

*Big Stone County Courthouse
20 S.E. Second Street
Ortonville, MN 56278-1544
Phone (612) 839-2537
County organized 1862 from Pierce County (which was abolished the same year)
Land records: Contact Recorder's Office
Naturalization records: Contact Minnesota Historical Society Research Center, 345 Kellogg Boulevard, West, Saint Paul, MN 55102-1906
Vital records: From 1881
Probate records: From 1881
Probate search service: $8.00 per hour; copies: $3.50 plus 25¢ per page, $8.00 minimum

Blue Earth County Courthouse
PO Box 8608
Mankato, MN 56002-8608
Phone (507) 625-3031
County organized 1853 from unorganized territory
Naturalization records: Contact Minnesota Historical Society Research Center, 345 Kellogg Boulevard, West, Saint Paul, MN 55102-1906

*Brown County Courthouse
PO Box 248
New Ulm, MN 56073
Phone (507) 359-7900; (507) 233-6653 County Recorder, Land Records; (507) 223-6657 County Recorder, Vital Records; (507) 233-6670 Court Administrator
County organized 1855 from Nicollet County
Land records: Contact County Recorder
Naturalization records: Contact Minnesota Historical Society Research Center, 345 Kellogg Boulevard, West, Saint Paul, MN 55102-1906
Vital records: Births and deaths from 1870 (prior records destroyed by fire); contact County Recorder
Probate records: Contact Court Administrator
Probate search service: $10.00 per hour (supply dates to be searched); copies: $5.00 each, $10.00 for certified copies, $10.00 minimum

*Carlton County Courthouse
PO Box 130
Carlton, MN 55718-0130
Phone (218) 384-4281
*County organized 1857 from Pine
County*
Land records: Contact Recorder
Naturalization records: Contact Clerk of
Court or Minnesota Historical Society
Research Center, 345 Kellogg
Boulevard, West, Saint Paul, MN
55102-1906
Vital records: Contact Clerk of Court
Probate records: Contact Clerk of Court

Carver County Courthouse
600 East Fourth Street
Chaska, MN 55318-2158
Phone (612) 448-3435
*County organized 1855 from Hennepin
County*
Naturalization records: Contact
Minnesota Historical Society
Research Center, 345 Kellogg
Boulevard, West, Saint Paul, MN
55102-1906

*Cass County Courthouse
Walker, MN 56484
Phone (218) 547-3300
County organized 1851, original county
Land records: From about 1887; contact
District Court; copies: $1.00 per page,
$1.00 per page for certified copies,
$3.00 minimum
Naturalization records: Only filing cards;
contact County Clerk or Minnesota
Historical Society Research Center,
345 Kellogg Boulevard, West, Saint
Paul, MN 55102-1906
Vital records: Births, deaths and
marriages from 1900 (only a few
recorded before 1900); copies: $11.00
for births, $8.00 for marriages and
deaths
Probate records: From 1896
Probate search service: $5.00; copies:
$3.50 for the first page and 25¢ for
each additional page, $5.00 for the
first certified page and 25¢ for each
additional certified page; "Any
research is a minimum of $5.00 per
hour."

*Chippewa County Courthouse
Montevideo, MN 56265
Phone (612) 269-7774
*County organized 1870 from Pierce
County (which was abolished in
1862)*
Land records: From 1870; contact
County Recorder
Naturalization records: Contact
Minnesota Historical Society
Research Center, 345 Kellogg
Boulevard, West, Saint Paul, MN
55102-1906

Vital records: Births, deaths and
marriages from 1870; contact Gail
Erickson, County Recorder; copies:
$11.00 for births, $8.00 for deaths and
marriages
Probate records: From 1870; contact
Probate Registrar, Court
Administrator's Office
Probate search service: $10.00 per hour
("If it's just a few names, there are no
charges"); "Please give us as much
information on the parties as they
have (father's name, mother's *maiden*
name, etc.)"

*Chisago County Courthouse
PO Box 126
Center City, MN 55012
Phone (612) 257-1300
*County organized 1851 from
Washington County*
Land records: Contact County Recorder's
Office
Naturalization records: Contact
Minnesota Historical Society
Research Center, 345 Kellogg
Boulevard, West, Saint Paul, MN
55102-1906
Vital records: Births and deaths from
1870, marriages from 1852; contact
County Court Administrator, Vital
Statistics Division; copies: $11.00 for
births, $8.00 for deaths and marriages
Probate records: From 1864; contact
County Court Administrator,
Genealogy Division
Probate search service: $10.00 per hour
for genealogy; copies: $3.50 for the
first page and 25¢ for each additional
page, $5.00 for the first certified page
and 25¢ for each additional certified
page; "Payment must be received with
request."

*Clay County Courthouse
PO Box 280
Moorhead, MN 56560
Phone (218) 299-5006
*County organized 9 March 1862; name
changed from Breckenridge County
in 1862*
Land records: Contact County Recorder
Naturalization records: Contact
Minnesota Historical Society
Research Center, 345 Kellogg
Boulevard, West, Saint Paul, MN
55102-1906
Vital records: Contact County Recorder;
copies: $11.00 for births, $8.00 for
deaths and marriages
Probate records: Contact Court
Administrator
Probate search service: no charge if
approximate year is given; copies:
$5.00 per document, $10.00 per
certified document

Clearwater County Courthouse
Bagley, MN 56621
Phone (218) 694-6177
*County organized 1902 from Beltrami
County*
Naturalization records: Contact
Minnesota Historical Society
Research Center, 345 Kellogg
Boulevard, West, Saint Paul, MN
55102-1906

*Cook County Courthouse
211 West Second Street
PO Box 1150
Grand Marais, MN 55604
Phone (218) 387-2282
*County organized 1874 from Lake
County*
Land records: Contact County Recorder
Naturalization records: Contact
Minnesota Historical Society
Research Center, 345 Kellogg
Boulevard, West, Saint Paul, MN
55102-1906
Vital records: From 1900; contact Court
Administrator
Vital records search service: $10.00 per
hour; copies: $11.00 for certified
births, $8.00 for certified deaths and
marriages and uncertified births
Probate records: From 1896; contact
Court Administrator
Probate search service: $10.00 per hour;
copies: $5.00 each, $10.00 for
certified copies

Cottonwood County Courthouse
900 Third Avenue
Windom, MN 56101-1645
Phone (507) 831-1905
*County organized 1857 from Brown
County*
Naturalization records: Contact
Minnesota Historical Society
Research Center, 345 Kellogg
Boulevard, West, Saint Paul, MN
55102-1906

*Crow Wing County Courthouse
Brainerd, MN 56401
Phone (218) 828-3970
*County organized 1857 from Cass and
Aitkin counties*
Land records: Contact County Recorder
Naturalization records: Contact
Minnesota Historical Society
Research Center, 345 Kellogg
Boulevard, West, Saint Paul, MN
55102-1906
Vital records: Contact County Treasurer
Probate records: Contact Court
Administrator
No probate search service; copies: $5.00
per document, $10.00 per certified
document

*Dakota County Government Center
1560 Highway 55 West
Hastings, MN 55033-2343
Phone (612) 438-4295; (612) 438-4319
Vital Statistics Department
County organized 1849, original county,
formerly called Dakotah County
Naturalization records: Contact
Minnesota Historical Society
Research Center, 345 Kellogg
Boulevard, West, Saint Paul, MN
55102-1906
Vital records: Births, deaths and
marriages from 1870, with a very few
marriages before 1870; contact Vital
Statistics Department
Vital records search service: $10.00 per
hour; copies: $11.00 for certified
copies of births, $8.00 for certified or
uncertified copies of deaths and
marriages or uncertified copies of
births, or for verification of
information; make checks payable to
Dakota County Treasurer-Auditor
Probate records: Contact District Court,
Division 1
No probate search service; copies: $3.50
for the first page and 25¢ for each
additional page, $5.00 for the first
certified page and 25¢ for each
additional certified page, $3.50
minimum

*Dodge County Courthouse
PO Box 38
Mantorville, MN 55955
Phone (507) 635-2321
County organized 1855 from Olmstead
County
Land records: Contact Donald O. Nyseth
Naturalization records: Contact Pauline
(Polly) Huse or Minnesota Historical
Society Research Center, 345 Kellogg
Boulevard, West, Saint Paul, MN
55102-1906
Vital records: Contact Pauline Huse
Probate records: Contact Pauline Huse
Probate search service: no charge unless
lengthy; copies: 25¢ per page for the
first ten pages and 10¢ for each
additional page, no minimum

*Douglas County Courthouse
305 Eighth Avenue West
Alexandria, MN 56308-1759
Phone (612) 762-2381
County organized 1858 from Todd
County
Land records: Contact County Recorder's
Office
Naturalization records: Contact
Minnesota Historical Society
Research Center, 345 Kellogg
Boulevard, West, Saint Paul, MN
55102-1906
Vital records: Contact County Recorder's
Office

Probate records: Contact Court
Administrator's Office
Probate search service: no charge;
copies: variable from 50¢ to $3.50,
50¢ minimum

*Faribault County Courthouse
North Main—PO Box 130
Blue Earth, MN 56013
Phone (507) 526-5142
County organized 1855 from Blue Earth
County
Land records: Contact Ms. Nancy Huff,
Recorder of Deeds
Naturalization records: From 1880s to
1920s; contact Court Administrator or
Minnesota Historical Society
Research Center, 345 Kellogg
Boulevard, West, Saint Paul, MN
55102-1906
Vital records: Contact Court
Administrator
Probate records: Contact Court
Administrator
Probate search service: no charge;
copies: $3.50 plus 25¢ per page, no
minimum

*Fillmore County Courthouse
101 Fillmore Street
Preston, MN 55965
Phone (507) 765-4701
County organized 1853, original county
Land records: Contact County Recorder's
Office
Naturalization records: Contact
Minnesota Historical Society
Research Center, 345 Kellogg
Boulevard, West, Saint Paul, MN
55102-1906
Vital records: Contact County Auditor's
Office; certified copies: $11.00 for
births, $8.00 for deaths and marriages
Probate records: Contact Court
Administrator's Office
Probate search service: no charge for
index search but a 50¢ charge for each
register needed

*Freeborn County Courthouse
411 South Broadway
Albert Lea, MN 56007
Phone (507) 377-5153
County organized 1855 from Blue Earth
and Rice counties
Land records: Contact County Recorder
Naturalization records: Contact
Minnesota Historical Society
Research Center, 345 Kellogg
Boulevard, West, Saint Paul, MN
55102-1906
Vital records: From 1870 to date; contact
Court Administrator
Probate records: Contact Court
Administrator

*Goodhue County Courthouse
Red Wing, MN 55066
Phone (612) 385-3006 County Assessor;
(612) 385-3148 County Recorder;
(612) 385-3051 Court Administrator
County organized with indefinite
boundaries on 5 March 1853 from
Wabasha County. After the
government survey of the greater
part of the county was completed, the
boundaries were defined in 1854.
The Half Breed Tract, however, had
not been included in the survey, and
it was later found that the starting
point of the boundaries described in
the act was in Wisconsin, a few miles
northeast of Frontenac. In general,
the boundary was as at present,
except that Central Point Township
was excluded, and the line between
Welch Township in Goodhue County
and Douglas Township in Dakota
County was extended due north to
the Mississippi River a few miles
southeast of Hastings. The present
boundaries were defined in 1855. A
bill was introduced in the Legislature
in 1858 to detach part of Goodhue,
Olmsted and Wabasha counties and
to form a new county to be called
Zumbrota. A committee to which it
was referred made an unfavorable
report, and the bill was never
brought to a vote. In 1861 the voters
defeated a proposition to attach that
part of Cannon Falls Township north
of the Cannon River to Dakota
County.
Land records: Contact Bradford R.
Johnson, County Assessor
Naturalization records: Contact
Minnesota Historical Society
Research Center, 345 Kellogg
Boulevard, West, Saint Paul, MN
55102-1906
Vital records: Contact Craig Anderson,
County Recorder
Probate records: Contact Lawrence H.
Peterson, Court Administrator
No probate search service; copies: 25¢
per page, no minimum

*Grant County Courthouse
Elbow Lake, MN 56531-0059
Phone (218) 685-4825
County organized 1868 from Stearns
County
Land records: Contact County Recorder
Naturalization records: Contact
Minnesota Historical Society
Research Center, 345 Kellogg
Boulevard, West, Saint Paul, MN
55102-1906
Vital records: Contact Court
Administrator
Probate records: Contact Court
Administrator

Probate search service: $2.00 per name; copies: $5.00

*Hennepin County Government Center
300 South Sixth Street
Minneapolis, MN 55487-0999
Phone (612) 348-3051 County Recorder; (612) 348-3070 Registrar of Titles; (612) 348-2791 Vital Records Section; (612) 348-3244 Clerk of Probate Court
County organized 1852, original county
Land records: Contact Property Tax and Public Records Department, County Recorder (Abstract), A-803 or Registrar of Titles (Torrens), A-803
Naturalization records: Contact Minnesota Historical Society Research Center, 345 Kellogg Boulevard, West, Saint Paul, MN 55102-1906
Vital records: Births and deaths, marriage licenses, ministerial credentials and notary filings; contact Vital Records Section, Public Service Level
Probate records: On microfiche from 1859; contact Mary Hawkinson, Clerk of Probate Court, C-400, Probate Court
Probate search service: no charge; copies: 50¢ per page, $7.00 for certified copies (includes nine pages), no minimum

*Houston County Courthouse
304 South Marshall Street
Caledonia, MN 55921-1324
Phone (507) 724-5211; (507) 724-5813 County Recorder; (507) 724-5806 Court Administrator; (507) 724-5550 FAX Court Administrator
County organized 1854 from Fillmore County
Land records: Contact Daryl A. Tessmer, County Recorder, PO Box 29, Caledonia, MN 55921-0029
Land records search service: $20.00 per hour; copies: 50¢ per page, $1.00 per certified page, $5.00 minimum
Naturalization records: Contact Minnesota Historical Society Research Center, 345 Kellogg Boulevard, West, Saint Paul, MN 55102-1906
Vital records: Births, deaths and marriages; contact County Recorder
Vital records search service: $20.00 per hour; copies: $11.00 for births, $8.00 for deaths
Probate records: Contact Darlene L. Larson, Court Administrator
Probate search service: $10.00 per hour; certified copies: $5.00 per document (includes search), $10.00 per certified document (includes search)

*Hubbard County Courthouse
Court Street
Park Rapids, MN 56470-1483
Phone (218) 732-3196 General Information/Auditor's Office; (218) 732-3552 Recorder's Office; (218) 732-5286 Court Administrator
County organized 1883 from Cass County
Land records: Contact Kathy Rossi, Recorder
Naturalization records: Contact Minnesota Historical Society Research Center, 345 Kellogg Boulevard, West, Saint Paul, MN 55102-1906
Vital records: Contact Recorder
Probate records: Contact LuAnn Bolton, Court Administrator

*Isanti County Courthouse
237 S.W. Second Avenue
Cambridge, MN 55008-1536
Phone (612) 689-1191 County Recorder; (612) 689-2292 County Administrator
County organized 1857 from Anoka County
Land records: From 1860s; contact County Recorder
Naturalization records: Contact Minnesota Historical Society Research Center, 345 Kellogg Boulevard, West, Saint Paul, MN 55102-1906
Vital records: From 1870s; contact Court Administrator; copies: $11.00 for births, $8.00 for deaths and marriages
Probate records: From 1873; contact County Administrator
Probate search service: $10.00 per hour; copies: depends on document length; $2.50 minimum for name search

*Itasca County Courthouse
123 Fourth Street, N.E.
Grand Rapids, MN 55744
Phone (218) 327-2870
County organized 1850, original county
Naturalization records: Contact Minnesota Historical Society Research Center, 345 Kellogg Boulevard, West, Saint Paul, MN 55102-1906
Vital records: Births, deaths and marriages from late 1890s; contact Court Administrator
Probate records: From late 1890s; contact Court Administrator
Probate search service: no charge unless very large request; copies: $5.00 per document, $10.00 per certified document

*Jackson County Courthouse
Jackson, MN 56143
Phone (507) 847-4400; (507) 847-2566 Probate

County organized 1857 from unorganized lands
Land records: From 1865; contact County Recorder
Naturalization records: Contact Minnesota Historical Society Research Center, 345 Kellogg Boulevard, West, Saint Paul, MN 55102-1906
Vital records: Births, deaths and marriages from 1870; contact David E. Johnson, Court Administrator, PO Box G, Jackson County Courthouse, Jackson, MN 56143
Probate records: From 1867
Probate search service: no charge; copies: $5.00 per document, $10.00 for certified copies

*Kanabec County Courthouse
18 North Vine
Mora, MN 55051-1342
Phone (612) 679-1022
County organized 1858 from Pine County
Land records: Yes
Naturalization records: Contact Minnesota Historical Society Research Center, 345 Kellogg Boulevard, West, Saint Paul, MN 55102-1906
Vital records: Yes
Probate records: Yes
Probate search service: $10.00 per hour; copies: variable, $10.00 minimum

*Kandiyohi County Courthouse
(505 West Becker, Willmar, MN 56201— location)
PO Box 736 (mailing address)
Willmar, MN 56210
Phone (612) 231-6223 County Recorder and Office of Vital Statistics
County organized 1858 from Meeker County, annexed Monongalia County in November 1870
Land records: From the mid 1850s; Contact Julie Gravley, County Recorder and Office of Vital Statistics; copies: 50¢ each
Naturalization records: Contact Minnesota Historical Society Research Center, 345 Kellogg Boulevard, West, Saint Paul, MN 55102-1906
Vital records: Births and deaths from the 1870s, marriages from the 1860s; contact County Recorder and Office of Vital Statistics; copies: $11.00 for births (except "confidential" births under 100 years old, which require the mother's permission), $8.00 for deaths and marriages

*Kittson County Courthouse
Hallock, MN 56728

Phone (218) 843-3632 Deputy Court
Administrator or Registrar
*County organized 8 April 1879 from
unorganized lands; name changed
from Pembina County in 1878*
Land records: Contact County Recorder,
PO Box 639, Hallock, MN 56728
Naturalization records: Contact
Minnesota Historical Society
Research Center, 345 Kellogg
Boulevard, West, Saint Paul, MN
55102-1906
Vital records: Contact Bart Johnson,
Deputy Court Administrator, PO Box
39, Hallock, MN 56728; certified
copies: $11.00 for births, $8.00 for
deaths and marriages
Probate records: Contact Jennifer
Boychuk, Registrar, PO Box 39,
Hallock, MN 56728
Probate search service: no charge;
copies: $5.00 each, $10.00 per
certified copy

*Koochiching County Courthouse
715 Fourth Street
International Falls, MN 56649
Phone (218) 283-6290; (218) 283-6260
Clerk of Court
*County organized 1906 from Itasca
County*
Land records: Contact Pam LaGoo,
County Recorder
Naturalization records: Contact Terry
Carew, Clerk of Court
Vital records: Contact Clerk of Court
Probate records: Contact Judge Peter
Hemstad or Secretary Mary Mahle
No probate search service; copies: 25¢
each, $5.00 per certified copy, no
minimum

*Lac qui Parle County Courthouse
600 Sixth Street
Madison, MN 56256-1233
Phone (612) 598-7444; (612) 598-3536
Court Administrator
*County organized 1863 north of the
Minnesota River, disestablished in
1868, then recreated in 1871 south of
the river*
Land records: Contact County Recorder's
Office, PO Box 132, Madison, MN
56256
Naturalization records: Contact
Minnesota Historical Society
Research Center, 345 Kellogg
Boulevard, West, Saint Paul, MN
55102-1906
Vital records: Contact Court
Administrator, PO Box 36, Madison,
MN 56256; copies: $11.00 for births,
$8.00 for deaths and marriages;
"Individuals may search the marriage
and death records, but do not have
access to births."

Probate records: Contact Court
Administrator
Probate search service: $10.00 per hour;
copies: $3.50 for the first page and
25¢ for each additional page, $5.00
for the first certified page and 25¢ for
each additional page, $2.50 minimum
"if our office searches records."

*Lake County Courthouse
601 Third Avenue
Two Harbors, MN 55616
Phone (218) 834-8311 County Recorder;
(218) 834-8330 Court Administrator;
(218) 834-8397 FAX, Court
Administrator; (218) 834-5581
*County organized 1856; name changed
from Doty County*
Land records: Contact County Recorder
Naturalization records: Contact
Minnesota Historical Society
Research Center, 345 Kellogg
Boulevard, West, Saint Paul, MN
55102-1906
Vital records: Births from 1888 to date,
deaths and marriages from 1891 to
date; contact Larry J. Saur, Court
Administrator; copies: $8.00 for
uncertified copies of births or certified
copies of deaths and marriages,
$11.00 for certified copies of births
Probate records: Contact Court
Administrator
Probate search service: $10.00 per hour;
copies: $5.00 per document, $10.00
per certified document

***Lake of the Woods County
Courthouse**
PO Box 808
Baudette, MN 56623-0808
Phone (218) 634-2836; (218) 634-1902
County Recorder; (218) 634-1451
Court Administrator (Vital Records);
(218) 634-1388 Court Administrator
(Probate)
*County organized 1923 from Beltrami
County*
Land records: Contact County Recorder
Naturalization records: Contact
Minnesota Historical Society
Research Center, 345 Kellogg
Boulevard, West, Saint Paul, MN
55102-1906
Vital records: Contact Court
Administrator
Probate records: From January 1923;
contact Court Administrator
Probate search service: $10.00 per hour;
copies: $5.00 for the first page and
25¢ for each additional page, no
minimum

*Le Sueur County Courthouse
PO Box 10
Le Center, MN 56057-0010
Phone (612) 357-2251 County Recorder

*County organized 1853 from
unorganized lands*
Land records: Contact David A. Sexe,
County Recorder, 88 South Park
Avenue, Le Center, MN 56057-1620
Land records search service: $5.00 per
hour; copies: 50¢ per page (from
microfiche originals), $1.00 per page
(plats), $1.00 per certified copy, plus
$1.00 minimum for postage
Naturalization records: Contact
Minnesota Historical Society
Research Center, 345 Kellogg
Boulevard, West, Saint Paul, MN
55102-1906
Vital records: Contact County Recorder's
Office; certified copies: $11.00 for
births, $8.00 for deaths and marriages
Probate records: Contact Court
Administrator
Probate search service: $8.00 per hour;
copies: $5.00 each, $10.00 for
certified copies

Lincoln County Courthouse
PO Box 29
Ivanhoe, MN 56142
Phone (507) 694-1529
*County organized 1873 from Lyon
County*
Naturalization records: Contact
Minnesota Historical Society
Research Center, 345 Kellogg
Boulevard, West, Saint Paul, MN
55102-1906

*Lyon County Courthouse
607 West Main
Marshall, MN 56258-3021
Phone (507) 537-6728
*County organized 1871 from Yellow
Medicine County*
Land records: Contact Recorder
Naturalization records: Contact Court
Administrator or Minnesota Historical
Society Research Center, 345 Kellogg
Boulevard, West, Saint Paul, MN
55102-1906
Vital records: Contact Court
Administrator
Probate records: Contact Court
Administrator
No probate search service; copies: $3.50
for the first page and 25¢ for each
additional page, $5.00 for the first
certified page and 25¢ for each
additional certified page, no
minimum; "Records destroyed by fire
1870–1874."

*Mahnomen County Courthouse
PO Box 379
Mahnomen, MN 56557-0379
Phone (218) 935-5669
*County organized 1906 from Norman
County*

Land records: Yes
Naturalization records: Contact
    Minnesota Historical Society
    Research Center, 345 Kellogg
    Boulevard, West, Saint Paul, MN
    55102-1906
Vital records: Yes
Probate records: Yes

*Marshall County Courthouse
208 East Collin Avenue
Warren, MN 56762-1693
Phone (218) 745-4851
County organized 1879 from Kittson
County
Land records: From 1879; contact
    Recorder's Office
Naturalization records: From 1883 to
    1965; contact Court Administrator's
    Office
Vital records: From 1883; contact Court
    Administrator's Office
Probate records: From 1883; contact
    Court Administrator's Office
Probate search service: no charge;
    copies: $3.50 for the first page and
    25¢ for each additional page, $5.00
    for the first certified page and 25¢ for
    each additional certified page; "Give
    name and year."

Martin County Courthouse
201 Lake Avenue
Fairmont, MN 56031
Phone (507) 238-3214
County organized 1857 from Faribault
County
Naturalization records: Contact
    Minnesota Historical Society
    Research Center, 345 Kellogg
    Boulevard, West, Saint Paul, MN
    55102-1906

*McLeod County Courthouse
830 11th East
Glencoe, MN 55336-2216
Phone (612) 864-5551
County organized 1856 from Carver
County
Land records: From 1856; contact
    Recorder's Office
Naturalization records: Contact
    Minnesota Historical Society
    Research Center, 345 Kellogg
    Boulevard, West, Saint Paul, MN
    55102-1906
Vital records: Births and deaths from
    1870, marriages from 1865; contact
    Recorder's Office
Probate records: From 1865; contact
    Court Administrator, Attn: Probate
    Clerk
Probate search service: $10.00 per hour;
    copies: $5.00 per document, $10.00
    per certified document

*Meeker County Courthouse
325 North Sibley Avenue
Litchfield, MN 55355
Phone (612) 693-2458; (612) 693-6112
    County Recorder or Court
    Administrator
County organized 1856 from Wright
County
Land records: Contact Elaine Lenhard,
    County Recorder
Naturalization records: Index only;
    contact County Clerk or Minnesota
    Historical Society Research Center,
    345 Kellogg Boulevard, West, Saint
    Paul, MN 55102-1906
Vital records: Births and deaths from
    1870, marriages from 1869; contact
    Allan Knutson, County Treasurer
Vital records search service: $10.00 per
    hour; certified copies: $11.00 for
    births, $8.00 for deaths and marriages
Probate records: Contact Court
    Administrator
No probate search service; copies: $1.00
    per page, $5.00 for the first certified
    page and 25¢ for each additional
    certified page

*Mille Lacs County Courthouse
635 Second Street, S.E.
Milaca, MN 56353-1305
Phone (612) 983-2561
County organized 1857 from Kanabec
County
Land records: Yes
Naturalization records: Contact
    Minnesota Historical Society
    Research Center, 345 Kellogg
    Boulevard, West, Saint Paul, MN
    55102-1906
Vital records: Yes
Probate records: Yes
No probate search service; copies: $5.00
    for the first page and 25¢ for each
    additional page, $5.00 minimum

Monongalia County
(see Kandiyohi County)

*Morrison County Administration
Buliding-Government Center
213 S.E. First Avenue
Little Falls, MN 56345-3196
Phone (612) 632-0145 County Recorder;
    (612) 632-0139 FAX, County
    Recorder
County organized 1856 from Benton
and Stearns counties
Land records: From 1860 (early years
    sketchy); contact Elda Mae (Bunny)
    Johnston, County Recorder
Land records search service: $20.00 per
    hour; copies: $1.00 per page in
    person, $2.00 plus SASE if mailed out
Naturalization records: Contact
    Minnesota Historical Society

Research Center, 345 Kellogg
    Boulevard, West, Saint Paul, MN
    55102-1906
Vital records: Births, deaths and
    marriages from 1870; contact County
    Recorder
Vital records search service: $20.00 per
    hour by mail; certified copies: $10.00
    for births, $8.00 for deaths and
    marriages
Probate records: From 1857; contact
    Linda Sinotte, Court Administrator's
    Office
Probate search service: $10.00 per hour;
    copies: 50¢ per page, no minimum

*Mower County Courthouse
201 First Street, N.E.
Austin, MN 55912
Phone (507) 437-9465
County organized 1855 from Fillmore
County
Land records: Contact County Recorder
Naturalization records: Contact
    Minnesota Historical Society
    Research Center, 345 Kellogg
    Boulevard, West, Saint Paul, MN
    55102-1906
Vital records: Contact County Recorder;
    copies: $11.00 for births, $8.00 for
    deaths
Probate records: Contact Court
    Administrator
No probate search service; copies: $3.50
    plus 25¢ per page, no minimum

*Murray County Courthouse
2500 28th Street
Slayton, MN 56172
Phone (507) 836-6148
County organized 1875 from Lyon
County
Land records: Contact Recorder's Office
Naturalization records: Contact
    Minnesota Historical Society
    Research Center, 345 Kellogg
    Boulevard, West, Saint Paul, MN
    55102-1906
Vital records: Contact Treasurer's Office
Probate records: Contact Clerk of Court's
    Office

*Nicollet County Courthouse
510 South Minnesota
Saint Peter, MN 56082-2508
Phone (507) 931-6800; (507) 931-9220
    FAX
County organized 1853 from
unorganized lands
Land records: Contact Kathy Conlon,
    Recorder's Office
Naturalization records: Contact
    Recorder's Office or Minnesota
    Historical Society Research Center,
    345 Kellogg Boulevard, West, Saint
    Paul, MN 55102-1906

Vital records: From 1870; contact Court Administrator's Office; copies: $11.00 for births, $8.00 for deaths and marriages

Probate records: From 1870; contact Recorder's Office

Probate search service: $10.00 per hour; certified copies: $5.00 each

Nobles County Courthouse

Worthington, MN 56187

Phone (507) 372-8263

County organized 1857 from Jackson County

Naturalization records: Contact Minnesota Historical Society Research Center, 345 Kellogg Boulevard, West, Saint Paul, MN 55102-1906

Norman County Courthouse

16 East Third Avenue

Ada, MN 56510-1362

Phone (218) 784-2101

County organized 1881 from Polk County

Naturalization records: Contact Minnesota Historical Society Research Center, 345 Kellogg Boulevard, West, Saint Paul, MN 55102-1906

*Olmsted County Government Center

151 Fourth Street, S.E.

Rochester, MN 55904-3710

Phone (507) 287-1444 County Recorder; (507) 285-8363 Court Administrator; (507) 285-8996 FAX, Court Administrator

County organized 1855 from unorganized lands

Land records: From 1855; contact County Recorder

Land records search service: $50.00 minimum, prepaid; copies: $1.00 per page

Naturalization records: Contact Minnesota Historical Society Research Center, 345 Kellogg Boulevard, West, Saint Paul, MN 55102-1906

Vital records: Births and deaths from 1870, marriages from 1855; contact County Recorder

Probate records: From about 1900; contact Jeanne A. Haben, Court Administrator, Fifth Floor

Probate search service: $5.00 per name for probate or judgment search, $4.00 per name for probate claim search; copies: $5.00 per document, $10.00 per document for certified copies; "All fees must be paid in advance; no searches done by telephone."

*Otter Tail County Courthouse

Junius Avenue

Fergus Falls, MN 56537

Phone (218) 739-2271, ext. 245

County organized 1858 from Pembina and Cass counties

Land records: From 1870; contact Wendy L. Metcalf, County Recorder, PO Box 867, Fergus Falls, MN 56538-0867; copies: $2.00 each

Naturalization records: Contact Minnesota Historical Society Research Center, 345 Kellogg Boulevard, West, Saint Paul, MN 55102-1906

Vital records: From 1870; contact County Recorder; copies: $11.00 for births, $8.00 for deaths and marriages

Probate records: Contact Court Administrator's Office, Probate Division, PO Box 417, Fergus Falls, MN 56537

No probate search service; copies: $3.50 plus 25¢ per page per document

*Pennington County Courthouse

Thief River Falls, MN 56701

Phone (218) 681-2522 County Recorder; (218) 681-2407 Court Administrator

County organized 1910 from Red Lake County

Land records: Contact County Recorder, PO Box 616, Thief River Falls, MN 56701

Naturalization records: Contact Minnesota Historical Society Research Center, 345 Kellogg Boulevard, West, Saint Paul, MN 55102-1906 or Barbara Beito, Court Administrator, PO Box 619, Thief River Falls, MN 56701 ("Records are at the Minnesota Historical Society, but I have index.")

Vital records: Contact Court Administrator

Probate records: Contact Court Administrator

Probate search service: no charge; copies: $5.00 each, $10.00 for certified copies

Pine County Courthouse

Pine City, MN 55063

Phone (612) 629-6781

County organized 1856 from unorganized lands, annexed Buchanan County in 1861

Naturalization records: Contact Minnesota Historical Society Research Center, 345 Kellogg Boulevard, West, Saint Paul, MN 55102-1906

*Pipestone County Courthouse

416 South Hiawatha Avenue

Pipestone, MN 56164-1566

Phone (507) 825-4494

County organized 1857 from Murray County; name changed from Rock County in 1862

Land records: From 1885; contact Mary Ann De Groot, County Recorder

Naturalization records: Contact Minnesota Historical Society Research Center, 345 Kellogg Boulevard, West, Saint Paul, MN 55102-1906

Vital records: From 1877; contact County Recorder

Probate records: From 1880; contact Linda Delany, Court Administrator's Office

Probate search service: no charge; copies: $3.50 for the first page and 25¢ for each additional page, $3.50 minimum

Polk County Courthouse

Crookston, MN 56716

Phone (218) 281-2332

County organized 1858 from Indian lands

Naturalization records: Contact Minnesota Historical Society Research Center, 345 Kellogg Boulevard, West, Saint Paul, MN 55102-1906

*Pope County Courthouse

Glenwood, MN 56334

Phone (612) 634-5301

County organized 1862 from Pierce County (which was abolished the same year)

Land records: Contact Recorder's Office

Naturalization records: Contact Minnesota Historical Society Research Center, 345 Kellogg Boulevard, West, Saint Paul, MN 55102-1906

Vital records: From 1870

Probate records: From 1870

Probate search service: $10.00; copies: $3.50 each, $5.00 per certified copy, no minimum

Ramsey County Courthouse

Saint Paul, MN 55102

Phone (612) 298-5980

County organized 1849, original county

Naturalization records: Contact Minnesota Historical Society Research Center, 345 Kellogg Boulevard, West, Saint Paul, MN 55102-1906

*Red Lake County Courthouse

Red Lake Falls, MN 56750

Phone (218) 253-2997 County Recorder; (218) 253-4281 Court Administrator

County organized 1896 from Polk County

Land records: Contact Jerry Thibert, County Recorder

Naturalization records: Contact Minnesota Historical Society Research Center, 345 Kellogg Boulevard, West, Saint Paul, MN 55102-1906

Vital records: Contact County Recorder

Probate records: Contact Duane Dargon, Court Administrator; copies: $5.00 per document, $10.00 per certified document

Redwood County Courthouse
PO Box 130
Redwood Falls, MN 56283-0130
Phone (507) 637-8325
County organized 1862 from Brown County
Naturalization records: Contact Minnesota Historical Society Research Center, 345 Kellogg Boulevard, West, Saint Paul, MN 55102-1906

*Renville County Courthouse
500 East DePue Avenue
Olivia, MN 56277-1396
Phone (612) 523-2071; (612) 523-1000 County Recorder's Office; (612) 523-2080 Court Administrator's Office
County organized 1855 from unorganized lands
Land records: Contact Auditor's Office and Registrar of Titles
Naturalization records: Contact Ellen Smith, County Recorder's Office or Minnesota Historical Society Research Center, 345 Kellogg Boulevard, West, Saint Paul, MN 55102-1906
Vital records: Contact County Recorder's Office
Probate records: Contact Joanne Erickson, Court Administrator's Office
Probate search service: no charge; copies: $5.00 each, $10.00 for certified copies

*Rice County Courthouse
218 N.W. Third Street
Faribault, MN 55021-5146
Phone (507) 332-6100
County organized 1853 from Nobles County
Naturalization records: Contact Minnesota Historical Society Research Center, 345 Kellogg Boulevard, West, Saint Paul, MN 55102-1906
Vital records: Births and deaths from 1870, marriages from 1856; contact Recorder
Probate records: From 1870s; contact Court Administrator

Probate search service: $10.00 per hour, $2.50 minimum; copies: $3.50 for the first page and 25¢ for each additional page, $5.00 for the first certified page and 25¢ for each additional certified page

*Rock County Courthouse
Luverne, MN 56156
Phone (507) 283-9501
County organized 1857 from Nobles County; name changed from Pipestone County in 1862
Land records: Contact Jere Ohme, County Recorder
Naturalization records: Contact Anna Mae Huiskes, Court Administrator or Minnesota Historical Society Research Center, 345 Kellogg Boulevard, West, Saint Paul, MN 55102-1906
Vital records: Contact Court Administrator
Probate records: Contact Court Administrator
Probate search service: $8.00 per hour; copies: $5.00 each; $10.00 for certified copies

Roseau County Courthouse
216 Center Street, West
Roseau, MN 56751-1494
Phone (218) 463-2541
County organized 1894 from Kittson County
Naturalization records: Contact Minnesota Historical Society Research Center, 345 Kellogg Boulevard, West, Saint Paul, MN 55102-1906

*Saint Louis County Courthouse
100 North Fifth Avenue West
Duluth, MN 55802
Phone (218) 726-2438 Court Administrator
County organized 1855 from Lake County (then called Doty County)
Land records: Deeds and titles from 1850s; contact Register of Deeds and Titles, Room 101
Naturalization records: Contact Minnesota Historical Society Research Center, 345 Kellogg Boulevard, West, Saint Paul, MN 55102-1906
Vital records: From 1870; contact Joseph M. Lasky, Court Administrator, Room 320; certified copies: $11.00 for births, $8.00 for deaths and marriages
Probate records: Contact Court Administrator, Room 301
Probate search service: $10.00 per hour; copies: $3.50 for the first page and 25¢ for each additional page, $5.00 for the first certified page and 25¢ for each additional page, no minimum

*Scott County Courthouse
Shakopee, MN 55379
Phone (612) 445-7750
County organized 1853 from Dakota County
Land records: Contact Recorder, Registrar of Titles, Room 113
Naturalization records: Contact Court Administrator, Room 212 or Minnesota Historical Society Research Center, 345 Kellogg Boulevard, West, Saint Paul, MN 55102-1906
Vital records: Contact County Recorder, Room 113
Probate records: Contact Court Administrator
Probate search service: no charge; copies: $5.00 per document, $10.00 per certified document

*Sherburne County Courthouse
13880 Highway 10
PO Box 318
Elk River, MN 55330-1692
Phone (612) 241-2800 County Administrator; (612) 241-2915 County Recorder's Office
County organized 25 February 1856 from Benton County
Land records: Land ownership, etc., records from 1856; contact Patricia Rasmusson, County Recorder, County Recorder's Office, Administration Building, PO Box 320, Elk River, MN 55330; copies: $1.00 each, $5.00 for certified copies
Naturalization records: Contact Minnesota Historical Society Research Center, 345 Kellogg Boulevard, West, Saint Paul, MN 55102-1906
Vital records: Births and deaths from 1870, marriage applications from 1856; contact County Recorder's Office
Probate records: From 1893; contact Lorayne Norgren, Court Administrator
Probate search service: $10.00 per hour; copies: $5.00 per document, $10.00 per certified document

*Sibley County Courthouse
400 Court Street
Gaylord, MN 55334
Phone (612) 237-5526 County Recorder
County organized 1853 from unorganized lands
Land records: Contact County Recorder
Land records search service: $20.00 per hour
Naturalization records: Contact Minnesota Historical Society Research Center, 345 Kellogg Boulevard, West, Saint Paul, MN 55102-1906

Vital records: Contact Court
Administrator
Vital records search service: $20.00 per
hour
Probate records: Contact County
Recorder

***Stearns County Administration
Center**
705 Courthouse Square
Saint Cloud, MN 56303
Phone (612) 259-3620; (612) 259-3855
County Recorder; (612) 259-3925
County License Center
*County organized 20 February 1855
from unorganized lands*
Land records: From 1855; contact
Patricia M. Overman, County
Recorder, Administration Center
Room 131, PO Box 186, Saint Cloud,
MN 56302; copies: $1.00 per page,
$5.00 minimum, $9.50 plus 50¢ for
certification for plats
Naturalization records: Contact
Minnesota Historical Society
Research Center, 345 Kellogg
Boulevard, West, Saint Paul, MN
55102-1906
Vital records: From 1870; contact County
License Center, PO Box 548, Saint
Cloud, MN 56302
Probate records: Yes
Probate search service: no charge;
copies: $3.50 for the first page and
25¢ for each additional page, $5.00
for the first certified page and 25¢ for
each additional certified page, no
minimum; "Need name and
approximate year of death."

*Steele County Courthouse
Owatonna, MN 55060
Phone (507) 451-8040, ext. 216 County
Recorder; (507) 451-8040, ext. 226
County Court; (507) 451-8040, ext.
232 Probate Court
*County organized 1855 from
unorganized territory*
Land records: Contact Rose
Branderhorst, County Recorder, PO
Box 487, Owatonna, MN 55060 ("The
County Recorder will not do phone
searches; we will do index searches
but only when our regular work is
caught up; so it would be best to come
to the office in person.")
Naturalization records: Contact
Minnesota Historical Society
Research Center, 345 Kellogg
Boulevard, West, Saint Paul, MN
55102-1906
Vital records: Contact County Court
Probate records: Contact Probate Court
Probate search service: no charge for
initial search; copies: $3.50 for the
first page and 25¢ for each additional
page, $5.00 for the first certified page

and 25¢ for each additional certified
page, no minimum

Stevens County Courthouse
PO Box 107
Morris, MN 56267-0107
Phone (612) 539-4764
*County organized 1862 from Pierce
County (which was abolished the
same year)*
Naturalization records: Contact
Minnesota Historical Society
Research Center, 345 Kellogg
Boulevard, West, Saint Paul, MN
55102-1906

*Swift County Courthouse
Benson, MN 56215
Phone (612) 843-3377 County Recorder;
(612) 843-3544 County Treasurer and
Registrar of Vital Statistics; (612)
843-2299 FAX, County Treasurer and
Registrar of Vital Statistics; (612)
843-2744 Court Administrator's
Office
*County organized 1870 from Chippewa
County*
Land records: Contact County Recorder's
Office
Naturalization records: Contact
Minnesota Historical Society
Research Center, 345 Kellogg
Boulevard, West, Saint Paul, MN
55102-1906
Vital records: Births from 1870; contact
Ronald A. Vadnais, County Treasurer
and Registrar of Vital Statistics, 301
14th Street, North, PO Box 50,
Benson, MN 56215
Vital records search service: $10.00 per
hour (no charge for minor assistance);
copies: $11.00 for births, $8.00 for
deaths
Probate records: From 1870; contact
Court Adminstrator's Office
Probate search service: $10.00 per hour;
copies: $3.50 for the first page and
25¢ for each additional page, $5.00
for the first certified page and 25¢ for
each additional certified page, no
minimum; "Dates must be given at the
time of the search."

*Todd County Courthouse
215 First Avenue, South
Long Prairie, MN 56347-1351
Phone (612) 732-4459; (612) 732-4469
Court Administrator
*County organized 1855 from Stearns
County*
Land records: Contact County Recorder
Naturalization records: Contact
Minnesota Historical Society
Research Center, 345 Kellogg
Boulevard, West, Saint Paul, MN
55102-1906

Vital records: Contact County Recorder
Probate records: Contact Court
Administrator
Probate search service: $10.00 per hour;
copies: $2.00 each, $2.00 minimum;
"If copies can be completed on copy
machine, 25¢ per copy."

Traverse County Courthouse
PO Box 428
Wheaton, MN 56296-0428
Phone (612) 563-4242
*County organized 1862 from Wilkin
County (then called Toombs County*
Naturalization records: Contact
Minnesota Historical Society
Research Center, 345 Kellogg
Boulevard, West, Saint Paul, MN
55102-1906

*Wabasha County Courthouse
625 Jefferson Avenue
Wabasha, MN 55981-1577
Phone (612) 565-3623 County Recorder;
(612) 565-4070 (Vital Records); (612)
565-3524 (Probate)
*County organized 1849, original county,
formerly called Wabashaw County*
Land records: Contact County Recorder
Naturalization records: Contact
Minnesota Historical Society
Research Center, 345 Kellogg
Boulevard, West, Saint Paul, MN
55102-1906
Vital records: Births and deaths from
1870, marriages from 1865; contact
David E. Meyer, Court Administrator
Probate records: From 1856; contact
Registrar
Probate search service: no charge;
copies: $5.00 per document, $10.00
per certified document

*Wadena County Courthouse
415 South Jefferson
Wadena, MN 56482-1596
Phone (218) 631-2362 County Recorder;
(218) 631-2852 Court Administrator
*County organized 1858 from Cass and
Todd counties*
Land records: From 1873; contact
County Recorder
Naturalization records: Contact
Minnesota Historical Society
Research Center, 345 Kellogg
Boulevard, West, Saint Paul, MN
55102-1906
Vital records: From 1880; contact County
Recorder
Probate records: Contact Court
Administrator's Office (Clerk of
Court)
Probate search service: no charge unless
it takes more than ¹/₂ hour, then $5.00
per hour; copies: $5.00 each, $10.00
for certified copies, no minimum

*Waseca County Courthouse
North State Street
Waseca, MN 56093
Phone (507) 835-0670 County Recorder;
   (507) 835-0540 Court Administrator
*County organized 1857 from Steele
   County ("most records in Steele
   County until 12 August 1858, some
   even later, until the county seat was
   moved from Wilton to Waseca in
   1870")*
Land records: From 1857; contact
   County Recorder
Naturalization records: Contact
   Minnesota Historical Society
   Research Center, 345 Kellogg
   Boulevard, West, Saint Paul, MN
   55102-1906
Vital records: From 1870, marriages from
   1858; contact Court Administrator
Probate records: From 1871, will books
   from 1858; contact Court
   Administrator
Probate search service: $10.00 per hour;
   copies: $5.00 each, $10.00 for
   certified copies, no minimum; "Items
   other than documents in the file can
   be copied for 15¢ per page."

***Washington County Government
   Center**
14900 North 61st Street
Stillwater, MN 55082-0006
Phone (612) 430-6756 County Recorder;
   (612) 430-6245 FAX, County
   Recorder; (612) 439-3220
County organized 1849, original county
Land records: Abstracts (Abstract
   Department) and titles (Torrens
   Department); contact Cindy
   Koosmann, County Recorder/
   Registrar of Titles, (14900 North 61st
   Street—location), PO Box 6 (mailing
   address), Stillwater, MN 55082-0006
Naturalization records: Contact
   Minnesota Historical Society
   Research Center, 345 Kellogg
   Boulevard, West, Saint Paul, MN
   55102-1906
Vital records: Contact Auditor-
   Treasurer's Office
Probate records: Contact Clerk
Probate search service: no charge;
   copies: $3.50 for the first page and
   25¢ for each additional page, $2.00
   for the first page of non-court
   documents and 25¢ for each
   additional page of non-court
   documents, no minimum

*Watonwan County Courthouse
Saint James, MN 56081
*County organized 1860 from Brown
   County*
Land records: Contact County Recorder
Naturalization records: Contact
   Minnesota Historical Society

Research Center, 345 Kellogg
   Boulevard, West, Saint Paul, MN
   55102-1906
Vital records: Contact Court
   Administrator
Probate records: Contact Court
   Administrator
Probate search service: no charge;
   copies: $3.50 for the first page and
   25¢ for each additional page, $5.00
   for the first certified page and 25¢ for
   each additional certified page, no
   minimum

*Wilkin County Courthouse
Breckenridge, MN 56520
Phone (218) 643-4012 County Recorder;
   (218) 643-5112 Treasurer; (218) 643-
   4972 Court Administrator
*County organized 1858 from Cass
   County; name changed from Toombs
   County to Andy Johnson County in
   1863; name changed from Andy
   Johnson County to Wilkin County in
   1868*
Land records: From 1872; contact
   County Recorder and Registrar of
   Titles, PO Box 29, Breckenridge, MN
   56520
Naturalization records: Contact
   Minnesota Historical Society
   Research Center, 345 Kellogg
   Boulevard, West, Saint Paul, MN
   55102-1906
Vital records: Births, deaths and
   marriages from 1874; contact
   Treasurer; copies: $11.00 for births,
   $8.00 for deaths and marriages
Probate records: From 1874; contact
   Court Administrator
No probate search service

*Winona County Courthouse
171 West Third Street
Winona, MN 55987-3102
Phone (507) 457-6340; (507) 457-6395
   Vital Statistics
*County organized 1854 from
   unorganized lands*
Land records: Contact County Recorder
Naturalization records: Contact
   Minnesota Historical Society
   Research Center, 345 Kellogg
   Boulevard, West, Saint Paul, MN
   55102-1906
Vital records: Births and deaths from
   1870, marriages from 1858; contact
   Vital Statistics
Vital records search service: $20.00 per
   hour; copies: $11.00 for certified
   copies of births, $8.00 for certified
   copies of deaths and marriages and
   non-certified copies of births
Probate records: Contact County Court
   Administrator
Probate search service: "Try to be as

reasonable as possible; cost will cover
copies and mailing expense."

*Wright County Courthouse
10 Second Street, N.W.
Buffalo, MN 55313-1187
Phone (612) 682-3900; (612) 682-7509
   County Auditor-Treasurer
*County organized 1855 from Becker
   County*
Land records: From 1857; contact
   County Recorder's Office
Naturalization records: Contact
   Minnesota Historical Society
   Research Center, 345 Kellogg
   Boulevard, West, Saint Paul, MN
   55102-1906
Vital records: Births from 1871 to 1899
   and from 1942 to 1981 open to the
   public (other years upon request,
   deaths from 1871 to date, marriages
   from 1858 to 1979 open to the public
   (from 1979 to date upon request);
   contact Darla M. Groshens, County
   Auditor-Treasurer, Vital Statistics/
   License Bureau, Room 160
Vital records search service: $20.00 per
   hour, $2.50 minimum, copies: $8.00
   for uncertified copies of births, $11.00
   for certified copies of births (includes
   search), $8.00 for certified copies of
   deaths and marriages (includes search,
   no uncertified copies available)
Probate records: From 1871; contact
   Probate Division of the Court
   Administrator's Office
Probate search service: no charge;
   copies: $1.00 per page, no minimum

*Yellow Medicine County Courthouse
415 Ninth Avenue
Granite Falls, MN 56241-1367
Phone (612) 564-2529 County
   Recorder's Office; (612) 564-3325
   Court Administrator
*County organized 1871 from Redwood
   County*
Land records: Contact County Recorder's
   Office
Naturalization records: Contact
   Minnesota Historical Society
   Research Center, 345 Kellogg
   Boulevard, West, Saint Paul, MN
   55102-1906
Vital records: Contact County Recorder's
   Office
Probate records: Contact Court
   Administrator
Probate search service: $10.00 per hour;
   copies: $5.00 per page, $10.00 per
   certified page

MISSISSIPPI

Capital: Jackson. Statehood: 10 December 1817 (annexed in 1783, became a separate territory in 1798 with extensions in 1804 and 1813)

Court System

Mississippi has about fifty Municipal Courts which handle municipal ordinance violations. Some 410 Justice Courts hear some civil actions, misdemeanors and felony preliminaries. Seventeen County Courts handle some civil actions, misdemeanors, felony preliminaries and juvenile matters in Adams, Bolivar, Coahoma, DeSoto, Forrest, Harrison, Hinds (judicial elections stayed by injunction), Jackson, Jones, Lauderdale, Leflore, Madison, Pike, Rankin, Warren, Washington and Yazoo counties.

The Circuit Court is the state's trial court of general jurisdiction and sits at the county seats within each circuit. First Judicial District: Alcorn, Itawamba, Lee, Monroe, Pontotoc, Prentiss and Tishomingo counties; Second Judicial District: Hancock, Harrison and Stone counties; Third Judicial District: Benton, Calhoun, Chickasaw, Lafayette, Marshall, Tippah and Union counties; Fourth Judicial District: Holmes, Humphreys, Leflore, Sunflower and Washington counties; Fifth Judicial District: Attala, Carroll, Choctaw, Grenada, Montgomery, Webster and Winston; Sixth Judicial District: Adams, Amite, Franklin, Jefferson and Wilkinson counties; Seventh Judicial District: Hinds and Yazoo counties; Eighth Judicial District: Leake, Neshoba, Newton and Scott counties; Ninth Judicial District: Claiborne, Issaquena, Sharkey and Warren counties; Tenth Judicial District: Clarke, Kemper, Lauderdale and Wayne counties; Eleventh Judicial District: Bolivar, Coahoma, Quitman and Tunica counties; Twelfth Judicial District: Forrest and Perry counties; Thirteenth Judicial District: Covington, Jasper, Simpson and Smith counties; Fourteenth Judicial District: Copiah, Lincoln, Pike and Walthall counties; Fifteenth Judicial District: Jefferson Davis, Lamar, Lawrence, Marion and Pearl River counties; Sixteenth Judicial District: Clay, Lowndes, Noxubee and Oktibbeha counties; seventeenth Judicial District: DeSoto, Panola, Tallahatchie, Tate and Yalobusha counties; Eighteenth Judicial District: Jones County; Nineteenth Judicial District: George, Greene and Jackson counties; Twentieth Judicial District: Madison and Rankin counties.

Mississippi's Chancery Courts sit in each county seat and deal with matters of equity, alimony and divorce, probate, mental competency, real estate titles, etc. First Judicial District: Alcorn, Itawamba, Lee, Monroe, Pontotoc, Prentiss, Tishomingo and Union counties; Second Judicial District: Jasper, Newton and Scott counties; Third Judicial District: DeSoto, Grenada, Montgomery, Panola, Tate and Yalobusha counties; Fourth Judicial District: Amite, Franklin, Pike and Walthall counties; Fifth Judicial District: Hinds County; Sixth Judicial District: Attala, Carroll, Choctaw, Kemper, Neshoba and Winston counties; Seventh Judicial District: Bolivar, Coahoma, Leflore, Quitman, Tallahatchie and Tunica counties; Eighth Judicial District: Hancock, Harrison and Stone counties; Ninth Judicial District: Humphreys, Issaquena, Sharkey, Sunflower, Warren and Washington counties; Tenth Judicial District: Forrest, Lamar, Marion, Pearl River and Perry counties; Eleventh Judicial District: Holmes, Leake, Madison and Yazoo counties; Twelfth Judicial District: Clarke and Lauderdale counties; Thirteenth Judicial District: Covington, Jefferson Davis, Lawrence, Simpson and Smith counties; Fourteenth Judicial District: Chickasaw, Clay, Lowndes, Noxubee, Oktibbeha and Webster counties; Fifteenth Judicial District: Copiah and Lincoln counties; Sixteenth Judicial District: George, Greene and Jackson counties; Seventeenth Judicial District: Adams, Claiborne, Jefferson and Wilkinson counties; Eighteenth Judicial District: Benton, Calhoun, Lafayette, Marshall and Tippah counties; Nineteenth Judicial District: Jones and Wayne counties; Twentieth Judicial District: Rankin County. The Mississippi Supreme Court handles appeals.

Courthouses

*Adams County Courthouse
PO Box 1006
Natchez, MS 39120-1006
Phone (601) 446-6684
County organized 1799 from the Old Natchez District, one of two areas to which the British acquired title by treaty with the Indians in 1765
Land records: From the 1800s; contact Chancery Clerk's Office
No land records search service
Probate records: From the 1800s; contact Chancery Clerk's Office
No probate search service; copies: 50¢ per page, $1.00 for certification, 50¢ minimum

Alcorn County Courthouse
PO Box 69
Corinth, MS 38834

Phone (601) 286-6265
County organized 1870 from Tippah, Tishomingo and Wilkinson counties

*Amite County Courthouse
PO Box 680
Liberty, MS 39645
Phone (601) 657-8022
County organized 1809 from Wilkinson County
Land records: Yes
Naturalization records: Yes
Vital records: Marriage licenses only
Probate records: Yes

*Attala County Courthouse
230 West Washington
Kosciusko, MS 39090
Phone (601) 289-2921
County organized 1833 from Choctaw Cession
Land records: Contact Chancery Clerk
Vital records: Marriages; contact Circuit Clerk; copies: $5.00 each
Probate records: Contact Chancery Clerk

*Benton County Courthouse
PO Box 218
Ashland, MS 38603-0218
Phone (601) 224-6300
County organized 1870 from Marshall and Tippah counties
Land records: From 1870
Naturalization records: No naturalization records
Vital records: No vital records
Probate records: From 1890
No probate search service; copies: 50¢ each, no minimum

Bolivar County Courthouse
Cleveland, MS 38732
Phone (601) 843-2071
County organized 1836 from Choctaw Cession

*Calhoun County Chancery Clerk's Office
PO Box 8
Pittsboro, MS 38951-0008
Phone (601) 983-3117
County organized 1852 from Chickasaw, Lafayette and Yalobusha counties
Land records: From 1923; contact Tommy Hallum, Chancery Clerk ("County courthouse burned 22 December 1922, destroying *all* records *except* for five books of abstracts of land deed records (indexed by land sections, but *not* indexed by surname), the 1921–1922 tax roll, and a very few deeds re-recorded after the courthouse burned; the abstract books are in the process of being indexed, but at present the

only way to check is by precise land location.")

Naturalization records: No naturalization records

Vital records: Marriages from 1923 (and several marriages prior to 1923, which were obtained elsewhere or re-recorded); contact Circuit Clerk's Office

Probate records: From 1923; contact Chancery Clerk's Office

Probate search service: no charge, but will be done only as time permits; copies: 50¢ per page, plus $1.00 for each certification, no minimum

Carroll County Courthouse
PO Box 291
Carrollton, MS 38917-0291
Phone (601) 237-9283
County organized 1833 from Choctaw Cession

*Chickasaw County Courthouse
Houston, MS 38851
Phone (601) 456-2513
County organized 1836 from Chickasaw Cession 1832
Land records: From 1861 ("County records were destroyed by Yankee troops in 1863; one deed book and a few tax rolls and a very few other items of this nature survived.")
Naturalization records: No naturalization records
Vital records: No vital records
Probate records: From 1861
No probate search service; copies: 50¢ per page

Choctaw County Courthouse
PO Box 250
Ackerman, MS 39735-0250
Phone (601) 285-6329
County organized 1833 from Chickasaw Cession 1832

*Claiborne County Courthouse
PO Box 449
Port Gibson, MS 39150-0449
Phone (601) 437-4992
County organized 1802 from Jefferson County
Land records: Contact Chancery Clerk's Office
Vital records: Name changes, correcting birth certificates; contact Chancery Clerk Office
Probate records: Contact Chancery Clerk's Office
Probate search service: $5.00; copies: 50¢ for each of the first twenty-five copies and 25¢ for each additional copy

*Clarke County Courthouse
PO Box M
Quitman, MS 39355-1013
Phone (601) 776-2126
County organized 1812 from Choctaw Cession
Land records: Yes
Probate records: Yes
No probate search service; copies: 50¢ per page, no minimum

*Clay County Courthouse
PO Box 815
West Point, MS 39773-0815
Phone (601) 494-3124
County organized 1872 from Chickasaw, Oktibbeha and Lowndes counties; name changed from Colfax County in 1876
Land records: From about 1862
Naturalization records: No naturalization records
Vital records: No vital records
Probate records: From 1872; contact Chancery Clerk
Probate search service: no charge; copies: 50¢ per page, $2.00 minimum

Coahoma County Courthouse
PO Box 98
Clarksdale, MS 38614-0098
Phone (601) 624-9411
County organized 1836 from Chickasaw Cession 1836

*Copiah County Courthouse
PO Box 507
Hazlehurst, MS 39083-0507
Phone (601) 894-3021
County organized 1823 from Hinds County
Land records: From 1823 (first Deed Book A lost when county seat moved)
Naturalization records: From 1823 to 1906 (indexed by W.P.A., found in minute books)
Vital records: No vital records
Probate records: From 1823
No probate search service ("will refer request to a genealogist"); copies: 50¢ each

Covington County Courthouse
PO Box 1679
Collins, MS 39428-1679
Phone (601) 765-4242
County organized 1819 from Lawrence and Wayne counties

*DeSoto County Courthouse
Hernando, MS 38632
Phone (601) 368-5011
County organized 1836 from Indian lands
Land records: From 1836; contact Chancery Clerk's Office or Genealogical Society of Desoto County, Mississippi, PO Box 632, Hernando, MS 38632-0632; copies from Genealogical Society: $1.00 per page
Naturalization records: A few naturalization records in probate court records, but have no index; contact Genealogical Society of Desoto County; copies: $1.00 per page
Vital records: No vital records
Probate records: Earlier probate records not indexed; contact Genealogical Society of Desoto County; copies: $1.00 per page

Forrest County Courthouse
316 Forest Street
Hattiesburg, MS 39403-0951
Phone (601) 582-3213
County organized 1906 from Perry County

*Franklin County Courthouse
PO Box 297
Meadville, MS 39653
Phone (601) 384-2330
County incorporated 1809 from Adams County
Land records: Deeds from 1806 (some books were destroyed in courthouse fire of 1876), mortgages and deeds of trust from 1806, land rolls from 1872
Naturalization records: No naturalization records
Vital records: Marriages; contact Circuit Clerk's Office
Probate records: Wills from 1877
Probate search service: no charge; copies: 50¢ per page, $1.00 for certification, no minimum

George County Courthouse
Courthouse Square
Lucedale, MS 39452
Phone (601) 947-4801
County organized 1811 from Greene and Jackson counties

Greene County Courthouse
PO Box 610
Leakesville, MS 39451-0610
Phone (601) 394-2377
County organized 1811 from Amite, Franklin and Wayne counties

*Grenada County Courthouse
PO Box 1208
Grenada, MS 38901-1208
Phone (601) 226-1821
County organized 1870 from Carroll, Tallahatchie and Yalobusha counties at Coffeeville, Mississippi
Land records: Yes

No land records search service (contact Mrs. J. W. (Ruth) Martin or Henry Heggie, local historians)
Naturalization records: No naturalization records
Vital records: No vital records
Probate records: Yes

Hancock County Courthouse
Bay Saint Louis, MS 39520
Phone (601) 467-5404
County organized 1812 from Mobile District

Harrison County Courthouse
Gulfport, MS 39502
Phone (601) 865-4001
County organized 1841 from Hancock and Jackson counties

***Hinds County Courthouse**
First Judicial District
PO Box 686
Jackson, MS 39205-0686
Second Judicial District
PO Box 88
Raymond, MS 39154
Phone (601) 968-6508 First Judicial District; (601) 857-8055 Second Judicial District
County organized 1821 from Choctaw Cession
Land records: "The original Hinds County Courthouse is in Raymond, Mississippi; they have all the records for the entire county up to 1870; at that time, the county built another courthouse at Jackson, Mississippi; Raymond Courthouse continued to keep the records for the western 2/3 of the county, and Jackson started keeping the records for the eastern 1/3 of the county."
Naturalization records: No naturalization records
Vital records: No vital records
Probate records: Yes
No probate search service; copies: 50¢ per page, no minimum

Holmes County Courthouse
PO Box 239
Lexington, MS 39095-0239
Phone (601) 834-2508
County organized 1833 from Yazoo county

***Humphreys County Courthouse**
PO Box 547
Belzoni, MS 39038-0547
Phone (601) 247-1740
County organized 1918 from Holmes, Washington, Yazoo and Sunflower counties

Land records: Contact Yvonne Champion, Chancery Clerk
Naturalization records: No naturalization records
Vital records: No vital records
Probate records: Contact Chancery Clerk
Probate search service: $5.00; copies: 50¢ per page (25¢ per page if you do the copying), $1.00 for certified copies, $5.00 minimum plus SAE

Issaquena County Courthouse
Mayersville, MS 39113
Phone (601) 873-2761
County organized 1844 from Washington County

***Itawamba County Courthouse**
201 West Main
Fulton, MS 38843-1153
Phone (601) 862-3421
County organized 1836 from Indian lands
Land records: Contact Clerk
Naturalization records: No naturalization records
Vital records: Marriages from 1836; contact Clerk
Probate records: From 1836; contact Clerk
No probate search service; copies: 50¢ each, no minimum

***Jackson County Courthouse**
PO Box 998
Pascagoula, MS 39568-0998
Phone (601) 769-3131
County organized 1812 from Mobile District
Land records: From 1875, although some records which were destroyed by two courthouse fires have been re-recorded back to the early 1800s; contact Chancery Clerk; copies: 50¢ per page, $3.00 and up for maps
Naturalization records: From 1875 (temporarily misplaced); contact Chancery Clerk
Vital records: Marriages from 1875; contact Chancery Clerk
Probate records: From 1875 (some earlier records re-recorded); contact Chancery Clerk
No probate search service; copies: 50¢ per page

***Jasper County Courthouse**
PO Box 406
Bay Springs, MS 39422
Phone (601) 764-3368
County organized 1833 from Indian lands
Probate records: Yes
No probate search service; copies: 25¢ per page

***Jefferson County Courthouse**
PO Box 145
Fayette, MS 39069-0145
Phone (601) 786-3021
County organized 1799 from Pickering County
Land records: Yes; copies: 50¢ per page (supply section, township and range)
Naturalization records: No naturalization records
Vital records: Yes
Probate records: Yes
Probate search service: $5.00; copies: 50¢ per page, no minimum

Jefferson Davis County Courthouse
PO Box 1137
Prentiss, MS 39474-1137
Phone (601) 792-4204
County organized 1906 from Covington and Lawrence counties

Jones County Courthouse
PO Box 1468
Laurel, MS 39441-1468
Phone (601) 428-0527
County organized 1826 from Covington and Wayne counties

Kemper County Courthouse
PO Box 188
De Kalb, MS 39328-0188
Phone (601) 743-2460
County organized 1833 from Indian lands

Lafayette County Courthouse
PO Box 1240
Oxford, MS 38655-1240
Phone (601) 234-7563
County organized 1836 from Chickasaw Cession 1832

***Lamar County Courthouse**
PO Box 247
Purvis, MS 39475-0247
Phone (601) 794-8504
County organized 1904 from Marion and Pearl River
Land records: From 1880; contact Clerk
Naturalization records: No naturalization records
Vital records: No vital records
Probate records: From 1905; contact Clerk
Probate search service: no charge if you make search; copies: 50¢ each (25¢ each if you do the copying); no minimum

***Lauderdale County Department of Archives and History, Inc.**
Court House Annex Building
PO Box 5511
Meridian, MS 39302

Phone (601) 482-9714
County organized 1833 from Choctaw Cession

Lawrence County Courthouse
PO Box 40
Monticello, MS 39654-0040
Phone (601) 587-7162
County organized 1814 from Marion County

*Leake County Courthouse
PO Box 72
Carthage, MS 39051-0072
Phone (601) 267-7372
County organized 1833 from Choctaw Cession 1830
Land records: Contact Chancery Clerk
Probate records: Contact Chancery Clerk
Probate search service: "We don't wish to do searches because of insufficient time, however we will for $20.00 per hour"; copies: $1.00 per page if mailed (25¢ per page if you do the copying), $10.00 minimum

*Lee County Courthouse
PO Box 1785
Tupelo, MS 38802-1785
Phone (601) 841-9100
County organized 1866 from Itawamba and Pontotoc counties
Land records: From 1867; contact Bill Benson, Chancery Clerk, PO Box 7127, Tupelo, MS 38802
Probate records: From 1867; contact Chancery Clerk
No probate search service; copies: 50¢ per page, no minimum

Leflore County Courthouse
PO Box 1468
Greenwood, MS 38930-1468
Phone (601) 453-1041
County organized 1871 from Carroll and Sunflower counties

*Lincoln County Courthouse
PO Box 555
Brookhaven, MS 39601-0555
Phone (601) 835-3435
County organized 1870 from Amite, Pike, Lawrence and Franklin counties
Land records: From 1893
Naturalization records: No naturalization records
Vital records: No vital records
Probate records: From 1893
No probate search service: "Will refer to private person"; copies: 50¢ per page

*Lowndes County Courthouse
PO Box 684
Columbus, MS 39703-0684

Phone (601) 329-5880; (601) 329-5900 Circuit Clerk's Office
County organized 1830 from Monroe County
Land records: From 1832; contact Charles J. Younger, Chancery Clerk
No land records search service (contact Mrs. H. C. Johnson, Jr., Ridge Road, Columbus, MS 39701); copies: 50¢ per page in advance
Naturalization records: No naturalization records
Vital records: Marriages; contact Circuit Clerk's Office
Probate records: Wills from 1832
No probate search service; copies: 50¢ per page in advance

Madison County Courthouse
PO Box 404
Canton, MS 39046-0404
Phone (601) 859-1177
County organized 1828 from Yazoo County

Marion County Courthouse
Columbia, MS 39429
Phone (601) 736-2691
County organized 1811 from Amite, Wayne and Franklin counties

Marshall County Courthouse
Holly Springs, MS 38635
Phone (601) 252-4431
County organized 1836 from Indian lands

Monroe County Courthouse
PO Box 578
Aberdeen, MS 39730-0578
Phone (601) 369-8143
County organized 1821 from Chickasaw Cession 1821

Montgomery County Courthouse
Winona, MS 38967
Phone (601) 283-2333
County organized 1871 from Carroll and Choctaw counties

Neshoba County Courthouse
PO Box 67
Philadelphia, MS 39350-0067
Phone (601) 656-3581
County organized 1833 from Choctaw Cession 1830

*Newton County Courthouse
PO Box 68
Decatur, MS 39327-0068
Phone (601) 635-2367
County organized 1836 from Neshoba County
Land records: From 1876; contact Janice Nelson, Chancery Clerk

Probate records: From 1876; contact Chancery Clerk
Probate search service: no charge; copies: 50¢ per page, no minimum

*Noxubee County Courthouse
PO Box 147
Macon, MS 39341-0147
Phone (601) 726-4243
County organized 1833 from Choctaw Cession 1830
Land records: From 1834
Naturalization records: No naturalization records
Vital records: No vital records
Probate records: From 1834; no photocopies of older, bound records

Oktibbeha County Courthouse
Starkville, MS 39759
Phone (601) 323-5834
County organized 1833 from Choctaw Cession 1830

Panola County Courthouse
151 Public Square
Batesville, MS 38606-2220
Phone (601) 563-3171
County organized 1836 from Indian lands

Pearl River County Courthouse
Poplarville, MS 39470
Phone (601) 795-2237
County organized 1890 from Hancock and Marion counties

*Perry County Courthouse
PO Box 198
New Augusta, MS 39462-0198
Phone (601) 964-3218
County organized 1820 from Greene County
Land records: Contact Chancery Clerk
Naturalization records: No naturalization records
Vital records: No vital records
Probate records: Contact Chancery Clerk
No probate search service; copies: 25¢ per page, no minimum

*Pike County Courthouse
PO Box 309
Magnolia, MS 39652-0309
Phone (601) 783-3362
County organized 1815 from Marion County
Land records: From 1882
Naturalization records: From 1882
Vital records: From 1882
Probate records: From 1882
Probate search service: no charge; copies: 25¢ per page, $1.00 for certification, no minimum

*Pontotoc County Courthouse
PO Box 209
Pontotoc, MS 38863-0209
Phone (601) 489-3800
County organized 1836 from Chickasaw Cession
Land records: Yes
Naturalization records: No naturalization records
Vital records: Marriage licenses
Probate records: Yes
No probate search service; copies: 25¢ per page, no minimum

*Prentiss County Courthouse
PO Box 477
Booneville, MS 38829-0477
Phone (601) 728-8151
County organized 1870 from Tishomingo County
Land records: Contact Chancery Clerk
Naturalization records: No naturalization records
Vital records: No vital records
Probate records: Contact Chancery Clerk

*Quitman County Courthouse
Marks, MS 38646
Phone (601) 326-2661
County organized 1877 from Coahoma, Panola Tallahatchie and Tunica counties
Land records: Deeds; contact Butch Scipper, Clerk of the Chancery Court
Land records search service: $40.00 per hour; copies: 50¢ per page, $1.00 for certification
Probate records: Wills; contact Clerk of the Chancery Court

Rankin County Courthouse
Brandon, MS 39042
Phone (601) 825-2217
County organized 1828 from Hinds County

*Scott County Courthouse
PO Box 630
Forest, MS 39074-0630
Phone (601) 469-1922
County organized 1833 from Choctaw Cession 1832
Land records: Contact James Edgar Johnston, Chancery Clerk
Naturalization records: No naturalization records
Vital records: No vital records
Probate records: Contact Chancery Clerk
No probate search service; copies: 50¢ each (25¢ each if you do the copying), no minimum

Sharkey County Courthouse
PO Box 218
Rolling Fork, MS 39159-0218
Phone (601) 873-2755

County organized 1876 from Warren, Washington and Issaquena counties

*Simpson County Courthouse
PO Box 367
Mendenhall, MS 39114-0367
Phone (601) 847-2626
County organized 1824 from Copiah County
Land records: Contact Donnie Caughman, Clerk of the Chancery Court, Chancery Clerk's Office; copies: 50¢ each, $1.00 for certified copies
Naturalization records: No naturalization records
Vital records: No vital records
Probate records: Contact Clerk of the Chancery Court; copies: 50¢ each, $1.00 for certified copies

*Smith County Chancery Clerk
PO Box 39
Raleigh, MS 39153
Phone (601) 782-9811
County organized 1833 from Indian lands
Land records: From 1892 (some deeds prior to 1892 re-recorded after 1892 fire) ("We do not have sufficient office force to permit us to run land indexes.")
Naturalization records: No naturalization records
Vital records: Marriages from 1912, no death records
Probate records: From 1892
Probate search service: $5.00; copies: $5.00 per page, no minimum

*Stone County Courthouse
PO Drawer 7
323 Cavers Avenue
Wiggins, MS 39577
Phone (601) 928-5266
County organized 1916 from Harrison County
Land records: Contact Jane C. O'Neal, Chancery Clerk; copies: 50¢ per page (25¢ per page if you do the copying), $1.00 for certified copies
Probate records: Contact Chancery Clerk
Probate search service: no charge; copies: 50¢ per page (25¢ per page if you do the copying), no minimum

Sunflower County Courthouse
PO Box 988
Indianola, MS 38751-0988
Phone (601) 887-4703
County organized 1844 from Bolivar County

Tallahatchie County Courthouse
PO Box H
Charleston, MS 38921-0330

Phone (601) 647-5551
County organized 1833 from Indian lands

Tate County Courthouse
201 Ward Street
Senatobia, MS 38668-2616
Phone (601) 562-5661
County organized 1873 from DeSoto, Marshall and Tunica counties

*Tippah County Courthouse
PO Box 99
Ripley, MS 38663-0099
Phone (601) 837-7374
County organized 1836 from Chickasaw Cession
Land records: From 1836
Vital records: From 1836 (partially destroyed 1864)
Probate records: From 1836 (partially destroyed 1864)
Probate search service: $10.00; copies: 25¢ per page, $10.00 minimum, covers postage

*Tishomingo County Courthouse
1008 Highway 25-S
Iuka, MS 38852-1020
Phone (601) 423-6021
County organized 1836 from Chickasaw Cession, divided 1870 into Alcorn, Prentiss and Tishomingo counties
Land records: From 1887 ("Present Tishomingo County records burned in 1887.")
Probate records: From 1887; contact Irene Barnes, Rt. 5, Box 210, Iuka, MS 38852
Probate search service: $5.00; copies: 25¢ per page, no minimum

*Tunica County Courthouse
PO Box 217
Tunica, MS 38676-0217
Phone (601) 363-2451
County organized 9 February 1836 by the Treaty of Pontotoc from Chickasaw Cession of 1832
Land records: Deeds from 3 February 1837; contact Susie White, Chancery Clerk
Vital records: No vital records
Probate records: From 13 December 1837; contact Chancery Clerk
Probate search service: $10.00; copies: 50¢ per page

Union County Courthouse
PO Box 847
New Albany, MS 38652-0847
Phone (601) 534-5284
County organized 1870 from Pontotoc and Tippah counties

*Walthall County Courthouse
PO Box 351
Tylertown, MS 39667-0351
Phone (601) 876-4947
County organized 1910 from Marion and Pike counties
Land records: From 1914
Naturalization records: No naturalization records
Vital records: No vital records
Probate records: From 1914
Probate search service: $5.00; copies: 50¢ each, no minimum

Warren County Courthouse
PO Box 351
Vicksburg, MS 39180-0251
Phone (601) 636-4415
County organized 1809 from the Old Natchez District

*Washington County Courthouse
PO Box 309
Greenville, MS 38702-0309
Phone (601) 332-1595
County organized 1827 from Warren and Yazoo counties
Land records: From 1827; contact Margaret P. Tucker, Chancery Clerk
Naturalization records: From 12 December 1890 until 1930s; contact Chancery Clerk
Vital records: No vital records
Probate records: From 1827; contact Chancery Clerk
No probate search service; copies: 75¢ per page, no minimum

*Wayne County Courthouse
Waynesboro, MS 39367
Phone (601) 735-2873
County organized 1809 from Washington County
Land records: From 1892; contact H. H. Hardee, Chancery Clerk
Probate records: From 1892; contact Chancery Clerk
Probate search service: no charge; copies: 50¢ each, no minimum

*Webster County Courthouse
PO Box 398
Walthall, MS 39771
Phone (601) 258-4131
County organized 1874 from Sumner and Montgomery counties
Land records: Contact Lady H. Doolittle, Chancery Clerk
Naturalization records: Contact Chancery Clerk
Vital records: Contact Chancery Clerk
Probate records: Contact Chancery Clerk
Probate search service: $5.00; copies: 50¢ per page, no minimum

Wilkinson County Courthouse
PO Box 516
Woodville, MS 39669-0516
Phone (601) 888-4361
County organized 1802 from Adams County

Winston County Courthouse
PO Box 188
Louisville, MS 39339-0188
Phone (601) 773-3631
County organized 1833 from Indian lands

*Yalobusha County Courthouse
PO Box 664
Water Valley, MS 38965-0664
Phone (601) 473-2091
County organized 1833 from Choctaw Cession 1830
Land records: Contact Bobby H. Clark, Chancery Clerk
Vital records: Marriages only; contact Chancery Clerk and Mary Sue Stevens, Circuit Clerk
Probate records: Contact Chancery Clerk
No probate search service; copies: 50¢ per page, $1.00 minimum

*Yazoo County Courthouse
PO Box 68
Yazoo City, MS 39194-0068
Phone (601) 746-2661
County organized 1823 from Hinds County
Land records: Contact Chancery Clerk's Office
Naturalization records: No naturalization records
Vital records: No vital records
Probate records: Contact Chancery Clerk's Office
No probate search service; copies: 50¢ per page (25¢ per page if you do the copying), no minimum

MISSOURI

Capital: Jefferson City. Statehood: 10 August 1821 (annexed as part of the Louisiana Purchase, 1803, became a separate territory in 1812)

Court System

Missouri has 114 counties and an independent city, Saint Louis, which is not contained within any county. The state's Circuit Courts were reorganized as of January 1979, eliminating the former Magistrate Court, Probate Court, Municipal Court and Hannibal and Cape Girardeau Courts of Common Pleas. The courts now consist of five divisions: the Circuit Division, with jurisdiction over civil and criminal cases; the Juvenile Division; the Associate Division, with jurisdiction over some civil cases, small claims cases, felony preliminaries, misdemeanors, etc.; the Probate Division; and the Municipal Divison.

First Judicial Circuit: Clark, Schuyler and Scotland counties; Second Judicial Circuit: Adair, Knox and Lewis counties; Third Judicial Circuit: Grundy, Harrison, Mercer and Putnam counties; Fourth Judicial Circuit: Atchison, Gentry, Holt, Nodaway and Worth counties; Fifth Judicial Circuit: Andrew and Buchanan counties; Sixth Judicial Circuit: Platte County; Seventh Judicial Circuit: Clay County; Eighth Judicial Circuit: Carroll and Ray counties; Ninth Judicial Circuit: Chariton, Linn and Sullivan counties; Tenth Judicial Circuit: Marion, Monroe and Ralls counties; Eleventh Judicial Circuit: Lincoln, Pike and Saint Charles counties; Twelfth Judicial Circuit: Audrain, Montgomery and Warren counties; Thirteenth Judicial Circuit: Boone and Callaway counties; Fourteenth Judicial Circuit: Howard and Randolph counties; Fifteenth Judicial Circuit: Lafayette and Saline counties; Sixteenth Judicial Circuit: Jackson County; Seventeenth Judicial Circuit: Cass and Johnson counties; Eighteenth Judicial Circuit: Cooper and Pettis counties; Nineteenth Judicial Circuit: Cole County; Twentieth Judicial Circuit: Franklin, Gasconade and Osage counties; Twenty-first Judicial Circuit: Saint Louis County; Twenty-second Judicial Circuit: City of Saint Louis; Twenty-third Judicial Circuit: Jefferson County; Twenty-fourth Judicial Circuit: Madison, Perry, Saint Francois, Sainte Genevieve and Washington counties; Twenty-fifth Judicial Circuit: Maries,

Phelps, Pulaski and Texas counties; Twenty-sixth Judicial Circuit: Camden, Laclede, Miller, Moniteau and Morgan counties; Twenty-seventh Judicial Circuit: Bates, Henry and Saint Clair counties; Twenty-eighth Judicial Circuit: Barton, Cedar, Dade and Vernon counties; Twenty-ninth Judicial Circuit: Jasper County; Thirtieth Judicial Circuit: Benton, Dallas, Hickory, Polk and Webster counties; Thirty-first Judicial Circuit: Greene County; Thirty-second Judicial Circuit: Bollinger and Cape Girardeau counties; Thirty-third Judicial Circuit: Mississippi and Scott counties; Thirty-fourth Judicial Circuit: New Madrid and Pemiscot counties; Thirty-fifth Judicial Circuit: Dunklin and Stoddard counties; Thirty-sixth Judicial Circuit: Butler and Ripley counties; Thirty-seventh Judicial Circuit: Carter, Howell, Oregon and Shannon counties; Thirty-eighth Judicial Circuit: Christian and Taney counties; Thirty-ninth Judicial Circuit: Barry, Lawrence and Stone counties; Fortieth Judicial Circuit: McDonald and Newton counties; Forty-first Judicial Circuit: Macon and Shelby counties; Forty-second Judicial Circuit: Crawford, Dent, Iron, Reynolds and Wayne counties; Forty-third Judicial Circuit: Caldwell, Clinton, Daviess, DeKalb and Livingston counties; Forty-fourth Judicial Circuit: Douglas, Ozark and Wright counties. The Court of Appeals and Supreme Court hear appeals from the lower courts.

The first provision for statewide registration of births and deaths was enacted 1 July 1883 when the State Board of Health was created for the supervision of such registrations. The act concerning birth and death registration was repealed in 1893 and registration ceased until 1910. The Missouri State Archives (600 West Main Street, PO Box 778, Jefferson City, MO 65102) has birth and death records for Andrew, Audrain, Barry, Barton, Bates, Benton, Bollinger, Butler, Cape Girardeau, Carroll, Cedar, Chariton, Clark, Clay, Clinton, Cole, Cooper, Dade, Dallas, Daviess, Dent, Gasconade, Gentry, Greene, Grundy, Harrison, Hickory, Holt, Howard, Iron, Jackson, Jefferson, Johnson, Knox, Laclede, Lawrence, Lewis, Linn, Livingston, Macon, Madison, Maries, Marion, Mercer, Miller, Moniteau, Monroe, Morgan, Newton, Nodaway, Oregon, Osage, Ozark, Perry, Phelps, Polk, Putnam, Ralls, Randolph, Ray, Reynolds, Ripley, Saint Clair, Saint Francois, Sainte Genevieve, Saline, Schuyler, Scotland, Scott, Shelby, Stoddard, Sullivan, Texas, Vernon, Warren, Washington, Webster and Worth counties; birth records only for Adair, Cass, Christian, DeKalb, Franklin, Howell, McDonald, Pemiscot, Pettis and Pike counties; and death records only for Buchanan and Lincoln counties.

Courthouses

*Adair County Courthouse
Kirksville, MO 63501
Phone (816) 665-3877
County organized 1841 from Macon County
Land records: Contact Clerk
Probate records: Contact Clerk
No probate search service; copies: 25¢ per page

*Andrew County Courthouse
Savannah, MO 64485
Phone (816) 324-3624
County organized 1841 from Platte Purchase
Land records: Contact Rose Lancey, Circuit Clerk
Vital records: Births and deaths from 1883 to 1893; contact Betty L. Williams, County Clerk
Probate records: Contact Judge L. Glen Zshud
No probate search service; copies: 50¢ each, no minimum

*Atchison County Courthouse
400 Washington Street
Rock Port, MO 64482
Phone (816) 744-2707
County organized 1845 from Holt County
Land records: From 1845; contact Sharon L. Taylor, Recorder, PO Box J, Rock Port, MO 64482
Land records search service: $4.00; copies: $1.00 per page
Naturalization records: Contact Sharon L. Taylor, Circuit Clerk ("We have found these in various places.")
Vital records: Deaths only from 1883 through 1893, marriages from 1845 to date; contact Sharon L. Taylor, Recorder; copies: $2.00 each, $9.00 for certification
Probate records: From 1845; contact Judge Kay G. Rosenbohm
Probate search service: $4.00; copies: $1.00 per page plus $1.00 for certification, $1.00 minimum; "It helps if they would send a SASE."

*Audrain County Courthouse
101 North Jefferson
Mexico, MO 65265-2769
Phone (314) 581-8211
County organized 1836 from Pike, Callaway and Ralls counties
Land records: Contact Collector's Office
Vital records: From 1883 to 1886 only; contact County Clerk's Office
Probate records: Contact Circuit Court, Division II

Probate search service: no charge; copies: 20¢ each, no minimum; "Please send SASE."

Barry County Courthouse
Cassville, MO 65625
Phone (417) 847-2561
County organized 1835 from Greene County

*Barton County Courthouse
Lamar, MO 64759
Phone (417) 682-3529
County organized 1855 from Jasper County
Land records: From 1857
Naturalization records: From about 1890 to 1940
Vital records: Births from 1833 to 1896, deaths from 1883 to 1899 (incomplete), marriages from 1866
Probate records: From 1866
Probate search service: "All charges vary by time involved in search; complete information provided decreases time involved"; copies: $1.00 per page, $2.00 for certified copies; "SASE *all* offices; no charge except postage for return if nothing found."

*Bates County Courthouse
Butler, MO 64730
Phone (816) 679-3611 Recorder of Deeds; (816) 679-5171 Circuit Clerk's Office; (816) 679-3371 County Clerk's Office; (816) 679-3311 Associate Circuit Court
County organized 1841 from Cooper County
Land records: From 1840 to date; contact Recorder of Deeds, PO Box 186, Butler, MO 64730
Naturalization records: Very few records from January 1867 to 1880; contact Circuit Clerk's Office, PO Box 288, Butler, MO 64730
Vital records: Births and deaths from 1883 to 1886; contact County Clerk's Office, 1 North Delaware, Butler, MO 64730
Probate records: From 1850 to date; contact Associate Circuit Court, 1 North Delaware, Butler, MO 64730

*Benton County Courthouse
PO Box 1238
Warsaw, MO 65355-1238
Phone (816) 438-7712 Circuit Clerk; (816) 438-7326
County organized 1835 from Cooper County
Land records: From 1837; contact Circuit Clerk, PO Box 775, Warsaw, MO 65355

Naturalization records: Contact Circuit Clerk

Vital records: Births and deaths from 1883 to 1888, marriages from 1839

Probate records: From 1854

No probate search service; copies: $2.00 each, no minimum; "Mail is worked as time allows."

Bollinger County Courthouse
Marble Hill, MO 63764
Phone (314) 238-2126
County organized 1851 from Cape Girardeau, Madison, Stoddard and Wayne counties

*Boone County Circuit Court
Daniel Boone Building
701 East Walnut
Columbia, MO 65201-4470
Phone (314) 874-7510; (314) 886-4090 Probate Division
County organized 1820 from Howard County
Land records: Contact Recorder of Deeds
Naturalization records: Contact Circuit Court
Probate records: Contact Probate Division, Circuit Court
Probate search service: no charge; copies: $1.00 per page (before 1900), $1.00 for the first page and 25¢ for each additional page (after 1900), no minimum, certified check or money order only; "Try to give us as much information about the person as possible; if you know the middle name or initial it would help a lot, plus the date or year that the person died in."

*Buchanan County Courthouse
411 Jules
Saint Joseph, MO 64501
Phone (816) 271-1437; (816) 271-1477 Probate Court
County organized 1838 from Platte Purchase
Land records: From 1839; contact Recorder's Office
No land records search service (contact Northwest Missouri Genealogical Society, 412 Felix Street, PO Box 382, Saint Joseph, MO 64502)
Naturalization records: Contact Circuit Clerk's Office
Vital records: Marriages from 1839; contact Recorder's Office
No vital records search service (contact Northwest Missouri Genealogical Society)
Probate records: From 1839; contact Probate Court
Probate search service: $10.00; copies: $1.00 per page, $1.00 minimum

Butler County Courthouse
PO Box 332
Poplar Bluff, MO 63901-0332
Phone (314) 785-8201
County organized 1849 from Wayne County

*Caldwell County Courthouse
PO Box 67
Kingston, MO 64650-0067
Phone (816) 586-2571
County organized 26 December 1836 from Ray County
Land records: Original land patents 1834, deeds from 1860 (plus records re-recorded after the courthouse fire of 1860), atlases (rural land owners); contact Charlene Ward, Deputy Recorder, PO Box 86, Kingston, MO 64650
Land records search service: no charge (extensive searches referred to Mrs. Marilyn Williams, Rt. 1, Box 38, Kingston, MO 64650); copies: $2.00 for the first page and $1.00 for each additional page
Naturalization records: From 1887 to about 1899 (only about ten in all); contact Beverly Graham, Circuit Clerk, PO Box 86, Kingston, MO 64650
Vital records: Marriages only; contact Deputy Recorder
Probate records: Contact Sue Adkison, Probate Clerk, PO Box 5, Kingston, MO 64650

Callaway County Courthouse
Fulton, MO 65251
Phone (314) 642-0730
County organized 1820 from Howard, Boone and Montgomery counties

Camden County Courthouse
1 Court Circle
Camdenton, MO 65020
Phone (314) 346-4440
County organized 1841 from Pulaski, Morgan and Benton counties

*Cape Girardeau County Administration Building
1 Barton Square
Jackson, MO 63755
Phone (314) 243-3547; (314) 243-8123 Recorder of Deeds; (314) 334-6249 Division 4
County organized 1812, original county
Land records: Contact Recorder of Deeds
Probate records: Contact Division 4—Judicial
No probate search service; copies: 15¢ each

*Carroll County Courthouse
Carrollton, MO 64633
Phone (816) 542-0615
County organized 1833 from Ray County
Land records: From 1833; copies: $1.00 each
Naturalization records: From 1833; copies: 35¢ each
Vital records: Births from 1883 to 1894, deaths from 1883 to 1890, marriages from 1833; copies: $2.00 for marriages

Carter County Courthouse
PO Box 517
Van Buren, MO 63965-0517
Phone (314) 323-4527
County organized 1859 from Ripley, Reynolds, Shannon and Oregon counties

*Cass County Courthouse
Harrisonville, MO 64701
Phone (816) 887-2393 Wade Archives; (816) 380-1510, (816) 380-1505, (816) 380-1506, (816) 380-1507 Recorder of Deeds; (816) 380-1580 Probate Office
County organized 1835 from Jackson County; name changed from Van Buren County in 1849
Land records: From December 1840 to September 1960; contact Harrisonville Chamber of Commerce, Wade Archives at Cass County Historical Society, 400 East Mechanic, PO Box 406, Harrisonville, MO 64701-0406. Land records from 1960; contact Recorder's Office, 100 East Wall, Harrisonville, MO 64701
Naturalization records: No naturalization records
Vital records: Marriages from 1835; contact Recorder's Office
Probate records: From 1836 to 1956; contact Wade Archives. From 1956; contact Probate Office, 100 East Wall, Harrisonville, MO 64701
No probate search service; copies: 50¢ each, $2.00 for certified copies

Cedar County Courthouse
PO Box 158
Stockton, MO 65785
Phone (417) 276-3514
County organized 1845 from Dade and Saint Clair counties

*Chariton County Courthouse
306 South Cherry
Keytesville, MO 65261
Phone (816) 288-3273 County Clerk
County organized 1820 from Howard County

Land records: Contact Recorder of Deeds
Naturalization records: Contact Circuit Clerk
Vital records: Births and deaths from 1883 to 1887; contact County Clerk. Marriage licenses; contact Recorder's Office; copies: $1.00 per page, $2.00 for certified copies
Probate records: From 1860 to date; contact Associate Probate Division
No probate search service; copies: $1.00 per page, $1.50 per certified page

Christian County Courthouse
Ozark, MO 65721
Phone (417) 485-6360
County organized 1859 from Taney, Greene and Webster counties

*Clark County Courthouse
Kahoka, MO 63445
Phone (816) 727-3283
County organized 1836 from Lewis County
Land records: Deeds and mortgages from 1836; copies: $1.00 each
Naturalization records: Very few naturalization records, some dating from about 1850
Vital records: Marriages from 1836; contact Mary D. Jones, 111 East Court, Kahoka, MO 63445; copies: $1.00 per page
Probate records: Contact County Probate and Assocate Division, 113 West Court, Kahoka, MO 63445
Probate search service: no charge, "but we can only do when time allows— we are under-staffed"; copies: $1.00 per page, no minimum

*Clay County Archives and Historical Library, Inc.
210 East Franklin Street
PO Box 99
Liberty, MO 64068-0099
Phone (816) 781-3611
County organized 1822 from Ray County
Land records: Index to original land grants
Naturalization records: From 1824 to 1902
Vital records: No birth or death records, marriages from the 1830s through the 1890s (with the exception of the 1840s), index to marriages from 1822 through 1915; contact County Recorder's Office
Probate records: From 1822 to 1989
Probate search service: $3.00 minimum; copies: $1.00 per page

*Clinton County Courthouse
Plattsburg, MO 64477
Phone (816) 539-3719 Recorder's Office

County organized 1833 from Clay and Ray counties
Land records: From 1833; contact Recorder's Office, PO Box 275, Plattsburg, MO 64477
Naturalization records: From 1883 to 1927; contact Recorder's Office
Vital records: A few births and deaths from 1833 to 1889, marriage records from 1833; contact Recorder's Office
Probate records: Contact Anna Richerson, Probate Clerk

*Cole County Courthouse
301 East High
Jefferson City, MO 65101-3208
Phone (314) 634-9177 Probate Division IV
County organized 1820 from Cooper County
Probate records: Wills and probate estates from 1834; contact Probate Division IV—Room 406
No probate search service; copies: $1.00 per page; "Give full name and date of death for search."

Cooper County Courthouse
200 Main
Boonville, MO 65233
Phone (816) 882-2114
County organized 1818 from Howard County

*Crawford County Courthouse
Steelville, MO 65565
Phone (314) 775-5048
County organized 1829 from Gasconade County
Land records: Contact Karen A. McPeters, PO Box 177, Steelville, MO 65565
Vital records: Marriages; contact Karen A. McPeters
Probate records: Contact Judge J. Kent Howald, PO Box B.C., Steelville, MO 65565

Dade County Courthouse
Greenfield, MO 65661
Phone (417) 637-2271
County organized 1841 from Polk and Barry counties

*Dallas County Courthouse
PO Box 436
Buffalo, MO 65622-0436
Phone (417) 345-2632
County organized 1841 from Polk County
Vital records: From 1883 to 1893; contact County Clerk; certified copies: $3.00 each
Probate records: Contact Clerk, PO Box 1150, Buffalo, MO 65622

No probate search service; copies: 50¢ per page, no minimum

*Daviess County Courthouse
Gallatin, MO 64640
Phone (816) 663-2641
County organized 1836 from Ray County
Land records: From 1837
Naturalization records: Some naturalization records in 1930s
Vital records: Births and deaths from 1883 to 1893, marriages from 1839
Probate records: From 1890
Probate search service: no charge; copies: 50¢ each, no minimum; "Certified copies vary from office to office."

*DeKalb County Courthouse
PO Box 248
Maysville, MO 64469-0248
Phone (816) 449-5402; (816) 449-2602
County organized 1845 from Clinton County
Land records: From 1845; contact Recorder of Deeds
Land records search service: no charge; copies: $1.00 per page
Naturalization records: From 1906 to 1923; contact Recorder of Deeds
Naturalization records search service: no charge; copies: $1.00 per page
Vital records: Some births from 1883 to 1887 (very incomplete); contact County Clerk's Office. Deaths from 1883 to 1891 and 1942 to 1943; contact Recorder of Deeds
Vital records search service: no charge; copies: $1.00 per page
Probate records: From 1878; contact Associate Circuit Court, Probate Division, Maysville, MO 64469
Probate search service: no charge; copies: $1.00 per page, no minimum

Dent County Courthouse
Salem, MO 65560-1298
Phone (314) 729-4144
County organized 1851 from Crawford and Shannon counties

Douglas County Courthouse
Ava, MO 65608
Phone (417) 683-4714
County organized 1857 from Ozark County

Dunklin County Courthouse
Kennett, MO 63857
Phone (314) 888-2796
County organized 1845 from Stoddard County

*Franklin County Courthouse
PO Box 311
Union, MO 63084-0311
Phone (314) 583-6355
County organized 1818 from Saint Louis County
Land records: Contact Assessor's Office, Union City Auditorium, 500 East Locust, Union, MO 63084
Vital records: Contact Recorder of Deeds
Probate records: Contact Judge Walter Murray, Court House Annex, PO Box 352, Union, MO 63084
No probate search service; copies: 35¢ each, no minimum

*Gasconade County Courthouse
119 East First Street
Hermann, MO 65041-0295
Phone (316) 486-2632 Recorder and Circuit Clerk's Office; (314) 486-5427 County Clerk; (314) 486-2321 Probate Office
County organized 1820 from Franklin County
Land records: From 1821; contact Recorder, Room 6
Naturalization records: From 1837 to 1949; contact Recorder
Vital records: Births from 1867 to 1900, deaths from 1883 to 1900; contact County Clerk, Room 2. Marriages from 1822; contact Recorder.
Vital records search service: no charge; copies: $1.00 per page, no minimum
Probate records: Contact Probate Clerk, Division IV, Associate Circuit Court, PO Box 176, Hermann, MO 65041
Probate search service: no charge; copies: $10.00 per page, no minimum

Gentry County Courthouse
Albany, MO 64402
Phone (816) 726-3618
County organized 1845 from Clinton County

*Greene County Courthouse
940 Boonville Avenue
Springfield, MO 65802
Phone (417) 868-4055; (417) 868-4068 Recorder of Deeds Office
County organized 1833 from Wayne and Crawford counties
Land records: Land tax records from 1833 to 1864 (with gaps) and from 1865, land transaction records; contact Recorder of Deeds Office
Vital records: Marriage licenses; contact Recorder of Deeds Office
Probate records: From 1833 to 1970
Probate search service: no charge; copies: 20¢ per page, $1.00 minimum if SASE not enclosed; "Genealogy Information: Green County Archives, 1126 Boonville Avenue, Springfield, MO 65802, (417) 868-4021."

Grundy County Courthouse
700 Main Street
Trenton, MO 64683-2063
Phone (816) 359-6305
County organized 1841 from Livingston and Ray counties

*Harrison County Courthouse
Bethany, MO 64424
Phone (816) 425-6424
County organized 1845 from Daviess and Ray counties
Land records: Contact Circuit Clerk—Recorder of Deeds; copies: $1.00 per instrument
Naturalization records: Contact Circuit Clerk—Recorder of Deeds
Vital records: Births and deaths from 1883 through 1893 only; contact County Clerk's Office. Marriages and divorces; contact Circuit Clerk—Recorder of Deeds
Probate records: Contact Marjorie Butz, Clerk, Circuit Court, Probate Division II Office
Probate search service: no charge; copies: 25¢ per page, $1.00 minimum; "Generally I do not answer letters as I do not have much time for doing genealogy research, but I do assist people when they come to the office; I will not copy complete files, only wills and other instruments with information relative to heirs, etc."

Henry County Courthouse
Clinton, MO 64735
Phone (816) 885-6963
County organized 1834 from Lafayette County; name changed from Rives County in 1841

Hickory County Courthouse
Hermitage, MO 65668
Phone (417) 745-6450
County organized 1845 from Benton and Polk counties

Holt County Courthouse
Oregon, MO 64473
Phone (816) 446-3303
County organized 1841 from Platte Purchase

*Howard County Courthouse
300 County Road 407
Fayette, MO 65248
Phone (816) 248-2284
County organized 1816 from Saint Louis and Saint Charles counties
Land records: Warranty deeds, deeds of trust, surveys from 1817; contact Louise Coutts, Court House Volunteer
Land records search service: no charge, but donation appreciated; copies: $2.00 per page

Naturalization records: From 1850 to 1906; contact Court House Volunteer
Naturalization records search service: no charge, but donation appreciated; copies: $2.00 per page
Vital records: A few births and deaths from 1883 to 1889, marriages from 1816; contact Court House Volunteer
Vital records search service: no charge, but donation appreciated; copies: $2.00 per page
Probate records: Estates, guardianships, intestates; contact Court House Volunteer
Probate search service: no charge, but donation appreciated; copies: $2.00 per page

*Howell County Courthouse
West Plains, MO 65775
Phone (417) 256-2591
County organized 1857 from Oregon County
Land records: From 1867; contact Recorder
Vital records: Births from 1883 to 1894, deaths from 1883 to 1893; contact Dennis K. VonAllman, County Clerk. Marriages; contact Recorder; certified copies: $2.00 each
Probate records: From 1867
No probate search service; copies: 25¢ per page from paper originals, $1.00 per page from microfiche originals, $1.50 for certified copies

*Iron County Courthouse
PO Box 42
Ironton, MO 63650-0042
Phone (314) 546-2912
County organized 1857 from Madison, Reynolds, Saint Francois, Wayne and Washington counties
Land records: From 1857
Naturalization records: Some naturalization records from 1887 to 1906
Vital records: Births and deaths from 1883 to 1887, marriages from 1857; certified copies: $2.00 each
Probate records: Yes
Probate search service: fee determined at time of search; copies: $1.00 to $1.50 per page, no minimum

*Jackson County Courthouse
308 West Kansas
Independence, MO 64050
Jackson County Courthouse
415 East 12th Street
Kansas City, MO 64106-2706
Phone (816) 881-3198 Land Records or Marriages, Kansas City; (816) 881-4478 Land Records, Independence; (816) 881-3913 Circuit Court; (816) 881-4608 Marriages, Independence; (816) 274-2000 Kansas City City

Hall; (816) 881-3242 County Clerk; (816) 881-3761 Probate Records, Kansas City; (816) 881-4553 Probate Records, Independence
County organized 1826 from Lafayette County
Land records: Yes; copies: $2.00 per page, $5.00 for plat maps, $1.00 for certification
Naturalization records: Early records; contact Circuit Court, Kansas City
Vital records: Marriages from 1881; contact Kansas City. Marriages from 1826; contact Independence. Deaths in the late 1800s; contact County Clerk. Births and deaths for Kansas City; contact Kansas City City Hall, 412 East Twelfth Street, Kansas City, MO 64106
Vital records search service from Courthouses: $3.00; copies: $2.00 for marriage applications and marriage licenses, $10.00 for certified marriage licenses
Probate records: Yes

*Jasper County Courthouse
Carthage, MO 64836
Phone (417) 358-0421 Recorder of Deeds; (417) 358-0416 County Clerk; (417) 358-0403 Circuit Court
County organized 1841 from Barry County
Land records: Contact Recorder of Deeds, Room 207, PO Box 387, Carthage, MO 64836
Naturalization records: No naturalization records
Vital records: A few births and deaths from 1883 through 1897 (none from 1898 to 1909); contact Marjorie S. Bull, County Clerk. Marriages; contact Recorder
Probate records: Contact Circuit Court, Probate Division Courthouse, Room 108, Carthage, MO 64836

*Jefferson County Courthouse
PO Box 100
Hillsboro, MO 63050-0100
Phone (314) 789-5414
County organized 1818 from Sainte Genevieve and Saint Louis counties
Land records: Contact Marlene Castle, Recorder of Deeds; copies: $2.00 and up
Vital records: Marriage licenses; contact Recorder of Deeds; copies: $2.00 and up

*Johnson County Courthouse
Warrensburg, MO 64093
Phone (816) 747-6811 Recorder of Deeds
County organized 1834 from Lafayette County
Land records: From 1835; contact Laurie

Mifflin, Recorder of Deeds, PO Box 32, Warrensburg, MO 64093
No land records search service; copies: $1.00 for the first page and 25¢ for each additional page of the same document
Vital records: Births and deaths from 1883 to 1893 only; contact County Clerk's Office. Marriages from 1835; contact Recorder of Deeds
Probate records: Contact Debby Boone Pryor, Clerk Circuit Court, Probate Division
Probate search service: $5.00; copies: $1.00 for the first page and 25¢ for each additional page, no minimum; "All payments to be made by money order only."

*Knox County Courthouse
Edina, MO 63537
Phone (816) 397-2184
County organized 1845 from Scotland County
Land records: From 1845
Naturalization records: From 1845
Vital records: From 1883 to 1890
Probate records: From 1845; contact County Clerk
No probate search service; copies: 25¢ each

*Laclede County Courthouse
Second and Adam Streets
Lebanon, MO 65536
Phone (417) 532-5471 County Clerk
County organized 1849 from Camden, Pulaski and Wright counties
Land records: Warranty deeds and mortgage records from 1849; contact Recorder. Platt books from 1912; contact County Clerk
Naturalization records: No naturalization records
Vital records: Births from 1884 to 1899; contact County Clerk. Marriages from 1865; contact Recorder
Probate records: From late 1800s; contact Lobby of the Courthouse
No probate search service; copies: 15¢ to 50¢ each, $1.50 for certified copies; "Cannot make copies of bound books."

*Lafayette County Courthouse
PO Box 357
Lexington, MO 64067-0357
Phone (816) 259-4315
County organized 1820 from Cooper County, called Lillard County in 1821, then Lafayette County in 1826
Land records: From 1821; contact County Recorder
Naturalization records: From 1821; contact Circuit Clerk
Vital records: No births or deaths
Probate records: From 1821; contact

Circuit Court—Probate Division, PO Box E, Lexington, MO 64067
Probate search service: $1.00 per legal-sized page, no minimum

Lawrence County Courthouse
Mount Vernon, MO 65712
Phone (417) 466-2638
County organized 1845 from Dade and Barry counties

*Lewis County Courthouse
Monticello, MO 63457
Phone (314) 767-5205
County organized 1833 from Marion County
Land records: Contact Recorder of Deeds, PO Box 97, Monticello, MO 63457
Naturalization records: Contact Circuit Clerk
Vital records: Births and deaths from 1883 through 1887 only
Probate records: Contact Probate Office
Probate search service: no charge; copies: $1.00 each, no minimum

Lincoln County Courthouse
201 Main Street
Troy, MO 63379-1127
Phone (314) 528-4415
County organized 1818 from Saint Charles County

*Linn County Courthouse
Linneus, MO 64653
Phone (816) 895-5417 County Clerk
County organized 1837 from Chariton County
Land records: From 1842; contact Recorder's Office
Naturalization records: From 1850 to 1930; contact Circuit Clerk's Office. Naturalization records from 1889; contact Circuit Clerk, 309 1/2 North Main, Brookfield, MO 64628
Vital records: A few births and deaths from 1883 to 1887; contact County Clerk. Marriages from 1842; contact Recorder's Office
Probate records: From 1850; contact Probate Office
Probate search service: $2.00; copies: $1.00 per page

Livingston County Courthouse
PO Box 803
Chillicothe, MO 64601
Phone (816) 646-2293
County organized 1837 from Carroll County

*Macon County Courthouse
PO Box 382
Macon, MO 63552

Phone (816) 385-2732 Recorder of Deeds; (816) 385-4631 Circuit Court; (816) 385-2913 County Clerk; (816) 385-3131 Probate Records

County organized 1837 from Randolph and Chariton counties

Land records: Contact Recorder of Deeds

Naturalization records: Contact Circuit Court

Vital records: Births and deaths from 1883 to 1893 only; contact County Clerk, PO Box 96, Macon, MO 63552. Marriages; contact Recorder of Deeds

Probate records; contact Probate Records, PO Box 491, Macon, MO 63552

*Madison County Courthouse
Court Square
Fredericktown, MO 63645
Phone (314) 783-2102 Circuit Clerk and Recorder's Office; (314) 783-2176 County Clerk's Office; (314) 783-3105 Associate and Probate Divisions

County organized 1818 from Sainte Genevieve and Cape Girardeau counties

Land records: From 1818 to date; contact Circuit Clerk and Recorder's Office; copies: $1.00 each

Naturalization records: From 1818 to date; contact Circuit Clerk and Recorder's Office; copies: $1.00 each

Vital records: Marriages from 1818 to date; contact Circuit Clerk and Recorder's Office. A few births and deaths from 1883 to 1893; contact County Clerk's Office; copies from Circuit Clerk and Recorder's Office: $1.00 each

Probate records: From 1822 to 1960; contact Mrs. Carol King, Associate and Probate Divisions of the Madison County Circuit Court Division III, PO Box 521, Fredericktown, MO 63645

Probate search service: no charge; copies: 25¢ per page, $12.75 for fifty-one-page master list of all files from 1822 to 1960, no minimum

*Maries County Courthouse
Vienna, MO 65582
Phone (314) 422-3338 Circuit Clerk and Recorder; (314) 422-3303 Probate

County organized 1855 from Gasconade, Osage and Pulaski counties

Land records: From 1855; contact Circuit Clerk and Recorder

Naturalization records: Thirteen naturalization records; from 1874 to 1906 (Lischine, Schanning, Spielhagen, Danuser, Kleinecke, Juergens, McKenzie, Hartman, Brockman, Segrist, Spielhagan, Dette and Dette); contact Historical Society of Maries County, PO Box 289, Vienna, MO 65582

Vital records: Marriages from 1881; contact Circuit Clerk and Recorder. Very few vital records; contact Record Room of Historical Society of Maries County

Probate records: From 1885

No probate search service; copies: 15¢ or 25¢ each; "I don't believe there is a set charge—people usually donate."

Marion County Courthouse
Palmyra, MO 63461
Phone (314) 769-2549

County organized 1826 from Ralls County

McDonald County Courthouse
PO Box 665
Pineville, MO 64856
Phone (417) 223-4717

County organized 1849 from Newton County

Mercer County Courthouse
Princeton, MO 64673
Phone (816) 748-3425

County organized 1845 from Grundy and Livingston counties

Miller County Courthouse
PO Box 12
Tuscumbia, MO 65082-0012
Phone (314) 369-2731

County organized 1837 from Cole and Pulaski counties

*Mississippi County Courthouse
PO Box 369
Charleston, MO 63834-0304
Phone (314) 683-2146; (314) 683-2104 Recorder of Deeds; (314) 683-6228 Probate Court

County organized 1845 from Scott County

Land records: Contact Recorder of Deeds

Naturalization records: Contact Recorder of Deeds

Vital records: No vital records

Probate records: Contact Probate Court

*Moniteau County Courthouse
California, MO 65018
Phone (314) 796-4661 County Clerk; (314) 796-2213 County Commission; (314) 796-4637 Assessor; (314) 796-2071 Circuit Clerk; (314) 796-4671 Probate Clerk

County organized 1845 from Cole and Morgan counties, annexed small part of Morgan County in 1881

Land records: From 1845; contact Assessor

Naturalization records: No naturalization records

Vital records: Births from 1883 to 1894

(incomplete), deaths from 1883 to 1887 (incomplete), marriages from 1845; contact Circuit Clerk

Probate records: From 1845; contact Probate Clerk

Probate search service: "Our personnel will do this if time permits"; copies: $1.00 per page, no minimum

*Monroe County Courthouse
300 North Main Street
Paris, MO 65275-1399
Phone (816) 327-5106 County Clerk; (816) 327-5220 Probate Clerk

County organized 1831 from Ralls County

Land records: County Court records, plat books, road maps; contact Sandy Carter, County Clerk. Land and warranty deeds; contact Gale Bierly, Circuit Clerk; copies from County Clerk: $15.00 plus postage for plat books, $1.00 for road maps

Vital records: Marriages; contact Circuit Clerk

Probate records: Contact Betty Hitchcock, Probate Clerk

Probate search service: $4.00; copies: $1.00 per page, 50¢ for seal

Montgomery County Courthouse
211 East Third
Montgomery City, MO 63361-1956
Phone (314) 564-3357

County organized 1818 from Saint Charles County

*Morgan County Recorder's Office
PO Box 687
Versailles, MO 65084
Phone (314) 378-4029

County organized 1833 from Cooper County

Land records: From 1833

Naturalization records: Mixed in with court records and are very hard to find

Vital records: Very few vital records, starting around 1880

Probate records: From 1833

Probate search service: no charge; copies: 50¢ per page, no minimum

*New Madrid County Courthouse
New Madrid, MO 63869
Phone (314) 748-2524; (314) 748-5146 Recorder; (314) 748-5556 Clerk

County organized 1812, original county

Land records: From 1805; contact Recorder

Naturalization records: No naturalization records

Vital records: Marriages from 1805; contact Recorder

Probate records: From 1806; contact Paula Scobey, Clerk

Probate search service: no charge; copies: 25¢ each, no minimum

*Newton County Courthouse
Neosho, MO 64850
Phone (417) 451-4540
County organized 1838 from Barry County
Land records: Contact Recorder of Deeds Office, PO Box 1307, Neosho, MO 64850
Probate records: Contact Division III
Probate search service: $5.00 per person; copies: $1.00 per page, no minimum

*Nodaway County Courthouse
Maryville, MO 64468
Phone (816) 582-2251; (816) 582-5711 Recorder's Office; (816) 582-5431 Circuit Clerk's Office; (816) 582-4221 Probate Clerk
County organized 1845 from Andrew County
Land records: Contact Donna Carmichael, Recorder's Office
Naturalization records: Contact Patrick O'Riley, Circuit Clerk's Office
Probate records: Contact Probate Clerk
Probate search service: no charge; copies: $1.00 per page, no minimum

*Oregon County Courthouse
PO Box 406
Alton, MO 65606-0406
Phone (417) 778-7475
County organized 1845 from Ripley County
Land records: Contact Recorder
Naturalization records: Contact Recorder
Vital records: Contact Recorder
Probate records: Contact Recorder

*Osage County Courthouse
PO Box 826
Linn, MO 65051
Phone (314) 897-3114 Circuit Clerk and Recorder; (314) 897-2139 County Clerk's Office; (314) 897-2136 Division III
County organized 1841 from Gasconade County
Land records: Contact Jerry Starke, Circuit Clerk and Recorder
Naturalization records: Contact Circuit Clerk and Recorder
Vital records: Births and deaths from 1882 to 1892; contact Wanda J. Bunch, County Clerk's Office. Marriages; contact Circuit Clerk and Recorder
Probate records: Contact Judge Ralph R. Voss, Associate Judge, Division III
No probate search service; copies: 25¢ each

Ozark County Courthouse
Gainesville, MO 65655
Phone (417) 679-3516
County organized 1841 from Taney County

Pemiscot County Courthouse
Caruthersville, MO 63830
Phone (314) 333-4203
County organized 1851 from New Madrid County

Perry County Courthouse
Perryville, MO 63775
Phone (314) 547-4242
County organized 1820 from Sainte Genevieve County

Pettis County Courthouse
415 South Ohio
Sedalia, MO 65301-4435
Phone (816) 826-5395
County organized 1833 from Saline and Cooper counties

*Phelps County Courthouse
Third and Rolla Streets
Rolla, MO 65401
Phone (314) 364-1891 Recorder's Office
County organized 1857 from Crawford County
Land records: From 1857; contact Recorder's Office
Naturalization records: To the early or mid-50s; contact Recorder's Office
Vital records: Births and deaths from 1882 to 1892
Probate records: From January 1858
Probate search service: no charge; copies: $1.00 per page, no minimum

*Pike County Courthouse
115 West Main
Bowling Green, MO 63334
Phone (314) 324-2412
County organized 1818 from Saint Charles County
Land records: Contact Recorder's Office
Naturalization records: No naturalization records
Vital records: No vital records
Probate records: Contact Probate Office
No probate search service; copies: 25¢ per page; "The Probate Office does not do index searches but will refer an individual to persons that do this kind of work."

*Platte County Courthouse
Platte City, MO 64079
Phone (816) 431-2232
County organized 1838 from Platte Purchase
Land records: From 1839; contact County Recorder

Naturalization records: Just a few naturalization records in storage; contact Circuit Clerk's Office
Vital records: One page of vital records in an old book
Probate records: From 1839; contact Probate Judge
Probate search service: no charge; copies: 25¢ each, no minimum

Polk County Courthouse
Bolivar, MO 65613
Phone (417) 326-4031
County organized 1835 from Greene and Laclede counties

*Pulaski County Courthouse
301 U.S. Highway 44 East
Waynesville, MO 65583
Phone (314) 774-2241
County organized 1833 from Crawford County
Land records: From 1903; contact Beth Carroll, Recorder of Deeds, Suite 202; copies: $1.00 per page
Naturalization records: Some old naturalization records
Vital records: No vital records
Probate records: From 1903; contact Wanda Swenson, Clerk; copies: 25¢ per page

*Putnam County Courthouse
Unionville, MO 63565
Phone (816) 947-2071 Recorder of Deeds and Circuit Clerk; (816) 947-2674 County Clerk; (816) 947-2117 Probate Court
County organized 1845 from Adair, Sullivan and Linn counties, annexed Dodge County in 1853
Land records: From 1848; contact Recorder of Deeds, Room 202
Naturalization records: From 1904 to 1905; contact Circuit Clerk, Room 202
Vital records: Births from 1883 to 1898; contact County Clerk. Marriages from 1850; contact Recorder of Deeds
Probate records: From 1845; contact Probate Court, Room 101
Probate search service: no charge; copies: $1.00 per page, no minimum

*Ralls County Courthouse
New London, MO 63459-0444
Phone (314) 985-7111
County organized 1820 from Pike County
Land records: Contact County Recorder of Deeds
Naturalization records: Contact Circuit Clerk
Vital records: Marriages; contact County Recorder of Deeds

Probate records: Contact Probate Clerk, New London, MO 63459-0466
Probate search service: $3.00; copies: $1.00 per page, no minimum

Randolph County Courthouse
South Main Street
Huntsville, MO 65259
Phone (816) 277-4717
County organized 1829 from Chariton and Ralls counties

*Ray County Courthouse
Richmond, MO 64085
Phone (816) 776-3184
County organized 1820 from Howard County
Land records: From 23 November 1820; contact Recorder of Deeds
Naturalization records: From 1903 to 1945; contact Circuit Clerk
Vital records: Births from 1884 to 1890, deaths from 1883 to 1886; contact County Clerk
Probate records: From 3 April 1821; contact Clerk Associate Division Circuit Court
Probate search service: $5.00 for up to three names; copies: 25¢ per page per side "with no charge until $5.00 index search is exhausted," $5.00 minimum

*Reynolds County Courthouse
Courthouse Square
PO Box 76
Centerville, MO 63633
Phone (314) 648-2494, ext. 38, 39, 44
County organized 1845 from Shannon County
Land records: From 1872 (courthouse burned in 1867)
Naturalization records: Photocopied and hand-written naturalization records in deed books
Vital records: Marriage records only 1872
Probate records: From 1872; contact Associate Judge Donald E. Lamb or Paula Gray, Clerk, Probate—Circuit Court
Probate search service: "We don't usually do this, only if time allows"; copies: $2.00 plus $1.00 per each additional page, $1.00 minimum

Ripley County Courthouse
Doniphan, MO 63935
Phone (314) 996-3215
County organized 1833 from Wayne County

Saint Charles County Courthouse
Third and Jefferson
PO Box 99
Saint Charles, MO 63301

Phone (314) 946-4694
County organized 1812, original county

*Saint Clair County Courthouse
PO Box 334
Osceola, MO 64776
Phone (417) 646-2226
County organized 29 January 1841 from Rives County
Land records: Yes
Naturalization records: Yes
Vital records: From 1883 to 1887 only
Probate records: Yes

*Saint Francois County Courthouse
1 North Washington Street
Farmington, MO 63640
Phone (314) 756-5411
County organized 1821 from Sainte Genevieve, Jefferson and Washington counties
Land records: Yes
Naturalization records: Yes
Vital records: Yes
Probate records: Yes

Saint Louis City Courthouse
Saint Louis, MO 63103
Phone (314) 622-4000
City organized 1764, made an independent city from Saint Louis County in 1804
Vital records: Births and deaths from 1825; contact City of Saint Louis, Vital Records, PO Box 14702, Saint Louis, MO 63178

Saint Louis County Courthouse
7900 Forsythe Boulevard
Clayton, MO 63105
Phone (314) 889-2016
County organized 1812, original county

Sainte Genevieve County Courthouse
55 South Third
Sainte Genevieve, MO 63670
Phone (314) 883-5589
County organized 1812, original county

Saline County Courthouse
Marshall, MO 65340
Phone (816) 886-3331
County organized 1820 from Cooper County

Schuyler County Courthouse
PO Box 187
Lancaster, MO 63548-0187
Phone (816) 457-3842
County organized 1845 from Adair County

Scotland County Courthouse
Memphis, MO 63555

Phone (816) 465-7027 Presiding Commissioner; (816) 465-8605 Clerk Circuit Court and ex officio Recorder of Deeds
County organized 1841 from Clark, Lewis and Shelby counties

*Scott County Courthouse
Benton, MO 63736
Phone (314) 545-3549; (314) 545-3551 Recorder of Deeds; (314) 545-3511 Probate Clerk
County organized 1821 from New Madrid County
Land records: Contact John J. Bollinger, Recorder of Deeds, PO Box 76, Benton, MO 63736
Naturalization records: Contact Recorder of Deeds
Vital records: No vital records
Probate records: Contact Probate Clerk
Probate search service: no charge; copies: 50¢ each, no minimum; "Inquiries answered on basis of clerk's time available."

*Shannon County Courthouse
PO Box 187
Eminence, MO 65466-0187
Phone (314) 226-3414 Presiding Commissioner; (314) 226-3315 Clerk Circuit Court and ex officio Recorder of Deeds
County organized 1841 from Ripley County
Land records: Contact Lucille Orchard, Recorder of Deeds, PO Box 148, Eminence, MO 65466

*Shelby County Courthouse
PO Box 186
Shelbyville, MO 63469-0186
Phone (314) 633-2181
County organized 1835 from Marion County
Land records: Contact Charles R. Wood, Clerk Circuit Court and Recorder of Deeds, PO Box 176, Shelbyville, MO 63469
Naturalization records: Contact Clerk Circuit Court and Recorder of Deeds
Vital records: Marriages; contact Clerk Circuit Court and Recorder of Deeds
Probate records: Contact Probate Clerk, PO Box 206, Shelbyville, MO 63469
Probate search service: no charge; copies: 50¢ each, no minimum

*Stoddard County Courthouse
Bloomfield, MO 63825
Phone (314) 568-3339
County organized 1835 from Cape Girardeau County
Land records: Contact Recorder's Office
Naturalization records: Contact Circuit Clerk's Office

Vital records: Births and deaths from 1883 to 1886; contact County Clerk's Office

Probate records: Contact Probate Office, Trust Building, Bloomfield, MO 63825

No probate search service; copies: 50¢ each, no minimum; "The Stoddard County Historical Society does some research work."

*Stone County Courthouse
PO Box 18
Galena, MO 65656
Phone (417) 357-6127
County organized 1851 from Taney County
Land records: Contact Cathy Shortt, Recorder of Deeds; copies: $2.00 each
Naturalization records: No naturalization records
Vital records: Marriages only; contact Recorder of Deeds; copies: $2.00 each
Probate records: Contact Judge Kirsch, Associate Circuit Court

Sullivan County Courthouse
Milan, MO 63556
Phone (816) 265-3786
County organized 1845 from Linn County

Taney County Courthouse
Forsyth, MO 65653
Phone (417) 546-2241
County organized 1837 from Greene County

Texas County Courthouse
210 North Grand
Houston, MO 65483-1224
Phone (417) 967-2112
County organized 1845 from Shannon and Wright counties

Vernon County Courthouse
Nevada, MO 64772
Phone (417) 667-3157
County organized 1851 from Bates County

Warren County Courthouse
116 West Main
Warrenton, MO 63383
Phone (314) 456-3331
County organized 1833 from Montgomery County

*Washington County Courthouse
102 North Missouri
Potosi, MO 63664
Phone (314) 438-4901
County organized 1813 from Sainte Genevieve County

Land records: Yes
Naturalization records: Yes
Vital records: Yes
Probate records: Yes

*Wayne County Courthouse
Greenville, MO 63944
Phone (314) 224-3221
County organized 1818 from Cape Girardeau and Lawrence counties
Land records: From December 1892; contact Circuit Clerk and Recorder's Office ("All records in the courthouse were destroyed by fire in December of 1892; a few of the land records were re-recorded, but not many.")
Vital records: Marriages; contact Circuit Clerk and Recorder's Office
Probate records: From December 1892; contact Associate and Probate Division of Circuit Court
Probate search service: no charge; copies: 25¢ per page, plus SASE, no minimum

*Webster County Courthouse
PO Box 529
Marshfield, MO 65706
Phone (417) 468-2173
County organized 1855 from Greene County
Land records: From 1855; contact Recorder of Deeds, PO Box 529, Marshfield, MO 65706
Vital records: Marriages only; contact Recorder's Office
Probate records: Contact Associate Division Probate
Probate search service: no charge; copies: $1.00 per page, no minimum

*Worth County Courthouse
PO Box L
Grant City, MO 64456-0530
Phone (816) 564-2219
County organized 1861 from Gentry County
Land records: Contact Peggy Hunt, Recorder
Land records search service: $4.00; copies: $1.00 per document
Naturalization records: From 1861
Vital records: From 1883 to 1893; contact Recorder
Probate records: Contact Carmetta Jackson, Court Clerk
Probate search service: $4.00; copies: $1.00 per document

*Wright County Courthouse
PO Box 39
Hartville, MO 65667-0098
Phone (417) 741-7121 Circuit Clerk; (417) 741-6780 FAX, Circuit Clerk
County organized 1841 from Pulaski County

Land records: From 1849 to date; contact Joe Chadwell, Circuit Clerk and Ex-officio Recorder of Deeds, or Becky Jones, Deputy Recorder
Naturalization records: No naturalization records
Vital records: No vital records
Probate records: From about 1900; contact Circuit Clerk or Deputy Recorder
Probate search service: no charge; copies: 25¢ per page, no minimum

MONTANA

Capital: Helena. Statehood: 8 November 1889 (settled border with Canada in 1818 and 1846, was part of Washington, Nebraska, Dakota and Idaho territories before becoming a separate territory in 1864)

Court System

Montana has four courts of limited jurisdiction: the Missoula Municipal Court, City Courts in ninety-three cities, Justice of the Peace Courts in each county and the Montana Water Court.

The District Court sits in each county seat and handles all felonies, juvenile matters and probate, as well as some misdemeanors, civil actions and appeals from lower courts. The court is divided into twenty districts. First Judicial District: Broadwater and Lewis and Clark counties; Second Judicial District: Silver Bow; Third Judicial District: Deer Lodge, Granite and Powell counties; Fourth Judicial District: Mineral, Missoula and Ravalli counties; Fifth Judicial District: Beaverhead, Jefferson and Madison counties; Sixth Judicial District: Park and Sweet Grass counties; Seventh Judicial District: Dawson, McCone, Prairie, Richland and Wibaux counties; Eighth Judicial District: Cascade County; Ninth Judicial District: Glacier, Pondera, Teton and Toole counties; Tenth Judicial District: Fergus, Judith Basin and Petroleum counties; Eleventh Judicial District: Flathead County; Twelfth Judicial District: Chouteau, Hill and Liberty counties; Thirteenth Judicial District: Big Horn, Carbon, Stillwater and Yellowstone counties; Fourteenth Judicial District: Golden Valley, Meagher, Musselshell and Wheatland counties; Fifteenth Judicial District: Daniels, Roosevelt and Sheridan counties; Sixteenth Judicial District: Carter, Custer, Fallon, Garfield, Powder River, Rosebud and Treasure counties; Seventeenth Judicial District: Blaine, Phillips and Valley counties; Eighteenth Judicial District: Gallatin County; Nineteenth Judicial District: Lincoln County; Twentieth Judicial District: Lake and Sanders counties. The Supreme Court in Helena hears appeals from all the lower courts.

Courthouses

*Beaverhead County Courthouse
2 South Pacific
Dillon, MT 59725-2713

Phone (406) 683-5245 County Commissioners; (406) 683-2642 County Clerk and Recorder; (406) 683-5831 Clerk of District Court
County organized 1864, original county
Land records: From 1864; contact County Clerk and Recorder; copies: 50¢ each plus SASE; prefer written requests
Naturalization records: From 1876 to 1929; contact Clerk of District Court; copies: none
Vital records: Births and deaths from 1900; contact County Clerk and Recorder; certified copies: $5.00 each for births, $3.00 each for deaths. Marriages from 1867; contact Sheila Brunkhorst, Clerk of District Court.
Vital records search service from Clerk of District Court: 50¢ per year; copies: 50¢ for each of the first five pages and 25¢ for each additional page
Probate records: From 1878; contact Clerk of District Court
Probate search service: 50¢ per year; copies: 50¢ for each of the first five pages and 25¢ for each additional page; "Will accept *written* requests only; please provide prepaid return postage."

*Big Horn County Courthouse
Hardin, MT 59034
Phone (406) 665-3520; (406) 665-1504 District Court Clerk
County organized 1913 from Rosebud and Yellowstone counties
Land records: Contact Clerk and Recorder; copies: 50¢ for the first page and 25¢ for each additional page
Naturalization records: To the mid-1950s only; contact District Court Clerk, 121 West Third Street, #221, PO Box H, Hardin, MT 59034
Vital records: Births and deaths; contact Clerk and Recorder; certified copies: $5.00 each for births (some restrictions apply), $3.00 each for deaths. Marriages; contact District Court Clerk.
Probate records: Contact District Court Clerk
Probate search service: 50¢ per year per name, $25.00 maximum; copies: 50¢ per page for each of the first five pages and 25¢ for each additional page, $2.00 for certification

*Blaine County Courthouse
PO Box 278
Chinook, MT 59523
Phone (406) 357-3250
County organized 1895 from Chouteau and Hill counties
Land records: Yes
Land records search service: 50¢ per year

per index; copies: 50¢ for the first page and 25¢ for each additional page
Naturalization records: Yes
Naturalization records search service: 50¢ per year per index; copies: 50¢ for the first page and 25¢ for each additional page
Vital records: Births and deaths (closed to the public)
Probate records: Yes
Probate search service: 50¢ per year per index; copies: 50¢ for the first page and 25¢ for each additional page

*Broadwater County Courthouse
515 Broadwater
Townsend, MT 59644
Phone (406) 266-3443
County organized 1897 from Jefferson and Meagher counties
Land records: Contact County Clerk and Recorder
Naturalization records: Contact Nellie B. Sayer, Clerk of Court
Vital records: Contact Clerk and Recorder
Probate records: Contact Clerk of Court
Probate search service: 50¢ per year, $25.00 maximum; copies: 50¢ for each of the first five pages and 25¢ for each additional page, $2.00 for certification

*Carbon County Courthouse
PO Box 887
Red Lodge, MT 59068
Phone (406) 446-1220 Clerk and Recorder; (406) 446-1225 Clerk of Court
County organized 1895 from Park and Yellowstone counties
Land records: Contact Clerk and Recorder
Naturalization records: Contact Clerk of Court
Vital records: Contact Clerk and Recorder or Clerk of Court
Probate records: Contact Clerk of Court

*Carter County Courthouse
PO Box 315
Ekalaka, MT 59324-0315
Phone (405) 775-8749
County organized 1917 from Custer County
Land records: Contact County Assessor
Naturalization records: Contact Clerk of District Court
Vital records: Contact Clerk and Recorder
Probate records: Contact Clerk of District Court
Probate search service: 50¢ per name per year, $25.00 maximum; copies: 50¢ for each of the first five pages and 25¢ for each additional page, plus postage for mailings, no minimum

*Cascade County Courthouse
Great Falls, MT 59401
Phone (406) 761-6700
County organized 1887 from Chouteau and Meagher counties
Land records: Contact County Assessor
Naturalization records: Limited naturalization records; contact U.S. District Court
Vital records: Contact Clerk and Recorder
Probate records: Contact Clerk of District Court
Probate search service: "full search, all books, $25.00 per name per year"; copies: 50¢ for each of the first five pages and 25¢ for each additional page; "Make checks payable to Clerk of Court."

*Chouteau County Courthouse
Fort Benton, MT 59442
Phone (406) 622-5151
County organized 1865, original county
Land records: Contact Clerk and Recorder Office
Naturalization records: Contact Clerk of Court Office
Vital records: Contact Clerk and Recorder Office
Probate records: Contact Clerk of Court Office
Probate search service: $7.00; copies: 50¢ each, $1.00 minimum; "Record search consists of Liens, Mortgages, etc."

*Custer County Courthouse
1010 Main Street
Miles City, MT 59301-3496
Phone (406) 232-7800
County organized 1865, original county
Land records: Mortgages, deeds, patents, homesteads; contact Clerk and Recorder
Land records search service: $7.00 for the first five years and 50¢ for each additional year searched and 50¢ for each book searched for the additional years
Naturalization records: Contact Clerk of Court
Vital records: Contact Clerk and Recorder
Vital records search service: $6.00 for births, $4.00 for deaths (includes certified copy); certified copies: $5.00 each for births (limited to relatives of the registrant with proof that the registrant died at least thirty years ago), $3.00 each for deaths (limited to relatives of registrants who died at least twenty years ago)
Probate records: Contact Clerk of Court

*Daniels County Courthouse
PO Box 247
Scobey, MT 59263

Phone (406) 487-5561
County organized 1920 from Valley County
Land records: From August 1920 (some transcribed records from July 1913); contact Clerk and Recorder; copies: 50¢ for the first page and 25¢ for each additional page
Vital records: Births and deaths from August 1920 ("some from before"); contact Clerk and Recorder. Marriages from 1920; contact Clerk of Court, PO Box 67, Scobey, MT 59263; certified copies: $5.00 each for births, $3.00 each for deaths (both confidential)
Probate records: From August 1920; contact Clerk of Court
Probate search service: 50¢ per year per name; copies: 50¢ each, $2.00 for certified copies, no minimum

*Dawson County Courthouse
207 West Bell Street
Glendive, MT 59330-1616
Phone (406) 365-3058 Clerk and Recorder
County organized 1865, original county
Land records: Contact Maurine Lenhardt, Clerk and Recorder
Land records search service: $10.00 per hour; copies: 25¢ each, $2.00 for certification
Naturalization records: Contact Ardelle Adams, Clerk of Court
Vital records: Births and deaths; contact Clerk and Recorder; copies: $5.00 each for births (restricted to registrant or parents, notarized application required), $3.00 each for deaths (notarized application required). Marriages; contact Clerk of Court
Probate records: Contact Clerk of Court
No probate search service; copies: 50¢ for each of the first five pages and 25¢ for each additional page, 50¢ minimum

*Deer Lodge County Courthouse
800 South Main Street
Anaconda, MT 59711-2999
Phone (406) 563-8421 Clerk and Recorder; (406) 563-8421, ext. 223 Clerk of District Court
County organized 1864, original county
Land records: From 1864; contact Clerk and Recorder
Land records search service: $5.00 for four or more names, $7.00 per document; copies: 50¢ for the first page and 25¢ for each additional page
Naturalization records: From the 1870s to the 1950s; contact Clerk District Court
Vital records: From 1898; contact Clerk and Recorder
Vital records search service: 50¢ per year; copies: $5.00 each for births,

$3.00 each for deaths (proof of relationship required)
Probate records: From 1870; contact Clerk of District Court
Probate search service: 50¢ per year, $5.00 maximum; copies: 50¢ for each of the first five pages and 25¢ for each additional page, $2.00 for certification, 50¢ minimum

*Fallon County Courthouse
10 West Fallon Avenue
Baker, MT 59313
Phone (406) 778-2883
County organized 1913 from Custer County
Land records: Contact Mary Lee Dietz, Clerk and Recorder; PO Box 846, Baker, MT 59313
Land records search service: 50¢ per year; copies: 50¢ for the first page and 25¢ for each additional page
Naturalization records: Contact Clerk of Court, PO Box 1521, Baker, MT 59313
Vital records: From about 1920; contact Clerk and Recorder
Vital records search service: 50¢ per year; certified copies: $5.00 each for births, $3.00 each for deaths (both confidential, but information can be verified)
Probate records: Contact Clerk of Court
Probate search service: no charge; copies: 50¢ for each of the first five pages and 25¢ for each additional page, no minimum

*Fergus County Courthouse
712 West Main
Lewistown, MT 59457-2562
Phone (406) 538-5119
County organized 1885 from Meagher County
Land records: From about 1818; contact Clerk and Recorder
Naturalization records: Contact Clerk of Courts
Vital records: From about 1877; contact Clerk and Recorder
Probate records: Contact Clerk of Courts
Probate search service: 50¢ per year, $25.00 maximum; copies: 50¢ for each of the first five pages and 25¢ for each additional page, no minimum; "School Records—County Superintendent of Schools."

*Flathead County Courthouse
Kalispell, MT 59901
Phone (406) 758-5526
County organized 1893 from Missoula County
Land records: Contact Clerk and Recorder, 800 South Main
Kalispell, MT 59901-5435

Vital records: Some vital records; contact Clerk and Recorder

*Gallatin County Courthouse
311 West Main
Bozeman, MT 59715-4576
Phone (406) 582-3050; (406) 582-2165 Clerk of District Court
County organized 1864, original county
Land records: Contact Clerk and Recorder, Room 204
Vital records: Births and deaths; contact Clerk and Recorder. Marriages; contact Clerk of District Court, 615 South 16th, Room 200, Bozeman, MT 59715
Probate records: Contact Clerk of District Court

*Garfield County Courthouse
PO Box 7
Jordan, MT 59337-0007
Phone (406) 557-2760
County organized 1919 from McCone and Valley counties
Land records: Yes
Naturalization records: Contact Clerk of Court's Office
Vital records: Births and deaths (both subject to restrictions)
Probate records: Contact Clerk of Court's Office

*Glacier County Courthouse
512 Main Street
Cut Bank, MT 59427-3016
Phone (406) 873-5063
County organized 1919 from Teton County
Land records: Contact Loretta Barron, Deputy Clerk and Recorder's Office
Naturalization records: Contact Marty Phippen, Clerk of Court
Vital records: Contact Gail Davis, Deputy Clerk and Recorder's Office ("Signing and filling out release form for birth and death certificates needed.")
Probate records: Contact Clerk of Court
Probate search service: $7.00; copies: 50¢ each, $7.00 minimum

*Golden Valley County Courthouse
107 Kemp
Ryegate, MT 59074
Phone (406) 568-2231
County organized 1920 from Musselshell and Sweet Grass counties
Land records: Patents
Naturalization records: No naturalization records
Vital records: Births from 1909, deaths from 1911
Probate records: Yes
Probate search service: 50¢ per name per

year, $25.00 maximum; copies: 50¢ for each of the first five pages and 25¢ for each additional page, $5.00 minimum

Granite County Courthouse
PO Box J
Philipsburg, MT 59858
Phone (406) 859-3771
County organized 1893 from Deer Lodge County

*Hill County Courthouse
Havre, MT 59501-3999
Phone (406) 265-5481
County organized 1912 from Chouteau County
Land records: Contact Clerk and Recorder; copies: 50¢ for the first page and 25¢ for each additional page
Naturalization records: Contact Clerk of District Court
Vital records: Contact Clerk and Recorder
No vital records search service; "Long form birth and death certificates require a questionnaire form completed and notarized; in some instances a court order is required."
Probate records: Contact Clerk of District Court
No probate search service; copies: $3.00 each

*Jefferson County Courthouse
PO Box H
Boulder, MT 59632
Phone (406) 225-4251
County organized 1864, original county

*Judith Basin County Courthouse
Stanford, MT 59479
Phone (406) 566-2301 Clerk and Recorder; (406) 566-2491 Clerk of Court
County organized 1920 from Fergus and Cascade counties
Land records: Contact Clerk and Recorder, Appraiser, Assessor
Naturalization records: To 1939
Vital records: Contact Clerk and Recorder or Clerk of Court
Probate records: Contact Clerk of Court
Probate search service: 50¢ per year; copies: 50¢ each, no minimum

*Lake County Courthouse
106 Fourth Avenue
Polson, MT 59860-2125
Phone (406) 883-6211
County organized 1923 from Flathead and Missoula counties
Land records: Contact Paddy Trusler, Land Services
Vital records: Contact Lorin Jacobson, Clerk and Recorder

Probate records: Contact Katherine Pedersen, Clerk of Court
Probate search service: $7.00; copies: 50¢ for each of the first five pages and 25¢ for each additional page, $1.00 minimum

*Lewis and Clark County Courthouse
316 North Park
Helena, MT 59601-5059
Phone (406) 443-1010
County organized 1864, original county
Land records: Yes
Naturalization records: Contact 228 Broadway, Helena, MT 59601
Vital records: Yes
Probate records: Contact 228 Broadway, Helena, MT 59601
Probate search service: 50¢ per year per name; copies: 50¢ for each of the first five pages and 25¢ for each additional page, no minimum

*Liberty County Courthouse
PO Box 549
Chester, MT 59522
Phone (406) 759-5365 Clerk and Recorder; (406) 759-5615 Clerk of Court
County organized 1920 from Chouteau County
Land records: Contact Clerk and Recorder, PO Box 459, Chester, MT 59522
Naturalization records: Contact Clerk of Court
Vital records: Contact Clerk and Recorder
Probate records: Contact Clerk of Court

*Lincoln County Courthouse
512 California Avenue
Libby, MT 59923-1942
Phone (406) 293-7781 Clerk and Recorder or Clerk of Court; (406) 293-8577 FAX, Clerk and Recorder
County organized 1909 from Flathead County
Land records: Contact Coral M. Cummings, Clerk and Recorder
Land records search service: 50¢ per year; copies: 50¢ for the first page and 25¢ for each additional page
Naturalization records: Contact Clerk of Court
Naturalization records search service: 50¢ per name per year, $25.00 maximum; copies: 50¢ for each of the first five pages and 25¢ for each additional page
Vital records: Contact Clerk and Recorder; copies: $5.00 each for births, $3.00 each for deaths
Probate records: Contact Clerk of Court
Probate search service: 50¢ per name per year, $25.00 maximum; copies: 50¢

for each of the first five pages and 25¢ for each additional page

Madison County Courthouse
110 West Wallace Street
PO Box 185
Virginia City, MT 59755
Phone (406) 843-5392
County organized 1864, original county

*McCone County Courthouse
PO Box 199
Circle, MT 59215-0199
Phone (406) 485-3505
County organized 1919 from Dawson and Richland counties
Land records: Contact Clerk and Recorder
Naturalization records: contact Clerk and Recorder
Vital records: Contact Clerk and Recorder (proof of relationship required)
Probate records: Contact Clerk and Recorder

Meagher County Courthouse
PO Box 309
White Sulphur Springs, MT 59645
Phone (406) 547-3612
County organized 1867, original county

*Mineral County Courthouse
PO Box 550
Superior, MT 59872-0550
Phone (406) 822-4541 Clerk and Recorder; (406) 822-4612 Clerk of District Court
County organized 1914 from Missoula County
Land records: Contact Clerk and Recorder
Land records search service: $5.00 per name; copies: 50¢ for the first page and 25¢ for each additional page
Naturalization records: No naturalization records
Vital records: Births and deaths; contact Clerk and Recorder (access restricted). Marriages; contact Clerk of District Court, PO Box 96, Superior, MT 59872
Vital records search service from Clerk of District Court: 50¢ per name per year; copies: 50¢ for each of the first five pages and 25¢ for each additional page
Probate records: Contact Clerk of District Court
Probate search service: 50¢ per name per year; copies: 50¢ for each of the first five pages and 25¢ for each additional page

*Missoula County Courthouse
Missoula, MT 59802-4292

Phone (406) 721-5700
County organized 14 December 1860, while part of Washington Territory, from Spokane County (all land east of longitude 115)
Land records: Contact County Clerk and Recorder
Naturalization records: Declarations of Intent from 1856 with admissions from 1869 through the late 1940s ("We have a very few listed through 1979, but those are sporadic"); contact Kathleen D. Breuer, Clerk of District Court
Vital records: Births and deaths from 1885; contact County Clerk and Recorder. Fairly complete marriage licenses from 1883; contact Clerk of District Court
Vital recorder search service from County Clerk and Recorder: $10.00 per hour; certified copies: $3.00 each ("The State of Montana Department of Health and Environmental Sciences does not permit public inspection of vital statistic indexes; genealogists will be given short-form death certificates for anyone who died from 1950 to present; this does not give family history other than birthplace for decedent and birth date; genealogists can receive a full copy if the death occurred before 1950; a birth certificate cannot be given to genealogists unless they have a certified copy of the person's death certificate for whom they are requesting a birth certificate.")
Probate records: From 1868 (with the most complete from 1889); contact Clerk of District Court
Probate search service: 50¢ per year searched, $25.00 maximum; copies: 50¢ for each of the first five pages and 25¢ for each additional page, $2.00 for certified copies; "also must include a SASE"

*Musselshell County Courthouse
PO Box 686
Roundup, MT 59072
Phone (406) 323-1104 Clerk and Recorder; (406) 323-1413 Clerk of District Court
County organized 1911 from Fergus and Yellowstone counties
Land records: Contact Clerk and Recorder
Naturalization records: From 1911; contact Clerk of District Court, PO Box 357, Roundup, MT 59072
Vital records: Births and deaths from 1911; contact Clerk and Recorder. Marriages from 1911; contact Clerk of District Court
Probate records: Contact Clerk of District Court

Probate search service: no charge; copies: 50¢ per page, $2.00 for certification

*Park County Courthouse
414 East Callendar
Livingston, MT 59047-2746
Phone (406) 222-6120, ext. 234 Clerk of District Court
County organized 1887 from Gallatin County
Land records: Contact Clerk and Recorder's Office
Naturalization records: From 1887; contact Clerk of District Court, PO Box 437, Livingston, MT 59047
Vital records: Marriage licenses from 1887; contact Clerk of District Court
Probate records: From 1887; contact Clerk of District Court
Probate search service: 50¢ per year, $25.00 maximum; copies: 50¢ for each of the first five pages and 25¢ for each additional page

*Petroleum County Courthouse
201 East Main
Winnett, MT 59087
Phone (406) 429-5311 Clerk and Recorder and Clerk of Court
County organized 1926 from Fergus County
Land records: From 1882; contact Clerk and Recorder
Naturalization records: No naturalization records
Vital records: From 1890; contact Clerk and Recorder or Clerk of Court
Probate records: From 1890; contact Clerk of Court
Probate search service: 50¢ per year up to $25.00; copies: 50¢ for each of the first five pages and 25¢ for each additional page, no minimum

*Phillips County Courthouse
314 South Second Avenue, West
Malta, MT 59538
Phone (406) 654-2429
County organized 1915 from Valley County
Land records: Contact Laurel N. Hines, Clerk and Recorder, PO Box U, Malta, MT 59538
Naturalization records: Contact Frances M. Webb, Clerk of Court, PO Box I, Malta, MT 59538
Vital records: Contact Clerk and Recorder
Probate records: Contact Clerk of Court
Probate search service: $7.00; copies: $1.00 each

*Pondera County Courthouse
20 Fourth Avenue, S.W.
Conrad, MT 59425-2340

Phone (406) 278-7681
*County organized 1919 from
Yellowstone County*
Land records: Contact Clerk and
Recorder
Naturalization records: Contact Clerk of
District Court
Vital records: Contact Clerk and
Recorder
Probate records: Contact Clerk of District
Court
Probate search service: $5.00 per person;
copies: 50¢ per page, $1.00 minimum

*Powder River County Courthouse
PO Box J
Broadus, MT 59317
Phone (406) 436-2657
*County organized 1919 from Custer
County*
Land records: From early 1800s; contact
Clerk and Recorder ("All land records
affecting present Powder River
County were transcribed from the
records of Custer County.")
Naturalization records: From 1919;
contact Clerk and Recorder
Vital records: From 1919; contact Clerk
and Recorder
Probate records: From 1919; contact
Clerk of District Court
Probate search service: 50¢ per year per
index; copies: 50¢ for each of the first
five pages and 25¢ for each additional
page, no minimum; "We also charge
postage costs."

*Powell County Courthouse
400 Missouri
Deer Lodge, MT 59722-1084
Phone (406) 846-3680
*County organized 1907 from Deer
Lodge County*
Land records: Contact Clerk and
Recorder's Office and/or Assessor's
Office
Naturalization records: Some old
naturalization records; contact Mary
Ann McKee, Clerk of Court
Vital records: Births and deaths; contact
Clerk and Recorder's Office
Probate records: Contact Clerk of Court
Probate search service: 50¢ per year,
$25.00 maximum; copies: 50¢ for
each of the first five pages and 25¢ for
each additional page, no minimum

*Prairie County Courthouse
PO Box 125
Terry, MT 59349-0125
Phone (406) 637-5575
*County organized 1915 from Custer,
Dawson and Fallon counties*
Land records: Contact Clerk and
Recorder
Naturalization records: Contact Clerk of
Court

Vital records: Contact Clerk of Court
Probate records: Contact Clerk of Court
Probate search service: $7.00; copies:
25¢ per page from paper original, 50¢
per page from microfilm original, no
minimum

*Ravalli County Courthouse
205 Bedford Street
Hamilton, MT 59840
Phone (406) 363-1900
*County organized 1893 from Missoula
County*
Land records: From about 1893 to date
(a few earlier); contact Betty T. Lund,
County Clerk and Recorder,
Courthouse Box 5002
No land records search service; copies:
50¢ per page
Vital records: Births and deaths from
1893 but incomplete until about 1920;
contact County Clerk and Recorder;
certified copies: $5.50 each for births
(restricted to the immediate family),
$3.50 each for deaths (records under
fifty years old restricted to the
immediate family)

*Richland County Courthouse
201 West Main
Sidney, MT 59270-4035
Phone (406) 482-1708 Clerk and
Recorder; (406) 482-1709 Clerk of
District Court
*County organized 1914 from Dawson
County*
Land records: From 1895 (transcribed
from Dawson County); contact Clerk
and Recorder; copies: 25¢ per page
Naturalization records: Contact Clerk of
District Court
Vital records: From 1915; contact Clerk
and Recorder; copies: 25¢ per page
(proof of relationship, registrant's date
of birth and names of parents
required)
Probate records: From 1915; contact
Clerk of District Court
Probate search service: no charge;
copies: 50¢ for each of the first five
pages and 25¢ for each additional
page, $2.00 for certification, $1.00
minimum

*Roosevelt County Courthouse
400 Second Avenue, South
Wolf Point, MT 59201-1605
Phone (406) 653-1590
*County organized 1919 from Sheridan
and Valley counties*
Land records: Contact Cheryl Hansen,
Clerk and Recorder, or County
Assessor
Naturalization records: Contact Clerk of
Court
Vital records: Contact Clerk and
Recorder

No vital records search service (must
have name, date of birth and parents'
names); copies: $1.00 each, $5.00 for
certified copies of births, $3.00 for
certified copies of deaths
Probate records: Contact Clerk of Court

Rosebud County Courthouse
PO Box 48
Forsyth, MT 59327
Phone (406) 356-2251
*County organized 1901 from Dawson
County*

*Sanders County Courthouse
Main Street
Thompson Falls, MT 59873
Phone (406) 827-4392
*County organized 1906 from Missoula
County*
Land records: Contact Clerk and
Recorder
Naturalization records: Contact Clerk of
District Court
Vital records: Contact Clerk and
Recorder
Probate records: Contact Clerk of District
Court
Probate search service: 50¢ per year;
copies: 50¢ for each of the first five
pages and 25¢ for each additional
page

*Sheridan County Courthouse
100 West Laurel Avenue
Plentywood, MT 59254-1619
Phone (406) 765-2310
*County organized 1913 from Valley
County*
Land records: Contact Bernice Van
Curen, Clerk and Recorder's Office
Naturalization records: Contact Clerk of
Court
Vital records: Contact Clerk and
Recorder's Office
Probate records: Contact Clerk of Court
Probate search service: 50¢ per year per
name; copies: 50¢ per page, no
minimum

*Silver Bow County Courthouse
155 West Granite
Butte, MT 59701-9256
Phone (406) 723-8262; (406) 723-8262,
ext. 306 Butte-Silver Bow Public
Archives
*County organized 1881 from Deer
Lodge County*
Land records: From 1881 to date; contact
Barbara Sullivan, Clerk and Recorder;
copies: 50¢ for the first page and 25¢
for each additional page (must furnish
names of owners and years of
ownership)
Naturalization records: Contact Butte-
Silver Bow Public Archives (17 West

Quartz, Butte, MT 59701—location),
PO Box 81 (mailing address), Butte,
MT 59703

Vital records: Births from about 1915 to
date (sketchy before 1915, but many
delayed certificates have been filed),
deaths from 1907 to date (sketchy
before 1907); contact Clerk and
Recorder; certified copies: $5.00 each
for births (must show proof of
relationship), $3.00 each for deaths
(must supply date of death within a
ten-year period). Marriages; contact
Lori Maloney, Clerk of the District
Court, Room 313. Births from 1906 to
1921, deaths from 1901 to 1917;
contact Butte-Silver Bow Public
Archives

Vital records search service from Clerk
of the District Court: 50¢ per name
per year, payable in advance; copies:
$1.00 each, $3.00 for certified copies

Probate records: Contact Clerk of the
Court; copies: 50¢ per page for each
of the first five pages and 25¢ for each
additional page plus postage, $2.00
for certification

*Stillwater County Courthouse
Columbus, MT 59019
Phone (406) 322-4546
***County organized 1913 from Sweet
Grass and Yellowstone counties***

Land records: Contact Clerk and
Recorder

Naturalization records: Contact Clerk of
District Court, PO Box 367,
Columbus, MT 59019

Vital records: Contact Clerk and
Recorder

Probate records: Contact Clerk of District
Court

Probate search service: $7.00; copies:
50¢ for each of the first five pages and
25¢ for each additional page, no
minimum

*Sweet Grass County Courthouse
PO Box 460
Big Timber, MT 59011
Phone (406) 932-5152
***County organized 1895 from Meagher,
Park and Yellowstone counties***

Land records: Contact Clerk and
Recorder

Naturalization records: Contact Clerk of
District Court, PO Box 698, Big
Timber, MT 59011

Vital records: Births and deaths; contact
Clerk and Recorder. Marriages;
contact Clerk of District Court

Probate records: Contact Clerk of District
Court

Probate search service: 50¢ per name;
copies: 50¢ for each of the first five
pages and 25¢ for each additional
page, no minimum

*Teton County Courthouse
PO Box 610
Choteau, MT 59422-0610
Phone (406) 466-2693 Clerk and
Recorder; (406) 466-2909 Clerk of
Court
***County organized 1893 from Chouteau
County***

Land records: Contact Clerk and
Recorder

Naturalization records: Contact Clerk of
Court (must have name of person and
approximate year)

Vital records: Contact Clerk and
Recorder

Probate records: Contact Clerk of Court

Probate search service: 50¢ per name per
year; copies: 50¢ for each of the first
five pages and 25¢ for each additional
page, 50¢ minimum

*Toole County Courthouse
226 First Street, South
PO Box 850
Shelby, MT 59474
Phone (406) 434-2271
***County organized 1914 from Teton
County***

Land records; contact Clerk and
Recorder

Naturalization records: Some records
before the 1960s; contact Clerk of
Court

Vital records: Contact Clerk and
Recorder

Probate records: Contact Clerk of Court

*Treasure County Courthouse
PO Box 392
Hysham, MT 59038
Phone (406) 342-5547
***County organized 1919 from Big Horn
County***

Land records: Contact County Clerk and
Recorder's Office

Naturalization records: Contact District
Court Office

Vital records: Contact County Clerk and
Recorder's Office

Probate records: Contact District Court
Office

No probate search service; copies: 50¢
for the first page and 25¢ for each
additional page, $2.00 for
certification, $2.00 minimum mail-out
charge

*Valley County Courthouse
501 Court Square
Glasgow, MT 59230-2405
Phone (406) 228-8221, ext. 21 Clerk and
Recorder; (406) 228-8221 Clerk of
Court
***County organized 1893 from Dawson
County***

Land records: Contact Clerk and
Recorder, 501 Court Square, #2

Land records search service: 50¢ per
page per name; copies: 50¢ for each
of the first five pages and 25¢ for each
additional page

Naturalization records: To 1979; contact
Clerk of Court, 501 Court Square, #6

Naturalization records

Land records search service: 50¢ per
page per name; copies: 50¢ for each
of the first five pages and 25¢ for each
additional page

Vital records: Contact Clerk and
Recorder

Vital records search service: 50¢ per
page per name; copies: 50¢ for each
of the first five pages and 25¢ for each
additional page

Probate records: Contact Clerk of Court

Probate search service: 50¢ per page per
name; copies: 50¢ for each of the first
five pages and 25¢ for each additional
page

*Wheatland County Courthouse
Harlowton, MT 59036
Phone (406) 632-4891
***County organized 1917 from Meagher,
Fergus and Sweet Grass counties***

Land records: Contact Clerk and
Recorder, Assessor, Appraiser

Naturalization records: Contact Clerk of
Courts

Vital records: Births and deaths; contact
Clerk and Recorder (proof of
relationship required). Marriages;
contact Clerk of Court

Probate records: Contact Clerk of Court

No probate search service; copies: 50¢
for each of the first five pages and 25¢
for each additional page, $2.00 for
certified copies, $1.50 plus postage
minimum

Wibaux County Courthouse
PO Box 310
Wibaux, MT 59353
Phone (406) 795-2410
***County organized 1914 from Dawson
County***

*Yellowstone County Courthouse
North 27th and Third North
Billings, MT 59101
Phone (406) 256-2785 Clerk and
Recorder; (406) 256-2860 Clerk of the
District Court
***County organized 1883 from Custer,
Gallatin and Meagher counties***

Land records: From 1881; contact Clerk
and Recorder; copies: 50¢ for the first
page and 25¢ for each additional page
of the same document

Naturalization records: Contact
Immigration and Naturalization
(Yellowstone County), Federal
Building, Room 5405, 316 North 26th

Street, Billings, MT 59101, (406) 657-6366

Vital records: Births from 1800, deaths from 1895; contact Clerk and Recorder; certified copies: $5.00 each for births, $3.00 each for deaths. Marriages; contact Clerk of District Court; copies: 50¢ each, $2.50 for certified copies, plus 50¢ postage unless SASE included

Probate records: Contact Clerk of District Court

Probate search service: 50¢ per name per year; copies: 50¢ for each of the first five pages and 25¢ for each additional page per case plus 50¢ postage unless SASE included, no minimum

NEBRASKA

Capital: Lincoln. Statehood: 1 March 1867 (annexed as part of the Louisiana Purchase, 1803, part of the Territory of Orleans and later the Missouri Territory until made a separate territory by the Kansas-Nebraska Act of 1854)

Court System

Nebraska has a separate Juvenile Court for Douglas, Lancaster and Sarpy counties and a Workers' Compensation Tribunal, but the bulk of its civil actions, probates, guardianships, adoptions, eminent domain matters, misdemeanors, traffic cases, municipal ordinance violations, felony preliminaries and juvenile matters are heard in the state's County Courts. First Judicial District: Johnson, Nemaha, Pawnee and Richardson counties; Second Judicial District: Cass, Otoe and Sarpy counties; Third Judicial District: Lancaster County; Fourth Judicial District: Douglas County; Fifth Judicial District: Butler, Hamilton, Polk, Saunders, Seward and York counties; Sixth Judicial District: Burt, Dodge, Thurston and Washington counties; Seventh Judicial District: Fillmore, Nuckolls, Saline and Thayer counties; Eighth Judicial District: Cedar, Dakota and Dixon counties; Ninth Judicial District: Antelope, Cuming, Knox, Madison, Pierce, Stanton and Wayne counties; Tenth Judicial District: Adams, Clay, Franklin, Harlan, Kearney, Phelps and Webster counties; Eleventh Judicial District: Hall and Howard counties; Twelfth Judicial District: Buffalo and Sherman counties; Thirteenth Judicial District: Arthur, Dawson, Hooker, Keith, Lincoln, Logan, McPherson and Thomas counties; Fourteenth Judicial District: Chase, Dundy, Frontier, Furnas, Gosper, Hayes, Hitchcock, Perkins and Red Willow counties; Fifteenth Judicial District: Boyd, Brown, Cherry, Holt, Keya Paha and Rock counties; Sixteenth Judicial District: Box Butte, Dawes, Grant, Sheridan and Sioux counties; Seventeenth Judicial District: Garden, Morrill and Scotts Bluff counties; Eighteenth Judicial District: Gage and Jefferson counties; Nineteenth Judicial District: Banner, Cheyenne, Deuel and Kimball counties; Twentieth Judicial District: Blaine, Custer, Garfield, Greeley, Loup, Valley and Wheeler counties; Twenty-first Judicial District: Boone, Colfax, Merrick, Nance and Platte counties.

The state's District Courts have general jurisdiction. Their districts are identical to the County Courts' districts with the ex-ception that Morrill County is in the Sixteenth Judicial District and Garden County is in the Nineteenth Judicial District. A Supreme Court is the court of last resort.

Courthouses

Adams County Courthouse
500 West Fifth
Room 109
Hastings, NE 68901
Phone (402) 461-7107
County organized 1867 from Clay County

*Antelope County Courthouse
Neligh, NE 68756
Phone (402) 887-4410
County organized 1871 from Pierce County
Land records: From 1875; contact Eleanor Holm, County Clerk
Naturalization records: From 1875; contact Nadene Hughes, Clerk of District Court
Vital records: Marriages from 1875; contact County Clerk
Probate records: From 1875; contact Barbara Zegers, Clerk Magistrate
No probate search service: "If we have to do the research, we base it on the amount of time it took us"; copies: 20¢ per page

Arthur County Courthouse
Arthur, NE 69121
Phone (308) 764-2208
County organized 1887 from unattached lands

*Banner County Courthouse
PO Box 67
Harrisburg, NE 69345-0067
Phone (308) 436-5265
County organized 1888 from Cheyenne County
Land records: Yes; copies: 25¢ each
Naturalization records: Some but not all; copies: 25¢ each
Vital records; Yes; copies: 25¢ each
Probate records: Yes; copies: 25¢ each

Blackbird County
(see Thurston County)

*Blaine County Courthouse
PO Box 136
Brewster, NE 68821
Phone (308) 547-2222
County organized 1885 from Custer County
Land records: Contact County Clerk

Naturalization records: Contact County
Clerk
Probate records: Contact County
Treasurer

*Boone County Courthouse
222 South Fourth Street
Albion, NE 68620-1258
Phone (402) 395-2055
*County organized 1871 from Platte
County*
Land records: Contact Register of Deeds
Naturalization records: Contact Clerk of
the District Court
Probate records: Contact County Court
Probate search service: $5.00; copies:
50¢ each, $5.00 minimum including
postage; "Very helpful if we had land
descriptions or approximate year."

Box Butte County Courthouse
PO Box 678
Alliance, NE 69301-0678
Phone (308) 762-6565
*County organized 1886 from
unorganized territory*

*Boyd County Courthouse
Butte, NE 68722
Phone (402) 775-2391
*County organized 1891 from an
unorganized area that was
transferred in 1882 from Dakota
Territory to Nebraska, but which,
according to the 1883 act adding it to
Holt County, required voter approval,
which the courts ruled was not done*
Land records: Contact Phyllis Black,
Register of Deeds, PO Box 26, Butte,
NE 68722
Naturalization records: Contact Phyllis
Black, County Clerk
Probate records: Contact Donald L.
Bursell, County Court
Probate search service: no charge;
copies: 25¢ each, no minimum

*Brown County Courthouse
148 West Fourth Street
Ainsworth, NE 69210
Phone (402) 387-2705 Combined Office
of County Clerk, Register of Deeds
and Clerk of District Court; (402)
387-2864 County Court Clerk
*County organized 1883 from
unorganized territory*
Land records: Contact Janet Huggins,
County Clerk/Register of Deeds
No land records search service; copies:
50¢ each, $1.50 per certified page,
plus postage
Naturalization records: W.P.A. index
cards only; contact Clerk of District
Court; copies: unavailable because of
the condition of the books

Vital records: Marriages; contact County
Clerk
No vital records search service; certified
copies: $6.00 each plus postage
Probate records: Contact County Court
Clerk
No probate search service; copies: 50¢
each plus postage, $1.50 per page for
certified copies of certain records;
"Fees are set by law in some matters."

*Buffalo County Courthouse
15th and Central Avenue
PO Box 1270
Kearney, NE 68848
Phone (308) 236-1226 County Clerk's
Office
*County organized 1855, original county.
However there are no county records
earlier than 1870. The county
business appears to have been
transacted by the officials of Hall
County before 1870, since few people
resided in Buffalo County*
Land records: Contact Margaret
Swanson, Register of Deeds
Naturalization records: Contact State
Archives Division, Nebraska State
Historical Society (1500 R Street,
Lincoln, NE 68508—location), PO
Box 82554 (mailing address), Lincoln,
NE 68501-2554
Vital records: Marriage records; contact
Roberta A. Nansel, County Clerk
Probate records: Contact Donna Dworak,
Clerk Magistrate, County Court
Probate search service: no charge (list
approximate date); copies: 25¢ per
page, 25¢ minimum

*Burt County Courthouse
111 North 13th Street
Tekamah, NE 68061-1043
Phone (402) 374-1955 County Clerk
County organized 1854, original county
Land records: Contact County Clerk, PO
Box 87, Tekamah, NE 68061
Naturalization records: Contact Clerk of
District Court
Vital records: Marriages only; contact
County Clerk
Probate records: Contact County Court,
PO Box 87, Tekamah, NE 68061

*Butler County Courthouse
451 Fifth Street
David City, NE 68632
Phone (402) 367-7430
*County organized 1857 from
unorganized territory*
Land records: Contact County Clerk
Naturalization records: Contact Clerk of
District Court
Vital records: Marriages only; contact
County Clerk
Probate records: Contact County Court

Cass County Courthouse
Fourth and Main Street
Plattsmouth, NE 68048
Phone (402) 296-2164
County organized 1854, original county

Cedar County Courthouse
Hartington, NE 68739
Phone (402) 254-7411
County organized 1855, original county

*Chase County Courthouse
PO Box 1299
Imperial, NE 69033-0310
Phone (308) 882-5266
*County organized 1889 from
unorganized territory*
Land records: Yes
Naturalization records: No naturalization
records
Vital records: No vital records
Probate records: Yes

*Cherry County Courthouse
PO Box 120
Valentine, NE 69201
Phone (402) 376-2771
*County organized 1883 from
unorganized territory*
Land records: Yes
Naturalization records: Yes
Vital records: Yes
Probate records: Contact County Court,
365 North Main, Valentine, NE 69201

*Cheyenne County Courthouse
PO Box 217
Sidney, NE 69162-0217
Phone (308) 254-2141 County Clerk;
(308) 254-2814 District Court; (308)
254-2150 Cheyenne County Historical
Association; (308) 254-2929 County
Court
*County created by proclamation in
August 1870 from unorganized
territory (containing the "paper"
counties of Lyon and Taylor, and
covering the entire south half of the
Panhandle, with the north half of the
Panhandle, then unorganized
territory, attached for judicial
purposes)*
Land records: Deeds, mortgages and
patent records from the 1860s,
grantor/grantee index; contact County
Clerk
Naturalization records: Contact District
Court
Vital records: Marriages from the late
1800s; contact Cheyenne County
Historical Association, Sixth and
Jackson, PO Box 596, Sidney, NE
69162
Probate records: Contact County Court

*Clay County Courthouse
111 West Fairfield
Clay Center, NE 68933-1499
Phone (402) 762-3463
*County organized 1855, original county
(according to Thorndale and
Dollarhide's* Map Guide to the U.S.
Federal Censuses, 1790–1920, *area
originally called Clay County is now
part of Lancaster and Gage counties,
while present-day Clay County
occupies area which was unattached
in 1860)*
Land records: Contact Janet Hajny,
County Clerk/Register of Deeds
Naturalization records: Contact Clerk of
District Court
Vital records: From 1917 to 1918;
contact County Clerk
Probate records: Contact County Court

*Colfax County Courthouse
411 East 11th Street
Schuyler, NE 68661-1940
Phone (402) 352-3434
*County organized 1869 from Platte
County*
Land records: Contact County Clerk/
Register of Deeds; copies: 25¢ per
page
Naturalization records: Contact Clerk of
District Court
Probate records: Contact County Judge's
Office
Probate search service: no charge;
copies: 25¢ each, no minimum

*Cuming County Courthouse
PO Box 290
West Point, NE 68788-0290
Phone (402) 372-6002 County Clerk
*County organized 1855 from Burt
County*
Land records: Contact County Clerk
No land records search service
Naturalization records: Contact Clerk
District Court, 200 South Lincoln,
West Point, NE 68788
Vital records: Marriages; contact County
Clerk
No vital records search service; copies:
35¢ each, $4.00 or $5.00 for certified
copies
Probate records: Contact County Court
Office

*Custer County Courthouse
431 South Tenth Avenue
Broken Bow, NE 68822-2001
Phone (308) 872-2221 Register of Deeds;
(308) 872-5701 County Clerk; (308)
872-2121 Clerk of District Court;
(308) 872-5761 County Court
*County organized 1877 from
unorganized territory*
Land records: Contact Register of Deeds

Naturalization records: Contact Clerk of
District Court
Vital records: Marriage licenses; contact
County Clerk
Probate records: Contact County Court
No probate search service; copies: 25¢
each

*Dakota County Courthouse
PO Box 39
Dakota City, NE 68731
Phone (402) 987-2126
County organized 1855, original county
Land records: Contact Register of Deeds
Vital records: Marriages; contact County
Clerk; certified copies: $5.00 each
Probate records: Contact County Judge
No probate search service; copies: 25¢
each

*Dawes County Courthouse
451 Main
Chadron, NE 69337
Phone (308) 432-0100
*County organized 1885 from Sioux
County*
Land records: Contact County Clerk's
Office—Register of Deeds; copies:
$1.00 per page, 50¢ for certification
Naturalization records: Contact Clerk of
the District Court
Vital records: Marriages; contact County
Clerk's Office; certified copies: $5.00
each
Probate records: Contact County Court
No probate search service; copies: $1.00
per page

*Dawson County Courthouse
PO Box 370
Lexington, NE 68850-0370
Phone (308) 324-2127
*County organized 1860 from Buffalo
County*
Land records: Contact Register of Deeds
Office
Naturalization records: Contact Clerk of
District Court
Vital records: Marriage licenses; contact
County Clerk's Office; copies: 50¢
each, $5.00 for certified copies, $2.00
for mailed copy
Probate records: Contact County Court
Probate search service: no charge;
copies: 25¢ each, $1.00 per page for
certification, no minimum; send
"name and date of death."

*Deuel County Courthouse
Chappell, NE 69129
Phone (308) 874-3308
*County organized January 1889 from
Cheyenne County*
Land records: From 1889
Naturalization records: From 1889
Vital records: No vital statistics

Probate records: Contact County Court
Probate search service: no charge;
copies: 10¢ per page, $1.00 per
certified page, no minimum

*Dixon County Courthouse
Ponca, NE 68770
Phone (402) 755-2208 County Clerk;
(402) 755-2881 Clerk of the District
Court; (402) 755-2355 County Court
County organized 1856, original county
Land records: Contact County Clerk, PO
Box 546, Ponca, NE 68770
Naturalization records: To the 1930s;
contact Clerk of the District Court, PO
Box 395, Ponca, NE 68770
Vital records: Marriages from 1872;
contact County Clerk
Probate records: Contact County Court,
PO Box 497, Ponca, NE 68770
Probate search service: no charge;
copies: 25¢ per page, $1.00 for
certification

*Dodge County Courthouse
435 North Park
Fremont, NE 68025
Phone (402) 727-2767
County organized 1855, original county
Land records: Contact Register of Deeds
Vital records: Marriages; contact County
Clerk
Probate records: Contact County Judge
No probate search service; copies: 50¢
each, $5.00 for certified copies, 25¢
minimum

*Douglas County Courthouse
1819 Farnam Street
Omaha, NE 68183
Phone (402) 444-7000; (402) 444-7152
Probate Division
*County organized 1854, original county,
later annexed part of Washington
County*
Probate records: From 1876; contact
County Court, Probate Division, 17th
and Farnam Street, Omaha, NE 68183
Probate search service: no charge;
copies: 25¢ per page, no minimum;
"Must give year of death or we will
not search."

Dundy County Courthouse
Benkelman, NE 69021
Phone (308) 423-2058
*County organized 1873 from
unorganized territory*

Emmett County
(see Knox County)

*Fillmore County Courthouse
Geneva, NE 68361
Phone (402) 759-4931

County organized 1871 from unorganized territory

Land records: From 1 July 1871; contact Carol L. Vejraska, County Clerk/Register of Deeds, Lock Box 307, Geneva, NE 68361

Naturalization records: Contact Clerk of District Court

Vital records: Marriages; contact County Clerk and Clerk of District Court

Probate records: Contact County Judge

No probate search service: "We refer searches to Fillmore County Genealogical Society"; copies: 35¢ each, $1.00 minimum

*Franklin County Courthouse
405 15th Avenue
Franklin, NE 68939-1309
Phone (308) 425-6202 and 6203 County Clerk, Election Commission, Clerk of the District Court, and Register of Deeds (four offices in one); (308) 425-6288 County Court

County organized 1867 from Kearney County

Land records: Contact Register of Deeds, PO Box 146, Franklin, NE 68939

Naturalization records: Contact Clerk of District Court, PO Box 146, Franklin, NE 68939

Probate records: Contact County Court, PO Box 174, Franklin, NE 68939

Probate search service: no charge; copies: 25¢ per page

*Frontier County Courthouse
Stockville, NE 69042
Phone (308) 367-8641

County organized 1872 from unorganized territory

Land records: Contact Twila P. Johnson County Clerk-Register of Deeds, PO Box 40, Stockville, NE 69042

Land records search service: $3.00 per name; copies: $1.00 per record

Naturalization records: Contact County Clerk-Register of Deeds; copies: unavailable

Vital records: No vital records

Probate records: Contact County Clerk Magistrate, PO Box 38, Stockville, NE 69042

*Furnas County Courthouse
PO Box 387
Beaver City, NE 68926-0387
Phone (308) 268-4145 County Clerk; (402) 471-2871 Clerk of District Court; (308) 268-4025 County Court

County organized 1873 from unorganized territory

Land records: Contact County Clerk

Naturalization records: Contact Clerk of District Court, PO Box 413, Beaver City, NE 68926

Probate records: Contact County Court/Clerk Magistrate, PO Box 373, Beaver City, NE 68926

Probate search service: $3.00 per name, copies: 50¢ each, 50¢ minimum; "The Furnas County Genealogical Society does most of the searching for us and they have their own fees."

*Gage County Courthouse
Sixth and Grant Streets
Beatrice, NE 68310
Phone (402) 228-3355

County organized 1855, original county

Land records: Contact Register of Deeds, PO Box 337, Beatrice, NE 68310; copies: $1.00 per page

Naturalization records: From 21 September 1871 to 15 February 1932; contact Clerk of District Court

Vital records: Marriages only from 1860; contact County Clerk's Office

Probate records: From 1860; contact County Court, PO Box 219, Beatrice, NE 68310

Probate search service: no charge; copies: 25¢ per page, no minimum

*Garden County Courthouse
Oshkosh, NE 69154
Phone (308) 772-3924

County organized 1909 from unorganized territory

Land records: Contact Lorie Koester, County Clerk, PO Box 486, Oshkosh, NE 69154

Probate records: Contact Sandra S. Schmid, Clerk Magistrate, PO Box 465, Oshkosh, NE 69154

*Garfield County Courthouse
PO Box 218
Burwell, NE 68823-0218
Phone (308) 346-4161

County organized 1884 from Wheeler County

Land records: Contact County Clerk

Naturalization records: No naturalization records

Vital records: No vital records

Probate records: Contact Clerk Magistrate

No probate search service: "Garfield County has an active Historical Society that may perform searches if contacted"; copies: 20¢ each

*Gosper County Courthouse
PO Box 136
Elwood, NE 68937
Phone (308) 785-2611

County organized 1873 from unorganized territory

Land records: From 1873; copies: 26¢ each, no minimum; "We are understaffed and pass any requests on to a private individual."

*Grant County Courthouse
County Clerk, Assessor, Register of Deeds, Clerk of District Court
PO Box 139
Hyannis, NE 69350
Phone (308) 458-2488

County organized 1887 from unorganized territory (in 1870 a "paper" county called Grant covered parts of present-day Lincoln, Frontier, Red Willow, Furnas, Gosper, Dawson, Hayes and Hitchcock counties, much of which area was known as Shorter County in 1860)

Land records: Contact County Assessor

Naturalization records: No naturalization records

Probate records: Contact County Court

No probate search service; copies: 20¢ each

*Greeley County Courthouse
PO Box 287
Greeley, NE 68842-0287
Phone (308) 428-3625; (308) 428-2705 Clerk Magistrate

County organized 1871 from Boone County

Land records: Contact County Clerk

Naturalization records: Contact County Clerk

Vital records: No vital records

Probate records: Contact Clerk Magistrate, PO Box 302, Greeley, NE 68842

Probate search service: no charge; copies: 25¢ per page, no minimum

Hall County Courthouse
121 South Pine
Grand Island, NE 68801-6076
Phone (308) 381-5080

County organized 1858, original county

*Hamilton County Courthouse
Aurora, NE 68818
Phone (402) 694-3443 County Clerk; (402) 694-3533 Clerk of District Court; (402) 694-6188 Clerk of County Court

County organized 1867 from York County

Land records: Contact County Clerk

Naturalization records: Contact Clerk of District Court, PO Box 201, Aurora, NE 68818

Vital records: Marriages; contact County Clerk

Probate records: From 1881; contact Clerk of County Court, PO Box 323, Lincoln, NE 68509-5007

Probate search service: no charge; copies: 25¢ per page, no minimum

*Harlan County Courthouse
Alma, NE 68920
Phone (308) 928-2173
*County organized 1871 from
    unorganized territory*
Land records: Yes
Naturalization records: Yes
Vital records: No vital records
Probate records: Contact County Judge
No probate search service; copies: 25¢
    per page

*Hayes County Courthouse
PO Box 67
Hayes Center, NE 69032-0067
Phone (308) 266-3413
*County organized 1877 from
    unorganized territory*
Land records: From late 1800s; contact
    Register of Deeds
Naturalization records: From 1907;
    contact Register of Deeds
Probate records: From 1892
Probate search service: no charge;
    copies: 25¢ per page, no minimum

*Hitchcock County Courthouse
Trenton, NE 69044
Phone (308) 334-5646
*County organized 1873 from
    unorganized territory*
Land records: Contact Margaret
    Pollmann, County Clerk, PO Box 248,
    Trenton, NE 69044-0248
Naturalization records: Contact County
    Clerk
Vital records: Contact County Clerk
Probate records: Contact County Judge
No probate search service; copies: 50¢
    per page, no minimum

*Holt County Courthouse
O'Neill, NE 68763
Phone (402) 336-1762
*County organized 1876 from Knox
    County*
Land records: Contact Register of Deeds,
    PO Box 329, O'Neill, NE 68763
Naturalization records: Contact Clerk of
    District Court, PO Box 755, O'Neill,
    NE 68763
Vital records: Marriages; contact County
    Clerk, PO Box 329, O'Neill, NE
    68763
Probate records: Contact M. Clark, Clerk
    Magistrate, County Court
No probate search service: "Genealogical
    Society, K. Manoucheri, PO Box 878,
    O'Neill, NE 68763, will do probate
    searches for $5.00 plus 25¢ each copy
    plus postage."

Hooker County Courthouse
PO Box 184
Mullen, NE 69152-0184
Phone (308) 546-2244

*County organized 1889 from
    unorganized territory*

*Howard County Courthouse
PO Box 25
Saint Paul, NE 68873-0025
Phone (308) 754-4343
*County organized 1871 from Hall
    County*
Land records: Contact RaNae Smith,
    County Clerk
Naturalization records: Contact Linda M.
    Scarborough, Clerk Magistrate,
    County Court
Probate records: Contact Clerk
    Magistrate
Probate search service: no charge;
    copies: 25¢ each, $1.50 for certified
    copies

Jackson County
(see Lincoln County)

*Jefferson County Courthouse
411 Fourth Street
Fairbury, NE 68352-2513
Phone (402) 729-5201 Register of Deeds;
    (402) 729-2019 Clerk of District
    Court; (402) 729-2323 County Clerk;
    (402) 729-2312 County Court
*County organized 1856 from Gage
    County (according to Thorndale and
    Dollarhide's* Map Guide to the U.S.
    Federal Censuses, 1790-1920, *area
    now called Jefferson County was
    called Jones County in 1860, and in
    1870 Jefferson County covered both
    present-day Jefferson County and
    present-day Thayer, which in 1860
    was called Nuckolls County)*
Land records: From 1871; contact Sandra
    Stelling, Register of Deeds; copies:
    $1.00 each
Naturalization records: From 1887;
    contact Katherine E. Young, Clerk of
    District Court; copies: 50¢ per page
Vital records: Marriages from 1869 only;
    contact Sandra Stelling, County Clerk;
    copies: $1.00 each
Probate records: From the 1870s; contact
    Tammie Duensing, County Court
Probate search service: no charge;
    copies: 25¢ each plus postage, no
    minimum

*Johnson County Courthouse
PO Box 416
Tecumseh, NE 68450-0416
Phone (402) 335-3246
County organized 1855, original county
Land records: Contact Clerk; copies: 25¢
    each
Naturalization records: Contact Clerk of
    the District Court; copies: 25¢ each
Vital records: Marriages only; contact
    Clerk; copies: 25¢ each

Probate records: Contact County Court
Probate search service; no charge;
    copies: $1.00 each, no minimum

Jones County
(see Jefferson County)

*Kearney County Courthouse
Minden, NE 68959
Phone (308) 832-2723 County Clerk/
    Register of Deeds; (308) 832-1742
    Clerk of District Court; (308) 832-
    2719 County Court
County organized 1860, original county
Land records: Contact Register of Deeds
Naturalization records: Contact Clerk of
    District Court
Probate records: Contact County Court
Probate search service: no charge;
    copies: $1.00 for the first copy and
    10¢ for each additional copy, no
    minimum

*Keith County Courthouse
PO Box 149
Ogallala, NE 69153-0149
Phone (308) 284-4726
*County organized 1873 from Lincoln
    County*
Land records: From 1873; contact
    County Clerk, PO Box 149, Ogallala,
    NE 69153
Vital records: Marriages; certified copies:
    $5.00 each
Probate records: Contact Judge, 511
    North Spruce, Ogallala, NE 69153
No probate search service; copies: 50¢
    each, $1.50 for certified copies, no
    minimum

*Keya Paha County Courthouse
PO Box 349
Springview, NE 68778
Phone (402) 497-3791
*County organized 1884 from Brown and
    Rock counties and part of the area
    transferred in 1882 from Dakota
    Territory*
Land records: Yes
Naturalization records: From 1886
Vital records: Marriages from 1886
Probate records: From 1886
Probate search service: no charge;
    copies: 15¢ each (8¹/₂" x 11"), 20¢
    each (8¹/₂" x 14"), no minimum

*Kimball County Courthouse
114 East Third Street
Kimball, NE 69145-1401
Phone (308) 235-2241 County Clerk
*County organized 1888 from Cheyenne
    County*
Land records: From 1889; contact
    Cathleen A. Sibal, County Clerk
Naturalization records: Contact State
    Historical Society

Vital records: Marriage licenses only; contact County Clerk; certified copies: $5.00 each

Probate records: Contact County Court

*Knox County Courthouse
Center, NE 68724
Phone (402) 288-4282
County established by the Territorial Legislature in 1857, original county; name changed from L'eau Qui Court County to Emmett County; name changed from Emmett County to Knox County in 1873
Land records: Contact Register of Deeds Office
Naturalization records: Contact Clerk of District Court Office
Probate records: Contact Virginia Buerman, County Clerk

*Lancaster County Courthouse
555 South Tenth
Lincoln, NE 68508-2803
Phone (402) 471-7481
County organized 1854, original county

L'eau Qui Court County
(see Knox County)

Lincoln County Courthouse
North Platte, NE 69101
Phone (308) 534-4350
County organized 1860 from unorganized territory (contained the "paper" counties of Grant and Jackson in 1870)

Logan County Courthouse
PO Box 8
Stapleton, NE 69163-0008
Phone (308) 636-2311
County organized 1885 from Custer County

*Loup County Courthouse
PO Box 187
Taylor, NE 68879-0187
Phone (308) 942-3135
County organized 1883 from unorganized territory
Land records: Contact County Clerk
No land records search service; copies 35¢ each
Naturalization records: Contact County Clerk
No naturalization records search service; copies 35¢ each
Probate records: Contact County Court, PO Box 146, Taylor, NE 68879
Probate search service: no charge with no copies issued; copies: $1.00 for the first page (includes search) and 50¢ for each additional copy, $1.00 minimum for search with one copy

Lyon County
(see Cheyenne County)

*Madison County Courthouse
PO Box 230
Madison, NE 68748-0230
Phone (402) 454-3311, ext. 165 County Court
County organized 1868 from Platte County
Land records: Contact Register of Deeds, PO Box 229, Madison, NE 68748; copies: 50¢ per page
Naturalization records: No naturalization records
Vital records: Contact County Clerk, PO Box 290, Madison, NE 68748
Probate records: From 1868; contact County Court
Probate search service: no charge; copies: 25¢ each, no minimum

McPherson County Courthouse
PO Box 122
Tryon, NE 69167-0122
Phone (308) 587-2363
County organized 1887 from Lincoln and Keith counties

*Merrick County Courthouse
PO Box 27
Central City, NE 68826-0027
Phone (308) 946-2881
County organized 1858, original county
Land records: From 1866; contact County Clerk's Office
Naturalization records: Contact Clerk of District Court
Vital records: Marriage from 1869; contact County Clerk's Office
Probate records: From 1875; contact County Judge Office, Attn: Beth Puller, Clerk Magistrate
Probate search service: $5.00; copies: 25¢ per page, $1.00 for certification, no minimum

Monroe County
(see Platte County)

*Morrill County Courthouse
PO Box 610
Bridgeport, NE 69336-0610
Phone (308) 262-0860
County organized November 1908 from Cheyenne County
Land records: From 1908; contact County Clerk
Naturalization records: From 1909 to 1945; contact Clerk District Court, PO Box 824, Bridgeport, NE 69336
Probate records: From 1908; contact Clerk Magistrate, County Court, PO Box 418, Bridgeport, NE 69336
No probate search service; copies: 25¢ per page, no minimum

*Nance County Courthouse
Fullerton, NE 68638
Phone (308) 536-2331
County organized 1879 from Merrick County, encompassing the entire former Pawnee Reservation
Land records: Contact County Clerk, PO Box 338, Fullerton, NE 68638
Naturalization records: Contact Clerk of District Court
Vital records: Marriage licenses; contact County Clerk
Probate records: Contact County Court
Probate search service: no charge; copies: 25¢ per page, no minimum; "Please state approximate date of death if available."

*Nemaha County Courthouse
1824 N Street
Auburn, NE 68305-2342
Phone (402) 274-4213
County organized 1855, original county
Land records: Contact County Clerk; copies: $1.00 each
Naturalization records: No naturalization records
Vital records: Marriage certificates; copies: $1.00 each
Probate records: Contact County Court

*Nuckolls County Courthouse
Nelson, NE 68961
Phone (402) 225-4361 County Clerk; (402) 225-4341 Clerk of the District Court; (402) 225-2371 County Court
County organized 1860 from unorganized territory; a county which was originally named Nuckolls is now Thayer County
Land records: Real estate ownership, deeds, plats, mortgages; contact County Clerk/Register of Deeds, PO Box 366, Courthouse, Nelson, NE 68961
No land records search service (contact Nuckolls County Genealogy Society, PO Box 324, Superior, NE 68978); copies: 50¢ per standard-sized page
Naturalization records: A limited amount of information; contact Clerk of the District Court, PO Box 362, Courthouse, Nelson, NE 68961
Vital records: Marriage licenses from 1872; contact County Clerk/Register of Deeds
No vital records search service; certified copies: $1.50 per page
Probate records: Contact County Court/ Judge, PO Box 372, Courthouse, Nelson, NE 68961
Probate search service: no charge ("This takes time, so we do it when we have the extra time"); copies: $1.00 per document

*Otoe County Courthouse
Nebraska City, NE 68410
Phone (402) 873-6439 Register of Deeds;
  (402) 873-3586 County Clerk
County organized 1854, original county
Land records: From 4 April 1855; contact
  Register of Deeds; copies: $1.00 each,
  no minimum
Naturalization records: Contact Clerk of
  the District Court
Vital records: Marriages from 1855;
  contact County Clerk, PO Box 249,
  Nebraska City, NE 68410; copies:
  $3.00 each, $5.00 for certified copies
Probate records: From 1854; contact
  Clerk Magistrate, County Court, 1021
  Central Avenue, Nebraska City, NE
  68410
Probate search service: no charge;
  copies: 25¢ per page, $1.00 for
  certification, no minimum; "Payment
  in advance of mailing copies."

*Pawnee County Courthouse
PO Box 431
Pawnee City, NE 68420-0431
Phone (402) 852-2962; (402) 852-2388
  County Court
County organized 1854, original county
Land records: From 1854; copies: $1.00
  each (if you do your own search),
  $2.50 for certified copies
Naturalization records: From 1871;
  copies: $1.00 each
Probate records: From 1857; contact
  County Court, PO Box 471, Pawnee
  City, NE 68420-0471
Probate search service: no charge;
  copies: 25¢ per page

*Perkins County Courthouse
PO Box 156
Grant, NE 69140-0156
Phone (308) 352-4643; (308) 352-4415
  County Judge's Office
*County organized 1887 from Keith
  County*
Land records: Contact County Clerk
Naturalization records: Some
  naturalization records from 1890 to
  1928; contact County Clerk
Probate records: Contact County Judge's
  Office
Probate search service: no charge;
  copies: 25¢ per page, no minimum

*Phelps County Courthouse
Holdrege, NE 68949
Phone (308) 995-4469; (308) 995-2281
  Clerk of District Court
*County organized 1873 from
  unorganized territory*
Land records: Contact County Clerk, PO
  Box 404, Holdrege, NE 68949-0404
Naturalization records: Contact Clerk of
  District Court, PO Box 462, Holdrege,
  NE 68949

Vital records: No vital records
Probate records: Contact County Court,
  PO Box 255, Holdrege, NE 68949
Probate search service: no charge;
  copies: 25¢ each plus postage, no
  minimum; "Please print or type names
  and dates."

*Pierce County Courthouse
111 West Court Street
Pierce, NE 68767
Phone (402) 329-4225; (402) 329-4335
  Clerk of Court
*County organized 1859 from Madison
  County*
Land records: Contact County Clerk
Naturalization records: Contact Clerk of
  District Court
Probate records: Contact County Court
No probate search service; copies: 25¢
  each

*Platte County Courthouse
2610 14th Street
Columbus, NE 68601-4929
Phone (402) 563-4904
*County created 1855 from Dodge
  County and was composed of the
  twenty-four miles square, or five
  hundred seventy-six square miles,
  included in townships 17, 18, 19 and
  20 North and ranges 1, 2, 3 and 4
  East of the sixth principal meridian.
  In 1858 it was made to include, in
  addition, all of Monroe County
  (which had been created in August
  1857, on the west, which was not
  comprised within the Pawnee Indian
  Reservation. In 1868 the County of
  Colfax was created by an act of the
  State Legislature, taking from Platte
  all of the eastern three ranges. After
  several changes made at different
  times, the southern boundary has
  been fixed, and it now remains at the
  south side of the South Channel of
  the Platte River, from the sixth
  principal meridian and at the south
  side of the North Channel of the
  river, westward from said line. Platte
  County now consists of townships 16,
  17, 18, 19 and 20 North and ranges
  1, 2, 3 and 4 West and 1 East of the
  sixth principal meridian*
Land records: Contact County Register
  of Deeds Office
Naturalization records: No naturalization
  records
Vital records: Marriages; contact Diane
  C. Pinger, County Clerk
No vital records search service; copies:
  50¢ each (date of marriage required)
Probate records: From 1869; contact
  County Court, PO Box 538,
  Columbus, NE 68602-0538

*Polk County Courthouse
Osceola, NE 68651
Phone (402) 747-5431
County organized 1856, original county
Land records: From 1870
Naturalization records: From 1876 to
  1943
Vital records: Marriages only
Probate records: From 1880
Probate search service: no charge;
  copies: 25¢ per page, no minimum;
  "By written request, include date of
  death."

*Red Willow County Courthouse
500 Norris Avenue
McCook, NE 69001-2006
Phone (308) 345-1552
*County organized 1873 from
  unorganized territory*
Land records: Contact Register of Deeds
Naturalization records: Contact Clerk of
  the District Court
Vital records: Marriages only; copies:
  75¢ each, $5.00 for certified copies
Probate records: Contact County Court
Probate search service: no charge;
  copies: 25¢ per page, no minimum

*Richardson County Courthouse
Falls City, NE 68355
Phone (402) 245-2911
County organized 1855, original county
Land records: From 1855 to date; contact
  Register of Deeds; copies: 50¢ per
  page
Naturalization records: Contact State
  Archives Division, Nebraska State
  Historical Society (1500 R Street,
  Lincoln, NE 68508—location), PO
  Box 82554 (mailing address), Lincoln,
  NE 68501-2554
Vital records: Marriages only from 1856
  to date; contact County Clerk;
  certified copies: $5.00 each
Probate records: From 1859 to date;
  contact County Court; copies: 25¢ per
  page, $1.00 for certification

*Rock County Courthouse
PO Box 367
Bassett, NE 68714-0367
Phone (402) 684-3933
*County organized 1888 from Brown
  County*
Land records: Contact Register of Deeds
Naturalization records: No naturalization
  records
Vital records: No vital records
Probate records: Contact County Judge,
  PO Box 249, Bassett, NE 68714

*Saline County Courthouse
PO Box 865
Wilber, NE 68465-0865
Phone (402) 821-2374

*County organized 18 February 1867
from Gage and Lancaster counties*
Land records: Contact Register of Deeds
Naturalization records: Contact Clerk of
District Court
Vital records: Marriages only; contact
Norma K. Ripa, County Clerk
Probate records: Contact County Court
Probate search service: no charge;
copies: 25¢ each, $5.00 minimum;
"Send $5.00 and we will refund
money we don't need."

*Sarpy County Courthouse
1210 Golden Gate Drive
Papillion, NE 68046-2845
Phone (402) 593-2106
County organized 1857, original county
Vital records: Marriage licenses from 1
January 1887; contact County Clerk's
Office. Marriage licenses before 1887;
contact Sarpy County Historical
Society
Probate records: Yes
Probate search service: no charge;
copies: $1.00 per page, no minimum

*Saunders County Courthouse
Wahoo, NE 68066
Phone (402) 443-8111 Register of Deeds
Office; (402) 443-8113; (402) 443-
8101 County Clerk; (402) 443-8119
County Court
*County organized 1856 from Sarpy and
Douglas counties*
Land records: Contact Register of Deeds
Office
Naturalization records: Contact Clerk of
the District Court
Probate records: Contact County Court
No probate search service; copies: 25¢
per page

Scotts Bluff County
1825 Tenth Street
Gering, NE 69341-2413
Phone (308) 456-6600
*County organized 1881 from Cheyenne
County*

*Seward County Courthouse
PO Box 190
Seward, NE 68434
Phone (402) 643-2883
*County organized 1867 from Lancaster
County*
Land records: From 1867
Vital records: Contact State Historical
Society
Probate records: Contact County Court
No probate search service; copies: 25¢
each, $5.00 for certified copies, no
minimum

*Sheridan County Courthouse
PO Box 39
Rushville, NE 69360-0039

Phone (308) 327-2633
*County organized 1885 from Sioux
County*
Land records: Yes
No land records search service
Naturalization records: No naturalization
records
Vital records: Marriages only
No vital records search service
Probate records: Contact County Court,
PO Box 430, Rushville, NE 69360
No probate search service

*Sherman County Courthouse
PO Box 456
Loup City, NE 68853-0456
Phone (308) 745-1513
*County organized 1871 from Buffalo
County*
Land records: From 1870s; contact
Margaret Dzingle, Clerk; copies: 50¢
per page
Naturalization records: From late 1800s;
contact Clerk
Vital records: No vital records
Probate records: From 1870s; contact
Carolyn Heil, Clerk Magistrate, PO
Box 55, Loup City, NE 68853
Probate search service: no charge;
copies: 25¢ per page, no minimum

Shorter County
(see Grant County)

*Sioux County Courthouse
Harrison, NE 69346
Phone (308) 668-2443 County Clerk;
(308) 668-2475 County Court
*County organized 1877 from
unorganized territory*
Land records: Contact County Clerk, PO
Box 158, Harrison, NE 69346
Naturalization records: Only a few
available; contact County Clerk
Probate records: Contact Clerk of County
Court, PO Box 477, Harrison, NE
69346
Probate search service: no charge;
copies: 25¢ per page, no minimum

*Stanton County Courthouse
804 Ivy Street
PO Box 14
Stanton, NE 68779
Phone (402) 439-2222
*County organized 1865 from Dodge
County*
Land records: From May 1868; contact
Clerk
Naturalization records: From 1871;
contact Clerk
Vital records: Marriage licenses from
June 1869; contact Clerk
Probate records: From late 1800s; contact
County Court
Probate search service: no charge;
copies: 25¢ per page, no minimum

Taylor County
(see Cheyenne County)

*Thayer County Courthouse
225 North Fourth
Hebron, NE 68370
Phone (402) 768-6126 County Clerk;
(402) 768-6116 Clerk District Court;
(402) 768-6325 County Court
*County organized 1872 from Jefferson
County; originally named Nuckolls
County*
Land records: Contact County Clerk, PO
Box 208, Hebron, NE 68370
Naturalization records: Contact Clerk
District Court, PO Box 297, Hebron,
NE 68370
Vital records: Dissolution of marriages;
contact Clerk District Court
Probate records: From 1871; contact
County Court, PO Box 94, Hebron,
NE 68370
Probate search service: no charge;
copies: 25¢ per page, $1.00 per
certified page, no minimum

*Thomas County Courthouse
Thedford, NE 69166
Phone (308) 645-2261; (308) 645-2266
County Court
*County organized 1887 from Blaine
County*
Land records: Contact County Clerk
Vital records: Marriages
Probate records: Contact County Court
Probate search service: $3.00; copies:
25¢ each, $1.00 minimum

*Thurston County Courthouse
PO Box G
Pender, NE 68047
Phone (402) 385-2343
*County organized 1865 from Burt
County; name changed from
Blackbird County in 1889*
Land records: Contact County Clerk
Naturalization records: Contact Clerk of
District Court
Vital records: Marriages; contact County
Clerk
Probate records: Contact County Court,
PO Box 129, Pender, NE 68047
Probate search service: no charge;
copies: $1.00 per page, no minimum

Valley County Courthouse
125 South 15th
Ord, NE 68862-1409
Phone (308) 728-3700
*County organized 1871 from
unorganized territory*

*Washington County Courthouse
1555 Colfax Street
Blair, NE 68008-2022
Phone (402) 426-6822

County organized 1854, original county
Land records: From 1854
Naturalization records: Contact State
  Historical Society
Vital records: Marriages only from 1867;
  contact County Clerk's Office; copies:
  25¢ each, $5.00 for certified copies
Probate records: From latter part of
  1800s; contact County Court, PO Box
  615, Blair, NE 68008
No probate search service; copies: 25¢
  per page, no minimum

Wayne County Courthouse
Wayne, NE 68787
Phone (402) 375-2288
*County organized 1867 from Thurston
  County*

*Webster County Courthouse
621 North Cedar
Red Cloud, NE 68970
Phone (402) 746-2716 County Clerk
*County organized 1871 from
  unorganized territory*
Land records: From 1872; contact
  County Clerk
Naturalization records: From 1872;
  contact County Clerk
Vital records: Marriages; copies: $2.00
  each
Probate records: From 1872; contact
  County Judge
Probate search service: no charge;
  copies: $1.00 each, no minimum;
  "Enclose SASE."

Wheeler County Courthouse
Bartlett, NE 68622
Phone (308) 654-3235
*County organized 1877 from Boone
  County*

*York County Courthouse
York, NE 68467
Phone (402) 362-7759
County organized 1855, original county
Land records: From 1855; copies: 25¢
  each
Naturalization records: Contact State
  Historical Society
Probate records: Contact County Judge

NEVADA

Capital: Carson City. Statehood: 31 October 1864 (ceded by Mexico in 1848, part of the Utah Territory from 1850 to 1861, when it became a separate territory)

Court System

Nevada has several Municipal Courts of limited jurisdiction in incorporated cities and towns. The state's Judicial Courts have limited jurisdiction over civil cases, misdemeanors and small claims. The District Courts which sit at each county seat have general jurisdiction over major civil cases, equity, probate and guardianship, felonies, misdemeanors and juvenile matters. First Judicial District: Carson City (which is an independent city, not located within a county) and Storey County; Second Judicial District: Washoe County; Third Judicial District: Churchill and Lyon counties; Fourth Judicial District: Elko County; Fifth Judicial District: Esmeralda, Mineral and Nye counties; Sixth Judicial District: Humboldt, Lander and Pershing counties; Seventh Judicial District: Eureka, Lincoln and White Pine counties; Eighth Judicial District: Clark County; Ninth Judicial District: Douglas County. The Supreme Court is the court of last resort.

Courthouses

*Carson City Courthouse
198 North Carson Street
Carson City, NV 89701
Phone (702) 887-2260
Ormsby County, original County, organized 1861, was consolidated with Carson City in 1969 to form the consolidated municipality
Vital records: Marriages; copies: $10.00
  maximum
Probate records: Contact Clerk
Probate search service: $1.00 per year;
  copies: $1.00 per page, no minimum

Churchill County Courthouse
190 West First Street
Fallon, NV 89406-3309
Phone (702) 423-5136
County organized 1861, original county

*Clark County Courthouse
200 South Third Street
Las Vegas, NV 89101-6112
Phone (702) 455-4011 Indexing/

Fileroom; (702) 455-4929 FAX,
  County Clerk
*County organized September 1909 from
  Lincoln County*
Land records: Contact County Recorder,
  309 South Third Street, PO Box
  551510, Las Vegas, NV 89155-1510
Vital records: Contact District Health
  Department, 625 Shadow Lane, Las
  Vegas, NV 89101. Marriage license
  applications; contact Loretta Bowman,
  County Clerk, (200 South Third
  Street, Third Floor—location), PO
  Box 551601 (mailing address), Las
  Vegas, NV 89155-1601; certified
  copies: $4.00 each. Marriage
  certificates; contact County Recorder;
  certified copies: $7.00 each (no
  personal checks accepted)
Probate records: Contact County Clerk
Vital records search service: $1.00 per
  year; copies: $1.00 per page, $3.00 for
  certification
Probate search service: $1.00 per year
  per name; copies: $1.00 per page, no
  minimum

*Douglas County
PO Box 218
Minden, NV 89423-0218
Phone (702) 782-9026 or (702) 782-9025
  Recorder's Office
County organized 1861, original county
Land records: From 1855; contact
  Recorder's Office; copies: $1.00 per
  page, $3.00 for certification per
  document
Vital records: Births from 1887 to 1923,
  deaths from 1887 to 1933; contact
  Recorder's Office, PO Box 218,
  Minden, NV 89423; copies: $1.00 per
  page, $3.00 for certification
Probate records: Contact Court Clerk's
  Office

*Elko County
571 Idaho Street
Elko, NV 89801-3770
Phone (702) 738-6526 County Recorder;
  (702) 738-3044 County Clerk
*County organized 1869 from Lander
  County*
Land records: Contact Jerry D. Reynolds,
  County Recorder, Room 103
No land records search service
Naturalization records: Contact County
  Clerk, Third Floor
Vital records: Births and deaths from
  1887 to 1915, marriages from 1869;
  contact County Recorder
Vital records search service: no charge if
  approximate dates are furnished
Probate records: From 1869; contact
  County Clerk
Probate search service: $1.00 per year
  per name; copies: $1.00 per page, no
  minimum

*Esmeralda County Courthouse
PO Box 547
Goldfield, NV 89013-0547
Phone (702) 485-6337 County Recorder;
(702) 485-6367 County Clerk
County organized 1861, original county
Land records: Contact County Recorder
Naturalization records: Contact County
Clerk
Probate records: Contact County Clerk

*Eureka County Courthouse
PO Box 677
Eureka, NV 89316-0677
Phone (702) 237-5262
*County organized 1873 from Lander
County*
Land records: Contact County Recorder
Naturalization records: Through the
1940s; contact County Clerk
Vital records: Contact County Recorder
Probate records: Contact County Clerk
Probate search service: $1.00 per year;
copies: $1.00 per page, $1.00
minimum

*Humboldt County Courthouse
50 West Fifth Street
Winnemucca, NV 89445-0352
Phone (702) 623-6343
County organized 1861, original county
Land records: Contact County Recorders
Office, City-County Complex,
Winnemucca, NV 89445
Naturalization records: Yes
Vital records: Contact Nancy Johnson,
Registrar of Vital Statistics, City-
County Complex, Winnemucca, NV
89445
Probate records: Contact Susan Harrer,
County Clerk
Probate search service: $1.00 per year;
copies: $1.00 per page, no minimum;
"Must be written request."

*Lander County Courthouse
315 South Humboldt Street
Battle Mountain, NV 89820
Phone (702) 635-5738
*County organized 1862 from Humboldt
and Saint Mary's counties*
Land records: Contact Clerk
Land records search service: $1.00 per
year; copies: $1.00 each, $3.00 for
certification
Naturalization records: Contact Clerk
Naturalization records search service:
$1.00 per year; copies: $1.00 each,
$3.00 for certification
Vital records: Contact Clerk
Vital records search service: $1.00 per
year; copies: $1.00 each, $3.00 for
certification
Probate records: Contact Clerk
Probate search service: $1.00 per year;
copies: $1.00 each, $3.00 for
certification

*Lincoln County Courthouse
PO Box 90
Pioche, NV 89043-0090
Phone (702) 962-5495 County Recorder/
Auditor; (702) 962-5390 County
Clerk
*County organized 1866 from Nye
County*
Land records: Contact County Recorder/
Auditor, PO Box 218, Pioche, NV
89043
Naturalization records: Contact County
Clerk
Vital records: Contact County Clerk
Probate records: Contact County Clerk
Probate search service: $1.00 per year;
copies: $1.00 each, no minimum

Lyon County Courthouse
PO Box 816
Yerington, NV 89447-0816
Phone (702) 463-3341
County organized 1861, original county

*Mineral County Courthouse
PO Box 1450
Hawthorne, NV 89415-1450
Phone (702) 945-2446
*County organized 1911 from Esmeralda
County*
Land records: Real property tax rolls;
contact County Clerk and Treasurer's
Office
Naturalization records: To 23 August
1957
Vital records: Marriages
Probate records: Contact County Clerk
and Treasurer
Probate search service: $1.00 per year
searched per name; copies: $1.00 per
page, no minimum

*Nye County Courthouse
PO Box 1031
Tonopah, NV 89049
Phone (702) 482-8127
*County organized 1864 from Esmeralda
County*
Land records: Contact County Recorder,
PO Box 111, Tonopah, NV 89049 or
County Assessor, PO Box 271,
Tonopah, NV 89049
Naturalization records: Through 1911;
contact County Clerk
Vital records: Contact County Recorder
Probate records: Contact County Clerk
Probate search service: $1.00 per year
searched; copies: $1.00 per page, no
minimum

Ormsby County
(see Carson City)

*Pershing County Courthouse
PO Box 820
Lovelock, NV 89419-0820

Phone (702) 273-2408 Recorder-Auditor;
(702) 273-2208 Clerk
*County organized 1919 from Humboldt
County*
Land records: Contact Recorder-Auditor,
PO Box 736, Lovelock, NV 89419
Naturalization records: From 1919 to
1960; contact Clerk
Probate records: Contact Clerk
Probate search service: $1.00 per year;
copies: $1.00 per page, no minimum

*Storey County Courthouse
Drawer D
Virginia City, NV 89440-0139
Phone (702) 847-0967 County Recorder
and Auditor; (702) 847-0969 Clerk-
Treasurer
County organized 1861, original county
Land records: Deeds from 1859 to date;
contact County Recorder and Auditor,
PO Box 493, Virginia City, NV 89440
Vital records: Births from 1887 to 1949,
deaths from 1887 to 1949, and
marriages (index from 1862); contact
County Recorder and Auditor.
Marriage licenses: Contact Doreen
Bacus, Clerk-Treasurer
Probate records: Contact Clerk-Treasurer

*Washoe County Courthouse
PO Box 11130
Reno, NV 89520-0027
Phone (702) 328-3661 County Recorder;
(702) 328-3260 County Clerk; (702)
328-2400 County Health Department;
(702) 328-3110 Court Clerk
*County organized 1861, original county;
in 1883 annexed Roop County
(called Lake County until 1862),
which was also an original county*
Land records: Contact County Recorder
Naturalization records: Contact Judi
Bailey, County Clerk
Vital records: Contact County Health
Department
Probate records: Contact Court Clerk
Probate search service: $1.00 per year
per case; copies: $1.00 per page, no
minimum

*White Pine County Courthouse
Campton Street
Ely, NV 89301
Phone (702) 289-3016 County Assessor;
(702) 289-2341 County Clerk
*County organized 1869 from Elko and
Lincoln counties*
Land records: Contact County Assessor
Naturalization records: Contact County
Clerk, PO Box 659, Ely, NV 89301
Probate records: Contact County Clerk
Probate search service: no charge;
copies: 50¢ per page, no minimum

NEW HAMPSHIRE

Capital: Concord. Statehood: 21 June 1788 (became a separate royal province in 1679, relinquished Vermont in 1782)

Court System

New Hampshire has several Municipal Courts of limited jurisdiction whose duties, since 1964, have been assumed by the District Courts as vacancies occur. The District Courts handle a variety of civil and criminal matters and have original juvenile jurisdiction. Auburn District: Auburn, Candia, Deerfield, Nottingham, Raymond and Northwood in Rockingham County; Berlin District: Berlin, Milan, Dummer, Cambridge and Success in Coos County; Claremont District: Claremont, Cornish, Unity, Charlestown, Acworth, Langdon and Plainfield in Sullivan County; Colebrook District: Colebrook, Pittsburg, Clarksville, Wentworth's Location, Errol, Millsfield, Columbia, Stewartstown, Stratford, Dix's Grant, Atkinson and Gilmanton Academy Grant, Second College Grant, Dixville, Erving's Location and Odell in Coos County; Concord District: Concord, Loudon, Canterbury, Dunbarton, Bow and Hopkinton in Merrimack County; Conway District: Conway, Bartlett, Jackson, Eaton, Chatham, Hart's Location, Albany, Madison and Hale's Location in Carroll County; Derry District: Derry, Chester, Londonderry and Sandown in Rockingham County; Dover District: Dover, Barrington and Madbury in Strafford County; Durham District: Durham and Lee in Strafford County; Exeter District: Exeter, Newmarket, Stratham, Newfields, Fremont, East Kingston, Kensington, Epping and Brentwood in Rockingham County; Franklin District: Franklin, Northfield, Danbury, Andover, Boscawen, Salisbury, Hill and Webster in Merrimack County; Goffstown District: Goffstown, Weare, New Boston and Francestown in Hillsborough County; Gorham District: Gorham, Shelburne, Randolph, Bean's Purchase, Martin's Location, Green's Grant, Pinkham's Grant, Thompson and Meserve's Purchase, Sargent's Purchase, Cutt's Grant, Bean's Grant, Crawford's Purchase, Low and Burbank's Grant and Chandler's Purchase in Coos County; Hampton District: Hampton, Hampton Falls, North Hampton, South Hampton and Seabrook in Rockingham County; Hanover District: Hanover, Orford and Lyme in Grafton County; Haverhill District: Haverhill, Bath, Landaff, Benton, Piermont

and Warren in Grafton County; Henniker District: Henniker, Warner and Bradford in Merrimack County; Hillsboro District: Hillsboro, Deering, Windsor, Antrim and Bennington in Hillsborough County; Hooksett District: Hooksett, Pembroke and Allenstown in Merrimack County; Jaffrey District: Jaffrey, Dublin, Fitzwilliam, Troy and Rindge in Cheshire County; Keene District: Keene, Stoddard, Westmoreland, Surry, Gilsum, Sullivan, Nelson, Roxbury, Marlow, Swanzey, Marlborough, Winchester, Richmond, Hinsdale, Harrisville, Walpole, Alstead and Chesterfield in Cheshire County; Laconia District: Laconia, Meredith, New Hampton, Gilford, Sanbornton, Tilton, Belmont, Alton, Gilmanton and Center Harbor in Belknap County; Lancaster District: Lancaster, Stark, Northumberland, Carroll, Whitefield, Dalton, Jefferson and Kilkenny in Coos County; Lebanon District: Lebanon, Enfield, Canaan, Grafton and Orange in Grafton County; Lincoln District: Lincoln, Woodstock and Livermore in Grafton County; Littleton District: Littleton, Monroe, Lyman, Lisbon, Franconia, Bethlehem, Sugar Hill and Easton in Grafton County; Manchester District: Manchester in Hillsborough County; Merrimack District: Merrimack and Bedford in Hillsborough County; Milford District: Milford, Brookline, Amherst, Mason, Wilton, Lyndeborough and Mont Vernon in Hillsborough County; Nashua District: Nashua, Hudson, Pelham, Hollis and Litchfield in Hillsborough County; New London District: New London, Wilmot, Newbury and Sutton in Merrimack County; Newport District: Newport, Grantham, Croydon, Springfield, Goshen, Sunapee, Lempster and Washington in Sullivan County; Ossipee District: Ossipee, Tamworth, Freedom, Effingham and Wakefield in Carroll County; Peterborough District: Peterborough, Hancock, Greenville, Greenfield, New Ipswich, Temple and Sharon in Hillsborough County; Pittsfield District: Pittsfield, Epsom, Barnstead and Chichester in Merrimack County; Plaistow District: Plaistow, Hampstead, Kingston, Newton, Atkinson and Danville in Rockingham County; Plymouth District: Plymouth, Bristol, Dorchester, Groton, Wentworth, Rumney, Ellsworth, Thornton, Campton, Waterville Valley, Ashland, Hebron, Holderness, Bridgewater and Alexandria in Grafton County; Portsmouth District: Portsmouth, Newington, Greenland, Rye and New Castle in Rockingham County; Rochester District: Rochester, Milton, New Durham, Farmington, Strafford and Middleton in Strafford County; Salem District: Salem and Windham in Rockingham County; Somersworth District: Somersworth and Rollinsford in Strafford County; Wolfeboro District: Brookfield, Moulton-

borough, Sandwich, Tuftonboro and Wolfeboro in Carroll County.

The Probate Court of New Hampshire has special jurisdiction over probate matters and sits in each county seat. The New Hampshire Superior Court is the court of general jurisdiction and sits at all the county seats (except Woodsville), plus Lancaster, Manchester and North Haverhill. The New Hampshire Supreme Court hears appeals at Concord.

For Provincial Deeds from about 1670 to 1772, titles to state-owned property, and probate from about 1650 to 1772, contact Division of Records Management and Archives, Department of State, 71 South Fruit Street, Concord, NH 03301-2410, (603) 271-2236, (603) 271-2272 FAX

Counties

*Belknap County Courthouse
PO Box 578
Laconia, NH 03247-0578
Phone (603) 524-3570; (603) 524-0618 Register of Deeds; (603) 524-0903 Register of Probate
County organized 1840 from Strafford County
Land records: Contact Rachel M. Normandin, Register of Deeds, 64 Court Street, PO Box 1343, Laconia, NH 03247
Naturalization records: Yes
Vital records: Contact individual town and city clerks
Probate records: Contact Estelle J. Dearborn, Register of Probate, 64 Court Street, PO Box 1343, Laconia, NH 03247
Probate search service: no charge; copies: $2.00 for the first page and 50¢ for each additional page, no minimum

*Carroll County Administration Building
Route 171
PO Box 152
Ossipee, NH 03864
Phone (603) 539-4872 Register of Deeds; (603) 539-4123 County Probate Court
County organized 1840 from Strafford, Coos and Grafton counties
Land records: Contact Lillian O. Brookes, Register of Deeds
No land records search service; copies: $1.00 per page
Vital records: Contact individual town and city clerks
Probate records: From 1840 to date ("The majority of our records prior to 1840 are at Strafford County"); contact Gail S. Tinker, Register of

Probate, County Probate Court, PO Box 419, Ossipee, NH 03864

Probate search service: no charge to find out if a named individual has a file; copies: $2.00 for the first page and 50¢ for each additional page (payable in advance), no minimum; "We need a check before we send out copies; call or write to request fee for a copying job."

*Cheshire County Courthouse

12 Court Street
PO Box 444
Keene, NH 03431
Phone (603) 352-0051; (603) 352-0403 Register of Deeds; (603) 357-7786 Register of Probate

County organized 1769, original county

Land records: Contact Evelyn Hubal, Register of Deeds, 33 West Street, Keene, NH 03431; copies: 50¢ per page

Naturalization records: Contact Superior Court (cases prior to 1918 are not indexed and not available for review except when case name and date are known)

Vital records: Contact individual town and city clerks

Probate records: Contact Elizabeth Minkler, Register of Probate

*Coos County Courthouse

148 Main Street
Lancaster, NH 03584
Phone (603) 788-2392 Register of Deeds; (603) 788-4900 Clerk of Court; (603) 788-2001 Register of Probate

County organized 1803 from Grafton County

Land records: Contact Margaret Frizzell, Register of Deeds

Naturalization records: Contact Superior Court

Vital records: Contact individual town and city clerks

Probate records: Contact Carol Reed, Register of Probate, County Probate Court

*Grafton County Courthouse

RR 1, Box 65
North Haverhill, NH 03774
Phone (603) 787-6941; (603) 787-6921 Register of Deeds; (603) 271-2236 Division of Records Management and Archives; (603) 271-2272 FAX, Division of Records Management and Archives; (603) 787-6931 Register of Probate

County organized 1769, original county

Land records: Contact Carol A. Elliott, Register of Deeds, PO Box 226, Woodsville, NH 03785. Deeds from 1772 to about 1840; contact Division

of Records Management and Archives, Department of State, 71 South Fruit Street, Concord, NH 03301-2410

Naturalization records: Contact Register of Probate

Vital records: Contact individual town and city clerks

Probate records: Contact Rebecca Wyman, Register of Probate

*Hillsborough County Courthouse

19 Temple Street
Nashua, NH 03060-3444
Phone (603) 882-6933 Registry of Deeds; (603) 882-7527 FAX, Register of Deeds; (603) 669-7410 Superior Court; (603) 882-1231 Register of Probate

County organized 1769, original county

Land records: Deeds from 1771; contact Judith A. MacDonald, Registrar, County Registry of Deeds, 19 Temple Street, PO Box 370, Nashua, NH 03061-0370; copies: $1.00 per page, $2.00 per certified document, plus postage

Naturalization records: Contact Superior Court, 300 Chestnut Street, Manchester, NH 03101

Vital records: Contact individual town and city clerks

Probate records: From 1771; contact Robert R. Rivard, Register of Probate, County Probate Court, PO Box P, Nashua, NH 03061

No probate search service; copies: available, no minimum

*Merrimack County Courthouse

163 North Main Street
Concord, NH 03301-5068
Phone (603) 228-0331; (603) 228-0101 Register of Deeds; (603) 224-9589 Register of Probate

County organized 1823 from Rockingham and Hillsborough counties

Land records: Contact Kathi Guay, Register of Deeds, PO Box 248, Concord, NH 03301-0248

Naturalization records: Contact Marshall A. Buttrick, Clerk

Vital records: Contact individual town and city clerks

Probate records: Contact Patricia Fraser, Register of Probate

No probate search service; copies: 50¢ per page, no minimum

*Rockingham County Courthouse

Hampton Road
Exeter, NH 03833
Phone (603) 772-4712 Register of Deeds; (603) 271-2236 Division of Records Management and Archives; (603) 271-2272 FAX, Division of Records

Management and Archives; (603) 772-3714 Superior Court; (603) 772-9347 Register of Probate

County organized 1769, original county

Land records: Contact Cathy Ann Stacey, Register of Deeds. Deeds from 1772 to about 1840; contact Division of Records Management and Archives, Department of State, 71 South Fruit Street, Concord, NH 03301-2410

Naturalization records: From 1780; contact Superior Court

Vital records; Contact individual town and city clerks

Probate records: Contact Charles K. Thayer, Register of Probate

Probate search service: $5.00; copies: $2.00 for the first page of will and 50¢ for each additional page of will, 50¢ per page for all other copies

*Strafford County Justice and Administration Building

259 County Farm Road
PO Box 799
Dover, NH 03820-0799
Phone (603) 742-1741 Register of Deeds; (603) 742-3065 County Superior Court Clerk; (603) 742-2550 Register of Probate

County organized 1769, original county

Land records: Contact Leo Lessard, Register of Deeds; copies: $1.00 per page

Naturalization records: Contact County Superior Court Clerk

Vital records: Contact individual town and city clerks

Probate records: Contact Kimberly Quint, Register of Probate

Probate search service: no charge; copies: "Varies by document and size of document," 50¢ minimum

Sullivan County Courthouse

24 Main Street
Newport, NH 03773-1520
Phone (603) 863-3450 Clerk of Court; (603) 863-2110 Register of Deeds; (603) 863-3150 Register of Probate

County organized 1827 from Cheshire County

Land records: From 1825 to date; contact Sharron A. King, Register of Deeds

Vital records: Contact individual town and city clerks

Probate records: Contact Diane M. Davis, Register of Probate

Cities and Towns

Town of Acworth
Town Clerk
PO Box 15
South Acworth, NH 03607
Phone (603) 835-6579 Town Clerk

Organized 1735/36 (Sullivan County)

Town of Albany
Town Clerk
PO Box 1767
Albany, NH 03818
Phone (603) 447-2877 Town Clerk
Organized 1833 (Carroll County)

Town of Alexandria
Town Clerk
Rt. 1, Box 807
Bristol, NH 03222
Phone (603) 744-3220; (603) 744-5024
    Town Clerk
Organized 1753 (Grafton County)

Town of Allenstown
Town Clerk
PO Box 231
Suncook, NH 03275
Phone (603) 485-4276; (603) 485-3111
    Town Clerk
Organized 1721 (Merrimack County)

Town of Alstead
Town Clerk
PO Box 33
Alstead, NH 03602
Phone (603) 835-2242 Town Clerk
Organized 1763 (Cheshire County)

*Town of Alton
Town Clerk
PO Box 637
Alton, NH 03809
Phone (603) 875-2101 Town Clerk
Organized 1796 (Belknap County)
Land records: No land records
Naturalization records: No naturalization
    records
Vital records: Yes
Probate records: No probate records

Town of Amherst
Town Clerk
PO Box 960
Amherst, NH 03031
Phone (603) 673-6041 Town Clerk
Organized 1760 (Hillsborough County)

Town of Andover
Town Clerk
PO Box 61
Andover, NH 03216
Phone (603) 735-5332 Town Clerk
Organized 1779 (Merrimack County)

Town of Antrim
Town Clerk
PO Box 248
Antrim, NH 03440

Phone (603) 588-6785; (603) 588-6700
    Town Clerk
Organized 1777 (Hillsborough County)

*Town of Ashland
Town Clerk
10 Highland Street
PO Box 517
Ashland, NH 03811
Phone (603) 968-4432 Town Clerk
Organized 1868 (Grafton County)
Vital records: Births before 1901, deaths
    and marriages before 1938 (open to
    the public upon completion of a
    written form)

Town of Atkinson
Town Clerk
21 Academy
PO Box 366
Atkinson, NH 03811
Phone (603) 362-5266; (603) 362-4920
    Town Clerk
Organized 1767 (Rockingham County)

**Atkinson and Gilmanton Academy
    Grant (unincorporated)**
(Coos County)

Town of Auburn
Town Clerk
PO Box 218
Auburn, NH 03032
Phone (603) 483-2281 Town Clerk
Organized 1845 (Rockingham County)

*Town of Barnstead
Town Clerk
PO Box 11
Center Barnstead, NH 03225
Phone (603) 269-4631 Town Clerk
Organized 1727 (Merrimack County)
Land records: No land records
Naturalization records: No naturalization
    records
Vital records: From 1868; contact Dawn
    Foss, Town Clerk
Vital records search service: $10.00
    (includes a certified copy of the
    record, if found)
Probate records: No probate records

*Town of Barrington
41 Province Lane
Barrington, NH 03825
Phone (603) 664-9007 Selectman's
    Office; (603) 664-5476 Town Clerk
Organized 1722 (Strafford County)
Land records: Contact Selectman's
    Office
Vital records: Contact Town Clerk;
    certified copies: $10.00 for the first
    copy and $6.00 for each additional
    copy

Town of Bartlett
Town Clerk
PO Box 141
Intervale, NH 03845
Phone (603) 356-2950; (603) 356-2300
    Town Clerk
Organized 1790 (Carroll County)

Town of Bath
Town Clerk
PO Box 30
Bath, NH 03740
Phone (603) 747-2454 Town Clerk
Organized 1761 (Grafton County)

Bean's Grant (unincorporated)
(Coos County)

Bean's Purchase (unincorporated)
(Coos County)

Town of Bedford
Town Clerk
24 North Amherst
Bedford, NH 03102
Phone (603) 472-5242; (603) 472-3550
    Town Clerk
*Organized 1733/34 (Hillsborough
    County)*

Town of Belmont
Town Clerk
PO Box 106
Belmont, NH 03220
Phone (603) 267-8145 Town Clerk
Organized 1859 (Belknap County)

Town of Bennington
Town Clerk
Bennington, NH 03442
Phone (603) 588-2189 Town Clerk
Organized 1842 (Hillsborough County)

Town of Benton
Town Clerk
Rt. 2, Box 348
Woodsville, NH 03785
Phone (603) 787-6541 Town Clerk
Organized 1764 (Grafton County)

City of Berlin
City Clerk
Main Street
Berlin, NH 03570
Phone (603) 752-2340 City Clerk
Organized 1771 (Coos County)

Town of Bethlehem
Town Clerk
Main Street
PO Box 394
Bethlehem, NH 03574

Phone (603) 869-3351; (603) 869-2293
Town Clerk
Organized 1774 (Grafton County)

Town of Boscawen
Town Clerk
High Street
Boscawen, NH 03303
Phone (603) 796-2426; (603) 796-2368
Town Clerk
Organized 1732 (Merrimack County)

*Town of Bow
Town Clerk
10 Grandview Road
Bow, NH 03304-3410
Phone (603) 225-2683 Town Clerk
Organized 1727 (Merrimack County)
Land records: No land records
Naturalization records: No naturalization
records
Vital records: Closed to the public
Probate records: No probate records

Town of Bradford
Town Clerk
PO Box 147
Bradford, NH 03221
Phone (603) 938-5900; (603) 938-2253
Town Clerk
Organized 1735/36 (Merrimack County)

*Town of Brentwood
Town Clerk
Rt. 1, Dalton Road
Exeter, NH 03833
Phone (603) 642-8817 Town Clerk
Organized 1742 (Rockingham County)
Vital records: From 1742 (missing from
1813 to 1825, lost in fire); contact
Phyllis Thompson, Town Clerk
Vital records search service: $10.00

Town of Bridgewater
Town Clerk
Rt. 2
Plymouth, NH 03264
Phone (603) 744-5055; (603) 968-7911
Town Clerk
Organized 1788 (Grafton County)

Town of Bristol
Town Clerk
PO Box 297
Bristol, NH 03222
Phone (603) 744-3354; (603) 744-8478
Town Clerk
Organized 1819 (Grafton County)

*Town of Brookfield
Town Clerk
PO Box 756
Brookfield, NH 03872
Phone (603) 522-3688; (603) 522-3231
Town Clerk (Mon 1:00–8:00)

Organized 1794 (Carroll County)
Vital records: Contact Virginia
McGinley, Town Clerk

*Town of Brookline
Town Clerk
PO Box 336
Brookline, NH 03033
Phone (603) 673-8933 Town Clerk
Organized 1769 (Hillsborough)
Land records: Some from 1758 but not
complete; contact Nancy Howard,
Town Clerk
Vital records: Some from 1758 but not
complete

Cambridge (unincorporated)
(Coos County)

Town of Campton
Town Clerk
PO Box 127
Campton, NH 03223
Phone (603) 726-3223 Town Clerk
Organized 1761 (Grafton County)

*Town of Canaan
PO Box 38
Canaan, NH 03741
Phone (603) 523-4501 Selectmen's
Office; (603) 523-7106 Town Clerk
Organized 1761 (Grafton County)
Land records: Contact Sherril Smith,
Secretary, Selectmen's Office
Naturalization records: No naturalization
records
Vital records: Contact Edward C. Morse,
Town Clerk; certified copies: $10.00
each (with proof of relationship)

Town of Candia
Town Clerk
74 High Street
Candia, NH 03034
Phone (603) 483-8101; (603) 483-5573
Town Clerk
Organized 1763 (Rockingham County)

Town of Canterbury
Town Clerk
PO Box 112
Canterbury, NH 03224
Phone (603) 783-9955 Town Clerk
Organized 1727 (Merrimack County)

*Town of Carroll
Town Clerk
PO Box 88
Twin Mountain, NH 03595
Phone (603) 846-5754 Selectmen's
Office; (603) 846-5494 Town Clerk
Organized 1772 (Coos County)
Land records: Contact Selectmen's
Office

Naturalization records: No naturalization
records
Vital records: From 1900
Vital records search service: $10.00
(includes copy)

Town of Center Harbor
Town Clerk
PO Box 140
Center Harbor, NH 03226
Phone (603) 253-4561 Town Clerk
Organized 1797 (Belknap County)

Town of Chandler's Purchase
(unincorporated)
Organized 1835 (Coos County)

*Town of Charlestown
Town Clerk
PO Box 834
Charlestown, NH 03603
Phone (603) 826-5821 Town Clerk
Organized 1735 (Sullivan County)
Vital records: Births, deaths and
marriages from the 1700s to date;
contact Debra J. Clark, Town Clerk-
Tax Collector
Vital records search service: $10.00
(includes certified copy if found,
births before 1901 and deaths and
marriages before 1938 open to the
public, newer records restricted to
those with a "direct and tangible
interest," including grandchildren,
nephews and nieces of the registrant)

*Town of Chatham
Town Clerk
Chatham, NH 04058
Phone (603) 694-3303 Town Clerk's
home
Organized 1767 (Carroll County)

Town of Chester
Town Clerk
PO Box 275
Chester, NH 03036
Phone (603) 887-4979; (603) 887-3636
Town Clerk
Organized 1720 (Rockingham County)

Town of Chesterfield
Town Clerk
PO Box 56
Chesterfield, NH 03443
Phone (603) 363-8071 Town Clerk
Organized 1735 (Cheshire County)

Town of Chichester
Town Clerk
Main Street
Chichester, NH 03264
Phone (603) 798-5350; (603) 798-5808
Town Clerk
Organized 1727 (Merrimack County)

City of Claremont
City Clerk
City Hall
Claremont, NH 03743
Phone (603) 542-6262; (603) 542-6371
    City Clerk
Organized 1764 (Sullivan County)

Town of Clarksville
Town Clerk
Rt. 1, Box 460
Pittsburg, NH 03592
Phone (603) 246-7751 Town Clerk
Organized 1792 (Coos County)

Town of Colebrook
Town Clerk
10 Bridge Street
Colebrook, NH 03576
Phone (603) 237-4070 Town Clerk
Organized 1762 (Coos County)

Town of Columbia
Town Clerk
Rt. 1, Box 523
Colebrook, NH 03576
Phone (603) 237-5225; (603) 237-8803
    Town Clerk
Organized 1762 (Coos County)

*City of Concord
City Clerk
41 Green Street
Concord, NH 03301
Phone (603) 225-8500 City Clerk
Organized 1659 (Merrimack County)
Land records: No land records
Naturalization records: No naturalization
    records
Vital records: Yes
Probate records: No probate records

Town of Conway
Town Clerk
PO Box 98
Center Conway, NH 03813
Phone (603) 447-3822 Town Clerk
Organized 1765 (Carroll County)

*Town of Cornish
Town Clerk
PO Box 183
Cornish Flat, NH 03746
Phone (603) 542-2845 Town Clerk
Organized 1763 (Sullivan County)
Vital records: Contact Reigh H. Rock;
    copies: 25¢ each, $10.00 for the first
    certified copy and $6.00 for each
    additional certified copy, $5.00
    minimum

**Town of Crawford's Purchase
    (unincorporated)**
Organized 1834 (Coos County)

Town of Croydon
Town Clerk
RFD 1
PO Box 315
Newport, NH 03773
Phone (603) 863-2054 Town Clerk's
    home
Organized 1763 (Sullivan County)

Cutt's Grant (unincorporated)
(Coos County)

Town of Dalton
Town Clerk
Rt. 2
Whitefield, NH 03598
Phone (603) 837-9821; (603) 837-9802
    Town Clerk
Organized 1784 (Coos County)

Town of Danbury
Town Clerk
Box 86A-Ragged Mountain Road
Danbury, NH 03230
Phone (603) 768-3313 Town Clerk
Organized 1795 (Merrimack County)

Town of Danville
Town Clerk
PO Box 753
Danville, NH 03819
Phone (603) 382-8253 Town Clerk
Organized 1760 (Rockingham County)

Town of Deerfield
Town Clerk
141 Middle Road
Deerfield, NH 03037
Phone (603) 463-8811 Town Clerk
Organized 1766 (Rockingham County)

*Town of Deering
Town Clerk
Rural Route, Box 166
Hillsboro, NH 03244
Phone (603) 464-3248 Town Clerk
Organized 1774 (Hillsborough County)
Land records: Subdivision plats only
    from 1975
Vital records: From about 1800 to date
    (from 1810 to 1830 missing)

*Town of Derry
Town Clerk
48 East Broadway
Derry, NH 03038
Phone (603) 432-6100; (603) 432-6105
    Town Clerk
Organized 1827 (Rockingham County)
Land records: From the 1820s
Naturalization records: No naturalization
    records
Vital records: From 1857
Probate records: No probate records

Dix's Grant (unincorporated)
(Coos County)

*Dixville (unincorporated)
(Coos County)

Town of Dorchester
Town Clerk
Rt. 1, Box 490
Rumney, NH 03266
Phone (603) 523-7088; (603) 786-9076
    Town Clerk
Organized 1791 (Grafton County)

City of Dover
City Clerk
288 Central Avenue
Dover, NH 03820
Phone (603) 742-3551 City Clerk
Organized 1623 (Strafford)

*Town of Dublin
Town Clerk
PO Box 62
Dublin, NH 03444
Phone (603) 563-8859 Town Clerk
Organized 1749 (Cheshire County)
Land records: No land records
Naturalization records: No naturalization
    records
Probate records: No probate records

Town of Dummer
Town Clerk
Rt. 1, Box 24
Milan, NH 03588
Phone (603) 449-2006; (603) 449-3408
    Town Clerk's home
Organized 1773 (Coos County)

Town of Dunbarton
Town Clerk
Rt. 2, Box 244
Dunbarton, NH 03301
Phone (603) 774-3541; (603) 774-3547
    Town Clerk
Organized 1735 (Merrimack County)

*Town of Durham
Town Clerk
15 Newmarket Road
Durham, NH 03824-2898
Phone (603) 868-5571; (603) 868-5577
    Town Clerk
Organized 1732 (Strafford County)
Land records: No land records
Naturalization records: No naturalization
    records
Vital records: Contact Linda Ekdahl,
    Town Clerk
Probate records: No probate records

Town of East Kingston
Town Clerk

PO Box 4
East Kingston, NH 03827
Phone (603) 642-8406; (603) 642-8794
   Town Clerk
Organized 1738 (Rockingham County)

*Town of Easton
Town Clerk
PO Box 741
Franconia, NH 03580
Phone (603) 823-8017 Town Hall; (603)
   823-5238 Town Clerk's home
Organized 1876 (Grafton County)
Land records: From 1988 at Clerk's
   home, other records at Town Hall
Naturalization records: No naturalization
   records
Vital records: From 1878 to date
Probate records: No probate records

Town of Eaton
Town Clerk
PO Box 42
Eaton Center, NH 03832
Phone (603) 447-2840 Town Clerk
Organized 1766 (Carroll County)

Town of Effingham
Town Clerk
PO Box 48
South Effingham, NH 03882
Phone (603) 539-7770; (603) 539-7551
   Town Clerk
Organized 1749 (Carroll County)

Town of Ellsworth
Town Clerk
PO Box 871
Plymouth, NH 03264-0871
Phone (603) 726-3195 Town Clerk
Organized 1769 (Grafton County)

*Town of Enfield
Town Clerk
PO Box 373
Enfield, NH 03748
Phone (603) 632-5001 Town Clerk
Organized 1761 (Grafton County)

Town of Epping
Town Clerk
54 Main Street
Epping, NH 03042
Phone (603) 679-8288 Town Clerk
Organized 1741 (Rockingham County)

*Town of Epsom
Town Clerk
Route 28N, Epsom Shoppes
Epsom, NH 03234
Phone (603) 736-4725; (603) 736-9300
   Town Clerk's home
Organized 1727 (Merrimack County)
Naturalization records: No naturalization
   records

Vital records: From 1850 to date
Vital records search service: $10.00
   (includes certified copy, must indicate
   the reason for the request)

*Town of Errol
Town Clerk
PO Box 74
Errol, NH 03579
Phone (603) 482-7747; (603) 482-3351
   Town Clerk
Organized 1774 (Coos County)

**Erving's Location (unincorporated)
(Coos County)**

*Town of Exeter
Town Clerk
10 Front Street
Exeter, NH 03833
Phone (603) 778-0591 Town Clerk
Organized 1638 (Rockingham County)
Land records: No land records
Naturalization records: No naturalization
   records
Vital records: Contact Linda Hartson
Vital records search service: $10.00
   (includes one certified copy); certified
   copies: $10.00 for the first copy and
   $6.00 for each additional copy
   (records after 1901 are not open to the
   public)
Probate records: No probate records

Town of Farmington
Town Clerk
Town Hall
Farmington, NH 03835
Phone (603) 755-2208; (603) 755-3657
   Town Clerk
Organized 1798 (Strafford County)

Town of Fitzwilliam
Town Clerk
PO Box 504
Fitzwilliam, NH 03447
Phone (603) 585-7791 Town Clerk
Organized 1752 (Cheshire County)

Town of Francestown
Town Clerk
PO Box 118
Francestown, NH 03043
Phone (603) 547-3469 Town Clerk
Organized 1772 (Hillsborough County)

Town of Franconia
Town Clerk
Rt. 1, Sawmill Lane
Franconia, NH 03580
Phone (603) 823-7752; (603) 823-8895
   Town Clerk
Organized 1764 (Grafton County)

*City of Franklin
City Clerk
316 Central Street
Franklin, NH 03235
Phone (603) 934-3900; (603) 934-3109
   City Clerk
Organized 1828 (Merrimack County)
Land records: No land records
Naturalization records: No naturalization
   records
Vital records: Yes
Vital records search service: $10.00
Probate records: No probate records

Town of Freedom
Town Clerk
PO Box 450
Freedom, NH 03836
Phone (603) 539-6323 Town Clerk
Organized 1831 (Carroll County)

*Town of Fremont
Town Clerk
167 Scribner Road
Fremont, NH 03044
Phone (603) 895-2226
Organized 1764 (Rockingham County)

Town of Gilford
Town Clerk
47 Cherry Valley Road
Gilford, NH 03246
Phone (603) 524-7438; (603) 524-3286
   Town Clerk
Organized 1812 (Belknap County)

Town of Gilmanton
Town Clerk
PO Box 10
Gilmanton, NH 03237
Phone (603) 364-5101 Town Clerk
Organized 1727 (Belknap County)

Town of Gilsum
Town Clerk
Surry Road, Box 93A
Gilsum, NH 03448
Phone (603) 357-0320 Town Clerk
Organized 1752 (Cheshire County)

Town of Goffstown
Town Clerk
16 Main
Goffstown, NH 03045
Phone (603) 497-3613 Town Clerk
*Organized 1733/34 (Hillsborough
   County)*

Town of Gorham
Town Clerk
Park Street
Gorham, NH 03581
Phone (603) 466-2744 Town Clerk
Organized 1779 (Coos County)

Town of Goshen
Town Clerk
PO Box 710
Goshen, NH 03752
Phone (603) 863-5655 Town Clerk
Organized 1791 (Sullivan County)

*Town of Grafton
Town Clerk
Rt. 4
Grafton, NH 03240
Phone (603) 523-7218; (603) 768-3638
    Town Clerk
Organized 1761 (Grafton County)

Town of Grantham
Town Clerk
PO Box 135
Grantham, NH 03753
Phone (603) 863-5608 Town Clerk
Organized 1761 (Sullivan County)

Green's Grant (unincorporated)
(Coos County)

Town of Greenfield
Town Clerk
PO Box 16
Greenfield, NH 03047
Phone (603) 547-3442; (603) 547-2782
    Town Clerk
Organized 1791 (Hillsborough County)

Town of Greenland
Town Clerk
575 Portsmouth
Greenland, NH 03840
Phone (603) 431-7111 Town Clerk
Organized 1721 (Rockingham County)

Town of Greenville
Town Clerk
Main Street
Greenville, NH 03048
Phone (603) 878-4155 Town Clerk
Organized 1872 (Hillsborough County)

*Town of Groton
Town Clerk
HC 58, Box 580-1
Groton, NH 03241
Phone (603) 744-8849 Town Clerk
Organized 1761 (Grafton County)
Naturalization records: No naturalization
    records
Vital records: Some (available for
    viewing at the discretion of the town
    clerk)

Hadley's Purchase (unincorporated)

Hale's Location (unincorporated)
(Carroll County)

Town of Hampstead
Town Clerk
PO Box 338
Hampstead, NH 03841
Phone (603) 329-5011; (603) 329-6840
    Town Clerk
Organized 1749 (Rockingham County)

Town of Hampton
Town Clerk
PO Box 1
Hampton, NH 03842
Phone (603) 926-6766 Town Clerk
Organized 1635 (Rockingham County)

*Town of Hampton Falls
Town Clerk
1 Drinkwater Road
Hampton Falls, NH 03844
Phone (603) 926-7101; (603) 926-4618
    Town Clerk
Organized 1722 (Rockingham County)
Vital records: Yes

Town of Hancock
Town Clerk
School Street
Hancock, NH 03449
Phone (603) 525-4441 Town Clerk
Organized 1779 (Hillsborough County)

Town of Hanover
Town Clerk
PO Box 483
Hanover, NH 03755
Phone (603) 643-4123 Town Clerk
Organized 1761 (Grafton County)

*Town of Harrisville
Town Clerk
PO Box 103
Harrisville, NH 03450
Phone 827-3331 Town Clerk
Organized 1870 (Cheshire County)

*Town of Hart's Location
Town Clerk
Route 302
Bartlett, NH 03812
Phone (603) 374-2436 Town Clerk
(Carroll County)
Land records: No land records
Naturalization records: No naturalization
    records
Vital records: From 1830 to date
Vital records search service: $10.00
Probate records: No probate records

Town of Haverhill
Town Clerk
Court Street
Woodsville, NH 03785
Phone (603) 747-2808 Town Clerk
Organized 1763 (Grafton County)

Town of Hebron
Town Clerk
Star Rt. 1, Box 286
East Hebron, NH 03232
Phone (603) 744-2631; (603) 744-5095
    Town Clerk
Organized 1792 (Grafton County)

Town of Henniker
Town Clerk
Henniker, NH 03242
Phone (603) 428-3240 Town Clerk
Organized 1735/36 (Merrimack County)

Town of Hill
Town Clerk
Rt. 1, Box 45
Hill, NH 03243
Phone (603) 934-5249; (603) 934-6737
    Town Clerk's home
Organized 1753 (Merrimack County)

*Town of Hillsborough
Town Clerk
PO Box 54
Hillsboro, NH 03244
Phone (603) 464-3422 Town Clerk
Organized 1735/36, incorporated 1772
    (Hillsborough County)
Land records: No land records
Naturalization records: No naturalization
    records
Vital records: Contact Town Clerk
Probate records: No probate records

*Town of Hinsdale
Town Clerk
15 Spring Street
Hinsdale, NH 03451
Phone (603) 336-5719 Town Clerk
Organized 1753 (Cheshire County)

Town of Holderness
Town Clerk
PO Box 446
Holderness, NH 03245
Phone (603) 968-3537; (603) 968-7536
    Town Clerk
Organized 1751 (Grafton County)

*Town of Hollis
Town Clerk
7 Monument Square
Hollis, NH 03049
Phone (603) 465-2064 Town Clerk
Organized 1746 (Hillsborough County)
Vital records: Yes

Town of Hooksett
Town Clerk
16 Main Street
Hooksett, NH 03106
Phone (603) 485-8471; (603) 498-9534
    Town Clerk
Organized 1822 (Merrimack County)

Town of Hopkinton
Town Clerk
PO Box 169
Contoocook, NH 03229
Phone (603) 746-3170; (603) 746-3180
Town Clerk
Organized 1735/36 (Merrimack County)

Town of Hudson
Town Clerk
12 School Street
Hudson, NH 03051
Phone (603) 889-1890 Town Clerk
Organized 1746 (Hillsborough County)

*Town of Jackson
Town Clerk
PO Box 268
Jackson, NH 03846
Phone (603) 383-4223 Office of the
Selectmen; (603) 383-9024 Town
Clerk
Organized 1800 (Carroll County)
Naturalization records: No naturalization
records
Vital records: Births, deaths and
marriages from 1889 through 1988

Town of Jaffrey
Town Clerk
Jaffrey, NH 03452
Phone (603) 532-8322 Town Clerk
Organized 1749 (Cheshire County)

Town of Jefferson
Town Clerk
Rt. 1, Box 162A
Jefferson, NH 03583
Phone (603) 586-4553; (603) 586-4364
Town Clerk
Organized 1765 (Coos County)

City of Keene
City Clerk
3 Washington Street
Keene, NH 03431
Phone (603) 352-5211; (603) 352-0133
City Clerk
Organized 1733 (Cheshire County)

Town of Kensington
Town Clerk
22 Trundle Bed Lane
Kensington, NH 03827
Phone (603) 772-5423 Town Clerk
Organized 1737 (Rockingham County)

Kilkenny (unincorporated)
(Coos County)

*Town of Kingston
Town Clerk
PO Box 657
Kingston, NH 03848

Phone (603) 642-3342; (603) 642-3112
Town Clerk
Organized 1694 (Rockingham County)
Land records: Yes
Naturalization records: No naturalization
records
Vital records: From 1700
Probate records: No probate records

City of Laconia
City Clerk
Beacon Street West
PO Box 489
Lanconia, NH 03247
Phone (603) 524-1520 City Clerk
Organized 1855 (Belknap County)

Town of Lancaster
Town Clerk
PO Box 151
Lancaster, NH 03584
Phone (603) 788-2306 Town Clerk
Organized 1763 (Coos County)

*Town of Landaff
Town Clerk
319 Jockey Hill Road
Landaff, NH 03585
Phone (603) 838-6220 Town Clerk (Tue
5:00–7:00); (603) 838-6353 answering
machine
Organized 1764 (Grafton County)

*Town of Langdon
Town Clerk
Rt. 1, Box 158A
Alstead, NH 03602
Phone (603) 835-2389 Town Clerk's
business; (603) 835-6036 Town
Clerk's home
Organized 1787 (Sullivan County)
Land records: Yes
Vital records: Yes (proof of relationship
required)

*City of Lebanon
City Clerk
51 North Park Street
PO Box 1207
Lebanon, NH 03766-4207
Phone (603) 448-4220; (603) 448-3054
City Clerk
Organized 1761 (Grafton County)
Land records: No land records
Naturalization records: No naturalization
records
Vital records: Births, deaths and
marriages; contact Dorothy J. Doyle,
City Clerk
Vital records search service: $10.00
(includes one copy, if found); certified
copies: $10.00 for the first copy and
$6.00 for each additional copy (for
births after 1901 or deaths and
marriages after 1938, requests must be
made in writing, with name of

registrant, date and place of birth,
mother's maiden name, purpose for
which the certificate is requested, and
the correspondent's relationship to the
registrant; ID may be required)
Probate records: No probate records

Town of Lee
Town Clerk
7 Mast Road
Durham, NH 03824
Phone (603) 659-2964 Town Clerk
Organized 1766 (Strafford County)

Town of Lempster
Town Clerk
PO Box 33
East Lempster, NH 03605
Phone (603) 863-3213 Town Clerk
Organized 1735/36 (Sullivan County)

*Town of Lincoln
PO Box 25
Lincoln, NH 03251
Phone (603) 745-8971 Town Clerk
Incorporated 1764 (Grafton County)
Land records: Yes
Naturalization records: No naturalization
records
Vital records: Yes
Probate records: No probate records

Town of Lisbon
Town Clerk
21 School Street
Lisbon, NH 03585
Phone (603) 838-2862 Town Clerk
Organized 1763 (Grafton County)

Town of Litchfield
Town Clerk
255 Charles Bancroft Highway
Litchfield, NH 03051
Phone (603) 424-4045 Town Clerk
Organized 1729 (Hillsborough County)

*Town of Littleton
Town Clerk
1 Union Street
Littleton, NH 03561
Phone (603) 444-3996; (603) 444-3995
Town Clerk
Organized 1764 (Grafton County)
Land records: Property cards and
assessments; contact Tax Collector's
Office
Naturalization records: No naturalization
records
Vital records: Contact Faye V. White,
Town Clerk
Vital records search service: $10.00
(includes one certified copy); certified
copies: $10.00 for the first copy and
$6.00 for each additional copy made
at the same time
Probate records: No probate records

Livermore (unincorporated)
(Grafton County)

Town of Londonderry
Town Clerk
268 Manmoth Road
Londonderry, NH 03053
Phone (603) 434-1133 Town Clerk
Organized 1722 (Rockingham County)

Town of Loudon
Town Clerk
PO Box 7329
Loudon, NH 03301
Phone (603) 783-4575 Town Clerk
Organized 1773 (Merrimack County)

**Lowe and Burbank's Grant
   (unincorporated)**
(Coos County)

Town of Lyman
Town Clerk
Rt. 1
Lisbon, NH 03585
Phone (603) 838-5522 Town Clerk
Organized 1761 (Grafton County)

*Town of Lyme
Town Clerk
Rt. 1, Box 153
Lyme, NH 03768
Phone (603) 795-2535 Town Clerk
Organized 1761 (Grafton County)
Land records: No land records
Naturalization records: No naturalization
   records
Vital records: From 1872 to date (a fire
   destroyed records previous to 1872)
Vital records search service: $10.00
   (includes one copy, if found)
Probate records: No probate records

Town of Lyndeborough
Town Clerk
PO Box 164
Lyndeborough, NH 03082
Phone (603) 654-9053 Town Clerk
Organized 1735 (Hillsborough County)

Town of Madbury
Town Clerk
13 Town Hall
Madbury, NH 03820
Phone (603) 742-5131 Town Clerk
Organized 1755 (Strafford County)

Town of Madison
Town Clerk
Rt. 113, Box 248
Madison, NH 03849
Phone (603) 367-4332; (603) 367-9931
   Town Clerk
Organized 1852 (Carroll County)

City of Manchester
City Clerk
904 Elm Street
Manchester, NH 03101
Phone (603) 624-6455 City Clerk
Organized 1735 (Hillsborough County)

*Town of Marlborough
Town Clerk
PO Box 487
Marlborough, NH 03455
Phone (603) 876-3751; (603) 876-4529
   Town Clerk
Organized 1752 (Cheshire County)
Land records: Yes
Naturalization records: No naturalization
   records
Vital records: Yes
Probate records: No probate records

Town of Marlow
Town Clerk
PO Box 39
Marlow, NH 03456
Phone (603) 446-2245 Town Clerk
Organized 1753 (Cheshire County)

Martin's Location (unincorporated)
(Coos County)

*Town of Mason
Selectman's Office
Darling Hill Road
Mason, NH 03048
Phone (603) 878-2070 Town Clerk
Organized 1749 (Hillsborough County)
Vital records: Scant records from 1850 to
   1900, more complete from 1900 to
   date
Vital records search service: $10.00
   (includes certified copy, after 1938
   limited to legal relatives, lawyers,
   etc.)

*Town of Meredith
Town Clerk
Main Street
Meredith, NH 03253
Phone (603) 279-4538 Town Clerk
Organized 1748 (Belknap County)
Land records: No land records
Naturalization records: No naturalization
   records
Vital records: Yes
Probate records: No probate records

*Town of Merrimack
Town Clerk
PO Box 27
Merrimack, NH 03054
Phone (603) 424-3651 Town Clerk
Organized 1746 (Hillsborough County)

Town of Middleton
Town Clerk
New Portsmouth Road
Union, NH 03887
Phone (603) 473-3968; (603) 473-2261
   Town Clerk
Organized 1749 (Strafford County)

Town of Milan
Town Clerk
PO Box 104
Milan, NH 03588
Phone (603) 449-3461 Town Clerk
Organized 1771 (Coos County)

Town of Milford
Town Clerk
Nashua Street
Milford, NH 03055
Phone (603) 673-2257; (603) 673-3403
   Town Clerk
Organized 1746 (Hillsborough County)

Town of Millsfield
Town Clerk
PO Box 48
Errol, NH 03579
Phone (603) 482-3305 Town Clerk
Organized 1774 (Coos County)

*Town of Milton
Town Clerk
(Route 125—location)
PO Box 310 (mailing address)
Milton, NH 03851-0310
Phone (603) 652-4501 Town Office;
   (603) 652-9414 Town Clerk
*Settled 1760, incorporated 1802; also
   called Milton Mills (Strafford
   County)*
Land records: Property records for
   taxation purposes (including copies of
   deeds); contact Town Office
Naturalization records: No naturalization
   records
Vital records: Births, deaths and
   marriages; contact Town Clerk
Probate records: No probate records

Town of Monroe
Town Clerk
Rt. 1, Box 279
PO Box 63
Monroe, NH 03771
Phone (603) 638-2644 Town Clerk
Organized 1854 (Grafton County)

Town of Mont Vernon
Town Clerk
PO Box 277
Mont Vernon, NH 03057
Phone (603) 673-6080 Town Clerk
Organized 1803 (Hillsborough County)

Town of Moultonborough
Town Clerk
PO Box 15
Moultonborough, NH 03254
Phone (603) 476-2347; (603) 476-5757
  Town Clerk
Organized 1763 (Carroll)

City of Nashua
City Clerk
229 Main Street
Nashua, NH 03061
Phone (603) 880-3300; (603) 880-3340
  City Clerk
Organized 1746 (Hillsborough County)

*Town of Nelson
Town Clerk
HCR 33, Box 660
Nelson, NH 03457
Phone (603) 847-9043 Town Clerk
Organized 1752 (Cheshire County)
Land records: Yes
Vital records: Yes

*Town of New Boston
Town Clerk
PO Box 250
Town Office
New Boston, NH 03070
Phone (603) 487-5571 Town Clerk (Mon,
  Wed & Fri 9:00-3:30)
*Organized 1735/36 (Hillsborough
  County)*
Land records: No land records
Naturalization records: No naturalization
  records
Vital records: Yes
Vital records search service: $10.00 per
  record (in advance, includes one copy,
  if found); certified copies: $10.00 for
  the first copy and $6.00 for each
  additional copy of the same record
  (births after 1902 and deaths and
  marriages after 1938, subject to
  restrictions)
Probate records: No probate records

*Town of New Castle
Town Clerk
PO Box 367
New Castle, NH 03854
Phone (603) 431-6710
Organized 1693 (Rockingham County)

*Town of New Durham
Town Clerk
PO Box 11
New Durham, NH 03855
Phone (603) 859-2091 Town Clerk
Organized 1749 (Strafford County)
Vital records: Contact Eloise Bickford

Town of New Hampton
Town Clerk
PO Box 214
New Hampton, NH 03256
Phone (603) 744-3559; (603) 744-3013
  Town Clerk
Organized 1765 (Belknap County)

*Town of New Ipswich
Town Clerk
30 Tricnit Road, Unit 9
New Ipswich, NH 03071
Phone (603) 878-3567 Town Clerk
*Organized 1735/36 (Hillsborough
  County)*
Land records: Yes
Naturalization records: No naturalization
  records
Vital records: Yes
Probate records: No probate records

*Town of New London
Town Clerk
PO Box 314
New London, NH 03257
Phone (603) 536-4821; (603) 526-4046
  Town Clerk
Organized 1753 (Merrimack County)
Land records: No land records
Naturalization records: No naturalization
  records
Vital records: Yes
Probate records: No probate records

Town of Newbury
Town Clerk
PO Box 28
South Newbury, NH 03272
Phone (603) 938-2115; (603) 938-2113
  Town Clerk
Organized 1753 (Merrimack County)

Town of Newfields
Town Clerk
PO Box 45
Newfields, NH 03856
Phone (603) 772-5070; (603) 772-3149
  Town Clerk
Organized 1849 (Rockingham County)

*Town of Newington
Town Clerk
205 Nimble Hill Road
Newington, NH 03801
Phone (603) 436-7640 Town Clerk
Organized 1764 (Rockingham County)
Vital records: Yes
Vital records search service: $10.00
  (proof of direct and tangible interest
  required)

Town of Newmarket
Town Clerk
Main Street
Newmarket, NH 03857
Phone (603) 659-3073 Town Clerk

Organized 1727 (Rockingham County)

Town of Newport
Town Clerk
15 Sunapee Street
Newport, NH 03773
Phone (603) 863-2224 Town Clerk
Organized 1753 (Sullivan County)

Town of Newton
Town Clerk
PO Box 85
Newton, NH 03858
Phone (603) 382-4405; (603) 382-4096
  Town Clerk
Organized 1749 (Rockingham County)

*Town of North Hampton
Town Clerk
PO Box 141
North Hampton, NH 03862
Phone (603) 964-8087; (603) 964-6029
  Town Clerk
*Organized 1738, became a town 1742
  (Rockingham County)*
Land records: Contact Selectmen's
  Office
Naturalization records: No naturalization
  records
Vital records: From the 1800s; contact
  Town Clerk's Office
Probate records: No probate records

*Town of Northfield
Town Clerk
21 Summer
Northfield, NH 03276
Phone (603) 286-4482 Town Clerk
Organized 1780 (Merrimack County)
Land records: No land records
Naturalization records: No naturalization
  records
Vital records: Yes; copies: $10.00 each
  (must show relationship for births
  after 1900 or deaths and marriages
  after 1937)
Probate records: No probate records

Town of Northumberland
Town Clerk
2 State Street
Groveton, NH 03582
Phone (603) 636-1451 Town Clerk
Organized 1761 (Coos County)

*Town of Northwood
Town Clerk
PO Box 314
Northwood, NH 03261-0314
Phone (603) 942-5586; (603) 942-5422
  Town Clerk
Organized 1773 (Rockingham County)
Land records: No land records
Naturalization records: No naturalization
  records

Vital records: Contact Arlene W. Johnson, Town Clerk; copies: $10.00 each (with statement of relationship)

Probate records: No probate records

Town of Nottingham
Town Clerk
PO Box 92
Nottingham, NH 03290
Phone (603) 679-5022 Town Clerk
Organized 1722 (Rockingham County)

Odell (unincorporated)
(Coos County)

Town of Orange
Town Clerk
Rt. 2, Box 137
Orange, NH 03741
Phone (603) 523-7054; (603) 523-4808 Town Clerk
Organized 1769 (Grafton County)

Town of Orford
Town Clerk
Orford, NH 03777
Phone (603) 353-4858 Town Clerk
Organized 1761 (Grafton County)

Town of Ossipee
Town Clerk
PO Box 67
Center Ossipee, NH 03814
Phone (603) 539-4181 Town Clerk
Organized 1785 (Carroll County)

*Town of Pelham
Town Clerk
6 Main Street
Pelham, NH 03076
Phone (603) 635-2040 Town Clerk
Organized 1746 (Hillsborough County)
Land records: Yes
Naturalization records: Yes
Vital records: Contact Linda Derby
Probate records: No probate records

Town of Pembroke
Town Clerk
145 Main Street
Suncook, NH 03275
Phone (603) 485-4747; (603) 485-9556 Town Clerk
Organized 1728 (Merrimack County)

*Town of Peterborough
Town Clerk
1 Grove Street
Peterborough, NH 03458
Phone (603) 924-3201; (603) 924-6633 Town Clerk
Organized 1737/38 (Hillsborough County)
Land records: Contact Assessor's Office

Naturalization records: No naturalization records

Vital records: Contact Town Clerk's Office

Probate records: No probate records

Town of Piermont
Town Clerk
PO Box 27
Piermont, NH 03779
Phone (603) 272-4840 Town Clerk
Organized 1764 (Grafton County)

Pinkham's Grant and Pinkham's Notch (unincorporated)
(Coos County)

*Town of Pittsburg
Town Clerk
PO Box 127
Pittsburg, NH 03592
Phone (603) 538-6697 Town Clerk
Organized 1840 (Coos County)
Land records: No land records
Naturalization records: No naturalization records
Vital records: From 1850; contact Joanne Carlson, Town Clerk
Vital records search service: $10.00; certified copies: $10.00 (records less than seventy-five years old are available only to relatives or those exhibiting a direct and tangible interest in the event)
Probate records: No probate records

Town of Pittsfield
Town Clerk
PO Box 98
Pittsfield, NH 03263
Phone (603) 435-6773 Town Clerk
Organized 1782 (Merrimack County)

Town of Plainfield
Town Clerk
Plainfield, NH 03781
Phone (603) 469-3201 Town Clerk
Organized 1761 (Sullivan County)

Town of Plaistow
Town Clerk
145 Main Street
PO Box 155
Plaistow, NH 03865
Phone (603) 382-8129 Town Clerk
Organized 1749 (Rockingham County)

Town of Plymouth
Town Clerk
Main Street
Plymouth, NH 03264
Phone (603) 536-1732 Town Clerk
Organized 1763 (Grafton County)

City of Portsmouth
City Clerk
1 Junkins Avenue
Portsmouth, NH 03801
Phone (603) 431-2000 City Clerk
Organized 1631 (Rockingham County)

*Town of Randolph
Town Clerk
Randolph, NH 03593
Phone (603) 466-5771 Town Clerk
Organized 1772 (Coos County)
Naturalization records: No naturalization records
Vital records: Births, deaths and marriages
Vital records search service: $10.00 (must show proof of relationship to registrant); certified copies: $10.00 each

*Town of Raymond
Town Clerk
4 Epping Street
Raymond, NH 03077
Phone (603) 895-4735 Town Clerk
Organized 1764 (Rockingham County)
Land records: Property records
Vital records: Yes

*Town of Richmond
Town Clerk
105 Old Homestead Highway
Richmond, NH 03470
Phone (603) 239-6202 Town Clerk (closed Tue, Thur P.M. and Fri)
Organized 1735 (Cheshire County)
Land records: No land records
Vital records: Yes
Vital records search service: $10.00 (must show direct and tangible interest in records after 1900)

*Town of Rindge
Town Clerk
Payson Hill Road
PO Box 11
Rindge, NH 03461-0011
Phone (603) 899-5181 Selectman's and Assessing Office; (603) 899-3354 Town Clerk
Organized 1736/37; incorporated 11 February 1768 (Cheshire County)
Land records: Assessing information; contact Selectman's and Assessing Office, PO Box 163, Rindge, NH 03461
Naturalization records: No naturalization records
Vital records: Births, deaths and marriages
Vital records search service: $7.00 plus SASE (on letterhead); copies: 75¢ per page, $5.00 minimum (records after 1939 restricted to immediate relatives)

*City of Rochester
City Clerk
31 Wakefield Street
Rochester, NH 03867
Phone (603) 332-2130 City Clerk
Organized 1722 (Strafford County)
Vital records: Contact Clerk of Courts,
    North Main Street, Rochester, NH
    03867

Town of Rollinsford
Town Clerk
PO Box 427
Rollinsford, NH 03869
Phone (603) 742-2510 Town Clerk
Organized 1849 (Strafford County)

*Town of Roxbury
Town Clerk
404 Branch Road
Roxbury, NH 03431
Phone (603) 352-4903 Town Clerk's
    home
Organized 1812 (Cheshire County)
Land records: No land records
Naturalization records: No naturalization
    records
Vital records: Yes; copies: $10.00 each
    plus SASE (with signed, written
    request, includes search)
Probate records: No probate records

*Town of Rumney
Town Clerk
RR 1, Box 119A
Rumney, NH 03266
Phone (603) 786-2237 Town Clerk (Mon,
    Wed & Thurs–Fri 9:00–1:00, Wed
    5:00–8:00
Organized 1761 (Grafton County)
Land records: Contact Selectmen's
    Office, PO Box 220, Rumney, NH
    03266
Vital records: Births before 1901, deaths
    and marriages before 1938; Contact
    Byron Merrill Library, Rumney, NH
    03266. Births from 1901 to date,
    deaths and marriages from 1938 to
    date; contact Linda Whitcomb, Town
    Clerk
Vital records search service from Town
    Clerk: $10.00 (includes one copy);
    copies: $10.00 for the first copy and
    $6.00 for each additional copy made
    at the same time (available only to
    immediate family of the registrant)

Town of Rye
Town Clerk
10 Central Road
Rye, NH 03870
Phone (603) 964-5523; (603) 964-8562
    Town Clerk
Organized 1726 (Rockingham County)

Town of Salem
Town Clerk
33 Geremonty
Salem, NH 03079
Phone (603) 893-5731 Town Clerk
Organized 1750 (Rockingham County)

*Town of Salisbury
Town Clerk
Old Coach Road
Salisbury, NH 03268
Phone (603) 648-2473 Town Clerk (Tue–
    Wed 9:00–11:00 & 6:30–8:30)
Organized 1736/37 (Merrimack County)
Vital records: Contact Dora Rapalyea,
    Town Clerk; certified copies: $10.00
    each

*Town of Sanbornton
Town Clerk
PO Box 124
Sanbornton, NH 03269
Phone (603) 286-4034 Town Clerk
*Organized 1748; incorporated 1770
    (Belknap County)*
Land records: No land records
Naturalization records: No naturalization
    records
Vital records: Births, deaths and marriage
    intentions from 1824 (older recorders
    are incomplete); contact Anne
    Ingemundsen, Town Clerk
Probate records: No probate records

Town of Sandown
Town Clerk
Town Hall
Sandown, NH 03873
Phone (603) 887-3646; (603) 887-4870
    Town Clerk
Organized 1756 (Rockingham County)

*Town of Sandwich
Town Clerk
Town Hall
PO Box 194
Center Sandwich, NH 03227
Phone (603) 284-7701; (603) 284-7113
    Town Clerk
Organized 1763 (Carroll County)

Sargent's Purchase (unincorporated)
(Coos County)

*Town of Seabrook
Town Clerk
PO Box 476
Seabrook, NH 03874
Phone (603) 474-3152 Town Clerk
Organized 1768 (Rockingham County)
Land records: From 1859 to date;
    Contact Virginia L. Small, Town Clerk
Vital records: From 1850 to date; Contact
    Town Clerk

**Second College Grant
    (unincorporated)**
(Coos County)

Town of Sharon
Town Clerk
Rt. 2, Box 312
Peterborough, NH 03458
Phone (603) 924-3656 Town Clerk
Organized 1791 (Hillsborough County)

*Town of Shelburne
Town Clerk
Philbrook Farm Inn
Shelburne, NH 03581
Phone (603) 466-2262 Selectman's
    Office; (603) 466-3831 Town Clerk
Organized 1769 (Coos County)
Land records: No land records
Naturalization records: No naturalization
    records
Vital records: Contact Constance P.
    Leger, Town Clerk
Probate records: No probate records

City of Somersworth
City Clerk
157 Main Street
Somersworthe, NH 03878
Phone (603) 692-4262 City Clerk
Organized 1754 (Strafford County)

Town of South Hampton
Town Clerk
Rt. 2, Main Avenue
South Hampton, NH 03827
Phone (603) 394-7696 Town Clerk
Organized 1742 (Rockingham County)

*Town of Springfield
Town Clerk
PO Box 87
Springfield, NH 03284
Phone (603) 763-4805 Town Clerk
Organized 1769 (Sullivan County)
Land records: Contact Cynthia C.
    Anderson, Town Clerk
Vital records: Contact Town Clerk;
    copies: $10.00 each (proof of
    relationship required)

*Town of Stark
Town Clerk
RFD 1, Box 388
Groveton, NH 03582
Phone (603) 636-2118; (603) 449-2572
    Town Clerk's home (Tue & Thur
    noon–5:00)
Organized 1774 (Coos County)
Vital records: Yes
Vital records search service: $3.00;
    certified copies: $10.00 each (must
    supply a reason for the request)

Town of Stewartstown
Town Clerk
PO Box 35
West Stewartstown, NH 03597
Phone (603) 246-3329 Town Clerk
Organized 1770 (Coos County)

Town of Stoddard
Town Clerk
Rt. 9
Stoddard, NH 03464
Phone (603) 446-3326; (603) 446-2203
    Town Clerk
Organized 1752 (Cheshire County)

Town of Strafford
Town Clerk
Rt. 1, Province Road
Strafford, NH 03884
Phone (603) 664-2192 Town Clerk
Organized 1820 (Strafford County)

Town of Stratford
Town Clerk
PO Box 266
North Stratford, NH 03890
Phone (603) 922-5536; (603) 922-5598
    Town Clerk
Organized 1762 (Coos County)

*Town of Stratham
Town Clerk
Town Office
10 Bunker Hill Avenue
Stratham, NH 03885
Phone (603) 772-4741 Town Clerk
Organized 1716 (Rockingham County)

Success (unincorporated)
Organized 1773 (Coos County)

Town of Sugar Hill
Town Clerk
PO Box 74
Sugar Hill, NH 03585
Phone (603) 823-8468 Town Clerk
Organized 1962 (Grafton County)

Town of Sullivan
Town Clerk
HCR 33, Box 228
Keene, NH 03431
Phone (603) 847-3316; (603) 352-1495
    Town Clerk
Organized 1787 (Cheshire County)

Town of Sunapee
Town Clerk
PO Box 303
Sunapee, NH 03782
Phone (603) 763-2212; (603) 763-2449
    Town Clerk
Organized 1768 (Sullivan County)

Town of Surry
Town Clerk
Rt. 2, Box 826
Keene, NH 03431
Phone (603) 352-3075; (603) 352-7798
    Town Clerk
Organized 1769 (Cheshire County)

*Town of Sutton
Town Clerk
PO Box 554
South Sutton, NH 03273
Phone (603) 927-4575 Town Clerk
Organized 1784 (Merrimack County)
Naturalization records: No naturalization
    records
Vital records: Yes

Town of Swanzey
Town Clerk
PO Box 12
East Swanzey, NH 03446
Phone (603) 352-7411 Town Clerk
Organized 1733 (Cheshire County)

Town of Tamworth
Town Clerk
PO Box 279
Tamworth, NH 03886
Phone (603) 323-7971 Town Clerk
Organized 1766 (Carroll County)

Town of Temple
Town Clerk
PO Box L 55
Temple, NH 03084
Phone (603) 878-1972; (603) 878-2709
    Town Clerk
Organized 1750 (Hillsborough County)

**Thompson and Meserve's Purchase
    (unincorporated)**
(Coos County)

*Town of Thornton
Town Clerk
Rt. 1, Box 830-B
Campton, NH 03223
Phone (603) 726-4232; (603) 726-3515
    Town Clerk
Organized 1763 (Grafton County)
Vital records: Yes

*Town of Tilton
Town Clerk
145 Main Street
Tilton, NH 03276
Phone (603) 286-4521; (603) 286-4425
    Town Clerk
Organized 1869 (Belknap County)
Land records: No land records
Vital records: Yes
Probate records: No probate records

*Town of Troy
Town Clerk
PO Box 249
Troy, NH 03465
Phone (603) 242-3845 Town Clerk
Organized 1815 (Cheshire County)
Vital records: Births, deaths and
    marriages from 1850 to date (with
    some gaps)
Vital records search service: $10.00

*Town of Tuftonboro
Town Clerk
PO Box 98
Center Tuftonboro, NH 03816
Phone (603) 569-4539 Town Clerk
*Organized 1750; incorporated 1795
    (Carroll County)*
Land records: No land records
Naturalization records: No naturalization
    records
Vital records: Yes
Probate records: No probate records

*Town of Unity
Town Clerk
HCR 66, Box 176A
Newport, NH 03773
Phone (603) 542-9665 Town Clerk
Organized 1764 (Sullivan County)
Vital records: Contact Peggy L. Austin,
    Town Clerk
Vital records search service: $10.00;
    certified copies: $10.00 for the first
    copy and $6.00 for each additional
    copy (must be a relative of a deceased
    registrant, provide a reason for the
    request, and supply positive ID for
    births)

*Town of Wakefield
Town Clerk
PO Box 279
Sanbornville, NH 03872
Phone (603) 522-6205; (603) 522-3327
    Town Clerk
*Organized 1749; incorporated 1774
    (Carroll County)*
Land records: No land records
Naturalization records: Discontinued
Vital records: Yes
Vital records search service: $3.00;
    certified copies: $10.00 each (proof of
    relationship required)
Probate records: No probate records

Town of Walpole
Town Clerk
PO Box 729
Walpole, NH 03608
Phone (603) 756-3672; (603) 756-3514
    Town Clerk
Organized 1736 (Cheshire County)

Town of Warner
Town Clerk
Rt. 2, Box 27AA
Warner, NH 03278
Phone (603) 456-3362 Town Clerk
Organized 1735/36 (Merrimack County)

Town of Warren
Town Clerk
Studio Road, Box 98
Warren, NH 03279
Phone (603) 764-5780 Town Clerk
Organized 1763 (Grafton County)

Town of Washington
Town Clerk
Rt. 3, Box 449
Hillsboro, NH 03244
Phone (603) 495-3667 Town Clerk
Organized 1735/36 (Sullivan County)

Town of Waterville Valley
Town Clerk
PO Box 267
Waterville Valley, NH 03223
Phone (603) 236-4730 Town Clerk
Organized 1829 (Grafton County)

Town of Weare
Town Clerk
PO Box 90
Weare, NH 03281
Phone (603) 529-7575 Town Clerk
Organized 1735 (Hillsborough County)

Town of Webster
Town Clerk
Rt. 5, Box 255
Penacook, NH 03303
Phone (603) 648-2389 Town Clerk
Organized 1860 (Merrimack County)

Town of Wentworth
Town Clerk
PO Box 44
Wentworth, NH 03282
Phone (603) 764-9411; (603) 764-5244
   Town Clerk
Organized 1766 (Grafton County)

Town of Wentworth's Location
Town Clerk
Rt. 16
Errol, NH 03579
Phone (603) 482-3285 Town Clerk's
   home
Organized 1797 (Coos County)

Town of Westmoreland
Town Clerk
Westmoreland, NH 03467
Phone (603) 399-4471 Town Clerk
Organized 1735/36 (Cheshire County)

Town of Whitefield
Town Clerk
7 Jefferson Road
Whitefield, NH 03598
Phone (603) 837-2551; (603) 837-9871
   Town Clerk
Organized 1774 (Coos County)

Town of Wilmot
Town Clerk
Cross Hill Road
Wilmot, NH 03287
Phone (603) 526-4674; (603) 536-4524;
   (603) 526-4802 Town Clerk
Organized 1807 (Merrimack County)

Town of Wilton
Town Clerk
PO Box 83
Wilton, NH 03086
Phone (603) 654-9451 Town Clerk
Organized 1749 (Hillsborough County)

Town of Winchester
Town Clerk
PO Box 512
Winchester, NH 03470
Phone (603) 239-6233 Town Clerk
Organized 1733 (Cheshire County)

Town of Windham
Town Clerk
3 North Lowell
Windham, NH 03087
Phone (603) 432-7732; (603) 434-5075
   Town Clerk
*Organized 1741/42 (Rockingham
   County)*

Town of Windsor
Town Clerk
Rt. 2, Box 170B
Hillsboro, NH 03244
Phone (603) 478-5215 Town Clerk
Organized 1798 (Hillsborough County)

*Town of Wolfeboro
Town Clerk
South Main, Box 1207
Wolfeboro, NH 03894
Phone (603) 569-3902 Tax Collector;
   (603) 569-5328 Town Clerk
Organized 1759 (Carroll County)
Land records: Contact Tax Collector
Naturalization records: No naturalization
   records
Vital records: Yes
Probate records: No probate records

Town of Woodstock
Town Clerk
Lost River Road
North Woodstock, NH 03262
Phone (603) 745-8752 Town Clerk
Organized 1763 (Grafton County)

NEW JERSEY

Capital: Trenton. Statehood: 18 December 1787 (ceded to England in 1644, became a royal province in 1702)

Court System

New Jersey's courts of limited jurisdiction include the New Jersey Municipal Courts, the New Jersey Surrogate's Office and New Jersey Tax Court. General jurisdiction is exercised by the New Jersey Superior Court which is divided into Appellate, Law and Chancery Divisions, which sit in fifteen vicinages. Vicinage One: Atlantic and Cape May counties; Vicinage Two: Bergen County; Vicinage Three: Burlington County; Vicinage Four: Camden County; Vicinage Five: Essex County; Vicinage Six: Hudson County; Vicinage Seven: Mercer County; Vicinage Eight: Middlesex County: Vicinage Nine: Monmouth County; Vicinage Ten: Morris and Sussex counties; Vicinage Eleven: Passaic County; Vicinage Twelve: Union County; Vicinage Thirteen: Hunterdon, Somerset and Warren counties; Vicinage Fourteen: Ocean County; Vicinage Fifteen: Cumberland, Gloucester and Salem counties. The New Jersey Supreme Court is the court of last resort.

New Jersey State Archives, 185 West State Street, CN 307, Trenton, NJ 08625-0307 has birth, death and marriage records, arranged by county, from 1 May 1848 to 30 April 1878, available for a $2.00 search/copy fee, as well as wills and inventories before 1901, deeds filed with the Secretary of State, mostly before 1790, marriage bonds or licenses filed with the Secretary before 1800. Vital records after 1 May 1878 are available from New Jersey Department of Health, State Registrar—Search Unit, Bureau of Vital Statistics, CN 370, Trenton, NJ 08625-0370.

Courthouses

*Atlantic County Clerk's Office
5901 Main Street
Mays Landing, NJ 08330
Phone (609) 625-4011 County Clerk's
   Office (Mon–Fri 8:30–4:30); (609)
   625-4011, ext. 5200 County
   Surrogate's Office
*County organized 1837 from Gloucester
   County*
Land records: Deeds from 1837 to date;

contact County Clerk; certified copies available

Naturalization records: Declarations of intention, court hearings, petitions for naturalization and verification of naturalization records; contact County Clerk

Vital records: Contact City or Township Clerk in the municipality where the event occurred

Probate records: Wills, estates, probate court matters; contact County Surrogate's Office, 5911 Main Street, Mays Landing, NJ 08330

Bergen County Justice Center
Main and Essex Streets
Hackensack, NJ 07601-7017
Phone (201) 646-2500
County organized 1683, original county
Vital records: Contact City or Township Clerk in the municipality where the event occurred

Burlington County Courthouse
49 Rancocas Road
Mount Holly, NJ 08060-1384
Phone (609) 265-5020; (609) 386-1636 West Jersey Proprietors
County organized 1694, original county
Land records: Deeds in Hunterdon area prior to 1714; contact West Jersey Proprietors, PO Box 158, Burlington, NJ 08016
Vital records: Contact City or Township Clerk in the municipality where the event occurred

*Camden County Courthouse
520 Market Street
Camden, NJ 08102-1375
Phone (609) 225-5323 County Register of Deeds and Mortgages (Mon–Fri 9:00–4:00); (609) 225-7223 County Clerk's Office; (609) 225-7275
County organized 1844 from Gloucester County
Land records: Contact Susan R. Rose, County Register of Deeds and Mortgages, Room 102; copies: $1.00 per page, $1.00 for certification
Naturalization records: From 1800 to 1933; contact Michael S. Keating, County Clerk, County Clerk's Office, Hall of Justice, Fifth Street and Mickle Boulevard, First Floor, Suite 150, Camden, NJ 08103-4001
Naturalization records search service: $10.00; copies: 75¢ for each of the first ten pages, 50¢ per page for each of the next ten pages and 25¢ for each additional page
Vital records: Contact City or Township Clerk in the municipality where the event occurred
Probate records: Contact Maria Barnabya

Greenwald, Surrogate, Office of the Surrogate, Hall of Justice, 101 South Fifth Street, Camden, NJ 08103

*Cape May County Courthouse
7 North Main Street
PO Box 5000
Cape May Court House, NJ 08210-5000
Phone (609) 465-1010 County Clerk; (609) 463-6666 Surrogate
County organized 1692
Land records: From 1692 (Liber of Deeds A, in vault, begins 1692 with deeds recorded as early as 1694); contact Angela F. Pulvino, County Clerk
Naturalization records: From 1896 through 1964; contact County Clerk. Naturalization records from 1964; contact Atlantic County
Vital records: Marriages from 1745 to 1878; contact County Clerk. Other vital records; contact City or Township Clerk in the municipality where the event occurred
Probate records: From 1804; contact W. Robert Hentges, Judge, Surrogate Court, Central Mail Room—DN-207. Probate records before 1804; contact New Jersey Archives, Trenton
Probate search service: no charge; copies: $3.00 per page

*Cumberland County Courthouse
Broad and Fayette
Bridgeton, NJ 08302
Phone (609) 451-8000
County organized 1748 from Salem County
Land records: From late 1700s; contact Gloria Noto, County Clerk
Naturalization records: From 1800; contact County Clerk
Vital records: Old Marriage Books A and B (first entry 1795); contact County Clerk. Other vital records; contact City or Township Clerk in the municipality where the event occurred
Probate records: Wills from 1803; contact Surrogate's Office

Essex County Hall of Records
465 Martin Luther King Boulevard
Newark, NJ 07102
Phone (201) 621-4916
County organized 1683, original county
Vital records: Contact City or Township Clerk in the municipality where the event occurred

Gloucester County Courthouse
1 North Broad Street
Woodbury, NJ 08096-7376
Phone (609) 853-3200
County organized 1686, original county
Vital records: Contact City or Township

Clerk in the municipality where the event occurred

*County of Hudson
Justice William J. Brennan Jr. Court House
583 Newark Avenue
Jersey City, NJ 07306
Phone (201) 795-6600 Court House; (201) 795-6131 County Clerk; (201) 795-6040 Vital Statistics; (201) 795-6377 Surrogate
County organized 22 February 1840 from Bergen County
Land records: Contact Kenneth Chmielewski, County Register, Hudson County Administration Building, 595 Newark Avenue, Jersey City, NJ 07306-2301
Naturalization records: From 1840 to 1989; contact Janet Haynes, County Clerk
Vital records: Contact County Registrar, County Administration Building. Other vital records; contact City or Township Clerk in the municipality where the event occurred
Probate records: Contact Donald W. De Leo, Surrogate, Surrogate's Court, County Administration Building
Probate search service: $3.00 per estate; copies: $3.00 per page, no minimum

*Hunterdon County Hall of Records
71 Main Street
Flemington, NJ 08822-0500
Phone (201) 788-1214 County Clerk
County organized 1714 from Burlington County
Land records: From 1785 to date, mortgages from 1766 to date; contact County Clerk; copies: $1.00 per page
Naturalization records: From 1808 to 1965; contact County Clerk; copies: $1.00 per page
Vital records: Contact City or Township Clerk in the municipality where the event occurred
Probate records: Contact Surrogate's Office

Mercer County Courthouse
PO Box 8068
Trenton, NJ 08650-0068
Phone (609) 989-6517
County organized 1838 from Hunterdon and Middlesex counties
Vital records: Contact City or Township Clerk in the municipality where the event occurred

Middlesex County Courthouse
1 John F. Kennedy
New Brunswick, NJ 08901-2153
Phone (201) 745-3040
County organized 1683, original county

Vital records: Contact City or Township Clerk in the municipality where the event occurred

Monmouth County Hall of Records
Main Street
PO Box 1255
Freehold, NJ 07728-1255
Phone (201) 431-7387; (908) 431-7324 County Clerk; (908) 431-7330 Surrogate
County organized 1683, original county
Land records: Deeds from 1665 to date; contact Jane G. Clayton, County Clerk, Hall of Records, Main Street, Freehold, NJ 07728; copies: 50¢ per page for each of the first ten pages, 25¢ per page for each of the next ten pages and 10¢ per page for each additional page
Naturalization records: From 1808 to 1991; contact County Clerk
Vital records: Marriage returns from 1790 to 1900. Other vital records; contact City or Township Clerk in the municipality where the event occurred
Probate records: From the mid-1800s, will books from 1875 to date; contact Marie S. Muhler, Surrogate, Hall of Records, PO Box 1265, Freehold, NJ 07728-1265

Morris County Courthouse
CN-900
Morristown, NJ 07960
Phone (201) 829-8226
County organized 1739 from Hunterdon County
Vital records: Contact City or Township Clerk in the municipality where the event occurred

Ocean County Courthouse
118 Washington Street
PO Box 2191
Toms River, NJ 08754-2191
Phone (908) 929-2018 County Clerk; (908) 349-4336 FAX, County Clerk; (800) 722-0291 County Clerk; (908) 341-1880 Ocean County Historical Society; (908) 929-2011 Surrogate's Court
County organized 1850 from Monmouth County
Land records: Contact M. Dean Haines, County Clerk
Naturalization records: Contact Ocean County Historical Society, Strickler Research Library, Historical Research Department, (26 Hadley Avenue, Toms River, NJ 08753—location), CN 2191 (mailing address), Toms River, NJ 08754
Vital records: Contact City or Township Clerk in the municipality where the event occurred

Probate records: Contact Surrogate's Court, Courthouse, Room 211, Toms River, New Jersey 08754

Passaic County Courthouse
77 Hamilton Street
Paterson, NJ 07505-2018
Phone (201) 881-4120
County organized 1837 from Bergen and Sussex counties
Land records: Contact County Clerk's Office
Naturalization records: Contact County Clerk's Office
Vital records: Contact Board of Health, 176 Broadway, Paterson, NJ 07505. Other vital records; contact City or Township Clerk in the municipality where the event occurred
Probate records: Contact County Clerk's Office

Salem County Courthouse
92 Market Street
Salem City, NJ 08079-1913
Phone (609) 935-7510, ext. 212 County Clerk
County organized 1694, original county
Land records: From 1688 to date; contact John W. Cawman, Clerk, 92 Market Street, PO Box 18, Salem, NJ 08079
Naturalization records: Contact County Clerk
Vital records: Marriage records from 1699 to 1912; contact County Clerk. Other vital records; contact City or Township Clerk in the municipality where the event occurred
Probate records: From 1804 to date; contact County Clerk

Somerset County Administration Building
20 Grove Street
PO Box 3000
Somerville, NJ 08876-1262
Phone (201) 231-7006; (908) 231-7013 County Clerk; (908) 231-7003 Surrogate
County organized 1688 from Middlesex County
Land records: Contact R. Peter Widin, County Clerk
Naturalization records: Contact County Clerk
Vital records: Contact City or Township Clerk in the municipality where the event occurred
Probate records: Contact Surrogate

Sussex County Hall of Records
4 Park Place
Newton, NJ 07860
Phone (201) 579-0900 County Clerk
County organized 1753 from Morris County

Land records: Deeds and mortgages from 1795; contact County Clerk
No land records search service; copies: $1.50 per page, no minimum
Naturalization records: From 1808 to 1989; contact County Clerk
No naturalization search service; copies: $1.50 per page, no minimum
Vital records: Marriages from 1795 through mid-1878, births and manumissions of slaves; contact County Clerk. Other vital records; contact City or Township Clerk in the municipality where the event occurred
Probate records: Wills, trusts, probate matters, divisions, etc.; contact Surrogate
Probate search service: no charge; copies: $3.00 per page, no minimum

Union County Courthouse
2 Broad Street
Elizabeth, NJ 07207
Phone (201) 527-4966; (201) 527-4787 Register of Deeds and Mortgages
County organized 1857 from Essex County
Land records: Deeds and mortgages from 1857; contact Joanne Rajoppi, Register of Deeds and Mortgages; copies: $1.50 per page; certified copies: $8.00 for the first page and $2.00 for each additional page
Vital records: Contact City or Township Clerk in the municipality where the event occurred

Warren County Courthouse
Belvidere, NJ 07823
Phone (201) 475-8000; (201) 475-6223 Surrogate's Court
County organized 1824 from Sussex County
Land records: From 1825; contact Terry Lee, County Clerk
Naturalization records: From 1825 to 1987; contact County Clerk
Vital records: Marriages from 1825 to 1875; contact County Clerk. Other vital records; contact City or Township Clerk in the municipality where the event occurred
Probate records: Contact Albert Rutt, Surrogate's Court, 116 Court House, Belvidere, NJ 07825
Probate search service: no charge (for one name, *must* have *first* and last names); copies: $3.00 per page plus SASE, no minimum; "Surrogate's records are indexed by a letter book for first letter of *last* name."

NEW MEXICO

Capital: Santa Fe. Statehood: 6 January 1912 (parts obtained through the annexation of Texas in 1845, the Gadsden Purchase of 1853 and the Treaty of Guadalupe-Hidalgo, 1850)

Court System

New Mexico has four courts of limited jurisdiction: Magistrate Courts (in every county except Bernalillo County), the Bernalillo County Metropolitan Court, Municipal Courts (in incorporated cities or towns with populations of 1000 or more), and Probate Courts (which sit in each county). The District Court has general jurisdiction. First Judicial District: Los Alamos, Rio Arriba and Santa Fe counties; second Judicial District: Bernalillo County; Third Judicial District: Doña Ana County; Fourth Judicial District: Guadalupe, Mora and San Miguel counties; Fifth Judicial District: Chaves, Eddy and Lea counties; Sixth Judicial District: Grant, Hidalgo and Luna counties; Seventh Judicial District: Catron, Sierra, Socorro and Torrance counties; Eighth Judicial District: Colfax, Taos and Union counties; Ninth Judicial District: Curry and Roosevelt counties; Tenth Judicial District: De Baca, Harding and Quay counties; Eleventh Judicial District: McKinley and San Juan counties; Twelfth Judicial District: Lincoln and Otero counties; Thirteenth Judicial District: Cibola, Sandoval and Valencia counties. The Court of Appeals and Supreme Court have appellate jurisdiction.

Courthouses

Bernalillo County Probate Court
1 Civic Plaza, N.W.
Albuquerque, NM 87102
Phone (505) 768-4247 Probate
County organized 1852, original county, annexed Santa Ana County 1876

*Catron County Courthouse
PO Box 507
Reserve, NM 87830
Phone (505) 533-6423; (505) 533-6400 County Clerk
County organized 1921 from Socorro County
Land records: From 1921; contact County Clerk, PO Box 197, Reserve, NM 87830

Naturalization records: No naturalization records
Vital records: Some vital records, not complete
Probate records: From 1921; contact County Clerk
Probate search service: no charge; copies: 10¢ per page, no minimum

*Chaves County Courthouse
401 North Main
Roswell, NM 88201-4726
Phone (505) 624-6614
County organized 25 February 1889 from Lincoln County
Land records: From 1890s; contact County Clerk, PO Box 580, Roswell, NM 88202
Naturalization records: No naturalization records
Vital records: Births and deaths from 1900s to 1961; contact County Clerk
Probate records: Contact Informal Probate Court, County Clerk's Office, PO Box 580, Roswell, NM 88202 or Formal Probate Court, Chaves County District Court, PO Box 1776, Roswell, NM 88202
Probate search service: no charge; copies: 25¢ per page, no minimum; "We will try to help you as much as we can; we do not do in depth searches; my staff does not have the time for such."

*Cibola County Courthouse
515 West High Street
Grants, NM 87020-2526
Phone (505) 287-8107; (505) 287-9431 County Clerk's Office
County organized 19 June 1981 from Valencia County
Land records: Contact County Clerk's Office; copies: 25¢ per page, $2.00 per document for certification
Naturalization records: No naturalization records
Vital records: No vital records
Probate records: Informal Probates; contact County Clerk's Office. Probate records; contact 13th Judicial District Court
No probate search service from County Clerk's Office; copies: 25¢ per page, $2.00 per document for certification

*Colfax County Courthouse
Raton, NM 87740
Phone (505) 445-5551 County Clerk
County organized 1869 from Mora County
Land records: From 1864; contact Barbara Castille, County Clerk, PO Box 159, Raton, NM 87740
Naturalization records: Contact District Court, PO Box 160, Raton, NM 87740

Probate records: From 1800; contact County Clerk (some also filed in District Court)
Probate search service: no charge; copies: 35¢ per page, 35¢ minimum, no restrictions

*Curry County Courthouse
PO Box 1822
Clovis, NM 88101
Phone (505) 763-5591
County organized 1909 from Quay and Roosevelt counties
Land records: From 1909; contact County Clerk, PO Box 1168, Clovis, NM 88102-1168
Naturalization records: Contact District Court Clerk
Probate records: From 1909; contact County Clerk
Probate search service: no charge; copies: 25¢ each, no minimum

*De Baca County Courthouse
PO Box 347
Fort Sumner, NM 88119
Phone (505) 355-2601 County Clerk
County organized 1917 from Chaves, Guadalupe and Roosevelt counties
Land records: From 1917; contact County Clerk ("Also have records when De Baca County was part of Chaves, Guadalupe and Roosevelt Counties.")
Naturalization records: No naturalization records
Vital records: Marriage licenses; contact County Clerk; copies: $1.50 each
Probate records: From 1917; contact County Clerk
No probate search service; copies: 30¢ per page, $1.30 for certified copies, no minimum

*Doña Ana County Courthouse
251 West Amador Avenue
Las Cruces, NM 88005-2893
Phone (505) 525-6659 County Clerk
County organized 1852, original county, annexed Arizona County 1861
Land records: From 1853; contact Ruben Ceballos, County Clerk, Room 103
Naturalization records: No naturalization records
Vital records: No vital records
Probate records: From 1853
Probate search service: no charge; copies: 15¢ per page, no minimum

Eddy County Courthouse
PO Box 1139
Carlsbad, NM 88221-1139
Phone (505) 887-9511
County organized 1887 from Lincoln County

*Grant County Courthouse
PO Box 898
Silver City, NM 88062-0898
Phone (505) 538-9581; (505) 538-2979
    County Clerk; (505) 388-1525
    Assessor; (505) 538-5240 Probate
    Judge; (505) 538-3250 District Court
County organized 1868 from Socorro
    County
Land records: Contact County Clerk or
    Assessor
Probate records: Contact County Clerk or
    Probate Judge. Formal probates;
    contact District Court
Probate search service: no charge;
    copies: 50¢ per page, no minimum

*Guadalupe County Courthouse
420 Parker Avenue
Santa Rosa, NM 88435
Phone (505) 472-3791
County organized 1891 from Lincoln
    and San Miguel counties
Land records: Yes
Probate records: Yes
Probate search service: $5.00; copies:
    25¢ per page, no minimum

*Harding County Courthouse
PO Box 1002
Mosquero, NM 87733-1002
Phone (505) 673-2301; (505) 673-2922
    FAX, County Clerk
County organized 1921 from Mora and
    Union counties
Land records: Contact Elizabeth
    Martinez, County Clerk; copies: 25¢
    per page, $1.00 for certification
Naturalization records: Contact County
    Clerk; copies: 25¢ per page, $1.00 for
    certification
Vital records: Marriage licenses; contact
    County Clerk; copies: $1.50 each
Probate records: Contact County Clerk;
    copies: 25¢ per page, $1.00 for
    certification

*Hidalgo County Courthouse
300 Shakespeare Street
Lordsburg, NM 88045-1939
Phone (505) 542-9213
County organized 1920 from Grant
    County
Land records: Contact Robert Kerr.
    Deeds, mortgages, etc.; contact
    Belinda Chavez
Probate records: Contact Hon. Norma
    Jean Richins
Probate search service: no charge;
    copies: 25¢ per page

*Lea County Courthouse
PO Box 4C
Lovington, NM 88260
Phone (505) 396-8521, ext. 229 County
    Clerk

County organized 1917 from Chaves
    and Eddy counties
Land records: Contact County Clerk, PO
    Box 1507, Lovington, NM 88260
Probate records: Contact County Clerk or
    District Court Clerk, PO Box 6C,
    Lovington, NM 88260
Probate search service: no charge;
    copies: 50¢ per page, no minimum

*Lincoln County Courthouse
300 Central Avenue
Carrizozo, NM 88301-0711
Phone (505) 648-2331
County organized 1869 from Socorro
    County
Land records: Deeds from 1869; contact
    County Clerk, PO Box 338,
    Carrizozo, NM 88301
Vital records: Marriages from 1882;
    contact County Clerk
Probate records: Informal probate records
    from 1880s; contact County Clerk.
    Other probate records; contact District
    Court, PO Box 725, Carrizozo, NM
    88301
Probate search service: no charge;
    copies: 25¢ per page, no minimum;
    "This office will do a brief search;
    extensive searches must be done by an
    abstract or title company."

Los Alamos County Courthouse
2300 Trinity Drive
Los Alamos, NM 87544-3051
Phone (505) 662-8010
County organized 1949 from Sandoval
    and Santa Fe counties

*Luna County Courthouse
PO Box 1838
Deming, NM 88031-1838
Phone (505) 546-0491
County organized 1901 from Doña Ana
    and Grant counties
Land records: From late 1800s; contact
    County Clerk
Naturalization records: No naturalization
    records
Vital records: Old birth and death index
    (incomplete), births from 1907 to
    1932, deaths from 1907 to 1941,
    marriages from 1901; contact County
    Clerk; certified copies: $1.50 each
Probate records: From 1901
No probate search service; copies: 50¢
    per page; "If you have probate
    number, we do make copies upon
    request."

*McKinley County Courthouse
PO Box 1268
Gallup, NM 87305
Phone (505) 863-6866
County organized 1899 from Bernalillo,
    Valencia and San Juan counties

Land records: Values; contact Assessor.
    Ownership transfers; contact Gloria A.
    Lente, County Clerk
Naturalization records: Contact Judge
    Joseph Rich, District Court, PO Box
    460, Gallup, NM 87305
Vital records: Contact County Clerk
Probate records: Contact County Clerk
Probate search service: $1.00 per year;
    copies: 50¢ per page, 50¢ for
    certification

Mora County Courthouse
PO Box 360
Mora, NM 87732
Phone (505) 387-5279
County organized 1859 from San
    Miguel County

*Otero County Courthouse
1000 New York Avenue
Alamogordo, NM 88310
Phone (505) 437-7427; (505) 437-4942
    County Clerk
County organized 1899 from Doña Ana,
    Lincoln and Socorro counties
Land records: From 1888 (not bonded for
    this search)
Naturalization records: No naturalization
    records
Vital records: No vital records
Probate records: From 1888
Probate search service: no charge;
    copies: 25¢ per page, $1.00 for
    certification, no minimum

*Quay County Courthouse
PO Box 1225
Tucumcari, NM 88401
Phone (505) 461-0510
County organized 1903
Land records: From 1892
Naturalization records: No naturalization
    records
Probate records: From 1892
Probate search service: no charge;
    copies: $1.00 for the first page and
    50¢ for each additional page, no
    minimum

Rio Arriba County Courthouse
PO Box 158
Tierra Amarilla, NM 87575
Phone (505) 588-7255
County organized 1852, original county

*Roosevelt County Courthouse
Portales, NM 88130
Phone (505) 356-8562
County organized 1903 from Chaves
    County
Land records: Contact Clerk
Naturalization records: No naturalization
    records
Vital records: No vital records
Probate records: Contact Clerk

*San Juan County Courthouse
Aztec, NM 87410
Phone (505) 334-9471
County organized 1887 from Rio Arriba County
Land records: From 1887
Naturalization records: No naturalization records
Vital records: Marriages from 1887
Probate records: Some are also kept at District Court
Probate search service: no charge; copies: 50¢ per page, no minimum

San Miguel County Courthouse
Las Vegas, NM 87701
Phone (505) 425-9331
County organized 1852, original county

Sandoval County Courthouse
PO Box 40
Bernalillo, NM 87004
Phone (505) 867-2209
County organized 1903 from Rio Arriba County

*Santa Fe County Courthouse
PO Box 1985
Santa Fe, NM 87504-1985
Phone (505) 984-5080; (505) 986-6281
County organized 1852, original county
Land records: Yes
Vital records: Marriages
Probate records: Yes

*Sierra County Courthouse
311 Date Street
Truth or Consequences, NM 87901-2362
Phone (505) 894-2840 County Clerk;
(505) 894-2516 FAX, County Clerk
County organized 1884 from Socorro County
Land records: From 1884; contact Lupe A. Carrejo, County Clerk
Probate records: From 1913; contact County Clerk
Probate search service: $2.00; copies: 25¢ per page

Socorro County Courthouse
PO Box 1
Socorro, NM 87801
Phone (505) 835-0589
County organized 1852, original county

Taos County Courthouse
PO Box 676
Taos, NM 87571
Phone (505) 758-8836
County organized 1852, original county

*Torrance County Courthouse
Estancia, NM 87016
Phone (505) 384-2221

County organized 1903 from Lincoln, San Miguel, Socorro and Santa Fe counties
Land records: From 1910; contact Clerk
Naturalization records: No naturalization records
Vital records: No vital records
Probate records: Contact Judge
No probate search service; copies: 25¢ each, no minimum

*Union County Courthouse
PO Box 430
Clayton, NM 88415-0430
Phone (505) 374-9491
County organized 1903 from Colfax, Mora and San Miguel counties
Land records: Contact Freida Birdwell, County Clerk
Naturalization records: No naturalization records
Vital records: No vital records
Probate records: Contact County Clerk
No probate search service; copies: 30¢ per page from paper originals, $1.00 per page from microfilm originals, no minimum

Valencia County Courthouse
PO Box 1119
Los Lunas, NM 87031
Phone (505) 865-9681
County organized 1852, original county

NEW YORK

Capital: Albany. Statehood: 26 July 1788 (Dutch settlement conquered by the English in 1664, became a royal province in 1685)

Court System

New York State has a number of courts of limited jurisdiction. The New York Court of Claims sits at Albany and hears claims against the state. Town and Village Justice Courts handle minor civil and criminal matters. New York District Courts are established only in Nassau and Suffolk counties and have jurisdiction over some civil matters and misdemeanors. The Criminal Court of the City of New York has trial jurisdiction over misdemeanors and violations, and the Civil Court of the City of New York has civil jurisdiction. New York City encompasses the counties of Bronx, Kings (Brooklyn), New York (Manhattan), Queens and Richmond (Staten Island). City Courts are established in cities outside the city of New York and have limited jurisdiction over civil cases and criminal jurisdiction over misdemeanors. Family Courts established in each county and New York City hear matters involving children and families and have concurrent jurisdiction with the Surrogate's Court in adoption cases. The Surrogate's Court hears cases involving probate. In some counties jurisdiction is handled by the County Court Judge.

The County Courts are established in every county except the five counties of New York City and have general jurisdiction over criminal offenses and some civil cases. The Supreme Court sits in every county seat and has general jurisdiction over cases beyond the jurisdiction of other courts. First Judicial District: New York County; Second Judicial District: Kings and Richmond counties; Third Judicial District: Albany, Columbia, Greene, Rensselaer, Schoharie, Sullivan and Ulster counties; Fourth Judicial District: Clinton, Essex, Franklin, Fulton, Hamilton, Montgomery, Saint Lawrence, Saratoga, Schenectady, Warren and Washington counties; Fifth Judicial District: Herkimer, Jefferson, Lewis, Oneida, Onondaga and Oswego counties; Sixth Judicial District: Broome, Chemung, Chenango, Cortland, Delaware, Madison, Otsego, Schuyler, Tioga and Tompkins counties; Seventh Judicial District: Cayuga, Livingston, Monroe, Ontario, Seneca, Steuben, Wayne and Yates counties; Eighth Judicial District: Allegany,

Cattaraugus, Chautauqua, Erie, Genesee, Niagara, Orleans and Wyoming counties; Ninth Judicial District: Dutchess, Orange, Putnam, Rockland and Westchester counties; Tenth Judicial District: Nassau and Suffolk counties; Eleventh Judicial District: Queens County; Twelfth Judicial District: Bronx County. Appeals are handled by the Supreme Court Appellate Division and the New York Court of Appeals.

Courthouses

*Albany County Courthouse
County Clerk's Office
16 Eagle Street
Albany, NY 12207-1019
Phone (518) 487-5100; (518) 487-5120 County Clerk; (518) 447-4500 Hall of Records; (518) 487-5393 Surrogate's Court
County organized 1683, original county
Land records: Current deeds, and mortgages; contact Thomas G. Clingan, County Clerk, Room 128. Atlases from 1860 to 1941, deeds from 1681 to 1765, city mortgages from 1870 to 1936; contact The Albany County Hall of Records, 250 South Pearl Street, Albany, NY 12202
Naturalization records: After 1961; contact County Clerk. Naturalizations and declarations of intent from 1827 to 1978; contact Hall of Records
Vital records: City marriage records from 1870 to 1936; contact Hall of Records. Births and deaths; contact city and town clerks: Albany, City Vital Statistics, City Hall, Room 107, Albany, NY 12207, (518) 434-5045; Altamont (518) 861-8554; Berne (518) 872-1448; Bethlehem (518) 439-4955; Coeymans (518) 756-2100; Cohoes (518) 237-7648; Colonie (518) 783-2734; Colonie (village) (518) 869-7562; Green Island (518) 273-0661; Green Island (village) (518) 273-2201; Guilderland (518) 356-1980; Knox (518) 872-2551; Menands (518) 434-2922; New Scotland (518) 439-4865; Ravena (518) 756-8233; Rensselaerville (518) 797-3798; Watervliet (518) 270-3810; Westerlo (518) 797-3111
Probate records: contact Surrogate Court. Wills from 1681 to 1765, index to wills and letters of administration from 1787 to 1895, surrogates court records from 1800 to 1840; contact Hall of Records

*Allegany County
Belmont, NY 14813
County organized 1806 from Genesee County

Land records: From 1806; contact County Clerk's Office; copies: 50¢ each, $1.00 minimum, $1.00 each for certified copies, $4.00 minimum
Naturalization records: Yes
Vital records: Marriages
Probate records: Wills, etc.
No probate search service

Bronx County Courthouse
851 Grand Concourse
Bronx, NY 10451-2937
Phone (212) 590-3644
County organized 1914 from New York County

*Broome County Courthouse
Binghamton, NY 13902
County organized 1806 from Tioga County
Land records: Contact County Clerk's Office, Broome County Office Building, Binghamton, NY 13902
Naturalization records: From 1850, with earlier records represented to a lesser extent; contact County Clerk's Office
Naturalization records search service: $5.00 for every two years searched by Martha Westbrook, County Records Manager, provided the necessary information is supplied; copies: 50¢ per page, $1.00 minimum
Vital records: Marriages from 1908 to 1934; contact County Clerk. Vital records are maintained by the individual towns
Probate records: Contact Marilyn Vescio, Surrogate Court Clerk, Surrogate Court Office, First Floor

Cattaraugus County Courthouse
303 Court Street
Little Valley, NY 14755-1028
Phone (716) 938-9111
County organized 1808 from Genesee County

Cayuga County Courthouse
160 Genesee Street
Auburn, NY 13021-3424
Phone (315) 253-1308
County organized 1799 from Onondaga County

Charlotte County
(see Washington County)

*Chautauqua County
Gerace Office Building
Mayville, NY 14757-1007
Phone (716) 753-4331 County Clerk; (716) 753-4339 Surrogate's Office
County organized 1808 from Genesee County
Land records: From 1811; contact Sandra

K. Sopak, County Clerk, PO Box 170, Mayville, NY 14757
Land records search service: $5.00 per two-year period searched; copies: $1.00 per page (copies of grantor and grantee indices not available)
Naturalization records: From the early 1800s through 1972; contact County Clerk
Naturalization records search service: $5.00 per name; copies: $1.00 per page
Vital records: Marriages from 1908 to April 1935; contact County Clerk's Office. Births, deaths and marriages; contact town or city clerk's office
Vital records search service: $5.00 per marriage; copies: $5.00 each
Probate records: From 1811; contact Willard W. Cass, Jr., Surrogate, Surrogate's Court, PO Box C, Mayville, NY 14757
Probate search service: $20.00 under twenty-five years, $53.00 for over twenty-five years, including certification ("We do not charge this for running our records to see if we have the estates"); copies: $1.00 per page, $1.00 minimum

*Chemung County Courthouse
210 Lake Street
Elmira, NY 14902-0588
Phone (607) 737-2920
County organized 1836 from Tioga County
Land records: Tioga County deeds from 1790 to 1835, Chemung County from 1836
Naturalization records: From 1860 to 1906
Vital records: Contact Registrar, County Health Department
Probate records: Contact Surrogate Court, 224 Lake Street, Elmira, NY 14902
Probate search service: $20.00 files under twenty-five years, $53.00 files over twenty-five years; copies: $1.00 per page, $4.00 per page certified; "Requests must be made in writing and appropriate fee paid prior to search."

*Chenango County Office Building
5 Court Street
Norwich, NY 13815-1676
Phone (607) 335-4575 County Clerk's Office; (607) 335-4515 Surrogate Court
County organized 1798 from Herkimer and Tioga counties
Land records: Contact Mary C. Weidman, County Clerk, County Clerk's Office; copies: $1.50 per page
Naturalization records: Contact County Clerk

Naturalization records search service: $5.00 per name for a two-year search; copies: $1.50 per page

Vital records: Marriages; contact County Clerk. Births, deaths and marriages; contact City or Town Clerk's Office of the town in which the event occurred: City of Norwich, Jody Zakrevsky, 31 East Main Street, Norwich, NY 13815, (607) 334-1220; Town of Afton, Carol A. Armstrong, 169 Main Street, Afton, NY 13730; Bainbridge, Deborah K. Hromada, 15 North Main Street, Bainbridge, NY 13733, (607) 967-3781; Columbus, Francis E. Aldrich, Rt. 1, Box 54B, Sherburne, NY 13460, (607) 847-8593; Coventry, Arlene R. Nickerson, Box 91, Bainbridge, NY 13733, (607) 656-8602; German, Ellen T. Maroney, Rt. 1, Box 266D, McDonough, NY 13801, (607) 656-4493; Greene, Barbara A. VanderBunt, PO Box 129, 51 Genesee Street, Greene, NY 13778, (607) 656-4191; Guilford, Jane P. Winchester, PO Box 135, Mount Upton, NY 13809, (607) 764-8375; Lincklaen, Judy M. Brown, HC 65, Box 451, DeRuyter, NY 13052, (315) 852-9802; McDonough, Cindy L. Paul, Rt. 1, Box 203, McDonough, NY 13801, (607) 647-5566; New Berlin, Dorothy M. Clark, 20 South Main Street, PO Box 308, New Berlin, NY 13411, (607) 847-8909; North Norwich, Loretta L. Smith, PO Box 404, North Norwich, NY 13814, (607) 334-9224; Norwich, Helen R. Bowers, Rt. 1, Box 10, Hale Street Extension, Norwich, NY 13815, (607) 334-6359; Otselic, Louise F. Perry, Town Hall, PO Box 275, South Otselic, NY 13155, (315) 653-7201; Oxford, Mary Houghtaling, PO Box 271, Oxford, NY 13830, (607) 843-6222; Pharsalia, Brenda L. Smith, HCR 67, Box 297A, South Plymouth, NY 13844, (607) 334-5203; Pitcher, Florence B. Livermore, 8033 Route 26, Box 13, Pitcher, NY 13136, (607) 863-3511; Plymouth, Nadine M. Adams, County Route 16, Box 118B, Plymouth, NY 13832, (607) 334-7271; Preston, Deanna J. Johnson, Rt. 2, Box 189, Oxford, NY 13830, (607) 336-5584; Sherburne, John McDaniel, 17 East State Street, Sherburne, NY 13460, (607) 674-6071; Smithville, Town Office, PO Box 171, Smithville Flats, NY 13841; Smyrna, Geraldine W. Day, Rt. 1, Box 14, (607) 627-6269; certified copies from County Clerk: $5.00 each

Probate records: Contact Surrogate Court

*Clinton County Government Center
137 Margaret Street
Plattsburgh, NY 12901

Phone (518) 565-4700
County organized 1788 from Washington County
Land records: From 1788; contact Bernard Amell, County Clerk
Naturalization records: Aliens Admitted Index and Records, naturalization records from about 1900; contact County Clerk
Vital records: Contact City Clerk, City Hall, Plattsburgh, NY 12901
Probate records: Contact Surrogate's Office

*Columbia County Courthouse
Hudson, NY 12534
Phone (518) 828-3339
County organized 1786 from Albany County
Land records: From mid 1800s
Naturalization records: From mid 1800s to 1934
Probate records: Contact Surrogate Court
No probate search service; copies: 25¢ per page, $1.00 minimum

*Cortland County Courthouse
Cortland, NY 13045
Phone (607) 753-5021 County Clerk
County organized 1808 from Onondaga County
Land records: Deeds and mortgages from 1808; contact County Clerk's Office, PO Box 5590, First Floor, Court House, Cortland, NY 13045
Naturalization records: From 1816 through early 1960s
Vital records: Marriages from 1908 to 1933 (earlier and later records filed with city and town clerks)
Probate records: From 1808; contact Honorable Charles J. Mullen, Jr., Surrogate's Court, Second Floor, Court House, Cortland, NY 13045

*Delaware County Courthouse
111 Main Street
Delhi, NY 13753-1212
Phone (607) 746-2123 County Clerk's Office; (607) 746-2126 Surrogate Court
County organized 1797 from Ulster and Otsego counties
Land records: From 1797 to date; contact Gary L. Cady, County Clerk, County Clerk's Office, PO Box 426, Delhi, NY 13753
Naturalization records: From early 1800s; contact County Clerk's Office
Vital records: Births, deaths and marriages from 1847 to 1848, marriages from 1874 to 1881 and from 1909 to 1935; contact County Clerk's Office
Probate records: From 1797 to date; contact Surrogate Court Clerk, Court House Square, Delhi, NY 13753

No probate search service

*Dutchess County Courthouse
10 Market Street
Poughkeepsie, NY 12601-3222
Phone (914) 431-2020
County organized 1683, original county
Land records: Contact County Clerk's Office, Record Room, Second Floor
No land records search service; copies: $5.00 per document, $6.00 per document for certified copies
Naturalization records: Contact County Clerk's Office
No naturalization records search service; copies: $5.00 per document, $6.00 per document for certified copies
Vital records: Marriage certificates from 1908 to 1935; contact County Clerk's Office
No vital records search service; copies: $5.00 per document, $6.00 per document for certified copies

*Erie County Courthouse
95 Franklin Street
Buffalo, NY 14202-3904
Phone (716) 846-8500; (716) 846-8865 County Clerk
County organized 1821 from Niagara County
Land records: Deeds; contact David J. Swarts, County Clerk, 25 Delaware Avenue, Buffalo, NY 14202
Land records search service: $5.00 per name for each two-year period or portion thereof, payable in advance by money order
Naturalization records: From 1827 to 1929; contact County Clerk
Naturalization records search service: $5.00 per name for each two-year period or portion thereof, payable in advance by money order
Vital records: Marriages from 1878 through 29 April 1935 (very few before 1878); contact County Clerk's Office. Birth and death records: contact City or Town Clerk's Office where the birth or death occurred
Vital records search service from County Clerk's Office: $5.00 per name for each two-year period or portion thereof, payable in advance by money order; copies: $5.00 each
Probate records: Contact Surrogate's Court

*Essex County Government Center
Elizabethtown, NY 12932
Phone (518) 873-6301, ext. 281; (518) 873-3600 Clerk's Office; (518) 873-3384 Surrogate's Clerk
County organized 1 March 1799 from Clinton County
Land records: Deeds from 1800; contact Joseph A. Provoncha, County Clerk

Naturalization records: Contact County Clerk

Vital records: Marriage licenses and certificates from 1909 to 1912 for all towns and births, deaths and marriages from 1847 to 1850 for the towns of Crown Point, Keene, Moriah, Schroon, Ticonderoga, Westport and Willsboro; contact County Clerk. Other vital records; contact town clerks' offices: Chesterfield (20 February 1802), Lynn Jarvis (518) 834-9042; Crown Point (23 March 1788), Linda Woods, Crown Point, NY 12928, (518) 597-3235; Elizabethtown (12 February 1798), Cindy Heald (518) 873-6555; Essex (4 April 1805), Grace Drummond (518) 963-7231; Jay (16 January 1798), Beatrice Furnia (518) 647-7782; Keene (19 March 1808), Inez Estes, Keene, NY 12942, (518) 576-4311; Lewis (4 April 1805), James E. Pierce, Lewis, NY 12950, (518) 873-6777; Minerva (17 March 1817), Jack Vanderwalker, Olmstedville, NY 12857, (518) 251-3395; Moriah (12 February 1808), Esther Waldron, Port Henry, NY 12974, (518) 546-3341; Newcomb (15 March 1828), James Montayne, Newcomb, NY 12852, (518) 582-3131; North Elba (13 December 1849), Barbara Whitney, Lake Placid, NY 12946, (518) 523-2162; North Hudson (12 April 1848), Sally Vinskus (518) 532-9273 (Clerk's Home), (518) 532-7666 (Town Hall); Saint Armand (23 April 1844), Connie Willette (518) 891-0536; Schroon (7 March 1804), Janice Tyrell, Schroon Lake, NY 12870, (518) 532-7737; Ticonderoga (20 March 1804), Wilma Ryan, Ticonderoga, NY 12883, (518) 585-6677; Westport (24 March 1815), Helen E. Collins, (518) 962-8360; Willsboro (7 March 1788), Beverly Moran, Willsboro, NY 12996, (518) 963-8933; Wilmington (22 March 1821), Judy A. Bowen, Wilmington, NY 12997, (518) 946-2105

Probate records: Contact Surrogate's Clerk

Probate search service: $25.00 for under 25 years, $70.00 for over 25 years; copies: 25¢ each, $5.00 for certified copies

*Franklin County Courthouse
63 West Main Street
Malone, NY 12953-1817
Phone (518) 483-6767
County organized 1808 from Clinton County
Land records: Deeds and mortgages from 1808 to date, lis pendens from 1820 to date, homestead exemptions of the 1830s, land tax records from the 1800s and early 1900s; contact County Clerk's Office

Naturalization records: Some naturalization records from 1825 to September 1953, declarations of intent from 1834; contact County Clerk's Office

Vital records: Marriages from 1908 to 1935; contact County Clerk's Office

Probate records: Contact Surrogate's Office

*Fulton County Courthouse
County Building
Johnstown, NY 12095-2331
Phone (518) 762-0555 County Clerk
County organized 1838 from Montgomery County
Land records: Contact County Clerk, PO Box 485, Johnstown, NY 12095

Naturalization records: Contact County Clerk

Vital records: Contact Registrar of Vital Statistics in each town/city

Probate records: Contact Surrogate Court

Probate search service: $20.00 up to twenty-five years, $53.00 over twenty-five years, includes certification; copies: $1.00, no minimum; "Oldest courthouse still in use—1776."

*Genesee County Courthouse
Main and Court Streets
Batavia, NY 14020
County organized 1802 from Ontario County
Land records: Deeds from 1802; contact County Clerk, PO Box 379, Batavia, NY 14020

Land records search service: $5.00 per name; copies: 50¢ per page, $1.00 minimum

Naturalization records: From 1834 to February 1962; contact County Clerk

Vital records: Marriages from 1908 to 1934; contact County Clerk. Births, deaths and marriages from 1880; contact local municipality

Probate records: From 1802; contact Surrogate; PO Box 462, Batavia, NY 14020

Probate search service: from $35.00 (estates under $10,000) up; copies: 25¢ per page, $5.00 per page for certified copies; "Please read about the local history first!"

*Greene County Courthouse
Main Street
Catskill, NY 12414
Phone (518) 943-2050
County organized 1800 from Albany and Ulster counties
Probate records: Contact County

Surrogate's Court, PO Box 469, Catskill, NY 12414

Probate search service: $20.00 under twenty-five years, $53.00 over twenty-five years; copies: 25¢ per page, no minimum; "We ask that requests be made in writing."

Hamilton County Office Building
Lake Pleasant, NY 12108
Phone (518) 548-7111
County organized 1816 from Montgomery County

Herkimer County Courthouse
PO Box 471
Herkimer, NY 13350-0471
Phone (315) 867-1002
County organized 1791 from Montgomery County

*Jefferson County Building
175 Arsenal Street
Watertown, NY 13601-2522
Phone (315) 785-3081
County organized 1805 from Oneida County
Land records: Deeds from 1795 (Oneida), 1805 (Jefferson), mortgages from 1805; contact Clerk's Office

Naturalization records: Through 1972; contact Clerk's Office. Earlier and later records filed with Town Clerks

Vital records: Marriages from 1908 to 1933 only; contact Clerk's Office

Probate records: Decedent's estates from 1847; contact Surrogate's Court

Kings County Courthouse
360 Adams Street
Brooklyn, NY 11201-3712
Phone (718) 643-5771
County organized 1683, original county

*Lewis County Courthouse
(7660 State Street, Lowville, NY 13367-1396—location)
PO Box 332 (mailing address)
Lowville, NY 13367-1432
Phone (315) 376-5333 County Clerk
County organized 1805 from Oneida County
Land records: From 1805; contact Jesse Schantz, County Clerk

Naturalization records: From 1808 to 1906; contact County Clerk

Vital records: From 1848 to 1850 (incomplete); contact County Clerk

Probate records: Contact County Clerk

Probate search service: $10.00 per name; copies: $1.00 per page, $3.00 minimum

*Livingston County Courthouse
2 Court Street
Geneseo, NY 14454-1048

Phone (716) 243-2500
County organized 1821 from Genesee and Ontario counties
Land records: From 1821; contact Clerk
Naturalization records: From early 1860s to 1954; contact Clerk
Vital records: No vital records
Probate records: From 1821; contact Toni A. Moore, Chief Clerk, Surrogate Court
Probate search service: $25.00 under twenty-five years, $70.00 over twenty-five years; copies: 25¢ per page, $5.00 for certified copies

*Madison County Courthouse
PO Box 607
Wampsville, NY 13163
Phone (315) 366-2261 County Clerk's Office
County organized 1806 from Chenango County
Land records: Contact County Clerk's Office, County Office Building, PO Box 668, Wampsville, NY 13163-0668
No land records search service
Naturalization records: Yes
Vital records: Marriages to 1920; contact County Clerk's Office
No vital records search service
Probate records: Contact Surrogate's Court
Probate search service: $20.00 under twenty-five years, $53.00 over twenty-five years; copies: $1.00 per page, no minimum

*Monroe County Office Building
39 West Main Street, Room 101
Rochester, NY 14614
Phone (716) 428-5151
County organized 1821 from Genesee and Ontario counties
Land records: From 1821; contact Clerk's Office
Naturalization records: From 1821; contact Clerk's Office

*Montgomery County
New County Office Building
Fonda, NY 12068
Phone (518) 853-3431
County organized 1772 from Albany County; name changed from Tryon County in 1784
Land records: Contact County Clerk
Naturalization records: Contact County Clerk
Vital records: Contact City of Amsterdam and town clerks' offices
Probate records: Contact Surrogate's Office, New Court House, Fonda, NY 12068
Probate search service: $20.00 under twenty-five years, $53.00 over

twenty-five years; copies: 25¢ each, $4.00 for certified copies; "Most genealogical records are filed in Montgomery County Department of History and Archives, Old Courthouse, Railroad Street, Fonda, NY 12068; we have the third largest collection of records for genealogical and historical research in the State of New York; telephone: (518) 853-3431 Violet Dake Fallone, County Historian and Archivist."

Nassau County Courthouse
1 West Street
Mineola, NY 11501-4812
Phone (516) 535-2663
County organized 1899 from Queens County

*New York County Courthouse
60 Centre Street
New York, NY 10007-1402
Phone (212) 374-4376 Division of Old Records (Tue & Thur 9:00-5:00); (212) 374-4781 Record Room
County organized 1683, original county
Land records: Contact New York City Register, Borough of Manhattan
Naturalization records: From 1794 to 1924; contact Coutny Clerk, 60 Centre Street, Room 161, New York, NY 10007
Naturalization search service: $10.00 (includes copy)
Vital records: Births before 1908, deaths before 1947, and marriages before 1938; contact New York City Municipal Archives, 31 Chambers Street, Room 103, New York, NY 10007. Births and deaths; contact Bureau of Vital Records, New York City Health Department, 125 Worth Street, New York, NY 10013
Probate records: Contact Surrogate's Office, Room 402, 31 Chambers Street, New York, NY 10007

*Niagara County Courthouse
Lockport, NY 14094
Phone (716) 439-7324 County Historian (Mon.–Fri. 9:00–4:00)
County organized 1808 from Genesee County
Land records: From 1821; contact Dorothy Rolling, County Historian, County Historian's Office, Civil Defense Building, 139 Niagara Street, Lockport, NY 14094-2740. Land records from 1808 to 1821; contact Erie County, Buffalo, NY.
Land records search service from County Historian (index to land owners prior to 1850): $10.00 per hour, $10.00 deposit required, made payable to Niagara County Treasurer; copies: 25¢ per page

Naturalization records: Contact County Clerk's Office
Vital records: Contact municipality where event occurred
Probate records: From 1821; contact Surrogate Department, Courthouse Building. Index of wills prior to 1880; contact County Historian. Probate records from 1808 to 1821; contact Erie County (formerly Niagara County)
Probate search service from Surrogate Department: $20.00 under twenty years, $53.00 over twenty years; copies: 25¢ per page. Probate search service from County Historian: $10.00 per hour, $10.00 deposit required, made payable to Niagara County Treasurer; copies: 25¢ per page

*Oneida County Courthouse
800 Park Avenue
Utica, NY 13501-2939
Phone (315) 798-5866 Surrogate's Court
County organized 1798 from Herkimer County
Probate records: From 1798; contact Martha R. Hoffman, Chief Clerk, Surrogate's Court
Probate search service: $25.00 under twenty-five years, $70.00 over twenty-five years; copies: 25¢ per page for short copies, 50¢ per page for long copies, $5.00 per page for certified copies

*Onondaga County Courthouse
County Clerk
401 Montgomery Street, Room 200
Syracuse, NY 13202
Phone (315) 435-2226 County Clerk; (315) 435-3241 Bureau of Vital Statistics; (315) 425-2101 Surrogate Court
County organized 1794 from Herkimer County
Land records: Contact County Clerk
Naturalization records: Contact County Clerk
Vital records: From 1865 to 1907, marriage certificates from 1908 to 1938; contact County Clerk. Births from 1873 to date (incomplete before 1914), deaths from 1873 to date, and marriage certificates from 1873 to 1907 for the city of Syracuse; contact Office of Vital Statistics, 421 Montgomery Street, Civic Center, Ninth Floor, Syracuse, NY 13202
Vital records search service from Office of Vital Statistics: $10.00 per hour or fractional part of an hour, payable with application; copies: $1.00 each (restrictions on birth records created within the last seventy-five years and death and marriage records created within the last fifty years are waived for direct descendants)

Probate records: Contact County
Surrogate Court, Room 209
Probate search service: $20.00 under
twenty-five years; $53.00 over
twenty-five years; copies: $4.00 per
page, no minimum; "Fees must be
paid in advance."

***Ontario County Records, Archives,
and Information Management
Services**
3969 County Road #46
Canandaigua, NY 14424
Phone (716) 396-4376
*County organized 1789 from
Montgomery County*
Land records: From 1789; contact Mary
Jo Barone, Assistant Records
Management Officer
Naturalization records: From 1803 to
1956; contact Assistant Records
Management Officer
Vital records: Marriages from 1908 to
1935; contact Assistant Records
Management Officer
Probate records: From 1789 to 1965;
contact Assistant Records
Management Officer
Probate search service: $15.00; copies:
50¢ per page, $1.00 minimum;
"Access to records may be denied if
information contained therein
constitutes an unwarranted invasion of
privacy."

Orange County Courthouse
255-275 Main Street
Goshen, NY 10924-1621
Phone (914) 294-5151
County organized 1683, original county

*Orleans County Courthouse
Courthouse Square
Albion, NY 14411-1449
Phone (716) 589-4457; (716) 589-5334
County Clerk; (716) 589-4457
Surrogate's Office
*County organized 1824 from Genesee
County*
Land records: From 1824; contact Carol
R. Lonnen, County Clerk
Naturalization records: Contact County
Clerk's Office
Vital records: Births, deaths and
marriages (villages have very few
marriage records); contact Town
Clerk: Albion (1883), Nancy Miles,
3665 Clarendon Road, Albion, NY
14411, (716) 589-7048; Barre (1884),
Joy Markle, West Barre Road, Albion,
NY 14411, (716) 589-5100; Carlton
(1847), Pamela E. Rush, 14341
Waterport-Carlton Road, Albion, NY
14411, (716) 682-4358; Clarendon
(1847), Jean Rockafellow, Church and
Fourth Section Road, PO Box 145,

Clarendon, NY 14429, (716) 638-
6371; Gaines (1883), Ruth Drew, Rt.
4, Ridge Road, Albion, NY 14411,
(716) 589-5833; Kendall (1881),
JoAnn Herman, 1873 Kendall Road,
Kendall, NY 14476, (716) 659-8721;
Murray (1884), Jennifer H.
Piedmonte, 16797 Lynch Road,
Holley, NY 14470, (716) 638-6570;
Ridgeway (1848), June Stalker, 410
West Avenue, Medina, NY 14103,
(716) 798-0730; Shelby (1882),
Mildred Green, 11248 Maple Ridge
Road, Medina, NY 14103, (716) 798-
3120; Yates (1883), Lawrence Brown,
8 South Main Street, Lyndonville, NY
14098, (716) 765-9716; Albion
Village (1887), Kathy Ludwick, 37
East Bank Street, Albion, NY 14411,
(716) 589-9176; Lyndonville Village
(1903), Debra Miller, 2 South Main
Street, Lyndonville, NY 14098, (716)
765-9385; Medina Village (1885), E.
Margaret Crowley, Village Building,
Medina, NY 14103, (716) 798-0710;
Holley Village (1898), Theresa Cary,
72 Public Square, Holley, NY 14470,
(716) 638-6367
Probate records: Some beginning in
1845; contact Surrogate's Office
Probate search service: "according to
how many years they have to search";
copies: $2.00 per page

*Oswego County Courthouse
East Second and Oneida Streets
Oswego, NY 13126
Phone (315) 349-3230
*County organized 1816 from Oneida
and Onondaga counties*

*Otsego County Offices
197 Main Street
Cooperstown, NY 13326-1129
Phone (607) 547-4276 County Clerk
*County organized 1791 from
Montgomery County*
Land records: From 1791; contact
Charlotte P. Koniuto, County Clerk,
Clerk's Office, 197 Main Street, PO
Box 710, Cooperstown, NY 13326
Naturalization records: From 1806 to
1889 and from 1895 to 1955
(incomplete); contact County Clerk
Vital records: Marriages from 1908 to
January 1935; contact County Clerk
Probate records: Contact County
Surrogate, Surrogate's Office

*Putnam County Courthouse
2 County Center
Carmel, NY 10512
Phone (914) 278-7209
*County organized 1812 from Dutchess
County*
Land records: Yes

Naturalization records: Yes
Vital records: Yes
Probate records: Yes

Queens County General Courthouse
88-11 Sutphin Boulevard
Jamaica, NY 11435
Phone (718) 520-3137
County organized 1683, original county

*Rensselaer County Courthouse
1600 Seventh Avenue
Troy, NY 12180-3409
Phone (518) 270-2700; (518) 270-4080
County Clerk
*County organized 1791 from Albany
County*
Land records: Yes
No land records search service
Naturalization records: Yes
No naturalization records copying service
Vital records: Births, deaths and
marriages; contact city or town clerk
Probate records: Contact Surrogate's
Court

*Richmond County Courthouse
18 Richmond Terrace
Staten Island, NY 10301-1935
Phone (718) 390-5386
County organized 1683, original county
Land records: From 1884 to 1929;
contact County Clerk's Office
Naturalization records: From 1907 to
1960 (covered by two liber indexes),
card index only from 1820 to 1906,
declarations of intention from about
1884 to 1929
Vital records: Contact Bureau of Vital
Statistics, 125 Worth Street, New
York, NY 10013
Probate records: Contact Surrogate's
Court

*Rockland County Courthouse
Main Street
New City, NY 10956
Phone (914) 638-5070; (914) 638-5330
Surrogate's Court
*County organized 1798 from Orange
County*
Land records: Contact County Clerk, 27
New Hempstead Road, New City, NY
10956
Naturalization records: Contact County
Clerk
Probate records: Contact Surrogate's
Court
Probate search service: $20.00 under
twenty-five years, $53.00 over
twenty-five years; copies: $4.00 per
page, no minimum

*Saint Lawrence County Courthouse
48 Court Street
Canton, NY 13617-1198

Phone (315) 379-2237
County organized 1802 from Clinton, Herkimer and Montgomery counties
Land records: From 1802; contact County Clerk
Naturalization records: From 1802; contact County Clerk
Vital records: Marriages from 1908 to 1936; contact County Clerk
Probate records: Contact Surrogate Court
No probate search service; copies: 50¢ per page, $1.00 minimum

*Saratoga County Courthouse
40 McMasters Street
Ballston Spa, NY 12020-1908
Phone (518) 885-5381
County organized 1791 from Albany County
Probate records: From 1791; contact Surrogate's Court
Probate search service: $20.00 under twenty-five years old, $53.00 over twenty-five years old; copies: $1.00 per page, no minimum

Schenectady County Courthouse
620 State Street
Schenectady, NY 12305-2113
Phone (518) 382-3220
County organized 1809 from Albany County

*Schoharie County Courthouse
300 Main Street
Schoharie, NY 12157
Phone (518) 295-8316 County Clerk's Office; (518) 295-8383 Surrogate's Court
County organized 1795 from Albany and Otsego counties
Land records: From 1797; contact County Clerk, PO Box 549, Schoharie, NY 12157-0549
Probate records: From 1791; contact Surrogate's Court, The Courthouse, 300 Main Street, PO Box 669, Schoharie, NY 12157
Probate search service: $25.00 for an estate which is less than twenty-five years old, $70.00 for an estate which is twenty-five years old or older; copies: 25¢ per page; "Fees are payable in advance; please submit SASE; many older records are in such poor condition that we are unable to photocopy them, and many are not accessible to examine at this time; we do expect at some date in the future to have our older records placed on microfilm, at which time copies will be available."

*Schuyler County Courthouse
Watkins Glen, NY 14891
Phone (607) 535-2132

County organized 1854 from Tompkins, Steuben and Chemung counties
Land records: Deeds from 1855, deeds from 1796 (transcribed from Chemung County), deeds from 1817 (transcribed from Tompkins County), deeds from 1798 (transcribed from Steuben County); contact County Clerk, PO Box 9, Watkins Glen, NY 14891-0009
Vital records: Some marriages from 1908 to 1935; contact County Clerk. Births and deaths; contact town and/or village clerks: Catharine, Nancy Williams, Grant Road, Odessa, NY 14869, (607) 594-2273; Cayuta, Debra VanGalder, Box 116, Conkrite Road, Cayuta, NY 14824, (607) 594-2507; Dix, Lela Gates, Madison Avenue, Watkins Glen, NY 14891, (607) 535-2525; Hector, Jane Coyle, 5097 Rt. 227, Burdett, NY 14818, (607) 546-5286; Montour, Louise Eckelberger, Havana Glen, Montour Falls, NY 14865, (607) 535-9476; Orange, Paula Reynolds, Rt. 1, Hornby Road, Beaver Dams, NY 14812, (607) 936-8571; Reading, Judith Brimmer, PO Box 5, Reading Center, NY 14876, (607) 535-7459; Tyrone, Helen Baxter, Rt. 2, Box 113B, Dundee, NY 14837
Probate records: Contact Shirley H. Craver, Chief Clerk, Surrogate's Court
Probate search service: $20.00 under twenty-five years, $53.00 over twenty-five years (with copies); copies: $1.00 per page, no minimum; "Please include SASE with inquiry; no estate, no charge."

*Seneca County Courthouse
48 West William Street
Waterloo, NY 13165-1338
Phone (315) 539-7531
County organized 1804 from Cayuga County
Land records: From 1804
Naturalization records: From 1830 to 1948
Vital records: Contact Registrar of each town
Probate records: From 1804; contact Ernest C. Humbert, Chief Clerk, Surrogate Court
Probate search service: $25.00 for under twenty-five years, $70.00 for over twenty-five years (for searching and certifying to any record for which search is made); copies: 25¢ per page for photocopies, $5.00 per page for certified copies, no minimum

*Steuben County Office Building
3 East Pulteney Square
Bath, NY 14810

Phone (607) 776-9631, est. 3207 County Clerk
County organized 1796 from Ontario County
Land records: Contact County Clerk, 3 East Pulteney Square, Bath, NY 14810
Naturalization records: Index only from the 1820s to the 1970s; contact County Clerk
Vital records: Computer list telling what clerk holds the death or marriage record from 1885 to the 1940s (some later); contact County Clerk. Births, deaths and marriages from 1885 to date; contact town, village or city clerks
Probate records: Special project: 1796 to circa 1900, computer indexed; contact County Clerk
Probate search service: one name, no charge; copies: $1.00 per page

Suffolk County Courthouse
County Center
Riverhead, NY 11901-3398
Phone (516) 548-3100
County organized 1683, original county

*Sullivan County Government Center
100 North Street
Monticello, NY 12701-1160
Phone (914) 794-3000
County organized 1809 from Ulster County
Land records: Yes
Naturalization records: Yes
Vital records: Yes
Probate records: Yes

*Tioga County Courthouse
Clifford Balliet, Records Management Officer
16 Court Street
Owego, NY 13827
Phone (607) 687-0135
County organized 1791 from Montgomery County

*Tompkins County Courthouse
320 North Tioga Street
Ithaca, NY 14850-4284
Phone (607) 274-5431 County Clerk; (607) 273-7272 County Health Department; (607) 277-0622 Surrogate Clerk's Office
County organized 1817 from Cayuga and Seneca counties
Land records: From 1817; contact County Clerk's Office; copies: $1.00 per page
Naturalization records: From 1895; contact County Clerk
Vital records: Births and deaths from 1880 (except Dreyden from 1887, Freeville from 1894, Ithaca births

from 1886 and deaths from 1893, Ulysses from 1922, and Trumansburg from 1914); contact Vital Records, County Health Department, 401 Harris B. Dates Drive, Ithaca, NY 14580-1386. Marriages from 1908; contact town clerks or City Chamberlain Office for Ithaca (from 1881)

Vital records search service from County Health Department: $6.00 per hour, includes abstract copy

Probate records: From 1817; contact Surrogate Clerk's Office

Probate search service: no charge unless person asks us to certify the search, then $20.00 if for under twenty-five years, $53 if over twenty-five years; copies: $1.00 per page, $4.00 per page for certified copies, no minimum; "We prefer to receive written requests, not telephone requests; requests for searches do not receive high priority unless accompanied by a check (since we must do a receipt when payment is received)."

Tryon County
(see Montgomery County)

*Ulster County Courthouse
240 Fair Street
Kingston, NY 12801-3806
Phone (914) 331-9300, ext. 252 County Clerk's Office
County organized 1683, original county
Land records: From 1685 to date; contact Albert Spada, County Clerk, County Clerk's Office, PO Box 1800, Kingston, NY 12401-0800
Land records search service: $5.00 for every two years searched, payable in advance; copies: 50¢ per page, payable in advance
Naturalization records: From 1800 to 1903 (index available, however some records are incomplete), petitions for naturalization before March 1992; contact County Clerk
Naturalization records search service: $5.00 for every two years searched, payable in advance; copies: 50¢ per page, payable in advance
Vital records: Marriages from 1903 to 1935; contact County Clerk. Births and additional marriage records; contact town or city clerk's office
Vital records search service from County Clerk: $5.00 for every two years searched, payable in advance; copies: 50¢ per page, payable in advance

*Warren County Courthouse
Warren County Municipal Center
Route 9
Lake George, NY 12845

Phone (518) 761-6427 County Clerk; (518) 761-6455 County Records Storage; (518) 761-6515 Surrogate's Court
County organized 1813 from Washington County
Land records: From 1813 to date; contact Caryl M. Clark, County Clerk, County Clerk's Office
Naturalization records: From 1813 to 1955; contact County Clerk or Pamela Vogel, County Records Storage
Vital records: Marriages from 1908 to 1935; contact County Clerk. Births, deaths and marriages; contact individual town clerks
Probate records: From 1813 to date; contact County Surrogate's Court

*Washington County Courthouse
383 Broadway
Fort Edward, NY 12828
Phone (518) 746-2136 County Archivist (Mon–Fri 9:00–4:30); (518) 746-2545 Surrogate Court Clerk
County organized 1772 from Albany County; name changed from Charlotte County in 1784; annexed towns of Cambridge and Easton from Albany County in 1791; settled boundary with Vermont in 1812
Land records: Deeds from 1794 to date, unrecorded conveyances from 1742 to 1870; contact Carol A. Senecal, County Archivist
Land records search service: $10.00 plus SASE; copies: $1.00 per page
Naturalization records: From 1794 to 1952, from December 1977 to October 1991 (restricted), and from 1991 (index to certificates held by INS); contact County Archivist
Naturalization records search service: $10.00 plus SASE; copies: $1.00 per page
Vital records: Births, deaths and marriages from 1848–1849, marriage licenses from 1908 to 1935; contact County Archivist. From 1881 to date; contact individual town clerks
Vital records search service from County Archivist: $10.00 plus SASE; copies: $1.00 per page
Probate records: From 1786 to 1900; contact County Archivist. Books of record and disposition of real property from 1900 to date; contact Mary Fraser, Surrogate Court Clerk
Probate search service from County Archivist: $10.00 plus SASE; copies: $1.00 per page

*Wayne County Courthouse
26 Church Street
Lyons, NY 14489-1134
Phone (315) 946-5400; (315) 946-5870

County Clerk; (315) 946-5430 Surrogate Court Clerk
County organized 1823 from Ontario and Seneca counties
Land records: Contact Linda Shaffer, County Clerk, County Office Building, 9 Pearl Street, PO Box 608, Lyons, NY 14489
Naturalization records: Contact County Clerk
Vital records: Births, deaths and marriages; contact individual town clerks: Arcadia, Hazel Herdman, 100 East Miller Street, Newark, NY 14513, (315) 331-1222; Butler, Robin Warrick, 4576 Butler Center Road, Wolcott, NY 14590, (315) 594-2719; Galen, Donna Carr, 106 Glasgow Street, PO Box 32, Clyde, NY 14433, (315) 923-7259; Huron, Shirley Eygnor, 10880 Lummisville Road, Wolcott, NY 14590, (315) 594-8074; Lyons, Sal J. Colatarci, 76 William Street, Lyons, NY 14489, (315) 946-6252; Macedon, Judy Gravino, 30 Main Street, Macedon, NY 14502, (315) 986-4177; Marion, Jolene Bender, 3823 North Main Street, Marion, NY 14505, (315) 926-4271; Ontario, Cathy Herzog, 1850 Ridge Road, Ontario, NY 14519, (315) 524-3441; Palmyra, Beverly Hickman, 201 East Main Street, Palmyra, NY 14522, (315) 597-5521; Rose, Christine Smith, North Main Street, North Rose, NY 14516, (315) 587-4418; Savannah, Julie Gansz, North Main Street, Savannah, NY 13146, (315) 365-2811; Sodus, Nancy DeHond, 14–16 Mill Street, Sodus, NY 14551, (315) 483-6934; Walworth, Marcia Englert, 3600 Lorraine Drive, Walworth, NY 14568, (315) 986-1400; Williamson, Esther Plyter, 4100 Ridge Road, Williamson, NY 14589, (315) 589-8100; Wolcott, Carol Reynolds, 16 Lake Avenue, PO Box 237, Wolcott, NY 14590, (315) 594-9431; copies: $5.00 each
Probate records: Contact Shirley Comella, Surrogate Court Clerk
Probate search service: $25.00 under twenty-five years, $70.00 over twenty-five years; copies: $1.00 per page, $5.00 for certified copies

Westchester County Records Center and Archives
2199 Saw Mill Rover Road
Elmsford, NY 10523
Phone (914) 285-3080
County organized 1683, original county
Land records: Yes
Probate records: Consolidated index; contact Surrogate Court, 111 Grove Street, Room 702, White Plains, NY 10601

*Wyoming County Courthouse
143 North Main Street
PO Box 70
Warsaw, NY 14569-1123
Phone (716) 786-8810; (716) 786-3703
   FAX, County Clerk
*County organized 1841 from Genesee
   County*
Land records: Contact Jean Krotz,
   County Clerk
Naturalization records: Some
   naturalization records for a limited
   period, petitions of intentions from
   1841; copies: 50¢ per page
Vital records: No vital records
Probate records: Contact William C.
   Beyer, Clerk, Surrogate's Court
Probate search service: $20.00 under
   twenty-five years, $53.00 over
   twenty-five years; copies: $1.00 per
   page, $4.00 for certified copies, no
   minimum

*Yates County Courthouse
County Office Building
110 Court Street
Penn Yan, NY 14527
Phone (315) 536-4221; (315) 536-5147
   County Historian
*County organized 1823 from Ontario
   County*
Land records: From 1788; contact
   Virginia H. Gibbs, County Historian,
   County Office Building, Room 3
Naturalization records: From 1823;
   contact County Historian
Vital records: Contact town and village
   clerks' offices
Probate records: From 1823; contact
   County Historian
Probate search service: $6.00 per hour;
   copies: $1.00 per page, no minimum

NORTH CAROLINA

Capital: Raleigh. Statehood: 21 November 1789 (part of the Carolina Grant of 1663, gave up claims to western lands in 1790, including eastern Tennessee, the State of Franklin)

Court System

North Carolina's District Courts handle some civil actions, domestic relations, divorces, misdemeanors, felony preliminaries and juvenile cases. First Judicial District: Camden, Chowan, Currituck, Dare, Gates, Pasquotank and Perquimans counties; Second Judicial District: Beaufort, Hyde, Martin, Tyrrell and Washington counties; Third Judicial District: Carteret, Craven, Pamlico and Pitt counties; Fourth Judicial District: Duplin, Jones, Onslow and Sampson counties; Fifth Judicial District: New Hanover and Pender counties; Sixth Judicial District: Bertie, Halifax, Hertford and Northampton counties; Seventh Judicial District: Edgecombe, Nash and Wilson counties; Eighth Judicial District: Greene, Lenoir and Wayne counties; Ninth Judicial District: Franklin, Granville, Person, Vance and Warren counties; Tenth Judicial District: Wake County; Eleventh Judicial District: Harnett, Johnston and Lee counties; Twelfth Judicial District: Cumberland and Hoke counties; Thirteenth Judicial District: Bladen, Brunswick and Columbus counties; Fourteenth Judicial District: Durham County; Fifteenth Judicial District A: Alamance County; Fifteenth Judicial District B: Chatham and Orange counties; Sixteenth Judicial District: Robeson and Scotland counties; Seventeenth Judicial District A: Caswell and Rockingham counties; Seventeenth Judicial District B: Stokes and Surry counties; Eighteenth Judicial District: Guilford County; Nineteenth Judicial District A: Cabarrus and Rowan counties; Nineteenth Judicial District B: Montgomery and Randolph counties; Twentieth Judicial District: Anson, Moore, Richmond, Stanly and Union counties; Twenty-first Judicial District: Forsyth County; Twenty-second Judicial District: Alexander, Davidson, Davie and Iredell counties; Twenty-third Judicial District: Alleghany, Ashe, Wilkes and Yadkin counties; Twenty-fourth Judicial District: Avery, Madison, Mitchell, Watauga and Yancey counties; Twenty-fifth Judicial District: Burke, Caldwell and Catawba counties; Twenty-sixth Judicial District: Mecklenburg County; Twenty-seventh Judicial District A: Gaston County; Twenty-seventh Judicial

District B: Cleveland and Lincoln counties; Twenty-eighth Judicial District: Buncombe County; Twenty-ninth Judicial District: Henderson, McDowell, Polk, Rutherford and Transylvania counties; Thirtieth Judicial District: Cherokee, Clay, Graham, Haywood, Jackson, Macon and Swain counties.

The Superior Courts, which sit at each county seat, are the courts of general jurisdiction. Division One: First through Eighth Judicial districts; Division Two: Ninth through Sixteenth Judicial districts; Division Three: Seventeenth through Twenty-third Judicial districts; Division Four: Twenty-fourth through Thirtieth Judicial districts. The Court of Appeals and Supreme Court have appellate jurisdiction.

The state began to record births and deaths in 1913.

Courthouses

*Alamance County Courthouse
Graham, NC 27253
Phone (910) 228-1312 County
   Switchboard; (910) 570-6860 Clerk's
   Office
*County organized 1848 from Orange
   County*
Land records: Contact Register of Deeds,
   118 West Harden Street, Graham, NC
   27253
Vital records: Contact Register of Deeds
Probate records: Contact Clerk of
   Superior Court
No probate search service; copies: $1.00
   for the first page and 25¢ for each
   additional page, no minimum

*Alexander County Courthouse
Taylorsville, NC 28681
Phone (704) 632-9332
*County organized 1850 from Iredell,
   Caldwell and Wilkes counties*
Land records: Contact County Tax Office
Vital records: Contact Register of Deeds
Probate records: Contact Clerk of
   Superior Court
Probate search service: no charge to
   individuals; copies: 25¢ per page, no
   minimum

Alleghany County Courthouse
PO Box 61
Sparta, NC 28675
Phone (919) 372-8949
*County organized 1859 from Ashe
   County*

*Anson County Courthouse
Wadesboro, NC 28170
Phone (704) 694-2796; (704) 694-3212
   Register of Deeds

County organized 1749 from Bladen County

Land records: From the early 1700s to date; contact Foye L. Ray, Register of Deeds, PO Box 352, Wadesboro, NC 28170

Land records search service: $2.00 per name; copies: $1.00 for the first page and 50¢ for each additional page from handwritten originals, 50¢ per page from typewritten originals, $3.00 for the first certified page and $1.00 for each additional certified page, plus SASE

Vital records: Births and deaths from 1913, marriages from 1868 (when courthouse burned); contact Register of Deeds

Vital records search service: $2.00 per name; certified copies: $3.00 each for births, deaths or marriages (available only to authorized persons), $1.50 each for marriage licenses, $1.00 each for uncertified copies of births and deaths, plus SASE

Probate records: Contact Clerk of Superior Court

No probate search service

Archdale County
(see Beaufort County)

Ashe County Courthouse
Jefferson, NC 28640
Phone (919) 246-8841
County organized 1799 from Wilkes County

*Avery County Courthouse
PO Box 640
Newland, NC 28657-0640
Phone (704) 733-8201
County organized 1911 from Caldwell, Mitchell and Watauga counties
Land records: Yes
Naturalization records: Yes
Vital records: Yes
Probate records: Yes

*Beaufort County Courthouse
PO Box 1027
Washington, NC 27889-1027
Phone (919) 946-2323 Register of Deeds
County organized 1705 from Bath District, which was organized 1696 and abolished in 1739; name changed from Archdale County in 1712
Land records: From 1696; contact John I. Morgan, Register of Deeds, PO Box 514, Washington, NC 27889
Naturalization records: No naturalization records
Vital records: From 1913; contact Register of Deeds

*Bertie County Courthouse
204 South Queens Street
Windsor, NC 27983-1822
Phone (919) 794-3039
County organized 1722 from Bath District
Land records: From 1722; contact Register of Deeds, PO Box 340, Windsor, NC 27983-0340
Vital records: Births and deaths from 1 October 1913, marriages from 1760; contact Register of Deeds
Probate records: Wills from 1763 to date; contact Clerk of Superior Court, PO Box 370, Windsor, NC 27983-0370

Bladen County Courthouse
PO Box 547
Elizabethtown, NC 28337
Phone (919) 862-3438
County organized 1734 from Bath District

Brunswick County Courthouse
PO Box 249
Bolivia, NC 28422-0249
Phone (919) 253-4331
County organized 1764 from New Hanover and Bladen counties

Buncombe County Courthouse
60 College Street
Asheville, NC 28801-2818
Phone (704) 251-6007
County organized 1792 from Burke and Rutherford counties (in 1812 annexed Walton County, which was formed in 1803 from Indian lands)

*Burke County Courthouse
PO Box 219
Morganton, NC 28655-0219
Phone (704) 433-4013; (704) 438-5450 Register of Deeds; (704) 438-5540 Clerk of Court
County organized 1777 from Rowan County
Land records: Deed transfers from 1865; contact Register of Deeds, PO Box 936, Morganton, NC 28680
No land records search service
Vital records: Births, deaths and marriages; contact Register of Deeds
No vital records search service
Probate records: Estate proceedings from 1865; contact Clerk of Court, PO Box 796, Morganton, NC 28680
No probate search service

Cabarrus County Courthouse
PO Box 70
Concord, NC 28026-0070
Phone (704) 786-4137
County organized 1792 from Mecklenburg County

*Caldwell County Courthouse
PO Box 1376
Lenoir, NC 28645-1376
Phone (704) 757-1375
County organized 1841 from Burke and Wilkes counties
Land records: Contact County Office Building
Naturalization records: Contact County Office Building
Vital records: Contact County Office Building
Probate records: Contact Clerk of Court

*Camden County Courthouse
Camden, NC 27921
Phone (919) 335-7942; (919) 335-4077 Register of Deeds
County organized 1777 from Pasquotank County
Land records: Contact Register of Deeds, PO Box 190, Camden, NC 27921
Vital records: Contact Register of Deeds; copies: 25¢ each, $3.00 for certified copies
Probate records: Contact Clerk Superior Court
No probate search service ("Any request is passed on to member of Historical Society"); copies: $1.00 for the first page and 25¢ for each additional page

*Carteret County Courthouse
Beaufort, NC 28516
Phone (919) 728-8500; (919) 728-8474 Register of Deeds
County organized 1722 from Bath District
Land records: Contact Register of Deeds, Courthouse Square, Administration Building, Beaufort, NC 28516
Vital records: Contact Register of Deeds; certified copies: $3.00 each (must be a member of the family)

*Caswell County Courthouse
PO Box 790
Yanceyville, NC 27379-0790
Phone (919) 694-4171
County organized 1777 from Orange County
Land records: From 1777; contact Register of Deeds, PO Box 98, Yanceyville, NC 27379
Vital records: From 1913 (some delayed births from 1880); contact Register of Deeds
Probate records: From 1777; contact Clerk's Office
No probate search service; copies: $1.00 for the first page and 25¢ for each additional page, no minimum; "I do not photocopy the probate records due to the fact that the records are in bound volumes and wear and tear on the books has nearly destroyed some

records; all probate records for Caswell are available from North Carolina Department of Archives."

*Catawba County Justice Center
Highway 321
Newton, NC 28658
Phone (704) 465-1573 Register of Deeds; (704) 464-5216 Clerk
County organized 1842 from Lincoln County
Land records: Contact Ruth Mackie, Register of Deeds, PO Box 65, Newton, NC 28658
Naturalization records: No naturalization records
Vital records: Contact Register of Deeds
Probate records: Contact Clerk's Office, PO Box 728, Newton, NC 28658
No probate search service; copies not available of index pages

*Chatham County Courthouse
PO Box 368
Pittsboro, NC 27312-0368
Phone (919) 542-3240
County organized 1842 from Orange County
Land records: Contact Register of Deeds
Vital records: Contact Register of Deeds
Probate records: Contact Clerk of Superior Court
No probate search service; copies: $1.00 for the first page and 25¢ for each additional page, no minimum

Cherokee County Courthouse
Peachtree Street
Murphy, NC 28906
Phone (704) 837-5527
County organized 1839 from Macon County

*Chowan County Courthouse
PO Box 588
Edenton, NC 27932
Phone (919) 482-2323
County organized 1672 from Albemarle District
Land records: Contact Anne Spruill, Register of Deeds, PO Box 487, Edenton, NC 27932; copies: $1.00 for the first page and 25¢ for each additional page, no minimum

*Clay County Courthouse
PO Box 118
Hayesville, NC 28904-0118
Phone (704) 389-8231
County organized 1861 from Cherokee County
Land records: From 1870; contact Melissa B. Roach, Register of Deeds; copies: 25¢ per page
Vital records: Births and deaths from

1913, marriages from 1890; contact Register of Deeds
Probate records: From 1890; contact Harold McClure, Clerk
No probate search service; copies: $1.00 for the first page and 25¢ for each additional page, no minimum

Cleveland County Courthouse
PO Box 1210
Shelby, NC 28151-1210
Phone (704) 484-4800
County organized 1841 from Rutherford and Lincoln counties

Columbus County Courthouse
Whiteville, NC 28472
Phone (919) 642-3119
County organized 1808 from Bladen and Brunswick counties

*Craven County Courthouse
PO Box 1187
New Bern, NC 28563-1187
Phone (919) 514-4774; (919) 514-4891 FAX
County organized 1712 from Bath District
Land records: Yes
Naturalization records: Yes
Vital records: Yes
Probate records: Yes

*Cumberland County Courthouse
117 Dick Street
Fayetteville, NC 28301-5749
Phone (910) 678-7775 Register of Deeds; (910) 678-2902 Clerk of Court
County organized 1754 from Bladen County
Land records: From 1754; contact George E. Tatum, Register of Deeds, PO Box 2039, Fayetteville, NC 28302-2039; copies: 25¢ per page, $3.00 for certified copies
Vital records: From 1913; contact Register of Deeds
Probate records: Contact Clerk of Superior Court
No probate search service

Currituck County Courthouse
PO Box 39
Currituck, NC 27929-0039
Phone (919) 232-2075
County organized 1672 from Albemarle District

Dare County Courthouse
PO Box 1849
Manteo, NC 27954-1849
Phone (919) 473-2950
County organized 1870 from Tyrrell, Hyde and Currituck counties

*Davidson County Courthouse
Lexington, NC 27293
Phone (704) 249-7011
County organized 1822 from Rowan County
Land records: Contact Register of Deeds; copies: varies
Naturalization records: Contact Clerk of Court
Vital records: Contact Register of Deeds
Probate records: Contact Clerk of Court
No probate search service; copies: $1.00 for the first page and 25¢ for each additional page

*Davie County Courthouse
140 South Main Street
Mocksville, NC 27028-2425
Phone (704) 634-5513
County organized 1836 from Rowan County
Land records: From 1836
Vital records: Births and deaths from 1913, marriages from 1836
Probate records: From 1836
Probate search service: no charge; copies: $1.00 for wills, no minimum

*Duplin County Courthouse
Kenansville, NC 28349
Phone (919) 296-1240
County organized 1749 from New Hanover County
Land records: From 1749; contact Joyce J. Williams, Register of Deeds, PO Box 970, Kenansville, NC 28349-0970
No land records search service; copies: $1.00 per page, $3.00 for the first certified page and $1.00 for each additional certified page
Vital records: Births and deaths from 1913, and a few marriages in the late 1800s; contact Register of Deeds
No vital records search service: copies: $1.00 per page, $3.00 per page for certified copies
Probate records: Contact Bertha Wholey, Clerk of Superior Court
No probate search service other than for copies; copies: $1.00 for the first page and 25¢ for each additional page, $2.00 certified copy, no minimum; "Need full name—no initials— approximate date of death."

*Durham County Judicial Building
201 East Main Street
Durham, NC 27701-3641
Phone (919) 560-0027 Clerk to the Board of County Commissioners
County organized 1881 from Orange and Wake counties
Land records: Contact Mrs. Ruth Garrett, Register of Deeds
Vital records: Deaths; contact Dr. John

D. Fletcher, Public Health Director, 414 East Main Street, Durham, NC 27701. Marriages; contact Register of Deeds

Probate records: Contact James Leo Carr, Clerk of Court

No probate search service; copies: $1.00 for the first page and 25¢ for each additional page, $5.00 minimum

*Edgecombe County Courthouse
Tarboro, NC 27886
Phone (919) 823-6161
County organized 1735 from Bertie County

Probate records: Old wills in book in Clerk's handwriting back to 1760 (originals in Department of Archives and History, Raleigh, NC), estate records from 1945

No probate search service; copies: $1.00 for the first page and 25¢ for each additional page, no minimum; "No copies can be made from old will books; we refer requests for old records to the Department of Archives and History."

*Forsyth County Hall of Justice
Winston-Salem, NC 27101
Phone (910) 727-2797; (910) 727-2903 Register of Deeds
County organized 1849 from Stokes County

Land records: Contact L. E. Speas, Register of Deeds, Hall of Justice, Room 208, PO Box 20639, Winston-Salem, North Carolina 27120-0639

Vital records: Births and deaths from 1913 to date, marriage licenses from 1849 to date; contact Register of Deeds

No vital records search service; copies: 50¢ each, $3.00 for certified copies

*Franklin County Courthouse
102 South Main Street
Louisburg, NC 27549-2523
Phone (919) 496-5104
County organized 1779 from Bute County, which was discontinued at that time

Probate records: Wills from 1776; contact Clerk of Court

No probate search service; copies: $1.00 for the first page and 25¢ for each additional page

*Gaston County Courthouse
PO Box 1578
Gastonia, NC 28053-1578
Phone (704) 866-3181, Register of Deeds; (704) 868-5800 County Clerk's Office
County organized 1846 from Lincoln County

Land records: From 1847; contact Register of Deeds

No land records search service; copies: 50¢ each

Naturalization records: No naturalization records

Vital records: From 1913; contact Register of Deeds

No vital records search service; certified copies: $3.00 each

Probate records: Contact County Clerk's Office, Gastonia, NC 28053

Gates County Courthouse
Gatesville, NC 27938
Phone (919) 357-1240
County organized 1778 from Chowan, Hertford and Perquimans counties

Glasgow County
(see Greene County)

Graham County Courthouse
PO Box 575
Robbinsville, NC 28771-0575
Phone (704) 479-3361
County organized 1872 from Cherokee County

*Granville County Courthouse
Oxford, NC 27565
Phone (919) 693-2649; (919) 693-6314 Register of Deeds
County organized 1746 from Edgecombe County

Land records: From 1746; contact Shirley E. Ford, Register of Deeds, PO Box 427, Oxford, NC 27565; copies: only available from 1900

Vital records: Births and deaths from 1913 to date (plus delayed births), and marriages from 1869 to date; contact Register of Deeds

No vital records search service

Probate records: Contact Clerk of Court's Office, PO Box 219, Oxford, NC 27565-0219

No probate search service; copies: 50¢ per legal-sized page, 25¢ per letter-sized page, no minimum

*Greene County Courthouse
PO Box 675
Snow Hill, NC 28580-0675
Phone (919) 747-3505
County organized 1791 from Dobbs County, when Dobbs County was dissolved and divided between Greene and Lenoir counties; name changed from Glasgow County in 1799

Land records: Yes
Naturalization records: Yes
Vital records: Yes
Probate records: Yes

*Guilford County Courthouse
PO Box 3427
Greensboro, NC 27402
Phone (919) 373-7556 Register of Deeds
County organized 1770 from Rowan and Orange counties

Land records: Deeds from 1771; contact Register of Deeds, PO Box 3427, Greensboro, NC 27402

Naturalization records: No naturalization records

Vital records: Births and deaths from 1913, marriages from 1865; contact Register of Deeds; copies: 50¢ each

Probate records: Contact County Clerk of Court's Office

Halifax County Courthouse
PO Box 66
Halifax, NC 27839
Phone (919) 583-5061
County organized 1758 from Edgecombe County

*Harnett County Courthouse
East Front Street
Lillington, NC 27546
Phone (910) 893-7540 Register of Deeds; (910) 893-5164 Clerk of Superior Court
County organized 1855 from Cumberland County

Land records: Contact Register of Deeds, PO Box 279, Lillington, NC 27546

Naturalization records: No naturalization records

Vital records: Contact Register of Deeds

Probate records: From 1920; contact Clerk of Superior Court, PO Box 849, Lillington, NC 27546

No probate search service

*Haywood County Courthouse
420 North Main Street
Waynesville, NC 28786
Phone (704) 452-6625
County organized 1808 from Buncombe County

Land records: From 1808; contact Register of Deeds Office

Vital records: Births and deaths from 1913, marriages from 1850; contact Register of Deeds Office

Henderson County Courthouse
244 Second Avenue, East
Hendersonville, NC 28739
Phone (704) 697-4808
County organized 1838 from Buncombe County

*Hertford County Courthouse
Winton, NC 27986
Phone (919) 358-7845
County organized 1759 from Chowan, Bertie and Northampton counties

Probate records: Contact Richart T. Vann,
Clerk of the Superior Court, PO Box
86, Winton, NC 27986

Probate search service: no charge;
copies: $1.00 for the first page and
25¢ for each additional page, $1.00
for certification; "The Hertford
County Court House burned down
twice, about 1830 and again in 1862;
our resources are limited except for
some old wills that were recopied and
put on record many years after the
death of a person."

Hoke County Courthouse
PO Box 410
Raeford, NC 28376
Phone (919) 875-8751
*County organized 1911 from
Cumberland and Robeson counties*

*Hyde County Courthouse
Swan Quarter, NC 27885
Phone (919) 926-3011 Register of Deeds;
(919) 926-4101 Clerk of Superior
Court
*County organized 1705 from Bath
District; name changed from
Wickham County in 1712*
Land records: Contact Register of Deeds,
PO Box 294, Swan Quarter, NC
27885
Vital records: Contact Register of Deeds
Probate records: Wills from late 1700s,
administration records from 1900s;
contact Clerk of Superior Court, PO
Box 337, Swan Quarter, NC 27885
No probate search service; copies: $1.00
for the first page and 25¢ for each
additional page, $1.00 minimum

*Iredell County Courthouse
PO Box 788
Statesville, NC 27677-0788
Phone (704) 878-3000
*County organized 1788 from Rowan
County*
Land records: Contact Register of Deeds,
PO Box 904, Statesville, NC 28687
Vital records: Births and deaths from
1915, marriages from 1855; contact
Register of Deeds; copies: "Earlier
records are in poor shape and cannot
be copied; originals are in North
Carolina Archives."

***Jackson County Justice and
Administration Center**
401 Grindstaff Cove Road
Sylva, NC 28779
Phone (704) 586-4055
*County organized 1851 from Haywood
and Macon counties*
Land records: From 1851; copies: 50¢
per page
Vital records: From 1913; copies: 50¢
per page

*Johnston County Courthouse
Smithfield, NC 27577-1049
Phone (919) 989-5160 Register of Deeds;
(919) 934-3191 Clerk of the Superior
Court
*County organized 1746 from Craven
County*
Land records: From 1600 to 1700s;
contact Phyllis N. Wall, Register of
Deeds, County Courthouse, PO Box
118, Smithfield, NC 27577; copies:
50¢ per page, $1.00 per map
Vital records: Births and deaths from
1913, marriages from 1600s; contact
Register of Deeds
Probate records: From late 1700s; contact
Will R. Crocker, Clerk of the Superior
Court, PO Box 297, Smithfield, NC
27577
No probate search service; copies: $1.00
for the first page and 25¢ for each
additional page, no minimum

*Jones County Courthouse
Jones and Market Streets
PO Box 280
Trenton, NC 28585
Phone (919) 448-7571
*County organized 1778 from Craven
County*
Land records: Yes
Naturalization records: Yes
Vital records: Yes
Probate records: Yes

*Lee County Courthouse
1400 South Horner Boulevard
Sanford, NC 27331
Phone (919) 774-4821 Register of Deeds;
(919) 708-4400 Clerk of Superior
Court
*County organized 1907 from Chatham
and Moore counties*
Land records: Contact Register of Deeds
Probate records: Contact County Clerk of
Superior Court
No probate search service; copies: $1.00
for the first page and 25¢ for each
additional page, no minimum

*Lenoir County Courthouse
130 South Queen Street
Kinston, NC 28501-4934
Phone (919) 523-2390
*County organized 1791 from Dobbs and
Craven counties, when Dobbs County
was dissolved and divided between
Greene and Lenoir counties*
Land records: Deeds, deeds of trust,
leases, etc.; contact Register of Deeds,
PO Box 3289, Kinston, NC 28502;
copies: $1.00 per page
Vital records: Births and deaths from
1914, marriages from 1873; contact
Register of Deeds

*Lincoln County Courthouse
Lincolnton, NC 28092
Phone (704) 732-3361
*County organized 1778 from Tyron
County, which was organized in 1768
and abolished in 1779*
Land records: Yes
Naturalization records: No naturalization
records
Vital records: Yes
Probate records: Yes
Probate search service: no charge;
copies: 50¢ per page, no minimum

*Macon County Courthouse
5 West Main Street
Franklin, NC 28734-3005
Phone (704) 524-6421, ext. 218, 219,
220, 221, 321 Register of Deeds
*County organized 1828 from Haywood
County*
Land records: From 1828; contact
Register of Deeds
Vital records: From 1 October 1913

*Madison County Courthouse
Marshall, NC 28753
Phone (704) 649-2531
*County organized 1851 from Yancey
and Buncombe counties*
Land records: Contact Register of Deeds,
PO Box 66, Marshall, NC 28753
Naturalization records: Contact Register
of Deeds
Vital records: Contact Register of Deeds
Probate records: Contact Register of
Deeds

*Martin County Governmental Center
PO Box 668
Williamston, NC 27892-0668
Phone (919) 792-1901 County Marriages
Office; (919) 792-1683 Register of
Deeds
*County organized 1774 from Tyrrell and
Halifax counties*
Land records: Real estate from 1771;
contact Mrs. Tina P. Manning,
Register of Deeds, PO Box 348,
Williamston, NC 27892; copies: 25¢
each
Vital records: Births and deaths from
1913 (many delayed birth certificates
which are before that time), marriages
from 1872; contact Register of Deeds
Probate records: Contact Mrs. Phyllis G.
Pearson, Clerk of the Superior Court,
PO Box 807, Williamston, NC 27892
No probate search service; copies: 25¢
each

*McDowell County Courthouse
1 South Main Street
Marion, NC 28752
Phone (704) 652-4727 Register of Deeds

County organized 1842 from Burke and Rutherford counties
Land records: Contact Marjorie C. McEntire, Register of Deeds
Naturalization records: No naturalization records
Vital records: Contact Register of Deeds
Probate records: Contact Clerk of Superior Court

Mecklenburg County Courthouse
PO Box 31787
Charlotte, NC 28231-1787
Phone (704) 342-6233
County organized 1762 from Anson County

*Mitchell County Courthouse
PO Box 354
Bakersville, NC 28705-0354
Phone (704) 688-2139
County organized 1861 from Burke, Caldwell, Yancey, McDowell and Watauga counties
Land records: Yes
Naturalization records: No naturalization records
Vital records: Yes
Probate records: Yes
No probate search service; copies: 25¢ per page, no minimum

*Montgomery County Courthouse
PO Box 425
Troy, NC 27371-0425
Phone (919) 576-4221
County organized 1778 from Anson County
Land records: Yes
Naturalization records: Yes
Vital records: Yes
Probate records: Yes

*Moore County Courthouse
Courthouse Square
Carthage, NC 28327
Phone (919) 947-5800
County organized 1784 from Cumberland County
Land records: Contact Register of Deeds, PO Box 1210, Carthage, NC 28327
Naturalization records: Contact Clerk of Court
Vital records: Contact Register of Deeds
Probate records: Contact Clerk of Court
No probate search service; copies: 50¢ per page

*Nash County Courthouse
Nashville, NC 27856-1255
Phone (919) 459-4141; (919) 459-9836 Register of Deeds
County organized 1777 from Edgecombe County
Land records: Deeds from 1777 to date;

contact Barbara W. Sasser, Register of Deeds
Vital records: Births from 1913 to date, deaths from 1911 to date, marriages from 1862 to date; contact Register of Deeds
Probate records: Wills and estates; contact Clerk of Court

New Hanover County Courthouse
320 Chestnut Street
Wilmington, NC 28401-4027
Phone (919) 341-7184
County organized 1729 from Bath and Clarendon districts

*Northampton County Courthouse
Main Street
Jackson, NC 27845
Phone (919) 534-2501
County organized 1741 from Bertie County
Land records: Contact PO Box 637, Jackson, NC 27845
Naturalization records: Contact Register of Deeds, PO Box 128, Jackson, NC 27845
Vital records: Contact Register of Deeds
Probate records: Contact Clerk of Court, Jefferson Street, Jackson, NC 27845

*Onslow County Courthouse
625 Court Street
Jacksonville, NC 28540-4797
Phone (910) 455-4458
County organized 1734 from Bath District
Land records: Contact Register of Deeds
Vital records: Contact Register of Deeds
Probate records: Contact Clerk of Superior Court
No probate search service; copies: $1.00 for the first copy and 25¢ for each additional page

*Orange County Courthouse
106 East Margaret Lane
Hillsborough, NC 27278-2546
Phone (919) 732-8181
County organized 1752 from the western portions of Bladen, Granville and Johnston counties
Land records: From 1754; contact Register of Deeds, Cameron Street, Hillsborough, NC 27278
Vital records: Births and deaths from 1913; marriage bonds from 1754
Probate records: From 1754; contact Joan Terry, Clerk of Superior court
No probate search service (must have book and page number of a specific document); copies: $1.00 for the first page and 25¢ for each additional page, $2.00 for certification

*Pamlico County Manager
PO Box 776
Bayboro, NC 28515-0776
Phone (919) 745-3133; (919) 745-4421 Register of Deeds; (919) 745-3881 Clerk of Court
County organized 1872 from Craven County; Lowland and Hobucken were in Beaufort County and were organized into Pamlico County in 1874
Land records: From 1872; contact Register of Deeds, PO Box 433, Bayboro, NC 28515
Vital records: Births and deaths from 1913, marriages from 1872; contact Register of Deeds
Probate records: Contact Clerk of Court

*Pasquotank County Courthouse
PO Box 39
Elizabeth City, NC 27909-0039
Phone (919) 335-0865; (919) 335-4367 Register of Deeds
County organized 1672 from Albemarle District
Land records: From 1700; contact Register of Deeds, PO Box 154, Elizabeth City, NC 27907; copies: 25¢ per 11" x 14" page, 50¢ per 14" x 17" page, $1.00 minimum
Vital records: Births and deaths from 1913 (a few born in city back to 1903), marriage licenses from 1867, marriage bonds from 1761 to 1866; contact Register of Deeds; copies: 25¢ each, $3.00 for certified copies, $1.00 minimum
Probate records: Contact North Carolina Department of Cultural Resources, Division of Archives and History, Raleigh, NC 27611

*Pender County Courthouse
PO Box 43
Burgaw, NC 28425
Phone (919) 259-1200
County organized 1875 from New Hanover County
Land records: Yes; copies: 25¢ each, $1.00 minimum
Naturalization records: No naturalization records
Vital records: Yes; certified copies: $3.00 each (must have proper authorization)

Perquimans County Courthouse
206 North Covent Garden
Hertford, NC 27944-1157
Phone (919) 426-5458
County organized 1672 from Albemarle District

Person County Courthouse
Roxboro, NC 27573
Phone (919) 599-0288

County organized 1791 from Caswell County

*Pitt County Courthouse
Third and Evans Streets
Greenville, NC 27834
Phone (919) 830-6302; (919) 830-6400
    Clerk Superior Court
County organized 1760 from Beaufort County
Land records: Contact Mrs. Annie G.
    Holder, Register of Deeds, PO Box
    64, Greenville, NC 27834
Vital records: Contact Register of Deeds
Probate records: From 1865; contact
    Miss Sandra Gaskins, Clerk Superior
    Court, PO Box 6067, Greenville, NC
    27835-6067
No probate search service; copies: $1.00
    for the first page and 25¢ for each
    additional page

*Polk County Courthouse
PO Box 308
Columbus, NC 28722-0308
Phone (704) 894-3301
County organized 1855 from Rutherford and Henderson counties
Land records: Yes
Naturalization records: Yes
Vital records: Yes
Probate records: Yes

*Randolph County Courthouse
145 Worth Street
Asheboro, NC 27203-5509
Phone (910) 318-6960
County organized 1779 from Guilford County
Land records: From 1779; contact Ann
    Shaw, Register of Deeds ("We do not
    have the time or personnel to do
    extensive genealogical research; I
    usually refer searchers to the
    Historical Society at the Asheboro
    Public Library, 201 Worth Street,
    Asheboro, NC 27203; they have a
    very elaborate set-up with copies of
    all of our records and more."); copies:
    50¢ per page plus SASE
Vital records: Births and deaths from
    1913, marriage bonds from 1779
Probate records: Contact Lynda B.
    Skeen, Clerk of Superior Court
No probate search service: "If someone
    needs this type of work done, they
    should contact the Randolph County
    Historical Society or hire a
    professional"; copies: $1.00 for the
    first page and 25¢ for each additional
    page, $1.00 minimum plus SASE

Richmond County Courthouse
Rockingham, NC 28379
County organized 1779 from Anson County

*Robeson County Courthouse
501 North Elm Street
Lumberton, NC 28358-5558
Phone (910) 671-3042
County organized 1786 from Bladen County
Land records: Deeds, deeds of trust, etc.;
    contact Joe B. Freeman, Register of
    Deeds, Box 22, Courthouse, Room
    102, Lumberton, NC 28358
No land records search service (contact
    Sam West, Rt. 5, Box 319,
    Lumberton, NC 28358); copies: 50¢
    each
Vital records: Contact Register of Deeds
    Office
Probate records: Contact Clerk of Court's
    Office
No probate search service

*Rockingham County Courthouse
PO Box 26
Wentworth, NC 27375-0026
Phone (910) 342-8820 Register of Deeds;
    (910) 342-8700 Clerk of Superior
    Court
County organized 1785 from Guilford County
Land records: From 1787; contact
    Ramona H. Page, Register of Deeds,
    PO Box 56, Wentworth, NC 27375
No land records search service (must
    have grantor, grantee, property
    involved and date of transaction);
    copies: 50¢ per page, $3.00 for the
    first certified page and $1.00 for each
    additional certified page, $1.00
    minimum
Vital records: Births and deaths from
    October 1913 (some delayed
    certificates for persons living in 1942
    and applying for registration),
    marriage licenses from 1868, marriage
    bond index to marriages on file in the
    Department of Archives and History
    in Raleigh; contact Register of Deeds.
    Marriage bonds from 1785 to 1868,
    marriage licenses from 1962; contact
    Archives of the North Carolina
    Historical Commission in Raleigh
No vital records search service from
    Register of Deeds (must have
    registrant's and parents' names and
    date and place of birth or registrant's
    name and date and place of death or
    names of bride and groom and date of
    marriage); copies available only to
    registrant, current spouse, sibling,
    child, parent, step-parent, grandparent
    or authorized agent)
Probate records: Cross index to wills
    from 1804, cross index to
    administrators and executors from
    1865, a book of old wills containing
    wills prior to 1804 ("A number of
    estate records are at the Archives in
    Raleigh"); contact North Carolina

State Archives, Department of
    Cultural Resources, Division of
    Archives and History, Archives and
    History—State Library Building, 109
    East Jones Street, Raleigh, NC 27601-
    2807
No probate search service

Rowan County Courthouse
202 North Main Street
Salisbury, NC 28144-4346
Phone (704) 636-0361
County organized 1753 from Anson County

*Rutherford County Courthouse
601 North Main Street
Rutherfordton, NC 28139-2511
Phone (704) 287-2211
County organized 1779 from Burke and Tyron counties, the latter of which was organized in 1768 and abolished in 1779
Land records: From the 1700s ("but we
    do not make copies of these very old
    records"); contact Register of Deeds,
    PO Box 551, Rutherfordton, NC
    28139
Vital records: Births and deaths from
    1913, marriages from 1700s; contact
    Register of Deeds
Probate records: Contact Clerk of Court,
    PO Box 630, Rutherfordton, NC
    28139

*Sampson County Courthouse
Main Street
Clinton, NC 28328
Phone (919) 592-6308
County organized 1784 from Duplin and New Hanover counties
Land records: From the mid-1700s;
    contact Mae H. Troublefield, Register
    of Deeds, (Courthouse, Main Street—
    location), PO Box 256 (mailing
    address), Clinton, NC 28328
No land records search service; copies:
    $2.00 per deed, $3.00 for certified
    copies
Naturalization records: No naturalization
    records
Vital records: Births and deaths from
    1913, and marriages from 1865;
    contact Register of Deeds; certified
    copies: $3.00 (identification needed to
    search vital records)
Probate records: Wills, estates and early
    court minutes; contact Clerk of
    Superior Court

*Scotland County Courthouse
PO Box 769
Laurinburg, NC 28353
Phone (919) 277-2575
County organized 1899 from Richmond County

Land records: Contact Jane P. Callahan, Register of Deeds
Naturalization records: Contact C. Whitfield Gibson, Clerk of Court
Vital records: Contact Register of Deeds
Probate records: Contact Clerk of Court

*Stanly County Courthouse
201 South Second Street
Albemarle, NC 28001-5747
Phone (704) 983-7204; (704) 982-2161 Clerk of Court
County organized 1841 from Montgomery County
Land records: From 1841; contact Cecil Almond, Register of Deeds, PO Box 97, Albemarle, NC 28002-0097
Naturalization records: No naturalization records
Vital records: Births and deaths from October 1913, marriages from mid-1800s
Probate records: Contact Clerk of Court
No probate search service; copies: $1.00 each, $1.00 minimum

*Stokes County Government Center
PO Box 20
Danbury, NC 27016
Phone (919) 593-2811
County organized 1798 from Surry County
Land records: Contact Register of Deeds, PO Box 67, Danbury, NC 27016
Vital records: Contact Register of Deeds
Probate records: Contact Clerk of Superior Court, PO Box 56, Danbury, NC 27016; copies: 25¢ per page

*Surry County Courthouse
Dobson, NC 27017
Phone (910) 386-9235 Register of Deeds; (910) 386-8131 Clerk of Superior Court
County organized 1770 from Rowan County
Land records: Contact Register of Deeds, PO Box 303, Dobson, NC 27017
Naturalization records: No naturalization records
Vital records: Contact Register of Deeds
Probate records: Contact Clerk of Superior Court, PO Box 345, Dobson, NC 27017

Swain County Courthouse
PO Box A
Bryson City, NC 28713-2001
Phone (704) 488-9273
County organized 1871 from Jackson and Macon counties

*Transylvania County Courthouse
12 East Main Street
Brevard, NC 28712

Phone (704) 884-3162 Register of Deeds
County organized 1861 from Jackson and Henderson counties
Land records: Deeds; contact Register of Deeds
Naturalization records: Contact Clerk of Court
Vital records: Births and deaths from 1914; contact Register of Deeds
Probate records: Wills; contact Clerk of Court
No probate search service; copies: 25¢ each, $3.00 for certified copies

*Tyrrell County Courthouse
PO Box 449
Columbia, NC 27925-0449
Phone (919) 796-2901
County organized 1729 from Albemarle District
Land records: Contact Register of Deeds; copies: 25¢ per page
Naturalization records: Contact Clerk of Court
Vital records: Contact Register of Deeds
Probate records: Contact Clerk of Court
Probate search service: no charge; copies: $1.00 for the first page and 25¢ for each additional page, no minimum

*Union County Courthouse
500 North Main Street
Monroe, NC 28110-4747
Phone (704) 283-3500
County organized 1842 from Mecklenburg and Anson counties
Land records: Contact Office of the Register of Deeds
Vital records: Contact Office of the Register of Deeds
Probate records: Contact Clerk of Superior Court
No probate search service

Vance County Courthouse
PO Box 2017
Henderson, NC 27536-2017
Phone (919) 492-2094
County organized 1881 from Franklin, Granville and Warren counties

*Wake County Courthouse
PO Box 550
Raleigh, NC 27602-0550
Phone (919) 755-6160
County organized 1770 from Cumberland, Johnston and Orange counties
Land records: Yes
Naturalization records: Yes
Vital records: Yes
Probate records: Yes

*Warren County Courthouse
109 South Main Street
Warrenton, NC 27589-1929
Phone (919) 257-3261
County organized 1779 from Bute County, which was discontinued at that time
Land records: From 1764; contact Register of Deeds, PO Box 506, Warrenton, NC 27589
Vital records: From 1913; contact Register of Deeds
Probate records: From 1764; contact Clerk of Court, PO Box 709, Warrenton, NC 27589
Probate search service: no charge for specific name; copies: $1.00 for the first page and 25¢ for each additional page, $1.00 minimum; "If search required, send as much information as possible."

*Washington County Courthouse
PO Box 1007
Plymouth, NC 27962-1007
Phone (919) 793-2325 Register of Deeds
County organized 1799 from Tyrrell County
Land records: Contact Elaine G. Davis, Register of Deeds
Naturalization records: No naturalization records
Vital records: Births and deaths from 1913, marriage index from 1851, marriage licenses from 1881; contact Register of Deeds; certified copies: $3.00 each (restricted to immediate family members)
Probate records: Contact Clerk of Court, PO Box 901, Plymouth, NC 27962
No probate search service; copies: 25¢ per page

*Watauga County Courthouse
842 West King Street
Boone, NC 28607
Phone (704) 265-8000; (704) 265-8052 Register of Deeds; (704) 265-5364 Clerk of Court
County organized 1849 from Ashe, Caldwell, Wilkes and Yancey counties
Land records: Contact Register of Deeds
Naturalization records: No naturalization records
Vital records: Contact Register of Deeds
Probate records: Contact Clerk of Court

*Wayne County Courthouse
224 East Walnut Street
Goldsboro, NC 27530
Phone (919) 731-1449
County organized 1779 from Craven and Dobbs counties
Land records: From 1779; contact Deborah C. Lane, Register of Deeds, PO Box 267, Goldsboro, NC 27533-0267

Naturalization records: Contact Clerk of
Court
Vital records: From November 1913;
contact Register of Deeds
Probate records: Contact Clerk of Court
Probate search service: no charge;
copies: $1.00 for the first page and
25¢ for each additional page, $1.00
minimum

Wickham County
(see Hyde County)

*Wilkes County Office Building
Wilkesboro, NC 28697
Phone (919) 651-7346
*County organized 1777 from Burke and
Surry counties*
Land records: Yes
Naturalization records: Yes
Vital records: Yes
Probate records: Yes

*Wilson County Courthouse
125 East Nash Street
Wilson, NC 27893
Phone (919) 399-2935
*County organized 1855 from
Edgecombe, Johnston, Wayne and
Nash counties*
Land records: From 1855; contact
Register of Deeds
Naturalization records: No naturalization
records
Vital records: Births and deaths from
1913, marriages from 1855; contact
Register of Deeds; copies: $1.00 each
for uncertified copies (available to
"anyone with a stamp stating certain
information), $3.00 each for certified
copies (restricted to parents, children,
spouse, siblings)

*Yadkin County Courthouse
Yadkinville, NC 27055
Phone (910) 679-8838
*County organized 1850 from Surry
County*
Probate records: Contact Clerk of Court,
PO Box 95, Yadkinville, NC 27055
No probate search service; copies: $1.00
for the first page and 25¢ for each
additional page

*Yancey County Courthouse
Burnsville, NC 28714
Phone (704) 682-6181 Register of Deeds;
(704) 682-2122 Clerk of Superior
Court
*County organized 1833 from Buncombe
and Burke counties*
Land records: Contact Register of Deeds,
Room #4

Naturalization records: No naturalization
records
Vital records: Contact Register of Deeds
Probate records: Contact Clerk of Court
No probate search service; copies: $1.00
for the first page and 25¢ for each
additional page, $1.00 minimum

NORTH DAKOTA

*Capital: Bismarck. Statehood: 2 Novem-
ber 1889 (part of Dakota Territory in 1861,
separated from South Dakota in 1889)*

Court System

North Dakota has several Municipal
Courts of limited jurisdiction. The North
Dakota County Courts used to handle some
civil actions, misdemeanors, preliminary
hearings, mental health cases, probate,
guardianship and small claims. As of 1
January 1995 the County Courts were
consolidated with the District Courts. The
District Courts have general jurisdiction but
do not sit at each county seat. East Central
Judicial District: Cass, Steele and Traill
counties at Fargo; Northeast Judicial Dis-
trict: Benson, Bottineau, Cavalier,
McHenry, Pembina, Pierce, Ramsey,
Renville, Rolette, Towner and Walsh coun-
ties at Devils Lake, Grafton and Rugby;
Northeast Central Judicial District: Grand
Forks, Griggs and Nelson counties at Grand
Forks; Northwest Judicial District: Burke,
Divide, McKenzie, Mountrail, Ward and
Williams counties at Minot and Williston;
South Central Judicial District: Burleigh,
Emmons, Grant, Kidder, Logan, McIntosh,
McLean, Mercer, Morton, Oliver, Sheridan,
Sioux and Wells counties at Bismarck,
Linton and Mandan; Southeast Judicial
District: Barnes, Dickey, Eddy, Foster, La
Moure, Ransom, Richland, Sargent and
Stutsman counties at Jamestown, Valley
City and Wahpeton; Southwest Judicial
District: Adams, Billings, Bowman, Dunn,
Golden Valley, Hettinger, Slope and Stark
counties at Dickinson and Hettinger. The
state's Supreme Court is the court of last
resort.

Courthouses

*Adams County Courthouse
Hettinger, ND 58639
Phone (701) 567-2460
*County organized 1885 from Stark
County*
Land records: From 1907
Naturalization records: Contact State
Archives and Historical Research
Library, State Historical Society of
North Dakota, North Dakota Heritage
Center, 612 East Boulevard Avenue,
Bismarck, ND 58505
Probate records: From 1907

Probate search service: no charge; copies: 25¢ per page, no minimum

Barnes County Courthouse
Valley City, ND 58072
Phone (701) 845-0708
County organized 1875 from Cass County

*Benson County Courthouse
Minnewaukan, ND 58351
Phone (701) 473-5332 Register of Deeds; (701) 473-5345 Clerk of District Court
County organized 1883 from Ramsey County
Land records: Contact Register of Deeds
Naturalization records: Contact State Archives and Historical Research Library, State Historical Society of North Dakota, North Dakota Heritage Center, 612 East Boulevard Avenue, Bismarck, ND 58505
Vital records: Contact Clerk of District Court
Probate records: Contact Clerk of District Court
Probate search service: no charge; copies: $1.00 per document, no minimum; "Pre-payment required before copies are mailed."

*Billings County Courthouse
Medora, ND 58645
Phone (701) 623-4491
County organized 1879 from unorganized territory
Land records: From 1886; contact Registrar
Naturalization records: Contact State Archives and Historical Research Library, State Historical Society of North Dakota, North Dakota Heritage Center, 612 East Boulevard Avenue, Bismarck, ND 58505
Vital records: Births from 1904, deaths from 1909 (both very incomplete)
Probate records: From 1896
Probate search service: no charge; copies: 50¢ per page, no minimum

*Bottineau County Courthouse
Bottineau, ND 58318
Phone (701) 228-3983; (701) 228-2786 Register of Deeds
County organized 1873 from unorganized territory
Land records: Contact Register of Deeds, 314 West Fifth Street, Bottineau, ND 58318; copies: $1.00 for each five pages or part thereof, $5.00 for the first two certified pages and $2.00 for each additional certified page
Naturalization records: Contact State Archives and Historical Research Library, State Historical Society of

North Dakota, North Dakota Heritage Center, 612 East Boulevard Avenue, Bismarck, ND 58505
Vital records: Incomplete vital records before 1944; contact Clerk of Courts
Probate records: From 1884; contact Clerk of Courts
Probate search service: no charge; copies: 25¢ per page, no minimum

Bowman County Courthouse
Bowman, ND 58623
Phone (701) 523-3450
County organized 1883 from Billings County

*Burke County Courthouse
PO Box 219
Bowbells, ND 58721
Phone (701) 377-2718; (701) 377-2020 FAX
County organized 1910 from Ward County
Land records: Contact Register of Deeds
Naturalization records: Contact State Archives and Historical Research Library, State Historical Society of North Dakota, North Dakota Heritage Center, 612 East Boulevard Avenue, Bismarck, ND 58505
Vital records: Marriages from 1910; contact Clerk of Court; copies: not available
Probate records: From 1910; contact Clerk of Court
Probate search service: no charge; copies: 50¢ per page, no minimum

*Burleigh County Courthouse
PO Box 5518
Bismarck, ND 58502-5518
Phone (701) 222-6711
County organized 1873 from Buffalo County, which was discontinued
Land records: Contact Registrar of Deeds
Naturalization records: No naturalization records
Vital records: Contact Clerk of District Court
Probate records: Contact Clerk of District Court
No probate search service; copies: 20¢ per page, no minimum

*Cass County Courthouse
207 Ninth Street, South
Fargo, ND 58103-1823
Phone (701) 241-5660 Clerk of District Court
County organized 1873, original county
Vital records: Marriage licenses from 24 March 1872; contact Linda J. Rogers, Clerk of District Court
Probate records: Probate and guardianship records from January 1899; contact Clerk of District Court

Probate search service: no charge; copies: 25¢ per page, $5.00 per certified page, no minimum

Cavalier County Courthouse
Langdon, ND 58249
Phone (701) 256-2124
County organized 1873 from Pembina County

*Dickey County Courthouse
309 North Second Street
Ellendale, ND 58436
Phone (701) 349-3249
County organized 1881 from La Moure County
Land records: Contact Register of Deeds
Naturalization records: Contact State Archives and Historical Research Library, State Historical Society of North Dakota, North Dakota Heritage Center, 612 East Boulevard Avenue, Bismarck, ND 58505
Vital records: Contact Clerk of District Court
Probate records: Contact Clerk of District Court
Probate search service: no charge; copies: $5.00 each, $5.00 minimum

*Divide County Register of Deeds-Clerk of Court
PO Box 68
Crosby, ND 58730-0068
Phone (701) 965-6831
County organized 1910 from Williams County
Land records: Contact Shirley Peterman, Register of Deeds
Naturalization records: Contact State Archives and Historical Research Library, State Historical Society of North Dakota, North Dakota Heritage Center, 612 East Boulevard Avenue, Bismarck, ND 58505
Vital records: Copies on file, but certified copies must be issued by state office
Probate records: Contact Shirley Peterman, Clerk of Court
Probate search service: no charge; copies: 25¢ per page, no minimum

Dunn County Courthouse
Manning, ND 58642
Phone (701) 573-4447
County organized 1883 from Howard County, which was discontinued

*Eddy County Courthouse
524 Central Avenue
New Rockford, ND 58356-1698
Phone (701) 947-2434
County organized 1885 from Foster County
Land records: Contact W. Jane Dunham,

Register of Deeds; certified copies: $5.00 each

Naturalization records: Contact State Archives and Historical Research Library, State Historical Society of North Dakota, North Dakota Heritage Center, 612 East Boulevard Avenue, Bismarck, ND 58505

Vital records: Contact W. Jane Dunham, Clerk of District Court

Probate records: Contact W. Jane Dunham, Clerk of District Court

Probate search service: $5.00 per certificate per person; copies: $1.00 per page out of records

*Emmons County Courthouse

Linton, ND 58552

Phone (701) 254-4812

County organized 1879 from unorganized territory

Land records: From August 1890; contact Clerk of Court, PO Box 905, Linton, ND 58552

Naturalization records: Contact State Archives and Historical Research Library, State Historical Society of North Dakota, North Dakota Heritage Center, 612 East Boulevard Avenue, Bismarck, ND 58505

Vital records: From 1903

Probate records: From 28 June 1884

Probate search service: 25¢ per person; copies: $1.00 per document, $5.00 for certified copies of documents, $1.00 minimum

*Foster County Courthouse

Carrington, ND 58421

Phone (701) 652-2441

County organized 1883 from Dakota Territory

Land records: Contact Auditor, PO Box 104, Carrington, ND 58421

Naturalization records: Contact Clerk of Court, PO Box 257, Carrington, ND 58421

Vital records: Contact Clerk of Court

Probate records: Contact Clerk of Court

*Golden Valley County Courthouse

PO Box 596

Beach, ND 58621

Phone (701) 872-4352

County organized 1912 from Billings County

Land records: Contact Register of Deeds

Naturalization records: Contact State Archives and Historical Research Library, State Historical Society of North Dakota, North Dakota Heritage Center, 612 East Boulevard Avenue, Bismarck, ND 58505

Probate records: Contact District Court

Probate search service: $5.00; copies: 25¢ per uncertified page, $5.00 per

certified document; "Any other problems, contact the District Court Administrator's Office, PO Box 1507, Dickinson, ND 58602-1507."

*Grand Forks District Court

PO Box 5939

Grand Forks, ND 58206-5939

Phone (701) 780-8238; (701) 780-8200 Auditor's Office

County organized 1873 from Pembina County

Land records: Contact Register of Deeds, PO Box 6, Grand Forks, ND 58206-0006; copies: $1.00 per page from paper originals, $2.00 per page from microform originals

Naturalization records: Contact State Archives and Historical Research Library, State Historical Society of North Dakota, North Dakota Heritage Center, 612 East Boulevard Avenue, Bismarck, ND 58505

Vital records: No vital records

Probate records: Contact Clerk of District Court, PO Box 5979, Grand Forks, ND 58206

Probate search service: $5.00; certified copies: $5.00 each

*Grant County Courthouse

Carson, ND 58529

Phone (701) 622-3615

County organized 1916 from Morton County

Land records: Contact Register of Deeds

Naturalization records: Contact Clerk of Court

Vital records: Contact Clerk of Court

Probate records: Contact Clerk of Court

No probate search service; copies: $5.00 for the first page and $2.00 for each additional page

*Griggs County Courthouse

PO Box 326

Cooperstown, ND 58425-0326

Phone (701) 797-2772

County organized 1881 from Foster County

Land records: Contact Register of Deeds, PO Box 237, Cooperstown, ND 58425

Naturalization records: Contact State Archives and Historical Research Library, State Historical Society of North Dakota, North Dakota Heritage Center, 612 East Boulevard Avenue, Bismarck, ND 58505

Vital records: From 1902 to 1943; contact Clerk of Court (must know the *place* of residence at birth or death—township, city—no alpha listings)

Probate records: Contact Clerk of Court

Probate search service: $5.00; copies: 25¢ per page, $5.00 for certified copies, minimum depends on circumstances; "No phone calls."

*Hettinger County Courthouse

Mott, ND 58646

Phone (701) 824-2545

County organized 1883 from Stark County

Land records: Contact Courthouse

Naturalization records: Contact State Archives and Historical Research Library, State Historical Society of North Dakota, North Dakota Heritage Center, 612 East Boulevard Avenue, Bismarck, ND 58505

Probate records: Contact Courthouse

Probate search service: $3.00; copies: 25¢ per page, no minimum

*Kidder County Courthouse

PO Box 66

Steele, ND 58482

Phone (701) 475-2672

County organized 1873 from Buffalo County, which was discontinued

Land records: Contact Alice Grove, Register of Deeds/Clerk of Court

Land records search service: $5.00

Naturalization records: Contact State Archives and Historical Research Library, State Historical Society of North Dakota, North Dakota Heritage Center, 612 East Boulevard Avenue, Bismarck, ND 58505

Probate records: Contact Register of Deeds/Clerk of Court

Probate search service: $5.00

*La Moure County Courthouse

La Moure, ND 58458

Phone (701) 883-4295; (701) 883-5304 Register of Deeds; (701) 883-5193 Clerk of Court

County organized 1873 from Pembina County

Land records: Contact Register of Deeds, PO Box 156, La Moure, ND 58458

Naturalization records: Contact State Archives and Historical Research Library, State Historical Society of North Dakota, North Dakota Heritage Center, 612 East Boulevard Avenue, Bismarck, ND 58505

Vital records: Contact Clerk of Court, PO Box 5, La Moure, ND 58458

Probate records: Contact Clerk of Court

Probate search service: $5.00 (include as much information as possible; copies: 10¢ per page, $5.00 for certified copies, no minimum

*Logan County Register of Deeds and Clerk of Court

PO Box 6

Napoleon, ND 58561-0006

Phone (701) 754-2751; (701) 754-2270

County organized 1873 from Buffalo County, which was discontinued

Land records: Contact Register of Deeds

Naturalization records: Contact State Archives and Historical Research Library, State Historical Society of North Dakota, North Dakota Heritage Center, 612 East Boulevard Avenue, Bismarck, ND 58505

Vital records: Marriages; copies: $1.00 each, $5.00 for certified copies

Probate records: Contact Clerk of Court

Probate search service: no charge; copies: $1.00 per page, $5.00 for certified copies, no minimum

*McHenry County Courthouse
407 Main Street, South
PO Box 57
Towner, ND 58788
Phone (701) 537-5729
County organized 1873 from Buffalo County, which was discontinued and whose records are in McHenry County; county organized by election on second Tuesday in May 1885

Land records: Patents, deeds and mortgages from 1800 to date; contact Register of Deeds; copies $1.00 per document

Naturalization records: Contact State Archives and Historical Research Library, State Historical Society of North Dakota, North Dakota Heritage Center, 612 East Boulevard Avenue, Bismarck, ND 58505

Probate records: Contact Clerk of Court

Probate search service: no charge; copies: $1.00 each, $1.00 minimum

*McIntosh County Courthouse
112 Northeast First
Ashley, ND 58413-0179
Phone (701) 288-3450
County organized 1883 from Logan County

Land records: Contact Register of Deeds

Naturalization records: Contact State Archives and Historical Research Library, State Historical Society of North Dakota, North Dakota Heritage Center, 612 East Boulevard Avenue, Bismarck, ND 58505

Vital records: Births, deaths and marriages; contact Gideon Becker, Clerk of District Court

Probate records: Contact Clerk of District Court

Probate search service: $5.00 per name for a written response; copies: 15¢ per page, $5.00 for certified copies, $2.00 minimum for mailing out a plain copy

*McKenzie County Courthouse
PO Box 543
Watford City, ND 58854-0543
Phone (701) 842-3451
County organized 1883 from Howard County, which was discontinued

*McLean County Courthouse
PO Box 1108
Washburn, ND 58577
Phone (701) 462-8541; (701) 462-3542 FAX
County organized 1883 from Stevens County

Land records: Contact Dwayne Oster, Register of Deeds

Naturalization records: Contact Mary Ann Anderson, Clerk of Court

Vital records: Contact Clerk of Court

Probate records: Contact Clerk of Court

*Mercer County Courthouse
PO Box 39
Stanton, ND 58571-0039
Phone (701) 745-3292
County organized 1875 from original territory; first records 30 August 1884

Land records: Contact Register of Deeds

Naturalization records: Contact State Archives and Historical Research Library, State Historical Society of North Dakota, North Dakota Heritage Center, 612 East Boulevard Avenue, Bismarck, ND 58505

Probate records: Contact Clerk of District Court

Probate search service: $5.00; copies: 25¢ to $1.00 depending on what it is, $5.00 each for certified copies, 25¢ minimum; "Postage prepaid."

Morton County Courthouse
210 Second Avenue, N.W.
Mandan, ND 58554-3124
Phone (701) 667-3355
County organized 1873 from original territory

*Mountrail County Courthouse
PO Box 69
Stanley, ND 58784
Phone (701) 628-2915; (701) 628-2945 Register of Deeds
County organized 25 January 1909 from Ward County

Land records: Contact Delores M. Marmon, Register of Deeds; copies: $1.00 for each two-page recorded document

Naturalization records: Contact State Archives and Historical Research Library, State Historical Society of North Dakota, North Dakota Heritage Center, 612 East Boulevard Avenue, Bismarck, ND 58505

Vital records: From 1909; contact Debra M. Nichols, Clerk of Court

Probate records: From 1909; contact Clerk of Court

Probate search service: no charge; copies: 25¢ per page, $5.00 for certified copies, no minimum

*Nelson County Clerk of Court/ Register of Deeds
PO Box 565
Lakota, ND 58344
Phone (701) 247-2462
County organized 1883 from Foster and Grand Forks counties

Land records: Contact Register of Deeds

Naturalization records: Contact State Archives and Historical Research Library, State Historical Society of North Dakota, North Dakota Heritage Center, 612 East Boulevard Avenue, Bismarck, ND 58505

Vital records: Contact Clerk of Court

Probate records: Contact Clerk of Court

Probate search service: $1.00; copies: 25¢ per page

Oliver County Courthouse
PO Box 166
Center, ND 58530-0166
Phone (701) 794-8748
County organized 1885 from Mercer County

Pembina County Courthouse
PO Box 160
Cavalier, ND 58220-0160
Phone (701) 265-8411
County organized 1867 from Indian lands

*Pierce County Courthouse
240 S.E. Second Street
Rugby, ND 58368-1830
Phone (701) 776-5206 Register of Deeds; (701) 776-6161 Clerk of Court
County organized 1887 from parts of Rolette, Bottineau and McHenry counties and all of De Smet County, annexed part of Church County in 1891

Land records: From 1889; contact Register of Deeds

Naturalization records: No naturalization records

Vital records: From 1943; contact Clerk of Court

Probate records: From 1889; contact Clerk of Court

Probate search service: $5.00 per name; copies: 15¢ per page

Ramsey County Courthouse
1029 Fourth Street
Devils Lake, ND 58301-2701
Phone (701) 662-7069
County organized 1873 from Pembina County

*Ransom County Courthouse
PO Box 668
Lisbon, ND 58054
Phone (701) 683-5823, ext. 20; (701) 683-5827 FAX

County organized 1873 from Pembina County
Land records: Contact Register of Deeds
Naturalization records: Contact State Archives and Historical Research Library, State Historical Society of North Dakota, North Dakota Heritage Center, 612 East Boulevard Avenue, Bismarck, ND 58505
Vital records: Marriage licenses; contact Clerk of District Court, PO Box 626, Lisbon, ND 58054
Probate records: Contact Clerk of District Court
Probate search service: no charge; copies: 20¢ per page

*Renville County Courthouse
PO Box 68
Mohall, ND 58761-0068
Phone (701) 756-6398
County organized 1873 from Pembina County
Land records: From 1910; contact Register of Deeds
Naturalization records: Contact State Archives and Historical Research Library, State Historical Society of North Dakota, North Dakota Heritage Center, 612 East Boulevard Avenue, Bismarck, ND 58505
Vital records: Township vital records from 1900 to about 1935, county vital records from 1935 (also at State Capitol)
Probate records: From 1910
Probate search service: no charge; copies: $1.00 per page, no minimum

Richland County Courthouse
418 Second Avenue North
Wahpeton, ND 58075
Phone (701) 642-7700
County organized 1873, original county

*Rolette County Courthouse
102 N.E. Second
Rolla, ND 58367
Phone (701) 477-3816
County organized 1873 from Buffalo County, which was discontinued (no population in 1880 census); county established 1884 or 1885
Land records: Contact Register of Deeds, PO Box 276, Rolla, ND 58367
Naturalization records: Contact State Archives and Historical Research Library, State Historical Society of North Dakota, North Dakota Heritage Center, 612 East Boulevard Avenue, Bismarck, ND 58505
Probate records: Contact Greta Monette, Clerk of Court, PO Box 460, Rolla, ND 58367
Probate search service: no charge; copies: 25¢ per page, $5.00 for the

first certified copy and $2.00 for each additional certified copy

*Sargent County Courthouse
PO Box 98
Forman, ND 58032-0098
Phone (701) 724-6241
County organized 1883 from Ransom County
Land records: Contact Register of Deeds, PO Box 176, Forman, ND 58032
Naturalization records: Contact State Archives and Historical Research Library, State Historical Society of North Dakota, North Dakota Heritage Center, 612 East Boulevard Avenue, Bismarck, ND 58505
Probate records: Contact Clerk of Court, PO Box 176, Forman, ND 58032
Probate search service: no charge; copies: 10¢ per page, no minimum

*Sheridan County Courthouse
PO Box 668
McClusky, ND 58463-0668
Phone (701) 363-2207
County organized 1873 from Buffalo County, which was discontinued
Land records: From 1909; contact Register of Deeds ("If asking for copies of deeds, mortgages, etc., please give complete description of land as to section, township and range.")
Naturalization records: Contact State Archives and Historical Research Library, State Historical Society of North Dakota, North Dakota Heritage Center, 612 East Boulevard Avenue, Bismarck, ND 58505
Vital records: Marriage licenses; copies: $1.00 each
Probate records: From 1909; contact Clerk of Court
Probate search service: no charge; copies: 25¢ per page or $1.00 per instrument if copy of a recording

*Sioux County Courthouse
Fort Yates, ND 58538
Phone (701) 854-3853
County organized 1915 from the Standing Rock Indian Reservation
Land records: Contact Register of Deeds
Naturalization records: No naturalization records
Vital records: No vital records
Probate records: Yes
Probate search service: $5.00; copies: 25¢ per page, no minimum

*Slope County Courthouse
PO Box NN
Amidon, ND 58620-0449
Phone (701) 879-6276

County organized 1915 from Billings County
Land records: Yes
Naturalization records: Contact State Archives and Historical Research Library, State Historical Society of North Dakota, North Dakota Heritage Center, 612 East Boulevard Avenue, Bismarck, ND 58505
Vital records: Not many births and deaths, some marriages
Probate records: Yes
Probate search service: $5.00; copies: $1.00 per page, no minimum; "SASE is always appreciated."

*Stark County Courthouse
PO Box 130
Dickinson, ND 58602-0130
Phone (701) 225-3211
County organized 1879 from unorganized territory
Land records: Contact Register of Deeds
Naturalization records: Contact Clerk of District Court
Vital records: Contact Clerk of District Court
Probate records: Contact Clerk of District Court
No probate search service; copies: 25¢ per page, no minimum

*Steele County Courthouse
Finley, ND 58230
Phone (701) 524-2790
County organized 1883 from Griggs County
Land records: Yes
Naturalization records: Yes
Vital records: Yes
Probate records: Yes

*Stutsman County Courthouse
511 Second Avenue, S.E.
Jamestown, ND 58401-4210
Phone (701) 252-9034 Register of Deeds; (701) 525-9042 Vital Statistics
County organized 1873 from Pembina County
Land records: From 1883; contact Karen Samek, Register of Deeds; copies: $1.00 each
Naturalization records: Contact State Archives and Historical Research Library, State Historical Society of North Dakota, North Dakota Heritage Center, 612 East Boulevard Avenue, Bismarck, ND 58505
Vital records: Births and deaths from 1882. Marriages; contact Clerk of District Court; copies from Clerk of District Court: $5.00 each
Probate records: From 1879; contact Clerk of District Court
Probate search service: no charge; copies: $5.00 each

Towner County Courthouse
Cando, ND 58324
Phone (701) 968-3424
County organized 1883 from Rolette
County

*Traill County Courthouse
Hillsboro, ND 58045
Phone (701) 436-4457 Register of Deeds;
(701) 436-4454 Clerk of Court
County organized 1875 from Grand
Forks County
Land records: Contact Register of Deeds,
PO Box 399, Hillsboro, ND 58045
Naturalization records: Contact State
Archives and Historical Research
Library, State Historical Society of
North Dakota, North Dakota Heritage
Center, 612 East Boulevard Avenue,
Bismarck, ND 58505
Vital records: From the 1900s; contact
Clerk of Court, PO Box 805,
Hillsboro, ND 58045
Probate records: Contact Clerk of Court

*Walsh County Courthouse
600 Cooper Avenue
Grafton, ND 58237-1542
Phone (701) 352-2851
County organized 1881 from Grand
Forks and Pembina counties
Land records: Deeds from 1882,
mortgages from 1881
Naturalization records: Contact State
Archives and Historical Research
Library, State Historical Society of
North Dakota, North Dakota Heritage
Center, 612 East Boulevard Avenue,
Bismarck, ND 58505
Vital records: From 1892
Probate records: From 1882
Probate search service: $5.00; copies:
25¢ per page, $5.00 for the first
certified copy and $2.00 for each
additional certified copy, 25¢
minimum

*Ward County Courthouse
Minot, ND 58701
Phone (701) 857-6460
County organized 1885 from Renville
County
Land records: Contact Eunice Lieninger,
Register of Deeds
Naturalization records: Contact State
Archives and Historical Research
Library, State Historical Society of
North Dakota, North Dakota Heritage
Center, 612 East Boulevard Avenue,
Bismarck, ND 58505
Probate records: Contact District Court
Probate search service: $5.00; "No
telephone requests."

Wells County Courthouse
PO Box 596

Fessenden, ND 58438-0596
Phone (701) 547-3122
County organized 1873 from Sheridan
County

*Williams County Courthouse
PO Box 2047
Williston, ND 58802-2047
Phone (701) 572-6373
County organized 1890 by absorbing
both Buford and Flannery counties
Land records: Contact Register of Deeds
Vital records: Contact Clerk of District
Court
Probate records: Contact Clerk of District
Court
Probate search service: no charge;
copies: 25¢ per page, $5.00 for the
first certified copy and $2.00 for each
additional certified copy, no minimum

OHIO

Capital: Columbus. Statehood: 1 March
1803 (official) (parts claimed by Virginia,
Connecticut and New York from 1609 to
1786, part annexed by the Treaty of Paris,
1783, included in the Northwest Territory
in 1787)

Court System

Ohio has four courts of limited jurisdiction. Municipal Courts have jurisdiction in lesser civil cases and in less serious criminal cases. Mayor's Courts are created in areas without Municipal Courts. A Court of Claims hears cases for claims against the state. County Courts have countywide limited jurisdiction in areas not under the Municipal Courts. These include: Adams, Ashtabula, Belmont, Brown, Butler, Carroll, Clermont, Columbiana, Darke, Erie, Fulton, Hardin, Harrison, Highland, Holmes, Jefferson, Mahoning, Meigs, Monroe, Montgomery, Morgan, Morrow, Muskingum, Noble, Paulding, Perry, Pike, Putnam, Sandusky, Trumbull, Tuscarawas, Vinton and Warren counties. The Ohio Courts of Common Pleas sit at each county seat and hear civil actions, domestic relations and all probate matters as well as felonies and juvenile cases. The Court of Appeals and Supreme Court have appellate jurisdiction.

Courthouses

*Adams County Courthouse
110 West Main
West Union, OH 45693-1347
Phone (513) 544-3286; (513) 544-2513
Recorder's Office; (513) 544-5547
County Board of Health; (513) 544-
2368 Probate Office
County organized 1797, original county
Land records: Contact Recorder's Office.
Abstracts of surveys of property
owners as early as 1814; contact
Dorothy Helton, The Adams County
Genealogical Society, PO Box 231,
West Union, OH 45693.
Naturalization records: No naturalization
records
Vital records: Contact County Board of
Health, 508 East Main Street, West
Union, OH 45693. Births and deaths
from 1888 to 1893, marriage licenses
from 1803 to 1833; contact Lesa J.
Scott and Louise McFarland, Deputy

Clerks, Probate Court; copies: $1.00 per page plus SASE. Marriages from 1797 to 1833; contact County Genealogical Society.

Probate records: Will book 1849–1860, index attached; contact Probate Office. Abstracts of guardianship and administration's bonds from 1856 to 1859, abstracts of estate settlements from 1850 to 1879, abstracts of guardianship from 1867 to 1878, index to estate inventories from 1810 to 1849; contact County Genealogical Society.

No probate search service; copies: 50¢ per page, $2.00 for certified copies; "In the year 1910 our courthouse burned."

*Allen County Courthouse
301 North Main Street
Lima, OH 45801-4456
Phone (419) 228-3700, ext. 276 Probate Division

County organized 1820 from Mercer County but remained attached to Darke County

Naturalization records: From March 1860 through December 1925; contact Research Clerk, Probate Division, Court of Common Pleas, Courthouse, Fourth Floor, PO Box 1243, Lima, OH 45802

Vital records: Births and deaths from 1867 through 1908, marriages from 1831 to date; contact Research Clerk; copies: $5.00 each for births and deaths, 75¢ each for marriages, $2.00 for certified copies of marriages, $2.75 for certified copies of marriage application, plus SASE

Probate records: Estates and guardianships from 1835 to date; contact Research Clerk

No probate search service; copies: 75¢ per page, plus SASE

*Ashland County Courthouse
West Second Street
Ashland, OH 44805
Phone (419) 282-4244 Recorder's Office; (419) 282-4242 Clerk of Courts; (419) 282-4332 Probate Court

County organized 24 February 1846 from the counties of Huron (Ruggles Township), Lorain (Sullivan and Troy townships), Richland (Vermillion, Montgomery, Orange, Green, Hanover, parts of Monroe, Mifflin and Clear Fork townships, also Milton and Clear Creek) and Wayne (Jackson, Perry, Mohican and Lake townships)

Land records: From 1846; contact Barbara J. Harding, County Recorder, Recorder's Office

Naturalization records: From 20 January 1860 through 21 April 1906; contact Probate Court. A few naturalization records for 1904, 1921, 1929, 1940, 1941, 1943, 1959; contact Juanita Wright, Clerk of Courts; copies: 35¢ each, $1.00 for certified copies

Vital records: Births and deaths from 1867 to 1908, marriages from 1846; contact Probate Court; copies: $3.00 each

Probate records: From 1852; contact Probate court

Probate search service: no charge, based on availability of time; copies: $1.00 per page by mail

*Ashtabula County Courthouse
25 West Jefferson Street
Jefferson, OH 44047-1027
Phone (216) 576-9090; (216) 576-3455 Probate Court

County organized 1807 from Trumbull County

Vital records: Births and deaths from 1867 through 1908, marriages from 1811 to date; contact Candy Baker, Deputy Clerk, Probate Court, 25 West Jefferson Street, Jefferson, OH 44047-1092; copies: $1.00 each, $5.00 for certified copies, plus SASE

*Athens County Courthouse
Athens, OH 45701-2888
Phone (614) 592-3219; (614) 592-3228 County Recorder; (614) 592-3242 Clerk of Courts; (614) 592-4431 Health Department; (614) 592-3251 Probate Judge

County organized 1805 from Washington County

Land records: Contact Julia M. Scott, County Recorder

Naturalization records: Contact Marge Mitchell, Clerk of Courts

Vital records: From 1909; contact Joe Kasler, City-County Health Department, 278 West Union Street, Athens, OH 45701. Births, deaths and marriages; contact Probate Judge Roger Jones

Probate records: Contact Probate Judge

Probate search service: no charge but only limited searches can be performed; copies: $1.00 per page, $3.00 for certified copies, no minimum

*Auglaize County Courthouse
Rt. 3
Wapakoneta, OH 45895-9803
Phone (419) 738-7896

County organized 14 February 1848 from Allen and Mercer counties

Land records: From 1848

Naturalization records: No naturalization records; contact Wright State University

Vital records: Births and deaths from 1867, marriages from 1848; copies: $3.00 each

Probate records: From 1848

No probate search service; copies: 50¢ per page

*Belmont County Courthouse
101 Main Street
Saint Clairsville, OH 43950-1224
Phone (614) 695-2121 Probate Division; (614) 695-1202 County Health Department; (614) 633-9752 Martins Ferry Health Department; (614) 676-6061 Bellaire Health Department

County organized 1801 from Jefferson County

Vital records: Births from 1867 to 20 August 1982, deaths from 1867 to 1808 and from 1940 to 20 August 1982, marriages from 1803 to date; contact John J. Malik, Jr., Probate Judge, Probate Division, Court of Common Pleas. Births from 1867 to date, deaths from 1917 to date (no records for 1922); contact County Health Department, Rt. 331, 68501 Bannock Road, Saint Clairsville, OH 43950. Births from 1909 to date and deaths from 1908 to date (some 1900); contact Martins Ferry Health Department, City Building, Martins Ferry, OH 43935; births and deaths from 1909 to date; contact Bellaire Health Department, City Building, Bellaire, OH 43906

No vital records search service (must know the exact name and date within a two-year period); certified copies from Probate Division: $3.00 each, money order only

Probate records: Contact Probate Division

No probate search service (must know the exact name and date within a two-year period); certified copies: $1.00 per page, money order only

*Brown County Courthouse
101 South Main
Georgetown, OH 45121
Phone (513) 378-3100

County organized 1817 from Adams and Clermont counties

Land records: Yes
Naturalization records: Yes
Vital records: Yes
Probate records: Yes

*Butler County Courthouse
130 High Street
Hamilton, OH 45011-2732
Phone (513) 867-5800; (513) 887-3192 County Recorder

County organized 1803 from Hamilton County

Land records: Contact Recorder's Office; copies: $1.00 per page
Naturalization records: From 1840 to 1977; contact Richard W. Creager, Manager, County Records Department, Probate Court; copies: $3.00 per page
Vital records: Births and deaths from 1868 to 1908, marriages from 1803 (applications not on file prior to 1905); contact County Records Department; certified copies: $7.00 for births and deaths, $2.00 for marriages
Probate records: Contact County Records Department
Probate search service: no charge if time permits; copies: $3.00 per page for wills, 50¢ per page for estates, $1.00 minimum; "Checks to Department."

*Carroll County Courthouse
Genealogy Department, Third Floor
Public Square
Carrollton, OH 44615
Phone (216) 627-2323
County organized 1832 from Columbiana, Harrison, Jefferson and Stark counties
Land records: From 1833 to date
Naturalization records: From 1833 to about 1900
Vital records: From 1867 to 1909
Probate records: From 1833 to date

*Champaign County Courthouse
200 North Main Street
Urbana, OH 43078
Phone (513) 652-2263 Recorder's Office; (513) 652-2108 Probate Court
County organized 1805 from Greene and Franklin counties
Land records: From 1805; contact Recorder's Office
Naturalization records: From 1805 to 1852 (in Minute Books); contact Clerk of Court. Naturalization records from 1852 to about 1906; contact Probate Court
Vital records: From 1867 to 1909; contact Sue Heatherly Birt, Probate Court Deputy Clerk; copies: $4.00 for births and deaths, $2.00 for marriages. Vital records from 1909; contact Health Department
Probate records: From 1805; contact Probate Court
Probate search service: $2.00; copies: 50¢ per page, no minimum; "Enclose a long SASE with every inquiry."

Clark County Courthouse
31 North Limestone
PO Box 10008
Springfield, OH 45502
Phone (513) 328-2458

County organized 1817 from Champaign, Madison and Greene counties

Clermont County Courthouse
76 South Riverside
Batavia, OH 45103-2602
Phone (513) 732-7300
County organized 1800, original county

*Clinton County Courthouse
46 South South Street
Wilmington, OH 45177-2214
Phone (513) 382-2103
County organized 1810 from Highland County
Land records: Contact Recorder's Office
Naturalization records: From 1880 to 1895
Vital records: Births and deaths from 1867 to 1908, marriages from 1810. Births and deaths from 1908; contact County Health Department
Probate records: Wills from 1810
No probate search service; copies: 25¢, 50¢ or $1.00 each, depending on the size of the page, 75¢ for certification; "We have a gentleman that comes to the court and takes our mail and answers it."

*Columbiana County Courthouse
105 South Market Street
Lisbon, OH 44432-1255
Phone (216) 424-9511
County organized 1803 from Jefferson and Washington counties
Land records: From 1803; contact Veronica E. Wolski, County Recorder; copies: $1.00 per page
Naturalization records: From 1860 to 1980; contact Carl L. Stacey, Clerk of Courts; copies: $1.00 per page
Vital records: From 1803; contact Clerk of Courts; copies: $1.00 per page. Births and deaths from 1867, marriages from 1803; contact Probate Court; copies: $7.00 each
Probate records: From 1803; contact Probate Court
No probate search service; copies: 50¢ per page from paper originals, $1.00 per page from microfilm originals, 50¢ for certification by stamp, $2.00 for certificate of copy

*Coshocton County Courthouse
318 Main Street
Coshocton, OH 43812
Phone (614) 622-2817 County Recorder; (614) 622-1837 Probate Court
County organized 1811 from Muskingum County
Land records: Contact Sandra Corder, County Recorder, 349 Main Street, PO Box 806, Coshocton, OH 43812;

copies: $1.00 per page, 50¢ for certification
Vital records: Births and deaths from 1867, marriages from 1811; contact Linda Manson, Deputy Clerk, Probate Court; copies: $5.00 for births and deaths before 1909, $2.00 for marriages
Probate records: Wills from 1811; contact Probate Court
Probate search service: $5.00; copies: $1.00 per page, $1.00 for certification

*Crawford County Courthouse
112 East Mansfield Street
Bucyrus, OH 44820-2386
Phone (419) 562-5876; (419) 562-8891 Probate Court
County organized 1820 from Old Indian Territory
Land records: Contact Recorder's Office
Naturalization records: Early and later records; contact Clerk of Courts. Other records, created between early and later records; contact Mrs. Randi K. Webber, Deputy Clerk, Probate Court
Vital records: Births and deaths from 1867 to 1908, marriage licenses from 1831 to date; contact Probate Court
Vital records search service: no charge on as-available basis; copies: $2.00, $5.00 for certification
Probate records: Estates from 1834 to date, guardianships; contact Probate Court
Probate search service: no charge on an as-available basis; copies: 50¢ per page, $1.00 for certification

*Cuyahoga County Courthouse
1 Lakeside Avenue
Cleveland, OH 44113
Phone (216) 443-7000
County organized 1808 from Geauga County
Land records: Contact Recorder, 1219 Ontario Street, Cleveland, OH 44113
Naturalization records: Contact Federal Courthouse, 201 Superior Avenue, Cleveland, OH 44113
Vital records: Contact City of Cleveland, City Hall, Lakeside Avenue, Cleveland, OH 44113
Probate records: Contact Probate Court

*Darke County Courthouse
Fourth and Broadway
Greenville, OH 45331
Phone (513) 548-2325; (513) 547-7390 County Recorder; (513) 873-2092 Wright State University; (513) 548-4196 County Health Department; (513) 547-7345 Probate Court
County organized 1809 from Miami County

Land records: From 1816; contact Alice Stephens, County Recorder

Land records search service: $2.00 per name; copies: $1.00 per page, no minimum

Naturalization records: Old naturalization records; contact Wright State University, Special Collections and Archives, Paul Laurence Dunbar Library, Dayton, OH 45435-0001

Vital records: From December 1908; contact County Health Department, 300 Garst Avenue, Greenville, OH 45331. Births and deaths from 1867 to December 1908, marriages from 1815 to date; contact Probate Court, 300 Garst Avenue, Greenville, OH 45331

Vital records search service from County Health Department: no charge; copies: $3.00 each, $7.00 each for certified copies, no minimum. Copies from Probate Court: 50¢ per page

Probate records: Contact Probate Court

Probate search service: no charge; copies: 50¢ per page, no minimum

*Defiance County Records Center
510 Court Street
Defiance, OH 43512
Phone (419) 782-8918 Records Center
County organized 1845 from Williams, Henry and Paulding counties

Land records: Original handwritten deeds/mortgages from 1845 to 1904, auditor's records from June 1845 to 1992; contact Records Center. Current records; contact Recorder's Office, Courthouse, 500 Court Street, Defiance, OH 43512-2157

Naturalizations: From 1872 to 1906, declarations of intent from 1885 to 1903; contact Records Center

Vital records: Births from 1867 to 1908 (part), unofficial births from 1856 to 1857, deaths from 1867 to March 1908, unofficial deaths from 1856 to 1857, marriage licenses from 1845 to 1994; contact Records Center; copies: $7.00 each for births and deaths, $2.00 for marriages, $3.00 for certified marriages. Births and deaths after 1907; contact Health Department, 197 C Island Parkway, Defiance, OH 43512; copies: $7.00 each for births and deaths.

Probate records: Estates from 1852 to 1994; contact Records Center

*Delaware County Courthouse
91 North Sandusky
Delaware, OH 43015-1703
Phone (614) 368-1800; (614) 548-7313
County organized 1808 from Franklin County
Land records: Yes
Naturalization records: Yes
Vital records: Yes
Probate records: Yes

*Erie County Courthouse
323 Columbus Avenue
Sandusky, OH 44870
Phone (419) 627-7786
County organized 1838 from Huron and Sandusky counties
Land records: Contact Recorder

Naturalization records: Contact Clerk of Courts

Vital records: Before 1908; contact Probate Court. Vital records from 1908; contact City-County Health Department, 420 Superior Street, Sandusky, OH 44870

Probate records: Contact Probate Court

Probate search service: no charge; copies: $1.00 each, no minimum

Fairfield County Courthouse
224 East Main
Lancaster, OH 43130-3842
Phone (614) 687-7030
County organized 1800 from Franklin County

*Fayette County Courthouse
110 East Court Street
Washington Court House, OH 43160-1355
Phone (614) 335-1770 County Recorder; (614) 335-6371 Clerk of Courts; (614) 335-0640 Probate Court
County organized 1810 from Ross and Highland counties
Land records: Deeds from 1810; contact County Recorder; copies: $1.00 per page

Naturalization records: From 1828 to 1852 and from 1906; contact Clerk of Courts. Naturalization records from 1852 to 1906; contact Probate Court.

Vital records: Births and deaths from 1867 to 1908, marriages from 1810; contact Probate Court; copies: $5.00 each for certified births and deaths, $1.00 per page for marriages, $2.00 per page for certified marriages. Births and deaths after 1908; contact Health Department, 317 South Fayette Street, Washington Court House, OH 43160; copies from Health Department: $2.00 each, $7.00 for certified copies.

Probate records: Wills and administrations from 1828; contact Probate Court

Probate search service: no charge; copies: $1.00 per page, no minimum; "A courthouse fire on 19 January 1828 destroyed estate records and common pleas court records."

*Franklin County
Hall of Justice
369 South High Street
Columbus, OH 43215-4516

Phone (614) 462-3322; (614) 462-3930 County Recorder; (614) 462-3894 Probate Court; (614) 645-7331 Columbus Health Department
County organized 1803 from Ross County

Land records: Contact County Recorder, 410 South High Street, Fourth Floor, Columbus, OH 43215

Naturalization records: From 1856 to 1876; Contact Ohio Historical Society, Archives-Library Division, I-71 and 17th Avenue, 1982 Velma Avenue, Columbus, OH 43211-2497

Vital records: Births and deaths from 1867 to 1908, marriages from 1803; contact William A. Reddington, General Referee, Probate Court, 373 South High Street, 22nd Floor, Columbus, OH 43215-6311; copies: $3.00 each. Births, deaths and marriages from 20 December 1908; contact Columbus Health Department, Vital Statistics, 181 South Washington Boulevard, Room 110, Columbus, OH 43215-4096

Probate records: Estates from 1800; contact Probate Court

Probate search service: $1.00 per ten-year search; copies: 75¢ for each of the first three pages and 25¢ for each additional page, $1.00 per page for certification; "Please send cashier's check or money order and SASE."

Fulton County Courthouse
210 South Fulton
Wauseon, OH 43567-1355
Phone (419) 337-9255
County organized 1850 from Lucas, Henry and Williams counties

*Gallia County Courthouse
Locust Street
Gallipolis, OH 45631
Phone (614) 446-4612 Probate Court
County organized 1803 from Washington County

Land records: Contact Recorder's Office

Naturalization records: Some naturalization records included in probate index; contact Probate Court

Vital records: Births and deaths from 1864 to 1952, marriages from 1803 to date; contact Probate Court; certified copies from Probate Court: $3.00 for births and deaths, $1.50 for marriages. Births and deaths from 1909 to date; contact County Health Department.

Probate records: Estates, wills, guardianships and miscellaneous records from 1803; contact Probate Court

Probate search service: about $5.00 per hour; copies: 25¢ per page, no minimum

*Geauga County Courthouse
100 Short Court Street
Chardon, OH 44024
Phone (216) 285-2222
*County organized 1805 from Trumbull
County*
Land records: Contact County Recorder,
Courthouse Annex
Naturalization records: From 1903 to
1944
Vital records: Births and deaths from
1867 to 1908, marriages from 1805 to
1919; contact Probate Court. Births
and deaths from 1908; contact Geauga
County Health Department. Marriages
from 1919; contact Probate Court.
Divorces from 1806; contact Clerk of
Courts
Probate records: Wills, estates, etc., from
1807; contact Probate Court
No probate search service; copies: $1.00
per page, no minimum; "We have
very little time to do any research for
people."

*Greene County Courthouse
45 North Detroit Street
Xenia, OH 45385
Phone (513) 376-5000; (513) 376-5270
County Recorder; (513) 376-5017
County Treasurer; (513) 376-5065
County Auditor; (513) 376-5290 Clerk
of Courts; (513) 376-5280 Probate
Clerk
*County organized 1803 from Hamilton
and Ross counties*
Land records: Contact Larry B. Morris,
County Recorder, James W. Schmidt,
County Treasurer, and Luwanna
Delaney, County Auditor
Naturalization records: No naturalization
records
Vital records: Births before 1912; contact
William Litterel, PO Box 156, Xenia,
OH 45385. Deaths and marriages;
contact Marsha Linkhart, Probate
Clerk
Probate records: Contact Probate Clerk

*Guernsey County Courthouse
Wheeling Avenue
Cambridge, OH 43725
Phone (614) 432-4026 Probate Court
*County organized 1810 from Belmont
County*
Land records: Contact County Recorder's
Office
Naturalization records: From 1864 to
1906; contact Probate Court; copies:
$1.00 per page
Vital records: Births and deaths from
1867 to 1909, marriages from 1812;
contact Probate Court; certified
copies: $2.00 for births or marriages
Probate records: From 1812; contact
Probate Court
Probate search service: no charge;

copies: $1.00 per page, $1.00 for
certification, no minimum; "Only
charged for copies if we find
anything; no phone requests; please
direct mail to Clerk of Probate Court."

*Hamilton County Courthouse
1000 Main Street
Cincinnati, OH 45202-1206
Phone (513) 632-6500; (513) 632-8585
Auditor; (513) 632-8644 County
Recorder; (513) 632-6014 County
Recorder's computer Dial-in Access
Information (need to set up an escrow
account before logging on); (513)
632-8746 Chief Deputy, Probate
Court; (513) 632-3364 Probate Court
*County organized 1790, original county;
fire destroyed many records in 1884*
Land records: Real estate tax records,
plat maps; contact Auditor, County
Administration Building, Room 304,
138 East Court Street, Cincinnati, OH
45202. Deeds from 1794, mortgages
and leases, 1939 WPA platting of
cemeteries, original subdivision maps
and atlases; contact Eve Bolton,
County Recorder, County
Administration Building, Room 205,
138 East Court Street, Cincinnati, OH
45202. Property tax records from
1883; contact Treasurer's Office (off
main foyer)
Land records search service: no charge
for index search (not permitted by law
to do title search or historical
searches); copies: $1.00 per page
Naturalization records: From 1869 to
1884, some declarations of intention
from 1846 to 1908; contact Chief
Deputy, Probate Court, Room 514.
Naturalization records from 1850 to
1893, declarations of intent; contact
Clerk of Courts Office, Room 315
Vital records: Births from 1846 to 1908,
deaths from 1882 to 1908, marriages
from 1817 to date; contact Chief
Deputy, Probate Court; copies: $7.00
each. Births and deaths outside the
city limits from 1909 to date; contact
Vital Statistics, 11499 Chester Road,
Suite 1500, Cincinnati, OH 45246.
Births from June 1874, deaths from
1865; contact Elm Street Health
Center, 1525 Elm Street, Cincinnati,
OH 45210; copies: $7.00 each. Births
and deaths of persons born or dying at
home; contact Saint Bernard City
Hall, 110 Washington Street. Vital
records from 1908; contact Norwood
Health Center, 2059 Sherman Avenue,
Norwood, OH 45212. Vital records
from 1899; contact Reading City Hall,
100 Market Street, Reading, OH
45215.
Probate records: Estate cases, wills from
1791 to date, guardianship records;
contact Chief Deputy, Probate Court

No probate search service; copies: $2.00,
$2.00 minimum; no telephone
requests to courthouse, enclose SASE;
courthouse destroyed in 1884 and
many records lost

*Hancock County Courthouse
300 South Main
Findlay, OH 45840-9039
Phone (419) 424-7044; (419) 424-7079
Probate Court
*County organized 1820 from Indian
lands, and attached to Wood County*
Land records: From 1830; contact
County Recorder
Naturalization records: Before 1906;
contact Ruth Troxel, Deputy Clerk,
Probate Court, 308 Dorney Plaza,
Findlay, OH 45840-3302. Some
naturalization records between 1907
and 1930; contact Clerk's Office.
Vital records: Births and deaths from
1867 to 1909, marriages from 1827;
contact Probate Court; copies from
Probate Court: $5.00 each for births
and deaths, $1.25 each for marriages
Probate records: Estates from 1825;
contact Probate Court
Probate search service: no charge;
copies: 25¢ per page, no minimum

*Hardin County Courthouse
1 Court House Square
Kenton, OH 43326
Phone (419) 673-6283; (419) 674-2278
*County organized 12 February 1820
from Indian lands by an act of the
Ohio legislature, but leaving it
attached to Logan County; made a
separate county in 1833; fire
destroyed records in 1853*

*Harrison County Courthouse
100 West Market Street
Cadiz, OH 43907
Phone (614) 942-8868 Probate Court
*County organized 1813 from Jefferson
and Tuscarawas counties*
Land records: Contact Tracy L. Boyer,
Recorder's Office
Naturalization records: Contact Diane
Mazeroski, Clerk of Courts
Vital records: Births and deaths from
1867, marriages from 1813; contact
Steven Ray Karto, Probate Court;
copies: $7.00 for certified births or
deaths
Probate records: Wills and estates from
1813; contact Probate Court
Probate search service: depends on
amount of time spent; copies: $1.00
per page, $2.00 for certified copies,
plus LSASE

Henry County Courthouse
660 North Perry

PO Box 546
Napoleon, OH 43545-1702
Phone (419) 592-4876
County organized 1820 from Indian lands and attached to Wood County

*Highland County Courthouse
105 North High Street
Hillsboro, OH 45133
Phone (513) 393-1981
County organized 1805 from Ross, Adams and Clermont counties
Land records: Some land records; contact Clerk
Vital records: From 1867 to 1909; contact Clerk
Probate records: Contact Clerk
No probate search service; copies: 25¢ per page, no minimum

*Hocking County Courthouse
1 East Main Street
Logan, OH 43138-1207
Phone (614) 385-5195 Commissioners Office; (614) 385-3022 Probate Office
County organized 1818 from Athens and Ross counties
Land records: Contact Recorder's Office
Naturalization records: Very limited naturalization records from 1863 to 1900; contact Probate Office
Vital records: Births from 1867 to 1943, deaths from 1867 to 1908, marriages from 1818; contact Probate Office
Probate records: From 1837; contact Probate Office
Probate search service: $2.00; copies: 50¢ each, no minimum; "Do not do searches over phone; must put request in writing including self-addressed envelope."

*Holmes County Courthouse
Probate Court, Court of Common Pleas or County Recorder
Millersburg, OH 44654
Phone (216) 674-0286
County organized 1824 from Coshocton County
Land records: From 1825; contact County Recorder
Naturalization records: From 1825 to 1850; contact Court of Common Pleas. Naturalization records from 1850; contact Probate Court
Vital records: From 1867 to 1908; contact Probate Court. Vital records from 1908; contact Health Department
Probate records: From 1855; contact Probate Court
No probate search service: most research done by local genealogist, Dave Marshall; copies: "according to type and whether they are certified."

*Huron County Courthouse
2 East Main Street
Norwalk, OH 44857
County organized 1815 from Indian lands
Land records: Contact County Recorder
Naturalization records: Before 1859; contact Common Pleas. From 1859; contact Probate Court
Vital records: Births and deaths from 1867 to 1908, marriages from 1815; contact Probate Court
Probate records: From March 1852; contact Probate Court
Probate search service: SASE; copies: $1.00 per page, $3.00 per record, $1.00 minimum

*Jackson County Courthouse
Jackson, OH 45640
Phone (614) 286-3301
County organized 1816 from Pike County
Land records: Deeds from 1816; contact County Recorder, 226 East Main Street, Suite 1, Jackson, OH 45640-1799; copies: $1.00 per page
Vital records: Births and deaths from 1867 to 1908, marriages from 1817 to date; contact Probate Court. Births and deaths after 1908; contact Health Department, Main Street, Jackson, OH 45640
Probate records: Wills from 1817 to date; contact Probate Court

*Jefferson County Courthouse
301 Market Street
Steubenville, OH 43952-2133
Phone (614) 283-8587 Deputy Clerk; (614) 283-6050 City of Steubenville Health Department; (614) 283-8530 Jefferson County Health Department
County organized 1797, original county
Land records: Yes
Naturalization records: Contact Deputy Clerk, Common Pleas Court, Probate Division
Vital records: Births and deaths from 1867 to 1908, marriages from 1803 to date (early records indexed by groom only, cross index begins 1976); contact Deputy Clerk. Births in Steubenville after 1908; contact City of Steubenville Health Department, 312 Market Street, Steubenville, OH 43952. Births in Jefferson County, outside the City of Steubenville, after 1908; contact Jefferson County Health Department, 814 Adams Street, Steubenville, OH 43952; copies: $7.00 each for certified copies of births and deaths, $3.00 for certified copies of marriages, $1.00 for uncertified copies of marriages
Probate records: Estates and guardianships from 1838 to date, wills

from 1798 to date, trust records from 1859 to date; contact Deputy Clerk; copies: $1.00 per page, $1.00 for certification

Knox County Courthouse
106 East High Street
Mount Vernon, OH 43050-3453
Phone (614) 397-2727
County organized 1808 from Fairfield County

Lake County Courthouse
PO Box 490
Painesville, OH 44077-0490
Phone (216) 352-6281
County organized 1840 from Geauga and Cuyahoga counties

Lawrence County Courthouse
Fifth and Park Avenue
Ironton, OH 45638
Phone (614) 533-4355
County organized 1815 from Gallia County

*Licking County Courthouse
Court House Square
Newark, OH 43055-9553
Phone (614) 349-6000 County Administration Building; (614) 349-6207 Clerk of Court of Common Pleas, Gen. Division; (614) 349-6138 Marriage License; (614) 349-6137 Probate Office
County organized 1808 from Fairfield County
Land records: Contact Recorder's Office, County Administration Building, 20 South Second Street, Newark, OH 43055
Naturalization records: Contact Clerk of Court of Common Pleas, County Administration Building
Vital records: Births and deaths from 1875 through 1908, marriages from 1808 to 1875; contact Probate Office
Probate records: Wills from 1875; contact Probate Office
No probate search service; copies: $1.00 if book and page number are known

Logan County Courthouse
PO Box 429
Bellefontaine, OH 43311-0429
Phone (513) 599-7275
County organized 1817 from Champaign County

*Lorain County Courthouse
308 Second Street
Elyria, OH 44035-5506
Phone (216) 329-5536; (216) 329-5148 County Recorder; (216) 329-5539 County Clerk of Court; (216) 329-

3785 County Board of Health; (216) 329-5175 Probate Division

County organized 26 December 1822 from Huron, Cuyahoga and Medina counties

Land records: Contact County Recorder, Administration Building, 226 Middle Avenue, Elyria, OH 44035

Naturalization records: Contact County Clerk of Courts

Vital records: Births and deaths from June 1867 to June 1908, marriages from 1843; contact County Board of Health, 9880 South Murray Ridge Road, Elyria, OH 44035

Probate records: From 1824; contact County Court of Common Pleas, Probate Division, 226 Middle Avenue, Elyria, OH 44035

Probate search service: no charge; copies: $1.00 per page, no minimum

*Lucas County Courthouse
700 Adams Street
Toledo, OH 43624
Phone (419) 245-4764 Probate Division
County organized 1835 from Wood County

Naturalization records: Contact Bowling Green State University, Center for Archival Collections, Fifth Floor, Jerome Library, Bowling Green, OH 43403-0175

Vital records; Births and deaths from 1865 to 1908, birth registrations from 1865 to date, marriages from 1835 to date; contact Probate Division. Births and deaths after 1908; contact Health Department

Probate records; Wills from 1865 to date, administrations from 1891 to date; contact Probate Division; copies: $1.00 per page, $2.00 per page for certified copies

*Madison County Courthouse
London, OH 43140
Phone (614) 852-0756 Probate Division
County organized 1810 from Fayette County

Land records: Contact Recorder's Office

Naturalization records: Some scattered naturalization records; contact Court of Common Pleas, Probate Division

Vital records: Births and deaths from 1867 to 1908, marriages from 1810; contact Probate Division. Births and deaths from 1908; contact County Health Department

Probate records: Wills, estates, guardianships from 1820; contact Deputy Clerk, Probate Division

Probate search service: no charge; copies: 50¢ per page, $1.00 for certification, no minimum; "We are not permitted to make change through the mail; requests for searches should

be *first*; *then*, if we find the record, we will notify the individual of costs for copies; upon receiving these costs we will send the copies."

*Mahoning County Courthouse
120 Market Street
Youngstown, OH 44503-1710
Phone (216) 740-2345 Recorder's Office; (216) 740-2104 Clerk of Courts; (216) 740-2114 Clerk; (216) 740-2314 Probate Court
County organized 1846 from Columbiana and Trumbull counties

Land records: "Deeds, etc., from our parent counties were recorded here when Mahoning County was founded"; contact County Recorder, Recorder's Office; copies: $1.00 per page

Naturalization records: Contact Clerk, 2801 Market Street, Youngstown, OH 44507

Vital records: Births and deaths from 1 April 1856 to 31 March 1857 and from 1 April 1864 to 20 December 1908, marriages from February 1846; contact Probate Department. Deaths from 1922; contact City Health Department, Division of Vital Statistics, Seventh Floor, City Hall, South Phelps Street, Youngstown, OH 44503

Probate records: On microfilm; contact Probate Department

No probate search service; copies: 50¢ per page, no minimum; "*No checks—cash or money order only, business size SASE a *must*; write for information about the record you are seeking before you send money.*"

*Marion County Courthouse
114 North Main Street
Marion, OH 43302-3030
Phone (614) 387-4521
County organized 1820 from Indian lands by an act of the Ohio legislature but remained attached to Delaware County; separated 1824 from Delaware County

Land records: From 1822 to date; contact Recorder's Office

Naturalization records: From 1860 to 1904; contact Ohio Historical Society, Archives-Library Division, I-71 and 17th Avenue, 1982 Velma Avenue, Columbus, OH 43211-2497 or Marion Public Library, 445 East Church Street, Marion, OH 43302

Vital records: Births and deaths from 1867 to 1908, marriages from 1824 to 1920; contact Ohio Historical Society or Marion Public Library

Probate records: From 1824; contact Probate Court

No probate search service; copies: $1.00 per page, no minimum

*Medina County Courthouse
93 Public Square
Medina, OH 44256-2205
Phone (216) 725-9703 Probate Division; (216) 723-9523 County Health Department
County organized 1812 from Portage County

Land records: From 1795

Naturalization records: From 1839

Vital records: Births and deaths from 1867 to December 1908, marriages from 1818; contact L. Thomas Skidmore, Judge, Court of Common Pleas, Probate Division. Births and deaths from 1909; contact County Health Department, 4800 Ledgewood Drive, Medina, OH 44256

Probate records: Estates, guardianships, trusts, etc. from 1833; contact Probate Division

No probate search service; copies: $1.00 per page, $2.00 for certified copies; "We would prefer a money order or check and no cash for each request."

*Meigs County Courthouse
Second Street
Pomeroy, OH 45769
Phone (614) 992-2895; (614) 992-3096 Probate and Juvenile Divisions
County organized 1819 from Gallia and Athens counties

Land records: Yes
Naturalization records: Yes
Vital records: Yes
Probate records: Yes
No probate search service; "Due to the overwhelming amount of genealogy requests and the work load of the Meigs County Probate and Juvenile Courts, it is impossible for either office to do any more genealogy research."

*Mercer County Courthouse
Recorder's Office or Probate Court
Celina, OH 45822
Phone (419) 586-3178
County organized 1820 from Darke County

Miami County Courthouse
201 West Main Street
Troy, OH 45373-3239
Phone (513) 335-8341
County organized 1807 from Montgomery County

*Monroe County Courthouse
County Recorder or Probate Court
101 North Main Street
Woodsfield, OH 43793

Phone (614) 472-0873; (614) 472-1654
Probate Court Judge
County organized 1813 from Belmont, Washington and Guernsey counties
Land records: From 1837; contact James N. Neuhart, County Auditor, or County Recorder
Naturalization records: From 1867 to 1885; contact F. V. Ballard, Probate Court Judge
Vital records: Births and deaths from 1867 to 1908, marriages from 1867; contact Probate Court Judge; copies: $5.00 each. Vital records from 1909; contact County Health Department, 47029 Moore Ridge Road, Woodsfield, OH 43793.
Probate records: From 1867; contact Probate Court Judge; copies: $1.00 per page, $1.00 per document for certification

*Montgomery County Administration Building
451 West Third Street
Dayton, OH 45422-0001
Phone (513) 225-4000
County organized 1803 from Hamilton and Ross counties
Vital records: Yes. Divorce records; contact Montgomery County Records Center, Reibold Building (Sixth Floor), 117 South Main Street, Dayton, OH 45402.
Probate records: Contact Montgomery County Courts Building, 41 North Perry Street, Dayton, OH 45422

*Morgan County Courthouse
19 East Main Street
McConnelsville, OH 43756-1172
Phone (614) 962-2861; (614) 962-4051 Recorder's Office
County organized 1817 from Washington County
Land records: Deeds; contact Recorder's Office
Naturalization records: Some naturalization records from early 1800s; contact Probate Division
Vital records: Births and deaths from 1867 to 1952, marriages from 1819
Probate records: Wills, executor and administration records from 1820; contact Probate Division
Probate search service: no charge; copies: 50¢ per page, no minimum

Morrow County Courthouse
Mount Gilead, OH 43338
Phone (419) 947-2085
County organized 1848 from Knox, Marion, Delaware and Richland counties

Muskingum County Courthouse
Zanesville, OH 43702
Phone (614) 455-7104
County organized 1804 from Washington and Fairfield counties

*Noble County Courthouse
Caldwell, OH 43724
Phone (614) 732-2969
County organized 11 March 1851 from Monroe, Morgan, Guernsey and Washington counties
Land records: Contact Recorder's Office
Naturalization records: Contact Probate Court and Clerk of Courts
Vital records: Births and deaths from 1867, marriages from 1851; contact Probate Court. Vital records from 1908; contact Health Department.
Probate records: Wills, estates and guardianships from 1851; contact Probate Court
Probate search service: $2.00 per category; copies: 50¢ each, $3.00–$7.00 for certification, $2.00 minimum (search fee); "Always include SASE."

*Ottawa County Courthouse
315 Madison Street
Port Clinton, OH 43452-1936
Phone (419) 734-4431
County organized 1840 from Erie, Sandusky and Lucas counties
Land records: From 1840; contact County Recorder
Naturalization records: Contact Ann Bowers, Center for Archival Collections, Bowling Green University, Fifth Floor Library, Bowling Green, OH 43403
Vital records: Before 1909; contact Probate Office. Vital records from 1909; contact Irene Cupp, Health Department.
Probate records: From 1840; contact Judge David Zeitzheim
Probate search service: no charge; copies: $1.00 per page, $1.00 for certification

Paulding County Courthouse
115 North Williams Street
Paulding, OH 45879
Phone (419) 399-2051
County organized 1820 from Indian lands and attached to Wood County

*Perry County Courthouse
New Lexington, OH 43764
Phone (614) 342-2494 County Recorder; (614) 342-5179 Board of Health; (614) 342-1493 Probate Court
County organized 1817 from Washington, Fairfield and Muskingum counties

Land records: Plats, liens, mortgages, oil and gas leases, armed service discharges; contact County Recorder, First Floor, Perry County Courthouse, PO Box 147, New Lexington, OH 43764-0147; copies: 50¢ per page
Naturalization records: From 1818; contact Probate Court, First Floor, Perry County Courthouse, PO Box 167, New Lexington, OH 43764-0167; copies: 75¢ per page
Vital records: Births and deaths from 1867 to 1925, marriages from 1818; contact Probate Court; copies: 75¢ per page for births and deaths, $5.00 for certified copies of births and deaths, 50¢ for marriages before 1900, 75¢ for marriages after 1900, $2.00 for certified copies of marriages. Births and deaths from 1908; contact Board of Health, Administration Building, Brown Street, New Lexington, OH 43764-0230; copies: $1.10 each, $7.00 for certified copies
Probate records: Wills, estates, guardianships, trusts, name changes, some divorces from 1818; contact Probate Court
No probate search service; copies: 75¢ per page

*Pickaway County Courthouse
Circleville, OH 43113
Phone (614) 474-3950 Probate Court
County organized 1810 from Ross, Fairfield and Franklin counties
Naturalization records: From 1860; contact Charlesa S. Canter, Chief Deputy Clerk, Probate Court
Vital records: Births and deaths from 1867, marriages from 1810; contact Probate Court
Probate records: Estates from 1810; contact Probate Court
Probate search service: no charge; copies: $1.00 per page, no minimum

*Pike County Courthouse
100 East Second
Waverly, OH 45690-1301
Phone (614) 947-2715
County organized 1815 from Ross, Highland and Scioto counties
Land records: Yes
Naturalization records: Yes
Vital records: Yes
Probate records: Yes
Probate search service: no charge; copies: $1.00

*Portage County Courthouse
203 West Main Street
Ravenna, OH 44266-2761
Phone (216) 296-6466
County organized 1807 from Trumbull and Jackson counties, officially formed 9 June 1808

Land records: Contact Administration
Building, 449 South Meridian,
Ravenna, OH 44266
Naturalization records: No naturalization
records
Vital records: No vital records
Probate records: Yes

Preble County Courthouse
Eaton, OH 45320
Phone (513) 456-8160
*County organized 1808 from
Montgomery and Butler counties*

*Putnam County Courthouse
245 Main Street
Ottawa, OH 45875-1968
Phone (419) 523-3656
*County organized 1820 from Indian
lands and attached to Wood County*
Land records: Yes
Naturalization records: Yes
Vital records: Yes
Probate records: Yes

*Richland County Courthouse
50 Park Avenue, East
Mansfield, OH 44902-1850
Phone (419) 774-5550
*County organized 1813 from Knox
County*
Land records: Yes
Naturalization records: Yes
Vital records: Births and deaths from
1865 to December 1908, marriages
from 1813
Probate records: From 1813

Ross County Courthouse
Chillicothe, OH 45601
Phone (614) 773-5115
County organized 1798, original county

*Sandusky County Courthouse
100 North Park
Fremont, OH 43420-2454
Phone (419) 334-6100; (419) 334-6161
Clerk of Courts; (419) 334-6377
Department of Health; (419) 334-6217
Court Administrator
*County organized 1820 from Huron
County*
Land records: Contact Judge John
Chambers, Probate Court
Naturalization records: Contact Alberta
Rathbun, Clerk of Courts
Vital records: Contact Ken Kerik,
Department of Health, H. C. 2000
Countryside Drive, Fremont, OH
43420
Probate records: Contact Michael Geiger,
Court Administrator
Probate search service: no charge;
copies: $1.00 plus $1.00 for
certification

Scioto County Courthouse
602 Seventh Street
Portsmouth, OH 45662-3948
Phone (614) 353-5111
*County organized 1803 from Indian
Territory*

*Seneca County Courthouse
81 Jefferson Street
Tiffin, OH 44883-2339
Phone (419) 447-4550; (419) 447-3121
Probate Division
*County organized 1820 from Indian
land and attached to Sandusky
County*
Vital records: Births and deaths from
1867 to 1908, marriages from 1841;
contact County Common Pleas Court,
Probate Division, 108 Jefferson Street,
Tiffin, OH 44883. Births and deaths
from 1908; contact County Health
District, 3100 State Route #100,
Tiffin, OH 44883.
Vital records search service from Probate
Division: $5.00; copies: $7.00 each
for births and deaths, $2.00 for
marriages, plus SASE

Shelby County Courthouse
Sidney, OH 45365
Phone (513) 498-7226
*County organized 1819 from Miami
County*

*Stark County Office Building
115 Central Plaza North
Canton, OH 44702
Phone (216) 438-0800; (216) 972-7670
Bierce Library; (216) 452-0665 Stark
County District Library; (216) 438-
0953 Probate Court, Records Center;
(216) 438-0753 Court of Common
Pleas, Probate Division
*County organized 1808 from Indian
Territory*
Naturalization records: From 1861 to
1903; contact Bierce Library, The
University of Akron, Second Floor,
Room 269, Buchtel Avenue, Akron,
OH 44325-1702 or Stark County
District Library, 715 Market Avenue,
North, Canton, OH 44702-1080
Vital records: Births and deaths from
1867 to 1908 and from 1939 to 1940,
death index to 1940, marriages from
1809 to 1901, marriage index from
1809 to about 1857; contact Bierce
Library. Births from 1867 to 1909
(microfilm), deaths from 1867 to 1908
(microfilm), marriages from 1809 to
1916 (early index from 1809 to 1874,
alphabetical index from 1858 to
1972); contact Stark County District
Library
Probate records: Administration record of
accounts, administration records

(estate files), administration records
index from 1809 to 1914 (microfilm),
applications, bonds and letters of
administration, assignee records,
assignments, executor's bonds and
letters of administration, files and
administration dockets index, guardian
records; contact Stark County District
Library. Will index from 1811 to
1942, wills from 1811 to the 1980s;
contact Stark County District Library.
Probate records, including estate case
files from 1920; contact Probate
Court, Records Center
No probate search service; copies: 50¢
per page; "Always include SASE."

*Summit County Courthouse
209 South High Street
Akron, OH 44308
Phone (216) 643-2512; (216) 643-2352
Probate Court Records Room; , (216)
375-2976 Akron Health Department;
(216) 745-6067 Barberton Health
Department; (216) 923-4891 County
Health Department
*County organized 1840 from Portage,
Medina and Stark counties*
Land records: Contact County Recorder,
Ohio Building, Fourth Floor, 175
South Main Street, Akron, OH 44308-
1355
Naturalization records: Contact County
Clerk of Courts, Naturalization
Department, 53 University Avenue,
Akron, OH 44308
Vital records: Births and deaths from
1869 through 1908, marriages from
1840; contact Kimberly Guldeman,
Records Supervisor, Probate Court,
Records Room; copies: $3.00 each for
births and deaths, $1.00 each for
marriages, $2.00 for certified
marriages. Vital records from 1908;
contact Akron Health Department, 177
South Broadway, Akron, OH 44308 or
Barberton Health Department, 571
West Tuscarawas Avenue, Barberton,
OH 44203, or County Health
Department, 1100 Graham Circle,
Cuyahoga Falls, OH 44221
Probate records: Estates, guardianships,
trusts from 1840; contact Probate
Court, Records Room
Probate search service: no charge, but
will not do extensive research (will
search one or two records); copies:
75¢ per page, $1.00 for certification,
no minimum; "We have a list of
researchers in the area to do
genealogical research; we are not
staffed to provide researching; fees
should be in the form of a money
order or certified check made out to
Summit County Probate Court."

*Trumbull County Courthouse
161 High Street, N.W.
Warren, OH 44481-1005
Phone (216) 841-0562
County organized 1800 from Jefferson County
Land records: Contact Clerk of Courts Office
Naturalization records: From 1800 to 1985; contact Margaret R. O'Brien, Clerk of Courts
Vital records: Contact Recorder's Office
Probate records: From 1805; contact Marci Matteo, Probate Court
Probate search service: no charge; copies: $1.00, $2.00 per certified page, no minimum

*Tuscarawas County Courthouse
Public Square
New Philadelphia, OH 44663
Phone (216) 364-8811
County organized 1808 from Jefferson County
Land records: Contact Recorder's Office
Naturalization records: To 1907; contact Probate Court
Vital records: Births from 1867 to 1908, deaths from 1867 to 1924, marriages from 1808; contact Probate Court; copies: $7.00 each for births and deaths, $2.00 for marriages
Probate records: Wills, estates, guardianships from 1808
No probate search service; copies: $1.00 per page, no minimum; "We do not have the staff to do extensive research for you; contact local genealogical society if you cannot come in yourself."

*Union County Courthouse
Marysville, OH 43040
Phone (513) 645-3100 Recorder's Office; (513) 645-3029 Probate Court
County organized 1820 from Franklin, Madison and Logan counties
Land records: From 1820 (few deeds before); contact Recorder's Office, County Office Building, 233 West Sixth Street, Marysville, OH 43040
Naturalization records: Some from 1860; contact Probate Court
Vital records: Births and deaths from 1867 to 1909, marriages from 1820 to date; contact Probate Court; copies: $3.00 for births and deaths
Probate records: From 1820; contact Probate Court
Probate search service: no charge; copies: 50¢ per page, $1.50 for certified copies

*Van Wert County Courthouse
Van Wert, OH 45891

Phone (419) 238-6159; (419) 238-2558 Recorder's Office
County organized 1820 from Indian Territory
Land records: From 1838; contact Recorder's Office
Naturalization records: From 1835 to 1854; contact Common Pleas Court. Naturalization records from 1855 to 1908; contact Probate Court. Naturalization records from 1908 to 1974; contact Clerk of Courts
Naturalization records search service: $3.00
Vital records: Births and deaths from 1867 to 1908, marriages from 1840; contact Probate Court. Vital statistics from 1908; contact Division of Vital Statistics
Vital records search service: $3.00
Probate records: Estates and wills from 1837, guardianships from 1873; contact Probate Court
Probate search service: $3.00

*Vinton County Courthouse
McArthur, OH 45651
Phone (614) 596-4571; (614) 596-4134 Recorder's Office; (614) 596-5233 Health Department; (614) 596-5480 Probate
County organized 1850 from Gallia, Athens, Ross, Hocking, Meigs and Jackson counties
Land records: Contact Recorder's Office
Naturalization records: Contact Historical Society, PO Box 141, McArthur, OH 45651
Vital records: Births, deaths and marriages; contact Health Department, State Route 93N, McArthur, OH 45651; copies: $7.00 plus SASE, exact information needed
Probate records: Yes
No probate search service; copies: 25¢ per page plus SASE

*Warren County Courthouse
320 East Silver Street
Lebanon, OH 45036-1816
Phone (513) 932-4040; (513) 932-1140 Recorder's Office; (513) 933-1228 Health Department; (513) 933-1180 Probate Court
County organized 1803 from Butler and Hamilton counties
Land records: Contact Recorder's Office
No land records search service; copies: $1.00 per page
Naturalization records: No naturalization records
Vital records: Contact Health Department, East Street, Lebanon, OH 45036
Probate records: Contact Probate Court, 310 East Silver Street, Lebanon, OH 45036

*Washington County Courthouse
205 Putnam Street
Marietta, OH 45750-3085
Phone (614) 373-6623 Probate Division
County organized 1788, original county
Land records: Contact Recorder's Office
Naturalization records: From 1859 to 1905; contact Deputy Clerk, Probate Court. Other naturalization records; contact Clerk of Courts Office; copies cannot be certified
Vital records: Births and deaths from 1867 to 20 December 1908, marriages from 1789; contact Deputy Clerk, Probate Court; certified copies: $5.00 each. Births and deaths from 1908; contact County Health Department, 342 Muskingum Drive, Marietta, OH 45750 or City Health Department 304 Putnam Street, Marietta, OH 45750
Probate records: From 1789; contact Deputy Clerk, Probate Court
Probate search service: no charge ("We must have dates and name"); copies: 50¢ for each of the first two pages and 25¢ for each additional page, $1.00 for certified copies, $1.00 minimum; "Send to Washington County Probate Court; we do NOT take personal checks."

*Wayne County Courthouse
107 West Liberty Street
Wooster, OH 44691
Phone (216) 263-3184
County organized 1786, original county; the present county was created in 1808 and organized in 1812
Land records: Contact Recorder's Office, 428 West Liberty Street, Wooster, OH 44691
Naturalization records: Contact Probate Judge
Vital records: Births and deaths from 1867 to April 1908, marriages from 1813; contact Probate Judge
Probate records: From 1813; contact Probate Judge
Probate search service: no charge; copies: 25¢ per page, no minimum; "should be as specific as possible."

Williams County Courthouse
Bryan, OH 43506
Phone (419) 636-2059
County organized 1820 from Indian land and attached to Wood County

*Wood County Courthouse
1 Courthouse Square
Bowling Green, OH 43402-2427
Phone (419) 354-9140; (419) 354-9230 Probate Division
County organized 1820 from Indian lands, Northwest Territory
Naturalization records: From 1859

through 1929 and one in 1960; contact Microfilm Department, Sue Kinder, County Recorder

Vital records: Births and deaths from 1867 through 1908, marriages from 1820; contact Clerk, Court of Common Pleas, Probate Division; certified copies: $7.00 each for births and deaths, $2.00 for abstracts of marriages. Vital records from 1908; contact County Health Department.

Probate records: Estates from 1821, guardianships from 1852; contact Clerk, Probate Division

No probate search service; copies: $1.00 per page, $1.00 for certification, no minimum

*Wyandot County Courthouse

109 South Sandusky Avenue
Upper Sandusky, OH 43351
Phone (419) 294-1432

County organized 1845 from Marion, Crawford, Hardin and Hancock counties

Vital records: Births and deaths from 1867 to 1908, marriages from 1845 to date; contact Probate Court, Second Floor. Births and deaths after 1908; contact County Health Department, 127 South Sandusky Avenue, Upper Sandusky, OH 43351; copies: $2.00 each for births and deaths, $7.00 each for certified copies of births and deaths, 50¢ each for complete marriage record (includes application, date issued, date married), $5.00 for certified copy of complete marriage record, $2.00 for marriage certificate (includes names, date married and by whom)

Probate records: Estate proceedings from 1845 to date; contact Probate Court; copies: 50¢ per page, $1.00 for certification

OKLAHOMA

Capital: Oklahoma City. Statehood: 16 November 1907 (annexed as part of the Louisiana Territory, 1803, except for the panhandle, Indian Territory created 1820, Oklahoma Territory created 1890, merged to form state)

Court System

Oklahoma's courts of limited jurisdiction include: Court of Tax Review, Court of Bank Review, Municipal Criminal Court of Record, Workers' Compensation Court, Municipal Court Not of Record, and Court on the Judiciary. The District Courts sit in each county seat and have general jurisdiction, including civil actions, probate, domestic relations, felonies, misdemeanors, and juvenile matters. First Judicial District: Beaver, Cimarron, Harper and Texas counties; Second Judicial District: Beckham, Custer, Ellis, Greer, Harmon and Roger Mills counties; Third Judicial District: Jackson, Kiowa, Tillman and Washita counties; Fourth Judicial District: Alfalfa, Blaine, Dewey, Garfield, Grant, Kingfisher, Major, Woods and Woodward counties; Fifth Judicial District: Comanche, Cotton, Jefferson and Stephens counties; Sixth Judicial District: Caddo and Grady counties; Seventh Judicial District: Oklahoma County; Eighth Judicial District: Kay and Noble counties; Ninth Judicial District: Logan and Payne counties; Tenth Judicial District: Osage County; Eleventh Judicial District: Nowata and Washington counties; Twelfth Judicial District: Craig, Mayes and Rogers counties; Thirteenth Judicial District: Delaware and Ottawa counties; Fourteenth Judicial District: Pawnee and Tulsa counties; Fifteenth Judicial District: Adair, Cherokee, Muskogee, Sequoyah and Wagoner counties; Sixteenth Judicial District: Haskell, Latimer and LeFlore counties; Seventeenth Judicial District: Choctaw, McCurtain and Pushmataha counties; Eighteenth Judicial District: McIntosh and Pittsburg counties; Nineteenth Judicial District: Bryan County; Twentieth Judicial District: Carter, Johnston, Love, Marshall and Murray counties; Twenty-first Judicial District: Cleveland, Garvin and McClain counties; Twenty-second Judicial District: Hughes, Pontotoc and Seminole counties; Twenty-third Judicial District: Lincoln and Pottawatomie counties; Twenty-fourth Judicial District: Creek, Okfuskee and Okmulgee counties; Twenty-fifth Judicial District: Atoka and Coal counties. Appeals are referred to the Court of Appeals, the Court of Criminal Appeals and the Supreme Court.

Courthouses

*Adair County Courthouse

Division Street and Highway 59
Stilwell, OK 74960
Phone (918) 696-7198 voice or FAX, County Clerk

County organized 1907 from Cherokee lands

Land records: Contact Carrie Philpott, County Clerk, PO Box 169, Stilwell, OK 74960

Land records search service: $5.00 per name; copies: $1.00 per page

*Alfalfa County Courthouse

Cherokee, OK 73728
Phone (405) 596-3158; (405) 596-3523 Court Clerk's Office

County organized 1907 from Woods County

Land records: From 1895; contact County Clerk's Office

Naturalization records: Contact Court Clerk's Office

Vital records: Marriages; contact Court Clerk's Office

Probate records: Contact Court Clerk's Office

Probate search service: $5.00; copies: $1.00 per page

*Atoka County Courthouse

200 East Court
Atoka, OK 74525-2045
Phone (405) 889-5157

County organized 1907 from Choctaw lands

Land records: Contact Troy Gammon, County Clerk; copies: $1.00 each

Probate records: Contact Helen Kroger, Court Clerk

*Beaver County Courthouse

PO Box 338
Beaver, OK 73932-0338
Phone (405) 625-3141

County organized 1890, original county

Land records: Contact County Clerk

Probate records: Contact Court Clerk, PO Box 237, Beaver, OK 73932

No probate search service; copies: $1.00 per page, no minimum

*Beckham County Courthouse

PO Box 428
Sayre, OK 73662
Phone (405) 928-3383; (405) 928-3330 Court Clerk

County organized 1907 from Roger Mills and Greer counties

Land records: From 1900
Vital records: No vital records
Probate records: Contact Court Clerk

Blaine County Courthouse
PO Box 138
Watonga, OK 73772-0138
Phone (405) 625-5890
County organized 1895, original county

Bryan County Courthouse
402 West Evergreen
Durant, OK 74701-4744
Phone (405) 924-2201
County organized 1907 from Chickasaw lands

*Caddo County Courthouse
PO Box 68
Anadarko, OK 73005
Phone (405) 247-6609 County Clerk;
(405) 247-3393 Court Clerk
County organized 6 August 1901, original county
Land records: Through 1 July 1993; contact J. T. McCasland, County Clerk
Naturalization records: Some citizenship records; contact Court Clerk, PO Box 10, Anadarko, OK 73005
Vital records: No vital records
Probate records: Contact County Clerk

Canadian County Courthouse
El Reno, OK 73036
Phone (405) 262-1070
County organized 1890, original county

Carter County Courthouse
County Clerk or Court Clerk
First and B Street, S.W.
Ardmore, OK 73401
Phone (405) 223-8162
County organized 1907 from Chickasaw lands

*Cherokee County Courthouse
213 West Delaware
Tahlequah, OK 74464-3639
Phone (918) 456-4121; (918) 456-0691 Court Clerk
County organized 1907 from Indian lands
Land records: From 1907; contact County Clerk
Vital records: Marriage licenses from 1907; contact M. Margaret Robbins, Court Clerk, Room 302; copies: $5.00 each
Probate records: From 1907; contact Court Clerk
Probate search service: $5.00 written; copies: $1.00 for the first page and 50¢ for each additional page, no minimum

*Choctaw County Courthouse
Hugo, OK 74743
Phone (405) 326-3778
County organized 1907 from Choctaw lands
Land records: Yes
Naturalization records: Yes
Vital records: No vital records
Probate records: Yes

*Cimarron County Courthouse
Boise City, OK 73933
Phone (405) 544-2251 County Clerk;
(405) 544-2221 Court Clerk
County organized 1907 from Beaver County
Land records: Contact County Clerk
Naturalization records: From May 1908 to February 1923; contact Court Clerk
Probate records: From February 1908; contact Court Clerk, PO Box 788, Boise City, OK 73933
Probate search service: $2.00 per quarter hour; copies: $1.00 for the first page and 50¢ for each additional page, no minimum

*Cleveland County Clerk
201 South Jones
Norman, OK 73069-6099
Phone (405) 366-0240 County Clerk;
(405) 321-6402 Court Clerk
County organized 1890 from Cherokee lands
Land records: From 1889; contact Pat Dodson, County Clerk; copies: $1.00 per page
Probate records: Contact Court Clerk, 200 South Peters, Norman, OK 73069
Probate search service: direct or reverse, no charge, if time allows; copies: $1.00 for the first page and 50¢ for each additional page, no minimum

*Coal County Courthouse
4 North Main Street
Coalgate, OK 74538-2832
Phone (405) 927-2103 County Clerk
County organized 1907 from Chickasaw lands
Land records: From 1907; contact County Clerk, Suite #1
Naturalization records: No naturalization records
Vital records: No vital records
Probate records: From 1907
No probate search service; copies: $1.00 per page, no minimum

*Comanche County Courthouse
315 S.W. Fifth Street
Lawton, OK 73501-4326
Phone (405) 353-4017 District Court Clerk
County organized 1901 from Cherokee lands

Land records: Contact County Clerk, Room 504
Naturalization records: From 28 June 1930 to 23 August 1982; contact Court Clerk
Vital records: Marriages; contact Court Clerk
Probate records: Contact Court Clerk
Probate search service: no charge, but must have a date (no ten-year searches); copies: $1.00 for the first page and 50¢ for each additional page

*Cotton County Courthouse
301 North Broadway Street
Walters, OK 73572-1271
Phone (405) 875-3026 County Clerk;
(405) 875-3029 Court Clerk
County organized 1912 from Comanche County
Land records: Contact County Clerk
Vital records: Some births and deaths; contact County Clerk
Probate records: Contact Court Clerk
No probate search service; copies: $1.00 per page, no minimum

*Craig County Courthouse
PO Box 397
Vinita, OK 74301
Phone (918) 256-2507
County organized 1907 from Cherokee lands
Land records: No land records
Naturalization records: No naturalization records
Vital records: No vital records
Probate records: No probate records

*Creek County Courthouse
Sapulpa, OK 74066
Phone (918) 224-0278
County organized 1907 from Creek lands
Land records: Contact County Clerk
No land records search service; copies: $1.00 each
Naturalization records: No naturalization records
Probate records: Contact Court Clerk
No probate search service; copies: $1.00 each

*Custer County Courthouse
Arapaho, OK 73620
Phone (405) 323-4420; (405) 323-3233 Court Clerk
County organized 1891, original county
Land records: Contact County Clerk, PO Box 300, Arapaho, OK 73620
Vital records: Marriages; contact Court Clerk, PO Box D, Arapaho, OK 73620
Probate records: Contact Court Clerk
Probate search service: $5.00 per name; copies: $1.00 per page, no minimum

*Delaware County Courthouse
PO Box 309
Jay, OK 74346-0309
Phone (918) 253-4432
County organized 1907 from Cherokee lands
Land records: Contact County Clerk; copies: $1.00 each
Naturalization records: No naturalization records
Vital records: No vital records
Probate records: Contact Court Clerk

*Dewey County Courthouse
PO Box 368
Taloga, OK 73667-0368
Phone (405) 328-5390
County organized 1892, original county
Land records: From 1892; contact County Clerk; copies: $1.00 per page
Naturalization records: No naturalization records
Probate records: From 1901; contact Court Clerk
Probate search service: no charge; copies: $1.00 for the first page and 50¢ for each additional page, no minimum

*Ellis County Courthouse
100 South Washington
Arnett, OK 73832-0257
Phone (405) 885-7301
County organized 1907 from Day (which was abolished) and Woodward counties
Land records: Contact County Clerk, PO Box 197, Arnett, OK 73832; copies: $1.00 per page, $1.00 per instrument for certification
Naturalization records: No naturalization records
Vital records: No vital records
Probate records: Contact Court Clerk, PO Box 217, Arnett, OK 73832
Probate search service: no charge; copies: $1.00 for the first page and 50¢ for each additional page; "Copies made only if money accompanies request."

*Garfield County Courthouse
Enid, OK 73701
Phone (405) 237-0227
County organized 1895, original county
Land records: Deeds and mortgages from 1893 to date; contact Register of Deeds; copies: $1.00 per page, no minimum
Probate records: Contact Court Clerk

Garvin County Courthouse
County Clerk
Pauls Valley, OK 73075
Phone (405) 238-2685; (405) 238-2772 County Clerk

County organized 1907 from Chickasaw lands

*Grady County Courthouse
PO Box 1009
Chickasha, OK 73023-1009
Phone (405) 224-5211
County organized 1907 from Caddo and Comanche counties
Land records: Contact County Clerk
Probate records: From 1907; contact Court Clerk
No probate search service; copies: $1.00 for the first page and 50¢ for each additional page, no minimum; "Requests for copies must be written."

Grant County Courthouse
Medford, OK 73759-1243
Phone (405) 395-2214
County organized 1895, original county

*Greer County Courthouse
Mangum, OK 73554
Phone (405) 782-2329
County organized 1890, original county
Land records: Contact County Clerk, PO Box 207, Mangum, OK 73554
Naturalization records: Contact Court Clerk
Probate records: Contact Court Clerk

Harmon County Courthouse
Hollis, OK 73550
Phone (405) 688-3658
County organized 1909 from Greer County

*Harper County Courthouse
PO Box 369
Buffalo, OK 73834-0369
Phone (405) 735-2012
County organized 1905 from Indian lands
Land records: Contact County Clerk; copies: $1.00 per page
Naturalization records: No naturalization records
Vital records: Marriages; contact Court Clerk
Probate records: Contact Court Clerk
Probate search service: no charge; copies: $1.00 for the first page and 50¢ for each additional page

*Haskell County Courthouse
202 East Main
Stigler, OK 74462-2439
Phone (918) 967-4352
County organized 1907 from Choctaw lands
Land records: Contact County Clerk; copies: $1.00 per page, $1.00 for certification

Naturalization records: No naturalization records
Probate records: Contact Court Clerk; copies: $1.00 per page, $1.00 for certification

*Hughes County Courthouse
Holdenville, OK 74848
Phone (405) 379-3211 Courthouse; (405) 379-5487 County Clerk; (405) 379-2884 Court Clerk
County organized 1907 from Creek lands
Land records: From 1907; contact Carol Gann, County Clerk, 200 North Broadway, Suite 5, Holdenville, OK 74848
Probate records: From 1907; contact Shirley Harkey, Court Clerk, PO Box 32, Holdenville, OK 74848
Probate search service: no charge; copies: $1.00 for the first page and 50¢ for each additional page

*Jackson County Courthouse
Altus, OK 73521
Phone (405) 482-4420
County organized 1907 from Greer County
Land records: Contact County Clerk, PO Box 515, Altus, OK 73522
Land records search service: $5.00; copies: $1.00 per page, $1.00 for certification
Naturalization records: Contact Court Clerk, Room 303
Naturalization records search service: $5.00; copies: $1.00 per page, $1.00 for certification
Probate records: Contact Court Clerk
Probate search service: $5.00; copies: $1.00 per page, $1.00 for certification

*Jefferson County Courthouse
220 North Main
Waurika, OK 73573-2234
Phone (405) 228-2241; (405) 228-2029 County Clerk
County organized 1907 from Comanche County
Land records: Deeds and mortgages from 1907; contact Doris Pilgreen, County Clerk
Probate records: Contact Court Clerk's Office
No probate search service; copies: $1.00 per page

*Johnston County Courthouse
Tishomingo, OK 73460
Phone (405) 371-3058
County organized 1907 from Chickasaw lands
Land records: From 1907; contact County Clerk, PO Box 338, Tishomingo, OK 73460

Vital records: Marriages from 1907; contact Court Clerk

Probate records: From 1907; contact Court Clerk

Probate search service: no charge; copies: $1.00 for the first page and 50¢ for each additional page, $1.00 minimum

*Kay County Courthouse

Newkirk, OK 74647

Phone (405) 362-2537 County Clerk; (405) 362-3350 Court Clerk's Office

County opened for settlement by land run on 16 September 1893; organized 1895, original county; first named "K" County

Land records: From 1893 to date; contact Mattie Kimbrel, County Clerk, PO Box 450, Newkirk, OK 74647

Land records search service: $3.00 if you have a legal description; copies: $1.00 per page

Naturalization records: From 1924 to 1960; contact Court Clerk's Office, PO Box 428, Newkirk, OK 74647

Vital records: Marriages; contact Court Clerk's Office

Vital records search service: $5.00 per name per type of record; copies: $1.00 for the first page and 50¢ for each additional page of the same instrument

Probate records: Probate and estates; contact Court Clerk's Office

Probate search service: $5.00 per name per type of record; copies: $1.00 for the first page and 50¢ for each additional page of the same instrument

*Kingfisher County Courthouse

101 South Main, Room #3

Kingfisher, OK 73750

Phone (405) 375-3887; (405) 375-3813 Court Clerk's Office

County organized 1890, original county

Naturalization records: Contact Court Clerk

Vital records: Marriages; contact Court Clerk

Probate records: Contact Court Clerk's Office

*Kiowa County Courthouse

Hobart, OK 73651

Phone (405) 726-5286 County Clerk; (405) 726-5125 Court Clerk

County organized 1901, original county

Land records: Contact County Clerk, PO Box 73, Hobart, OK 73651; copies: $1.00 per page

Naturalization records: From 1906 to 1955; contact Court Clerk, PO Box 854, Hobart, OK 73651

Vital records: Marriages from September 1901; contact Court Clerk

Probate records: From August 1901; contact Court Clerk

Probate search service: $5.00; copies: $1.00 for the first page and 50¢ for each additional page, 50¢ for certification, plus SASE

*Latimer County Courthouse

109 North Central, Room 200

Wilburton, OK 74578-2440

Phone (918) 465-2011

County organized 1907 from Choctaw lands

Land records: Contact County Clerk

Vital records: No vital records

Probate records: From 1906

Probate search service: no charge; copies: $1.00 for the first page and 50¢ for each additional page

*LeFlore County Courthouse

PO Box 607

Poteau, OK 74953-0607

Phone (918) 647-2527; (918) 647-5738 County Clerk; (918) 647-3181 Court Clerk

County organized 1907 from Choctaw lands

Land records: Contact County Clerk, PO Box 218, Poteau, OK 74953

Probate records: Contact Court Clerk, PO Box 688, Poteau, OK 74953

*Lincoln County Courthouse

PO Box 126

Chandler, OK 74834-0126

Phone (405) 258-1264

County organized 1891, original county

Land records: Contact County Clerk; copies: $1.00 per page

Naturalization records: From late 1890s until 1907; contact Court Clerk

Vital records: Marriages; contact Court Clerk

Probate records: Contact Court Clerk

Probate search service: no charge; copies: $1.00 for the first page and 50¢ for each additional page, no minimum

*Logan County Courthouse

301 East Harrison

Guthrie, OK 73044

Phone (405) 292-0266 County Clerk's Office; (405) 282-0123 Court Clerk

County organized 1891, original county

Land records: Contact Mary Lou Orndorff, County Clerk's Office, Suite 102

Land records search service: must have direct or indirect records by name and legal description, if known

Naturalization records: Contact Barbara Hayes, Court Clerk, Suite 201

Probate records: Contact Court Clerk

*Love County Courthouse

405 West Main Street

Marietta, OK 73448-2848

Phone (405) 276-3059

County organized 1907 from Chickasaw lands

Land records: Contact County Clerk; copies: $1.00 per page

Naturalization records: No naturalization records

Vital records: Marriages: contact Court Clerk; copies: $1.00 per page

Probate records: Contact Court Clerk; copies: $1.00 per page

*Major County Courthouse

East Broadway

Fairview, OK 73737

Phone (405) 227-4732

County organized 1909 from Woods County

Land records: From 1908; contact County Clerk's Office

Naturalization records: From 1908 to 1928; contact Court Clerk's Office

Vital records: No vital records

Probate records: From 1908

Probate search service: no charge; copies: $1.00 for the first page and 50¢ for each additional page, no minimum

*Marshall County Courthouse

Madill, OK 73446

Phone (405) 795-3165; (405) 795-3220 County Clerk; (405) 795-3278 Court Clerk

County organized 1907 from Chickasaw lands

Land records: From about 1907; contact Glenda Bobbitt, County Clerk, Room 101

No land records search service: copies: $1.00 per page, $1.00 for certified copies

Vital records: Marriages; contact Wanda Pearce, Court Clerk

Probate records: Contact Court Clerk

No probate search service; copies: $1.00 per page, $1.00 minimum

*Mayes County Courthouse

Pryor, OK 74361

Phone (918) 825-0639

County organized 1907 from Indian lands

Land records: Contact Office of County Clerk, PO Box 97, Pryor, OK 74362

Naturalization records: No naturalization records

Vital records: No vital records

Probate records: Contact Office of Court Clerk, PO Box 867, Pryor, OK 74362

Probate search service: no charge; copies: $1.00 for the first page and 50¢ for each additional page, $1.00 minimum

*McClain County Courthouse
PO Box 629
Purcell, OK 73080
Phone (405) 527-3117
County organized 1907 from Chickasaw lands
Land records: Contact Phyllis Bennett, County Clerk
Land records search service: $3.00 per name; copies: $1.00 each
Naturalization records: No naturalization records
Vital records: No vital records
Probate records: Contact Court Clerk
Probate search service: $10.00 per name; copies: $1.00 for the first page and 50¢ for each additional page

*McCurtain County Courthouse
PO Box 1078
Idabel, OK 74745
Phone (405) 286-7428; (405) 286-2370 County Clerk; (405) 286-3693 Court Clerk
County organized 1907 from Choctaw lands
Land records: Deeds and mortgages; contact County Clerk
Probate records: Contact Court Clerk, PO Box 1038, Idabel, OK 74745
Probate search service: no charge; copies: $1.00 for the first page and 50¢ for each additional page, no minimum

McIntosh County Courthouse
PO Box 108
Eufaula, OK 74432-0108
Phone (918) 689-2362
County organized 1907 from Indian lands

*Murray County Courthouse
Sulphur, OK 73086
Phone (405) 622-3920 County Clerk; (405) 622-3223 Court Clerk
County organized 1907 from Chickasaw lands
Land records: Contact County Clerk, PO Box 442, Sulphur, OK 73086
Probate records: Contact Court Clerk

*Muskogee County Courthouse
PO Box 2307
Muskogee, OK 74402-2307
Phone (918) 682-9601
County organized 1907 from Cherokee lands
Land records: Contact County Clerk, PO Box 1008, Muskogee, OK 74402
Probate records: Contact Court Clerk, PO Box 1350, Muskogee, OK 74402
Probate search service: no charge; copies: $1.50 for the first page and 50¢ for each additional page, 50¢ for certification, no minimum

*Noble County Courthouse
300 Courthouse Drive, Box #11
Perry, OK 73077
Phone (405) 336-2141 County Clerk; (405) 336-5187 Court Clerk
County organized 1897 from Indian lands
Land records: Final certificates from the U.S., U.S. patents, deeds, mineral deeds, etc. from 1892; contact Ronita Coldiron, County Clerk
Land records search service: $5.00 per name; copies: $1.00 per page, $1.00 per page for certification
Naturalization records: Some naturalization records from 1893; contact Marilyn M. Mills, Court Clerk, 300 Courthouse Drive, Box #14, Perry, OK 73077
Naturalization records search service: $5.00 per name; copies: $1.00 for the first page and 50¢ for each additional page per instrument
Vital records: Marriages from 1893; contact Court Clerk
Vital records search service: $5.00 per name; copies: $1.00 for the first page and 50¢ for each additional page per instrument
Probate records: From 1893; contact Court Clerk
Probate search service: $5.00 per name; copies: $1.00 for the first page and 50¢ for each additional page per instrument

*Nowata County Courthouse
229 North Maple Street
Nowata, OK 74048-2654
Phone (918) 273-0175; (918) 273-2480 County Clerk; (918) 273-0127 Probate
County organized 1907 from Cherokee lands
Land records: Contact Teresa Jackson, County Clerk; copies: $1.00 per page, $1.00 for certification
Naturalization records: No naturalization records
Vital records: No vital records
Probate records: Yes

Okfuskee County Courthouse
PO Box 26
Okemah, OK 74859-0026
Phone (918) 623-0939
County organized 1907 from Creek lands

*Oklahoma County Courthouse
320 N.W. Robert S. Kerr
Oklahoma City, OK 73102-3441
Phone (405) 236-2727; (405) 278-1539 Registrar of Deeds; (405) 278-1722 Court Clerk
County organized 1891, original county
Land records: Contact Registrar of Deeds

Probate records: Contact Tom Petuskey, Court Clerk, 409 Oklahoma County Office Building, Oklahoma City, OK 73102
Probate search service: no charge; copies: $1.00 for the first page and 50¢ for each additional page, no minimum

*Okmulgee County Courthouse
314 West Seventh Street
Okmulgee, OK 74447
Phone (918) 756-0788 County Clerk; (918) 756-3042 Court Clerk
County organized 1907 from Creek lands
Land records: Contact Frances L. Smith, County Clerk, PO Box 904, Okmulgee, OK 74447; copies: $1.00 per page, $1.00 for certification
Naturalization records: No naturalization records
Vital records: No vital records
Probate records: Contact Linda Beaver, Court Clerk
No probate search service; copies: $1.00 for the first page and 50¢ for each additional page, no minimum

*Osage County Courthouse
PO Box 87
Pawhuska, OK 74056-0087
Phone (918) 287-2615
County organized 1907 from Osage Indian lands
Land records: From 1907; contact County Clerk's Office; copies: $1.00 each
Naturalization records: No naturalization records
Vital records: Marriage licenses; contact Court Clerk's Office
Probate records: Contact Court Clerk's Office
No probate search service; copies: $1.00 per page, no minimum

Ottawa County Courthouse
Miami, OK 74354
Phone (918) 542-9408
County organized 1907 from Indian lands

Pawnee County Courthouse
500 Harrison Street, Room 202
Pawnee, OK 74058
Phone (918) 762-3741
County organized 1897 from Indian lands

*Payne County Courthouse
Sixth and Husband
Stillwater, OK 74074
Phone (405) 624-9300
County organized 1890, original county

Land records: Contact County Clerk, PO Box 7, Stillwater, OK 74076
Naturalization records: No naturalization records
Vital records: No vital records
Probate records: Contact Court Clerk, Room 308
No probate search service; copies: $1.00 for the first page and 50¢ for each additional page, plus certification, $1.00 minimum

*Pittsburg County Courthouse
McAlester, OK 74501
Phone (918) 423-6865
County organized 1907 from Choctaw lands
Land records: No search service; copies: $1.00 per page; "We do not do genealogy searches."

*Pontotoc County Courthouse
Thirteenth and Broadway
Ada, OK 74820
Phone (405) 332-1425
County organized 1907 from Choctaw lands
Land records: Yes

*Pottawatomie County Courthouse
325 North Broadway
Shawnee, OK 74801
Phone (405) 273-8222
County organized 1891 as Pottawatomie-Shawnee County, original county; later named Pottawatomie County
Land records: Contact Nancy Bryce, County Clerk
Land records search service: no charge for index search; copies: $1.00 per page
Naturalization records: Contact County Clerk
Vital records: Marriage licenses; contact Billie Clark, Court Clerk
Probate records: Contact Court Clerk
No probate search service; copies: $1.00 per page

Pushmataha County Courthouse
203 S.W. Third
Antlers, OK 74523-3899
Phone (405) 298-2512
County organized 1907 from Indian lands

*Roger Mills County Courthouse
PO Box 708
Cheyenne, OK 73628
Phone (405) 497-3366
County organized 1895, original county; annexed part of Day County when it was abolished in 1907
Land records: Tract, indirect/direct, grantor/grantee records; contact

County Clerk and Recorder; copies: $1.00 per page
Probate records: Contact Court Clerk's Office
Probate search service; copies: $1.00 for the first page and 50¢ for each additional page, no minimum

Rogers County Courthouse
219 South Missouri
Claremore, OK 74017-7832
Phone (918) 341-0585
County organized 1907 from Cherokee lands

Seminole County Courthouse
Wewoka, OK 74884
Phone (405) 257-2450
County organized 1907 from Seminole lands

Sequoyah County Courthouse
120 East Chickasaw Street
Sallisaw, OK 74955-4655
Phone (918) 775-5539
County organized 1907 from Cherokee lands

*Stephens County Courthouse
Duncan, OK 73533
Phone (405) 255-0977 County Clerk; (405) 255-8460 Court Clerk
County organized 1907 from Comanche County
Land records: Contact County Clerk, PO Box 1998, Duncan, OK 73534
Land records search service: no charge; copies: $1.00 each
Probate records: Contact Court Clerk
Probate search service: $5.00 per search; copies: $1.00 for the first page and 50¢ for each additional page, no minimum

*Texas County Courthouse
Guymon, OK 73942
Phone (405) 338-3141 County Clerk; (405) 338-3003 Court Clerk
County organized 1907 from Beaver County
Land records: Contact County Clerk, PO Box 197, Guymon, OK 73942-0197
No land records search service (must have book and page number); copies: $1.00 per page
Probate records: Contact Court Clerk, PO Box 1081, Guymon, OK 73942

*Tillman County Courthouse
PO Box 992
Frederick, OK 73542
Phone (405) 335-3421 County Clerk; (405) 335-3023 Court Clerk
County organized 1907 from Comanche lands

Land records: Contact County Clerk; copies: $1.00 per page, $1.00 per instrument for certification
Naturalization records: Ten or twelve naturalization records from during World War II; contact Lois Kent, District Court Clerk, PO Box 116, Frederick, OK 73542. Other naturalization records; contact District Court Clerk in Lawton, OK or District Court Clerk in Altus, OK
Vital records: Contact District Court Clerk
Probate records: Contact District Court Clerk
No probate search service; copies: $1.00 for the first page and 50¢ for each additional page of same instrument, $1.00 minimum

*Tulsa County Courthouse
500 South Denver
Tulsa, OK 74103-3826
Phone (918) 584-0471
County organized 1907 from Creek lands
Probate records: From 1907; contact Sue McLearan, Supervisor
Probate search service: $5.00 per name; copies: $1.00 for the first page and 50¢ for each additional page, 50¢ for certification, no minimum

Wagoner County Courthouse
307 East Cherokee
Wagoner, OK 74467-4729
Phone (918) 485-2141
County organized 1907 from Creek lands

*Washington County Courthouse
420 South Johnstone
Bartlesville, OK 74003-6605
Phone (918) 337-2840 County Clerk; (918) 337-2870 Court Clerk
County organized 1907 from Cherokee lands
Land records: Contact County Clerk
Naturalization records: Contact Court Clerk
Vital records: Contact Court Clerk
Probate records: Contact Court Clerk

*Washita County Courthouse
PO Box 380
Cordell, OK 73632
Phone (405) 832-3548 County Clerk; (405) 832-3836 Court Clerk
County organized 1897 from Indian lands
Land records: Contact County Clerk, PO Box 380, Cordell, OK 72632
Land records search service: must have complete name, year, and legal description (section, township, range) of the land, if known

Naturalization records: Some naturalization records to about 1907 (indexed); contact Court Clerk, PO Box 397, Cordell, OK 73632

Naturalization records search service: no charge for a single record in a known year, $5.00 for more extensive searches; copies: $1.00 for the first page and 50¢ for each additional page

Vital records: Marriage applications/certificates from 1892 to date (indexed); contact Court Clerk

Vital records search service: no charge for a single record in a known year, $5.00 for more extensive searches; copies: $1.00 for the first page and 50¢ for each additional page

Probate records: From 1903 to date; contact Court Clerk

Probate search service: no charge for a single record in a known year, $5.00 for more extensive searches; copies: $1.00 for the first page and 50¢ for each additional page

*Woods County Courthouse
PO Box 386
Alva, OK 73717
Phone (405) 327-2126; (405) 327-0998 County Clerk
County organized 1893, original county
Land records: Contact County Clerk; copies: $1.00 per page

Naturalization records: Contact Court Clerk, PO Box 924, Alva, OK 73717

Vital records: No vital records

Probate records: Contact Court Clerk

Probate search service: no charge; copies: $1.00 for the first page and 50¢ for each additional page

*Woodward County Courthouse
1600 Main Street
Woodward, OK 73801-3046
Phone (405) 256-8097
County organized 1907 from Indian lands
Land records: From 1893 to date; contact Ron Hohweiler, County Clerk, 1600 Main Street, Woodward, OK 73801-3051

Naturalization records: Contact Court Clerk

Vital records: Marriages; contact Court Clerk

Probate records: Contact Court Clerk

OREGON

Capital: Salem. Statehood: 14 February 1859 (annexed when Great Britain relinquished claim in 1846, became a separate territory 14 August 1848, including all lands north of the 42nd parallel and west of the Rockies)

Court System

Oregon has some 145 Municipal Courts of limited jurisdiction. Nine County Courts have probate jurisdiction in Gilliam, Grant, Harney, Malheur, Sherman and Wheeler counties, and have juvenile jurisdiction in Crook, Gilliam, Harney, Jefferson, Morrow, Sherman and Wheeler counties. Justice Courts in Baker, Columbia, Curry, Douglas, Gilliam, Grant, Harney, Hood River, Jackson, Klamath, Lake, Lane, Lincoln, Linn, Malheur, Marion, Morrow, Sherman, Tillamook, Washington and Wheeler counties handle most civil actions, misdemeanors and traffic matters. District Courts in twenty-eight counties (all except Baker, Gilliam, Grant, Harney, Lake, Malheur, Sherman and Wheeler counties) have jurisdiction over some criminal cases, some civil cases, traffic violations and small claims. The District Courts in Curry, Hood River and Wasco counties hear probate cases. The state's Tax Court has statewide jurisdiction over tax cases.

The Circuit Courts have general jurisdiction and sit at each county seat. First Judicial District: Jackson County; Second Judicial District: Lane County; Third Judicial District: Marion County; Fourth Judicial District: Multnomah County; Fifth Judicial District: Clackamas County; Sixth Judicial District: Morrow and Umatilla counties; Seventh Judicial District: Gilliam, Hood River, Sherman, Wasco and Wheeler counties; Eighth Judicial District: Baker and Grant counties; Ninth Judicial District: Harney and Malheur counties; Tenth Judicial District: Union and Wallowa counties; Eleventh Judicial District: Crook, Deschutes and Jefferson counties; Twelfth Judicial District: Polk and Yamhill counties; Thirteenth Judicial District: Klamath and Lake counties; Fourteenth Judicial District: Josephine County; Fifteenth Judicial District: Coos and Curry counties; Sixteenth Judicial District: Douglas County; Seventeenth Judicial District: Lincoln County; Nineteenth Judicial District: Clatsop, Columbia and Tillamook counties; Twentieth Judicial District: Washington County; Twenty-first Judicial District:

Benton and Linn counties. The Court of Appeals and Supreme Court hear appeals.

Courthouses

*Baker County Courthouse
1995 Third Street
Baker, OR 97814-3363
Phone (503) 523-6414
County organized 1862 from unorganized territory
Land records: Contact Assessor's Office

Probate records: Contact Circuit Court

Probate search service: no charge; copies: 25¢ per page, $1.00 minimum

*Benton County Courthouse
180 N.W. Fifth
Corvallis, OR 97330-4728
Phone (503) 757-6855 County Assessor; (503) 757-6831 Department of Records and Elections; (503) 757-6825 Court Civil Division
County organized 1847, original county
Land records: Contact County Assessor's Office, 121 N.W. Fourth Street, Corvallis, OR 97330. Deeds and mortgages; contact Department of Records and Elections, 120 N.W. Fourth Street, Corvallis, OR 97330

Land records search service from Department of Records and Elections: $3.75 per name; copies: 25¢ each

Vital records: Births and deaths from 1907 to 1944; contact Department of Records and Elections

Vital records search service: $3.75 per name; copies: 25¢ each

Probate records: Contact Court Civil Division, PO Box 1870, Corvallis, OR 97339

No probate search service; copies: 25¢ per page, $3.75 for certification, no minimum

*Clackamas County Courthouse
807 Main Street
Oregon City, OR 97045
Phone (503) 655-8551 County Clerk
County organized 1843, original county
Land records: From 1856; contact John R. Kauffman, County Clerk, Recording Department, Room 104

No land records search service; copies: $4.00 for the first page and 25¢ for each additional page of the same document, $3.75 per document for certification

Naturalization records: Contact Archives Division, Secretary of State, 800 Summer Street, N.E., Salem, OR 97310

Vital records: Marriages from 1847; contact County Clerk

No vital records search service; copies: $4.00 for the first page and 25¢ for each additional page of the same document, $3.75 per document for certification

Clatsop County Courthouse
Astoria, OR 97103
Phone (503) 325-8511
County organized 1844, original county

*Columbia County Courthouse
Saint Helens, OR 97051
Phone (503) 397-3796
County organized 1854 from Washington County
Land records: Deeds and mortgages from the 1800s; contact Betty Huser, County Clerk
Naturalization records: Some naturalization records; contact County Clerk; no copies
Vital records: Marriages from 1800s; contact County Clerk
Probate records: From 1880; contact County Clerk
Probate search service: $3.75; copies: 25¢ per page, no minimum

*Coos County Courthouse
250 North Baxter Street
Coquille, OR 97423-1899
Phone (503) 396-3121, ext. 241 or 229 County Clerk
County organized 1853 from Umpqua and Jackson counties
Land records: Contact County Clerk
Naturalization records: Some indexes on file; contact County Clerk
Vital records: Births and deaths; contact Health Department. Marriages; contact Circuit Court Clerk
Probate records: Before 1 January 1983; contact County Clerk. Probate records after 1 January 1983; contact Circuit Court Clerk
No probate search service; copies: $3.75 plus 25¢ per page, no minimum

*Crook County Courthouse
300 East Third Street
Prineville, OR 97754-1949
Phone (503) 447-6555
County organized 1882 from Wasco and Grant counties
Land records: Contact Clerk
Naturalization records: Contact Clerk
Vital records: Old births and deaths to about 1950; contact Clerk's Office
Probate records: Contact Circuit Court
Probate search service: "Any records search prior to August 1986 we refer to private research person"; copies: 25¢ per page, $3.75 for certification, no minimum

*Curry County Courthouse
Gold Beach, OR 97444
Phone (503) 247-7011, ext. 209 County Clerk
County organized 1855 from Coos County
Land records: Contact Reneé Kolen, County Clerk, 450 North Ellensburg, PO Box 746, Gold Beach, OR 97444-0746; copies: 25¢ per page
Naturalization records: From 1856 to 1907; contact County Clerk; copies: 25¢ per page
Vital records: Marriages; contact County Clerk; copies: 25¢ per page

*Deschutes County Courthouse
1164 N.W. Bond Street
Bend, OR 97701-1905
Phone (503) 388-6570
County organized 1916 from Crook County
Land records: Deeds from 1882 to date, mortgages from 1897 to date, plats, mine claims; contact Mary Sue "Susie" Penhollow, County Clerk, Administration Building, 1130 N.W. Harriman, Bend, OR 97701
Land records search service: $3.75; copies: 25¢ per page
Naturalization records: Petitions from 1917 to 1970; contact County Clerk
Naturalization records search service: $3.75; copies: 25¢ per page
Vital records: Marriage applications from 1947 to date, some death certificates (in deeds); contact County Clerk. Marriage applications from 1916 to 1947; contact Archives
Vital records search service: $3.75; copies: 25¢ per page
Probate records: Contact Circuit Court Records

Douglas County Courthouse
1036 S.E. Douglas
Roseburg, OR 97470-3317
Phone (503) 672-3311
County organized 1852 from Umpqua County, which was organized in 1851 and whose remnant, after Coos County was broken off in 1855, was annexed to Douglas County in 1862

*Gilliam County Courthouse
221 South Oregon Street
PO Box 427
Condon, OR 97823
Phone (503) 384-2311
County organized 1885 from Wasco County
Land records: Contact County Clerk
Naturalization records: Limited, incomplete naturalization records; contact County Clerk
Vital records: No vital records

Probate records: Contact County Clerk
Probate search service: $3.75; copies: 25¢ per page, $3.75 per document minimum ("if we have to find it")

*Grant County Courthouse
PO Box 220
Canyon City, OR 97820-0220
Phone (503) 575-0059
County organized 1864 from Harney County
Land records: Deeds, mortgages, land patents from 1864
Naturalization records: Cannot be photocopied
Vital records: Births and deaths from 1915 to 1948, marriages from 1872
Probate records: From 1864
Probate search service: $3.75; copies: 25¢ each, no minimum

*Harney County Courthouse
450 North Buena Vista
Burns, OR 97720
Phone (503) 573-6641
County organized 1889 from Grant County
Land records: Yes; certified copies: $3.75 per instrument
Naturalization records: Discontinued
Vital records: Marriage licenses
Probate records: Yes
Probate search service: $12.50; copies: $1.00 per page, no minimum

*Hood River County Courthouse
309 State Street
Hood River, OR 97031-2093
Phone (503) 386-1442 Records Department; (503) 386-3535 Circuit Court
County organized 1908 from Wasco County
Land records: Deeds, mortgages, etc.; contact Assessment and Records Department
Land records search service: $3.75; copies: 25¢ each, $3.75 for certification
Naturalization records: Very few naturalization records
Vital records: Marriages from July 1908; contact Records Department
Probate records: Contact Trial Court Clerk
Probate search service: no charge; copies: 25¢ per page

*Jackson County Courthouse
10 South Oakdale
Medford, OR 97501-2952
Phone (503) 776-7258
County organized 1852 from Wasco County
Land records: Deeds from 1908; contact

Kathleen S. Beckett, Clerk and Recorder
Vital records: Marriages from 1970. Marriages from 1800s; contact Archives, 320 Antelope Road, White City, OR 97501. Births from 1980, deaths from 1967; contact County Health Department, 1313 Maple Grove Drive, Medford, OR 97501.
Probate records: Contact Circuit Court, Justice Building, 100 South Oakdale, Medford, OR 97501

*Jefferson County Courthouse
75 S.E. C Street
Madras, OR 97741-1707
Phone (503) 475-2449 Board of Commissioners
County organized 1914 from Crook County
Land records: Contact County Clerk
Land records search service: $3.75; copies: 50¢ per page from microfilm originals
Naturalization records: Contact County Clerk
Naturalization records search service: $3.75; copies: 50¢ per page from microfilm originals
Probate records: Contact Trial Court Clerk, Circuit Court

Josephine County Courthouse
N.W. Sixth and C
Grants Pass, OR 97526
Phone (503) 474-5221
County organized 1856 from Jackson County

Klamath County Courthouse
316 Main Street
Klamath Falls, OR 97601-6347
Phone (503) 882-2501
County organized 1882 from Lake County

Lake County Courthouse
513 Center Street
Lakeview, OR 97630-1539
Phone (503) 947-2421
County organized 1874 from unorganized territory

Lane County Courthouse
125 East Eighth Avenue
Eugene, OR 97401-2922
Phone (503) 687-4203
County organized 1851 from Linn and Benton counties

*Lincoln County Courthouse
225 West Olive Street
Newport, OR 97365-3811
Phone (503) 265-4121 County Clerk's Office

County organized 1893 from Benton County
Land records: Contact County Clerk's Office, Room 201; copies: 25¢ per page
Naturalization records: No naturalization records; contact County Clerk's Office
Vital records: Marriages only; contact County Clerk's Office
Probate records: Contact State Court Administration Office, Room 202

*Linn County Courthouse
PO Box 100
Albany, OR 97321-0031
Phone (503) 967-3831 County Clerk
County organized 1847, original county
Land records: From 1850; contact County Clerk
Naturalization records: From July 1855 to November 1956 via Clerk's accession number; contact Archives Division, Secretary of State, 800 Summer Street, N.E., Salem, OR 97310
Vital records: Births and deaths from 1903 to 1915 and 1921 to 1945; contact Archives. Marriages from 1847; contact County Clerk
Probate records: Contact Circuit Court Records, PO Box 1749, Albany, OR 97321

*Malheur County Courthouse
251 B Street, South
Vale, OR 97918
Phone (503) 473-5123
County organized 1887 from Baker County
Land records: From 1887
Naturalization records: No naturalization records
Vital records: No vital records
Probate records: From 1887
Probate search service: $3.75; copies: 25¢ per page, no minimum

*Marion County Courthouse
Salem, OR 97301
Phone (503) 588-5225
County organized 1843, original county
Land records: Contact County Clerk's Office
Probate records: Contact State of Oregon, County Courthouse

*Morrow County Courthouse
PO Box 338
Heppner, OR 97836-0338
Phone (503) 676-9061, ext. 18 County Clerk; (503) 676-5264 Circuit Court Trial Court Clerk
County organized 1885 from Umatilla County
Land records: Contact Office of the County Clerk

Naturalization records: Contact Office of the County Clerk
Vital records: Contact Office of the County Clerk
Probate records: Contact Circuit Court Trial Court Clerk
Probate search service: no charge; copies: 25¢ each, no minimum

*Multnomah County Courthouse
1021 S.W. Fourth
Portland, OR 97204-1110
Phone (503) 248-3277
County organized 1854 from Clackamas and Washington counties
Probate records: Yes
Probate search service: no charge; copies: 25¢ per page, no minimum; "Need complete name and approximate date of death and/or case number."

*Polk County Courthouse
850 Main Street
Dallas, OR 97338-3116
Phone (503) 623-9217
County organized 1845, original county
Land records: Contact County Surveyor, 751 S.W. Clay Street, Dallas, OR 97338. Deeds from 1856, mortgages, leases; contact Clerk's Office, Room 201
Vital records: Deaths (indexed under direct deeds), marriages from 1849; contact Clerk's Office
Probate records: From 1926; contact Room 301. Probate records before 1926; contact Archives Division, Secretary of State, 800 Summer Street, N.E., Salem, OR 97310.
Probate search service: $12.50; copies: 25¢ per page, no minimum

Sherman County Courthouse
500 Court Street
PO Box 365
Moro, OR 97039-0365
Phone (503) 565-3606
County organized 1889 from Wasco County

*Tillamook County Courthouse
201 Laurel Avenue
Tillamook, OR 97141-2394
Phone (503) 842-3402
County organized 1853 from Clatsop, Polk and Yamhill counties
Land records: Contact County Clerk
Vital records: Marriages; contact County Clerk
Probate records: Contact Circuit Court
No probate search service; copies: 25¢ per page, $3.75 for certified copies

*Umatilla County Courthouse
216 S.E. Fourth Avenue
Pendleton, OR 97801-2500
Phone (503) 276-7111; (503) 278-0341
    State Courts Office
County organized 1862 from Wasco
    County
Land records: From 1862 to date; contact
    Clerk's Office
Naturalization records: Scattered records
    from various years; contact Jolene
    Meadows, County Archives; copies:
    25¢ per page
Vital records: No vital records
Probate records: Contact State Courts
    Office

*Union County Courthouse
1100 L Avenue
La Grande, OR 97850-2121
Phone (503) 963-1001
County organized 1864 from Umatilla
    County
Land records: Contact County Assessor
    and County Clerk
Naturalization records: Contact County
    Clerk
Vital records: Births from 1922 to 1944,
    deaths from 1921 to 1944, marriages
    from 1864 to date; contact County
    Clerk
Probate records: Contact County Circuit
    Court
Probate search service: $12.00; $12.00
    minimum

*Wallowa County Courthouse
101 South River Street
Enterprise, OR 97828-0170
Phone (503) 426-4543 County Clerk
County organized 1887 from Union
    County
Land records: Contact Charlotte McIver,
    County Clerk, Room 100, Door 16;
    copies: $3.75 per book pulled plus
    25¢ per page copied
Naturalization records: Contact County
    Clerk; copies: $3.75 per book pulled
    plus 25¢ per page copied
Vital records: Contact County Clerk;
    copies: $3.75 per book pulled plus
    25¢ per page copied
Probate records: Contact County Clerk;
    copies: $3.75 per book pulled plus
    25¢ per page copied

*Wasco County Courthouse
511 Washington Street
The Dalles, OR 97058
Phone (503) 296-2207; (503) 296-6159
    County Clerk
County organized 1854, created from
    the original Champoeg District by
    the Territorial Legislature; it
    embraced all of Oregon east of the
    Cascade Range, most of Idaho, and
    parts of Montana and Wyoming

Land records: From 1854; contact
    County Clerk
Land records search service: no charge;
    copies: $4.00 for the first page of each
    document and 25¢ for each additional
    page
Naturalization records: Contact Archives
    Division, Secretary of State, 800
    Summer Street, N.E., Salem, OR
    97310
Vital records: Marriages from 1854;
    contact County Clerk
Vital records search service: no charge;
    copies: $4.00 for the first page of each
    document and 25¢ for each additional
    page
Probate records: From 1854; contact
    Trial Court Clerk
Probate search service: no charge;
    copies: 25¢ per page

*Washington County Public Services
    Building
155 North First Avenue
Hillsboro, OR 97124
Phone (503) 648-8741 Department of
    Assessment and Taxation; (503) 648-
    8879 Probate; (503) 648-8767 Trial
    Court Administrator
County organized 1843, original county
Land records: From 1850; contact
    Recording Section, Department of
    Assessment and Taxation—County
    Clerk, Mapping and Records Division,
    Mail Stop #9, 155 North First Avenue,
    Suite 130, Hillsboro, OR 97124
Land records search service: $3.75 per
    document plus 25¢ per page; copies:
    50¢ each for self-made copies, which
    cannot be certified, $3.75 for certified
    copies
Naturalization records: Contact State of
    Oregon Court Services, Circuit and
    District Courts of Oregon
Probate records: Contact State of Oregon
    Court Services
No probate search service; copies: 25¢
    per page, $3.75 for certification; "All
    fees payable in advance."

*Wheeler County Courthouse
PO Box 327
Fossil, OR 97830-0327
Phone (503) 763-2400
County organized 1899 from Crook,
    Gilliam and Grant counties
Land records: From 1899; contact Judy
    L. Potter, County Clerk
Naturalization records: From 1899
Vital records: Abstracts only of vital
    records; contact County Clerk
Probate records: From 1899; contact
    County Clerk
Probate search service: $3.75 per file;
    copies: 25¢ per page up to legal size,
    no minimum; "For extensive searches
    the charge is $15.00 per hour."

*Yamhill County Courthouse
535 East Fifth Street
McMinnville, OR 97128
Phone (503) 434-7518
County organized 1843, original county
Land records: Deeds from 1853,
    mortgages and plats; contact County
    Clerk
Land records search service: $15.00 per
    hour; copies: 25¢ per page
Vital records: Marriages from 1854;
    contact County Clerk
Vital records search service: $15.00 per
    hour; certified copies: $10.00 each
Probate records: From 1852; contact
    Trial Court Office
Probate search service: no charge;
    copies: 25¢ per page, $3.75 for
    certification, no minimum

PENNSYLVANIA

Capital: Harrisburg. Statehood: 12 December 1787 (obtained royal charter in 1681, Mason-Dixon Line settled 1763–1767)

Court System

Philadelphia has a Municipal Court and a Traffic Court, and Pittsburgh has a Magistrates Court. These three courts, along with the District Justice Courts, which exist in magisterial districts throughout the state except in Philadelphia County, have limited jurisdiction over lesser civil and minor criminal offenses. The Court of Common Pleas, which sits at each county seat, has general jurisdiction over all civil and criminal matters. The Orphans Court Division handles probate. Each of the state's sixty Judicial Districts has one county except the following: Seventeenth Judicial District: Snyder and Union counties; Twenty-sixth Judicial District: Columbia and Montour counties; Thirty-seventh Judicial District: Forest and Warren counties; Thirty-ninth Judicial District: Franklin and Fulton counties; Forty-first Judicial District: Juniata and Perry counties; Forty-fourth Judicial District: Sullivan and Wyoming counties; Fifty-ninth Judicial District: Cameron and Elk counties. The Commonwealth Court hears cases involving the government and its agencies. Superior Court hears some intermediate appeals, and the Supreme Court is the court of last resort.

Courthouses

*Adams County Courthouse
111–117 Baltimore Street
Gettysburg, PA 17325-2312
Phone (717) 334-6781
County organized 1800 from York County
Land records: From 1800; contact Betty H. Pitzer, Register and Recorder
Naturalization records: Contact Patricia A. Funt, Prothonotary's Office
Vital records: Contact Peggy J. Breighner, Clerk of Courts
Probate records: Contact Register and Recorder
Probate search service: $5.00 per hour, $3.00 minimum; copies: 25¢ per page, $9.00 for the first page of certified documents and $4.00 for each additional certified page, plus LSASE

*Allegheny County Office Building
542 Forbes Avenue
Pittsburgh, PA 15219
Phone (412) 350-4220 Recorder of Deeds; (412) 350-4210 Prothonotary; (412) 350-5378 Clerk of Courts; (412) 350-4188 Register of Wills (birth and death records); (412) 350-4177 Register of Wills (marriage records)
County organized 1788 from Washington and Westmoreland counties
Land records: Deeds; contact Recorder of Deeds, Room 101
Naturalization records: Contact Prothonotary, City-County Building, 414 Grant Avenue, Pittsburgh, PA 15219 and Clerk of Courts, County Courthouse, Pittsburgh, PA 15219
Vital records: Births, deaths and marriage licenses; contact Register of Wills, City-County Building, 414 Grant Street, Pittsburgh, PA 15219-2471
Probate records: Wills; contact Register of Wills

*Armstrong County Courthouse
Market Street
Kittanning, PA 16201
Phone (412) 543-2500
County organized 1800 from Allegheny, Lycoming and Westmoreland counties
Land records: Contact Beverly A. Casella, Acting Recorder of Deeds
Naturalization records: Contact Nancy Heilman, Prothonotary
Vital records: Contact Beverly A. Casella, Acting Clerk of Orphans Court
Probate records: Contact Beverly A. Casella, Acting Register of Wills
No probate search service; copies: $1.00 per page by mail, plus SASE, no minimum; "Very helpful to have names spelled correctly and approximate dates."

*Beaver County Courthouse
Beaver, PA 15009
Phone (412) 728-5700
County organized 1800 from Allegheny and Washington counties
Land records: Contact Recorder of Deeds/Tax Assessment
Naturalization records: Contact Prothonotary
Vital records: Contact Register of Wills
Probate records: Contact Register of Wills
Probate search service: cost varies; copies: $1.00 per page

*Bedford County Courthouse
203 South Julieanna Street
Bedford, PA 15522-1714

Phone (814) 623-4836 Register and Recorder; (814) 623-4833 Prothonotary
County organized 9 March 1771 from Cumberland County
Land records: Deeds from 1771; contact Gerald A. Yoder, Register and Recorder (search requires first and last names)
Naturalization records: Contact Glenora Faupel, Prothonotary
Vital records: Births and deaths from 1852 to 1854 and from 1893 to 1905, marriage licenses from 1852 to 1854 and from 1885; contact Prothonotary's Office
Probate records: Wills from 1771; contact Recorder's Office and Register of Wills
Probate search service: no charge (require first and last names); copies: 50¢ per page plus postage, no minimum

*Berks County Courthouse
633 Court Street, 13th Floor
Reading, PA 19601
Phone (215) 378-8000; (215) 378-8015 Recorder of Deeds; (215) 378-8039 Prothonotary; (215) 378-8048 Register of Wills
County organized 1751 from Bucks, Lancaster and Philadelphia counties
Land records: From 1752; contact Recorder of Deeds
Naturalization records: From 1798; contact Prothonotary (Chief Clerk—Civil Division Courts)
Probate records: From 1752; contact Register of Wills
Probate search service: $5.00; copies: $1.00 per page, no minimum

Blair County Courthouse
423 Allegheny Street
Holidaysburg, PA 16648-2022
Phone (814) 695-5541
County organized 1846 from Bedford and Huntingdon counties

*Bradford County Courthouse
301 Main Street
Towanda, PA 18848-1824
Phone (717) 265-5700
County organized 1810 from Luzerne and Lycoming counties
Land records: Deeds and mortgages from 1812, oil leases from September 1930; contact Register and Recorder's Office; copies: 50¢ per page
Naturalization records: From 1840; contact Prothonotary's Office
Vital records: Births from 1893 through 1905, deaths from 1895 through 1905, marriages from 1885; contact Register and Recorder's Office; copies: 50¢ per page

Probate records: Wills from 1812 (indexed by decedent's name or by executor/administrator); contact Register and Recorder's Office; copies: 50¢ per page

Probate search service: $10.00; copies: 50¢ per page, no minimum; "Please send a SASE."

*Bucks County Courthouse
Main and Court Street
Doylestown, PA 18901
Phone (215) 348-2911
County organized 1682, original county
Land records: Contact Edward R. Gudknecht, Recorder of Deeds
Naturalization records: Contact Charles L. Worthington, Prothonotary
Vital records: Contact Barbara G. Reilly, Register of Wills
Probate records: Contact Register of Wills
Probate search service: $10.00 estate charge; copies: $1.00 per page, $10.00 minimum

*Butler County Courthouse
336 South Main Street
Butler, PA 16001-5978
Phone (412) 285-4731
County organized 1800 from Allegheny County
Land records: Deeds and other instruments for the transfer of interest in land; contact Recorder of Deeds Office
Naturalization records: Contact Prothonotary's Office
Vital records: No vital records
Probate records and estate administration: Contact Register of Wills and Clerk of Courts Office
No probate search service

Cambria County Courthouse
South Center Street
Ebensburg, PA 15931
Phone (814) 472-5440
County organized 1804 from Bedford, Huntingdon and Somerset counties

*Cameron County Courthouse
Fifth Street
Emporium, PA 15834
Phone (814) 486-2315
County organized 1860 from Clinton, Elk, McKean and Potter counties
Land records: From 1860; contact David J. Reed, Recorder of Deeds
Naturalization records: From 1860 to 1907; contact Prothonotary
Vital records: From 1860 to 1907
Probate records: From 1860; contact Register of Wills
No probate search service; copies: 50¢ per page, $2.00 minimum

*Carbon County Courthouse
Broadway
Jim Thorpe, PA 18229
Phone (717) 325-2651 Recorder of Deeds; (717) 325-2261 Register of Wills/Clerk of Orphans Court
County organized 13 March 1843 from Monroe and Northampton counties
Land records: Deeds, mortgages, assignments, leases, etc.; contact Andrew J. Snoha, Recorder of Deeds, PO Box 87, Jim Thorpe, PA 18229; copies: 50¢ per page, $1.50 for certification
Naturalization records: Contact County Archives and Records Service, Courthouse, PO Box 129, Jim Thorpe, PA 18229
Vital records: Births from 1892 through 1905, marriages from 1 October 1885; contact Register of Wills/Clerk of Orphans Court, Courthouse, PO Box 286, Jim Thorpe, PA 18229
Vital records search service: $12.00 per hour, $7.00 for ¹/₂ hour or less; copies: 25¢ per page from paper originals, 50¢ per page from microfilm originals
Probate records: Wills from December 1843; contact Register of Wills/Clerk of Orphans Court
Probate search service: $12.00 per hour; copies, $7.00 for ¹/₂ hour or less: 25¢ per page from paper originals, 50¢ per page from microfilm originals.
Probate search service from County Archives and Records Services: $20.00 per individual name (supply approximate birth and death dates), includes index to wills and administrations, deed and mortgage indexes, Orphans Court index, naturalization records, indexes to the Court of Quarter Sessions, burial records from Spanish American War to World War II, birth, death and marriage records, and mapping (original land owners), and includes up to 25 pages of copies; additional copies: 50¢ per page

*Centre County Courthouse
Bellefonte, PA 16823-3003
Phone (814) 355-6700
County organized 1800 from Huntingdon, Lycoming, Mifflin and Northumberland counties
Land records: Contact Hazel M. Peters, Recorder of Deeds
Naturalization records: Contact David L. Immel, Prothonotary
Vital records: Births from 1893 to 1905; contact Roger A. Bierly, Register of Wills
Probate records: Contact Register of Wills
Probate search service: no charge; copies: costs vary

*Chester County Archives and Records Services
117 West Gay Street
West Chester, PA 19380
Phone (215) 334-6760; (215) 344-6000 Recorder of Deeds Office, Prothonotary's Office, Clerk of Orphans Court, or Register of Wills
County organized 1682, original county
Land records: Deeds from about 1716 to 1805. Deeds after 1805; contact Recorder of Deeds Office, Chester County Courthouse, Market and High Streets, West Chester, PA 19380
Naturalization records: From 1798 to 1906. Naturalization records after 1900; contact Prothonotary's Office, Chester County Courthouse, Market and High Streets, West Chester, PA 19380
Vital records: Births and deaths from 1852 to 1855 and 1893 to 1906, marriages from 1852 to 1855 and 1885 to 1930. Marriages after 1930; contact Clerk of Orphans Court, Chester County Courthouse, Market and High Streets, West Chester, PA 19380
Vital records search service from courthouse: $5.00 for three years (includes copy of the record if found)
Probate records: From 1714 to 1923. Probate records after 1923; contact Register of Wills, Chester County Courthouse, Market and High Streets, West Chester, PA 19380
Probate search service: no charge; copies: $5.00 per file, up to fifteen pages, and 35¢ for each additional page, $5.00 minimum; "Please give sufficient reference information (name(s), date, location, etc.); make check payable to the 'Chester County Archives.'"

*Clarion County Courthouse
Main Street
Clarion, PA 16214
Phone (814) 226-4000
County organized 1839 from Armstrong and Venango counties
Land records: From 1840; contact Recorder's Office
Naturalization records: To late 1800s; contact Prothonotary's Office
Vital records: Births and deaths from 1893 to 1906, marriages from 1885; contact Recorder's Office
Probate records: From 1840; contact Recorder's Office
Probate search service: $5.00; copies: $1.00 per page, plus SASE, no minimum

*Clearfield County Courthouse
2 Market Street
PO Box 361

Clearfield, PA 16830-0316
Phone (814) 765-2641
County organized 1804 from Lycoming and Northumberland counties
Land records: From 1804; contact Karen L. Starck, Register and Recorder
Naturalization records: From 1850; contact Prothonotary
Vital records: Births and deaths from 1893 to 1905, marriages from 1885; contact Register and Recorder
Probate records: From 1820; contact Register and Recorder
No probate search service; copies: 50¢ per page

*Clinton County Courthouse
PO Box 928
Lock Haven, PA 17745
Phone (717) 893-4000; (717) 893-4020 Register and Recorder
County organized 21 June 1839 from Centre and Lycoming counties
Land records: From 1839; contact Barbara G. Muthler, Registrar and Recorder; copies: $1.00 for the first page and 50¢ for each additional page
Naturalization records: Contact Prothonotary
Vital records: Births and deaths from 1893 through 1905; marriages from 1885 to date (no general index); contact Register and Recorder; copies: $1.00 for the first page and 50¢ for each additional page
Probate records: From 1839; contact Registrar and Recorder
Probate search service: no charge; copies: $1.00 for the first page and 50¢ for each additional page

*Columbia County Courthouse
PO Box 380
Bloomsburg, PA 17815
Phone (717) 784-1991
County organized 1813 from Northumberland County
Land records: Contact Tax Records
Naturalization records: Contact Prothonotary/Clerk of Courts
Vital records: From 1893 to 1905; contact Prothonotary/Clerk of Courts
Probate records: From 1813; contact Register of Wills
No probate search service; copies: 25¢ each, no minimum

*Crawford County Courthouse
903 Diamond Park
Meadville, PA 16335-2677
Phone (814) 336-1151
County organized 1800 from Allegheny County
Land records: Contact Register and Recorder
Naturalization records: Contact

Prothonotary; copies: 50¢ per page
Vital records: From 1893 through 1905; contact Clerk of Courts
Probate records: Contact Register and Recorder
Probate search service: usually no charge; copies: $2.00 per page, no minimum

Cumberland County Courthouse
Hanover Street
Carlisle, PA 17013
Phone (717) 249-1133
County organized 1750 from Lancaster County

*Dauphin County Courthouse
Front and Market Streets
PO Box 1295
Harrisburg, PA 17108-1295
Phone (717) 255-2741; (717) 255-2802 Recorder of Deeds; (717) 255-2697 Prothonotary; (717) 255-2657 Register of Wills
County organized 1785 from Lancaster County
Land records: From 1785; contact Phil Spaseff, Recorder of Deeds
Naturalization records: From 1845 (except 1900 to 1917 inclusive filed with Clerk of Court, Federal Courthouse, Scranton, PA); contact Stephen Farina, Prothonotary
Vital records: Births and deaths from 1893 to 1906, marriages from 1885; contact Jane D. Marfizo, Register of Wills and Clerk of the Orphans Court Division
Probate records: From 1785; contact Register of Wills and Clerk of the Orphans Court Division
Probate search service: $10.00 per individual; copies: $1.00 per page; "We duplicate from original documents."

*Delaware County Courthouse
West Front Street
Media, PA 19063
Phone (610) 891-4000; (610) 891-5983 Records Facility Manager
County organized 1789 from Chester County
Land records: From 1935; contact Assessment, Planning
Naturalization records: From 1800; contact John J. Stubbs, Records Facility Manager, Building #19, Fair Acres, Lima, PA 19037
Probate records: From 1789; contact Records Facility

*Elk County Courthouse
PO Box 314
Ridgway, PA 15853-0314

Phone (814) 776-5349 Register and Recorder and Clerk of Orphans Court
County organized 1843 from Clearfield, Jefferson and McKean counties
Land records: From 1843 to date; contact Recorder of Deeds
Naturalization records: From 1944 to date; contact Prothonotary, PO Box 237, Ridgway, PA 15853
Vital records: Births and deaths from 1893 to 1905; contact Register of Wills. Births and deaths from 1906 to date; contact Vital Records, PO Box 1528, New Castle, PA 16103
Probate records: From 1843 to date; contact Register of Wills

*Erie County Courthouse
140 West Sixth Street
Erie, PA 16501-1011
Phone (814) 451-6000
County organized 1800 from Allegheny County
Land records: Contact Recorder of Deeds
Naturalization records: Contact Prothonotary
Vital records: Contact Prothonotary
Probate records: Contact Register of Wills
Probate search service: $5.00; copies: $1.00 each, no minimum

*Fayette County Courthouse
61 East Main Street
Uniontown, PA 15401-3514
Phone (412) 437-4525; (412) 430-1238 Recorder of Deeds; (412) 430-1206 Register of Wills
County organized 1783 from Westmoreland County
Land records: Contact David Malosky, Recorder of Deeds
Naturalization records: Contact Edward Brady
Vital records: Contact Michael Frick, Register of Wills
Probate records: Contact John V. Schroyer
Probate search service: no charge (must have given name and surname and approximate dates); copies: 50¢ per page, no minimum

*Forest County Courthouse
PO Box 423
Tionesta, PA 16353
Phone (814) 755-3526
County organized 1848 from Jefferson and Venango counties
Land records: From 1857; contact Recorder
Naturalization records: Dates are questionable; contact Prothonotary
Vital records: Births from 1893 to 1905, deaths from 1893 to 1907, marriages from 1885; contact Clerk of Orphans Court

Probate records: From 1855; contact
Register of Wills
Probate search service: $5.00; copies:
25¢ per page, $1.00 minimum

*Franklin County Courthouse
157 Lincoln Way, East
Chambersburg, PA 17201-2211
Phone (717) 264-4125
*County organized 1784 from
Cumberland County*
Land records: Contact Register and
Recorder
Naturalization records: Contact
Prothonotary
Vital records: Contact Clerk of Courts
Probate records: Contact Register and
Recorder
No probate search service; copies: 25¢
per page, $1.00 minimum

*Fulton County Courthouse
201 North Second Street
McConnellsburg, PA 17233
Phone (717) 485-4212
*County organized 1850 from Bedford
County*
Land records: From 1850; contact
Prothonotary's Office
Naturalization records: From 1843 to
1915; contact Prothonotary's Office
Vital records: Births and deaths from
1895 to 1905; contact Prothonotary's
Office
Probate records: From 1850; contact
Prothonotary's Office (Prothonotary,
Recorder of Deeds, Register of Wills
and Clerk of Courts all held by same
office holder)
Probate search service: no charge;
copies: 25¢ each for regular-sized
copies, 50¢ for large copies, $1.00
minimum

*Greene County Courthouse
Waynesburg, PA 15370-9998
Phone (412) 852-5283 Register and
Recorder
*County organized 1796 from
Washington County*
Land records: Deeds, mortgages, leases,
agreements, right of ways, etc. from
1796 to date; contact Shirley
McDougal, Recorder's Office
Naturalization records: From 1796 to
early 1900s; contact Prothonotary's
Office
Vital records: Births and deaths from
1893 to 1915, marriages from 1885;
contact Clerk of Courts; copies: $4.00
for births, $3.00 for deaths, $5.00 for
marriages
Probate records: From 1796 to date;
contact Recorder's Office
Probate search service: no charge (need
first and last names); copies: $5.00 for

the first page and 50¢ for each
additional page

*Huntingdon County Courthouse
223 Penn Street
Huntingdon, PA 16652
Phone (814) 643-3091; (814) 643-2740
Recorder of Deeds and Register of
Wills and Clerk of Orphans Court;
(814) 643-1610 Prothonotary
*County organized 1787 from Bedford
County*
Land records: From 1787 to date; contact
Recorder of Deeds
Naturalization records: From 1787;
contact Prothonotary
Vital records: Births and deaths from
1894 to 1905, marriages from October
1885 to date; contact Clerk of
Orphans Court
Probate records: From 1787 to date;
contact Register of Wills

*Indiana County Courthouse
825 Philadelphia
Indiana, PA 15701-3934
Phone (412) 465-3860 Register and
Recorder; (412) 465-3855
Prothonotary and Clerk of Courts
*County organized 1803 from Lycoming
and Westmoreland counties*
Land records: From 1803; contact
Register and Recorder
Naturalization records: From 1806 to
1958; contact Prothonotary and Clerk
of Courts
Vital records: Births and deaths from
1893 to 1905; contact Register and
Recorder
Probate records: From 1803; contact
Register and Recorder
No probate search service; copies: 25¢
per page, $3.00 minimum

*Jefferson County Courthouse
200 Main Street
Brookville, PA 15825-1236
Phone (814) 849-8031; (814) 849-1610
Register and Recorder; (814) 849-
1606 Prothonotary
*County organized 1804 from Lycoming
County*
Land records: From 1828 to date; contact
Diane Maihle Kiehl, Recorder of
Deeds
Land records search service: $5.00 per
name; copies: 50¢ per page plus $2.50
for mailing
Naturalization records: Contact Kae
Ploucha, Prothonotary
Vital records: From 1893 to 1906;
contact Diane Maihle Kiehl, Clerk of
the Orphans Court
Vital records search service: $5.00 per
name; copies: 50¢ per page plus $2.50
for mailing

Probate records: From 1828 to date;
contact Diane Maihle Kiehl, Register
of Wills
Probate search service: $5.00 per name;
copies: 50¢ per page plus $2.50 for
mailing

Juniata County Courthouse
PO Box 68
Mifflintown, PA 17059-0068
Phone (717) 436-8991
*County organized 1831 from Mifflin
County*

*Lackawanna County Courthouse
North Washington Avenue
Scranton, PA 18503
Phone (717) 963-6723
*County organized 1878 from Luzerne
County*
Land records: From 1878; contact
Genealogical Research Society of
Northeastern Pennsylvania, Inc.
(GRSNP), PO Box 175, Olyphant, PA
18447-0175
Land records search service: $5.00 per
name and/or event for society
members, $10.00 for non-members,
payable in advance, plus LSASE
Naturalization records: From 5 October
1866 to 1906; contact GRSNP
Naturalization records search service:
$5.00 per name and/or event for
society members, $10.00 for non-
members, payable in advance, plus
LSASE
Vital records: Births and deaths,
marriages from 1885; contact GRSNP
Vital records search service: $5.00 per
name and/or event for society
members, $10.00 for non-members,
payable in advance, plus LSASE
Probate records: Yes; contact GRSNP
Probate search service: $5.00 per name
and/or event for society members,
$10.00 for non-members, payable in
advance, plus LSASE

Lancaster County Courthouse
50 North Duke Street
Lancaster, PA 17602-2805
Phone (717) 299-8300; (717) 299-8319
Archives Division
*County organized 1729 from Chester
County*
Land records: From 1729; contact
Richard Galbreath, Director of Office
of Records and Archives Services,
Ground Floor of Old Court House, PO
Box 3450, Lancaster, PA 17603-1881
Vital records: Births from 1893 to 1907
for Lancaster County, from 1881 to
1906 for Lancaster City, marriages
from 1885; contact Office of Records
and Archives Services
Probate records: Contact Register of
Wills

*Lawrence County Courthouse
Court Street
New Castle, PA 16101
Phone (412) 658-2541
County organized 1849 from Beaver and Mercer counties
Land records: Contact Recorder of Deeds' Office
Naturalization records: Contact Prothonotary's Office
Vital records: Births and deaths from 1893 to 1905, marriages; contact Prothonotary's Office. Births and deaths from 1905 to date; contact Bureau of Vital Statistics, The Central Building, 101 South Mercer Street, Fourth Floor, New Castle, PA 16101
Probate records: Contact Register of Wills; copies: $1.00 for the first page (includes mail search) and 50¢ for each additional page

*Lebanon County Courthouse
400 South Eighth Street
Lebanon, PA 17042-6794
Phone (717) 274-2801
County organized 1815 from Dauphin and Lancaster counties
Land records: Contact Recorder of Deeds
Naturalization records: From about 1861 to date; contact Prothonotary's Office
Vital records: Births from 1893 through 1906, marriages from 1885 to date; contact Register of Wills, Orphans Court
Probate records: Contact Register of Wills Office

*Lehigh County Courthouse
455 Hamilton Street
Allentown, PA 18105
Phone (215) 820-3000
County organized 1812 from Northampton County
Land records: Yes
Naturalization records: Yes
Vital records: Yes
Probate records: Yes

*Luzerne County Courthouse
600 North River Street
Wilkes-Barre, PA 18702-2685
Phone (717) 825-1500
County organized 1786 from Northumberland County
Land records: Contact Recorder of Deeds
Naturalization records: Contact Prothonotary
Vital records: Births; contact Register of Wills
Probate records: Contact Register of Wills
Probate search service: $5.00 per search; copies: $1.00 per page

*Lycoming County Courthouse
48 West Third Street
Williamsport, PA 17701-6519
Phone (717) 327-2258
County organized 1795 from Northumberland County
Land records: From 1795; contact Annabel Miller, Register and Recorder
Naturalization records: From 1804 to 1956; contact William J. Burd, Prothonotary
Vital records: Births from 1893 to 1905, deaths from 1893 to 1898, marriages from 1885; contact Register and Recorder
Probate records: From 1850; contact Register and Recorder
Probate search service: $5.00; copies: 25¢ per page, $1.00 minimum

*McKean County Courthouse
Main Street
PO Box 202
Smethport, PA 16749
Phone (814) 887-5571, ext. 250 Recorder of Deeds; (814) 887-5571, ext. 270 Prothonotary; (814) 887-5571 Register of Wills
County organized 1804 from Lycoming County
Land records: Contact Betty Comes, Recorder of Deeds
Naturalization records: Contact Bonnie Moore, Prothonotary
Vital records: Marriage licenses; contact Carol P. Christensen, Register of Wills; certified copies: $10.00 each for licenses, $15.00 each for applications
Probate records: Contact Register of Wills
Probate search service: no charge; copies: $1.00 per page, $10.00 for the first certified page and $5.00 for each additional certified page, no minimum

*Mercer County Courthouse
South Diamond Street
Mercer, PA 16137
Phone (412) 662-3800
County organized 1800 from Allegheny County
Land records: Contact Marilyn L. Felesky, Recorder of Deeds
Naturalization records: Contact Elizabeth F. Fair, Prothonotary
Vital records: Contact Marie V. Forsyth, Clerk of Courts and Clerk of Orphans Court
Probate records: Contact Marie V. Forsyth, Register of Wills, 112 Mercer County Courthouse

Mifflin County Courthouse
20 North Wayne Street
Lewistown, PA 17044-1770
Phone (717) 248-6733

County organized 1789 from Cumberland and Northumberland counties

*Monroe County Courthouse
Courthouse Square
Stroudsburg, PA 18360
Phone (717) 424-5100
County organized 1836 from Northampton and Pike counties
Land records: Contact Dennis W. Deshler, Recorder of Deeds
Naturalization records: Contact Joyce A. Reese, Prothonotary
Vital records: Contact Prothonotary
Probate records: Contact Dennis W. Deshler, Register of Wills
Probate search service: no charge for one name if time warrants; copies: 25¢ per page; "Old records all on microfiche up to end of 1981; reader-printers are available; 1981 to present files may be used from file folders."

Montgomery County Courthouse
Norristown, PA 19404
Phone (215) 278-3000
County organized 1784 from Philadelphia County

*Montour County Courthouse
29 Mill Street
Danville, PA 17821-1945
Phone (717) 271-3012
County organized 1850 from Columbia County
Land records: From 1850; contact Register and Recorder's Office
Naturalization records: From 1850 to 1940; contact Suzanne M. Tinsley, Prothonotary
Vital records: Births and deaths from 1893 to 1905, marriage licenses from 1885; contact Suzanne M. Tinsley, Clerk of Court and Clerk of Orphans Court
Probate records: From 1850; contact Register and Recorder's Office
Probate search service: $5.00; copies: 50¢ each, no minimum

Northampton County Courthouse
Seventh and Washington Streets
Easton, PA 18042-7401
Phone (215) 253-4111
County organized 1752 from Bucks County

*Northumberland County Courthouse
Sunbury, PA 17801-3408
Phone (717) 988-4100
County organized 1772 from Bedford, Berks, Cumberland, Lancaster and Northampton counties
Land records: From 1772; contact Frederick F. Reed, Recorder

Naturalization records: Contact Prothonotary

Vital records: Contact Recorder

Probate records: From 1772; contact Frederick F. Reed, Register of Wills

No probate search service; copies: 25¢ each, $2.00 minimum

*Perry County Courthouse
PO Box 223
New Bloomfield, PA 17068
Phone (717) 582-2131
County organized 1820 from Cumberland County
Land records: From 1820
Naturalization records: From 1904 to 1973; contact Prothonotary, PO Box 325, New Bloomfield, PA 17068
Vital records: Births from 1893 to 1918
Probate records: From 1820
Probate search service: $2.00; copies: 50¢ per page plus 25¢ per ounce postage and handling, no minimum

Philadelphia County Courthouse
City Hall
Philadelphia, PA 19107-3209
Phone (215) 686-3462
County organized 1682, original county

*Pike County Courthouse
412 Broad Street
Milford, PA 18337-1511
Phone (717) 296-7613
County organized 1814 from Wayne County
Land records: From 1814
Naturalization records: No naturalization records
Vital records: Births and deaths from 1895 to 1905 only
Probate records: From 1820
No probate search service; copies: 25¢ (in person only)

*Potter County Courthouse
1 East Second Street, Room 22
Coudersport, PA 16915
Phone (814) 274-8290
County organized 1804 from Lycoming County
Land records: Yes
Naturalization records: Yes
Vital records: Yes
Probate records: Yes

*Schuylkill County Courthouse
401 North Second Street
Pottsville, PA 17901-2528
Phone (717) 622-5570
County organized 1811 from Berks and Northampton counties
Vital records: Births and deaths from 1893 to 1905, marriages from 1885 to date; contact George A. Uritis, Register of Wills and Clerk of the

Orphans Court; certified copies: $4.00 each for births, $3.00 each for deaths and marriages, plus SASE

Probate records: Wills from 1811 to date, estates (minors' and decedents', indexed from 1888 to date), Orphans Court proceedings (indexed from 1888 to date); copies: 50¢ per page

*Snyder County Courthouse
PO Box 217
Middleburg, PA 17842-0217
Phone (717) 837-4202
County organized 1855 from Union County
Land records: From 1855; contact Harvey J. Kreamer, Jr., Recorder of Deeds
Naturalization records: No naturalization records
Vital records: Births and deaths from 1893 to 1905 inclusive, marriages from 1885; contact Teresa J. Berger, Prothonotary
Probate records: From 1855; contact Harvey J. Kreamer, Jr., Register of Wills
No probate search service; copies: 50¢ each for regular-sized copies, $1.00 each for oversized copies, no minimum

*Somerset County Courthouse
111 East Union Street
Somerset, PA 15501
Phone (814) 443-1434
County organized 1795 from Bedford County
Land records: Contact Pat Brant, Recorder of Deeds
Naturalization records: Contact Sandra Miller Hickton, Prothonotary
Vital records: Births and deaths from 1893 to 1906 (a few for 1907 and 1908), marriages from 10 October 1885 to date; contact Linda Jo Berkey, Register of Wills
Probate records: From 1795 to date; contact Register of Wills
Probate search service: no charge; copies: 50¢ each, $5.00 for certified copies, plus SASE

Sullivan County Courthouse
Laporte, PA 18626
Phone (717) 946-5201
County organized 1847 from Lycoming County

*Susquehanna County Courthouse
PO Box 218
Montrose, PA 18801
Phone (717) 278-4600, ext. 110 Recorder's Office
County organized 1810 from Luzerne County

Land records: Deeds from 1810, mortgages from 1813; contact Recorder's Office ("Need a first name when looking up deeds and mortgages, also an approximate year")

Naturalization records: Contact Prothonotary

Vital records: Births and deaths from 1893 to 1906, marriages from 1885; contact Recorder's Office

Probate records: From 1810; contact Recorder's Office

Probate search service: $5.00; copies: $2.00 per page

*Tioga County Courthouse
116–188 Main Street
Wellsboro, PA 16901-1410
Phone (717) 724-9260 Register and Recorder; (717) 724-9281 Prothonotary
County organized 26 March 1804 from Lycoming County (townships and dates of organization: Tioga from Lycoming 1808; Delmar from Lycoming 1808; Deerfield from Delmar 1814; Elkland from Delmar 1814; Covington from Tioga, February 1815; Jackson from Tioga, September 1815; Sullivan from Covington, February 1816; Lawrence from Tioga and Elkland, December 1816; Charleston from Delmar, December 1820; Westfield from Deerfield, December 1821; Middlebury from Delmar and Elkland, September 1822; Liberty from Delmar and Covington, February 1823; Shippen from Delmar, February 1823; Richmond from Covington, February 1824; Morris from Delmar, September 1824; Rutland from Jackson and Sullivan, February 1828; Chatham from Deerfield, February 1828; Farmington from Elkland, February 1830; Union from Sullivan, February 1830; Gaines from Shippen, March 1838; Bloss from Covington, June 1841; Clymer (formerly Middlebury) from Westfield and Gaines, December 1850; Ward from Sullivan and Union, February 1852; Elk from Delmar and Morris, February 1856; Osceola from Elkland, December 1854; Nelson from Elkland, December 1857; Hamilton from Bloss, December 1872; Duncan from Delmar, Charleston and Morris, December 1873; Brookfield from Westfield 1827; Putnam from Covington Township and Borough 1 October 1918) (boroughs and dates: Wellsboro from Delmar, May 1830; Lawrenceville from Lawrence, May 1831; Covington from Covington Township, May 1831; Elkland from Elkland Township, May 1831;

Knoxville from Deerfield, May 1850; Mansfield from Richmond, February 1857; Mainesburg from Sullivan, February 1859; Tioga from Tioga Township, February 1860; Fall Brook from Ward, August 1864; Westfield from Westfield Township, January 1867; Blossburg from Bloss, August 1871; Roseville from Rutland, August 1876; Nelson from Nelson Township; Osceola from Osceola Township, November 1882; Liberty from Liberty Township, July 1893)

Land records: Deeds from 1807, mortgages from 1812; contact Nancy C. Kimble, Register of Deeds, Recorder of Wills, and Clerk of Orphans Court

Land records search service: $5.00 per surname; copies: $2.00 per page, $1.50 for certification

Naturalization records: Contact Prothonotary

Vital records: Births and deaths from 1893 to 1905, marriage licenses from 1885; contact Register and Recorder

Vital records search service: $5.00 per name; copies: $7.00 each

Probate records: Wills and administrations from 1806; contact Register and Recorder

Probate search service: $40.00 per surname (from Tioga County Historical Society, 120 Main Street, PO Box 724, Wellsboro, PA 16901, includes grantee and grantor deeds index 1807–1874, wills and administrations 1807–1880, Orphans Court 1807–1880, alien records 1813–1903, marriage licenses 1885–1905, and births and deaths 1893–1905), $5.00 per name (from Register and Recorder); copies: $7.00 for the first certified page and $3.00 for each additional certified page

*Union County Courthouse
103 South Second Street
Lewisburg, PA 17837-1903
Phone (717) 524-8761 Registrar; (717) 524-8751 Prothonotary and Clerk of Courts
County organized 1813 from Northumberland County
Land records: Grantor/grantee records; contact Registrar
Naturalization records: From 1813 to 1956; contact Prothonotary
Vital records: Births and deaths from 1893 to 1905, marriage licenses from 1885; contact Clerk of the Orphans Court
Probate records: Wills and letters of administration; contact Registrar
Probate search service: $5.00; copies: $1.00 per page, $5.00 minimum (includes search), plus LSASE

*Venango County Courthouse
Franklin, PA 16323
Phone (814) 432-9534 Register and Recorder; (814) 432-9576 Prothonotary and Clerk of Courts
County organized 1800 from Allegheny and Lycoming counties
Land records: From 1805; contact Sue A. Buchan, Register of Wills, Recorder of Deeds, Clerk of Orphans Court Division
Naturalization records: From 1806 to 1929; contact Peggy L. Miller, Prothonotary and Clerk of Courts
Vital records: Births and deaths from 1893 through 1905 inclusive, marriages from 1 October 1885; contact Register of Wills, Recorder of Deeds, Clerk of Orphans Court Division
Probate records: From 1805; Register of Wills, Recorder of Deeds, Clerk of Orphans Court Division
Probate search service: cost determined by amount and kind of work to be done; copies: 50¢ per page plus postage, no minimum

*Warren County Courthouse
204 Fourth Street
Warren, PA 16365-2318
Phone (814) 723-7550
County organized 1800 from Allegheny and Lycoming counties
Land records: From 1819; contact Recorder of Deeds
Naturalization records: From 1847 to 1969; contact Prothonotary
Vital records: From 1893 through 1905; contact Clerk of Orphans Court
Probate records: From 1819; contact Register of Wills
Probate search service: $5.00; copies: $1.00 per page; "Must be paid in advance with SASE for return of papers."

Washington County Courthouse
100 West Beau Street
Washington, PA 15301-4402
Phone (412) 228-6700
County organized 1781 from Westmoreland County

*Wayne County Courthouse
925 Court Street
Honesdale, PA 18431-1996
Phone (717) 253-5970, ext. 200
County organized 1798 from Northampton County
Land records: From 1798; contact Ginger Golden, Register and Recorder
Naturalization records: From 1798 through 1956; contact Edmund J. Rose, Prothonotary and Clerk of Courts

Vital records: From 1893 to 1906; contact Prothonotary and Clerk of Courts
Probate records: From 1798; contact Register and Recorder
No probate search service; copies: 50¢ per page, no minimum; "Some records are missing due to a flood."

*Westmoreland County Courthouse
301 Courthouse Square
Greensburg, PA 15601-2405
Phone (412) 830-3000; (412) 830-3177 Register of Wills
County organized 1773 from Bedford County
Land records: From 1773; contact Jeanne C. Griffith, Recorder of Deeds, Recorder of Deeds Office, 503 Courthouse Square, PO Box 160, Greensburg, PA 15601
Naturalization records: Copies and dockets for cases from 20 September 1902 to 20 January 1907, petitions from 1874 to date, and a group of volumes listing immigrants and their naturalizations in alphabetical order; contact Ron Diehl, Prothonotary, Room 501; copies: $2.00 per page
Vital records: Births and deaths from 1893 to 1905, marriages from 1885 to date; contact Register of Wills Office; certified copies: $5.00 each
Probate records: From 1773 to date; contact Register of Wills Office
Probate search service: $3.00 minimum per will (must have both first and last names, and approximate date); copies: 50¢ per page plus postage

Wyoming County Courthouse
Courthouse Square
Tunkhannock, PA 18657-1216
Phone (717) 836-3200
County organized 1842 from Luzerne County

*York County Courthouse
28 East Market Street
York, PA 17401-1501
Phone (717) 771-9675; (717) 771-9727 County Archives
County organized 1749 from Lancaster County
Land records: Contact Recorder of Deeds
Naturalization records: Contact County Archives, Fourth Floor
Vital records: Contact Orphans Court and Register of Wills
Probate records: Contact Register of Wills
No probate search service; copies: $1.00 per page, no minimum

RHODE ISLAND

Capital: Providence. Statehood: 29 May 1790 (officially called Rhode Island and Providence Plantations, chartered 1663)

Court System

Rhode Island has Municipal Courts of limited jurisdiction in Coventry, North Providence, Pawtucket, Providence, and Warwick. Probate Courts, whose judges are appointed by the mayor or town council, exist in thirty-six towns: Barrington, Bristol, Burrillville, Central Falls, Charlestown, Coventry, Cranston, Cumberland, East Greenwich, East Providence, Exeter, Foster, Glocester, Hopkinton, Jamestown, Johnston, Lincoln, Little Compton, Middletown, Narragansett, Newport, North Providence, North Smithfield, Pawtucket, Portsmouth, Providence, Richmond, Scituate, Smithfield, South Kingston, Tiverton, Warren, Warwick, West Greenwich, West Warwick, Westerly and Woonsocket. Family Court sits in Kent, Newport, Providence and Washington counties to hear domestic and juvenile cases, and sits in Bristol County and the city of Woonsocket for juvenile matters only.

District Courts sit in places designated by the chief judge and hear some civil actions, small claims, mental health matters, housing code violations, misdemeanors, felony arraignments and administrative agency appeals. First Division: Bristol County; Second Division: Newport County; Third Division: Kent County; Fourth Division: Washington County; Fifth Division: cities of Pawtucket and Central Falls and the towns of Lincoln and Cumberland; Sixth Division: cities of Providence and East Providence; Seventh Division: city of Woonsocket and the towns of Burrillville, Glocester, Smithfield and North Smithfield; Eighth Division: city of Cranston and the towns of North Providence, Johnston, Scituate and Foster. The Superior Court sits at Bristol, Newport, Providence, South Kingston, Warwick, Westerly and Woonsocket and has general jurisdiction over civil and felony actions. The Supreme Court hears appeals.

Note that town records, vital records, probate records, and land records are not held at the county level.

Counties

Bristol County Courthouse
Bristol, RI 02809
County organized 1747 from Newport County

Third Division, District Court (Kent County)
Cranston, RI 02910
Phone (401) 821-1740
County organized 1750 from Washington County

Newport County Courthouse
Newport, RI 02840
County organized 1703, original county

Providence County Courthouse
Providence, RI 02903
County organized 1703, original county

Washington County Courthouse
4800 Tower Hill Road
Wakefield, RI 02879
Phone (401) 783-5441
County organized 1729 from Newport County
Naturalization records: Contact Oliver Stedman Government Center, District Court

Towns, Cities and Probate Courts

Barrington Probate Court
514 Main Street
Warren, RI 02885
Town incorporated 1770

*Bristol Probate Court
Bristol, RI 02809
Phone (401) 253-7000
Town incorporated 1680
Land records: From 1746
Naturalization records: Yes
Vital records: From 1600s
Probate records: From 1700s
No probate search service; copies: 50¢ per page, no minimum

*Burrillville Probate Court
Town of Burrillville
105 Harrisville Main Street
Harrisville, RI 02830
Phone (401) 568-4300
Town incorporated 1806
Land records: From 1806
Vital records: From 1806
Probate records: From 1806
No probate search service; copies: $1.50 per page, $20.00 minimum

*Central Falls Office of the City Clerk
580 Broad Street
Central Falls, RI 02863
City incorporated 1895
Land records: Yes
Naturalization records: No naturalization records
Vital records: Certified copies only: $5.00 per individual
Probate records: Yes
Probate search service: 25¢ per year as time allows; photocopies not available due to the age of the books involved; typed copies: $15.00 minimum; "When requests are made any and all information about the person(s) should be included, i.e., date of event, spouse, children, parents, etc."

*Charlestown Town Clerk's Office
Town of Charlestown
4540 South County Trail
Charlestown, RI 02813
Phone (401) 364-1200 Town Clerk, Clerk of Probate Court
Town incorporated 1738
Land records: Land evidence from 1738
Naturalization records: No naturalization records
Vital records: From 1738
No vital records search service; certified copies: $12.00 each
Probate records: From about 1767
No probate search service; copies: $1.00 per page, $2.00 for certification, no minimum

Coventry Probate Court
1075 Main Street
Coventry, RI 02816
Town incorporated 1741

Cranston Probate Court
City Hall
Cranston, RI 02910
City incorporated 1754

*Cumberland Probate Court
45 Broad Street
Cumberland, RI 02864
Phone (401) 728-2400
Town incorporated 1747
Land records: Contact Marianne B. Mulholland, CMC, Town Clerk
Land records search service: first ½ hour free, $15.00 per hour thereafter; copies: 15¢ per page
Naturalization records: No naturalization records
Vital records: Contact Town Clerk (proof of relationship required for certified copies)
Vital records search service: first ½ hour free, $15.00 per hour thereafter; copies: 15¢ per page
Probate records: Contact Town Clerk

Probate search service: first ¹/₂ hour free, $15.00 per hour thereafter; copies: 15¢ per page

East Greenwich Probate Court
PO Box 111
East Greenwich, RI 02818
Town incorporated 1677

*East Providence Probate Court
145 Taunton Avenue
East Providence, RI 02914
City incorporated 1863
Land records: From 1862
Naturalization records: No naturalization records
Vital records: From 1862
Probate records: From 1862
Probate search service: no charge; copies: 75¢ per page, no minimum

*Exeter Probate Court
675 Ten Rod Road
Exeter, RI 02822
Phone (401) 294-3891
Town incorporated 1742
Land records: Contact Deputy Town Clerk
Naturalization records: No naturalization records
Vital records: Contact Deputy Town Clerk
Probate records: Contact Deputy Town Clerk

*Foster Probate Court
181 Howard Hill Road
Foster, RI 02825
Phone (401) 392-9200
Town incorporated 1781
Land records: From 1781
Vital records: From 1781
Probate records: From 1781
No probate search service; copies: $1.50 per page

*Glocester Town Hall
1145 Putnam Pike
PO Box B
Glocester, RI 02814-0702
Phone (401) 568-6206
Town incorporated 1731
Land records: From 1730; contact Barbara E. Robertson, Town Clerk/ Probate Clerk
Vital records: From 1730s; contact Town Clerk/Probate Clerk (for public use only 100 years back)
Probate records: From 1797; contact Town Clerk/Probate Clerk
No probate search service; certified copies: $5.00 for the first page and $1.00 for each additional page

*Hopkinton Town Clerk
1 Town House Road
Hopkinton, RI 02833
Phone (401) 377-7777 Town Clerk
Town incorporated 1757
Land records: From 1757; contact Jenarita F. Aldrich, CMC, Town Clerk
Land records search service: no charge for index search; copies: 15¢ per page from old records, $1.50 per page from current records, no minimum
Naturalization records: No naturalization records
Vital records: From 1757; contact Town Clerk; certified copies: $12.00 each, but will provide information from public records (births and marriages over 100 years old or deaths over 50 years old) and will assist in searching protected records provided there is a vested interest.
Probate records: From 1757; contact Town Clerk
Probate search service: no charge for index search; copies: 15¢ per page from old records, $1.50 per page from current records, no minimum

Jamestown Probate Court
71 Narragansett Avenue
Jamestown, RI 02835
Town incorporated 1678

Johnston Probate Court
1385 Hartford Avenue
Johnston, RI 02919
Town incorporated 1759

*Lincoln Town Clerk
100 Old River Road
Lincoln, RI 02865
Phone (401) 333-1100
Town incorporated 1871
Land records: From 1895
Naturalization records: No naturalization records
Vital records: From 1895 ("Must show proof of membership in genealogy society to search vitals")
Probate records: From 1895
No probate search service; copies: $1.50; "All records before 1895 in Central Falls."

*Little Compton Probate Court
PO Box 523
Little Compton, RI 02837
Town incorporated 1682
Land records: Yes
Naturalization records: No naturalization records
Vital records: Yes
Probate records: Yes
No probate search service; copies: $1.00 per page, no minimum

*Middletown Probate Court
350 East Main Road
Middletown, RI 02840
Town incorporated 1743
Land records: From 1743
Vital records: From 1743
Probate records: From 1730
Probate search service: no charge; copies: 50¢ per page, $2.00 per page for certification, no minimum

*Narragansett Office of the Town Clerk
25 Fifth Avenue
Narragansett, RI 02882
Phone (401) 789-1044, ext. 245
Town incorporated 22 March 1888
Land records: From 1888
Naturalization records: No naturalization records
Vital records: From 1888
Probate records: From 1888
Probate search service: no charge (within reason); copies: $1.00 per page, no minimum

Newport Probate Court
Washington Square
Newport, RI 02840
Phone (401) 846-5556
Town incorporated 1639

*New Shoreham Town Clerk
Block Island, RI 02807
Phone (401) 466-3200
Town incorporated 1661 (established 1664 as Block Island)
Land records: Grantor/grantee books, land evidence records from 1675 to date, mortgage index from 1675, mortgage book from 1872, land trust, etc.
Land records search service: first ¹/₂ hour free, $15.00 per hour thereafter; copies: 15¢ per page, $1.50 and $3.00 per instrument for certified copies
Naturalization records: From 1889 to 1910
Naturalization records search service: first ¹/₂ hour free, $15.00 per hour thereafter; copies: 15¢ per page, $1.50 and $3.00 per instrument for certified copies
Vital records: Births, deaths and marriages from 1849
Vital records search service: first ¹/₂ hour free, $15.00 per hour thereafter; copies: 15¢ per page, $1.50 and $3.00 per instrument for certified copies
Probate records: From 1798 to date, bonds and letters, inventories and accounts, wills, etc.
Probate search service: first ¹/₂ hour free, $15.00 per hour thereafter; copies: 15¢ per page, $1.50 and $3.00 per instrument for certified copies

*North Kingston Town Clerk
80 Boston Neck Road
North Kingstown, RI 02852
Phone (401) 294-3331
Town incorporated 1674
Land records: From late 1600s to date
No land records search service (must
    know book and page); contact Town
    Clerk's Office, Attention Land
    Records; copies: $1.50 per page
Naturalization records: No naturalization
    records
Vital records: From about 1674 to date
    (some damaged by a fire at the town
    Hall); contact Town Clerk's Office,
    Attention Vitals Clerk
Vital records search service: $12.00 for
    two consecutive calendar years, and
    50¢ for each additional year (includes
    copy); certified copies: $12.00 for the
    first copy and $7.00 for each
    additional copy of the same record
Probate records: From the late 1600s to
    date

North Providence Probate Court
Town Hall
2000 Smith Street
North Providence, RI 02904
Phone (401) 232-0900
Town incorporated 1765

*North Smithfield Probate Court
North Smithfield, RI 02876
Town incorporated 1871
Land records: Land evidence records
    from 1871; copies: $1.50
Naturalization records: Only on voter
    registration information
Vital records: From 1871
Probate records: From 1871
Probate search service: no charge;
    copies: $1.50 each, no minimum; "We
    do not research by phone request."

Pawtucket Probate Court
City Hall
Pawtucket, RI 02860
City incorporated 1862
Naturalization records: Contact Supreme
    Court Judicial Archives, Pawtucket,
    RI 02860

Portsmouth Probate Court
2200 East Main Road
Portsmouth, RI 02871
City incorporated 1638

Providence Probate Court
250 Benefit
Providence, RI 02903-2719
Phone (401) 277-3220
City incorporated 1636

*Richmond Town Clerk
5 Townhouse Road
Wyoming, RI 02898
Phone (401) 539-2497
Town incorporated 1747
Land records: From 1747 to date; copies:
    $1.50 per page
Naturalization records: No naturalization
    records
Vital records: From 1747 to date (open to
    the public to 1910 only, open to
    genealogists to present)
Probate records: From 1747 to date

*Scituate Probate Court
Town Hall
195 Danielson Pike
PO Box 328
North Scituate, RI 02857-0328
Phone (401) 647-2822
Town incorporated 1731
Land records: From 1731 to date
Naturalization records: From 1731 to
    date
Vital records: From 1731 to date
Probate records: From 1731 to date

*Smithfield Probate Court
64 Farnum Pike
Smithfield, RI 02917
Phone (401) 233-1000
Town incorporated 1731
Vital records: Yes; copies: $1.50 for the
    first page and $1.00 for each
    additional page, $3.00 for certification
    (restricted to those showing proof of
    relationship)
Probate records: Contact Flora A.
    Simeone, Probate Clerk; copies: $1.50
    for the first page and $1.00 for each
    additional page, $3.00 for certification

***Probate Court, Town of South
  Kingston**
180 High Street
Wakefield, RI 02879
Phone (401) 789-9331
Town incorporated 1723
Land records: Contact Town Clerk
No land records search service (contact
    Merideth Sorozan, 262 Spring Grove
    Road, Chepachet, RI 02814); copies:
    $1.50 per page, $3.00 per document
    for certification
Naturalization records: No naturalization
    records
Vital records: From 1850; contact Town
    Clerk
No vital records search service; copies:
    $1.50 per page, $3.00 per document
    for certification (ID and proof of
    relationship required, access restricted
    for births and marriages under one
    hundred years old and deaths under
    fifty years old)
Probate records: Contact Probate Clerk

No probate search service; copies: $1.50
    per page, $3.00 per document for
    certification

Tiverton Probate Court
Tiverton, RI 02878
Town incorporated 1747

*Warren Probate Court
Warren, RI 02885
Phone (401) 245-7340
Town incorporated 1747
Land records: From 1700s to date;
    contact Town Clerk
Naturalization records: "Only here for
    safekeeping"; contact Town Clerk
Vital records: From 1850 to date ("Only
    those more than 100 years old
    accessible"); contact Town Clerk
Probate records: Yes; contact Town Clerk

*Warwick Probate Court
3275 Post Road
Warwick, RI 02886
Phone (401) 738-2000
*Town founded 1642; city incorporated
1931*
Land records: From 1642, indexed;
    contact Marie T. Bennett, City Clerk
Vital records: From 1850, indexed;
    contact City Clerk
Probate records: From about 1899,
    indexed; contact City Clerk
Probate search service: no charge;
    copies: $1.50 per page plus $3.00 for
    certification, no minimum

*West Greenwich Probate Court
280 Victory Highway
West Greenwich, RI 02817
Phone (401) 397-5016
Town incorporated 1741
Land records: Contact Town Clerk
Vital records: Contact Town Clerk
Probate records: Contact Probate Clerk
No probate search service; copies: $1.50
    per page, no minimum

*West Warwick Probate Court
1170 Main Street
West Warwick, RI 02893-2144
Phone (401) 822-9200
Town incorporated November 1913
Land records: From November 1913
Naturalization records: No naturalization
    records
Vital records: From November 1913
Probate records: From November 1913
No probate search service; copies: $1.50
    per page

*Westerly Probate Court
Town Clerk's Office
Town Hall
45 Broad Street
Westerly, RI 02891

Phone (401) 348-2500
Town incorporated 1669
Land records: From 1669
Naturalization records: From late 1800s
Vital records: From 1600s–1700s
Probate records: From 1600s–1700s
No probate search service; "Due to the
    pressure of business in this office it is
    impossible to devote any time to
    researching the 'old records.'"

*Woonsocket Probate Court
169 Main Street
Woonsocket, RI 02895
Phone (401) 762-6400
City incorporated 1867
Land records: Contact John R. Reynolds,
    City Clerk
Vital records: Contact City Clerk
Probate records: Contact Probate Clerk
Probate search service: $5.00 per name;
    copies: $1.50 per page, $5.00 for
    certified copies

SOUTH CAROLINA

*Capital: Columbia. Statehood: 23 May
1788 (included in the Carolina Grant of
1663, ceded western lands in 1787)*

Court System

South Carolina's Municipal Courts have
limited jurisdiction to try offenses for which
the penalty is under $200 or thirty days
imprisonment. Over three hundred Magistrate Courts have jurisdiction over civil
matters under $1,000 and criminal matters
similar to the Municipal Courts. Probate
Courts in each county handle estates,
guardianships, and mental health issues.
Family Court sits at each county seat and
has jurisdiction over marriage, divorce, custody, support, etc. South Carolina's Circuit
Court has general jurisdiction and sits in
each county seat. First Judicial Circuit:
Calhoun, Dorchester and Orangeburg counties; Second Judicial Circuit: Aiken,
Bamberg and Barnwell counties; Third Ju-
dicial Circuit: Clarendon, Lee, Sumter and
Williamsburg counties; Fourth Judicial
Circuit: Chesterfield, Darlington, Dillon
and Marlboro counties; Fifth Judicial Cir-
cuit: Kershaw and Richland counties; Sixth
Judicial Circuit: Chester, Fairfield and
Lancaster counties; Seventh Judicial Cir-
cuit: Cherokee and Spartanburg counties;
Eighth Judicial Circuit: Abbeville, Green-
wood, Laurens and Newberry counties;
Ninth Judicial Circuit: Berkeley and
Charleston counties; Tenth Judicial Circuit:
Anderson and Oconee counties; Eleventh
Judicial Circuit: Edgefield, Lexington,
McCormick and Saluda counties; Twelfth
Judicial Circuit: Florence and Marion coun-
ties; Thirteenth Judicial Circuit: Greenville
and Pickens counties; Fourteenth Judicial
Circuit: Allendale, Beaufort, Colleton,
Hampton and Jasper counties; Fifteenth
Judicial Circuit: Georgetown and Horry
counties; Sixteenth Judicial Circuit: Union
and York counties. Its judicial circuits are
the same as those for the Family Courts. A
Court of Appeals and Supreme Court hear
appeals.

In 1683 three "counties" were laid out
in South Carolina: Berkeley, Colleton and
Craven counties. Carteret (later changed to
Granville) was added somewhat later. How-
ever, no records were kept in the counties.
In 1706 "parishes" took the place of the
former counties. In 1768 the area was di-
vided into seven "judicial districts": Charles
Town, Beaufort, George Town, Cheraws,
Camden, Orangeburg and Ninety Six.
Pickney and Washington districts were

added in 1793. In 1798 the nine districts
were divided into twenty-four. Camden
District: Lancaster, Chester, Fairfield,
Kershaw, Sumter and York; Ninety Six
District: Abbeville, Edgefield, Newberry,
Pendleton, Greenville, Laurens, Spartan-
burg and Union; Cheraws District: Ches-
terfield, Darlington and Marlborough;
Georgetown District: George Town and
Marion; Charles Town District: Charles-
town and Colleton; Orangeburg District:
Barnwell and Orangeburg; Beaufort Dis-
trict: no change. Between 1800 and 1858
Richland was taken from Kershaw,
Williamsburg from Georgetown, Horry
from Georgetown, Lexington from
Orangeburg, Anderson and Pickens from
Pendleton, and Clarendon from Sumter.
Some of these districts had been organized
as "counties" within their parent districts
prior to being formally designated as districts in their own right. In 1868 all districts
were renamed counties.

Courthouses

*Abbeville County Clerk of Court
PO Box 99
Abbeville, SC 29620-0099
Phone (803) 459-5074
*County organized 1785 from Ninety Six
    District*
Land records: From 1873 to date (older
    records burned while in storage);
    contact Jennifer M. Roosmann, Clerk
    of Court, PO Box 99, Abbeville, SC
    29620; copies: send LSASE for price
    quote. Plats from 1780 to 1788 from
    the Old Ninety-Six District collection;
    contact Probate Court, PO Box 70,
    Abbeville, SC 29620; copies: $2.00
    each on 11" x 17" sheets
Naturalization records: No naturalization
    records
Vital records: Marriages from 1911 to
    date; contact Probate Court
No vital records search service (must
    have name of groom, maiden name of
    bride and year of marriage); copies:
    $5.00 each
Probate records: Wills from 1776 to date;
    inventories and accounts from 1783
Probate search service: $5.00 for out-of-
    state requests (send LSASE for price
    quote); copies: 50¢ per side plus $1.50
    handling for each file, pack or volume

*Aiken County Courthouse
PO Box 583
Aiken, SC 29802-0583
Phone (803) 642-2099 Clerk of Court;
    (803) 642-1707 Judgments; (803)
    642-1706 Civil Suits; (803) 642-1702
    Criminal Record; (803) 642-1710
    Family Court (divorces); (803) 642-

2076 Register Mesne Conveyance;
(803) 642-2001 Probate Judge
*County organized 1871 from Edgefield
County*
Land records: Contact Register Mesne
Conveyance, PO Box 537, Aiken, SC
29802
Vital records: Marriage licenses; contact
Probate Judge, PO Box 1576, Aiken,
SC 29802
Probate records: Estates; contact Probate
Judge
No probate search service; copies: 25¢
per page, $1.00 for certification

Allendale County Courthouse
PO Box 126
Allendale, SC 29810-0126
Phone (803) 584-2737
*County organized 1919 from Barnwell
and Hampton counties*

Anderson County Courthouse
PO Box 8002
Anderson, SC 29622
Phone (803) 260-4053
*County organized 1826 from Pendleton
District, which was abolished at that
time*

*Bamberg County Courthouse
PO Box 150
Bamberg, SC 29003-0150
Phone (803) 245-2025
*County organized 1897 from Barnwell
County*
Land records: From 1897; contact Clerk
of Court; copies: 50¢ per page, $2.00
for certification

*Barnwell County Courthouse
PO Box 723
Barnwell, SC 29812-0723
Phone (803) 259-3485
*County organized 1798 from
Orangeburg District*
Land records: Yes
Vital records: Contact County Health
Department, Allen Street, Barnwell,
SC 29812
Probate records: Contact Probate Court,
Room 112, Courthouse, Barnwell, SC
29812
Probate search service: no charge;
copies: 50¢ per page

*Beaufort County Courthouse
Beaufort, SC 29901
Phone (803) 525-7300
County organized 1764, original district
Land records: Contact Register Mesne
Conveyance Office
Naturalization records: Contact Health
Department
Vital records: Contact Health Department
Probate records: Contact Probate Court

*Berkeley County Courthouse
223 North Live Oak Drive
Moncks Corner, SC 29461-2331
Phone (803) 761-6900, ext. 4085
Register Mesne Conveyance; (803)
761-6900, ext. 6003 Birth and Death
Records; (803) 761-6900, ext. 5201
Probate Court
*County organized 1882 from Charleston
District*
Land records: Deeds, mortgages and
liens from 1882; contact Register
Mesne Conveyance
Naturalization records: No naturalization
records
Vital records: Births and deaths
(restricted to registrant, parents,
guardians or legal representatives);
contact County Health Department.
Marriages; contact Probate Court,
300B California Avenue, Moncks
Corner, SC 29461
Probate records: Wills and estates,
guardianships and conservatorships;
contact Probate Court, 300B
California Avenue, Moncks Corner,
SC 29461

*Calhoun County Courthouse
302 South Railroad Avenue
Saint Matthews, SC 29135-1452
Phone (803) 874-3524
*County organized 1908 from Lexington
County*
Land records: Contact Clerk of Court,
PO Box 1226, Gaffney, SC 29342
Vital records: Marriage licenses; contact
Clerk of Court, PO Box 1226,
Gaffney, SC 29342; certified copies:
$2.00 each
Probate records: Contact Probate Court,
PO Box 22, Gaffney, SC 29342
No probate search service; copies: 25¢
per page

Charleston County Courthouse
2144 Melbourne
Charleston, SC 29402
Phone (803) 723-6724; (803) 740-5860
*County organized 1769, as Charles
Town and later Charlestown, an
original district*

*Cherokee County Courthouse
PO Box 866
Gaffney, SC 29342
Phone (803) 487-2562
*County organized 1897 from Union and
York counties*
Land records: From the 1700s; contact
Clerk; copies: $1.50 for the first two
pages and $1.00 for each additional
page
Vital records: Births and deaths from
1853, marriages from the 1700s;
contact Clerk; copies: $1.50 for the

first two pages and $1.00 for each
additional page
Probate records: From the 1700s; contact
Clerk; copies: $1.50 for the first two
pages and $1.00 for each additional
page

*Chester County Courthouse
PO Box 580
Chester, SC 29706-0580
Phone (803) 385-2605 Clerk of Court;
(803) 385-2604 Judge of Probate
*County organized 1785 from Camden
District*
Land records: Contact Clerk of Court
Naturalization records: Contact Clerk of
Court
Vital records: Births and deaths from
1915; contact County Health
Department, 129 Wylie Street,
Chester, SC 29706. Marriage records
from 1911; contact Judge of Probate
Probate records: Contact Judge of
Probate
No probate search service; copies: 50¢
per page

*Chesterfield County Courthouse
200 West Main Street
Chesterfield, SC 29709
Phone (803) 623-2574
*County organized 1798 from Cheraws
District*
Land records: Deeds and mortgages;
contact Clerk's Office
Naturalization records: No naturalization
records
Vital records: No vital records
Probate records: Contact Probate Judge's
Office

*Clarendon County Courthouse
PO Drawer E
Manning, SC 29102-0136
Phone (803) 435-4444
*County organized 1855 from Sumter
District*
Land records: Yes
Naturalization records: Yes
Vital records: Yes
Probate records: Yes

*Colleton County Courthouse
PO Box 620
Walterboro, SC 29488-0620
Phone (803) 549-5791
*County organized 1798 from Charleston
District*
Land records: From about 1865 to date;
contact Linda Carter, Clerk of Court
Office, Register Mesne Conveyance
Office
Land records search service: no charge;
copies: 25¢ each
Naturalization records: No naturalization
records

Vital records: Contact Health
Department, Benson Street,
Walterboro, SC 29488
Probate records: Contact Probate Court,
Washington Street, Walterboro, SC
29488

*Darlington County Courthouse
Darlington, SC 29532-3213
Phone (803) 393-3836
*County organized 1785 from Cheraws
District*
Land records: From 1806; contact Clerk
of Court
Naturalization records: From about 1845
to about 1890; contact Darlington
County Historical Commission, 204
Hewitt Street, Darlington, SC 29532
Vital records: Marriages only from 1911;
contact Probate Judge
Probate records: From about 1789;
contact County Historical
Commission
Probate search service: no charge;
copies: $1.00 for the first page and
50¢ for each additional page, plus
$2.50 for mailing first fifty pages, no
minimum

*Dillon County Courthouse
PO Box 1220
Dillon, SC 29536-1220
Phone (803) 774-1425 Clerk of Court;
(803) 774-5611 Health Department;
(803) 774-1423 Probate
*County organized 1910 from Marion
County*
Land records: Contact Clerk of Court
Naturalization records: No naturalization
records
Vital records: Contact Health
Department, West Hampton Street,
Dillon, SC 29536
Probate records: Contact PO Box 189,
Dillon, SC 29536
Probate search service: $1.00 per year;
copies: $5.00, no minimum

*Dorchester County Courthouse
101 Ridge Street
Saint George, SC 29477-2443
Phone (803) 563-0196
*County organized 1868 from Ninety Six
District*
Land records: Contact RMC
Vital records: Contact Health Department
Probate records: Contact Jim Wylie,
Probate Judge
Probate search service: no charge;
copies: 25¢ per page

*Edgefield County Courthouse
129 Courthouse Square
Edgefield, SC 29824
Phone (803) 637-4080

*County organized 1785 from Ninety Six
District*
Land records: From 1839 to date

*Fairfield County Courthouse
PO Drawer 299
Winnsboro, SC 29180
Phone (803) 635-1411
*County organized 1785 from Camden
District*
Land records: Yes
No land records search service
Naturalization records: Yes
No naturalization records search service
Vital records: Yes
No vital records search service
Probate records: Yes
No probate search service

Florence County Courthouse
180 North Irby Street
Florence, SC 29501-3456
Phone (803) 665-3031
*County organized 1888 from Marion,
Darlington, Williamsburg and
Clarendon counties*

Georgetown County Courthouse
715 Prince Street
Georgetown, SC 29440-3631
Phone (803) 546-5011
County organized 1769, original district

*Greenville County Courthouse
East North Street
Greenville, SC 29601-2121
Phone (803) 467-8551 Clerk of Court;
(803) 467-8873 County Vital Records;
(803) 467-8873
*County organized 1798 from Ninety Six
District*
Land records: From the 1700s to date;
contact Ms. Donnie Tankersley,
Register Mesne Conveyance Office,
301 University Ridge, Suite 1300,
Greenville, SC 29601; copies: 50¢
each
Naturalization records: No naturalization
records
Vital records: Marriage licenses from
1911 to date; contact 3101 University
Ridge, Suite 1200, Greenville, SC
29601. Births and deaths from 1915 to
date; contact County Vital Records,
PO Box 2507, Greenville, SC 29602
No vital records search service from
County Vital Records: must have
names, date and place (restricted to
family members, legal guardians or
representative with proof of
relationship)
Probate records: From 1800 to date;
contact County Probate Court, 3101
University Ridge, Suite 1200,
Greenville, SC 29601

*Greenwood County Courthouse
528 Monument
Greenwood, SC 29646-2643
Phone (803) 942-8625 Probate Court
*County organized 3 June 1897 from
Abbeville and Edgefield counties*
Vital records: Marriage licenses from
1895; contact Jayne M. Bell, Office
Manager, Probate Court, PO Box
1210, Greenwood, SC 29648
No vital records search service
Probate records: From 1895; contact
Probate Court
No probate search service; certified
copies: $5.00 for the first page and
25¢ for each additional page of the
same document, plus at least $1.00 for
mailing, no minimum; "Fee for copies
to precede copies' being mailed."

*Hampton County Courthouse
PO Box 7
Hampton, SC 29924-0007
Phone (803) 943-7510
*County organized 1878 from Beaufort
County*
Land records: Yes
Naturalization records: Yes
Vital records: No births or deaths
Probate records: Yes

*Horry County Courthouse
PO Box 677
Conway, SC 29526-0677
Phone (803) 248-6247; (803) 248-1275
Register Mesne Conveyance; (803)
248-1270 Clerk of Court
*County organized 1802 from
Georgetown District*
Land records: Contact Register Mesne
Conveyance, PO Box 470, Conway,
SC 29526
Naturalization records: Contact Billie G.
Richardson, Clerk of Court
Vital records: Contact Health
Department, Elm Street, Conway, SC
29526
Probate records: Yes

Jasper County Courthouse
PO Box 248
Ridgeland, SC 29936-0248
Phone (803) 726-8832
*County organized 1912 from Beaufort
and Hampton counties*

*Kershaw County Courthouse
1121 Broad Street
Camden, SC 29020
Phone (803) 425-1527
*County organized 1798 from Camden
District*
Land records; Contact Clerk of Court,
Room 313
Vital records: Contact County Health
Department, 1116 Church Street,
Camden, SC 29020

Probate records: Contact Probate Judge's Office, Room 302

*Lancaster County Courthouse
PO Box 1809
Lancaster, SC 29720
Phone (803) 285-1581
County organized 1798 from Camden District
Land records: Contact Tax Assessor
Naturalization records: Contact Clerk of Court
Vital records: Contact Health Department, PO Box 817, Lancaster, SC 29720
Probate records: From 1860; contact Probate Judge, PO Box 1028, Lancaster, SC 29720
Probate search service: $10.00; copies: $1.00 per page, $10.00 minimum

Laurens County Courthouse
PO Box 287
Laurens, SC 29360-0287
Phone (803) 984-3538
County organized 1785 from Ninety Six District

*Lee County Courthouse
Courthouse Square
Bishopville, SC 29010
Phone (803) 484-5341 Clerk of Court and Probate Judge
County organized 1902 from Darlington and Kershaw counties
Land records: Contact James I. Davis, Clerk of Court, PO Box 281, Bishopville, SC 29010
Probate records: Contact Catherine Harris, Probate Judge, Rt. 1, Box 166-B, Bishopville, SC 29010

Lexington County Courthouse
Lexington, SC 29072
Phone (803) 359-8212
County organized from 1804 Orangeburg District

Marion County Courthouse
PO Box 295
Marion, SC 29571-0295
Phone (803) 423-6500
County organized 1800 with boundaries identical with those of Liberty County, created 1798 within Georgetown District

*Marlboro County Courthouse
PO Box 996
Bennettsville, SC 29512-0996
Phone (803) 479-8391
County organized 1798 from Cheraws District
Land records: Deeds; contact Clerk of Court's Office

Vital records: Contact County Health Department
Probate records: Estates and wills; contact Probate Judges' Office
No probate search service; copies: 25¢ per page; "The above is subject to change."

McCormick County Courthouse
Clerk of Court
133 South Mine Street, Room 102
McCormick, SC 29835
Phone (803) 465-2195
County organized 1914 from Edgefield County

Newberry County Courthouse
PO Box 278
Newberry, SC 29108-0278
Phone (803) 276-3494
County organized 1785 from Ninety Six District

*Oconee County Courthouse
PO Box 678
Walhalla, SC 29691
Phone (803) 638-4280
County organized 1868 from Pickens County
Land records: Contact Salli Smith, Clerk of Court
Naturalization records: No naturalization records
Vital records: Contact Clerk of Court
Probate records: Contact Sandra Orr, Probate Judge
No probate search service; copies: 50¢ per page, 50¢ minimum

*Orangeburg County Courthouse
PO Box 9000
Orangeburg, SC 29116-9000
Phone (803) 533-6280
County organized 1769, original district
Land records: From 1865; contact Register Mesne Conveyance
No land records search service; copies: 50¢ per page, $1.00 per document minimum
Probate records: From 1865; contact Judge of Probate
Probate search service: no charge; copies 50¢ per page, $1.00 minimum; "All records in courthouse were destroyed by fire in 1865; fees may be increased in the near future—amounts yet to be determined."

Pickens County Courthouse
PO Box 215
Pickens, SC 29671-0215
Phone (803) 878-7809
County organized 1826 from Pendleton District, which was abolished at that time

*Richland County Courthouse
1701 Main Street
PO Box 1781
Columbia, SC 29202
Phone (803) 748-4684
County organized 1799 from Kershaw District
Land records: Contact Register Mesne Conveyance Office. Additional records; contact County Archives, 2020 Hampton Street, Columbia, SC 29201
Probate records: Contact Judge of Probate, 1701 Main Street, Columbia, SC 29201

Saluda County Courthouse
Courthouse Square
Saluda, SC 29138-1444
Phone (803) 445-3303
County organized 1896 from Edgefield County

*Spartanburg County Judicial Center
180 Magnolia Street
PO Box 5666
Spartanburg, SC 29304
Phone (803) 596-2526 County Administration; (803) 596-2414 Register Mesne Conveyance; (803) 596-3337 Spartanburg Health Department; (803) 596-2556 Probate Judge
County organized 1785 from Ninety Six District
Land records: Contact Martha West, Register Mesne Conveyance, 366 North Church Street, Spartanburg Administrative Building, Spartanburg, SC 29303
Naturalization records: Contact Carolyn Mabry, Spartanburg Health Department, 151 East Wood Street, Spartanburg, SC 29303
Vital records: Births and deaths; contact Spartanburg Health Department. Births and marriages; contact Judge Raymond Eubanks, Probate Judge; copies: $5.00 each
Probate records: Contact Probate Judge
Probate search service: $5.00 per search; copies: 50¢ per page

*Sumter County Courthouse
141 North Main Street
Sumter, SC 29150-4965
Phone (803) 773-1581
County organized 1798 from Camden District
Probate records: Contact Probate Court
Probate search service: no charge; copies: $1.00 for the first page and 50¢ for each additional page, no minimum; "Records prior to 1900s are on microfiche."

*Union County Courthouse
PO Box 200
Union, SC 29379-0200
Phone (803) 427-0391
County organized 1798 from Ninety Six District
Land records: From 1785; contact County Clerk of Court
Naturalization records: No naturalization records
Vital records: Contact County Health Department, Thompson Boulevard, Union, SC 29379. Marriage records from 1911; contact Probate Court
Probate records: From late 1700s; contact Probate Court
No probate search service; copies: 20¢ per page plus postage and handling

*Williamsburg County Courthouse
PO Box 86
Kingstree, SC 29556-0086
Phone (803) 354-6855
County organized 1802 from Georgetown District
Land records: Contact Clerk of Court
Naturalization records: No naturalization records
Probate records: Contact Judge Gamble, Probate Judge's Office, Courthouse Square, Kingstree, SC 29556

York County Courthouse
PO Box 649
York, SC 29745-0649
Phone (803) 684-8505
County organized 1798 from Camden District

SOUTH DAKOTA

Capital: Pierre. Statehood: 2 November 1889 (part of Dakota Territory in 1861)

Court System

South Dakota Magistrate Courts have limited jurisdiction over civil suits, small claims, mental health matters, misdemeanors, ordinance violations, etc. They are divided into circuits which are identical to those of the Circuit Courts, which sit at each county seat and have concurrent jurisdiction with the Magistrate Courts, plus exclusive jurisdiction over felony cases and civil cases involving land title or boundary disputes, domestic relations, probate and juvenile hearings. First Judicial Circuit: Bon Homme, Charles Mix, Clay, Douglas, Hutchinson, Lincoln, Turner, Union and Yankton counties; Second Judicial Circuit: Minnehaha County; Third Judicial Circuit: Beadle, Brookings, Clark, Codington, Deuel, Grant, Hamlin, Hand and Kingsbury counties; Fourth Judicial Circuit: Aurora, Brule, Buffalo, Davison, Hanson, Jerauld, Lake, McCook, Miner, Moody and Sanborn counties; Fifth Judicial Circuit: Brown, Campbell, Day, Edmunds, Faulk, Marshall, McPherson, Roberts, Spink and Walworth counties; Sixth Judicial Circuit: Bennett, Gregory, Haakon, Hughes, Hyde, Jackson, Jones, Lyman, Mellette, Potter, Stanley, Sully, Todd (attached to Tripp) and Tripp counties; Seventh Judicial Circuit: Custer, Fall River, Pennington and Shannon (attached to Fall River) counties; Eighth Judicial Circuit: Butte, Corson, Dewey, Harding, Lawrence, Meade, Perkins and Ziebach counties.

Lay magistrates, some of whom are clerks of Circuit Courts, can hear some uncontested civil actions and guilty pleas. The Supreme Court is the court of last resort.

Courthouses

*Aurora County Courthouse
Plankinton, SD 57368
Phone (605) 942-7161 Register of Deeds; (605) 942-7165 Clerk of Courts
County created by an act of legislature 22 February 1879 and organized 8 August 1881 from land that had been part of Hanson County (what was later Davison, Jerauld and Cragin counties); organization ratified

November 1882; in 1881 annexed the western tier of townships from Davison County (Township 109 is now part of Jerauld County; Cragin County was organized in 1873 and abolished in 1879)
Land records: Contact Arlene Koch, Register of Deeds, PO Box 334, Plankinton, SD 57368
Naturalization records: Contact Clerk of Courts
Vital records: Contact Register of Deeds
Probate records: Contact Clerk of Courts
Probate search service: $2.00 per name; copies: 10¢ per page plus postage charge if there are a lot of pages, no minimum

Beadle County Courthouse
Huron, SD 57350
Phone (605) 353-7165
County organized 1879 from Spink and Clark counties

Bennett County Courthouse
Main Street
Martin, SD 57551
Phone (605) 685-6969
County organized 1909 from Indian lands

Bon Homme County Courthouse
Tyndall, SD 57066
Phone (605) 589-3382
County organized 1862 from Charles Mix County

*Brookings County Courthouse
314 Sixth Avenue
Brookings, SD 57006-2041
Phone (605) 692-6284
County organized 1862 from unorganized territory
Land records: From the 1870s
Naturalization records: No naturalization records
Vital records: From 1905
Probate records: Contact Clerk of Courts

*Brown County Courthouse
111 S.E. First Avenue
Aberdeen, SD 57401-4203
Phone (605) 622-2266
County organized 1879 from Beadle County
Land records: Contact Register of Deeds, PO Box 1307, Aberdeen, SD 57401
Vital records: Contact Register of Deeds
Probate records: Contact Register of Deeds and Clerk of Courts
Probate search service: $4.00; copies: $1.00 per page, no minimum

*Brule County Courthouse
300 South Courtland

Chamberlain, SD 57325-1508
Phone (605) 734-5443
County organized 1875 from Buffalo County
Land records: Contact Register of Deeds
Naturalization records: Contact Clerk of Courts
Vital records: Contact Register of Deeds
Probate records: Contact Clerk of Courts

*Buffalo County Courthouse
PO Box 174
Gann Valley, SD 57341-0174
Phone (605) 293-3239
County organized 1873 from territorial county; first county officials appointed 5 January 1885 at Gann Valley
Land records; Contact Sheila Sinkie, Register of Deeds; copies: $1.00 plus 20¢ per page for each page after five, $2.00 for certified copies, $10.00 for the first page of plats and $5.00 for the second page
Naturalization records: Contact Clerk of Courts
Vital records: Births and deaths from 1905 to date, burials from 1941 to date; contact Register of Deeds; copies: $7.00 for certified copies of births and deaths, $5.00 for certified copies of marriages, $3.00 for the first page of coroner's records and $2.00 for each additional page
Probate records: Contact Clerk of Courts

*Butte County Courthouse
839 Fifth Avenue
Belle Fourche, SD 57717
Phone (605) 892-2912
County organized 1883 from Harding County
Land records: Contact Register of Deeds; copies: $1.00 per document (up to five pages) and 20¢ for each additional page
Naturalization records: No naturalization records
Vital records: Contact Register of Deeds; copies: $7.00 each for births and deaths, $5.00 each for marriages
Probate records: Contact Clerk of Courts, PO Box 237, Bellefourche, SD 57717

*Campbell County Courthouse
Second and Main
Mound City, SD 57646
Phone (605) 955-3505 Register of Deeds; (605) 955-3308 FAX, Register of Deeds; (605) 955-3536 Clerk of Court
County organized 1873 from Buffalo County, when the legislature of Dakota Territory divided the territory into counties; surveyed 1883 and 1884, when settlers began to arrive; first board of county commissioners appointed 1883 and met 17 April 1884
Land records: Contact Joyce Krokel, Register of Deeds, PO Box 148, Mound City, SD 57646-0148; copies: $1.00 per instrument, $2.00 per instrument for certified copies
Naturalization records: From 1884 to 1942; contact Kathleen E. Fuehrer, Clerk of Court, PO Box 146, Mound City, SD 57646-0146
Vital records: Births from 1905 (earliest delayed birth from 1883), deaths from 1905, marriage licenses from 10 May 1890; contact Register of Deeds; certified copies: $7.00 for births and deaths, $5.00 for marriages
Probate records: From 1891 to date
Probate search service: $2.00 per name; copies: 25¢ per page

Charles Mix County Courthouse
Lake Andes, SD 57356
Phone (605) 487-7511
County organized 1862, original county

*Clark County Courthouse
PO Box 294
Clark, SD 57225-0294
Phone (605) 532-5851; (605) 532-5363 Register of Deeds
County formed 1873, organized 1881
Land records: Contact Janet Hurlbut, Register of Deeds; copies: $1.00 per instrument
Naturalization records: No naturalization records
Vital records: Births and deaths from 1905, marriages from the 1890s; contact Register of Deeds; certified copies: $7.00 for births and deaths, $5.00 for marriages
Probate records: From 1882; contact Roberta Heim, Clerk of Courts Office
Probate search service: $2.00; copies: 20¢ each

*Clay County Courthouse
PO Box 403
Vermillion, SD 57069-0403
Phone (605) 624-2281; (605) 624-2871 Register of Deeds or Clerk of Courts
County organized 1862 from unorganized territory
Land records: From 1870; contact Register of Deeds, PO Box 536, Vermillion, SD 57069
Naturalization records: From 1867; contact Clerk of Courts, PO Box 377, Vermillion, SD 57069
Vital records: From 1905; contact Register of Deeds
Probate records: From 1875; contact Clerk of Courts
Probate search service: $2.00; copies: 10¢ per page, $2.00 for certification, $2.00 minimum

*Codington County Courthouse
Watertown, SD 57201
Phone (605) 886-4850
County organized 1877 from Indian lands
Land records: Contact Register of Deeds/ Director of Equalization
Vital records: Contact Register of Deeds
Probate records: Contact Clerk of Courts
Probate search service: no charge; copies: 20¢ each, no minimum

*Corson County Courthouse
200 First Street, East
McIntosh, SD 57641
Phone (605) 273-4201
County organized 1909 from Dewey County
Land records: Yes; copies: $1.00 each, $2.00 for certified copies
Naturalization records: Yes; certified copies: $2.00 each
Vital records: Yes; copies: $1.00 each, $2.00 for certified copies
Probate records: Yes
No probate search service; copies: 25¢ per page, $2.00 for certified copies

Custer County Courthouse
420 S.W. Mount Rushmore
Custer, SD 57730-1934
Phone (605) 673-4816
County organized 1875 from Indian lands

*Davison County Courthouse
200 East Fourth Street
Mitchell, SD 57301-2631
Phone (605) 996-2450
County organized 1873 from Hanson County
Land records: Contact Register of Deeds
Naturalization records: No naturalization records
Vital records: Contact Register of Deeds
Probate records: Contact Clerk of Courts, PO Box 927, Mitchell, SD 57301
Probate search service: $2.00; copies: two for 25¢ plus postage, no minimum

*Day County Courthouse
710 West First Street
Webster, SD 57274-1397
Phone (605) 345-3102
County organized 1879 from Clark County
Land records: Contact Register of Deeds
Naturalization records: Contact Clerk of Courts
Vital records: Contact Register of Deeds
Probate records: Contact Clerk of Courts
No probate search service; copies: 10¢ per page, no minimum

Deuel County Courthouse
PO Box 125
Clear Lake, SD 57226
Phone (605) 874-2120
County organized 1862 from Brookings County

*Dewey County Courthouse
Timber Lake, SD 57656
Phone (605) 865-3661 Register of Deeds; (605) 865-3566 Clerk of Courts; (605) 865-3672 Auditor
County organized 1873 from Indian lands
Land records: Contact Register of Deeds; copies: 25¢ per page, $2.00 for the first five pages and 25¢ for each additional page of the same instrument for certified copies
Naturalization records: Contact Clerk of Courts
Vital records: Contact Register of Deeds and/or Clerk of Courts; certified copies: $7.00 each
Probate records: Contact Clerk of Courts
Probate search service: $2.00; copies: 25¢ per page, $2.00 for certified copies

Douglas County Courthouse
Armour, SD 57313
Phone (605) 724-2585
County organized 1873 from Charles Mix County

*Edmunds County Courthouse
Ipswich, SD 57451
Phone (605) 426-6671
County organized 1873 from Buffalo County
Land records: Contact Director of Equalization, PO Box 247, Ipswich, SD 57451
Naturalization records: Contact Clerk of Courts, PO Box 384, Ipswich, SD 57451
Vital records: Contact Register of Deeds, PO Box 386, Ipswich, SD 57451
Probate records: Contact Clerk of Courts
Probate search service: $2.00 and up; copies: 10¢ or 15¢ per page, no minimum

*Fall River County Courthouse
906 North River Street
Hot Springs, SD 57747-1387
Phone (605) 745-5132
County organized 1883 from Custer County
Land records: Contact Register of Deeds
Naturalization records: No naturalization records
Vital records: Contact Register of Deeds
Probate records: Contact Clerk of Courts
Probate search service: $2.00 per name; copies: $2.00 per certified copy of each document, $2.00 minimum

Faulk County Courthouse
Faulkton, SD 57438
Phone (605) 598-6223
County organized 1873 from Buffalo County and unorganized territory

*Grant County Courthouse
210 East Fifth Avenue
Milbank, SD 57252-2433
Phone (605) 432-5482
County organized 1873 from Codington and Deuel counties
Land records: Contact Register of Deeds Office
Naturalization records: From about 1895; contact LaVona Van de Voort, Clerk-Magistrate, PO Box 509, Milbank, SD 57252
Vital records: Contact Register of Deeds Office
Probate records: From about 1895; contact Clerk-Magistrate
Probate search service: no charge; copies: 20¢ per page, no minimum

Gregory County Courthouse
Burke, SD 57523
Phone (605) 775-2665
County organized 1862 from Yankton County

*Haakon County Courthouse
Philip, SD 57567
Phone (605) 859-2627
County organized 1914 from Stanley County
Land records: Contact Register of Deeds, PO Box 100, Philip, SD 57567
Naturalization records: Contact Clerk of Courts, PO Box 70, Philip, SD 57567
Vital records: Contact Register of Deeds
Probate records: Contact Clerk of Courts
Probate search service: $2.00; copies: 20¢ per page, no minimum

*Hamlin County Courthouse
PO Box 237
Hayti, SD 57241
Phone (605) 783-3751
County organized 1873 from Deuel County
Land records: Contact Register of Deeds
Naturalization records: Contact Clerk of Courts
Vital records: Contact Register of Deeds
Probate records: Contact Clerk of Courts
Probate search service: $2.00; copies: 15¢ per letter-sized page, 20¢ per legal-sized page, $2.00 minimum plus SASE

*Hand County Courthouse
415 West First Avenue
Miller, SD 57362-1346
Phone (605) 853-3337 Clerk of Courts; (605) 853-3512 Register of Deeds

County created 1873; organized 1882
Land records: From 1881; contact Register of Deeds; copies: 50¢ per page, $2.00 per instrument for certification
Naturalization records: No naturalization records; contact State Archives
Vital records: Births and deaths from July 1905 (some delayed births registered), marriages from 1883; contact Register of Deeds; certified copies: $7.00 each for births and deaths, $5.00 each for marriages
Probate records: Contact Clerk of Courts
Probate search service: $2.00 per name; copies: 20¢ per page

Hanson County Courthouse
Alexandria, SD 57311
Phone (605) 239-4446
County organized 1873 from Buffalo and Deuel counties

*Harding County Courthouse
PO Box 26
Buffalo, SD 57720-0026
Phone (605) 375-3351
County organized 1909 from Butte County
Land records: From 1909 (numerical and alphabetical); contact Register of Deeds
Naturalization records: No naturalization records
Vital records: Contact Register of Deeds
Probate records: Contact Clerk of Courts
Probate search service: $2.00; copies: $1.00 per page, $2.00 for certified copies

*Hughes County Courthouse
104 East Capital
Pierre, SD 57501-2589
Phone (605) 224-7891 Register of Deeds
County organized 26 November 1880 from Buffalo County
Land records: Contact Register of Deeds
Vital records: Contact Register of Deeds

*Hutchinson County Courthouse
Olivet, SD 57052
Phone (605) 387-4217 Register of Deeds or Clerk of Courts
County organized 1862 from unorganized territory, in 1879 annexed Armstrong County, which was created in 1871
Land records: Contact Register of Deeds, 140 Euclid, Room 37, Olivet, SD 57052; copies: $1.00 per document
Vital records: Contact Register of Deeds; certified copies: $7.00 each for births and deaths, $5.00 each for marriages
Probate records: Contact Clerk of Courts, PO Box 7, Olivet, SD 57052
Probate search service: $2.00 per name; copies: 10¢ per page, no minimum

*Hyde County Courthouse
PO Box 306
Highmore, SD 57345-0306
Phone (605) 852-2512
*County organized 1873 from Buffalo
County*
Land records: Contact Register of Deeds
Office, 112 Commercial, S.E.,
Highmore, SD 57345
Land records search service: $2.00 in
advance
Naturalization records: Contact Alfred F.
Jetty, Clerk of Courts
Vital records: Contact Register of Deeds
Office
Probate records: Contact Clerk of Courts

*Jackson County Courthouse
Kadoka, SD 57543
Phone (605) 837-2420 Register of Deeds;
(605) 837-2121 Clerk of Courts
*County organized 1914 from Stanley
County; in 1976 annexed
Washabaugh County, which was
organized 1883 from Indian lands
and continued as an Indian
reservation*
Land records: Contact Register of Deeds,
PO Box 249, Kadoka, SD 57543;
certified copies: $1.00 each
Naturalization records: Contact Clerk of
Courts, PO Box 128, Kadoka, SD
57543; certified copies: $2.00 each
Vital records: Contact Register of Deeds;
certified copies: $5.00 each
Probate records: Contact Clerk of Courts
Probate search service: no charge;
copies: 15¢ each, $2.00 for certified
copies, no minimum

*Jerauld County Courthouse
Wessington Springs, SD 57382
Phone (605) 539-1221 Register of Deeds;
(605) 539-1202 Clerk of Courts
*County organized 1883 from Aurora
County*
Land records: Deeds from 1884; contact
Register of Deeds; copies: $1.00 each,
$2.00 for certified copies
Naturalization records: From 1884;
contact Clerk of Courts
Vital records: From 1905; contact
Register of Deeds (proof of
relationship required)
Probate records: From 1905; contact
Clerk of Courts
Probate search service: $2.00 per name;
copies: 20¢ per page, no minimum; no
telephone requests

Jones County Courthouse
Murdo, SD 57559
Phone (605) 669-2361
*County organized 1916 from Lyman
County*

*Kingsbury County Courthouse
PO Box 196
De Smet, SD 57231
Phone (605) 854-3832
*County organized 1873 from Hanson
County*
Land records: Contact Register of Deeds,
PO Box 146, De Smet, SD 57231
Naturalization records: Not available
Vital records: From 1905; contact
Register of Deeds
Probate records: Contact Clerk of Courts,
PO Box 176, De Smet, SD 57231
Probate search service: $2.00; copies:
20¢ per page, no minimum

*Lake County Courthouse
PO Box 447
Madison, SD 57042-0447
Phone (605) 256-4876
*County organized 1873 from Brookings
and Hanson counties*
Land records: Contact Register of Deeds,
PO Box 266, Madison, SD 57042
Naturalization records: Contact Clerk of
Courts
Vital records: From 1 July 1905; contact
Register of Deeds
Probate records: Contact Clerk of Courts
Probate search service: no charge;
copies: 25¢ per page, no minimum

Lawrence County Courthouse
644 Main Street
Deadwood, SD 57732-1124
Phone (605) 578-2040
*County organized 1875 from
unorganized territory*

*Lincoln County Courthouse
100 East Fifth Street
Canton, SD 57013-1732
Phone (605) 987-5661 Register of Deeds;
(605) 987-5891 Clerk of Courts
*County organized 1867 from
Minnehaha County*
Land records: Contact Register of Deeds;
copies: $1.00 each, $2.00 for certified
copies
Naturalization records: First papers from
1870, second papers to 1941; contact
Clerk of Courts
Vital records: Births and deaths from
1905 (delayed births from 1870),
marriages from 1873; contact Register
of Deeds; certified copies: $5.00 each
Probate records: From June 1880; contact
Clerk of Courts
Probate search service: $2.00 per name;
copies: 15¢ each for short pages, 20¢
for long pages, $2.00 for certified
copies, no minimum

*Lyman County Courthouse
Kennebec, SD 57544
Phone (605) 869-2277

*County organized 1873 from
unorganized territory*
Land records: Contact Jean A. Brakke,
Register of Deeds, PO Box 98,
Kennebec, SD 57544; copies: $1.00
per document plus 20¢ per page for
each page after five, $2.00 for
certified copies
Vital records: Births and deaths; contact
Register of Deeds; certified copies:
$7.00 each
Probate records: Contact Clerk of Courts,
c/o Janice A. Lien, PO Box 235,
Kennebec, SD 57544
Probate search service: $2.00; copies:
25¢ each, $2.00 minimum

*Marshall County Courthouse
PO Box 130
Britton, SD 57430
Phone (605) 448-5213
*County organized 1885 from Day
County*
Land records: Contact Register of Deeds
Land records search service: $2.00;
copies: 10¢ each, $2.00 for certified
copies

*McCook County Courthouse
Salem, SD 57058
Phone (605) 425-2781
*County organized 1873 from Hanson
County*
Land records: Contact Director of
Equalization
Naturalization records: Contact Clerk of
Courts
Vital records: Contact Register of Deeds
Probate records: Contact Clerk of Courts
Probate search service: $2.00; copies:
20¢ per page, no minimum

*McPherson County Courthouse
PO Box L
Leola, SD 57456
Phone (605) 439-3151 Register of Deeds;
(605) 439-3361 Clerk of Courts
*County organized 1873 from Buffalo
County*
Land records: From 1884; contact
Register of Deeds, PO Box 129,
Leola, SD 57456-0129; copies: $1.00
each
Naturalization records: From 1884 to
1943; contact Clerk of Courts, PO
Box 248, Leola, SD 57456-0248
Vital records: From 1905; contact
Register of Deeds; certified copies:
$7.00 each
Probate records: From 1887; contact
Clerk of Courts
Probate search service: $2.00; copies 30¢
per page, $2.25 certified, no minimum

Meade County Courthouse
1425 Sherman
Sturgis, SD 57785-1452

Phone (605) 347-4411
County organized 1889 from Lawrence County

*Mellette County Courthouse
PO Box C
White River, SD 57579-0403
Phone (605) 259-3230
County organized 1909 from Tripp County
Land records: Contact Register of Deeds, PO Box 183, White River, SD 57579
Naturalization records: Contact Clerk of Courts, PO Box 257, White River, SD 57579
Vital records: Contact Register of Deeds; copies: $7.00 for births and deaths
Probate records: Contact Clerk of Courts
No probate search service; copies: 25¢ each

*Miner County Courthouse
401 North Main
PO Box 265
Howard, SD 57349
Phone (605) 772-5621 Register of Deeds; (605) 772-4612 Clerk of Courts
County organized 1873 from Hanson County
Land records: Contact Register of Deeds, PO Box 546, Howard, SD 57349
Naturalization records: Contact Clerk of Courts
Vital records: Contact Register of Deeds
Probate records: Contact Clerk of Courts

*Minnehaha County Courthouse
415 North Dakota Avenue
Sioux Falls, SD 57102-0136
Phone (605) 335-4223 Register of Deeds; (605) 339-6418 Clerk of Courts
County organized 1862 from territorial county
Land records: From 1870; contact Register of Deeds
Vital records: Some vital records from late 1800s but not complete; contact Register of Deeds; certified copies: $7.00 each
Probate records: Contact Clerk of Courts
Probate search service: $2.00; copies: 20¢ per page, no minimum but must enclose SASE

Moody County Courthouse
PO Box 152
Flandreau, SD 57028
Phone (605) 997-3181
County organized 1873 from Brookings and Minnehaha counties

*Pennington County Courthouse
315 Saint Joseph Street
PO Box 230
Rapid City, SD 57709-0230
Phone (605) 394-2575

County organized 1875 from unorganized territory
Land records: Contact Register of Deeds, 315 Saint Joseph Street, Rapid City, SD 57701
Vital records: Contact Register of Deeds
Probate records: Contact Clerk of Circuit Court, Seventh Judicial Circuit, Pennington County Courthouse, PO Box 230, Rapid City, SD 57709
Probate search service: no charge; copies: 25¢ each, no minimum

*Perkins County Courthouse
Bison, SD 57620
Phone (605) 244-5626
County organized 1909 from Harding and Butte counties
Land records: Contact Jean Smith, Register of Deeds, PO Box 127, Bison, SD 57620
Land records search service: $4.00; copies: 25¢ each for 8½" x 11", 50¢ each for 11" x 14"
Naturalization records: Yes
Vital records: Contact Register of Deeds
Vital records search service: $5.00; certified copies: $7.00 each
Probate records: From 1908
Probate search service: $2.00; copies: 25¢ each for letter-sized copies, 50¢ for legal-sized copies, $2.00 minimum; "Written requests only."

Potter County Courthouse
201 South Exene
Gettysburg, SD 57442-1521
Phone (605) 765-9472
County organized 1875 from Buffalo County

*Roberts County Courthouse
411 Second Avenue East
Sisseton, SD 57262-1403
Phone (605) 698-3395; (605) 698-7152 Register of Deeds
County organized 1883 from Grant County
Land records: Contact Register of Deeds
Naturalization records: No naturalization records
Vital records: Births, deaths and marriages; contact Register of Deeds; certified copies: $7.00 each for births and deaths, $5.00 each for marriages
Probate records: Contact Clerk of Courts
Probate search service: $2.00 by mail (no random searches; will search only specific names); copies: 15¢ per page, $2.00 per document for certification, no minimum

*Sanborn County Courthouse
Woonsocket, SD 57385
Phone (605) 796-4516 Register of Deeds; (605) 796-4515 Clerk of Courts

County organized 1883 from Miner County
Land records: Contact Register of Deeds, PO Box 295, Woonsocket, SD 57385
Naturalization records: Cannot be photocopied
Vital records: Contact Register of Deeds
Probate records: Contact Clerk of Courts, PO Box 56, Woonsocket, SD 57385
Probate search service: $2.00; copies: 25¢ per page, no minimum

*Shannon County Courthouse
c/o Fall River County Courthouse
906 North River Street
Hot Springs, SD 57747-1387
Phone (605) 745-3996
County organized 1875 from territorial county, in 1943 reannexed Washington County, which was organized in 1883 from Shannon County
Land records: Contact Register of Deeds
Naturalization records: No naturalization records
Vital records: Contact Register of Deeds
Probate records: Contact Clerk of Courts
Probate search service: $2.00 per name; copies: $2.00 per certified copy of each document, $2.00 minimum

*Spink County Courthouse
210 East Seventh Avenue
Redfield, SD 57469-1266
Phone (605) 472-1825; (605) 472-1922 Clerk of Courts Office
County organized 1873 from Hanson and Walworth counties
Land records: Contact Register of Deeds; copies: $1.00 for each of the first five pages and 20¢ for each additional page
Naturalization records: From 1884; contact Clerk of Courts Office
Vital records: Contact Register of Deeds; certified copies: $7.00 each for births and deaths, $5.00 each for marriages
Probate records: From 1928; contact Clerk of Courts
Probate search service: $2.00; copies: 15¢ per page plus postage, no minimum; "Our records are alphabetized, so most of the time dates are not necessary."

Stanley County Courthouse
PO Box 595
Fort Pierre, SD 57532
Phone (605) 223-2673
County organized 1873 from unorganized territory

*Sully County Courthouse
Onida, SD 57564
Phone (605) 258-2535
County organized 1873 from Potter County

Land records: Contact Register of Deeds
Naturalization records: Contact Clerk of Courts
Vital records: Contact Register of Deeds
Probate records: Contact Clerk of Courts

*Todd County Courthouse
c/o Tripp County Courthouse
200 East Third Street
Winner, SD 57580-1806
Phone (605) 842-2266; (605) 842-2208 Register of Deeds
County organized 1909 from Indian lands
Land records: From 1909; contact Register of Deeds Office; copies: $1.00 per instrument (up to five pages) and 20¢ for each additional page
Naturalization records: From 1909; contact Clerk of Courts
Vital records: From 1909; contact Register of Deeds; certified copies: $7.00 per document
Probate records: From 1907; contact Clerk of Courts
Probate search service: $2.00; copies: 10¢ per page, no minimum

*Tripp County Courthouse
200 East Third Street
Winner, SD 57580-1806
Phone (605) 842-2266; (605) 842-2208 Register of Deeds
County organized 1873 from unorganized territory
Land records: From 1909; contact Register of Deeds Office; copies: $1.00 per instrument (up to five pages) and 20¢ for each additional page
Naturalization records: From 1909; contact Clerk of Courts
Vital records: From 1909; contact Register of Deeds; certified copies: $7.00 per document
Probate records: From 1907; contact Clerk of Courts
Probate search service: $2.00; copies: 10¢ per page, no minimum

*Turner County Courthouse
Main Street
PO Box 368
Parker, SD 57053
Phone (605) 297-3115; (605) 297-3153; (605) 773-3804 South Dakota State Historical Society
County organized 1871 from Lincoln County and part of the now-defunct Jayne County
Land records: From 1871; contact Carol J. Viet, Register of Deeds, PO Box 485, Parker, SD 57053-0485
Land records search service: no charge, but must have legal description of the land; copies: $1.00 per document

Naturalization records: From 1887; contact South Dakota State Historical Society, South Dakota Archives, Cultural Heritage Center, 900 Governors Drive, Pierre, SD 57501-2217
Vital records: From July 1905; contact Register of Deeds
Vital records search service: no charge, but must have first, middle, and last name of child, father's name, mother's maiden name, place of birth for birth certificate; decedent's full name, date and place of death for death certificate; full names of bride and groom, date and place of marriage for marriage certificate; certified copies: $7.00 each for births and deaths, $5.00 for marriages, payable in advance
Probate records: From 1884; contact Clerk of Courts, PO Box 446, Parker, SD 57053. From May 1927 through March 1949; contact Record Storage, East Hiway Bypass, Pierre, SD 57501
Probate search service: $2.00 per name; copies: 25¢ each, no minimum

Union County Courthouse
PO Box 757
Elk Point, SD 57025-0757
Phone (605) 356-2132
County organized 1862 from unorganized territory

*Walworth County Courthouse
PO Box 199
Selby, SD 57472-0199
Phone (605) 649-7878
County organized 1873 from territorial county
Land records: Contact Register of Deeds, PO Box 159, Selby, SD 57472
Naturalization records: No naturalization records
Vital records: Contact Register of Deeds
Probate records: Contact Clerk of Courts, PO Box 328, Selby, SD 57472
No probate search service; copies: $1.00 per page

Washabaugh County
(see Jackson County)

Washington County
(see Shannon County)

*Yankton County Courthouse
PO Box 155
Yankton, SD 57078-0137
Phone (605) 668-3438
County organized 1862 from territorial county
Probate records: From 1905
Probate search service: $2.00 per name; copies: 20¢ per page, no minimum;

"Correct name on probate and year it was filed would be helpful in locating the file."

*Ziebach County Courthouse
Main Street
PO Box 68
Dupree, SD 57623
Phone (605) 365-5157; (605) 365-5165 Register of Deeds; (605) 365-5159 Clerk of Courts
County organized 1911 from Pennington County
Land records: Contact Register of Deeds; copies: $1.00 per page, $2.00 per certified page
Naturalization records: Contact Clerk of Courts
Vital records: Contact Register of Deeds; certified copies: $7.00 each for births and deaths, $5.00 each for marriages
Probate records: Contact Clerk of Courts
Probate search service: $2.00; copies: 25¢ per page, no minimum

TENNESSEE

Capital: Nashville. Statehood: 1 June 1796 (acknowledged as part of the U.S. by Great Britain in 1783, eastern part constituted the State of Franklin, 1784 to 1788; North Carolina relinquished its claims in 1790)

Court System

Tennessee has more than 300 Municipal Courts in home-rule municipalities that hear city ordinance violations and various other matters. Special Juvenile Courts have been set up in some fourteen counties, exercising authority otherwise given to the General Sessions Courts. Davidson and Shelby counties have Probate Courts, whose duties are elsewhere handled by the General Sessions Courts. The General Sessions Courts sit at each county seat and have limited jurisdiction over civil controversies and some misdemeanors, as well as conducting preliminary felony hearings and, in some counties, presiding over probate and juvenile matters.

In 1984 the State Trial Courts were divided into thirty-one judicial districts, consisting of the Criminal Courts, the Chancery Courts and the Circuit Courts, sitting at each county seat. Thereby the Law and Equity Courts of Gibson, Montgomery and Sullivan counties became Chancery Courts, and the Law and Equity Court of Dyer County became a Circuit Court. Criminal Courts, having original jurisdiction over criminal matters, are established in thirteen of the thirty-one judicial districts in the state (marked with a superscript 1—[1]). Chancery Courts, having jurisdiction over all equity matters (over $50), most civil cases (except torts), divorce and adoption, as well as some probate matters, exist in twenty-five judicial districts (marked below with a superscript 2—[2]). Circuit Courts have general jurisdiction in each of the thirty-one judicial districts.

First Judicial District[1,2]: Carter, Johnson, Unicoi and Washington counties; Second Judicial District[1,2]: Sullivan County; Third Judicial District[1,2]: Greene, Hamblen, Hancock and Hawkins counties; Fourth Judicial District[2]: Cocke, Grainger, Jefferson and Sevier counties; Fifth Judicial District: Blount County; Sixth Judicial District[1,2]: Knox County; Seventh Judicial District[2]: Anderson County; Eighth Judicial District[1,2]: Campbell, Claiborne, Fentress, Scott and Union counties; Ninth Judicial District[1,2]: Loudon, Meigs, Morgan and Roane counties; Tenth Judicial District[1,2]: Bradley, McMinn, Monroe and Polk counties; Eleventh Judicial District[1,2]: Hamilton County; Twelfth Judicial District[2]: Bledsoe, Franklin, Grundy, Marion, Rhea and Sequatchie counties; Thirteenth Judicial District[1,2]: Clay, Cumberland, DeKalb, Overton, Pickett, Putnam and White counties; Fourteenth Judicial District: Coffee County; Fifteenth Judicial District[1,2]: Jackson, Macon, Smith, Trousdale and Wilson counties; Sixteenth Judicial District[2]: Cannon and Rutherford counties; Seventeenth Judicial District[2]: Bedford, Lincoln, Marshall and Moore counties; Eighteenth Judicial District[1,2]: Sumner County; Nineteenth Judicial District[2]: Montgomery and Robertson counties; Twentieth Judicial District[1,2]: Davidson County; Twenty-first Judicial District: Hickman, Lewis, Perry and Williamson counties; Twenty-second Judicial District: Giles, Lawrence, Maury and Wayne counties; Twenty-third Judicial District: Cheatham, Dickson, Houston, Humphreys and Stewart counties; Twenty-fourth Judicial District[2]: Benton, Carroll, Decatur, Hardin and Henry counties; Twenty-fifth Judicial District[2]: Fayette, Hardeman, Lauderdale, McNairy and Tipton counties; Twenty-sixth Judicial District[2]: Chester, Henderson and Madison counties; Twenty-seventh Judicial District[2]: Obion and Weakley counties; Twenty-eighth Judicial District[2] Crockett, Gibson and Haywood counties; Twenty-ninth Judicial District[2]: Dyer and Lake counties; Thirtieth Judicial District[1,2]: Shelby County; Thirty-first Judicial District: Van Buren and Warren counties. Appeals are heard by the Court of Appeals, Court of Criminal Appeals and Supreme Court.

Courthouses

*Anderson County Courthouse
Clinton, TN 37716
Phone (615) 457-5400
County organized 1801 from Grainger and Knox counties
Land records: From 1802; contact Mary S. Harris, County Historian, Room 204 Vault
Naturalization records: No naturalization records
Vital records: Births from 1891 to 1899, from 1909 to 1912 and from 1925 to 1938, deaths from 1909 to 1912 (all incomplete), marriages from 1838 to date; contact County Historian
Probate records: From 1830 to date; contact County Historian
Probate search service: $5.00; copies: 25¢ per page, no minimum

*Bedford County Courthouse
1 Public Square
Shelbyville, TN 37160
Phone (615) 684-5719 Register of Deeds; (615) 684-1921 County Clerk; (615) 684-1672 Chancery Court Clerk
County organized 1807 from Rutherford County and Indian lands
Land records: From the early or mid-1800s; contact Donnetta Hurt, Register of Deeds, Suite 102
Vital records: Births from 1909 to 1911, and from 1925 to 1939, deaths from 1925 to 1939, marriages from 1 January 1861 to date; contact Kathy K. Prater, County Clerk, Suite 100; copies: $2.00 each, $4.00 for certified copies
Probate records: From 1861 to 31 August 1982; contact County Clerk; copies: $1.00 per page, $2.00 each for certified copies. After 1 September 1982; contact Howard Barton, Chancery Court Clerk, Suite 302

*Benton County Courthouse
PO Box 8
Camden, TN 38320-0008
Phone (901) 584-6053
County organized 1835 from Henry and Humphreys counties
Naturalization records: No naturalization records
Vital records: Marriage licenses from 1852 to date; contact Rosanne K. Gaskin, County Clerk
Vital records search service: $5.00
Probate records: To 1984; contact County Clerk. From 1984; contact Chancery Clerk

*Bledsoe County Courthouse
Pikeville, TN 37367
Phone (615) 447-2137
County organized 1807 from Roane County and Indian lands
Land records: From 1908 to date (most earlier records destroyed by fire); contact Neva Hale, Register of Deeds
No land records search service
Probate records: Wills (one will book and some old court minutes have been restored, but cannot be copied); contact Register of Deeds

Blount County Courthouse
Maryville, TN 37803
Phone (615) 982-4391
County organized 1795 from Knox County

Bradley County Courthouse
PO Box 46
Cleveland, TN 37364-0046
Phone (615) 479-9654
County organized 1836 from Indian lands

Campbell County Courthouse
PO Box 13
Jacksboro, TN 37757-0013
Phone (615) 562-4985
County organized 1806 from Anderson and Claiborne counties

Cannon County Courthouse
Woodbury, TN 37190
Phone (615) 563-4278
County organized 1836 from Rutherford, Warren and Smith counties

*Carroll County Courthouse
PO Box 110
Huntingdon, TN 38344-0110
Phone (901) 986-1952 Register of Deeds; (901) 986-1990 Health Department; (901) 986-1960 County Clerk; (901) 986-1920 Clerk and Master
County organized 1821 from Western District (Indian lands)
Land records: Contact Judy Baker, Register of Deeds
Vital records: Contact Health Department. Marriages from 1838; contact Carolyn Lutz, County Clerk
Probate records: Contact Kenneth Todd, Clerk and Master

Carter County Courthouse
Elizabethton, TN 37643
Phone (615) 543-2431
County organized 1796 from Washington County; name changed from Carteret County

*Cheatham County Courthouse
100 Public Square
Ashland City, TN 37015-1711
Phone (615) 792-4317 Register of Deeds; (615) 792-5179 County Clerk; (615) 792-4620 Chancery Court
County organized 1856 from Dickson, Montgomery, Davidson and Robertson counties
Land records: Contact Register of Deeds
Vital records: Marriages from 1956 to date; contact W. J. Hall, County Clerk, Room 115; copies: 25¢ each (from old records only), $1.00 for certified copies
Probate records: Wills and testaments from 1856 to 1982; contact County Clerk; copies: $1.00 per page. From 1982; contact Chancery Court
Probate search service from Chancery Court: no charge; copies: $2.00 per page, $2.00 for certification, no minimum

Chester County Courthouse
Henderson, TN 38340
Phone (910) 989-2233

County organized 1879 from Hardeman, Henderson, Madison and McNairy counties

Claiborne County Courthouse
PO Box 173
Tazewell, TN 37879-0173
Phone (615) 626-3283
County organized 1801 from Grainger and Hawkins counties

*Clay County Courthouse
PO Box 218
Celina, TN 38551-0218
Phone (615) 243-2249
County organized 1870 from Jackson and Overton counties
Land records: Contact Ray Frogge, Register of Deeds
Probate records: Contact Corinne McLerran, Clerk and Master

*Cocke County Courthouse
Newport, TN 37821
Phone (615) 623-6176; (615) 623-7540 Register of Deeds; (615) 623-6176 County Clerk Office; (615) 623-3321 Clerk and Master
County organized 1797 from Jefferson County
Land records: Contact Mr. Paul Lee, Register of Deeds
Vital records: Marriages from 1877 to date; contact Janice Butler, County Clerk; copies of open records: $1.00 each, $2.00 for certified copies
Probate records: Contact Mr. Charles Chesteen, Clerk and Master

*Coffee County Courthouse
101 West Fort Street
Manchester, TN 37355
Phone (615) 728-3024 County Executive; (615) 728-3371 Register of Deeds; (615) 728-2002 Clerk and Master
County organized 1836 from Bedford, Franklin and Warren counties
Land records: Deeds from 1835; contact Mrs. Betty M. Majors, Chairman, County Records Commission, 111 Oak Park Drive, Tullahoma, TN 37388 or Ellen P. Vaughn, Register of Deeds, PO Box 786, Manchester, TN 37355
Naturalization records: In Minute Books; contact County Records Commission
Vital records: Very few vital records, for scattered years; contact County Records Commission
Probate records: Will Books from 1835, Chancery Court Minute Books (and loose papers, also covering dower, ex parte) from 1872 (some scattered cases from 1850 to 1872), County Court Minute Books (and loose papers, probate, dower, ex parte) from

about 1865; contact County Records Commission or Ben G. Jenkins, PO Box 5, Manchester, TN 37355
Probate search service: no charge; copies: 25¢ each, no minimum; "Only Will Books have usable indices; the County Records Commission has a volunteer group who will, time permitting, check the above, as the county officials do not have time to do research; this group is also cleaning, filing and preparing an all-name index to the loose papers prior to their being microfilmed by the Tennessee State Archives; this is an on-going project, and, because of its magnitude, will be some years in completion."

Crockett County Courthouse
Alamo, TN 38001
Phone (901) 696-5451
County organized 1871 from Dyer, Gibson, Haywood and Madison counties

*Cumberland County Courthouse
Main Street
Crossville, TN 38555-9428
Phone (615) 484-8212
County organized November 1855 from Bledsoe, Fentress, Morgan, Putnam, Rhea, Roane, Van Buren and White counties; boundary lines established by 1856
Land records: From 1856 (sketchy before 1905 courthouse fire); contact County Registrar and Tax Assessor
Naturalization records: No naturalization records
Vital records: Contact County Court Clerk
Probate records: Contact Clerk and Master

*Davidson County Courthouse
Nashville, TN 37201
Phone (615) 862-6790
County organized 1783 (Middle Tennessee) by act of North Carolina
Land records: From 1784 to date; contact Felix Z. Wilson, II, County Register, Room 103

Decatur County Courthouse
PO Box 488
Decaturville, TN 38329-0488
Phone (901) 852-2231
County organized 1845 from Perry County

DeKalb County Courthouse
Smithville, TN 37166
Phone (615) 597-5177
County organized 1837 from Cannon, Warren, White, Wilson and Jackson counties

*Dickson County Courthouse
Charlotte, TN 37036
Phone (615) 789-4171
County organized 1803 from
Montgomery and Robertson counties
Land records: Contact Clyde Buckner,
Register of Deeds
Probate records: Contact William E.
Brazzell, County Clerk
No probate search service; "I most times
turn it over to someone and set the
charges by them."

Dyer County Courthouse
PO Box 1360
Dyersburg, TN 38025-1360
Phone (901) 285-1490
County organized 1823 from Western
District (Indian lands)

*Fayette County Courthouse
1 Court Square
Somerville, TN 38068
Phone (901) 465-2851 County Register;
(901) 465-3529 Circuit Court Clerk;
(901) 465-2871 County Clerk; (901)
465-2461 Clerk and Master of
Chancery Court
County organized 1824 from Shelby and
Hardeman counties
Land records: Contact Edward Pattat,
Register of Deeds, PO Box 99,
Somerville, TN 38068
Naturalization records: Early
naturalization records; contact Jimmie
German, Circuit Court Clerk, PO Box
177, Somerville, TN 38068
Vital records: Marriages; contact Dell
Graham, County Clerk, PO Box 218,
Somerville, TN 38068-0218
Probate records: Contact Barbara Walls,
Clerk and Master of Chancery Court,
PO Drawer 220, Somerville, TN
38068
Probate search service: no charge;
copies: 30¢ each.

Fentress County Courthouse
PO Box C
Jamestown, TN 38556-0200
Phone (615) 879-8014
County organized 1823 from Overton,
White and Morgan counties

Franklin County Courthouse
Winchester, TN 37398
Phone (615) 967-2541
County organized 1807 from Rutherford
County and Indian lands

*Gibson County Courthouse
Trenton, TN 38382
Phone (901) 855-7613
County organized 1823 from Western
District (Indian lands)

Land records: Contact Charles Lovell,
Tax Assessor
Naturalization records: No naturalization
records
Vital records: Contact County Clerk,
Clerk and Master at Humboldt and
Trenton, and Circuit Clerk
Probate records: Contact Clerk and
Master, Trenton
No probate search service; copies: 50¢
per page, no minimum

*Giles County Courthouse
PO Box 678
Pulaski, TN 38478-0678
Phone (615) 363-1509; (615) 363-8434
Old Records Department
County organized 1809 from Maury
County
Land records: Deeds from 1810 to 1900,
Survey-Entry from 1828 to 1848, tax
books from 1875, tax lists 1812 and
1836; contact Old Records
Department
Land records search service: $10.00;
copies: 25¢ per page (back and front)
Naturalization records: No naturalization
records
Vital records: Marriages from 1865 to
1900 (a few early marriages before
1865); contact Old Records
Department
Vital records search service: $10.00;
copies: 25¢ per page (back and front)
Probate records: Will books from 1860 to
1900, some early loose wills,
Chancery Court Original Court Cases
from the 1830s, some County Court
loose records and cases; contact Old
Records Department
Probate search service: $10.00; copies:
25¢ per page (back and front)

Grainger County Courthouse
Rutledge, TN 37861
Phone (615) 828-3511
County organized 1796 from Hawkins
County

Greene County Courthouse
Greeneville, TN 37743
Phone (615) 639-5321
County organized 1783 from
Washington County

Grundy County Courthouse
Altamont, TN 37301
Phone (615) 692-3622
County organized 1844 from Franklin
and Warren counties

*Hamblen County Courthouse
511 West Second N Street
Morristown, TN 37814-3964
Phone (615) 586-1993

County organized 1870 from Grainger,
Hawkins and Jefferson counties
Land records: Contact Jim Clawson,
Register of Deeds
Naturalization records: No naturalization
records
Vital records: Contact County Clerk
Probate records: Contact County Clerk
Probate search service: per time charge;
copies: 10¢ per page, $2.00 for
certified copies, no minimum

Hamilton County Courthouse
105 County Courthouse
Chattanooga, TN 37402
Phone (615) 757-2185
County organized 1819 from Rhea
County and Indian lands, and in
January 1920 annexed James
County, which was organized 1871
from Hamilton and Bradley counties

Hancock County Courthouse
Main Street
Sneedville, TN 37869
Phone (615) 733-4475
County organized 1844 from Claiborne
and Hawkins counties

Hardeman County Courthouse
100 North Main
Bolivar, TN 38008-2322
Phone (901) 658-3541
County organized 1823 from Hardin
County and Western District (Indian
lands)

Hardin County Courthouse
Main Street
Savannah, TN 38372
Phone (901) 925-3921
County organized 1819 from Western
District (Indian lands), to run to the
Mississippi, but eleven days later
Shelby County was organized from
Hardin County

*Hawkins County Courthouse
150 Washington Street
Rogersville, TN 37857-3346
Phone (615) 272-7002
County organized 1786 from Sullivan
County
Land records: Contact Gale Carpenter,
Register of Deeds
Naturalization records: Contact Holly
Jaynes, Circuit Court Clerk
Probate records: From 1787 through
1982; contact Donna Alvis, County
Clerk. Probate records from 1982;
contact Shirley Graham, Clerk and
Master.
No probate search service from the
County Clerk's Office; copies: 25¢ per
page, $2.00 for certified copies

*Haywood County Courthouse
1 North Washington
Brownsville, TN 38012-2557
Phone (901) 772-1432
County organized 1823 from Western District (Indian lands)
Land records: Contact Register of Deeds
Naturalization records: Contact County Clerk
Vital records: Contact County Clerk
Probate records: Contact Clerk and Master
Probate search service: depends on amount of research; copies: 25¢ each, no minimum

Henderson County Courthouse
Lexington, TN 38351
Phone (901) 968-2856
County organized 1821 from Western District (Indian lands)

*Henry County Courthouse
PO Box 24
Paris, TN 38242-0024
Phone (901) 642-4081 Register of Deeds; (901) 642-0162 Assessor of Property; (901) 642-2412 County Clerk's Office
County organized 1821 from Western District (Indian lands)
Land records: Contact Alice Webb, Register of Deeds, PO Box 44, Paris, TN 38242 or Albert Wade, Assessor of Property, PO Box 564, Paris, TN 38242
Vital records: Marriages; contact Jerry D. Bomar, County Clerk
Probate records: Contact County Clerk

Hickman County Courthouse
Public Square
Centerville, TN 37033
Phone (615) 729-2621
County organized 1807 from Dickson County

Houston County Courthouse
PO Box 388
Erin, TN 37061-0388
Phone (615) 289-3141
County organized 1871 from Dickson, Montgomery, Stewart and Humphreys counties

Humphreys County Courthouse
Waverly, TN 37185
Phone (615) 296-7671
County organized 1809 from Stewart County

*Jackson County Courthouse
PO Box 346
Gainesboro, TN 38562-0346
Phone (615) 268-9212
County organized 1801 from Smith County and Indian lands

Land records: Contact Bill West, Register of Deeds
Probate records: Contact Mildred Demis, County Clerk
Probate search service: $1.00; copies: 15¢ each

*Jefferson County Courthouse
Dandridge, TN 37725
Phone (615) 397-2935
County organized 1792 from Greene and Hawkins counties
Land records: Contact Carroll Bales, PO Box 58, Dandridge, TN 37725
Vital records: Marriages; contact R. E. Farrar, III, County Clerk, PO Box 710, Dandridge, TN 37725-0710
Probate records: Contact County Clerk
Probate search service: $2.00; copies: $1.00 each; "SASE helpful."

*Johnson County Courthouse
222 West Main Street
Mountain City, TN 37683-1612
Phone (615) 727-7841 Register of Deeds; (615) 727-9633 County Clerk; (615) 727-7853 Clerk and Master
County organized 1836 from Carter County
Land records: From 1836; contact James Lefler, Register of Deeds
Land records search service: no charge
Naturalization records: No naturalization records
Vital records: Marriages from 1836; contact Danny Cullop, County Clerk
Vital records search service: no charge
Probate records: Wills from 1836; contact County Clerk
Probate search service: no charge

*Knox County Archives
(East Tennessee Historical Center, 314 West Clinch Avenue, Knoxville, TN 37902-2203—location)
500 West Church Avenue (mailing address)
Knoxville, TN 37902-2505
Phone (615) 544-5741 Archives; (615) 544-4144 County Health Department
County organized 1792 from Greene and Hawkins counties
Land records: Warranty Deeds from 1779 to 1929; contact Archives; Warranty Deeds after 1929; contact County Register of Deeds, Suite 225, City/County Building, 400 Main Avenue, Knoxville, TN 37902; copies from Archives: $1.00 for the first page and 50¢ for each additional page, $1.00 for certification
Naturalization records: From the late 1800s and early 1900s (most in the Circuit Court loose papers); contact Archives; copies: $1.00 for the first page and 50¢ for each additional page, $1.00 for certification

Vital records: Births from 1881 and from 1908 to 1925, deaths from 1908 to 1912 and from 1925 to 1939, marriages from 1792 to 1993 (bonds, licenses, applications, indexes); contact Archives. Marriages from 1992 to date; contact County Clerk, Marriage Records, Courthouse, 300 Main Avenue, Knoxville, TN 37902. Long certificates of births in Knoxville or Knox County from August 1975 to date, short certificates of births from 1949 to date in all of Tennessee, deaths from 1973 to date for Knoxville or Knox County; contact County Health Department, 925 Cleveland Place, Knoxville, TN 37919; copies from Archives: $1.00 for the first page and 50¢ for each additional page, $1.00 for certification
Probate records: Wills from 1796 to 1991 (indexed from 1792 to 1979), settlements administration (estate) books from 1792 to 1982 (missing from 1884 to 1890), probate cases from 1939 to 1955, guardian settlement papers, administrators settlement papers, administrators bonds, executors settlement papers, executors bonds; contact Archives; copies: $1.00 for the first page and 50¢ for each additional page, $1.00 for certification

Lake County Courthouse
Church Street
Tiptonville, TN 38079
Phone (901) 253-7582
County organized 1870 from Obion County

Lauderdale County Courthouse
Ripley, TN 38063
Phone (901) 635-2561
County organized 1835 from Dyer, Tipton and Haywood counties

*Lawrence County Courthouse
PO Box NBU #2
Lawrenceburg, TN 38464
Phone (615) 762-7700; (615) 762-2407 Mrs. Coffey
County organized 1817 from Hickman and Maury counties
Land records: Historical records; contact Mrs. F. L. Coffey, Jr., 200 Parkes Avenue, Lawrenceburg, TN 38464
Probate records: Historical records; contact Mrs. F. L. Coffey, Jr., 200 Parkes Avenue, Lawrenceburg, TN 38464

*Lewis County Courthouse
Hohenwald, TN 38462
Phone (615) 796-3378
County organized 1843 from Hickman,

Maury, Wayne and Lawrence counties
Land records: Contact Robert G. Johnston, Assessor of Property
Vital records: Contact Kenneth R. Turnbow, County Clerk
Probate records: Contact Janet Williams, Clerk and Master
Probate search service: $2.00; copies: $1.00 per page, no minimum; "Please send as much information as possible."

Lincoln County Courthouse
PO Box 577
Fayetteville, TN 37334-0577
Phone (615) 433-2454
County organized 1809 from Bedford County

Loudon County Courthouse
Loudon, TN 37774
Phone (615) 458-3314
County organized 1870 from Blount, Monroe, McMinn and Roane counties

*Macon County Courthouse
Lafayette, TN 37083
Phone (615) 666-2333
County organized 1842 from Smith and Sumner counties
Land records: Deeds; contact Register of Deeds Office
Naturalization records: No naturalization records
Vital records: Marriage records from April 1901
Probate records: From 1901
Probate search service: $5.00; copies: 50¢ each, no minimum

*Madison County Courthouse
100 East Main Street
Jackson, TN 38301-6299
Phone (901) 423-6022; (901) 423-6106 Office of Property Assessor; (901) 423-6028 Register; (901) 423-6023 County Clerk and Probate Clerk
County organized 1821 from Western District (Indian lands)
Land records: Contact Office of Property Assessor, Room 112
Vital records: Contact Register, Room 112. Old marriage licenses; contact Freddie Pruitt, County Clerk, Room 105; certified copies available (or photocopies of original documents but not of "old books")
Probate records: Contact Freddie Pruitt, Probate Clerk, Room 105
Probate search service: $10.00 for five years search; copies: $1.00 per page, $2.00 for certification, $10.00 minimum

Marion County Courthouse
Courthouse Square
Jasper, TN 37347
Phone (615) 942-2515
County organized 1817 from Western District (Indian lands)

*Marshall County Courthouse
Public Square
Lewisburg, TN 37091
Phone (615) 359-4933 Register of Deeds; (615) 359-1072 County Clerk
County organized 1836 from Giles, Bedford, Lincoln and Maury counties
Land records: From 1836; contact Barbara Simmons, Register of Deeds, 205 Marshall County Courthouse
Naturalization records: No naturalization records
Vital records: No vital records
Probate records: From 1836; contact Rebecca F. Stockman, County Clerk, 207 Marshall County Courthouse
Probate search service: $5.00; copies: 30¢ per page, no minimum

*Maury County Courthouse
Public Square
Columbia, TN 38401
Phone (615) 381-3690
County organized 1807 from Williamson County and Indian lands
Land records: Contact L. Wayne White, Register of Deeds; copies: 50¢ per page
Vital records: From 1807; contact Ed Harlan, County Executive
Probate records: Contact Shirley Napier, Clerk and Master
No probate search service; copies: 25¢ each, no minimum

*McMinn County Courthouse
Athens, TN 37303
Phone (615) 745-4440 County Clerk; (615) 745-1923 Circuit Court
County organized 1819 from Cherokee Indian lands
Land records: Contact Register of Deeds
Vital records: Marriages from 1820; contact County Clerk
Probate records: Contact Circuit Court

McNairy County Courthouse
Selmer, TN 38375
Phone (901) 645-3511
County organized 1823 from Hardin County

*Meigs County Courthouse
PO Box 218
Decatur, TN 37322-0218
Phone (615) 334-5747

County organized 1836 from Hamilton, McMinn, Rhea and Roane counties

*Monroe County Archives
105 College Street
Madisonville, TN 37354
Phone (615) 442-3981
County organized 1819 from Hiwassee Purchase, Indian lands
Land records: From 1819 to date (published through 1846); contact Lynn McConkey, County Genealogist
Naturalization records: From 1858 to date (in County Court Minutes Books); contact County Genealogist
Vital records: Births and deaths from 1908 to 1925 (published), marriages from 1838 to date; contact County Genealogist
Probate records: Wills from 1824 to date (published from 1824 to 1945); contact County Genealogist

Montgomery County Courthouse
Clarksville, TN 37042
Phone (615) 648-5711
County organized 1796 by the division between Montgomery and Robertson counties of Tennessee County, which had been organized in 1788 from Davidson County and was then abolished, and whose records were deposited with Montgomery County

Moore County Courthouse
Lynchburg, TN 37352
Phone (615) 759-7346
County organized 1871 from Bedford, Franklin, Lincoln and Coffee counties

Morgan County Courthouse
Main Street
Wartburg, TN 37887
Phone (615) 346-3480
County organized 1817 from Roane County, and in 1903 annexed part of Anderson County

*Obion County Courthouse
Union City, TN 38261
Phone (901) 885-9351 Register of Deeds; (901) 885-3831 County Clerk; (901) 885-2562 Chancery Court
County organized 1823 from Western District (Indian lands)
Land records: Contact Register of Deeds
Vital records: Marriages and some births and deaths; contact County Clerk
Probate records: Contact Chancery Court

Overton County Courthouse
Livingston, TN 38570
Phone (615) 823-5630

County organized 1806 from Jackson County and Indian lands

*Perry County Courthouse
PO Box 16
Linden, TN 37096-0016
Phone (615) 589-2216
County organized 1821 from Hickman and Humphreys counties (petitioned for formation 1819, legislation passed 1820, first court held the first Monday of January 1821)
Land records: From 1841 (only reconstructed records available from before courthouse fire of 1865, but most records saved from fire of 1928); contact Perry County Public Library, Rt. 10, Box 3A, Linden, TN 37096
Land records search service: donation; copies 15¢ per page
Vital records: Births and deaths from 1912
Vital records search service: donation; copies 15¢ per page
Probate records: Yes
Probate search service: donation; copies 15¢ per page

*Pickett County Courthouse
PO Box 5
Byrdstown, TN 38549-0005
Phone (615) 864-3879
County organized 1879 from Fentress and Overton counties
Land records: Contact Tax Assessor
Naturalization records: Contact County Agent, Community Center, Byrdstown, TN 38549
Vital records: Contact County Clerk
Probate records: Contact County Clerk
Probate search service: no set rate; copies: 25¢ per page, no minimum

*Polk County Courthouse
Benton, TN 37307
Phone (615) 338-4526
County organized 1839 from Bradley and McMinn counties
Land records: Contact Register of Deeds
Naturalization records: No naturalization records
Vital records: Marriages; contact County Clerk
Probate records: Contact Clerk and Master

Putnam County Courthouse
Cookeville, TN 38501
Phone (615) 526-7106
County organized 1842 from Smith, White, DeKalb, Overton and Jackson counties

Rhea County Courthouse
1475 Market Street
Dayton, TN 37321

Phone (615) 775-7808; (615) 775-1881
County organized 1807 from Roane County

*Roane County Courthouse
Records Department
PO Box 643
Kingston, TN 37763
Phone (615) 376-5578
County organized 1801 from Knox County and Indian lands
Land records: Deeds from 1801; certified copies: $5.00 each
Vital records: Marriages from 1801
Probate records: Wills and estates from 1803
Probate search service: $3.00; certified copies: $5.00 each; "Need approximate dates and SASE included with letter."

*Robertson County Courthouse
Springfield, TN 37172
Phone (615) 384-5895
County organized 1796 by the division between Montgomery and Robertson counties of Tennessee County, which had been organized in 1788 from Davidson County and was then abolished, and whose records were deposited with Montgomery County
Land records: Contact Register of Deeds, Courthouse Annex, Springfield, TN 37172
Naturalization records: Contact County Archives, 600 South Locust Street, Springfield, TN 37172
Vital records: Births and deaths from 1908, marriages from 1839 to 1975; contact County Archives
Probate records: From 1796 to 1975; contact County Archives
Probate search service: $2.00; copies: 50¢ per page, no minimum

*Rutherford County Judicial Building
20 Public Square North
Murfreesboro, TN 37130
Phone (615) 898-7799
County organized 1803 from Davidson, Williamson and Wilson counties
Land records: Contact Register, 1 Public Square South
Probate records: Contact Judge of Probate
No probate search service

*Scott County Courthouse
PO Box 69
Huntsville, TN 37756
Phone (615) 663-2000; (615) 663-2355; (615) 663-2440 Clerk
County organized 1849 from Fentress, Morgan, Anderson and Campbell counties
Land records: Contact Johnny Zachary, Assessor of Property

Probate records: Contact Jan Burress, Clerk

*Sequatchie County Courthouse
PO Box 595
Dunlap, TN 37327-0595
Phone (615) 949-2522
County organized 1857 from Hamilton County (and previously from Bledsoe, Marion and Grundy counties)
Land records: Deed books from 1858
Vital records: A few births in 1881 and from 1908 to early 1940; a few deaths in 1881 and from 1908 to 1938; marriages from 1858
Probate records: Some probate records in old court minutes and fairly complete to present; contact Clerk and Master
Probate search service: no charge; copies: 25¢ per page plus postage, no minimum; "Clerks are busy; a delay in answering is sometimes necessary."

*Sevier County Courthouse
125 Court Avenue
Sevierville, TN 37862
Phone (615) 453-5502
County organized 1794 from Jefferson County (territory south of River Ohio), effective 4 July 1796
Land records: Deeds from January 1846 to date, survey books from April 1824 to March 1903 (indexed)
No land records search service (must have specific name and date)
Naturalization records: No naturalization records
Vital records: No vital records
Probate records: From April 1856 (after courthouse burned 26 March 1856) to date
No probate search service (must have specific name and date)

*Shelby County Courthouse
140 Adams
Memphis, TN 38103-2018
Phone (901) 576-5000
County organized 1819 from Hardin County, eleven days after its parent county was organized
Land records: Contact Register, 160 North Mid-America Mall #519, Memphis, TN 38103
Vital records: Contact Health Department, 814 Jefferson, Memphis, TN 38105
Probate records: Contact Clerk
Probate search service: $1.00 per name; copies: $2.00 for wills, $2.00 for certification, $3.00 for letters, no minimum

Smith County Courthouse
Carthage, TN 37030
Phone (615) 735-9833

County organized 1799 from Sumner County and Indian lands

Stewart County Courthouse
PO Box 67
Dover, TN 37058-0067
Phone (615) 232-7616
County organized 1803 from Montgomery County

*Sullivan County Courthouse
Blountville, TN 37617
Phone (615) 323-7137
County organized 1779 from Washington County
Land records: Contact Mary Lou Duncan, Register of Deeds
Vital records: Marriages; contact Gay B. Feathers, County Clerk or Bill Ray, Sullivan County Health Department, Blountville, TN 37617
Probate records: Contact Mrs. Dorothy Dulaney, Clerk and Master and Probate Clerk

*Sumner County Archives
155 East Main Street
Gallatin, TN 37066
Phone (615) 452-0037
County organized 1786 from Davidson County (North Carolina), becoming part of the Territory South of the River Ohio (popularly called the Southwest Territory) from its creation in May 1790 until Tennessee became a state in 1796
Land records: From 1786 to August 1965 (on microfilm)
Naturalization records: Within court minute books
Vital records: Voter registration cards back to 1920 which contain birth dates (some from 1890), scattered births from 1908 to 1939, scattered deaths from 1881 to 1938 (births and deaths not mandated until 1914), marriage bonds from 1786 to date
Probate records: From 1786 to 1985 in book and in loose court packets
Probate search service: $5.00 plus SASE (requests must be specific in nature); copies: 50¢ per page from original documents, 15¢ per page from letter-sized published material, 25¢ per page from legal-sized published material

*Tipton County Courthouse
PO Box 528
Covington, TN 38019-0528
Phone (901) 476-2438
County organized 1823 from Western District (Indian lands)
Land records: Contact Pam Deed, County Clerk

Naturalization records: Contact County Clerk
Vital records: Contact County Clerk
Probate records: Contact County Clerk

*Trousdale County Courthouse
PO Box 69
Hartsville, TN 37074
Phone (615) 374-2906
County organized 1870 from Macon, Smith, Wilson and Sumner counties
Land records: Contact Registrar
Naturalization records: Contact Clerk
Vital records: Contact Clerk and Master
Probate records: Contact Clerk and Master
No probate search service; copies: $1.00 per page, $3.00 minimum

*Unicoi County Courthouse
PO Box 340
Erwin, TN 37650-0340
Phone (615) 743-3381
County organized 1875 from Washington and Carter counties
Vital records: Births from 1909 to 1912 and from 1925 to 1939, deaths from 1909 to 1911, marriages
Probate records: Yes
Probate search service: $2.00; copies: $1.00 per page

Union County Courthouse
PO Box 395
Maynardville, TN 37807-0395
Phone (615) 992-8043
County organized 1850 from Anderson, Campbell, Grainger, Claiborne and Knox counties

*Van Buren County Courthouse
PO Box 126
Spencer, TN 38585-0126
Phone (615) 946-2121
County organized 1840 from Bledsoe, Warren and White counties
Land records: From 1840
Vital records: Some births and deaths, marriages
Probate records: From 1840
Probate search service: no charge; copies: 50¢ per page, no minimum; "We have no personnel for such except County Historian, Mr. Earl J. Madewell, Rt. 1, Spencer, TN 38585."

*Warren County Courthouse
Public Square
McMinnville, TN 37110
Phone (615) 473-2623; (615) 473-2233 James A. Dillon, Jr., County Historian, PO Box 563, McMinnville, TN 37110
County organized 1807 from White, Jackson and Smith counties, and Indian lands

Land records: Deed books from 1808 (excluding Books "X" and "T", destroyed during Civil War); contact Betty Bryant, Tax Assessor or Donnie Starkey, Registrar
Vital records: Marriages from 1852 (prior records destroyed during Civil War); contact County Court Clerk
Probate records: Wills from 1827; contact Richard McGregor, Clerk and Master
No probate search service; copies: 25¢ each plus postage

Washington County Courthouse
Jonesboro, TN 37659
Phone (615) 753-6211
County organized 1777, original county by act of North Carolina

Wayne County Courthouse
Waynesboro, TN 38485
Phone (615) 722-3653
County organized 1817 from Hickman and Humphreys counties

*Weakley County Courthouse
Dresden, TN 38225
Phone (901) 364-2285
County organized 1823 from Western District (Indian lands)
Land records: Contact Register of Deeds
Probate records: Contact Clerk and Master
Probate search service; copies: 50¢ per page

White County Courthouse
Sparta, TN 38583
Phone (615) 836-3203
County organized 1806 from Jackson and Smith counties

*Williamson County Preservation of Records
510 Columbia Avenue
PO Box 1006
Franklin, TN 37065-1006
Phone (615) 790-5412
County organized 1799 from Davidson County
Land records: Deeds from 1800 to 1889
Land records search service: $5.00 per name (includes copies of up to ten pages, if record is found)
Naturalization records: Yes
Vital records: Marriage licenses and bonds from 1800 to 1879
Probate records: Wills (and probates) from 1800 to 1948, guardian bonds and settlements from 1859 to 1954, inventories, sales, estates
Probate search service: $5.00 per name (includes copies of up to ten pages, if record is found)

*Wilson County Courthouse
PO Box 176
Lebanon, TN 37087
Phone (615) 444-0314; (615) 443-2611
Register of Deeds
*County organized 1799 from Sumner
County*
Land records: From 1793 to date; contact
Margie Trice, Register of Deeds

TEXAS

*Capital: Austin. Statehood: 29 December
1845 (declared independence from Mexico
as the Republic of Texas on 2 March 1836,
boundaries fixed by the Treaty of Guadalupe-Hidalgo, 1848)*

Court System

Texas has some 839 Municipal Courts
and 948 Justice of the Peace Courts which
have limited jurisdiction over minor matters. Probate matters are dealt with either
in the District Courts or Constitutional
County Courts except in the special Probate Courts organized in Bexar, Dallas,
Galveston, Harris and Tarrant counties.
County Courts at Law, organized primarily
in metropolitan counties, relieve the Con-
stitutional County Courts of some of their
responsibilities: Anderson, Angelina, Aus-
tin, Bastrop, Bell, Bexar, Brazoria, Brazos,
Caldwell, Calhoun, Cameron, Cherokee,
Collin, Comal, Dallas, Denton, Ector, Ellis,
El Paso, Fort Bend, Galveston, Grayson,
Gregg, Guadalupe, Harris, Harrison, Hays,
Henderson, Hidalgo, Houston, Hunt,
Jefferson, Johnson, Kerr, Kleberg, Liberty,
Lubbock, McLennan, Medina, Midland,
Montgomery, Moore, Nacogdoches, Nolan,
Nueces, Orange, Panola, Parker, Polk, Pot-
ter, Randall, Reeves, Rusk, Smith, Starr,
Tarrant, Taylor, Tom Green, Travis, Val
Verde, Victoria, Walker, Waller, Webb,
Wichita, Williamson and Wise counties.

The Constitutional County Courts in
each county have probate jurisdiction (except in counties with Probate Courts), jurisdiction over misdemeanors involving
fines over $200 or sentences under two
years, criminal jurisdiction (except where
a Criminal District Court exists), and appellate jurisdiction over the Municipal and
Justice of the Peace Courts. The District
Courts have general jurisdiction, which
varies somewhat from district to district.
Most exercise both criminal and civil jurisdiction, but in Dallas, Jefferson and
Tarrant counties Criminal District Courts
exist. Special Family District Courts exist
in Districts 300 to 330 and 360.

There are 364 Judicial Districts, some
of which cover more than one county, or a
single county may contain as many as fifty-
eight districts. First Judicial District: Jasper, Newton and Tyler counties; 2nd:
Cherokee; 3rd: Anderson, Henderson and
Houston; 4th: Rusk; 5th: Bowie and Cass;
6th: Fannin, Lamar and Red River; 7th:
Smith; 8th: Delta, Franklin, Hopkins and
Rains; 9th: Montgomery, Polk, San Jacinto

and Waller; 9th (2nd): Montgomery, Polk,
San Jacinto and Trinity; 10th: Galveston;
11th: Harris; 12th: Grimes, Leon, Madison
and Walker; 13th: Navarro; 14th: Dallas;
15th: Grayson; 16th: Denton; 17th: Tarrant;
18th: Johnson and Somervell; 19th:
McLennan; 20th: Milam; 21st: Bastrop,
Burleson, Lee and Washington; 22nd:
Caldwell, Comal and Hays; 23rd: Brazoria,
Matagorda and Wharton; 24th: Calhoun, De
Witt, Goliad, Jackson, Refugio and
Victoria; 25th: Colorado, Gonzales,
Guadalupe and Lavaca; 25th (2nd): Colo-
rado, Gonzales, Guadalupe and Lavaca;
26th: Williamson; 27th: Bell and Lampasas;
28th: Kenedy, Kleberg and Nueces; 29th:
Palo Pinto; 30th: Wichita; 31st: Gray,
Hemphill, Lipscomb, Roberts and Wheeler;
32nd: Fisher, Mitchell and Nolan; 33rd:
Blanco, Burnet, Llano, Mason and San
Saba; 34th: Culberson, El Paso and
Hudspeth; 35th: Brown, Coleman and
Mills; 36th: Aransas, Bee, Live Oak,
McMullen and San Patricio; 37th: Bexar;
38th: Medina, Real and Uvalde; 39th:
Haskell, Kent, Stonewall and Throck-
morton; 40th: Ellis; 41st: El Paso; 42nd:
Callahan, Coleman and Taylor; 43rd:
Parker; 44th: Dallas; 45th: Bexar; 46th:
Foard, Hardeman and Wilbarger; 47th:
Armstrong, Potter and Randall; 48th:
Tarrant; 49th: Webb and Zapata; 50th:
Baylor, Cottle, King and Knox; 51st: Coke,
Irion, Schleicher, Sterling and Tom Green;
52nd: Coryell; 53rd: Travis; 54th:
McLennan; 55th: Harris; 56th: Galveston;
57th: Bexar; 58th: Jefferson; 59th: Grayson;
60th: Jefferson; 61st: Harris; 62nd: Delta,
Franklin, Hopkins and Lamar; 63rd:
Edwards, Kinney, Terrell and Val Verde;
64th: Castro, Hale and Swisher; 65th: El
Paso; 66th: Hill; 67th: Tarrant; 68th: Dal-
las; 69th: Dallam, Hartley, Moore and
Sherman; 70th: Ector; 71st: Harrison; 72nd:
Crosby and Lubbock; 73rd: Bexar; 74th:
McLennan; 75th: Liberty; 76th: Camp,
Morris and Titus; 77th: Freestone and
Limestone; 78th: Wichita; 79th: Brooks and
Jim Wells; 80th: Harris; 81st: Atascosa,
Frio, Karnes, La Salle and Wilson; 82nd:
Falls and Robertson; 83rd: Brewster, Jeff
Davis, Pecos, Presidio, Reagan and Upton;
84th: Hansford, Hutchinson and Ochiltree;
85th: Brazos; 86th: Kaufman and
Rockwall; 87th: Anderson, Freestone, Leon
and Limestone; 88th: Hardin and Tyler;
89th: Wichita; 90th: Stephens and Young;
91st: Eastland; 92nd: Hidalgo; 93rd:
Hidalgo; 94th: Nueces; 95th: Dallas; 96th:
Tarrant; 97th: Archer, Clay and Montague;
98th: Travis; 99th: Lubbock; 100th: Carson,
Childress, Collingsworth, Donley and Hall;
101st: Dallas; 102nd: Bowie and Red River;
103rd: Cameron and Willacy; 104th: Taylor; 105th: Kenedy, Kleberg and Nueces;
106th: Dawson, Gaines, Garza and Lynn;
107th: Cameron and Willacy; 108th: Potter; 109th: Andrews, Crane and Winkler;

110th: Briscoe, Dickens, Floyd and Motley; 111th: Webb; 112th: Crockett, Pecos, Reagan, Sutton and Upton; 113th: Harris; 114th: Smith and Wood; 115th: Marion and Upshur; 116th: Dallas; 117th: Nueces; 118th: Glasscock, Howard and Martin; 119th: Concho, Runnels and Tom Green; 120th: El Paso; 121st: Terry and Yoakum; 122nd: Galveston; 123rd: Panola and Shelby; 124th: Gregg; 125th: Harris; 126th: Travis; 127th: Harris; 128th: Orange; 129th: Harris; 130th: Matagorda; 131st: Bexar; 132nd: Borden and Scurry; 133rd: Harris; 134th: Dallas; 135th: Calhoun, De Witt, Goliad, Jackson, Refugio and Victoria; 136th: Jefferson; 137th: Lubbock; 138th: Cameron and Willacy; 139th: Hidalgo; 140th: Lubbock; 141st: Tarrant; 142nd: Midland; 143rd: Loving, Reeves and Ward; 144th: Bexar; 145th: Nacogdoches; 146th: Bell; 147th: Travis; 148th: Nueces; 149th: Brazoria; 150th: Bexar; 151st: Harris; 152nd: Harris; 153rd: Tarrant; 154th: Lamb; 155th: Austin, Fayette and Waller; 156th: Aransas, Bee, Live Oak, McMullen and San Patricio; 157th: Harris; 158th: Denton; 159th: Angelina; 160th: Dallas; 161st: Ector; 162nd: Dallas; 163rd: Orange; 164th: Harris; 165th: Harris; 166th: Bexar; 167th: Travis; 168th: El Paso; 169th: Bell; 170th: McLennan; 171st: El Paso; 172nd: Jefferson; 173rd: Henderson; 174th: Harris; 175th: Bexar; 176th: Harris; 177th: Harris; 178th: Harris; 179th: Harris; 180th: Harris; 181st: Potter and Randall; 182nd: Harris; 183rd: Harris; 184th: Harris; 185th: Harris; 186th: Bexar; 187th: Bexar; 188th: Gregg; 189th: Harris; 190th: Harris; 191st: Dallas; 192nd: Dallas; 193rd: Dallas; 194th: Dallas; 195th: Dallas; 196th: Hunt; 197th: Cameron and Willacy; 198th: Concho, Kerr, Kimble, McCulloch and Menard; 199th: Collin; 200th: Travis; 201st: Travis; 202nd: Bowie; 203rd: Dallas; 204th: Dallas; 205th: Culberson, El Paso and Hudspeth; 206th: Hidalgo; 207th: Caldwell, Comal and Hays; 208th: Harris; 209th: Harris; 210th: Culberson, El Paso and Hudspeth; 211th: Denton; 212th: Galveston; 213th: Tarrant; 214th: Nueces; 215th: Harris; 216th: Bandera, Gillespie, Kendall and Kerr; 217th: Angelina; 218th: Atascosa, Frio, Karnes, La Salle and Wilson; 219th: Collin; 220th: Bosque, Comanche and Hamilton; 221st: Montgomery; 222nd: Deaf Smith and Oldham; 223rd: Gray; 224th: Bexar; 225th: Bexar; 226th: Bexar; 227th: Bexar; 228th: Harris; 229th: Duval, Jim Hogg and Starr; 230th: Harris; 231st: Tarrant; 232nd: Harris; 233rd: Tarrant; 234th: Harris; 235th: Cooke; 236th: Tarrant; 237th: Lubbock; 238th: Midland; 239th: Brazoria; 240th: Fort Bend; 241st: Smith; 242nd: Castro, Hale and Swisher; 243rd: El Paso; 244th: Ector; 245th: Harris; 246th: Harris; 247th: Harris; 248th: Harris; 249th: Johnson and

Somervell; 250th: Travis; 251st: Potter and Randall; 252nd: Jefferson; 253rd: Chambers and Liberty; 254th: Dallas; 255th: Dallas; 256th: Dallas; 257th: Harris; 258th: Polk, San Jacinto and Trinity; 259th: Jones and Shackelford; 260th: Orange; 261st: Travis; 262nd: Harris; 263rd: Harris; 264th: Bell; 265th: Dallas; 266th: Erath; 267th: Calhoun, De Witt, Goliad, Jackson, Refugio and Victoria; 268th: Fort Bend; 269th: Harris; 270th: Harris; 271st: Jack and Wise; 272nd: Brazos; 273rd: Sabine, San Augustine and Shelby; 274th: Caldwell, Comal, Guadalupe and Hays; 275th: Hidalgo; 276th: Camp, Marion, Morris and Titus; 277th: Williamson; 278th: Grimes, Leon, Madison and Walker; 279th: Jefferson; 280th: Harris; 281st: Harris; 282nd: Dallas; 283rd: Dallas; 284th: Montgomery; 285th: Bexar; 286th: Cochran and Hockley; 287th: Bailey and Parmer; 288th: Bexar; 289th: Bexar; 290th: Bexar; 291st: Dallas; 292nd: Dallas; 293rd: Dimmit, Maverick and Zavala; 294th: Van Zandt and Wood; 295th: Harris; 296th: Collin; 297th: Tarrant; 298th: Dallas; 299th: Travis; 300th: Brazoria; 301st: Dallas; 302nd: Dallas; 303rd: Dallas; 304th: Dallas; 305th: Dallas; 306th: Galveston; 307th: Gregg; 308th: Harris; 309th: Harris; 310th: Harris; 311th: Harris; 312th: Harris; 313th: Harris; 314th: Harris; 315th: Harris; 316th: Hutchinson; 317th: Jefferson; 318th: Midland; 319th: Nueces; 320th: Potter; 321st: Smith; 322nd: Tarrant; 323rd: Tarrant; 324th: Tarrant; 325th: Tarrant; 326th: Taylor; 327th: El Paso; 328th: Fort Bend; 329th: Wharton; 330th: Dallas; 331st: Travis; 332nd: Hidalgo; 333rd: Harris; 334th: Harris; 335th: Bastrop, Burleson, Lee and Washington; 336th: Fannin and Grayson; 337th: Harris; 338th: Harris; 339th: Harris; 340th: Tom Green; 341st: Webb; 342nd: Tarrant; 343rd: Aransas, Bee, Live Oak, McMullen and San Patricio; 344th: Chambers; 345th: Travis; 346th: El Paso; 347th: Nueces; 348th: Tarrant; 349th: Anderson and Houston; 350th: Taylor; 351st: Harris; 352nd: Tarrant; 353rd: Travis; 354th: Hunt and Rains; 355th: Hood; 356th: Hardin; 357th: Cameron and Willacy; 358th: Ector; 359th: Montgomery; 360th: Tarrant; 361st: Brazos; 362nd: Denton. Appeals are heard by the Court of Appeals, the Court of Criminal Appeals and Supreme Court.

Certificates of births within the last fifty years and deaths within the last twenty-five years, subject to restrictions, namely limited to a legal representative, personal representative or agent, an immediate family member (parent, child, sibling, spouse, grandparent, legal guardian or conservator), or the registrant, who has a direct and tangible interest in the record and who shall have a significant legal relationship to the person whose record is requested. A legal representative is defined as any individual, attorney, funeral director, or other represen-

tative acting under contract for the requester, when the requester is not the applicant; or is one bearing an affidavit, authorizing that person, agent, genealogist, or other representative to make application on behalf of the registrant or member of the immediate family for the record or information requested.

Courthouses

*Anderson County Courthouse
500 North Church Street
Palestine, TX 75801
Phone (214) 723-7432
County organized 1846 from Houston County
Land records: From 1846; contact Clerk
Naturalization records: No naturalization records
Vital records: Births and deaths from 1903, marriages from 1846; contact Clerk
Probate records: From 1846; contact Clerk
Probate search service: $5.00; copies: $1.00 per page, no minimum

*Andrews County Courthouse
Andrews, TX 79714
Phone (915) 524-1426
County organized 1876 from Bexar County
Land records: Contact F. Wm. Hoermann, County Clerk, PO Box 727, Andrews, TX 79714
Vital records: Contact County Clerk
Probate records: Contact County Clerk
Probate search service: no charge; copies: $1.00 per page, $5.00 for certification, no minimum

*Angelina County Clerk
PO Box 908
Lufkin, TX 75902-0908
Phone (409) 634-8339
County organized 1846 from Nacogdoches County
Land records: From 1846; contact Jo Ann Chastain, County Clerk
Land records search service: $10.00; copies: $1.00 per page, plus $1.00 for certification on Real Property
Naturalization records: No naturalization records
Vital records: Births from 1928, deaths from 1904 (some delayed further back); contact County Clerk; certified copies: $9.00 each (births within the last fifty years and deaths within the last twenty-five years, subject to restrictions, no genealogists unless they have a certified letter from parent or qualified legal representative)

Probate records: From 1838
No probate search service

Aransas County Courthouse
301 Live Oak
Rockport, TX 78382-2744
Phone (512) 729-7430
County organized 1871 from Refugio County

Archer County Courthouse
PO Box 458
Archer City, TX 76351
Phone (817) 574-4615
County organized 1858 from Fannin County

Armstrong County Courthouse
PO Box 309
Claude, TX 79019-0309
Phone (806) 226-2081
County organized 1876 from Bexar County

*Atascosa County Courthouse
Circle Drive
Jourdanton, TX 78026
Phone (512) 769-2511
County organized 1856 from Bexar County
Land records: From 1856; contact Laquita Hayden, County Clerk, Room 6-1
Naturalization records: No naturalization records
Vital records: From 1856; contact County Clerk (births within the last fifty years and deaths within the last twenty-five years, subject to restrictions)
Probate records: From 1856
Probate search service: no charge; copies: $1.00 per page

*Austin County Courthouse
1 East Main
Bellville, TX 77418-1521
Phone (409) 865-5911
County organized 1836 from Old Mexican Municipality
Land records: From 1833; contact County Clerk; copies: $1.00 per page, $5.00 for certification
Naturalization records: From 1854; contact County Clerk and District Clerk
Vital records: From 1903; contact County Clerk; copies: $1.00 per page, $5.00 for certification
Probate records: From 1837; contact County Clerk; copies: $1.00 per page, $5.00 for certification

*Bailey County Courthouse
300 South First
Muleshoe, TX 79347
Phone (806) 272-3044

County formed without officials 1876 from Bexar County, organized 1917
Land records: From 1882; contact County Clerk
Naturalization records: No naturalization records
Vital records: From 1919; contact County Clerk
Probate records: From 1919; contact County Clerk
Probate search service: $5.00; copies: $1.00 per page, no minimum

*Bandera County Courthouse
Bandera, TX 78003
Phone (512) 796-3332
County organized 1856 from Uvalde County
Land records: From 1856
Naturalization records: Very few naturalization records
Vital records: Some vital records from 1856, but most are after 1903
Probate records: Some probate records from 1856
Probate search service: $5.00; copies: $1.00 each; "We prefer to look them up for the person in our older records because of the condition of the books—very old."

*Bastrop County Courthouse
803 Pine Street
Bastrop, TX 78602-0577
Phone (512) 321-4443
County organized 1836 from Old Mexican Municipality
Land records: From 1837; contact Shirley Wilhelm, County Clerk, PO Box 577, Bastrop, TX 78602
Naturalization records: From about 1837; contact County Clerk. Some records: contact District Clerk
Vital records: From 1903; contact County Clerk (not open to the public, but clerks will check for names)
Probate records: From 1837; contact County Clerk
Probate search service: no charge; copies: $1.00 per page; "We do not do searches over the phone; a request must be in writing and include a SASE for an answer."

Baylor County Courthouse
Seymour, TX 76380
Phone (817) 888-3322
County organized 1858 from Fannin County

*Bee County Courthouse
105 West Corpus Christi
Beeville, TX 78102-5627
Phone (512) 358-3664
County organized 1857 from Goliad and Refugio counties

Land records: From 1858; contact Julia V. Torres, County Clerk, Room #103
Naturalization records: No naturalization records
Vital records: From 1903; contact County Clerk
Probate records: From 1859; contact County Clerk
Probate search service: $5.00 per estate name; copies: $1.00 and $2.00 (small and large books), no minimum; "Fees due before copies are issued."

*Bell County Courthouse
Belton, TX 76513
Phone (817) 933-5160
County organized 1850 from Milam County
Land records: From 1850 to date; contact County Clerk, PO Box 480, Belton, TX 76513
Land records search service: $5.00 per name; copies: $1.00 per page
Naturalization records: Contact District Clerk, 104 South Main, Belton, TX 76513
Vital records: From 1903 to date; contact County Clerk
Vital records search service: $5.00 per name; copies: $1.00 per page
Probate records: From 1850 to date; contact County Clerk
Probate search service: $5.00 per name; copies: $1.00 per page

*Bexar County Courthouse
San Antonio, TX 78285-5100
Phone (512) 220-2011 Clerk's Offices; (512) 220-2201 Archives Department; (512) 220-2587 Archivist
County organized 1835 from Old Mexican Municipality
Land records: From 1736 (Spanish, Mexican, Republic, and up-to-date)
Naturalization records: From 1837 to 1890
Vital records: Church records of San Fernando Cathedral, others
Probate records: From Spanish, Mexican period, up-to-date also
Probate search service: $5.00 for the first five years and $1.00 for each additional year; copies: $1.00 per page, no minimum; "Deeds and Archives in Basement of Courthouse."

*Blanco County Courthouse
PO Box 65
Johnson City, TX 78636-0065
Phone (512) 868-7357
County created on 11 February 1858 from Burnet, Comal, Gillespie and Hays counties
Land records: Contact Clerk
Naturalization records: Contact Clerk
Vital records: Births and deaths from

1903, marriages from 1876; contact
Clerk
Probate records: From 1876
Probate search service: $5.00 per search;
copies: $1.00 per page; "Our
courthouse burned in 1876; we have
nothing before then."

Borden County Courthouse
Gail, TX 79738
Phone (915) 856-4312
*County organized 1876 from Bexar
County*

Bosque County Courthouse
PO Box 617
Meridian, TX 76665-0617
Phone (817) 435-2201
*County organized 1854 from McLennan
County*

*Bowie County Courthouse
New Boston, TX 75570
Phone (214) 628-2571
*County organized 1840 from Red River
County*
Vital records: Births, delayed births,
deaths, marriage licenses; contact
County Clerk, PO Box 248, New
Boston, TX 75570; copies: $9.00 each
for births, deaths and marriages,
$25.00 for delayed births; "Must have
name and dates in order to do
searches."

*Brazoria County Clerk
111 East Locust, Suite 200
Angleton, TX 77515
Phone (409) 849-5711, ext. 1355
*County organized 1836 from Old
Mexican Municipality*
Land records: Contact County Clerk
Vital records: Contact County Clerk
Probate records: Contact County Clerk
Probate search service: $5.00; copies:
$1.00 per page, no minimum

Brazos County Courthouse
300 East 26th Street, #314
Bryan, TX 77803
Phone (409) 775-7400
*County organized 1841 from
Washington County*

*Brewster County Courthouse
PO Drawer 119
Alpine, TX 79831
Phone (915) 837-3366
*County organized 1887 from Presidio
County*
Land records: From 1877; contact Berta
R. Martinez, County Clerk
Naturalization records: No naturalization
records
Vital records: Births and deaths from

1903, marriages from 1887; contact
County Clerk
Probate records: From 1887; contact
County Clerk
Probate search service: $9.00 each;
copies: $1.00 per page, no minimum

*Briscoe County Courthouse
PO Box 375
Silverton, TX 79257-0375
Phone (806) 823-2131, ext. 4
*County organized 1876 from Bexar
County*
Land records: Contact Bess McWilliams,
Clerk
Naturalization records: Contact Clerk
Vital records: Contact Clerk
Probate records: Contact Clerk
Probate search service: $5.00; copies:
$1.00 per page, no minimum

Brooks County Courthouse
Falfurrias, TX 78355
Phone (512) 325-3053
*County organized 1911 from Starr and
Zapata counties*

*Brown County Courthouse
200 South Broadway
Brownwood, TX 76801-3136
Phone (915) 643-2594
*County organized from Caldwell County
by an act of the legislature, passed 27
August 1856; after the election of 21
March 1857, the county lines were
found not to be exact; boundaries
corrected and a second election held
2 August 1858*
Land records: From 1880; contact
Margaret Woods, County Clerk
Land records search service: no charge;
copies: $1.00 per page
Naturalization records: No naturalization
records
Vital records: Births and deaths from
1903, marriages from 1880; contact
County Clerk
Vital records search service: no charge
(births within the last fifty years and
deaths within the last twenty-five
years, subject to restrictions)
Probate records: From 1880; contact
County Clerk
Probate search service: no charge;
copies: $1.00 per page, no minimum

*Burleson County Courthouse
Caldwell, TX 77836
Phone (409) 567-4326
*County organized 1846 from Milam and
Washington counties*
Land records: Contact County Clerk, PO
Box 57, Caldwell, TX 77836
Naturalization records: Contact District
Clerk
Vital records: Delayed births, marriages

from 21 September 1846; contact
County Clerk
Probate records: Contact County Clerk
Probate search service: no charge at this
time, "however our searching time is
limited"; copies: $1.00 per page, no
minimum

Burnet County Courthouse
220 South Pierce Street
Burnet, TX 78611-3136
Phone (512) 756-5420
*County organized 1852 from Travis
County*

*Caldwell County Courthouse
Lockhart, TX 78644
Phone (512) 398-2428
*County organized 1848 from Gonzales
County*
Land records: Contact County Clerk
Naturalization records: Contact District
Clerk
Vital records: Contact County Clerk
Probate records: Contact County Clerk
No probate search service; copies: $1.00
each, no minimum

Calhoun County Courthouse
211 South Ann
Port Lavaca, TX 77979-4249
Phone (512) 552-2954
*County organized 1846 from Victoria
County*

*Callahan County Courthouse
Baird, TX 79504
Phone (915) 854-1217
*County organized 1877 from Milam and
Travis counties*
Land records: From 1877; contact
County Clerk, 400 Market Street,
Suite 104, Baird, TX 79504
Vital records: Births and deaths from
1903 (early years are sketchy),
marriages from 1877; contact County
Clerk
Probate records: From 1877; contact
County Clerk
Probate search service: $6.00; copies:
$1.00 per page, $5.00 for certification,
no minimum; "We need full names
and an approximate date for any
record we search."

*Cameron County Courthouse
PO Box 2178
Brownsville, TX 78522-2178
Phone (512) 544-0815 County Clerk,
Recording Department; (512) 544-
0817 County Clerk; (512) 544-0826
County Clerk, Courts Department
*County organized 1848 from Nueces
County*
Land records: Contact County Clerk,
Recording Department

Vital records: Contact County Clerk
Probate records: Contact County Clerk,
  Courts Department
Probate search service: $5.00; copies:
  $1.00 per page, no minimum

*Camp County Courthouse
126 Church Street
Pittsburg, TX 75686-1346
Phone (214) 856-2731
*County organized 1874 from Upshur
  County*
Land records: From 1874; contact
  Clerk's Office, Room #102
Vital records: Births, deaths and
  marriages from 1903; contact Clerk's
  Office; copies: $9.00 each for births
  and deaths, $7.00 each for marriages
Probate records: From 1894; contact
  Clerk's Office
Probate search service: no charge;
  copies: 50¢ per page, no minimum

Carson County Courthouse
PO Box 487
Panhandle, TX 79068-0487
Phone (806) 537-3873
*County organized 1876 from Bexar
  County*

*Cass County Courthouse
Linden, TX 75563
Phone (214) 756-5071
*County organized 1846 from Bowie
  County; name changed from Davis
  County in 1871*
Land records: From 1846; contact Wilma
  O'Rand, County Clerk, PO Box 468,
  Linden, TX 75563-0468
Vital records: From early 1900s; contact
  County Clerk
Probate records: From 1846; contact
  County Clerk
Probate search service: $5.00 per search;
  copies: $1.00 per page, no minimum

Castro County Courthouse
100 East Bedford
Dimmitt, TX 79027-2643
Phone (806) 647-3338
*County organized 1876 from Wheeler
  County*

*Chambers County Courthouse
PO Box 728
Anahuac, TX 77514-0728
Phone (409) 267-8309
*County organized 1858 from Jefferson
  and Liberty counties*
Land records: From 1 January 1875
Naturalization records: No naturalization
  records
Vital records: From 1903
Probate records: From 1 January 1875;
  contact Norma W. Rowland

Probate search service: no charge;
  copies: $1.00 each, no minimum

*Cherokee County Courthouse
Rusk, TX 75785
Phone (214) 683-2350
*County organized 1846 from
  Nacogdoches County*
Land records: From 1846; contact
  County Clerk, PO Drawer 420;
  copies: $1.00 per page
Vital records: Births and deaths from
  1903, marriages from 1846; contact
  County Clerk; copies: $9.00 each for
  births, $2.00 each for non-certified
  deaths before 1950, $9.00 each for
  certified deaths before 1950 or any
  deaths after 1950, $2.00 each for non-
  certified marriage licenses before
  1950, $5.00 each for certified
  marriage licenses before 1950 or any
  marriages after 1950
Probate records: From 1839
Probate search service: $5.00; copies:
  $1.00 per page

*Childress County Courthouse
Courthouse Box 4
Childress, TX 79201-3755
Phone (817) 937-6143
*County organized 1887 from Bexar and
  Fannin counties*
Land records: Contact Clerk
Land records search service: $10.00;
  copies: $1.00 per page, $5.00 for
  certification
Vital records: Contact Clerk
Vital records search service: $10.00;
  copies: $1.00 per page, $5.00 for
  certification
Probate records: Contact Clerk
Probate search service: $10.00; copies:
  $1.00 per page, $5.00 for certification,
  no minimum

*Clay County Courthouse
PO Box 548
Henrietta, TX 76365-0548
Phone (817) 538-4631
*County organized 1857 from Cooke
  County*
Land records: From 1870s
Naturalization records: Proceedings
  discontinued 1917; contact District
  Clerk
Vital records: From 1903
Probate records: From 1873
Probate search service: no charge;
  copies: $1.00 per page

Cochran County Courthouse
Morton, TX 79346
Phone (806) 266-5450
*County organized 1876 from Bexar
  County*

*Coke County Courthouse
PO Box 150
Robert Lee, TX 76945-0150
Phone (915) 453-2631
*County organized 1889 from Tom Green
  County*
Land records: Contact County Clerk
Vital records: Contact County Clerk
Probate records: Contact County Clerk
Probate search service: no charge;
  copies: $1.00 per page, $5.00 for
  certification, no minimum

Coleman County Courthouse
PO Box 591
Coleman, TX 76834-0591
Phone (915) 625-2889
*County organized 1858 from Travis
  County*

*Collin County Courthouse
McKinney, TX 75069
Phone (214) 548-4100
*County organized 1846 from Fannin
  County*
Land records: From 1846; contact
  County Clerk, 210 McDonald Street,
  Suite 124, McKinney, TX 75069
Naturalization records: No naturalization
  records
Vital records: From 1903; contact County
  Clerk
Probate records: From about 1858;
  contact County Clerk
No probate search service; copies: $1.00
  per page, no minimum

*Collingsworth County Courthouse
Wellington, TX 79095-3037
Phone (806) 447-2408
*County organized 1876 from Bexar and
  Fannin counties*
Land records: Deeds from 1890s
Land records search service: $5.00 each;
  copies: $1.00 per page
Vital records: From 1890s
Vital records search service: $5.00 each;
  copies: $1.00 per page
Probate records: From 1890s; contact
  County Clerk, Room 3
Probate search service: $5.00; copies:
  $1.00 per page, no minimum

Colorado County Courthouse
PO Box 68
Columbus, TX 78934
Phone (409) 732-2155
*County organized 1836 from Old
  Mexican Municipality*

*Comal County Courthouse
100 Main Plaza, Suite 104
New Braunfels, TX 78130-5144
Phone (512) 620-5513
*County organized 1846 from Bexar and
  Gonzales counties*

Land records: From 1846; contact
County Clerk's Office
Naturalization records: From 1847;
contact District Clerk's Office,
Courthouse Annex. Index to the
naturalization records; contact County
Clerk's Office
Vital records: Births and deaths from
1903, marriages from 1846; contact
County Clerk's Office
Probate records: From 1846; contact
County Clerk's Office
Probate search service: $5.00 per name;
copies: $1.00 per page, no minimum

*Comanche County Courthouse
Comanche, TX 76442-3264
Phone (915) 356-2655
*County organized 1856 from Bosque
and Coryell counties*
Land records: From 1856
Naturalization records: No naturalization
records
Vital records: Births and deaths from
1903, marriages from 1856; copies:
$7.50 each for births and deaths,
$3.00 each for marriages
Probate records: From 1856
No probate search service; copies: $1.00
per page

*Concho County Courthouse
(Hwy 83—location)
PO Box 98 (mailing address)
Paint Rock, TX 76866-0098
Phone (915) 732-4321 County and
District Clerk
*County organized 1858 from Bexar
County*
Land records: Contact Hon. Margaret T.
Taylor, County and District Clerk;
copies: $1.00 per page, $5.00 for
certification
Vital records: Births, deaths and marriage
licenses; contact County and District
Clerk; copies: $9.00 each for births
and deaths

*Cooke County Courthouse
Gainesville, TX 76240
Phone (817) 668-5420
*County organized 1848 from Fannin
County*
Land records: From 1850; contact
County Clerk's Office
Naturalization records: From late 1890s;
contact District Clerk's Office
Vital records: From 1903
Probate records: From 1850s
Probate search service: no charge;
copies: $1.00 each (uncertified), no
minimum; "Be as specific on dates as
possible."

*Coryell County Courthouse
Main Street
Gatesville, TX 76528

Phone (817) 865-5016
*County organized 1854 from Bell and
McLennan counties*
Land records: Contact Barbara Simpson,
County Clerk, PO Box 237,
Gatesville, TX 76528
Land records search service: $10.00 per
index; copies: $1.00 per page,
certified copies: $5.00 for the first
page and $1.00 for each additional
page (money order only)
Vital records: Births and deaths; contact
County Clerk; copies: $9.00 (money
order only, births within the last fifty
years and deaths within the last
twenty-five years, subject to
restrictions)
Probate records: Contact County Clerk
Probate search service: $10.00 per index;
copies: $1.00 per page, $5.00 for the
first page of certified copies and $1.00
for each additional page (money order
only)

*Cottle County Courthouse
PO Box 717
Paducah, TX 79248
Phone (806) 492-3823
*County organized 1892 [sic] from
Childress County [other sources say
organized 1876; first federal census:
1880]*
Land records: From 1892
Vital records: All births that were
reported (but many were born at home
and not reported; lots of delayed
births were recorded in the 1940s),
death records not complete before
1929
Probate records: All are indexed and
complete
Probate search service: $5.00; copies:
$1.00 per page

*Crane County Courthouse
PO Box 578
Crane, TX 79731-0578
Phone (915) 558-3581 County and
District Clerk
*County organized 1927 [sic] from Ector
County [other sources say organized
1887 from Tom Green County; first
federal census: 1890]*
Vital records: Births and Deaths; contact
Maxine Willis, District and County
Clerk (births within the last fifty years
and deaths within the last twenty-five
years, subject to restrictions)
Probate records: Contact District and
County Clerk
Probate search service: $5.00; copies:
$1.00 per page, $5.00 per certificate

*Crockett County Courthouse
PO Box C
Osona, TX 76943-2502
Phone (915) 392-2022

*County organized 1875 from Bexar
County*
Vital records: Contact County Clerk
Probate records: Contact County Clerk
Probate search service: $10.00; copies:
$1.00 each, no minimum

*Crosby County Courthouse
Crosbyton, TX 79322
Phone (806) 675-2334
*County organized 1876 from Baylor
County [sic; other sources say
organized from Garza County]*
Land records: Contact County Clerk, PO
Box 218, Crosbyton, TX 79322;
copies: $1.00 per page
Vital records: From 1886; contact County
Clerk
Probate records: From 1886; contact
County Clerk
Probate search service: no charge;
copies: $1.00 per page, no minimum

*Culberson County Courthouse
PO Box 158
Van Horn, TX 79855-0158
Phone (915) 283-2058
*County organized 1911 from El Paso
County*
Land records: Yes
Land records search service: $5.00 per
name; copies: $1.00 per page
Naturalization records: No naturalization
records
Vital records: Yes
Vital records search service: $5.00 per
name; copies: $1.00 per page
Probate records: Yes
Probate search service: $5.00 per name;
copies: $1.00 per page

*Dallam County Courthouse
PO Box 1352
Dalhart, TX 79002-1352
Phone (806) 249-4751
*County organized 1876 from Bexar
County*
Land records: Deeds, deed of trust, etc.,
all indexed by name
Naturalization records: No naturalization
records
Vital records: Some vital records
(Dalhart is in two counties—Dallam
and Hartley; the hospital is located in
Hartley County, where most births and
deaths occur)
Probate records: Yes
Probate search service: no charge;
copies: $1.00 per page, no minimum;
"Give as much information as
possible—names, dates, etc."

Dallas County Courthouse
500 Main Street
Dallas, TX 75202-3507
Phone (214) 749-8131

*County organized 1846 from
   Nacogdoches County*

*Dawson County Courthouse
PO Box 1268
Lamesa, TX 79331-1268
Phone (806) 872-3778
*County organized 1858 from Bexar
   County*
Land records: Contact County Clerk's
   Office
Vital records: Contact County Clerk's
   Office
Probate records: Contact County Clerk's
   Office
Probate search service: no charge;
   copies: $1.00 per page, no minimum

*Deaf Smith County Courthouse
Hereford, TX 79045-5515
Phone (806) 364-1746
*County organized 1876 from Bexar
   County*
Land records: From 1876; contact
   County Clerk, Room 203
Naturalization records: No naturalization
   records
Vital records: From 1876; contact County
   Clerk
Probate records: From 1876; contact
   County Clerk
Probate search service: $2.00; copies:
   $1.00 per page, no minimum

Delta County Courthouse
200 West Dallas Avenue
Cooper, TX 75432-1726
Phone (214) 395-4110
*County organized 1870 from Lamar
   County*

*Denton County Courthouse
Denton, TX 76202
Phone (817) 565-8501 County Clerk
*County organized 1846 from Fannin
   County*
Land records: From 1876; contact
   County Clerk, PO Box 2187, Denton,
   TX 76202-2187
Naturalization records: Early
   naturalization records; contact
   Historical Museum
Vital records: From 1903, some delayed
   births from 1870s; contact County
   Clerk
Probate records: From 1876; contact
   County Clerk
Probate search service: $5.00 for the first
   five years and $1.00 for each
   additional year; copies: $1.00 per
   page; "No personal checks; all money
   orders or cashier's check."

*De Witt County Courthouse
307 North Gonzales Street
Cuero, TX 77954-2970

Phone (512) 275-3724
*County organized 1846 from Goliad,
   Gonzales and Victoria counties*
Land records: From 1846
Naturalization records: From 1846
Vital records: From 1903, some births
   registered during 1873 to 1876 and
   probate births (cities of Cuero and
   Yoakum have births and deaths from
   1951)
Probate records: From 1846; contact Ann
   Drehr, County Clerk
Probate search service: no charge;
   copies: $1.00 per page, no minimum

*Dickens County Courthouse
Dickens, TX 79229
Phone (806) 623-5531
*County organized 1876 from Bexar
   County*
Land records: Deeds from 1891; contact
   Yvonne "Tookie" Cash, County and
   District Clerk, PO Box 120, Dickens,
   TX 79229
Naturalization records: From 1891;
   contact County and District Clerk
Vital records: Births and deaths from
   1901, marriages from 1891; contact
   Clerk (births within the last fifty years
   and deaths within the last twenty-five
   years, subject to restrictions)
Probate records: From about 1900
Probate search service: $5.00; copies:
   $1.00 per page, no minimum

Dimmit County Courthouse
103 North Fifth
Carrizo Springs, TX 78834-3101
Phone (512) 876-3569
*County organized 1858 from Bexar and
   Maverick counties*

*Donley County Courthouse
Clarendon, TX 79226-2020
Phone (806) 847-3436
*County organized 1876 from Jack
   County*
Land records: From 1882; contact Fay
   Vargas, County Clerk, PO Drawer U,
   Clarendon, TX 79226
Land records search service: $5.00 per
   name; copies: $1.00 per page
Vital records: Births from 1878, deaths
   from 1903, marriages from 1882;
   contact County Clerk
Vital records search service: $5.00 per
   name; certified copies: $9.00 each
Probate records: From 1886; contact
   County Clerk
Probate search service: $5.00; copies:
   $1.00 per page, over thirty pages: 85¢
   for the first page and 15¢ for each
   additional page, no minimum

*Duval County Courthouse
San Diego, TX 78384

Phone (512) 279-3322; (512) 279-3322,
   ext. 271 County Clerk
*County organized 1858 from Live Oak,
   Starr and Nueces counties*
Land records: Contact Oscar Garcia, Jr.,
   County Clerk, PO Box 248, San
   Diego, TX 78384; copies: $1.00 each,
   $1.00 for certification
Naturalization records: No naturalization
   records
Vital records: From 1800; contact Ana L.
   Baez, Deputy County Clerk; copies:
   $8.00 each for long form of birth
   certificate and death certificate, $5.00
   each for birth cards or marriage
   certificates; request for birth
   certificate must include name, date of
   birth and parents; for death certificate:
   name and date of death; for marriage
   certificate: names of husband and wife
   and date of marriage
Probate records: From 1800; contact
   Delia L. Martinez, County Clerk's
   Office
Probate search service: no charge;
   copies: $1.00 per page, no minimum

*Eastland County Clerk
PO Box 110
Eastland, TX 76448-0110
Phone (817) 629-8622
*County organized 1858 from Bosque,
   Coryell and Travis counties*
Land records: From 1873
Naturalization records: No naturalization
   records
Vital records: Births and deaths from
   1903 (other than delayed records),
   marriages from 1873; certified copies:
   $9.00 each for births and deaths,
   $5.00 each for marriages (births
   within the last fifty years and deaths
   within the last twenty-five years,
   subject to restrictions)
Probate records: From 1873
No probate search service; copies: $1.00
   per page plus $5.00 for certification,
   no minimum

*Ector County Courthouse
Odessa, TX 79763
Phone (915) 335-3045
*County organized 1887 from Tom Green
   County*
Land records: Contact Barbara Bedford,
   County Clerk, PO Box 707, Odessa,
   TX 79760
Naturalization records: No naturalization
   records
Vital records: Births, deaths and
   marriages
Probate records: Yes
Probate search service: no charge;
   copies: $1.00 per page, no minimum

*Edwards County Courthouse
PO Box 184
Rocksprings, TX 78880-0184
Phone (512) 683-2235
County organized 1858 from Bexar County
Land records: Contact Dorothy R. Hatley, County and District Clerk
Vital records: Contact County and District Clerk (certified copies only)
Probate records: Contact County and District Clerk
Probate search service: $5.00 per name; copies: $1.00 each; "Send cash or check."

*Ellis County Courthouse
Waxahachie, TX 75165-3759
Phone (214) 923-5000 Courthouse; (214) 923-5070 Clerk
County organized 1849 from Navarro County
Land records: Deeds from 1845; contact Cindy Polley, County Clerk, Ellis County Records Building, 117 West Franklin, PO Box 250, Waxahachie, TX 75165-0250
Land records search service: $5.00 for five-year search per name; photocopies: 50¢ per page if made by individual in person, $1.00 per page if made by office staff, no minimum, $5.00 for certification
Naturalization records: Contact Billie Fuller, District Clerk, Courthouse, Second Floor
Vital records: Births from 1903 (unless delayed birth), deaths from 1903, marriages from 1850; contact County Clerk
Vital records search fee: $9.00 per birth, death or marriage, includes certified copy if found
Probate records: Estates and wills from 1845; contact County Clerk
Probate search service: $5.00 for five-year search per name; photocopies: 50¢ per page if made by individual in person, $1.00 per page if made by office staff, no minimum, $5.00 for certification; "Must have dates and names in order to check any of the above."

El Paso County Courthouse
500 East San Antonio
ElPaso, TX 79901-2421
Phone (915) 546-2071
County organized 1850 from Bexar County

*Erath County Courthouse
Stephenville, TX 76401-4219
Phone (817) 965-1482 County Clerk
County organized 1856 from Bosque and Coryell counties

Land records: Deeds from 1867; contact Nelda Crockett, County Clerk
Vital records: Births (also delayed records before 1903) and deaths from 1903, marriages (recorded in the county where the license was purchased) from 1869; contact County Clerk; certified copies: $9.00 each (includes search; births within the last fifty years and deaths within the last twenty-five years, subject to restrictions; restricted records may be made available to a properly qualified applicant, with positive identification, upon submission of a written, signed application that fully identifies the record)
Probate records: From 1876; contact County Clerk
Probate search service: $2.00; copies: $1.00 per page plus $5.00 for certification; "We cannot make extensive searches but will search for any record if names and dates are supplied; enclosing a SASE with any request for information will get you a reply."

*Falls County Courthouse
PO Box 458
Marlin, TX 76661-0458
Phone (817) 883-2061
County organized 1850 from Limestone and Milam counties
Land records: From 1835; contact Clerk; copies: $1.00 per page
Naturalization records: No naturalization records
Vital records: Births and deaths from 1903, marriages from 1854; contact Clerk; copies: $1.00 per page for genealogy
Probate records: From 1880; contact Clerk
Probate search service: fee not available; copies: $1.00 per page, no minimum

*Fannin County Courthouse
Bonham, TX 75418
Phone (214) 583-7486
County organized 1837 from Red River County
Land records: From 1838
Naturalization records: Some naturalization records
Vital records: From 1903
Probate records: From 1838
No probate search service; copies: $1.00 per page

*Fayette County Courthouse
151 North Washington Street
La Grange, TX 78945
Phone (409) 968-3251
County organized 1837 from Bastrop and Colorado counties

Land records: From 1838; contact Carolyn Kubos Roberts, County Clerk, PO Box 59, La Grange, TX 78945
Naturalization records: From 1850, indexed; contact District Clerk
Vital records: From 1903; contact County Clerk
Probate records: From 1838; contact County Clerk
Probate search service: $5.00; copies: $1.00 per page, no minimum

Fisher County Courthouse
Roby, TX 79543
Phone (915) 776-2401
County organized 1876 from Bexar County

*Floyd County Courthouse
PO Box 476
Floydada, TX 79235-0476
Phone (806) 983-3236
County organized 1876 from Bexar County
Land records: Contact County Clerk
Vital records: Contact County Clerk
Probate records: Contact County Clerk
Probate search service: no charge; copies: $1.00 per page, $1.00 minimum

*Foard County Courthouse
PO Box 539
Crowell, TX 79227
Phone (817) 684-1365
County organized 1891 from Cottle, Hardeman, King and Knox counties
Land records: Contact County Clerk
Land records search service: $10.00; copies: $1.00 per page
Naturalization records: Contact County Clerk
Vital records: From 1903; contact County Clerk
Vital records search service: $10.00; copies: $1.00 per page
Probate records: From 1893; contact County Clerk
Probate search service: $10.00; copies: $1.00 per page, no minimum

*Fort Bend County Courthouse
PO Box 520
Richmond, TX 77469-0520
Phone (713) 342-3411
County organized 1837 from Austin County
Naturalization records: No naturalization records
Vital records: Births from 1900, delayed births from late 1800s, deaths from 1903, marriages from 1837; contact Dianne Wilson, County Clerk's Office
Probate records: From 1838; contact County Clerk's Office

Probate search service: $2.00 per name; copies: $1.00 per page, $2.00 for certified copies, no minimum; "Please give the years to be searched; we do not do searches for last name only; we need a first name, also."

*Franklin County Clerk
PO Box 68
Mount Vernon, TX 75457-0068
Phone (903) 537-4252
County organized 1875 from Titus County
Land records: From 1849
Naturalization records: No naturalization records
Vital records: Births and deaths from 1903, marriages from 1875
Probate records: From 1875
Probate search service: $5.00 per name; copies: $1.00 per page, $1.00 for certification, no minimum

*Freestone County Clerk
Courthouse Annex
PO Box 1017
Fairfield, TX 75840-1017
Phone (903) 389-2635
County organized 1850 from Limestone County
Land records: From 1851; contact Mary Lynn White, County Clerk
Naturalization records: Before 1910; contact District Clerk's Office
Vital records: Births and deaths from 1903; certified copies: $9.00 each (births within the last fifty years and deaths within the last twenty-five years, subject to restrictions)
Probate records: From 1851
No probate search service; copies: $1.00 per page

Frio County Courthouse
PO Box X
Pearsall, TX 78061-1423
Phone (512) 334-2214
County organized 1858 from Bexar and Uvalde counties

*Gaines County Courthouse
Seminole, TX 79360-4341
Phone (915) 758-4003
County organized 1876 from Bexar County
Land records; From 1906; contact County Clerk's Office
Land records search service: no charge; copies: $1.00 per page, $9.00 per certified page
Vital records: Births, deaths and marriage licenses from 1906; contact County Clerk's Office
Vital records search service: no charge; copies: $1.00 per page, $9.00 per certified page (births within the last

fifty years and deaths within the last twenty-five years, subject to restrictions)
Probate records: From 1906; contact County Clerk's Office
Probate search service: no charge; copies: $1.00 per page, $9.00 per certified page

*Galveston County Courthouse
PO Box 2450
Galveston, TX 77553
Phone (409) 766-2210
County organized 1838 from Brazoria County
Land records: From 1838 (index under the grantors' and grantees' names, not by property description)
Naturalization records: Some naturalization records in 1879, and applications. Later records; contact District Court
Vital records: Births and deaths from June 1903 to February 1909 for city and county, births and deaths from 1941 to 1951 for City of Galveston or Texas City; contact County Clerk's Office. Births and deaths from 1910 to 1941 for City of Galveston and births and deaths from Bolivar; contact City Hall, Galveston, TX 77553. Births and deaths from November 1954 from Memorial Hospital; contact City Hall, City Registrar, PO Box 2608, Texas City, TX 77590
Probate records: From 1838
Probate search service: $5.00; copies: $1.00 per page, $1.00 for certification per instrument; "We do not bill."

Garza County Courthouse
Post, TX 79356-3242
Phone (806) 495-3535
County organized 1876 from Bexar County

*Gillespie County Courthouse
101 West Main, Unit #13
Fredericksburg, TX 78624
Phone (210) 997-6515
County organized 1846 from Bexar County
Land records: Contact Doris Lange, County Clerk; copies: $1.00 per page
Naturalization records: Contact Barbara Meyer, District Clerk, 101 West Main, Unit #3, Fredericksburg, TX 78624
Vital records: Births from 1846, deaths from 1903, marriages and marriage index from 1850; contact County Clerk; copies: $9.00 each for births and deaths, $6.00 each for marriages (births within the last fifty years and deaths within the last twenty-five years, subject to restrictions)
Probate records: Contact County Clerk

No probate search service; copies: $1.00 per page

Glasscock County Courthouse
PO Box 190
Garden City, TX 79739-0190
Phone (915) 354-2371
County organized 1887 from Tom Green County

*Goliad County Courthouse
PO Box 5
Goliad, TX 77963-0005
Phone (512) 645-3294
County organized 1836 from Old Mexican Municipality
Land records: From the late 1800s (after courthouse fire of June 1870); contact Gail M. Turley, District and County Clerk
Land records search service: $5.00 per name and index searched; copies: $1.00 per page, $5.00 for certification
Naturalization records: To 1915; contact District and County Clerk
Naturalization search service: $5.00 per name and index searched; copies: $1.00 per page, $5.00 for certification
Vital records: Births and deaths from 1903, with some from the late 1800s, marriages from 1876; contact District and County Clerk
Vital records search service: $5.00 per name and index searched; certified copies: $9.00 each for births and deaths (births within the last fifty years and deaths within the last twenty-five years, subject to restrictions)
Probate records: Contact District and County Clerk
Probate search service: $5.00 per name and index searched; copies: $1.00 per page, $5.00 for certification

Gonzales County Courthouse
Gonzales, TX 78629
Phone (512) 672-2435
County organized 1836 from Old Mexican Municipality

*Gray County Courthouse
200 North Russell Street
Pampa, TX 79065-6442
Phone (806) 669-8004
County organized 1876 from Bexar County
Land records: From 1880s (some prior)
Naturalization records: No naturalization records
Vital records: Yes
Probate records: Contact Wanda Carter, County Clerk, PO Box 1902, Pampa, TX 79065
No probate search service; copies: $1.00 per page

*Grayson County Courthouse
100 West Houston
Sherman, TX 75090
Phone (903) 813-4243 County Clerk
County organized 1846 from Fannin County
Land records: From 1846, contact Sara Jackson, County Clerk; certified copies: $5.00 per document plus $1.00 per page, plus $1.00 if staff makes the copy
Vital records: From 1900; contact County Clerk
Vital records search service: $5.00 for five-year search per name; copies: $9.00 each for births and deaths, $5.00 each for marriage licenses
Probate records: From 1900; contact County Clerk
No probate search service; copies: $1.00 per page, certification $5.00 per document or $2.00 per page

Gregg County Courthouse
PO Box 3049
Longview, TX 75606-3049
Phone (214) 758-6181
County organized 1873 from Rusk and Upshur counties

*Grimes County Courthouse
PO Box 209
Anderson, TX 77830
Phone (409) 873-2662
County organized 1846 from Montgomery County
Land records: From 1837; contact County Clerk
Naturalization records: From 1892; contact District Clerk
Vital records: From 1903; contact County Clerk
Probate records: From 1847; contact County Clerk
No probate search service; copies: 75¢ each, $1.00 per certified page plus $1.00 for certification

*Guadalupe County Courthouse
101 East Court Street
Seguin, TX 78155
Phone (512) 379-4188
County organized 1846 from Bexar and Gonzales counties
Land records: From 1854; contact Lizzie M. Lorenz, County Clerk
Naturalization records: From 1887 to 1906; contact District Clerk
Vital records: From 1933; contact County Clerk (births within the last fifty years and deaths within the last twenty-five years, subject to restrictions)
Probate records: From 1854; contact County Clerk
No probate search service; copies: $1.00 each, $5.00 for certification, no minimum

*Hale County County Clerk
500 Broadway, Room 140
Plainview, TX 79073
Phone (806) 293-8482 County Clerk; (806) 293-8482, ext. 261 Deputy for Vital Records
County organized 1876 from Bexar County
Land records: From 1884; contact Diane Williams, County Clerk
Land records search service: $5.00; copies: $1.00 each, $5.00 per document for certification
Vital records: Contact Nora Tipton, Deputy for Vital Statistics
Vital records search service: $10.00 for three names; certified copies: $9.00 each for births and deaths (births within the last fifty years and deaths within the last twenty-five years, subject to restrictions)
Probate records: From 1908; contact County Clerk
Probate search service: $5.00; copies: $1.00 each, $5.00 per document for certification

Hall County Courthouse
Memphis, TX 79245-3341
Phone (806) 259-2511
County organized 1876 from Bexar County

*Hamilton County Courthouse
Hamilton, TX 76531
Phone (817) 386-3518
County created 22 January 1858 and organized 2 June 1858, being part of the Milam Land District of Texas and developed from parts of Bosque, Lampasas and Comanche counties
Land records: From 1852; contact Virginia Lovell, County Clerk
Naturalization records: Contact District Clerk's Office
Vital records: From 1903 (incomplete until 1939); contact County Clerk
Probate records: From 1878
Probate search service: $5.00; copies: $1.00 each, no minimum

*Hansford County Clerk
PO Box 397
Spearman, TX 79081-0397
Phone (806) 659-4100
County organized 1876 from Bexar County
Land records: Contact County Clerk; copies: $1.00 per page
Vital records: Contact County Clerk
Probate records: Contact County Clerk; copies: $1.00 per page

*Hardeman County Courthouse
Quanah, TX 79252
Phone (817) 663-2901

County organized 1858 from Fannin County
Land records: From 1871; contact Clerk
Naturalization records: No naturalization records
Vital records: From 1903
Probate records: From 1886
Probate search service: no charge; copies: 25¢ per page, $1.00 for certified copies

*Hardin County Courthouse
PO Box 38
Kountze, TX 77625-0038
Phone (409) 246-5185
County organized 1858 from Jefferson and Liberty counties
Land records: Contact Dee Hatton, County Clerk
Vital records: Contact County Clerk
Probate records: Contact County Clerk
Probate search service: $5.00; copies: $1.00 per page, no minimum, $5.00 per certification; "Need to know date of death."

*Harris County Clerk's Office
PO Box 1525
Houston, TX 77251-1525
Phone (713) 221-6411 Beverly Kaufman, County Clerk
County organized 1836 from Austin and Liberty counties (Old Mexican Municipality); name changed from Harrisburg County
Land records: From 1836 to date
Naturalization records: From 1892 through 1905
Vital records: County births from 1903 to date, city births from October 1941 through April 1951
Probate records: From 1836 to date

*Harrison County Courthouse
Marshall, TX 75671
Phone (903) 938-4858
County organized 1839 from Shelby County
Land records: From 1839
Vital records: Most vital records from 1903
Probate records: From about 1840
No probate search service; copies: $1.00 per page, no minimum

Hartley County Courthouse
PO Box 22
Channing, TX 79018-0022
Phone (806) 235-3582
County organized 1876 from Bexar County

Haskell County Courthouse
PO Box 905
Haskell, TX 79521
Phone (817) 864-2451

*County organized 1858 from Fannin
and Milam counties*

*Hays County Courthouse
San Marcos, TX 78666
Phone (512) 396-2601
*County organized 1848 from Travis
County*
Land records: From 1848; contact
Ronnie Dannelley, County Clerk
Naturalization records: A few
naturalization records in deed records;
contact County Clerk
Vital records: Births and deaths from
1903; contact County Clerk. Births in
City of San Marcos from 1950;
contact City Registrar
Probate records: Contact County Clerk
Probate search service: no charge;
copies: $1.00 per page, no minimum;
"Need to know approximate date of
death."

*Hemphill County Courthouse
PO Box 867
Canadian, TX 79014-0867
Phone (806) 323-6212
*County organized 1876 from Bexar
County*
Land records: Real estate records from
1887; contact Davene Hendershot,
County and District Clerk
Naturalization records: A few
naturalization records in early 1900s;
contact County and District Clerk
Vital records: From 1896 (a few)
Probate records: From 1887
Probate search service: $1.00 and up,
depending on length; copies: 50¢ per
page, no minimum

*Henderson County Courthouse
Athens, TX 75751
Phone (903) 675-6140 County Clerk
*County organized 1846 from Houston
County*
Land records: Deeds; contact Gwen
Moffeit, County Clerk, PO Box 632,
Athens, TX 75751; copies: $1.00 per
page
Vital records: Births, deaths and marriage
licenses; copies: $9.00 each for births
and deaths, $3.00 each for marriage
licenses

Hidalgo County Courthouse
PO Box 58
Edinburg, TX 78540-0058
Phone (512) 383-2751
*County organized 1852 from Cameron
County*

*Hill County Courthouse
Hillsboro, TX 76645
Phone (817) 582-2161

*County organized 1853 from Navarro
County*
Land records: From 1860; contact
County Clerk's Office, PO Box 398,
Hillsboro, TX 76645-0398
Vital records: Births from 1875, deaths
from 1903, marriages from 1878;
contact County Clerk's Office
Probate records: From late 1800s (about
the 1890s); contact County Clerk's
Office
Probate search service: no charge;
copies: $1.00 per page, $1.00
minimum

*Hockley County Courthouse
Levelland, TX 79336
Phone (806) 894-3185 County Clerk;
(806) 894-8527 District Clerk
*County organized 1921 [sic; other
sources say organized 1876; first
federal census: 1880 with no
population]*
Land records: Contact Mary K. Walker,
County Clerk, Box 13, Courthouse,
Levelland, TX 79336
Naturalization records: Contact Wynelle
Donnell, District Clerk, Box 16,
Courthouse, Levelland, TX 79336
Vital records: Contact County Clerk
Probate records: Contact County Clerk
Probate search service: no charge;
copies: $1.00 per page, no minimum

*Hood County Courthouse
PO Box 339
Granbury, TX 76048-0339
Phone (817) 579-3222 County Clerk
*County organized 1865 from Johnson
County*
Land records: From 1865; contact
County Clerk
Land records search service: $5.00;
copies: $1.00 each, no minimum;
certification fee: $5.00 plus $1.00 per
page
Naturalization records: Yes
Vital records: From 1903; contact County
Clerk
Vital records search service: $5.00;
copies: $1.00 each, no minimum;
certification fee: $5.00 plus $1.00 per
page
Probate records: Contact County Clerk
Probate search service: $5.00; copies:
$1.00 each, no minimum; certification
fee: $5.00 plus $1.00 per page; "No
phone search."

*Hopkins County Courthouse
PO Box 288
Sulphur Springs, TX 75482-0288
Phone (214) 885-3929
*County organized 1846 from Lamar and
Nacogdoches counties*
Land records: From 1846; contact Mary
Attlesey, County Clerk

Naturalization records: No naturalization
records
Vital records: From 1903; contact County
Clerk
Probate records: From 1846; contact
County Clerk
Probate search service: $10.00 per hour;
copies: $1.00 per page, no minimum

*Houston County Courthouse
PO Box 370
Crockett, TX 75835
Phone (409) 544-3255
*County organized 1837 from
Nacogdoches County*
Land records: From 1881; contact
County Clerk
Vital records: From 1903; contact County
Clerk
Probate records: From 1859; contact
County Clerk
No probate search service; copies: $1.00
per page, no minimum

Howard County Courthouse
PO Box 1468
Big Spring, TX 79721-1468
Phone (915) 263-7247
*County organized 1876 from Bexar
County*

*Hudspeth County Courthouse
Sierra Blanca, TX 79851
Phone (915) 369-2301
*County organized 1917 from El Paso
County*
Land records: Official land records from
1917, however they do have
transcribed records from El Paso
County
Naturalization records: No naturalization
records
Vital records: Births, deaths and
marriages from 1917
Probate records: From 1917; contact
County Clerk's Office, PO Drawer A,
Sierra Blanca, TX 79851
Probate search service: no charge;
copies: $1.00 per page, no minimum

*Hunt County Courthouse
PO Box 1316
Greenville, TX 75403-1316
Phone (903) 408-4130 County Clerk
*County organized 1846 from Fannin
and Nacogdoches counties*
Land records: From 1846; contact Jimmy
P. Hamilton, County Clerk
Vital records: Births and deaths from
1903 (delayed births from the 1800s),
marriages from 1846; contact County
Clerk; copies: $9.00 each for births,
deaths and marriages (births within
the last fifty years and deaths within
the last twenty-five years, subject to
restrictions)

Probate records: From 1847; contact
County Clerk
Probate search service: $5.00 for five-
year search; copies: $1.00 per page,
$5.00 for certification, no minimum

*Hutchinson County Courthouse
PO Box 1186
Stinnett, TX 79083-0526
Phone (806) 878-4002
*County organized 1876 from Bexar
County*
Land records: Deeds from 1875; contact
Carol Ann Herbst, County Clerk
Naturalization records: No naturalization
records
Vital records: Births and deaths from
1927; contact County Clerk (proof of
relationship required with application
for copies of births and deaths)
Probate records: From 1927; contact
County Clerk
Probate search service: $5.00 for each
name searched; copies: $1.00 per
page, no minimum

Irion County Courthouse
Mertzon, TX 76941
Phone (915) 835-2421
*County organized 1889 from Tom Green
County*

*Jack County Courthouse
100 Main Street
Jacksboro, TX 76458
Phone (817) 567-2111
*County organized 4 July 1857 from
Cooke County*
Land records: Deeds from 1858
Naturalization records: From 1900;
contact District Clerk's Office
Vital records: Births and deaths from
1903, marriage licenses from 1858
Probate records: From 1858
Probate search service: $5.00; copies:
depends on the copy, no minimum

Jackson County Courthouse
115 West Main Street
Edna, TX 77957-2733
Phone (512) 782-3563
*County organized 1836 from Old
Mexican Municipality*

*Jasper County Archives Library
138 East Houston Street
Jasper, TX 75951
Phone (409) 384-6441
*County organized 1836 from Old
Mexican Municipality*

*Jeff Davis County Courthouse
PO Box 398
Fort Davis, TX 79734-0398
Phone (915) 426-3251

*County organized 1887 from Presidio
County*
Land records: Yes
Naturalization records: Yes
Vital records: Yes
Probate records: Yes

Jefferson County Courthouse
1149 Pearl Avenue
Beaumont, TX 77701-3619
Phone (409) 835-8475
*County organized 1836 from Old
Mexican Municipality*

Jim Hogg County Courthouse
Hebbronville, TX 78361
Phone (512) 527-4031
*County organized 1913 from Brooks
and Duval counties*

*Jim Wells County Courthouse
Alice, TX 78332-4845
Phone (512) 668-5702
*County organized 1911 from Nueces
County*
Land records: From 1911; contact
Arnoldo Gonzalez, County Clerk, PO
Box 1459, Alice, TX 78333
Naturalization records: No naturalization
records
Vital records: A few vital records in
delayed records from early 1900s
Probate records: From 1911
Probate search service: no charge;
copies: $1.00 per page, no minimum

Johnson County Courthouse
Cleburne, TX 76031
Phone (817) 641-4421
*County organized 1854 from McLennan
and Navarro counties*

*Jones County Courthouse
PO Box 552
Anson, TX 79501-0552
Phone (915) 823-3762
*County organized 1881 from Bexar and
Bosque counties*
Land records: From 1881 ("We do not do
this regularly, but if only a few
requests, will look when we have
time"); contact Margaret Jones,
County Clerk
Naturalization records: No naturalization
records
Vital records: Births and deaths from
1903; contact County Clerk
Probate records: Contact County Clerk
Probate search service: "If only one or
two names to search will do at our
time when can, and let you know the
number of pages"; copies: $1.00 per
page, $2.00 minimum

*Karnes County Clerk's Office
101 North Panna Maria Avenue, Suite 9
Karnes City, TX 78118-2959
Phone (210) 780-3938 County Clerk;
(210) 780-2562 District Clerk
*County organized 1854 from Goliad
County*
Land records: From 1854; contact
Elizabeth Swize, County Clerk
Naturalization records: From 1880;
contact District Clerk
Vital records: Births, deaths and
marriages from 1903; contact County
Clerk
Probate records: From 1854; contact
County Clerk

*Kaufman County Courthouse
Kaufman, TX 75142
Phone (214) 932-4331
*County organized 1848 from Van Zandt
County*
Land records: From 1840s (for search,
need year in which deed transaction
was done)
Naturalization records: One book of
naturalization records
Vital records: Births from 1870s (if put
on by affidavit), deaths from 1903 (for
search, need years)
Probate records: From middle 1800s
Probate search service: $5.00 for a ten-
year span; copies: $1.00 per page,
$5.00 for certification, $5.00
minimum (search fee)

Kendall County Courthouse
Boerne, TX 78006
Phone (512) 249-9343
*County organized 1862 from portions of
Blanco and Kerr counties*

*Kenedy County Courthouse
PO Box 7
Sarita, TX 78385-0007
Phone (512) 294-5220
*County organized 1911 from Hidalgo
and Cameron counties; name
changed from Willacy County in
1921, at which time a new Willacy
County was created from Cameron
and Hidalgo counties and a 1.4-mile
strip of old Willacy*
Land records: From 1849; contact
Barbara B. Turcotte, County Clerk
and District Clerk
Vital records: From 1912; contact County
Clerk and District Clerk
Probate records: From 1860; contact
County Clerk and District Clerk
Probate search service: $5.00; copies:
$1.00 per page, no minimum

*Kent County Courthouse
PO Box 9
Jayton, TX 79528-0009

Phone (806) 237-3881
County organized 1876 from Bexar County
Land records: From 1892
Vital records: From 1903 (a few delayed births earlier than that)
Probate records: From 1893
Probate search service: $5.00; copies: $1.00 per page; certification: $5.00 plus $1.00 per page

*Kerr County Courthouse
700 Main Street
Kerrville, TX 78028-5389
Phone (512) 257-6181
County organized 1856 from Bexar County
Land records: From 1856; contact County Clerk
Naturalization records: Very few naturalization records from 1858 to 1862, declarations of intent to become U.S. Citizen from 1876 to 1906; contact County Clerk
Vital records: Births from 1875, deaths from 1903, marriages from 1856; contact County Clerk
Probate records: From 1856; contact County Clerk
Probate search service: no charge; copies: 50¢ per page, $1.00 per page certified plus $1.00 for certification, no minimum

*Kimble County Courthouse
501 Main
Junction, TX 76849-4763
Phone (915) 446-3353
County organized 1858 from Bexar County
Land records: From 1884; contact Elaine Carpenter, County Clerk
Land records search service: $5.00
Vital records: Births, deaths and marriages from 1900; contact County Clerk
Vital records search service: $5.00; copies: $9.00 each for births and deaths, $5.00 each for marriages
Probate records: From 1884; contact County Clerk
Probate search service: $5.00; copies: $1.00 per page

King County Courthouse
Guthrie, TX 79236
Phone (806) 596-4412
County organized 1850 from Fannin County

*Kinney County Courthouse
PO Drawer 9
Brackettville, TX 78832-0009
Phone (512) 563-2521 County Clerk
County organized 1873 from Bexar County

Land records: From 1841; contact Dora Elia Sandoval, County Clerk
Land records search service: $10.00 per name per record group; copies: $1.00 per page
Vital records: Births, deaths and marriages; contact County Clerk
Vital records search service: $10.00 per name per record group; certified copies: $9.00 each for births and deaths, $5.00 each for marriages (births within the last fifty years and deaths within the last twenty-five years, subject to restrictions)
Probate records: From about 1841; contact County Clerk
Probate search service: $10.00 per name per record group; copies: $1.00 per page

*Kleberg County Courthouse
PO Box 1327
Kingsville, TX 78364-1327
Phone (512) 595-8548 Clerk
County organized 1913 from Nueces County
Land records: From 1913; contact Sam D. Deanda, County Clerk
Vital records: From 1913; contact County Clerk (photo I.D. required for birth certificates)
Probate records: From 1913; contact Sam D. Deanda, County Clerk
Probate search service: $5.00 per name; copies: $1.00 per page

*Knox County Courthouse
Benjamin, TX 79505
Phone (817) 454-2441
County organized 1858 from Fannin County
Land records: Contact County Clerk, PO Box 196, Benjamin, TX 79505
Naturalization records: No naturalization records
Vital records: Births from 1905, deaths from 1910, marriages from 1886; contact County Clerk
Probate records: Contact County Clerk
Probate search service: no charge; copies: $1.00 per page, no minimum

*Lamar County Courthouse
119 North Main
Paris, TX 75460-4265
Phone (214) 737-2420
County organized 1840 from Red River County
Land records: From 1836; copies: $1.00 per page, $5.00 per document for certification
Vital records: Births from 1903, delayed births from the 1800s, deaths from 1903 but were not required by the state until 1940
No vital records search service (must provide full names, dates and places,

and proof of relationship); certified copies: $9.00 each for births and deaths, $8.00 each for marriages, $1.00 each for uncertified copies of marriages
Probate records: From 1836
No probate search service; copies: $1.00 per page, $1.00 for certification, $20.00 deposit

*Lamb County Courthouse
Littlefield, TX 79339-3366
Phone (806) 385-5173
County organized 1876 from Bexar County
Land records: Contact Bill Johnson, County Clerk, Room 103, Box 3
Vital records: Contact County Clerk
Probate records: Contact County Clerk
Probate search service: no charge; copies: $1.00 per page plus $1.00 for certification, no minimum

*Lampasas County Courthouse
PO Box 231
Lampasas, TX 76550-0231
Phone (512) 556-8271
County organized 1856 from Bell and Travis counties
Land records: Deeds only; contact Office of the County Clerk, PO Box 347, Lampasas, TX 76550. Ad valorem tax records; contact County Appraisal District Office
Naturalization records: No naturalization records
Vital records: Births and deaths; contact Office of the County Clerk
Probate records: From 1856; contact Office of the County Clerk
Probate search service: no charge, unless very time consuming; copies: $1.00 per page, $5.00 for certification, if needed, no minimum

*La Salle County Courthouse
PO Box 340
Cotulla, TX 78014-0340
Phone (512) 879-2117
County organized 1880 from Bexar and Webb counties
Land records: From 1881; contact County Clerk
Naturalization records: Yes
Vital records: From 1881; contact County Clerk
Probate records: From 1881; contact County Clerk
Probate search service: no charge unless extensive search; copies: $1.00 per page, no minimum; "Fee must be paid in advance."

*Lavaca County Courthouse
Hallettsville, TX 77964
Phone (512) 798-3612

County organized 1846 from Colorado, Victoria and Jackson counties
Land records: Direct and reverse land records from 1846; contact Henry J. Sitka, County Clerk, PO Box 326, Hallettsville, TX 77964
No land records search service (must have record volume and page reference or a specific name and date for transaction, no copies of indexes)
Naturalization records: Just one volume from about the 1880s; contact County Clerk
Naturalization search service: $5.00 per for up to five names per record
Vital records: Births from 1859, deaths from 1903, marriages from 1847; contact County Clerk
No birth or death records search service (must have specific names and dates), $5.00 for search of marriage records; certified copies: $9.00 each for births and deaths, $5.00 each for marriages, $1.00 each for uncertified copies of marriages (births within the last fifty years and deaths within the last twenty-five years, subject to restrictions)
Probate records: From 1847; contact County Clerk
Probate search service: no charge for a single name and date; copies: $1.00 each, no minimum

*Lee County Courthouse
PO Box 419
Giddings, TX 78942-0419
Phone (409) 542-3684
County organized 1874 from Bastrop, Burleson, Washington and Fayette counties
Land records: From 1874; contact County Clerk
Naturalization records: From 1874; contact County Clerk and District Clerk
Vital records: From 1903; contact County Clerk
Probate records: From 1874; contact County Clerk
Probate search service: $5.00; copies: $1.00 per page, no minimum

*Leon County Courthouse
PO Box 98
Centerville, TX 75833-0098
Phone (903) 536-2352
County organized 1846 from Robertson County
Land records: From 1848; contact County Clerk
Naturalization records: No naturalization records
Vital records: Births and deaths from 1903, marriages from 1885; contact County Clerk
Probate records: From 1846; contact County Clerk

Probate search service: no charge; copies: $1.00 per page, no minimum

Liberty County Courthouse
1923 Sam Houston
Liberty, TX 77575-4815
Phone (409) 336-8071
County organized 1836 from Bexar County

*Limestone County Courthouse
200 West State Street
Groesbeck, TX 76642-1702
Phone (817) 729-5504
County organized 1846 from Robertson County
Land records: From about 1900; copies: $1.00 per page
Vital records: Births from 1900, deaths from 1903, marriages from 1873; copies: $9.00 each for births and deaths, $6.00 each for marriages
Probate records: From 1900
No probate search service (must have dates and names); copies: $1.00 per page, no minimum

*Lipscomb County Courthouse
Lipscomb, TX 79056
Phone (806) 862-3091 County and District Clerk
County organized 1876 from Bexar County
Land records: Contact Coeta Sperry, County and District Clerk, PO Box 70, Lipscomb, TX 79056
Naturalization records: From 1925 to 1926; contact County and District Clerk
Vital records: Contact County and District Clerk
Probate records: Contact County and District Clerk
Probate search service: $5.00; copies: $1.00 per page, no minimum; "SASE."

Live Oak County Courthouse
PO Box 280
George West, TX 78022-0280
Phone (512) 449-1624
County organized 1856 from Nueces County

*Llano County Clerk
107 West Sandstone
Llano, TX 78643
Phone (915) 247-4455
County organized 1856 from Bexar County
Land records: From 1880 to date

*Loving County Courthouse
PO Box 194
Mentone, TX 79754
Phone (915) 377-2441

County organized 1887 from Tom Green County

*Lubbock County Courthouse
Lubbock, TX 79401-3420
Phone (806) 741-8089; (806) 741-8035 County Clerk; (806) 762-6411 City Health Department
County organized 1891 [sic] from Baylor County [other sources say organized 1876; first federal census: 1880]
Land records: Contact Ann Davidson, County Clerk, PO Box 10536, Lubbock, TX 79408 (no search service)
Vital records: Contact County Clerk. Births and deaths within the city from 1 June 1951; contact City Health Department, PO Box 2548, Lubbock, TX 79408.
Probate records: Contact County Clerk
Probate search service: $5.00 per name; copies: $1.00 per page, no minimum

Lynn County Courthouse
PO Box 1256
Tahoka, TX 79373-1256
Phone (806) 998-4750
County organized 1876 from Bexar County

*Madison County Courthouse
101 West Main
Madisonville, TX 77864
Phone (409) 348-2638
County organized 1854 from Montgomery, Walker, Grimes and Leon counties
Land records: From 1873; contact Joyce M. Coleman, County Clerk, Room 102; copies: $1.00 per page, $5.00 per instrument for certified copies
Vital records: From 1903; contact County Clerk; copies: $9.00 each; "Records are closed to public, need as much information as possible for us to search."
Probate records: From 1873; contact County Clerk
Probate search service: $5.00; copies: $1.00 per page, $5.00 per instrument for certified copies, no minimum

*Marion County Courthouse
PO Box F
Jefferson, TX 75657-0420
Phone (214) 665-3971
County organized 1860 from Cass County
Land records: From 1860; contact Mrs. Clairece Ford, County Clerk
Naturalization records: Very few old ones; contact Janie McCay, District Clerk, 102 West Austin Street, Room 301, Jefferson, TX 75657
Vital records: From 1903 (very few in

earlier years); contact County Clerk (births within the last fifty years and deaths within the last twenty-five years, subject to restrictions)

Probate records: From 1860; contact County Clerk

Probate search service: $5.00 for index search; copies: $1.00 per page, no minimum

*Martin County Courthouse
Stanton, TX 79782
Phone (915) 756-3412 District and County Clerk
County organized 1876 from Bexar County
Land records: From 1883; contact Susie Hull, District and County Clerk, PO Box 906, Stanton, TX 79782
Vital records: Births from 1885, deaths from 1910 and marriages from 1885; contact District and County Clerk
Vital records search service: no charge; copies: $1.00 each for births over fifty years old, deaths over twenty-five years old or marriages, $9.00 each for certified copies of births and deaths, $5.00 each for certified copies of marriages
Probate records: From 1888; contact District and County Clerk
Probate search service: no charge; copies: $1.00 per page, no minimum

Mason County Courthouse
PO Box 702
Mason, TX 76856-0702
Phone (915) 347-5253
County organized 1858 from Bexar County

*Matagorda County Courthouse
1700 Seventh Street
Bay City, TX 77414-5034
Phone (409) 244-7680
County organized 1836 from Old Mexican Municipality
Land records: From early 1800s
Vital records: From 1903
Probate records: From early 1800s
No probate search service; copies: $1.00 per page, no minimum

Maverick County Courthouse
Eagle Pass, TX 78853
Phone (512) 773-2829
County organized 1856 from Kenedy County

*McCulloch County Courthouse
Brady, TX 76825
Phone (915) 597-2355
County organized 1856 from Bexar County
Land records: From 1875

Naturalization records: No naturalization records
Vital records: From 1903 (earlier for delayed)
Probate records: From 1876
No probate search service; copies: $1.00 per page plus certification if required, no minimum; "Names and dates are required."

*McLennan County Courthouse
Waco, TX 76701-1364
Phone (817) 757-5000
County organized 1850 from Milam, Robertson and Navarro counties
Land records: Contact County Clerk
Naturalization records: Contact District Clerk
Vital records: Contact County Clerk
Probate records: Contact County Clerk
No probate search service; copies: $7.50, no minimum

*McMullen County Courthouse
PO Box 235
Tilden, TX 78072-0235
Phone (512) 274-3215
County organized 1858 from Bexar and Live Oak counties
Land records: From 29 November 1871
Naturalization records: From 1877
Vital records: From 1903
Probate records: From 1877
Probate search service: $5.00; copies: $1.00 each, no minimum

Medina County Courthouse
Hondo, TX 78861
Phone (512) 426-5381
County organized 1848 from Bexar County

Menard County Courthouse
Menard, TX 76659
Phone (915) 396-4682
County organized 1858 from Bexar County

*Midland County Courthouse
200 West Wall Suite 105
Midland, TX 79701-4620
Phone (915) 688-1059 County Clerk
County organized 1885 from Tom Green County
Land records: Need date of transaction and name of buyer and seller, do not index under property description; copies: $1.00 per page, $1.00 for certification
Naturalization records: No naturalization records
Vital records: Births and deaths (closed to public, will assist in finding same if have name of person and date of birth or death), marriages (need name of male and female and date of

marriage); copies: $7.50 each for births and deaths, $2.00 each for marriage licenses
Probate records: Open to the public except for mentally ill cases or alcoholic cases
Probate search service: no charge; copies: $1.00 per page, $1.00 for certification; "Please send cash, cashier's check or money order; we cannot accept personal checks (out of town checks)."

*Milam County Courthouse
100 South Fannin
Cameron, TX 76520-4216
Phone (817) 697-6596
County organized 1836 from Old Mexican Municipality
Land records: From 1874
Naturalization records: Contact District Clerk
Vital records: Some vital records from 1878
Probate records: From 1874
Probate search service: no charge if not too many; copies: $1.00 per page

*Mills County Courthouse
PO Box 646
Goldthwaite, TX 76844-0646
Phone (915) 648-2711
County organized 1887 from Brown, Comanche, Lampasas and Hamilton counties
Land records: From 1836
Naturalization records: Until 1925
Vital records: From 1903
Probate records: From 1887
No probate search service; copies: $1.00 per page; "Do not do genealogy research."

*Mitchell County Courthouse
PO Box 1166
Colorado City, TX 79512-1166
Phone (915) 728-3481
County organized 1881 from Bexar County
Land records: Contact Clerk; copies: $1.00 per page
Vital records: Births and deaths; contact Clerk; certified copies: $9.00 for the first copy and $3.00 for each additional copy of the same record (births within the last fifty years and deaths within the last twenty-five years, subject to restrictions)
Probate records: Contact Clerk
Probate search service: "$5.00 over five names per request"; copies: $1.00 per page plus $5.00 to certify

*Montague County Clerk
PO Box 77
Montague, TX 76251-0077
Phone (817) 894-2461

County organized 1857 from Cooke County
Land records: Grantor and grantee indexes from 1873
Naturalization records: No naturalization records
Vital records: Births and deaths from 1903, marriages from 1873; copies: $9.00 each for births and deaths, $6.00 each for certified copies of marriages, $1.00 each for plain copies of marriages ("When requesting birth and death records we require name of person, birth date, place of birth, parents' names and the reason for needing this record"; births within the last fifty years and deaths within the last twenty-five years, subject to restrictions)
Probate records: From 1873
Probate search service: no charge; copies: $1.00 each, $1.00 for certification

*Montgomery County Courthouse
300 North Main Street
PO Box 959
Conroe, TX 77305
Phone (409) 539-7885
County organized 1837 from Washington County
Land records: Yes
Naturalization records: No naturalization records
Vital records: Births and deaths from 1903
Probate records: From 1838
Probate search service: $5.00; copies: $1.00 per page for plain copies, $2.00 per page for certified copies, no minimum

*Moore County Courthouse
715 Dumas Avenue
Courthouse, Room 202
Dumas, TX 79029
Phone (806) 935-5588
County organized 1876 from Bexar County
Land records: Contact County Clerk Office
Vital records: Contact County Clerk Office
Probate records: Contact County Clerk Office

*Morris County Courthouse
500 Broadnax Street
Daingerfield, TX 75638-1304
Phone (903) 645-3911
County organized 1875 from Titus County
Land records: Transcribed from Titus County from 1849; contact County Clerk
Naturalization records: No naturalization records

Vital records: Births and deaths from 1904 (closed to the public, we will check), marriages from about 1875; contact County Clerk. Divorces; contact District Clerk; copies: $9.00 each for births, deaths and marriage licenses
Probate records: From 1875; contact County Clerk
Probate search service: "We do it as a courtesy unless it takes more time than we can afford, then we advise"; copies: $1.00 per plain copy, no minimum

*Motley County Courthouse
Matador, TX 79224
Phone (806) 347-2621
County organized 1876 from Bexar County
Land records: Deeds, deeds of trust, releases; contact County Clerk
Vital records: Births, deaths and marriage licenses; contact County Clerk
Probate records: Contact County Clerk
Probate search service: $10.00 per estate; copies: $1.00 per page plus $1.00 for certification

*Nacogdoches County Courthouse
101 West Main Street
Nacogdoches, TX 75961-5119
Phone (409) 560-7733
County organized 1836 from Old Mexican Municipality
Land records: From 1833
Vital records: From 1903, some delayed birth records back into the 1800s
Probate records: From 1838
No probate search service; copies: $1.00 per page, $1.00 minimum

*Navarro County Courthouse
300 West Third Avenue
Corsicana, TX 75110
Phone (214) 654-3035; (214) 872-3656 Mildred Duncan
County organized 1846 from Robertson County
Land records: Contact Mildred Duncan, 516 West Third Avenue, Corsicana, TX 75110
Naturalization records: Contact Mildred Duncan
Vital records: Contact Mildred Duncan
Probate records: Contact Mildred Duncan
Probate search service: $5.00 per hour; copies: $1.00 per page, no minimum

*Newton County Courthouse
PO Box 484
Newton, TX 75966-0484
Phone (409) 379-5341
County organized 1846 from Jasper County
Land records: From 1846; contact County Clerk

Naturalization records: Contact District Clerk
Vital records: From 1903; contact County Clerk
Probate records: From 1846; contact County Clerk
Probate search service: no charge; copies: $1.00 per page, no minimum

*Nolan County Clerk
PO Drawer 98
Sweetwater, TX 79556
Phone (915) 235-2462
County organized 1876 from Bexar County
Land records: From 1880; contact Elsie Pierce, County Clerk
Land records search service: $5.00 per name
Naturalization records: No naturalization records
Vital records: From 1880; contact County Clerk
Vital records search service: $5.00 per name
Probate records: From 1881; contact County Clerk
Probate search service: $5.00 per name; copies: $1.00 per page, no minimum; "We do not do extensive searches; to search our index, names and dates are required; persons may do own searches."

Nueces County Courthouse
901 Leopard
Corpus Christi, TX 78401-3606
Phone (512) 888-0580
County organized 1846 from San Patricio County

*Ochiltree County Courthouse
511 South Main Street
Perryton, TX 79070-3154
Phone (806) 435-8100
County organized 1876 from Bexar County
Land records: Deeds; contact County Clerk's Office (no search service)
Vital records: Yes
Probate records: Yes
Probate search service: no charge; copies: $1.00 per page, no minimum

*Oldham County Clerk
PO Box 360
Vega, TX 79092-0360
Phone (806) 267-2667
County organized 1876 from Jack County
Land records: Yes
Land records search service: $5.00
Naturalization records: Yes
Naturalization records search service: $5.00
Vital records: Births and deaths

Vital records search service: $5.00; copies: birth certificates available to the public on or after the fiftieth anniversary of the date on which the record was filed, $11.00 each; death certificates available on or after the twenty-fifth anniversary of the date on which the record was filed, $9.00 each
Probate records: Yes
Probate search service: $5.00; copies: $1.00 per page, $5.00 for certified copies

*Orange County Courthouse
801 Division Street
Orange, TX 77630-6321
Phone (409) 883-7740
County organized 1852 from Jefferson County
Land records: From 1852
Naturalization records: No naturalization records
Vital records: Births and deaths from 1903 for those who were born or died outside of city limits; copies: $7.50 each for births and deaths
Probate records: From 1852
No probate search service; copies: $1.00 per page

*Palo Pinto County Clerk
PO Box 219
Palo Pinto, TX 76072
Phone (817) 659-1277
County organized 1856 from Navarro County
Land records: From 1857; contact Bobbie Smith, County Clerk
Naturalization records: No naturalization records
Vital records: Births and deaths from 1903, marriages from 1857; contact County Clerk
Probate records: From 1857; contact County Clerk
Probate search service: no charge; copies: $1.00 per page plus $5.00 for certification, payable in advance, no minimum

*Panola County Courthouse Building
Room 201
Carthage, TX 75633
Phone (214) 693-0302
County organized 1846 from Harrison and Shelby counties
Land records: From 1846
Naturalization records: No naturalization records
Vital records: From 1903, some delayed births before 1903 (births within the last fifty years or deaths within the last twenty-five years, subject to restrictions)
Probate records: From 1846
Probate search service: $10.00; copies:

$1.00 per page, no minimum; "Have to have approximate date for all searches."

Parker County Courthouse
1112 Santa Fe Drive
Weatherford, TX 76086-5827
Phone (817) 594-7461
County organized 1855 from Bosque and Navarro counties

Parmer County Courthouse
PO Box 356
Farwell, TX 79325-0356
Phone (806) 481-3691
County organized 1876 from Bexar County

Pecos County Courthouse
103 West Callahan Street
Fort Stockton, TX 79735-7101
Phone (915) 336-7555
County organized 1871 from Presidio County

*Polk County Clerk
PO Drawer 2119
Livingston, TX 77351
Phone (409) 327-6804 County Clerk
County organized 1846 from Liberty County
Land records: From 1846; contact Barbara Middleton, County Clerk
Land records search service: $10.00 per name
Vital records: From 1903; contact County Clerk
Probate records: From 1846; contact County Clerk
Probate search service: $10.00; copies: $1.00 per page

Potter County Courthouse
511 South Taylor
Amarillo, TX 79101-2437
Phone (806) 379-2250
County organized 1876 from Bexar County

*Presidio County Courthouse
PO Box 789
Marfa, TX 79843-0789
Phone (915) 729-4812
County organized 1850 from Bexar County
Land records: A few land records from 1832, most from late 1880s
Land records search service: $5.00; copies: $1.00 per page plus $1.00 for certification
Vital records: A few births from 1868, most from 1903, deaths from 1903. The City of Marfa has some birth records of the 1950s; copies: $7.50 each for births and deaths, $5.00 each

for marriage licenses; "No telephone requests honored; need written request of person for self or relative to include parents' names, date of birth or death, place of birth or death, purpose for which birth certificate is to be used, and form of birth certificate needed— I.D. Card or long form."
Probate records: From 1878
Probate search service: $5.00

Rains County Courthouse
PO Box 187
Emory, TX 75440-0187
Phone (214) 473-2461
County organized 1870 from Hopkins and Hunt counties

Randall County Courthouse
PO Box 660
Canyon, TX 79015-0660
Phone (806) 655-7001
County organized 1876 from Bexar County

Reagan County Courthouse
PO Box 100
Big Lake, TX 76932-0100
Phone (915) 884-2442
County organized 1903 from Tom Green County

*Real County Courthouse
PO Box 656
Leakey, TX 78873-0656
Phone (210) 232-5202
County organized 1913 from Bandera, Edwards and Kerr counties
Land records: Yes; copies: $1.00 per page, $5.00 per document for certification
Naturalization records: No naturalization records
Vital records: Births and deaths; copies: $9.00 each for births and deaths (births within the last fifty years and deaths within the last twenty-five years, subject to restrictions)
Probate records: Yes; copies: $1.00 per page, $5.00 per document for certification

*Red River County Courthouse
400 North Walnut Street
Clarksville, TX 75426
Phone (214) 427-2401
County organized 1836 from Old Mexican Municipality
Land records: From 1835; contact Mary Hausler, County Clerk
Naturalization records: Not very many naturalization records from 1839
Vital records: From 1903
Probate records: From 1835
Probate search service: $5.00 per name

with approximate date that you want searched; copies: $1.00 per page; $6.00 minimum (search and copy); "When making a request for a search of the records be specific as to name and date of search."

*Reeves County Courthouse
PO Box 867
Pecos, TX 79772-0867
Phone (915) 445-5467
County organized 1885 from Pecos County
Land records: From 1885 (no search service)
Naturalization records: No naturalization records
Vital records: From 1885
Probate records: From 1885
Probate search service: $10.00; copies: $1.00 each, no minimum

*Refugio County Courthouse
PO Box 704
Refugio, TX 78377-0704
Phone (512) 526-2233
County organized 1856 from Old Mexican Municipality
Land records: From 1835; contact Janelle Morgan, County Clerk
Naturalization records: From 1854; contact County Clerk
Vital records: Births, deaths and marriage licenses from 1903 to 1974; contact County Clerk
Vital records search service: $10.00; copies: $9.00 each for births and deaths, $5.00 each for marriage licenses
Probate records: From 1840; contact County Clerk
Probate search service: $10.00; copies: $1.00 per page, no minimum

Roberts County Courthouse
PO Box 477
Miami, TX 79059-0477
Phone (806) 868-2341
County organized 1876 from Bexar County

*Robertson County Courthouse
PO Box 1029
Franklin, TX 77856-1029
Phone (409) 828-4130
County organized 1837 from Bexar County
Land records: From 1838; contact County Clerk
Naturalization records: Contact District Clerk, PO Box 250, Franklin, TX 77856
Vital records: From 1903; contact County Clerk
Probate records: From 1836; contact County Clerk

Probate search service: no charge; copies: $1.00 per page, $5.00 for certification, no minimum

*Rockwall County Courthouse
Rockwall, TX 75087
Phone (214) 771-5141
County organized 1873 from Kaufman County
Land records: From 1873
Naturalization records: No naturalization records
Vital records: From 1873
Probate records: From 1873
Probate search service: $5.00; copies: $1.00 each, no minimum

*Runnels County Courthouse
600 Courthouse Square
Hutchings and Broadway
PO Box 189
Ballinger, TX 76821-0189
Phone (915) 365-2720
County organized 1858 from Coleman County
Land records: From 1880
No land records search service (must have grantor or grantee and year of transaction; copies: $1.00 per page plus $5.00 for certification
Vital records: From 1880; copies: $9.00 each for births and deaths (births within the last fifty years and deaths within the last twenty-five years, subject to restrictions)
Probate records: From 1880
Probate search service: no charge; copies: $1.00 per page plus $5.00 for certification

*Rusk County Courthouse
PO Box 758
Henderson, TX 75653-0758
Phone (903) 657-0330
County organized 1843 from Nacogdoches County
Land records: From 1844
Naturalization records: No naturalization records
Vital records: Births and deaths from 1904, marriages from 1844
Probate records: From 1844
Probate search service: no charge; copies: $1.00 per page, no minimum

Sabine County Courthouse
Hemphill, TX 75948
Phone (409) 787-3786
County organized 1836 from Old Mexican Municipality

*San Augustine County Courthouse
106 Courthouse
San Augustine, TX 75972
Phone (409) 275-2452

County organized 1836 from Old Mexican Municipality
Land records: From 1834
Vital records: Births from late 1800s, deaths from 1903
Probate records: From 1838
Probate search service: $5.00; copies: $1.00 per page plus $5.00 if certified

*San Jacinto County Courthouse
PO Box 669
Coldspring, TX 77331
Phone (409) 653-2324 County Clerk
County organized 1870 from Liberty County
Land records: Deeds from 1800; contact Joyce Hogue, County Clerk
Vital records: Births, deaths and marriages from 1870; contact County Clerk; copies: $9.00 each for births and deaths
Probate records: Wills from 1800; contact County Clerk
No probate search service; copies: $1.00 per page, no minimum

*San Patricio County Courthouse
PO Box 578
Sinton, TX 78387-0578
Phone (512) 364-2490
County organized 1836 from Old Mexican Municipality
Land records: From 1846
Naturalization records: No naturalization records
Vital records: Births and deaths from 1903
Probate records: From 1847
Probate search service: no charge; copies: $1.00 each, $1.00 for certification, no minimum

San Saba County Courthouse
San Saba, TX 76877
Phone (915) 372-3635
County organized 1856 from Bexar County

Schleicher County Courthouse
Eldorado, TX 76936
Phone (915) 853-2833
County organized 1887 from Crockett County

*Scurry County Clerk
1806 25th Street, Suite 300
Snyder, TX 79549-2530
Phone (915) 573-5332
County organized 1876 from Bexar County
Land records: Contact Frances Billingsley, County Clerk
No land records search service (contact local abstract companies)
Vital records: Births and deaths; contact

County Clerk; certified copies: $9.00
each, with documentary evidence
Probate records: Contact County Clerk
Probate search service: no charge;
copies: $1.00 per page, no minimum

*Shackelford County Courthouse
PO Box 247
Albany, TX 76430-0247
Phone (915) 762-2232
*County organized 1858 from Bosque
County*
Land records: Contact Frances Wheeler,
County and District Clerk
Naturalization records: No naturalization
records
Vital records: Contact County and
District Clerk
Probate records: Contact County and
District Clerk

*Shelby County Courthouse
PO Box 592
Center, TX 75935-0592
Phone (409) 598-6361 County Clerk
*County organized 1836 from Old
Mexican Municipality*
Land records: From 1882 (after
courthouse fire); contact Peaches
Conway, County Clerk
Land records search service: $9.00,
applied to cost of copies, if record is
found; copies: $2.00 per page, $5.00
per instrument for certification
Naturalization records: No naturalization
records
Vital records: Births, deaths after the late
1920s and marriages from 1882 to
date; contact County Clerk; certified
copies: $9.00 each
Probate records: Contact County Clerk
Probate search service: $9.00, applied to
cost of copies, if record is found;
copies: $2.00 per page, $5.00 per
instrument for certification

Sherman County Courthouse
PO Box 270
Stratford, TX 79084-0270
Phone (806) 396-2371
*County organized 1876 from Bexar
County*

*Smith County Courthouse
PO Box 1018
Tyler, TX 75710-1018
Phone (903) 535-0630
*County organized 1846 from
Nacogdoches County*
Land records: From 1846; contact
County Clerk
Vital records: Rural births from 1903,
deaths from 1875, marriage licenses;
contact County Clerk. City births and
deaths; contact City of Tyler, 815
North Broadway, Tyler, TX 75702

Probate records: From 1846; contact
County Clerk
Probate search service: $5.00; copies:
$1.00 per page, $1.00 minimum

*Somervell County Courthouse
PO Box 1098
Glen Rose, TX 76043-1098
Phone (817) 897-4427
*County organized 1875 from Hood
County*
Land records: From 1875
Naturalization records: No naturalization
records
Vital records: Births and deaths from
1903
Probate records: From 1800
Probate search service: no charge;
copies: $1.00 per page, no minimum

*Starr County Courthouse
Britton Avenue
Rio Grande City, TX 78582
Phone (512) 487-2954
*County organized 1848 from Nueces
County*
Land records: Filing of deeds, deeds of
trust, liens, release of liens, oil & gas
mineral leases, cemetery deeds, etc.;
contact Omar J. Garza, County Clerk,
Room 201; copies: $1.00 per page,
$5.00 for certification
Naturalization records: Contact Juan E.
Saenz, District Clerk
Vital records: Births, deaths and marriage
licenses; contact County Clerk;
copies: $9.00 for each birth or death
certificate or certified copy of
marriage license
Probate records: Contact County Clerk
Probate search service: no charge;
copies: $1.00 per page, no minimum

Stephens County Courthouse
Breckenridge, TX 76024
Phone (817) 559-3700
*County organized 1858 from Bosque
County, formerly Buchanan County*

*Sterling County Courthouse
PO Box 55
Sterling City, TX 76951-0055
Phone (915) 378-5191
*County organized 1891 from Tom Green
County*
Land records: Contact Clerk
Vital records: From 1902; contact Clerk
Probate records: Contact Clerk
No probate search service; copies: $1.00
per page, no minimum

Stonewall County Courthouse
PO Box P
Aspermont, TX 79502-0914
Phone (817) 989-2272

*County organized 1876 from Fannin
County*

Sutton County Courthouse
PO Box 481
Sonora, TX 76950-0481
Phone (915) 387-3815
*County organized 1887 from Wood
County*

Swisher County Courthouse
Tulia, TX 79088-2245
Phone (806) 995-3294
*County organized 1876 from Bexar
County*

*Tarrant County Courthouse
100 West Weatherford Street
Fort Worth, TX 76196
Phone (817) 334-1195
*County organized 1849 from Navarro
County*
Land records: Deeds from 1876 (date of
courthouse fire), plats from 1876;
contact Mr. Bill Erwin, Supervisor,
Central Records
Naturalization records: Contact
University of Texas at Arlington,
Special Collections, University
Library, Arlington, TX 76019
Vital records: Births from 1876, deaths
from 1903, marriages from 1876;
contact Bertha Bible, Supervisor
Probate records: From 1876; contact Jane
Skiffington, Assistant Chief Deputy.
Pre-1876 probate records, contact
Records Management Center for
originals or Fort Worth Public Library
for microfilm copies
Probate search service: no charge;
copies: $1.00 per page plus $1.00 for
certification, no minimum; "Money in
advance and cause number if
available."

Taylor County Courthouse
Abilene, TX 79608
Phone (915) 677-1711
*County organized 1858 from Bexar
County*

Terrell County Courthouse
PO Box 410
Sanderson, TX 79848-0410
Phone (915) 345-2391
*County organized 1905 from Pecos
County*

Terry County Courthouse
Brownfield, TX 79316-4328
Phone (806) 637-8551
*County organized 1876 from Bexar
County*

Throckmorton County Courthouse
PO Box 309
Throckmorton, TX 76083-0309
Phone (817) 849-2501
County organized 1858 from Bosque County

Titus County Courthouse
Mount Pleasant, TX 75455
Phone (214) 572-8891
County organized 1846 from Red River County

***Tom Green County Courthouse**
124 West Beauregard Avenue
San Angelo, TX 76903-5835
Phone (915) 659-6553
County organized 1874 from Bexar County
Land records: Contact Judith Hawkins, County Clerk
Naturalization records: Contact U.S. District Clerk, 33 East Twohig Avenue, San Angelo, TX 76903
Vital records: Contact County Clerk
Probate records: Contact County Clerk
Probate search service: $5.00 per name; copies: $1.00 per page, $5.00 per instrument for certification

***Travis County Courthouse**
1000 Guadalupe
Austin, TX 78701-2336
Phone (512) 473-9188 Recording Division; (512) 473-9595 Probate Division
County organized 1840 from Bastrop County
Land records: From 1840 to date; contact County Clerk, Recording Division, PO Box 1748, Austin, TX 78767
Land records search service: $10.00 per name per ten-year period per index (grantor or grantee index); copies: $1.00 per page plus $5.00 per document for certification
Naturalization records: From 1903; contact County Clerk
Naturalization records search service: $10.00 per name per ten-year period; copies: $1.00 per page plus $5.00 per document for certification
Vital records: Births and deaths for all of Travis County and the city of Austin from 1903 to 1917 and from 1941 to 1956, births and deaths for Travis County outside the city limits of Austin from 1917 to 1941 and from 1956 to date, marriage licenses from 1840 to date; contact County Clerk. Births and deaths within the city of Austin from 1917 to 1941 and from 1956 to date; contact City of Austin Health Department, 15 Waller Street, Austin, TX 78702
Vital records search service from County Clerk: $11.00 each for birth records,

$9.00 each for death records, $10.00 per name per ten-year period per index (male or female index) for marriage records; copies: $1.00 per page plus $5.00 per document for certification of marriage records (births within the last fifty years and deaths within the last twenty-five years, subject to restrictions)
Probate records: From 1845 to date; contact County Clerk, Probate Division, PO Box 1748, Austin, TX 78767
Probate search service: $5.00 per name per ten-year period; copies: $1.00 per page plus $5.00 per document for certification, no minimum; "Payment must be received before service can be performed; checks and correspondence addressed to Travis County Clerk."

***Trinity County Courthouse**
PO Box 456
Groveton, TX 75845-0456
Phone (409) 642-1208
County organized 1850 from Houston County
Land records: From 1800s, index from 1900; contact Elaine Ingram Lockhart, County Clerk
Naturalization records: Contact County Clerk
Vital records: From 1903; contact County Clerk
Probate records: From 1900s; contact County Clerk
No probate search service; copies: $1.00 each, no minimum

***Tyler County Courthouse**
110 Courthouse
Woodville, TX 75979-5245
Phone (409) 283-2281
County organized 1846 from Liberty County
Land records: From 1840s
Land records search service: $5.00; copies: $1.00 per page
Naturalization records: No naturalization records
Vital records: From 1850s
Vital records search service: $5.00
Probate records: From 1840s
Probate search service: $5.00 per search; copies: $1.00 per page, no minimum

Upshur County Courthouse
Gilmer, TX 75644
Phone (214) 843-3083
County organized 1846 from Harrison and Nacogdoches counties

***Upton County Courthouse**
PO Box 465
Rankin, TX 79778-0465
Phone (915) 693-2861

County organized 1887 from Tom Green County
Land records: Contact Phyllis Stephens, County Clerk
Vital records: Contact County Clerk; copies: $9.00 each for births, deaths and marriages
Probate records: Contact County Clerk
No probate search service; copies: $1.00 per page plus $1.00 for certification, no minimum; "Copies are not provided until payment is made."

***Uvalde County Courthouse**
PO Box 284
Uvalde, TX 78802-0284
Phone (512) 278-6614
County organized 1850 from Bexar County
Land records: From 1856
Land records search service: $10.00 per name per ten-year period; copies: $1.00 per page, $5.00 per document for certification
Naturalization records: No naturalization records
Vital records: From 1856
Vital records search service: $9.00 per name for births and deaths, $8.00 per name for marriages (includes one certified copy)
Probate records: From 1856
Probate search service: $10.00 per name; copies: $1.00 per page, $5.00 per document for certification, no minimum

***Val Verde County Courthouse**
PO Box 1267
Del Rio, TX 78841-1267
Phone (512) 774-3611
County organized 1885 Kinney and Pecos counties
Land records: From 1885
Probate records: From June 1885
Probate search service: $5.00 per name; copies: $1.00 each, no minimum; "Fee on any service must be paid before delivery of service."

***Van Zandt County Courthouse**
PO Box 515
Canton, TX 75103-0515
Phone (214) 567-6503
County organized 1848 from Henderson County
Land records: Yes
Vital records: Yes
Probate records: Yes
Probate search service: $5.00; copies: $1.00

***Victoria County Courts Building**
(115 North Bridge—location)
PO Box 2410
Victoria, TX 77901-6513

Phone (512) 575-4558 County Judge;
(512) 575-1478 County Clerk
*County organized 1836 from Old
Mexican Municipality*
Land records: From 1838; contact Val D.
Huvar, County Clerk
Naturalization records: From 1870,
which is very limited; contact County
Clerk. Federal and District Clerk's
Office have some naturalization
records, also
Vital records: From 1903; contact County
Clerk
Vital records search service: births and
deaths closed to the public, but will
"check on one or more" for
researchers
Probate records: From 1838; contact
County Clerk
Probate search service: $5.00 prepaid;
copies: $1.00 per page plus $5.00 for
the certificate, no minimum

*Walker County Courthouse
1100 University
Huntsville, TX 77340-4631
Phone (409) 291-9500
*County organized 1846 from
Montgomery County*
Land records: From 1846; contact James
D. Patton, County Clerk, PO Box 210,
Huntsville, TX 77342-0210
Naturalization records: Contact District
Clerk
Vital records: Births and deaths from
1903, marriages from 1846; contact
County Clerk
Probate records: From 1846; contact
County Clerk
Probate search service: $5.00; copies:
$1.00 per page plus $1.00 for
certification, no minimum

Waller County Courthouse
836 Austin Street
Hempstead, TX 77445-4667
Phone (409) 826-3357
*County organized 1873 from Austin
County*

*Ward County Courthouse
Monahans, TX 79756
Phone (915) 943-3294
*County organized 1892 [sic] from Tom
Green County [other sources say
organized 1887; first federal census:
1890]*
Land records: Contact Pat V. Finley,
County Clerk, County Clerk's Office
Vital records: Contact County Clerk's
Office
Probate records: Contact County Clerk's
Office
Probate search service: $5.00 per search
per name; copies: $1.00 per page plus
$1.00 per certificate, no minimum;

"Fee must accompany written request;
NO personal checks, NO food store
money orders; bank or U.S. Post
Office Checks or money orders *only*."

*Washington County Courthouse
Washington County Courthouse
Brenham, TX 77833
Phone (409) 277-6200
*County organized 1836 from Texas
Municipality*
Land records: From 1837 to date;
Contact Beth A. Rothermel, County
Clerk
Land records search service: $5.00 per
name; copies: $1.00 per page
Naturalization records: Contact Blondean
Kuecker, District Clerk, 100 East
Main, Suite 300, Brenham, TX 77833
Vital records: Births and deaths from
1903 to date, marriages from 1837 to
date; contact County Clerk
Vital records search service: $5.00 per
name; copies: $1.00 per page (picture
I.D. or two other forms of I.D.
required)
Probate records: From 1837 to date;
contact County Clerk
Probate search service: $5.00 per name;
copies: $1.00 per page

Webb County Courthouse
204 McPherson Drive
Laredo, TX 78041-2712
Phone (512) 727-7272
*County organized 1848 from Bexar
County*

*Wharton County Courthouse
PO Box 69
Wharton, TX 77488
Phone (409) 532-2381
*County organized 1846 from Colorado
and Jackson counties*
Land records: Contact County Clerk
Naturalization records: Contact District
Clerk
Vital records: Contact County Clerk
Probate records: Contact County Clerk
No probate search service; copies: $1.00
per page

*Wheeler County Courthouse
PO Box 465
Wheeler, TX 79096-0465
Phone (806) 826-5544
*County organized 1876 from Bexar
County*
Land records: From early 1900s
Vital records: From early 1900s
Probate records: From early 1900s
Probate search service: "We do not
search for you unless you request a
specific name"; copies: $1.00 per
page; "You are welcome to use our
records for your own search."

Wichita County Courthouse
PO Box 1679
Wichita Falls, TX 76307-1679
Phone (817) 766-8100
*County organized 1858 from Fannin
County*

*Wilbarger County Courthouse
1700 Wilbarger Street
Vernon, TX 76384-4742
Phone (817) 552-5486
*County organized 1858 from Bexar
County*
Land records: From 1881
Naturalization records: No naturalization
records
Vital records: From 1890
Probate records: From 1900
Probate search service: $5.00; copies:
$1.00 per page, $5.00 minimum

Willacy County Courthouse
Raymondville, TX 78580-3533
Phone (512) 689-2710
*County organized 1921 from Cameron
and Hidalgo counties and a 1.4-mile
strip of a former Willacy County,
which was renamed Kenedy County
at the same time that the new county
was created*

*Williamson County Courthouse
County Clerk
PO Box 18
Georgetown, TX 78627-0018
Phone (512) 930-4315
*County organized 1848 from Milam
County*
Land records: From 1848
No land records search service
Vital records: From 1903
No vital records search service
Probate records: From 1848
No probate search service; copies: $1.00
per page

*Wilson County Clerk
PO Box 27
Floresville, TX 78114-0027
Phone (210) 393-7308 County Clerk
*County organized 1860 from Bexar
County*
Land records: Contact Eva S. Martinez,
County Clerk
Naturalization records: No naturalization
records
Vital records: Contact County Clerk
(proof of relationship required)
Probate records: Contact County Clerk
No probate search service (must have
names and dates); copies: $1.00 each,
no minimum

*Winkler County Courthouse
PO Box 1007
Kermit, TX 79745-1007

Phone (915) 586-3401
County organized 1887 from Tom Green County
Land records: From 1883; contact Ruth Godwin, County Clerk (no title searches made on real estate without volume and page numbers)
Vital records: From 1912; contact County Clerk
Probate records: From 1912; contact County Clerk
Probate search service: $5.00 per single name; copies: $1.00 per page, $1.00 for certification

*Wise County Courthouse
PO Box 359
Decatur, TX 76234-0359
Phone (817) 627-3351
County organized 1856 from Cooke County
Land records: From 1852; contact Clerk; copies: $1.00 each
Naturalization records: No naturalization records
Vital records: From 1903; contact Clerk
Vital records search service: $9.00 (includes one copy; requires a properly completed application for certified copies)
Probate records: From 1882; contact Clerk
Probate search service: no charge; copies: $1.00 each

*Wood County Clerk
PO Box 338
Quitman, TX 75783-0338
Phone (214) 763-2711
County organized 1850 from Van Zandt County
Land records: From 1879 to date
Naturalization records: No naturalization records
Vital records: From 1903 or 1904 to date
Probate records: From 1879 to date

*Yoakum County Courthouse
PO Box 309
Plains, TX 79355-0309
Phone (806) 456-2721
County created 1876 from Bexar County; organized 1907
Land records: Contact County Clerk
Vital records: Births, deaths and marriage licenses; contact County Clerk
No vital records search service (must furnish name of child or decedent, year of birth or death); certified copies: $9.00 each for births or deaths, $3.00 each for marriage licenses
Probate records: Contact County Clerk
Probate search service: $5.00 by Clerk's Office; copies: $1.00 per page, no minimum

*Young County Courthouse
PO Box 218
Graham, TX 76046-0218
Phone (817) 549-8432
County organized 1856 from Bosque County
Land records: From March 1854
Vital records: Births and deaths from 1903
Probate records: From 1876
Probate search service: $5.00 per name; copies: $1.00 per page

Zapata County Courthouse
Zapata, TX 78076
Phone (512) 765-4331
County organized 1858 from Starr and Webb counties

*Zavala County Courthouse
Crystal City, TX 78839-3547
Phone (512) 374-2331 County Clerk
County organized 1884 from Uvalde and Maverick counties
Land records: From 1886 to date; contact Teresa P. Flores, County Clerk
Naturalization records: No naturalization records
Vital records: From 1900 to date; contact County Clerk (births within the last fifty years and deaths within the last twenty-five years, subject to restrictions)
Probate records: From 1900 to date; contact County Clerk

UTAH

Capital: Salt Lake City. Statehood: 4 January 1896 (annexed by the Treaty of Guadalupe-Hidalgo, 1848, became a territory in 1850 from the provisional State of Deseret, south of the 42nd parallel and west of the Rockies)

Court System

Utah has about 180 Justice of the Peace Courts which hear lesser civil cases, small claims, some misdemeanors and felony preliminaries. Juvenile Court sits at each county seat and has special jurisdiction; its six districts are different from either the Judicial Districts of the District Court or the Circuits of the Circuit Court. Circuit Court handles some civil cases, some criminal cases and some small claims, and sits in each county seat (some of them as secondary locations), except Farmington in Davis County and Parowan in Iron County. First Circuit: Box Elder County; Second Circuit: Cache and Rich counties; Third Circuit: Morgan and Weber counties; Fourth Circuit: Davis County; Fifth Circuit: Salt Lake and Summit counties; Sixth Circuit: Tooele County; Seventh Circuit: Daggett, Duchesne and Uintah counties; Eighth Circuit: Juab, Utah and Wasatch counties; Ninth Circuit: Beaver, Iron, Millard and Washington counties; Tenth Circuit: Garfield, Kane, Piute, Sanpete, Sevier and Wayne counties; Eleventh Circuit: Carbon and Emery counties; Twelfth Circuit: Grand and San Juan counties.

District Court sits at each county seat and hears criminal felonies, review of administrative agencies, and all civil matters not heard by the lower courts. First Judicial District: Box Elder, Cache and Rich counties; Second Judicial District: Davis, Morgan and Weber counties; Third Judicial District: Salt Lake, Summit and Tooele counties; Fourth Judicial District: Juab, Millard, Utah and Wasatch counties; Fifth Judicial District: Beaver, Iron and Washington counties; Sixth Judicial District: Garfield, Kane, Piute, Sanpete, Sevier and Wayne counties; Seventh Judicial District: Carbon, Daggett, Duchesne, Emery, Grand, San Juan and Uintah counties. The Court of Appeals and Supreme Court hear appeals.

Courthouses

Beaver County Courthouse
Beaver, UT 84713
Phone (801) 438-2552
County organized 1856 from Iron and Millard counties

*Box Elder County Courthouse
1 Main Street
Brigham City, UT 84302-4357
Phone (801) 734-2031
County organized 1856 from unorganized territory
Land records: Contact LuAnn Adams, County Recorder/Clerk
Naturalization records: Contact LuAnn Adams, County Recorder/Clerk
Probate records: Contact District Court
Probate search service: $4.00 per hour; copies: 25¢ per page, $2.00 per page certification

*Cache County Courthouse
179 North Main
Logan, UT 84321
Phone (801) 752-3542
County organized 4 April 1857 from unorganized territory
Land records: Contact County Recorder
Naturalization records: No naturalization records
Vital records: Marriages; contact County Clerk, 170 North Main, Logan, UT 84321-4541. Births and deaths; contact Bear River Health Department, 655 East 1300 North, Logan, UT 84321
Probate records: Contact Clerk of the District Court, Hall of Justice, 140 North 100 West, Logan, UT 84321

*Carbon County Courthouse
120 East Main
Price, UT 84501-3046
Phone (801) 637-4700
County organized 1894 from Emery County
Land records: Contact Recorder
Naturalization records: Contact Clerk
Vital records: Marriages; contact Clerk
Probate records: Contact District Court, 149 East First South, Price, UT 84501

*Daggett County Courthouse
PO Box 219
Manila, UT 84046
Phone (801) 784-3154; (801) 784-3210; (801) 784-3335 FAX
County organized 1918 from Uintah County
Land records: Yes
Naturalization records: Yes
Vital records: Marriages
Probate records: Yes

*Davis County Courthouse
PO Box 618
Farmington, UT 84025
Phone (801) 451-4402; (801) 451-3224 Recorder's Office; (801) 451-3214 County Clerk; (801) 451-3337 Health Department; (801) 451-3206 District Court
County organized 1850 from Salt Lake County
Land records: From 1886; contact Recorder's Office
Naturalization records: From 1905 to 1925; contact County Clerk
Vital records: Births and deaths from 1972; contact County Health Department. Marriages from June 1888; contact County Clerk
Probate records: Contact Second District Court
Probate search service: $10.00 per hour; copies: 25¢ per page

*Duchesne County Courthouse
PO Drawer 270
Duchesne, UT 84021
Phone (801) 738-2435, ext. 170 Recorder's Office; (801) 738-2435, ext. 114 County Clerk; (801) 738-2468 Court Clerk
County organized 5 January 1915 from Wasatch County
Land records: From 1875; contact Recorder's Office
No land records search service (can be accessed with a legal description or a name)
Naturalization records: Only what may have been recorded by certain individuals; contact Recorder's Office
Vital records: Marriage licenses from 1915; contact Pat Stratton, County Clerk
Probate records: From 1915; contact Probate Clerk Office
Probate search service: no charge; copies: 25¢ per page plus postage, no minimum

*Emery County Courthouse
Castle Dale, UT 84513
Phone (801) 381-2465
County organized 1880 from Sanpete and Sevier counties
Land records: Yes
Probate records: Yes
Probate search service: available; copies: available

*Garfield County Courthouse
PO Box 77
Panguitch, UT 84759
Phone (801) 676-8826
County organized 9 March 1882 from Iron, Kane and Sevier counties
Land records: Contact Les Barker, Recorder

Naturalization records: No naturalization records
Vital records: Marriage licenses only; contact County Clerk; copies: $6.00 each
Probate records: Contact Dawna Barney, Court Clerk
Probate search service: $8.00 per hour; copies: 50¢ per page, no minimum

*Grand County Courthouse
125 East Center
Moab, UT 84532-2449
Phone (801) 259-1333 Recorder
County organized 1890 from Emery and Uintah counties
Land records: Contact Recorder
Naturalization records: No naturalization records
Vital records: No vital records
Probate records: Contact District Court Clerk
Probate search service: no charge; copies: 25¢ per page, no minimum

*Iron County Courthouse
68 South 100 East
Parowan, UT 84761
Phone (801) 477-8350 County Recorder; (801) 477-8340 County Clerk; (801) 586-7440 Fifth District Court
County organized 1850 from unorganized territory; name changed from Little Salt Lake County in 1850
Land records: Contact Dixie B. Matheson, County Recorder
Naturalization records: Contact David I. Yardley, County Clerk
Vital records: Marriage licenses from 1896 to date; contact County Clerk
Probate records: Contact Fifth District Court
Probate search service: $7.65 per hour; copies: 25¢ each, no minimum

*Juab County Courthouse
160 North Main
Nephi, UT 84648-1412
Phone (801) 623-0271
County organized 1852, original county
Land records: From 1890
Naturalization records: From 1900 to 1905
Vital records: From 1898 to 1905
Probate records: From 1890
Probate search service: $7.50 per hour; copies: 25¢ per page, no minimum

*Kane County Courthouse
76 North Main
Kanab, UT 84741
Phone (801) 644-2551
County organized 1864 from Washington County
Land records: Contact Recorder's Office

Naturalization records: No naturalization records

Vital records: No vital records

Probate records: Contact Court Clerk's Office; copies: 25¢ per page plus postage

*Millard County Courthouse
Fillmore, UT 84631
Phone (801) 743-6223
County organized 1851 from Juab County
Land records: Contact County Recorder
Probate records: Contact County Clerk
Probate search service: no charge for one name, one time, otherwise $5.00 per hour; copies: 25¢ per page plus postage costs; "Call for instructions."

*Morgan County Courthouse
48 West Young Street
Morgan, UT 84050
Phone (801) 829-6811
County organized 1862 from Davis and Summit counties
Land records: Contact Debbie Weaver, Recorder
Naturalization records: No naturalization records
Vital records: Marriage licenses only; contact County Clerk's Office
Probate records: Contact District Court
Probate search service: no charge; copies: 25¢ per page, $2.00 per document plus 50¢ per page for certified copies, plus postage, no minimum

Piute County Courthouse
21 North Main
Junction, UT 84740
Phone (801) 577-2840
County organized 1865 from Sevier County

Rich County Courthouse
Randolph, UT 84064
Phone (801) 793-2415
County organized 1864, original county; name changed from Richland County

Salt Lake County Courthouse
240 East Fourth South
Salt Lake City, UT 84111-2804
Phone (801) 535-7541
County organized 1849, original county; name changed from Great Salt Lake County in 1868
Vital records: Births and deaths; contact 610 South 200 East, Salt Lake City, UT 84111

*San Juan County Courthouse
Monticello, UT 84535

Phone (801) 587-2231
County organized 1880 from Kane County
Land records: Contact Louise Jones, Recorder
Naturalization records: No naturalization records
Vital records: No vital records
Probate records: Contact Gail Johnson, Clerk
Probate search service: $2.00 per name/ $7.00 per hour; copies: 50¢ each, $2.00 minimum

*Sanpete County Courthouse
160 North Main
Manti, UT 84642-1266
Phone (801) 835-2131
County organized 1849, original county
Land records: Contact County Recorder
Vital records: Births and deaths from 1898 to 1905, marriages; contact County Clerk
Probate records: Contact County Clerk
Probate search service: $10.00 per hour (longer than ten minutes); copies: 15¢ to 25¢ per page, $2.00 per document plus 25¢ per page for certified copies, no minimum

Sevier County Courthouse
250 North Main
Richfield, UT 84701-2158
Phone (801) 896-9262
County organized 1865 from Sanpete County

*Summit County Courthouse
PO Box 128
Coalville, UT 84017-0128
Phone (801) 336-4451 Recorder
County organized 1854 from Salt Lake County
Land records: From 1856 to date; contact Alan Spriggs, Recorder
No land records search service; copies: 50¢ per page, $2.00 each for plats up to 18" x 18", $4.00 each for larger plats
Naturalization records: Contact County Clerk
Vital records: Contact County Clerk
Probate records: Contact County Clerk
Probate search service: $7.65 per hour after ten minutes; copies: 25¢ per page, no minimum; "Fees paid in advance."

*Tooele County Courthouse
47 South Main
Tooele, UT 84074-2131
Phone (801) 882-5550
County organized 1849, original county; includes Shambip County, which was abolished in 1862
Land records: Yes

Naturalization records: Early naturalization records only
Vital records: Births and deaths from 1897 to 1905
Probate records: Contact District Court
Probate search service: $6.00 per hour; copies: 25¢ each, no minimum

*Uintah County Courthouse
147 East Main
Vernal, UT 84078
County organized 1880 from Wasatch County
Land records: Contact Recorder's Office
Naturalization records: No naturalization records
Probate records: Contact District Court Office

*Utah County Building
Provo, UT 84601
Phone (801) 370-8116 District Court
County organized 1849, original county; includes Cedar County, which was abolished in 1862
Land records: Yes
Naturalization records: No naturalization records
Vital records: Yes
Probate records: Contact Fourth Judicial District Court, PO Box 1847, 125 North 100 West, Provo, UT 84603
Probate search service: $8.00 per hour plus SASE; copies: 25¢ each, no minimum

*Wasatch County Courthouse
25 North Main Street
Heber City, UT 84032-1827
Phone (801) 654-3211; (801) 654-4676 Court Clerk
County organized 1870 from Salt Lake and Utah counties
Land records: Contact Recorder's Office
Naturalization records: Contact Recorder's Office
Vital records: Marriage licenses and some births; contact Clerk's Office
Probate records: Contact Court Clerk's Office

*Washington County Administration Building
197 East Tabernacle
Saint George, UT 84770-3473
Phone (801) 634-5712
County organized 1856 from unorganized territory
Land records: Contact County Recorder
Naturalization records: Contact County Clerk
Vital records: Marriage licenses only; contact County Clerk
Probate records: Contact Fifth District Court Clerk, Hall of Justice, 220 North 200 East, Saint George, UT 84770

Probate search service: $2.00 per hour; copies: 15¢ each

*Wayne County Courthouse
18 South Main
Loa, UT 84747
Phone (801) 836-2731; (801) 836-2765
   Recorder
County organized 1892 from Piute County
Land records: Contact Recorder
Vital records: From 1898 to 1947; contact Clerk
Probate records: From 1898; contact Clerk
Probate search service available; copies: 50¢ per page, $6.00 for certified copies, no minimum

*Weber County Courthouse
Municipal Building
Ogden, UT 84401
Phone (801) 399-8455
County organized 1849, original county

VERMONT

Capital: Montpelier. Statehood: 4 March 1791 (claims relinquished by Massachusetts in 1781, by New Hampshire in 1782, and by New York in 1790, although Vermont asserts that it was an "independent republic" from 1777 until it joined the U.S. in 1791)

Court System

Vermont's Probate Court is divided into eighteen districts. It sits at the county seats in Addison, Caledonia, Chittenden, Franklin, Grand Isle, Lamoille, Orange, Orleans and Washington Districts. The Probate Court in Bennington District sits at Bennington and includes the towns of Bennington, Glastenbury, Pownal, Readsboro, Searsburg, Shaftsbury, Stamford and Woodford; Essex District sits at Island Pond; Fair Haven District sits at Fair Haven and includes the towns of Benson, Castleton, Fair Haven, Hubbardton, Pawlet, Poultney, Sudbury, Wells and West Haven; Hartford District sits at Woodstock and includes the towns of Barnard, Bethel, Bridgewater, Hartford, Hartland, Norwich, Pomfret, Rochester, Royalton, Sharon, Stockbridge and Woodstock; Manchester District sits at Manchester and includes the towns of Arlington, Dorset, Landgrove, Manchester, Peru, Rupert, Sandgate, Sunderland and Winhall; Marlboro District sits at Brattleboro and includes the towns of Brattleboro, Dover, Dummerston, Guilford, Halifax, Marlboro, Newfane, Stratton, Somerset, Vernon, Wardsboro, Whitingham and Wilmington; Rutland District sits at Rutland City and includes the towns of Brandon, Chittenden, Clarendon, Danby, Ira, Mendon, Middletown Springs, Mount Holly, Mount Tabor, Pittsfield, Pittsford, Proctor, Rutland Town, Rutland City, Sherburne, Shrewsbury, Tinmouth, Wallingford and West Rutland; Westminster District sits at Bellows Falls and includes the towns of Athens, Brookline, Grafton, Jamaica, Londonderry, Putney, Rockingham, Townshend, Westminster and Windham; Windsor District sits at North Springfield and includes the towns of Andover, Baltimore, Cavendish, Chester, Ludlow, North Springfield, Plymouth, Reading, Springfield, Weathersfield, West Windsor, Weston and Windsor.

The District Courts have limited jurisdiction over civil, criminal and juvenile matters and are organized into three multicounty units, with each county constituting a district within the unit, and two special units: Brandon (at the town of Brandon, having jurisdiction over the Brandon Training School, a mental health facility) and Waterbury (at Barre, exercising mental health jurisdiction only). Unit One: Bennington, Rutland, Windham and Windsor Circuits (at Bennington, Rutland, Brattleboro and White River Junction); Unit Two: Addison, Chittenden, Orange and Washington Circuits (at Middlebury, Burlington, Chelsea and Barre); Unit Three: Caledonia, Essex, Franklin, Grand Isle, Lamoille and Orleans Circuits (at Saint Johnsbury, Saint Albans, North Hero, Hyde Park and Newport). Superior Court sits at each county seat and has general jurisdiction over criminal and civil actions, real estate and domestic relations. The Supreme Court is the court of last resort.

The town offices house land records and vital records.

Counties

Addison County Courthouse
Route 7 South
5 Court Street
Middlebury, VT 05753-1405
Phone (802) 388-4237
County organized 1785 from Rutland and Chittenden counties
Naturalization records: Contact Public Records Division, General Services Division, U.S. Route 2, Middlesex, PO Drawer 33, Montpelier, VT 05633-7601
Probate records: Contact Addison Probate District (see address pg. 349)

*Bennington County Courthouse
207 South Street
Bennington, VT 05201-0157
Phone (802) 447-2700
County organized 1779, original county
Land records: Glastenbury (unorganized town) land records from 1833
Naturalization records: Contact Public Records Division, General Services Division, U.S. Route 2, Middlesex, PO Drawer 33, Montpelier, VT 05633-7601
Vital records: Glastenbury vital records from 1833
Probate records: Contact Bennington Probate District (see address below) or Manchester District Probate Court (see address pg. 350)

Caledonia County Courthouse
27 Main Street
Saint Johnsbury, VT 05819-2637
Phone (802) 748-3813
County organized 1792 from unorganized territory

Naturalization records: Contact Public Records Division, General Services Division, U.S. Route 2, Middlesex, PO Drawer 33, Montpelier, VT 05633-7601

Probate records: Contact Caledonia Probate District (see address pg. 350)

*Chittenden County Courthouse
175 Main Street
PO Box 187
Burlington, VT 05402
County organized 1787, original county
Naturalization records: Contact Public Records Division, General Services Division, U.S. Route 2, Middlesex, PO Drawer 33, Montpelier, VT 05633-7601

Probate records: Contact Chittenden Probate District (see address pg. 350)

*Essex County Courthouse
Guildhall, VT 05905
Phone (802) 676-3910
County organized 1792 from unorganized territory
Naturalization records: Contact Public Record Division, General Services Division, U.S. Route 2, Middlesex, PO Drawer 33, Montpelier, VT 05633-7601

Vital records: Kept only for unorganized Towns and Government of Essex County; contact Ellen R. Ramsdell, Clerk, Essex Superior Court, PO Box 75, Guildhall, VT 05905

Probate records: Contact Essex District Probate Court (see address pg. 350)

Franklin County Courthouse
Church Street
Saint Albans, VT 05478
Phone (802) 524-2739
County organized 1792 from Chittenden County
Naturalization records: Contact Public Records Division, General Services Division, U.S. Route 2, Middlesex, PO Drawer 33, Montpelier, VT 05633-7601

Probate records: Contact Franklin Probate District (see address pg. 350)

Grand Isle County Courthouse
PO Box 7
North Hero, VT 05474-0007
Phone (802) 372-8350
County organized 1802 from Franklin County
Naturalization records: Contact Public Records Division, General Services Division, U.S. Route 2, Middlesex, PO Drawer 33, Montpelier, VT 05633-7601

Probate records: Contact Grand Isle Probate District (see address pg. 350)

*Lamoille County Courthouse
PO Box 303
Hyde Park, VT 05655-0303
Phone (802) 888-2207
County organized 1835 from Orleans and Chittenden counties
Land records: Limited and badly indexed land records
Naturalization records: To the year transferred to Burlington and Saint Albans
Probate records: Contact Lamoille Probate District (see address pg. 350)

*Orange County Court
Rt. 1, Box 30
Chelsea, VT 05038-9746
Phone (802) 685-4610
County organized 1781 from Windsor and Caledonia counties
Land records: From 1771 to 1850 (most land records in Town Clerks' Offices)
Naturalization records: Contact Public Records Division, General Services Division, U.S. Route 2, Middlesex, PO Drawer 33, Montpelier, VT 05633-7601
Vital records: No vital records
Probate records: From 1781; contact Orange District Probate Court (see address pg. 351)

*Orleans County Courthouse
83 Main Street
PO Box 787
Newport, VT 05855-0787
Phone (802) 334-3344
County organized 1792, original county
Land records: Contact each individual town
Naturalization records: To 1990; contact Clerk
Vital records: Contact each town
Probate records: Contact Register, Orleans Probate District (see address pg. 351)

*Rutland Superior Court
83 Center Street
Rutland, VT 05701-4017
Phone (802) 775-0114
County organized 1781, original county
Naturalization records: Contact Public Records Division, General Services Division, U.S. Route 2, Middlesex, PO Drawer 33, Montpelier, VT 05633-7601
Probate records: Contact Rutland Probate Court (see address below) or Fair Haven Probate Court (see address pg. 351)

*Washington County Courthouse
PO Box 426
Montpelier, VT 05602-0426
Phone (802) 223-2091

County organized 1810 from Addison and Orange counties
Land records: No land records
Naturalization records: Contact Public Records Division, General Services Division, U.S. Route 2, Middlesex, PO Drawer 33, Montpelier, VT 05633-7601
Vital records: No vital records
Probate records: Contact Washington Probate District (see address pg. 351)

*Windham Superior Court
PO Box 207
Newfane, VT 05345
Phone (802) 365-7979
County organized 1779, original county
Land records: Contact town clerks where land is located
Naturalization records: Contact Public Records Division, General Services Division, U.S. Route 2, Middlesex, PO Drawer 33, Montpelier, VT 05633-7601
Vital records: Contact town clerks
Probate records: Contact Marlboro Probate District (see address pg. 350) or Westminster District Probate Court (see address pg. 351)

*Windsor County Clerk
12 The Green
PO Box 458
Woodstock, VT 05091-1212
Phone (802) 457-2121
County organized 1781, original county
Land records: No land records
Naturalization records: Contact Public Records Division, General Services Division, U.S. Route 2, Middlesex, PO Drawer 33, Montpelier, VT 05633-7601 and Vermont Historical Society, Pavilion Office Building, 109 State Street, Montpelier, VT 05609-0901
Vital records: No vital records
Probate records: Contact Windsor District Probate Court (see address below) or The Hartford District Probate Court (see address pg. 351)

Probate Districts

(probate records only)

Addison Probate District
Marble Works
Middlebury, VT 05753-1405
Phone (802) 388-2612
Probate records: For all of Addison County, including City of Vergennes and the towns of Addison, Bridport, Bristol, Cornwall, Ferrisburg, Goshen, Granville, Hancock, Leicester,

Lincoln, Middlebury, Monkton, New
Haven, Orwell, Panton, Ripton,
Salisbury, Shoreham, Starksboro,
Waltham, Weybridge and Whiting

*Bennington Probate District
207 South Street
PO Box 65
Bennington, VT 05201-0065
Phone (802) 447-2705
Land records: No land records
Naturalization records: No naturalization
    records
Vital records: No vital records
Probate records: From the 1770s for the
    towns of Bennington, Glastenbury,
    Pownal, Readsboro, Searsburg,
    Shaftsbury, Stamford and Woodford
    (remainder of Bennington County
    covered by Manchester District
    Probate Court); contact Debbie J.
    Briggs, Register
No probate search service; copies: 25¢
    per page, $1.00 minimum

Bradford Probate District
(consolidated into Orange District
    Probate Court)

Caledonia Probate District
27 Main Street
Saint Johnsbury, VT 05819-2637
Phone (802) 748-6605
Probate records: For all of Caledonia
    County, including the towns of Barnet,
    Burke, Danville, Groton, Hardwick,
    Kirby, Lyndon, Newark, Peacham,
    Ryegate, Saint Johnsbury, Sheffield,
    Stannard, Sutton, Walden, Waterford
    and Wheelock

*Chittenden Probate District
175 Main Street
PO Box 511
Burlington, VT 05402
Phone (802) 864-7481
Land records: No land records
Naturalization records: No naturalization
    records
Vital records: No vital records
Probate records: For all of Chittenden
    County, including Buel's Gore, Essex
    Junction, City of Burlington, City of
    Winooski and the towns of Bolton,
    Charlotte, Colchester, Essex,
    Hinesburg, Huntington, Jericho,
    Milton, Richmond, Saint George,
    Shelburne, South Burlington,
    Underhill, Westford and Williston;
    contact Probate Register, Probate
    Court
Probate search service: no charge;
    copies: 25¢ per page, $1.00 minimum;
    "Prepaid—we cannot bill."

*Essex District Probate Court
(Main Street—location)
PO Box 426 (mailing address)
Island Pond, VT 05846
Phone (802) 723-4770
Land records: No land records
Naturalization records: No naturalization
    records
Vital records: No vital records
Probate records: Estates, trusts and
    guardian estates from about 1869
    (index cards for the prior years) for all
    of Essex County, including Avery's
    Gore, Warner's Grant, Warren's Gore
    and the towns of Averill, Bloomfield,
    Brighton, Brunswick, Canaan,
    Concord, East Haven, Ferdinand,
    Granby, Guildhall, Lemington, Lewis,
    Lunenburg, Maidstone, Norton and
    Victory; contact Marilyn W. Maxwell,
    Probate Judge, or Joan G. Watson,
    Register of Probate. Probate records:
    From 1791 to 1855; contact Public
    Records Division, General Services
    Division, U.S. Route 2, Middlesex,
    PO Drawer 33, Montpelier, VT
    05633-7601
Probate search service: no charge;
    copies: 25¢ per page, $1.00 minimum

*Fair Haven Probate Court
3 North Park Place
Fair Haven, VT 05743
Phone (802) 265-3380
Land records: No land records
Naturalization records: No naturalization
    records
Vital records: No vital records
Probate records: From 1797 for the
    towns of Benson, Castleton, Fair
    Haven, Hubbardton, Pawlet, Poultney,
    Sudbury, Wells and West Haven
    (remainder of Rutland County covered
    by Rutland Probate Court); contact
    Mrs. Maureen F. Clement, Register
No probate search service; copies: 25¢
    per page, $1.00 minimum

Franklin Probate District
Church Street
Saint Albans, VT 05478
Phone (802) 524-7948
*County organized 1792 from Chittenden
County*
Probate records: For all of Franklin
    County, including Saint Albans City
    and the towns of Bakersfield,
    Berkshire, Enosburg, Fairfax,
    Fairfield, Fletcher, Franklin, Georgia,
    Highgate, Montgomery, Richford,
    Saint Albans, Sheldon and Swanton

Grand Isle Probate District
PO Box 7
North Hero, VT 05474-0007
Phone (802) 372-8350
Probate records: From 1820 for all of

Grand Isle County, including the
towns of Alburg, Isle La Motte, Grand
Isle, North Hero and South Hero;
contact the Clerk
No probate search service; copies: 10¢
each

*The Hartford District Probate Court
PO Box 275
Woodstock, VT 05091
Phone (802) 457-1503 Clerk
Probate records: Estates, adoptions
    (confidential), trust, guardianships and
    change of names for the towns of
    Barnard, Bethel, Bridgewater,
    Hartford, Hartland, Norwich, Pomfret,
    Rochester, Royalton, Sharon,
    Stockbridge and Woodstock
    (remainder of Windsor County
    covered by Windsor District Probate
    Court); contact Twila B. Nemkovich,
    Clerk
Probate search service: 25¢ per page,
    $1.00 minimum

*Lamoille Probate District
PO Box 102
Hyde Park, VT 05655
Phone (802) 888-3306
Land records: No land records
Naturalization records: No naturalization
    records
Vital records: Corrections only
Probate records: For all of Lamoille
    County, including the towns of
    Belvidere, Cambridge, Eden, Elmore,
    Hyde Park, Johnson, Morristown,
    Stowe, Waterville and Wolcott from
    1837; contact Register, Lamoille
    Probate Court
Probate search service: no charge;
    copies: 25¢ per page, $1.00 minimum

*Manchester District Probate Court
Rt. 7, Box 446
Manchester, VT 05254
Phone (802) 362-1410
District organized 1771
Land records: No land records
Naturalization records: No naturalization
    records
Vital records: No vital records
Probate records: From 1771 for the
    towns of Arlington, Dorset,
    Landgrove, Manchester, Peru, Rupert,
    Sandgate, Sunderland and Winhall
    (remainder of Bennington County
    covered by Bennington Probate
    District); contact Jane P. Robertson,
    Register
Probate search service: no charge;
    copies: 25¢ per page, $1.00 minimum

*Marlboro Probate District
West River Road
PO Box 523
Brattleboro, VT 05302

Phone (802) 257-2898

Land records: No land records

Naturalization records: No naturalization records

Vital records: No vital records

Probate records: For the towns of Brattleboro, Dover, Dummerston, Guilford, Halifax, Marlboro, Newfane, Stratton, Somerset, Vernon, Wardsboro, Whitingham and Wilmington (remainder of Windham County covered by Westminster District Probate Court)

*Orange District Probate Court

Rt. 1, Box 30

Chelsea, VT 05038-9746

Phone (802) 685-4610

Consolidated Randolph (organized 1781) and Bradford districts 1 June 1994

Land records: No land records

Naturalization records: No naturalization records

Vital records: No vital records

Probate records: For all of Orange County, including the towns of Bradford, Braintree, Brookfield, Chelsea, Corinth, Fairlee, Newbury, Orange, Randolph, Strafford, Thetford, Topsham, Tunbridge, Vershire, Washington, West Fairlee and Williamstown; contact Dorothy Fuchs, Register

*Orleans Probate District

83 Main Street

PO Box 787

Newport, VT 05855-0787

Phone (802) 334-2711; (802) 334-3366

Probate records: For all of Orleans County, including Newport City and the towns of Albany, Barton, Brownington, Charleston, Coventry, Craftsbury, Derby, Glover, Greensboro, Holland, Irasburg, Jay, Lowell, Morgan, Newport, Troy, Westfield and Westmore; contact Register

Probate search service: varies; copies: 25¢ per page, $1.00 minimum for document of less than four pages

*Randolph District Courthouse

(consolidated into Orange District Probate Court)

Rutland Probate Court

83 Center Street

PO Box 339

Rutland, VT 05701-4017

Phone (802) 775-0114; (802) 775-0115

Probate records: For Rutland City and the towns of Brandon, Chittenden, Clarendon, Danby, Ira, Mendon, Middletown Springs, Mount Holly,

Mount Tabor, Pittsfield, Pittsford, Proctor, Rutland, Sherburne, Shrewsbury, Tinmouth, Wallingford and West Rutland (remainder of Rutland County covered by Fair Haven Probate Court)

Probate search service: no charge for check of index; copies: 25¢ per page, $1.00 minimum

*Washington Probate District

PO Box 15

Montpelier, VT 05601-0015

Phone (802) 828-3405

Land records: No land records

Naturalization records: No naturalization records

Vital records: No vital records

Probate records: For all of Washington County, including Barre City, City of Montpelier and the towns of Barre, Berlin, Cabot, Calais, Duxbury, East Montpelier, Fayston, Marshfield, Middlesex, Moretown, Northfield, Plainfield, Roxbury, Waitsfield, Warren, Waterbury, Woodbury and Worcester

Probate search service: no charge; copies: 25¢ per page

*Westminster District Probate Court

PO Box 47

Bellows Falls, VT 05101-0047

Phone (802) 463-3019

District organized 1700s

Probate records: From the 1700s for the towns of Athens, Brookline, Grafton, Jamaica, Londonderry, Putney, Rockingham, Townshend, Westminster and Windham (remainder of Windham County covered by Marlboro Probate District)

Probate search service: no charge; copies: 25¢ per page, $1.00 minimum; "Fees must be paid in advance."

*Windsor District Probate Court

(Route 106, Cota Fuel Building—location)

PO Box 402 (mailing address)

North Springfield, VT 05150-0402

Phone (802) 886-2284

District organized 1763

Vital records: Corrections of birth, marriage or death certificates from Middlesex and Burlington

Probate records: Estates, guardianships, adoptions for the towns of Andover, Baltimore, Cavendish, Chester, Ludlow, Plymouth, Reading, Springfield, Weathersfield, West Windsor, Weston and Windsor (remainder of Windsor County covered by The Hartford District Probate Court); contact Brenda S. Neronsky, Register

Probate search service: no charge; copies: 25¢ per page, $1.00 minimum

Towns and Cities

(land and vital records only)

*Town of Addison

RD 1

Vergennes, VT 05491

Phone (802) 759-2020

Formed 1761 (Addison Probate District, Addison County)

Land records: Contact Jane B. Grace, Town Clerk

Land records search service: $5.00 per hour; copies: $1.00 per page, $6.00 per page for certified copies

Naturalization records: No naturalization records

Vital records: Births, deaths and marriages; contact Town Clerk

Land records search service: $5.00 per hour; copies: $1.00 per page, $6.00 per page for certified copies

Probate records: No probate records

*Town of Albany

c/o Town Clerk

PO Box 284

Albany, VT 05820-0284

Phone (802) 755-6100

Formed 1782 (Orleans Probate District, Orleans County)

Land records: Yes

Land records search service: $5.00 per hour; copies: $1.00 per page

Naturalization records: No naturalization records

Vital records: Yes

Vital records search service: $5.00 per hour; copies: $1.00 per page

*Town of Alburg

PO Box 346

Alburg, VT 05440

Phone (802) 796-3468

Formed 1781 (Grand Isle Probate District, Grand Isle County)

Land records: From about 1792 to date; contact Town Clerk

Land records search service: no charge

Naturalization records: No naturalization records

Vital records: From about 1792 to date

Vital records search service: no charge

Probate records: No probate records

*Town of Andover

Rural Route 1, Box 179

Chester, VT 05143

Phone (802) 875-2765

Formed 1761 (Windsor District Probate Court, Windsor County)

Land records: Yes

Naturalization records: No naturalization
      records
Vital records: Yes
Probate records: No probate records

Town of Arlington
PO Box 186
Arlington, VT 05250
Formed 1761 (Manchester District
      Probate Court, Bennington County)

Town of Athens
c/o Miriam Sonderquist, Town Clerk
Rt. 3, Box 195C
Chester, VT 05143
Phone (802) 869-3370
Formed 1780 (Westminster District
      Probate Court, Windham County)
Land records: Yes
Naturalization records: No naturalization
      records
Vital records: Yes
Probate records: No probate records

Town of Averill (unorganized)
Formed 1762 (Essex District Probate
      Court, Essex County)

Avery's Gore
(Essex District Probate Court, Essex
      County)

*Town of Bakersfield
c/o Town Clerk
PO Box 203
Bakersfield, VT 05441
Phone (802) 827-4495
Formed 1791 (Franklin Probate
      District, Franklin County)
Land records: Yes
Vital records: Yes

*Town of Baltimore
RD 4, Box 365
Chester, VT 05143
Phone (802) 263-5419
Formed 1793 (Windsor District Probate
      Court, Windsor County)
Land records: Yes
Naturalization records: No naturalization
      records
Vital records: Yes
Probate records: No probate records

*Town of Barnard
PO Box 274
Barnard, VT 05031
Phone (802) 234-9211
Formed 1761 (The Hartford District
      Probate Court, Windsor County)
Land records: From 1781 to date
Naturalization records: No naturalization
      records
Vital records: From 1774 to date
Probate records: No probate records

*Town of Barnet
PO Box 15
Barnet, VT 05821
Phone (802) 633-2256
Formed 1763 (Caledonia Probate
      District, Caledonia County)
Land records: From 1783; copies: 25¢
      each, $5.00 each for certified copies
Naturalization records: No naturalization
      records
Vital records: From 1783; copies: 25¢
      each, $5.00 each for certified copies
Probate records: No probate records

*Barre City
Box 418
Barre, VT 05641
Phone (802) 479-9391
Formed 1894 (Washington Probate
      District, Washington County)
Land records: Yes
Vital records: Yes

*Barre Town
Municipal Building
Websterville, VT 05678
Phone (802) 479-9391
Formed 1781 (Washington Probate
      District, Washington County)

*Town of Barton
PO Box R
Barton, VT 05822
Phone (802) 525-6222
Formed 1789 (Orleans Probate District,
      Orleans County)
Land records: Yes
Naturalization records: No naturalization
      records
Vital records: Yes
Probate records: No probate records

Town of Belvidere
Belvidere Center, VT 05442
Formed 1791 (Lamoille Probate
      District, Lamoille County)

Town of Bennington
205 South Street
Bennington, VT 05201
Formed 1749 (Bennington Probate
      District, Bennington County)

Town of Benson
PO Box 163
Benson, VT 05731
Formed 1780 (Fair Haven Probate
      Court, Rutland County)

Town of Berkshire
Rt. 1
Enosburg Falls, VT 05450
Formed 1781 (Franklin Probate
      District, Franklin County)

*Town of Berlin
Rt. 4, Box 2375
Montpelier, VT 05602
Phone (802) 229-9298
Formed 1763 (Washington Probate
      District, Washington County)
Land records: Contact Dorothy B.
      Hartman, Town Clerk; copies: 50¢
      each
Naturalization records: No naturalization
      records
Vital records: Contact Town Clerk;
      certified copies: $5.00 each
Probate records: No probate records

*Town of Bethel
c/o Town Clerk
(South Main Street—location)
Rural Route 2, Box 85 (mailing address)
Bethel, VT 05032
Phone (802) 234-9722
Formed 1779 (The Hartford District
      Probate Court, Windsor County)
Land records: Yes
Land records search service: $5.00 per
      hour; copies: $1.00 per page
Naturalization records: No naturalization
      records
Vital records: Yes
Vital records search service: $5.00 per
      hour; certified copies: $5.00 each
Probate records: No probate records

*Town of Bloomfield
PO Box 336
North Stratford, NH 03590
Phone (802) 962-5191
Formed 1762 (Essex District Probate
      Court, Essex County)

Town of Bolton
Rt. 1
Waterbury, VT 05676
Formed 1763 (Chittenden Probate
      District, Chittenden County)

Town of Bradford
Main Street
Bradford, VT 05033
Formed 1770 (Orange District Probate
      Court, Orange County)

*Town of Braintree
c/o Janice L. Thresher, Town Clerk
Rt. 1, Box 316A
Randolph, VT 05060
Phone (802) 728-9787
Formed 1781 (Orange District Probate
      Court, Orange County)
Land records: From 1781 to date
Land records search service: $5.00 per
      hour; copies: $1.00 per record, $6.00
      per page for certified copies
Naturalization records: No naturalization
      records

Vital records: From 1857 to date
Vital records search service: $5.00 per hour; copies: $5.00 each
Probate records: No probate records

*Town of Brandon
49 Center Street
Brandon, VT 05733
Phone (802) 247-5721
Formed 1761 (Rutland Probate Court, Rutland County)
Land records: From 1761 to date; copies: $1.00 per page
Naturalization records: No naturalization records
Vital records: Births from 1775, deaths from 1803, marriages from 1795
Probate records: No probate records

*Town of Brattleboro
c/o Annette L. Cappy, Town Clerk
230 Main Street
Brattleboro, VT 05301
Phone (802) 254-4541
Formed 1753 (Marlboro Probate District, Windham County)
Land records: From 1753
Naturalization records: No naturalization records
Vital records: From 1753
Probate records: No probate records

*Town of Bridgewater
c/o Town Clerk's Office
PO Box 14
Bridgewater, VT 05034
Phone (802) 672-3334
Formed 1761 (The Hartford District Probate Court, Windsor County)
Land records: Yes; copies: $1.00 per page
Naturalization records: No naturalization records
Vital records: Yes; certified copies: $5.00 each
Probate records: No probate records

*Town of Bridport
PO Box 27
Bridport, VT 05734-0027
Phone (802) 758-2483
Formed 1761 (Addison Probate District, Addison County)
Land records: From 1760
Naturalization records: No naturalization records
Vital records: From 1748
Probate records: No probate records

*Town of Brighton
PO Box 377
Island Pond, VT 05846
Phone (802) 723-4405
Formed 1781 (Essex District Probate Court, Essex County)

Land records: From 1832 to date; copies: 25¢ each
Vital records: From 1860 to date; copies: 25¢ each

Town of Bristol
1 South Street
Bristol, VT 05443
Formed 1762 (Addison Probate District, Addison County)

Town of Brookfield
PO Box 423
Brookfield, VT 05636
Formed 1781 (Orange District Probate Court, Orange County)

Town of Brookline
c/o Joyce Rogers, Town Clerk
PO Box 943
Newfane, VT 05345
Phone (802) 365-7537
Formed 1794 (Westminster District Probate Court, Windham County)

*Town of Brownington
Rt. 2, Box 158
Orleans, VT 05860
Phone (802) 754-8401
Formed 1790 (Orleans Probate District, Orleans County)
Land records: Yes
Naturalization records: No naturalization records
Vital records: Yes
Probate records: No probate records

Town of Brunswick
Rt. 1, Box 470
Guildhall, VT 05905
Formed 1761 (Essex District Probate Court, Essex County)

Buel's Gore
(Chittenden Probate District, Chittenden County)

Town of Burke
West Burke, VT 05871
Formed 1782 (Caledonia Probate District, Caledonia County)

*City of Burlington
Office of the City Clerk
Room #20, City Hall
Burlington, VT 05401
Phone (802) 865-7131
Formed 1763 (Chittenden Probate District, Chittenden County)
Land records: Yes
Naturalization records: No naturalization records
Vital records: Yes
Probate records: No probate records

*Town of Cabot
c/o Christopher Kaldor, Town Clerk
PO Box 36
Cabot, VT 05647
Phone (802) 563-2279
Formed 1781 (Washington Probate District, Washington County)

Town of Calais
PO Box 35
Calais, VT 05648
Formed 1781 (Washington Probate District, Washington County)

Town of Cambridge
Jeffersonville, VT 05464
Formed 1781 (Lamoille Probate District, Lamoille County)

*Town of Canaan
PO Box 159
Canaan, VT 05903
Phone (802) 266-3370
Formed 1782 (Essex District Probate Court, Essex County)
Land records: From 1796 to date
Naturalization records: No naturalization records
Vital records: From 1857 to date
Probate records: No probate records

*Town of Castleton
c/o Town Clerk
PO Box 115
Castleton, VT 05735
Formed 1761 (Fair Haven Probate Court, Rutland County)
Land records: Yes
Naturalization records: No naturalization records
Vital records: Yes
Probate records: No probate records

*Town of Cavendish
PO Box 126
Cavendish, VT 05145
Phone (802) 226-7292
Formed 1761 (Windsor District Probate Court, Windsor County)
Land records: Yes
Naturalization records: No naturalization records
Vital records: Yes
Probate records: No probate records

*Town of Charleston
c/o Jeannine Bennett, Clerk/Treasurer
HCR 61, Box 26
West Charleston, VT 05872
Phone (802) 895-2814
Chartered as Town of Navy 1780, name changed to Charleston 1825 (Orleans Probate District, Orleans County)
Land records: From 1780 to date; copies: $1.00 per page, $2.00 minimum per deed

Naturalization records: No naturalization records
Vital records: From 1803 to date; certified copies: $5.00 each
Probate records: No probate records

*Town of Charlotte
c/o Mary Bonn, Town Clerk
PO Box 119
Charlotte, VT 05445
Formed 1762 (Chittenden Probate District, Chittenden County)
Land records: Yes; copies: $1.00 per page of recorded documents, $5.00 for certified copies
Vital records: Yes; copies: $1.00 per page of recorded documents, $5.00 for certified copies

*Town of Chelsea
PO Box 266
Chelsea, VT 05038
Phone (802) 685-4460
Formed 1781 (Orange District Probate Court, Orange County)
Land records: Yes
Naturalization records: No naturalization records
Vital records: Yes
Probate records: No probate records

Town of Chester
PO Box 86
Chester Depot, VT 05144
Formed 1754 (Windsor District Probate Court, Windsor County)

Town of Chittenden
Chittenden, VT 05737
Formed 1780 (Rutland Probate Court, Rutland County)

*Town of Clarendon
PO Box 30
North Clarendon, VT 05759
Phone (802) 775-4274
Formed 1761 (Rutland Probate Court, Rutland County)
Land records: Yes
Naturalization records: No naturalization records
Vital records: Yes
Probate records: No probate records

*Town of Colchester
172 Blakely Road
PO Box 55
Colchester, VT 05446
Phone (802) 655-0811
Formed 1763 (Chittenden Probate District, Chittenden County)
Land records: From 1922. Land records prior to 1922: contact Winooski City Clerk's Office

Land records search service: $2.00 per hour; copies: $1.00 per page
Vital records: From 1922. Vital records prior to 1922: contact Winooski City Clerk's Office
Vital records search service: $2.00 per hour; copies: $2.00 each, $5.00 for certified copies

*Town of Concord
c/o Town Clerk
Main Street, Box 316
Concord, VT 05824
Phone (802) 695-2220
Formed 1781 (Essex District Probate Court, Essex County)

Town of Corinth
c/o Town Clerk
Corinth, VT 05039
Phone (802) 439-5850
(Orange District Probate Court, Orange County)

*Town of Cornwall
Rural Delivery 4, Box 680
Middlebury, VT 05753
Phone (802) 462-2919
Formed 1761 (Addison Probate District, Addison County)
Land records: Yes
Naturalization records: No naturalization records
Vital records: Yes
Probate records: No probate records

*Town of Coventry
PO Box 158
Coventry, VT 05825
Phone (802) 754-2288
Formed 1761 (Orleans Probate District, Orleans County)
Land records: From 1913 to date; contact Town Clerk
Land records search service: $5.00 per hour; copies: $1.00 per page, $6.00 each for uncertified copies; $2.00 minimum
Vital records: From 1913 to date; contact Town Clerk
Vital records search service: $5.00 per hour; certified copies: $5.00 each (application must be filed)

Town of Craftsbury
Craftsbury, VT 05826
Formed 1781 (Orleans Probate District, Orleans County)

*Town of Danby
Box 231, School Street
Danby, VT 05739
Phone (802) 293-5136
Formed 1761 (Rutland Probate Court, Rutland County)

*Town of Danville
PO Box 183
Danville, VT 05828
Phone (802) 684-3352
Formed 1786 (Caledonia Probate District, Caledonia County)
Land records: Contact Clerk; copies: $1.00 per page, no minimum
Naturalization records: No naturalization records
Vital records: Contact Clerk; certified copies: $5.00 each, no minimum, no restrictions on public records

*Town of Derby
PO Box 25
Derby, VT 05829
Phone (802) 766-4906
Formed 1779 (Orleans Probate District, Orleans County)
Land records: From 1800 to date; copies: $1.00 per page
Naturalization records: No naturalization records
Vital records: From 1800 to date; certified copies: $5.00 per page
Probate records: No probate records

Town of Dorset
Mad Tom Road
East Dorset, VT 05253
Formed 1761 (Manchester District Probate Court, Bennington County)

Town of Dover
c/o Virginia Carruthers, Town Clerk
PO Box 527
West Dover, VT 05356
Phone (802) 464-5100
Formed 1764 (Marlboro Probate District, Windham County)

*Town of Dummerston
c/o Janice C. Duke, Town Clerk
Rt. 2, Box 199
Putney, VT 05346
Phone (802) 257-1496
Formed 1753 (Marlboro Probate District, Windham County)
Land records: From the late 1700s
Vital records: From the late 1700s

Town of Duxbury
Rt. 2, Box 1260
Waterbury, VT 05676
Formed 1763 (Washington Probate District, Washington County)

Town of East Haven
PO Box 43
East Haven, VT 05837
Formed 1790 (Essex District Probate Court, Essex County)

Town of East Montpelier
PO Box 157
East Montpelier, VT 05651
Formed 1848 (Washington Probate District, Washington County)

Town of Eden
PO Box 3
Eden Mills, VT 05653
Formed 1781 (Lamoille Probate District, Lamoille County)

Town of Elmore
Lake Elmore, VT 05657
Formed 1781 (Lamoille Probate District, Lamoille County)

*Town of Enosburg
PO Box 465
Enosburg Falls, VT 05450
Phone (802) 933-4421
Formed 1780 (Franklin Probate District, Franklin County)
Land records: Contact Carolyn Stimpson, Town Clerk
Vital records: Contact Town Clerk; certified copies: $5.00 each

Town of Essex
81 Main Street
Essex Junction, VT 05452
Formed 1763 (Chittenden Probate District, Chittenden County)

*Town of Fair Haven
North Park Place
Fair Haven, VT 05743
Phone (802) 265-3610
Formed 1779 (Fair Haven Probate Court, Rutland County)
Land records: Contact Town Clerk
Vital records: Contact Town Clerk
Probate records: No probate records

*Town of Fairfax
Box 27, Hunt Street
Fairfax, VT 05454
Phone (802) 849-6111
Formed 1763 (Franklin Probate District, Franklin County)
Land records: From the late 1700s
Naturalization records: No naturalization records
Vital records: From the late 1700s
Probate records: No probate records

*Town of Fairfield
c/o G. F. Longway, Town Clerk
PO Box 5
Fairfield, VT 05455
Formed 1763 (Franklin Probate District, Franklin County)
Land records: Yes
Land records search service: $5.00 (no title searches)

Naturalization records: No naturalization records
Vital records: Yes; certified copies: $5.00
Probate records: No probate records

*Town of Fairlee
PO Box 95
Fairlee, VT 05045
Phone (802) 333-4363
Formed 1761 (Orange District Probate Court, Orange County)
Land records: Contact Georgette Wolf-Ludwig, Town Clerk; copies: $1.00 per page
Naturalization records: No naturalization records
Vital records: Contact Town Clerk; copies: $1.00 per page
Probate records: No probate records

Town of Fayston
Rt. 1, Box 1594
Moretown, VT 05660
Formed 1782 (Washington Probate District, Washington County)

Town of Ferdinand (unorganized)
Formed 1761 (Essex District Probate Court, Essex County)

*Town of Ferrisburg
Main Street, Box 6
Ferrisburg, VT 05456
Phone (802) 877-3429
Formed 1762 (Addison Probate District, Addison County)
Land records: Yes
Naturalization records: No naturalization records
Vital records: Yes
Probate records: No probate records

*Town of Fletcher
Rt. 1, Box 1550
Cambridge, VT 05444
Phone (802) 849-6616
Formed 1781 (Franklin Probate District, Franklin County)

Town of Franklin
PO Box 82
Franklin, VT 05457
Formed 1789 (Franklin Probate District, Franklin County)

Town of Georgia
Rt. 2
Saint Albans, VT 05478
Formed 1763 (Franklin Probate District, Franklin County)

Town of Glastenbury (unorganized)
Formed 1761 (Bennington Probate District, Bennington County)

*Town of Glover
c/o Town Clerk
PO Box 226
Glover, VT 05839
Phone (802) 525-6227
Formed 1783 (Orleans Probate District, Orleans County)
Land records: Yes
Vital records: Yes

*Town of Goshen
Rural Route 3, Box 3384
Goshen, VT 05733
Phone (802) 247-6455
Formed 1792, organized 1814 (Addison Probate District, Addison County)
Land records: Yes
Naturalization records: No naturalization records
Vital records: Yes
Probate records: No probate records

Town of Grafton
c/o Cynthia W. Gibbs, Town Clerk
Town Hall
Grafton, VT 05146
Phone (802) 843-2419
Formed 1754 (Westminster District Probate Court, Windham County)

*Town of Granby
PO Box 126
Granby, VT 05840
Phone (802) 328-3611
Formed 1761 (Essex District Probate Court, Essex County)
Land records: Contact Town Clerk
Naturalization records: No naturalization records
Vital records: Contact Town Clerk
Probate records: No probate records

Town of Grand Isle
9 Hyde Road
Grand Isle, VT 05458
Phone (802) 372-8830
Formed 1769 (Grand Isle Probate District, Grand Isle County)
Land records: From 1795 to date; contact Town Clerk
Naturalization records: No naturalization records
Vital records: From 1820 to date (sketchy from 1779 to 1820); contact Town Clerk
Probate records: No probate records

*Town of Granville
Box 66
Granville, VT 05747
Phone (802) 767-4403
Formed 1781 (Addison Probate District, Addison County)

*Town of Greensboro
PO Box 115
Greensboro, VT 05841
Phone (802) 533-2911
Formed 1781 (Orleans Probate District, Orleans County)
Land records: From the early 1800s (some earlier records, destroyed by fire, were replaced)
Land records search service: $5.00 per hour; copies: $1.00 each
Naturalization records: No naturalization records
Vital records: Yes
Vital records search service: $5.00 per hour

*Town of Groton
314 Scott Highway
Groton, VT 05046
Phone (802) 584-3276
Formed 1789 (Caledonia Probate District, Caledonia County)
Land records: Yes
Vital records: Yes

Town of Guildhall
PO Box 27
Guildhall, VT 05905
Formed 1761 (Essex District Probate Court, Essex County)

*Town of Guilford
c/o Barbara B. Oles, Town Clerk
Rt. 3, Box 255
Brattleboro, VT 05301
Phone (802) 254-6857
Formed 1754 (Marlboro Probate District, Windham County)
Land records: From the late 1760s to date
Naturalization records: No naturalization records
Vital records: From the late 1760s to date
Probate records: No probate records

*Town of Halifax
c/o Laura Sumner, Town Clerk
PO Box 45
West Halifax, VT 05358
Phone (802) 368-7390
Formed 1750 (Marlboro Probate District, Windham County)
Land records: Yes
Land records search service: $5.00 per hour; copies: $1.00 per page, $2.00 minimum
Naturalization records: No naturalization records
Vital records: Yes
Vital records search service: $5.00 per hour; certified copies: $5.00 each

Town of Hancock
Hancock, VT 05748

Formed 1781 (Addison Probate District, Addison County)

*Town of Hardwick
Hardwick Town Clerk
PO Box 523
Hardwick, VT 05843
Phone (802) 472-5971
Formed 1781 (Caledonia Probate District, Caledonia County)
Land records: From 1795
Land records search service: $5.00 per hour by Clerks Office personnel
Vital records: From 1795
Vital records search service: $5.00 per hour by Clerks Office personnel

*Town of Hartford
c/o Town Clerk
Municipal Building, 15 Bridge Street
White River Junction, VT 05001
Phone (802) 295-2785
Formed 1761 (The Hartford District Probate Court, Windsor County)
Land records: From 1761 to date
No land records search service; records open to the public during business hours at $2.00 per hour research fee; copies: $1.00 per page
Vital records: From 1857 to date
No vital records search service; records open to the public during business hours at $2.00 per hour research fee; copies: $5.00 each

*Town of Hartland
c/o Clyde A. Jenne, Town Clerk
PO Box 349
Hartland, VT 05048
Phone (802) 436-2444
Chartered 1761, formed 1763 (The Hartford District Probate Court, Windsor County)
Land records: From 1780 to date
Land records search service: $5.00 per hour, $2.00 minimum
Vital records: From 1780 to date
Vital records search service: $5.00 per hour, $2.00 minimum

Town of Highgate
PO Box 67
Highgate Center, VT 05459
Formed 1763 (Franklin Probate District, Franklin County)

*Town of Hinesburg
PO Box 133
Hinesburg, VT 05461
Phone (802) 482-2281
Chartered 1762, formed 1763 (Chittenden Probate District, Chittenden County)
Land records: Contact Office of the Town Clerk and Treasurer; copies: $1.00 each

Naturalization records: No naturalization records
Vital records: Contact Office of the Town Clerk and Treasurer (must complete vital records application form and state relationship)
Probate records: No probate records

*Town of Holland
Rt. 1, Box 37
Derby Line, VT 05830
Phone (802) 895-4440 Town Clerk
Formed 1787; first town meeting 1805 (Orleans Probate District, Orleans County)
Land records: From 1805; copies: $1.00 per page, $2.00 minimum
Naturalization records: No naturalization records
Vital records: From 1805; certified copies: $5.00 each (application required)
Probate records: No probate records

*Town of Hubbardton
Rural Route 1, Box 2828
Fair Haven, VT 05743
Phone (802) 273-2951
Formed 1764 (Fair Haven Probate Court, Rutland County)
Land records: Yes
Vital records: Yes

Town of Huntington
Rt. 1, Box 171A
Huntington, VT 05462
Formed 1762 (Chittenden Probate District, Chittenden County)

*Town of Hyde Park
c/o Town Clerk
PO Box 98
Hyde Park, VT 05655
Phone (802) 888-2300
Formed 1781 (Lamoille Probate District, Lamoille County)
Land records: From the late 1700s to date; copies: $1.00 per page, $5.00 per certified page
Vital records: From the early 1800s to date; copies: $1.00 per page, $5.00 per certified page

*Town of Ira
c/o Town Clerk
RFD 1, West Road
West Rutland, VT 05777-9738
Formed 1780 (Rutland Probate Court, Rutland County)

*Town of Irasburg
PO Box 51
Irasburg, VT 05845
Phone (802) 754-2242
Formed 1781 (Orleans Probate District, Orleans County)

Land records: Contact Town Clerk
Naturalization records: No naturalization records
Vital records: From about 1865; contact Town Clerk
Probate records: No probate records

*Town of Isle La Motte
PO Box 135
Isle La Motte, VT 05463
Formed 1779 (Grand Isle Probate District, Grand Isle County)
Land records: Yes
Naturalization records: No naturalization records
Vital records: Yes; certified copies: $5.00 each
Probate records: No probate records

*Town of Jamaica
c/o Bonnie West, Town Clerk
PO Box 173
Jamaica, VT 05343
Phone (802) 874-4681
Chartered 1780, formed 1792 (Westminster District Probate Court, Windham County)
Land records: From 1780 to date
Naturalization records: No naturalization records
Vital records: From 1780 to date
Probate records: No probate records

Town of Jay
Rt. 2, Box 136
Jay, VT 05859
Formed 1792 (Orleans Probate District, Orleans County)

Town of Jericho
PO Box 67
Jericho, VT 05465
Formed 1763 (Chittenden Probate District, Chittenden County)

*Town of Johnson
PO Box 383
Johnson, VT 05656
Phone (802) 635-2611; (802) 635-9523 FAX
Formed 1792 (Lamoille Probate District, Lamoille County)
Land records: Contact Helen W. Neill, Town Clerk; copies: $2.00 per document
Naturalization records: No naturalization records
Vital records: Contact Town Clerk; copies: $1.00 each, $5.00 each for certified copies
Probate records: No probate records

*Town of Kirby
Rt. 2
Lyndonville, VT 05851
Phone (802) 626-9386

Formed 1790 (Caledonia Probate District, Caledonia County)
Land records: From 1808 to date; contact Wanda Grant
Land records search service: $5.00 per hour; copies: 50¢ per page
Naturalization records: No naturalization records
Vital records: From 1808 to date; contact Wanda Grant
Vital records search service: $5.00 per hour (must state reasons for search); certified copies: $5.00 per page

Town of Landgrove
Rt. 1
Landgrove, VT 05148
Formed 1780 (Manchester District Probate Court, Bennington County)

Town of Leicester
Rt. 2
Brandon, VT 05733
Formed 1761 (Addison Probate District, Addison County)

*Town of Lemington
c/o Diana Ouimette, Town Clerk
Rt. 1, Box 183
Canaan, VT 05903
Formed 1762 (Essex District Probate Court, Essex County)

Town of Lewis (unorganized)
Formed 1762 (Essex District Probate Court, Essex County)

*Town of Lincoln
Rt. 1, Box 1830
Bristol, VT 05443
Phone (802) 453-2980
Formed 1780 (Addison Probate District, Addison County)
Land records: From 1798 to date; contact Sandra Rhodes, Town Clerk
Land records search service: $2.00 per hour; copies: 15¢ per page
Naturalization records: No naturalization records
Vital records: From 1868 to date; contact Town Clerk
Vital records search service: $2.00 per hour; copies: 15¢ per page
Probate records: No probate records

Town of Londonderry
PO Box 118
South Londonderry, VT 05115
Phone (802) 824-3356
Formed 1780 (Westminster District Probate Court, Windham County)

*Town of Lowell
c/o Town Clerk
PO Box 7
Lowell, VT 05847

Phone (802) 744-6559
Formed 1791 (Orleans Probate District, Orleans County)
Land records: From 1791; copies: $1.00 each
Vital records: From the late 1850s to date

Town of Ludlow
PO Box 307
Ludlow, VT 05149
Formed 1791 (Windsor District Probate Court, Windsor County)

Town of Lunenberg
PO Box 54
Lunenberg, VT 05906
Formed 1763 (Essex District Probate Court, Essex County)

Town of Lyndon
20 Park Avenue, Box 167
Lyndonville, VT 05851
Phone (802) 626-5785
Formed 1780 (Caledonia Probate District, Caledonia County)
Land records: Yes
Land records search service: $2.00 per hour plus cost of copies, appointments helpful
Vital records: Yes (identification required)

*Town of Maidstone
(Route 102, Maidstone, VT 05905—location)
PO Box 118 (mailing address)
Guildhall, VT 05905
Phone (802) 676-3210
Formed 1761 (Essex District Probate Court, Essex County)
Land records: Contact Susan Irwin, Clerk
Land records search service: $5.00 per hour; copies: $1.00 each, $2.00 minimum
Vital records: Births from 1768 to 1927, from 1898 to 1913 and from 1894 to 1916, deaths from 1847 to 1858 and from 1786 to 1927, marriages from 1796 to 1926 and from 1860 to 1886; contact Clerk. Births, marriages and deaths from 1891 to 1893; contact Registrar
Vital records search service: $5.00 per hour, certified copies: $5.00 each (no restrictions)

Town of Manchester
c/o Town Clerk
PO Box 909
Manchester Center, VT 05255
Phone (802) 362-1315
Formed 1761 (Manchester District Probate Court, Bennington County)
Land records: Yes; copies: $1.00 per page
Naturalization records: No naturalization records

Vital records: Yes (may require
   identification)
Naturalization records: No naturalization
   records

*Town of Marlboro
c/o Nora Wilson, Town Clerk
PO Box E
Marlboro, VT 05344
Phone (802) 254-2181
*Formed 1751 (Marlboro Probate
   District, Windham County)*
Land records: Yes; copies: $1.00 per
   page, $2.00 minimum, $6.00 per page
   for certified copies
Naturalization records: No naturalization
   records
Vital records: Yes; copies: $5.00 per page
Probate records: No probate records

Town of Marshfield
Marshfield, VT 05658
*Formed 1790 (Washington Probate
   District, Washington County)*

Town of Mendon
Rt. 2, Box 8780
Rutland, VT 05701
*Formed 1781 (Rutland Probate Court,
   Rutland County)*

*Town of Middlebury
c/o Town Clerk
Municipal Building
Middlebury, VT 05733
Phone (802) 388-4041
*Formed 1761 (Addison Probate District,
   Addison County)*
Land records: Yes
Naturalization records: No naturalization
   records
Vital records: Yes
Probate records: No probate records

*Town of Middlesex
Rt. 3, Box 4600
Montpelier, VT 05602
Phone (802) 223-5915
*Formed 1763 (Washington Probate
   District, Washington County)*
Land records: From 1790 to date
Naturalization records: No naturalization
   records
Vital records: From about 1790
Probate records: No probate records

Town of Middletown Springs
Middletown Springs, VT 05757
*Formed 1784 (Rutland Probate Court,
   Rutland County)*

*Town of Milton
PO Box 18
Milton, VT 05468

Phone (802) 893-7344
*Formed 1763 (Chittenden Probate
   District, Chittenden County)*
Land records: Yes
Vital records: Yes

Town of Monkton
Rt. 1, Box 204
North Ferrisburg, VT 05473
*Formed 1762 (Addison Probate District,
   Addison County)*

*Town of Montgomery
PO Box 356
Montgomery Center, VT 05471
Phone (802) 326-4719
*Formed 1789 (Franklin Probate
   District, Franklin County)*
Land records: From 1802 to date
Naturalization records: No naturalization
   records
Vital records: From 1815 to date
Probate records: No probate records

City of Montpelier
City Hall
Main Street
Montpelier, VT 05602
*Formed 1781 (Washington Probate
   District, Washington County)*

Town of Moretown
Rt. 1, Box 635
Moretown, VT 05660
*Formed 1763 (Washington Probate
   District, Washington County)*

Town of Morgan
Morgan, VT 05853
*Formed 1780 (Orleans Probate District,
   Orleans County)*

Town of Morristown
PO Box 398
Morrisville, VT 05661
*Formed 1781 (Lamoille Probate
   District, Lamoille County)*

Town of Mount Holly
School Street, Box 10
Mount Holly, VT 05658
*Formed 1792 (Rutland Probate Court,
   Rutland County)*

*Town of Mount Tabor
Rt. 1, Box 32
Danby, VT 05739
Phone (802) 293-5282
*Formed 1761 (Rutland Probate Court,
   Rutland County)*
Land records: From 8 July 1788
Naturalization records: No naturalization
   records
Vital records: Births from 27 July 1827

to date, deaths from 1 January 1792 to
date, marriages from 10 May 1804 to
date
Probate records: No probate records

Town of Navy
(see Town of Charleston)

Town of New Haven
Rt. 1, Box 4
New Haven, VT 05472
*Formed 1761 (Addison Probate District,
   Addison County)*

Town of Newark
Rt. 1
West Burke, VT 05871
*Formed 1781 (Caledonia Probate
   District, Caledonia County)*

Town of Newbury
PO Box 126
Newbury, VT 05051
*Formed 1763 (Orange District Probate
   Court, Orange County)*

Town of Newfane
c/o Sandra Dowley, Town Clerk
PO Box 36
Newfane, VT 05345
Phone (802) 365-7772
*Formed 1753 (Marlboro Probate
   District, Windham County)*
Vital records: From the 1700s for
   Newfane, South Newfane and
   Williamsville

Newport City
74 Main
Newport, VT 05855
*Formed 1917 (Orleans Probate District,
   Orleans County)*

Newport Town
PO Box 85
Newport Center, VT 05857
*Formed 1802 (Orleans Probate District,
   Orleans County)*
Land records: No land records (contact
   Newport City)
Vital records: No vital records (contact
   Newport City)

Town of North Hero
PO Box 38
North Hero, VT 05474
*Formed 1779 (Grand Isle Probate
   District, Grand Isle County)*

*Town of Northfield
c/o Town Clerk's Office
26 South Main Street
Northfield, VT 05663

Phone (802) 485-5421
**Formed 1781 (Washington Probate
District, Washington County)**
Land records: For Northfield and
Northfield Falls; contact Laurence T.
Robinson, Town Clerk, or Debra J.
Russo, Assistant Town Clerk; copies:
$1.00 per page, 25¢ to 50¢ each for
maps, etc.
Naturalization records: No naturalization
records
Vital records: Contact Town Clerk
Vital records search service: $5.00 per
hour; copies: $1.00 per page, $5.00
for certified copies
Probate records: No probate records

Northfield Falls
(see Town of Northfield)

*Town of Norton
c/o M. E. Nelson, Town Clerk
Norton, VT 05907
**Formed 1779 (Essex District Probate
Court, Essex County)**
Land records: Warranty deeds, quit-claim
deeds and mortgage deeds
Vital records: Births, deaths and
marriages
Probate records: Probate decrees of
distribution

*Town of Norwich
c/o Karen Porter, Town Clerk
PO Box 376
Norwich, VT 05055
Phone (802) 649-1419
**Formed 1761 (The Hartford District
Probate Court, Windsor County)**
Land records: Yes
Land records search service: $5.00 per
hour; copies: $1.00 per page, $6.00
per page for certified copies
Naturalization records: No naturalization
records
Vital records: From 1761 to date
Vital records search service: $5.00 per
hour; copies: $5.00 per page
Probate records: No probate records

Town of Orange
PO Box 233
East Barre, VT 05649
**Formed 1781 (Orange District Probate
Court, Orange County)**

Town of Orwell
PO Box 32
Orwell, VT 05760
**Formed 1763 (Addison Probate District,
Addison County)**

*Town of Panton
Rt. 3
PO Box 174
Vergennes, VT 05491

Phone (802) 475-2333
**Formed 1761 (Addison Probate District,
Addison County)**
Land records: Yes; copies: $1.00 each
Naturalization records: No naturalization
records
Vital records: Yes; certified copies: $5.00
each
Probate records: No probate records

*Town of Pawlet
c/o Town Clerk
PO Box 128
Pawlet, VT 05761-0128
Phone (802) 325-3309
**Formed 1761 (Fair Haven Probate
Court, Rutland County, Town of
Pawlet)**
Land records: From 1765; copies: $1.00
per page
Naturalization records: No naturalization
records
Vital records: From 1762
Probate records: No probate records

Town of Peacham
PO Box 244
Peacham, VT 05862
Phone (802) 592-3218
**Formed 1763 (Caledonia Probate
District, Caledonia County)**
Land records: Contact Clerk
Naturalization records: No naturalization
records
Vital records: Contact Clerk
Probate records: Copies only; contact
Clerk

Town of Peru
Peru, VT 05152
**Formed 1761 (Manchester District
Probate Court, Bennington County)**

*Town of Pittsfield
PO Box 556
Pittsfield, VT 05762
Phone (802) 746-8313
**Formed 1781 (Rutland Probate Court,
Rutland County)**
Land records: Yes
Naturalization records: No naturalization
records
Vital records: Yes

Town of Pittsford
PO Box 8
Pittsford, VT 05763
**Formed 1761 (Rutland Probate Court,
Rutland County)**

Town of Plainfield
Rt. 2, Box 100
Plainfield, VT 05667
**Formed 1788 (Washington Probate
District, Washington County)**

*Town of Plymouth
HC 70, Box 39A
Plymouth, VT 05056
Phone (802) 672-3655
**Formed 1761 (Windsor District Probate
Court, Windsor County)**
Land records: Contact Town Clerk's
Office
Land records search service: $2.00 per
hour; copies: $1.00 per page
Naturalization records: No naturalization
records
Vital records: Contact Town Clerk's
Office
Vital records search service: $2.00 per
hour; certified copies: $5.00 each
Probate records: No probate records

Town of Pomfret
PO Box 286
North Pomfret, VT 05053
**Formed 1761 (The Hartford District
Probate Court, Windsor County)**

*Town of Poultney
c/o Patricia A. McCoy, Town Clerk
86–88 Main Street
Poultney, VT 05764
Phone (802) 287-5761
**Formed 1761 (Fair Haven Probate
Court, Rutland County)**
Land records: From 1862 (when records
were destroyed by fire) to date;
copies: $1.00 per page
Naturalization records: No naturalization
records
Vital records: From 1862 to date; copies:
$1.00 per page

Town of Pownal
Rt. 1, Box 41
Pownal, VT 05261
**Formed 1760 (Bennington Probate
District, Bennington County)**

Town of Proctor
Main Street
Proctor, VT 05765
**Formed 1886 (Rutland Probate Court,
Rutland County)**

*Town of Putney
c/o Anita M. Coomes, Town Clerk
PO Box 233
Putney, VT 05346
Phone (802) 387-5862
**Formed 1753 (Westminster District
Probate Court, Windham County)**
Land records: From earliest records to
date; contact Town of Putney Archives
Naturalization records: No naturalization
records
Vital records: From earliest records to
date; contact Town of Putney Archives
Probate records: No probate records

Town of Randolph
PO Drawer B
Randolph, VT 05060
Formed 1781 (Orange District Probate Court, Orange County)

*Town of Reading
c/o Ms. Gene G. Goodhouse, Assistant
  Town Clerk
PO Box 72
Reading, VT 05062
Phone (802) 484-7250
Formed 1761 (Windsor District Probate Court, Windsor County)
Land records: From 1786 to date
Land records search service: $5.00 per
  hour, $25.00 maximum; copies: $1.00
  per page, $6.00 per page for certified
  copies
Naturalization records: No naturalization
  records
Vital records: From 1786 to date
Vital records search service: $5.00 per
  hour, $25.00 maximum; certified
  copies: $5.00 each
Probate records: No probate records

*Town of Readsboro
PO Box 246
Readsboro, VT 05350
Phone (802) 423-5405
Formed 1764 (Bennington Probate District, Bennington County)
Land records: Contact Mary
  Franceschette, Town Clerk; copies:
  $2.00 per deed
Vital records: Contact Town Clerk

*Town of Richford
PO Box 236
Richford, VT 05476
Phone (802) 848-7751
Formed 1780 (Franklin Probate District, Franklin County)
Land records: Yes
Naturalization records: No naturalization
  records
Vital records: Yes
Probate records: No probate records

*Town of Richmond
PO Box 285
Richmond, VT 05477
Phone (802) 434-2221
Formed 1794 (Chittenden Probate District, Chittenden County)
Land records: Yes
Land records search service: $2.00 per
  hour; copies: $1.00 per page
Vital records: Yes
Vital records search service: no charge

Town of Ripton
PO Box 10
Ripton, VT 05766

Formed 1781 (Addison Probate District, Addison County)

Town of Rochester
School Street, Box 238
Rochester, VT 05767
Formed 1781 (The Hartford District Probate Court, Windsor County)

*Town of Rockingham
c/o Rita M. Bruce, Town Clerk
The Square
PO Box 339
Bellows Falls, VT 05101
Phone (802) 463-3964
Formed 1753 (Westminster District Probate Court, Windham County)
Land records: Yes
Naturalization records: No naturalization
  records
Vital records: From about 1850 to date
Probate records: No probate records

Town of Roxbury
PO Box 53
Roxbury, VT 05669
Formed 1781 (Washington Probate District, Washington County)

*Town of Royalton
PO Box 680
South Royalton, VT 05068
Phone (802) 763-7207
Formed 1769 (The Hartford District Probate Court, Windsor County)

Town of Rupert
PO Box 140
West Rupert, VT 05776
Formed 1761 (Manchester District Probate Court, Bennington County)

Rutland City
City Hall, Box 969
Rutland, VT 05701
Formed 1892 (Rutland Probate Court, Rutland County)

Rutland Town
PO Box 225
Center Rutland, VT 05736
Formed 1761 (Rutland Probate Court, Rutland County)

*Town of Ryegate
PO Box 332
Ryegate, VT 05042
Formed 1763 (Caledonia Probate District, Caledonia County)
Land records: Contact Town Clerk
Vital records: Contact Town Clerk
Probate records: No probate records

*Saint Albans City
100 North Main Street
PO Box 867
Saint Albans, VT 05478
Phone (802) 524-1501
Formed 1902 (Franklin Probate District, Franklin County)
Land records: Yes
Vital records: Yes
Vital records search service: by mail
  only; copies: $5.00 each

*Town of Saint Albans
PO Box 37
Saint Albans Bay, VT 05481
Phone (802) 524-2415
Formed 1763 (Franklin Probate District, Franklin County)
Land records: From 1897 to date (see
  Saint Albans City for records before
  1897)
Naturalization records: No naturalization
  records
Vital records: From 1897 to date;
  certified copies: $5.00 each
Probate records: No probate records

Town of Saint George
Rt. 2, Box 455
Williston, VT 05495
Formed 1763 (Chittenden Probate District, Chittenden County)

Town of Saint Johnsbury
34 Main Street
Saint Johnsbury, VT 05819
Formed 1786 (Caledonia Probate District, Caledonia County)

*Town of Salisbury
Salisbury, VT 05769
Phone (802) 352-4228
Formed 1761 (Addison Probate District, Addison County)
Land records: Yes
Vital records: Yes

*Town of Sandgate
Rt. 1, Box 2466
Sandgate, VT 05250
Phone (802) 375-9075
Formed 1761 (Manchester District Probate Court, Bennington County)
Land records: Contact Town Clerk
Land records search service: $5.00 per
  hour; copies: $1.00 each
Naturalization records: No naturalization
  records
Vital records: Contact Town Clerk
Vital records search service: $5.00 per
  hour; certified copies: $5.00 each
Probate records: Some probate records;
  contact Town Clerk
Probate records search service: $5.00 per
  hour; copies: $1.00 each

*Town of Searsburg
PO Box 157
Wilmington, VT 05363
Phone (802) 464-8081
*Formed 1781 (Bennington Probate
   District, Bennington County)*
Land records: From 1833 to date; contact
   Clerk
Land records search service: $5.00 per
   hour; copies: $1.00 per page
Vital records: From the 1830s to date;
   contact Clerk
Vital records search service: $5.00 per
   hour; certified copies: $5.00 per page

Town of Shaftsbury
PO Box 196
Shaftsbury, VT 05262
*Formed 1761 (Bennington Probate
   District, Bennington County)*

Town of Sharon
PO Box 8
Sharon, VT 05065
*Formed 1761 (The Hartford District
   Probate Court, Windsor County)*

*Town of Sheffield
c/o Kathy Newland, Town Clerk
PO Box 165
Sheffield, VT 05866
Phone (802) 626-8862
*Formed 1793 (Caledonia Probate
   District, Caledonia County)*
Land records: From 1793 to date
Vital records: From 1793 to date

Town of Shelburne
PO Box 88
Shelburne, VT 05482
*Formed 1763 (Chittenden Probate
   District, Chittenden County)*

Town of Sheldon
PO Box 66
Sheldon, VT 05483
*Formed 1763 (Franklin Probate
   District, Franklin County)*

*Town of Sherburne
c/o Sherburne Town Clerk
PO Box 429
Killington, VT 05751
Phone (802) 422-3243
*Formed 1761 (Rutland Probate Court,
   Rutland County)*
Land records: Yes
Vital records: Yes

Town of Shoreham
PO Box 11
Shoreham, VT 05770
*Formed 1761 (Addison Probate District,
   Addison County)*

Town of Shrewsbury
PO Box 658
Cuttingsville, VT 05738
*Formed 1761 (Rutland Probate Court,
   Rutland County)*

Town of Somerset (unorganized)
*Formed 1761 (Marlboro Probate
   District, Windham County)*

Town of South Burlington
575 Dorset Street
South Burlington, VT 05401
*Formed 1864 (Chittenden Probate
   District, Chittenden County)*

*Town of South Hero
PO Box 175
South Hero, VT 05486
*Formed 1779 (Grand Isle Probate
   District, Grand Isle County)*

South Newfane
(see Town of Newfane)

Town of Springfield
96 Main Street
Springfield, VT 05156
*Formed 1761 (Windsor District Probate
   Court, Windsor County)*

*Town of Stamford
Rural Route 1, Box 718, Main Road
Stamford, VT 05352
Phone (802) 694-1361
*Formed 1753 (Bennington Probate
   District, Bennington County)*
Land records: Contact Town Clerk
Land records search service: $5.00 per
   hour
Naturalization records: No naturalization
   records
Vital records: Contact Town Clerk
Vital records search service: $5.00 per
   hour; certified copies: $5.00 each
Probate records: No probate records

Town of Stannard
c/o Town Clerk
Greensboro Bend, VT 05842
*Formed 1798 (Caledonia Probate
   District, Caledonia County)*

*Town of Starksboro
c/o Cheryl Estey, Town Clerk
PO Box 91
Starksboro, VT 05487
Phone (802) 453-2639
*Formed 1780 (Addison Probate District,
   Addison County)*
Land records: Deeds; copies: $1.00 per
   page
Vital records: From 1857

Town of Stockbridge
PO Box 39
Stockbridge, VT 05772
*Formed 1761 (The Hartford District
   Probate Court, Windsor County)*

Town of Stowe
PO Box 248
Stowe, VT 05672
*Formed 1763 (Lamoille Probate
   District, Lamoille County)*

*Town of Strafford
PO Box 27
Strafford, VT 05072
Phone (802) 765-4411
*Formed 1761 (Orange District Probate
   Court, Orange County)*
Land records: From 1761 to date
Naturalization records: No naturalization
   records
Vital records: Some from 1761 to 1857
   and all registered from 1857 to date
Probate records: No probate records

Town of Stratton
c/o Andrew W. King, Town Clerk
PO Box 166
West Wardsboro, VT 05360
Phone (802) 896-6140
*Formed 1761 (Marlboro Probate
   District, Windham County)*

Town of Sudbury
Rt. 1
Sudbury, VT 05733
*Formed 1763 (Fair Haven Probate
   Court, Rutland County)*

Town of Sunderland
PO Box 176
East Arlington, VT 05252
*Formed 1761 (Manchester District
   Probate Court, Bennington County)*

*Town of Sutton
c/o Dorreen S. Devenger, Town Clerk
PO Box 106
Sutton, VT 05867
Phone (802) 467-3377
*Formed 1782 (Caledonia Probate
   District, Caledonia County)*

*Town of Swanton
PO Box 711
Swanton, VT 05488
Phone (802) 868-4421
*Formed 1763 (Franklin Probate
   District, Franklin County)*
Land records: Yes
Land records search service: $2.00 per
   hour
Vital records: Yes
Vital records search service: $2.00 per
   hour

*Town of Thetford
c/o Roberta C. Howard, Town Clerk
PO Box 126
Thetford Center, VT 05075
Phone (802) 785-2922
*Formed 1761 (Orange District Probate
    Court, Orange County)*
Land records: Yes; copies: $1.00 each
Vital records: Yes

*Town of Tinmouth
c/o Gail Fallar, Town Clerk
Rural Route 1, Box 551
Wallingford, VT 05773
Phone (802) 446-2498
*Formed 1761 (Rutland Probate Court,
    Rutland County)*
Land records: From 1761 to date
Naturalization records: No naturalization
    records
Vital records: From the late 1700s to date
Probate records: Whatever is recorded

Town of Topsham
c/o Town Clerk
West Topsham, VT 05086
*Formed 1763 (Orange District Probate
    Court, Orange County)*

Town of Townshend
c/o Janet A. Sleeper, Town Clerk
PO Box 223
Townshend, VT 05353
Phone (802) 365-7300
*Formed 1753 (Westminster District
    Probate Court, Windham County)*

Town of Troy
PO Box 30
North Troy, VT 05869
*Formed 1801 (Orleans Probate District,
    Orleans County)*

*Town of Tunbridge
c/o Helen O'Donnell, Town Clerk
PO Box 6
Tunbridge, VT 05077
Phone (802) 889-5521
*Chartered 3 September 1761 (Orange
    District Probate Court, Orange
    County)*
Land records: From 9 May 1780 to date,
    proprietors' records from 1782 to
    1809 (Vol. A) and from 1788 to 1847
    (Vol. B); copies: 10¢ per page
Naturalization records: No naturalization
    records
Vital records: Births, deaths and
    marriages from 1700 to date; copies:
    $5.00 each
Probate records: Some interspersed
    within the land records

*Town of Underhill
PO Box 32
Underhill Center, VT 05490

Phone (802) 899-4434; (802) 899-2137
    FAX
*Formed 1763 (Chittenden Probate
    District, Chittenden County)*
Land records: Contact Clerk
Naturalization records: No naturalization
    records
Vital records: Contact Clerk
Probate records: No probate records

*City of Vergennes
City Hall
120 Main Street
PO Box 35
Vergennes, VT 05491
Phone (802) 877-2841
*Incorporated 1788 (Addison Probate
    District, Addison County)*
Land records: Yes; copies: $1.00 per
    page for land records, 15¢ per 8½" x
    11" page, 20¢ per 8½" x 14" page,
    25¢ per 11" x 17" page
Vital records: Yes

*Town of Vernon
c/o Sandra B. Harris, Town Clerk
PO Box 116
Vernon, VT 05354
Phone (802) 257-0292; (802) 254-3561
    FAX
*Formed 1672 (Marlboro Probate
    District, Windham County)*

Town of Vershire
Rt. 1, Box 66-C
Vershire, VT 05079
*Formed 1781 (Orange District Probate
    Court, Orange County)*

*Town of Victory
HCR 60, Box 511
North Concord, VT 05858
Phone (802) 328-2400
*Formed 1781 (Essex District Probate
    Court, Essex County)*
Land records: Yes
Naturalization records: No naturalization
    records
Vital records: Yes
Probate records: No probate records

Town of Waitsfield
Rt. 1, Box 390
Waitsfield, VT 05673
*Formed 1782 (Washington Probate
    District, Washington County)*

Town of Walden
c/o Town Clerk
Walden, VT 05873
Phone (802) 563-2220
*Formed 1761 (Caledonia Probate
    District, Caledonia County)*

Town of Wallingford
Rt. 1, Box 57
Wallingford, VT 05773
Phone (802) 446-2336
*(Rutland Probate Court, Rutland
    County)*

*Town of Waltham
Office of Clerk and Treasurer
PO Box 175
Vergennes, VT 05491
Phone (802) 877-3641
*Formed 1764, organized 20 March 1797
    (Addison Probate District, Addison
    County)*
Land records: From 1797 to date
Land records search service: $5.00 per
    hour
Naturalization records: No naturalization
    records
Vital records: From 1868 to date
Vital records search service: $5.00 per
    hour
Probate records: No probate records

Town of Wardsboro
c/o Ruth-Ann Bailey, Town Clerk
PO Box 48
Wardsboro, VT 05355
Phone (802) 896-6055
*Formed 1780 (Marlboro Probate
    District, Windham County)*

Warner's Grant
*(Essex District Probate Court, Essex
    County)*

Town of Warren
PO Box 337
Warren, VT 05674
*Formed 1789 (Washington Probate
    District, Washington County)*

Warren'sGore
*(Essex District Probate Court, Essex
    County)*

Town of Washington
Rt. 1, Box 22
Washington, VT 05675
*Formed 1781 (Orange District Probate
    Court, Orange County)*

Town of Waterbury
51 South Main
Waterbury, VT 05676
*Formed 1763 (Washington Probate
    District, Washington County)*

*Town of Waterford
c/o Town Clerk
Lower Waterford, VT 05848
Phone (802) 748-2122

Formed 1780 (Caledonia Probate District, Caledonia County)
Land records: Yes
Vital records: Yes
Vital records search service: $2.00 per hour by other than clerk, $5.00 per hour by clerk; copies: 25¢ each, $5.00 for certified copies

*Town of Waterville
PO Box 132
Waterville, VT 05492-0132
Formed 1824 (Lamoille Probate District, Lamoille County)
Land records: Some from 1824
Naturalization records: No naturalization records
Vital records: Some from 1824 but not in detail

Town of Weathersfield
PO Drawer E
Ascutney, VT 05030
Formed 1761 (Windsor District Probate Court, Windsor County)

Town of Wells
PO Box 585
Wells, VT 05774
Formed 1761 (Fair Haven Probate Court, Rutland County)

Town of West Fairlee
PO Box 615
West Fairlee, VT 05083
Formed 1797 (Orange District Probate Court, Orange County)

Town of West Haven
West Haven Center, VT 05743
Formed 1792 (Fair Haven Probate Court, Rutland County)

*Town of West Rutland
c/o Jayne L. Pratt, Town Clerk
234–6 Main
PO Box 115
West Rutland, VT 05777
Phone (802) 438-2204
Formed 1886 (Rutland Probate Court, Rutland County)
Land records: From 1887 to date
Land records search service: $5.00; copies: $1.00 each
Naturalization records: No naturalization records
Vital records: From 1887 to date
Land records search service: $5.00; copies: $1.00 each
Probate records: No probate records

Town of West Windsor
PO Box 6
Brownsville, VT 05037

Formed 1848 (Windsor District Probate Court, Windsor County)

*Town of Westfield
Rural Route 1, Box 171
Westfield, VT 05874
Formed 1780 (Orleans Probate District, Orleans County)
Land records: From about 1800
Naturalization records: No naturalization records
Vital records: From 1857 to date
Probate records: No probate records

*Town of Westford
Rural Route 1, Box 30
Westford, VT 05494
Phone (802) 878-4587
Formed 1763 (Chittenden Probate District, Chittenden County)
Land records: Yes
Naturalization records: No naturalization records
Vital records: Yes
Probate records: No probate records

*Town of Westminster
c/o Janette U. Holton, Town Clerk
PO Box 271
Westminster, VT 05158
Phone (802) 722-4091
First township granted in Vermont, named Township No. 1 in 1736, incorporated as Westminster by the Province of New Hampshire 1752 (Westminster District Probate Court, Windham County)
Land records: Yes; copies: $1.00 per page, $2.00 minimum
Naturalization records: Few
Vital records: Yes; certified copies: $5.00 each
Probate records: Some

*Town of Westmore
Rural Route 2, Box 854
Orleans, VT 05860
Phone (802) 525-3007
Formed 1781 (Orleans Probate District, Orleans County)

*Town of Weston
c/o Town Clerk
PO Box 98
Weston, VT 05161
Phone (802) 824-6645
Formed 1799 (Windsor District Probate Court, Windsor County)
Land records: Yes
No land records search service; copies: $1.00 per page
Naturalization records: No naturalization records
Vital records: Yes

No vital records search service
Probate records: No probate records

*Town of Weybridge
Rural Delivery 1
Middlebury, VT 05753
Phone (802) 545-2450
Formed 1761 (Addison Probate District, Addison County)
Land records: Contact Karen B. Curavoo, Town Clerk's Office
Naturalization records: No naturalization records
Vital records: Contact Town Clerk's Office
Probate records: No probate records

*Town of Wheelock
c/o Audrey Smith, Town Clerk
PO Box 428
Lyndonville, VT 05951
Phone (802) 626-9094 voice or FAX
Formed 1785 (Caledonia Probate District, Caledonia County)
Land records: From 1785 to date (indexed)
Naturalization records: No naturalization records
Vital records: From 1857 (date of fire which destroyed older records)
Probate records: No probate records

*Town of Whiting
29 South Main Street
Whiting, VT 05778
Phone (802) 623-7813
Formed 1763 (Addison Probate District, Addison County)

*Town of Whitingham
c/o Earle S. Holland, Jr., Town Clerk
PO Box 529
Jacksonville, VT 05342-0529
Phone (802) 368-7887
Formed 1770 (Marlboro Probate District, Windham County)
Land records: Yes
Land records search service: $5.00; copies: $1.00 per page, $6.00 per page for certified copies, $2.00 minimum
Vital records: Yes
Vital records search service: $5.00; certified copies: $5.00 each

*Town of Williamstown
PO Box 646
Williamstown, VT 05679
Phone (802) 433-5455
Formed 1781 (Orange District Probate Court, Orange County)
Land records: From the 1700s to date
Naturalization records: No naturalization records
Vital records: From the 1700s to date
Probate records: No probate records

Williamsville
(see Town of Newfane)

*Town of Williston
c/o Arlene H. Degree, Town Clerk
7822 Williston Road
Williston, VT 05495
Phone (802) 878-5121
Formed 1763 (Chittenden Probate District, Chittenden County)
Land records: From 1763
Naturalization records: No naturalization records
Vital records: From 1763
Probate records: No probate records

*Town of Wilmington
c/o Janice Karwoski, Town Clerk
Box 217, Main Street
Wilmington, VT 05363
Phone (802) 464-5836
Formed 1751 (Marlboro Probate District, Windham County)
Land records: Yes
Naturalization records: No naturalization records
Vital records: Yes
Probate records: No probate records

Town of Windham
c/o Carol C. Merritt, Town Clerk
PO Box 109
South Windham, VT 05359
Phone (802) 874-4211
Formed 1761 (Westminster District Probate Court, Windham County)

*Town of Windsor
PO Box 47
Windsor, VT 05089
Formed 1761 (Windsor District Probate Court, Windsor County)

Town of Winhall
Bondville, VT 05340
Formed 1761 (Manchester District Probate Court, Bennington County)

City of Winooski
27 West Allen Street
Winooski, VT 05404
Formed 1921 from Town of Colchester (Chittenden Probate District, Chittenden County)

*Town of Wolcott
Main Street
PO Box 100
Wolcott, VT 05680
Phone (802) 888-2746
Formed 1781 (Lamoille Probate District, Lamoille County)

Town of Woodbury
PO Box 123
Woodbury, VT 05681
Formed 1781 (Washington Probate District, Washington County)

Town of Woodford
HCR 65, Box 600
Bennington, VT 05201
Formed 1753 (Bennington Probate District, Bennington County)

*Town of Woodstock
c/o Town Clerk
29 Central, Box 155
Woodstock, VT 05091
Formed 1761 (The Hartford District Probate Court, Windsor County)

*Town of Worcester
Vermont Route 12 (Worcester Village Road)
PO Drawer 161
Worcester, VT 05682
Phone (802) 223-6942
Chartered 1763, organized 1803 (Washington Probate District, Washington County)
Land records: From 1803
Naturalization records: No naturalization records
Vital records: From 1827
Probate records: No probate records

VIRGINIA

Capital: Richmond. Statehood: 25 June 1788

Court System

Virginia has had independent cities since Williamsburg was chartered in 1722. As of 1980 they are now officially outside county boundaries. Three previously incorporated cities are now absorbed into counties: Manchester, formed 1874, merged into Richmond County in 1910; South Norfolk, formed 1921, merged with all of Norfolk County in 1962 to form the city of Chesapeake; Warwick, formed 1952 from all of Warwick County, merged into the city of Newport News in 1957. Also, Elizabeth City County merged with the city of Hampton in 1952, and Princess Anne County merged with the city of Virginia Beach in 1962.

Virginia's Juvenile and Domestic Relations Courts sit in all county seats and independent cities but are not courts of record; their district boundaries are the same as for the General District Court. The District Courts hear some civil actions, plus misdemeanors, ordinance violations, traffic and felony preliminaries. First Judicial District: city of Chesapeake; Second Judicial District: city of Virginia Beach; Second Judicial District A: Accomack and Northampton counties; Third Judicial District: city of Portsmouth; Fourth Judicial District: city of Norfolk; Fifth Judicial District: cities of Franklin and Suffolk and counties of Isle of Wight and Southampton; Sixth Judicial District: cities of Emporia and Hopewell and counties of Brunswick, Greensville, Prince George, Surry and Sussex; Seventh Judicial District: city of Newport News; Eighth Judicial District: city of Hampton; Ninth Judicial District: cities of Poquoson and Williamsburg and counties of Charles City, Gloucester, James City, King and Queen, King William, Mathews, Middlesex, New Kent and York; Tenth Judicial District: city of South Boston and counties of Appomattox, Buckingham, Charlotte, Cumberland, Halifax, Lunenburg, Mecklenburg and Prince Edward; Eleventh Judicial District: city of Petersburg and counties of Amelia, Dinwiddie, Nottoway and Powhatan; Twelfth Judicial District: city of Colonial Heights and county of Chesterfield; Thirteenth Judicial District: city of Richmond; Fourteenth Judicial District: Henrico County; Fifteenth Judicial District: city of Fredericksburg and counties of Caroline,

Essex, Hanover, King George, Lancaster, Northumberland, Richmond, Spotsylvania, Stafford and Westmoreland; Sixteenth Judicial District: city of Charlottesville and counties of Albemarle, Culpeper, Fluvanna, Goochland, Greene, Louisa, Madison and Orange; Seventeenth Judicial District: Arlington County; Eighteenth Judicial District: city of Alexandria; Nineteenth Judicial District: cities of Falls Church and Fairfax and Fairfax County; Twentieth Judicial District: Fauquier, Loudoun and Rappahannock counties; Twenty-first Judicial District: city of Martinsville and counties of Henry and Patrick; Twenty-second Judicial District: city of Danville and counties of Franklin and Pittsylvania; Twenty-third Judicial District: cities of Roanoke and Salem and Roanoke County; Twenty-fourth Judicial District: cities of Bedford and Lynchburg and counties of Amherst, Bedford, Campbell and Nelson; Twenty-fifth Judicial District: cities of Buena Vista, Clifton Forge, Covington, Lexington, Staunton and Waynesboro and counties of Alleghany, Augusta, Bath, Botetourt, Craig, Highland and Rockbridge; Twenty-sixth Judicial District: cities of Harrisonburg and Winchester and counties of Clarke, Frederick, Page, Rockingham, Shenandoah and Warren; Twenty-seventh Judicial District: cities of Galax and Radford and counties of Carroll, Floyd, Grayson, Montgomery, Pulaski and Wythe; Twenty-eighth Judicial District: city of Bristol and counties of Smyth and Washington; Twenty-ninth Judicial District: Bland, Buchanan, Dickenson, Giles, Russell and Tazewell counties; Thirtieth Judicial District: city of Norton and counties of Lee, Scott and Wise; Thirty-first Judicial District: cities of Manassas and Manassas Park and county of Prince William.

The Circuit Court has general civil and criminal jurisdiction and sits in Judicial Circuits which are the same as the District Courts' Judicial Districts, except that the Second Judicial Circuit includes both the Second Judicial District and the Second Judicial District A. The Court of Appeals and the Supreme Court hear appeals.

Courthouses

Accawmack County
(see Northampton County)

*Accomack County Courthouse
Accomac, VA 23301
Phone (804) 787-3776
County organized 1663 from Northampton County
Land records: Yes
Naturalization records: Yes
Vital records: Yes

Probate records: Yes
No probate search service; contact Mrs. Mary Francis Carey, C.G., New Church, VA 23415, (804) 824-4615

*Albemarle County Courthouse
501 East Jefferson Street, Court Square
Charlottesville, VA 22901
Phone (804) 972-4083; (804) 972-4084
County organized 1744 from Goochland County
Land records: From 1744 to date; contact Circuit Court Clerk's Office
Naturalization records: No naturalization records
Vital records: From 1780 to date; contact Circuit Court Clerk's Office (prior to 1780 contact Goochland County)
Probate records: From 1744 to date; contact Circuit Court Clerk's Office

*Alexandria (Independent City) Courthouse
301 King Street
Alexandria, VA 22314-3211
Phone (703) 838-4550
Alexandria County organized 1801 from part of the District of Columbia which had been ceded by Virginia to the federal government in 1791, being then part of Fairfax County; in 1846 the county was retroceded back to Virginia, and the area was renamed Arlington County in March 1920; the city of Alexandria was separated from the county in 1920
Land records: From 1782; contact Clerk
Vital records: Marriage licenses only from 1870; contact Clerk
Probate records: From 1797; contact Clerk
No probate search service; copies: $1.00 for each of the first two pages and 50¢ for each additional page per document; "Some of the older books cannot be photocopied due to age; they must either be copied by hand or by using a camera."

*Alleghany County Courthouse
266 West Main Street
PO Box 670
Covington, VA 24426
Phone (703) 965-1730
County organized 1822 from Bath and Botetourt counties, Virginia, and Monroe County (now West Virginia)
Land records: From 1822 (records include independent city of Covington)
No land records search service; copies: 50¢ per page
Vital records: From 1822 (records include independent city of Covington); certified copies: $2.50 per page

Probate records: From 1822 (records include independent city of Covington)
No probate search service; copies: 50¢ per page

*Amelia County Clerk of Circuit Court
PO Box 237
Amelia Court House, VA 23002
Phone (804) 561-2128
County organized 1734 from Brunswick and Prince George counties
Land records: Yes
Naturalization records: No naturalization records
Vital records: Yes
Probate records: Yes

*Amherst County Courthouse
100 E Street
PO Box 462
Amherst, VA 24521
Phone (804) 929-9321
County organized 1761 from Albemarle County
Land records: Contact Circuit Court Clerk
Vital records: Marriages only; contact Circuit Court Clerk
Probate records: Contact Circuit Court Clerk
Probate search service: no charge; copies: $1.00 per page

*Appomattox County Circuit Court
PO Box 672
Appomattox, VA 24522-0672
Phone (804) 352-5275
County organized 1845 from Buckingham, Campbell, Charlotte and Prince Edward counties
Land records: From 1892; contact B. K. Williams, Clerk
Naturalization records: No naturalization records
Vital records: Marriages from 1892; contact Clerk; copies: $5.00
Probate records: From 1892; contact Clerk
No probate search service; copies: 50¢ per page, no minimum

Arlington County Courthouse
1400 North Courthouse Road
Arlington, VA 22201-2622
Phone (703) 558-2105
Alexandria County organized 1801 from part of the District of Columbia which had been ceded by Virginia to the federal government in 1791, being then part of Fairfax County; in 1846 the county was retroceded back to Virginia, and the area was renamed Arlington County in March 1920

*Augusta County Courthouse
6 East Johnson Street
Staunton, VA 24401-4301
Phone (703) 245-5321
County organized 1745 from Orange County
Land records: Deeds from November 1745, land tax records from 1786, survey books from 1745 to about 1840; contact John B. Davis, Clerk, PO Box 689, Staunton, VA 24402-0689
Naturalization records: From 1790 to 1900 (must be searched for); contact Clerk
Vital records: Births and deaths from 1853 to 1896, marriages from 1785; contact Clerk; certified copies only: an additional $2.00 per record for certification
Probate records: From 1745; contact Clerk
Probate search service: "Do not do extensive searches—charge only for copies in brief searches"; copies: 50¢ per page, no minimum

*Bath County Courthouse
PO Box 180
Warm Springs, VA 24484-0180
Phone (703) 839-2361
County organized 1790 from Augusta and Botetourt counties, Virginia, and Greenbrier County (now West Virginia)
Land records: From 1791
Vital records: Births from 1853 to 1950, deaths from 1853 to 1912
Probate records: Wills from 1791
Probate search service: depends on amount of time involved; copies: $1.00 for each of the first two pages and 50¢ for each additional page per instrument, no minimum

Bedford (Independent City)
PO Box 807
Bedford, VA 24523-0807
Phone (703) 586-8974
Land records: Contact Bedford County Courthouse (see address below)
Vital records: Contact Bedford County Courthouse
Probate records: Contact Bedford County Courthouse

*Bedford County Courthouse
122 East Main Street
PO Box 235
Bedford, VA 24523
Phone (703) 586-7632
County organized 1753 from Albemarle and Lunenburg counties. City organized September 1968.
Land records: Deeds from 1754; contact Clerk of Courts; copies: 50¢ per page

Naturalization records: No naturalization records
Vital records: Births from 1853, deaths from 1853, marriages from 1754; contact Clerk of Courts; copies: $3.00 each
Probate records: From 1754; contact Clerk of Courts
Probate search service: yes; copies: 50¢ per page, no minimum, "We do not do family history."

Bland County Courthouse
PO Box 295
Bland, VA 24315-0295
Phone (703) 688-4562
County organized 1861 from Giles, Tazewell and Wythe counties

*Botetourt County Courthouse
PO Box 219
Fincastle, VA 24090-0219
Phone (703) 473-8274 Clerk's Office
County organized 1769 from Augusta and Rockbridge counties
Land records: From 1770; contact Tommy L. Moore, Clerk of Circuit Court; copies: 50¢ per page
Naturalization records: A few naturalization records recorded in the Court Order Books; contact Clerk of Circuit Court
Vital records: Births and deaths from 1853 to 1870, marriages from 1770; contact Clerk of Circuit Court; copies: $2.00 each
Probate records: From 1770; contact Clerk of Circuit Court
Probate search service: no charge for cursory search; copies: 50¢ per page, no minimum; "Court Order and Minute Books from 1770, Surveyor's Records from 1799."

Bristol (Independent City) Courthouse
497 Cumberland
Bristol, VA 24201-4394
Phone (703) 466-2221

*Brunswick County Clerk's Office
Circuit Court of Brunswick County
216 North Main Street
Lawrenceville, VA 23868
Phone (804) 848-2215 Clerk's Office; (804) 848-4307 FAX
County organized 1732 from Prince George, Isle of Wight and Surry counties
Land records: Maps, survey plats from 1902, deed books from 1732, and deed of trust books; contact V. Earl Stanley, Jr., Clerk
Vital records: Marriages from 1732; contact Clerk
Probate records: From 1732; contact Clerk
No probate search service (must have at

least name(s), type of transaction and general time period); copies: 50¢ each, $1.00 minimum, plus SASE

*Buchanan County Courthouse
PO Drawer 950
Grundy, VA 24614-0950
Phone (703) 935-6500
County organized 1858 from Tazewell and Russell counties
Land records: Yes
Naturalization records: Yes
Vital records: Yes
Probate records: Yes

*Buckingham County Circuit Court
Malcolm Booker, Jr., Clerk
Highway 60
PO Box 107
Buckingham, VA 23921
Phone (804) 969-4734; (804) 969-2043 FAX
County organized 1758 from Albemarle and Appomattox counties
Land records: From 1869
Naturalization records: No naturalization records
Vital records: From 1869 to 1918
Probate records: From 1869

Buena Vista (Independent City) Courthouse
2039 Sycamore Avenue
Buena Vista, VA 24416-3123
Phone (703) 261-6121

*Campbell County Courthouse
PO Box 7
Rustburg, VA 24588
Phone (804) 332-5161; (804) 847-0961, ext. 126
County organized 1782 from Bedford County
Land records: Contact Deborah Hughes, Clerk
Naturalization records: No naturalization records
Vital records: Contact Clerk
Probate records: Contact Clerk
Probate search service: no charge; copies: $1.00 per page, no minimum

Caroline County Courthouse
Bowling Green, VA 22427
Phone (804) 633-5800
County organized 1728 from Essex, King and Queen and King William counties

Carroll County Courthouse
PO Box 515
Hillsville, VA 24343-0515
Phone (703) 728-3331
County organized 1842 from Grayson and Patrick counties

*Charles City County Circuit Court
PO Box 86
Charles City, VA 23030
Phone (804) 829-9211
County organized 1634, original county
Land records: From 1789
Vital records: From 1850
Probate records: From 1790
Probate search service: no charge;
copies: $1.00 per page, no minimum

Charles River County
(see York County)

*Charlotte County Courthouse
PO Box 38
Charlotte Court House, VA 23923
Phone (804) 542-5147 Clerk
County organized 1765 from Lunenburg County
Land records: Deeds from 1765; contact
Stuart B. Fallen, Clerk, Circuit Court
Vital records: Marriages from 1765
Probate records: Wills from 1765
No probate search service; copies: $1.00
per page, no minimum; "We check
will, deed, marriages for specific
name and date."

Charlottesville (Independent City) Courthouse
PO Box 911
Charlottesville, VA 22902-0911
Phone (804) 971-3101

*City of Chesapeake Circuit Court of Chesapeake
PO Box 15205
Chesapeake, VA 23328-5205
Phone (804) 547-6111 Clerk
*City organized 1 January 1963 and
merged with remaining part of
Norfolk County, which was
organized in 1691 from Lower
Norfolk County (which was formed
in 1637 from New Norfolk County)
and from the city of South Norfolk
(which was incorporated in 1921)*
Land records: Deeds from 1637; contact
Lillie M. Hart, Clerk
Vital records: Births from 1853 to 1917
(not complete), deaths from 1853 to
1917 and from 1870 to 1917 (not
complete), marriage bonds from 1706
to 1850 (not complete), marriages
from 1850 (not complete); contact
Clerk
Probate records: Wills from 1637 to 1755
and from 1756 (not complete)
Probate search service: no charge;
copies: 50¢ per page, $1.00 minimum;
"Must send check or money order
with request."

*Chesterfield County Circuit Court
PO Box 125
Chesterfield, VA 23832-0125
Phone (804) 748-1209 Record Room
County organized 1749 from Henrico County
Land records: From 1749; contact
Record Room
Naturalization records: No naturalization
records
Vital records: Marriages from 1771;
contact Record Room
Probate records: From 1749; contact
Record Room
Probate search service: no charge for a
five-year span; copies: 50¢ per page,
no minimum

Chickacoun Indian District
(see Northumberland County)

*Clarke County Courthouse
PO Box 189
Berryville, VA 22611-0189
Phone (703) 955-5116
County organized 1836 from Frederick County
Land records: Contact Circuit Court
Clerk
Naturalization records: No naturalization
records
Vital records: Marriages; contact Circuit
Court Clerk
Probate records: Contact Circuit Court
Clerk

*Clifton Forge Circuit Court
PO Box 27
Clifton Forge, VA 24422-0027
Phone (703) 863-5091
City organized 1906
Land records: From 1906; contact Clerk
of Circuit Court
Naturalization records: No naturalization
records
Vital records: Marriages only from 1906;
contact Clerk of Circuit Court
Probate records: From 1906; contact
Clerk of Circuit Court
No probate search service; copies: 50¢
per page, no minimum

*Colonial Heights Circuit Court
401 Temple Avenue
PO Box 3401
Colonial Heights, VA 23834
Phone (804) 520-9365
*City organized 1928, made independent
as of 1 February 1961*
Land records: From 1 February 1961;
contact Stacy L. Stafford, Clerk,
Circuit Court
Naturalization records: No naturalization
records
Vital records: No vital records

Probate records: From 1 February 1961
No probate search service; copies: 50¢
per page

*Covington (Independent City)
City Hall
158 North Court Avenue
Covington, VA 24426
City organized 1952
Land records: From 1822; contact
Alleghany County Courthouse (see
address above)
Vital records: From 1822; contact
Alleghany County Courthouse
Probate records: From 1822; contact
Alleghany County Courthouse

*Craig County Courthouse
PO Box 185
New Castle, VA 24127
Phone (703) 864-6141
*County organized 1851 from Botetourt,
Giles and Roanoke counties,
Virginia, and Monroe County (now
West Virginia)*
Land records: From 1864; contact P. B.
Elmore, Clerk
Naturalization records: No naturalization
records
Vital records: Births and deaths from
1864 to 1896; contact Clerk
Probate records: From 1851; contact
Clerk
Probate search service: no charge ("Due
to our small staff we can only do these
as time allows"); copies: 50¢ per page

*Culpeper County Courthouse
Culpeper, VA 22701
County organized 1748 from Orange County
Land records: Yes
Probate records: Yes
No probate search service

*Cumberland County Clerk's Office
PO Box 8
Cumberland, VA 23040
Phone (804) 492-4442 Clerk of Circuit
Court
County organized 1749 from Goochland County
Land records: From 1749; contact Clerk
of Circuit Court
Naturalization records: From 1917 to
1925; contact Clerk of Circuit Court
Vital records: Births and deaths from
1853 to the 1880s (varies), marriages
from 1749; contact Clerk of Circuit
Court
Probate records: From 1749; contact
Clerk of Circuit Court
Probate search service: no charge unless
research is extensive; copies: 50¢ per
page, no minimum

*Danville (Independent City) Courthouse
212 Lynn Street
Danville, VA 24543
Phone (804) 799-5168
City organized 1793
Land records: From 15 May 1841
No land records search service; copies: 50¢ per page, no minimum
Naturalization records: No naturalization records
Vital records: Marriage licenses only from 13 July 1841
No vital records search service; copies: 50¢ per page, no minimum
Probate records: From 16 July 1857
No probate search service; copies: 50¢ per page, no minimum; "All records are open to the public."

*Dickenson County Courthouse
c/o Joe Tate, Clerk of Circuit Court
PO Box 190
Clintwood, VA 24228
Phone (703) 926-1616
County organized 1880 from Buchanan, Russell and Wise counties
Land records: Yes
No land records search service, but will look up records; copies: 50¢ per page, $2.00 for certification
Naturalization records: No naturalization records
Vital records: Marriage licenses and one book of old births and deaths
No vital records search service, but will look up records; copies: 50¢ per page, $2.00 for certification
Probate records: Yes
No probate search service, but will look up records; copies: 50¢ per page, $2.00 for certification

*Dinwiddie County Courthouse
Dinwiddie, VA 23841
Phone (804) 469-4540
County organized 1752 from Prince George County
Land records: From 1833; contact Annie L. Williams, Clerk, PO Box 63, Dinwiddie, VA 23841
Naturalization records: From 1903 to 1916; contact Clerk
Vital records: Only a few births and deaths from 1865 to 1896, marriages; contact Clerk; copies: $3.00 for marriages
Probate records: From 1833; contact Clerk
No probate search service; copies: 25¢ per page, $2.00 for certified copies

District of Columbia
(see Alexandria City and Arlington County)

Dunmore County
(see Shenandoah County)

Elizabeth City County
(City of Hampton)

Emporia (Independent City) Courthouse
Emporia, VA 23847
Phone (804) 634-3332

*Essex County Courthouse
PO Box 445
Tappahannock, VA 22560-0445
Phone (804) 443-3541
County organized 1692 from Old Rappahannock County, which was organized 1656 from Lancaster County and abolished 1692
Land records: Deeds from 1656
Naturalization records: No naturalization records
Vital records: Births and deaths from 1853 to about 1912, marriages from 1804 to date
Probate records: Wills from 1656

*Fairfax (Independent City) Court Clerk's Office
Fairfax, VA 22030
Phone (703) 385-7866 Court Clerk
Land records: No land records; contact Fairfax County Circuit Court (see address below)
Naturalization records: No naturalization records; contact Fairfax County Circuit Court
Vital records: No vital records; contact Fairfax County Circuit Court
Probate records: No probate records; contact Fairfax County Circuit Court

*Fairfax County Circuit Court
4110 Chain Bridge
Fairfax, VA 22030-4009
Phone (703) 246-4168 Archives Section; (703) 246-2770 General Information
County organized 1742 from Prince William and Loudoun counties
Land records: From 1742 (some early years missing)
Naturalization records: Very spotty naturalization records from 1785 to 1900
Vital records: Births, deaths and marriages from 1853 (incomplete except for marriages)
Probate records: From 1742
Probate search service: no charge; copies: 50¢ each, 25¢ each for seniors and students, no minimum

Falls Church (Independent City) Courthouse
300 Park
Falls Church, VA 22046-3301

Phone (703) 241-5001

*Fauquier County Courthouse
40 Culpeper Street
PO Box 985
Warrenton, VA 22186-0985
Phone (703) 347-8610
County organized 1759 from Prince William County
Land records: Grantor/grantee indices from 1759; contact Clerk's Office
Vital records: Births and deaths from 1853 to 1896 and 1913 to 1916, marriages from 1759; contact Clerk's Office; ("Early official records of births and deaths in Virginia are almost nonexistent, as the recording was not required by law; by an act passed in 1853, the state required the recording of vital statistics; birth records were not routinely filed during the period 1896 to 1912")
Probate records: From 1759
Probate search service: no charge; copies: $1.00 for each of the first two pages and 50¢ for each additional page

Fincastle County
(see Montgomery and Washington counties)

*Floyd County Courthouse
Floyd, VA 24091
Phone (703) 745-4158
County organized 1831 from Montgomery and Franklin counties
Land records: From 1831; copies: 50¢ per page
Naturalization records: No naturalization records
Vital records: Births and deaths from 1853 to 1873, marriages from 1831; copies: $2.50 each for marriages
Probate records: From 1831
No probate search service (name provided for private search); copies: 50¢ per page plus SASE

*Fluvanna County Courthouse
Palmyra, VA 22963
County organized 1777 from Albemarle County
Land records: From 1777
Vital records: Births and deaths from 1853 to 1896, marriages from 1777
Probate records: From 1777
No probate search service; copies: about $1.00 per page

*Franklin (Independent City) Courthouse
c/o Bobbie B. Johnson, Clerk
207 West Second Avenue
Franklin, VA 23851-1713
Phone (804) 562-8500

Land records: No land records
Naturalization records: No naturalization records
Vital records: No vital records
Probate records: No probate records
"We are not a court of record; our records would be in Southampton County Circuit Court."

*Franklin County Courthouse
PO Box 567
Rocky Mount, VA 24151
Phone (703) 483-3065
County organized 1786 from Bedford, Henry and Patrick counties
Land records: Yes
No land research search service
Naturalization records: No naturalization records
Vital records: No vital records
Probate records: Yes
No probate search service (must give book and page); copies: $1.00 per page, $2.00 for certification

*Frederick County Circuit Court
5 North Kent Street
Winchester, VA 22601
Phone (703) 667-5770 Clerk
County organized 1743 from Orange County
Land records: From 1743; contact George B. Whitacre, Clerk
Naturalization records: No naturalization records
Vital records: Births from 1853 to 1912, deaths from 1853 to 1896, marriages from 1782; contact Clerk
Probate records: Wills from 1743
No probate search service; copies: 50¢ per page, no minimum; "We do not do extensive research work or copying; if they have Book and Page Numbers for one or two instruments we will copy at a reasonable rate; otherwise we refer to a local genealogist, Rebecca H. Good, 30 West 13th Street, Front Royal, VA 22630."

*Fredericksburg (Independent City) Circuit Court
PO Box 359
Fredericksburg, VA 22404-0359
Phone (703) 372-1066
City organized 1782
Land records: From 1782 (all loose papers are sealed during reformatting and indexing project); contact Sharon S. Mitchell, Clerk
Naturalization records: No naturalization records
Vital records: Marriages from 1782; contact Clerk
Probate records: From 1782; contact Clerk
No probate search service (referred to

local researchers who charge for their services); copies: 50¢ per page, no minimum.

*Galax (Independent City)
123 North Main Street
Galax, VA 24333-2907
Phone (703) 236-3441
Land records: No land records; contact Carroll County Courthouse (see address above) or Grayson County Courthouse (see address below)
Naturalization records: No naturalization records; contact Carroll County Courthouse or Grayson County Courthouse
Vital records: No vital records; contact Carroll County Courthouse or Grayson County Courthouse
Probate records: No probate records; contact Carroll County Courthouse or Grayson County Courthouse

*Giles County Courthouse
120 North Main Street
Pearisburg, VA 24134-1625
Phone (703) 921-2525
County organized 1806 from Montgomery, Tazewell and Wythe counties, Virginia, and Monroe County (now West Virginia)
Land records: Deeds, etc., from 1806
Naturalization records: No naturalization records
Vital records: Births and deaths from 1855 to 1896, marriages from 1806
Probate records: From 1806
Probate search service: "We do not have a particular fee; research service limited due to small size of staff"; copies: 50¢ per page, no minimum

*Gloucester County Courthouse
PO Box 329
Gloucester, VA 23061-0329
Phone (804) 693-4042
County organized 1651 from York County
Land records: Contact Clerk of Circuit Court, PO Box N, Gloucester, VA 23061
Naturalization records: No naturalization records
Vital records: No vital records
Probate records: Contact Clerk of Circuit Court
No probate search service; copies: $1.00 per page

*Goochland County Courthouse
PO Box 196
Goochland, VA 23063-0196
Phone (804) 556-5353
County organized 1727 from Henrico County
Land records: From 1728; contact D.

Louis Parrish, Jr., Clerk of Circuit Court
Naturalization records: No naturalization records
Vital records: No vital records
Probate records: From 1728; contact Clerk of Circuit Court
Probate search service: $5.00; copies: $1.00 per page, no minimum

*Grayson County Courthouse
129 Davis Street
Independence, VA 24348-9602
Phone (703) 773-2231
County organized 1793 from Wythe and Patrick counties
Land records: From 1793; contact Clerk of Circuit Court, PO Box 130, Independence, VA 24348
Naturalization records: No naturalization records
Vital records: Marriages from 1793; contact Clerk of Circuit Court
Probate records: From 1793; contact Clerk of Circuit Court
No probate search service; copies: 50¢ per page, $2.00 for certification

*Greene County Courthouse
PO Box 386
Stanardsville, VA 22973-0386
Phone (804) 985-5208
County organized 1838 from Orange County
Land records: From 1838; contact Maric C. Durrer, Clerk, Circuit Court, PO Box 386, Stanardsville, VA 22973
No land records search service (must have complete names); copies: 50¢ per page
Naturalization records: No naturalization records
Vital records: Births and deaths from 1838 to the late 1800s (not complete), marriage licenses from 1838; contact Clerk
No vital records search service (must have complete names); copies: 50 per page for births and deaths, $2.00 each for marriage licenses
Probate records: From 1838 to the late 1800s, probate of wills from 1838 to date
No probate search service (must have complete names); copies: 50¢ per page, no minimum

*Greensville County Courthouse
337 South Main Street
Emporia, VA 23847-2027
Phone (804) 348-4215
County organized 1780 from Brunswick and Sussex counties
Land records: Contact Robert C. Wrenn, Clerk
Naturalization records: No naturalization records

Vital records: Marriages; contact Clerk
Probate records: Contact Clerk
Probate search service: no charge;
copies: $1.00 per page, no minimum

Halifax County Courthouse
PO Box 786
Halifax, VA 24558-0786
Phone (804) 476-2141
County organized 1752 from Lunenburg County

*Clerk's Office of Circuit Court of the City of Hampton, Virginia
101 King's Way
PO Box 40
Hampton, VA 23669-0040
Phone (804) 727-6105
On 1 July 1952 the City of Hampton absorbed Elizabeth City County, which was formed in 1634, original county
Land records: Deeds from 1689 to 1699 (incomplete and not indexed) and from 1865 (complete)
Naturalization records: No naturalization records
Vital records: Marriages
Probate records: Wills from 1689 to 1699 (incomplete and not indexed), from 1701 to 1859 (restored and indexed in 1968), and from 1865 (complete)
Probate search service: no charge ("We do not research unindexed records prior to 1865"); copies: $1.00 for each of the first two pages and 50¢ for each additional page, no minimum

Hanover County Courthouse
Hanover, VA 23069
Phone (804) 537-6000
County organized 1720 from New Kent

Harrisonburg (Independent City) Courthouse
Rockingham Courthouse
Harrisonburg, VA 22801
Phone (703) 434-6776

*Henrico County Courthouse
Parham and Hungary Spring Roads
PO Box 27032
Richmond, VA 23273-0001
Phone (804) 672-5468; (804) 672-4202
County organized 1634, original county
Land records: Deeds from 1781; contact Yvonne G. Smith, Clerk of the Circuit Court
Vital records: Marriages from 1900 to date; contact Clerk of the Circuit Court
Probate records: Wills from 1781 to date; contact Clerk of the Circuit Court

Henry County Courthouse
Martinsville, VA 24114

Phone (703) 638-3961
County organized 1777 from Pittsylvania and Patrick counties

*Highland County Courthouse
PO Box 190
Monterey, VA 24465
Phone (703) 468-2447
County organized 1847 from Bath County, Virginia, and Pendleton County (now West Virginia)
Land records: Yes
Naturalization records: No naturalization records
Vital records: Births from 1853 to 1896 and from 1912 to 1917, deaths from 1853 to 1870 and from 1912 to 1917, marriages from 1847
Probate records: Yes
Probate search service: no charge; copies: $1.00 per page, no minimum

*City of Hopewell Circuit Court
100 East Broadway, Room 251
Hopewell, VA 23860
Phone (804) 541-2239 Clerk of Circuit Court
City organized 1 July 1916
Land records: From 1 July 1916; contact Clerk of Circuit Court, PO Box 354, Hopewell, VA 23860
Probate records: From 1 July 1916; contact Clerk of Circuit Court
Probate search service: no charge; copies: $1.00 for the first page and 50¢ for each additional page, plus SASE

*Isle of Wight County Courthouse
Circuit Court Clerk
Isle of Wight, VA 23397
Phone (804) 357-3191
County organized 1634 from Upper Norfolk (which was organized 1636 from New Norfolk County and renamed Nansemond County 1642/3); name changed from Warrossauosacke County in 1637
Land records: Yes
Naturalization records: No naturalization records
Vital records: Marriages
Probate records: Yes
No probate search service ("The Court Clerk does not have a research staff, however, if the person can provide the book and page number they will copy and send"; copies: 50¢ per page, no minimum; "The Court Clerk staff can assist in the location of a local genealogist."

*James City County Courthouse
PO Box 3045
Williamsburg, VA 23187
Phone (804) 229-2552

County organized 1634, original county

*King and Queen County Courthouse
King and Queen Courthouse, VA 23085-0067
Phone (804) 785-2460
County organized 1691 from New Kent County
Land records: From 1864; contact Samuel C. Winn, Clerk of Circuit Court, PO Box 67, King and Queen Courthouse, VA 23085 ("All records prior to 1865 destroyed by fire")
Naturalization records: No naturalization records
Probate records: From 1864; contact Clerk of Circuit Court
No probate search service; copies: $1.00 per page, $1.00 minimum

*King George County Courthouse
c/o Charles V. Mason, Clerk of the Circuit Court
PO Box 105
King George, VA 22485
Phone (703) 775-3322
County organized 1721 from Richmond and Westmoreland counties
Land records: From 1721
Naturalization records: No naturalization records
Vital records: Very few, scattered vital records
Probate records: From 1721
Probate search service: no charge; copies: 50¢ per page, $2.00 minimum

*King William County Courthouse
PO Box 216
King William, VA 23086
Phone (804) 769-2311
County organized 1702 from King and Queen County
Land records: From 1885 (date of courthouse fire)
No land records search service
Naturalization records: No naturalization records
Vital records: No vital records
Probate records: From 1885
No probate search service

Lancaster County Courthouse
Lancaster, VA 22503
Phone (804) 462-5611
County organized 1651 from York and Northumberland counties

*Lee County Courthouse
c/o Charles Calton, Circuit Court Clerk
PO Box 326
Jonesville, VA 24263
Phone (703) 346-7763
County organized 1793 from Russell and Scott counties

Land records: From 1793
Naturalization records: No naturalization records
Vital records: From 1857 to 1875
Probate records: From 1793
Probate search service: $10.00; copies: 25¢ per page, no minimum

*Lexington (Independent City) Courthouse
300 East Washington Street
Lexington, VA 24450-2720
Phone (703) 463-7133
Probate records: For the City of Lexington, contact Rockbridge County Circuit Court, Court (see address pg. 374)

Logan County
(see Tazewell County)

*Loudoun County Clerk of the Circuit Court
(18 North King Street—location)
PO Box 550 (mailing address)
Leesburg, VA 22075-0550
Phone (703) 777-0270
County organized 1757 from Fairfax County
Land records: Yes
No land records search service (must have full name and time period)
Naturalization records: Very few from the early to mid-1800s, unindexed
No naturalization records search service
Probate records: Yes
No probate search service; copies: 50¢ per page, no minimum; "I know of one individual who is a member of the Historical Society, who may be willing to do some research: Mrs. Mary Fishback, 20 North Street, N.E., Leesburg, VA 22075."

Louisa County Courthouse
PO Box 160
Louisa, VA 23093-0160
Phone (703) 967-0401
County organized 1742 from Hanover County

Lower Norfolk County
(see cities of Chesapeake and Virginia Beach)

*Lunenburg County Courthouse
c/o Clerk, Circuit Court
Lunenburg, VA 23952
Phone (804) 696-2230
County organized 1746 from Brunswick County
Land records: Yes
Naturalization records: Only one or two Orders of Naturalization on record in the Order Books

Vital records: Yes
Probate records: Yes

*Lynchburg (Independent City) Courthouse
PO Box 4
Lynchburg, VA 24505-0004
Phone (804) 847-1590
City organized 1805
Land records: Contact Clerk of Circuit Court
Naturalization records: No naturalization records
Vital records: Marriages and divorces only (no births and deaths); contact Clerk of Circuit Court
Probate records: Contact Clerk of Circuit Court
No probate search service; copies: 50¢ per page, $2.00 for certification, no minimum

*Madison County Courthouse
Main Street
PO Box 220
Madison, VA 22727
Phone (703) 948-6888
County organized 1793 from Culpeper County
Land records: From 1793; contact John M. Powell, Clerk
Naturalization records: No naturalization records
Vital records: Marriages only from 1793; contact Clerk
Probate records: From 1793; contact Clerk
No probate search service ("We refer all requests to local genealogist")

*Manassas (Independent City)
c/o Prince William County
9311 Lee Avenue
Prince William, VA 22110
Phone (703) 335-6015
Land records: Deeds from 1731; contact Clerk of Circuit Court
Naturalization records: No naturalization records
Vital records: Marriages from 1859; contact Clerk of Circuit Court
Probate records: From 1731
Probate search service: $10.00; copies: 50¢ per page, no minimum

Manassas Park City Hall
1 Park Center Court
103 Manassas Drive
Manassas Park, VA 22111
Phone (703) 361-8800
Land records: Contact Prince William County Courthouse
Vital records: Contact Prince William County Courthouse
Probate records: Contact Prince William County Courthouse

City of Manchester
(see City of Richmond)

Martinsville (Independent City) Courthouse
Martinsville, VA 24112
Phone (703) 638-3971

Mathews County Courthouse
Court Street
Mathews, VA 23109
Phone (804) 725-2550
County organized 1791 from Gloucester County

Mecklenburg County Courthouse
PO Box 307
Boydton, VA 23917-0307
Phone (804) 738-6191
County organized 1765 from Lunenburg County

*Middlesex County Courthouse
Saluda, VA 23149
Phone (804) 758-5317
County organized 1673 from Lancaster County
Land records: From 1675; contact County Research Department
Naturalization records: No naturalization records
Vital records: Marriages from 1742; contact County Research Department
Probate records: From 1674; contact County Research Department
Probate search service: $1.00 per name; copies: $1.00 for each of the first two pages and 50¢ for each additional page; $1.00 minimum

Monroe County, West Virginia
(see Alleghany and Giles counties)

*Montgomery County Circuit Court
PO Box 209
Christiansburg, VA 24073
Phone (703) 382-5700
County organized 1777 from Fincastle (organized 1772 from Botetourt County and abolished 1777), Botetourt and Pulaski counties
Land records: From 1773 to date
Land records search service: no detailed searches or a lot of requests at one time; copies: 50¢ per page
Naturalization records: No naturalization records
Vital records: From 1853 to 1868 only
Vital records search service: no detailed searches or a lot of requests at one time; copies: 50¢ per page
Probate records: From 1773 to date
No probate search service (contact Dorothy S. Kessler, PO Box 67, Fincastle, VA 24090); copies: 50¢ per page

Nansemond County
(see City of Suffolk and Isle of Wight
and Southampton counties)

Nelson County Courthouse
Lovingston, VA 22949
Phone (804) 263-4245
*County organized 1808 from Amherst
County*

*New Kent County Courthouse
PO Box 98
New Kent, VA 23124-0050
Phone (804) 966-9601
*County organized 1654 from York and
James City counties*
Land records: From 1865; contact Clerk
of Circuit Court, PO Box 98, New
Kent, VA 23124
Naturalization records: No naturalization
records
Vital records: Deaths and marriages from
1865; contact Clerk of Circuit Court
Probate records: From 1865; contact
Clerk of Circuit Court
No probate search service; copies: 50¢
per page, no minimum; "Payment
must be received before copies are
mailed."

New Norfolk County
(see cities Chesapeake and Suffolk, and
Isle of Wight County)

**Newport News (Independent City)
Courthouse**
2400 Washington Avenue
Newport News, VA 23607-4305
Phone (804) 247-8691
*In 1957 absorbed the city of Warwick,
which had been organized in 1952
from all of Warwick County. Warwick
County was organized in 1642
(original county) and called Warwick
River County until later that same
year*
Land records: From 1863 (date of fire)
Naturalization records: Contact Virginia
State Library and Archives, 11th
Street at Capitol Square, Richmond,
VA 23219-3491
Vital records: Marriages from 1863
Probate records: From 1863

**Norfolk (Independent City)
Courthouse**
100 Saint Paul Boulevard
Norfolk, VA 23501
Phone (804) 441-2471

Norfolk County
(see cities of Chesapeake and
Portsmouth)

*Northampton County Courthouse
Clerk of Circuit Court
PO Box 36
Eastville, VA 23347
Phone (804) 678-0465
*County organized 1634, original county;
name changed from Accawmack
County 1642/3*
Land records: Contact Kenneth F.
Arnold, Clerk of Circuit Court
Probate records: Contact Clerk of Circuit
Court
Probate search service: no charge, time
permitting; copies: 50¢ per page

*Northumberland County Courthouse
PO Box 217
Heathsville, VA 22473
Phone (804) 580-3700
*County organized 1648 from
Chickacoun Indian District*
Land records: Deeds from 1650 (from
1672 to 1706 missing unless re-
recorded and from 1729 to 1738
missing), land tax from 1850; contact
Steve Thomas, Clerk of the Circuit
Court
Naturalization records: Denizations (in
Colonial era) in order books; contact
J. Steve Thomas, Clerk of the Circuit
Court
Vital records: Some early births (and a
few deaths) of the Saint Stephens
parish from 1661 to 1810, no births of
the Wicomico parish for this period,
births from 1853 to 1896, deaths from
1861 to 1895, some marriages from
1735 to 1795, marriage bonds from
1783 to 1850, unindexed register of
minister's returns from 1850 to 1853,
marriages from 1854; contact Clerk of
the Circuit Court
Probate records: From 1650 (with some
missing years as land records); contact
Clerk of the Circuit Court; copies:
$1.00 per page if envelope and
postage are sent, no minimum;
"Please send an envelope, self-
addressed, large enough to include all
records requested; include sufficient
postage; since the General Index for
both wills and deeds does not
commence until 1750, one must know
the Record Book and page in
requesting documents before 1750; in
requesting documents after 1750, give
full name and approximate dates; for
those requesting genealogical
research, they will be given names of
genealogists to contact."

City of Norton
(see Wise County/Norton City)

*Nottoway County Courthouse
Nottoway, VA 23955

Phone (804) 645-9043
*County organized 1789 from Amelia
County*
Land records: From 1789 to 1842 and
from 1865; contact Clerk
Naturalization records: No naturalization
records
Vital records: No vital records
Probate records: From 1789 to 1842 and
from 1865; contact Clerk
Probate search service: $5.00; copies:
$1.00 per page, no minimum

Old Rappahannock County
(see Essex and Richmond counties)

*Orange County Courthouse
PO Box 230
Orange, VA 22960
Phone (703) 672-4030
*County organized 1734 from
Spotsylvania County*
Land records: From 1734; contact Clerk
of Circuit Court
Naturalization records: No naturalization
records
Vital records: Marriages from 1857;
contact Clerk of Circuit Court
Probate records: From 1734; contact
Clerk of Circuit Court
No probate search service; copies: 50¢
per page, no minimum

*Page County Circuit Court
116 South Court Street
Luray, VA 22835-1224
Phone (703) 743-4064
*County organized 1831 from
Rockingham and Shenandoah
counties*
Land records: Contact Luther E. Miller,
Clerk
No land records search service: copies:
50¢ per page
Probate records: Contact Clerk
No land records search service: copies:
50¢ per page

*Patrick County Courthouse
PO Box 148
Stuart, VA 24171-0148
Phone (703) 694-7213
*County organized 1791 from Henry
County*
Land records: From 1791; contact Susan
C. Gray, Clerk of Circuit Court
Vital records: Births from 1853 to 1896,
deaths from 1853 to 1870, marriages
from 1791; contact Clerk of Circuit
Court
Probate records: From 1791; contact
Clerk of Circuit Court
No probate search service; copies: 50¢
per page, additional fee for certified
copies

Pendleton County, West Virginia
(see Highland County)

**Petersburg (Independent City)
Courthouse**
Union and Tabb Streets
Petersburg, VA 23803
Phone (804) 733-2301

*Pittsylvania County Courthouse
PO Box 31
Chatham, VA 24531-0031
Phone (804) 432-2041
*County organized 1767 from Halifax
County*

*Poquoson (Independent City)
830 Poquoson Avenue
Poquoson, VA 23662-1733
Phone (804) 868-3510
City organized 1975
"Poquoson does not have a courthouse;
we share this service with the County
of York, and this inquiry should be
directed to them."

**Portsmouth (Independent City) Circuit
Court**
601 Crawford Street
Portsmouth, VA 23704
Phone (804) 393-8671
*City organized 1958 from Norfolk
County*
Land records: Yes; copies: 50¢ per page,
no restrictions
Vital records: Yes; copies: 50¢ per page,
no restrictions
Probate records: Yes; copies: 50¢ per
page, no restrictions

Powhatan County Courthouse
3834 Old Buckingham Road
Powhatan, VA 23139-7019
Phone (804) 598-5600
*County organized 1777 from
Cumberland and Chesterfield
counties*

Prince Edward County Courthouse
PO Box 304
Farmville, VA 23901-0304
Phone (804) 392-5145
*County organized 1754 from Amelia
County*

*Prince George County Courthouse
PO Box 98
Prince George, VA 23875-0098
Phone (804) 733-2640
*County organized 1703 from Charles
City County*
Land records: From 1710 to 1728, from
1787 to 1792, and from 1842 to date;
contact Clerk

Naturalization records: Contact Clerk
Vital records: Contact Clerk
Probate records: Contact Clerk

*Prince William County
PO Box 191
9311 Lee Avenue
Prince William, VA 22110
Phone (703) 335-6015
*County organized 1731 from King
George and Stafford counties*
Land records: Deeds from 1731; contact
Clerk of Circuit Court
Naturalization records: No naturalization
records
Vital records: Marriages from 1859;
contact Clerk of Circuit Court
Probate records: From 1731
Probate search service: $10.00; copies:
50¢ per page, no minimum

Princess Anne County
(see Virginia Beach)

*Pulaski County Courthouse
Third Street
Pulaski, VA 24301
Phone (703) 980-8888
*County organized 1839 from
Montgomery and Wythe counties*
Land records: From 1839
Naturalization records: No naturalization
records
Vital records: Births and deaths from
1853 to 1933, marriages from 1854 to
1933; copies: $2.00 for marriages
Probate records: From 1839
No probate search service; copies: $1.00
per page, no minimum

***Radford (Independent City)
Courthouse**
619 Second Street
Radford, VA 24141-1431
Phone (703) 731-3610
City organized 1892
Land records: From 1892
Vital records: Marriage licenses (if
obtained licenses in Radford, if living
in Radford at the time)
Probate records: Yes
No probate search service; copies: 50¢
per page

*Rappahannock County Clerk's Office
PO Box 517
Washington, VA 22747-0517
Phone (703) 675-3621
*County organized 1833 from Culpeper
County (not to be confused with Old
Rappahannock County, with county
seat at Lancaster, which was
organized 1656 from Lancaster
County and abolished 1692)*
Land records: Yes

Naturalization records: No naturalization
records
Vital records: A few births and deaths
(1850s and 1890s), marriage licenses
from 1833
Probate records: From 1833
No probate search service

*Richmond (Independent City)
John Marshall Courts Building
800 East Marshall Street
Richmond, VA 23219
*In late 1910 annexed the city of
Manchester, which was incorporated
in 1874*
Land records: Contact Circuit Court
Probate records: Contact Circuit Court

*Richmond County Courthouse
Court Street
PO Box 956
Warsaw, VA 22572
Phone (804) 333-3781
*County organized 1692 from Old
Rappahannock County, which was
organized 1656 from Lancaster
County and abolished 1692*
Land records: From 1692
Naturalization records: No naturalization
records
Vital records: Church registers from 1672
to 1800 includes births, deaths and
marriages
Probate records: From 1699
Probate search service: refer to State
Library; copies: 50¢ to 75¢ per page,
$1.00 minimum plus SASE

**Roanoke (Independent City)
Courthouse**
215 Church Avenue, S.W.
Roanoke, VA 24011-1517
Phone (703) 981-2333

*Roanoke County Courthouse
PO Box 1126
Salem, VA 24153-1126
Phone (703) 387-6205
*County organized 1838 from Botetourt
and Montgomery counties*
Land records: Contact Steven A.
McGraw, Clerk
Naturalization records: No naturalization
records
Vital records: Marriages but no deaths;
contact Clerk
Probate records: Contact Clerk
Probate search service: $5.00; copies:
50¢ per page, no minimum; "All
record searches must be in writing;
with a limited staff there may be
delays in responding to the search
requests."

*Rockbridge County Circuit Court
Courthouse Square
2 South Main Street
Lexington, VA 24450
Phone (703) 463-2232
*County organized 1778 from Augusta
and Botetourt counties*
Land records: From 1778 to date; ("We
do not have manpower to do general
index searches for land records, etc.")
Naturalization records: Some recorded in
an old order book (unsure of the
number)
Vital records: Births from 1853 to 1896
(very limited), deaths from 1853 to
1870 (very limited), marriages from
1778 to date
Probate records: From 1778 to date
No probate search service; copies: $1.00
for each of the first two pages and 50¢
for each additional page, no
minimum; "Our office is not staffed to
do genealogical research; we will
assist persons who come to our office
but can answer mailed requests only
when time allows (usually during
summer months); requests for
copywork received through the mail
must be accompanied by SASE and
should request specific documents."

*Rockingham County Courthouse
Circuit Court Square
Harrisonburg, VA 22801
Phone (703) 434-4455
*County organized 1778 from Augusta
County*
Land records: From 1778
Naturalization records: No naturalization
records
Vital records: No vital records
Probate records: From 1778
No probate search service; copies: 50¢
each, no minimum

Russell County Courthouse
PO Box 435
Lebanon, VA 24266
Phone (703) 889-8023
*County organized 1786 from
Washington County*

*Salem (Independent City) Courthouse
PO Box 891
Salem, VA 24153-0891
Phone (703) 375-3067
Land records: From 1968
Vital records: From 1968
Probate records: From 1968

Scott County General District Court
104 Jackson Street East, #9
Gate City, VA 24251
Phone (703) 386-7341
*County organized 1814 from Lee,
Russell and Washington counties*

*Shenandoah County Courthouse
PO Box 406
Woodstock, VA 22664-0406
Phone (703) 459-6150
*County organized 1772 from Frederick
County; name changed from
Dunmore County in 1778*
Land records: From 1772 to date; contact
Clerk
Vital records: Births and deaths from
1853 to 1869 (some years missing),
marriages from 1772 to date; contact
Clerk ("We can do certification of
marriages on record in indexes";
originals filed at Virginia State
Library and Archives, 11th Street at
Capitol Square, Richmond, VA 23219-
3491, copies from microfilm available
from Shenandoah County Historical
Society, c/o Shenandoah County
Library, 300 Stoney Creek Boulevard,
Edinburg, VA 22824)
Probate records: From 1772 to date;
contact Research Team
Probate search service: $5.00 per search
(includes up to five copies from Will
Book A–F only); copies: $1.00 each

*Smyth County Courthouse
PO Box 1025
Marion, VA 24354-1025
Phone (703) 783-7186
*County organized 1832 from
Washington and Wythe counties*
Land records: Contact Circuit Court
Clerk
Probate records: Contact Circuit Court
Clerk
Probate search service: $15.00 per hour;
copies: $1.00 per page, $2.00
minimum

South Boston (Independent City)
PO Box 417
South Boston, VA 24592-0417
Phone (804) 572-3621

Southampton County Courthouse
Courtland, VA 23837
Phone (804) 653-2200
*County organized 1749 from Isle of
Wight and Nansemond counties*

*Spotsylvania County Courthouse
PO Box 96
Spotsylvania, VA 22553-0096
Phone (703) 582-7090
*County organized 1721 from Essex,
King and Queen and King William
counties*
Land records: Contact Linda Jo Johnson,
Circuit Court Clerk
Naturalization records: Contact Circuit
Court Clerk
Vital records: Contact Circuit Court
Clerk

Probate records: Contact Circuit Court
Clerk

*Stafford County Circuit Court Clerk
PO Box 69
Stafford, VA 22555
Phone (703) 659-8750
*County organized 1664 from
Westmoreland County*
Land records: Yes (mostly post-war).
Pre-war records; contact Virginia State
Library and Archives, 11th Street at
Capitol Square, Richmond, VA 23219-
3491
Naturalization records: No naturalization
records
Vital records: No vital records
Probate: Yes (mostly post-war). Pre-war
records; contact Virginia State Library
and Archives, 11th Street at Capitol
Square, Richmond, VA 23219-3491

***Staunton (Independent City)
Courthouse**
Circuit Court Clerk's Office
PO Box 1286
Staunton, VA 24402-1286
Phone (703) 332-3874
Land records: From 1802
Naturalization records: No naturalization
records
Vital records: Some old births and deaths
from 1853 to 1898
Probate records: From 1802

Suffolk (Independent City) Courthouse
441 Market Street
Suffolk, VA 23434-5237
Phone (804) 934-3111
*City organized 1 January 1974 from
Nansemond County (which was
called Upper Norfolk County from its
organization in 1636 from New
Norfolk County until 1642/3)*

Surry County Courthouse
PO Box 65
Surry, VA 23883-0065
Phone (804) 294-5271
*County organized 1652 from James City
County*

*Sussex County Courthouse
PO Box 1337
Sussex, VA 23884-0337
Phone (804) 246-5511
*County organized 1754 from Surry
County*
Land records: Deeds from 1754; contact
Clerk of Circuit Court
Naturalization records: Interspersed in
court minutes (not readily available);
contact Clerk of Circuit Court
Vital records: Births and deaths from
1853 to 1869 and 1892 to 1896,

marriages from 1754; contact Clerk of Circuit Court; copies: $3.00 for marriages

Probate records: From 1754; contact Clerk of Circuit Court

Probate search service: generally no charge; copies: $1.00 for each of the first two pages and 50¢ for each additional page, no minimum; "A limit of five archival records per customer copied at one time."

*Tazewell County Courthouse
PO Box 968
Tazewell, VA 24651
Phone (703) 988-7541
County organized 1800 from Logan, Russell, Washington and Wythe counties
Land records: Deeds from 1800; contact Circuit Court Clerk's Office
Vital records: Births and deaths from 1853 to 1870, marriages from 1800; contact Circuit Court Clerk's Office
Probate records: Wills from 1800; contact Circuit Court Clerk's Office
No probate search service; copies: $1.00 for each of the first two pages and 50¢ for each additional page per document; "Office employees are forbidden to do index searches."

Upper Norfolk County
(see City of Suffolk and Isle of Wight County)

*Virginia Beach Circuit Court Clerk's Office
2401 Courthouse Boulevard
Virginia Beach, VA 23456
Phone (804) 427-4181
In 1963 absorbed Princess Anne County, which was formed in 1691 from Lower Norfolk County
Land records: From 1691 to date; contact J. Curtis Fruit, Clerk
Naturalization records: No naturalization records
Vital records: Marriage licenses from 1821 to date; contact Clerk
Probate records: From 1691 to date; contact Clerk

*Warren County Circuit Court
1 East Main Street
Front Royal, VA 22630-3382
Phone (703) 635-2435
County organized 1836 from Frederick and Shenandoah counties
Land records: From 1836; contact William A. Hall, Clerk
Naturalization records: No naturalization records
Vital records: From 1836 to 1895; contact Clerk

Probate records: From 1836; contact Clerk
No probate search service; copies: 50¢ per page, $1.00 minimum

Warrossauosacke County
(see Isle of Wight County)

City of Warwick
(see City of Newport News)

Warwick County
(see City of Newport News)

Warwick River County
(see City of Newport News)

*Washington County Circuit Court
111 North Court Street
Abingdon, VA 24210
Phone (703) 628-5568; (703) 628-3761
County organized 1777 from Fincastle (organized 1772 from Botetourt County and abolished 1777) and Montgomery counties
Land records: From about 1778
Naturalization records: No naturalization records
Vital records: Marriages
Probate records: From 1778
No probate search service; copies: 50¢ per page, $1.00 for certified copies, 50¢ minimum; "We prefer you get a genealogist to do the research."

*City of Waynesboro
PO Box 910
Waynesboro, VA 22980-0748
Phone (703) 942-6616
City organized 1 May 1948 from Augusta County
Land records: From 1 May 1948; contact Jeanette J. Akers, Clerk of Circuit Court; copies: 50¢ per page
Naturalization records: No naturalization records
Vital records: Marriages; contact Clerk of Circuit Court; copies: 50¢ per page
Probate records: contact Clerk of Circuit Court; copies: 50¢ per page

*Westmoreland County Courthouse
PO Box 307
Montross, VA 22520
Phone (804) 493-0108
County organized 1653 from Northumberland County
Land records: From 1653; contact Mrs. Doris R. Moss, Clerk
Naturalization records: Contact Clerk ("We may have some but do not know dates")
Vital records: Births and deaths from 1855 to 1895; contact Clerk

Probate records: Wills from 1653; contact Clerk
Probate search service: "We usually don't charge to look, but for copies"; copies: $2.00 for each of the first four pages and 50¢ for each additional page, $2.00 minimum; "We do research when we have time, so there may be a delay in getting an answer because we haven't had the time to look it up."

Williamsburg (Independent City) Courthouse
401 Lafayette Street
Williamsburg, VA 23185
Phone (804) 229-4821

*Winchester (Independent City) Circuit Court
Frederick-Winchester Judicial Center
5 North Kent Street
Winchester, VA 22601-5037
Phone (703) 667-5770 Clerk of Circuit Court
City founded 1744, chartered as independent city in 1872
Land records: From 1790; contact Michael M. Foreman, Clerk of Winchester Circuit Court
Naturalization records: Contact Virginia State Library and Archives, 11th Street at Capitol Square, Richmond, VA 23219-3491
Vital records: Marriages from 1790 (very incomplete until 1853, complete from 1866); contact Clerk of Winchester Circuit Court
Probate records: From 1790; contact Clerk of Winchester Circuit Court
No probate search service; copies: 50¢ per page, no minimum; "We will copy pages of specific requests when name, book and page number given; to have individual research done, contact Historical Society."

*Wise County/Norton City Courthouse
PO Box 1248
Wise, VA 24293-1248
Phone (703) 328-6111 Clerk of the Circuit Court
County organized 1856 from Lee, Russell and Scott counties
Land records: Deeds; contact Gracie G. Hensky, Acting Clerk of the Circuit Court, Wise County/City of Norton
Naturalization records: No naturalization records
Vital records: Marriages; contact Clerk of the Circuit Court
Probate records: Contact Clerk of the Circuit Court
No probate search service; copies: 50¢ per page.

*Wythe County Circuit Court Building
225 South Fourth Street
Wytheville, VA 24382
Phone (703) 228-6644 Clerk
County organized 1790 from
    Montgomery and Grayson counties
Land records: From 1790; contact
    Hayden H. Horney, Clerk of the
    Circuit Court
No land records search service: contact
    Mary B. Kegley, PO Box 134,
    Wytheville, VA 24382 or Mrs. W. T.
    Trevillian, 665 West Washington
    Street, Wytheville, VA 24382
Naturalization records: No naturalization
    records
Vital records: Only one Birth and Death
    Record Book ("It starts 1853 for a
    span of about 10 to 12 years"); contact
    Clerk of the Circuit Court
No naturalization records search service
    (contact Ms. Kegley or Mrs.
    Trevillian)
Probate records: From 1790; contact
    Clerk of the Circuit Court
No probate search service (contact Ms.
    Kegley or Mrs. Trevillian); copies:
    $1.00 per page from large-format,
    early books, 50¢ per page from small
    books

York County Courthouse
PO Box 532
Yorktown, VA 23690-0532
Phone (804) 898-0200
County organized 1634, original county;
    name changed from Charles River
    County in 1642

WASHINGTON

Capital: Olympia. Statehood: 11 November 1889 (territory organized 2 March 1853 out of Oregon Territory, including the present-day states of Washington, Idaho and Montana, west of the Rockies)

Court System

Washington has some 136 Municipal and Police Courts with limited jurisdiction over municipal ordinance violations. Seventy-one District Courts, having jurisdiction over some civil actions, small claims, misdemeanors, traffic and felony preliminaries, serve Washington's thirty-nine counties, sitting in each county seat and elsewhere. Those Distict Courts which are the only one in their county sit at the county seat and are named after the county; for example, Asotin District Court in Asotin County. The following counties have more than one District Court within their boundaries: Adams County: Othello and Ritzville District Courts; Clallam County: Clallam District Courts No. 1 (at Port Angeles) and No. 2 (at Forks); Douglas County: Douglas (at East Wenatchee) and Bridgeport Branch District Courts; Grays Harbor County: Grays Harbor District Courts No. 1 (at Montesano) and No. 2 (at Aberdeen); King County: Airport (at Seattle), Aukeen (at Auburn), Bellevue, Federal Way, Issaquah, Mercer Island, Northeast King (at Redmond), Renton, Roxbury (at Seattle), Seattle, Shoreline (at Seattle) and Vashon Island District Courts; Kittitas County: Lower Kittitas (at Ellensburg) and Upper Kittitas (at Cle Elum) District Courts; Klickitat County: East Klickitat (at Goldendale) and West Klickitat (at White Salmon); Pacific County: North Pacific (at South Bend) and South Pacific (at Long Beach) District Courts; Pierce County: Pierce District Courts No. 1 (at Tacoma), No. 2 (at Gig Harbor), No. 3 (at Eatonville) and No. 4 (at Buckley); Snohomish County: Cascade (at Arlington), Everett, Evergreen (at Monroe) and South Snohomish (at Lynwood) District Courts; Spokane County: Cheney, Deer Park, Millwood (at Spokane) and Spokane District Courts; Walla Walla County: College Place and Walla Walla District Courts; Whitman County: Whitman (at Colfax) and Pullman Branch District Courts; Yakima County: Sunnyside, Toppenish and Yakima District Courts.

Superior Court sits at each county seat and has general jurisdiction over all civil matters except small claims, probate, divorce, criminal and juvenile matters. Seven of the thirty judicial districts include more than one county: Asotin-Columbia-Garfield, Benton-Franklin, Chelan-Douglas, Ferry-Pend Oreille-Stevens, Island-San Juan, Klickitat-Skamania and Pacific-Wahkiakum. The Court of Appeals and Supreme Court hear appeals.

Courthouses

*Adams County Courthouse
210 West Broadway
Ritzville, WA 99169-1860
Phone (509) 659-0090
County organized 1883 from Whitman
    County
Land records: From 1879 to date; contact
    County Auditor
Land records search service: $8.00 per
    hour; copies: $1.00 each, $3.00 for
    certified copies
Naturalization records: Contact County
    Clerk
Vital records: Births and deaths from
    1891 to 1907; contact County Auditor
Probate records: Contact County Clerk
Probate search service: $8.00 per hour;
    copies: $1.00 each, $3.00 for certified
    copies

*Asotin County Courthouse
PO Box 159
Asotin, WA 99402-0159
Phone (509) 243-4181
County organized 1883 from Garfield
    County
Land records: Contact Assessor
Probate records: Yes
Probate search service: $8.00 per hour;
    copies: statutory fee

Benton County Courthouse
PO Box 190
Prosser, WA 99350-0190
Phone (509) 786-4278
County organized 1855, original county

*Chelan County Courthouse
PO Box 3025
Wenatchee, WA 98801-0403
Phone (509) 664-5380
County organized 1899 from Kittitas
    and Okanogan counties
Land records: Only as awarded through
    litigation
Naturalization records: No naturalization
    records
Vital records: Adoptions (confidential)
Probate records: From 1900
Probate search service: $20.00 minimum;
    copies: $2.00 for the first page and
    $1.00 for each additional page, $2.00
    minimum

*Clallam County Courthouse
223 East Fourth Street
Port Angeles, WA 98362-3098
Phone (360) 417-2000
County organized 1854 from Jefferson County
Land records: Deeds: Contact Auditor
Naturalization records: Contact County Clerk
Vital records: Births, deaths and marriages to 1907 (not complete); contact Auditor
Probate records: Contact County Clerk
Probate search service: $8.00 per hour; copies: $2.00 for the first page and $1.00 for each additional page

*Clark County Courthouse
1200 Franklin Street
PO Box 5000
Vancouver, WA 98666-5000
Phone (206) 699-2291 Assessor; (206) 699-2292 County Clerk; (206) 695-9215 Health Department
County organized 1845, original county
Land records: Contact Assessor
Naturalization records: Contact County Clerk
Vital records: Contact Health Department
Probate records: Contact County Clerk
Probate search service: $8.00; copies: $2.00 for the first page and $1.00 for each additional page; "If papers leave Clerk's office they need to be certified."

*Columbia County Courthouse
341 East Main Street
Dayton, WA 99328-1361
Phone (509) 382-4541 Auditor; (509) 382-4321 Clerks
County organized 1875 from Walla Walla County
Land records: From 1864; contact Auditor
Naturalization records: From 1875 to 1942 (index only)
Vital records: Births and deaths from July 1891 to July 1906; contact Auditor
Probate records: From 1875; contact Clerks
Probate search service: $20.00 per hour, $8.00 minimum; copies: $1.00 per page

*Cowlitz County Hall of Justice
312 S.W. First Street
Kelso, WA 98626-1798
Phone (360) 577-3010 Assessor; (360) 577-3016 County Clerk
County organized 1854, original county
Land records: Contact County Assessor's Office, 207 North Fourth Avenue, Kelso, WA 98626
Probate records: Index to wills from 6 December 1878, probate fee book

from 13 February 1894; contact Peggy J. Bogdon, County Clerk, Room 233
Probate search service: $20.00 per hour, $10.00 per name minimum (especially for pre-1925 records); copies: $1.00 per page, $1.00 for certification of pleadings

*Douglas County Courthouse
PO Box 516
Waterville, WA 98858-0516
Phone (509) 745-8529
County organized 1883 from Lincoln County
Probate records: Yes
Probate search service: $8.00 per hour; copies: $2.00 for the first page and $1.00 for each additional page

*Ferry County
PO Box 498
Republic, WA 99166-0498
Phone (509) 775-5200 Auditor; (509) 775-5232 Clerk's Office
County organized 1899 from Stevens County
Land records: From 1898; contact Auditor's Office; copies: $1.00 per page
Land records search service: $8.00 per hour; copies: $1.00 per page, $2.00 for certification
Naturalization records: From 1920 to 1930 only; contact Clerk
Vital records: Marriages from 1898; contact Auditor's Office
Vital records search service: $8.00 per hour; copies: $1.00 per page, $2.00 for certification
Probate records: Contact Clerk's Office
Probate search service: $8.00 per hour; copies: 50¢ per page, no minimum

Franklin County Courthouse
1016 North Fourth Avenue
Pasco, WA 99301-3706
Phone (509) 545-3525
County organized 1883 from Whitman County

*Garfield County Courthouse
PO Box 915
Pomeroy, WA 99347-0915
Phone (509) 843-1411 Auditor; (509) 843-3731 Clerk
County organized 1881 from Columbia County
Land records: Contact Donna Deal, Auditor, PO Box 278, Pomeroy, WA 99347
Naturalization records: Contact Betty Capwell, Clerk
Vital records: Births from 1891 to 1952, deaths from 1891 to 1955; contact Auditor

Probate records: From 1882; contact Clerk
Probate search service: no charge; copies: 25¢ per page

*Grant County Law and Justice Center
PO Box 37
Ephrata, WA 98823-0037
Phone (509) 754-2011 Clerk
County organized 24 February 1909 from Douglas County
Land records: Deeds, etc.; contact Auditor's Office. Land records; contact County Assessor
Naturalization records: Contact Gorden E. Harris, Clerk
Vital records: Contact County Health District. Marriage licenses; contact Auditor
Probate records: Contact Clerk
Probate search service: $8.00 per hour per name; copies: $2.00 for the first page and $1.00 for each additional page, no minimum

*Grays Harbor County
100 West Broadway
PO Box 590
Montesano, WA 98563-0590
Phone (360) 249-4121 Assessor; (360) 249-4232 County Auditor; (360) 249-3842 County Clerk
County organized 1855, original county; name changed from Chehalis County in 1915
Land records: Current ownership records, but no history of ownership; contact F. Paul Easter, Assessor, PO Box 470, Montesano, WA 98563-0470. Chain of title; contact Verna Spatz, County Auditor, PO Box 751, Montesano, WA 98563
No land records search service (contact Coast Title and Escrow, Inc., 211 East Market Street, Aberdeen 98520)
Probate records: From 1856 (microfilm used); contact Jackie Busse, County Clerk, PO Box 711
No probate search service; copies: $2.00 for the first page and $1.00 for each additional page, $8.00 minimum for written report

*Island County Courthouse
PO Box 5000
Coupeville, WA 98239
Phone (206) 679-7359
County organized 1854, original county
Land records: Contact Auditor/Assessor/Treasurer
Probate records: Contact Clerk
Probate search service: $20.00 per hour; copies: $2.00 for the first page and $1.00 for each additional page per document; "No personal checks."

*Jefferson County Courthouse
PO Box 1220
Port Townsend, WA 98368
Phone (206) 385-9100; (206) 385-9105
Assessor; (206) 385-9115 Auditor;
(206) 385-9125 Superior Court
County organized 1854, original county
Land records: Contact Assessor
Naturalization records: From 1854 to
September 1906; contact County
Clerk
Vital records: Births and deaths to 1907;
contact Auditor
Probate records: Contact Superior Court
Probate search service: $8.00 per hour;
copies: $1.00 for the first page and
50¢ for each additional page, $2.00
for the first certified page and $1.00
for each additional certified page,
$8.00 minimum

*King County Courthouse
Superior Court Clerk
516 Third Avenue
Seattle, WA 98104
Phone (206) 296-1540 Records and
Elections Division; (206) 296-7300
Assessor's Office
County organized 1852, original county
Land records: All real estate documents
of encumbrance or transfer; contact
Jane Hague, Manager of Records and
Elections Division, Records Section,
311 King County Administration
Building, 500 Fourth Avenue, Seattle,
WA 98104. Precise legal description,
tax account numbers, brief sales
history and assessed value; contact
Assessor's Office, Seventh and Eighth
Floor, King County Administration
Building
Probate records: Contact Superior Court
Clerk
No probate search service; copies: $2.00
for the first page and $1.00 for each
additional page; "Correspondence
requests: $8.00."

*Kitsap County Courthouse
614 Division Street
Port Orchard, WA 98366-4614
Phone (206) 876-7164
*County organized 1857 from Jefferson
County*
Land records: Contact Assessor
Probate records: Contact County Clerk
Probate search service: $8.00; copies:
$1.00 per page, $2.00 per document
for certification, no minimum

*Kittitas County Courthouse
205 West Fifth Avenue
Ellensburg, WA 98926-2887
Phone (509) 962-6811
*County organized 1883 from Yakima
County*

Land records: Appraisals of land; contact
Assessor. Land ownership, deeds,
plats, surveys; contact Auditor
Naturalization records: From 1889;
contact Clerk
Vital records: Contact Auditor
Probate records: From 1889; contact
Clerk
Probate search service: $8.00 per hour;
copies: $1.00 per page

*Klickitat County Courthouse
205 South Columbus Avenue
Goldendale, WA 98620-9286
Phone (509) 773-4001 Auditor; (509)
773-5744 County Clerk
*County organized 1859, original county
(or from Clark County)*
Land records: From 1866; contact Nancy
J. Evans, Auditor, Room 203
Land records search service: $8.00 per
hour; copies: $1.00 per page, $3.00
for certified copies
Naturalization records: From March 1889
to 1906; contact County Clerk's
Office, Room 204
Vital records: Births from 1882 to July
1907, deaths from 1891 to 12 March
1907, marriages; contact Auditor
Vital records search service: $8.00 per
hour; copies: $3.00 each
Probate records: From January 1880;
contact Clerk's Office
Probate search service: $8.00 per hour;
copies: $2.00 for the first page and
$1.00 for each additional page, $3.00
for the first certified page and $1.00
for each additional certified page, no
minimum

*Lewis County Courthouse
344 West Main
Chehalis, WA 98532-1922
Phone (360) 740-1156 Auditor; (800)
562-6130 Auditor; (360) 740-1163
Recording Department
County organized 1845, original county
Land records: Plats, surveys; contact
Gary E. Zandell, Auditor, 351 N.W.
North Street, PO Box 29, Chehalis,
WA 98532-0029
Land records search service: $8.00 per
name; copies: $1.00 per page, $2.00
per document for certification
Naturalization records: No naturalization
records
Vital records: Births and deaths before 1
June 1907; contact Auditor. Marriage
licenses; contact Recording
Department, Auditor's Office; copies:
$11.00 each. Births and deaths from
1954 to date; contact County Health
Department, 360 N.W. North Street,
Chehalis, WA 98532; copies: $11.00
each
Probate records: Contact Donna Karvia,

County Clerk, 360 N.W. North Street,
Chehalis, WA 98532

*Lincoln County Courthouse
450 Logan Street
Davenport, WA 99122-9501
Phone (509) 725-1401
*County organized 1883 from Spokane
County*
Naturalization records: Contact County
Clerk's Office
Probate records: Contact County Clerk's
Office
Probate search service: $8.00 per hour,
$4.00 minimum; copies: 25¢ per page,
$2.00 for certified documents plus
$1.00 per page

*Mason County Courthouse
Fourth and Alder
Shelton, WA 98584
Phone (206) 427-9670 Auditor
*County organized 1854 from Thurston
County; name changed from
Sawanish County in 1864*
Land records: Washington Territorial
Records from 1858 to 1889, Statehood
records from 1890; contact Auditor's
Office, Courthouse Annex II, 411
North Fifth Street, Shelton, WA 98584
Naturalization records: No naturalization
records ("Clerk's Office transferred
Mason County's records to
Department of Naturalization in
Tacoma, WA")
Vital records: Births from 1891 to 1906,
deaths from 1891 to 1905, marriages
from 1892; contact Auditor's Office
Probate records: From 1890; contact
Clerk's Office
Probate search service: $8.00 per hour,
$4.00 minimum; copies: $2.00 for the
first page and $1.00 for each
additional page plus SASE, no
minimum

*Okanogan County
PO Box 72
Okanogan, WA 98840-0072
Phone (509) 422-3650
*County organized 2 February 1888 from
the west part of Stevens County*
Land records: Contact Jim Hand, County
Assessor's Office
Naturalization records: Some
naturalization records, none after
1976; contact County Clerk
Probate records: From 1895; contact
County Clerk
Probate search service: $8.00 per hour;
copies: 50¢ per page, no minimum

Pacific County Courthouse
PO Box 67
South Bend, WA 98586-0067
Phone (206) 875-6541

County organized 1854, original county

*Pend Oreille County Courthouse

PO Box 5015
Newport, WA 99156-5015
Phone (509) 447-3185 Auditor; (509) 447-2435 County Clerk
County organized 1911 from Stevens County

Land records: Information concerning land; contact Assessor's Office. Statutory warranty deeds, quit claim deeds, easements, agreements, plats, liens, mortgages, UCCs, patent records, quartz locations, mining locations, lis pendens and water right locations; contact Ann Swenson, Auditor

Land records search service from Auditor: $8.00 per hour; copies: $1.00 per page, $2.00 per document for certification, $5.00 for the first page of surveys or plats and $3.00 for each additional page

Vital records: Marriages; contact Auditor
Vital records search service: $8.00 per hour; copies: $8.00 each
Probate records: Contact County Clerk's Office, 229 South Garden Avenue, Newport, WA 99156
Probate search service: $8.00 per hour; copies: $2.00 for the first page and $1.00 for each additional page, no minimum

*Pierce County Courthouse

Clerk's Office
930 Tacoma Avenue South
Tacoma, WA 98402-2102
Phone (206) 475-9555 Assessor-Treasurer; (206) 591-7455 Clerk's Office—Divorces; (206) 591-6413 Health Department; (206) 591-7461 Clerk's Office—Probate
County organized 1853, original county
Land records: Contact Assessor-Treasurer, 2401 South 35th, Tacoma, WA 98409
Land records search service: $10.00; copies: $1.00 for the first page and $1.00 for each additional page, no minimum
Naturalization records: No naturalization records
Vital records: Births and divorces; contact Health Department, 3629 South D Street, Tacoma, WA 98408-6897
Vital records search service: $10.00; copies: $1.00 for the first page and $1.00 for each additional page, no minimum
Probate records: Contact Clerk's Office
Probate search service: $10.00; copies: $1.00 for the first page and $1.00 for each additional page, no minimum

*San Juan County Courthouse

350 Court Street
Friday Harbor, WA 98250
Phone (206) 378-2163 County Clerk and ex-officio Clerk of San Juan Superior Court; (206) 378-2161 County Auditor
County organized 1873 from Whatcom County
Land records: Contact County Assessor. Surveys and plat maps; contact Si A. Stephens, County Auditor, 350 Court Street, PO Box 638, Friday Harbor, WA 98250; copies: $1.00 per page, $2.00 per document for certification, $1.50 per page for reduced size surveys and plats
Naturalization records: No naturalization records ("Old records sent to State Archives.")
Vital records: Marriages to July 1907; contact County Auditor; copies $1.00 each, $11.00 for certified copies
Probate records: From 1800s and early 1900s; contact State Archives at Western Washington University, Bellingham. Recent probate records: Contact County Clerk's Office
Probate search service: $8.00 per hour; copies: $2.00 for the first page and $1.00 for each additional page, $8.00 minimum

*Skagit County Courthouse

PO Box 837
Mount Vernon, WA 98273-0837
Phone (206) 336-9440
County organized 1883 from Whatcom County
Land records: Contact Treasurer or Assessor
Probate records: Contact Phyllis Coole-McKeehen, Clerk
Probate search service: $20.00 per hour per name (prepaid); copies: $2.00 for the first page and $1.00 for each additional page, $2.00 per document for certification

*Skamania County Courthouse

PO Box 790
Stevenson, WA 98648-0790
Phone (509) 427-5141
County organized 1854 from Clark County
Land records: Contact Assessor
Naturalization records: Contact Clerk
Vital records: Marriages; contact Auditor. Dissolutions; contact Clerk
Probate records: Contact Clerk
Probate search service: $8.00 per hour; copies: $2.00 for the first page and $1.00 for each additional page, no minimum

*Snohomish County

3000 Rockefeller
Everett, WA 98201
Phone (206) 388-3483 County Auditor; (206) 339-5280 County Health District; (206) 388-3466 County Clerk
County organized 1861 from Island County
Land records: Contact County Auditor, Recording and Filing, First Floor Administration Building, 3000 Rockefeller, M/S 204, Everett, WA 98201
Vital records: Contact County Health District, Vital Statistics, 3020 Rucker, Everett, WA 98201
Probate records: Contact County Clerk, Room 246 Mission Building, 3000 Rockefeller, Everett, WA 98201
Probate search service: $12.00 for 1 to 10 names, $16.00 for 11 to 15 names, $20.00 for 16 to 20 names; copies: $2.00 for the first page and $1.00 for each additional page of document, no minimum; "The Clerk's Office cannot accept personal checks; cashier's check or money order acceptable; SASE requested."

*Spokane County Courthouse

West 1116 Broadway
Spokane, WA 99201
Phone (509) 456-2270 Auditor's Office; (509) 456-3671 Vital Records; (509) 456-2211 Clerk's Office
Spokane County created 29 January 1858 in the legislature's 1858–59 session, from Walla Walla County; Missoula County (now Montana) created 7 May 1860, from all land east of longitude 115 (eastern third of Spokane County); Stevens County created 20 January 1863, with Stevens County attached to Spokane County for judicial purposes; Washington Territory divided by Congress 3 March 1863, with all east of longitude 117 and the Snake River in Idaho Territory, thus shrinking Stevens County so that Spokane County was eliminated 19 January 1864 and annexed to Stevens County; Spokane County recreated 30 October 1879
Land records: Contact Auditor's Office
Land records search service: $8.00 per hour; copies: $1.00 per page, $2.00 for certification
Vital records: Contact West 1101 College, Spokane, WA 99201
Probate records: Contact County Clerk's Office, PO Box 470, Spokane, WA 99210-0470
Probate search service: $8.00; copies: $2.00 for the first page and $1.00 for each additional page; "Please enclose SASE."

*Stevens County Courthouse
PO Box 189
Colville, WA 99114
Phone (509) 684-3751
Spokane County created 29 January 1858 in the legislature's 1858-59 session, from Walla Walla County; Missoula County (now Montana) created 7 May 1860, from all land east of longitude 115 (eastern third of Spokane County); Stevens County created 20 January 1863, with Stevens County attached to Spokane County for judicial purposes; Washington Territory divided by Congress 3 March 1863, with all east of longitude 117 and the Snake River in Idaho Territory, thus shrinking Stevens County so that Spokane County was eliminated 19 January 1864 and annexed to Stevens County; Spokane County recreated 30 October 1879
Land records: Contact Tim Gray, County Auditor
Land records search service: $8.00 per hour, $4.00 minimum; copies: $1.00 per page, $2.00 for certification

*Thurston County Courthouse
2000 Lakeridge, S.W.
Olympia, WA 98502-6045
Phone (206) 754-3800
County organized 1852 from Lewis County
Land records: Contact Auditor
Naturalization records: No naturalization records
Vital records: Births and deaths from 1890 to 1907, marriages from 1852; contact Auditor or Thurston County Health Department, 529 West Fourth, Olympia, WA 98501
Probate records: Contact Clerk

Wahkiakum County Courthouse
PO Box 116
Cathlamet, WA 98612-0116
Phone (206) 795-3558
County organized 1854 from Lewis County

*Walla Walla County Courthouse
315 West Main Street
Walla Walla, WA 99362-2838
Phone (509) 527-3221 County Clerk
County organized 1854 at the first session of the Washington Territorial Legislature, original county
Land records: From 1860; contact County Auditor's Office, PO Box 1856, Walla Walla, WA 99362
Land records search service: $8.00 per hour per name; copies: $1.00 per page
Naturalization records: From 1800s to September 1906; contact Washington

State Archives, Eastern Regional Branch, J.F.K., Library N1584, Eastern Washington University, Cheney, WA 99004-2495. Records from September 1906 to September 1950 moved to Yakima, WA. Must request certificates from Spokane, WA
Vital records: Marriages from 1862 to date
Probate records: From 1800s; contact County Clerk, PO Box 836, Walla Walla, WA 99362
Probate search service: $20.00 per hour; copies: $2.00 for the first page and $1.00 for each additional page

Whatcom County Courthouse
311 Grand Avenue
Bellingham, WA 98225-4038
Phone (206) 676-6777
County organized 1854 from Island County

*Whitman County Courthouse
Main and Island
PO Box 390
Colfax, WA 99111-0390
Phone (509) 397-6240
County created 29 November 1871 from Stevens County, organized 1 January 1872 by an 1871 act of the legislature
Land records: Contact Clerk's Office; copies: 25¢ per page
Naturalization records: Contact Clerk's Office; copies: 25¢ per page
Vital records: Contact Clerk's Office; copies: 25¢ per page
Probate records: Contact Clerk's Office; copies: 25¢ per page

*Yakima County Courthouse
(Second and East "B" Streets—location)
128 North "B" Street, Room 323 (mailing address)
Yakima, WA 98901
Phone (509) 575-4048 Auditor; (509) 575-4120 Clerk's Office
County organized 1865 from Indian Territory
Land records: From the late 1800s to date by name, date only—no legal description; contact Auditor, 128 North Second Street, Room 117
Land records search service: $8.00 per hour; copies: $1.00 per page, $2.00 per document for certification
Naturalization records: Limited records retained; contact Kim M. Eaton, County Clerk, Office of County Clerk and Ex-Officio Clerk of Superior Court
Vital records: Births and deaths before 1907, marriages from the late 1800s to date
Vital records search service: $8.00 per hour (please submit correct spelling of

names and approximate dates); copies: $1.00 per page, $2.00 per document for certification
Probate records: Contact Office of County Clerk and Ex-Officio Clerk of Superior Court
Probate search service: $20.00 per hour (please submit correct spelling of names and approximate dates); copies: 10¢ per page, minimum, $2.00 for the first certified page and $1.00 for each additional certified page

WEST VIRGINIA

Capital: Charleston. Statehood: 20 June 1863 (part of Virginia until the Civil War)

Court System

West Virginia has about fifty-five Magistrate Courts and fifty-four Municipal Courts of limited jurisdiction. The Court of Claims hears damage claims against the government and claims made under the Crime Victims Compensation Act. The County Commissions, formerly the County Courts, are established in every county to administer probate, mental commitments, guardianships, etc.

Thirty-one Circuit Courts have general jurisdiction in civil and criminal matters. The following Judicial Circuits include more than one county: First Judicial Circuit: Brooke, Hancock and Ohio counties; Second Judicial Circuit: Marshall, Tyler and Wetzel counties; Third Judicial Circuit: Doddridge, Pleasants and Ritchie counties; Fourth Judicial Circuit: Wirt and Wood counties; Fifth Judicial Circuit: Calhoun, Jackson and Roane counties; Eleventh Judicial Circuit: Greenbrier, Monroe, Pocahontas and Summers counties; Fourteenth Judicial Circuit: Braxton, Clay, Gilmer and Webster counties; Nineteenth Judicial Circuit: Barbour and Taylor counties; Twenty-first Judicial Circuit: Grant, Mineral and Tucker counties; Twenty-second Judicial Circuit: Hampshire, Hardy and Pendleton counties; Twenty-third Judicial Circuit: Berkeley, Jefferson and Morgan counties; Twenty-fifth Judicial Circuit: Boone and Lincoln counties; Twenty-sixth Judicial Circuit: Lewis and Upshur counties; Twenty-ninth Judicial Circuit: Mason and Putnam counties; Thirty-first Judicial Circuit: Berkeley, Jefferson and Morgan counties. Note that the Twenty-third and Thirty-first Judicial Circuits are the same. The Supreme Court of Appeals is the court of last resort.

Courthouses

Barbour County Courthouse
PO Box 310
Philippi, WV 26416-0310
Phone (304) 457-2232
County organized 1843 from Harrison, Lewis and Randolph counties

*Berkeley County Courthouse
100 West King Street (Public Square, corner of King and Queen Streets)
Martinsburg, WV 25401-3210
Phone (304) 264-1927
County organized 1772 from Frederick County (now Virginia)
Land records: Deeds from 1772 (books 14, 22, 28, 37, 42, 56 and the last half of 59 and 62 lost), land grants from 1772, surveyor's records from 1771, land books from 1782 to 1900 (last not open to the public); contact John W. Small, Jr., Clerk
No land records search service
Vital records: Births and deaths from 1865 to date, marriage bonds from 1781 to 1870 (originals not open to the public, but available in printed form); contact Clerk
No vital records search service
Probate records: From 1772 (will books 11, 17, 18, 19 and 20 lost, some lost wills re-recorded), inventories and settlements of accounts (listed separately from will books after the Civil War), guardian bonds from 1776 to 1847 and from 1865 to 1873 (not open to the public); contact Clerk
No probate search service

Boone County Courthouse
Madison, WV 25130
Phone (304) 369-3925
County organized 1847 from Cabell, Kanawha and Logan counties

*Braxton County Courthouse
PO Box 486
Sutton, WV 26601
Phone (304) 765-2833
County organized 1836 from Kanawha, Lewis, Nicholas and Randolph counties
Land records: From 1836; contact County Clerk
Land records search service: no charge
Naturalization records: No naturalization records
Vital records: Births and deaths from 1853, marriages from 1856; contact County Clerk
Vital records search service: no charge; copies: $2.00 each
Probate records: From 1836; contact County Clerk
Probate search service: no charge; copies: $1.50 for the first two pages and $1.00 for each additional page, no minimum; "We do not search the indexes without specific periods of time within the request."

*Brooke County Courthouse
632 Main Street
Wellsburg, WV 26070

Phone (304) 737-3661
County organized 1796 from Ohio County
Land records: Deeds; contact Sylvia J. Benzo, County Clerk, County Clerk's Office; copies: $3.00 for the first two pages of deeds and 50¢ for each additional page, plus stamps, $2.00 each for plats up to 120 square inches and 1¢ for each additional square inch
Naturalization records: Contact County Circuit Clerk's Office
Vital records: Births and deaths from 1853, marriages from 1797; copies: $2.00 each; contact County Clerk's Office
Probate records: Wills from 1797, letters of administration; contact County Clerk's Office
No probate search service; copies: $1.00 each, $1.50 to certify long form

Cabell County Courthouse
Huntington, WV 25701
Phone (304) 526-8625
County organized 1809 from Kanawha County

*Calhoun County Courthouse
PO Box 230
Grantsville, WV 26147
Phone (304) 354-6725 County Clerk
County organized 1856 from Gilmer County
Land records: Grantor and grantee; contact Richard Kirby, County Clerk
Naturalization records: No naturalization records
Vital records: Births, deaths and marriages; contact Clerk
Probate records: Wills; contact Clerk
Probate search service: no charge (supply names and dates); copies: $1.50 for the first two pages and $1.00 for each additional page of the same document, $1.50 minimum

*Clay County Courthouse
PO Box 190
Clay, WV 25043
Phone (304) 587-4259
County organized 1858 from Braxton and Nicholas counties
Land records: From 1858
Vital records: From 1858
Probate records: From 1858
No probate search service; copies: $1.50 for the first two pages and $1.00 for each additional page, $1.50 minimum

*Doddridge County Courthouse
118 East Court Street
West Union, WV 26456
Phone (304) 873-2631
County organized 1845 from Harrison, Tyler, Ritchie and Lewis counties

Land records: From 1845; contact
County Clerk's Office
Vital records: Births, deaths and
marriages from 1845; contact County
Clerk's Office; copies: $1.50 each
Probate records: From 1845; contact
County Clerk's Office
No probate search service; copies: $1.50
for the first two pages and $1.00 for
each additional page

*Fayette County Courthouse
Fayetteville, WV 25840
Phone (304) 574-1200
*County organized 1831 from Kanawha,
Greenbrier, Nicholas and Logan
counties*
Land records: From 1830s
Naturalization records: No naturalization
records
Vital records: Births and deaths from
1866, marriages from 1831
Probate records: Yes
No probate search service; copies: $1.50
for the first two pages and $1.00 for
each additional page, $1.50 minimum;
"Need date of death, name of
decedent."

*Gilmer County Courthouse
Glenville, WV 26351
Phone (304) 462-7641
*County organized 1845 from Lewis and
Kanawha counties*
Land records: From 1845; contact
County Clerk's Office
Vital records: From 1853; contact County
Clerk's Office
Probate records: From 1845; contact
County Clerk's Office
Probate search service: no charge (no
genealogy searches, but will look up
specific items when pertinent
information is provided); copies:
$1.50 for the first two pages and
$1.00 for each additional page, no
minimum

*Grant County Courthouse
5 Highland Avenue
Petersburg, WV 26847-1705
Phone (304) 257-4422
*County organized 1866 from Hardy
County*
Land records: From 1866; contact
County Clerk's Office
Naturalization records: From 1866;
contact Circuit Clerk's Office
Vital records: From 1866; contact County
Clerk's Office
Probate records: From 1866; contact
County Clerk's Office
No probate search service; copies: 25¢
for each of the first ten pages and 15¢
for each additional page, 25¢
minimum

*Greenbrier County Courthouse
PO Box 506
Lewisburg, WV 24901-0506
Phone (304) 647-6602
*County organized 1778 from
Montgomery and Botetourt counties
(now Virginia)*
Land records: From late 1700s
Naturalization records: No naturalization
records
Vital records: From 1853
Probate records: From late 1700s
Probate search service: $5.00; copies:
$1.00 per standard page or $1.00 per
reduced page, no minimum

*Hampshire County Courthouse
Romney, WV 26757
Phone (304) 822-5112
*County organized 1754 from Frederick
and Augusta counties (now Virginia)*
Land records: Deeds from 1754
Naturalization records: No naturalization
records
Vital records: Births, deaths and marriage
records from 1865
Probate records: From 1754 (although
some of these are missing)
Probate search service: no charge;
copies: $1.50 for the first two pages
and $1.00 for each additional page, no
minimum; "We need names and dates
before we will research any record."

*Hancock County Courthouse
102 North Court Street
New Cumberland, WV 26047
Phone (304) 564-3311; (304) 564-4059
FAX
*County organized 1848 from Brooke
County*
Land records: Contact County Clerk and
Assessor
Naturalization records: Contact Circuit
Clerk
Vital records: Contact County Clerk
Probate records: Contact County Clerk
No probate search service; copies: $1.50
for the first two pages and $1.00 for
each additional page, $1.50 minimum

*Hardy County Courthouse
PO Box 540
Moorefield, WV 26836-0540
Phone (304) 538-2929
*County organized 1786 from Hampshire
County*
Land records: Yes
Naturalization records: No naturalization
records
Vital records: Yes
Probate records: Yes
Probate search service: $5.00; copies:
$1.50 for the first two pages and
$1.00 for each additional page, $1.50
minimum; "We do very little

genealogy research; we refer requests
to a local genealogist."

*Harrison County Courthouse
301 West Main
Clarksburg, WV 26301-2909
Phone (304) 624-8611
*County organized 1784 from
Monongalia, Randolph and Ohio
counties*
Land records: From 1800s
Naturalization records: No naturalization
records
Vital records: Births and deaths from
1853, marriages from 1700s; copies:
$2.00 per page
Probate records: From 1881
No probate search service; copies: $1.50
for the first two pages and $1.00 for
each additional page

*Jackson County Courthouse
c/o Jeff Waybright, Clerk
PO Box 800
Ripley, WV 25271
Phone (304) 372-2011
*County organized 1831 from Kanawha,
Mason and Wood counties*
Land records: From 1831
Naturalization records: No naturalization
records
Vital records: Births and deaths from
1853, marriages from 1831 (no
restrictions)
Probate records: From 1831
No probate search service: copies: $1.50
for the first two pages and $1.00 for
each additional page

*Jefferson County Courthouse
PO Box 208
Charles Town, WV 25414
Phone (304) 728-3215
*County created from Berkeley County in
an act passed by the General
Assembly of Virginia 8 January 1801
(area contained in Virginia's
Northumberland County, 1648–1652,
Lancaster County 1652–1656, Old
Rappahannock County 1656–1691,
Essex County 1691–1720,
Spotsylvania County 1720–1734,
Orange County 1734–1738,
Frederick County 1738–1772, and
Berkeley County 1772–1801)*
Land records: From 1801; copies: $1.00
per page
Naturalization records: Contact Circuit
Clerk, PO Box 584, Charles Town,
WV 25414
Vital records: Births and deaths from
1853, marriages from 1801; copies:
$1.00 per page
Probate records: Wills from 1801; copies:
$1.00 per page

*Kanawha County Courthouse
PO Box 3226
Charleston, WV 25332-3226
Phone (304) 357-0130
County organized 1789 from Greenbrier County (now West Virginia) and Montgomery County (now Virginia)
Land records: From 1790; contact Alma Y. King, Clerk
Vital records: Births and deaths from 1853, marriages from 1854; contact Clerk
Probate records: Wills from 1790; contact Clerk

*Lewis County Commission
PO Box 87
Weston, WV 26452-0076
Phone (304) 269-3371
County organized 1816 from Harrison and Randolph counties
Land records: From early 1800s; contact Mary Lou Myers, County Clerk
Naturalization records: Contact Randolph County
Vital records: Births and deaths from 1853, marriages from early 1800s; copies: $2.00 each
Probate records: From early 1800s
Probate search service: $5.00; copies: $1.50 for the first two pages and $1.00 for each additional page, no minimum

*Lincoln County Courthouse
c/o Donald C. Whitten, County Clerk
(8000 Court Street—location)
PO Box 497 (mailing address)
Hamlin, WV 25523
Phone (304) 824-3336
County organized 1867 from Boone, Cabell and Kanawha counties
Land records: Yes
Naturalization records: Yes
Vital records: Yes
Probate records: Yes

*Logan County Courthouse
Logan, WV 25601
Phone (304) 752-2000
County organized 1824 from Cabell and Kanawha counties, and Giles and Tazewell counties (now Virginia)
Land records: Yes
Naturalization records: No naturalization records
Vital records: Yes
Probate records: Yes
Probate search service: no charge; copies: $1.50 for the first two pages and $1.00 for each additional page, $1.50 minimum

Marion County Courthouse
Fairmont, WV 26554
Phone (304) 367-5440

County organized 1842 from Harrison and Monongalia counties

Marshall County Courthouse
PO Box 459
Moundsville, WV 26041-0459
Phone (304) 845-1220
County organized 1835 from Ohio County

Mason County Courthouse
Point Pleasant, WV 25550
Phone (304) 675-1997
County organized 1804 from Kanawha County

McDowell County Courthouse
PO Box 967
Welch, WV 24801-0967
Phone (304) 436-6587
County organized 1858 from Tazewell County (now Virginia)

*Mercer County Courthouse
Courthouse Square
Princeton, WV 24740
Phone (304) 487-8311
County organized 1837 from Giles and Tazewell counties (now Virginia)
Land records: From 1837
Naturalization records: No naturalization records
Vital records: From 1853
Probate records: From 1853
No probate search service; copies: $1.50 for the first two pages and $1.00 for each additional page

*Mineral County Commission
150 Armstrong Street
Keyser, WV 26726-0250
Phone (304) 788-3924
County organized 1866 from Hampshire County
Land records: From 1865; contact Clerk of County Commission; copies: $1.50 for the first two pages and $1.00 for each additional page
Naturalization records: No naturalization records
Vital records: Births, deaths and marriages from 1865; contact Clerk of County Commission
No vital records search service (must have date of event within two or three years); copies: $1.50 each
Probate records: Wills from 1865; contact Clerk of County Commission; copies: $1.50 for the first two pages and $1.00 for each additional page

*Mingo County Commission
PO Box 1197
Williamson, WV 25661-1197
Phone (304) 235-1638

County organized 1895 from Logan County
Land records: Contact Assessor, Tax Department, County Clerk
Naturalization records: Contact Circuit Clerk
Vital records: Contact County Clerk
Probate records: Contact County Clerk
No probate search service; copies: $1.50 for the first two pages and $1.00 for each additional page, no minimum; "Records are public, you may search."

*Monongalia County Courthouse
243 High Street
Morgantown, WV 26505-5491
Phone (304) 291-7230 County Clerk
County organized 1776 from District of West Augusta
Land records: Some land records in 1700s, Thelma J. Gibson, Clerk
No land records search service (contact Monongalia County Historical Society, PO Box 127, Morgantown, WV 26505)
Vital records: Births and deaths from 1853, marriages from 1796; contact Clerk
No vital records search service
Probate records: Some probate records from the 1700s; contact Clerk
No probate search service; copies: $1.50 for the first two pages and $1.00 for each additional page; "We do not have anyone employed to do genealogy research."

*Monroe County Courthouse
PO Box 350
Union, WV 24983
Phone (304) 772-3096
County organized 1779 from Greenbrier County (now West Virginia) and Botetourt County (now Virginia)
Land records: Yes
No land records search service; copies: $1.00 each
Naturalization records: Yes
No naturalization records search service; copies: $1.00 each
Vital records: Yes
No vital records search service; copies: $1.00 each
Probate records: Yes
No probate search service; copies: $1.00 each

Morgan County Courthouse
Fairfax Street
Berkeley Springs, WV 25411
Phone (304) 258-2774
County organized 1820 from Berkeley and Hampshire counties

Nicholas County Courthouse
Summersville, WV 26651
Phone (304) 872-3630

County organized 1818 from Greenbrier, Kanawha and Randolph counties

*Ohio County Courthouse
City County Building
1500 Chapline Street, Room 205
Wheeling, WV 26003-3553
Phone (304) 234-3656
County organized 1776 from Augusta County
Land records: Deed books from 1778; copies: 50¢ per page (no copies of index records)
Naturalization records: No naturalization records, just index ("All records kept in Library in Morgantown, WV")
Vital records: Births and deaths from 1853 ("Births were not required to be recorded until 1923, some we have, others we don't"), marriages from 1790
Vital records search service: $1.00 per name; certified copies: $2.00 each
Probate records: Settlements from 1777, wills from late 1700s
No probate search service (contact Wheeling Area Genealogical Society, 2237 Marshall Avenue, Wheeling, WV 26003); copies: 50¢ per page (no copies of index records), no minimum

*Pendleton County Courthouse
Franklin, WV 26807
Phone (304) 358-2505
County organized 1788 from Hardy County (now West Virginia) and Augusta and Rockingham counties (now Virginia)
Land records: From 1788
Vital records: Births and deaths from 1853, marriages from 1800
Probate records: From 1789
No probate search service; copies: $1.00 per page, $1.50 minimum

*Pleasants County Courthouse
301 Court Lane
Saint Marys, WV 26170
Phone (304) 684-7542
County organized 1851 from Ritchie, Tyler and Wood counties
Land records: Contact Shirley Roby, County Clerk, Room 101
Naturalization records: Contact Gail Mote, Circuit Clerk
Vital records: Contact County Clerk
Probate records: Contact County Clerk
Probate search service: no charge, but accurate years must be provided; copies: $1.50 for the first two pages and $1.00 for each additional page, $1.50 each for certified copies

*Pocahontas County Courthouse
900C Tenth Avenue
Marlinton, WV 24954-1333

Phone (304) 799-4549
County organized 1821 from Pendleton, Randolph and Greenbrier counties (now West Virginia) and Bath County (now Virginia)
Land records: From 1822
Naturalization records: From 1904 to 1929; contact Circuit Clerk's Office
Vital records: Births from 1854, deaths from 1853
Probate records: From 1822
Probate search service: 50¢ per name; copies: $1.50 for the first two pages and $1.00 for each additional page per document, no minimum

Preston County Courthouse
101 West Main
Kingwood, WV 26537-1121
Phone (304) 329-0070
County organized 1818 from Monongalia and Randolph counties

*Putnam County Courthouse
PO Box 508
Winfield, WV 25213-0508
Phone (304) 586-9292
County organized 1848 from Kanawha, Mason and Cabell counties
Land records: From 1848; contact Clerk
Vital records: From 1848; contact Clerk
Probate records: From 1848; contact Clerk
Probate search service: $2.00 per name; copies: $1.50 for the first two pages and $1.00 for each additional page

*Raleigh County Courthouse
Beckley, WV 25801
Phone (304) 255-9123
County organized 1850 from Fayette County
Land records: Contact Assessor
Naturalization records: Contact Circuit Clerk
Vital records: From 1853; contact County Clerk
Probate records: From 1853; contact County Clerk
Probate search service: no charge; copies: $1.50 for the first two pages and $1.00 for each additional page, $2.00 each for certified copies; "We only check years that the incident occurred, we don't do genealogical searches."

Randolph County Courthouse
Elkins, WV 26241
Phone (304) 636-0543
County organized 1787 from Harrison County

*Ritchie County Courthouse
115 East Main Street
Harrisville, WV 26362

Phone (304) 643-2164 Clerk
County organized 1843 from Harrison, Lewis and Wood counties
Land records: From 1853; contact Linda B. Maze, County Clerk
Vital records: From 1853; contact County Clerk
Probate records: From 1853; contact County Clerk
No probate search service; copies: $1.50 for the first two pages and $1.00 for each additional page

*Roane County Courthouse
PO Box 69
Spencer, WV 25276
Phone (304) 927-2860
County organized 1856 from Gilmer, Jackson and Kanawha counties
Land records: Contact County Clerk; copies: $1.50 for the first two pages and $1.00 for each additional page
Naturalization records: No naturalization records
Vital records: Contact County Clerk; copies: $2.00 each
Probate records: Contact County Clerk
Probate search service: $1.00 per name per book; copies: $1.50 for the first two pages and $1.00 for each additional page, no minimum

*Summers County Courthouse
PO Box 97
Hinton, WV 25951-0097
Phone (304) 466-3770
County organized 1871 from Greenbrier, Monroe and Mercer counties
Land records: From 1871; contact County Clerk
Vital records: From 1871; contact County Clerk
Probate records: From 1871; contact County Clerk
Probate search service: no charge; copies: $1.50 for the first two pages and $1.00 for each additional page, no minimum

Taylor County Courthouse
Grafton, WV 26354
Phone (304) 265-1401
County organized 1844 from Harrison, Barbour and Marion counties

*Tucker County Courthouse
Parsons, WV 26287
Phone (304) 478-2414
County organized 1856 from Randolph County
Land records: From 1856; contact Nina B. Buchanan, County Clerk
Naturalization records: Contact Allen D. Judy, Circuit Clerk

Vital records: From 1856; contact County Clerk

Probate records: From 1856; contact County Clerk

Probate search service: $5.00; copies: $1.50 for the first two pages and $1.00 for each additional page, $1.50 minimum

*Tyler County Courthouse
PO Box 66
Middlebourne, WV 26149-0066
Phone (304) 758-2102
County organized 1814 from Ohio County
Land records: Contact Clerk and Assessor's Office
Vital records: From 1853; contact Clerk's Office
Probate records: Contact Clerk's Office
Probate search service: fees depending on the research; copies: $1.50 for the first two pages and 50¢ for each additional page, $2.00 each for certified copies, $1.50 minimum

Upshur County Courthouse
Buckhannon, WV 26201
Phone (304) 472-1068
County organized 1851 from Randolph, Barbour and Lewis counties

*Wayne County Courthouse
Wayne, WV 25570
Phone (304) 272-6371
County organized 1842 from Cabell County
Land records: Deeds from 1842; contact County Clerk, PO Box 248, Wayne, WV 25570
Naturalization records: No naturalization records
Vital records: Births, deaths and marriages from 1853; contact County Clerk
Probate records: Supplemental fiduciary (list of heirs) from 1909, appraisements from 1878, settlements from 1886, wills from 1843; contact County Clerk
Probate search service: no charge; copies: $1.50 for the first two pages and $1.00 for each additional page, $1.50 minimum

*Webster County Commission
2 Court Square, Room G-1
Webster Springs, WV 26288
Phone (304) 847-2508
County organized 1860 from Braxton, Nicholas and Randolph counties
Land records: Contact Terry J. Payne, Clerk
Naturalization records: Contact Clerk
Vital records: Births, deaths and marriages; contact Clerk; copies: $1.50 each

*Wetzel County Courthouse
PO Box 156
New Martinsville, WV 26155-0156
Phone (304) 455-8224; (304) 455-8217
County organized 1846 from Tyler County
Land records: From 1846; contact County Clerk's Office; copies: $1.50 for the first two pages and $1.00 for each additional page
Naturalization records: From 1846; contact Circuit Clerk's Office
Vital records: Births, deaths and marriage licenses from 1846; contact County Clerk's Office; copies: $2.00 each
Probate records: From 1846; contact County Clerk's Office
No probate search service (will look up a name but will not do index searches; contact Wetzel County Genealogical Society, PO Box 464, New Martinsville, WV 26155-0464, which charges $10.00 per half day); copies: $1.50 for the first two pages and $1.00 for each additional page, no minimum

*Wirt County Courthouse
PO Box 53
Elizabeth, WV 26143-0053
Phone (304) 275-4271
County organized 1848 from Jackson and Wood counties
Land records: Contact County Clerk
Vital records: Contact County Clerk
Probate records: Contact County Clerk
No probate search service; copies: $1.50 for the first two pages and $1.00 for each additional page, no minimum

*Wood County Courthouse
Parkersburg, WV 26101
Phone (304) 424-1850
County organized 1798 from Harrison and Kanawha counties
Land records: From 1798
Naturalization records: No naturalization records
Vital records: From 1801
Probate records: From 1880
Probate search service: no charge; copies: $1.50 for the first two pages and $1.00 for each additional page, no minimum

*Wyoming County Courthouse
PO Box 309
Pineville, WV 24874-0309
Phone (304) 732-8000
County organized 1850 from Logan County
Land records: From 1850; contact D. Michael Goode, Clerk
Naturalization records: Contact Jack Lambert, Clerk, Circuit Clerk's Office, PO Box 190, Pineville, WV 24874; copies: 25¢ per page

Vital records: From 1850; contact Clerk
Probate records: From 24 January 1931; contact Clerk
No probate search service; copies: $1.50 for the first two pages and $1.00 for each additional page

WISCONSIN

Capital: Madison. Statehood: 29 May 1848 (recognized as part of the U.S. by great Britain in 1783, claims relinquished by Virginia, Massachusetts and Connecticut, in the Northwest Territory 1787, Indiana Territory 7 May 1800, Illinois Territory 3 February 1809, Michigan Territory 18 April 1818, and organized as a separate territory in 20 April 1836)

Court System

Wisconsin has over 200 Municipal Courts with limited jurisdiction over local ordinances. There are sixty-nine Circuit Courts with general jurisdiction which sit at each county seat except in the following combined districts: Buffalo-Pepin at Alma, Forest-Florence at Crandon, and Shawano-Menominee at Shawano. The Court of Appeals and Supreme Court hear appeals.

Courthouses

*Adams County Courthouse
PO Box 219
Friendship, WI 53934
Phone (608) 339-4206
County organized 1848 from Portage County
Land records: Deeds from 1853; contact Alma Thurber, Register of Deeds; copies: $2.00 each
Naturalization records: No naturalization records
Vital records: Births from 1860, deaths from 1876, marriages from 1859; contact Register of Deeds; copies: $10.00 each for births, $7.00 each for deaths and marriages

*Ashland County Courthouse
201 West Second Street
Ashland, WI 54806-1638
Phone (715) 682-7008 Register of Deeds; (715) 682-7016 Clerk of Circuit Court; (715) 682-7009 Probate
County organized 1860 from unorganized territory
Land records: Contact Wendell Friske, Register of Deeds
Naturalization records: From 1890; contact Kathleen Colgrove, Clerk of Circuit Court
Vital records: From 1890; contact Register of Deeds

Probate records: From 1890; contact Jean F. Stolarzyk
Probate search service: $4.00 per name; copies: $1.00 per page, no minimum

Bad Ax County
(see Vernon County)

*Barron County Courthouse
Barron, WI 54812-9801
Phone (715) 537-6210
County organized 1859; name changed from Dallas County in 1869
Land records: Contact Donna M. Miller, Register of Deeds, 330 East LaSalle Avenue, Barron, WI 54812
Naturalization records: Contact Area Research Center, University of Wisconsin—Stout, Menomonie, WI 54751
Vital records: Contact Register of Deeds
Probate records: Contact Judge's Office

*Bayfield County Courthouse
PO Box 878
Washburn, WI 54891
Phone (715) 373-5508
County organized 1845 from Ashland County; name changed from LaPointe County in 1866
Land records: Contact Tax Lister's Office
Naturalization records: Contact Register of Deeds
Vital records: Contact Register of Deeds
Probate records: Contact Clerk of Courts
Probate search service: $5.00; copies: $1.25 per page

*Brown County Office Building
PO Box 1600
Green Bay, WI 54305-5600
Phone (414) 448-4471 Tract Index; (414) 448-4160 Clerk of Courts; (414) 448-4470 Register of Deeds; (414) 448-4275 Register in Probate
County organized 1818 from territorial county, annexed part of Shawano and Oconto counties in 1919
Land records: Contact Tract Index, Brown County Office Building, 111 North Jefferson Street, PO Box 23600, Green Bay, WI 54305-3600
Naturalization records: From 1940; contact Clerk of Courts, Brown County Courthouse, PO Box 23600, Green Bay, WI 54305-3600. Before 1940; contact Area Research Center, University of Wisconsin—Green Bay, Seventh Floor, Library Learning Center, Special Collections, 2420 Nicolet Drive, Green Bay, WI 54311-7001
Vital records: Births from 1746, deaths from 1834, marriages from 1821; contact Cathy Williquette Breunig,

Register of Deeds, 305 East Walnut Street, Room 260, PO Box 23600, Green Bay, WI 54305-3600; copies: $8.00 each for births, $5.00 each for deaths and marriages (cashier's check or money order)
Probate records: Contact Register in Probate, Brown County Courthouse, Room 160
Probate search service: $4.00; copies: $1.00 per page; "All county offices require the fee before we search or issue copies of documents."

*Buffalo County Courthouse
Alma, WI 54610
Phone (608) 685-4940
County organized 6 July 1853 from Jackson County to include all of what is now Trempealeau County, west of the line between ranges 7 and 8, south of the Buffalo River and north of the line between townships 18 and 19, enlarged in 1854 north to the line between townships 24 and 25, west to the Chippewa River, south to the Mississippi and the line between townships 18 and 19
Land records: Contact Donna J. Carothers, Register of Deeds, PO Box 28, Alma, WI 54610; copies: $2.00 for the first page and $1.00 for each additional page, 25¢ per document for certification
Naturalization records: Contact Rosella Urness, Clerk of Court
Vital records: Contact Register of Deeds; certified or uncertified copies: $10.00 each for births, $7.00 each for deaths and marriages (certified copies restricted to persons with a "direct and tangible interest" in the records)
Probate records: Contact Circuit Court, Renee Pronschinske, Register in Probate

*Burnett County Courthouse
7410 County Road K
Siren, WI 54872
Phone (715) 349-2183 Register of Deeds; (715) 349-2177 Register in Probate
County organized 1856 from Polk County
Land records: Contact Register of Deeds, #103; copies: $2.00 for the first page and $1.00 for each additional page
Naturalization records: No naturalization records
Vital records: Contact Register of Deeds; certified copies: $1.00 each for births, $7.00 each for deaths and marriages
Probate records: Contact Register in Probate, #110
Probate search service: $4.00; copies: $1.00 per page, $1.00 minimum

*Calumet County Courthouse
206 Court Street
Chilton, WI 53014-1127
Phone (414) 849-2361
County organized 1836 from territorial county
Land records: Contact Donna Schommer, Register of Deeds
Naturalization records: No naturalization records
Vital records: Contact Register of Deeds
Probate records: Contact Register of Probate

*Chippewa County Courthouse
711 North Bridge Street
Chippewa Falls, WI 54729-1876
Phone (715) 726-7927 Register of Deeds; (715) 726-7758 Clerk of Court; (715) 726-7737 Register of Probate
County organized 1845 from Crawford County (not to be confused with a former Chippewa County which existed at the time of the 1830 census, covering much of what is now Ashland, Bayfield, Douglas, Iron and Vilas counties)
Land records: Contact Register of Deeds
Naturalization records: Contact Clerk of Court
Vital records: Contact Register of Deeds
Probate records: Contact Register of Probate

*Clark County Courthouse
517 Court Street
Neillsville, WI 54456-1971
Phone (715) 743-5162 Register of Deeds; (715) 743-5173 Register in Probate
County organized 1853 from Marathon County
Land records: Contact Eugene Oberle, Register of Deeds, PO Box 384, Neillsville, WI 54456; copies: $2.00 for the first page and $1.00 for each additional page of the same document
Naturalization records: Incomplete before 1895; contact Register of Deeds
Vital records: Incomplete before 1905; contact Register of Deeds; certified or uncertified copies: $10.00 each for births, $7.00 each for deaths and marriages
Probate records: From 1874; contact Register in Probate ("Files prior to 1901 are on microfilm at State Historical Society")
Probate search service: $4.00, presently; copies: 15¢ each, no minimum

*Columbia County Courthouse
PO Box 177
Portage, WI 53901-0177
Phone (608) 742-2191
County organized 1846 from Portage, Brown and Crawford counties

Land records: From 1828 to date; contact Register of Deeds, PO Box 133, Portage, WI 53901; copies: $2.00 for the first page and $1.00 for each additional page of the same document
Naturalization records: Contact Clerk of Circuit Court, PO Box 405, Portage, WI 53901
Vital records: From the 1850s; contact Register of Deeds
Vital records search service: $10.00 for births, $7.00 for deaths and marriages (includes one copy, if the record is found)
Probate records: Contact Register in Probate, PO Box 221, Portage, WI 53901
Probate search service: $4.00 (cost of search applied to copies); copies: $1.00 per page, no minimum

*Crawford County Courthouse
220 North Beaumont Road
Prairie du Chien, WI 53821
Phone (608) 326-0219
County organized 26 October 1818 from territorial county
Land records: Contact Florence Erickson, Register of Deeds
Naturalization records: Contact Donna Steiner, Clerk of Courts
Vital records: Contact Register of Deeds
Probate records: Contact Joan Hurda, Register in Probate
No probate search service; copies: $2.00 per page, no minimum

Dallas County
(see Barron County)

*Dane County City-County Building
210 Martin Luther King, Jr. Boulevard
Madison, WI 53709
Phone (608) 266-4121; (608) 266-4141 Register of Deeds
County organized 1839 from Iowa County
Land records: Deeds, mortgages, land contracts, satisfactions, etc., from 1835 to date; contact Jane Licht, Register of Deeds, Room 110; copies: $2.00 for the first page and $1.00 for each additional page, 25¢ for certification. Land records; contact Planning and Development, Room 116
Naturalization records: Contact The State Historical Society of Wisconsin, 816 State Street, Madison, WI 53706
Vital records: From the 1850s to date (early records incomplete); contact Register of Deeds; certified or uncertified copies: $1.00 for births and $7.00 for deaths and marriages (certified copies restricted to persons with a "direct and tangible interest" in the records)

Probate records: Contact Probate Court, Room 305

*Dodge County Courthouse
127 East Oak Street
Juneau, WI 53039
Phone (414) 386-3600; (414) 386-3720 Register of Deeds
County organized 1836 from territorial county
Land records: From 1877 (date of fire); contact Doris Westra, Register of Deeds
No land records search service (contact Jeanne Dornfeld, W4402 Raasch's Hill Road, Horicon, WI 53032); copies: $2.00 for the first page and $1.00 for each additional page
Naturalization records: Index cards to naturalization records. Original records; contact Citizenship Records, Area Research Center, University of Wisconsin—Oshkosh, Forrest R. Polk Library, Elmwood Avenue, Oshkosh, WI 54901
Vital records: Births, deaths and marriages: copies: $10.00 each for births, $7.00 each for deaths and marriages (certified copies restricted to persons with a "direct and tangible interest" in the records)
Probate records: From 1840s; contact Register in Probate
Probate search service: $4.00 each; copies: $1.00 each, no minimum

*Door County Courthouse
421 Nebraska Street
PO Box 670
Sturgeon Bay, WI 54235-0670
Phone (414) 743-5511
County organized 1851 from Brown County
Land records: From 1857
Naturalization records: Contact the University of Wisconsin, Green Bay
Vital records: From 1857 (not a lot of records in the late 1800s); contact Register of Deeds; copies: $10.00 each for births, $7.00 each for deaths and marriages (certified copies restricted to persons with a "direct and tangible interest" in the records)
Probate records: From 1863
Probate search service: $4.00; copies: $1.00 each, no minimum

*Douglas County Courthouse
1313 Belknap Street
Superior, WI 54880-2730
Phone (715) 394-0341; (715) 394-0359; (715) 392-0463 Probate Court
County created by an act of legislature on 8 February 1854 from unorganized territory
Land records: Contact Diane Preston,

Register of Deeds and/or Raymond H. Somerville, County Clerk

Naturalization records: Contact Area Research Center, Superior Public Library, 1530 Tower Avenue, Superior, WI 54880

Vital records: Contact Register of Deeds; certified copies (restricted to persons with a "direct and tangible interest" in the records): $10.00 each for births, $7.00 each for deaths and marriages, $1.00 each for uncertified copies

*Dunn County Courthouse
800 Wilson Avenue
Menomonie, WI 54751-2717
Phone (715) 232-1228 Register of Deeds; (715) 232-1449 Register in Probate
County organized 1854 from Chippewa County

Land records: Contact Register of Deeds ("The Register of Deeds Office will not do land or vital record searches over the telephone; the office does not have the staff to handle verbal requests; please send SASE with requests; the fee should be sent, and if a record is found a copy will be sent")

Naturalization records: Contact Area Research Center, University of Wisconsin—Stout, Menomonie, WI 54751

Vital records: Contact Register of Deeds; copies: $8.00 each for births, $5.00 each for deaths and marriages

Probate records: Contact Register in Probate

Probate search service: $4.00; copies: $1.00 per page, no minimum

*Eau Claire County Courthouse
721 Oxford Avenue
Eau Claire, WI 54703-5481
Phone (715) 839-5106; (715) 839-4745 Register of Deeds; (715) 839-4823 Register in Probate
County organized 1856 from Clark County

Land records: From 1856

Naturalization records: Contact Clerk of Court

Vital records: From 1907; contact Register of Deeds; copies: $10.00 each for births, $7.00 each for deaths and marriages

Probate records: Contact Register in Probate

Probate search service: $4.00; copies: $1.00 per page, $3.00 for certification, no minimum

*Florence County Courthouse
501 Lake Avenue
PO Box 410
Florence, WI 54121-0410
Phone (715) 528-3201 County Clerk;

(715) 528-4252 Register of Deeds; (715) 528-3205 Clerk of Court
County organized 1882 from Marinette and Oconto counties

Land records: Contact Rita McMullen, Register of Deeds

Naturalization records: Contact Clerk of Court

Vital records: Contact Register of Deeds

Probate records: Contact Clerk of Court

*Fond du Lac County Courthouse
160 South Macy Street
Fond du Lac, WI 54935-4241
Phone (414) 929-3000; (414) 929-3084 Register in Probate
County organized 1836 from territorial county

Land records: Contact Register of Deeds; copies: $2.00 for the first page and $1.00 for each additional page

Naturalization records: Contact Citizenship Records, University of Wisconsin—Oshkosh, Polk Library, Elmwood Avenue, Oshkosh, WI 54901

Vital records: Contact Register of Deeds

Vital records search service: $10.00 (applied to cost of copy if found); copies: $10.00 each for births, $7.00 for deaths and marriages

Probate records: Contact Register in Probate, PO Box 1355, Fond du Lac, WI 54936-1355

Probate search service: $4.00; copies: $1.00 per page, no minimum; "Send searching fee and summary of what information you want; we will advise as to what we have and cost of copies."

Forest County Courthouse
Crandon, WI 54520
Phone (715) 478-2422
County organized 1885 from Langlade and Oconto counties

Grant County Courthouse
130 West Maple
Lancaster, WI 53813-1625
Phone (608) 723-2675
County organized 1836 from Iowa County

*Green County Courthouse
1016 16th Avenue
Monroe, WI 53566
Phone (608) 328-9430; (608) 328-9439 Register of Deeds
County organized 1836 from Iowa County

Land records: Real estate records from 1837; contact Marilyn Neuenschwander, Register of Deeds; copies: $2.00 for the first page and $1.00 for each additional page, 25¢ for certification

Naturalization records: Contact Wisconsin Room—Karrmen Library, University of Wisconsin—Platteville, 1 University Plaza, Platteville, WI 53818; certified copies: $3.50 each

Vital records: Legitimate births from 1852, deaths from 1874, marriages from 1843 (incomplete before 1 June 1907); contact Register of Deeds; certified or uncertified copies: $10.00 each for births, $7.00 each for deaths and marriages (certified copies restricted to persons with a "direct and tangible interest" in the records)

Probate records: Contact Register in Probate

Probate search service: $4.00 per name; copies: $1.00 per page, no minimum

*Green Lake County Courthouse
492 Hill Street
Green Lake, WI 54941
Phone (414) 294-4021 Register of Deeds; (414) 294-4044 Register in Probate Office
County organized 1858 from Marquette District

Land records: From 1845; contact Register of Deeds

Naturalization records: Area Research Center, University of Wisconsin—Oshkosh, Forrest R. Polk Library, Oshkosh, WI 54901

Vital records: Births and deaths from 1876, marriages from 1852; contact Register of Deeds

Probate records: Contact Register in Probate Office

*Iowa County Courthouse
222 North Iowa Street
Dodgeville, WI 53533-1557
Phone (608) 935-5628 Register of Deeds
County organized 1829 from territorial county

Land records: From 1835 (grantee/grantor index only); contact Marian J. Raess, Register of Deeds

Land records search service: no charge, as time permits; copies: $2.00 for the first page and $1.00 for each additional page

Naturalization records: Naturalization index from 1835 to 1906; contact Clerk of Courts Office

Vital records: Births and deaths from 1877 (a few earlier), marriages from 1849 (most are indexed by groom only); contact Register of Deeds

Probate records: From 1830s; contact Register in Probate. Some wills and final judgments for estates recorded in land records; contact Register of Deeds

No probate search service; copies: $1.00 per page

Iron County Courthouse
300 Taconite Street
Hurley, WI 54534
Phone (715) 561-3375
County organized 1893 from Ashland and Oneida counties

*Jackson County Courthouse
Black River Falls, WI 54615
Phone (715) 284-0201
County organized 11 May 1853 from Crawford and La Crosse counties
Land records: Contact Treasurer or Tax Lister
Naturalization records: Contact Claudia Singleton, Clerk of Circuit Court
Vital records: Contact Shari Marg, Register of Deeds
Probate records: Contact Kathy Powell, Register in Probate
Probate search service: $4.00; copies: $1.00 each, no minimum

Jefferson County Courthouse
320 South Main Street
Jefferson, WI 53549-1718
Phone (414) 674-2500
County organized 1836 from Dodge and Waukesha counties

*Juneau County Courthouse
Mauston, WI 53948
Phone (608) 847-9311 Real Property Description Office; (608) 847-9355 Clerk of Courts Office; (608) 847-9325 Register of Deeds Office; (608) 847-9346 Register in Probate Office
County organized 1856 from Adams County
Land records: Contact Real Property Description Office
Naturalization records: Contact Clerk of Courts Office
Vital records: Contact Register of Deeds Office
Probate records: Contact Register in Probate Office
Probate search service: $4.00; copies: $1.00 per page, $3.00 certified

*Kenosha County Courthouse
1010 56th Street
Kenosha, WI 53140
Phone (414) 653-2414 Register of Deeds—Real Estate; (414) 653-2444 Register of Deeds—Vitals
County organized 1850 from Racine County
Land records: Contact Louise I. Principe, Register of Deeds; copies: $2.00 for the first page and $1.00 for each additional page, $3.00 each for plats, 25¢ for certification
Naturalization records: Contact Clerk of Courts. Old records; contact

University of Wisconsin—Parkside Library.
Vital records: Contact Register of Deeds; copies: $10.00 each for births, $7.00 each for deaths and marriages
Probate records: Contact Register in Probate
No probate search service

Kewaunee County Courthouse
613 Dodge Street
Kewaunee, WI 54216
Phone (414) 388-4410
County organized 1852 from Manitowoc County

*La Crosse County Courthouse
400 North Fourth Street
La Crosse, WI 54601-3227
Phone (608) 785-9581; (608) 785-9882 Register in Probate
County organized 1851 Crawford County
Land records: From 1851; contact Real Property Lister, Land, Title, Mapping Department
Naturalization records: Contact University of Wisconsin—La Crosse, Murphy Library, Area Research Center, 1725 State Street, La Crosse, WI 54601. If the Library does not have necessary records, contact La Crosse County Clerk of Courts
Vital records: From late 1800s; contact Register of Deeds
Probate records: From the late 1890s; contact Register in Probate, Room 312
Probate search service: $4.00; copies: $1.00 per page, no minimum

*Lafayette County Courthouse
PO Box 40
Darlington, WI 53530-0040
Phone (608) 776-4838 Register of Deeds Office
County organized 1846 from Iowa County
Land records: Government entry book from 1835; contact Register of Deeds Office
Naturalization records: Contact Karrmen Library, Platteville, WI
Vital records: Births from 1855 ("very sparse, not good until 1900"), deaths from 1876, marriages from 1847; contact Register of Deeds Office
Probate records: Through 1960; contact Area Research Center, University of Wisconsin—Platteville, Wisconsin Room—Elton S. Karrmann Library, 1 University Plaza, Platteville, WI 53818-3099
Probate search service: $4.00; copies: $1.00 per page, no minimum; "If mailed out, payment is required before."

*Langlade County Courthouse
800 Clermont Street
Antigo, WI 54409-1985
Phone (715) 627-6200; (715) 627-6209 Register of Deeds; (715) 346-3726 Area Research Center; (715) 627-6213 Register in Probate
County organized 1879 from Oconto County
Land records: From 1883 to date; contact Register of Deeds; copies: $2.00 for the first page and $1.00 for each additional page
Naturalization records: Contact Arthur Fish, Area Research Center, University of Wisconsin—Stevens Point, Learning Resources Center, Stevens Point, WI 54481
Vital records: Contact Register of Deeds; copies: $1.00 each for births, $7.00 each for deaths and marriages
Probate records: Contact Register in Probate
Probate search service: $4.00 per file; copies: $1.00 per page

LaPointe County
(see Bayfield County)

*Lincoln County Courthouse
1110 East Main Street
Merrill, WI 54452-2577
Phone (715) 536-0312; (715) 536-0318 Register of Deeds
County organized 1874 from Marathon County
Land records: Contact Joel Lang, Register of Deeds
Naturalization records: Area Research Center, University of Wisconsin—Stevens Point, Learning Resources Center, Stevens Point, WI 54481
Vital records: Contact Register of Deeds; copies: $10.00 each for births, $7.00 each for deaths and marriages
Probate records: Contact Register in Probate
Probate search service: $4.00; copies: 25¢ per page, no minimum; "Enclose SASE."

*Manitowoc County Courthouse
1010 South Eighth Street
Manitowoc, WI 54220-5392
Phone (414) 683-4000; (414) 683-4013 Register of Deeds; (414) 683-4015 Register in Probate
County organized 1836 from territorial county
Land records: From the early 1800s; contact Preston F. Jones, Register of Deeds, PO Box 421, Manitowoc, WI 54221-0421
Naturalization records: Contact Area Research Center, Library Learning Center, University of Wisconsin—

Green Bay, 2420 Nicolet Drive, Green Bay, WI 54301-7001

Vital records: Births, deaths and marriages from the 1850s; contact Register of Deeds

Probate records: Probate files from 1850; contact Jo Ann Monka, Register in Probate

Probate search service: $4.00; copies: $1.00 per page, $1.00 minimum; "We will review file and advise requester of documents we feel will be of genealogical value."

*Marathon County Courthouse
500 Forest Street
Wausau, WI 54403-5568
Phone (715) 847-5000 Courthouse switchboard; (715) 847-5214 Register of Deeds
County organized 1850 from Portage County
Land records: Contact Michael J. Sydow, Register of Deeds
Naturalization records: Contact Clerk of Court
Vital records: Contact Register of Deeds; copies: $10.00 each for births, $7.00 each for deaths and marriages
Probate records: Contact Register in Probate
Probate search service: $4.00 per name; copies: $1.00 per page, no minimum; "Return postage appreciated; old probate files stored in basement, not available for immediate review."

*Marinette County Courthouse
1926 Hall
Marinette, WI 54143-1728
Phone (715) 735-3371
County organized 1879 from Oconto County
Land records: Contact Florence Magnuson, Register of Deeds
Naturalization records: Contact Clerk of Court
Vital records: Contact Register of Deeds
Probate records: Contact Register in Probate
Probate search service: $4.00; fee for copies, no minimum

*Marquette County Courthouse
Montello, WI 53949
Phone (608) 297-9114
County organized 1836 from Marquette District
Land records: From 1836; contact Register of Deeds, PO Box 236, Montello, WI 53949
Naturalization records: No naturalization records
Vital records: From 1870, better records after 1911; contact Register of Deeds
Probate records: Contact Register in Probate

Probate search service: $4.00, but depends on extent of search; copies: $1.25 each

Menominee County Courthouse
800 Wilson Avenue
Keshena, WI 54135
Phone (715) 799-3311
County organized 1961 from Shawano and Oconto counties

*Milwaukee County Courthouse
901 North Ninth Street
Milwaukee, WI 53233
Phone (414) 278-4000 Register of Deeds (land); (414) 278-4003 Register of Deeds (vital records); (414) 278-4444 Register in Probate
County organized from the Northwest Territory; by an act of the Michigan Territorial Legislature, Milwaukee County became a distinct political division in August 1835, some eight months before the Territory of Wisconsin was created
Land records: Contact Register of Deeds
Naturalization records: Contact Milwaukee County Historical Society, Milwaukee, WI
Vital records: Contact Register of Deeds
Probate records: Contact Register in Probate, Room 207
Probate search service: $4.00; copies: $1.00 per page, no minimum

*Monroe County Courthouse
112 South Court Street
Sparta, WI 54656
Phone (608) 269-8705 County Clerk; (608) 269-8716 Register of Deeds; (608) 269-8701 Register in Probate
County organized 1854 from unorganized territory
Land records: Contact Vicky Jo Dutton, Register of Deeds, 112 South Court Street, PO Box 195, Sparta, WI 54656
Land records search service: $5.00 plus SASE; copies: $2.00 for the first page and $1.00 for each additional page of the same document
Naturalization records: Contact Area Research Center, University of Wisconsin—La Crosse, Eugene W. Murphy Library, 1631 Pine Street, La Crosse, WI 54601
Vital records: Births from 1850, deaths from 1867, marriages from 1854; contact Register of Deeds; copies: $10.00 each for births, $5.00 each for deaths and marriages (send for application form first, certified copies restricted to persons with a "direct and tangible interest" in the records)
Probate records: From the early 1870s; contact Susan K. Giudice, Register in Probate, 112 South Court Street, PO Box 165, Sparta, WI 54656

Probate search service: $4.00; copies: 50¢ per page, no minimum; "Please include a SASE for use in returning information."

*Oconto County Courthouse
300 Washington Street
Oconto, WI 54153-1621
Phone (414) 834-6807 Register of Deeds; (414) 834-6839 Register in Probate
County organized 1851 from Brown County
Land records: Contact Register of Deeds
Naturalization records: Contact Area Research Center, University of Wisconsin—Green Bay
Vital records: Births and deaths from 1872, marriages from 1855; contact Register of Deeds
Probate records: Contact Register in Probate
Probate search service: $4.00; copies: $1.00 per page, no minimum; "Payment in advance; mentals, adoptions and juvenile files are sealed and not for public view."

*Oneida County Courthouse
Oneida Avenue
PO Box 400
Rhinelander, WI 54501-0400
Phone (715) 369-6150
County organized 1885 from Lincoln County
Land records: Contact Thomas H. Leighton, Register of Deeds; copies: $1.00 per page
Naturalization records: Contact University of Wisconsin—Stevens Point, Stevens Point, WI 54481
Vital records: Contact Register of Deeds; copies: $10.00 each for births, $7.00 each for deaths and marriages (proof of relationship required)
Probate records: Contact Register in Probate
Probate search service: $4.00; copies: $1.00 per page, no minimum

*Outagamie County Courthouse
410 South Walnut Street
Appleton, WI 54911-5936
Phone (414) 832-5095 Register of Deeds; (414) 832-5601 Register in Probate
County organized 1851 from Brown County
Land records: From 1851; contact Grace Herb, Register of Deeds
Naturalization records: Through 1906; contact University of Wisconsin—Green Bay
Vital records: Not required by law until 1907; contact Register of Deeds; copies: $10.00 each for births, $7.00 each for deaths and marriages (certified copies restricted to persons

with a "direct and tangible interest" in the records)

Probate records: From 1855; contact Register in Probate

Probate search service: $4.00; copies: $1.00 per page, no minimum; "Not all of our records are kept at the courthouse so we may not be able to supply file the day of the search."

*Ozaukee County Administration Center
121 West Main Street
PO Box 994
Port Washington, WI 53074-0994
Phone (414) 284-8260 Register of Deeds; (414) 284-8100 FAX, Register of Deeds

County organized 1853 from Washington County

Land records: Contact Ronald A. Voigt, Register of Deeds

No land records search service

Naturalization records: Contact Register of Deeds

No naturalization records search service

Vital records: Contact Register of Deeds

No vital records search service; copies: $10.00 each for births, $7.00 each for deaths and marriages

Probate records: Contact Register in Probate, 1201 South Spring Street, Port Washington, WI 53074

*Pepin County Courthouse
770 Seventh Avenue West
Durand, WI 54736-1627
Phone (715) 672-8857

County organized 1858 from Chippewa County

Land records: Deeds, mortgages, land contracts, etc.; contact Register of Deeds

Naturalization records: Contact Clerk of Court

Naturalization records search service: $5.00

Vital records: Contact Register of Deeds

Probate records: Contact Register in Probate

Probate search service: $4.00; copies: $1.00 each, $4.00 certified, no minimum other than search fee

Pierce County Courthouse
414 West Main Street
PO Box 119
Ellsworth, WI 54011-0119
Phone (715) 273-3531

County organized 1853 from Saint Croix County

*Polk County Courthouse
Balsam Lake, WI 54810
Phone (715) 485-3161 Register of Deeds;

(715) 485-3099 FAX, Register of Deeds

County organized March 1853 from Saint Croix County

Land records: From about 1854 to date; contact Bonnie Hallberg, Register of Deeds, 100 Polk Plaza, PO Box 576, Balsam Lake, WI 54810; copies: $2.00 for the first page and $1.00 for each additional page

Naturalization records: Contact Clerk of Courts Office

Vital records: Births, deaths and marriages from about 1865 to date; certified or uncertified copies: $10.00 each for births, $7.00 each for deaths and marriages (certified copies restricted to persons with a "direct and tangible interest" in the records)

Probate records: Contact Register in Probate's Office

*Portage County Courthouse
1516 Church Street
Stevens Point, WI 54481
Phone (715) 346-1351

County organized 1836 from territorial county in the area now occupied by much of Columbia County, expanded northward in 1841 (into territory from Crawford County), and Columbia County detached in 1846

Land records: Contact Kevin Shibilski, Register of Deeds, Land Description Office

Naturalization records: Contact Clerk of Courts Office

Vital records: Contact Register of Deeds Office

Probate records: Contact Terrie Gagas, Circuit Court Branch II

*Price County Courthouse
126 Cherry Street
Phillips, WI 54555
Phone (715) 339-3325

County organized 1879 from Chippewa and Lincoln counties

Land records: Contact Register of Deeds

Naturalization records: Contact Clerk of Courts

Vital records: Contact Register of Deeds

Probate records: Contact Register in Probate

*Racine County Courthouse
730 Wisconsin Avenue
Racine, WI 53403-1238
Phone (414) 636-3862; (414) 636-3208 Register of Deeds

County organized 1836 from territorial county

Land records: Contact Register of Deeds

Naturalization records: No naturalization records

Probate records: From 1836

Probate search service: $4.00; copies: $1.00 per page

Richland County Courthouse
PO Box 337
Richland Center, WI 53581
Phone (608) 647-2197

County organized 1842 from Crawford, Sauk and Iowa counties

*Rock County Courthouse
51 South Main Street
Janesville, WI 53545-3951
Phone (608) 757-5650 Register of Deeds

County organized 1836 from territorial county

Land records: From 1830; contact Donna L. Berkley, Register of Deeds, 51 South Main Street, Janesville, WI 53545

Naturalization records: From 1839; contact Wayne Pfister, Clerk of Courts

Vital records: Births from 1860, deaths from 1873, marriages from 1849; contact Register of Deeds

Vital records search service: $10.00 for births, $7.00 for deaths and marriages (includes one copy, if found)

Probate records: Index from 1850; contact Steve Meyer, Register in Probate. Probate records from Files #1 through 20394; contact Rock County Historical Society, 10 South High Street, Janesville, WI 53545.

Probate search service: $4.00; copies: 25¢ per page plus SASE

Rusk County Courthouse
311 East Miner Avenue
Ladysmith, WI 54848-1829
Phone (715) 532-2100

County organized 1901 from Chippewa County

*Saint Croix County Courthouse
911 Fourth Street
Hudson, WI 54016-1656
Phone (715) 386-4600; (715) 386-4650 Register of Deeds; (715) 386-4618 Register in Probate

County organized 1840 from territorial county

Naturalization records: Contact State Historical Society, Madison, WI

Vital records: Contact Register of Deeds

Probate records: Contact Register in Probate

Probate search service: $4.00; copies: $1.00 per page, $3.00 certification fee, no minimum

*Sauk County Courthouse
515 Oak Street
Baraboo, WI 53913-2416
Phone (608) 355-3288 Register of Deeds; (608) 355-3226 Register in Probate

County organized 1840 from territorial county
Land records: Contact Mary Klingenmeyer, Register of Deeds
Vital records: Contact Register of Deeds
Probate records: Contact Carmen Green, Register in Probate

*Sawyer County Courthouse
406 Main
Hayward, WI 54843
Phone (715) 634-4867 Register of Deeds; (715) 634-3564 Mapping Department; (715) 634-4886 Judge/Register in Probate
County organized 1883 from Ashland and Chippewa counties
Land records: Contact Register of Deeds, PO Box 686, Hayward, WI 54843 and Mapping Department, PO Box 441, Hayward, WI 54843
Naturalization records: Contact Register of Deeds
Vital records: Contact Register of Deeds
Probate records: Contact Judge/Register in Probate, PO Box 447, Hayward, WI 54843

Shawano County Courthouse
311 North Main Street
Shawano, WI 54166-2145
Phone (715) 526-9150
County organized 1853 from Oconto County

*Sheboygan County Courthouse
615 North Sixth Street
Sheboygan, WI 53081-4612
Phone (414) 459-3023
County organized 1836 from territorial county
Land records: From 1836; contact Darlene J. Navis, Register of Deeds, Room 106
Naturalization records: Contact Clerk of Courts
Vital records: From the 1840s; contact Register of Deeds
Vital records search service: $7.00; copies: $7.00 each, $10.00 each for certified copies of births, $7.00 each for certified copies of deaths and marriages (satisfactory proof of identity required)
Probate records: From the 1800s to the 1950s; contact Register of Deeds. Probate records: Contact Register of Probate
No probate search service; copies: $2.00 per page from Register of Deeds

*Taylor County Courthouse
224 South Second Street
Medford, WI 54451

Phone (715) 748-1483 Register of Deeds; (715) 748-1465 Real Property Lister; (715) 748-1425 Clerk of Court; (715) 748-1435 Register in Probate
County organized 1875 from Clark and Lincoln counties
Land records: Contact Register of Deeds or Real Property Lister
Naturalization records: Contact Clerk of Court
Naturalization records search service: $5.00; copies: $1.25 per page
Vital records: Contact Register of Deeds
Probate records: Contact Toni Matthias, Register in Probate
Probate search service: $5.00; copies: $1.00 per page

*Trempealeau County Courthouse
Whitehall, WI 54773
Phone (715) 538-2311
County created as Trempe a l'eau by an act approved 24 January 1854 from Chippewa County (north of the Buffalo River), Jackson County (south of the Buffalo River, east of the line between ranges 7 and 8, and north of the line between townships 18 and 19), Buffalo County (south of the Buffalo River, west of the line between ranges 7 and 8, and north of the line between townships 18 and 19), and La Crosse County (south of the line between townships 18 and 19); boundaries adjusted with La Crosse County along the Black River and with Buffalo County along the Trempealeau and Mississippi rivers in 1857
Land records: Contact Register of Deeds
No land records search service by mail
Naturalization records: Area Research Center, University of Wisconsin—La Crosse, Eugene W. Murphy Library, 1631 Pine Street, La Crosse, WI 54601
Vital records: Contact Register of Deeds
No vital records search service by mail; certified copies: $10.00 for births, $7.00 for deaths and marriages (application must be completed and fee paid in advance, restricted to immediate family)
Probate records: Contact Register in Probate
Probate search service: $4.00, "as work load permits"; copies: $1.00 per page

*Vernon County Courthouse
PO Box 46
Viroqua, WI 54665
Phone (608) 637-3568 Register of Deeds Office
County organized 1851 from Richland and Crawford counties; name

changed from Bad Ax County in 1862
Land records: From the late 1850s to date; contact Register of Deeds Office
Naturalization records: Contact Clerk of Court
Vital records: From the late 1860s to date (scattered early records); contact Register of Deeds Office
Probate records: Contact Register in Probate

Vilas County Courthouse
PO Box 369
Eagle River, WI 54521-0369
Phone (715) 479-3600
County organized 1893 fron Oneida County

*Walworth County Courthouse
Courthouse Square
PO Box 1001
Elkhorn, WI 53121
Phone (414) 741-4241
County organized 1836 from territorial county
Land records: Grantor/grantee index from 1839; contact Clerk
Naturalization records: Contact University of Wisconsin—Whitewater, Whitewater, WI 53910
Vital records: Births from 1856, deaths from 1873, marriages from 1839; contact Clerk
Probate records: Contact Register in Probate, Room 202
Probate search service: $4.00 per name; copies: $1.00 per page, no minimum

*Washburn County Courthouse
Shell Lake, WI 54871
Phone (715) 468-7808; (715) 468-2960 Register in Probate
County organized 1883 from Burnett County
Land records: Contact Sandra I. Johnson, Register of Deeds, PO Box 607, Shell Lake, WI 54871
Vital records: Contact Register of Deeds
Probate records: Contact Register in Probate, PO Box 316, Shell Lake, WI 54871
Probate search service: $4.00; copies: $1.00 per page, no minimum

*Washington County Courthouse
432 East Washington Street
PO Box 1986
West Bend, WI 53095-7986
Phone (414) 335-4318 Register of Deeds; (414) 335-4333 Register in Probate
County organized 1836 from territorial county
Land records: Contact Dorothy C.

Gonnering, Register of Deeds, Room 2084

Naturalization records: Area Research Center, University of Wisconsin—Milwaukee, The Golda Meir Library, 2311 East Hartford Avenue, PO Box 604, Milwaukee, WI 53201

Vital records: Contact Register of Deeds; certified copies: $10.00 each for births, $7.00 each for deaths and marriages

Probate records: Contact Register in Probate, Room 3008

*Waukesha County Courthouse
515 West Moreland Boulevard
Waukesha, WI 53188-2428
Phone (414) 548-7583 Register of Deeds
County organized 1846 from Milwaukee County

Land records: From 1840 to date; contact Michael J. Hasslinger, Register of Deeds, 1320 Pewaukee Road, Room 110, Waukesha, WI 53188

Vital records: Births from 1860, deaths from 1872, marriages from 1846; contact Register of Deeds; copies: $10.00 each for births and deaths, $7.00 each for deaths and marriages (certified copies restricted to persons with a "direct and tangible interest" in the records). Transcripts of births recorded at the Waukesha County Courthouse from 1846 to 1879, some copies of courthouse birth records (not complete) from the 1890s to 1961, annual Vital Records Books (including birth announcements, obituaries and cemetery records, marriage licenses and anniversaries) from 1973 to date; marriages from 1836 to 1866, miscellaneous newspaper accounts of weddings and anniversaries from 1859 to 1972, marriage license applications from 1899 to 1958; contact Waukesha County Museum, Research Center, (101 West Main Street, Waukesha, WI 53186—location), PO Box 833 (mailing address), Waukesha, WI 53187

Probate records: Contact Register in Probate, Third Floor

*Waupaca County Courthouse
811 Harding Street
PO Box 307
Waupaca, WI 54981
Phone (715) 258-6250 Register of Deeds; (715) 258-6425 Register in Probate
County organized 1851 from Winnebago and Brown counties

Land records: From 1852; contact Register of Deeds

Naturalization records: No naturalization records

Vital records: From 1852; contact Register of Deeds (proof of relationship required)

Probate records: From 1860; contact Nancy Virnig, Register in Probate

*Waushara County Courthouse
Wautoma, WI 54982
Phone (414) 787-4631
County organized 1851 from Marquette County

Land records: From 1852; contact Register of Deeds Office

Naturalization records: No naturalization records

Vital records: Births and deaths from 1876, marriages from 1852; contact Register of Deeds Office

*Winnebago County Courthouse
415 Jackson Street
Oshkosh, WI 54901-4751
Phone (414) 236-4882 Register of Deeds
County organized 1840 from Brown County

Land records: From 1864; contact Susan Winninghoff, Register of Deeds, 415 Jackson Street, PO Box 2808, Oshkosh, WI 54903-2808

No land records search service

Naturalization records: Contact Area Research Center, University of Wisconsin—Oshkosh, Forrest R. Polk Library, Oshkosh, WI 54901

Vital records: Births from 1838, deaths from 1876, marriages from 1867 (all records sparse before July 1907); contact Register of Deeds

Vital records search service: $10.00 for births and $7.00 for deaths or marriages (includes one copy, must have approximate date of the event, within a five-year span)

Probate records: Contact Register of Probate

Probate search service: $4.00 per name; copies: $1.00 per page, no minimum; "We do not do genealogy research in person or by mail; local genealogists will do research for a fee."

*Wood County Courthouse
400 Market Street
Wisconsin Rapids, WI 54494
Phone (715) 421-8455 Register of Deeds; (715) 421-8495 Clerk of Circuit Court; (715) 421-8523 Register in Probate
County organized 1856 from Portage County

Land records: Contact Rene Krause, Register of Deeds

Naturalization records: From 1856; contact Edward J. Hellner, Clerk of Circuit Court

Vital records: Births and deaths; contact Register of Deeds

Probate records: Contact Sherry Masephol, Register in Probate

Probate search service: $4.00 per file; copies: $1.00 per page; "The search fee must be sent in before the records will be looked up, and copies will not be mailed until the copying fee is received."

WYOMING

Capital: Cheyenne. Statehood: 10 July 1890 (annexed as part of the Louisiana Purchase, 1803, territory gained from Great Britain in 1846 and from Texas in 1850, became a separate territory in 1868)

Court System

Wyoming has Municipal Courts in incorporated cities and towns with local jurisdiction. Justice Courts have limited jurisdiction in counties where there are no County Courts: Big Horn, Crook, Hot Springs, Johnson, Niobrara, Park, Platte, Sublette, Teton, Washakie and Weston counties. County Courts are required in counties with populations over 30,000, but may be established in smaller counties with the consent of the state legislature.

The District Court has general jurisdiction in civil, criminal and juvenile matters and sits at each county seat. First Judicial District: Laramie County; Second Judicial District: Albany and Carbon counties; Third Judicial District: Lincoln, Sweetwater and Uinta counties; Fourth Judicial District: Johnson and Sheridan counties; Fifth Judicial District: Big Horn, Hot Springs, Park and Washakie counties; Sixth Judicial District: Campbell, Crook and Weston counties; Seventh Judicial District: Natrona County; Eighth Judicial District: Converse, Goshen, Niobrara and Platte counties; Ninth Judicial District: Fremont, Sublette and Teton counties. The Supreme Court is the court of last resort.

Courthouses

*Albany County Courthouse
Laramie, WY 82070-3836
Phone (307) 721-2541 County Clerk; (307) 721-2508 Clerk of the District Court
County organized 1868, original county
Land records: From January 1869; contact Jackie R. Gonzales, County Clerk
Naturalization records: From early 1900; contact Clerk of the District Court
Probate records: From 1889; contact Clerk of the District Court
Probate search service: no charge; copies: $1.00 for the first page and 50¢ for each additional page

*Big Horn County Courthouse
Basin, WY 82410
Phone (307) 568-2357
County organized 1896 from Fremont, Johnson and Sheridan counties
Land records: Contact Ellen Cowan Whipps, County Clerk
Vital records: Marriages; contact County Clerk
Probate records: Contact Donette Martin, Clerk of Court, PO Box 670, Basin, WY 82410
Probate search service: no charge; copies: $1.00 for the first page and 50¢ for each additional attached page, 50¢ for certification of each document, no minimum; "All fees must be prepaid before we will mail out any requested documents."

*Campbell County Courthouse
500 South Gillette Avenue
Gillette, WY 82716-4239
Phone (307) 682-7285 County Clerk and Recorder
County organized 1911 from Crook and Weston counties
Land records: From late 1800s; contact County Clerk and Recorder, PO Box 3010, Gillette, WY 82717-3010; copies: $1.00 per page, $2.00 per instrument for certification
Vital records: Marriages from 1913; contact County Clerk and Recorder
Probate records: From 1913; contact Clerk of District Court
Probate search service: no charge; copies: $1.00 for the first page and 50¢ for each additional page, no minimum

*Carbon County Courthouse
Fifth and Spruce
Rawlins, WY 82301
Phone (307) 328-2668
County organized 1868, original county
Land records: From 1868; contact Clerk and Recorder, PO Box 6, Rawlins, WY 82301
Naturalization records: Contact Clerk of District Court
Probate records: Contact Clerk of District Court
Probate search service: no charge (written requests only, none by phone); copies: $1.00 for the first page and 25¢ for each additional page, 50¢ per page for certification, no minimum

*Converse County Courthouse
PO Box 990
Douglas, WY 82633-0990
Phone (307) 358-2061; (307) 358-3165 Clerk of District Court
County organized 1888 from Albany County

Land records: From 1888; contact County Clerk
Naturalization records: From late 1890s and early 1900s to 2 April 1941 (all files not complete)
Vital records: Marriages only from 1888; contact County Clerk
Probate records: From 1892; contact Clerk of District Court, PO Box 189, Douglas, WY 82633-0189
Probate search service: no charge; copies: 25¢ per page, 50¢ for certification plus $1.00 for the first certified page and 50¢ for each additional certified page, no minimum

*Crook County Courthouse
PO Box 37
Sundance, WY 82729-0037
Phone (307) 283-1323; (307) 283-2523 Clerk of the District Court
County organized 1875
Land records: From beginning
Naturalization records: From 1885; contact Clerk of the District Court, PO Box 904, Sundance, WY 82729
Probate records: Contact Clerk of District Court
Probate search service: no charge; copies: $1.00 for the first page and 50¢ for each additional page, no minimum; "SASE."

*Fremont County Courthouse
450 North Second Street, Room 220
Lander, WY 82520
Phone (307) 332-2405
County organized 1884 from Sweetwater County

Goshen County Courthouse
PO Box 160
Torrington, WY 82240
Phone (307) 532-4051
County organized 1911 from Laramie and Platte counties

Hot Springs County Courthouse
Thermopolis, WY 82443-2729
Phone (307) 864-3515
County organized 1911 from Fremont County

Johnson County Courthouse
76 North Main
Buffalo, WY 82834-1847
Phone (307) 684-7272
County organized 1875 from Pease County

*Laramie County Courthouse
1902 Carey Avenue
Cheyenne, WY 82001
Phone (307) 638-4350 County Clerk; (307) 638-4270 Clerk of District Court

County organized 1867, original county
Land records: Contact County Clerk
Naturalization records: Contact U.S. District Court of Wyoming, PO Box 727, Cheyenne, WY 82001
Probate records: Contact Clerk of District Court
No probate search service; copies: $1.00 for the first page and 50¢ for each additional page

*Lincoln County Courthouse
Kemmerer, WY 83101-3141
Phone (307) 877-9056
County organized 1911 from Uinta County
Land records: Contact Marsha Moe, County Clerk, PO Box 670, Kemmerer, WY 83101
Naturalization records: Contact Kenneth Roberts, Clerk of the District Court, PO Drawer 510, Kemmerer, WY 83101
Probate records: From 1911 to 1960; contact Archives, Cheyenne, WY. Probate records from 1960; contact Clerk of the District Court.
Probate search service: no charge; copies: $1.00 for the first page and 50¢ for each additional page, no minimum

*Natrona County Courthouse
200 North Center
Casper, WY 82601-1949
Phone (307) 235-9200
County organized 1888 from Carbon County
Land records: Natrona County land records from 1890, Carbon County transcripts from 1887; contact County Clerk, PO Box 863, Casper, WY 82602
Naturalization records: From 1907; contact Clerk of District Court, PO Box 3120, Casper, WY 82602
Vital records: Marriages only from 1890; contact County Clerk
Probate records: From 1892; contact Clerk of District Court
Probate search service: no charge; copies: $1.00 for the first page and 50¢ for each additional page, no minimum; "Payment in advance."

*Niobrara County Courthouse
424 South Elm
PO Box 420
Lusk, WY 82225
Phone (307) 334-2211
County organized 1911 from Converse County
Land records: From patent; copies: $1.00 per page
Vital records: Marriages; copies: $1.00 each, $8.00 for certified copies

Probate records: Contact Clerk of Court

*Park County Clerk
PO Box 1060
Cody, WY 82414-1060
Phone (307) 587-5548; (307) 587-2204, extension 204
County organized 1909 from Big Horn County
Land records: Yes
Naturalization records: Old records; contact Clerk of District Court, PO Box 1960, Cody, WY 82414
Probate records: Contact Clerk of District Court

Platte County Courthouse
PO Box 728
Wheatland, WY 82201-0728
Phone (307) 322-3555
County organized 1911 from Laramie County

*Sheridan County Courthouse
224 South Main
Sheridan, WY 82801
Phone (307) 674-6822 County Clerk; (307) 674-4821 Clerk of Court
County organized 1888 from Johnson County
Land records: Contact County Clerk, Suite B-2
Land records search service: $5.00 per name; copies: 50¢ for the first page and 25¢ for each additional page
Naturalization records: Contact Clerk of Court, Suite B-11
Naturalization records search service: $5.00 per name (records over fifty years old are open to the public); copies: 50¢ for the first page and 25¢ for each additional page
Probate records: Contact Clerk of Court
Probate search service: $5.00 per name; copies: 50¢ for the first page and 25¢ for each additional page

*Sublette County Courthouse
21 South Tyler Street
Pinedale, WY 82941
Phone (307) 367-4372
County organized 1921 from Fremont and Lincoln counties
Land records: Contact County Clerk, PO Box 250, Pinedale, WY 82941
Vital records: Marriages; contact County Clerk's Office
Probate records: Contact Clerk of District Court, PO Box 292, Pinedale, WY 82941
Probate search service: no charge; copies: $1.00 for the first page and 50¢ for each additional page, no minimum

*Sweetwater County Courthouse
PO Box 730
Green River, WY 82935-0730
Phone (307) 875-2611; (307) 872-6400 County Clerk
County organized 1869, original county
Land records: Contact Loretta Bailiff, County Clerk; copies: $1.00 per page, $2.00 for certification
Naturalization records: Contact District Court
Vital records: Marriages; contact County Clerk; certified copies: $5.00 each
Probate records: Contact District Court

Teton County Courthouse
PO Box 1727
Jackson, WY 83001-1727
Phone (307) 733-4430
County organized 1921 from Lincoln County

*Uinta County Courthouse
225 Ninth Street
Evanston, WY 82930-3415
Phone (307) 789-1780
County organized 1869, original county
Land records: Contact County Clerk, PO Box 810, Evanston, WY 82931
Naturalization records: Contact Clerk of Court, PO Drawer 1906, Evanston, WY 82931
Probate records: Contact Clerk of Court

*Washakie County Courthouse
PO Box 260
Worland, WY 82401-0260
Phone (307) 347-6491
County organized 1911 from Big Horn County
Land records: Contact County Clerk or County Assessor
Naturalization records: Contact Clerk of Court
Probate records: Contact Clerk of Court
No probate search service; copies: $1.00 for the first page and 50¢ for each additional page, $1.00 minimum

*Weston County Courthouse
1 West Main
Newcastle, WY 82701-2106
Phone (307) 746-4744
County organized 1890 from Crook County
Land records: Contact County Clerk

AMERICAN SAMOA

Capital: Pago Pago. Granted to the U.S. by treaty in 1899

Courthouse

The High Court of American Samoa
Courthouse
Pago Pago, AS 96799
Phone (684) 633-4131 Robert Gorniak, Clerk

GUAM

Capital: Agana. Ceded December 1898

Courthouse

*Superior Court of Guam
Guam Judiciary Building
120 West O'Brien Drive
Agana, GU 96910
Phone (671) 475-3420
Organized 1945
Land records: Contact Department of Land Management
Naturalization records: Contact District Court of Guam
Vital records: Contact Department of Public Health and Social Services
Probate records: Limited jurisdiction from 1945 to 1974, general jurisdiction from 1974 to date; contact Alfredo M. Borlas, Clerk of Court
Probate search service: $1.00 per year plus $10.00 retrieval fee; copies: 50¢ per page, $1.00 for certification per document

PUERTO RICO

Capital: San Juan. Ceded 10 December 1898

Court System

Puerto Rico's Justice of the Peace Courts and Municipal Courts handle civil investigations, probable cause hearings, warrants and summonses, but hold no trials. The District Courts have general jurisdiction over certain misdemeanors and violations and over lesser civil actions, including torts, contracts, real property rights and domestic relations. The Superior Courts (in twelve districts) hear major civil actions, juvenile and criminal matters and have exclusive jurisdiction over estates. The Supreme Court hears appeals.

Courthouses

*Aguadilla Superior Court
Centro Judicial
Progreso Street, Box 1010
Aguadilla, PR 00605
Phone (809) 891-0115 Chief Clerk
Land records: Contact Fernando Castillo-Velez, Chief Clerk
Naturalization records: Contact Chief Clerk
Vital records: Contact Chief Clerk
Probate records: Contact Chief Clerk

Aibonito Superior Court
18th Street—Bo. Robles
Urb. El Roble
Aibonito, PR 00609
Phone (809) 735-7201 Lucia Santiago Rivera, Chief Clerk

*Arecibo Superior Court
Rotario Avenue
Box 1238
Arecibo, PR 00613
Phone (809) 878-0060 Chief Clerk
Land records: Contact María del Carmen Cruz, Chief Clerk; copies: $1.00 each (money order payable to Secretario de Hacienda)
Naturalization records: Contact Chief Clerk
Vital records: Contact Chief Clerk
Probate records: Contact Chief Clerk

Bayamon Superior Court
State Highway #2
Corner Estaban Padilla, Box 60-619
Bayamon, PR 00619
Phone (809) 780-8402 Rosa M. Carrillo Batista, Chief Clerk

Caguas Superior Court
Highway 9
Corner Rafael Cordero
Caguas, PR 00625
Phone (809) 744-0953 Nelly Gonzalez Cabrera, Chief Clerk

Carolina Superior Court
Chief Clerk
Carolina, PR 00630
Phone (809) 752-6810 Chief Clerk

Guayama Superior Court
McArthur Street
Guayama, PR 00654
Phone (809) 864-1202 Edna Ramos de Alicea, Chief Clerk

Humacao Superior Court
Atanacio Cuadra Street
Humacao, PR 00661
Phone (809) 852-5370 Midlenia Santiago-Colon, Chief Clerk

Mayaguez Superior Court
Leon Street, Corner Nenadich
Box 97
Mayaguez, PR 00708
Phone (809) 832-6340 Gladys Falu Olivencia, Chief Clerk

Ponce Superior Court
State Highway #1, Box 1791
Ponce, PR 00733
Phone (809) 840-7380 Paulita Colon Rivera, Clerk

San Juan Superior Court
Munoz Rivera Avenue
Corner Coll y Toste, Stop 35 1/2
PO Box 887
Hato Rey, PR 00919
Phone (809) 763-0590 Maria M. Pou, Chief Clerk

Utuado Superior Court
Box 950
New Avenue
Utuado, PR 00761
Phone (809) 894-2476 Edwin Barreiro Figueroa, Chief Clerk

VIRGIN ISLANDS

Capital: Charlotte Amalie. Acquired 1917

Court System

The Virgin Islands' Territorial Courts are courts of general jurisdiction. The U.S. District Court for the District of the Virgin Islands handles all appeals.

Courthouses

Territorial Court of the Virgin Islands, Division of Saint Thomas-Saint John
PO Box 70
Charlotte Amalie
Saint Thomas, VI 00801
Phone (809) 774-6680 Viola E. Smith, Administrator/Clerk of the Court

Territorial Court of the Virgin Islands, Division of Saint Croix
PO Box 9000
Kingshill
Saint Croix, VI 00850
Phone (809) 774-6680 Viola E. Smith, Administrator/Clerk of the Court

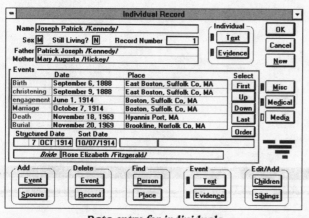
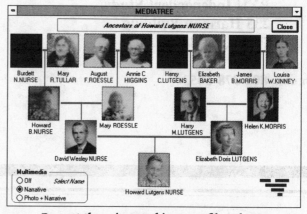
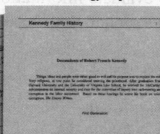

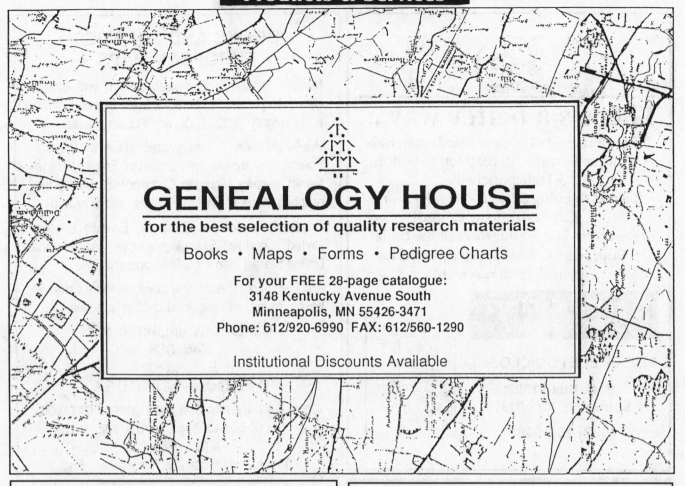